M000312876

The Making of the Medieval Middle East

The Making of the Medieval Middle East

RELIGION, SOCIETY, AND SIMPLE BELIEVERS

Jack Tannous

PRINCETON UNIVERSITY PRESS
Princeton & Oxford

Copyright © 2018 by Princeton University Press

Published by Princeton University Press,
41 William Street, Princeton, New Jersey 08540

In the United Kingdom: Princeton University Press,
6 Oxford Street, Woodstock, Oxfordshire OX20 1TR

press.princeton.edu

All Rights Reserved

ISBN 978-0-691-17909-4

LCCN 2018939251

British Library Cataloging-in-Publication Data is available

Editorial: Fred Appel and Thalia Leaf

Production Editorial: Debbie Tegarden

Text Design: Leslie Flis

Jacket Design: Leslie Flis

Jacket art: Twelfth-century illumination from a manuscript of *The Heavenly Ladder* by St. John Klimakos (Sinai Greek 418). By permission of Saint Catherine's Monastery, Mount Sinai, Egypt

Production: Jacquie Poirier

Publicity: Kathryn Stevens

Copyeditor: Eva Jaunzems

This book has been composed in Linux Libertine

Printed on acid-free paper. ∞

Printed in the United States of America

1 3 5 7 9 10 8 6 4 2

In memory of Jamileh Tannous

مَنْ آمَنَ بي وإنْ ماتَ فسَيَحْيا

ܫܪܓܐ ܕܦܓܪܐ. ܐܝܬܝܗ̇ ܥܝܢܐ. ܐܢ ܥܝܢܟ ܗܟܝܠ
ܬܗܘܐ ܦܫܝܛܐ. ܐܦ ܟܠܗ ܦܓܪܟ ܢܗܝܪ ܗ̱ܘ

Contents

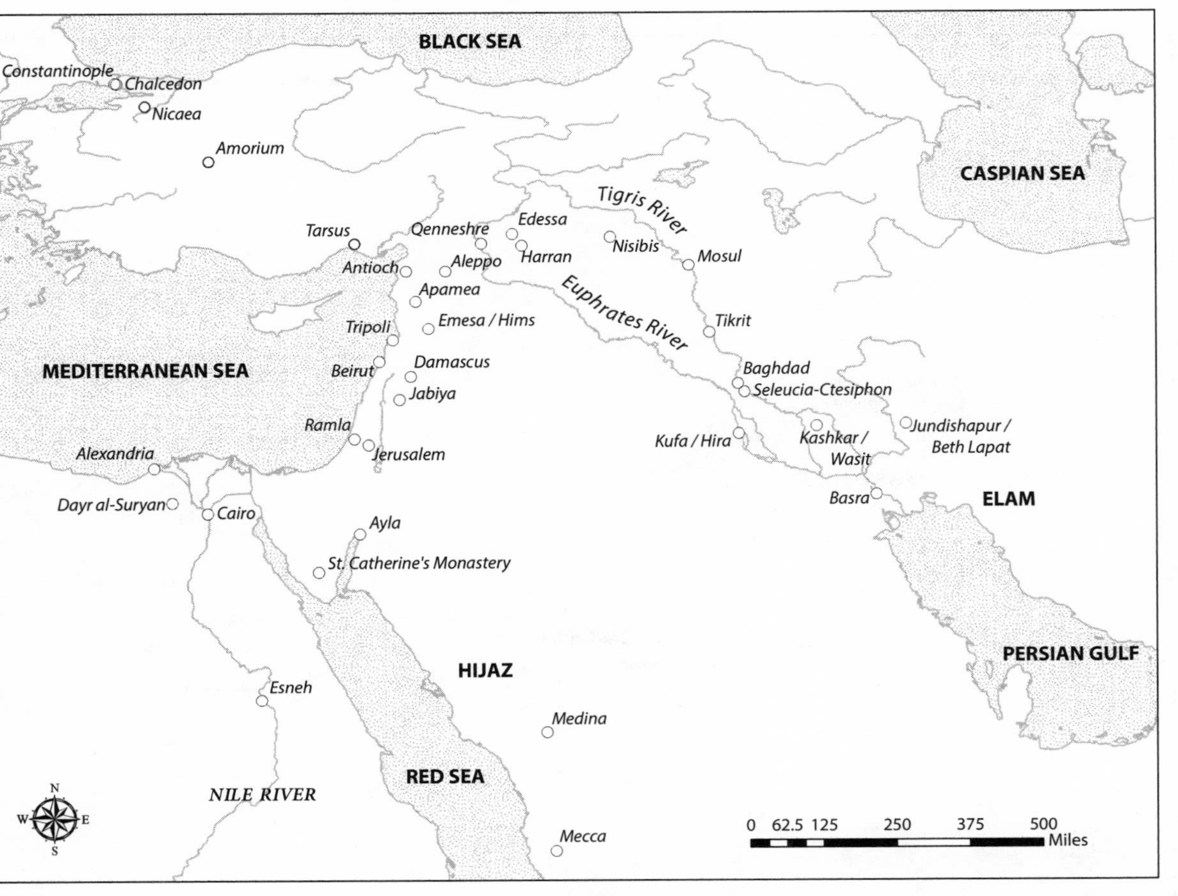

Map 1. The Middle East

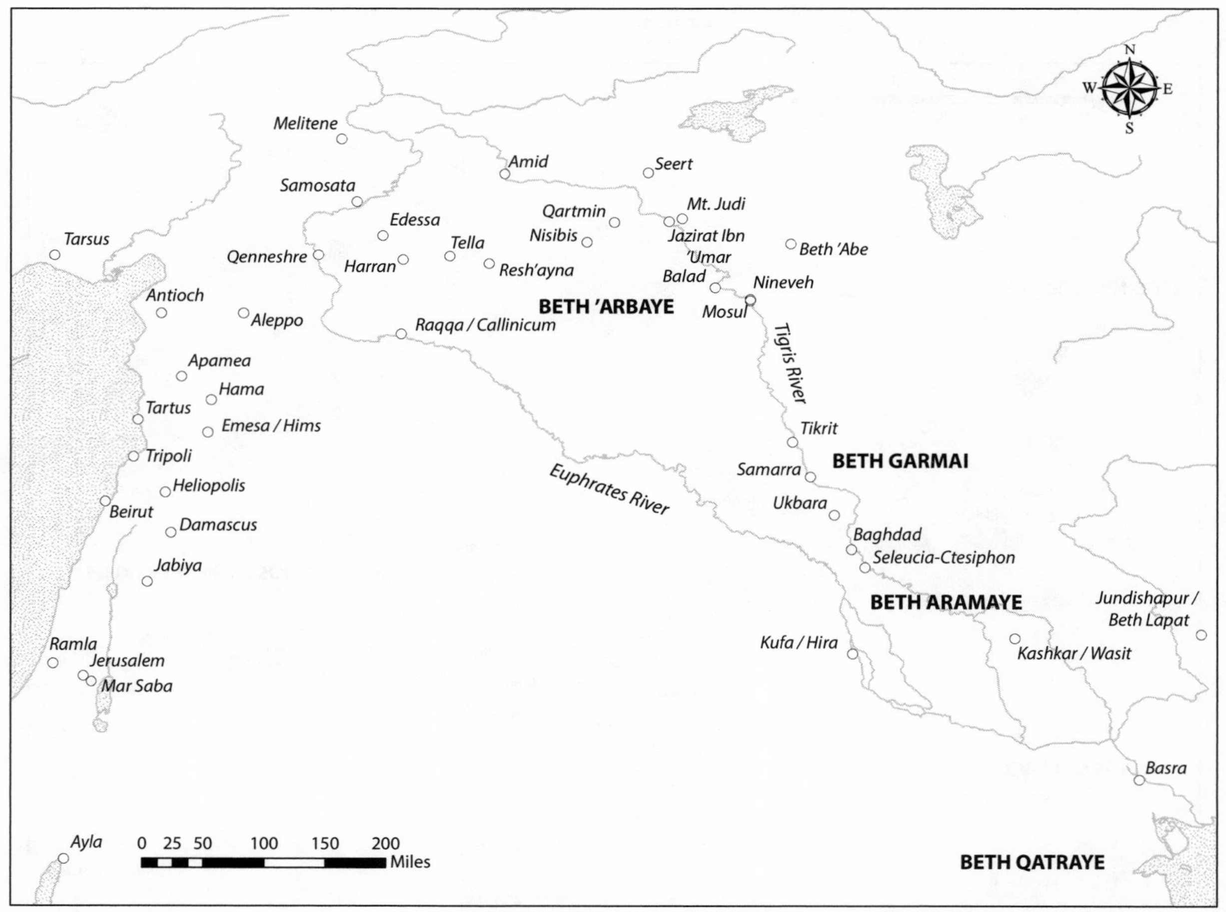

Map 2. The Core Regions of Syriac Christianity

Preface

The origins of this book lie in two questions that have engaged me for a very long time. The first is a persistent and longstanding curiosity I have had about what it would have meant in the late Roman and medieval worlds for people with little or no education to belong to a church whose identity was articulated in part through councils that created definitions and creeds which deployed sophisticated theological concepts.

The second question rises from a sense of puzzlement I first started having as an undergraduate at the University of Texas around the end of the last century. It was there that I began to be intrigued by a very simple, yet profoundly consequential, transformation: how did the Middle East go from being the birthplace of Christianity and eventually a largely Christian region, to being one where Christianity was a minority religion, if it had any presence at all?

Like all abiding interests, these questions had a personal connection: my grandfather, born in Mandatory Palestine, left school in the fourth grade to help support his family, in which there were eleven children. I never met him—he died before I was born—but I have been told he could read, though not a great deal. One of my great uncles told me that he once had an argument with my grandfather about whether the world was flat. My grandfather believed that it was (if it were round, he argued, all the water would fall off).

These two questions ran parallel in my mind for years, but I gradually recognized that the second could not be properly addressed without considering the first. When thinking about questions of de-Christianization, apostasy, conversion, and Islamization, I came to realize that I had implicitly assumed, as did most of the scholarly literature I was reading, that medieval Christians and Muslims were uniformly learned, like the churchmen and *'ulāmā'* whose literary remains have formed the subject of historical and theological study in Western universities for centuries. But what would it mean for these questions if most Christians had no formal education, theological or otherwise? What if the erudite churchmen and Muslim religious authorities that scholars have traditionally studied were the exception, not the rule? It was a simple and obvious point, but its implications for how we understood confessional belonging and religious change in the Middle East were potentially vast.

The book that follows represents an attempt to deal with a number of related historical problems, but it is these two persistent questions—the nature and significance of nonelite Christianity and the mechanics and pace of de-Christianization/Islamization—that are at its root. So, too, is a desire to understand the place that Christian communities have in the Middle East, both medieval and contemporary.

In the years since I first began to think about these issues, the Second Iraq War, the Syrian Civil War, and the rise of the Islamic State, among other things, have combined to devastate much of the Middle East's Christian population, with communities in Syria and Iraq undergoing the second Middle Eastern Christian genocide in a century and Christians in Egypt regularly experiencing horrific acts of violence. The question of Christian-Muslim relations, another fundamental concern of this book, will not cease to be an important one in our lifetimes or those of our children and grandchildren. As this project has drawn to a close, however, this violence and the immigration it fuels have made increasingly likely the possibility that Christian-Muslim relations in the Middle East, the very place where these contacts first began, may become a concern only for students of the past, and not for those living in the present. And although I study the past, I live in the present. It has given me great sadness therefore to realize that we stand before a rich world that is on the verge of being lost.

Princeton, New Jersey
All Saints' Day, 2017

The Making of the Medieval Middle East

Introduction

This book is about the world the Arabs encountered when they conquered the Middle East in the mid-seventh century and the world those conquests created. The importance of the Arab conquests for the history of the Middle East and, indeed, for the history of the subsequent fourteen hundred years, needs no emphasis. Apart from the rise and triumph of Christianity, no other event in the first millennium rivals them in significance. A majority of the population of the world today is affected in profound ways, daily, by these two events.

For all its importance, however, this period has been remarkably resistant to the writing of a compelling and persuasive unified account that does equal justice to the religious landscape of the region and to its changes under both Roman and Arab rule. On the Roman side, one easily gets lost in a thicket of ecclesiastical labels and rarefied Greek theological terms. The fact that these terms, when rendered into Syriac—a dialect of Aramaic that served as the literary language for much of the Middle East's Christian population at this time—might mean different things to different Christian confessions does not help matters, nor does the fact that many of the labels used to refer to various groups can be regarded as offensive. It is a period rich in historical importance but also abounding in opportunities for perplexity.

The appearance of Muslims on the scene adds another layer of potential confusion. The emergence of Islam along with its controversies and civil wars brings with it befuddling Arabic names, competing precedence claims, and tribal genealogical assertions and relations that seem, to the uninitiated, as arcane as they are apparently consequential. The Islamic tradition has left us remarkably detailed—even at times awkwardly intimate—information about the Prophet Muḥammad, and yet accounts of early Islamic history have frequently been mired in interminable and intractable debates about how much, if anything, we can believe of the traditional Muslim account of Islamic origins. More significant than this or that report about the Prophet's behavior or activities are the bigger questions that haunt the field: Did the Qur'ān actually originate in Muḥammad's lifetime, in Western Arabia? Can we even speak of 'Islam' as a phenomenon before the late seventh century?

In the last several decades, it has become increasingly common for scholars to attempt to bring together the late antique and early Islamic worlds.[1] In this

[1] The literature is increasingly vast and rich. See, e.g., A. al-Azmeh, *The Emergence of Islam in Late Antiquity: Allāh and His People* (New York, 2014) and R. G. Hoyland, ed., *The Late Antique World of Early*

book, I will try to do this as well, but I hope to offer a slightly different approach from a number of previous attempts. I will proceed from a basic assumption that if we want to understand how Arab conquerors related to the traditions of the populations they conquered and, more specifically, how Christians and Muslims interacted with one another, we must first understand Christian-Christian interactions, for the Middle East, in the several centuries before the birth of the Prophet, witnessed the irreparable fracturing of its Christian community and the development of rival and competing churches.

Looking at intra-Christian relations in the late Roman period will take us to a still more antecedent question: What did most of the population of the Middle East actually make of the disputes that had so divided the Christian communities of the region and which fill the pages of manuals of church history? What did it mean to be a Christian for most people, and what importance was accorded to intra-Christian religious differences? These questions will lead us to a whole host of further questions. Was there a layering of knowledge that could be found in the Christian community—that is, did some members know more than others? The answer to this last question is obvious, but it leads to a further question whose answer is not so immediately clear: What were the consequences of such a layering?

In order to understand the world that the Arab conquests created, I want to suggest, we need to first understand the world they found. And to understand that world, we need to attempt to understand the religious attitudes and

Islam: Muslims among Christians and Jews in the East Mediterranean (Princeton, 2015), the latter one volume of more than two dozen that have been published in the landmark series, edited by Lawrence Conrad and Jens Scheiner, *Studies in Late Antiquity and Early Islam*. G. Fowden, *Before and after Muḥammad: The First Millennium* (Princeton, 2014), represented an ambitious attempt at reperiodization. H. Kennedy, 'Islam,' in G. W. Bowersock, P. Brown, and O. Grabar, *Late Antiquity: A Guide to the Postclassical World* (Cambridge, Mass./London, 1999), pp. 219–37, is a classic statement of the continuities and discontinuities between the late antique and Islamic periods. Av. Cameron, 'Patristic Studies and the Emergence of Islam,' in B. Bitton-Ashkelony, T. de Bruyn, and C. Harrison, eds., *Patristic Studies in the Twenty-First Century* (Turnhout, 2015), pp. 249–78, provided an overview of attempts at viewing Islam within late antiquity and advocated greater integration of patristic and early Islamic studies. A. Borrut and F. M. Donner, eds., *Christians and Others in the Umayyad State* (Chicago, 2016), can be taken as representative of an increasingly prominent tendency among scholars to focus on non-Muslims in medieval Muslim empires. Decades before this trend picked up steam, of course, Peter Brown's *World of Late Antiquity* (London, 1971) had already set the rise of Islam firmly in the context of the later Roman world. The tendency to set the origins of Islam in the late antique period has been especially notable in Qur'ānic studies. Among an abundance of publications, see, e.g., A. Neuwirth's, *Der Koran als Text der Spätantike: ein europäischer Zugang* (Berlin, 2010); Neuwirth, 'Locating the Qur'an' and Early Islam in the "Epistemic Space" of Late Antiquity,' in C. Bakhos and M. Cook, eds., *Islam and Its Past: Jahiliyya, Late Antiquity, and the Qur'an* (Oxford, 2017), pp. 165–85; G. S. Reynolds, ed., *The Qur'ān in Its Historical Context* (London/New York, 2008); Reynolds, ed., *New Perspectives on the Qur'ān: The Qur'ān in Its Historical Context* 2; and N. Schmidt, N. K. Schmidt, and A. Neuwirth, eds., *Denkraum Spätantike: Reflexionen von Antiken im Umfeld des Koran* (Wiesbaden, 2016).

behaviors of most of its inhabitants and how those attitudes and behaviors affected the leaders of the Christian churches. It is these leaders who have left us the texts we study in order to try to understand this world.

A great deal of this book will be an effort to put flesh on the unseen contexts that swirl around such texts. These contexts were there when the texts were written, but they escape our notice easily; once supplied, however, they cast many things into new light. The great majority of Christians in the Middle East, I will suggest in Part I of this book, belonged to what church leaders referred to as 'the simple.' They were overwhelmingly agrarian, mostly illiterate, and likely had little understanding of the theological complexities that split apart the Christian community in the region. 'Simple' here does not connote 'simple-minded,' as it might in some varieties of English, nor should it be understood as a category restricted to the laity: there were monks, priests, and even bishops who were simple believers. The men who wrote the texts we study lived their lives among these simple believers: they fed them and ate with them, they prayed with them and for them, they taught and healed them, and they had the responsibility of pastoral care for them. A key to understanding the world that the Arabs found is the recognition that it was overwhelmingly one of simple, ordinary Christians; and that it was a world fracturing into rival groups on the basis of disagreements that most of those Christians could not fully understand.

I will attempt to show how this paradox can help explain the shape that Middle Eastern Christianity had in the centuries after the Council of Chalcedon took place in AD 451 and before the Arab conquests covered in Part II of this book. There was, during this period, fierce competition for the loyalties of simple, everyday Christians among leaders of the various Christian movements in the Middle East. This competition helped fuel debates, the composition of polemics, the translation of texts, the creation of educational institutions, and the development of a Syriac-language syllabus of study (among Miaphysites) in the seventh century. In this regard, it might be helpful to recall the competition between Catholic and Protestant missionaries in the nineteenth-century Middle East and the educational consequences it had for the region, especially Lebanon.[2]

Because the question of continuity/discontinuity between the periods of Roman and Arab rule in the Middle East has been a topic of such great interest to so many, I will pause for a brief "Interlude" between Parts II and III to look at it more closely, focusing especially on the question of continuity when

[2] On Catholic-Protestant competition in the Middle East, see, e.g., the brief overview in A. de Dreuzy, *The Holy See and the Emergence of the Modern Middle East: Benedict XV's Diplomacy in Greater Syria (1914–1922)* (Washington, D.C., 2016), pp. 218–21.

seen through the prism of Syriac sources and the unique non-imperial, non-state-centered perspective that they offer.[3] The intense competition among religious elites for the allegiances of simple Christians led to a series of remarkable intellectual continuities in the Syriac-speaking world across the sixth to ninth centuries, a time that has traditionally been seen as one of great cultural rupture.

In Part III, I will arrive at the question of how Arab conquerors and settlers fit into the landscape sketched out in the first two sections of the book. Here, I will emphasize that when thinking about the history of the Middle East in the early period of Muslim rule, one needs to constantly supply another context often invisible in the Arabic texts we read about the period: that of the non-Muslims who formed the overwhelming demographic majority of the region for centuries after the Arab conquests. The Christian communities of the Middle East are the ones with which I am most familiar, and it is for this reason (as well as for reasons of space) that I have focused primarily on them rather than on Jews, Zoroastrians, or others; the story of how Muslims related to these other non-Muslim groups is an important one that I will leave to scholars more learned than I. Discussions of Christian-Muslim interaction have customarily focused on actual interactions—there is a rich body of scholarship that has located, classified, and analyzed instances of Christian-Muslim encounter [4]—but in Part III, I will attempt to look first at what 'Christian' and 'Muslim' meant in the seventh and eighth centuries before asking questions about how Christians and Muslims related to one another. As in Parts I and II, my focus will be on the level of the ordinary, simple believers who were the great mass of both Christians and Muslims living in the Middle East in the early medieval period.

Crucially, in this early period of Muslim rule, we also need to recognize that most of the Prophet's notional followers, including many of the leaders of the early Muslim state, were people who had converted late in his life for apparently this-worldly reasons, often en masse. These late converts, many of whom rebelled against the leadership of the Prophet's community after his death and had to be forced back into the fold by means of military violence, likely had little deep understanding of Muḥammad's message or the full im-

[3] Cf. the remarks in M. Debié and D.G.K. Taylor, 'Syriac and Syro-Arabic Historical Writing, c. 500–c. 1400,' in S. Foot and C. F. Robinson, eds., *The Oxford History of Historical Writing*, vol. 2: *400–1400* (Oxford, 2012), p. 156: 'Syriac historiography is a rare example of non-étatist, non-imperial, history writing.'

[4] Most notable perhaps are R. G. Hoyland, *Seeing Islam as Others Saw It: A Survey and Evaluation of Christian, Jewish, and Zoroastrian Writings on Early Islam* (Princeton, 1997) and the monumental series edited by David Thomas and others, *Christian-Muslim Relations: A Bibliographic History*, vols. 1–11 (Leiden/Boston, 2009–) (hereafter *CMR*).

plications of what it meant to belong to the religious community he founded. Indeed, those implications and Islam itself were still being worked out in this period. One of the keys to thinking about the earliest Christian-Muslim interactions, I will therefore suggest, is to keep in mind that we are dealing with a setting in which simple Christians were meeting late mass converts and their descendants, even as Islam itself was being elaborated as a full-fledged way of living in the world.

Keeping our focus on simple believers, Christian and Muslim, will also give us what I hope is a different perspective on the question of the gradual conversion from Christianity to Islam of much of the Middle East's population over the course of the Middle Ages. Whatever the social and economic benefits and consequences—and these often will have been significant—when viewed from the standpoint of ordinary religious believers, a conversion from Christianity to Islam may not have been as momentous, in religious terms, as one might expect. We are dealing with a world, I will suggest, in which one could become a Muslim and still hold on to many Christian practices and even beliefs.

Here an obvious but basic point should be emphasized. We should resist the easy assumption that the beliefs and practices of the contemporary Muslim (or Christian) population of the Middle East in an era of printing, satellite television, the Internet, and attempted universal public education will have been substantially similar to those of most of the medieval Muslim (or Christian) population of the region. We need to think away the ability of the state and religious institutions to use modern mass communication and education to create a uniformity of religious belief and understanding. As a useful analogy, it might be helpful to recall that '[e]ven in a country such as France, which had centuries-long traditions of political frontiers and where norms of proper usage had been developing for centuries, probably not much more than 50 percent of French men and women spoke French as their native language in 1900.'[5] The understanding and practice of Islam by most medieval Middle Eastern Muslims will have been quite different from that of the literate, television-watching, Internet and social-media using Muslim population in the cities of the Middle East today.[6] It will also have been different from the beliefs found expressed in the medieval texts we study. As is the case also with Christian writings of the late antique and early medieval periods, when it comes to Islamic religious documents, we need to learn to see the

[5] P. J. Geary, *The Myth of Nations: The Medieval Origins of Europe* (Princeton, 2002), p. 31.

[6] J. Grehan, *Twilight of the Saints: Everyday Religion in Ottoman Syria and Palestine* (New York, 2014) is a very suggestive study. Though based in the late Ottoman period, Grehan's arguments about the nature of religious understanding and practice for most inhabitants of the Middle East could be applied to earlier periods as well.

invisible context of simple, ordinary adherents swirling around the things we read.

The question of the motivations, meaning, and consequences of conversion will be a major focus of Part III of this book. At the end of Part III, I will take up the question of how Muslims related to the religious traditions of the people they now ruled. This was a world where, very literally, the mosque was in the shadow of the church. Following Albrecht Noth, I will suggest that the precarious demographic and cultural situation that conquering Muslims found themselves in led to attempts, reflected in a variety of *ḥadīth*, to limit contact with Christians and Jews and discourage imitation of their behavior and religious practices. Alongside such attempts at proscription, however, can be set other putatively Prophetic utterances, which seemed to grant approval to seeking information from Christians and Jews. What is more, it is possible to identify various figures who did just this. Furthermore, scholars have long noted a variety of wide-ranging continuities between late antique Christian practices and later Muslim practices and beliefs.

Part IV takes up the question of the process by which this great host of late antique ideas, habits, and at times even texts, entered into what Patricia Crone termed 'the bloodstream of Islam.' The field of medieval Middle Eastern history is commonly understood to be Islamic history, an unspoken and sectarian conflation that relegates the non-Muslim population to what is usually, at best, the shadows of whatever image of the period we are given. Social history provides a key approach for recovering the role that non-Muslims played in making the world that scholars of the region in this period study. Moreover, the question of how Muslims related to the traditions of the religious communities they now found themselves ruling provides a vehicle for making the story of the Middle East under Muslim rule less overtly elitist and confessional—that is, one that focuses on more than just its hegemonic Muslim minority and concerns itself with all of the region's inhabitants.

In attempting to tell this story, I have made use of a large number of sources, in various languages, and belonging to a variety of genres. In order to keep the book from becoming any longer than it already is, I have tried to keep issues of *Quellenkritik* to a minimum and have instead chosen to offer some reflections on my approach to the sources in Appendix I.

* * *

Much of what follows will be an attempt to tell the religious history of the late antique and medieval Middle East from perspectives that are typically not privileged or which are often traditionally ignored or relegated to some sort of inferior status. Chronologically, my main focus will be roughly the years 500–1000, that is, from the era of Anastasius and Justinian in the post-Chalcedonian Roman Empire up to the pre-Crusader Abbasid period, but I will use evidence from other periods as well; geographically, I will concentrate on the Fertile Crescent—Syria, Palestine, and Iraq—but other regions, most notably Egypt, will also appear. Before the Arab conquests, my main emphasis will be on the simple, uneducated Christian and how he or she related to the theological debates that occupied the leaders of their church. I will focus on the Aramaic-speaking Christian population of the Middle East, not just those authors who wrote in Greek. In the period of Muslim rule, I will be particularly interested in the Christian population of the Middle East, the population which must have been a large majority in much of the region but whose existence and importance often silently vanishes after the conquests.

The result of pushing these perspectives from the margins toward the center will be, I hope, a narrative that subverts deeply ingrained tendencies in the historiography of this period. This book has two fundamental goals: first, to argue against adopting a heavily theological understanding of the Christian communities in the post-Chalcedonian Middle East as well as against a strongly doctrinally focused understanding of Christian-Muslim interactions. And second, to de-center Islam within medieval Middle Eastern history and de-sectarianize the subject by undermining the common understanding that the history of the medieval Middle East is synonymous with the problems and questions of Islamic history. If modern European historians now commonly speak of 'transnational histories,' historians of the medieval Middle East should strive for 'transconfessional histories' that explicitly reject the unstated millet system which has traditionally governed how the field has operated, a system that gives Islam, a minority religion, pride of place in the region's medieval history and dissertations focused on Islamic topics distinct preference in hiring decisions for academic positions. Apart from distorting contemporary understandings—both in the Middle East and in the West—of the role and importance of non-Muslims in the history of the medieval Middle East, this historiographic millet system distorts how we view medieval Islam itself. For properly understanding the Middle East's politically dominant medieval Muslim population requires understanding that it is precisely that: a hegemonic minority whose members were descended from non-Muslim converts, one which elaborated and articulated its positions on a host of issues in conversation and competition with the non-Muslims whom they ruled over, lived alongside of, were frequently related to, and often explicitly defined themselves against ideologically. Another challenge should be kept in mind as well: the East Roman Empire, an overt and thoroughgoing Christian state, represented the chief ideological, political, and military rival of the state governed by Muḥammad's successors in the centuries after his death. Both internally and externally, non-Muslims were competitors, and they were seen as such.

This book ultimately represents an attempt at writing a nonelitist, desectarianized religious history of the late Roman and early medieval Middle East, one that takes seriously the existence of a layering or continuum of knowledge and engagement in religious communities and which is concerned with the lived religious experience of all the region's inhabitants, not just that of select members of politically hegemonic groups. Scholars have written many erudite books and articles about learned Christians, Jews, and Muslims in this period. But these were figures who would have constituted a fraction of their respective communities. What happens if we ask about everyone else?

PART I

Simple Belief

CHAPTER 1

Theological Speculation and Theological Literacy

> However, it was inevitable that in the great number of people overcome by the Word [sc. by Christianity], because there are many more vulgar and illiterate people than those who have been trained in rational thinking, the former class should far outnumber the more intelligent.
>
> —Origen[1]

> [Celsus] says that 'some do not even want to give or to receive a reason for what they believe and use such expressions as 'Do not ask questions; just believe'; and 'Thy faith will save thee'. And he affirms that they say: 'The wisdom in the world is an evil, and foolishness a good thing.' My answer to this is that if every man could abandon the business of life and devote his time to philosophy, no other course ought to be followed but this alone.... However, if this is impossible, since, partly owing to the necessities of life and partly owing to human weakness, very few people are enthusiastic about rational thought, what better way of helping the multitude could be found other than that given to the nations by Jesus?
>
> —Origen[2]

In the period beginning with the controversy between Cyril and Nestorius in 428 and ending with the Third Council of Constantinople in 680–681, the Christian community of the Middle East splintered into separate and competing churches as a result of disagreements over theological speculation. There was chronic and irresolvable controversy as to how many natures, persons, energies, and wills there were in the Incarnate Christ.

The failure to reach consensus on these issues was not for a lack of trying. Ecumenical councils were called on at least five occasions—in 431, 449, 451, 553, and 680–681—with vast distances traveled and large sums of money expended in attempts to broker a resolution of sharp theological conflicts. Apart

[1] Origen, *Contra Celsum* 1.27 (ed. M. Borret, *Origène: Contre Celse. Tome I (Livres I et II)* [SC 132] [Paris, 2005], pp. 148, 150; translation taken from H. Chadwick, *Origen: Contra Celsum* [Cambridge, 1953], p. 27; I have slightly altered Chadwick's use of upper and lower cases).

[2] Origen, *Contra Celsum* 1.9 (ed. Borret [SC 132], pp. 98–100; ET taken from Chadwick, *Origen: Contra Celsum*, p. 12). For discussion of this passage, see P. W. Martens, *Origen and Scripture: The Contours of the Exegetical Life* (Oxford/New York, 2012), pp. 27–28.

from such spectacular efforts, for centuries Roman emperors attempted in a variety of ways—always ultimately unsuccessful—to get churchmen to come to agreement about the mechanics of how the human and the divine fit together in the person of Christ. Even Sasanian rulers[3] and, later, Muslim Caliphs and authorities,[4] at times could be drawn into Christian doctrinal wrangling. Churches were seized and plundered. Proponents of this view or that were exiled, mutilated, and even killed. The Roman army might be deployed to attempt to enforce doctrinal consent and unity,[5] and on at least one occasion an Umayyad Caliph sent an army to try to do the same.[6] The various distinct churches that emerged in the Middle East as a result of the theological controversies that took place in the period bookended by the Councils of Ephesus (431) and Constantinople III (680–681) identified themselves and their rivals on the basis of their Christological stances. Neither violence nor persuasion proved capable of bringing about resolution and reconciliation. Stubbornly, the issues resisted concord.

In this region, more so than any other, a variety of distinct and competing churches eventually developed: there were Chalcedonians, who accepted the Definition of the Council of Chalcedon (AD 451) and held that Christ was incarnate in two natures. There were Miaphysites, who rejected Chalcedon (but accepted the Second Council of Ephesus [AD 449], which would be rejected by supporters of Chalcedon) and held that he was incarnate in one.[7]

[3] Khusro II held a dispute between Miaphysites and members of the Church of the East in 612. See *Khuzistan Chronicle*, p. 23 (ed. I. Guidi, *Chronica Minora, Pars Prior* [CSCO Syr. III.4] [Paris, 1903]; ET available in Greatrex and Lieu, *The Roman Eastern Frontier and the Persian Wars.* Part 2, *AD 363–630: A Narrative Sourcebook* [London, 2002], p. 233). Also, see below, n. 140 in this chapter and Chapter 4, nn. 31, 35.

[4] See, e.g., the debate 'concerning faith' held between Maronites and Miaphysites held before Mu'āwiya, ca. 659: *Maronite Chronicle*, p. 70 (ed. E. W. Brooks, *Chronica Minora, Pars Secunda* [CSCO III.4] [Paris/Leipzig, 1904]; ET available in A. Palmer et al., *The Seventh Century in the West-Syrian Chronicles* [Liverpool, 1993], p. 30). The *History of the Patriarchs of Alexandria* 1.16 (ed. B. Evetts, *History of the Patriarchs of the Coptic Church of Alexandria* [PO 5.1] [Paris, 1910], pp. 288–89) records an assembly of Severan, Gaianite, Chalcedonian, and other bishops convoked by the Umayyad governor 'Abd al-'Azīz in Alexandria. Among other things, 'Abd al-'Azīz would censure their 'want of agreement in the doctrines of religion.' This happened at the time of Leontius's overthrow of Justinian II in 695 (translation Evetts, p. 289).

[5] See, e.g., *Chronicle to 846*, p. 225 (ed. E. W. Brooks, *Chronica Minora, Pars Secunda* [CSCO III.4] [Paris/Leipzig, 1904], p. 225) and Chapter 2, nn. 57–58.

[6] Marwān II used both military force and financial penalties to try to suppress Monotheletism in Syria and impose Dyotheletism around 744/745. For the incident, see Michael the Great, *Chronicle* 11.13 (ed. J.-B. Chabot, *Chronique de Michel le Syrien, patriarche Jacobite d'Antioche, 1169–99* [Paris, 1899–1910], 4.467 [Syriac] = 2.511 [French]). For the dating of this incident, see J. Gribomont, 'Documents sur les origines de l'Église maronite,' *PdO* 5 (1974), p. 122.

[7] It is their strong insistence that Christ had one nature—*mia physis*—that has led scholars to refer to members this church as 'Miaphysites.' A famous slogan of Cyril of Alexandria had affirmed that there

The Church of the East, the largest and most important Christian community in the Sasanian Empire and across the expanse of Asia, also held that Christ was incarnate in two natures but would eventually affirm that he was also incarnate in two hypostases as opposed to the Chalcedonian view that he was only incarnate in one hypostasis.[8] Among Chalcedonians, there would be a split in the seventh century between those who believed that Christ had one will and one energy (Monotheletes) and those who held that he had two wills and two energies (Dyotheletes), with the former developing into the Maronite Church and the latter developing into what are called today the Rūm Orthodox.[9]

---

was one nature in God the Word incarnate. This celebrated statement had its origins in a line in Athanasius' *Ad Iouianum*, a text that was later charged with being an Apollinarian forgery. For the text in (Ps-?) Athanasius, see H. Lietzmann, *Apollinaris von Laodicea und seine Schule: Texte und Untersuchungen* (Tübingen, 1904), p. 251.1–2; Justinian's charge of Apollinarian forgery against this letter can be found in *Contra monophysitas*, PG 86 (1), cols. 1125–28. Lietzmann's discussion of the forgery is in *Apollinaris von Laodicea*, pp. 119–21.

[8] For the evolution of the Church of the East's views on the nature of the Incarnation over the course of the sixth century, see G. J. Reinink, 'Tradition and the Formation of the 'Nestorian' Identity in Sixth- to Seventh-Century Iraq,' *Church History and Religious Culture* 89 (2009), pp. 217–50. It was around 561 that theologians in the Church of the East began to affirm the view that the incarnate Christ had two *hypostaseis*, a stance that contradicted Chalcedon's assertion that he had one *hypostasis*; see A. Guillaumont, 'Un colloque entre orthodoxes et théologiens nestoriens de Perse sous Justinien,' *Comptes-rendus des séances de l'Académie des Inscriptions et Belles-Lettres, Paris* (1970), pp. 206–207; Guillaumont, 'Justinien et l'Église de Perse,' *Dumbarton Oaks Papers* 23 (1969–1970), pp. 61–62; and see L. van Rompay, 'Pawlos of Nisibis,' in *GEDSH*, p. 324.

[9] The welter of different names used to refer to the various eastern Christian communities has long been a source of confusion and bewilderment. Though 'West Syrian' also includes the Chalcedonian communities of the Middle East, in what follows, I will use it primarily to refer to what is today called the Syrian Orthodox Church. I will also refer to the latter as Miaphysites, though they have also been at times referred to as 'Jacobites,' and 'Monophysites.' I will use 'East Syrian' to refer to members of the ecclesiastical community known as the Church of the East, today at times referred to as Assyrian Orthodox or, in Arabic, *Ashūrī*. (The Chaldeans, in Arabic, *Kaldān*, are an Eastern Rite of the Roman Catholic Church and also belong to the East Syrian tradition.) At times, however, I will also refer to them as 'Nestorians,' usually because this word is used by a text under discussion, but also where it is useful to highlight the Dyophysite doctrinal stance of this church. In such instances, 'Nestorian' should not be taken pejoratively, and it is useful to remember that by the time of Shahdost in the first part of the eighth century, members of the Church of the East were calling themselves 'Nestorians' (see L. Abramowski and A. E. Goodman, *A Nestorian Collection of Christological Texts: Cambridge Library Ms. Oriental 1319*, vol. 2 [Cambridge, 1972], p. xxviii). I will refer to those Christians who accepted the Council of Chalcedon as 'Chalcedonians.' This latter group includes both Monotheletes and Dyotheletes. There is no longer a Monothelete church in the Middle East, but the Maronite Church, strongest in Syria and Lebanon, but with an historical presence also in Cyprus and Israel, has its origins as a Monothelete community. The Dyothelete Chalcedonian church corresponds to the Middle Eastern group referred to today in Arabic as the *Rūm* Orthodox and also includes its Catholic Eastern Rite analogue, the *Rūm Kāthūlīk* or Melkite Church. Confusingly, in the period that this book covers, 'Melkite' can be used to refer to Dyothelete Chalcedonians, i.e., *Rūm, simpliciter*, who are not part of an Eastern Rite of the Roman Catholic Church in the sense that the Melkites of today are. Important discussions of these issues of nomenclature include: S. P. Brock, 'The "Nestorian" Church: A Lamentable Misnomer,' *Bulletin of the John Rylands*

These divisions are only the best known: among Miaphysites, there were as many as twelve different groups, the most prominent being Severan Miaphysites and the Julianist Miaphysites,[10] called such by scholars on account of their most important thinkers, Severus of Antioch (d. 536) and Julian of Halicarnassus (d. ca. 527). The Church of the East never experienced a split like that of the Chalcedonians or the Miaphysites, but the Christological (and other) teachings of Henana of Adiabene in the late sixth and early seventh centuries led to fierce disputes within the church and dealt the School of Nisibis, its premier theological training institution, a severe blow from which it never recovered.[11]

And yet, for all their apparent importance, the intensity of the controversies puzzles modern readers. How could late ancient Christians get so worked up about what seem, to many people today at least, to be rather rarefied metaphysical concepts and concerns? Was believing that Christ had two wills rather than one will worth losing one's hand and one's tongue over, as Maximus the Confessor did? Why, in the late 620s, did the Emperor Heraclius reportedly order that the nose and ears be cut off anyone who did not accept the Council of Chalcedon, an ecclesiastical gathering that had been held nearly three centuries earlier?[12]

The questions become even more pressing if we think about the population of the late antique and early medieval Middle East and eastern Mediterranean. It was overwhelmingly agrarian with higher-level religious instruction and

University Library of Manchester 78 (1996), pp. 23–35; D. W. Winkler, 'Miaphysitism: A New Term for Use in the History of Dogma and in Ecumenical Theology,' *The Harp* 10 (1997), pp. 33–40; S. H. Griffith, '"Melkites," "Jacobites" and the Christological Controversies in Arabic in Third/Ninth-Century Syria,' in D. R. Thomas, ed., *Syrian Christians under Islam: The First Thousand Years* (Leiden/Boston/Köln, 2001), pp. 9–55; F. Millar, 'The Evolution of the Syrian Orthodox Church in the Pre-Islamic Period: From Greek to Syriac?,' *JECS* 21 (2013), pp. 50–58; and S. P. Brock, 'Miaphysite, Not Monophysite!', *Cristianesimo nella storia* 37 (2016), pp. 45–54, which responded to P. Luisier, 'Il miafisismo, un termine discutibile della storiografia recente. Problemi teologici ed ecumenici,' *Cristianesimo nella storia* 35 (2013), pp. 297–307.

[10] Timothy, Presbyter of Constantinople, writing perhaps in the early eighth century, listed twelve different types of Miaphysites. See his *De iis qui ad ecclesiam accedunt*, PG 86.1, cols. 52–68. See T. Hainthaler, *Christ in Christian Tradition*, vol. 2, pt. 3: *The Churches of Jerusalem and Antioch from 451 to 600*, trans. M. Ehrhardt (Oxford, 2013), pp. 387–88, for discussion of the groups listed by Timothy. For a date of composition around 600, see C. Schmidt's entry, 'Timothy of Constantinople,' in *DECL*, p. 589, but for an early eighth century date, see F. Carcione, 'Il "De iis qui ad ecclesiam accedunt" del presbitero constantinopolitano Timoteo. Una nuova proposta di datazione,' *Studi e ricerche dull'Oriente cristiano* 14 (1991), pp. 309–20.

[11] See the events described in *Chronicle of Seert* 2.74 (ed. and trans. A. Scher [and R. Griveau], *Histoire Nestorienne [Chronique de Séert]* [PO 13.4] [Paris, 1919], pp. 187–93) and the charge of Theopaschism leveled in Babai the Great, *History of George the Priest*, p. 495 (ed. P. Bedjan, *Histoire de Mar-Jabalaha, de trois autres patriarches, d'un prêtre et de deux laïques nestoriens* [Paris, 1895]).

[12] Michael the Great, *Chronicle* 11.3 (ed. Chabot, 4.410 [Syriac] = 2.412).

sophisticated theological literature likely not in great supply (or any supply) in most areas. Though scholars have typically focused on works written by learned churchmen, Christian communities included everything from mountain tribes to suburban peasants, most of whom would not have had access to the training or the books needed to understand the debates that separated the churches to which they ostensibly belonged.[13] What did most Christians make of these disputes? Did the society of the late antique Middle East resemble something like an advanced seminar in patristic theology and Christology run amok?

THE QUESTION OF LITERACY

The question of literacy complicates things further. To be sure, measuring literacy, however understood,[14] in the ancient world is a notoriously tricky business, and in the end all attempts at measurement must remain little more than conjectures based on anecdotes and an evidentiary foundation that is, to put it generously, incomplete and fragmentary.[15] But scholars have found the urge to estimate, even on wobbly bases, irresistible. One famous study suggested the upper limits of literacy in the western provinces of the Roman world in the late Republic and the later Roman period at between 5 and 10 percent.[16]

[13] To give just one example at present: what would the Christological debates have meant to those Christians under the authority of the seventh-century (East Syrian) David, bishop of Kurdish tribes in northern Iraq? For David as *apesqopā d-kartwāyē*, see Thomas of Marga, *Monastic History* 2.24 (ed. and trans. E.A.W. Budge, *The Book of Governors: The Historia Monastica of Thomas, Bishop of Margâ A.D. 840, Edited from Syriac Manuscripts in the British Museum and Other Libraries* [London, 1893], 1.99 [Syriac] = 2.225 [ET]). On the meaning of *kartwāyē* here and the location of these tribes north of Arbela, see J. P. Margoliouth, *Supplement to the Thesaurus Syriacus of R. Payne Smith, S.T.P.* (Oxford, 1927), s.v. ܟܪܬܘܝܐ (p. 173). More generally on David, see A. Baumstark, *Geschichte der Syrischen Literatur* (Bonn, 1922), pp. 205–206.

[14] See the useful and brief discussion of the meanings of literacy by Rosamond McKitterick in her introduction to *The Uses of Literacy in Early Medieval Europe*, ed. R. McKitterick (Cambridge/New York, 1990), pp. 2–6, and see the studies by MacDonald and Hanna cited below (n. 22).

[15] In many instances, Vindolanda and the sites of Egyptian papyrus discoveries are stretched to cover the entire ancient world. G. Woolf, 'Literacy,' in A. K. Bowman, P. Garnsey, and D. Rathbone, eds., *The Cambridge Ancient History*, 2nd ed., vol. 11: *The High Empire, A.D. 70–192* (Cambridge, 2000), pp. 875–97, provides a useful overview of literacy in the Roman world and the various issues involved in trying to understand it.

[16] W. V. Harris, *Ancient Literacy* (Cambridge, Mass., 1989), p. 272; see p. 267 for the suggestion that literacy in Italy was less than 15 percent. For Harris's discussion of literacy in late antiquity, which he suggests declined from the levels of the high empire (p. 321), see pp. 285–322. For reactions to Harris's work, see J. H. Humphrey, ed., *Literacy in the Roman World* (Ann Arbor, 1991). R. P. Duncan-Jones, 'Age-Rounding, Illiteracy and Social Differentiation in the Roman Empire,' *Chiron* 7 (1977), pp. 333–53, used the phenomenon of age-rounding in death inscriptions to argue for rates of illiteracy in the Roman

Another estimate of literacy among Christians in the first several centuries AD suggested that no more than 10 percent were able to 'read, criticize, and interpret' Christian literature in this time.[17]

Looking at the Middle East in more recent periods provides additional suggestive numbers.[18] Adult literacy in Egypt may have been 1% in 1830 and may have risen to 3% by 1850 as a result of the educational reforms of Muḥammad 'Alī.[19] In the early twentieth century, 25% of Muslim men and at most 5% of Muslim women were literate in Syrian Tripoli, despite decades of Ottoman attempts at improving education.[20] The village of Qilqilya had a literacy rate of 10% in 1915, and in 1931 a British survey found that only 20% of the male population of Palestine was literate, even after 10 years of attempts at improving education in the Mandate.[21] There are ways, of course, of complicating such figures,[22] but even optimistic assessments—whether based on educated conjecture about what the ancient world may have been like or on the grounds of more recent evidence from the region—leave literacy rates in our world depressingly low, even if some will nevertheless classify it as a 'literate society.'[23] In the fifth-century *Teaching of Addai*, in fact, universal literacy was

---

empire that were likely higher than 70 percent. For a study of age-rounding in Egypt specifically, see Duncan-Jones, 'Age-Rounding in Greco-Roman Egypt,' *Zeitschrift für Papyrologie und Epigraphik* 33 (1979), pp. 169–77.

[17] See H. Y. Gamble, *Books and Readers in the Early Church: A History of Early Christian Texts* (New Haven/London, 1995), p. 5. At 231, Gamble suggests 15–20 percent as an upper limit of Christian literacy (and see p. 10 for a suggested upper limit of 10–15 percent).

[18] See also the table in Harris, *Ancient Literacy*, p. 23.

[19] For this, see E. R. Toledano's article, 'Muḥammad 'Alī Pasha,' in *EI2*, vol. 7, p. 427.

[20] See Grehan, *Twilight of the Saints*, p. 53. The literacy rates among Christians educated in foreign missionary schools were considerably higher, though the precise numbers cannot be known for sure (pp. 53–54).

[21] Grehan, *Twilight of the Saints*, pp. 54-56.

[22] See M.C.A. Macdonald, 'Literacy in an Oral Environment,' in P. Bienkowski, C. Mee, and E. Slater, eds., *Writing and Ancient Near Eastern Society: Papers in Honour of Alan R. Millard* (New York/London, 2005), pp. 45–114. K. Hopkins, 'Conquest by Book,' in *Literacy in the Roman World*, pp. 133–58, has a much more optimistic take on levels of literacy, even in towns and villages, and J. L. Maxwell, *Christianization and Communication in Late Antiquity: John Chrysostom and His Congregation in Antioch* (Cambridge/New York, 2006), pp. 98–104, also argues for greater levels of literacy than are commonly assumed. N. Hanna, 'Literacy among Artisans and Tradesmen in Ottoman Cairo,' in C. Woodhead, ed., *The Ottoman World* (Milton Park, Abingdon, Oxford/New York, 2012), pp. 319–31, should be consulted when looking at any estimates of Middle Eastern literacy from the Ottoman period. One can point to certain times and places that were exceptional, too. For instance: A. G. McDowell, 'Daily Life in Ancient Egypt,' *Scientific American* 275.6 (1996), pp. 100–105, suggested that at certain points in the period between 1275 and 1075 BC, most of the males in the village of Deir el-Medina were literate, though in ancient Egypt more generally, literacy rates were likely at 1 to 2 percent (see esp. p. 101).

[23] See MacDonald, 'Literacy in an Oral Environment,' p. 45, and the brief discussion in R. S. Bagnall, *Everyday Writing in the Graeco-Roman East* (Berkeley/Los Angeles/London, 2011), pp. 2–3. For a vivid evocation of the ubiquity of literacy in the Greco-Roman world and the suggestion that 'These were

seen as something that would only be realized in the eschaton. 'At that time,' Addai the Apostle is reported to have preached to the nobles and people of Edessa and its environs:

> Their manner of life will be represented in their own persons and their bodies will become parchment skins for the books of justice. There will be no one there who cannot read, because in that day everyone will read the writings of his own book. He will hold a reckoning of his deeds in the fingers of his hands. Moreover, the unlearned (*hedyoṭē*) will know the new writing of the new language. No one will say to his companion, 'read this for me,' because teaching and instruction will rule over all people.[24]

But late Roman Christians were not living in the Last Day, and our picture is further complicated if we pause to ask where it was that that they did actually live. Scholars have debated the nature of the audience for late antique homilies and the ability of these audiences to understand the content of sermons,[25] but we should never forget that most late antique Christians did not live in cities—they lived in rural areas. And however low urban literacy would have been, rural literacy rates were likely even lower.[26] What is more, literacy rates among women, who would have been a significant percentage of the Christian population, will almost certainly have been lower than those of men.[27]

---

profoundly literate socieities, despite the relatively small number of functional literates and probably much smaller number of deeply literate people of whom we have evidence,' see T. Morgan, *Literate Education in the Hellenistic and Roman Worlds* (Cambridge, 1998), pp. 1–2 (quote at 2).

[24] *Teaching of Addai*, p. *23 (ed. G. Phillips in G. Howard, *The Teaching of Addai* [Chico, Calif., 1981]; the ET is that of Howard, p. 47). I am grateful to Muriel Debié for bringing this passage to my attention.

[25] See R. MacMullen, 'The Preacher's Audience (AD 350-400),' *JTS* 40 (1989), pp. 503–11 and P. Rousseau, '"The Preacher's Audience": A More Optimistic View,' in T. W. Hillard, R. A. Kearsley, C.E.V. Nixon, and A. M. Nobbs, eds., *Ancient History in a Modern University*, vol. 2: *Early Christianity, Late Antiquity and Beyond* (New South Wales/Grand Rapids/Cambridge, 1998), pp. 391–400; E. G. Clark, 'Pastoral Care: Town and Country in Late-Antique Preaching,' in T. S. Burns and J. W. Eadie, eds., *Urban Centers and Rural Contexts in Late Antiquity* (East Lansing, 2001), pp. 265–84; and W. Mayer, 'John Chrysostom and His Audiences: Distinguishing Different Congregations at Antioch and Constantinople,' *Studia Patristica* 31 (1997), pp. 70–75.

[26] See Harris, *Ancient Literacy*, pp. 17, 190–93, for the connection between illiteracy and rusticity; but on the unknowability of rates of rural literacy, also see the sage remarks of Macdonald, 'Literacy in an Oral Environment,' p. 83. C. Hezser, *Jewish Literacy in Roman Palestine* (Tübingen, 2001), pp. 170–76, is a careful and expert discussion of the question of urban vs. rural rates of literacy in Palestine. Though dealing with a slightly earlier period, Alan Millard's discussion of literacy in Galilee and whether it should be considered a rural 'backwater' so far as reading and writing are concerned, is instructive when thinking about rural areas more generally, the importance of mobility, and the limitations of our source base. See his *Reading and Writing in the Time of Jesus* (New York, 2000), pp. 179–82.

[27] Though of course some women will have been literate as well: Origen, for instance, made use of

The lack of learning outside the cities would have had consequences for the nature, quality, and availability of Christian teaching in nonurban areas.[28] When we use homilies to understand late ancient Christianity, we also often forget that they were an 'urban phenomenon,'[29] while the world we are dealing with was primarily rural. Those who live in the cities, John Chrysostom wrote, enjoy constant teaching, but those who live in the countryside do not benefit from such bounty: 'They do not hear the tongue of teachers regularly.'[30] Chrysostom would even rebuke landowners for providing a variety of buildings for the villages and estates they owned—baths and markets, for instance—but building no churches on them.[31] To be sure, there was preaching to be found in the countryside—in North Africa, Augustine preached in both rural areas

---

females who had been trained in writing beautifully in the writing out of his works; see Eusebius, *Ecclesiastical History* 6.23.2 (ed. E. Schwartz, T. Mommsen [and F. Winkelmann], *Eusebius Werke* 2.2: *Die Kirchengeschichte* [Berlin, 1999], p. 570). In the Syriac milieu, we might point to the Miaphysite Simeon the Mountaineer, who in the mid-sixth century taught those who had been tonsured, 'boys and girls equally,' how to write and the Psalms and the scriptures; see John of Ephesus, *Lives of the Eastern Saints* 16 (ed. and trans. E. W. Brooks, *John of Ephesus. Lives of the Eastern Saints* [PO 17.1] [Paris, 1923], p. 246 [my translation], and cf. Chapter 9, nn. 55–62, below). In *Lives of the Eastern Saints* 12 (ed. Brooks [PO 17.1], 171), Euphemia memorizes the Psalter and teaches her daughter the Psalms, too, 'for her daughter also had while she was a child been splendidly trained in the psalms and in the Scriptures and in handwriting' (translation Brooks). The East Syrian *Canons of Marutha* stipulated that female monastics—known as 'daughters of the covenant'—should be trained in the reading of the Scriptures and in the service of the Psalms; see *Canons of Marutha* 41.2 (ed. A. Vööbus, *Syriac and Arabic Documents Regarding Legislation Relative to Syrian Asceticism* [Stockholm, 1960], p. 125). The Miaphysite collection of *Canons for Nuns* 9, dating to the eighth century or earlier, forbade female monastics from writing a letter without the permission of their abbess (ed. and trans. Vööbus, *Syriac and Arabic Documents*, p. 67). On the question of female scribes, especially in an early Christian context, see K. Haines-Eitzen, 'Girls Trained in Beautiful Writing: Female Scribes in Roman Antiquity and Early Christianity,' *JECS* 6 (1998), pp. 629–46, and Haines-Eitzen, *Guardians of Letters: Literacy, Power, and the Transmitters of Early Christian Literature* (Oxford, 2000), pp. 41–52.

[28] Though we should be cautious not reflexively to identify it with someone living in the country, it nevertheless bears pointing out that referring to someone as 'rustic' in Syriac was a way of stating that they were ignorant. See M. Sokoloff, *A Syriac Lexicon: A Translation from the Latin, Correction, Expansion, and Update of C. Brockelmann's Lexicon Syriacum* (Winona Lake, Ind. /Piscataway, N.J., 2009), s.v. ܩܘܪܝܐ (p. 1344); cf. also the meanings in Y. A. Manna, *Qāmūs kaldānī-ʿarabī* (Beirut, 1975), s.v. ܩܘܪܝܘܬܐ (p. 699).

[29] On the urban character of homilies, see P. Allen and W. Mayer, 'Computer and Homily: Accessing the Everyday Life of Early Christians,' *Vigiliae Christianae* 47 (1993), pp. 260, 261–67 (quote from 260).

[30] Οἱ μὲν γὰρ τὰς πόλεις οἰκοῦντες συνεχοῦς ἀπολαύουσι διδασκαλίας, οἱ δὲ ἐν ἀγροικίᾳ ζῶντες, οὐ τοσαύτης μετέχουσιν ἀφθονίας... Οὐκ ἀκούουσι διδασκάλων γλώττης ἐκεῖνοι διηνεκῶς. For this reason, Chrysostom said, God had given rural areas more martyrs. See John Chrysostom, *De Sanctis Martryibus*, PG 50, col. 647. Cf. J. Bingham, *Origines ecclesiasticae: or, The Antiquities of the Christian Church* (London, 1856), vol. 2, p. 715 [14.4.9].

[31] John Chrysostom, *Homilies on the Acts of the Apostles* 18.4 (PG 60 cols.146–47; ET by J. Walker, J. Sheppard, H. Browne, and G. B. Stevens available in *NPNF*, ser. 1, vol. 11, pp. 117–18). On this passage, see Clark, 'Town and Country in Late-Antique Preaching,' p. 275.

and urban contexts,[32] as did other urban bishops, as well as rural bishops and apparently even rural clergy[33]—but instruction in rural areas cannot have been of the same standard, quantity, or quality as that available in urban centers.[34] The practice of preachers reading out or reusing edited versions of sermons written by their bishops or by some great authority also points to situations where clergy needed help in fulfilling teaching expectations or lacked confidence in their own knowledge.[35]

Another complication arises from the very basic problem ecclesiastical leaders faced of simply making sure each church had a priest. Among the canons attributed to Marutha of Maipherqat and claiming to have their origin at the East Syrian Synod of Seleucia-Ctesiphon of 410, are a series that describes the duties of the chorepiscopus. The job of these rural bishops included circulating through the countryside and visiting churches and monasteries, as well as appointing qualified visitors who would look after these same churches and monasteries.[36] One of their responsibilities was to make sure that there were clergy supplied everywhere they were needed. 'Let him see,' one canon instructed,

> if perhaps there are villages that are lacking and in need of priests. Let him work in them and not leave the villages to conduct themselves according to disgraceful customs. There are villages in which there are no Sons of the Covenant [i.e., ascetics] from whom they can make priests, [so] let him bring brothers out from the monasteries or the churches under his authority and make [them priests]. Let him not leave churches or monasteries without priests so that the altars are not treated shamefully and the holy sanctuaries do not remain without a service

[32] See Clark, 'Town and Country in Late-Antique Preaching,' pp. 268–70.

[33] L. Dossey, *Peasant and Empire in Christian North Africa* (Berkeley, 2010), pp. 153–62. As an indication of the nature of central oversight of villages in a Syriac context, we might point to the *Canons of Marutha*, which specified that the consecrated ascetics of the villages—referred to as the *bnay qyāmā*, 'sons and daughters of the covenant'—were to meet their bishop twice a year, once at the beginning of winter and once after Easter. Monks were to meet their bishop once a year. Heads of monasteries were to meet him three times a year. *Canons of Marutha* 27.1-3 (ed. and trans. Vööbus, *Syriac and Arabic Documents*, pp. 122–23). On the history of these canons, which may contain material that goes back to 410 as well as later material, and which were taken up into the West Syrian tradition, see pp. 115–18.

[34] Dossey, *Peasant and Empire in Christian North Africa*, pp. 153–62, uses the presence of simple language and agrarian metaphors as one possible indication of a sermon's having been preached to a rural or rather humble audience.

[35] Cf. Dossey, *Peasant and Empire in Christian North Africa*, p. 170.

[36] *Canons of Marutha* 25.4, 5 (ed. and trans. Vööbus, *Syriac and Arabic Documents*, pp. 119–20). On the chorepiscopus, see Henry Chadwick's succinct remarks in H. Chadwick, *The Role of the Christian Bishop in Ancient Society* (Berkeley, 1980), p. 2; and see further P. Wood, 'The Chorepiscopoi and Controversies over Orthopraxy in Sixth-Century Mesopotamia,' *Journal of Ecclesiastical History* 63 (2012), pp. 446–57.

> and especially so that they do not have Christians in name but [who] in deeds are like pagans because they do not have pastors.[37]

If the chorepiscopus found, in the course of his visitation, that the churches and monasteries of a certain place were lacking monks and nuns, one of his assigned tasks was to persuade parents to set some of their sons and daughters aside as 'children of the covenant' (*bnay qyāmā*). These were to be dedicated to churches and monasteries and educated in doctrine and instruction so that 'at their hands, the churches and monasteries will be strengthened.'[38]

But finding properly trained clergy in rural areas was no doubt a challenge: also, in the fifth century, Rabbula of Edessa forbade periodeutes (the rural representatives of bishops) from advancing to the priesthood 'a man of ill fame, [or] those who are under the yoke of slavery and have not been liberated.'[39] The *Canons of Marutha* forbade villagers from selecting 'whomever they want to be priest for themselves.'[40] Another canon attributed to Marutha stipulated that 'churches of cities' should not lack female monastics. No such requirement was made, however, for churches outside of cities.[41] Indeed, shortfalls in the supply and quality of clergy in rural churches would be a constant problem: centuries later, the *Nomocanon* of the medieval East Syrian bishop 'Abdisho' bar Brikha (d. 1318) suggested that church leaders expected different abilities from a person who was a deacon in a city and a person who was a deacon in a village. If a person did not have a knowledge of the Scriptures, 'Abidsho' wrote—specifying by this the lectionary readings, the New Testament (*ḥdattā*), and the letters of Paul—he could not be appointed a deacon in a city. But if necessity required it, a person could be appointed deacon in a village merely because he was able to recite the Psalms.[42]

The consequences of poor religious instruction in rural areas can be seen in Augustine's work *On Catechizing the Uninstructed*, in which he discussed how a teacher should take into account the makeup of his audience when

[37] *Canons of Marutha* 25.7 (ed. Vööbus, *Syriac and Arabic Documents*, pp. 120–21). My translation.

[38] *Canons of Marutha* 26.2–4 (ed. Vööbus, *Syriac and Arabic Documents*, p. 122). My translation.

[39] Rabbula of Edessa, *Rules and Admonitions for Priests and Ascetics* 13 (ed. J. J. Overbeck, *S. Ephraemi Syri*... [Oxford, 1865], p. 216; ET taken from R. H. Connolly, 'Some More Early Syrian Rules,' *Downside Review* 25 [1906], p. 302).

[40] *Canons of Marutha* 40.1 (ed. Vööbus, *Syriac and Arabic Documents*, p. 124; my translation).

[41] *Canons of Marutha* 41.1 (ed. Vööbus, *Syriac and Arabic Documents*, p. 125; my translation).

[42] 'Abdisho' bar Brikho, *Nomocanon* 6.4.3 (ed. A. Mai, *Scriptorum veterum nova collectio e Vaticanis codicibus edita*, vol. 10 [Rome, 1838], p. 275 [Syriac] = 112 [Latin translation]). Rabbula required that a copy of the separated Gospels (as opposed to the Diatessaron) be kept and read in every church, though we cannot know the extent to which this rule was observed. See his *Rules and Admonitions for Priests and Ascetics* 42 (ed. Overbeck, *S. Ephraemi Syri*..., p. 220; translation available in Connolly, 'Some More Early Syrian Rules,' p. 305).

giving instruction: The nature of one's listeners, Augustine noted, determined the manner in which one should speak as a teacher. 'It likewise makes a great difference,' he wrote,

> ... whether there are few present or many; whether learned or unlearned, or a mixed audience made up of both classes; whether they are townsfolk or countryfolk, or both together; or a gathering in which all sorts and conditions of men are represented.[43]

The evidence of Augustine's sermons themselves indicates that he followed his own advice: careful study suggests that he typically pitched his messages to a wealthier, propertied audience, but on special feast days, when there would have been a broader swath of society present, he may have modified his way of speaking.[44] In the handful of his surviving rural sermons, in fact, we can see Augustine employing language and metaphors that would be especially suitable for an agrarian audience.[45]

Even if we were to assume that there were well-trained, highly literate and informed clergy in urban and rural areas alike throughout the Middle East, we would nevertheless have to consider the question of whether people actually went to church and what, if anything, they got out of their attendance. But levels of church attendance in our period are impossible to gauge.[46] And, if we suppose they were high, frequent complaints about congregants' misbehavior—doing everything from making business transactions, to talking during the service, to gawking at women, to shoving and kicking as they lined up to take the Eucharist—should give us pause before assuming any kind of correlation between church attendance and levels of Christian knowledge or seriousness of engagement with Christianity.[47]

[43] Augustine, *On the Catechizing the Uninstructed* 15 (ed. J. Bauer, *Sancti Aurelii Augustini De fide rerum invisibilium*... [CCSL 46] [Turnhout, 1969] p. 147; ET by J. P. Christopher taken from his *The First Catechetical Instruction* [*De Catechizandis Rudibus*] [Westminster, Md./London, 1962], p. 50).

[44] Dossey, *Peasant and Empire in Christian North Africa*, pp. 149–53.

[45] Dossey, *Peasant and Empire in Christian North Africa*, pp. 156–57. On the simple character of the sermons of Maximus of Turin and Caesarius of Arles preached to rural audiences, see C. P. Jones, *Between Pagan and Christian* (Cambridge, Mass., 2014), p. 102.

[46] See A. Olivar, *La predicación cristiana antigua* (Barcelona, 1991), pp. 744–60, for a discussion of preaching and church attendance in the first six Christian centuries that collects a large amount of evidence for both good and poor attendance of sermons. Maxwell, *Christianization and Communication in Late Antiquity*, pp. 133–36, discusses church attendance for Chrysostom's sermons and congregations specifically.

[47] People leaving church before the Eucharist: John Chrysostom, *On the Incomprehensible Nature of God* 3 (ed. A.-M. Malingrey, *Jean Chrysostome: Sur l'incompréhensibilité de Dieu*, vol. 1: *Homélies I-V* [SC 28bis] [Paris, 1970], p. 216; English available in P. W. Harkins, *St. John Chrysostom: On the Incomprehensible Nature of God* [Washington, D.C., 1982], p. 110 [3.32 in the English translation]). Talking during the consecration: John Chrysostom, *On the Incomprehensible Nature of God* 4.36 (ed. Malingrey, *Jean*

The social ramifications of disagreement over theological speculation are therefore amplified by several factors—the rural and agrarian nature of much of the Christian population of the Roman world, the character and (non-) availability of clergy, and the question of literacy. What is more, the sort of literacy I am interested in is not the ability to slowly scrawl one's name at the bottom of a papyrus legal document: I am interested in theological literacy and the ability of ordinary, everyday believers and nonspecialists to understand the Christological issues that led to the formation of separate and distinct Christian churches. However we want to define literacy and whatever percentage of late Roman society we want to say was literate, the level of *theological* literacy will have been much lower.

LITERACY AND THEOLOGICAL LITERACY

Here it is important to make several further distinctions: a person could have been deeply acquainted with traditional *paideia*, having an ability to read and write more than one language, and yet still lack awareness of the contents of the Christian tradition. Such a person could have been very literate and yet, theologically, at least in terms of Christian theology, illiterate. Gregory the Elder, the father of Gregory Nazianzen is a case in point. Not long after his conversion to Christianity, he was made a priest. According to his son's funeral oration, it was only after becoming a priest that Gregory began to study the scriptures seriously: 'though a late student of such matters,' Gregory Nazianzen stated, [his father] 'gathered together so much wisdom within a short time that he was in no wise excelled by those who had spent the greatest toil upon

Chrysostome: Sur l'incompréhensibilité de Dieu, p. 256; ET in Harkins, *St. John Chrysostom: On the Incomprehensible Nature of God*, p. 129. Cf. Bingham, *Origines ecclesiasticae: or, The Antiquities of the Christian Church*, vol. 2, pp. 734–35 [14.4.30], for this and examples of complaints about the behavior of church attendees.) Shoving, kicking, hitting, shouting, while approaching to take the Eucharist: John Chrysostom, *De Baptismo Christi* 4, PG 49, col. 370 (Cf. Malingrey, *Jean Chrysostome: Sur l'incompréhensibilité de Dieu*, p. 356, n. 1). Leaving church early, chattering idly during the service, looking at women, making business deals, slandering each other and the priest during the service: Anastasius of Sinai, *Homilia de sacra synaxi*, PG 89, cols. 829, 832. See the detailed summary of this passage in J. Haldon, 'The Works of Anastasius of Sinai: A Key Source for the History of Seventh-Century East Mediterranean Society and Belief,' in Av. Cameron and L. I. Conrad, *The Early Medieval Near East: Problems in the Literary Source Material* (Princeton, 1990), p. 133, n. 48. Leaving church early to socialize and using the church sanctuary as a meeting place: Leontius of Neapolis, *Life of John the Almsgiver* 42 (ed. H. Gelzer, *Leontios' von Neapolis Leben des heiligen Johannes des Barmherzigen, Erzbischofs von Alexandrien* [Freiburg/Leipzig, 1893], pp. 83–84; ET available in E. Dawes and N. H. Baynes, *Three Byzantine Saints: Contemporary Biographies translated from Greek* [Oxford, 1948], p. 250. For the Greek text of this passage in the 'long recension' of this *vita*, see A. J. Festugière and L. Rydén, eds. and trans., *Vie de Syméon le Fou et Vie de Jean de Chypre* [Paris, 1974], pp. 387 [Greek] = 508–509 [FT] = chapter 45).

them.'[48] Being made bishop with such little background in Christian ministry was not necessarily an exceptional event: the New Testament in fact had warned against making recent converts into bishops (1 Timothy 3:6), and the Council of Nicaea sought to stop the practice of elevating those who had only just been baptized to the priesthood or the episcopacy.[49] We nonetheless know the names of a number of bishops who were elevated to the episcopacy very shortly after their baptism, or even while still catechumens.[50] In other cases, people who sought ordination in order to obtain some sort of financial or personal gain undoubtedly will have come to their position of authority without a great knowledge of the Christian tradition. Such were the priests whom Gregory Nazianzen derisively referred to as those 'who only begin to study religion when appointed to teach it.'[51]

At the same time, those Christians who had basic functional literacy might also be considered theologically illiterate or theologically unschooled, at least so far as debates over theories of the Incarnation were concerned, if they were not conversant in and trained in the technical language of Christian theological argumentation and speculation. In this regard, we need to keep in mind that the texts that contained the ideas over which Christians were disagreeing might be written in very high theological or philosophical registers.[52] Being able to read a treatise by Leontius of Byzantium and understanding it is not the same thing as being able to write or read a label on an amphora, nor is it the same as having a basic understanding of Christian moral teachings, a knowledge of biblical stories, or a strong grasp of the concrete events of Christian salvation history—that Christ was born of a Virgin, suffered under Pontius

[48] Gregory of Nazianzus, *Orations* 18.16 (PG 35, col. 1004; I have used the translation by C. G. Browne and J. E. Swallow from *NPNF*, ser. 2, vol. 7 [Oxford/New York, 1894], p. 259).

[49] Council of Nicaea, *Canons* 2 (ed. and trans. P.-P. Joannou, *Discipline générale antique*, vol. 1.1 [Grottaferrata (Roma), 1962], pp. 24–25). On the habit of choosing as leaders rich men with dubious Christian credentials over poor men with good ones, see Chadwick, *The Role of the Christian Bishop*, p. 9.

[50] Bingham, *The Antiquities of the Christian Church*, vol. 1, pp. 45–46 [1.10.5–7], contains a rich collection of examples of presbyters, deacons, readers, laymen, and newly-baptized who were elevated to the episcopacy.

[51] Gregory of Nazianzus, *Orations* 21.9 (Ed. and trans. J. Mossay, *Grégoire de Nazianze. Discours 20–23* [SC 270] [Paris, 1980], pp. 126 = 127 [FT]; I have used the ET by Browne and Swallow from *NPNF*, ser. 2, vol. 7, p. 271).

[52] This held true even for texts that were not explicitly theological: for example: Severus might have to explain to one of his readers the grammar of a passage in a letter written by John bar Aphtonia (Severus of Antioch, *Select Letters* 8.5 [*Letter to Andrew the Reader and Notary*] [ed. and trans. E. W. Brooks, *The Sixth Book of the Select Letters of Severus, Patriarch of Antioch, in the Syriac Version of Athanasius of Nisibis* (London, 1902–1904), 1.2.470–71 (Syriac) = 2.2.415–17 (ET)]) and George of the Arabs would have to explain difficult passages in a letter of Jacob of Edessa (George, Bishop of the Arab Tribes, *Letter 8*, BL Add. 12,154, fols. 273a–278a [and see Chapter 7, n. 62]).

Pilate, was crucified, dead and buried, rose from the grave, and so on.[53] The ease of understanding basic Christianity was something that even pagans commented upon,[54] but speculation about the numbers of natures, hypostases, *prosopa*, wills, and energies in the Incarnate Christ was something quite different. How many Christians in the sixth or seventh or eighth centuries would have understood what precisely Severus of Antioch was getting at when he asked an opponent: 'How then, do you presume to call the gathering together of the hypostases according to a natural union "two natures", that is, two hypostases united, when you do not perceive as a result of the union one entity in composition?'[55] The sophisticated Christological polemic present in the sermons of Severus has in fact prompted the question: 'If we may expect something of the faithful of a metropolis like Antioch, one can still ask whether the comments on theological concepts were really understood and led to religious deepening.'[56]

ACCESS TO BOOKS?

Apart from the question of reading (or hearing) and understanding, there is the question of availability: how many would even have access to a book

[53] See H. J. Carpenter, 'Popular Christianity and the Theologians in the Early Centuries,' *JTS* 14 (1963), pp. 294–310, for an attempt to retrieve the theological views of laymen in the second and third centuries based on extant textual evidence, esp. 296–300, where he describes what he terms its 'moralism, institutionalism, and practical and historical interest in theology.'

[54] See Galen's comment, preserved in Arabic, in R. Walzer, *Galen on Jews and Christians* (Oxford, 1949), p. 15 (Arabic text on p. 16). On Galen's comments on Christians, preserved in Arabic, see S. Gerö, 'Galen on the Christians: A Reappraisal of the Arabic Evidence,' *OCP* 56 (1990) pp. 371–11.

[55] Severus of Antioch, *Ad Nephalium*, Or. 2, p. 18 (ed. J. Lebon, *Severi Antiocheni orationes ad Nephalium. Eiusdem ac Sergii Grammatici epistulae mutuae* [CSCO 119: SS 64] [Louvain, 1949]; ET taken from P. Allen and C.T.R. Hayward, *Severus of Antioch* [London/New York, 2004], p. 64).

[56] H.-J. Höhn in A. Grillmeier and T. Hainthaler, *Christ in Christian Tradition*, vol. 2: *From the Council of Chalcedon (451) to Gregory the Great (590–604)*. Part 2: *The Church of Constantinople in the Sixth Century*. Trans. J. Cawte and P. Allen (London/Louisville, 1995), p. 147. On Christological polemic in Severus's homilies, see F. Alpi, 'Sévère d'Antioche, prédicateur et polémiste: qualification et disqualification des adversaires dogmatiques dans les *Homélies cathédrales*,' in P. Nagy, M.-Y. Perrin, and P. Ragon, *Les controverses religieuses entre débats savants et mobilisations populaires : monde chrétien, antiquité tardive–XVIIe siècle* (Mont-Saint-Aignan, 2011), pp. 33–45. On this question, see the remarks in P. Allen, 'The Homilist and the Congregation: A Case-Study of Chrysostom's Homilies on Hebrews,' *Augustinianum* 36 (1996), pp. 401–402 and also Allen, 'Severus of Antioch as a Source for Lay Piety in Late Antiquity,' in M. Maritano, ed. *Historiam perscrutari. Miscellanea di studi offerti al prof. Ottorino Pasquato* (Rome, 2002), p. 712. Although dealing with a much later period, the observations of Keith Thomas about illiteracy and 'religious and political activism and Noncomformity' are nevertheless very interesting: 'such people were often in the forefront of religious and political upheaval.... In the mid-seventeenth century... illiteracy was compatible with a high degree of religious heterodoxy.' See 'The Meaning of Literacy in Early Modern England,' in G. Baumann, ed., *The Written Word: Literacy in Transition*, (Oxford, 1986), pp. 104–105.

containing the works of Severus?[57] Though a number of his theological and controversial writings were available in Syriac, 'they were copied only rarely and not often quoted.'[58] Modern scholars have easy access to a range and variety of writings that would have exceeded what was available to all but a few in the periods they study. Writing probably in the first part of the eighth century, the Miaphysite George, Bishop of the Arab Tribes (d. 724), stated that he had written his commentary on the liturgy especially for people like himself who were not able constantly to be reading the books of past Christian authorities, 'either because they are not available to them or because not everyone can grasp the elevated thought of the Fathers.'[59] Jacob of Edessa (d. 708), George's older contemporary and friend, at one point wrote that he was unable to answer a question because he did not have the necessary biblical commentaries with him.[60] Severus himself reported that he had difficulty completing and correcting his polemical work against the Chalcedonian grammarian John of Caesarea, because it was a job that 'needed a great number of books.' He worked, he wrote, as he moved about and 'appropriate testimonies and arguments from books were not available to me in every place.'[61] In the late eighth and early ninth century, the East Syrian catholicos Timothy I was regularly engaged in attempts to get hold of various patristic and philosophical works to which he did not have access.[62] If leading bishops and patriarchs could not procure the texts they would have liked to have at hand, what are we to assume about individuals at lower levels within church hierarchies, let alone of rural laity?

[57] On the availability of Christian books in the first five Christian centuries, see Gamble, *Books and Readers*, pp. 82–143. C. Mango, 'The Availability of Books in the Byzantine Empire, A.D. 750–850,' in C. Mango and I. Ševčenko, eds., *Byzantine Books and Bookmen: A Dumbarton Oaks Colloquium* (Washington, D.C., 1975), pp. 29–45, looks at a later period. J. T. Walker, 'Ascetic Literacy: Books and Readers in East-Syrian Monastic Tradition,' in H. Börm and J. Wiesehoefer, eds., *Commutatio et Contentio: Studies in the Late Roman, Sasanian, and Early Islamic Near East in Memory of Zeev Rubin* (Düsseldorf, 2010), esp. 333–37, deals with book ownership among East Syrian monks.

[58] L. van Rompay, 'Severus, Patriarch of Antioch (512–538), in the Greek, Syriac, and Coptic Traditions,' *Journal of the Canadian Society for Syriac Studies* 8 (2008), p. 7.

[59] George, Bishop of the Arab Tribes, *Commentary on the Liturgy*, p. *3 (ed. and trans. R. H. Connolly and H. W. Codrington, *Two Commentaries on the Jacobite Liturgy by George Bishop of the Arab Tribes and Moses Bar Kepha, together with the Syriac Anaphora of St. James and a Document Entitled The Book of Life* [London/Oxford, 1913]. My translation, but an ET is also available on p. 1).

[60] BL Add. 12,172, fols. 100a–100b. See below, Chapter 7, n. 34.

[61] Rebutting Chalcedonians demanded investigating the patristic witnesses they used and showing that they had been taken out of context or falsely attributed; sometimes, Severus lamented, required books were simply not to be found. See Severus of Antioch, *Letters* (*Letter 34, To Elisha*), pp. 100–103 (quote at 100), in E. W. Brooks, ed. and trans., *A Collection of Letters of Severus of Antioch, from Numerous Syriac Manuscripts* (PO 12.2) (Paris, 1919). The ET used here is mine. (For this point, cf. Allen and Hayward, *Severus of Antioch*, p. 27).

[62] See the evidence in Chapter 8, below.

But even having access to books, or at least the Scriptures, was no guarantee that a person would have an interest in studying them. 'Tell me,' John Chrysostom asked his congregation, 'who of you that stand here, if he were required, could repeat one Psalm, or any other portion of the divine Scriptures? There is not one.' There were, it would seem, some laymen who felt that it was not their job to read and study the Bible: 'But what is the answer to these charges?' Chrysostom went on: "I am not," you will say, "one of the monks, but I have both a wife and children and the care of a household."'[63] In the seventh century, mention of Marutha of Tikrit (d. 649) and others traveling to study prompted the Miaphysite writer Denḥā to scold his readers about their own interest in learning: 'When we therefore hear these things, my brothers,' he wrote,

> How do we not deserve punishment and complete condemnation, if these holy men persevered, exhausted and afflicted, in various places over a long period of time in order to attain knowledge of the Holy Scriptures and Orthodox teachers, but we, staying in our cities and in our houses are not diligent to teach ourselves or our children and give them instruction in the divine teachings? Neither do we concern ourselves with hearing the reading of the Scriptures which are always read out in the churches on Sundays and holy feast days.[64]

Like Chrysostom, Denḥā was disappointed in those who were content to leave study and learning to certain members of the clergy. At the end of the tenth century, the laments of Ps.-Samuel of Qalamūn's *Apocalypse* about what would come to pass in the last days can be read as a commentary on his views of what was happening in his own time in Egypt. He sounded notes similar to what we have already heard from other church leaders:

> They spend more time in places of conversation where there is food and drink than they do in the church of God. They will be sitting in the streets of the markets, taking interest in the matters of the world and not concerned at all in the church. It will not occur to their hearts that the Scripture portions are being read and are escaping their notice—even also the Gospel they will not hear. They

[63] John Chrysostom, *Homilies on Matthew* 2.5 (PG 57, col. 30; ET by G. Prevost taken from *NPNF*, ser. 1, vol. 10 [New York, 1888], p. 13 [2.9–10 in the English translation]; I have slightly altered the English translation). Cf. A. von Harnack, *Bible Reading in the Early Church*, trans. J. R. Wilkinson (London/New York, 1912), pp. 125–26. This passage was already being cited as evidence for low levels of private scripture reading in the early modern period; see J. Scholefield, ed., *The Works of James Pilkington, B.D., Lord Bishop of Durham* (Cambridge, 1842), p. 609. On the question of the access to books in Theodore, Diodore, and Chrysostom, see also the brief comments in R.C. Hill, *Reading the Old Testament in Antioch* (Atlanta, 2005), p. 12 (and cf. 47–50 for Antioch more generally).

[64] Denḥā, *Life of Marutha*, p. 71 (ed. F. Nau, *Histoires d'Ahoudemmeh et de Marouta, métropolitains jacobites de Tagrit et de l'Orient (VIe et VIIe siècles), suivies du traité d'Ahoudemmeh sur l'homme* [PO 3.1] [Paris, 1905]).

> will only show up in church at the conclusion of the liturgy. Some of them will do works they should not, since they are preoccupied with their own affairs and so miss the scripture portions. They will come to the church and take the Gospel and ask about the passage which was read and stand in a corner and read it alone and make themselves a law.[65]

One might point out, of course, that it is often the job of church leaders to be unhappy about the behavior and moral state of their flocks. Granting this, however, such passages nevertheless raise the question of just how many Christians were deeply interested in what went on in, and was taught by, their churches—if and when they attended.

What is more, the words of Ps.-Samuel, Denḥā, and Chrysostom's rhetorical layman should not lead us to imagine that the clergy were necessarily more engaged in the Christian faith than the laity, or even that they would know the Scriptures that well: 'Let the monk who knows only one Psalm,' one church canon stipulated, 'repeat the same one in all the prayers.'[66] Philoxenus of Mabbug (d. 523) lamented that people became monks for a variety of 'unhealthy reasons'—among them, escaping debt or slavery, parental coercion, or abuse from one's wife,[67] and Severus of Antioch grumbled that many people were treating ordination to the priesthood as if it were a trade, something they could do to earn money. For them it was the same as being a metalworker or a carpenter or doing some other job, 'as if it were unlawful for us here to procure the necessities of life from any office other than this.'[68]

[65] Ps.-Samuel of Qalamūn, *Apocalypse*, p. 379 (ed. and trans. J. Ziadeh, 'L'Apocalypse de Samuel, supérieur de Deir-el-Qalamoun,' *ROC* 20 [1915–1917]; FT available on p. 391). On this text and its date, see A. Papaconstantinou, '"They Shall Speak the Arabic Language and Take Pride in It": Reconsidering the Fate of Coptic after the Arab Conquest,' *LM* 120 (2007), pp. 273–99.

[66] *Rules for the Monks in Persia* 22 (ed. and trans. Vööbus, *Syriac and Arabic Documents*, p. 92; my translation). A slightly different ET by Vööbus is available, p. 92. These canons were transmitted by Bar Hebraeus (d. 1286). Compare this rule with the anonymous Karshūnī collection of monastic rules, named by Vööbus the *Anonymous Rules for the Monks*, 22: 'The monk who knows one Psalm only shall repeat that Psalm in all the prayers' (p. 112, my translation) and with the East Syrian Isho' bar Nun's (d. 828) stipulation: 'If a monk knows well only one single Psalm, he shall fill his time with it; but if he knows well many Psalms, thus he shall not fill his time with only one, but shall find satisfaction in all' (Canon 13, translation by Vööbus, p. 202).

[67] Philoxenus of Mabbug, *Discourses* 3 (ed. E.A.W. Budge, *The Discourses of Philoxenus Bishop of Mabbôgh* [London, 1894], vol. 1, p. 70 [Syriac] = vol. 2, p. 66 [ET], though for this translation, see R. Kitchen, *The Discourses of Philoxenos of Mabbug: A New Translation and Introduction* [Collegeville, MN, 2013], p. 53). Note *Canons of Marutha* 54.27, 28, 30, 32, 33 suggest a number of other motivations for becoming a monk, many of which do not stem from what might be considered reasons of sincere religious motivation (ed. Vööbus, *Syriac and Arabic Documents Regarding Legislation Relative to Syrian Asceticism*, pp. 144–45).

[68] Severus would also complain that men who had come to Antioch from Constantinople and its environs were writing him a steady stream of letters, seeking ordination and not realizing the financial

Lay knowledge of sophisticated doctrines might be suspect: The *Teaching of the Apostles*, a text written in Greek in the third century but which enjoyed a long afterlife in Syriac, prohibited a layman or a widow from teaching: 'Indeed, when they speak without the knowledge of doctrine, they bring blasphemy against the word.'[69] Gregory of Nazianzen devoted an entire oration to arguing that there was an order in the Christian community, and that teaching and speaking about God should be a task reserved for only certain persons. For Gregory, the truly humble person was the one 'who shows restraint in discussing God' and knows when 'to admit his ignorance.' He or she 'yields to the one who has been charged with speaking and accepts the fact that another is more spiritually endowed and has made greater progress in contemplation.' There was a danger when one who was not a teacher sought to give instruction or to debate theological ideas: 'Once we get our hands on a little glory,' Gregory complained, 'and often not even that, by managing to memorize at random two or three phrases of Scripture, and these hopelessly out of context... we are forced into the impossible position of rejecting Moses and identifying with the godless scoundrels Dathan and Abiram' (cf. Numbers 16:1–35).[70] In the late seventh century, in fact, when the Quinisext Council forbade a layperson from teaching in pubic, it would invoke Gregory's ideas.[71]

Christians who could read and did possess books nevertheless might show an alarming lack of interest in what those books contained. Chrysostom complained that dice were more commonly found in Christian homes than Christian books, and that those did have books never consulted them, using them as objects of pride rather than study: 'They tie up their books, and keep them always put away in cases, and all their care is for the fineness of the parch-

---

strain it would put on an already over-burdened church. Severus of Antioch, *Select Letters* 1.5 (*Letter to Timostratus*) (ed. and trans. Brooks, 1.1.45–48 [Syriac] = 2.1.41–44 [ET]. This ET is taken from Allen and Hayward, *Severus of Antioch*, pp. 139).

[69] *Teaching of the Apostles* 15 (ed. and trans. A. Vööbus, *The Didascalia Apostolorum in Syriac* [CSCO 407-408: SS 179-180] [Louvain, 1979] p. 158 [Syriac] = p. 144 [ET]). The ET used here is that of Vööbus. See (CSCO 401: SS 175) pp. *11–*69 for a discussion of the 41 different manuscripts Vööbus used for his edition. On this passage, see M.-Y. Perrin, 'À propos de la participation du peuple fidèle aux controverses doctrinales dans l'antiquité tardive: considerations introductives,' *Antiquité tardive* 9 (2001), p. 191, and cf. Chadwick, *The Role of the Christian Bishop*, p. 14. R. Gryson, 'The Authority of the Teacher in the Ancient and Medieval Church,' *Journal of Ecumenical Studies* 19 (1982), pp. 179–180, notes that from the mid-third century onward evidence increasingly suggests that ordained priests exclusively took over the office of teaching in the church.

[70] Gregory of Nazianzus, *Orations* 32.19, 17 (ed. C. Moreschini, *Grégoire de Nazianze. Discours 32-37* [SC 318] [Paris, 1985], pp. 122, 124, 126; ET from M. Vinson, *St. Gregory Nazianzus: Select Orations* [Washington, D.C., 2003], p. 205, p. 203). For Gregory's attitudes in this sermon, see J. Maxwell, 'The Attitudes of Basil and Gregory of Nazianzus toward Uneducated Christians,' *Studia Patristica* 47 (2010), p. 119.

[71] Council in Trullo, *Canons* 64 (ed. Joannou, *Discipline générale antique*, vol. 1.1, pp. 201–202).

ments, and the beauty of the letters, but not for reading them.'[72] There were also those for whom church teachings were simply a means to some other end. We hear condemnations of people who might adopt whatever doctrine passed for orthodoxy in the name of advancing a career,[73] and there are reports of men making charges of religious heresy not out of conviction but rather so that they could seize the houses and property of those they were accusing of rejecting the council of Chalcedon.[74] Such considerations should give us pause before assuming that the ordinary Christian would have had a strong understanding of the theological issues at stake in the formation of separate churches. The same reservations hold for members of the clergy as well.

GREGORY OF NYSSA

But when the question arises of what the average person, a nonspecialist, would have or actually could have understood when it came to the sophisticated Christian theological debates that convulsed Roman society from the fourth century onward, that question is inevitably, and sometimes almost exclusively addressed by making reference to Gregory of Nyssa's (d. after 386) celebrated statement that the alleys, streets, and squares of Constantinople were filled with talk over the Arian controversy and that clothing peddlers, money changers, and grocers seemed more interested in asking their customers what they made of various Arian slogans than they were in transacting business.[75] It is a proof text with a long and esteemed pedigree—Gibbon, Hegel, and others have invoked it since it was first adduced as a piece of evidence by John Jortain in the eighteenth century.[76] It has had an unfortunately distorting effect on these discussions.

[72] John Chrysostom, *Homilies on John* 32.3 (PG 59, cols. 186–87; ET by G. T. Stupart taken from *NPNF*, ser. 1, vol. 14 [New York, 1889], p. 114). Cf. Scholefield, ed., *The Works of James Pilkington*, p. 609.

[73] See *Codex Justinianus* 1.5.18.5 (ed. P. Krueger, *Corpus Iuris Civilis*, vol. 2: *Codex Iustinianus* [Berlin, 1906], p. 57; ET based on the work of F. H. Blume available in B. W. Frier et al., eds., *The Codex of Justinian: A New Annotated Translation with Parallel Latin and Greek Text*, vol. 1 [Cambridge, 2016], p. 213). For this point, see A. Kaldellis, *Prokopios: The Secret History with Related Texts* (Indianapolis, 2010), p. 53, n. 82. Procopius may in fact be a rare example of one such figure who speaks explicitly about his lack of interest in the Christological controversies.

[74] John of Ephesus, *Ecclesiastical History* 5.21 (ed. E. W. Brooks, *Iohannis Ephesini historiae ecclesiasticae pars tertia* [CSCO III.3] [Paris, 1935], pp. 271–72).

[75] Gregory of Nyssa, *Oration on the Divinity of the Son and the Holy Spirit*, p. 121 (ed. E. Rhein in *Gregorii Nysseni Opera* 10.2 [Leiden/New York/København/Köln, 1996]; an ET is available in R. Lim, *Public Disputation, Power, and Social Order in Late Antiquity* [Berkeley, 1995], p. 149). For a rejection of the alleged connection between circus factions in Constantinople and Christological stances, see A. Cameron, *Circus Factions: Blues and Greens at Rome and Byzantium* (Oxford, 1976), pp. 126–53.

[76] See the discussion of M. Cassin, '*De deitate filii et spiritus sancti et in Abraham*,' in V. H. Drecoll

When thinking about this famous passage, we should remember that the levels of literacy and theological awareness in the capital city of the Eastern Roman Empire will likely have been much higher than they were in say, Upper Egypt, northern Syria, the small towns and villages of Anatolia, or the mountains of Lebanon. But Constantinople was no more the Eastern Roman Empire than London is the United Kingdom, New York City the United States of America, or Cairo the whole of Egypt. We should always attempt to resist embracing the easy solipsism of the metropole, especially in a context where there were vastly more people living in rural places than there were in Constantinople.

Rather than simply reading Gregory's words literally and taking them to represent the experience of the entire population of the whole Roman world, we might seek out other contexts that might be applied to help us better understand their meaning. Neil McLynn, for instance, has suggested that Gregory's statement reflects his own personal experience as 'the representative of an unpopular party' walking the streets of Constantinople, and not as a description of normal experience and conversation in the city.[77] Alternatively, in addition to seeing the passage as a 'rhetorical exaggeration,' Matthieu Cassin has suggested that it should be read as an artifice that Gregory used to warn of the social danger that would ensue if the boundaries of heresy and orthodoxy were not clearly defined and affirmed. The city would descend into a chaos of religious debate.[78]

We should keep in mind other pieces of evidence from Constantinople, too, which might limit the scope of the implications given to Gregory's famous passage. 'I know indeed that what now has been said cannot by many be comprehended,' John Chrysostom told his congregation after attempting to explain the co-eternity of the Father and the Son. 'Therefore it is that in many places we avoid agitating questions of human reasonings, because the rest of the people cannot follow such arguments, and if they could, still they have nothing firm or sure in them.'[79] I am more interested here in Chalcedon than

---

and M. Berghaus, eds., *Gregory of Nyssa: The Minor Treatises on Trinitarian Theology and Apollinarism* (Leiden/Boston, 2011), pp. 285–86.

[77] N. McLynn, 'Christian Controversy and Violence in the Fourth Century,' *Kodai* 3 (1992), pp. 33–34. See the comments on this argument in Cassin, '*De deitate filii et spiritus sancti et in Abraham*,' pp. 286–87.

[78] Cassin, '*De deitate filii et spiritus sancti et in Abraham*,' pp. 287–88. See also the discussion of various interpretations of this text in Perrin, 'À propos de la participation des fidèles aux controverses doctrinales,' pp. 188–189.

[79] John Chrysostom, *Homilies on John* 4.2 (PG 59, col. 48; the ET used here is that of G. T. Stupart, taken from *NPNF*, ser. 1, vol. 14, p. 17). For this, see Maxwell, *Christianization and Communication in Late Antiquity*, p. 97.

Nicaea, and though the issues being debated in the aftermath of Chalcedon were different from those to which Chrysostom referred, they were no less complex and difficult to understand. In terms of the issues at stake at Nicaea (and Constantinople I), as well as Chalcedon, Gregory's experience in the capital city can hardly have been typical.

LITERACY, THEOLOGICAL LITERACY, AND THE CLERGY

With this said, not all Christians, of course, were illiterate, theologically or otherwise. There were some who were supremely literate and indeed masters of the Christian tradition. They read works of great sophistication written by both Christians and pagans, and they composed their own works of great erudition and beauty. Those who wrote in Syriac translated medical, philosophical, scientific, and a vast number of theological works from Greek into Syriac. Neither were all Christians cut off from access to books containing sophisticated theological ideas.[80] But in speaking about such theologically literate Christians, we should be careful how we describe them. I have already mentioned reasons why we should not assume that being a member of the clergy meant that one was theologically literate.[81] If Jacob of Edessa felt the need to write out a scholion with detailed instructions for how a priest should celebrate a liturgy because, in his words, 'we see certain priests inappropriately and

[80] For overviews of Christian libraries, one can consult the following: W. E. Scudamore, 'Libraries,' in W. Smith and S. Cheetham, eds., *DCA*, vol. 2, pp. 985–88; J. de Ghellinck, 'Bibliothèques,' in *DSp*, vol. 1, cols. 1589–1606, esp. 1591–1600; C. Wendel, 'Bibliothek,' *RAC*, vol. 2, cols. 231–74, esp. 246–61; H. Leclercq, 'Bibliothèques,' in *DACL*, vol. 2.1, cols. 842–904; C. Wendel and W.Göber. 'IV. Die Kirche auf Griechisch-Römischem Boden,' pp. 128–39, as well as V. Burr, 'Der byzantinische Kulturkreis,' pp. 146–87 in F. Milkau and G. Leyh, eds., *Handbuch der Bibliothekswissenschaft*, vol. 3.1: *Geschichte der Bibliotheken* (Wiesbaden, 1955); Gamble, *Books and Readers*, pp. 144–202; and N. Wilson, 'Libraries in Byzantium and the West,' in *St Catherine's Monastery at Mount Sinai: Its Manuscripts and Their Conservation: Papers Given in Memory of Professor Ihor Ševčenko* (London, 2011), pp. 17-19 (for the medieval period). For libraries containing pagan authors and from a slightly earlier period, G. W. Houston, 'Papyrological Evidence for Book Collections and Libraries in the Roman Empire,' in W. A. Johnson and H. N. Parker, eds., *Ancient Literacies: The Culture of Reading in Greece and Rome* (Oxford/New York, 2009), pp. 243–67, is a good discussion.

[81] Note Gregory Nazianzen's lament about the possibility of a bishop's being theologically ignorant in *Orations* 21.24 (PG 35, col. 1109; ET by Browne and Swallow available in *NPNF*, ser. 2, vol. 7, p. 276). It was only at the Second Council of Nicaea in 787 that a requirement was made for bishops to know a certain amount about the Bible and church canons, Second Council of Nicaea, *Canons* 2 (ed. Joannou, *Discipline générale antique*, vol. 1.1, pp. 248–50, esp. 249). See the discussion of episcopal eligibility, accompanied by extensive citations, in A.W. Haddan's article, 'Bishop,' in *DCA*, vol. 1, pp. 219–20 and especially the discussion of the 'literary qualifications' of a bishop in E. Hatch's article, 'Orders, Holy,' in *DCA*, vol. 2, pp. 1487–88, where a great number of relevant witnesses are collected.

negligently drawing near to this divine service,'[82] and the Miaphysite bishop Moshe bar Kepha (d. 903) could write of the liturgical mistakes of priests who were 'untrained and ill-instructed' or 'uninstructed' or 'uninstructed and ignorant of the mysteries of the Christians,' what should we assume about the level of such clergymen's theological and not just ritual knowledge?[83] Priests aside, even being a bishop did not necessarily imply that a person was in fact literate, much less theologically literate.[84] One of the bishops present at the Council of Chalcedon, in fact, was illiterate.[85]

Over the course of late antiquity, this would gradually change. Or, at the least, the ideal of what a clergyman's level of knowledge should be evolved.[86] The East Syrian Synod of Mar Isaac in 410 attempted to set some minimal standards for ordination, decrying 'this vile and lax custom which has perversely taken place, of those who are youths with no instruction in the Scriptures having hands laid upon them with ease and speed and no discernment.' The synod ordered that no one younger than thirty was to be made a priest. A person 'simple in learning' (*hedyoṭ b-yulpānā*) who could not recite the Psalter was not even to be allowed appointment as a subdeacon.[87]

[82] Harvard Syriac 47, fol. 162v (the scholion is fols. 162v–163r).

[83] Moshe bar Kepha, *Commentary on the Liturgy*, pp. *28, *54, *62 (ed. and trans. Connolly and Codrington, *Two Commentaries on the Jacobite Liturgy*. I have used the ET of Connolly and Codrington, pp. 36, 61, 69). Note the sixth-century Miaphysite bishop Sergius bar Karya's observation that, despite the fact that the received tradition of the Fathers held that a priest could only add oil to the consecrated Myron if he had permission from the bishop to do so, 'priests are doing this everywhere.' See BL Add. 17,193, fol. 36a.

[84] The possibility of a bishop being illiterate is raised in *Apostolic Church Order* 16 (ed. and trans. J. P. Arendzen, 'An Entire Syriac Text of the "Apostolic Church Order,"' *JTS* O.S. 3 [9] [1901], pp. 68 [Syriac] = p. 69 [ET]). For the Greek text and English translation, see A. Stewart Sykes, *The Apostolic Church Order: The Greek Text with Introduction, Translation and Annotation* (Strathfield, NSW, 2006), p. 97 (Greek) = 109 (ET). A similar possibility is raised in *Apostolic Constitutions* 2.1 (ed. M. Metzger, *Les constitutions apostoliques* [SC 320] [Paris, 1985], p. 144; ET by W. Whiston and J. Donaldson available in *ANF*, vol. 7 [Buffalo, 1886], p. 396). On this, see C. Rapp, *Holy Bishops in Late Antiquity* (Berkeley, 2005), p. 179, who understands ἀγράμματος as 'illiterate,' (on the potential meanings of this word, however, cf. Gamble, *Books and Readers*, p. 9). In the Syriac version of the *Teaching of the Apostles*, this passage reads: 'But if it is possible, let him be instructed and able to teach but if he does not know letters (ܐܢܕܝܢ ܠܐ ܝܕܥ ܣܦܪܐ), he shall be capable and skillful in the word; and let him be advanced in years' (Translation A. Vööbus; for this text and translation, see Vööbus, ed. and trans., *The Didascalia Apostolorum in Syriac* [CSCO 401–402: SS 175–76] [Louvain, 1979], p. 52 [Syriac] = p. 44 [ET]. Here I have used Vööbus's translation).

[85] For this (and much more), see Chadwick, *The Role of the Christian Bishop*, p. 9.

[86] Peter Brown has suggested to me that increasing requirements of theological literacy among the ordained could also be interpreted as a way for church leaders to eliminate from the clergy those who—e.g., members of the *curiales*—might have been able to read and had an education, but who viewed ordination as a source of prestige and were not terribly interested in religious matters.

[87] Synod of Mar Isaac, *Canons* 16 (ed. J.-B.Chabot, *Synodicon Orientale* [Paris, 1902], pp. 29–30 [Syriac] = 269 [FT]).

It was not just the East Syrians who showed concern for the qualifications of their clergy. In the sixth century, John of Ephesus gave a vivid picture of the pains John of Tella (d. 538) took as he made the fateful decision to start large-scale ordinations of Miaphysite priests. Dozens, even hundreds, we are told, would come to him each day. John was a flurry of pastoral action teaching, admonishing, and most importantly ordaining new clergy. He was, John of Ephesus tells us,

> performing the ordinations after careful investigation and many testimonies given, subjecting every man to a careful examination and test in reading the Scriptures and repeating the psalms, and ability to write their names and signatures, not admitting anyone whomsoever who did not sign his name, and, if anyone was incapable of doing so, he would bid him learn... while he also inquired and learned who were the men of knowledge in all the districts, and he would send and fetch them, and give them instructions, and hand them the impress of his name and his monogram, themselves to see by investigation who were fit to become priests, and to write and send them to him, that he might not perform ordinations at random.[88]

Such a picture is undoubtedly an idealized and exaggerated one—we should not forget all of the factors we have considered that would have made achieving such a uniformly educated and capable clergy very difficult, if not impossible—but John's actions match well with other evidence that begins to appear in the sixth century about attitudes towards clerical literacy: rules among Chalcedonians against ordaining the illiterate to the priesthood[89] and references in an East Syrian context to those who had been unable to attain an ecclesiastical rank on account of their 'lack of training.'[90] We can therefore suggest that by this period, among Miaphysites, Chalcedonians, and East Syrians alike, it was increasingly unlikely that a bishop or even a clergyman would be totally unlettered.

But although notions of what was the ideal level of educational attainment for a clergyman had begun evolving by the sixth century, as late as the 620s

[88] John of Ephesus, *Lives of the Eastern Saints* 24 (ed. and trans. Brooks [PO 18.4] [Paris, 1924], pp. 316–17; the translation is that of Brooks).

[89] Justinian, *Novels* 6.4 (ed. R. Schoell and G. Kroll, *Corpus Iuris Civilis*, vol. 3: *Novellae* [Berlin, 1912], p. 42; an ET by F. Blume is available online at: http://www.uwyo.edu/lawlib/blume-justinian/ajc-edition-2/novels/1-40/novel%206_replacement.pdf). Also see *Novels* 123, c. 12 (ed. Schoell and Kroll, *Novellae*, p. 604), which forbade anyone being ordained to the clergy unless he 'knows letters.' (ET by Blume available here: http://www.uwyo.edu/lawlib/blume-justinian/ajc-edition-2/novels/121-140/novel%20123_replacement.pdf). For this, see Hatch, 'Orders, Holy,' p. 1487.

[90] See Synod of Ezekiel (AD 576), *Canons* 34 (ed. Chabot, *Synodicon Orientale*, p. 127 [Syriac] = 386 [FT]). Note that Chabot translated *lā mdarshuthon* as 'manque d'éducation.' Similarly, see Sokoloff, *A Syriac Lexicon*, p. 718, s.v. ܡܕܪܫܘܬܐ, where *lā mdarshutā* is understood to mean 'lack of erudition.'

or early 630s, it was still possible to find the Emperor Heraclius exiling Cyrus, the Chalcedonian bishop of Edessa, to Cyprus after discovering that he struggled to read the Gospel. 'O man,' the Emperor is supposed to have asked him, 'How did you become a bishop and you cannot read the Gospel well?' While on Cyprus, one of the things Heraclius wanted Cyrus to do was learn how to read.[91] One of the points for which the Miaphysite patriarch Julian (sed. 687–708) was praised was that 'he only advanced to the episcopate those who were trained in divine teaching and wisdom and adorned with spiritual behavior.'[92] Even as late as 790, we find that the Miaphysites had elected as their patriarch a man named Joseph (sed. 790–792) who, we are told, had an impressive stature, but when people 'tasted his speech, he was found to be simple (*brirā*) and they wanted to return him to his monastery.'[93]

In regions with competing churches that had rival hierarchies, the ranks of those with sufficient education to serve in the episcopate or even the priesthood must have been stretched.[94] Such was the case, for instance, in North Africa, where hundreds of episcopal sees, combined with both Donatist and Catholic hierarchies, meant that there were not enough elites to fill all the bishoprics: 'In fact, quite a significant number of North African bishops came from the lower class of *coloni* (tenant farmers), whose education was little more than rudimentary.'[95]

If being in the clergy did not guarantee that one would fully understand the issues of Chalcedon or even have a strong grasp of the Christian tradition, the converse, being a layperson, did not mean that one was illiterate, theologically or otherwise.[96] The theologically literate were a small subset of the literate,

[91] 'Go now,' the emperor continued, 'to this island and enter into it and learn to read and other matters from the affairs of the church.' Maḥbūb b. Qusṭanṭīn, *Kitāb al-'Unwān*, p. 207 (ed. A.-A. Vasiliev, *Kitab al-'unvan (Histoire universelle, écrite par Agapius de Menbidj)* [PO 8.3] [Paris, 1912]).

[92] Bar Hebraeus, *Ecclesiastical History* 1.55 (ed. Abbeloos and Lamy, vol. 1, col. 295).

[93] Michael the Great, *Chronicle* 12.3 (ed. Chabot, 4.483 [Syriac] = 3.10). Or 'perceived his speech. . . .'

[94] Though a highly confessionalized setting, characterized by competition between groups may, as we will see later, have led to a rise in levels of literacy.

[95] See Rapp, *Holy Bishops in Late Antiquity*, p. 178, for this point about the pool of potential bishops and the quote. See more generally, 173–78, for a discussion of this important phenomenon of 'Bishops of Modest Background,' which has informed and guided what I have written here. But for N. Africa having more bishoprics than anywhere else in the empire, see Dossey, *Peasant and Empire*, p. 125.

[96] Athanasius bar Gummaye, an Edessene elite who lived in the time of the Caliph 'Abd al-Malik (reg. 685–705) and who was 'well instructed in the books of the church and those of the pagans' (*barrāyē*), would be an example of a theologically literate layman: see Michael the Great, *Chronicle* 11.16 (ed. Chabot, *Chronique* 4.447–48 [Syriac] = 2.475–76 [French]; on Athanasius and his family, see now M. Debié, 'Christians in the Service of the Caliph: Through the Looking Glass of Communal Identities,' in Borrut and Donner, *Christians and Others*, pp. 53–71). So would Tribunus, a sixth-century layman who knew Greek and Syriac and worshipped and read the Scriptures in both languages and even lived in a monastic community, though he did not receive ordination; see John of Ephesus, *Lives of the Eastern*

and their numbers included both lay and clergy. In a world that was fracturing over theological speculation that few seemed equipped to properly understand, what means did these people have for spreading their views in a society such as the one I have been describing?

MEANS OF INSTRUCTION

Even if a person could not read Severus, there were other settings where he or she might encounter his ideas or those of his theological opponents: reading was not the only way a person might acquire knowledge, and we should not set up literacy as a red herring—people spoke with one another and ideas were communicated orally. In the order of salvation, we should remember, hearing held a privileged place. Faith, the Apostle Paul wrote, cometh by hearing (Romans 10:17); he did not write that it came by reading. Most obviously, if one was unable to read, he or she could nevertheless learn through listening to someone else read, and there is evidence that in late antiquity Christians did just this.[97] St. Augustine took up a book and read at his moment of conversion, but it was hearing the Gospel of Matthew read out in church that inspired St. Anthony to take up a life of asceticism.[98] At the root of the

Saints 44 (ed. Brooks [PO 18.4], pp. 459–668). The Emperor Justinian could also be considered a theologically literate layman.

[97] See the remarks and evidence in N. Horsfall, 'Statistics or State of Mind?' in *Literacy in the Roman World*, pp. 73–74, along with the observation in Gamble, *Books and Readers*, p. 205. Early modern England can serve as a useful point of comparison: see the observations and evidence in Thomas, 'The Meaning of Literacy in Early Modern England,' p. 107. Note the passage in the *Teaching of Addai*, quoted above (Chapter 1, n. 24), where it is stated that at the Last Day a person will not ask his friend to read things for him. When they appear in the *Teaching of Addai*, texts invariably are read out to their audience or addressee and not read privately by an individual. For example: Abgar's letter to Jesus is read out to Jesus (*3/7); the reports of the deeds worked by Christ through the Apostles, written by the Apostles to James and the Christians in Jerusalem, were read out in the congregation there (*17/35); Addai writes a letter to Narses, the king of the Assyrians, and he 'hears' it (*37/75); Abgar sends Tiberius a letter and Tiberius has it read out in his presence (*38/77) (page numbers refer to the Syriac text edited by G. Phillips and the ET by G. Howard in *The Teaching of Addai*). Note also the negative assessment by Ps.-Samuel of Qalamūn (Chapter 1, n. 65), of those who 'stand in a corner and read [the Scripture] alone and make themselves a law.' Reading could be understood as a communal or group experience. Note also the observation in E. A. Clark, *Reading Renunciation: Asceticism and Scripture in Early Christianity* (Princeton, 1999), p. 49: '... inability to read did not exclude the uneducated from Christian culture ...'.

[98] Athanasius, *Life of Anthony* 2 (Syriac text in R. Draguet, *La vie primitive de S. Antoine conservée en syriaque* [CSCO 417: SS 183] [Louvain, 1980] pp. 8–9). The Greek of these passages can be found in PG 26, cols. 841, 844 [= G.J.M. Bartelink, ed., *Vie d'Antoine* [SC 400] [Paris, 2004], p. 132]; ET of the Greek available R.C. Gregg, *Athanasius: The Life of Antony and the Letter to Marcellinus* [Mahwah, N.J., 1980], p. 31).

idea of 'catechesis,' we should remember, is the notion of oral instruction or teaching by mouth.[99]

For most Christians, the preeminent site of theological instruction will have been the liturgy: it was here that one heard the Scriptures read, it was here that the great events of salvation history were commemorated, and it was here that one heard repeated at each Eucharistic celebration the story of Christ's death and resurrection. It was here, too, that one could encounter the distinctive theological doctrines that separated one confession from another: when John the Almsgiver became the Chalcedonian patriarch of Alexandria in 609, 'he found only seven churches maintaining the services of the Orthodox liturgy'—that is, using the shorter version of the *Trisagion*—'and by much diligence he succeeded in increasing the number to seventy. . . .'[100] But more than even a longer or shorter version of the *Trisagion*, the liturgies of the various competing churches would eventually contain Christologically distinct language and be imbued with their particular theologies.[101] An important aspect, in fact, of the separation of Christian communities in the Middle East was the gradual evolution of distinct liturgies for each of the respective Christian groups.[102] Surviving homilies show that Christological ideas might be communicated in preaching to a wider audience, at least by some speakers,[103] and the copying, circulation, and public reading of homilies by important figures like Severus or Jacob of Sarugh will have spread the ideas of these men to

[99] See the comment in O. Pasquato and H. Brakmann's article 'Ketechese (Katechismus)' in *RAC*, vol. 20 (Stuttgart, 1950–), col. 424.

[100] *Life of John the Almsgiver* 5 (ed. H. Delehaye, 'Une vie inédite de Saint Jean l'Aumonier,' *AB* 45 [1927], p. 21; ET taken from Dawes and Baynes, *Three Byzantine Saints*, p. 201). On the authorship of this text, see most conveniently, Dawes and Baynes, pp. 195–96, and H. Chadwick, 'John Moschus and His Friend Sophronius the Sophist,' *JTS* 25 (1974), p. 50, esp. n. 4.

[101] See A. Baumstark, *On the Historical Development of the Liturgy*, trans. F. West (Collegeville, MN, 2011), p. 166. In the case of the Syrian Orthodox church, the *sedrē* prayers of its offices, sometimes as old as perhaps the sixth century, are rich repositories of theology. On the theological importance of the *sedro* and its alteration in the Uniate printing of the Mosul fenqitho, see S. Plathottathil, 'Themes of Incarnation in the Sedrē for the Period of Sūborō-Yaldō according to Mosul Fenqitho,' *PdO* 36 (2011), pp. 287–97, esp. 290–92.

[102] See my "Greek Canons and the Syrian Orthodox Liturgy," in B. Bitton-Ashkelony and D. Krueger, eds. *Prayer and Worship in Eastern Christianities, 6th to 11th Centuries* (London/New York, 2017), pp. 151–80.

[103] On late antique sermons, especially as a vehicle for communicating doctrinal information, see the groundbreaking work of P. M. Forness, 'Preaching and Religious Debate: Jacob of Serugh and the Promotion of his Christology in the Roman Near East.' PhD diss., Princeton Theological Seminary, 2016. J. Maxwell, 'Popular Theology in Late Antiquity,' in L. Grig, ed., *Popular Culture in the Ancient World* (Cambridge, 2017), pp. 277–95, offers a rich exploration of the theological information conveyed in martyrs sermons, and, moreover, makes a compelling argument for theological knowledge and engagement among ordinary Christians, and against any attempts at setting 'popular religion' and 'theology' in opposition to one another.

audiences which may have never had the chance to hear them in person or who lived after their deaths.[104] What is more, the ferment of the Christological controversies led to the introduction, at some point in the early sixth century, of the practice of reciting the Nicene-Constantinopolitan creed in the liturgy.[105] Once this practice spread, the creed would have been widely memorized in a liturgical context and therefore was not quite as limited in its circulation by the high cost of parchment or by an inability to read.[106] Even before the introduction of the creed, the words of the liturgy already contained within them a summary of Christian belief.[107] Catechesis, where available, would have provided systematic teaching about basic Christian theological and moral teachings.[108] Furthermore, acclamations or slogans, like the famous 'One nature of God the Word Incarnate,' might encapsulate in one sentence a theological position and serve as literal rallying cries.[109] Visually, the changing of images of bishops in churches and monasteries signaled to the faithful those leaders whose teaching was approved,[110] something which could also be learned from

[104] See, e.g., Gennadius of Marseilles, *Lives of Illustrious Men* 58 (ed. E. C. Richardson, *Hieronymus liber De viris inlustribus; Gennadius liber De viris inlustribus* [Leipzig, 1896], p. 81), on Cyril of Alexandria's being recommended for declamation by Greek bishops. In his own lifetime, Severus made provision for his sermons to be read out by others (see Chapter 2, n. 103). The existence of homilaries also points to this practice of copying, collecting, and reading out the homilies of venerated and respected teachers. The *vita* of a Christian holy man might also be used to spread Christological doctrine; for one example of this, see G. J. Reinink, 'Babai the Great's Life of George and the Propagation of Doctrine in the Late Sasanian Empire,' in J. W. Drijvers and J. W. Watt, eds., *Portraits of Spiritual Authority: Religious Power in Early Christianity, Byzantium and the Christian Orient* (Leiden, 1999), pp. 171–94.

[105] On the history of the introduction of the creed into the liturgy, see R. F. Taft, *The Great Entrance: A History of the Transfer of Gifts and Other Pre-Anaphoral Rites of the Liturgy of St. John Chrysostom* (Rome, 1975), pp. 400–405, and W. Kinzig, 'The Creed in the Liturgy: Prayer or Hymn?' in A. Gerhards and C. Leonhard, eds., *Jewish and Christian Liturgy and Worship: New Insights into Its History and Interaction* (Leiden/Boston, 2007), pp. 229–46, esp. 234–42.

[106] On the cost of parchment and books, see N. G. Wilson, 'Books and Readers in Byzantium,' in Mango and Ševčenko, eds., *Byzantine Books and Bookmen*, pp. 1–4, though books made from papyrus may have been cheaper than those made from parchment: see M. Mullett, 'Writing in Early Medieval Byzantium,' in R. McKitterick, ed., *The Uses of Literacy in Early Medieval Europe* (Cambridge, 1990), p. 158, and Gamble, *Books and Readers*, pp. 43–48.

[107] Cf. Taft, *The Great Entrance*, pp. 404–405.

[108] For a systematic overview of Christian catechetical material from the first seven centuries A.D., see O. Pasquato and H. Brakmann's 'Ketechese (Katechismus)' in *RAC*, vol. 20, cols. 422–96.

[109] See for instance the mixture of political and theological acclamations that took place at the Second Council of Ephesus in 449: *Acts of the Second Council of Ephesus*, pp. 15–21 (ed. J.P.G. Flemming, *Akten der Ephesinischen Synode vom Jahre 449: Syrisch. Abhandlungen der Königlichen Gesellschaft der Wissenschaften zu Göttingen, Philologisch-Historische Klasse*, N.F. 15.1. [Berlin, 1917]; ET available in S.G.F. Perry, *The Second Synod of Ephesus, together with Certain Extracts Relating to it, from Syriac Mss. Preserved in the British Museum* [Dartford, 1881], pp. 45–54). On acclamations, see P.R.L. Brown, *Power and Persuasion in Late Antiquity: Towards a Christian Empire* (Madison, Wisc., 1992), pp. 149–50.

[110] John of Ephesus, *Ecclesiastical History* 1.11, 2.27, 2.34 (ed. Brooks [CSCO SS III.3], pp. 11, 91–92,

the names of those previous leaders prayed for in the diptychs of various communities.[111]

In addition to the words of the liturgy, music and hymnody played important roles in providing religious instruction to everyday Christians. If we turn for a moment to the theological controversies that wracked the Christian community before the disagreement between Cyril and Nestorius, we learn that Arius himself was said to have composed songs that could be sung while people were sailing, while they were working at a mill, while they were travelling, and in other everyday settings.[112] And Arius was not the only Christian author to put hymns to sailing songs in the fourth century.[113] Decades after Arius had died, Arians in Constantinople were using the nocturnal chanting of hymns to propagate their message, and John Chrysostom, 'fearing lest any more of the simple (ἁπλουστέρων) should be drawn away from the church by such kind of hymns' had Nicenes do their own night-chanting, complete with imperially financed silver crosses. The competing chanting led to violence and even deaths.[114] Further east, Ephrem the Syrian, the greatest of all Syriac poets, was reputed to have taken up the writing of hymns in the fourth century to counteract the spread of dangerous theological ideas through the popularity of the songs of Harmonius, the supposed son of Bardaisan, the third-century Aramaic-speaking Christian thinker who would be a theological *bête noire* for

---

100; ET available in R. Payne Smith, *The Third Part of the Ecclesiastical History of John Bishop of Ephesus* [Oxford, 1860], pp. 9, 135, 145).

[111] See, e.g., John of Ephesus, *Ecclesiastical History* 2.11 (ed. Brooks [CSCO SS III.3], p. 73; ET in Payne Smith, *The Third Part*, pp. 108–109); also, cf. 1.41, 2.34. For more examples of the importance of prayers of remembrance for identity, see Ps.-Zacharias Rhetor, *Chronicle* 7.7, 7.8 (ed. E.W. Brooks, *Historia Ecclesiastica Zachariae Rhetori vulgo adscripta II* [CSCO 84: SS 39], pp. 39 [7.7], 42, 47 [7.8]; ET available in F.J. Hamilton and E.W. Brooks, *The Syriac Chronicle Known as That of Zachariah of Mitylene* [London, 1899], pp. 168 [7.7], 171, 175 [7.8]); and Severus of Antioch, *Select Letters* 1.24 ('To Theoteknos') (ed. and trans. Brooks, 1.194 [Syriac] = 2.1.84 [ET]). Note that when the East Syrian Patriarch Isho'yahb II of Gdala met Heraclius at Aleppo and celebrated several liturgies for him, he would do so only on the condition that Heraclius allow him to omit the name of Cyril from the diptychs; the Romans, in turn, wanted the names of Theodore, Diodore, and Nestorius omitted. See *Chronicle of Seert* 2.93 (ed. Scher [and Griveau] [PO 13.4], pp. 238–40) and cf. Chapter 3, n. 70.

[112] Philostorgius, *Church History* 2.2 (ed. J. Bidez and F. Winkelmann, *Philostorgius Kirchengeschichte* [3rd edition] [Berlin, 1981], p. 13; ET available in P. R. Amidon, *Philostorgius: Church History* [Atlanta, 2007], p. 16). C. R. Galvão-Sobrinho, *Doctrine and Power: Theological Controversy and Christian Leadership in the Later Roman Empire* (Berkeley, 2013), pp. 47–65, is an excellent discussion of the various ways in which theological ideas were disseminated to larger audiences of ordinary people by Arius and his supporters in Alexandria.

[113] See M. L. West, 'The Metre of Arius' *Thalia*,' *JTS* 33 (1982), p. 105.

[114] Eventually, the Arians were prohibited from their night music. See Socrates, *Ecclesiastical History* 6.8 (ed. G. C. Hansen, *Sokrates Kirchengeschichte* [Berlin, 1995], pp. 325–26. ET taken from E. Walford(?) and A. C. Zenos in *NPNF*, ser. 2, vol. 2 [New York, 1890], p. 144).

Christians well into the Islamic period.[115] Miaphysites remembered the sixth-century Chalcedonian poet Isaac of Antioch as having 'introduced the heresy of Nestorianism into Edessa' and having composed verse homilies (*mēmrē*) that 'mocked Christ.'[116] The East Syrian Narsai (d. ca. 500), by contrast, was remembered for using his metrical homilies to communicate the ideas of Theodore of Mopsuestia to a wider audience.[117] In fact, Narsai was said to have written *mēmrē* in order to counteract the efforts of the Miaphysite Jacob of Sarugh (d. 521), who had begun 'to compose his heresy and error hypocritically by the way of the *mēmrē*, which he composed, since through the pleasant composition of enticing sounds he drew the bulk of the people from the Glorious One.' Narsai's response, the East Syrian historian Barhadbshabba reported, was to 'set down the true opinion of orthodoxy in the manner of *mēmrē*, fitted upon sweet tones. He combined the meaning of the scriptures according to the opinion of the holy fathers in pleasant antiphons in the likeness of the blessed David.'[118] According to the anonymous author of a *vita* of Severus of Antioch, the famous bishop composed songs for the people of Antioch with a number of goals in mind: to draw them into church and away from the theater, to encourage them to love God, to teach them doctrine and precise dogma, to instruct them in the Scriptures, and to exhort them to good works, among other things.[119]

And though I have stressed the rural and agrarian nature of much late antique Christianity, this should be further nuanced, and attention should be paid to just where it was that people were living: 'the Late Roman East was studded with rural settlements,' it has been pointed out, 'it was a landscape of villages.'[120] It was in these villages that farmers typically lived, and there is

[115] See Sozomen, *Ecclesiastical History* 3.16 (ed. J. Bidez and G. C. Hansen, *Sozomenus Kirchengeschichte* [Berlin, 1960], pp. 128–29; ET by C. D. Hartranft available in P. Schaff and H. Wace, eds., *NPNF*, ser. 2, vol. 2, p. 296]). On the question of Harmonius's (non-) existence, see H.J.W. Drijvers, *Bardaiṣan of Edessa* (Assen, 1966), pp. 180–83.

[116] See the marginal note preserved in the *Chronicle to 846* (ed. Brooks [CSCO SS III.4], p. 217, n. 1). There are three or perhaps four different writers who are known as 'Isaac of Antioch'; on this particular Isaac, see the article 'Isḥaq of Edessa,' by E. G. Matthews, Jr. in *GEDSH*, p. 213.

[117] Barhadbshabba, *The Cause of the Foundation of the Schools*, pp. 68–69 (ed. A. Scher, *Mar Barhadbšabba 'Arbaya, évêque de Halwan (VIe siècle). Cause de la fondation des écoles* [PO 4.4] [Paris, 1908]; ET available in A. H. Becker, *Sources for the History of the School of Nisibis* [Liverpool, 2008], p. 151).

[118] Barhadbshabba, *Ecclesiastical History* 31 (ed. F. Nau, *La seconde partie de l'Histoire de Barhadbešabba 'Arbaïa et controverse de Théodore de Mopsueste avec les Macédoniens* [PO 9.5] [Paris, 1913], p. 124; translation taken from Becker, *Sources for the History of the School of Nisibis*, p. 69, though I have slightly altered Becker's capitalization).

[119] Ps.-John bar Aphtonia, *Life of Severus*, pp. 160–61 (ed. M.-A. Kugener, *Sévère, patriarche d'Antioche* [PO 2.3] [Paris, 1904]).

[120] M. Decker, *Tilling the Hateful Earth: Agricultural Production and Trade in the Late Antique East*

plenty of evidence throughout late antiquity of farmers paying for churches and their adornment in villages.[121] Furthermore, even though there may have been settings in which rural fairs meant that the people living in larger villages had no need to travel to cities,[122] we should still remember that, more generally, there was a flourishing trade connecting countryside and cities. This constant movement of goods and people will have provided opportunities for some inhabitants of the countryside to be exposed to theological speculation in urban areas.[123] Chrysostom, for instance, might make reference to simple agrarian workers from rural areas and Aramaic-speakers from the countryside among his audience,[124] and we have evidence of Christian holy men and scholars moving between cities and the countryside.[125] Though a largely agrarian and nonurban population, the Christians of the Middle East were not cut off from or unaware of the world of the city.[126]

(Oxford/New York, 2009), p. 33. On the nature of the rural landscape in Syria and Palestine in late antiquity, see *ibid.*, pp. 28–79. For villages specifically, see the overviews in P.-L. Gatier, 'Villages du Proche-Orient protobyzantin (4ème–7ème s.). Étude régionale,' in G.R.D. King and Av. Cameron, eds., *The Byzantine and Early Islamic Near East*, vol. 2: *Land Use and Settlement Patterns* (Princeton, 1994), pp. 17–48 and C. Wickham, *Framing the Early Middle Ages: Europe and the Mediterranean, 400–800* (Oxford/New York, 2005), pp. 443–59.

[121] See Decker, *Tilling the Hateful Earth*, pp. 33, 45 (farmers living primarily in villages); p. 71 (farmers financing churches or church plate).

[122] Cf. the comments of Libanius, *Orations* 11.230 (ed. R. Foerster, *Libanii opera*, vol. 1.2 [Leipzig, 1903], pp. 517–18; ET available in A. F. Norman, *Antioch as a Centre of Hellenic Culture as Observed by Libanius* [Liverpool, 2000], p. 54). On this passage, see Decker, *Tilling the Hateful Earth*, p. 232.

[123] For a rich discussion of late antique Levantine overland trade see Decker, *Tilling the Hateful Earth*, pp. 228–57; esp. 242–43 for the large movement of grain from hinterlands to cities in Syria. M. Whittow, 'How Much Trade was Local, Regional, and Inter-regional? A Comparative Perspective on the Late Antique Economy,' *Late Antique Archaeology* 10 (2013), pp. 133–65, argued 'most trade was local and regional, but with inter-regional trade reaching even into the homes of peasant farmers' (quote at 160). See, too, Hezser's observation (*Jewish Literacy in Roman Palestine*, p. 176): 'Business relations and mobility between rural and urban areas will have been paralleled by a flow of "traditional knowledge," whatever its nature and form, from city to countryside and *vice versa*,' and her invocation of a 'cultural continuum from city to country.'

[124] John Chrysostom, *Baptismal Instructions* 8.1–6 (simple rural Aramaic speakers who were both teachers and farmers) (ed. A. Wenger, *Huit catéchèses baptismales inédites* [SC 50] [Paris, 1957], pp. 247–51; ET available in P. W. Harkins, *St. John Chrysostom: Baptismal Instructions* [Westminster, Md./London, 1963], pp. 119–21); and *Homilies on the Statues* 19.1–2 (Aramaic-speaking farmers) (PG 49, cols. 188–190; ET by W.R.W. Stephens available in P. Schaff, ed., *A Select Library of the Nicene and Post-Nicene Fathers of the Christian Church*, vol. 9: *Saint Chrysostom: On the Priesthood; Ascetic Treatises; Select Homilies and Letters; Homilies on the Statues* [New York, 1889], pp. 464–66 [19.2–6 in English translation]). On the presence of rural ascetics in Chrysostom's audience, see the lengthy discussion in F. van de Paverd, *St. John Chrysostom, The Homilies on the Statues: An Introduction* (Rome, 1991), pp. 255–89.

[125] On Athanasius Gamolo and Jacob of Edessa and the question of urban/rural relations, see below, Chapter 8, p. 216.

[126] One might even go so far as to question the usefulness of an urban/rural distinction in the Roman world. For a discussion of urban-rural relationships (in an earlier period) that breaks down the notion

Such were some of the ways that theological speculation might reach a wider audience, even in a largely agrarian world where rates of literacy were low. And we know that theological speculation did in fact reach larger audiences. Examples of public acclamations—reports of between eighteen and twenty thousand people chanting Christological slogans at the Emperor Justinian in the Hippodrome of Constantinople,[127] or of a large crowd chanting for long hours in the church of Holy Wisdom in Constantinople in 518, demanding that the patriarch John anathematize Severus of Antioch and proclaim allegiance to the Council of Chalcedon[128]—suggest that some ordinary Christians, at least in large cities, had an awareness of Christological controversies and could participate in them even if they did not necessarily have a full understanding of all the theological nuances at stake. We find another such example when we read that, as Severus approached Antioch in 512, having finally accepted the request that he become its patriarch, a large number of people 'of every rank' poured out of the city to meet him and began chanting against the Council of Chalcedon.[129] The use of theological slogans provided ordinary, nonelite Christians similar avenues of involvement.[130] Controversies surrounding the wording of the liturgy offer further evidence for such engagement. Most notable in this regard was the dispute over the longer and shorter versions of the *Trisagion*—that is, over whether 'who was crucified for us' should be added after the phrase 'Holy God, Holy Mighty, Holy Immortal' in the liturgy. Disagreements over the thrice-holy hymn became a proxy for disagreements over Chalcedon (and later, an important confessional marker among different Chalcedonian groups in the Monothelete controversy). Even a parrot

---

of a sharp Roman urban/rural divide and suggests frequent and common interaction, see T. A. Robinson, *Who Were the First Christians? Dismantling the Urban Thesis* (New York, 2017), pp. 65–90.

127 Michael the Great, *Chronicle* 9.22 (ed. Chabot, 4.285 [Syriac] = 2.204).

128 See the description of the events, complete with extensive translations from the acts of the Synod of Constantinople of 536, in A. A. Vasiliev, *Justin the First: An Introduction to the Epoch of Justinian the Great* (Cambridge, Mass., 1950), pp. 137–41.

129 Ps.-John bar Aphtonia, *Life of Severus*, p. 157 (ed. Kugener [PO 2.3]; ET taken from S. P. Brock, *Two Early Lives of Severos, Patriarch of Antioch* (Liverpool, 2013), p. 125). I am grateful to Yonatan Moss for bringing this incident to my attention. On this incident, see also W. Frend, *The Rise of the Monophysite Movement: Chapters in the History of the Church in the Fifth and Sixth Centuries* (Cambridge, 1972), p. 221.

130 This was perhaps especially the case in the Trinitarian controversies of the fourth century, when various groups might be associated with a particular theological catchphrase or expression. See, e.g., an example of what R.P.C. Hanson termed 'a theology of slogans or catchphrases, bandied about for propaganda purposes,' written by Lucifer of Calaris in *The Search for the Christian Doctrine of God: The Arian Controversy 318–381* (Edinburgh, 1988) p. 515, and *passim* more generally for various theological slogans used in the course of the controversy. By comparison, see Thomas's observations on the importance of proverbs, maxims, and rhymes among the illiterate of early modern England: 'The Meaning of Literacy in Early Modern England,' pp. 107–108.

in Antioch was taught to recite the longer version of the hymn. Isaac of Antioch witnessed the parrot and commemorated it in a late-fifth century Syriac poem that runs to more than a thousand verses. Such was the bird's celebrity that before he had even seen it, Isaac wrote, he had heard about it; he also reported crowds of people gathering to hear its singing.[131] As late as the seventh or eighth century, the Dyothelete Chalcedonian Constantine of Harran wrote a letter in Syriac to Chalcedonians who were upset by the use of the shorter version of the Trisagion in the liturgy.[132] Apart from such conflicts over the liturgy, we also have reports of disagreements between parents and children over Christian orthodoxy[133] that suggest ordinary believers engaged with these questions, as do formulas of excommunication that were to be pronounced by a convert switching from one Christian group to another.[134] Viewed together,

[131] For the homily, see Isaac of Antioch, *On the Bird Who Would Cry Out, 'Agios O Theos' in the City of Antioch*, pp. 737–88 (ed. P. Bedjan, *Homiliae S. Isaaci, Syri Antiocheni* [Paris/Leipzig, 1903]); for Isaac hearing about the bird before singing and for crowds gathered to hear the bird, see p. 741. On this verse homily, see M. van Esbroeck, 'The Memra on the Parrot by Isaac of Antioch,' *JTS* 47 (1996), pp. 464–76 (van Esbroeck comments on the poem's length at 464). On the *Trisagion* more generally, see S. Janeras, 'Les Byzantins et le Trisagion christologique,' in *Miscellanea liturgica in onore di sua eminenza il Cardinale Giacomo Lercaro, arcivescovo di Bologna, presidente del 'Consilium' per l'applicazione della costituzione sulla sacra liturgia*, vol. 2 (Rome/New York, 1967), pp. 469–99; Janeras, 'Le Trisagion: une formule brève en liturgie comparée,' in R. F. Taft and G. Winkler, eds., *Comparative Liturgy Fifty Years after Anton Baumstark (1872–1948): Acts of the International Congress, Rome, 25–29 September 1998* (Rome, 2001), pp. 495–562; and S. P. Brock, 'The Thrice-Holy Hymn in the Liturgy,' *Sobornost /Eastern Churches Review* 7 (1985), pp. 24–34, note especially p. 29, where Brock adduces the example of the parrot as well as the practice of naming one of the thieves crucified next to Christ as Demas (from ὁ σταυροθεὶς *δι' ἡμᾶς*) as indicating that Christological disagreements could be viewed in a lighthearted way. For the Trisagion in the Monothelete controversy, see my 'In Search of Monotheletism,' *Dumbarton Oaks Papers* 68 (2014), *passim.* The 'we break heavenly bread' controversy in the Miaphysite church is another example of a liturgical dispute that had Christological implications and overtones, in this instance, between Severans and Julianists. On the controversy, see J.-M. Sauget, 'Vestiges d'une célébration gréco-syriaque de l'Anaphore de Saint Jacques,' in C. Laga, J. A. Munitiz, and L. van Rompay, eds., *After Chalcedon: Studies in Theology and Church History Offered to Professor Albert Van Roey for His Seventieth Birthday* (Leuven, 1985), pp. 309–45, esp. 335–44. For these examples and more, including further bibliography, see my, 'Greek Kanons and the Syrian Orthodox Liturgy,' in B. Bitton-Ashkelony and D. Krueger, eds., *Prayer and Worship in Eastern Christianities, 5th to 11th Centuries* (London/New York, 2017), p. 152.

[132] For Constantine of Harran and the fragments of his *Anagnosticon* preserved in the *Apologetic Letter* of Elia to Leo of Harran, see A. van Roey, 'Trois auteurs chalcédoniens syriens: Georges de Martyropolis, Constantin et Léon de Harran,' *Orientalia Lovaniensia Periodica* 3 (1972), pp. 129, 131–32, 143–44. Van Roey later published Elia's entire *Apologetic Letter*, for which see van Roey, ed. and trans., *Eliae epistula apologetica ad Leonem, syncellum Harranensem* (CSCO 469-470: SS 201–202) (Leuven, 1985). On this work, see also van Roey's earlier study, 'La lettre apologétique d'Élie à Léon, syncelle de l'évêque chalcédonien de Harran,' *LM* 57 (1944), pp. 1–52, as well as U. Possekel, 'Christological Debates in Eighth-Century Harran: The Correspondence of Leo of Harran and Eliya,' in M. E. Doerfler et al., eds., *Syriac Encounters: Papers from the Sixth North American Syriac Symposium, Duke University, 26–29 June 2011* (Leuven, 2015), pp. 345–68.

[133] See the material collected in my 'In Search of Monotheletism,' p. 32.

[134] See, e.g., the anathema contained in BL Add. 12,156 (dated to AD 562), fols. 61a–61b, to be used

such evidence suggests that some people, and not just theological elites only, took religious questions and Christological differences quite seriously.

LINGERING QUESTIONS

And yet, such reports, however suggestive, leave pestering questions: How precisely did the ordinary Christian relate to the theological debates that ultimately defined the church he or she chose? Was the ordinary Christian's allegiance to this or that confession based on considered reflection and precise doctrinal understanding, or was it based on something else, like loyalty to a local holy man or bishop whose sanctity and judgment about such matters was held in reverence and trust?[135] Or perhaps on the veneration of a particular figure in the past who had been strongly associated with one stance or another,[136] or even on something as decidedly nontheological as a change of sides to gain the upper hand following a disagreement within a community?[137] None of these options, of course, was mutually exclusive.

What is more, when it came to the question of actually understanding theological speculation, an urban-rural distinction may not have been ultimately of great significance. In terms of theological awareness and understanding, how different would an illiterate village stonemason have been from an illiterate urban craftsman? Or a farmer who lived in a city from a farmer who

---

by a person converting to Miaphysitism from Chalcedonianism, Nestorianism, Julianism, and other 'heresies.' According to its rubric, the anathema had been used in Egypt. *CBM*, vol. 2, p. 643 (no. 12) has a brief description and prints the rubric; the anathemas are followed by a prayer of Timothy Aelurus for those returning to Miaphysitism from Dyophysitism. An order of reconciliation for heretics by the East Syrian catholicos, Timothy I (d. 823), can be found in O. Braun, ed., *Tiomthei Patriarchae I: Epistulae* (CSCO 74: SS 30) (Paris, 1914), pp. 33–34. P.-P. Joannou, *Discipline générale antique (IVe-IXe s.). Index analytique aux CCO, CSP, CPG* (Grottaferrata [Rome], 1964), cols. 288–89, s.v. 'reconciliatio haereticorum,' summarizes a great deal of Greek canonical material on the reconciliation of heretics through the use of written declarations and also through baptism.

[135] The King of Nobatia's reported decision to follow a Miaphysite form of Christianity was not explicitly doctrinal/theological—he expressed it in terms of wanting to imitate Theodosius of Alexandria rather than the 'wicked faith' of Justinian. See John of Ephesus, *Ecclesiastical History* 4.7 (ed. Brooks [CSCO SS III.3], p. 186; ET taken from Payne Smith, *The Third Part*, p. 255). See also the case of Euthymius and the Council of Chalcedon in Cyril of Scythopolis, *Life of Euthymius* 27 (ed. E. Schwartz, *Kyrillos von Skythopolis* [Leipzig, 1939], pp. 41–45; ET available in R. M. Price, *The Lives of the Monks of Palestine by Cyril of Scythopolis* [Kalamazoo, Mich., 1991], pp. 37–41). (See Chapter 3, n. 38).

[136] See below for an example of the Severan-Julianist reunion thwarted not by theology but by an unwillingness to anathematize past figures.

[137] E.g., the case of the switch of the Miaphysite monk Elisha' and 70 associates to Chalcedonianism within the context of a communal dispute in Michael the Great, *Chronicle* 9.15 (ed. Chabot, 4.270 [Syriac] = 2.177–78).

lived in a village?[138] A rural craftsman may have donated money to help build a church, but does that mean he (or his priest) understood debates over the Hypostatic Union? And even if many villages in Syria were connected to major cities via trade, was there necessarily a strong connection between the movement of pottery or foodstuffs and the movement, not just of sophisticated theological ideas, but also of the understanding of those ideas? Food is much easier to transport and consume than high-level theological speculation. Inhabitants of cities may have been more keenly aware of the existence of competing churches, but simply knowing difference existed—even being able to repeat a theological slogan—and having sufficient understanding to evaluate that difference and the deeper issues underlying the slogan is an entirely different matter.

Moreover, how did the two poles on the spectrum of intellectual understanding and engagement in doctrinal disagreements relate to one another? What did the bishop who fiercely opposed Chalcedon expect from the ploughboy or artisan who did not understand the issues at stake? Conversely, what did the laborer, the sum of whose literacy might consist in being able slowly to sign his name, make of the debates over one nature or two, or one will or two, in the Incarnate Christ? And what about those who had more awareness of the controversies than people who were completely theologically unschooled, but whose understanding fell far short of that of the learned theologian whose texts can now be found printed in the *Patrologia Graeca*? When physical violence erupted in the churches of Constantinople around 510 over the singing of the longer version of the *Trisagion*, were those who were throwing punches in church motivated by horror at the theological implications of adding 'who was crucified for us' to the thrice-holy hymn?[139] What will a person who had been going to one of the sixty-three churches of Alexandria whose liturgy the Chalcedonian John the Almsgiver changed in the early seventh century so that it no longer included the words 'who was crucified for us' have made of the change? Will that person have gone, by virtue of the change in the liturgy in his or her local church, from being a Miaphysite to a

[138] Gatier, 'Villages du Proche-Orient protobyzantin,' p. 36, mentions the professions found in villages and notes: 'Cependent les habitants de villages sont presque uniquement des agriculteurs.' For farmers living in cities, see Decker, *Tilling the Hateful Earth*, p. 33, n. 17. Cf. also Walter Scheidel's discussion of the nature of Greco-Roman urbanization his article 'Demography,' in W. Scheidel, I. Morris, and R. Saller, eds., *The Cambridge Economic History of the Greco-Roman World* (Cambridge, 2008), pp. 74–80, especially, 77, where he suggests that in all but the very largest Greek cities, most of the population was engaged in agrarian pursuits.

[139] For the incident, see Theophanes, *Chronicle* AM 6003 (ed. C. de Boor, *Theophanis: Chronographia*, vol. 1 [Leipzig, 1883], p. 154; ET available in C. Mango and R. Scott, trans., *The Chronicle of Theophanes Confessor: Byzantine and Near Eastern History, AD 284–813* [Oxford, 1997], p. 235).

Chalcedonian? What will a farmer in Iraq have made of the statement of faith presented by leaders of the Church of the East to Khusro II in 612: 'It is not possible,' they wrote, 'for the one who assumes to be the thing assumed and for that which is assumed to be the assumer, for God the Word is revealed as a human being who has put on clothes and his human nature is seen by creation in the order of his humanity, through a unity which is not divisible'?[140]

Let us now look more closely at how persons ranging from the theologically literate to the theologically illiterate related to the questions raised by Chalcedon and how they related to one another. There was a layering of understanding of these issues in the Christian community: keeping this spectrum before us will be key to making sense of the religious landscape of the post-Chalcedonian world.

[140] *Statement of Faith of 612*, p. 565 (ed. Chabot, *Synodicon Orientale*, p. 565 [Syriac] = 583 [French]). On the use of clothing language to express theological ideas in the Syriac tradition, see S. P. Brock, 'Clothing Metaphors as a Means of Theological Expression in Syriac Tradition,' in M. Schmidt and C. Friedrich, *Typus, Symbol, Allegorie bei den östlichen Vätern und ihren Parallelen im Mittelalter. Internationales Kolloquium, Eichstätt 1981* (Regensburg, 1982), pp. 11–38.

CHAPTER 2

The Simple and the Learned

My brothers, our faith would be the most unfair thing in the world if it applied only to sophisticates and those with a flair for language and logic. It would then of necessity remain beyond the reach of most persons, like gold and silver and all the other things considered valuable here below in great popular demand; and what would be near and dear to God would be that which is placed high and touches only a few, while anything close enough to be grasped by the multitude would be scorned and rejected. When even among human beings the more fair minded would not behave in such a way as to find pleasure only in outstanding distinctions rather than call for those within our power to achieve, you surely cannot expect that God would act at all otherwise.

Gregory of Nazianzus[1]

It is quite clear that not all that can be grasped by the intellect of a teacher can also be grasped by the intellect of the public being taught.

Anastasius of Sinai[2]

Rather, each word of our Lord has its own form, and each form has its own members, and each member has its own character. Each individual understands according to his capacity and interprets as it is granted him.

Ephrem the Syrian[3]

In every religion every level of devoutness must have its appropriate form of expression which has no sense at a lower level. This doctrine, which means something at a higher level, is null and void for someone who is still at the lower level; he *can* only understand it *wrongly* and so these words are *not* valid for such a person.

Ludwig Wittgenstein[4]

[1] Gregory of Nazianzus, *Orations* 32.26 (ed. Moreschini [SC 318], p. 140; ET taken from M. Vinson, *St. Gregory of Nazianzus: Select Orations* [Washington, D.C., 2003], pp. 209–10).

[2] Anastasius of Sinai, *Questions and Answers* 66 (ed. M. Richard and J. A. Munitiz, *Anastasii Sinaitae Quaestiones et responsiones* [Turnhout/Leuven, 2006], p. 118; ET taken from J. A. Munitiz, *Anastasios of the Sinai. Questions and Answers* [Turnhout, 2011], p. 179). NB: Anastasius is here speaking about the subject of the plague and its origin.

[3] Ephrem the Syrian, *Commentary on the Diatessaron* 7.22. The ET is taken from S. P. Brock, *The Luminous Eye: The Spiritual World Vision of Saint Ephrem*, rev. ed. (Kalamazoo, 1992), p. 49. See also L. Leloir, *Commentaire de l'Évangile concordant ou Diatessaron* (SC 121) (Paris, 1966), pp. 151–52.

[4] L. Wittgenstein, *Culture and Value*, ed. G. H. von Wright and H. Nyman, trans. P. Winch, rev. ed. (Oxford, 1998), p. 32.

Let me begin with two anecdotes that can help us think about how the theologically informed related to the theologically uninformed in the Christian community of the post-Chalcedonian world. In 616, a reunion was achieved between the Syrian and Egyptian Miaphysite churches, which had been in schism since the late sixth century. The inclusion of the names of the deceased patriarchs Peter of Callinicus and Damian of Alexandria in the diptychs of their respective churches, however, proved to be a potential stumbling block. It was eventually agreed that the Egyptians would continue to proclaim the name of Damian in their services and the Syrians would proclaim the name of Peter in their services, and the two groups would communicate with one another. The Miaphysite patriarch of Antioch, Athanasius Gamolo, instructed Cyriacus of Amid:

> If there are simple brothers who are not certain of the actions and accommodations and are alarmed at the name placed at the end of the synodicon, you should persuade everyone, being a wise person (*ḥakkimā*) who is more expert than many, on our behalf, on behalf of those with us, and moreover, on behalf of the truth, for we have not done anything that does not agree with the approved ways of the Fathers.[5]

Nearly two centuries later, in 798, efforts at achieving a union between Severan and Julianist Miaphysites fell apart over the unwillingness of the Julianists to anathematize Julian of Halicarnassus, the sixth-century originator of their particular Miaphysite interpretation of the Incarnation. Gabriel, the patriarch of the Julianists, was, the anonymous (Severan) Miaphysite *Chronicle to 813* reported, won over to the Severan understanding of this doctrine, but knew that condemning Julian would cause a problem among his followers: 'You should know,' he told the Severans, 'that many of [my] adherents, from simplicity or from ignorance, or, as it would be more true to say... from the custom which has become inveterate to them, object to this same thing, to anathematizing Jul[ian] specially.' The refusal of the Severans to compromise on the question of anathematizing of Julian led to the collapse of the attempt at uniting these two major strands of Miaphysitism.[6] In both cases, significant portions of groups separated ecclesiastically were more concerned about veneration of certain individuals than they were about theological issues. Personal loyalty to an esteemed figure, or to the memory of such a figure, was more important than doctrine.

[5] Michael the Great, *Chronicle* 10.26 (ed. Chabot, *Michel le Syrien*, 4.399 [Syriac] = 2.393 [French]).

[6] *Chronicle to 813*, p. 253 (ed. E. W. Brooks, in E. W. Brooks, I. Guidi, and J.-B. Chabot, eds., *Chronica Minora, Pars Tertia* [CSCO SS 3.4] [Paris, 1905]; ET taken from E. W. Brooks, 'A Syriac Fragment,' *ZDMG* 54 [1900], p. 225).

Athanasius Gamolo spoke of 'simple brothers' (*aḥē pshiṭē*) being disturbed at the inclusion of certain names in prayers, and Gabriel spoke of the 'simplicity' (*pshiṭutā*) of his followers as being a possible explanation for their refusal to anathematize Julian. Such language was not coincidental. By the time of these two incidents, church leaders had been referring to ordinary Christians as 'simple'—ἁπλούστεροι or ἰδιῶται in Greek[7]—for centuries. The same was the case in Syriac: a simple, or uneducated, or guileless, or naïve person was a *pshiṭā* or *hedyoṭā*, that is, an ἰδιώτης. Christians across the theological spectrum, writing in both Greek and Syriac, would employ this language to refer to ordinary, uneducated believers. It was a label that Miaphysites and Chalcedonians would use, and members of the Church of the East would use it, too.[8] The same idea can be found also in Christian Arabic.[9]

The notion of simplicity and of the simple believer had, in fact, a complex history, both Christian and non-Christian, and was in use long before the Council of Chalcedon.[10] In the first centuries of Christian history, pagans attacked Christians for being simple, uneducated, and credulous,[11] but Christians

[7] Other synonyms included ἠλιθίος and ἀκέραιος. There was no difference in meaning between ἁπλοῦς and the frequently used comparative ἁπλούστερος. For all of this and an analysis of these words, see M. Hirschberg, *Studien zur Geschichte der simplices in der Alten Kirche. Ein Beitrag zur Problem der Schichtungen in der menschlichen Erkenntnis* (Berlin, 1944), pp. 3, 7–9. NB: In Syriac texts translated from Greek, one can at times see *yattir pshiṭin* ('the more simple'), rather than rather than *pshiṭē* ('the simple'). See, e.g., Severus of Antioch, *Select Letters* V.11 ('To John, John the Presbyter, and Others') (ed. and trans. Brooks, 1.2.379 [Syriac] = 2.2.336 [English]) and V.14 ('To John and Philoxenus and Thomas') (1.2.393 = 2.2.349). This likely represents a calque on the Greek ἁπλούστεροι. For an analysis of terminology relating to simple believers in Origen, G. af Hällström, *Fides Simpliciorum according to Origen of Alexandria* (Helsinki, 1984), pp. 11–19, is very valuable.

[8] See, for instance, *Synod of Dadisho'* [AD 424], p. 47.12 (ed. Chabot, *Synodicon Orientale*, p. 291 [French]), and *Synod of Isho'yahb I* [AD 585], *Canons* 9 (ed. Chabot, *Synodicon Orientale*, p. 145.31 [Syriac] = 407 [French]). For Miaphysites and Chalcedonians, see below.

[9] See *Chronicle of Seert* 2.72 (ed. Scher [and Griveau] [PO 13.4], p. 185), where certain people, dressed in the garb of monks, were leading astray those who were 'weak in knowledge.' See, too, Ps.-Theophilus of Alexandria, *Homily on SS Peter, Paul, Repentance, and Anba Athanasius*, p. 389 (ed. and trans. H. Fleisch, 'Une homélie de Théophile d'Alexandrie en l'honneur de St Pierre et de St Paul,' *ROC* 30 [1935–1936]), where heretics confuse the heart of the 'simple' (*sādij* [i.e., *sādhij*]) king Constantine in order to drag him into their error. Cf. also M. N. Swanson, 'A Copto-Arabic Catechism of the Later Fatimid Period: "Ten Questions That One of the Disciples Asked His Master,"' *PdO* 22 (1997), p. 481.

[10] Latin writers referred to the simple as *simplices*. On the history of the idea of *simplicitas*, see O. Hiltbrunner, *Latina Graeca: Semasiologische Studien über Lateinische Wörter im Hinblick auf ihr Verhältnis zur griechischen Vorbildern* (Bern, 1958), pp. 15–105, esp. 85–105, for its Christian usages. And cf. also J. Amstutz, *Haplotēs; eine begriffsgeschichtliche Studie zum jüdisch-christlichen Griechisch* (Bonn, 1968). af Hällström, *Fides Simpliciorum according to Origen of Alexandria* studies the *simplices* in the thought of Origen.

[11] See, e.g., Minucius Felix, *Octavius*, 5.4, 8.4 (ed. B. Kytzler, *M. Minuci Felicis. Octavius* [Stuttgart, 1992], pp. 3, 6–7; ET available in G. W. Clarke, *The Octavius of Marcus Minucius Felix* [New York/Paramus, N.J., 1974], pp. 56, 63). Origen, *Contra Celsum*, 1.27, 3.55 (ed. Borret [SC 132], pp. 148, 150 (1.27) and ed. M. Borret, *Origène: Contre Celse. Tome II (Livres III et IV)* [SC 136] [Paris, 1968], pp. 128, 130 [3.55]; ET

themselves would also acknowledge their simplicity[12] and take pride in the triumph of the Christian message over the wisdom of the world.[13] Christianity was a philosophy that was open to everyone[14] and brought with it 'the paradox of the uneducated but spiritually aware peasant.'[15] Christ had made simple fishermen into apostles and teachers and, before that, shepherds into kings and prophets.[16] 'With his simple teaching,' (*yulpānā pshiṭā*), Jacob of Sarugh wrote, 'he has conquered the entire world. He has chosen the simple (*hedyoṭē*), even the poor, for its proclamation.'[17] Simple believers were in very good company: both the Greek and Syriac New Testaments referred to Peter and John as 'unschooled' (ἀγράμματοί/*lā yād'in seprā*) and 'ordinary' (ἰδιῶται/*hedyoṭē*) men, and yet they had been bold in speaking to the religious leaders of their day.[18] Stories were told suggesting that a Christian with simple faith could defeat (and convert) even learned philosophers skilled in debate.[19] Labeling someone 'simple' could also be a polemical tool,[20] and the notion of the

available in Chadwick, *Origen: Contra Celsum*, pp. 27, 165). Eusebius, *Preparation for the Gospel* 1.1.11 (ed. K. Mras and É. des Places, *Die Praeparatio Evangelica* [Eusebius Werke 8.1] [Berlin, 1982], pp. 7–8; ET available in E. H. Gifford, *Preparation for the Gospel* [Oxford, 1903], p. 4). Clarke, *The Octavius of Marcus Minucius Felix*, p. 183, has a rich collection of citations of charges that early Christians were simple and uneducated.

[12] See, e.g., Athenagoras, *Supplicatio pro Christianis* 11.4 (ed. B. Pouderon, *Supplique au sujet des chrétiens; et, Sur la résurrection des morts* [SC 379] [Paris, 1992], p. 106; English translation by B.P. Pratten in *ANF*, vol. 2 [New York, 1885], p. 134). For many more references, see C. J. Cadoux, *The Early Church and the World* (reprint, Edinburgh/New York, 1955), pp. 319–320.

[13] The *locus classicus* of this idea is 1 Corinthians 1:18–28, but it can be easily found throughout Christian literature. See, e.g., Athanasius, *Orations against the Arians* 1.43 (PG 26, cols. 100–101; ET by J. H. Newman, available in *NPNF*, ser. 2, vol. 4 [New York, 1892], p. 331) and also John Chrysostom, *Homilies on the Statues* 19.1 (PG 49, cols. 189–190; ET by W.R.W. Stephens available in *NPNP*, ser. 1, vol. 9 [New York, 1889], p. 465 [= 19.3 in the ET]). Cf. Maxwell, 'The Attitudes of Basil and Gregory of Nazianzus toward Uneducated Christians,' pp. 117–19.

[14] See Tatian, *Oratio ad Graecos* 32 (ed. M. Marcovich, *Tatiani Oratio ad Graecos, Theophili Antiocheni Ad Autolycumi* [Berlin/New York, 1995], pp. 60–61; ET by J. E. Ryland available in *ANF*, vol. 2 [Buffalo, 1885], p. 78).

[15] Clark, 'Pastoral Care: Town and Country in Late Antique Preaching,' p. 277. Note the command in Eph. 6:5 and Col. 3:22 that slaves should obey their masters in 'simplicity of heart' (ἐν ἁπλότητι τῆς καρδίας and ἐν ἁπλότητι καρδίας).

[16] 'He has chosen the weak and despised, just as the Apostle said [cf. 1 Cor. 1:27], and now he has called me who am lowly.' See the letter of Anthimus to Theodosius, Miaphysite patriarch of Alexandria, preserved in Michael the Great, *Chronicle* 9.25 (ed. Chabot, 4.294 = 2.218).

[17] Or 'his proclamation.' See Jacob of Sarugh, *Homily on Faith* (ed. P. Bedjan, *Homiliae Selectae Mar-Jacobi Sarugensis*, vol. 3 [Paris, 1907], p. 622). I am grateful to Philip Forness for this reference.

[18] Cf. Acts 4:13 (here I use the New International Version translation and the Syriac is from the Peshitta).

[19] See the story in Rufinus, *Ecclesiastical History* 10.3 (ed. Mommsen, in *Eusebius Werke 2.2: Die Kirchengeschichte*, pp. 961–63; ET in P. R. Amidon, *Rufinus of Aquileia: History of the Church* [Washington, D.C., 2016], pp. 381–83). For this, see Chadwick, *The Role of the Christian Bishop*, p. 14.

[20] E.g., Ḥabīb called Philoxenus of Mabbug *saklā w-hedyoṭā*, 'foolish and a simpleton.' See Philoxenus

simple believer played an important role in the language Christian leaders used to discuss teachings they opposed. Accusing adversaries of leading the simple astray was a well-worn tactic: Paul himself had spoken of those who lead astray the hearts 'of the innocent' (Romans 16:18),[21] and Christian writers for centuries afterwards would charge their opponents with doing the same. One marker of the heretic was that he seduced the simple into false belief.[22]

Such charges serve as a reminder that, in addition to their actual existence, the simple in late antiquity and the early Middle Ages also led a rhetorical one, and these two groups—real simple believers and rhetorical ones—were not always the same: the expectation that ordinary Christians would muddle more complicated matters of theology proved useful to Christian leaders in various ways. In the context of competition over believers, chalking any loss to an opposing side up to the 'simple' being poached away by opponents acting mendaciously was an obvious way to help maintain the appearance of an intellectually compelling doctrinal position. What would it mean for one's views if people were leaving them for those of rivals on the basis of careful consideration? Augustine pointed to the presence of large numbers of *imperiti*—uninstructed and ignorant—as the reason for Manichean missionary success among North African Catholics and also to deflect Manichean attacks on particular Catholic behaviors: it was only the uninstructed who acted in this way.[23]

---

of Mabbug, *Mēmrē against Ḥabīb*, 10.186 (ed. M. Brière and F. Graffin, *Sancti Philoxeni episcopi Mabbugensis dissertationes decem de Uno e sancta Trinitate incorporato et passo (Mêmrê contre Habib). IV. Dissertationes 9a, 10a* [PO 40.2] [Turnhout, 1980], p. 150.8).

[21] τῶν ἀκάκων in Greek and *pshiṭē* in the Peshitta. For Severus of Antioch citing this passage, see *Select Letters* II.3 ('To the Orthodox in Emesa') (ed. and trans. Brooks, 1.1.257 [Syriac] = 2.1.229 [English]). Other instances of Severus using the language of the 'simple' when speaking about false teachers include: I.1 ('To Constantine the Bishop') (1.1.4, 6 = 2.1.5, 7); I.11 ('To the Archimandrite of the Monastery of Bassus') (1.1.57 = 2.1.51); V.11 ('To John, John the Presbyter, and Others') (1.2.379 = 2.2.336); V.13 ('To Proclus and Eusebona') (1.2.387 = 2.2.343; NB: here he cites Basil, speaking about those who deceive the *bririn*, 'the innocent'). See also the next note. Similarly, in 2 Corinthians 11:3, Paul wrote that he feared the minds of Christians in Corinth would be led astray from simplicity (τῆς ἁπλότητος/*pshiṭutā*) to Christ.

[22] The charge that heretics lead or seduce the simple astray, or otherwise unsettle them, is ubiquitous. See, e.g., Athanasius, *Epistle to the Monks* (PG 26, col. 1188); Athanasius, *Orations against Arians* 1.8 (PG 26, col. 23); Gregory of Nazianzus, *Orations* 21.22 (ed. Mossay [SC 270], p. 156); John Chrysostom, *In Illud:* Pater, si possibile est, transeat 1 (PG 51, col. 31); *Letter of the Bishops and Priests of Armenia to Proclus, Bishop of Constantinople*, p. 594, ln. 11 (ed. P. Bedjan, *Nestorius. Le Livre d'Héraclide de Damas* [Paris/Leipzig, 1910]); Michael the Great, *Chronicle* 12.8 (ed. Chabot, 4.495–96 [Syriac] = 3.32). See also the passage from Severus of Antioch discussed in Y. Moss, 'The Rise and Function of the Holy Text in Late Antiquity: Severus of Antioch, The Babylonian Talmud, and Beyond,' in Bitton-Ashkelony et al., eds., *Patristic Studies in the Twenty-First Century*, p. 530. For this rhetoric in Gregory Nazianzen and Basil, see Maxwell, 'The Attitudes of Basil and Gregory of Nazianzus toward Uneducated Christians,' pp. 120–22.

[23] See P. Brown, 'Augustine and a Practice of the *imperiti*,' in G. Madec, ed., *Augustin Prédicateur*

Polemically, ascribing an opponent's doctrinal transgressions to simplicity or lack of learning provided that opponent an 'out,' as it were, for his erroneous belief, without the need to accuse him of malicious error. Socrates described Anthropomorphite debates in Alexandria in the late fourth and early fifth century over whether God existed in a body as a case of the uneducated making theological mistakes: 'Very many of the more simple ascetics,' he wrote, 'asserted that God is corporeal, and has a human figure: most others condemn[ed] their judgment, and contended that God is incorporeal, and free of all form whatever.'[24] Like Socrates, Cassian used simplicity as an explanation of the doctrinal choices of Anthropomorphites. The rejection by a great number of monks of Theophilus's anti-Anthropomorphite festal letter of 399 was, he wrote, quite bitter 'owing to their simplicity and error.'[25] One prominent supporter of Anthropomorphite views of God was a certain Abba Sarapion who had spent decades in Scetis and who was regarded as superior to nearly all the monks there in both his personal ascetic virtue and time spent in the desert. In fact, according to Cassian, resistance in Scetis to Theophilus's anti-Anthropomorphite festal letter was in part a function of Sarapion's rejection of Theophilus's teaching on the subject. Sarapion's views, however, were not an example of willful unbelief: they were eventually changed by the persuasive efforts of a certain Photinus from Cappadocia. When the venerable old ascetic converted to the truth, Cassian and others were delighted 'that the Lord had not permitted a man of such age and crowned with such virtues, and one who erred only from ignorance and rustic simplicity, to wander from the path of the right faith up to the very last....'[26]

For Socrates and for Cassian, charging Sarapion and other Anthropomorphite monks with acting from an evil impulse in their beliefs would have been implausible: these were men who were widely acknowledged to have devoted their lives to self-denial, prayer, and personal holiness. This is perhaps why

---

(395–411): actes du Colloque International de Chantilly (5-7 septembre 1996) (Paris, 1998), p. 372. I am grateful to Peter Brown for pointing out this particular use of the notion of simplicity to me. The charge that converts away from a religious group were simple and being led astray has a long history. For its use by Middle Eastern church leaders to describe Protestant converts in the nineteenth century, see U. S. Makdisi, *Artillery of Heaven: American Missionaries and the Failed Conversion of the Middle East* (Ithaca, N.Y., 2008), p. 183.

[24] Socrates, *Ecclesiastical History* 6.7 (ed. Hansen, *Sokrates Kirchengeschichte*, p. 322. ET taken from Zenos in *NPNF*, ser. 2, vol. 2, p. 142). On the Anthropomorphite controversy, see E. Clarke, *The Origenist Controversy: The Cultural Construction of an Early Christian Debate* (Princeton, 1992), pp. 43–84.

[25] John Cassian, *Conferences*, 10.2 (ed. M. Petschenig, *Iohannis Cassiani Conlationes XXIIII* [Vienna, 1886], p. 287; the ET by E.C.S. Gibson is taken from *NPNF*, ser. 2, vol. 11 [New York, 1894], p. 401). For analysis of this story, see C. Stewart, *Cassian the Monk* (New York/Oxford, 1998), pp. 86–90.

[26] John Cassian, *Conferences*, 10.3 (ed. Petschenig, *Iohannis Cassiani Conlationes XXIIII*, pp. 288–89; ET by Gibson taken from *NPNF* ser. 2, vol. 11, p. 402).

even though he believed that Sarapion's 'grievous error' was 'conceived... by the craft of most vile demons,' Cassian did not suggest that Sarapion himself was demonically motivated in his support of Anthropomorphite views.[27] But of course, those supporting Anthropomorphite views were much more than just simple, uneducated monks: the Anthropomorphite viewpoint was one that took specific stances on a host of sophisticated theological issues—the nature of prayer, questions of Christology and the Trinity, and debates arising out of Nicaea.[28] What a claim of simplicity provided in this instance was another, less inflammatory 'error theory,' as it were, which a writer could invoke to explain why a particular person held to aberrant views if an accusation of malign motivation was not fitting.

The 'way out' that a claim of simplicity provided rhetorically would prove useful even in interreligious polemics.[29] Possibly in response to Christian polemical pressure,[30] Muslims from the mid-eighth century onward (beginning of the second century AH), started to explain references to the *ummiyyūn* in the Qur'ān and to Muḥammad himself as being *ummī* in terms of illiteracy rather than taking these to refer to non-Jews or to people who had not been the recipients of divine revelation.[31] Perhaps reflecting this development, the Christian *Legend of Sergius Baḥīrā* in the early ninth century would describe the entirety of the Arabs among whom the Christian monk Baḥīrā lived as 'barbarians and simple (*pshiṭē*),'[32] or 'ignorant and simple and uneducated'

[27] John Cassian, *Conferences* 10.4 (ed. Petschenig, *Iohannis Cassiani Conlationes XXIIII*, p. 289; ET by Gibson taken from taken from *NPNF* ser. 2, vol. 11, p. 402).

[28] See P. A. Patterson's attempt at retrieving Anthropomorphite views in *Visions of Christ: The Anthropomorphite Controversy of 399 CE* (Tübingen, 2012). I am grateful to Peter Brown for referring me to this book and to the story of Sarapion more generally.

[29] E.g., note H.J.W. Drijvers's comments on the *Doctrina Addai*'s portrayal of the Jews as having crucified Christ out of ignorance and on the lack of antagonism in the text towards Jews (and Manichees) in his 'Jews and Christians at Edessa,' *Journal of Jewish Studies* 36 (1985), p. 95.

[30] Cf. the observation and suggestion of S. H. Griffith, 'The Prophet Muhammad, His Scripture and His Message according to Christian Apologies in Arabic and Syriac from the First Abbasid Century,' in T. Fahd, ed., *La vie du prophète Mahomet* (Paris, 1983), p. 145.

[31] E.g., Q 3:20, 3:75; 7:157, 158; 62:2. On the development in understanding *ummiyyūn* and *ummī*, see I. Goldfeld, 'The Illiterate Prophet (*Nabī Ummī*): An Inquiry into the Development of a Dogma in Islamic Tradition,' *Der Islam* 57 (1980), pp. 58–67. On the meaning of *ummī*, see R. Paret, *Der Koran: Kommentar und Konkordanz* (Stuttgart, 1980), pp. 21–22; E. Goffroy, 'Ummī,' in *EI2*, vol. 10, pp. 863–64; R. Blachère, *Introduction au Coran*, 2nd ed. (Paris, 1959), pp. 6–8; T. Nöldeke, F. Schwally, G. Bergsträsser, and O. Pretzl, *The History of the Qur'ān* (trans. W. H. Behn) (Leiden/Boston, 2013), pp. 11–13; S. W. Zwemer, 'The "Illiterate" Prophet: Could Mohammed Read and Write?' *Moslem World* 11 (1921), pp. 344–63; and S. Günther's article, 'Ummī,' in *EQ*, vol. 5, pp. 399–403.

[32] *Legend of Sergius Baḥīrā* 1.5, p. 256 (East Syrian recension; ed. and trans. B. Roggema, *The Legend of Sergius Baḥīrā. Eastern Christian Apologetics and Apocalyptic in Response to Islam* (Leiden/Boston, 2009), p. 356; my translation) and cf. 20, 'the Sons of Ishmael were uncivilized (*brirē*) pagans, like horses without a bridle' (East Syrian Recension, p. 298 [translation Roggema]).

(*brirē wa-pshiṭē w-hedyoṭē*);[33] Muḥammad, for his part, was portrayed as 'uneducated' (*brirā*)[34] and 'humble and simple' (*makkikā wa-pshiṭā*).[35] In Acts 4:13, the Apostles, as we have seen, were described as 'not knowing letters' (*lā yād'in seprā*), and in the *Legend*, we find Muḥammad telling the Monk Baḥīrā, 'I am unschooled', (*seprā lā yāda' (e)nā*), literally, 'I do not know letters.'[36] Muḥammad's lack of education and the ignorance of the Arabs provided the author of the text with a way of rejecting Muslim claims that Muḥammad was a prophet and showing that Christianity was superior to Islam, while still maintaining a positive estimation of those claims: an illiterate person with a simple disposition, the Prophet was taught about divine matters by a Christian monk and given a true yet diluted understanding of Christianity; it was only later after Muḥammad's death that Ka'b al-Aḥbār, a Jew, corrupted and changed the Prophet's message, making it supercessionist with respect to Christianity and filling the Qur'ān with errors and false teaching.[37] An ascription of simplicity allowed one more easily to offload the blame for theological error when directly attacking the person in error was not plausible, practical, or, as in the case of Christians living under Muslim rule, prudent.

THE LEARNED AND THE SIMPLE

Such rhetorical usages aside, if there indeed existed an expectation that there would be a hierarchy of knowledge and expertise in the Christian community, we run into the problem of how we might best speak about it. We could speak of 'ordinary' Christians and use language of 'simple believers' and 'theological elites,' or people who were 'theologically literate,' and those who were

[33] *Legend of Sergius Baḥīrā* 1.5 (West Syrian recension, ed. Roggema, p. 318). At 6.4 (p. 330), the Arabs among whom Muḥammad lives are 'ignorant and simple' (*brirē wa-pshiṭē*).

[34] *Legend of Sergius Baḥīrā* 12.5 (East Syrian recension, ed. Roggema, p. 270; cf. West Syrian recension, p. 338).

[35] *Legend of Sergius Baḥīrā* 16.16 (East Syrian recension; ed. Roggema, p. 284; the translation is Roggema's; cp. with West Syrian recension, p. 354).

[36] *Legend of Sergius Baḥīrā* 16.16 (East Syrian recension; ed. Roggema, p. 278; cp. with West Syrian recension, p. 348, where Muḥammad says, 'I have not read a book and I do not know anything.') Also cp. the use of this expression in the *Apostolic Constitutions* 2.1 (see Chapter 1, n. 84). M. P. Penn, *Envisioning Islam: Syriac Christians and the Early Muslim World* (Philadelphia, 2015), p. 111, esp. n. 32 (p. 225), collected references to Muḥammad's illiteracy and simplicity in the *Legend*. Contrast these affirmations about the Apostles and Muḥammad with John 7:15, where Jesus's opponents ask 'How does this one know letters when he has not studied?' (*yāda' seprā kad lā ilep*/γράμματα οἶδεν μὴ μεμαθηκώς).

[37] For Ka'b's corruptions, see *Legend of Sergius Baḥīrā* 9.1-6, 21, 22 (East Syrian recension, ed. Roggema, pp. 268, 302–308; West Syrian recension, pp. 332–34). For the text's presentation of Islam as a 'simplified version of Christianity suitable for pagan Arabs,' see B. Roggema, 'The Legend of Sergius Baḥīrā,' in *CMR*, vol. 1, p. 602.

'theologically illiterate' or 'theologically unschooled.' But there are other choices one might make: 'learned' and 'unlearned,' or 'popular' and 'elite,' to name only a few options. Speaking of clergy versus the laity would not be quite accurate, since there were priests, monks, and even bishops who were illiterate, theologically and otherwise, just as there could be laity who were highly literate, theologically and otherwise. There were also clergy who had only recently been laymen, and some clergy and religious, as we will see later in this book, were known to engage in practices that many might want to classify as 'popular.'

In the New Testament, the author of Hebrews distinguished between those who were teachers and ate solid food and those who were like infants, needing rudimentary instruction and whose food was milk (Hebrews 5:12–6:1); similarly, Paul wrote to the Corinthians that he had to address them as infants rather than spiritual people and feed them with milk rather than solid food (1 Corinthians 3:1–3; cf. also 1 Thessalonians 2:7). If we look to Arabic and Syriac sources, a variety of categories can be found: Ḥabīb b. Khidma Abū Rā'iṭa al-Takrītī (d. 830), among the first Miaphysites to write important works of theology in Arabic, spoke of the 'learned' (*'uqalā'*) and the 'ignorant' (*juhalā'*),[38] while the Jewish Saadia Gaon (d. 942) contrasted the views of the Christian masses (*'awāmmihim*) and those of their elites (*khawāṣṣihim*) when critiquing the doctrine of the Trinity.[39] Another Miaphysite, Yaḥyā b. 'Adī (d. 974), contrasted the Trinitarian views of the 'ignorant' (*juhhāl*) among the Christians with those of the 'learned' (*'ulamā'*) and those 'possessed of understanding in their teaching' (*dhawū al-fahm bi-madhhabihim*).[40] Isaac of Antioch and other

[38] Abū Rā'iṭa al-Takrītī, *Min qawl Abī Rā'iṭa al-Takrītī al-Suryānī usquf Naṣībīn mustadillan bihi 'alā ṣiḥḥat al-Naṣrāniyya*, p. 162 (ed. G. Graf, *Die Schriften des Jacobiten Ḥabīb ibn Ḫidma Abū Rā'iṭa* [CSCO 130–31: SA 14–15] [Louvain, 1951] = p. 197 [GT]; cf. S. Toenies Keating, *Defending the "People of Truth" in the Early Islamic Period: The Christian Apologies of Abū Rā'iṭah* [Leiden/Boston, 2006], p. 342 [Arabic] = 343 [ET]). On the categories of 'learned' and 'ignorant' in Abū Rā'iṭa, see further K. Samir, 'Liberté religieuse et propogation de la foi chez les théologiens arabes chrétiens du IXe siècle et en Islam,' *Tantur Yearbook* (1980–1981), p. 104, who suggests the language echoes Romans 1:14.

[39] Sa'īd b. Yūsuf, *Kitāb al-amānāt wa-'l-i'tiqādāt*, p. 86 (ed. S. Landauer, *Kitâb al-amânât wa'l-I'tiqâdât* [Leiden, 1880]). 'I do not intend this response for their masses (*'awāmmihim*), for their common people only know the Trinity as embodied (*al-tathlīth al-mujassam*).... I intend, rather, my response for their elite (*khawāṣṣihim*) who claim that they believe in the Trinity with insight and precision.' (ET also available in S. Rosenblatt, *The Book of Beliefs and Opinions* [New Haven, 1948], p. 103). The contrast between the common people and the elites could be found in Muslim authors as well. See, e.g., the ninth-century al-Jāḥiẓ speaking about the *'āmma* and the *khāṣṣa* in his *al-'Uthmāniyya*, p. 250 (ed. 'A. al-Salām Muḥammad Hārūn [Miṣr, 1955]; ET available in C. Pellat, *The Life and Works of Jāḥiẓ*, trans. D. M. Hawke [London, 1969], pp. 78–79).

[40] Yaḥyā b. 'Adī, *Maqāla fī tabyīn al-wajh alladhī 'alayhi yaṣiḥḥu al-qawl fī 'l-Bārī', jalla wa-ta'ālā, innahu jawhar wāḥid dhū thalāth khawāṣṣ tusammīhā al-Naṣārā aqānīm*, p. 45 (ed. and trans. A. Périer, *Petits traités apologétiques de Yaḥyâ ben 'Adî* [Paris, 1920]). For these examples of Saadia (see previous

Syriac authors juxtaposed the 'wise' or 'learned' (*ḥakkimē*) and the 'simple' (*hedyoṭē*).[41] This was not merely a Middle Eastern concern, either: in the medieval West, Peter Lombard's discussion of the faith of the simple in his *Sentences* meant that the topic became a regular subject of theological discussion and instruction.[42]

There are a number of options. But all of this language can be problematic insofar as it suggests a two-tiered model of Christian society, with elites concerned about academic seminar-room-style debates, while those outside the seminar room operated in a different religious world entirely, one unconcerned with ideas. Such a model, whatever its usefulness in other contexts might be, would here be entirely misleading.[43] Rather than a two-tiered world, we are instead dealing with a world in which there was a continuum of understanding and engagement with doctrinal questions, one where there were both clergy who were theologically unschooled and laity who were theologically literate. What is more, there was, as we shall see, interaction between people at different stages on the continuum, and it is this interaction that helps to explain many of the most important features of the post-Chalcedonian Christian Middle East.

Importantly, underlying disputes over sophisticated theological doctrines there were often extremely practical, everyday concerns, related to systems of devotion and views of salvation that touched all Christians, not just the theologically literate.[44] The late ancient church was not a modern university

---

note) and Yaḥyā, see H. A. Wolfson, 'Saadia on the Trinity and the Incarnation,' in M. Ben-Horin, B. D. Weinryb, and S. Zeitlin, eds., *Studies and Essays in Honor of Abraham A. Neuman* (Leiden, 1962), pp. 547–48, who suggests that both writers are referring to Tritheists.

[41] Isaac of Antioch, *Second Mēmrā on Beth Hur, Which Was Taken Captive*, p. 603, lnn. 12, 14 (ed. Bedjan, *Homiliae S. Isaaci, Syri Antiocheni*). See the contrasting use of *ḥakkimē* and *hedyoṭā* in Aphrahat, *Demonstrations* 14.42 (ed. J. Parisot, *Patrologia Syriaca*, vol. 1 [Paris, 1894], col. 693.18–19). *Hedyoṭ* and *ḥakkim* are also contrasted in John of Ephesus, *Ecclesiastical History* 5.2 (ed. Brooks [CSCO SS III.3], p. 254, lnn. 19–20). A similar contrast can be found in the letter of Athanasius Gamolo to Cyriacus of Amid (see n. 5 in this chapter). See, too, the contrast between *hakkimā*, *ḥakkimē*, and *hedyoṭā* in Jacob of Sarugh, *Homily on Faith*, p. 631, lnn. 4–9 (ed. P. Bedjan, *Homiliae Selectae Mar-Jacobi Sarugensis*, vol. 3). For Nonnus of Nisibis contrasting the *ḥakkimē* and the *saklē* ('stupid,' 'foolish'), see his *Apologetic Treatise*, p. *31 (ln. 2) (ed. A. van Roey, *Traité apologétique: étude, texte et traduction* [Louvain, 1948]). I am grateful to Philip Forness for the reference to Jacob of Sarugh and to Kristian Heal for the reference to Aphrahat.

[42] See P. Biller, 'Intellectuals and the Masses: Oxen and She-Asses in the Medieval Church,' in J. H. Arnold, ed., *The Oxford Handbook of Medieval Christianity* (Oxford, 2014), pp. 323–39.

[43] See, e.g., Varro's contrast between mythical, natural, and civil theology in Augustine, *City of God* 6.5 (ed. B. Dombart and A. Kalb with FT by G. Combès in *La cité de Dieu* [Oeuvres de Saint Augustin 34] [Paris, 1959], pp. 64–69; ET available in R. W. Dyson, *Augustine. The City of God against the Pagans* [Cambridge/New York, 1998], p. 247).

[44] On the Arian controversy, see, e.g., R. C. Gregg and D. E. Groh, 'The Centrality of Soteriology in Early Arianism,' *Anglican Theological Review* 59 (1977), pp. 260–78 and Gregg and Groh, *Early Arianism:*

seminar, and we can only view these debates as logomachies if we study the *lex credendi* apart from the *lex orandi*, that is, if we understand 'orthodoxy' as a question only of right belief and not also of correct worship. But we do the latter only at our own peril: We must never forget that the theological elites who fought doctrinal wars lived lives dominated by pastoral concerns and saturated with prayer, fasting, and worship. It was out of the ground of these lived experiences that their doctrinal concerns grew. Much as sophisticated regional cuisines of the modern era represent refined versions of peasant food,[45] so too the religious concerns at stake in the complicated theological disputes of the elites in our period were, at base, substantially the same as those of everybody else. To draw an analogy from a later period: few religious experts in the eighteenth century were as learned as the Jesuits, and yet it has been argued Jesuit missionaries working among rural populations in Germany 'shared with the people what might be termed a culture of the miraculous.'[46] The 'worlds' of the learned Christian and the simple Christian were one and the same.[47]

A View of Salvation (Philadelphia, 1981). For the dispute between Cyril and Nestorius, see H. Chadwick, 'Eucharist and Christology in the Nestorian Conflict,' *JTS* 2 (1951), pp. 145–64, and for its aftermath, see P.T.R. Gray, 'From Eucharist to Christology: The Life-Giving Body of Christ in Cyril of Alexandria, Eutyches and Julian of Halicarnassus,' in I. Perczel, R. Forrai, and G. Geréby, eds., *The Eucharist in Theology and Philosophy: Issues of Doctrinal History in East and West from the Patristic Age to the Reformation* (Leuven, 2005), pp. 23–35. For the thought of the important Miaphysite Philoxenus of Mabbug, see D. A. Michelson, *The Practical Theology of Philoxenos of Mabbug* (Oxford, 2014). On the Monothelete controversy, see my remarks in 'In Search of Monotheletism,' pp. 64–67. For the relationship between Christology and mysticism in the thought of the seventh-century figure Sahdona, see O. Ioan, 'Martyrius-Sahdona: la pensée christologique, clé de la théologie mystique,' in A. Desreumaux, ed., *Les mystiques syriaques* (Paris, 2011), pp. 45–61. The comments of A. Louth, *Modern Orthodox Thinkers: From the* Philokalia *to the Present* (Downer's Grove, 2015), p. 3, on the patristic understanding of theology are also helpful to think with here.

[45] Cf. R. Laudan, *Cuisine and Empire: Cooking in World History* (Berkeley, 2013), p. 325: 'Cooks refined peasant dishes as nineteenth-century chefs had refined foreign dishes.' For Origen comparing doctrine with food, see *Contra Celsum* 7.59.

[46] T. Johnson, 'Blood, Tears and Xavier-Water: Jesuit Missionaries and Popular Religion in the Eighteenth-Century Upper Palatinate,' in B. Scribner and T. Johnson, eds., *Popular Religion in Germany and Central Europe, 1400–1800* (Basingstoke/New York, 1996), pp. 182–203, quote at 202.

[47] To say the concerns were the same is not, of course, to say that all levels shared a similar concern about matters of theological speculation. To assert, for instance, that worries about Eucharistic piety were one of the driving factors behind the dispute between Cyril and Nestorius is not to assert that both ordinary Christians and learned theologians were keenly interested in the propriety of using Theopaschite language. It is to argue, rather, that the Eucharist was important to ordinary and elite alike, and that the latter cared about Theopaschite language because they believed that its use (or non-use) affected how one viewed the Eucharist. In other words, people ultimately cared about Theopaschite language because they cared about the Eucharist.

G. Wainwright, *Doxology: The Praise of God in Worship, Doctrine, and Life: A Systematic Theology* (New York, 1980), is a contemporary systematic theology with a strong emphasis on the relationship between the *lex credendi* and *the lex orandi*. Stephen Shoemaker's description of the relationship between

A LAYERING OF KNOWLEDGE?

Most inquiries into the question of simplicity of belief or the idea of the simple believer have focused on the first four centuries of Christian history.[48] At present, however, I am more interested in the period after Chalcedon (451) than in the first centuries of Christianity and pagan-Christian relations.[49] Although the notion of the simple believer was used both polemically and rhetorically—as an indication of the power of the notion of the 'simple,' someone as erudite as George, Bishop of the Arab Tribes, a bilingual and perhaps even trilingual figure who translated and commented on Aristotle in Syriac, might even rhetorically refer to himself as a *hedyoṭā*,[50] and the great poet Jacob of Sarugh might compare himself to one[51]—what interests me here is the reality

---

popular Marian devotion and the formal treatment of Marian dogma provides a nice historical illustration of the relationship between doctrine and piety; see his *Mary in Early Christian Faith and Devotion* (New Haven/London, 2016), pp. 238–40. Though not dealing with theology, Teresa Morgan's discussion of the relationship between popular morality and the ethical doctrines of philosophical schools in the Roman Empire is also interesting to think with; see *Popular Morality in the Early Roman Empire* (Cambridge, 2007), pp. 274-299. L. A. Smoller, "'Popular' Religious Culture(s),' in Arnold, ed., *The Oxford Handbook of Medieval Christianity*, pp. 340–56, provides a useful discussion of the problems that attach to discussions of 'popular' (as opposed to elite) religion and questions our ability to even 'speak confidently of a single shared religious culture shared by all European Christians' (p. 351).

Alister McGrath has suggested that doctrine should be understood as serving four different functions: as 'social demarcation,' 'interpretation of narrative,' 'interpretation of experience,' and as 'truth claim.' See his *The Genesis of Doctrine: A Study in the Foundation of Doctrinal Criticism* (Grand Rapids/Cambridge/Vancouver, 1997), pp. 35–72. To make a crude generalization, historians have tended to view doctrine primarily in terms of the social role it has played, while theologians have been more concerned with its truth claims and their bases. One approach, of course, does not preclude or exclude the other, and it is an obvious point that doctrine will have played a social role for some precisely because they believed that it contained truth claims. Evaluating any such doctrinal truth claims, Christian or Muslim, is beyond the scope of this book (and my competence); nevertheless, for an important critique of sociological approaches to the study of religion as well as historical research that views religious phenomena primarily through a sociological lens, see J. Milbank, *Theology and Social Theory: Beyond Secular Reason*, 2nd ed. (Oxford/Malden, Mass., 2006), pp. 101–44.

[48] Perrin, 'À propos de la participation du peuple fidèle aux controverses doctrinales,' provides an invaluable overview and discussion of much of this literature.

[49] An attempt to look at some of the issues raised here in the context of Chalcedon can be found in W.H.C. Frend, 'Popular Religion and Christological Controversy in the Fifth Century,' in G. J. Cuming and D. Baker, eds., *Studies in Church History*, vol. 8 (Cambridge, 1971), pp. 19–29, reprinted in W.H.C. Frend, *Religion Popular and Unpopular in the Early Christian Centuries* (London, 1976), no. XVII.

[50] George, Bishop of the Arab Tribes, *Letter 4* (To Joshua the Hermit) (BL Add. 12.154, fol. 249b) and *Letter 10* (To John the Stylite) (BL Add., 12,154, fol. 284a). It is worth remembering that in 2 Corinthians 1:12, Paul had already written, 'For our boast is this, the testimony of our conscience, that we behaved in the world with simplicity (ἐν ἁπλότητι/*d-ba-pshiṭutā*) and godly sincerity, not by earthly wisdom but by the grace of God, and supremely so toward you' (ESV). Note also the positive use of ἁπλότης/*pshiṭutā* in Romans 12:8, 2 Cor. 8:2, 9:11, 9:13.

[51] Jacob of Sarugh, *Homily on Mar Ephrem* 11 (ed. and trans. J. Amar, *A Metrical Homily on Mar*

that underlies its use: the idea that within the Christian community, there might be a layering of knowledge, different levels of understanding and engagement with sophisticated and complex doctrines.[52] Recognizing that there was a layering of knowledge in the late antique Christian community—and that this layering was something Christian leaders recognized and spoke about—allows us to phrase the questions that I raised at the end of Chapter 1 in the language of texts from the late Roman world: How did simple believers relate to the disputes resulting from Chalcedon? Why would an ordinary person choose one confession over another?

THE SIMPLE AND CHALCEDON

We can begin an answer to such questions with a basic presupposition: many people, maybe most, never made a conscious choice of one confession over another. These controversies and the ecclesiastical splits they engendered lasted for centuries. After a certain point, theology was no longer the most important factor motivating the ecclesiastical separation for many—if it ever had been. One went to a Chalcedonian or Miaphysite church simply because that was what one's parents had done, not out of a conscious choice made after evaluating competing understandings of the Incarnation. Church attendance, we should recognize, must have been preeminently a local affair, so it is quite possible, and even likely, that one's parents (or forbears) never made a decision for or against Chalcedon either. They followed whatever their local priest or church did.

There were, in fact, a whole host of nontheological factors that might incline a person toward one confession or another. One was violence or the threat of violence: 'He heard some people, those attached to material things,' Elias, the biographer of the prominent Miaphysite John of Tella (d. 537) wrote,

> who shunned and despised spiritual things, saying, 'If the imperial edict should also come here requiring that we accept the Council of Chalcedon, then we

Ephrem by Mar Jacob of Sarug [PO 47.1] [Turnhout, 1995], p. 26). 'Simple' could even take on a moral connotation: see Bar Hebraeus, *Ecclesiastical History* 1.80 (ed. J. B. Abbeloos and T. J. Lamy, *Gregorii Barhebraei Chronicon Ecclesiasticum* [Paris/Louvain, 1872–1877], vol. 1, col. 439), where Ignatius of Melitene (d. 1063) is described as being educated in Greek and Syriac letters, like Jacob of Edessa and Thomas of Harkel, and also trained in rhetoric and grammar, but is also called 'simple (*pshiṭā*) and innocent (*tammimā*) and merciful and renunciant.'

[52] See, e.g., Origen, *Contra Celsum* 7.60 (ed. M. Borret, *Origène Contra Celse. Tome IV: (Livres VII et VIII)* [SC 150] [Paris, 1969], pp. 154, 156; ET available in Chadwick, *Origen: Contra Celsum*, pp. 445–46) and Gregory of Nazianzus, *Orations* 32.11 (ed. Moreschini [SC 318], pp. 108, 110; ET available in Vinson, *Select Orations*, p. 199).

> would easily persuade [John] to accept it, since this is nothing. There are none who can really stand against the imperial order![53]

The imperial order was not something to be taken lightly.[54] The sixth-century Miaphysite *vita* of Barṣawmā (d. 456) claimed that only a few bishops at Chalcedon actually held erroneous beliefs (i.e., only a few bishops actually supported the theology of Chalcedon), but 'because they feared the emperor, they sought to please him.'[55] This was an era in which force was used as a means of persuasion when it came to Christology. We have Miaphysite reports that Asclepius, the metropolitan of Edessa (sed. 518–524) tortured monks 'mercilessly' to make them accept Chalcedon.[56] Ephrem of Antioch (sed. 527–545) and Abraham bar Kayli, Chalcedonian bishop of Amid, were reported to have compelled people to accept the Council of Chalcedon while accompanied by Roman forces.[57] Ephrem, in fact, was remembered for having spent 18 years going about the region of Edessa with 'barbarian troops,' destroying

[53] Elias, *Life of John of Tella*, pp. 54–55 (ed. E. W. Brooks, *Vitae virorum apud Monophysitas celeberrimorum. Pars prima* (CSCO SS III.25) [Paris, 1907], pp. 54–55; ET taken from J. R. Ghanem, 'The Biography of John of Tella (d. A.D. 537) by Elias: Translated from the Syriac with a Historical Introduction and Historical and Linguistic Commentaries,' [PhD diss., University of Wisconsin, 1970], pp. 64–65). But contrast this view with that of the Marzban later in the *Life* who says he would resist a hypothetical order from the King of Kings to change his beliefs, even if it meant having his two sons murdered before him (Brooks, *Vitae virorum*, p. 73; Ghanem, 'The Biography of John of Tella,' pp. 84–85).

[54] On the reverence with which an emperor, his edicts, and even his image were viewed and treated in the later Roman world, cf. C. Kelly, 'Emperors, Government and Bureaucracy,' in Av. Cameron and P. Garnsey, eds., *The Cambridge Ancient History*, vol. 13: *The Late Empire, A.D. 337–425* (Cambridge, 1998), pp. 139–150; on the importance of loyalty to the emperor, cf. also M. McCormick, 'Emperor and Court,' in Av. Cameron, B. Ward-Perkins, and M. Whitby, eds., *The Cambridge Ancient History*, vol. 14: *Late Antiquity: Empire and Successors, A.D. 425–600* (Cambridge, 2000), p. 144. The 'royal' or 'imperial' decree referred to in the previous footnote was the *puqdānā d-malkā* (CSCO SS III.25, p. 55.4): for other examples of the imperial edict being difficult to resist and forcing Christian leaders to act, see, e.g., Ps.-John bar Aphtonia, *Life of Severus*, pp. 154.2 (*puqdānā d-malkā*), 156.1 (*puqdānā malkāyā*) (ed. Kugener [PO 2.3]).

[55] 'For they feared the power (*shulṭānā*) of humans more than the power (*shulṭānā*) of God.' Dioscorus, by contrast, 'did not fear the might (*shulṭānā*) of kings and did not accept the despicable doctrine of the unbelievers' (cf. Matthew 10:28; Acts 4:19–20, 5:29). For these quotations, I have relied on the digitized version of an unnumbered Syriac manuscript that was held in the Syrian Orthodox Church of St. George in Aleppo, but of whose current whereabouts I am unsure. The quotations occur on fols. 98b–99a (on fearful bishops), 99b (on Dioscorus). A summary of the *Life* was published in F. Nau, 'Résumé de monographies syriaques: Barṣauma, Abraham de la Haute Montagne, Siméon de Kefar 'Abdin, Yaret l'Alexandrin, Jacques le reclus, Romanus, Talia, Asia, Pantaléon, Candida, Sergis et Abraham de Caškar,' *ROC* 18 (1913), pp. 270–76, 379–89; 19 (1914), pp. 113–34, 278–89. For this quote, cf. *ROC* 19 (1914), p. 131. More generally on this *vita*, see L. van Rompay's article 'Barṣawmo,' in *GEDSH*, p. 59, and A. Palmer, 'The West-Syrian Monastic Founder Barṣawmo: A Historical Review of the Scholarly Literature,' in P. Bruns and H. O. Luthe, eds., *Orientalia Christiana: Festschrift für Hubert Kaufhold zum 70. Geburtstag* (Wiesbaden, 2013), pp. 399–414.

[56] Michael the Great, *Chronicle* 9.16 (ed. Chabot, 4.270 = 2.179).

[57] *Chronicle to 846*, p. 225 (ed. Brooks [CSCO III.4], p. 225).

monasteries, uprooting altars, and persecuting Miaphysites,[58] and a number of graphic horrors involving religious coercion were associated with Abraham.[59] Being on the wrong side of an ecclesiastical disagreement also meant that one's options might well be limited in seeking recourse for violence: Heraclius did not permit Miaphysites to enter into his presence and did not accept their complaints about the seizure of their churches.[60]

Even being at the highest levels of church leadership did not make one safe: Euphrasius, patriarch of Antioch (sed. 521–526), initially 'removed from the diptychs both the Synod of Chalcedon and the name of Hormisdas, the Pope of Rome.' But '[a]fterwards in fear he proclaimed the four synods.'[61] Miaphysites later looked back upon this period as a time of episcopal pusillanimity: 'The bishops in all the cities of the empire of the Romans,' Michael the Great (d. 1199) wrote about the reign of the staunch Chalcedonian Justinian, 'were weak, apart from the see of Alexandria, which itself after a period of twenty years was subjugated to the heresy of the Dyophysites by means of Paul.'[62]

There were other considerations as well. One was money: according to Michael the Great, when Justinian issued an order in the sixth century proclaiming that all soldiers who did not accept Chalcedon would be deprived of their pay and of military honors, most simply accepted the Synod.[63] Leontius

[58] Michael the Great, *Chronicle* 9.16 (ed. Chabot, 4.272 = 2.181). A more detailed description of the violence associated with Ephrem's 'descent to the East' can be found in *Zuqnin Chronicle*, pp. 38–44 (ed. I.-B. Chabot, *Incerti auctoris chronicon anonymum Pseudo-Dionysianum vulgo dictum* [CSCO 104: SS 53] [Paris, 1933]; ET available in A. Harrak, *The Chronicle of Zuqnīn*, Parts III and IV: *A.D. 488–775* [Toronto, 1999], pp. 64–67).

[59] See *Zuqnin Chronicle*, pp. 32–38 (ed. Chabot [CSCO 104: SS 53]; ET available in Harrak, *The Chronicle of Zuqnīn*, pp. 60–64). Note especially the story of Cyrus, the Miaphysite priest whose teeth were pulled out and who was eventually burned alive: *Zuqnin Chronicle*, pp. 34–36 (= Harrak, *The Chronicle of Zuqnīn*, p. 62) and cf. the shortened version of this story in Michael the Great, *Chronicle* 9.16 (ed. Chabot, 4.272 [Syriac] = 2.181). On Bar Kayli's infamous reputation, see V. Menze, *Justinian and the Making of the Syrian Orthodox Church* (Oxford, 2008), pp. 116–17, 235–45.

[60] And it was for this reason that God brought about the Arab conquests: see Michael the Great, *Chronicle* 11.4 (ed. Chabot, 4.410 = 2.412–413) and cf. S. P. Brock, 'Syriac Views of Emergent Islam,' in G.H.A. Juynboll, ed., *Studies in the First Century of Islamic Society* (Carbondale and Edwardsville, Ill., 1982), pp. 10–11.

[61] Theophanes, *Chronicle* AM 6013 (ed. de Boor, vol. 1, p. 167; ET taken from Mango and Scott, *The Chronicle of Theophanes Confessor*, p. 254).

[62] Michael the Great, *Chronicle* 9.29 (ed. Chabot, 4.308 [Syriac] = 2.243-244). The Paul in question was a Chalcedonian who was bishop from 538-542. In my translation, I follow Chabot who here understood the Syriac ܐܪܦܘ as 'se montrérent pusillanimes.' The situation during what has traditionally been referred to as the 'Arian' controversy is useful to think with by comparison: see the collection of material assembled by Cardinal Newman about bishops in the fourth century and their wavering relationship to Nicaea in J. H. Newman, 'On Consulting the Faithful in Matters of Doctrine,' *Rambler* 1 (N.S.) (1859), pp. 219–27.

[63] See Michael the Great, *Chronicle* 9.16 (ed. Chabot, pp. 270–71 [Syriac] = 2.180), where three exceptions who were martyred for their refusal are mentioned. NB: I understand ܐܢܘܢܐ (cf. ἀννώνα) here to

of Jerusalem wrote of various non-theological factors that might incline a person to holding on to his or her confession. There were, for example, 'passionate attachment to heresiarchs' and the 'ties of ancestry, family, or place which tie some people indissolubly to heterodoxy.' Leontius also mentioned 'means of gains or certain life-benefits that make it hard to tear us away from superstition, and that gradually persuade us to overlook the great gain, orthodoxy with contentment.'[64] There was also a certain amount of ideological inertia at play: once one had been established in a certain ecclesiastical setting and community, a host of everyday practical concerns might make it difficult to shift to a new one.

What of doctrine? Did it matter? For some of the simple, it did not. At the end of the Chalcedonian Leontius of Jerusalem's *Testimonies of the Saints*, there is a story about an actor captured by Christian Arabs that can serve to illustrate this.[65] The actor was putatively a Chalcedonian, but this affiliation had no great significance to him. He was, Leontius wrote, 'of our persuasion only in that, when he went to church, he gathered with us, though to tell the truth he did so without realizing there was any difference between Christians.'[66] Some Christians were simply not aware of the differences in confession.

But others were: we have examples of disagreement even within families over the question of Chalcedon—the most famous example, of course, being the disagreement between Justinian and Theodora, if indeed their disagreement was not feigned for reasons of political usefulness. In such instances, however, we need to probe further to ascertain the precise nature of that engagement with the question of Chalcedon.

One might consider doctrine important but be unable to articulate and defend the views of one's church in a compelling manner. In 560 the Emperor Justinian summoned *scholastici*, *grammatici*, monks, and shipmasters from Alexandria and Egypt to debate questions of the Incarnation at his court in Constantinople. Unlike the actor in Leontius's *Testimonies*, these Miaphysite shipmasters—who, according to John of Ephesus, were in charge of delivering

mean 'pay,' but it can also refer to food. See J. Payne Smith, *A Compendious Syriac Dictionary* (Oxford, 1903), s.v. ܐܢܘܢܐ and cf. Chabot's rendering: 'rations.'

[64] Leontius of Jerusalem, *Testimonies of the Saints*, p. 152 (ed. and trans. P.T.R. Gray, *Leontius of Jerusalem. Against the Monophysites: Testimonies of the Saints and Aporiae* [Oxford, 2006]; I have used the ET of Gray, p. 153).

[65] On this story as not being part of Leontius's original *Testimonies of the Saints*, see Gray, *Leontius of Jerusalem*, pp. 38–39. But for the view that this passage was written by Leontius and that Leontius should be dated to the seventh century, see D. Krausmüller, 'Leontius of Jerusalem: A Theologian of the Seventh Century,' *JTS* 52 (2001), pp. 637–57.

[66] Leontius of Jerusalem, *Testimonies of the Saints*, pp. 158–61 (ed. and trans. Gray, *Leontius of Jerusalem*; the translation I have used here is that of Gray, quote at 161).

wheat from Alexandria to the capital city—had a consciousness of their confessional affiliation. The importance of their occupation also suggests that they had some level of literacy.[67] But literacy and an awareness that one did not accept the Council of Chalcedon did not translate into an ability to articulate and defend one's faith: 'After a lengthy talk, they said to [the Emperor],' John wrote, ' "Because we are people who struggle with the sea and are not experienced in debate, if you wish, give an order, and when we return the next time, monastical fathers, *scholastici*, as well as *grammatici*, versed in the Scriptures and the rest of the city's officials will come with us. In this way, all the questions concerning the Faith will be examined and discussed." '[68] The shipowners' begging off from debate may have been an attempt to save face and extract themselves from a tricky situation once they realized they were in over their heads, but at the same time it pointed to a reality as well: their job was to move grain across the Mediterranean—it was not to critique the theological stance of learned theologians. Confronted with such theologians, they simply called in expert help.[69]

The reaction of the shipmasters should not be taken to mean that debates or discussions between those ordinary Christians who did care about religious difference never occurred. Quite the contrary.[70] 'But is there not some method or other,' the Chalcedonian Anastasius of Sinai (d. ca. 700) was asked, 'by which

[67] In Syriac, they were referred to as ܢܘܩܠܪܐ. For a discussion of the ναύκληρος and its various possible meanings—including 'captain,' 'shipmaster,' and 'shipowner,'—see A. I. Connolly in G.H.R. Horsley, *New Documents Illustrating Early Christianity: A Review of the Greek Inscriptions and Papyri Published in 1979* (North Ryde, N.S.W., 1987), pp. 116–17.

[68] *Zuqnin Chronicle*, pp. 136–37 (ed. Chabot [CSCO 104: SS 53]; ET taken from Harrak, *The Chronicle of Zuqnīn*, p. 131). ET also available in W. Witakowski, *Pseudo-Dionysius of Tel-Mahre: Chronicle* Part III (Liverpool, 1996), pp. 121–22. For John of Ephesus as the source of this report in the *Zuqnin Chronicle*, see W. Witakowski, 'Sources of Pseudo-Dionysius for the Third Part of his Chronicle,' *Orientalia Suecana* 40 (1991), p. 267 (under Lm 871).

[69] It is perhaps confusing that the shipowners wanted to bring *scholastici* and *grammatici* to support their position when such figures were already there in the story—but this curious fact, along with the fact that John of Ephesus singles out the shipowners specifically as believers, suggests that the first group of *scholastici* and *grammatici* referred to were supporters of Chalcedon; Justinian asked them to discuss the matter of Chalcedon with these non-Chalcedonian shipowners from Alexandria. They end by offering to bring their own experts to the discussion. Compare with the reported response of the Emperor Marcian in the Miaphysite *History of Dioscorus*, when he was urged to accept the *Tome* of Leo: 'I fear doing this lest my kingdom acquire a great sin. For it is bodily that I have been entrusted with the empire, but the bishops, spiritually. I know a certain monk in Scetis, which is in the Thebaid of Egypt, whose name is John. [In] everything that he says, I have found his words to be trustworthy, so now I am sending to him and I will ask whether it is the will of God that I accept the *Tome* of Leo or whether I should leave the faith as it is.' See Ps.-Theopistus, *History of Dioscorus* 8 (ed. F. Nau, 'Histoire de Dioscore,' *JA* 10 [1903], pp. 48–49 [Syriac] = 266 [French]). On this early sixth-century *vita*, see C. Lange, 'Dioscurus of Alexandria in the Syriac *vita* of Theopistus,' *The Harp* 19 (2006), pp. 341–51.

[70] On Chrysostom's preaching equipping ordinary Christians for debate, see Maxwell, *Christianization and Communication in Late Antiquity*, pp. 115–16.

an uneducated person may confute the heretic?' Anastasius counseled that the uneducated person should employ an argument that a Chalcedonian with no training in public speaking had recently used in a debate with Severans and Gaianites in Alexandria: the fact that God had given control over all the holy sites of the Old and New Testament to Chalcedonians was proof that it was they who possessed the truly orthodox faith.[71]

Anastasius's recommendation points us to an important reality: arguments and debates took place among ordinary believers over the question of Chalcedon—but these disputes were not always of a purely doctrinal nature, nor indeed did they necessarily have anything to do with doctrine at all. The 'uneducated person' Anastasius was advising was an ἰδιώτης, and the problem of the theologically uninstructed defending themselves dialectically was not one confined to Chalcedonian circles: John Rufus reported an incident in which a Chalcedonian priest and a zealous yet unlearned Miaphysite villager—a *hedyoṭā*, that is, an ἰδιώτης—had a dispute over the faith: the priest ordered the Miaphysite to take communion from him or leave the village. Their debate over right belief was settled not by reasoned arguments, but by starting a fire and placing their hands in it to see whose hand came out unscathed. 'They drew near the fire,' John reported, 'and placed their hands in. The hand of the priest was burned up, immediately and without delay, but that of the believing Orthodox layman remained without injury.'[72] In Pamphylia, a debate between Miaphysite and Chalcedonian monks eventually led to both sides starting a fire: the *Tome* of Leo was thrown in, as was the profession of Chalcedon and an encyclical with a Miaphysite profession. The Miaphysite encyclical was preserved in the midst of the flame, while the *Tome* and the words of Chalcedon went up in smoke. The Chalcedonian monks, John Rufus reported, repented, fled from their error, and became zealous for the Miaphysite faith.[73]

[71] Anastasius of Sinai, *Questions and Answers* 69 (ed. Richard and Munitiz, *Anastasii Sinaitae Quaestiones et responsiones*, pp. 121–22 [quote from p. 121]; translation taken from Munitiz, *Questions and Answers*, pp. 184–86 [quote from p. 184]). For a similar argument used in favor of Chalcedon in the twelfth century, see Dionysius bar Salibi, *Against the Melkites* 6 (ET in A. Mingana, ed. and trans., *Woodbrooke Studies*, vol. 1 [Cambridge, 1927], pp. 42–45 [English] = 78 [Syriac]; quotations at pp. 42 [= 79], 45 [=80]). For a related argument used against Jews, also in the seventh century, see *Trophies of Damascus* 2.2.1 (ed. G. Bardy, *Les trophées de Damas: controverse judéo-chrétienne du VIIe siècle* [PO 15.2] [Paris, 1920], pp. 47–48). For the suggestion that 'the holy places had gained theological weight as proof for theological doctrines,' already in the fifth century and discussion of how Miaphysites dealt with the reality of Chalcedonian control of these sites, see C. B. Horn, *Asceticism and Christological Controversy in Fifth-Century Palestine: the Career of Peter the Iberian* (Oxford, 2006), pp. 322–31 (quote at 322).

[72] John Rufus, *Plerophories* 47 (ed. F. Nau, *Jean Rufus, évêque de Maïouma. Plérophories* [PO 8.1] [Paris, 1912] pp. 98–100, quote on p. 100).

[73] John Rufus, *Plerophories* 45 (ed. Nau [PO 8.1] p. 98).

These were Miaphysite stories—but appeals to heat or fire were used by both sides to make their case, and they point to the fact that rigorous reasoning or clever questioning were not the only means of settling theological disagreements.[74] The Chalcedonian John Moschus reported the story of two stylites in Cilicia, one Chalcedonian and one Miaphysite, who debated over the nature of the faith. It seemed the Miaphysite had bested the Chalcedonian, but the final arbiter was not the relative strengths of their arguments: it was the Eucharist. The Chalcedonian requested that the Miaphysite send him a portion of his Eucharist. When the Chalcedonian received it, he placed it in boiling water and it promptly dissolved. After the Chalcedonian placed his own Eucharist in boiling water, however, the water cooled down.[75] Another story related by John Moschus had a Miaphysite stylite become a Chalcedonian after an encounter with Ephrem, the staunchly Chalcedonian patriarch of Antioch whom we have already encountered. The stylite initially had suggested that both he and Ephrem walk into a fire and judge the truth of their relative positions by seeing who would emerge unscathed. Ephrem settled the issue, however, by throwing his cloak into a fire that was built before the stylite's column; three hours later, when the fire had burned out, the cloak was retrieved, perfectly intact and unharmed.[76]

Stories such as these must have circulated widely throughout the Middle East—John Rufus, for instance, wrote in Greek, but his *Plerophories* were translated into Syriac and Coptic,[77] and John Moschus wrote in Greek, but at least

[74] It is also worth keeping in mind that disputes between pagans and Christians had been settled by nonintellectual means as well—see, e.g., Sozomen, *Ecclesiastical History* 7.20, where pagans blamed the failure of the Nile to flood at its normal time on the prohibition of sacrifices. The Nile did, however, eventually flood, and the flood was so enormous that a number of pagans became Christians.

[75] John Moschus, *Spiritual Meadow* 29 (PG 87, cols. 2876–77; ET in J. Wortley, *The Spiritual Meadow* [Collegeville, MN, 1992], pp. 20–21). On Eucharistic stories in John Rufus's *Plerophories*, which can be viewed as providing a pro-Miaphysite counter to these types of tales, see P. Booth, *Crisis of Empire: Doctrine and Dissent at the End of Late Antiquity* (Berkeley, 2014), pp. 38–40.

[76] John Moschus, *Spiritual Meadow* 36 (PG 87, cols. 2884–85; ET in Wortley, *The Spiritual Meadow*, pp. 25–26). For these stories and their contrast with the *Plerophories* of John Rufus, see Booth, *Crisis of Empire*, pp. 130–31. It should be kept in mind, too, that Christians also used fire to establish religious truth in disputes with pagans. See, e.g., *Chronicle of Seert* 2.31 (ed. Scher [PO 7.2], p. 81) and *Life of John of Daylam* 20 (ed. S. P. Brock, 'A Syriac Life of John of Dailam,' *PdO* 10 [1981–82], p. 138 [Syriac] = 147 [ET]). Perhaps all such stories should be seen, ultimately, as evocations of the stories of Shadrach, Meshach, and Abednego in Daniel 3 and Elijah and the prophets of Baal in 1 Kings 18.

[77] For fragments of the *Plerophories* in Coptic, see T. Orlandi, *Koptische Papyri theologischen Inhalts* (Vienna, 1974), pp. 110–20, and Orlandi, 'Un frammento delle Pleroforie in Copto,' *Studi e Ricerche sull'Oriente Cristiano* 2 (1979), pp. 3–12. Note that Michael the Great was still repeating John Rufus's stories nearly six hundred years after they were first written: see Michael the Great, *Chronicle* 8.11 (ed. Chabot, 4.203–15 = 2.69-88). The eighth-century *Zuqnin Chronicle* also incorporated material from the *Plerophories*. See the analysis in W. Witakowski, *The Syriac Chronicle of Pseudo-Dionysius of Tel-Maḥrē: A Study in the History of Historiography* (Uppsala, 1987), p. 133.

portions of his *Spiritual Meadow* were translated into Syriac.[78] There might also be rival stories about the fate of well-known proponents of this view or that: according to Chalcedonians, the bishops Asclepius of Edessa and Euphrasius of Antioch were taken up into heaven. Miaphysites, however, spread the story that they had fallen into a cauldron of pitch in the earthquake that struck Antioch in 526 and their bones were stripped of flesh. God, however, preserved their faces at the edge of the cauldron in order to make their identities and their error known.[79]

The popularity of these kinds of dueling stories points to the fact that an appeal to the miraculous or to a powerful figure provided an alternative justification for adopting a particular doctrinal stance or for associating with one communion as opposed to another: debating dialectically, citing the Bible, or researching patristic *testimonia* were not for everyone. What is more, doctrinal disputes no doubt caused confusion among many of those who were aware of them but lacked the ability to evaluate competing claims.[80] The variety of different Christian groups making similar claims threatened to overwhelm: 'But truly, Abba, all the sects speak like that . . . ,' a certain Theophanes from Dara in northern Mesopotamia told a Chalcedonian monk named Cyriacus at the lavra of Kalamon in the Holy Land, 'that if you are not in communion with us, you are not being saved. I am a simple person (ταπεινός) and really do not

[78] A Syriac translation of parts of the *Spiritual Meadow* was available in the now-destroyed Codex Syriacus I (Hiersemann 500/2.11). For its brief description by Anton Baumstark, see *Katalog 500: Orientalische Manuskripte (Karl Hiersemann)* (Leipzig, 1922), pp. 4–5 (no. 11); and cf. the description of the same manuscript in an earlier catalog (*Hiersemann 487* [Leipzig, 1921], p. 65, no. 11 = Hiersemann 487/255a, written when Baumstark had not yet realized that the manuscript's attribution to Palladius was erroneous). On the Hiersemann manuscripts, see B. Outtier, 'Le sort des manuscrits du "Katalog Hiersemann 500,"' *AB* 93 (1975), pp. 377–80 and W. Strothmann, 'Die orientalischen Handschriften der Sammlung Mettler (Katalog Hiersemann 500),' in W. Voigt, ed., XIX. *Deutscher Orientalistentag vom 28. September bis 4. Oktober 1975 in Freiburg im Breisgau: Vorträge* (Wiesbaden, 1977), pp. 285–93. For surviving fragments of Codex Syriacus I in Mingana Syriac 656 and Milan Chabot 34, see P. Géhin, 'Manuscrits sinaïtiques dispersés III: les fragments syriaques de Londres et de Birmingham,' OC 94 (2010), pp. 47–48.

[79] Michael the Great, *Chronicle* 9.16 (ed. Chabot, 4.273 = 2.182–83).

[80] Cf. the reported bewilderment of a pagan contemplating conversion to Christianity and unable to decide which Christian group's competing claim was in fact true: John Chrysostom, *Homilies on the Acts of the Apostles* 33.4 (PG 60, cols. 243–44; ET by J. Walker, J. Sheppard, and H. Browne available in *NPNF*, ser. 1, vol. 11, pp. 210–11). For this passage, cf. R. MacMullen, 'The Historical Role of the Masses in Late Antiquity,' in MacMullen, *Changes in the Roman Empire: Essays in the Ordinary* (Princeton, 1990), p. 275. Bar Hebraeus reported that in the fourth century Themistius attempted to calm the emperor's anger over Christian division by writing an oration (*mēmrā*) in which he said, 'No one should be amazed that the Christians are divided in their religion, for among the pagans there are 300 sects. Indeed, God himself wills that He be glorified in various ways, for that which may be known of Him is not easily comprehended' (Bar Hebraeus, *Ecclesiastical History* 1.31 [ed. Abbeloos and Lamy, *Gregorii Barhebraei Chronicon Ecclesiasticum*, vol. 1, cols. 107, 109]).

know what to do. Pray to the Lord that by a deed he will show me which is the true faith.'

Theophanes had sought out the help of Cyriacus in dealing with impure thoughts and after receiving it had told the monk that back home he communicated with Nestorians. Cyriacus, hearing that Theophanes was part of a Nestorian community 'became very concerned about the destruction of the brother,' and urged him to join the true church—the Chalcedonian church—the only place he might find salvation. Cyriacus was able, John Moschus reported, to bring Theophanes to Chalcedonianism by showing him a vision of hell in which Nestorius, Severus, Eutyches, Arius, and other heretics could be seen in the midst of fire. 'This place is prepared for heretics and for those who blaspheme against the holy Mother of God,' a radiant apparition told him. 'If you find this place to your liking, then stay with the doctrine you now hold. If you have no wish to experience the pains of this chastisement, proceed to the holy catholic church in which the elder teaches. For I tell you that if a man practise every virtue and yet not glorify [God] correctly, to this place he will come.'[81]

Such stories, however, created their own problems: How could one evaluate competing miracle or visionary claims? How could church leaders respond to stories that seemed to support the truth of their rivals' position? 'Some people,' the Chalcedonian Leontius of Jerusalem wrote, 'invent a different justification than these for their disobedience to the truth.' Rather than carefully examining doctrines to see if they were true, they looked for symbols of divine approval: 'This is what they say,' he wrote:

> When certain people who hold to the same opinion as they do—some of them living in the flesh, and some who have passed on—have been seen to possess the gift of healings and of signs from God, how could the opinion held among them not be pleasing to God? It is clear, after all, that divine powers operate on the basis of hearing and teaching God's correct faith.

Arians and Nestorians, Leontius admitted, could perform wonders, but he cautioned that this should in no way be interpreted as pointing to the truth of the doctrines they taught.[82]

Leaders had to provide explanations to make sense of how God might be at work in groups that were supposed to be in error. Scripture provided useful examples: even Balaam and the Witch of Endor were able to perform signs

[81] John Moschus, *The Spiritual Meadow* 26 (PG 87, cols. 2872–73; ET taken from Wortley, *The Spiritual Meadow*, p. 18).

[82] Leontius of Jerusalem, *Testimonies of the Saints*, p. 156 (ed. and trans. Gray, *Leontius of Jerusalem*; the ET is that of Gray, p. 157). For a comparison of Leontius of Jerusalem and Severus of Antioch's attitudes toward the probative value of miracles for doctrine, see Moss, 'The Rise and Function of the Holy Text in Late Antiquity,' p. 538, n. 44.

and wonders, Anastasius of Sinai counseled one of his questioners, and other 'unworthy persons' had done similarly. 'It is necessary to realize this,' he wrote, 'so that when you see that some sign has been performed, by some decision of God, through heretics or unbelievers, you not be shaken in the right-thinking faith because of signs and wonders.' There were other explanations for how a heretic or unbeliever might be able to work a miracle as well. Perhaps God was allowing it to happen to test one's faith. Alternatively, it may have been the faith of the person healed rather than the faith of the healer that was responsible for the wonder. 'Therefore,' Anastasius advised, 'do not think that it is very important if you happen to see some unworthy person or someone of erroneous faith working a sign.'[83]

An appeal to fire or to the miraculous works of a holy person was a simple tactic that allowed one to avoid discussions of natures, *prosopa*, and *hypostaseis* and yet still know which claim of Christian truth was the right one. The existence of such an alternate route of verification points, moreover, to the fact that the choice of which side of the Chalcedonian divide one stood on was not always a function of one's considered opinion about questions of natures in the Incarnate Christ.[84] This is precisely what we would expect if there was a layering of knowledge in the Christian community: understandings of Chalcedon and reasons for accepting or rejecting it varied in accordance with a variety of factors, some doctrinal, but many not.

The recognition of a layering of knowledge in the Christian community helps us to understand how the simple related to the question of Chalcedon, but it also brings to the front another question I raised at the end of Chapter 1: how did the theologically informed—those people whose Christological stances were most likely the result of consideration of the question of Chalcedon on its own terms—relate to everyone else?

ACCOMMODATING THE SIMPLE

One consequence of a layering of knowledge in the Christian community was that theological elites would have to accommodate their message to their audi-

[83] Anastasius of Sinai, *Questions and Answers* 62 (ed. Richard and Munitiz, *Quaestiones et responsiones*, pp. 112–13; ET taken from Munitiz, *Questions and Answers*, pp. 174–75).

[84] On the conversion of Philoxenus of Mabbug to Miaphysitism, which may have been an example of an intellectually motivated shift from one confession to another, see A. de Halleux, *Philoxène de Mabbog. Sa vie, ses écrits, sa théologie* (Louvain, 1963), pp. 28–29. The conversion of Dāwūd b. Marwān (also known as al-Muqammiṣ) (fl. late ninth/early tenth century) from Judaism to Christianity under the influence of the Christian philosopher Nānā (likely the Miaphysite Nonnus of Nisibis) is another potential example of an intellectual conversion. See al-Qirqisānī, *Kitāb al-anwār wa-'l-marāqib*, vol. 2 (ed. L. Nemoy) (New York, 1939), p. 44.

ence: indeed, the idea that God had accommodated his message to humanity and that the message of Christianity itself should, in turn, be accommodated to its audience, was a powerful one with a long pedigree that stretched deep into the Christian past.[85] The difference between a churchgoer's understanding of Christianity and that of his priest or bishop could be dramatic. In the early fifth century, Synesius of Cyrene famously wrote about the stark differences between his beliefs and those of everyday Christians and his unwillingness to teach things he did not believe.[86] In the sixth century, Hypatius, bishop of Ephesus (sed. 531–ca. 538), a contemporary of Severus of Antioch, spoke of the need to accommodate the simple believers under his authority when it came to the question of images and statues in a church: we 'allow even material adornment in the sanctuaries,' he (or a later iconophile interpolator)[87] wrote, 'not because we believe that God considers gold and silver and silken vestments and gem-studded vessels venerable and sacred but because we permit each order of the faithful to be guided and led up to the divine being in a manner appropriate to it.'[88]

Above, we saw that Severus of Antioch used music to give the people of Antioch Christian instruction. In this, (Ps.-)John bar Aphtonia wrote, he was

[85] On the history of the notion of divine accommodation in Judaism and Christianity, see S. D. Benin, 'The "Cunning of God" and Divine Accommodation,' *Journal of the History of Ideas* 45 (1984), pp. 179–91 and Benin, *The Footprints of God: Divine Accommodation in Jewish and Christian Thought* (Albany, N.Y., 1993). The notion of divine accommodation has become associated with the thought of John Calvin. For the classical and patristic roots of Calvin's ideas, see A. Huijgen, *Divine Accommodation in John Calvin's Theology: Analysis and Assessment* (Göttingen, 2011), pp. 47–92. For a modern example of a prominent Christian thinker explicitly speaking of his attempts to accommodate his message to a mass audience not trained in sophisticated theology, see C. S. Lewis, 'Rejoinder to Dr. Pittenger,' *The Christian Century* 75 (November 26, 1958), pp. 1359–61.

[86] Synesius of Cyrene, *Letter 105* (ed. A. Garzya, *Synésios de Cyrène.* vol. 3: *Correspondence. Lettres LXIV-CLVI* [Paris, 2003], pp. 239–40; ET available in A. FitzGerald, *The Letters of Synesius of Cyrene* [London, 1926], pp. 200–201). In this instance, it is important to keep in mind the very real possibility that Synesius was perhaps playing up the extent to which his beliefs differed from those of his flock as part of a clever attempt to prevent Theophilus of Alexandria from using Synesius's deviations from standard Christian belief as a pretext for deposing him at a future date.

[87] See P. Speck, 'ΓΡΑΦΑΙΣ Η ΓΛΥΦΑΙΣ. Zu dem Fragment des Hypatios von Ephesos über die Bilder,' in R.-J. Lilie and P. Speck, eds., *Varia* I (Bonn, 1984), pp. 211–72, esp. pp. 213–41. That this famous passage by Hypatius may actually date to the eighth century, to the conflict between Iconoclasts and Iconophiles, rather than its traditional date in the sixth, does not affect my argument. It in fact only strengthens it: I am not here interested in the question of the value and use of images in a Christian devotional context, but rather in the idea that God had accommodated his message to humanity and that the message of Christianity in turn itself should be accommodated to its audience. This latter notion had roots stretching back well before the Christian conflict over icons.

[88] Hypatius of Ephesus, *Miscellaneous Enquiries* (ed. F. Diekamp, *Analecta Patristica. Texte und Abhandlungen zur Griechischen Patristik* [Rome, 1938], p. 128; ET taken from P. J. Alexander, 'A Note on Image Worship in the Sixth Century,' *The Harvard Theological Review* 45 [1952], p. 180). P. Brown, 'Images as a Substitute for Writing,' in E. Chrysos and I. Wood, eds. *East and West: Modes of Communication* (Leiden/Boston, 1999), p. 17, places this text in an eighth-century context.

acting like God, who had allowed the Children of Israel to continue to offer sacrifices that they had grown accustomed to in Egypt, only now to Him, rather than banishing them.[89] Even the transmission of Severus's works reflects the complexities and the intellectual spectrum of the audience of Christian believers: in the case of his *Letter to the Deacon of Anastasia*, the Coptic, Arabic, and Syriac recensions of the text are different. The Coptic and Arabic, transmitted via a liturgical text, omit his patristic proof texts, whereas the Syriac recension, transmitted in the context of his letter collection, maintains them. This has led to the suggestion that the 'Copto-Arabic tradition caters for a general public who attended church, while the Syriac is aimed more at a scholarly audience.'[90]

Jacob of Edessa (d. 708) offers a particularly vivid example of how a church leader might relate to the simple over whom he had pastoral responsibilities. Jacob was one of the greatest intellects of the Syriac-speaking Miaphysite tradition and is a figure with whom we will spend a great deal of time in coming chapters. He was an elitist when it came to imparting certain kinds of information in a teaching capacity: in a letter to John, the Stylite of Litarb, Jacob wrote that he responded with few words to the subjects of John's inquiry, 'although I know that they need many words.' 'But know well,' he continued, 'I have intentionally kept them short and withheld because I judge that matters such as these [should not be] spoken to everyone.'[91]

For Jacob, dissimulation in the name of the spiritual well-being of weaker brethren was actually to be encouraged: his brand of spiritual elitism that was the product of a pastoral concern for weaker believers. John, Jacob noted, was a person who had many people asking him about the things he himself had written to Jacob about. As a result, Jacob wrote, 'I will set down the same rule for you: be vigilant and do not give what is holy to dogs and throw pearls before swine... do not speak to everyone about those things which are mystical and which should not be spoken of in front of everybody.'[92]

[89] See Chapter 1, n. 119. For more on divine and accommodation and sacrifice, see S. D. Benin, 'Sacrifice as Education in Augustine and Chrysostom,' *Church History* 52 (1983), pp. 7–20.

[90] See Allen and Hayward, *Severus of Antioch*, p. 32.

[91] Such pastoral prudence was not unique to Jacob; see, e.g., Timothy II (Aelurus), *Letter to Claudianus*, p. 346 (fol. 36b, col. a) (ed. and trans. R. Y. Ebied and L. R. Wickham, 'A Collection of Unpublished Syriac Letters of Timothy Aelurus,' *JTS* 21 [1970], p. 368 [English]). Note also Augustine's speculation as to why Ambrose read without speaking in *Confessions* 6.3 (ed. L. Verheijen, *Sancti Augustini Confessionum libri XIII* [Turnholt, 1981], p. 75; ET available in H. Chadwick, *Saint Augustine: Confessions* [Oxford, 1991], p. 93) (Cf. Rousseau, 'The Preacher's Audience': A More Optimistic view,' p. 395). Cf. also the references in G.W.H. Lampe, *A Patristic Greek Lexicon* (Oxford/New York, 1961), s.v. συγκατάβασις (p. 1267).

[92] Jacob of Edessa, *Letter 14 to John, the Stylite of Litarb*. BL Add. 12,172, fol. 126b. Syriac text also in J. Tannous, 'Syria between Byzantium and Islam: Making Incommensurables Speak,' (PhD diss., Princeton University, 2010), p. 196, n. 496 (hereafter, *SBI*).

In a different letter, Jacob informed the Stylite that 'there are many things in the laws of the Spirit which are written and true, but which we should not offer answers about to everyone who asks concerning them… showing prudence on account of the [enquirer's] insufficiency, seeing that perhaps when he hears the precision of the response, not only will he not receive healing with respect to what he asks, but also with respect to what is [already] living and sound within him—everything will die and perish.' Sometimes, Jacob reminded John, when weak and incapable people hear difficult things, they simply leave the faith. As evidence, he quoted John 6:66. 'Consider,' he therefore told him,

> what it is I am saying to you and let these secret things be for you alone and for your soul and your heart and your mind and your conscience. I do not know what more I should say. Do not tell me what you have written to me: 'I have shown these things to many people, and they have been troubled at them in bewilderment.' To what end do you act this way and show forth these things? For what purpose are they made to doubt and caused to have difficulty and made ill? You see that not everybody is sufficient [to deal with] an idea and not everybody can bear it. Nor does everybody possess a mind which is nourished and beneficial. Instead, sometimes something deadly will come upon those who hear [such things]. Have you not looked upon the seed which fell upon the shallow and rocky ground? As soon as the sun shone and waxed hot against it, it immediately withered [cf. Matthew 13:5]. Know [this], if what I am saying is agreeable to you, and learn to be prudent in places and to say one thing instead of something [else] to various people out of good judgment, either 'I don't know,' or 'I have not learned this matter precisely,' as you get a sense for a person's inability [to deal with difficult matters]. Do not answer each person everything he asks of you and give the bone of a bull to an infant, so that he runs away and you become for him a cause of loss, or we choke him off when he is still one of those who is in need of milk [cf. Hebrews 5:12–14].[93]

Jacob in fact believed that in being less than fully forthcoming in his answers to weaker brethren, he was in very good company. Both Athanasius of Alexandria and Basil of Caesarea, he suggested, had done precisely the same thing. Athanasius had knowingly made the false claim that there was no writing before the Flood. Basil, for his part, had made the inaccurate claim that there was no wine before the Flood. Both had done so with noble intent—Athanasius because he wanted to undercut the authenticity of the Book of Enoch, which

[93] Jacob of Edessa, *Letter 2, to John, the Stylite of Litarb*. BL Add. 12,172, fol. 81b. Syriac text also available in *SBI*, p. 197, n. 498.

was being used by people who were teaching dangerous doctrines; Basil, to encourage those who were fasting to also abstain from wine.[94] For Jacob, being in the role of a Christian leader necessarily involved an element of spiritual paternalism: like a doctor, one had to do what was good for the health of the patient.[95]

We have other examples, albeit slightly less vivid, of bishops adapting their message to their hearers. When Basil preached on the six days of creation, Gregory of Nyssa wrote, he was speaking to a full church and out of necessity he made his sermon appropriate for his audience.[96] Among those present were many who could understand the lofty things he spoke about, Gregory noted, but there were even more who were not suited to examining his more subtle points: simple men (ἄνδρες ἰδιῶται), artisans who worked in humble trades, women untrained in such areas of learning, youths, and old people.[97] John Chrysostom's sermons show that he was aware of the different levels of understanding and ability in his large congregations and tried to preach in a way that would be engaging to all. But they suggest he was also confident that everyday Christians from humble backgrounds could learn and memorize things they heard him say.[98] In his catechetical lectures, John's rough contemporary, Theodore of Mopsuestia, attempted to make his teaching of the more lofty points of theology more easily intelligible by covering only a small portion of the more difficult topics in each session.[99] In the West, we have already seen Augustine's advice that catechetical instruction should be adjusted to the level of those present.[100] We also might point to Ambrose's baptismal sermons, *On*

[94] Jacob of Edessa, *Letter 13, to John the Stylite.* Syriac text in W. Wright, 'Two Epistles of Mār Jacob, Bishop of Edessa,' *Journal of Sacred Literature and Biblical Record* 10 (1867), pp. ܟܘ – ܠ. FT available in F. Nau, 'Traduction des lettres XII et XIII de Jacques d'Édesse (exégèse biblique),' *ROC* 10 (1905), pp. 206-208.

[95] See Jacob of Edessa, *Letter 13, to John the Stylite* (ed. Wright, 'Two Epistles of Mār Jacob, Bishop of Edessa,' p. ܟܗ), for Jacob's describing Athanasius acting like a 'wise and crafty physician' who forbids the sick from all foods, both beneficial and harmful, in order to keep the patient from harm, in this case, the harm of bad books. For other instances of Jacob equating the job of bishop with that of a physician, see, e.g., his third letter to John of Litarb (BL Add. 12,172, fol. 82a; on the same page, he also refers to Cyril of Alexandria as a 'wise physician of souls'), as well as his fifth letter to John of Litarb, BL Add. 12,172, fol. 85a.

[96] Κατάλληλον ἐξανάγκης [i.e., ἐξ ἀνάγκης] ἐποιεῖτο τοῖς δεχομένοις τὸν λόγον.

[97] Gregory of Nyssa, *Apologia in hexaemeron* 4 (ed. G.H. Forbes, *Sancti Patris Nostri Gregorii Nysseni...* [Burntisland, 1855], p. 8). Compare this statement with Basil's own comments about the presence of artisans in his audience in his *Homilies on the Hexaemeron* 3.1 (ed. E. A. de Mendieta and S. Y. Rudberg, *Basilius von Caesarea: Homilien zum Hexaemeron* [Berlin, 1997], p. 39; FT in S. Giet, *Homélies sur l'hexaéméron* [SC 26] [Paris, 1949], p. 191).

[98] See Maxwell, *Christianization and Communication in Late Antiquity*, pp. 95–98.

[99] See the analysis in D. L. Schwartz, *Paideia and Cult: Christian Initiation in Theodore of Mopsuestia* (Washington, D.C., 2013), pp. 105–107.

[100] In addition to the passage cited above (Chapter 1, n. 43), see more generally Augustine's com-

the Sacraments. Aimed at an audience both educated and uneducated, they are so unlike his other work that questions have long been raised about whether they were truly written by Ambrose.[101]

Sometimes leaders would make adjustments for a potentially hostile audience. Severus wrote his response to the Chalcedonian grammarian John of Caesarea while in exile, yet he made it read as if he had written it in Antioch: 'The beginning of the treatise,' he wrote a priest named Elisha, 'I have put in such a form, in order that I may seem to have prepared this while I was living in Antioch, lest perhaps these great adversaries might kindle a greater flame of prejudice against me, if they perceived that this had been composed by me in exile.' But even if he had written the work in exile, Severus stated, he had begun working on it while he was still in Antioch.[102]

In the event that he was addressing an audience with supporters of the Council of Chalcedon who might be upset with some of his statements, Severus might also adapt his message: 'Now I suppose that the preface of the same sermon which was written by us on the holy Simeon [the Stylite],' he wrote in a letter to a certain Stephen, 'will be troublesome to you, inasmuch as it is not acceptable to the Byzantines,'—that is, to Chalcedonians—'but it is easy for you to use the three or four sections which are placed at the beginning, to leave out those things which are troublesome, and to read out in connected narrative the things which remain.'[103]

In most of the examples above, the message adaptation that church leaders were engaged in was not related to the question of Chalcedon, but they are nevertheless suggestive. The notion of accommodation gives us an answer to the question of what a Christian leader, one who was not only literate but theologically literate, would have expected of the ploughboy with respect to the subtler points of Christian theological speculation: perhaps not very much. The story of the actor and the Arabs appended to the end of Leontius of Jerusalem's *Testimonies of the Saints* illustrates this point well. We have seen that

ments in *On the Catechizing of the Uninstructed* 15 (ed. Bauer, pp. 147–48; ET in Christopher, *The First Catechetical Instruction*, pp. 37–38) and cf. Clark, 'Town and Country in Late-Antique Preaching,' pp. 278–79.

[101] See Clark, 'Town and Country in Late-Antique Preaching,' p. 279, and see Rousseau, '"The Preacher's Audience": A More Optimistic View', pp. 398–400, for an analysis of a passage from *On the Sacraments* which shows how Ambrose combined both elite rhetoric and an appeal to a broad audience in the text.

[102] Severus of Antioch, *Letters* (*Letter 34, To Elisha*), p. 104 (ed. and trans. Brooks [PO 12.2]). The ET used here is that of Brooks.

[103] Severus of Antioch, *Select Letters* 8.1 (*Letter to Stephen the Reader*) (ed. Brooks, 1.2.440-442 [Syriac]). I have used the ET here from Allen and Hayward, *Severus of Antioch*, p. 143. For this homily, see *Cathedral Homilies* (M. Brière and F. Graffin, eds., *Les Homiliae Cathedrales de Sévère d'Antioche* [PO 36.4] [Turnhout, 1974], pp. 74–105.

the actor, putatively a Chalcedonian, went to church not knowing that there were differences between Christians. His captors, according to the story, also shared the actor's level of confessional indifference. They 'traditionally shared the heresy of the Jacobites,' Leontius (or his anonymous continuator) wrote,

> who themselves give pride of place to one nature in the Lord. These Jacobites were the first to make a practice of travelling with the Arabs in the desert and ministering to them in every way. These men neither knew of, nor taught, precision about or comparison between doctrines held by different Christian groups. Rather they were converted to the ideas of Jacob [Baradaeus], taking the imprint of these ideas without any examination, much in the way of the Persians who were converted by the ideas of Nestorius.[104]

The Miaphysite monks who converted Arabs to Christianity without teaching them the particular characteristics of Miaphysite doctrine and how it differed from competing options were in good company: despite the existence of Chalcedonian and Miaphysite doctrinal and, eventually, liturgical distinguishing characteristics, a certain pragmatism in these areas might also prevail, even at the highest levels of the Miaphysite movement. When John of Ephesus, the celebrated Miaphysite bishop, converted thousands of pagans to Christianity in sixth-century Asia Minor, they were converted not to a Miaphysite understanding of Christianity but to a Chalcedonian one. It was the Chalcedonian Emperor Justinian who had spent large sums and given baptismal clothes in support of John's mission, Michael the Great reported, and 'for this reason they were instructed in the doctrine of Chalcedon, for the holy one [i.e., John] by whom they were made disciples thought it right and better that they should leave the error of paganism, even if it was to Chalcedonianism.'[105] Surviving Miaphysite sources consider the Christian community of Himyar to be Miaphysite; surviving Greek sources, however, regard them as Chalcedonians.[106] But the question should be asked: Would they actually have self-identified as either? And if they had, what would that have looked like in practice?

Such was the expectation that leaders might accommodate their message to the audience that some Christians would invoke it to explain the nature of

[104] Leontius of Jerusalem, *Testimonies of the Saints*, pp. 158–61 (ed. and trans. Gray, *Leontius of Jerusalem*; the translation I have used here is that of Gray, quote at 161). On the question of authorship, see n. 65 in this chapter.

[105] Michael the Great, *Chronicle* 9.24 (ed. Chabot, 4.287–88 = 2.207). For discussion of this passage and its historical plausibility, see Menze, *Justinian and the Making of the Syrian Orthodox Church*, pp. 258–59.

[106] See L. van Rompay's article, 'Ḥimyar,' in *GEDSH*, pp. 197–98 and see further van Rompay, 'The Martyrs of Najran: Some Remarks on the Nature of the Sources,' in J. Quaegebeur, ed., *Studia Paulo Naster oblata II: Orientalia Antiqua* (Leuven, 1982), pp. 301–309.

Muḥammad's preaching. We have already seen that the *Legend of Sergius Baḥīrā*, a text likely originating in the early ninth century, portrayed Muḥammad as a simple person who received a simplified understanding of Christian truth tailored for a simple Arab audience, but this notion (minus the alleged later corruption of Kaʿb al-Aḥbār) can be found already in the early eighth-century *Dispute between a Muslim and a Monk of Bēt Ḥālē*. When pressed for his estimation of Muḥammad, the Christian monk expressed the view that Muḥammad had been a 'wise and God-fearing man, who freed you from the worship of demons, and caused you to know the one true God.' Why then, his Muslim interlocutor responded, did he not teach his followers about the Trinity? 'You should know, O man,' the monk responded

> that a child when he is born, because he does not possess fully-formed senses (capable) of receiving whole good, they feed him with milk for two years, and (only) then do they give him food (consisting) of bread. So also Muḥammad, because he saw your childishness and your lack of knowledge, he first caused you to know the one true God—teaching which he received from Sergius Baḥira. Because you were childlike in knowledge he did not teach you about the mystery of the Trinity, so that you should not go astray after multiple gods. For you might perhaps have said, 'Since Muḥammad proclaimed three, let us make seven others, since ten would be even more powerful!' and (so) you would have run after the worship of carved-idols, as previously.[107]

Later, in the early 780s, the East Syrian patriarch Timothy I would employ a similar argument about Muḥammad in his disputation with the Caliph al-Mahdī. It was, Timothy argued, 'human weakness' that held Muḥammad back from teaching the fullness of the mystery of the Trinity to his followers—not Muḥammad's limitation, but that of his followers. Accustomed to thinking in terms of many idols and gods, Timothy suggested, his hearers would have interpreted language about the Father, Son, and Holy Spirit, in a polytheistic way. It was because he knew it would be a stumbling block to his idolatrous listeners that Muḥammad did not plainly teach about God's triune nature, leaving instead only indirect hints and symbols of it in the Qur'ān.[108]

[107] *Disputation between a Muslim and a Monk of Bēt Ḥālē* 31–34 (ed. and trans. D.G.K. Taylor, in 'The Disputation between a Muslim and a Monk of Bēt Ḥālē: Syriac Text and Annotated English Translation,' in S. H. Griffith and S. Grebenstein, eds., *Christsein in der islamischen Welt: Festschrift für Martin Tamcke zum 60. Geburtstag* [Wiesbaden, 2015], pp. 223–24; the translation is that of Taylor). On this passage, see Roggema, *The Legend of Sergius Baḥīrā*, p. 158; and on this text, see most conveniently her 'The Disputation between a Monk of Bēt Ḥālē and an Arab Notable,' in *CMR*, vol. 1, pp. 268–73.

[108] Timothy I, *Disputation with al-Mahdī* (*Letter 59*), 16.89–16.91 (ed. M. Heimgartner, *Timotheos I., Ostsyrischer Patriarch. Disputation mit dem Kalifen al-Mahdī* [CSCO 631–32: SS 244–45] [Louvain, 2011], pp. 113–14 [Syriac] = 16.89 [German]; ET available in A. Mingana, *Woodbrooke Studies:* vol. 2: *Timothy's*

A LAYERING OF KNOWLEDGE AND THE QUESTION OF DOCTRINE

Islam will occupy our attention later. For now, my concern is how a layering of knowledge—a continuum of different levels of understanding—in the Christian community affected attitudes towards Chalcedon. There is, as we shall see in subsequent pages, abundant evidence that the attitude of the actor and of the Christian Arabs toward the importance of doctrinal difference in the story at the end of Leontius's *Testimonies*, like the pragmatism of John of Ephesus, was not uncommon, so I will not belabor it here. Such a stance towards doctrinal difference is precisely the sort of thing we might expect to be widespread if the late antique and early medieval world had very low levels of literacy and even lower levels of theological literacy and was overwhelmingly agrarian. A knowledge of Christological slogans, or moral codes, or of the concrete events of Christian salvation history as encapsulated in creeds that were easily remembered and retold, was one thing. But expecting nomads or agrarian laborers to have considered views on the finer points of theological speculation would be something quite different. 'Each order of the faithful' (ἑκάστην τῶν πιστῶν τάξιν), to use the expression of (Ps.-) Hypatius, had different levels of engagement with the doctrinal questions by which their leaders defined their communities.[109]

Apology for Christianity; The Lament of the Virgin; The Martyrdom of Pilate [Cambridge, 1928], p. 68). On this text, see B. Roggema, 'Letter 59 (Disputation with the Caliph al-Mahdī),' in *CMR*, vol. 1, pp. 522–26. For the similarity of this argument with the argument in the *Disputation between a Muslim and a Monk of Bēt Ḥālē*, I follow Roggema, *The Legend of Sergius Baḥīrā*, p. 158. Penn, *Envisioning Islam*, p. 110, also made the connection.

[109] Note Palladius' report that Pachomius put his monks into groups according to the letters of the Greek alphabet: 'They followed a special meaning which was given to the letters. "To the simpler and less worldly (τοῖς μὲν ἁπλουστέροις καὶ ἀκεραιοτέροις) you shall assign the iota; but to the more difficult and headstrong, the chi." And so he fitted the letters to each order according to their state of life and disposition; but only the more spiritual ones knew the meaning of each symbol.' See *Lausiac History* 32.4–5 (ed. C. Butler, *The Lausiac History of Palladius: The Greek Text* [Cambridge, 1904], pp. 90–91; ET taken from R. T. Meyer, *Palladius: the Lausiac History* [Westminster, Md., 1965], p. 93). For the Syriac of this passage, τοῖς μὲν ἁπλουστέροις καὶ ἀκεραιοτέροις is rendered *trīṣē wa-pshīṭē* (righteous and simple). See 'Ananisho', *The Book of Paradise* 33.6 (ed. and trans. E.A.W. Budge, *The Book of Paradise* [London, 1904], 2.180 [Syriac] = 1.215-216 [ET]). Cf. also Origen, *Contra Celsum* 2.64 (ed. Borret [SC 132], pp. 434, 436), which noted that though 'Jesus was one... to those who saw him he did not appear alike to all.... his appearance was not just the same to those who saw him, but varied according to their individual capacity.' Christ, Origen pointed out, explained the meaning of his parables, which had been kept hidden from the crowds who heard them, to his disciples in private (cf. Mark 4:10-20, 33-34): 'just as those who heard the explanation of the parables had a greater capacity to hear than those who heard the parables without any explanations, so also was this the case with their vision.' ET taken from Chadwick, *Origen: Contra Celsum*, p. 115.

The layering of awareness of and engagement with the doctrinal disputes that religious leaders were engaged in meant that being a leader in the Christian community would entail juggling the concerns of both learned and unlearned believers alike. Like Severus, Jacob, and others, leaders would have to accommodate the members of their flock who did not fully comprehend the issues that were at stake. In this instance, the accommodation we are dealing with is a doctrinal one.

The fifth-century Miaphysite patriarch of Alexandria, Timothy II ('Aelurus'), provides a vivid example of such doctrinal accommodation. In a collection of originally Greek letters preserved in Syriac, Timothy II spoke in ways that are familiar to students of late antique literature of the danger that heretics posed to simple believers.[110] As we have already seen, people might switch from one confession to another, and Timothy offered his own guidelines for how a person who had previously believed that the Incarnate Christ had two natures might be able to enter into communion. Any person who had received ordination—from a deacon all the way to a bishop—was to anathematize in writing the Council of Chalcedon and the *Tome* of Leo. He was, moreover, to show repentance for a year, during which time he was to desist from carrying out any type of priestly activity.[111] Timothy, however, did not have the same set of expectations for everyone who wanted to join his Miaphysite communion. People who had received ordination were expected to make anathemas in writing or, at the least, sign an anathema with their own hand,[112] but there was no expectation of anything written from a Christian who had been taking part in the Eucharist of the Dyophysites but had not been ordained.

In fact, for the laity, Timothy's expectations were quite modest. 'I exhort you, dear friends,' he wrote in a letter to Palestine from his exile in Gangra, 'to be diligent, in so far as you are able, in saving those who are seduced'—here referring to simple believers who had been seduced into the Dyophysite communion.

> If, therefore, one of the simple (*pshiṭin*) comes to you, confessing the holy faith of the consubstantial Trinity, and desirous of being in communion with you who acknowledge our Lord's fleshly consubstantiality with us—I entreat you, not to

[110] Timothy II (Aelurus), *Letter to the City of Alexandria*, pp. 337 (fol. 32a, col. C), 338 (fol. 32b, col. C) (ed. Ebeid and Wickham, 'A Collection of Unpublished Syriac Letters of Timothy Aelurus.' For the English translations of Ebied and Wickham, see pp. 358, 359). About this letter, see p. 330.

[111] Timothy II (Aelurus), *Letter to Egypt, Thebaid, and Pentapolis*, see pp. 341–42 (fols. 34a, col. C–34b, cols. A-B) (ed. Ebied and Wickham, 'A Collection of Unpublished Syriac Letters of Timothy Aelurus.' ET at pp. 362–63).

[112] See Timothy II (Aelurus), *Letter to Egypt, Thebaid, and Pentapolis*, p. 342 (fol. 34b, col. A) (ed. Ebied and Wickham, 'A Collection of Unpublished Syriac Letters of Timothy Aelurus.' ET at p. 363).

> constrain those who hold such views as these with other words, nor require from them additional verbal subtleties, but leave such people to praise God and bless the Lord in the simplicity (*pshiṭutā*) and innocence of their hearts. For it was not against people like this that the holy fathers decreed anathemas, but against those who consider themselves to be something, and against those who are bereft of instruction and unstable, who pervert the divine Scriptures and the words of the holy fathers, interpreting them perversely, to their own destruction and the destruction of those who are obedient to them. It is against these that the holy fathers decreed anathemas. Anyone who does not abuse the saints touching this declaration: "I confess that our Lord is our brother and that he was of the same fleshly stock as us for the sake of our salvation"—accept such a one in our Lord, building him up yourselves on your holy faith.[113]

Timothy's doctrinal requirements were actually something all of the major competing and rival churches agreed upon: a belief in the Trinity and that the Incarnate Christ was fully human.[114] Such expectations were both pastoral and realistic: for most people, requiring that they evaluate competing theories of the Incarnation would have been simply asking too much. The Chalcedonian Leontius of Jerusalem, writing perhaps in the seventh century, would even grant that people who acted in good faith and affirmed wrong doctrines because they actually believed they were correct would escape God's judgment for false belief: 'If we really judged by our own unaided judgement,' he wrote,

> without any kind of clouding of our judgement by prejudices for or against, that their views are truer, more reasonable, stronger, and wiser, then we who're pressing these opponents of ours so hard would actually be so bold as to say that, even if the people led astray by them should think wrong things because a doctrine enunciated by our opponents seemed to them to be more worthy of God, they won't be condemned for heterodoxy on that day when God judges the secrets of our hearts.[115]

[113] Timothy II (Aelurus), *Letter to Faustinus the Deacon*, pp. 343–44 (fols. 35a, col. C-35b, col. A) (ed. Ebied and Wickham, 'A Collection of Unpublished Syriac Letters of Timothy Aelurus.' I have used the ET of Ebied and Wickham at pp. 365–66, but made some alterations). On this letter and Palestine as its likely destination, see p. 331.

[114] That such a doctrinal standard would have been acceptable to nearly the entire spectrum of post-Chalcedonian Christological options is evident by consulting the chart in Brock, 'The "Nestorian" Church: A Lamentable Misnomer,' p. 27. Note that the catechetical work intended for lay people discussed by Swanson in 'A Copto-Arabic Catechism of the Later Fatimid Period,' was apparently popular among Copts, Syrian Orthodox, and Chalcedonians; see esp. pp. 475, 481.

[115] Leontius of Jerusalem, *Testimonies of the Saints*, p. 150 (ed. and trans. Gray, *Leontius of Jerusalem*. The translation I have used here is that of Gray, p. 151).

Such moderation could also be found in the Church of the East: East Syrian patriarch Timothy I (d. 823) took an approach similar to the Miaphysite Timothy II's when discussing the question of whether to rebaptize a heretic who was joining the Church of the East. Those who affirmed Christ's humanity but denied his divinity should be rebaptized, he wrote, as should those who affirmed Christ's divinity but denied his humanity. Those who denied both Christ's humanity and divinity were not even heretics: they were pagans. But those who confessed both Christ's divinity and his humanity, but spoke of Christ's union in a different way from the Orthodox—in terms of natures or hypostases rather than in terms of the will or the *prosopa*—their baptism was a baptism indeed, even if one tarnished by heretical faith. For Timothy I, neither followers of Severus, that is, Miaphysites, nor Chalcedonians were to be rebaptized.[116] In both the case of the Miaphysite Timothy II and the East Syrian Timothy I, there was a recognition that a simple confession of Christ's full humanity and full divinity could serve as a sort of minimalist baseline. Choosing correctly from among the various theories of how such a union actually worked was not as important as believing that the phenomenon the theories were trying to explain was truly the case.

Basic expectations like these were not unique to the post-Chalcedonian world. The Trinitarian debates of the fourth century had reached similar levels of sophistication and complexity, such that properly understanding them was beyond the grasp of most nonspecialists, then or now.[117] In this case also, leaders might not demand that their congregations fully comprehend the questions being debated. 'Try not to trouble yourself over the precise nature of the Father,' Gregory Nazianzen had counseled his listeners,

[116] Timothy I, *Extracts on Whether to Rebaptize Jacobites and Marcionites, from Various Letters*, pp. 30–32 (ed. Braun [CSCO 74: SS 30] [Paris, 1914]). Similar ideas could be found in other confessions: see, e.g., Timothy, Presbyter of Constantinople, *De iis qui ad ecclesiam accedunt*, PG 86.1, cols. 40C–41A (Timothy was a Chalcedonian) and Council in Trullo, *Canons* 95 (ed. Joannou, *Discipline générale antique*, vol. 1.1, pp. 230–33), and also, e.g., Paris Syriac 100, a sixteenth-century Chalcedonian manuscript, which notes that Manichees and Arians had to be rebaptized, but Miaphysites and members of the Church of the East had to disown their previous belief; see H. Zotenberg, *Manuscrits orientaux. Catalogues des manuscrits syriaques et sabéens (mandaïtes) de la Bibliothèque nationale* (Paris, 1874), p. 58. More generally on the question of rebaptism, see W. B. Marriott's article, 'Baptism, iteration of,' in Smith and Cheetham, eds., DCA, vol. 1, pp. 172–73 and G. Bareille's article, 'Baptême des hérétiques (controverse relative au),' in *Dictionnaire de théologie catholique*, eds. A Vacant and E. Mangenot, vol. 2 (Paris, 1905), cols. 219–33. More recently, see the discussion in Y. Moss, *Incorruptible Bodies: Christology, Society, and Authority in Late Antiquity* (Oakland, Calif., 2016), pp. 65–74.

[117] Perrin, 'À propos de la participation du peuple fidèle aux controverses doctrinales,' is an excellent overview of both secondary literature and primary source material related to the question of popular awareness of and participation in theological disputes in the pre-Nicene and Nicene periods.

> the existence of his only-begotten Son, the glory and the power of the Spirit, the single divinity and splendor in the Three, the indivisible nature as well as confession, glory, and hope of those who truly believe. Try to keep to the words that you have known from childhood; leave sophisticated language to the more advanced. It is enough for you to have the foundation; leave it to the craftsman to build on it. It is enough to strengthen your *heart* with simple bread; leave the rich dishes to the rich. No reasonable person can condemn you for not providing a lavish feast, only for failing to offer some bread and water, whether to a disciple of Christ or anyone else, if you possibly can.[118]

It was in this same oration that Gregory spelled out a strong notion that the Christian community, like nature itself, was characterized by a certain order: 'neither does one see dolphins ploughing furrows or the ox gliding through the waves, just as one does not see the sun waxing or waning by night nor the moon blazing brightly by day.'[119] There were certain things that all Christians held in common, Gregory suggested, including the Scriptures, basic Christian teaching, and even 'the greatest gift of all, the recognition of the Father, the Son, and the Holy Spirit, and the confession of our highest hope.' But for Gregory, there were also types of spiritual knowledge that were not available to everyone and, for that reason, were not as important: 'As for the gifts that are above these, though more precious because of their rarity, they are secondary because they are not vital, for the things without which one cannot be a Christian are more useful than those accessible to only a few.'[120]

THE PARADOX OF CHALCEDON

We return to a fundamental point of tension: the Christian communities of the Middle East in the centuries after Chalcedon and on the eve of the Arab conquests were largely agrarian and (theologically) illiterate, and yet they came to define themselves communally by reference to disagreements over sophisticated theological speculation that very few people could fully understand, much less critically evaluate. For this reason, classifying the Christian communities of the Middle East by reference to their attitudes toward theories

[118] Gregory of Nazianzus, *Orations* 32.21 (ed. Moreschini [SC 318], pp. 128, 130; ET from Vinson, *Select Orations*, p. 206).

[119] Gregory of Nazianzus, *Orations* 32.9 (ed. Moreschini [SC 318], p. 102; ET from M. Vinson, *Select Orations*, p. 197).

[120] Gregory of Nazianzus, *Orations* 32.23 (ed. Moreschini [SC 318], p. 134; ET from Vinson, *Select Orations*, pp. 207–208).

of the Incarnation beyond the grasp of nearly all Christians in this period (or any period) casts very little light on the nature and meaning of Christianity in this crucial time. It does, however, raise the question of how the simple related to these debates and how their leaders related to the simple.

Even if a bishop did not expect of the simple believers under his spiritual care 'verbal subtleties' about doctrine, as Timothy II put it, but was instead content to 'leave such people to praise God and bless the Lord in the simplicity and innocence of their hearts,' the spiritual health and welfare of these Christians was nevertheless still his responsibility. A difference between the beliefs of the theologically literate and those of the simple was not something unique to Christianity,[121] but in the Christian case, leaders had to look out for and protect the spiritual health of those under their charge. What was a leader to do about those under his authority who did not treat the doctrines by which their communities were defined with the same seriousness as he did himself? What should his attitude be toward the simple believers under the care of other Christian leaders whom he regarded as in error? Moreover, what did confessional difference mean to simple believers who understood that it existed but who did not have the same comprehension of doctrine as their leaders?

Appreciating the consequences of this tension between simple believers and elites who based communal definitions on sophisticated disagreements is fundamental to understanding the religious dynamics of the world that Chalcedon created. And the world that Chalcedon created was the world that the Arabs would find in the seventh century when they conquered the Middle East: the world in which Islam emerged and in which it crystalized was a world of simple believers.

If we want therefore to understand the shape that both Middle Eastern Christianity and Islam came to have and how they related to one another, we must focus on this relationship between simple believers and the theological elite who wrote the texts we study and who, in fact, provide us with almost all that we know about simple believers. We must take seriously the religious consequences of a largely agrarian, illiterate population of Christians. Without keeping the simple before us, we cannot properly understand those whose job it was to look out for them. Without keeping the simple in front of us, we cannot understand what it meant to be a Christian for the vast majority of people who identified as such.

Underlying the pages that follow will be a simple (if the expression may be forgiven) conviction: keeping the question of the simple constantly and relent-

[121] Cf. A. D. Nock, 'Studies in the Graeco-Roman Beliefs of the Empire,' *The Journal of Hellenic Studies* 45 (1925), p. 90, n. 56, and Nock, *Sallustius: Concerning the Gods and the Universe* (Cambridge, 1926), p. xliii, n. 23.

lessly before us will cast many of the central religious and cultural questions and phenomena of the late antique and early medieval Middle East in a new and different light.

With the simple in mind, therefore, let us now turn in more detail to the world that Chalcedon created.

PART II

Consequences of Chalcedon

CHAPTER 3

'Confusion in the Land'

> What if our subjects seem to shrug their shoulders at the questions that interest us? Does it mean we need to ask different questions? Or can apparent indifference itself be a significant clue about the past?
>
> Tara Zahra[1]

At some point in what was probably the year 688, Jacob of Edessa confronted Julian, the Miaphysite patriarch of Antioch, about the problem of widespread neglect of canon law in the church.[2] The encounter was a dramatic one. Jacob had gone to the monastery where the patriarch Julian lived to resign his post as bishop of Edessa. It was apparently not a happy exchange. 'Before he left,' a short *vita* of Jacob reported,

> he had argued with the Patriarch and bishops about their observing ecclesiastical canons, but nobody listened to him at all. Instead, they were counseling him to consent to all things according to the age and happenings. On account of this, he brought forth the book of ecclesiastical canons and burned it with fire before the door of the patriarchal monastery, crying out and saying: 'It is these canons which are trampled upon by you and not observed that I am burning like things which are superfluous and useless.'[3]

By this point, Jacob had been bishop over Edessa for four years. 'He had been subjected to many troubles by people who had been banned by him from exercising their ministry because of their uncanonical actions,' Michael the

[1] T. Zahra, 'Imagined Noncommunities: National Indifference as a Category of Analysis,' *Slavic Review* 69 (2010), p. 93.

[2] Portions of this chapter and the entire second section of this book appeared in my article, 'You Are What You Read: Qenneshre and the Miaphysite Church in the Seventh Century,' in P. J. Wood, *History and Identity in the Late Antique Near East* (Oxford/New York, 2013), pp. 83–102.

[3] For the *vita*, see Michael the Great, *Chronicle* 11.15 (ed. Chabot, 4.445–46 = 2.471–72). My translation, but see the ET in S. P. Brock, *A Brief Outline of Syriac Literature* (Kottayam, 1997), p. 269. The monastery was quite likely Qenneshre: in the *Life* of Theodota of Amid, we see Patriarch Julian living at the monastery of Qenneshre. See *Life of Theodota of Amid*, St Mark's Jerusalem 199, fol. 547b (for the Syriac, see Mardin 275/8, pp. 486–87). Note that in the late seventh century, when the Maphrian Denḥā had a disagreement with certain bishops and the people of Tikrit, he and his adversaries went to meet the patriarch Julian. Bar Hebraeus does not explicitly say that Julian was living in Qenneshre, but he does state that Denḥā went there at this point, spending two years in the monastery; see *Ecclesiastical History* 2.32 (ed. Abbeloos and Lamy, vol. 3, cols. 147, 149).

Great noted, 'and also by others whom he had expelled and driven out of the Church of God.'[4] It was Jacob's anger at the situation that led him to quit his job as bishop—he resigned his post when 'his zeal and fervor of mind did not allow him to put up with' this state of affairs, Michael observed.[5]

Jacob of Edessa (whom we have already encountered in Part I) was no simple believer. He was, rather, one of the greatest polymaths to ever write in Syriac and one of the most learned men in the early eighth-century Middle East. Jacob belonged to what he regarded as the Orthodox Church, though scholars today typically refer to it as the 'Miaphysite' church, in order to distinguish it from other churches that also referred to themselves as 'Orthodox.' Jacob was perhaps the most learned Miaphysite in the world in his day, with a deep knowledge of the Christian tradition in both Greek and Syriac—and much more as well. As a young man, he had gone to Alexandria and there, Michael the Great noted, 'amassed knowledge of the sciences.'[6] Among other things, Jacob translated Aristotle's *Categories* into Syriac and revised Syriac translations of the Greek Old Testament, as well as the *Cathedral Homilies* and *Hymns* of Severus of Antioch. Jacob wrote the earliest surviving grammar we have in Syriac and a *Chronicle*, too. He composed biblical commentaries and scholia, has left us more than fifty letters, and was also active in translating and redacting a number of liturgical texts.[7]

What is important for us at present is that Jacob was a stickler for rules. His concern for the proper observance and enforcement of canons was in accord with a larger pattern in his life. In a letter written to scribes, for instance, he detailed the exact way in which he wanted certain words and expressions to be written out. He even specified how dots should be copied. Jacob was insistent that things be done his way, even when his manner of doing things was idiosyncratic. 'They should not write "Solomon" ܫܠܝܡܘܢ (*shleymun*) according to their custom,' he wrote at one point, spelling out the name 'Solomon'

[4] Michael the Great, *Chronicle* 11.15 (ed. Chabot, 4.445 = 2.471–72). ET taken from Brock, *A Brief Outline*, p. 269.

[5] Michael the Great, *Chronicle* 11.15 (ed. Chabot, 4.445 = 2.472). ET taken from Brock, *A Brief Outline*, p. 269.

[6] Michael the Great, *Chronicle* 11.15 (ed. Chabot, 4.445 = 2.471). ET taken from Brock, *A Brief Outline*, p. 268.

[7] On Jacob, see Michael the Great, *Chronicle* 11.15 (ed. Chabot, 4:445–46 = 2.471–72); Baumstark, *Geschichte*, pp. 248–56; A. Salvesen's article, 'Ya'qub of Edessa' in *GEDSH*, pp. 432–33, and B. ter Haar Romeny, ed., *Jacob of Edessa and the Syriac Culture of His Day* (Leiden/Boston, 2008). In this last volume, to J. van Ginkel's overview of fifty of Jacob's letters in "Greetings to a Virtuous Man: The Correspondence of Jacob of Edessa," pp. 78–81, should be added a recently discovered fifty-first letter of Jacob, the fragmentary *Letter to Domeṭ*, which is edited and translated in S. P. Brock and L. van Rompay, *Catalogue of the Syriac Manuscripts and Fragments in the Library of Deir al-Surian, Wadi al-Natrun (Egypt)* (Leuven, 2014), pp. 397–98.

as it is always written in Syriac, 'in the place of my own ܫܘܠܘܡܘܢ (*shulumun*),' spelling out 'Solomon' in a peculiar way that no one else in the Syriac tradition does. 'I know quite well what it is I have written.'[8]

After Jacob quit his job as bishop of Edessa, an old man named Ḥabīb was appointed bishop in his place. Ḥabīb evidently had a different style of leadership. He was, according to Michael, 'a serene and kind old man.'[9] Jacob himself went to the monastery of Mar Jacob of Kayshum and, apparently still upset with the state of both the laity and the leadership of his community, wrote two treatises: one against the pastors of the church, the other against transgressors of ecclesiastical laws and canons.[10] Jacob's treatise against pastors has been lost, but excerpts from the twelfth chapter of his work against those who transgress canons have been preserved in two different manuscripts in the British Library.[11] What survives of the twelfth chapter of this otherwise-lost treatise casts light on Jacob's understanding of the very nature of Christianity and the importance of the law to its true practice. It also reflects Jacob's view of the social situation among Christians in northern Syria in the late seventh century. For this reason, let us stop for a moment to consider it.

For Jacob, Christianity as a religion was actually older than any other religion—paganism, Judaism, 'barbarianism,'—it was something as old as creation itself. Christianity was nothing more than the covenant between God and humans.[12] This covenant between God and humans had been established a number of different times—six, to be precise: God established a covenant with Adam in Eden when he commanded him not to eat the fruit of the tree; the covenant was established a second time with Adam and his children after

[8] Jacob of Edessa, *Letter on Orthography*, p. *6 (ed. G. Phillips, *A Letter by Mār Jacob, Bishop of Edessa, on Syriac Orthography* [London/Edinburgh, 1869]; my translation, but Philips' ET is on p. 5). This text was also published in J.-P. P. Martin, ed., *Jacobi episcopi Edesseni epistola ad Georgium episcopum Sarugensem de orthographia syriaca* (Paris, 1869).

[9] Michael the Great, *Chronicle* 11.15 (ed. Chabot, 4.446 = 2.472); ET taken from Brock, *A Brief Outline*, p. 269.

[10] Michael the Great, *Chronicle* 11.15 (ed. Chabot, 4.446 = 2.472)

[11] See BL Add., 12,154, fols. 164b–168a and BL Add. 17,193, fols. 58a–61a (cf. also Baumstark, *Geschichte*, p. 254, n. 7). What remains of this text has now been published by Michael Penn in 'Jacob of Edessa's Defining Christianity: Introduction, Edition, and Translation,' *Journal of Eastern Christian Studies* 64 (2012): 175–99.

[12] Jacob of Edessa, *Treatise against Those Who Transgress Ecclesiastical Canons*, p. 183 (Syriac text in Penn, 'Jacob of Edessa's Defining Christianity'; Syriac text from BL Add. 12,154, fol. 165a, previously edited and translated in *SBI*, p. 216, n. 522). It is not clear whether Jacob has a specific religious group or religion in mind when he refers to *barbrāyutā*, 'barbarianism,' or 'barbarism.' See Penn's comment, p. 180, n. 16, on the possibility that this may refer to Muslims. For Arabs or Saracens referred to as 'barbarians,' *barbrāyē* in the Syriac version of the *Forty Martyrs of Sinai*, see Appendix II, n. 51, and cf. also, M.-A. Kugener, 'Sur l'emploi en Syrie, an VIe siècle de notre ère, du mot "barbare" dans le sens de "arabe,"' *Oriens Christianus* 7 (1907), pp. 408–12.

Adam's sin; the covenant was established a third time with Noah and his children; a fourth time, with Abraham and Isaac; a fifth time, with the children of Israel by means of Moses. The sixth establishment of the covenant was done by God himself, in the person of Christ.[13] This represented the grand climax of the relationship between God and humanity, and it was from this event that the canons of the church ultimately derived.

The seventh and final covenant between God and humanity, Jacob wrote, will come at the end of the world, when God judges each person according to his or her deeds and rewards or punishes him or her accordingly. The time of the coming of the seventh covenant will be like that of the previous six: when God sees His covenant being disregarded and sees that nobody is observing His law, He visits his people and renews it. Jacob believed that such was the situation in his own day. 'Although the same Person establishes it with humanity as established the sixth,' he wrote, 'this is nevertheless clear: He does not always establish a covenant with us peacefully, but He will rather establish with us this seventh covenant in a frightening and forceful and intolerable manner.'[14] The laxity that Jacob saw around him meant that the advent of the seventh and final age of the world was at hand, that God would have to act, yet again, and that a dramatic and violent end, associated with God's reappearance on earth, was quite possibly approaching.

We can perhaps see what Jacob meant if we turn to a short apocalypse which, it has been suggested, Jacob himself may have not only have translated from Greek into Syriac but may in fact have written—indeed, in 687, a year before his fiery resignation from the episcopacy.[15] This short apocalypse, prefaced to and included in a canonical work known as the *Testament of Our Lord*, has Jesus appear to the Disciples after the Resurrection. They ask Christ to tell them of the signs of the end times, so that they will be able to tell the believers at that time in order for them to be aware and be saved.[16] In response, Jesus

[13] Jacob of Edessa, *Treatise against Those Who Transgress Ecclesiastical Canons*, pp. 183–84 (Syriac text in Penn, 'Jacob of Edessa's Defining Christianity'; Syriac text from BL Add. 12,154, 165a–165b and BL Add. 17,193, fol. 58b, previously edited and translated in *SBI*, p. 217, n. 523).

[14] Jacob of Edessa, *Treatise against Those Who Transgress Ecclesiastical Canons*, p. 185 (Syriac text in Penn, 'Jacob of Edessa's Defining Christianity'; Syriac text from BL Add. 12,154, fol. 165b, previously edited and translated in *SBI*, p. 218 [Syriac in n. 522]).

[15] Han Drijvers has argued that a short apocalypse prefaced to the *Clementine Octateuch* was, along with the Octateuch itself, a text containing a large number of ecclesiastical canons, the work of Jacob of Edessa. See H. J.W. Drijvers, 'The Testament of Our Lord: Jacob of Edessa's Response to Islam,' *Aram* 6 (1994), pp. 104–14, esp. p. 107. On the question of Jacob's translation of the *Clementine Octateuch* into Syriac from Greek, see the discussion in H.G.B. Teule, 'Jacob of Edessa and Canon Law,' in ter Haar Romeny, ed., *Jacob of Edessa and the Syriac Culture of his Day*, pp. 85–86, and cf. also H. Kaufhold, 'Sources of Canon Law in the Eastern Churches,' in W. Hartmann and K. Pennington, eds., *The History of Byzantine and Eastern Canon Law to 1500* (Washington, D.C.), pp. 242–43.

[16] There is no critical edition of the *Testamentum Domini* and at least five different versions of the

describes famines, wars, political events, and portents in the heavens that will signal that the end is nigh. But it is Jesus's description of the state of the churches just prior to the end times that offers us a clue as to how Jacob himself may have viewed the church of his own day:

> There will be many disturbances in the assemblies and among the nations and in the churches, for wicked shepherds will rise up, unjust, despisers, greedy, lovers of pleasure, lovers of profit, lovers of money, full of words, boasters, arrogant, perverts, empty, effeminate, vainglorious, who come like adversaries against the ways of the Gospel and who flee from the narrow gate [cf. Matthew 7:13] and who cast away from themselves everyone who is wounded and have no pity on My wound. They reject every word of truth and treat every path of piety with contempt. They do not mourn over their sins. Therefore, unbelief, the hatred of brothers, wickedness, presumption, bitterness, contempt, jealousy, enmity, contentions, acts of theft, acts of oppression, drunkenness, debauchery, wantonness, excess, fornication, and all acts which oppose the commandments of life will be spread throughout the nations, for mournfulness and humility and peace and acts of mercy and gentleness and poverty and pity and weeping will flee from many because the shepherds heard of these things but did not practice them, nor did they show forth My commandments, being [instead] examples of wickedness among the people. And there will come a time when people from among them will deny Me and will cause confusion in the land and will trust in worldly kings; but those who persevere to the end in my name will be saved [cf. Mt. 24:13]. At that time, they will set down commandments for humans that are not according to the Scripture and commandment,[17] those things with which the Father is pleased, and my elect and holy ones will be rejected by them and will be called unclean among them. But these are orthodox, pure, earnest, gentle, merciful, earnest, pleasant....[18]

In the *Testament of Our Lord*, Christ himself spoke of pastors not obeying His commandments, and regardless of whether Jacob actually wrote the text (or merely was responsible for translating it into Syriac),[19] this emphasis on obey-

---

apocalyptic portion of it have been published: see Drijvers, 'The Testament of Our Lord,' pp. 104–105, 110, for discussion of these various publications and also see CPG, vol. 1, pp. 234–35

[17] For the disagreement of various manuscripts on the wording of this phrase, see J. P. Arendzen, 'A New Syriac Text of the Apocalyptic Part of the "Testament of the Lord,"' *JTS* (1901), p. 409, n. 1.

[18] *Testament of Our Lord*, pp. 3–4 (ed. and trans. A. Vööbus, *The Synodicon in the West Syrian Tradition I* [CSCO 367–68; SS 161–62] [Louvain, 1975], pp. 28-29 [ET]; my translation. The ET by Vööbus should be used with caution and checked against the Syriac text). For this passage and Jacob, cf. Drijvers, 'The Testament of Our Lord,' pp. 111–12.

[19] D.G.K. Taylor, 'The Patriarch and the Pseudepigrapha: Extra-Biblical Traditions in the Writings of Cyriacus of Tagrit (793–817),' in F. Briquel-Chatonnet, ed., *Sur les pas des Araméens chrétiens. Mélanges offerts à Alain Desreumaux* (Paris, 2010), p. 54, doubted Drijvers' claim that Jacob was the author of the

ing the commandments of Christ can be read in light of Jacob's *Treatise against Those Who Transgressed Ecclesiastical Canons.* In that treatise, Jacob showed an understanding of Christianity in which the commandments and teaching of Christ were at the absolute center. Indeed, in all the various divine covenants that had existed—from Adam, through Noah and Moses, and on to Christ—relations between God and humans had been governed by the need of humans to observe God's laws and commandments. Even before the coming of Christ, people who looked forward to his advent could, Jacob asserted, be called Christians.[20]

Apparently, some people in Jacob's day held to the view that merely having correct belief was sufficient to make one a Christian; this was a view that Jacob strongly rejected. Being a Christian demanded both proper belief *and* proper action. Neither one of these was optional: 'This is a complete description of Christianity, and this is the canon and definition which explains it,' Jacob wrote.

> Along with an Orthodox faith which is in God, it demands the doing of good works, being distant from evil activity and wronging [others], and the keeping of the laws and commandments of God. It is not in accordance with the empty belief of the transgressors of the law, who erroneously assert that Orthodox faith alone suffices us for salvation, apart from keeping the laws and apart from praiseworthy action and pure and chaste behavior... perfect Christianity is not faith alone, nor is it only action, but rather the two of them together.[21]

Troubled by his times, Jacob went so far as to explicitly define what exactly Christianity was.

> Definition of Christianity: We say therefore that Christianity is the covenant of God which is with humans, which is perfected by means of Orthodox faith in God and by means of a knowledge and confession of the Economy which God the Word suffered on our behalf when He became human, and by means of being born again through water and the Spirit [cf. John 3:5] and partaking in the sufferings and death of the only begotten Word, our Lord Jesus Christ, and

apocalypse attached to the *Testament of Our Lord* and has argued strongly and persuasively against it: see further his 'The Authorship of the Apocalyptic Section of the *Testament of Our Lord* Reconsidered,' forthcoming.

[20] Jacob of Edessa, *Treatise against Those Who Transgress Ecclesiastical Canons,* pp. 187–88 (ed. Penn, 'Jacob of Edessa's Defining Christianity'; for an ET of this passage and the edited Syriac text [on the basis of BL Add. 12,154, fol. 166b], see also *SBI,* p. 221 [and n. 532]).

[21] Jacob of Edessa, *Treatise against Those Who Transgress Ecclesiastical Canons,* pp. 189–90 (ed. Penn, 'Jacob of Edessa's Defining Christianity'; Syriac text from BL Add. 12,154, fols. 167a–167b previously edited in *SBI,* p. 223, n. 535).

> by means of receiving His holy Body and Blood, and by means of a pure and holy way of life, which imitates Christ as much as it is possible for a human to imitate Christ. It [sc. the covenant] is fulfilled through the observation of the laws and commandments of God and through the hope and expectation of the resurrection of human bodies from among the dead and of the judgment and recompense of the world which is to come.[22]

For Jacob, Christianity was that by which 'we are distinguished and different from all the pagan nations and the Jews, those who are in error and wicked and without law.'[23] To deny the canons, therefore, was to surrender nothing less than one's Christian identity. Little wonder, then, that Jacob took these rules of the Church with utmost seriousness and left behind a sizeable body of material relating to their proper observation. As we have seen, he even went so far as to translate canon law from Greek into Syriac.[24]

JACOB'S CANONS AS A WINDOW INTO SEVENTH-CENTURY SYRIAN SOCIETY

We should not write off Jacob's treatises as mere literary exercises. His fondness for rules and his insistence upon the strict observation of church canons and laws made him something of a difficult character for his contemporaries, but these same qualities make him a goldmine for the social historian today. It is, in fact, our good fortune that Jacob took ecclesiastical law so seriously, for his canons shed much light on certain aspects of society in Umayyad-ruled Syria, affording us an especially rich perspective on what was going on among the great number of Christians living there at the time who have left us no texts and are otherwise largely invisible to the historian's gaze. Moreover, as we shall see, the picture they give us is corroborated by what we find in other places.

[22] Jacob of Edessa, *Treatise against Those Who Transgress Ecclesiastical Canons*, pp. 188–89 (ed. Penn, 'Jacob of Edessa's Defining Christianity'; Wright published this text, on the basis of BL Add. 17,193, in *CBM* vol. 2, pp. 996–97 and Syriac text from BL Add. 12,154, fols. 166b–67a, edited and translated in *SBI*, p. 222 [text at n. 533]).

[23] Jacob of Edessa, *Treatise against Those Who Transgress Ecclesiastical Canons*, p. 189 (ed. Penn, 'Jacob of Edessa's Defining Christianity'; Syriac text from BL Add. 12,154, fol. 167a edited and translated in *SBI*, p. 222, n. 534).

[24] Drijvers argued that Jacob identified his own story with the plight of Cyprian in the third century. For this and Jacob's translation of canon law into Syriac, see Drijvers, 'Testament of Our Lord,' pp. 108–10 and D. Kruisheer, 'A Bibliographical Clavis to the Works of Jacob of Edessa (revised and expanded), in ter Haar Romeny, ed., *Jacob of Edessa and the Syriac Culture of His Day*, pp. 286–87.

In what follows, I will especially rely on Jacob's replies to dozens of questions asked him by the priest Addai.[25] If we assume that these canons were motivated by real-life situations of which he was aware, either through personal experience or through reports, then what we have here is a remarkable view of just what was actually happening 'on the ground' as Miaphysite Christians in Syria interacted with both other non-Miaphysite Christian groups and non-Christians who were their neighbors.[26] Viewed from the perspective of the canons and other sources, the situation outside the world of theological dispute was, in Jacob's opinion, messy and chaotic. The implications of differing on the finer points of Christology do not seem to have sunk in with certain segments of the Christian population. The image that emerges from Jacob's canons aligns well with that which can be detected in other seventh and early eighth-century sources. These various pieces of evidence suggest that we are dealing with a society where a separation between competing and rival churches has taken place at an ideological level, but where the actual day-to-day implications of the intellectual and doctrinal partition of the Christian community have not been fully worked out. In other words, the simple believers of Syria had not achieved the distinct confessional identity of at least some of their leaders. The lag-time separating ideological and on-the-ground partitions is reflected in the frequent displeasure and anger expressed by Jacob.

By the time Jacob was writing his canonical replies, supporters and opponents of Chalcedon had (notionally) been at odds, sometimes violently, in the Middle East for nearly two hundred and fifty years. And yet it seems as if

[25] We alas know little about Adai apart from the fact that he was a priest (*qashshishā*). Addai was also referred to as a 'lover of labors,' (*rāḥem 'amlē*), that is, a φιλόπονος. This Syriac calque on the Greek term was used especially in the seventh and eighth centuries by and in reference to philhellenic Miaphysite scholars and could be a term that denoted polymathy, great erudition, and might also indicate a knowledge of Greek; Jacob called himiself a *rāḥem 'amlā*, for instance—see the colophon attached to his revision of Paul of Edessa's translation of the *Hymns* of Severus in E. W. Brooks, *James of Edessa: The Hymns of Severus of Antioch and Others* (PO 7.5) (Paris, 1911), p. 389.

Seventy-one of Addai's questions to Jacob were published by P. de Lagarde, *Reliquiae Iuris Ecclesiastici Antiquissimae Syriace* (Osnabrück, 1967) pp. *117–*43 (see p. *117 for a reference to Addai as a *qashshishā* and *rāḥem 'amlē*) and T. J. Lamy, *Dissertatio de Syrorum fide et disciplina in re eucharistica* (Louvain, 1859), pp. 98–171. Harvard Syriac 93 and Mardin 310 contain two additional rulings by Jacob in this collection, in addition to a number of other canons of Jacob and further answers to more questions by Addai. For this information, see Hoyland, *Seeing Islam*, pp. 601–608. A. Vööbus, *Syrische Kanonessammlungen: Ein Beitrag zur Quellenkunde*, I: *Westsyrische Originalurkunden*, 1, B (CSCO 317: Subsidia 38) (Louvain, 1970), pp. 273–98 is the most detailed discussion of the complicated manuscript transmission of Jacob's canonical material. H. Teule in *CMR*, vol. 1, pp. 227–31, offers the clearest available presentation of this material. Teule, 'Jacob of Edessa and Canon Law,' provides a skilled overview of Jacob's canons, their reception in the later Syriac tradition, and their most important themes.

[26] Cf. Teule, 'Jacob of Edessa and Canon Law,' pp. 86–93 (NB: 89-90). Teule also used Jacob's canonical and question and answer material to offer a brief sketch of certain aspects of Jacob's contemporary religious setting (93–99).

Miaphysite and Chalcedonian clergy were nevertheless often on friendly terms. If, Addai asked, it happens out of necessity that a believing clergyman sits at the table with a heretical clergyman, what should take place? Should the Orthodox person say the blessing and the heretic eat, or vice versa?[27] But it was not always, apparently, necessity that made such situations unavoidable. In another question, Addai wanted to know whether it was appropriate for an Orthodox monk and ascetic to have as a friend a heretical monk and ascetic who was not a family member? Could they live next to one another and share in everything except for the liturgy? 'Loving our Lord and keeping His commandments and those of His Apostles,' Jacob answered, 'and loving a heretic and having interaction with him—the two things at the same time are not possible. It is, therefore, not right.'[28]

Jacob's canons suggest that extensive contact and interaction between Christians belonging to rival confessions affected every aspect of Christian practice. Addai had spoken of sharing everything save the Eucharist, but were people sharing even this, the most important marker of Christian unity and division? There was certainly worry among ecclesiastical leaders that people might take communion in rival churches. To depart for a moment from Syria, we find that John the Almsgiver, the Chalcedonian patriarch of Alexandria (sed. 609–619) was adamant that Chalcedonians under his authority not take communion with Miaphysites, 'even if,' he is reported to have told them,

> you remain without communicating all your life, if through stress of circumstances you cannot find a community of the Catholic Church.... For 'communion,' he said, has been so called because he who has 'communion' has things in common and agrees with those with whom he has 'communion.' Therefore I implore you earnestly, children, never go near the oratories of the heretics in order to communicate there.[29]

In a confessionally diverse city like Alexandria, the odds were no doubt high that many Christians under his jurisdiction had in fact visited a church where the Definition of Chalcedon was not viewed authoritatively. Proscribing members of one's church from setting foot in a rival church likely stemmed in part

[27] *Questions Which Addai the Priest and Lover of Labors Asked Jacob, the Bishop of Edessa* 53 (ed. Lamy, *Dissertatio*, p. 152, which contains misprints; see Mardin 310, fol. 203b for a better Syriac version). The Syriac text from Mardin 310, with an English translation, can also be found in *SBI*, p. 224, n. 538.

[28] *Questions Which Addai the Priest and Lover of Labors Asked Jacob, the Bishop of Edessa* 54 (ed. Lamy, *Dissertatio*, pp. 152, 154).

[29] Leontius of Neapolis, *Life of John the Almsgiver* 42 (ed. Gelzer, *Leontios' von Neapolis*, pp. 85–86; ET taken from Dawes and Baynes, *Three Byzantine Saints*, p. 251). For the 'longer recension,' see Festugière and Rydén, eds., *Vie de Syméon le Fou et Vie de Jean de Chypre*, pp. 398–99 [Greek] = 510–11 [FT] = chapter 49.

from a recognition that proximity to a rival Eucharist increased the odds that one would take it.

If we return now to Syria, we find evidence that people were in fact taking communion in rival churches. In the early eighth-century *vita* of Theodota of Amid (d. 698), a Miaphysite holy man active in northern Syria in the second half of the seventh century, the protagonist found a man in the monastery of Mar Sergius the Broad, learning the Psalms who was a secret Nestorian. 'This man is a Nestorian,' Theodota told the Abbot, 'and you trample upon the law of God when you give him the Eucharist and seat him at the table of life.' The abbot and monks nevertheless disregarded his warning. The Nestorian was a carpenter, and they did not want to send him away. The Nestorian was eventually sent out from the monastery, but it took a demon dramatically possessing the heretic and boasting at his joy in having spiritually damaged the monks by improperly taking communion to force the issue.[30] John the Almsgiver had ordered that members of his church stay away from the churches of rivals, and this anecdote from Theodota's *vita* illustrates just what might happen if they did not.

Importantly, worries about the presence of people from rival confessions in a different group's monasteries and churches would continue long after Theodota and Jacob's day: in 794, the patriarch Cyriacus (sed. 793–817) issued a canon condemning not just laymen but also clergy who went to the monasteries and churches of other confessions. 'Priests and deacons or laymen or women,' his canon stated,

> who go to the churches of the Nestorians, Chalcedonians or the Julianists and give there their gifts or their tithes or their vows or give them wives—these priests and deacons shall fall from their ranks. The laymen and women shall not enter the church and shall not participate in the holy mysteries.[31]

Especially notable here is the point that clergy and not just laymen were identified in this canon. As in the story of Theodota's crypto-Nestorian, who was knowingly being given communion by the members of a monastery, being ordained did not mean that one observed strict ecclesiastical separation.

We do not know the level of literacy, theological or otherwise, of the priests and deacons who were engaged in the behaviors that provoked Cyriacus' condemnation, but even the seriousness with which the literate and the scribes took Christological disagreements is called into question by Jacob's canons.

[30] For the incident, see St Mark's Jerusalem 199, fols. 553a–53b. The Syriac text is available in Mardin 275/8, pp. 520–24. NB: 'Nestorian' here might mean 'Chalcedonian.'

[31] *Canons of Patriarch Cyriacus (AD 794)* 14 (ed. and trans. Vööbus, *The Synodicon in the West Syrian Tradition* II [CSCO 375–76: SS 163–64] [Louvain, 1976], p. 10 [Syriac] = 12 [ET]). I have used the translation of Vööbus. On this canon, see Possekel, 'Christological Debates in Eighth-Century Harran,' p. 355.

Is it right, Addai asked Jacob, for an Orthodox monk to write out questions and answers that help the heretics against the Orthodox faith in exchange for money or some other form of compensation? The 'questions and answers' Addai spoke of likely referred to a particular post-Chalcedonian genre of Christological polemic that used aporetic questions to reduce one's opponent to confusion and absurdity.[32] Such a one, Jacob wrote, was a betrayer of the faith of Christ, even if he did not sell him for thirty pieces of silver like the first traitor.[33] Elsewhere Jacob spoke of a scribe who wrote out books for heretics as 'a second Judas.'[34]

It should perhaps come as no surprise that there was also confusion as to whether a Miaphysite should abide by the canons of heretics. Is it appropriate, Addai asked, that we keep a heretical canon? No, Jacob, responded, not even if it is justly and rightly stated.[35] Apparently, it was the switching of allegiances by individuals that was causing at least part of the confusion about jurisdiction and the applicability of canons and ecclesiastical decrees across competing communions. To take one example: 'Shall we receive,' asked John, the Stylite of Litarb, another one of Jacob's correspondents, 'a heretic who has been excommunicated by his superior because of his transgression, and who wants to be with us?'[36] 'An Orthodox man,' John also reported to Jacob, 'has been excommunicated by a heretical bishop. What should he do?'[37]

[32] On this genre, see A. Grillmeier, *Christ in Christian Tradition* II,1: *From the Council of Chalcedon (451) to Gregory the Great (590–604)*, pp. 82–84, 86–87.

[33] *Questions Which Addai the Priest and Lover of Labors Asked Jacob, the Bishop of Edessa* 55 (ed. Lamy, *Dissertatio*, p. 154).

[34] Bar Hebraeus, *Nomocanon* 7.8 (ed. P. Bedjan, *Nomocanon Gregorii Barhebraei* [Pairs/Leipzig, 1898], p. 102). NB: This canon may represent an abridgement/condensation of the one cited in the previous note. The British Library contains a Miaphysite lectionary that a stylite named Samuel copied and bound in 1089 near Alexandria (BL Add. 14,490); it also contains an East Syrian—that is, 'Nestorian'—lectionary that the same Samuel bound, also in 1089 (BL Add. 14,491); see *CBM*, vol. 1, 159–61 and *CBM*, vol. 1, 179–81, respectively. See also See Ibn Abī Dāwūd, *Kitāb al-masāḥif*, p. 133 (ed. A. Jeffery [Cairo, 1936]), where there are reports of early Muslims having Qur'āns written out for them by Christians, and also Ibn al-Nadīm, *Fihrist*, vol. 1, p. 264 (ed. G. Flügel [Leipzig, 1871–1872]), for the claim of Yaḥyā b. 'Adī, the famous Miaphysite philosopher, that he had written out with his own hand two copies of the Qur'ānic commentary of al-Ṭabarī.

[35] *Questions Which Addai the Priest and Lover of Labors Asked Jacob, the Bishop of Edessa*, p. 259 (ed. Vööbus, *The Synodicon in the West Syrian Tradition I* [CSCO 367–68: SS 161–62], p. 236 [ET]). Addai did not specify which canon he had in mind, but note that in his thirteenth-century work on canon law, Bar Hebraeus would cite the Council of Chalcedon as an authority. See, for example, *Nomocanon* 9.1, 9.10 (ed. Bedjan, *Nomocanon Gregorii Barhebraei*, pp. 77, 109) and see Bedjan's listing of Chalcedon as a source, p. 2.

[36] *Questions of All Kind, Which John the Stylite Asked the Venerable Jacob, the Teacher* 24 (ed. Vööbus [CSCO 367–68: SS 161–62], p. 244 [Syriac] = 224 [ET]). The ET here is that of Vööbus; ET also available in *SBI*, p. 227, n. 543. John of Litarb was a learned Miaphysite active in the first half of the eighth century and also a correspondent of George, Bishop of the Arab Tribes (d. 724); see most conveniently, Baumstark, *Geschichte*, pp. 258–59.

[37] *Questions of All Kind, Which John the Stylite Asked the Venerable Jacob, the Teacher* 26 (ed. Vööbus,

Confessional loyalties could vary, even within a family, from one generation to another. Addai wanted to know if it was lawful for Orthodox children to make memorials and celebrate Eucharists for their parents who were heretics and who had died in heresy. What if, he went on, the parents were heretics, but gave their son to the Orthodox to become a monk? Here we have an indication that putative sectarian boundaries apparently did not impede the donation of children to monasteries. This situation no doubt was the result of the fact that people's allegiances were likely more often to their local church, monastery, or holy man than they were to a particular confession.[38] Jacob's answer to the question of Orthodox children making memorials for heretical parents was nuanced. If the parents had been supporters and proponents of the heresy, no Eucharists or memorials should be celebrated. If, however, they had been among the 'simple people' and had held to the heresy out of a 'certain custom' and 'not out of wickedness,' then the question of whether such memorial services might be celebrated in their honor was left to the judgment of the children.[39]

Children and parents might have opposing Christological loyalties; so, too, might servants and masters. John, the Stylite of Litarb, asked Jacob about the case of a person who had been the servant of a heretic. Though the servant suffered abuse from his heretical master because of his beliefs, he never denied them. What profit would such a person have?[40] Cases like this may not have been rare: perhaps a century earlier, John Moschus recorded the story of a wealthy Miaphysite merchant who had a Chalcedonian agent in his employ. The merchant and a number of other Miaphysites would eventually convert

The Synodicon in the West Syrian Tradition I [CSCO 367–68: SS 161–62] p. 245 [=225 (ET)]). The ET is from Vööbus with slight modification; ET also available in *SBI*, p. 227, n. 544.

[38] For example: the news of Euthymius's acceptance of the Council of Chalcedon, Cyril of Scythopolis reported, would have been enough to sway all the monks of the Judean desert to accept Chalcedon as well had it not been for the Miaphysite patriarch Theodosius's activities: Cyril of Scythopolis, *Life of Euthymius* 27 (ed. Schwartz, *Kyrillos von Skythopolis*, pp. 41–45; ET available in Price, *Lives of the Monks of Palestine*, pp. 37–41). In the Miaphysite *History of Dioscorus*, the Emperor Marcian, when confronted with the decision of whether he should accept the *Tome* of Leo, was unsure of what to do and therefore sought out the counsel of a certain monk named John in Scetis as to whether accepting it was the will of God. The *History* claimed that Nestorians bribed the messenger sent by the emperor to change John's message and encourage Marcian to accept the *Tome*. See Ps.-Theopistus, *History of Dioscorus* 8 (ed. Nau, 'Histoire de Dioscore,' pp. 48–50 [Syriac] = 266–67 [French]) (and cf. Chapter 2, n. 69).

[39] The responsum (part of the *Further Questions which the Priest Addai Asked*) in Mardin 310, fols. 212b–213b. Harvard 93, fols. 25a–26a contains a longer version of the same canon. Because it is damaged, the full text needs to be reconstructed using materials from Harvard 93 and Mardin 310. For this text, and an English translation, see *SBI*, p. 228, n. 545. Bar Hebraeus, *Nomocanon* 6.2 (ed. Bedjan, *Nomocanon*, pp. 73–74) contains a shorter version of this canon.

[40] *Questions of All Kind, Which John the Stylite Asked the Venerable Jacob, the Teacher* 21 (ed. Vööbus [CSCO 367–68: SS 161–62], p. 243 [= p. 223 (ET)]). Another ET can be found in *SBI*, p. 229, n. 546.

to Chalcedonianism when it was discovered that pieces of the Eucharist the agent had set aside in a special box had grown shoots after being locked away for a year.[41]

In such a world, where ecclesiastical affiliations might shift within families and from generation to generation, it is not hard to imagine that there might be what one might call confessional code-switching, where a person would claim allegiance to one group or another depending on the circumstances in which he found himself in, much like a multilingual person shifts between languages depending on the context.[42] The *Codex Justinianus*'s worry about people changing confessional allegiance for the purpose of getting a government position points to the very real possibility of such switching.[43] One thing is clear: people were moving back and forth between different church groups. And this was not just going on in rural areas and far away from the centers of doctrinal power. There was confessional shape-shifting going on under the noses and in the company of the most elite theological elements of society.

To take one vivid example: nearing the end of his life at the close of the seventh century, Theodota of Amid encountered a confessional code-switcher near the famous monastery of Qenneshre, the intellectual heart of the Syriac-speaking Miaphysite movement in the seventh century and a place we will encounter later in this book. A foreigner from Beth Garmai, an area in northern Iraq, this old man was among the people from the monastery who came out to meet Theodota. Though the *Life* notes that he was honored by the monks of Qenneshre and by no less than the Miaphysite patriarch Julian as a holy man, Theodota saw through his projected identity and publicly called him out as not being a true believer. Though some of the monks doubted Theodota's accusations, the suspect eventually came clean: he was baptized a Nestorian but, going deaf because of ear problems, he had agreed to 'strip off' his baptism—presumably be circumcised—if a Jewish doctor would give him treatment. Theodota was right, yet again.[44] Baptized Nestorian, a convert to Judaism, and

[41] John Moschus, *Spiritual Meadow* 79 (PG 87, cols. 2936–37; ET in Wortley, *The Spiritual Meadow*, pp. 63–64).

[42] I am influenced here by Peter Burke's comments on 'occasionalism' on pp. 94–96 of his *What is Cultural History?* (Cambridge/Malden, MA, 2004) and also by conversations with Richard Payne.

[43] See Chapter 1, n. 73.

[44] 'So the venerable elders and all the brothers asked that apostate and he said to them, "Yes, indeed, my Brothers. The Holy Spirit has spoken through this man. He is a true prophet. For I was baptized with the baptism of Nestorius and when I became a man, my ears grew deaf and I could not hear. When, therefore, I approached a Jewish doctor, he said to me, 'If you do not strip off your baptism, it will not be possible for you to be healed.' So I said to him, 'Do with me whatever you want.' And he did with me according to his will. For this reason, I am fasting so that God will have mercy on me." ' St Mark's Jerusalem, 199, fols. 559a–b. The Syriac text of this incident, which is lacunose, can be found in Mardin 275/8, pp. 566–68.

living among the spiritual elites and highest leadership of the Miaphysite church, he had identified with a number of different religious communities over the course of his life. This particular incident, one in which a crypto-Nestorian lived among the leaders of the Syriac-speaking Miaphysite church, suggests, too, that even at the highest levels of the Miaphysite movement, there might be a certain amount of inconsistency, with some being less rigid and intransigent than others when it came to doctrinal difference. After all, when Jacob confronted Patriarch Julian about rampant nonobservance of canons in the church, no less an authority than the patriarch himself had told him to go along with the times.

The *Life* of Theodota gives us another report of a confessional code-switcher. Earlier in the story, Theodota had gotten word of a *faux* holy man going about the region of the Arsanias River (the modern Murad Su in Eastern Turkey) claiming to be Theodota himself. He would mix with the heretics and act as a heretic, the text tells us; and similarly, he would mix with the Orthodox and act as an Orthodox. The *Life* suggests that the real motivation of this Pseudo-Theodota was the large amount of gold he was amassing. The false holy man was eventually confronted by the real Theodota, who exposed his deception. Demons possessed him and he confessed publicly his true theological colors. 'I am a Nestorian,' he wailed before Theodota, 'I do not agree with the Orthodox, nor with the Chalcedonians.' Theodota drove out the demons that possessed the man, and he became properly Orthodox.[45] Now Miaphysite, now Chalcedonian, now Nestorian: confessional shape-shifting was easy, common, and perhaps even lucrative in this environment.[46]

In the same way, Jacob's canons speak of Orthodox children celebrating memorials for their heretical parents and heretical parents donating their children to Orthodox monasteries, but the Orthodox-heretical divide might exist also in the same generation, in fact within the same person, and this diverse ecclesiastical heritage might provide another opportunity for confes-

[45] St Mark's Jerusalem 199, fol. 554b. For the Syriac, see Mardin 275/8, pp. 532–34 (the Syriac text is lacunose).

[46] Although the case is slightly different, mention might also be made of a Christian named Severus who claimed to be Moses and thereby took much gold and other forms of property from Jews in Syria. See *Zuqnin Chronicle*, pp. 173–74 (ed. Chabot [CSCO 104: SS 53]; ET available in Harrak, *The Chronicle of Zuqnīn*, pp. 163–64); Michael the Great, *Chronicle* 11.19 (ed. Chabot, 4.456 = 2.490); Theophanes, *Chronicle* AM 6213 (ed. de Boor, vol. 1, p. 401; ET available in Mango and Scott, *The Chronicle of Theophanes Confessor*, p. 554). Marutha of Mosul, who claimed to be a wonderworker, consecrated altars, crosses, and priests in his own name, and attracted many Christians from the Jazira in the year 770 (AG 1081), is another example of a holy man who was viewed negatively by other religious leaders. For reports on Marutha, see *Chronicle to 819*, p. 19 (ed. A. Barsaum, *Chronicon anonymum ad A.D. 819 pertinens* [CSCO SS 3.14] [Paris, 1920]) and *Chronicle to 846*, p. 237 (ed. Brooks [CSCO Syr. III.4]; ET by Brooks available in his 'A Syriac Chronicle of the Year 846,' *ZDMG* 51 [1897], p. 587).

sional code-switching. Such individuals defied easy categorization and had multiple potential ecclesiastical loyalties that exasperated more institutionally-embedded church leaders. For reasons like these, it should come as no surprise, that marrying one's daughter to a member of a rival church was something that leaders frowned upon.[47] Children of marriages between people belonging to different and rival churches might show loyalties to both or perhaps to neither; and either outcome could be problematic.

We have a good example of such a figure from a Syriac source originating in Iraq. In a letter written while he was bishop of Nineveh and during the Byzantine occupation of northern Iraq after 628, East Syrian catholicos Isho'yahb III (d. ca. 658) bemoaned the construction of a Miaphysite church near the dung heap outside one of the gates of Nineveh by a group of people whom he referred to as the 'dung of the church.' The leader of this group of people, Isho'yahb noted, had an Orthodox (i.e., East Syrian/Nestorian) father and a heretical mother. This individual, Isho'yahb observed with disdain, went from his mother's doctrine to his father's doctrine, and then to 'true paganism' and intercommunion with heretics.[48] Fear of the authorities drove him back to orthodoxy (i.e., the Church of the East), but once the fear had subsided, he returned 'like a dog to his vomit' (cf. Proverbs 26:11, 2 Peter 2:22) to his old ways and to actively supporting the work of heretical agitators. For such a person, confessional allegiance seems to have been a function of many things and a concern for true doctrine was, at best, only one of them.

The confessional movements of this half-Miaphysite, half-Nestorian leader were not unique. Isho'yahb angrily lamented that among those helping in the construction of this Miaphysite church and supporting its activities were former Nestorians who had become Miaphysites. They were, he wrote, the ancient offspring of that heresy and belonged to it both by their nature and by their volition. Miaphysites were even being helped by people who had converted

[47] See the regulation contained in the revised shorter of the two Syriac recensions of the *Teaching of the Apostles* (3.20): 'It is not lawful for a Christian to give a woman to any kind of marriage with a Nestorian or with a people out of our fold, nor to a heretic, nor to those who are strange to us in faith' (ed. M. D. Gibson, *The Didascalia Apostolorum in English, Translated from Syriac* [London, 1903], pp. *33 [Syriac] = 22 [ET]; I have used here Gibson's translation). On the two different recensions of the *Teaching of the Apostles*, see Vööbus, *The Didascalia Apostolorum in Syriac* (CSCO 402: SS 176), pp. *33–*67. Also note that the Seventy-Second Canon of the Quinisext Council forbade marriage between Orthodox individuals (male or female) and heretics (male or female). See Council in Trullo, *Canons* 72 (ed. Joannou, *Discipline générale antique*, vol. 1.1, pp. 209–10).

[48] Compare this with Maximus the Confessor's alleged heritage in the Syriac *Life* written by George of Resh'ayna: Maximus' father was a Samaritan and his mother was the daughter of a Persian Jew—religiously 'mixed' families were dangerous. See George of Resh'ayna, *Life of Maximus Confessor* 1 (ed. S. P. Brock, 'An Early Syriac Life of Maximus the Confessor,' *AB* 91 [1973], p. 302 = 314 [ET]). I am grateful to Peter Brown for this point.

away from their confession: Isho'yahb observed that the prosperity of the Miaphysite community was in part the result of help from former Miaphysites who had converted to the religion of the rulers but who were still aiding their former brethren. This, clearly, was an environment in which people were moving around quite freely between confessions, Christian and non-Christian, and where religious identity might be used instrumentally.[49]

Variability in personal identities was mirrored by shifts in the ownership of real estate and church property: churches and church vessels changed hands between rival groups, and this raised its own series of questions that Jacob confronted in his canons. What should be done, Addai asked, to a priest who takes an altar and its vessels from Chalcedonians and then gives them back?[50] John the Stylite reported to Jacob an instance of zealous Miaphysites seizing a church from heretics. Before a bishop was able to pray in it, they had held a liturgy in the church and celebrated a Eucharist. There was also the opposite situation: a church of the Miaphysites seized by the heretics and then retaken by the Orthodox and used for a service before a bishop could say the appropriate prayers. What did Jacob make of such cases?[51] Individual conversions between confessions might happen: in another letter, Isho'yahb III complained about a foolish man (who had previously been a Nestorian) who was 'received in the great city of the heretics' (i.e., Tikrit) and who partook in their mysteries as well as in their faith.[52] There were also instances of mass conversions from one confession to another. If an entire village of heretics returns to the true faith, John tells Jacob, what should we now do with their mysteries?[53] This possibility of such large-scale shifting of allegiances was a noteworthy feature of the landscape we are dealing with: in letters written perhaps a century later, ca. 791–792, the Nestorian patriarch Timothy I would report that thirteen churches and more than two thousand people in the (Iraqi) city of Najran (near Kufa), had rejected their former Julianism and joined the Church of the East. Twenty-five men had come to Timothy—priests and deacons, along with a

[49] Isho'yahb III, *Letters* I.44 (To Gabriel), pp. 82–83 (ed. R. Duval, *Īšō'yahb III Patriarcha: Liber Epistularum* [CSCO: Syr. II.64] [Paris, 1904–1905], pp. 63–64 [=LT]). A LT can be also be found in J. S. Assemani, *BO*, vol. 3.1, p 115. Full ET can be found in *SBI*, p. 233, n. 553. For a discussion of this letter and its historical context (after the Byzantine conquest of northern Iraq in 628), see J.-M. Fiey, 'Īšō'yaw le Grand: Vie du caltholicos nestorien Īšō'yaw III d'Adiabène (580–659),' *OCP* 35 (1969), pp. 327–29.

[50] *Questions Which Addai the Priest and Lover of Labors Asked Jacob, the Bishop of Edessa*, p. 259 (ed. Vööbus [CSCO 367–68: SS 161–62], p. 236 [ET]); my translation available in *SBI*, p. 234, n. 554.

[51] *Questions of All Kind, which John the Stylite Asked the Venerable Jacob, the Teacher* 25 (ed. Vööbus [CSCO 367–68: SS 161–62], p. 244 [= 224 (ET)]). My translation available in *SBI*, p. 234, n. 555.

[52] Isho'yahb III, *Letters* II.17 (To Aba), p. 165 (ed. Duval [CSCO: Syr. II.64]; p. 122 [=LT]); cf. Fiey, 'Īšō'yaw le Grand,' p. 329, n. 1.

[53] *Questions of All Kind, Which John the Stylite Asked the Venerable Jacob, the Teacher* 23 (ed. Vööbus [CSCO 367–68: SS 161–62], pp. 243–44 [= 224 (ET)]). My translation available in *SBI*, p. 235, n. 557.

great number of common people—requesting a bishop be consecrated for them, and Timothy was happy to be of help.[54]

Aiding and abetting putative rivals was not a problem either, at least for some. In Job of Beth Man'am's *Life* of Simeon of the Olives (d. 734), we have a curious case of groups supposed to be enemies actually helping one another out when it came to building churches—at least to a point. Simeon's attempts to build a church outside of Nisibis were hampered by Nestorian priests. Their tactic? They forbade Nestorians from working on the building of the church, either with or without pay. For at least some 'Nestorians' there seems to have been nothing objectionable in helping to build a church to be used by Miaphysites.[55] In the case of the construction of the church in Nineveh that elicited Isho'yahb III's ire, he lamented the support that heretics (i.e., Miaphysites) were receiving from those among 'our people'; planning to go to Tikrit himself to speak with the rulers about the intolerable situation, Isho'yahb expected little if any help from local Nestorians. With one exception, a man named Kabab, they were all helpers of the wicked heretics.[56] This is the brick and mortar equivalent of Miaphysite scribes writing out theological polemics for their Christian rivals.

Given that people were willing to subordinate the importance of Chalcedon and precise Christological doctrines to other concerns in their self-presentation and behavior, it should come as no surprise that at the level of the sacraments and church ritual, there seems to have been sharing and overlap between people supposed to be holding opposing Christologies: Addai's questions

[54] For this, see Timothy I, *Letters* 27 (to Rabban Sergius), p. 151 (ed. Braun [CSCO 74: SS 30]) and his reference to this event in his *Letters* 41 ('To the Monks of Mar Maroun'), p. ܡܘ [*46] 'as for the well-known city of Najran… in the year that just passed, thirteen churches were united with us (*etḥayyad 'amman*), a group that exceeds 2,000 people in number' (ed. Bidawid, *Les lettres du patriarche nestorien Timothée I*; for the date of the letter to Sergius and a FT of this passage from Timothy's letter to the monks of Mar Maroun, see p. 60). NB: Timothy's letter clearly identifies this Najran as the Najran near Hira and not the Najran in South Arabia. On this Najran, see J.-M. Fiey, *Pour un Oriens Christianus Novus. Répertoire des diocèses syriaques orientaux et occidentaux.* (Beirut/Stuttgart, 1993), see pp. 247–48. Centuries before this, Theodoret of Cyrrhus (d. ca. 466) claimed to have brought eight villages of Marcionites, a village of Eunomians, and another full of Arians to correct belief in the course of his episcopal ministry: Theodoret of Cyrrhus, *Letters* 81 (To the Consul Nonnus) (ed. Y. Azéma, *Théodoret de Cyr. Correspondence* II [SC 98] [Paris, 1965], p. 197; ET by B. Jackson available in *NPNF*, ser. 2, vol. 3 [New York, 1892], p. 277).

[55] Mardin 8/259, fols. 112b–113a (section 22 in my translation). On this *vita*, see A. Palmer and J. Tannous, 'Life of Simeon of the Olives,' in *CMR*, vol. 5, pp. 615–19, as well as my 'The Life of Simeon of the Olives: A Christian Puzzle from Islamic Syria,' in J. Kreiner and H. Reimitz, eds., *Motions of Late Antiquity: Essays on Religion, Politics, and Society in Honour of Peter Brown* (Turnhout, 2016), pp. 309–30.

[56] Isho'yahb III, *Letters* I.44 (To Gabriel), p. 83 (ed. Duval [CSCO: Syr. II.64]; p. 64 [=LT]). See Fiey, 'Īšō'yahw le Grand,' p. 329, for discussion of Isho'yahb's planned trip to Tikrit. *SBI*, p. 237, n. 560, contains further translations from this letter.

reflect a milieu in which Miaphysite priests were performing rites for Christians who, strictly speaking, belonged to heretical and rival churches. This was due in part to the problem that neither the Chalcedonians nor the Miaphysites were, it seems, able to supply clergy to all of the people who agreed with them doctrinally. Is it right, Addai asked Jacob, for us to be escorts in the funeral processions of heretics and to bury them? According to Jacob, if the person who died was in a city or a village where there are clerics who agreed with his doctrine, and the deceased had not asked for an Orthodox (i.e., Miaphysite) burial, then he should not receive one. But if there were no heretical clergy nearby, then Miaphysite clergy should bury him, regardless of whether he had requested such a burial.[57] There were simply not enough priests to go around. Another one of Jacob's canons informs us that a number of priests were required to perform the Eucharist in many villages in a single day.[58] We see this manpower dilemma in the *Life* of Theodota when he comes across a boy in a village who is so ill that the villagers have already dug his grave. They beg Theodota to stay with them, because they have no priest to escort the boy's funeral procession.[59] Concern about the doctrinal purity of priests was a luxury available only to those who had an abundance of clergy from which to choose; what was important was the existence and availability of a clergyman as an all-around ritual practitioner.[60]

Addai also wanted to know from Jacob whether it was appropriate for an Orthodox clergyman or monk to take part in the funeral procession of a 'heretical Chalcedonian,' along with lay people, though abstaining from chanting while processing. Furthermore, was it right for the Miaphysites to allow Chalcedonian clerics to take part in Orthodox funeral processions, also while refraining from chanting?[61]

What if, Addai asked, an Orthodox clergyman found himself in the company of Chalcedonians who had no priest and who wanted him to administer their own Eucharist to them? If the Orthodox priest did not enter the altar of the

[57] *Questions Which Addai the Priest and Lover of Labors Asked Jacob, the Bishop of Edessa* 60 (ed. Lamy, *Dissertatio*, pp. 158, 160, which contains typos). Mardin 310, fols. 204b–205a, gives a superior text. For it and an English translation, see *SBI*, p. 237, n. 561. For this passage, cf. the LT of Lamy, *Dissertatio*, pp. 159, 161. Bar Hebraeus, *Nomocanon* 6.1 (ed. Bedjan, *Nomocanon*, p. 70), contains a shortened version of this canon.

[58] Jacob of Edessa, *Canons*, Mardin 310, fols. 210a–b. For the Syriac text and an English translation, see *SBI*, p. 238, n. 562.

[59] St Mark's Jerusalem 199, fol. 554a. For the Syriac, see Mardin 275/8, p. 529.

[60] I am grateful to Peter Brown for this point and this turn of phrase.

[61] *Questions Which Addai the Priest and Lover of Labors Asked Jacob, the Bishop of Edessa* 61 (ed. Lamy, *Dissertatio*, pp. 160, 162). Mardin 310, fol. 205a, is free from Lamy's typos. For the Syriac text and an English translation, see *SBI*, p. 239, n. 565. Bar Hebraeus, *Nomocanon* 6.1 (ed. Bedjan, *Nomocanon*, p. 70) contains a shortened version of this canon.

heretical Chalcedonians and if he did not himself communicate, would this be acceptable?[62] George, Bishop of the Arabs, Jacob's contemporary and friend, has left us a canon stipulating that a priest or a deacon who gives the Eucharist to heretics is to be deposed,[63] and we have seen examples from the *Life* of Theodota of clergy knowingly and unknowingly giving the mysteries to people whom they should have excluded. Writing in perhaps 684,[64] Miaphysite patriarch Athanasius of Balad condemned Orthodox priests who knowingly and willingly baptized Nestorians, Julianists, and other heretics, and who gave them the Eucharist.[65] These practices would continue to be problems for church leaders: Patriarch George of Beʿeltan (sed. 758–789/790) excommunicated presbyters and deacons who gave communion to heretics and similarly excommunicated anyone who 'baptize[d] his son in the temple of the heretics.'[66] Not long afterward, the patriarch Cyriacus in 794 condemned priests and deacons who baptized Nestorians, Chalcedonians, and Julianists.[67] The on-the-ground realities of a confessionally mixed world meant that such predicaments were abiding ones: even Severus of Antioch permitted Miaphysites who were high officials in the government to attend Chalcedonian services and listen to the lections and the prayers if their jobs required it.[68]

[62] *Questions Which Addai the Priest and Lover of Labors Asked Jacob, the Bishop of Edessa* 64 (ed. Lamy, *Dissertatio*, p. 162): 'Addai: if it is right for an Orthodox clergyman who, when found to be with Chalcedonians and they are speaking to him, to give to them from their Eucharist which is kept with them, but they do not have a clergyman with them to take and give to them, while he [sc. the Orthodox priest] does not communicate and does not enter their altar. Jacob: He should not at all do something like this. Indeed, he who is persuaded to do something like this should receive punishment like a heretic.'

[63] Bar Hebraeus, *Nomocanon* 4.3 (ed. Bedjan, *Nomocanon*, p. 42): 'George: A priest or a deacon who gives the Eucharist to the heretics shall be deposed.'

[64] For this date, see the marginal note in Mardin 310, fol. 183b. Also, cf. A. Vööbus, *Syrische Kanonsessammlungen: Ein Beitrag zur Quellenkunde* I. *Westsyrische Originalurkunden* 1, A (CSCO 307: Subsidia 35) (Louvain, 1975), p. 201.

[65] Athanasius of Balad, *Letter on Eating the Sacrifices of the Hagarenes*, p. 130 (ed. F. Nau, 'Littérature canonique syriaque inédite,' *ROC* 14 (1909), p. 130). Mardin 310, fols. 184b–85a, an eighth-century ms. is the oldest witness to the text (see Vööbus, *Syrische Kanonsessammlungen: Ein Beitrag zur Quellenkunde* I, pp. 200–201) and is slightly different from Nau's printed text. For the Syriac text and an ET, see *SBI*, p. 240, n. 569. This text is also edited in R. Y. Ebied, 'The Syriac Encyclical Letter of Athanasius II, patriarch of Antioch, Which Forbids the Partaking of the Sacrifices of the Muslims' in P. Bruns and H. O. Luthe, eds., *Orientalia Christiana: Festschrift für Hubert Kaufhold zum 70. Geburtstag* (Wiesbaden, 2013) p. 173 (= 174 [ET]).

[66] *Canons of the Patriarch George* 11, 21 (ed. and trans. Vööbus, *The Synodicon in the West Syrian Tradition* II [CSCO 375-376: SS 163–64] [Louvain, 1976], pp. 4, 5 [Syriac] = p. 5, 6 [ET]; the translation is mine.).

[67] *Canons of Patriarch Cyriacus (AD 794)* 9 (ed. and trans. Vööbus, *The Synodicon in the West Syrian Tradition* II [CSCO 37–76: SS 163–64], p. 10 [Syriac] = 12 [ET]).

[68] Severus of Antioch, *Select Letters* 4.10 ('To Caesaria') (ed. Brooks, 1.2.304–306; ET available in Allen and Hayward, *Severus of Antioch*, pp. 146–48).

When pressed to justify just why it was that the Eucharist of another confession should not be taken, one response might be that the Eucharist of heretics was no such thing. Confined by the Emperor Constans II to a convent in Constantinople, Maximus the Confessor reportedly urged the nuns not to take communion from the Monothelete abbot in charge 'on the grounds that the Holy Spirit had not descended on it.'[69] This was a view shared across confessions. 'How could the Holy Spirit hover over an ordinary altar which it had not consecrated?' the bishop Barṣawmā of Susa is supposed to have written to the patriarch Isho'yahb II of Gdala (sed. 628–45), criticizing the East Syrian leader's behavior on a visit he had made to Roman territory that included celebrating several liturgies for the Emperor Heraclius in Aleppo and giving communion to him and other Chalcedonians. 'No! By my life,' Barṣawmā continued, 'it did not descend upon your Eucharist on an altar of Constantinople!'[70] This notion that rival altars lacked the divine presence seems to have been a common one: 'Is the altar of heretics,' the student asks a teacher in a Miaphysite theological dialogue contained in Paris Syriac 111, 'bereft of the Holy Spirit and is it the dwelling place of Satan?'[71] Despite such suggestions of the Spirit's absence from rival Eucharists, whatever boundaries certain leaders might have liked to have established between people holding opposing Christological views were not so clear when it came to real life and the ad-

[69] Michael the Great, *Chronicle* 11.9 (ed. Chabot, 4.427 = 2.436). Translation by S. P. Brock from 'An Early Syriac Life of Maximus the Confessor,' p. 339. On the relationship between this passage from Michael's *Chronicle* and the now mutilated and lost ending of the seventh-century Syriac *Life* of Maximus and a parallel passage in the *Chronicle to 1234*, see Brock's comments, pp. 330–32. For the passage in the *Chronicle to 1234*, which states that Maximus 'was ordering them to not receive the Eucharist the Abbas, their master, was offering up, for he was saying, "The Holy Spirit does not descend upon it,"' see *Chronicle to 1234*, p. 266 (ed. J-B. Chabot, *Anonymi Chronicon ad annum Christi 1234 pertinens* [CSCO SS III.14] [Paris, 1920]; ET also available in Brock, p. 339).

[70] *Chronicle of Seert* 2.94 (ed. Scher [and Griveau] [PO 13.4], p. 252). For this example, see Brock, 'An Early Syriac Life of Maximus the Confessor,' p. 339, n. 1. One point of contention (p. 240) was that Isho'yahb had, at the request of Heraclius, not mentioned the names of Diodore, Theodore, and Nestorius in his liturgy. Note also Barṣawmā's suggestion (p. 250), 'If you consecrated the Eucharist in Constantinople on an altar that you had consecrated or which your bishops had consecrated then, by my life, your Eucharist would be holy and your sacrifice accepted and the sins on behalf of which you offered up the Eucharist would have been forgiven.' In the Miaphysite *History of Dioscorus*, a brilliant light dramatically descends upon the altar when Dioscorus utters the *epiclesis*, and those present at the Eucharist fall on the ground like dead men. 'Do you think that these things have only taken place or will only take place today?' Dioscorus asks Paphnutius afterwards. 'I speak the truth to you, that whenever I offer up the Eucharist of the Orthodox, in whatever place, all these things which you have seen attend and are gathered there [the voices of angels had also been audible earlier in the service]. And these are what God reveals to you today because you believe that the faith which I fight for is true and orthodox. . . .' Ps.-Theopistus, *History of Dioscorus* 19 (ed. Nau, 'Histoire de Dioscore,' pp. 98–99 [Syriac] = 302–303 [French]).

[71] Edited in C. Kayser, *Die Canones Jakob's von Edessa* (Leipzig, 1886), p. 3 (GT at 34). On this manuscript, see Zotenberg, *Manuscrits orientaux*, p. 72, no. 19.

ministration of the most important ritual and sacramental acts in the Christian faith. Life trumped ideology.

This, then, is the confessional landscape we see through the lens of Syriac sources of the sixth, seventh, and eighth centuries. The lives of members of rival Christian communities were closely intertwined, as were the lives of their clergy. Miaphysite priests were giving the Eucharist to Nestorians and Julianists and also to other heretics, presumably Chalcedonians. Miaphysite priests were filling in and administering the Eucharist of the Chalcedonians to Chalcedonians when there were no Chalcedonian priests to be found. Miaphysite monasteries were knowingly hosting heretics and giving them communion. Even the Miaphysite patriarch and monks of the most important monastery in the Miaphysite church could admire a holy man who was (at least allegedly) a crypto-Nestorian-turned-Jew. Miaphysites were leading funeral processions for Chalcedonians and burying them. Chalcedonians were seizing Miaphysite church buildings and Miaphysites were seizing Chalcedonian church buildings. Structures might change hands more than once. Liturgical vessels were going back and forth between communities. Nestorians were helping build Miaphysite churches. Chalcedonian and Miaphysite ascetics were living together. Chalcedonians might have Miaphysite servants. Chalcedonian parents donated their children to Miaphysite monasteries, and their children would hold Miaphysite memorial services for them when they had passed away.

In such a world, it seems that just about anything was possible. Indeed, in a situation like this, what exactly is the use of labels like 'Orthodox' or 'heretic,' 'Chalcedonian' or 'Nestorian'? As a predictor of patterns of social behavior, interaction and association, they will not have been very reliable. When John of Litarb wrote Jacob a letter full of canonical questions, Jacob took his time in responding. One of his reasons was a sense of the futility of the endeavor: 'I say,' he wrote to John, 'that at this point there is no necessity at all, not even for one canon, since no one observes the canons.'[72] The first question in the *Questions and Answers* of Jacob's Chalcedonian contemporary, Anastasius of Sinai, perhaps reflects similar confusion among the laity when it came to sorting out where the truth stood among competing claims in such a milieu. 'What,' the anonymous questioner asked, 'is the sign of the true and perfect Christian?'[73] How was one to know?

As for Jacob, he seems to have been extremely unhappy with the people over whom he had authority. As we have seen, during his first stint as bishop

[72] Jacob of Edessa, *Letter to John, the Stylite of Litarb*, p. 46 (ed. K.-E. Rignell, *A Letter from Jacob of Edessa to John the Stylite of Litarab Concerning Ecclesiastical Canons* [Lund, 1979]; my translation, but see Rignell's ET at 47).

[73] Anastasius of Sinai, *Questions and Answers* 1 (ed. Richard and Munitiz, p. 5).

of Edessa, which lasted four years, he is reported to have forbidden a number of priests from performing the liturgy and to have expelled many other people from the church because of their lawlessness, before finally giving up in the face of widespread disregard for the canons.[74] Jacob had burned the book of canon law for a reason. He was exasperated.

SACRAMENTAL DISCIPLINE

Going over our sources, we can locate a number of factors that would have made the enforcement of sacramental discipline difficult in the seventh century and would have contributed to the situation we have just described. A person might not even know the confessional affiliation of the priest or church where he or she was taking communion; or actually might be unaware that taking communion across confessional boundaries was frowned upon by leaders,[75] a confusion no doubt compounded by the fact that churches, as we have seen, might change hands between confessions.[76] Another factor may have been the physical indistinguishability of clergy from different confessions.[77] A celebrant himself might not even be aware of confessional differences.[78] Moreover, before the Chalcedonian liturgy underwent Byzantinization—that is, before Chalcedonian communities throughout the Middle East shifted from their local

[74] Michael the Great, *Chronicle* 11.15 (ed. Chabot, 4.445 = 2.471–72).

[75] See the story of the Syrian from Constantinople who returns home to Syria and takes communion from local Severan monks, not realizing that this was something he should not be doing: John Moschus, *Spiritual Meadow* 188 (PG 87, cols. 3065, 3068; ET available in Wortley, *The Spiritual Meadow*, p. 161).

[76] For Chalcedonians seizing Miaphysite churches, see, e.g., Michael the Great, *Chronicle* 10.23, 11.3, 11.5 (ed. Chabot, 4.386, 4.410, 4.414 = 2.372, 2.412–13, 2.419); on the Eucharistic consequences of Domitian's seizures, see *Qenneshre Fragment*, p. 385 (ed. and trans. M. Penn, 'Demons Gone Wild: An Introduction, and Translation of the Syriac Qenneshre Fragment,' *OCP* 79 [2013], p. 396 [ET]). For Miaphysites taking Chalcedonian churches and monasteries in Egypt, see Michael the Great, *Chronicle* 11.8 (4.423 = 2.433). For Miaphysites seizing East Syrian monasteries, see *Khuzistan Chronicle*, p. 22 (ed. Guidi [CSCO Syr. III.4]). For evidence from Jacob of Edessa, see above, nn. 50–51, and cf. W. G. Young, *Patriarch, Shah and Caliph* (Rawalpindi, 1974), pp. 96–97.

[77] One of the changes introduced to East Syrian monasticism by Abraham of Kashkar (d. 588) and Abraham of Nathpar was that they 'differentiated between the garments of [Orthodox] monks and the garments of the heretics, for [since] the days of Mar Awgen and his followers, monks had dressed in the garb of the people of Egypt.' See *Chronicle of Seert* 2.31 (ed. Scher [PO 7.2] [Paris, 1911], p. 80; and compare this to *Chronicle of Seert* 2.18 [p. 43]).

[78] John Moschus recorded the story of an elder who 'had learned the eucharistic rite from heretics but, as he was unlearned in theological matters, when he offered (the eucharist) he spoke the prayer in all simplicity and innocence, unaware that he was at fault.' The elder changed his manner of celebration after the propriety of an intervention by a 'brother who was skilled in theology' was confirmed by angels who were present every time the elder celebrated (*The Spiritual Meadow*, 199 [PG 87, col. 3088; ET taken from Wortley, *The Spiritual Meadow*, p. 177]).

liturgies to that of Constantinople starting around the end of the first millennium AD, Chalcedonian and Miaphysite liturgies, both based on the liturgy of Antioch, would have been quite similar (especially among Monotheletes, who kept the longer version of the Trisagion into the Middle Ages and afterward[79]), and the differences between the liturgical experience in the two communions would not have been great.[80] Reports of religious leaders having statements of faith put up outside of churches or monasteries suggest that the ambiguity that must have existed was recognized as a problem by some.[81] Even in instances where people knew that priests held different Christological positions and stopped taking communion from certain clergymen on this basis, other kinds of fellowship might be continued.[82]

[79] See the eleventh-century defense of the longer version of the *Trisagion* by the Monothelete Thomas of Kafarṭāb in his *Ten Chapters*, pp. 157–163 (ed. and trans. C. Chartouni, *Le traité des dix chapitres de Thomas de Kfarṭāb: un document sur les origines de l'Église maronite* [Beirut, 1986], pp. 105–12 [FT]). For the Maronites using the longer version into the late sixteenth century, see Janeras, 'Le Trisagion, une forumle brève en liturgie comparée,' p. 550.

[80] On liturgical Byzantinization, see J. Nasrallah, 'The Liturgy of the Melkite Patriarchs from 969 to 1300,' in S. F. Johnson, ed., *Languages and Cultures of Eastern Christianity: Greek* (Surrey, England, 2015), pp. 507–32 (an ET of Nasrallah, 'La liturgie des Patriarcats melchites de 969 à 1300,' *OC* 71 [1987], pp. 156–81). On liturgical Byzantinization with special reference to Jerusalem, see D. Galadza, *Worship of the Holy City in Captivity: The Liturgical Byzantinization of the Orthodox Patriarchate of Jerusalem After the Arab Conquests (8th–13th c.)* (Excerpta ex dissertation ad doctoratum; Rome, 2013) and Galadza, 'Liturgical Byzantinization in Jerusalem: Al-Biruni's Melkite Calendar in Context,' *Bollettino della Badia Greca di Grottaferrata* 7 (2010), pp. 69–85. For the Byzantinization of the Chalcedonian liturgy of Antioch, the studies of H. Husmann are foundational. See especially his, 'Eine alte orientalische christliche Liturgie: Altsyrisch-Melkitisch,' *OCP* 42 (1976), pp. 156–96. On the importance of taking liturgical separation into account when discussing the separation of the various Middle Eastern churches, see my 'Greek Kanons and the Syrian Orthodox Liturgy.'

[81] After the death of Henana of Adiabene (ca. 610), George the Priest, one of his leading opponents, posted a statement on the door of his church forbidding anyone who agreed with the 'error of Henana' and who did not accept the tradition of the church in the territory of the Persians and agree with the teaching of Diodore, Theodore, and Nestorius, from taking communion within. See Babai the Great, *History of George the Priest*, pp. 503–504 (ed. Bedjan, *Histoire de Mar-Jabalaha*). See, too, Severus of Antioch's letter to Naunus, the Bishop of Seleucia, in which he ordered that a 'superscription of the faith should be put up before the gate' of a monastery—that of St. Thomas at Seleucia Pieria—where Nestorians had been receiving communion. The superscription, Severus noted, was 'after the model of the other monasteries of the orthodox.' (ET from Brooks, *The Sixth Book of the Select Letters of Severus* 7.4 [1.2:423–24 (Syriac text) = 2.2:376 (Brooks's translation)]).

[82] I. E. Rahmani, ed., *Studia Syriaca*, vol. 3: *Vetusta Documenta Liturgica* (Charfeh, 1908), contains an anonymous work, *Chapters written by the Easterners [who] Presented Their Questions to the Holy Fathers*. One of these (§43, p. 22) was 'concerning brothers [i.e., monks] whose priests are heretics from the followers of Julian [of Halicarnassus], and who have separated themselves from them and do not communicate with them in the mysteries because they have come to the true faith, and who have requested to be allowed to serve with them the service of the Psalms and to eat with them the common meal. [Answer:] They should have kindness for them and compassion with them that perhaps with God's help, their priests will feel shame and be returned to the truth, [rather] than the brothers themselves, not enduring in perfection, return to the depths of heresy. There should be a witness to this concerning

What happened when Christian communities were formed on the basis of disagreements about theological speculation that most Christians simply could not understand fully or properly? We have now found part of an answer: many people paid little or only selective heed to the communal borders being set up on the basis of these disagreements. Indeed, we might suggest that a good number of these people may not have even known that such boundaries existed.

Historians are very fond of speaking of instances of 'boundary crossing' and 'fluid' religious situations: but should it be considered an act of 'boundary crossing' if one, like the putatively Chalcedonian actor we met in Leontius's story in Chapter 2, is not aware that a boundary has been erected? Communal boundaries are not natural features of a landscape, like rocks or rivers or mountains; they are socially established conventions that are only as good as the religious and catechetical institutions that exist to tell people they are there. Rather than speaking of distinct churches, we might suggest that into the seventh and even eighth centuries, the various confessional movements which resulted from Chalcedon, strongest in certain urban and monastic centers, were still sorting themselves out on the ground, even if they had undergone a definite separation at the level of doctrine and ideology. Rather than acts of boundary maintenance, we can then see Jacob's responses to Addai as examples of boundary drawing.

BOUNDARIES, INFERENCES, AND IGNORANCE

The evidence above, however, should not be understood to be an argument that nobody in the sixth, seventh, or eighth centuries cared about ecclesiastical difference. Some—most notably, many of the ecclesiastical writers we have from this period—obviously did. And in a world where there was a spectrum of engagement with Christological doctrines, there certainly were people who viewed the confessional stance of the priest who administered the Eucharist and performed baptisms as very important.[83] When we meet examples of

them from a trustworthy person from their village that they are not taking communion with them [the Julianist priests].'

[83] See, e.g., the story of people from Antioch, of all social standing, coming out to meet Severus in 512 and chanting that they have long wanted to take the Eucharist and have their children baptized in Ps.-John bar Aphtonia, *Life of Severus*, p. 157 (ed. Kugener [PO 2.3]; available in Brock, *Two Early Lives*, p. 125). For Miaphysite *scholastici* studying in Beirut refraining from taking the Eucharist from local bishops and in the local Chalcedonian church, see John Rufus, *Plerophories* 78 (ed. Nau [PO 8.1], pp. 134–35). For this, also see Frend, *The Rise of the Monophysite Movement*, p. 62, n. 5. See also reports of people beginning to take communion separately on account of the Chalcedonian Paul of Antioch ('the Jew'; sed. 519–521) in

people either observing or ignoring ecclesiastical boundaries, however, we need to be careful about inferring from this behavior that the person in question actually understood the theological issues at stake.[84]

What is more, it needs to be acknowledged that any given instance of reported boundary crossing should not be taken as direct evidence of ignorance of those boundaries. Some people may have been unaware of these communal boundaries. And some may not have fully understood them or may not properly have apprehended the reasons why church leaders sought to erect them. But some may have known confessional borders existed, with varying levels of understanding of the boundaries' justifications, and simply have chosen to ignore them.

This latter suggestion points us to an important consideration: another factor at play in the various anecdotes met in this chapter is the reality that a person's identity might have included being a (Miaphysite) Christian, or (East Syrian) Christian, or (Chalcedonian) Christian (though he or she will have, probably simply regarded himself or herself as an Orthodox Christian). But the inhabitants of the late Roman Middle East were other things as well—they were soldiers, farmers, merchants, carpenters, blacksmiths, tailors, shepherds, herdsmen, weavers, craftsmen, laborers, and so on. They were parents, husbands, wives, sisters, brothers, sons, daughters. They belonged to clans. They were from specific towns, cities, and regions. They spoke Greek, or one of a variety of dialects of Aramaic, or Arabic, or Persian, or two or more of these. They might be sedentary, semi-nomadic, or nomadic.

In other words, each individual's identity was comprised of more than the one axis of their religious and confessional identification. And the religious component of a person's identity was not necessarily the most important in any given situation, nor should we assume it was always the most predictive

Michael the Great, *Chronicle* 9.15 (ed. Chabot, 4.269 = 2.176). For a question to the Chalcedonian Anastasius of Sinai about carrying the Eucharist in a *skevophorion* while travelling, so as not to take communion from a heretic, see his *Questions and Answers* 64 (ed. Richard and Munitiz, pp. 114–15; ET and commentary in Munitiz, *Questions and Answers*, p. 176). For further examples of conscientiousness about taking communion across confessional lines, see R. F. Taft, 'Home-Communion in the Late Antique East,' in C. V. Johnson, ed., *Ars Liturgiae: Worship, Aesthetics and Praxis: Essays in Honor of Nathan D. Mitchell* (Chicago, 2003), pp. 3–4, and E. Wipszycka, 'How Insurmountable Was the Chasm between Monophysites and Chalcedonians?' in L. Arcari, ed., *Beyond Conflicts: Cultural and Religious Cohabitations in Alexandria and Egypt between the 1st and the 6th Century CE* (Tübingen, 2017), pp. 214–15.

[84] One thinks of Daniel Defoe's statement about attitudes among some Protestants toward the Roman Catholic Church: 'There be many who cry out against popery who know not whether it be a man or a horse.' I cannot find the source of this quote, but for its attribution to Defoe, see J. Dunn, 'The Politics of Locke in England and America in the Eighteenth Century,' in J. W. Yolton, ed., *John Locke: Problems and Perspectives: A Collection of New Essays* (London, 1969), p. 48. I am grateful to Michael Cook for bringing this quote to my attention.

of patterns of behavior. What this means is that in any instance of putative confessional boundary crossing, we have to entertain the possibility that a part of what we are seeing is the privileging of one aspect of a person's identity over his or her confessional identification—a parent's worry for his or her sick child, for instance, might be more important than the confessional concerns that would dictate he or she not take that child to a holy man belonging to a different church. In some instances, what we are witnessing may be not the result of ignorance of or indifference to the existence of boundaries, or of poorly understood boundaries or an incomplete understanding the importance of boundaries, but the result instead of an individual favoring particular personal concerns and desires over larger confessional agendas, agendas that were rooted in either theological commitments or in the brute sociological necessities that dictated the need for some sort of communal separation in order to maintain the identity, integrity, and continuity of a particular religious group. Such a point, however, raises a further question, unanswerable given our sources, of whether the triumph of personal agendas over doctrinally rooted communal ones was itself ultimately the result of an individual not really understanding the theological issues at stake and their import.[85]

Granting such additional nuances, however, it remains clear that serious problems resulted when church boundaries based on sophisticated theological speculation were imposed on a world that was unable to properly understand that speculation. In this chapter we have met one of the most pressing issues confronting church leaders in the Middle East in the wake of Cyril's fateful dispute with Nestorius: confessional chaos and disorder among the simple. What was the solution?

[85] For a sophisticated discussion of the interplay of Christian and other identities in a late antique context, see É. Rebillard, *Christians and Their Many Identities in Late Antiquity, North Africa, 200–450 CE* (Ithaca/London, 2012).

CHAPTER 4

Contested Truths

We have just seen one of the most common ways in which people dealt with doctrinal difference in the post-Chalcedonian world: they didn't. For many, the distinctions that church leaders like Jacob wanted to enforce were either simply unknown, of selective concern, of secondary or tertiary concern, or of no apparent importance at all.

But there were other ways in which disagreement was handled: violence, for example, was one. We have seen instances where brutal displays of force were employed to attempt to compel rejectionists to accept the Council of Chalcedon.[1] Such violence was not always state-sponsored, either, and it could occur at a local level.[2] Though we do have examples of Muslim authorities attempting to put their thumbs on the scale in favor of one Christian group or another,[3] in the Muslim-ruled Middle East of Jacob's day sustained imperial violence aimed at giving one Christian group the advantage over another was not an option in the same way it had been under Christian figures like Justinian or Heraclius. In the end, Muslim rulers were Muslims, not Christians, and the rifts stemming from Chalcedon were Christian problems.

Another route a Christian leader might take was persuasion and argument. This option took its most notable form in disputes and in the abundant polemical literature that emerged in the post-Chalcedonian Middle East.[4] Indeed, a

[1] See, e.g., Chapter 2, nn. 54–59. Michael the Great also credited the spread of Dyotheletism, like the spread of Chalcedonianism more generally, to 'the sword' (*Chronicle* 11.13 [ed. Chabot, 4.437 = 2.457]).

[2] Note the Chalcedonian priest who threated Epiphanius, a Miaphysite monk, with beatings, persecution, and exile if he did not communicate at his church: John Rufus, *Plerophories* 48 (ed. Nau [PO 8.1], pp. 100–102).

[3] See Chapter 6, n. 9. After their alleged defeat by Maronites in a dispute before Muʿāwiya in 659, Muʿāwiya had the Miaphysites pay him a large sum of gold each year as protection from Maronite persecution. See *Maronite Chronicle*, p. 70 (ed. Brooks [CSCO III.4]); ET in Palmer, *The Seventh Century in the West-Syrian Chronicles*, p. 30 and cf. n. 32 in this chapter.

[4] I use 'polemical literature' here to mean any sort of writing that was controversial in nature and aimed at refuting or criticizing the views of rival Christian groups or, alternately, any sort of literature that sought to define and vindicate the views of one's own group in opposition to the views of rivals. For the argument that 'the genre of "polemics" itself did not exist as such in the Middle Ages, and one might well affirm that "medieval polemic" is a largely artificial category based on postmedieval divisions,' see R. Szpiech, 'Introduction' in Szpiech, ed., *Medieval Exegesis and Religious Difference:*

culture of debate was part of the landscape of this period before the sixth century and well after it; debates might be between Christians and non-Christians, as well as both formal and informal;[5] and it is a traditional scholarly focus on this form of dealing with post-Chalcedonian religious difference that can be credited for giving the impression that the late Roman Middle East was an enormous patristic seminar run amok.

The tendency toward dispute was a result of several factors: the religious diversity of the Middle East, coupled with the Christian impulse to mission and conversion, and a belief in the exclusive truth of its religious claims. In the post-Chalcedonian world which concerns us here, the confessional confusion that existed among simple believers in the Middle East meant that there was a fierce battle on the ground between theological elites for the loyalty and adherence of ordinary Christians who were not firmly attached to any one church, and whose confessional identity was activated only selectively, if at all.[6] In a Sasanian context there was an additional impetus for dispute: Zoroastrian apostates were supposed to be imprisoned for a year, during which Zoroastrian religious scholars were to give them arguments to counter their reasons for turning to a new confession and attempt to remove any doubts they had. The renegade was only to be killed if these attempts at reconversion failed.[7] It is not surprising, therefore, to find debates between Christian converts and Zoroastrians featuring prominently in hagiographic literature from areas under Persian rule.[8]

Commentary, Conflict, and Community in the Premodern Mediterranean (New York, 2015), pp. 8–9 (quote at p. 9).

[5] See H. Cancik, 'Antike Religionsgespräch,' in G. Schörner, D. S. Erker, eds., *Medien religiöser Kommunikation im Imperium Romanum* (Stuttgart, 2008), pp. 15–25. Lim, *Public Disputation, Power, and Social Order in Late Antiquity*, sets Christian disputation, especially in the fourth century, in a broader late antique and Greco-Roman context. For a rich collection of studies on religious controversy in Syriac specifically, see F. Ruani, ed., *Les controverses religieuses en syriaque* (Paris, 2016).

[6] On the selective or intermittent activation of Christian identity, see Rebillard, *Christians and Their Many Identities, passim.*

[7] See *Letter of Tansar*, p. 42 (trans. M. Boyce, *The Letter of Tansar* [Rome, 1968]). Also, cf. *Mainyo-i-khard* 15.16-26, where one of the markers of 'Good government' is that 'if *there* be any one who shall stay *away* from the way of God, then it orders him to make a return thereto, and make him a prisoner, and brings *him* back to the way of God. . . .' (ed. and trans. E. W. West, *The Book of the Mainyo-i-khard* [Stuttgart/London, 1871], p. 148; the translation is that of West). On this passage in the *Mainyo-i-Khard*, see P. Bruns, 'Beobachtungen zu den Rechtsgrundlagen der Christenverfolgungen im Sasanidenreich,' *Römische Quartalschrift für christliche Altertumskunde und für Kirchengeschichte* 103 (2008), pp. 89–92 and pp. 107–108 for the passage in the *Letter of Tansar.*

[8] See, e.g., the debates that feature in the *vita* of Yazdpaneh, a Zoroastrian from Karka d-Ledan who converted to Christianity and eventually was martyred in the reign of Khusro I: *History of Mar Yazdpaneh*, pp. 396–97, 402–403 (ed. Bedjan, *Histoire de Mar-Jabalaha*).

WRITTEN DISAGREEMENT

There is evidence for controversial literature being written in Syriac not long after Chalcedon by members of all the major confessional movements. The Chalcedonian Samuel of Edessa was writing in Syriac against Nestorians, Eutychians, and followers of Timothy II of Alexandria within decades of the council;[9] the important Miaphysite Philoxenus of Mabbug wrote a lengthy set of discourses against a learned Dyophysite monk named Ḥabīb in the late fifth century;[10] and the East Syrian catholicos Aqaq (sed. 484–485/6) wrote a treatise on faith 'in which he exposed the faults of those who believe in one nature in Christ.'[11] Controversial works could take the shape of *florilegia*,[12] and polemic might also be found in other genres, such as exegesis.[13] Translation can also be viewed as an example of polemical creation: Paul of Callinicum's translation of controversial works by Severus of Antioch from Greek into Syriac in 528 (and perhaps later), for example, was itself an act that made available in the Syriac language more material that could be used in interconfessional disputes.[14]

[9] Gennadius, *Lives of Illustrious Men* 83 (ed. Richardson, pp. 89–90)

[10] The entirety of Philoxenus's work against Ḥabīb was published over the course of decades. See M. Brière, *Philoxène de Mabboug. De uno e sancta Trinitate incorporato et passo (*Dissertationes I et II*)* (PO 15.4) (Paris, 1927); M. Brière and F. Graffin, eds., *Sancti Philoxeni episcopi Mabbugensis dissertationes decem de uno e sancta Trinitate incorporato et passo. Dissertationes* 3a, 4a, 5a (PO 38.3) (Turnhout, 1977); Brière and Graffin, eds., *Sancti Philoxeni episcopi Mabbugensis dissertationes decem de Uno e sancta Trinitate incorporato et passo (Mêmrê contre Habib).* III. *Dissertationes 6a, 7a, 8a* (PO 39.4) (Turnhout, 1979); Brière and Graffin, eds., *Sancti Philoxeni episcopi Mabbugensis dissertationes decem de Uno e sancta Trinitate incorporato et passo (Mêmrê contre Habib).* IV. *Dissertationes 9a, 10a* (PO 40.2) (Turnhout, 1980) (cf. D. A. Michelson, 'A Bibliographic Clavis to the Works of Philoxenos of Mabbug,' *Hugoye* 13 [2010], p. 302). For other controversial writings by Philoxenus, see the various works of 'chapters' against different positions or persons enumerated in de Halleux, *Philoxène de Mabbog. Sa vie, ses écrits, sa théologie*, pp. 178–87.

[11] *Chronicle of Seert* 2.8 (ed. Scher [PO 7.2], p. 21).

[12] See, e.g., I. Rucker, *Florilegium Edessenum anonymum (syriace ante 562)* (Munich, 1933) and also the description of BL Add. 12,155 in *CBM*, 2.921–55, an eighth-century (Severan) Miaphysite manuscript that contains extensive catenae against a variety of different 'heresies,' including Julianists. More generally, see Baumstark, *Geschichte*, pp. 176–77. A. Grillmeier, *Christ in Christian Tradition.* vol. 2: *From the Council of Chalcedon (451) to Gregory the Great (590–604)*, trans. P. Allen, and J. Cawte (London/Oxford, 1987), pp. 63–70, surveys Miaphysite florilegia in Greek, Syriac, Armenian, Coptic, and Arabic; 71–73 details collections of Nestorian florilegia.

[13] See, e.g., D.G.K. Taylor, 'The Great Psalm Commentary of Daniel of Salah,' *The Harp* 11–12 (1998–1999), p. 38 and Taylor, 'The Christology of the Syriac Psalm Commentary (AD 541/2) of Daniel of Salah and the "Phantasiast" Controversy,' *Studia Patristica* 35 (2001), pp. 508–15.

[14] For Paul's translations, see most conveniently, Baumstark, *Geschichte*, p. 160. It has been commonly assumed that Paul also translated Severus's works against Sergius the Grammarian into Syriac

The transmission of the Greek writings of figures like Severus, Timothy II of Alexandria, and others into Syriac serves as a reminder that into at least the eighth century, many of the leaders of the Miaphysite church in Syria were actually bilingual and carried out controversial and theological activities in Greek, even if the vicissitudes of transmission mean that they now appear to us as Syriac figures.[15] In other words, focusing only on Syriac-language texts misses part of the picture when it comes to interconfessional polemics. The same culture of dispute existed contemporaneously in different languages—late antiquity was, as Averil Cameron has put it, 'a world full of talk.'[16] We should therefore remember that debates were going on among Greek-speakers in the Middle East, as well, and that polemical texts could easily move back and forth between Greek and Syriac.[17] For this reason, controversial works written in Greek by Middle Eastern Chalcedonian figures like Anastasius of Sinai[18] and John Damascene[19] (both of whom were known in Syriac translation),[20] and many others, should be kept in mind when we are thinking of interconfessional disputes in a Syriac milieu.

---

and, more recently, Daniel King has argued that the *Philalethes* was translated by Paul as well; for this see D. King, 'Paul of Callinicum and his Place in Syriac Literature,' *LM* 120 (2007), pp. 330–31.

[15] The Miaphysite patriarch Athanasius Gamolo (d. 631) is one such figure. Athanasius engaged in theological negotiations with the Emperor Heraclius (see Michael the Great, *Chronicle* 11.2–3 [ed. Chabot, 4.403–404, 404–408, 409–410 = 2.401–403, 405–408, 412]) and also was involved in the negotiations with Anastasius of Alexandria that ended the Tritheist schism between the Miaphysite churches of Egypt and Syria (see Michael the Great, *Chronicle* 10.26, 11.2 [ed. Chabot, 4.391–92, 401 = vol. 2.381, 403]). The *Doctrina Patrum* 22.13, 22.14 (ed. F. Diekamp, *Doctrina patrum de incarnatione verbi* [Münster in Westf., 1907], pp. 141–48) preserves excerpts of a Greek work, *Against Athanasius, the Pseudo-Bishop of the Severans*, written by Eubulus of Lystra against a statement of faith given by Athanasius to Heraclius, and Sophronius of Jerusalem attacked Athanasius as well (*Synodical Letter* 2.6.1 [ed. R. Riedinger and trans. P. Allen, *Sophronius of Jerusalem and Seventh-Century Heresy: The Synodical Letter and Other Documents* (Oxford/New York, 2009), pp. 144–45]).

[16] See Av. Cameron, *Dialoguing in Late Antiquity* (Washington, D.C., 2014), p. 23.

[17] See the examples of polemical questions moving between Greek and Syriac in my 'Between Christology and Kalām? The Life and Letters of George, Bishop of the Arab Tribes' in G. A. Kiraz, ed., *Malphono w-Rabo d-Malphone: Studies in Honor of Sebastian P. Brock* (Piscataway, N.J., 2008) pp. 671–716.

[18] E.g., his *Capita vi contra Monotheletas* (CPG 7756) and his *Captia xvi contra Monophysitas* (CPG 7757). Beck called Anastasius's Ὁδηγός 'ein Handbuch zur Bekämpfung der Häresien' and judged it one of the most important examples of later Chalcedonian polemics against Miaphysites. Anastasius also apparently wrote a now-lost work against Nestorians and two works against Jews. For this information and the quote, see H.-G. Beck, *Kirche und Theologische Literatur* (Munich, 1959), pp. 442–43.

[19] See Beck, *Kirche und Theologische Literatur*, pp. 477–78. John's polemical works include, *De haeresibus* (CPG 8044), *Contra Iaocbitas* (CPG 8047), *Dialogus contra Manichaeos* (CPG 8048), *De duabus in Christo voluntatibus* (CPG 8052), *Adversus Nestorianos* (CPG 8053), and *De fide contra Nestorianos* (CPG 8054).

[20] For Maximus's *Eulogii Alexandrini capita vii* (CPG 7697, no. 23b), see P. Bettiolo, *Una raccolta di opuscoli Calcedonensi: Ms. Sinaï Syr. 10* (CSCO 403: SS 177) (Louvain, 1979), pp. 6–7. For a description of the unpublished text of Anastasius's *Homily on Psalm 6* in Vatican Syriac 369, see J.-M. Sauget, 'Deux

The controversial literature generated by the conflict over Chalcedon, in both Greek and Syriac, was enormous; and it continued to be written for centuries; the list examples of intra-Christian and intrareligious polemics could very easily be expanded.[21] But focusing on such texts alone—or even bringing into the picture the great number of texts we know were written but which have not been survived[22] and pointing out that groups such as the Julianists must have had their own extensive controversial literature which has also perished[23]—would nevertheless give us an incomplete view of the nature and scope of religious disagreement in the post-Chalcedonian world. At best, it would furnish only a more finely detailed view of a picture of which a significant portion has been lost. What is more, such texts would give us insight into only one end of the spectrum of religious dispute in general, and issues related to Chalcedon more specifically—the most elite and sophisticated one.

ORAL DISAGREEMENT

Focusing only on written polemics also misses the fact that more important than textual controversy will have been oral discussion and disagreement. There were of course high-profile debates held before rulers. In 527, Justinian and Justin reportedly had held a dispute between the East Syrian Paul the Persian and a Manichee named Photinus,[24] and in 532, Justinian held conversa-

homéliaires syriaques de la Bibliothèque Vaticane,' *OCP* 27 (1961), p. 423 (no. 54). Vatican Syriac 369 only contains part of the homily, but Hiersemann 500/2 (= Louvain G-197), fols. 81v–94r, which was destroyed during the Second World War, contained the entire work; see *Katalog 500: Orientalische Manuskripte (Karl Hiersemann)*, p. 5. Elia, an eighth-century Chalcedonian convert to Miaphysitism, cited John Damascene's *Dialectica* (CPG 8041), *Expositio Fidei* (CPG 8043), and *Contra Jacobitas* (CPG 8047) in his *Apologetic Letter* to Leo of Harran, a Chalcedonian. For citations of John Damascene, see the Index Patristicus to van Roey's Latin translation (CSCO 470: SS 202), p. 79, s.n. Iohannes Damascenus; Van Roey, p. 30, n. 103, suggested that Elia was using a Syriac translation and was not simply translating directly into Syriac while reading the Greek, though the latter may of course be a possibility.

21 See further the numerous debates discussed in Cameron, *Dialoguing in Late Antiquity*, pp. 23–38. J. T. Walker, *The Legend of Mar Qardagh: Narrative and Christian Heroism in Late Antique Iraq* (Berkeley, 2006), pp. 164–80, expertly traces the development of a culture of debate in the late antique Middle East. Grillmeier, *Christ in Christian Tradition*, vol. 2.1, pp. 20–89, provides an exhaustive overview of the rich amount of polemical material that exists, from all parts of the theological spectrum, relating to the question of Chalcedon.

22 'Abdisho' bar Brikha's *Mēmrā on Ecclesiastical Books* (ed. Assemani, *BO*, 3.1, pp. 3–362), for example, contains references to a large number of polemical works written by members of the Church of the East in the post-Chalcedonian period, most of which no longer survive.

23 See the comments in R. Draguet, *Julien d'Halicarnasse et sa controverse avec Sévère d'Antioche sur l'incorruptibilité du corps du Christ* (Louvain, 1924), pp. 257–58, and dogmatic fragments of Julian's work edited at *5–*43.

24 Paul the Persian, *Dispute with Photinus the Manichaean*, PG 88, cols. 529–52. There are a number

tions between Chalcedonians and Miaphysites.[25] The emperor also once invited leaders from the Church of the East to debate Chalcedonians at his court, an event that took place over the course of three days in perhaps 562 or 563.[26] And it was not only before Roman rulers that disputes took place: at one point in the middle part of the sixth century, for instance, the Tritheists Conon of Tarsus and Eugene of Seleucia held a four-day-long disputation with the Miaphysites John of Ephesus and Paul of Beth Ukkamē before the Chalcedonian patriarch of Constantinople.[27] The East Syrian patriarch Shila (sed. 503–523) publicly confounded Miaphysites in the presence of the Arab ruler, al-Mundhir b. Nuʿmān in Hira.[28] Later in the same century, Hira witnessed another religious dispute when the Lakhmid ruler Nuʿmān III (reg. 580-602) ordered a disputation between East Syrians and Miaphysites be held in his presence.[29] Farther east, Khusro I held a debate between Miaphysites and East Syrians,[30] and in 612, Khusro II held yet another disputation at his court between Miaphysite and East Syrian leaders.[31] In the earliest period of Muslim rule in Syria, two Miaphysite bishops came to Damascus in June of 659, and held a dispute on faith with representatives of the Maronites in the presence of Muʿāwiya,[32] and a Syriac text preserves what purports to be a religious discussion held between

---

of different figures referred to as 'Paul the Persian,' who may or may not be identical. See P. Bruns, 'Wer war Paul der Perser?' *Studia Patristica* 45 (2010), pp. 263–68. On the debate and the question of Paul, see also S.N.C. Lieu, *Manichaeism in the Later Roman Empire and Medieval China: A Historical Survey* (Manchester and Dover, NH, 1985), pp. 171–73

[25] On the Miaphysite-Chalcedonian conversations of 532, see S. P. Brock, 'The Orthodox-Oriental Orthodox Conversations of 532,' *Apostolos Varnavas* 41 (1980), pp. 219–28 and Brock, 'The Conversations with the Syrian Orthodox under Justinian (532),' *OCP* 47 (1981), pp. 87–121.

[26] *Chronicle of Seert* 2.32 (ed. Scher [PO 7.2], pp. 187–88). For this date and the view that this debate between Chalcedonians and East Syrians is the same as that reported in Barhadbshabba, *Cause of the Foundation of the Schools*, 32 (ed. Nau [PO 9.5], p. 142]; ET available in A. Becker, *Sources for the Study of the School of Nisibis* [Liverpool, 2008], p. 83), see Guillaumont, 'Un colloque entre orthodoxes et théologiens nestoriens de Perse sous Justinien,' pp. 201–203 and Guillaumont, 'Justinien et l'Église de Perse,' pp. 50–51, and cf. Walker, *The Legend of Mar Qardagh*, p. 174, n. 35.

[27] Bar Hebraeus, *Ecclesiastical History* 1.45 (ed. Abbeloos and Lamy, vol. 1, col. 227).

[28] *Chronicle of Seert* 2.22 (ed. Scher [PO 7.2], pp. 51–52). For Shila's dates, see *GEDSH*, p. 482.

[29] Peter the Solitary, *Life of Sabrishoʿ*, pp. 323, 325–27 (ed. Bedjan, *Histoire de Mar-Jabalaha*).

[30] John of Ephesus, *Ecclesiastical History* 6.20 (ed. Brooks [CSCO III.3], pp. 316–18; ET in Payne Smith, *The Third Part*, pp. 418–20).

[31] See *Khuzistan Chronicle*, p. 23 (ed. Guidi [CSCO Syr. III.4]; ET available in Greatrex and Lieu, *The Roman Eastern Frontier and the Persian Wars*, p. 233). For the East Syrian statement of faith, polemics against Theopaschites, and answers to two questions posed to them by Miaphysites from this debate, see Chabot, ed., *Synodicon Orientale*, 562–80 (= 580–98 [French]). On the importance of the disputation of 612 in the formation of a 'Nestorian' identity in the Church of the East, see Reinink, 'Tradition and the Formation of the 'Nestorian' Identity in Sixth- to Seventh-Century Iraq.'

[32] *Maronite Chronicle*, p. 70 (ed. Brooks [CSCO III.4], ET in A. Palmer, *The Seventh Century in the West-Syrian Chronicles*, p. 30).

a Muslim emir and the Miaphysite patriarch John, which may or may not have occurred in 639 or 644.[33]

The line between debating orally and writing polemics was a thin one and easily crossed: 'Not only by word,' Babai the Great wrote of George the Priest, 'but also in writings did he take apart and bring to nothing the wicked teaching of the Theopaschites and the Chaldeanism of Henana.'[34] The dispute with Miaphysites before Khusro II in 612, in which George had played a leading role, was actually carried out both in writing and orally.[35] Gabriel 'the Cow,' a member of the Church of the East in the middle and later part of the seventh century, disputed with the monks of the Miaphysite monastery of Qartmin and responded to their polemics in writing. Gabriel was also supposed to have held a dispute with the Nestorian renegade Sahdona in Edessa.[36]

DOCTRINAL PRIZE FIGHTERS

Celebrated and enormously learned representatives of various rival groups typically played starring roles in such debates. And here we meet another important feature of the post-Chalcedonian landscape: the confessional champion who battled heretics and non-Christians alike, defending the truth of his

[33] *Disputation between John and the Emir* (ed. F. Nau, 'Un colloque du patriarche Jean avec l'émir des Agaréens,' *JA* 11 (1915), pp. 248–56). For a date of AD 639, see Nau, 'Un Colloque,' p. 227; for 644, see H. Lammens, 'A propos d'un colloque entre le patriarche Jacobite Jean 1er et 'Amr ibn al-'Āṣi,' *JA* 11 (1919), p. 98. For this text as being a fictional construct from the early eighth century, see G. J. Reinink, 'The Beginnings of Syriac Apologetic Literature in Response to Islam,' *OC* 77 (1993), pp. 171–87. Against Reinink, see H. Suermann, 'The Old Testament and the Jews in the Dialogue between the Jacobite patriarch John I and 'Umayr ibn Sa'd al-Anṣārī,' J. P. Monferrer-Sala, ed., *Eastern Crossroads: Essays on Medieval Christian Legacy* (Piscataway, N.J., 2007), pp. 131–41. This text has most recently been reedited and published with an ET in M. P. Penn, 'John and the Emir: A New Introduction, Edition and Translation,' *LM* 121 (2008), pp. 65–91. Penn, pp. 68–69, argued strongly for a late seventh or early eighth century date (pp. 69-77), but B. Roggema, 'Pour une lecture des dialogues islamo-chrétiens en syriaque à la lumière des controverses internes à l'islam,' in Ruani, ed., *Les controverses religieuses en syriaque*, pp. 263–69, has more recently (and quite persuasively) sought to place the text in the seventh century. More generally, Roggema, 'The Disputation of John and the Emir,' in *CMR*, vol. 1, pp. 782–85, summarizes the text and the differing theories that have been put forth about its dating.

[34] Babai the Great, *History of George the Priest*, p. 496 (ed. Bedjan, *Histoire de Mar-Jabalaha*). On this *vita* and the importance of correct doctrine in it, see Reinink, 'Babai the Great's Life of George.'

[35] Babai the Great, *History of George the Priest*, pp. 515–17 (ed. Bedjan, *Histoire de Mar-Jabalaha*). For a discussion of the relationship between Khusro's questions as found in the *History of George the Priest*, the *Synodicon Orientale*, and Cambridge Ms. Oriental 1319, see Abramowski and Goodman, *A Nestorian Collection of Christological Texts*, vol. 2, xliii–xliv. On the oral and literary in this dispute, see the comments of Walker, *The Legend of Mar Qardagh*, p. 178.

[36] See Thomas of Marga, *Monastic History* 2.18 (ed. Budge, 1.90–92 [Syriac] = 2.211–212 [ET]). On Gabriel, see also Baumstark, *Geschichte*, p. 222.

church's doctrinal stance. In this world, part of the job of a church leader was defending one's community against competitors and rivals.[37] Babai the Great (d. 628), Thomas of Marga observed, was that rare figure in whom are found all the qualities needed in a bishop: he interpreted the Scripture and commented on and researched the writings of the Fathers. The first ability, however, that Thomas listed Babai as having was *drāshā d-luqbal hērēsis* ('disputing against heresies').[38] Similarly, among the virtues of the mid-sixth-century East Syrian catholicos Narsai was that he had 'a fine understanding of disputation.'[39] Around the year 700, when Elia bar Gufna, the Miaphysite bishop of Harran, passed away, Simeon of the Olives was elected to succeed him because, Simeon's *vita* reported,

> there was no one in the church who was greater than Mar Simeon, for he was able to respond to all debates and questions, seeing as there survived in Ḥarran the old leaven of the worship of idols and of the Roman teachings of the Manichaeans who were living in the city of Ḥarran and in the regions which were around it. They appeared like tares among the wheat in the land of Syria.[40]

Simeon was, in fact, 'extremely frightening and terrifying' to the *barrāyē*—that is, 'outsiders,' i.e., 'pagans'—of Edessa and Harran, and he was credited with converting a number of Jews, pagans, and Manichees to Christianity.[41] Every major confession in our period could boast of its own intellectual ships of war—among Chalcedonians, for instance, Anastasius of Sinai lived in the Sinai but traveled to Egypt and Syria to dispute with heretics[42] and John Moschus and Sophronius were remembered as having engaged in a 'war of dialectics, setting their own wisdom against that of the mad followers of Severus and the other unclean heretics' in Egypt.[43]

[37] This expectation would continue: note Bar Hebraeus's (d. 1286) comment that, upon being made bishop, it was necessary to engage in disputation and argument with the leaders of other confessions, Christian and non-Christian. Bar Hebraeus, *Book of the Dove* 4 (ed. P. Bedjan, *Ethicon; seu, Moralia Gregorii Barhebraei* [Paris/Leipzig, 1898], p. 577; ET available in A. J. Wensinck, *Bar Hebraeus's Book of the Dove, together with Some Chapters from his Ethikon* [Leiden, 1919], p. 60). Bar Hebraeus went on to note, however, that he would come to reject disputing with other Christians. On this passage, cf. H.G.B. Teule, 'It Is Not Right to Call Ourselves Orthodox and the Other Heretics: Ecumenical Attitudes in the Jacobite Church in the Time of the Crusaders,' in K. N. Ciggaar and H.G.B. Teule, eds., *East and West in the Crusader States: Context - Contacts - Confrontations* II. *Acta of the Congress Held at Hernen Castle in May 1997* (Leuven, 1999), pp. 20–22.

[38] Thomas of Marga, *Monastic History* 1.28 (ed. Budge, p. 1.53 [Syriac] = 2.93 [ET]).

[39] *Chronicle of Seert* 2.25 (ed. Scher [PO 7.2], p. 56).

[40] Mardin 8/259, fol. 115v. The anonymous *Chronicle to 819* (ed. Barsaum [CSCO SS 3.14], p. 13) gives the date of Simeon's consecration as bishop of Harran as AG 1011, i.e., AD 700.

[41] Mardin 8/259, fol. 119r.

[42] See Beck, *Kirche und Theologische Literatur*, p. 442, and N. Marinides, 'Lay Piety in Byzantium, ca. 600–730' (PhD diss., Princeton University, 2014), pp. 337, 354–55.

[43] '... they' delivered many villages, very many churches, and monasteries, too, like good shepherds

At times we get more detailed pictures of how such confessional champions operated. Most famous is perhaps Simeon, 'the Persian Debater,' a Miaphysite active in Sasanian lands in the first half of the sixth century.[44] Simeon was a theological streetfighter who traveled widely debating heretics. In fact, he was so formidable in debate that, John of Ephesus claimed, Nestorian leaders and teachers 'dreaded to open their mouth and speak in a district in which his presence had been reported.' If Simeon learned of Nestorians starting debates with Miaphysites in an area, he would 'suddenly spring up and be present there.' Not only did Simeon debate and convert heretics, he also converted Zoroastrians, even prominent ones, and pagans.[45]

We have portrayals of other confessional champions as well; for instance, Mar Aba (d. 552), an East Syrian catholicos and a contemporary of Simeon. Aba's *vita* is filled with instances of victorious encounters with pagans and heretics. Not long after his conversion, for example, we are told that one of the reasons Mar Aba wanted to visit the Roman Empire was to debate a man named Sergius who 'had the doctrine of Arius and was mixed up with paganism.' Aba wanted to debate Sergius in order to 'to confirm the true faith.'[46] Previously, while in Arzun, Aba had 'returned many heretics to the true faith.'[47] In Alexandria, he is said to have brought many pagans, heretics, and people involved in astrology to true Christianity.[48] In Athens, when 'sophists holding the doctrine of the outsiders'—that is, pagans—'heard his teaching, they came near to the knowledge of the truth and burned the books of the pagans which they possessed.' News of this conversion, we are told, 'went out into all the land of Achaea.' Heretics there were 'defeated by his teaching,' because Aba was skillfully dismantling their arguments, and they therefore sought to kill him.[49]

Back in the Sasanian Empire, Aba was eventually elected head of the Church of the East, and the success of his ministry led to repeated run-ins with Zoroastrian leaders over his efforts at converting Magians to Christianity.[50] The

---

saving sheep from the jaws of these evil beasts. . . .' Leontius of Neapolis, *Life of John the Almsgiver* 32 (ed. Gelzer, *Leontios' von Neapolis*, p. 64; ET taken from Dawes and Baynes, *Three Byzantine Saints*, pp. 242–43. For the 'longer recension,' see Festugière and Rydén, eds., *Vie de Syméon le Fou et Vie de Jean de Chypre*, pp. 383 [Greek] = 490 [FT] = chapter 33).

[44] On Simeon, see Walker, *The Legend of Mar Qardagh*, pp. 175–76.

[45] John of Ephesus, *Lives of the Eastern Saints* 10 (ed. and trans. Brooks [PO 17.1], pp. 140–41, 152; English translations are by Brooks). Note, also, p. 158, Simeon also wrote treatises against Nestorians, Manichees, Bardaisanites, and Eutychians.

[46] *History of Mar Aba*, pp. 217–18 (ed. Bedjan, *Histoire de Mar-Jabalaha*).

[47] *History of Mar Aba*, p. 217 (ed. Bedjan, *Histoire de Mar-Jabalaha*).

[48] *History of Mar Aba*, pp. 218–19 (ed. Bedjan, *Histoire de Mar-Jabalaha*).

[49] *History of Mar Aba*, p. 221 (ed. Bedjan, *Histoire de Mar-Jabalaha*).

[50] *History of Mar Aba*, pp. 221, 228–29, 238, 256, 259–60 (ed. Bedjan, *Histoire de Mar-Jabalaha*).

Chronicle of Seert, in fact, preserves an account of a disputation between Aba and an elite Magian held in the presence of the Sasanian ruler, Khusro I.[51] Aba not only converted Zoroastrians, he encouraged others to do the same.[52] We know the names of some of Aba's disciples, and one of them, Theodore of Merv, wrote a book containing various arguments at Aba's request.[53] Though the book is no longer extant, its contents were quite possibly religious polemic.

The anger Aba's activities provoked among the Zoroastrian religious leadership led to his exile to a village that was a stronghold of Magianism; even there, Aba continued to debate and proselytize.[54] At other points in his *vita* we find him converting a chief mobed to Christianity[55] as well as many heretics who visited him when the 'King of the Arabs' came to pay his respects to the Sasanian ruler.[56]

STORIES AS WEAPONS

It is a notable feature of stories of confessional champions that they never lose their disputes. Similarly, whatever the outcome of actual formal debates, it is surely no coincidence that the winning side in a disputation inevitably belonged to the same confession as the writer reporting it.[57] What we are in fact dealing with in hagiographic accounts of confessional champions or reports of interconfessional disputes is a subspecies of the sort of dueling stories we encountered in Chapter 2. Like the tale of a hand that did not burn when placed in a fire, the account of a doctrinal champion who humiliated the leader of a rival church, when told and retold, could affirm in a powerful way the truth of a particular confession's doctrinal position. In such stories, in fact, we can see the world of the learned and the world of the simple unite: hagiographic

[51] *Chronicle of Seert* 2.28–2.29 (ed. Scher [PO 7.2], pp. 72–75).

[52] *History of Mar Aba*, p. 254 (ed. Bedjan, *Histoire de Mar-Jabalaha*).

[53] 'Abdisho' bar Brikha, *Mēmrā on Ecclesiastical Books* 77 (ed. Assemani, *BO*, 3.1, p. 147) and *Chronicle of Seert* 2.30 (ed. Scher [PO 7.2], p. 79). Also see Assemani, *BO*, 3.1, p. 86, n. 1, and Baumstark, *Geschichte*, pp. 122–23.

[54] *History of Mar Aba*, p. 244 (ed. Bedjan, *Histoire de Mar-Jabalaha*).

[55] *History of Mar Aba*, pp. 260–61 (ed. Bedjan, *Histoire de Mar-Jabalaha*).

[56] *History of Mar Aba*, pp. 269–71 (ed. Bedjan, *Histoire de Mar-Jabalaha*).

[57] The Miaphysite-Chalcedonian discussions before Justinian in 532 are a rare example of a dialogue where we have information from both sides. Note Brock's observation: 'Reading the accounts of the discussions of 532 as reported by the two sides one can readily enough see that each party has given a biased account of what must have taken place, dwelling on points where they felt they had scored, and passing over in silence awkward moments. . . .' See 'The Conversations with the Syrian Orthodox under Justinian,' p. 120.

reports of doctrinal prize fighters and their exploits could serve as nondoctrinal proof of the truth of one's confession. At times, we can even see both sophisticated and unsophisticated styles of debate united in a single figure: in the *History of Mar Yawnan*, for instance, a text set in the fourth century but likely written in the seventh or eighth, the protagonist defeated Magians in a debate and then stripped down, walked into a fire, and sat in its midst for a long time, uninjured, while his opponents refused to enter in.[58] The truth of Christianity was shown through both dialectics and an ordeal.[59]

Theodore Abū Qurrah (d. ca. 820), a Chalcedonian confessional champion, illustrates well how stories of confessional champions and their debates could become polemical tools in their own right. Theodore, who traveled the Middle East engaging in interconfessional and interreligious controversies and disputes in Greek, Syriac, and Arabic, is one of the most important figures in the Arabic-language Chalcedonian tradition. Miaphysite reactions to Theodore ranged from Michael the Great's hostile depiction of him as a pseudo-expert and poseur who was soundly defeated by the young Miaphysite confessional champion Nonnus of Nisibis,[60] to an implicit acknowledgement of Theodore's formidable dialectical powers: in the Miaphysite recension of an Arabic dispute text, purporting to record a debate between Theodore and the Caliph al-Ma'mūn, the Christian protagonist has been changed from the Chalcedonian Theodore to the Miaphysite Simeon of the Olives.[61]

[58] For the story of this debate, see Mar Zadoy, *History of Mar Yawnan*, pp. 516–18 (ed. Bedjan, *AMS*, vol. 1). The *History of Mar Yawnan* (BHO 527–30) has traditionally been dated to the fourth century, but more recently has been redated to the seventh and eighth by Richard Payne in 'Monks, Dinars and Date Palms: Hagiographical Production and the Expansion of Monastic Institutions in the Early Islamic Persian Gulf,' *Arabian Archaeology and Epigraphy* 22 (2011), pp. 97–111. A translation of the *History of Mar Yawnan* by S. P. Brock is now available. See his 'The History of Mar Yawnan,' in M. Kozah et al., eds., *An Anthology of Syriac Writers from Qatar in the Seventh Century* (Piscataway, N.J., 2015), pp. 1–42.

[59] Similarly, a single person might vindicate the truth of both Christianity and of a particular confession by multiple means. The sixth-century *vita* of the non-Chalcedonian Barṣawmā (d. 456) has the protagonist debate a Samaritan in Sebastia who has studied the (Mosaic) law and then heal the man's daughter, prompting her conversion to Christianity (*Miracle 54*, pp. 114–15); later, in a Samaritan village, Barṣawmā has another debate with Samaritans, using only the Books of Moses as the basis for discussion. After Barṣawmā heals a child, many Samaritans become Christians (*Miracle 56*, p. 118). Later in the *vita*, the plan of some bishops to gather a number of clergymen together to anathematize Barṣawmā is thwarted by a deacon who tells them that Barṣawmā had healed him (*Miarcle 80*, p. 282). Note that the *vita* earlier highlights Barṣawmā's simplicity: 'Now the Blessed Barṣawmā was up till this point guiless (*tammimā*) by nature, simple (*wa-brirā*) in the speech of his tongue, and inexperienced (*w-hedyoṭā*) in the training of human writing. But he was wise in the Lord, for the beginning of wisdom is the fear of the Lord [cf. Proverbs 9:10].' For these quotes, see Nau, 'Résumé de monographies syriaques': quote translated from *ROC* 18, p. 276; *Miracle 56* = *ROC* 19, p. 118; *Miracle 54* = *ROC* 19, pp. 114–15; *Miracle 80* = *ROC* 19, p. 282.

[60] Michael the Great, *Chronicle* 12.8 (ed. Chabot, 4.495-496 = 3.32-33).

[61] On the Miaphysite and Chalcedonian recensions of Abū Qurrah's *Debate* with the Caliph al-

Michael the Great's hostile account of Theodore's activity reads as a sort of anti-hagiography: it is clearly inaccurate in its portrayal of Theodore's Christological positions and perhaps in other details as well.[62] But, however distorted Michael's depiction of Theodore, was it any more inaccurate than John of Ephesus's depiction of Simeon the Persian Debater, or that of the anonymous author of Mar Aba's *vita*? Not likely. These accounts were all highly biased—even bordering on legendary—but in clearly different confessional directions. What would a Zoroastrian or Miaphysite depiction of Mar Aba have looked like? Or an East Syrian account of Simeon the Persian Debater?

As with reports of debates, when it came to confessional champions, different groups had different versions of the same events: Michael the Great claimed that the Miaphysite Nonnus of Nisibis had bested Theodore in debate, but Chalcedonians remembered the opposite, that it was Theodore who had defeated the Armenian Miaphysite.[63] Both sides could appeal to dialectical heroes for vindication.

And just as the stories of fire-based ordeals or miraculous Eucharists found in John Rufus and John Moschus were translated into different languages and still being recopied and circulated centuries after they were first recorded, stories of confessional champions, too, remained in circulation: the *vita* of Mar Aba was written in Syriac, but as we have seen, the eleventh-century Arabic *Chronicle of Seert* reported the story of Mar Aba's vanquishing of Magians by argument and fire.[64] Similarly, another version of the debate between Mar Awgen, Yawnan, and the Magians found in the Syriac *History of Mar Yawnan* can also be found in the Arabic *Chronicle of Seert*.[65]

'If I am questioned about the faith by heretics,' one of the questions posed to the Chalcedonian Anastasius of Sinai in the later seventh century went, 'and I do not know how to explain dogma, what shall I do?'[66] Knowing that a powerful figure had been able to defeat a leader of an opposing church in a

Ma'mūn, see D. Bertaina, 'An Arabic Account of Theodore Abu Qurra in Debate at the Court of Caliph al-Ma'mun: A Study in Early Christian and Muslim Literary Dialogues,' PhD diss., Catholic University of America, 2007, pp. 365–70. For the text of the West Syrian introduction and conclusion to the *Debate*, see I. Dick, *Mujādalat Abī Qurrah ma'a al-mutakallimīn al-muslimīn fī majlis al-khalīfa al-Ma'mūn* (Aleppo, 2007), pp. 121–24.

[62] See J. C. Lamoreaux, *Theodore Abū Qurrah* (Provo, 2005), pp. xii–xvi, esp. xiv–xv. One thinks, too, of the radically different views of a figure like Barṣawmā in the Miaphysite and Chalcedonian traditions. On this, see Palmer, 'The West-Syrian Monastic Founder Barṣawmo.'

[63] For a medieval Georgian chronicle claiming Theodore's victory over an Armenian opponent in a dispute it records, see van Roey, *Traité apologétique*, p. 16; cf. Lamoreaux, *Theodore Abū Qurrah*, p. xvi.

[64] *Chronicle of Seert* 2.28 (ed. Scher [PO 7.2], pp. 72–75).

[65] *Chronicle of Seert* 1.35 (ed. Scher [PO 5.2], pp. 135–36).

[66] Anastasius of Sinai, *Questions and Answers* 68 (ed. Richard and Munitiz, p. 120; ET taken from Munitiz, *Questions and Answers* p. 182). Cf. Chapter 6, n. 90.

public dispute—even if one could not repeat the arguments (which are often not recorded in depictions of confessional champions), much less evaluate them—or that God had miraculously shown the views of one's own church to be true and that of an opposing group's to be false, was one way of dealing with this challenge.

FILLING OUT THE SPECTRUM

Was this therefore a world with two camps—sophisticated doctrinal champions who wrote polemics against one another and who engaged in formal disputes on the one hand, and on the other, people who told stories about the victories of such prize fighters or of fire sparing this hand or that? Or, for good measure, we can even add a third camp: people who were either unaware of or not terribly concerned about the controversies coming out of Chalcedon? Was there anything else? There was. The dichotomy between the simple and the learned should not be drawn too sharply. It would be better, rather, to think of a continuum or a spectrum of different levels of engagement and understanding existing in the various Christian communities.

Here an additional distinction might be helpful: I have suggested that the late Roman world was characterized by very high rates of theological illiteracy, but theological illiteracy should not be confused with rampant anti-intellectualism or with a widespread lack of what might be termed 'theological curiosity.' Such curiosity can exist and indeed flourish even where formal training and rigorous instruction in a particular tradition of theological inquiry and reasoning is not available. Anyone can be theologically curious and theologically interested, regardless of where he or she lives and what he or she does in life, and—this needs to be emphasized—pointing out that the great mass of religious believers in the late antique and early medieval Middle East were illiterate and theologically uneducated is not the same as claiming that these people had no interest in religious questions, or that they had no intellectual cravings. Theological literacy typically requires some combination of teachers, institutions, and books; theological curiosity, awareness, and interest require none of these. We saw in Chapter 2, for instance, the story of shipmasters who engaged in Christological debate at the court of Justinian in 560, before telling the emperor that they were in over their heads and offering to call in expert help.[67] In the last chapter, we found Timothy I writing of two thousand Julianists in Najran joining the Church of the East and noting that

[67] See Chapter 2, nn. 67–69

among those from these converts who had come to him asking for a new bishop to be consecrated, was 'a great mass of people,' in addition to clergymen. Here were ordinary laymen who cared enough about theological and confessional matters to want a bishop from their new church.[68]

Can we find evidence of such people—those who were theologically engaged and yet not experts? To use language from Chapter 2, where should we look for those who were not quite simple believers—perhaps 'simpler believers'—but who, at the same time, fell somewhat short of being among the learned? If there was, as I suggested in Part I of this book, a layering of knowledge and engagement with doctrinal questions in general, and with Chalcedon specifically, in the Christian community, where might we find those in the middle?

We can start by suggesting that simmering beneath the more spectacular courtly encounters, formal controversial treatises, or literary set pieces that appear in our surviving texts was an untold number of small-scale, local, and unrecorded religious encounters and disagreements. What historians and theologians study is only the most elite tip of a much larger iceberg. People did discuss religious ideas and religious difference. These discussions might employ the sorts of stories we have already seen—stories of miraculous ordeals or re-tellings of the deeds of a dialectically skilled specialist who vanquished an opponent—but they might also be more doctrinally oriented, even if they lacked the sort of learned expertise that a confessional champion might possess. For some people were interested in theological difference and ideas, and they did talk about such things. In the fifth century, for instance, Valentinian III forbade Eutychians and Apollinarians from gathering groups, publicly or privately, to discuss their doctrines; he even fined those who, out of a desire to acquire knowledge, listened to heresies being talked about.[69] Writing in probably the early eighth century, the Miaphysite George, Bishop of the Arab Tribes, described an incident at a gathering in which a certain pagan boasted about astrology and the power of the stars in guiding the world; provoked by the unnamed pagan's boasts, George responded at length.[70] In the early ninth cen-

[68] *Sogā d-quṭnā d-ʿammā.* Timothy I, *Letters* 27 (to Rabban Sergius) (ed. Braun [CSCO 74: SS 30], p. 151) and cf. Chapter 3, n. 54. In an Arabic-speaking context, Timothy's use of *ʿammā* ('people'), especially as it is used in this passage, can possibly be understood as corresponding to the Arabic *al-ʿāmma* ('people'), which is commonly contrasted with *al-khāṣṣa* ('the elite') and used to refer to common, ordinary people.

[69] *Codex Justinianus* 1.5.8.8 and 1.5.8.11 (ed. Krueger, *Corpus Iuris Civilis*, vol. 2: *Codex Iustinianus*, p. 52; ET based on the work of F. H. Blume available in B. W. Frier et al., eds., *The Codex of Justinian: A New Annotated Translation*, p. 199).

[70] For the Syriac text, see E. Sachau, *Verzeichniss der syrischen Handschriften der Königlichen Bibliothek zu Berlin*, vol. 2 (Berlin, 1899), pp. 720–21 (from Berlin Syriac 236/Sachau 121, fol. 109b). An ET can be found in my, 'Between Christology and Kalām,' pp. 713–14. It is not clear whether the *ḥanpē* referred to in this passage are Arabs, pagans, or Zoroastrians. George was aware of Zoroastrian astrological

tury, the area around the tetrapylon at Edessa, in front of the ancient church, was called, Michael the Great reported, 'Bēt Shabtā': 'elders and leaders would gather there after the *ṣaprā* service [in the morning], engrossed in intellectual (*mlilē*) questions from ecclesiastical and pagan books until mealtime.'[71]

Unfortunately, most of this small-scale talk has now passed into oblivion. An East Syrian monk, for example, named Rabban Qusra lived in the sixth century, in the reign of Khusro I. Originally from Nineveh, he spent time in Adiabene and even Jerusalem before settling on a mountain near Nineveh where, the *Book of Chastity* informs us, 'heretics, [presumably Miaphysites] who were living there frequently beat him.'[72] Rabban Qusra, however, was also remembered for converting a number of Miaphysites in Nineveh to the 'true faith,' that is, to the Church of the East.[73] Between being beaten by Miaphysites and converting them, his interactions with members of this rival group must have been multifaceted—to say the least. The precise contents of his conversations with Miaphysites are sadly unavailable, and so we do not have direct access to what sorts of things would have made a religious case more or less persuasive, or what sorts of arguments or miraculous deeds might have motivated a rural inhabitant of the Sasanian Empire to change his or her traditional confessional adherence. We are similarly in the dark about the precise nature of the interactions that took place when Titus, the bishop of Hdatta, 'expelled the Jacobites from [Hdatta], disgraced them through his debates and baptized a number of its inhabitants as well as Jews,'[74] and about other controversial and missionary encounters whose only remaining trace is a line or two in a medieval chronicle.[75]

---

practices (see Chapter 9, n. 20) and East Syrian texts commonly refer to Zoroastrians as 'pagans' and Zoroastrianism as 'paganism,' making use of the word *ḥanpā* and its derivatives: see, e.g., *History of Karka d-Beth Slokh*, p. 514, ln. 21 (*ḥanpē*, 'pagans,' as Zoroastrians) (ed. Bedjan, *AMS*, vol. 2); Babai the Great, *History of George the Priest*, p. 435, ln. 15 (*ḥanpāyā*, 'pagan,' used adjectivally to refer to George's pre-Christian, Persian/Zoroastrian name); p. 436, ln. 3 (*ḥanputā*, 'paganism,' used to identify George's sister's name while she was still 'in paganism,' i.e., before she was a Christian—cp. with p. 564, ln. 6); p. 523, lnn. 7, 17 (a Zoroastrian as a *ḥanpā*, 'pagan'); *Martyrdom of Gregory Pirangushnasp* (ed. Bedjan, *Histoire de Mar-Jabalaha*), p. 347, ln. 8 (*ḥanpē*, 'pagans,' as Zoroastrians), p. 349, ln. 2 (*ḥanputā*, 'paganism,' as Zoroastrianism), etc.

[71] Michael the Great, *Chronicle* 12.13 (ed. Chabot, 4.514 = 3.61-62). A mosque was built on the spot of the tetrapylon around AG 1136 (= AD 825), Michael reported.

[72] Isho'dnaḥ of Basra, *The Book of Chastity* 50 (ed. and trans. J.-B. Chabot, *Le livre de la chasteté composé par Jésusdenah, évêque de Baçrah* [Rome, 1896], p. 32 [Syriac] = p. 28 [FT]).

[73] See *Chronicle of Seert* 2.40 (ed. Scher [PO 7.2], p. 107).

[74] *Chronicle of Seert* 2.64 (ed. Scher [and Griveau] [PO 13.4], p. 153). For Titus of Hdatta being active in the time of the catholicos Ezekiel (sed. 567 or 570–581), see Isho'dnaḥ of Basra, *The Book of Chastity* 54 (ed. Chabot, p. 34 [Syriac] = p. 30 [FT]).

[75] For example, Jacob of Beth 'Ābe who, according to the *Chronicle of Seert* 2.56 (ed. Scher [and Griveau] [PO 13.4], p. 142), 'converted a number of people [who were heretics] and turned many from

A saint's *vita* provides us with an example of what such minor-league religious discussions may have looked like: At some time in the late eighth or early ninth century, the Chalcedonian Dyothelete Timothy of Kākhushtā learned the craft of woodworking from Monothelete Maronites in a monastery. Timothy, however, was doing more than just learning a trade. 'As he worked,' Timothy's *Life* reports, 'the monks would gather about him. He did not restrain himself from informing them that just as Christ has two natures, so also he has two wills.' When the elders of the monastery saw what Timothy was up to, they disapproved, but the saint did not back down. 'Timothy began to exhort them from the Gospel and enlighten them from the divine and holy scriptures, adducing for them testimonials with manifest proofs. They, however, did not accept his teaching and would not even listen to his words, but their hearts became hard and their understanding became blind.'[76] In a world awash in different and competing Christian groups with overlapping and intertwined lives, can we doubt that such small-scale encounters might have taken place when confessionally aware individuals crossed paths?

Apart from pointing to suggestive figures like Rabban Qusra, how might we show that this lost level of disputes actually existed? And if it did, how can we recover it? How do we find the batting averages and numbers of runs batted in of the seventh century's minor league players? It is a difficult task, but not an impossible one, though at best our evidence can only be fragmentary. The problem is the oral nature of these discussions and arguments. Is there a way to conjure up the ghosts of conversations past?

THE GHOSTS OF CONVERSATIONS PAST

One way, perhaps, is through letters. If we view letters, at least some of them, as 'residues of conversations' we can, perhaps, find in them indications of the sort of confessional discussions I have been talking about.[77] When some spiritual perplexity or challenge arose, one contacted one's bishop. In a letter to the bishops Sergius of Cyrrhus and Marion of Sura, Severus noted that he had

the worship of idols' (I follow Scher's understanding of *talmadha* here, in the sense of converting ('il convertit plusieurs [hérétiques]').

[76] *Life of Timothy of Kākhushtā* 12.3–12.4 ('Saidnaya Version'; ed. and trans. J. C. Lamoreaux and C. Cairala, *The Life of Timothy of Kākhushtā* [PO 48.4] [Turnhout, 2000], p. 116 (Arabic) = 117 [ET]; the translation here is that of Lamoreaux and Cairala). On this *vita*, see P. Wood, 'Christian Authority under the Early Abbasids: The Life of Timothy of Kakushta,' *Proche-Orient Chrétien* 61 (2011), pp. 258–74.

[77] I owe the phrase 'residues of conversation' and this insight to John-Paul Ghobrial.

not yet had the time to write against the latest work of Julian of Halicarnassus. The epistolary pressures crowding in on him were unyielding: 'During the whole time of the summer,' he wrote, 'I have never ceased being worried by constant letters from men who in various ways ask different questions at different times, and beg to have now scriptural expressions, now doctrinal theories explained to them.'[78]

In our period, the letters of George, Bishop of the Arab Tribes, to provide precisely the kinds of residues we might expect if the confessional landscape of his day was anywhere nearly as muddled and unstable as I have tried to suggest. The first three of George's eleven extant letters are about rather dry Christological polemic. At least three things about them, however, merit observation in the context of this discussion.

One is their style. They are written in a punchy, aporetic manner. The opponent is relentlessly presented with a series of dilemmas that methodically reduce his Christological position to one of hopeless absurdity. This is a style of Christological dispute that made its appearance in the Near East within fifty years of Chalcedon and which became widespread in Greek and in Syriac.[79] Aporetic questions were weapons used by Chalcedonians, Miaphysites—both Severan and Julianist—as well as Nestorians to wreak havoc on their opponents.[80] Even Tritheists used them.[81] When Jacob labeled a Miaphysite scribe who wrote out questions and answers that helped Chalcedonian doctrine a 'second Judas,' as we saw in Chapter 2, he was quite probably referring to these sorts of aporetic questions. As an indicator of the ubiquity of such po-

[78] 'Also the loneliness of solitude, and the fact that I have not men at hand to serve as scribes when I want it in addition to the other things hinder me from writing.' Severus of Antioch, *Select Letters* V.15 (To Sergius and Marion) (ed. and trans. Brooks, 1.2.404–405 [Syriac] = 2.2.358–359 [English]). I have used here the translation of Brooks. For this passage, see Allen and Hayward, *Severus of Antioch*, p. 26.

[79] For a bibliographic listing of examples of Greek Christological *aporiai* see Grillmeier, *Christ in Christian Tradition*, vol. 2.1, pp. 86–87.

[80] For examples of collections of aporetic questions in Syriac from different Christological perspectives, see M. A. Cook, 'The Origins of "Kalām,"' *BSOAS* 43 (1980), p. 38–40. For an example of a Julianist use of aporetic questions, see the citations of the now-lost *Solution to Julianist Questions* by the Chalcedonian Syriac writer, George of Martyropolis, preserved in the *Apologetic Letter* of Elia, a Chalcedonian-turned-Miaphysite. For citations of George's *Solution to Julianist Questions* (as well as his *Solution to Miaphysite Questions*), see the Index Patristicus to van Roey's Latin translation (CSCO 470: SS 202), pp. 78–79, s.n. Georgius Martryopolitanus. Vatican Syriac 135, fols. 80b–87a, contains an anonymous work, *Solutions to Manichaean Blasphemies written by one of the Followers of Julian, from the Village of Saqra*, which contains both answers to aporetic questions the unnamed Julianist had written out in a small booklet and also aporetic questions aimed at Julianist teaching.

[81] For a Severan Miaphysite response to questions posed by Tritheists, see BL Add. 14,533, fols. 89b–98b (description in *CBM*, 2.969–970, no. 8); no. 10 [fol. 100b–101a] contains questions to be used against Tritheists [descripton p. 970]).

lemics, the earliest Islamic theology, when it appeared, would take this very distinctive aporetic form.[82]

The second point of interest about these letters is that sources for at least some of them are identifiable. A number of the questions George responded to in his first letter and in the appendices to it can be shown to exist also in a variety of Greek and Syriac Chalcedonian sources, sometimes with conflicting attributions of authorship.[83] This suggests they were circulating widely throughout the Middle East. Here is yet another indication of the popularity of this form of argumentation.

The third point of interest about these questions brings us back to the problem of 'the ghosts of conversations past.' These letters give us fleeting hints at precisely the sort of minor-league religious discussions I have just been speaking about. George's first letter is written to a certain Mar Mari, who is the Abbot of the important monastery of Tell 'Ada in northern Syria. Mari sent George a set of twenty-two Chalcedonian aporetic questions asking for a response to them.[84] Written as an alphabetical acrostic, the document that Mari sent George had no doubt been presented either to him or to one of his monks by a Chalcedonian. Here we have the faint whiff of some sort of polemical encounter; we also see that debate provided the opportunity to show one's intellectual and theological virtuosity—a motive we should never underestimate when thinking about doctrinal clashes.

In George's second letter, written to a deacon named Barhadbshabba, the smell of dispute becomes stronger. George began his letter to Barhadbshabba by noting that a certain Chalcedonian 'from among those who are puffed up with worldly power' had asked a group of Miaphysite monks a pointed doctrinal question. As George reported it, the Chalcedonian had

> asked men in a [certain] place who had put on the modest monastic habit a certain little question, and when a response was not made as it should have been, he went away, babbling about these heretical boasts. [Because of this] you asked of me that when I had seen it, I should make a reply to that little question.[85]

In writing to George for help with this question, Barhadbshabba was doing the same thing that the Alexandrian shipowners had done when they found themselves unable to adequately defend their positions in debate at Justinian's

[82] Cook, 'The Origins of "Kalām,"' pp. 32–43 and see my 'Between Christology and Kalām? The Life and Letters of George, Bishop of the Arab Tribes.'

[83] See my 'Between Christology and Kalām?' pp. 688–702.

[84] BL Add., 12,154, fol. 222b.

[85] BL Add. 12,154, fol. 237b.

court: he reached out to a learned expert. The entire incident of the arrogant Chalcedonian and the Miaphysite monks he confounded would have been completely lost to us had Barhadbshabba not written to George. We have here precisely the sort of conversational echo of a large informal layer of dispute and discussion that we have been seeking.

George's third letter, 'a response to a certain other heretical question that was presented to him by the elder Mar Joshua, a hermit who is in the village of Anab,' is really an excerpt from a longer letter written to a hermit named Joshua. What we have extant picks up where George begins to answer the questions of theological opponents. The cause for writing here again seems to be polemical pressure from some flavor of Dyophysite, another case of friction arising when confessionally aware individuals crossed paths. 'Concerning those heretics who ask us, "Do you confess that the Word and His flesh have one substance or two?"' George writes, 'we must ourselves ask and respond to them like this...,' and then George embarks on another aporetic dismantling of the opposition.[86]

We can catch additional glimpses of lost controversial exchanges in other places. In the words of a (partially preserved) letter written by Jacob of Edessa to the deacon Barhadbshabba, there are echoes of now-lost heated back-and-forths of the seventh and eighth-centuries: 'We will ask them,' Jacob repeats over and over, each time introducing a new problem in Chalcedonian theology.[87] A treatise written by the East Syrian patriarch Makikha, surviving in a Karshūnī manuscript in Cambridge, contains Syriac quotations from a letter Jacob wrote to the Chalcedonians of Harran. Jacob, like George, was very aware of the Chalcedonian theological challenge.[88]

In his canonical responses, in fact, the questions Jacob entertains embrace the entire Christian East. I have not yet mentioned Armenians, but they also come in for harsh treatment at his hands: Jacob accused them of keeping Jewish observances; having Julianists and Jews as teachers; and agreeing with Chalcedonians in some practices, with Nestorians in others, and with Arabs

[86] BL. Add. 12,154, fols. 241b–242a (Syriac text also in *SBI*, p. 253, n. 594).

[87] See Jacob of Edessa, *Letter to the Deacon Barhadbshabba*, BL Add., 14,631, fols. 16a–16b. The text is lacunose and hard to make out in some places, but significant portions can still be read, most notably the constant refrain, 'let us ask them....' For excerpts from what can be read of the Syriac text and an ET of them, see *SBI*, p. 253, n. 595.

[88] Karshūnī is Arabic written in the Syriac script. The two fragments are preserved in Syriac with a Karshūnī translation in a Karshūnī treatise written by the patriarch Makikha, in Cambridge Add. 2889, fols. 272b–273b. For their text and an English translation, see *SBI*, p. 254, n. 596. On Makkikā, see Assemani, *BO*, vol. 3.1, p. 552. A Syriac version of this complete text by Jacob was apparently contained in the now-destroyed collection of manuscripts at the Monastery of Seert. See the entry for MS Seert Syriac 69 (no. 12) in A. Scher, *Catalogue des manuscrits syriaques et arabes conservés dans la bibliothèque épiscopale de Séert (Kurdistan)* (Mosul, 1905), p. 53.

in still others.[89] They, too, were part of the confessional kaleidoscope of the seventh and early eighth centuries and they, too, were participants in the kinds of low-level disagreements that are at issue here. In his fourth letter, George took up the question of whether one should pour water into the cup at the Eucharist. Joshua the Hermit, his correspondent, had encountered difficulties directly related to this question. 'Now, since a certain Armenian was demanding of you,' he noted

> as you wrote, that you prove for him from the Gospel that there was water in that cup Our Lord gave to his disciples, or that we should pour water into that cup, let it be demanded of him that he prove from the Gospel that there was no water in that cup or that we should not put water into the cup of Mysteries. But perhaps he will say that it is written in the Gospel that Our Lord said to his disciples, 'Truly, truly, I say unto you, I will not drink from this fruit of the vine until I drink it anew with you in the Kingdom of God.' And it is claimed that based on the fact that He said, 'the fruit of the vine,' it is that [the wine] of that cup was pure wine and not mixed with water. But let us listen one more time. What now? Now, in the Kingdom of God—that is, in the time after His Resurrection—when Our Savior was eating and drinking with his disciples (in accordance with the divine plan, in order to confirm his Resurrection) and when He remained with them 40 days, as it is written [cf. Acts 1:3], was he drinking unmixed wine each time He and His disciples were eating and drinking? Who is so brainless so as to speak in this way, save the person who claims that that cup Our Lord took and gave thanks and said a blessing over and had His disciples drink from had no wine in it but only water? But if a person wanted to properly refute this reprehensible doctrine, he would need many words and even his own treatise.[90]

We know nothing about the nameless Armenian who had confronted Joshua or what sort of polemical resources he had available to him—though George's exact contemporary, the Armenian catholicos Yovhannēs Awjnec'i (sed. 718–729), the author of a number of treatises against heretics, also composed a text 'on leaven and water in the liturgy.'[91] The point of dispute was evidently very much a live one in the early eighth century, and here we only catch a glimpse of it in passing. This is another ghost of a conversation past.

[89] See the excerpt of Jacob contained in Paris Syriac 11, edited in Kayser, *Die Canones Jakob's von Edessa*, pp. 3–4 (GT at 34–35; ET available in *SBI*, p. 255, n. 597).

[90] See BL Add., 12,154, fol. 257a (Syriac text also in *SBI*, p. 256, n. 598).

[91] See R. W. Thomson, *A Bibliography of Classical Armenian Literature to 1500 AD* (Turnhout, 1995), p. 218.

These 'residues' extended well beyond the individual Christian churches. The increase in controversial Christian literature aimed at Jews in the seventh century has been long noted,[92] and we have traces of polemical conversations held with pagans and Muslims, too: disagreement and dispute over religious matters did not stop at the boundaries of the Christian faith. A seventh-century manuscript in the British Library, for example, preserves a set of aporetic questions for Christians to use against pagans—worshippers of the sun.[93]

THE LIMITS OF DEBATE?

In Chapter 3, we encountered people for whom the doctrinal differences resulting from Chalcedon were of little or only selective importance. Here, however, we have met other ways in which people handled and attempted to resolve doctrinal disagreement—through violence, but most notably through discussion, debate, disagreement, and the narration of stories that vindicated the truth of their church's stance. It is undeniable that, if we are interested in the ways in which Christians dealt with doctrinal difference in the post-Chalcedonian world, discussion, debate, and storytelling are a very important part of the picture.

This is the case because there were members of the various rival Christian communities who were in fact confessionally aware and theologically curious. The learned and the simple were not two distinct camps, informational haves and have-nots: they existed on a spectrum and along a continuum. And when confessionally aware individuals on one part of the spectrum came into contact with confessionally aware individuals on a different (and rival) part of the spectrum who were able to ask them questions they could not answer, help would be sought. Such encounters and the requests they generated were one of the factors driving the composition of controversial, question-and-answer, and instructional texts by church leaders.

It is in the context of these sorts of everyday encounters—the types of minor-league polemical exchanges we glimpse in passing references in the letters of George of the Arabs, or the kinds of discussions that regularly took

[92] See the comments in Av. Cameron, 'The Jews in Seventh-Century Palestine,' *Scripta Classical Israelica* 13 (1994), p. 79 and Cameron, 'Byzantines and Jews: Some Recent Work on Early Byzantium,' *Byzantine and Modern Greek Studies* 20 (1996), pp. 258–63, 265–70. More generally, V. Déroche, 'La polémique anti-judaïque au VIe et au VIIe siècle un mémento inédit, les *Képhalaia*,' *Travaux et mémoires* 11 (1991), pp. 275–311, is important for anti-Jewish polemics in this period.

[93] See BL Add. 14,533, fols. 138b–139a. Cf. also Cook, 'The Origins of "*Kalām*,"' p. 38. For the date of this manuscript, see Wright, *CBM*, vol. 2, p. 489.

place at the tetrapylon in Edessa—that we should perhaps also locate the telling of stories of confessional champions besting the learned representatives of a rival church in debate, and miraculous tales of one confession's doctrine being vindicated by supernatural means.[94] The written accounts we have of these kinds of stories should be viewed as particular textual instantiations of a broader variety of such tales that existed orally and were told by confessionally aware believers to members of rival churches or members of their own communions in order to point to the truth of their church's doctrinal stance. And the importance of such stories as controversial tools should not be underestimated. Nestorius himself complained of how the partisans of Cyril told stories of dreams they had had about him, of how they astonished listeners with accounts of visions and revelations they had had from saints concerning him, and of prophecies they contrived, all to discredit him. Not only Christians, but even pagans seem to have been moved by such reports. 'They were persuading everyone concerning all the things they were seeing,' he noted bitterly, 'making themselves out to be angels of light.'[95]

The propagandistic nature of these stories raises the question of what tools a theologically-aware church leader might have at his disposal to address the confused situation we found in Chapter 3. In a world of simple believers, debate and polemic will have ultimately been of more limited usefulness, for a variety of reasons. Many people, perhaps most, I suggested in Part I, did not choose their confession on the basis of doctrinal considerations. Many will not even have chosen their confession at all: it was something they will have been born into, or which was the result of the accidents of geography—their confession was that of their local church, if they even had a local church. And in the case of those who had a strong attachment to a certain confession, we should not

[94] Other contexts are of course possible, as well, most obviously a monastic one. When Dioscorus met with Paphnutius, the head of the Pachomian community at Tabennisi, the *History of Dioscorus* reports that they spent a good deal of time recounting edifying stories: 'They spoke with one another about the stories of the holy fathers who were before them: our father [sc. Dioscorus], concerning the archbishops and their steadfast ways of life, and concerning Cyril, the archbishop, and concerning the Samaritan woman who came to believe in Our Lord Jesus Christ at his own hands [cf. Jn. 4]. And Abba Paphnutius was telling of the miracles and wonders of the fathers who were before him: about Abba Pachomius, and Pẹtronius, and Theodore. He spoke many things about Aba Shenoudin, how he grew up and was trained in speaking eloquently from his youth, and how he rode on a chariot of clouds when he passed through the air [coming] from the capital city.' Ps.-Theopistus, *History of Dioscorus* 17 (ed. Nau, 'Histoire de Dioscore,' pp. 93–94 [Syriac] = 298–99 [French]). On the contexts of folk stories in Rabbinic literature, see G. Hasan-Rokem, *Web of Life: Folklore and Midrash in Rabbinic Literature* (Stanford, 2000).

[95] Nestorius, *Bazaar of Heracleides*, p. 374 (ed. P. Bedjan, *Nestorius. Le Livre d'Héraclide de Damas* [Paris/Leipzig, 1910]; my translation, but ET also available in G. R. Driver and L. Hodgson, *The Bazaar of Heracleides* [Oxford, 1925], p. 271). For this, see also Nau in *PO* 8.1, p. 7. Ironically, Severus of Antioch would complain to Julian of Halicarnassus about the use of dreams and visions to show the truth of Julian's teaching. See Moss, 'The Rise and Function of the Holy Text in Late Antiquity,' p. 530.

infer from that attachment that they had necessarily arrived at their position based upon considered reflection on a certain theory of the Incarnation. The effectiveness of dialectical approaches to managing confessional difference will have been further limited by the fact that, as I also suggested in Part I, most people did not have the theological formation, literacy, leisure time, and access to books necessary to properly understand the issues raised by Chalcedon and evaluate competing doctrinal stances.

Even debates and discussions that utilized stories of ordeals or employed appeals to legendary accounts of confessional champions vindicating this or that church's theological stance will have had been less than fully effective. If a person's confessional adherence was the result of nondoctrinal factors, how successful could arguments that referenced doctrine—even indirectly through stories of ordeals—be in influencing and encouraging behavior?

A church leader like Jacob might employ polemics, persuasion, even stories, written and oral, to try to bring order to his confessionally messy world. But this will not have been enough. Such methods will likely have been persuasive only to a select portion of the Christian community. What about everyone else? If we keep in mind the full spectrum of the simple and the learned, were there other tools at a church leader's disposal as well?

CHAPTER 5

Power in Heaven and on Earth

State-sponsored or local violence, the seizure of churches and purging of monasteries, arguments, debates, polemics, and stories, even the use of economic incentives to manage doctrinal disagreement and counter confessional chaos and conflict—all of these means shared one thing in common—they paled in comparison with the most powerful tool for community formation that Christian leaders had at their disposal: the sacraments, particularly the Eucharist.

The sacraments united the simple and the learned alike. They were not subject to vicissitudes of availability, of intelligibility, or of anything else that might limit the effectiveness of other means of persuasion and community formation. Constantly, physically present (in theory, at least) wherever there were communities of Christians, they impinged on the lives of all on a regular basis.[1] The sacraments went to the heart of what the lived experience of being a Christian was in a very tactile and tangible way. Apart from their ubiquity—and in part because of it—having control over the sacraments offered a figure like Jacob a range of tools whose effectiveness and power far exceeded that of even the most skilled debater, polemicist, or storyteller, and indeed exceeded the power of threats of violence as well.

But having control over the sacraments in a world of simple believers was easier said than done. And the sacraments were not without their own unique difficulties. First and foremost, precisely because of their ubiquity and perceived great power, in contexts where sophisticated doctrinal disagreement had fractured the Christian community and theological illiteracy was the norm among the laity and the clergy—which is to say, in most places in our period—the sacraments threatened to become detached from any confessional framework and to foster a certain confessional indifference: what became important in such contexts was not the doctrinal stance of the person administering the

[1] The question of how frequently clergy and laity actually communicated is not one to which a clear answer can be given, but it should nevertheless be acknowledged. On this issue, especially in the context of areas under the authority of the East Roman ruler and the patriarchate of Constantinople, see R. F. Taft, 'The Decline of Communion in Byzantium and the Distancing of the Congregation from the Liturgical Action: Cause, Effect, or Neither?' in S.E.J. Gerstel, ed., *Thresholds of the Sacred. Architectural, Art Historical, Liturgical, and Theological Perspectives on Religious Screens, East and West* (Washington, D.C., 2006), pp. 27–50. On the question of how often the Eucharist was available on a regular basis, see Taft, *Beyond East and West: Problems in Liturgical Understanding* (Washington, D.C., 1984), pp. 61–80 ('The Frequency of the Eucharist throughout History').

sacraments, but rather the sacraments themselves. This was exactly what we saw happening in Chapter 3—there were people who cared more about having access to the Eucharist than they did about ecclesiastical affiliation based on Christological speculation. The challenge the sacraments therefore represented for church leaders in the post-Chalcedonian Middle East was that they might work to undermine the integrity of the distinct and competing confessions that leaders were attempting to form, at least at the level of everyday life—arguably the most important level of all.

In what follows, I want to explore the lives that sacraments and Christian symbols lived in a world of simple believers. In this world, the Eucharist was much more than a Mystery one took at church, and baptism was much more than a rite of Christian initiation. Seeing the enormous power ascribed to these things and others will help us understand why they could help produce the sort of confessional indifference—and consequent confessional chaos—among the simple that so exercised church leaders like Jacob. Understanding the extra-ecclesial life of the sacraments will also help us understand why controlling them might prove fundamental to forming a communal vessel that, so to speak, did not have leaks and why controlling them was ultimately much, much more powerful than any dialectical argument.

To accomplish this task, we will need to return to the precious canonical material Jacob has left us. It offers a remarkable glimpse of religious behavior in the seventh and eighth centuries in Syria. Before we step into this world, however, several points should be made.

First: we should remember that what are commonly referred to as Jacob's 'canons' are not exactly canons in the sense that that word might normally be used; in many instances, what they are, in fact, are answers to questions written to him by other Christians. In other words, they are responses to actual, real-life situations and incidents.

Second: precisely for this reason, we must resist the temptation to view Jacob's canons as ethnographic reports of bizarre and abnormal practices unique to certain parts of Syria in a particular period. We are not dealing with singularities. The sorts of behaviors Jacob's canons describe were utterly normal and quite widespread, not only during his lifetime, but also before it and afterward.[2] In writing his responses, Jacob was playing the familiar role of an authority figure reacting in expected ways to practices that had been around for a long time. This was a dance of consultation and opinion-issuing whose

[2] For similar examples based on other bodies of ancient Christian evidence, see, e.g., F. R. Trombley, 'The Council in Trullo (691–92): A Study in the Canons Relating to Paganism, Heresy, and the Invasions,' *Comitatus: A Journal of Medieval and Renaissance Studies* 9 (1978), pp. 1–18; see also the large amount of Greek and Latin patristic material collected in Bingham, *Origines ecclesiasticae*, vol. 2, pp. 938–49 [16.5]. See also Chapter 9, n. 98.

steps had been written centuries before. What is unique, perhaps, about Jacob and his questions and answers is their extraordinary vividness and detail.

With these caveats in mind, let us now turn our attention more closely to the profile of the sacraments that emerges from Jacob's writings.

"THIS IS MY BODY"

Strategies for distinguishing one Christian group from another can take on a number of different forms: doctrinal, liturgical, creedal, among others. An inescapable reality, however, was that the creation of a separate church, a well-defined community of Christian worshippers, on the ground, in the real physical world—as opposed to a church in a strictly doctrinal sense, 'on paper,'—required both institutions and manpower. It required institutions for training manpower. The question is: How could one win hearts and minds in the seventh century, and then keep them won? How could someone like Jacob put a stop to the sort of behaviors we found him criticizing in Chapter 3?

Jacob had no state to enforce his vision of Christian orthodoxy. What he did have was words. We have just seen the great variety of polemical and controversial texts and stories that were employed in intraconfessional warfare in the post-Chalcedonian world. A leader like Jacob might make use of these—and Jacob did.[3] A leader could also tar someone with pejorative labels: Jacob did this, too. He might accuse someone of engaging in 'Jewish' behavior, for instance.[4] 'Pagan,'[5] 'Heretic,'[6] 'Strangers to the Church,'[7] and 'Arab'[8] were other labels used to describe a those who deviated from Jacob's norm and ideal. More

[3] For Jacob's letter to the Chalcedonians of Harran, see Chapter 4, n. 88; for his criticisms of the Armenians, Chapter 4, n. 89. For Jacob's *mēmrā On Faith and Against Nestorians*, see C. M. Ugolini, *Iacobi Edesseni de fide adversus Nestorium Carmen* (Rome, 1888). A new edition and translation is now available in A. Shemunkasho, 'A Verse-Homily Attributed to Jacob of Edessa: On Faith and Contra Nestorius,' in G. Y. Ibrahim and G. A. Kiraz, eds., *Studies on Jacob of Edessa* (Piscataway, N.J., 2010), pp. 107–141. More generally, for Jacob's polemical writings, see Baumstark, *Geschichte*, p. 254.

[4] Cf., e.g., Jacob of Edessa, *Canons*, Mardin 310, fol. 210a, where he criticizes Christians following 'Jewish observances.' Cp. with Canon 18 in Vööbus ed. and trans., *The Syndicon in the West Syrian Tradition* I [CSCO 367–368: SS 161–162], p. 271 [Syriac] = 246 [ET].

[5] Jacob of Edessa, *Canons*, Mardin 310, fol. 208b (Syriac text in *SBI*, p. 290, n. 683): 'Priests should not say many prayers with incense and draw out and produce prayers like the pagans, standing in opposition to the statement of Our Lord [cf. Matthew 6:7]. Instead, it is enough for them that they say one modest prayer for the edification of the people.' Also see Mardin 310 fol. 212a.

[6] *Questions Which Addai the Priest and Lover of Labors Asked Jacob, the Bishop of Edessa*, Mardin 310, fol. 203a (those who baptize the *nāqushā* are heretics and strangers to the church).

[7] *Questions Which Addai the Priest and Lover of Labors Asked Jacob, the Bishop of Edessa* 46 (ed. Lamy, *Dissertatio*, p. 146). (And see note above).

[8] Kayser, *Die Canones Jacob's von Edessa*, pp. 3–4, on the Armenians (cf. Chapter 4, n. 89).

important, Jacob also had the mysteries. He could punish a Christian who did not meet his expectations ecclesiastically, most dramatically by cutting that person off from the Eucharist, a course of action he frequently prescribed in his canons.[9]

Cutting a person off from the Eucharist was no small thing, either, for this was a world where a major source of religious authority was power—not political, but spiritual power.[10] At the base of and driving the spiritual economy of the seventh century were very concrete, real-life human concerns: anxiety over personal and family health, worry over crops and cattle, apprehension for the safety of travelers, a need for the forgiveness of sins. In the face of forces beyond its control, human finitude reached out for help in coping with the material uncertainties and challenges of life. 'Sleep fled from eyes,' the poet Cyrillona wrote at the end of the fourth century in a poem about invasions, locusts, and other afflictions:

And people abandoned
their homes.
Your churches became
as amphorae
and were filled up by multitudes
without number.
They saw the bow that was drawn,
and the tremors,
and wrath unsheathed
like a sword.
They rushed to take refuge
in baptism,
the people who
had been delaying it.
They came for washing
and received life;
They grasped the cross
and wrath abated.

[9] E.g., Lamy, *Dissertatio*, pp. 108, 136, 142, 148; Kayser, *Die Canones Jacob's von Edessa*, p. 21; Mardin 310, fol. 202b. Cf. Peter Brown's observations on the Council of Macon in Chadwick, *The Role of the Christian Bishop*, p. 44.

[10] Spiritual power might be even more effective than political power: note *Chronicle of Seert* 2.27 (ed. Scher [PO 7.2], p. 71), where Mar Aba writes a letter to the Christians of Jundishapur excommunicating them and ordering them to open the gates of the city to the Khusro's army, which was seeking to put down a rebellion led by his son. When the Christians did as Aba had ordered, the *Chronicle* noted, '[t]he people and Khusro marveled at the excellence of their obedience and their fear of excommunication.'

The king walked together
with the beggar
And begged for mercy
from the Most High.
He abased himself
and set aside his glory;
he wept with a groan
and poured out his tears.[11]

In our period, such dynamics remained unchanged. The *Life* of Theodota of Amid ends with a prayer for those who would come to visit the place of his death after he had passed away. Reportedly composed by Theodota at the end of his life in AD 698, it gives us a vivid picture of the kinds of human needs and worries that ordinary seventh-century Christians faced and that their religious systems had to provide means of effectively confronting and dealing with if those systems were to maintain their plausibility and appeal. 'Grant that person, my Lord,' Theodota asked, on behalf of future pilgrims to his shrine,

> mercies and the forgiveness of sins. And keep his family and his possessions and his crops.
>
> O Lord God, do not hold back this request which I ask of you: that everyone over whom losses arise, or for whom disease falls upon his beasts, or for whom there is illness in his flock or among his bulls or in whatever he possesses, and who then makes a vow and comes in Your name and the name of Your Mother and Your saints and in the name of my frailty makes a vigil, at that point, You, O Lord, cause to pass from his household every chastising rod which is coming against it and cover everything he owns with Your mercy. Bless his possessions that he might thank You, since You have answered him.
>
> O Lord, Our Lord, do for me this favor: that everyone who has a fever or the shivers or who has a throbbing head, and who comes into the presence of Your saints and who makes a vigil and who prays in Your name and in my name: Grant him that he goes away sound and rejoicing.
>
> Yes, O God! My Lord, grant me this request which I have asked from Your mercy and grant, O Lord, that I be mighty against the demons and after my departure from here, drive away the evil spirits from all those who are sealed with the sign of Your cross. And as for everyone who has a demon and calls

[11] Cyrillona, *On the Scourges*, ln. 476–503 (ed. and trans. C. Griffin, *The Works of Cyrillona* [Piscataway, N.J., 2016], pp. 176–79; I have used the translation of Griffin). On this poem, see Griffin, *Cyrillona: A Critical Study and Commentary* (Piscataway, N.J., 2016), pp. 179–230.

Your holy name and my name, cleanse him, O Lord, and let him go away from my body parts set free from servitude to Satan.

O Lord, it is in You that I have sought refuge. Grant me what I have asked of You, that every household or village or region may offer a Eucharist for Your holy name and for mine. Hold back from them hail and locusts and worms and blight and heat and disease and every kind of wrath, unto the ages. Amen.

Yes, O Lord God, do this favor for me: that everyone who goes out into a foreign land and everyone who travels in the road and is violently attacked and falls into the hands of robbers, or over whom waves rise in the sea or who is thrown in jail and who makes a vow and who comes and makes a vigil in Your name and in the name of the saints who are placed here in my contemptible name: Grant him his request, whatever he asks of You, and give him refuge in Your abundant mercy.[12]

Reading through Jacob's canons make clear that there was a widespread perception, among both clergy and laity, that the Eucharist and church ritual had enormous power to affect and deal with precisely the sorts of worries and trials that Theodota names in his prayer. The person who had control over these things would have control over a great deal. The state had only the power to kill the body, but a Christian priest, armed with the sacraments, had power to heal the body and deliver it from hell. In other words, even though Jacob may have lacked the power of the state to enforce his beliefs, he nevertheless had considerable means at his disposal for shaping the behavior of the Christian laity, so long as he maintained authority over the administration of the Eucharist.

Many of the practices we will observe later in this book—practices like proclaiming a young virgin to be the mother of a locust, or making the walls of a home out of bull dung[13]—had as their object dealing with precisely the sorts of problems outlined in Theodota's prayer. Though these particular practices were undertaken by Christians, they did not necessarily employ Christian symbols. The Eucharist and other channels of the sacred available to the Christian clergy, however, offered a rich field of possibilities for combating precisely the same sorts of afflictions with explicitly Christian resources. And unsurprisingly, we can see from Jacob's canons that the Eucharist and other Christian

[12] St Mark's Jerusalem 199, fols. 562a–62b. For the Syriac, see Mardin 275/8, pp. 586–88 (the Syriac is lacunose).

[13] For the case of the locust, see Chapter 9, n. 39. For bull dung, see *Questions Which Addai the Priest and Lover of Labors Asked Jacob, the Bishop of Edessa* 42 (ed. Lamy, *Dissertatio*, p. 140): 'Addai: Concerning those who take refuge in the dung of bulls and make it into walls for their houses for the protection and deliverance of their belongings from sickness. Jacob: Such people are with the worshippers of impurity.'

means of mediating the sacred were employed in a number of different settings as weapons against undesirable realities—things like locusts, drought, sickness, or the inability to have children.

The Eucharist in particular had apotropaic power. People took its elements, tied them up into knots, and used them as amulets. They wore them on their bodies like phylacteries; or even around their necks, along with the cross or with the bones of saints. For protection, they would place the sacred elements in beds, in the walls of houses, in vineyards, in gardens, and other places for physical protection. And practices such as these were not confined to a supposedly superstitious and ignorant laity, either. Jacob made provisions for the punishment of both clergy and lay people who engaged in them; all persons who did such things were to be held back from communion for a period of at least three years.[14] Eucharists might be celebrated in a wide variety of places, as Addai asked, '[Is it] appropriate for a Eucharist to be offered up on a mountain or in vineyards or in gardens or in sheep and goat folds, for the protection of these things?' Jacob's answer was nuanced: 'On a mountain—if it this is necessary,' he wrote,

> it is not forbidden and moreover, there is nothing blameworthy in a Eucharist being celebrated on behalf of believers who are in need of it. But as for in vineyards and fields or in [enclosures] for beasts that do not speak—goats or sheep or cattle or horses—if it is for the sake of a gathering of believers who are found there that the Eucharist is celebrated, nothing prohibits that this take place, just as in chapels, the holy ones of God are separated off. But if [the Eucharists are celebrated] for the protection of speechless things which are nearby, although those who are doing this are doing it in faith, I do not judge that it is appropriate nor do I permit that it take place because, as I have stated, the celebration of these holy mysteries is for the sake of the salvation of souls—of those who are alive and of those who have passed away—and it is not for the protection of cattle or the healing of speechless animals, even if when celebrating the mysteries, we supplicate God, who cares for the living, even for the protection of livestock and for the fruitfulness of the harvest.[15]

Just being placed in close proximity to the Eucharist was enough to give an object a special charge of healing power. 'Water or oil which is placed under the Table of Salvation in faith while the Mysteries are being celebrated,' Jacob

[14] *Questions Which Addai the Priest and Lover of Labors Asked Jacob, the Bishop of Edessa* 9 (ed. Lamy, *Dissertatio*, pp. 106, 108. NB: This printing contains errors; for a corrected version and English translation, see *SBI*, p. 293, n. 689).

[15] *Questions Which Addai the Priest and Lover of Labors Asked Jacob, the Bishop of Edessa* 11 (ed. Lamy, *Dissertatio*, p. 110, 112).

wrote, 'is not forbidden from being given for the healing of the sick when they request it. The same holds also for the dirt of the altar—but for drinking and eating and not that they place it upon themselves or sprinkle it on their beds or cribs or on top of their possessions.' Neither was it permitted to put such things in the walls of houses or in beds.[16] People were requesting permission to take portions of the Eucharist back to their houses; Jacob, however, would only allow this if the elements were being taken to a sick person there. If a sick person was in need of the Eucharist, cabbage leaves, grape leaves, or pieces of bread might be used to carry it; afterwards, these things could be eaten as one way of disposal. Eating the Eucharist itself, Jacob noted, was helpful for healing both soul and body.[17] Another strategy for dealing with illness was to uproot a certain thorny plant called the *genneshyā* in the name of a sick person and offer him the Eucharist while reciting Psalms. This was apparently being done by priests and monks, in addition to laypeople.[18] People tried to get hold of pieces of the Eucharistic bread before it had been consecrated and offered up in a church service; there seems to have been a belief that even bread with a consecration in its future had power: 'Should a person be given a portion (κολλύρα) of the bread that has been brought into the sanctuary before a Eucharist has been offered up from it?' Addai asked. As he almost always did, Jacob answered in the negative.[19]

The power of the Eucharist extended beyond the earthly sphere of behavior: it was believed to be able to affect the saints and people who were now departed. The Quinisext Council forbade giving the sacraments to dead bodies.[20] 'I want to find out about a priest,' Addai asked Jacob, 'who places the Eucharist next to the holy bones of martyrs, inside their urn (γοῦρνα), so that they do not work or show a miracle at his error when he is brought before them and takes an oath on them.'[21] Some people went so far as to believe that the bones

[16] Kayser, *Die Canones Jacob's von Edessa*, p. 14. See also *Questions Which Addai the Priest and Lover of Labors Asked Jacob, the Bishop of Edessa* 12 (ed. Lamy, *Dissertatio*, p. 112). ET of both these texts available in *SBI*, p. 295, n. 691.

[17] *Questions Which Addai the Priest and Lover of Labors Asked Jacob, the Bishop of Edessa*, Mardin 310, fols. 196a-197b (Syriac text and an ET in *SBI*, p. 295, n. 692). Also see Lamy, *Dissertatio*, p. 110. Kayser, *Die Canones Jacob's von Edessa*, p. 13, has a slightly different version, an ET of which can be found in *SBI*, p. 295, n. 692. For the Eucharist as healing both body and soul, see Lamy, *Dissertatio*, p. 112.

[18] *Questions Which Addai the Priest and Lover of Labors Asked Jacob, the Bishop of Edessa* 38 (ed. Lamy, *Dissertatio*, p. 136). ET available in *SBI*, p. 296, n. 693).

[19] *Questions Which Addai the Priest and Lover of Labors Asked Jacob, the Bishop of Edessa*, Mardin 310, fols. 199a–b. The Syriac text and full ET in *SBI*, p. 296, n. 694.

[20] Council in Trullo, *Canons* 83 (ed. Joannou, *Discipline générale antique*, vol. 1.1, p. 220; ET by H.R. Percival in *NPNF*, ser. 2, vol. 14 [New York, 1905], p. 401). Cf. also John Chrysostom, *In epistulam i ad Corinthos argumentum et homiliae* 40.1 (PG 61, col. 347).

[21] *Questions Which Addai the Priest and Lover of Labors Asked Jacob, the Bishop of Edessa* 20 (ed. Lamy, *Dissertatio*, p. 122). See also Mardin 310, fol. 199a, the Syriac text of which is in *SBI*, p. 297, n. 696.

of saints that healed the sick would stop their curative work if a Eucharist were celebrated in the sanctuary where they were stored; this was a view that Jacob rejected.[22] The Eucharist also was reputed to have the power of warding off demons. Anastasius of Sinai wrote of a woman who, attacked by an unclean spirit while passing through a filthy location reacted with equanimity: in her hand, she was carrying a piece of the Eucharist. She stretched forth her palm and opened it up and the demon sped off as soon as he saw what she was holding.[23]

By their association and contact with the Eucharist, other elements in the church might acquire powers as well. These powers might be curative and could help combat physical pain. Addai asked, whether it was

> appropriate for a priest to carry to a sick person, to his house, an empty holy chalice so that he can press it into his side for him because it is hurting him? Or [can he bring] the wrapping [ζωνάριον] of the Holy Table so that it can bind up [a woman] who is in distress with the pains of birth. Or [can he bring] the precious book of the holy Gospel?[24]

The Eucharist might be used to help animals and not just humans: Addai wanted to know 'whether it [was] right for the clergy to place the refuse of the sanctuary and the sweepings in a cistern of water from which animals drink.'[25] Water poured into the chalice after communion to clean it out was seen as possessing the Blood of God, as was anything else that might fall into the cup before it had been cleaned with a sponge.[26]

The view that the Eucharist and other sacred Christian objects had special power was of course not unique to Jacob. The Chalcedonian Anastasius of Sinai, Jacob's exact contemporary, recounted a number of similar stories where this can also be seen. For instance: A man who had been put in charge of the prison in Babylon (in Egypt) told him that among his prisoners were some sorcerers. He would visit them in private and interview them, writing down and passing information from them to his superiors. At one point, the oldest

[22] *Questions Which Addai the Priest and Lover of Labors Asked Jacob, the Bishop of Edessa* 21 (ed. Lamy, *Dissertatio*, pp. 122, 124). See also Mardin 310, fol. 199a.

[23] Anastasius of Sinai, *Narrations Beneficial for the Soul* II.4 (ed. A. Binggeli, 'Anastase le Sinaïte: récits sur le Sinaï et récits utiles à l'âme. Édition, traduction, commentaire [PhD diss., Paris, 2001], 1.222 [Greek] = 2.534 [French] [= C-2 in S. Heid, 'Die C-Reihe erbaulicher Erzählungen des Anastasios vom Sinai im *Codex Vaticanus Graecus* 2592,' *OCP* 74 [2008], p. 80]).

[24] *Questions Which Addai the Priest and Lover of Labors Asked Jacob, the Bishop of Edessa*, Mardin 310, fol. 198a. Syriac text and full ET in *SBI*, p. 298, n. 699.

[25] *Questions Which Addai the Priest and Lover of Labors Asked Jacob, the Bishop of Edessa*, Mardin 310, fols. 198a–b. Syriac text and full ET in *SBI*, p. 298, n. 700.

[26] Jacob of Edessa, *Canons*, Mardin 310, fols. 210a–b (For Syriac text and translation see SBI, p. 238, n. 562).

of the sorcerers pulled him aside in private and advised him to take precautionary measures: 'Never sit down,' he warned him, 'to examine us four sorcerers unless you have first taken communion and are wearing a cross around your neck. For the others are evil people and want to hurt you, but if you do as I have told you, neither they nor anybody else can injure you.'[27] Anastasius himself and some associates healed an Armenian afflicted with an evil spirit by forcibly hanging a silver cross with a piece of the True Cross in it around the tormented man's neck.[28] Another story recounts that before he was burned, a Jewish sorcerer named Daniel admitted that his spells never had any power over Christians who took communion every day.[29] When the devil sought to do harm to another monk, his point of attack was the Eucharist: he planted doubt in the monk's mind as to whether the bread and wine of the Eucharist was the actual Body and Blood of Christ. Persuaded, the monk stayed in his cell and did not attend the liturgy to communicate.[30] John of Bostra, a chartularius from Damascus interviewed four demon-possessed young women in the region of Antioch. 'What things do you fear from Christians?' he asked them.

> They said to him, 'In truth, you have three great things: One, which you wear around your necks; one, where you are washed in the church; one, which you eat in the church service.' John the servant of Christ then perceived that they had spoken about the precious Cross, and concerning Holy Baptism and about

[27] Anastasius of Sinai, *Narrations Beneficial for the Soul* II.14 (ed. Binggeli, 1.235 [Greek]= 2.550 [French] [= §48 in F. Nau, ed., 'Le texte grec des récits utiles à l'âme d'Anastase (le Sinaïte),' *OC* 3 (1903), p. 68; French summary available in idem, 'Les récits inédits du moine Anastase. Contribution à l'histoire du Sinai au commencement du VIIe siècle (traduction française),' *Revue de l'institut catholique de Paris* 1 (1902), p. 140]).

[28] Anastasius of Sinai, *Narrations Beneficial for the Soul* II.5 (ed. Binggeli, 1.223 [Greek] = 2.535 [FT] [= §45 in Nau, ed., 'Le texte grec des récits utiles à l'âme d'Anastase (le Sinaïte),' pp. 65–66; French summary in Nau, 'Les récits inédits du moine Anastase,' pp. 138-139]). ET available in D. Caner, *History and Hagiography from the Late Antique Sinai* (Liverpool, 2010), p. 196.

[29] Anastasius of Sinai, *Narrations Beneficial for the Soul* II.16 (ed. Binggeli, 1.238 [Greek] = 2.553 [FT] [= §50 in Nau, ed. 'Le texte grec des récits utiles à l'âme d'Anastase (le Sinaïte),' p. 70; French summary in Nau, 'Les récits inédits du moine Anastase,' pp. 141–42]). According to Anastasius, this story took place about the same time as the one before it, which happened ten years before the Arab conquest of Cyprus.

[30] Anastasius of Sinai, *Narrations Beneficial for the Soul* 52 (ed. Nau, 'Le texte grec des récits utiles à l'âme d'Anastase (le Sinaïte),' pp. 75–77; summary in Nau, 'Les récits inédits du moine Anastase,' pp. 144–45]). A subsequent vision from God during a church service convinces the monk that the bread and wine actually are the Body and Blood of Christ and the doubt is banished. NB: Though it was not attributed to Anastasius, Nau nevertheless edited this story as part of Anastasius' *Narrations Beneficial for the Soul.* For its attribution to Theophilus of Alexandria, see *CPG*, vol. 2, p. 131 (CPG 2666). Bingelli did not edit this story as part of his edition of the *Narrations*; see his discussion of Nau's edition in 'Anastase le Sinaïte,' p. 166.

> Holy Communion. He asked them again, saying, 'Then which of these three things do you fear most?' Then they answered him and said: 'In truth, if you observe properly when you communicate, none of us has power to injure a Christian.'[31]

In Anastasius's world, a church building itself might even have power, as we learn from a story he heard from an elderly monk in Jerusalem. There was a layman who was constantly sitting in the portico of the Church of the Resurrection, though he spent his time neither begging nor praying. At a certain point, the monk came and sat by the man and asked him why he was there. 'In truth, my Lord and Father,' the man told the monk, 'on account of my sins. I am a sorcerer, and lest I suffer disturbance from the demons, I always flee for refuge to the Holy Anastasis. A demon would not dare to enter the gate of the portico and trouble me, but I always see them standing outside, waiting for me.'[32]

The Eucharist was of course the most important ritual and mystery in the church—it was this rite that some people were apparently taking as paradigmatic, conforming all other church rituals to it, to Jacob's chagrin: "It is not right for uneducated people who love conflict,' he wrote

> to seek that the other, holy and sacramental parts of the services be organized in the figure and according to the canons of the consecration of the holy Eucharist and in the likeness of what is arranged in it. They should rather know that each part has an ecclesiastical ordering and an ancient tradition of the church. Each has been set down and arranged in a particular and separate and distinct way and not all of them have the same content. The things of the Eucharist are in a certain manner, and the things of baptism are in a separate and particular manner. In this way, the things of the Holy Myron [sc. the oil used to anoint at Baptism] are therefore [to be] in a distinct and different manner.[33]

But it was not just the Eucharist that might be used for health or to ward off unwanted evils: baptism was a potent tool as well. Addai wanted to know 'whether it [was] appropriate for a priest to give some of the waters of baptism after the candidates are baptized to women for them to put in their houses for

[31] Anastasius of Sinai, *Narrations Beneficial for the Soul* II.20 (ed. Binggeli, 1.250 [Greek] = 2.565 [FT] [= §53 in Nau, ed., 'Le texte grec des récits utiles à l'âme d'Anastase (le Sinaïte),' pp. 78–79; brief French summary in Nau, 'Les récits inédits du moine Anastase,' p. 144]).

[32] Anastasius of Sinai, *Narrations Beneficial for the Soul* II.6 (ed. Binggeli, p. 1.224 [Greek] = 2.536–537 [FT] [= §46, ed. Nau, 'Le texte grec des récits utiles à l'âme d'Anastase (le Sinaïte),' p. 66; French summary in Nau, 'Les récits inédits du moine Anastase,' p. 139]).

[33] Jacob of Edessa, *Canons*, Mardin 310, fols. 211a–b. Syriac text in *SBI*, p. 301, n. 708.

healing or for the purposes of sprinkling.'[34] There was apparently a notion current that the power baptism conferred might extend to nonhuman objects. The wooden clapper known as the *nāqushā*—or 'semantron'—might have the sacrament administered to it. Addai asked about 'those who baptize the wood of the *nāqushā* in the waters of baptism.' Jacob's response was scathing:

> If those who [have] the audacity to do this foul thing—to dip insentient wood in the water of baptism and make the Christian mystery a laughingstock—belonged to our household, there would have been something to say. But since they are heretics and strangers to the church, 'what do I have to do with judging outsiders'? [1 Cor. 5:12][35]

This baptism was not simply for the sake of baptism, however. There was a human purpose in mind: Addai wanted to know 'whether it [was] appropriate for us to strike the *nāqushā* and to bring out the cross and the consecrated elements against a hail cloud.'[36] Here, Jacob showed a bit more latitude: 'Those who baptized the *nāqushā* baptized it on account of this,' he wrote,

> so that they can put the clouds to flight, as they say, when they strike it. Believers, however, who strike a *nāqushā* against a hail cloud, are not to bring it forth as something that has been baptized, nor as something able to give it flight. Instead, let them bring it out in faith, in order to implore God that he have mercy upon them, and when they [also] bring out the Cross of Christ and the consecrated elements, that they may make supplication with them. Let them also beat the *nāqushā* for this reason: in order to summon the people and for them to be moved to remorse by means of its sound. Therefore, those who do these things in faith are not worthy of reproach.[37]

[34] *Questions Which Addai the Priest and Lover of Labors Asked Jacob, the Bishop of Edessa*, Mardin 310, fol. 198b. Syriac text and full ET in *SBI*, p. 301, n. 709.

[35] *Questions Which Addai the Priest and Lover of Labors Asked Jacob, the Bishop of Edessa* 51 (ed. Lamy, *Dissertatio*, p. 150). This translation is made from Mardin 310, fol. 203a; its Syriac text can be found in *SBI*, p. 301, n. 710. The people here apparently did not belong to Jacob's church—they were presumably Chalcedonians. The fact that Addai asked about their practices can be taken as another indication of cross-confessional awareness in this period. I am grateful to Luke Yarbrough for discussion of this passage with me.

[36] In the medieval West, bells were also seen to be effective in driving away hail and other types of bad weather. See the citation of William Durand (d. 1296) in M. E. Garceau, 'God and his Saints in Medieval Catalunya: A Social History,' (PhD diss., Princeton University, 2009), p. 34, n. 115. I am grateful to Peter Brown for this point. For the use of domestic bells in the West to ward off bad weather, as well as their baptism, see also S. Cheetham's article, 'Bells,' in Smith and Cheetham, eds., *DCA*, vol. 1, pp. 184–86, esp. 185–86.

[37] *Questions Which Addai the Priest and Lover of Labors Asked Jacob, the Bishop of Edessa* 52 (ed. Lamy, *Dissertatio*, pp. 150, 152). This translation is made from Mardin 310, fol. 203a; its Syriac text can be found in *SBI*, p. 302, n. 712.

Aside from baptism and the Eucharist, there were other sacramental elements that might be used as instruments of power. There were priests, for instance, who were using the oil of the Myron—to counter evil spirits: Addai asked 'whether it [was] appropriate for a priest to give the holy Myron to believers who ask, so they can put it in the ear of the person who is afflicted by evil, or that they might anoint him with it.'[38] The 'blessings of saints'—oil that had been in contact with the relics of a holy person—were also being used for defense. Addai asked 'whether it is right for those who at one point took refuge in God and in His saints and brought the blessings of the saints to a field or to a vineyard on account of locusts or worms or scorpions or another scourge, that they fight and drive away the locust or kill the worm or scorpions.' Jacob's response was here again nuanced: 'If it is the case that they do this while doubting the power of God,' he wrote,

> that he is sufficient to help them, they act wickedly and the place of refuge is empty for them and it was not necessary for them to bring the blessings of the saints. If, however, they brought the blessings as people who believe, like diligent and zealous people, and not doubting the power of God, they would have stood as much as possible and driven out the enemy. The act of going out according to their ability and driving away the locust or killing the worms in a vineyard or weevils or scorpions in a field of wheat does not cause loss to their faith or to them, nor does it bring them any sort of reproach. Now if a person says this [sc. that we should bring the blessings of the saints into fields and vineyards to combat locusts, worms, scorpions, etc.], I think we should class him either with the lazy or with those who know and are believers.[39]

The Psalter was another weapon that was in use. 'Concerning a priest who speaks words from the Psalter and [then] hail does not fall on the lands of his village that year,' Addai wanted to know, 'whether it is on his account that it does not fall, or because of chance, and it does not fall because of his decision?' This practice was strongly rejected: 'He himself is not a priest,' Jacob responded,

[38] *Questions Which Addai the Priest and Lover of Labors Asked Jacob, the Bishop of Edessa,* Mardin 310, fols. 198b–99a. Syriac text and full ET in *SBI,* p. 303, n. 714. For Jacob and the Myron, see S. P. Brock, 'Jacob of Edessa's Discourse on the Myron,' OC 63 (1979), pp. 20-36.

[39] *Questions Which Addai the Priest and Lover of Labors Asked Jacob, the Bishop of Edessa,* Mardin 310, fol. 207b. Syriac text also in *SBI,* p. 303, n. 715. Compare this with the report that the East Syrian Abraham of Kashkar (d. 588) gave water he had blessed to residents of a mountain village that was experiencing problems with locusts. The residents poured the blessed water into the water they used to irrigate their lands and the locusts went away. See *Chronicle of Seert* 2.18 (ed. Scher [PO 7.2], p. 42).

> he should be classed with the group which they have just spoken about [i.e., non-Christians]. Now, so that we know the judgment of God, we will answer concerning these things with precision, in the following way: it is not possible. Now perhaps, either there did not chance to be hail there in that year—for it is by all means not the case that every year this takes place—or this was ordained by God when He wanted to send upon them the error upon which they had relied and turn them over to a reprobate mind, as it is written.' [cf. Romans 1:24, 26, 28][40]

Medieval lectionaries contain readings for times of drought,[41] for earthquakes,[42] for famine,[43] for the plague,[44] and for times of God's wrath.[45] There were hymns and prayers that were used on similar occasions.[46] Indeed, we even have a hymn book, copied in 675, likely in the hand of Jacob of Edessa himself, which contains hymns dealing with divine wrath and suffering and hymns for times of drought.[47]

In short, the power residing in holy, divinized materials was believed to function apart from the ecclesiastical settings that defined these materials and gave them their original meaning. These items were being repurposed and they were being used outside of their original cultic and sacramental contexts. And although Jacob condemned most such uses of the Eucharist and other sacred items as tools to cope with forces beyond human control, these were nevertheless *Christian* responses, which had a place on one part of the spectrum of responses available to people living in the seventh century. We get a brief

[40] *Questions Which Addai the Priest and Lover of Labors Asked Jacob, the Bishop of Edessa* 37 (ed. Lamy, *Dissertatio*, p. 136). See also, Kayser, *Die Canones Jacob's von Edessa*, p. 21: 'And a priest who speaks words from David [i.e., the Psalter] so that hail not fall on a field is one who leads astray.' Mingana Syriac 281, written around AD 1780, is a Psalter that was apparently used for a variety of similar purposes. See its description in A. Mingana, *Catalogue of the Mingana Collection of Manuscripts*, vol. 1 (Cambridge, 1933), col. 550.

[41] E.g., BL Add. 14,492 (East Syrian, written in AD 862), no. 36 (*CBM*, vol. 1, p. 179); BL Add. 12,139 (West Syrian, written in AD 1000), no. 49; BL Add. 17,923 (East Syrian, perhaps written in AD 1074), no. 157 (*CBM*, vol. 1, p. 187); BL Add. 14,491 (East Syrian, repaired in AD 1089), no. 52 (*CBM*, vol. 1, p. 181).

[42] E.g., BL Add. 14,491, no. 55 (*CBM*, vol. 1, p. 181) and BL Ad. 14,492 (East Syrian, written in AD 862), no. 37 (*CBM*, vol. 1, p. 179).

[43] E.g., BL Add. 17,923, no. 159 (*CBM*, vol. 1, p. 187).

[44] E.g., BL Add. 17,923, no. 160 (*CBM*, vol. 1, p. 187).

[45] Cf. e.g., BL Add. 12,139 (no. 50) (*CBM*, vol. 1, p. 157).

[46] E.g., BL Add. 12,148 (West Syrian service book, written in 1007) no. 19, which contains an 'order of hymns and prayers, in time of wrath and scarcity of rain' (for Wright's description, see *CBM*, vol. 1, p. 265).

[47] BL Add. 17,134 (West Syrian, written in AD 675) 28a (hymns for times of suffering), 28b (hymns for drought). See *CBM*, vol. 1, p. 334 for references to these hymns and pp. 330–39 for a description of the manuscript.

sense of some of the non-Christian options that also were available when Addai asks, somewhat cryptically, about 'those who make wild animals not eat from their vineyards and feral beasts not take from their cattle.' Jacob's response was harsh: 'Such people are condemned,' he wrote,

> and strangers to the Church. They have done this having relied on demons to shut the mouths of the animals. Indeed, they [demons] also are in reality eager to show that they help those who have gone astray after them in these things which they have relied upon them for.[48]

Those who were doing such things likely did not see themselves as relying on satanic power to secure their desired ends; important for us here, however, is the point that whatever it was such people were doing seems to have made use of resources that were explicitly Christian to produce the desired effects.

Christian sacred objects and symbols were being used—however improperly, by Jacob's lights—to try to achieve good purposes. But they might also be used intentionally to commit evil. Addai gives the example of two men,

> neither one of whom knows incantations or how to write or read, when they have a dispute and make noise and come to the point of great enmity, and one of them goes and draws lines[?] on the reliquaries of the saints and the tomb of the lepers in the name of his enemy, and also under the table of the altars in sanctuaries and hands him over[?] there and he becomes sick and gets injured or is afflicted by evil: if this is the case, will he get sick? If it happens, will he get ill or will something evil happen to him?

Jacob's response was lengthy, but he granted that this might in fact happen, due to God's permitting demonic activity: 'At one point,' he wrote,

> people who gave themselves to error and who, having walked in all waywardness, went astray from the truth and from the path which is straight and well-trod, made themselves strangers to God and to his worship. But we have learned from the Holy Apostle that we are not to judge those who are outside (cf. 1 Cor. 5:12), therefore we shall gladly leave things such as these and the affairs of these people and we will not even mention their names on our lips, nor their deeds. Now, if someone among the believers is found to be doing these things, let him be judged like one who practices auguries, and let him be condemned like a murderer, on account of the fact that he [sc. his target] might be injured. This

[48] *Questions Which Addai the Priest and Lover of Labors Asked Jacob, the Bishop of Edessa* 46 (ed. Lamy, *Dissertatio*, pp. 144, 146). NB: Lamy, p. 144, n. 2, notes that the manuscript reads حخدمي but that he has corrected it to هخبمي at the beginning of Addai's question. I have preferred the original reading here.

> [is a possibility], I will say, because the demons are fighting at all times and against everything in order to carry out what they have taught and God, for His part, often lets humans, for the sake of their benefit, be chastised by means of the evil of others, and He will pronounce that which is precisely in accord with His laws—the righteous destruction of those who have done evil according to His just and incomprehensible judgements—while we do not pry into things which are above us. [49]

Anastasius of Sinai has left us a report about a priest in Cyprus, in the late 630s, who became a sorcerer and went so far in his depravity as to eat with unchaste women and sorcerers, using patens and other vessels employed in the Eucharist. Unlike in Addai's case, where God permitted this abuse, it would appear that in this instance the limits of divine toleration had been reached. Put on trial by church authorities for his gross abuses, the priest acknowledged that once he became a sorcerer (φάρμακος), an angel from God would bind him to a pillar and the angel himself would celebrate the Eucharist and administer it to the people, only letting the priest go once the service had been completed.[50]

The Eucharist and the vessels used to administer it were treated with all the care that radioactive material today receives. Theodota of Amid's *Life* records with admiration how, having caught the already-communicated Eucharistic elements after they had been vomited out—along with other food—by a sick woman, the holy man bowed and took them again.[51] The same extreme veneration for the Eucharist and anything associated with it comes through in Jacob's canons. Cautious to make sure that it was being handled appropriately, Addai asked him many questions. Could a layman or a woman take the Eucharist out of the paten with their own hand because of the vessel's weight and depth and the priest not being close by to give the element?[52] I have already mentioned the use of cabbage leaves, grape leaves, and pieces of unblemished bread to carry the Eucharist outside of the sanctuary. We know that this was

[49] *Questions Which Addai the Priest and Lover of Labors Asked Jacob, the Bishop of Edessa,* Mardin 310, fols. 207a–b. Syriac text also in *SBI,* p. 304, n. 717; I am unsure about some parts of this translation. Hoyland, *Seeing Islam,* p. 602, interprets *neḥrūq ḥerqē* to mean 'determines curses.'

[50] Anastasius of Sinai, *Narrations Beneficial for the Soul* II.15 (ed. Binggeli, 1.236-237 [Greek] = 2.551–52 [FT] [= §49 Nau, ed., 'Le texte grec des récits utiles à l'âme d'Anastase (le Sinaïte),' pp. 69–70; French summary in Nau, 'Les récits inédits du moine Anastase,' p. 141]). This story is supposed to have taken place about ten years before the Arab conquest of Cyprus.

[51] St Mark's Jerusalem 199, fol. 551a. For the Syriac, see Mardin 275/8, p. 507.

[52] *Questions Which Addai the Priest and Lover of Labors Asked Jacob, the Bishop of Edessa* 3 (ed. Lamy, *Dissertatio,* p. 100). Jacob responded, 'It is right for them to take the pearl of the mystery from the paten and place it in their mouth; [for] look! it is by no means the case that those who have done this have done something [belonging to] the priesthood.'

done because Addai had asked Jacob whether it was acceptable to do so. According to Jacob, it was; people would also use writing materials or clean cloths to convey the Eucharist to the sick, who presumably could not make it to church. After their use to carry the elements, these things were burned. If the cabbage leaf was not eaten afterward, it was to be burned as well.[53] If the Eucharistic wine were accidentally spilled, more drastic measures had to be taken: 'Now some put water on the place,' Jacob noted,

> wishing to flood and clean with it a drop of the holy blood which has fallen, but others place burning coals on the spot, eager to dry it up. It is, however, neither the former nor the latter [which should be done]. They have not been able to remove the holy drop from the place. Indeed, their aim was that it not be stepped upon; therefore, better than these [options] would be for that spot to be scraped, if possible with a knife—it would be more suitable—and then let it be placed either in fire or in another location. But if it is not possible [to do this], let these other alternatives [sc. pouring water or placing burning coals on the spot] take place, it being known that the power of the sacred elements is not being stepped upon and not being despised and that it does not attach to the floor, but rather to the souls of believers.[54]

A priest carrying the Eucharist from one place to another was not allowed to put it in a bag on a beast of burden and then ride on top of it; he was supposed to carry it on his shoulder.[55] Dirt and sweepings from the sanctuary were to be buried in a field or perhaps put into a cistern of water from which only humans would drink; Jacob opposed the practice I have already mentioned of placing them in a cistern from which animals drank.[56] A priest who had the audacity to throw a consecrated host that had grown moldy into a cistern of water was to be deposed. The water of the cistern was to be kept and only used as a source of drink for believers. After the water was all gone, the mud in the cistern was to be taken out and buried in a clean spot in a field.[57] Altars were even more precious. 'Regarding altars which have been broken up, in whatever way,' Jacob wrote, 'if there is a certain portion of them or a spot

[53] *Questions Which Addai the Priest and Lover of Labors Asked Jacob, the Bishop of Edessa* 10 (ed. Lamy, *Dissertatio*, p. 110). See also Mardin 310, fols. 196a–96b; and Kayser, *Die Canones Jacob's von Edessa*, p. 13.

[54] Mardin 310, fols. 201b–202a. Syriac text and full ET also in *SBI*, p. 306, n. 722.

[55] Kayser, *Die Canones Jacob's von Edessa*, p. 13. Full ET available in *SBI*, p. 307, n. 723

[56] *Questions Which Addai the Priest and Lover of Labors Asked Jacob, the Bishop of Edessa*, Mardin 310, fols. 198a–98b (and see n. 25 in this chapter). Compare this practice of burying with the report that 'Uthmān buried alternate codices of the Qur'ān between the Prophet's tomb and the minbar in Medina in Ibn Abī Dāwūd, *Kitāb al-maṣāḥif*, p. 34.

[57] Mardin 310, fol. 198b. Syriac text and full ET also in *SBI*, p. 307, n. 725.

which has not been broken, let them be thoroughly and finely broken up and deeply buried in the earth with care so that they will not be uncovered.'[58] Jacob was even concerned about what would be done with the material from which a chalice was made in the event it broke. Addai asked '… whether priests should sell the glass of holy chalices which have broken, or whether people should form pots (καλδάρια) from the tin of the cups? Jacob would brook no such thing. 'Not one of these things should take place,' he wrote.

> Instead, the glass of chalices which have been broken should be again finely broken up and buried deeply in the earth. As for tin, let it be given to Christian craftsmen and let them rework it for the same service of the sacred elements. But it is not lawful for a person to make [something] of it [sc. the tin] for some other human use. The one who dares to do [this] will receive an ecclesiastical rebuke, for Moses did not permit the bronze of the censers of Dathan and Abiram—though they were wicked men and enemies of the commandments of God—to be for a human use, but instead he ordered that an altar be made from it and that it be placed in the house of the Lord, inasmuch as that bronze had already been consecrated when those wicked men acted insolently and rose up audaciously before the Lord in order to burn incense [cf. Numbers 16:37–38].[59]

An altar even had the ability to sanctify images of pagan gods. 'There are people,' Jacob wrote,

> who, only looking upon the beauty of the fabrics and the excellence of the image on them, make from them coverings for the Holy Table without examination. On the fabrics, however, are found inscribed pagan, repulsive stories of the gods and goddesses of the Greeks, and the image of foul and disgusting interactions which are not to be spoken of. It has happened that these things—which it is not appropriate for Christians to look upon—have been found to be made into coverings for the Holy Altar. Now I myself have seen this repugnant thing on the Holy Table, and with difficulty, I persuaded those who owned it to tear it up and bury it in the earth. From this experience, I have come to the point of writing these things to you and of showing that it is not right that there be depicted on the Table upon which Christ—Who brings to an end and wipes out idols and their sacrifices and Who is the purifier of all uncleanliness—idols and their sacrifices and all the pollution and filth of the error of the gods and goddesses of the pagans. Therefore, it is not right that this take place without examination

[58] Mardin 310, fol. 200a. Syriac text and full ET also in *SBI*, p. 307, n. 726.

[59] *Questions Which Addai the Priest and Lover of Labors Asked Jacob, the Bishop of Edessa*, Mardin 310, fols. 201a–b. Syriac text also in *SBI*, p. 308, n. 727.

> and discernment: namely, that on account of the fineness of the fabric and the excellence of the weave and of the image which is on it, it be [used] for the sacred elements, for it is more profitable that the Holy Altar be used without any covering at all than with these things. [60]

What is important here is that even though Jacob had the pagan textile used as an altar covering removed, he also had it buried—in other words, it was given the same disposal as other items that had been associated with the Eucharist.

Other sacred vessels received similar careful treatment. Addai asked about 'vials of marble or glass into which the Myron has been placed, some of which have been broken and some of which are dirty and stale and smell awful, what should happen to them?' Jacob insisted they not be used for any profane purpose:

> . . . if they are broken up and made of glass, let them be buried in the earth with nobody having the audacity to sell some of their glass to glass workers. If they are made of tin or silver, let them be given to Christian craftsmen and they will restore them and re-make them for the use of the holy Myron. If they are not broken, but dirty and rancid and foul smelling, let them be thoroughly washed in the baptismal font and then used for the same purpose.[61]

Similarly, Addai asked about 'the marble containers or vials of blessings—or other vessels—which have either been broken or are dirty, or which are foul and bad-smelling, or the contents of which have completely dried up: What should we do with them?' Jacob insisted that these containers be handled with the utmost care: 'Let the vessels of the blessings of the saints not remain neglected this way in the churches,' he wrote,

> such that, on account of their filthiness or something else which is not good and pleasing, they be a source of shame for Christians. Instead, if they are broken, let them be buried in the earth. If they are intact, let them be washed with diligence in a clean place and let them be [used] for the same thing—either the oil of prayer or for something like this. If a person wants to use them for the holy Myron, nothing prevents this when they have been thoroughly washed. But those [containers] of the Myron should not be used for the blessings of the saints.[62]

[60] Jacob of Edessa, *Canons*, Mardin 310, fols. 208a–b. Syriac text in *SBI*, p. 308, n. 728. (Cp. with Canon 1 in Vööbus ed. and trans. [CSCO 367–68: SS 161–62], p. 269 [Syriac] = 245 [ET]).

[61] *Questions Which Addai the Priest and Lover of Labors Asked Jacob, the Bishop of Edessa*, Mardin 310, fols. 200b–201a: Syriac text in *SBI*, p. 309, n. 729 (cf. Lamy, *Dissertatio*, pp. 130, 132).

[62] *Questions Which Addai the Priest and Lover of Labors Asked Jacob, the Bishop of Edessa*, Mardin 310, fol. 201a. Syriac text in *SBI*, p. 309, n. 729.

As important as all these various items were, however, it was the Eucharist that was preeminent. And given its enormous power, it should come as no surprise that Jacob would be concerned with controlling just who could administer the Eucharist and where it could be taken. This was a charged issue as it also involved holy persons and ascetics and not simply ordinary lay persons. Stylites should not celebrate the Eucharist on their pillars, nor should they convene congregations for the liturgy there.[63] Recluses and solitaries were only allowed to celebrate the Eucharist under extreme circumstances.[64] In accordance with an ancient custom, it was appropriate for God-fearing laymen and chaste women to take the Eucharist to sick people in their homes.[65] It was only lawful for male deacons to put the Body into the cup; female deacons were not allowed to do this. Theirs was to look after sick women.[66] Addai had asked also about people taking the empty chalice into homes or the wrapping (ζωνάριον) of the altar to help combat the physical pain of a sick person or of a woman giving birth; for Jacob this was unacceptable. It was not even appropriate for a sick person to come into church and touch the sacred vessels in an attempt to find a cure. He would, however, permit a priest to take the Gospel into a home and press it against a sick person.[67]

But some people were going too far in restricting access to the Eucharist. Midwives were being kept out of church and prevented from taking the Eucharist after helping women give birth. This was a practice Jacob rejected.[68] Women who had given birth to boys were being kept from church for forty days after delivery; in the case of girls, it was eighty days. Jacob, for his part, ordered that they be allowed into church as soon as they had risen from their beds and washed themselves.[69]

By Jacob's day, Christians had worked out a variety of strategies for dealing with sickness, demon possession, and other difficulties; and non-Christians, too, were aware of the curative resources uniquely available to priests and

[63] Jacob of Edessa, *Canons*, Mardin 310, fol. 209a. Syriac text and ET in *SBI*, p. 310, n. 731. (Cp. with Canon 7 in Vööbus ed. and trans. [CSCO 367–68: SS 161–62], p. 270 [Syriac] = 245 [ET]).

[64] Jacob of Edessa, *Canons*, Mardin 310, fol. 209a. Syriac text and ET in *SBI*, p. 310, n. 732. (Cp. with Canon 8 in Vööbus ed. and trans. [CSCO 367–68: SS 161–62], p. 270 [Syriac] = 245–46 [ET]).

[65] *Questions Which Addai the Priest and Lover of Labors Asked Jacob, the Bishop of Edessa* 9 (ed. Lamy, *Dissertatio*, pp. 106, 108). (cf. n. 14 in this chapter).

[66] *Questions Which Addai the Priest and Lover of Labors Asked Jacob, the Bishop of Edessa*, Mardin 310, fol. 199b: Syriac text and full ET in *SBI*, p. 310, n. 734. Jacob's next responsum, fols. 199b–200a (Lamy, *Dissertatio*, p. 126), enumerates the responsibilities of a deaconess; full ET in *SBI*, n. 734.

[67] *Questions Which Addai the Priest and Lover of Labors Asked Jacob, the Bishop of Edessa*, Mardin 310, fol. 198a.

[68] Jacob of Edessa, *Canons*, Mardin 310, fols. 209b–10a: Syriac text and full ET in *SBI*, p. 311, n. 736. (Cp. with Canon 18 in Vööbus ed. and trans. [CSCO 367–68: SS 161–62], p. 271 [Syriac] = 246 [ET]).

[69] Jacob of Edessa, *Canons*, Mardin 310, fol. 210a: Syriac text and full ET in *SBI*, p. 311, n. 737. (Cp. with Canon 18 in Vööbus ed. and trans. [CSCO 367–68: SS 161–62], p. 271 [Syriac] = 246 [ET]).

holy men. 'It was not only his co-religionists who marveled at his way of life,' Peter the Solitary wrote of Sabrisho' (d. 604),

> which was aided by the good Lord who loves his servants, but also even the pagans (*ḥanpē*) and Jews were amazed at the power that accompanied him. It was possible to see the afflicted from every region frequenting his holy cave to be healed from their sicknesses and to receive the blessing of his blessed right hand and going back in joy, bearing the fruits of the labor of his prayer: the healing of secret and open afflictions.[70]

Similarly, the *Life of Mar Shabbay* reported that 'some of the Magian notables would rush to [Shabbay], not just to be healed and get rid of afflictions, but also to see the wonderful miracles he was proclaiming in the name of Christ. . . .'[71]. Everyone had to grapple with such challenges in his or her life—these were ecumenical concerns, in the broadest sense.[72] In the same vein, we find John of Litarb asking Jacob whether it was appropriate for a Christian priest to give the blessings of the saints or a special mixture of dust and oil called the *ḥnānā* to Hagarenes—that is, Muslims—or to pagans who were afflicted by evil spirits so that they might be healed. By all means, Jacob replied, it was appropriate, very appropriate, that such blessings not be held back from these non-Christians. Let them be given the blessings for whatever sickness. God's granting them healing would be a clear proof of Christianity's truth.[73] The ability to win a religious dispute was one thing; miraculous healing, however, was another and much more persuasive argument for one's confessional position.

GATEKEEPERS TO THE HOLY

Controlling access to the holy could help in nondoctrinal matters as well: Addai wrote to Jacob of a certain priest 'whose house is robbed and who enters

[70] Peter the Solitary, *Life of Sabrisho'*, pp. 296–97 (ed. Bedjan, *Histoire de Mar-Jabalaha*).

[71] *Life of Shabbay* 6 (ed. and trans, S. P. Brock, 'A West Syriac Life of Mar Shabbay (Bar Shabba), Bishop of Merv, ' in D. Bumazhnov, E. Grypeou, T. B. Sailors, and A. Toepel, eds., *Bibel, Byzanz und Christlicher Orient: Festschrift für Stephen Gerö zum 65. Geburtstag* [Leuven, 2011], p. 274 = 266 [English]; the ET used here is that of Brock). Brock, p. 264, suggests that the West Syrian recension of the *Life of Shabbay*, in its present state, dates to some point after the seventh century but also notes that it seems to contain earlier material.

[72] For the interreligious nature of magic bowl use, which provides an interesting comparison, see the comments of S. Shaked, 'Manichaean Incantation Bowls in Syriac,' *JSAI* 24 (2000) pp. 65–66.

[73] Jacob of Edessa, *Letter to John, the Stylite of Litarb*, p. 52 (ed. Rignell). Rignell's ET, p. 53, should be used with caution. For my translation, see *SBI*, p. 312, n. 738. For the *ḥnānā* as a mixture of oil, water, and dust compounded with saints' relics for the purpose of healing, see R. Payne Smith, ed., *Thesaurus Syriacus*, vol. 1 (Oxford, 1879), cols. 1315–16.

into his church and puts out the lamps and overturns the holy table and brings out the sacks of [the relics] of the holy martyrs and hangs them under the sky and sprinkles ash on the urns of the holy martyrs, demanding vengeance from the one who stole his wealth and says: "A lamp will not be lit in church and the altar will not be set right and these saints will not enter in from the rain and the ash will not be cleaned off their urns until they show who despoiled my house."'[74] Although the priest's act was aimed at obtaining help from the saints, he had also effectively set an embargo on the holy in his own village in order to smoke out the thieves. Here is a very vivid and immediate illustration of the sort of leverage that a clergyman could have over his community by exercising his authority over the points where the power of the sacred entered the realm of human existence. Those who held the keys to the Eucharist were gatekeepers who controlled access to the power of the holy.[75]

And the power that the sacraments had was not just temporal—it extended to the next life. Writing around 690, Anastasius of Sinai repeated the story of a priest who, suspended from the liturgy by his bishop, went to a different region, where pagans abused him and cut his head off for being a Christian. When the period of persecution came to an end, the Christians of the region dedicated a church to the priest, and his body was placed in a chest. At the consecration of the church, however, each time the bishop began to say the prayers of the liturgy, the box containing the martyr's body moved out of the church on its own accord. As night was coming on, the martyr appeared to the bishop and made a request: 'Have the goodness to make haste to such-and-such a city, to my bishop, and make him loose me from my penalty, for he banned me from the liturgy and I am unable to minister with you. And while I have taken up the crown of martyrdom, I have nevertheless not seen the face of Christ, on account of my being under excommunication.'[76] In excommunicating a believer, a Christian clergyman had even the power to deny a martyr direct access to Christ in the next life. No secular authority could wield such power.[77]

[74] *Questions Which Addai the Priest and Lover of Labors Asked Jacob, the Bishop of Edessa* 45 (ed. Lamy, *Dissertatio*, p. 144). Full ET available in *SBI*, p. 313, n. 740.

[75] For the use of saints' relics as a means whereby the religious might enforce their will on others in the tenth and eleventh-century medieval West, see P. Geary, 'L'humiliation des saints,' *Annales. Histoire, Sciences sociales* 34 (1979), pp. 27–42. I am grateful to Peter Brown for this reference.

[76] Anastasius of Sinai, *Narrations Beneficial for the Soul* II.27 (ed. Binggeli, p. 1.260 [Greek] = 2.575 [FT] [= §54, in Nau, ed., 'Le texte grec des récits utiles à l'âme d'Anastase (le Sinaïte),' pp. 80–81; quote on p. 81]).

[77] See the story in *Chronicle of Seert* 2.16 (ed. Scher [PO 7.2], pp. 39–40) of a dispute between two women over whether one stole a necklace from the other. A priest was involved and asked to excommunicate the one who had stolen it. He refused, but did make a pronouncement that the Word of God obligated the one who took the necklace to return it. The priest had barely finished making this statement when a mouse appeared with the necklace in its mouth. 'It threw the necklace before them, went

THE SACRAMENTS AND BORDERS

Most important for the question at hand, however, is the power the sacraments had to effect and erect confessional boundaries. If he could exert control over the nodes where the sacred intersected with everyday human life—in the Myron, in the blessings of the saints, and, preeminently, in the Eucharist—Jacob, or any church leader, would have enormous power to enforce their views. After the disciples of Henana of Adiabene, for example, had been defeated by George the Priest in discussions of Henana's doctrines, they were refused the Eucharist in George's community until they had anathematized Henana 'and all his wicked teaching.'[78]

If in trying to understand the nature of Christianity in the centuries after Chalcedon and before the Arab invasions we focus on doctrinal issues, it becomes easy to forget that celebrating the mysteries went to the very heart of the church's institutional mission and to what clergy were called to do. In dealing with new priests, Jacob wrote that a periodeute was to admonish them to honor the mysteries with great care.[79] Moreover, a priest was only permitted to leave the altar to which he had been consecrated in the event of unbearable distress and persecution.[80] But the perceived power of the sacraments made them resistant to confessionalization: as we have just seen, their appeal might even extend to competing religious groups, like Jews, pagans, and Muslims. In fact, later in this book we will find Muslims throughout the medieval period seeking to have their children baptized. Great power, exercised without knowledge, would lead to the confessional chaos I have attempted to identify as one of the central problems confronting the post-Chalcedonian Christian leadership of churches throughout the Middle East.

Priests had to have at least some instruction if they were to know how to properly carry out this central duty. Indeed, 'uneducated' was a term Jacob would use in his canons to explain the occurrence of aberrant behavior and violations of the canons.[81] In the short apocalypse that came at the beginning

off a little distance, split open, and died,' the *Chronicle* reported. 'I have related this marvelous tale,' the anonymous author wrote, 'so that the ignorant will not despise the word of God or the excommunication of priests.' The circulation of stories such as this clearly served to reinforce the seriousness with which excommunication was taken.

[78] Babai the Great, *History of George the Priest*, p. 503 (ed. Bedjan, *Histoire de Mar-Jabalaha*).

[79] Jacob of Edessa, *Canons*, Mardin 310, fol. 208b. Syriac text and full ET in *SBI*, p. 316, n. 742.

[80] Jacob of Edessa, *Canons*, Mardin 310, fol. 208b. Syriac text and ET in *SBI*, p. 316, n. 743. (Cp. with Canon 5 in Vööbus ed. and trans. [CSCO 367–68: SS 161–62], p. 270 [Syriac] = 245 [ET]).

[81] Jacob of Edessa, *Canons*, Mardin 310, fol. 210a (on uneducated and insane priests who keep women out of church after they have birth; see *SBI*, p. 311, n. 737 for text and translation) and Mardin 310, fol.

of Jacob's translation of *The Testament of Our Lord*, the disciples implored Jesus to tell them 'how to administer the Mysteries of the Church.' Because, they continued, 'we want to learn from your word, our Savior and Perfecter, without omission, how the chief of the consecrated elements and all those who serve in Your Church should be pleasing in Your sight.'[82]

Even if Jacob was not the author of this brief apocalypse but had only translated it, the very fact of his rendering of it into Syriac and attaching it to the *Testament of Our Lord* as a sort of preface to a work on canon law points to his recognition that a priest, if he was to administer the sacraments properly, had to be taught just what it was that Jesus had commanded about the Holy Things.[83] And it was here, at the point of instruction and training, that Miaphysites, Nestorians, Chalcedonians, and others might articulate the doctrinal distinctions that differentiated them from other, rival groups. Jesus's response to the disciples in this apocalypse included an emphasis on giving the Eucharist to the proper people:

> See that you do not give my holy things to dogs and do not throw pearls before swine [cf. Matthew 7:6] as I have commanded you many times. Give not my Eucharist [*quddāshā*][84] to degraded and wicked men who do not carry my cross and are not subject (to me). My commandments shall be derided among them and it shall be to him that is embittered and does not do them and answers my words unprofitably for the destruction of their souls.[85]

By cutting a person off from the Eucharist and other mediators of holy power, a church leader could deny access to the most potent tools available to individuals in the seventh century for coping with challenges and scourges outside of normal human control. But exclusion from access to the holy required priests who would agree with the doctrinal views on the basis of which such a decision was made and legitimated, and who would subsequently do the excluding.

A church leader like Jacob could not be in every church at the same time: herein lay the challenge of creating a church that would be distinct, on the

211a (uneducated people who are lovers of dispute [ܐ̈ܢܫܝܢ ܠܐ ܪ̈ܕܝܐ ܘܪ̈ܚܡܝ ܚܪܝܢܐ] are trying to make other rites—e.g., baptism and the consecration of the Myron—conform to the rite of the consecration of the Eucharist; cf. n. 33 in this chapter).

[82] *Testament of Our Lord*, p. 8 (ed. Vööbus [CSCO 367-368: SS 161-162], p. 32 [ET]). My construal is made with reference to that of Vööbus but differs from his.

[83] See Chapter 3, n. 19, on the question of Jacob's authorship of this apocalypse.

[84] Or, *qudshā*: 'holy thing.'

[85] *Testament of Our Lord*, p. 9 (ed. Vööbus [CSCO 367–68: SS 161–62], p. 33 [ET]; the Syriac is somewhat obscure and the translation used here is that of Vööbus with my own alterations). Cf. H.J.W. Drijvers, 'The Testament of Our Lord: Jacob of Edessa's Response to Islam,' *Aram* 6 (1994), p. 113.

ground, in a largely agrarian world with low rates of literacy and even lower rates of theological literacy. How could a church leader control what was going on in the churches under his authority on a day-to-day basis? How could one achieve sacramental discipline in a world of simple believers? As we have already seen, when John the Almsgiver became the Chalcedonian patriarch of Alexandria in the early seventh century, he reportedly changed the liturgy in sixty-three of the city's churches to make it conform to Chalcedonian rather than Miaphysite usage. Such an alteration will have required the cooperation (or replacement) of a large number of local priests—perhaps the reason why his *vita* noted how careful John was to verify the orthodoxy of those whom he ordained.[86]

Doing this in a city like Alexandria would have been challenge enough; how much more difficult, then, to ensure the success of such a venture in rural contexts? In the absence of a chain of authority based on doctrinal consensus, there would likely have been precisely the sort of rampant slippage in implementation that had so exasperated Jacob and driven him to burn the book of canon law and quit his post of bishop. In a world of simple believers, the power of the sacraments eclipsed the importance of disputed theological speculation. But in such a world, as I have suggested, the sacraments could be quite unruly. Without an obedient, trained clergy possessed of a particularly Miaphysite identity and consciousness, there could never be any hope for a truly (sociologically) distinct church.

The creation of a well-defined Miaphysite leadership and clergy therefore required a formation and education that would differentiate them from the clergy of rival communions. Such considerations were critical for Chalcedonians and East Syrians as well: famous stories of Jacob Baradaeus or John of Tella ordaining a Miaphysite clergy in the sixth century assume that the default position of clergy in a place like Syria would have been a Chalcedonian one. But it is not clear that the default position of most village clergy would have been any firm or considered stance on Chalcedon, for or against.

The Eucharist lay at the center of the formation of Christian communities. The shape that those communities took, however, would depend on to whom the priests administering the mysteries chose to give it. In the most concrete, local, and real-life terms, therefore, the lineaments of a particular Christian community were a function of the formation of its priesthood and the decisions its priests made with respect to who participated in a church's sacramental life. We saw in Chapter 1 that, beginning in the sixth century, it was

[86] *Life of John the Almsgiver* 5 (ed. Delehaye, 'Une vie inédite de Saint Jean l'Aumonier,' p. 21; ET available in Dawes and Baynes, *Three Byzantine Saints*, pp. 201–202). Cf. Chapter 1, n. 100.

increasingly common to find some sort of literacy as prerequisite for ordination among various Christian confessions,[87] and this was surely no coincidence: in a world of simple believers, confessionalization, and increasing sectarian contention, education was of fundamental importance for creating and maintaining a distinct church. This was the case because, as have seen in this chapter, one result of the power of the sacraments was an indifference among the simple, both lay and clergy, to disagreements over theological speculation: what was important was the sacrament itself, not the confessional identity of the priest administering it or his bishop. Any explanation of the confessional chaos we encountered in Chapter 3 must include the enormous perceived power of the sacraments as a major factor, in addition to widespread theological illiteracy. An educated clergy was one of the surest ways to counter the sectarian indifference that underlay such chaos. The sacraments were part of the problem, but they could also be part of the solution: having confessionally aware priests was the most effective means to harness the power of the sacraments in the service of forming a distinct Christian community.

Our efforts to understand the ramifications of the fallout from Chalcedon in a world of simple believers lead us, therefore, to the question of schools and the nature of the instruction that took place in them.

[87] Cf. Chapter 1, nn. 86–93.

CHAPTER 6

Competition, Schools, and Qenneshre

We have seen now several features of the post-Chalcedonian landscape of a Middle East populated with simple Christians: confessional indifference and confusion, a variety of types of polemics and controversy, and the importance (and unruliness) of the Eucharist. In this chapter, I want to look at yet another aspect of the world after Chalcedon: the spread of schools.

Before we can understand the spread of Christian schools, however, we must first pause and attempt to understand the intense confessional competition driving their creation. The rivalries underlying this competition were a consequence of the diversity of Christian confessional stances and the incomplete ecclesiastical and communal separation that existed on the ground between various factions. The object of this competition was simple believers, Christians who likely had a poor understanding, if any, of the theological issues separating the various churches and whose confessional allegiance was, consequently, very much up for grabs. Though there were certainly exceptions, it would not be a stretch to suggest that most simple Christians likely cared more about having access to central Christian mysteries—most notably the Eucharist and baptism—than they did about whether their priests held correct beliefs in matters of Christology. Claims made by church leaders that the Holy Spirit did not descend upon heretical altars can be read as an attempt to make communion in rival churches less attractive, though such claims were likely of uneven efficacy.

The existence of large numbers of simple believers has been a feature of Christianity throughout its existence—in the Latin West, for instance, various medieval teachers and leaders discussed the minimum amount the simple needed to believe in order to be saved.[1] But what made the late Roman and early medieval Middle Eastern case different from that of the Latin West in

[1] See N. Tanner and S. Watson, 'Least of the Laity: The Minimum Requirements for a Medieval Christian,' *Journal of Medieval History* 32 (2006), pp. 395–423, esp. 399–403. This idea is not unique to Christianity. Cp., e.g., with the *Kitāb farḍ ṭalab al-ʿilm* of Abū Bakr Muḥammad b. al-Ḥusayn al-Ājurrī (d. AH 360/AD 970), which was about the knowledge that each Muslim was required to have and not permitted to be ignorant of. For a description of this work, see W. Ahlwardt, *Verzeichnis der arabischen Handschriften* [Berlin, 1887], vol. 1, pp. 39–40, and cf. C. Brockelmann, *GAL*, vol. 1, p. 329. Cp. too, L. Lehmhaus, '"Were not understanding and knowledge given to you from Heaven?" Minimal Judaism and the Unlearned "Other" in *Seder Eliyahu Zuta*,' *Jewish Studies Quarterly* 19 (2012), pp. 230–58, for a discus-

the same period was the presence of multiple competing churches, each with its own episcopal hierarchy, monasteries, clergymen, holy men, saints, and claims of continuity with the apostolic past. No other region in the Christian world had the same density of ancient churches and rival claims.

We should not underestimate the powerful effect that this diversity and difference might have. 'There passed by us once,' the East Syrian catholicos Sabrisho' I (sed. 596–604) was reported to have said about an incident early in his life,

> a certain deceiver from the filthy-named heresy of the Marcionites, whose Nazirite clothing professed the appearance of continence and people who were misled, the children of misfortune, were rushing to be 'blessed' by him—according to their foolish supposition—and even a few of the simple believers (*hedyoṭē mhaymnē*) joined them in this fatal allurement concealed in a deadly monastic robe.... I thought to myself: "Whether this stranger to the truth is so completely honored by stupid people or whether a person conducts himself in the true faith according to the law, what honor is not due to God?" And from that day, I put it in my mind to draw near to the life of virtue.[2]

It was the sight of simple believers seeking out the blessing of a holy man whom he himself regarded as heretical that prompted Sabrisho' to set off down a path that culminated in his being the head of the East Syrian Church. In a world where there were many competing claims to *Christian* truth, the confusion that this could cause in certain quarters was something that church leaders had to deal with in order to maintain the integrity of their communities, or, indeed, to achieve communal integrity in the first place.[3]

Christianity is and was a missionary religion and attempts at winning simple believers into one's confession meant that church leaders were constantly in a position of playing both ecclesiastical defense and offense. The most obvious motivation for expanding the size of one's church (in addition to preventing sheep-stealing by opponents) was the conviction that one's communion held the truth. And the truth mattered, not only in this life, but

---

sion of a suggested 'core religion or "minimal Judaism"' that might unify Rabbinic and non-Rabbinic Jews in the early medieval *Seder Eliyahu Zuta*.

[2] Paul the Solitary, *Life of Sabrisho'*, pp. 288–89 (ed. Bedjan, *Histoire de Mar-Jabalaha*).

[3] The challenge of the holy lives of 'heretics' was a problem for church leaders before our period, as well. See e.g., Origen, *Homilies on Ezekiel* 7.3 for his comments on the threat posed by Marcionites and Valentinians whose doctrine was false but whose conduct was exemplary: 'But to my way of thinking,' he wrote, 'the heretic with a good life is much more dangerous.' Through their good conduct, such men could more easily entice people into following their harmful teachings (ed. W. A. Baehrens in M. Borret, *Homélies sur Ezéchiel* [Paris, 1989], pp. 254, 256, 258 [quote at 254]; ET by T. P. Scheck taken from *Origen: Homilies 1-14 on Ezekiel* [New York/Mahwah, N.J., 2010], p. 101).

especially in the next: as John Moschus's story of Cyriacus and Theophanes in Chapter 2 reminds us, there was a belief among (at least some) church leaders that getting the doctrine of the Incarnation wrong potentially meant fire and chastisement in the life to come.[4] Getting the Eucharist right mattered, too. The holy mysteries were celebrated, Jacob stated, for the salvation of souls.[5] The stakes could hardly have been higher.

The Arab conquests of the Middle East in the third and fourth decades of the seventh century had the effect of intensifying interconfessional rivalry by virtue of leveling the competitive playing field. In Syria and Palestine (and Egypt), there was no longer an imperially backed church that had a firm position on Christological questions and that enjoyed an advantage over its rivals: the Roman state was gone, and along with it its distorting effect on ecclesiastical struggles. When we read of Maronites and Miaphysites holding a debate concerning faith before Muʿāwiya in 659,[6] we can ask: would such a dispute have taken place if Syria were still under Roman control and Constans II's *Typos* was in effect, especially if the debate covered the question of the number of wills in the Incarnate Christ? The Miaphysite tradition would later claim that Theodoric, the brother of Heraclius, had planned to carry out a persecution of Miaphysites in Syria if Heraclius were victorious fighting against the Arabs; in fact, a Chalcedonian stylite allegedly guaranteed him victory if he promised to 'wipe out' the followers of Severus.[7] The Arab victory meant that this persecution never happened. Even if these stories are legendary, Arab victory nevertheless certainly put an end to Constantinople's attempts at enforcing doctrinal harmony and conformity in the Middle East. One of the traditional explanations for the end of the Monothelete controversy, we should recall, has been that the loss of the Middle Eastern parts of the Roman Empire meant that separated Miaphysite (and Monothelete) communities were no longer the emperor's problem to solve.

After the Arab conquests, the situation throughout the Middle East returned to what it had been previously for Christians in Sasanian-ruled territories: the various Christian groups now attempted to win the favor and support of non-Christian authorities against their rivals, both within their churches and in competing ones.[8] In the mid-740s, for instance, Theophylact bar Qanbara, the

[4] See Chapter 2, n. 81.

[5] See Lamy, *Dissertatio*, col. 110 and Chapter 5, n. 15.

[6] *Maronite Chronicle*, p. 70 (ed. Brooks [CSCO III.4]).

[7] Michael the Great, *Chronicle* 11.5 (ed. Chabot, 4.415 = 2.418).

[8] Cf. the observation of Hoyland in *Seeing Islam*, p. 179, and, in addition to the examples cited below, see those adduced in Hoyland, 'Introduction: Muslims and Others,' in R. Hoyland, ed., *Muslims and Others in Early Islamic Society* (Aldershot, 2004), p. xvii.

Dyothelete bishop of Harran, was able to get Marwān II to send an army to accompany him to the monastery of Mar Maron, where he attempted to force the monks to accept the doctrine of Christ's two wills and to reject the longer version of the *Trisagion.*[9] Such attempts had been going on since the earliest period of Muslim rule. The East Syrian catholicos Maremeh (sed. 646–649) was said to have been elected on account of his having aided the Muslim army that captured Mosul,[10] and his successor Isho'yahb III (sed. 649–659) was remembered for going every Friday to ask Arab rulers about his affairs and those of the Christians.[11] During Isho'yahb's time as patriarch, we find churchmen with whom he was engaged in disputes making unsuccessful attempts to enlist Arab authorities as help against him[12] and Miaphysites claiming that their missionary success against East Syrian communities had been aided by the 'command' of Arab authorities—a view that Isho'yahb rejected.[13] Another seventh-century catholicos, Henanisho' (sed. 685–699), was said to have had many enemies who sought the help of the Muslim authorities to unseat him; one, called John the Leper, reportedly spent four years lobbying 'Abd al-Malik and his companions against the catholicos, spending money as part of his effort, and finally was able to get the Caliph to depose Henanisho' and name John catholicos in his stead.[14] Muslim rulers played a role in Miaphysite church affairs as well: Patriarch Severus bar Mashqa (sed. ca. 668–684) was remembered for prosecuting the affairs of the church 'with a great deal of harshness,' as Michael the Great reported, 'for he was a severe man and he had power (*ḥaylā*) from the King of the Arabs.'[15]

[9] Michael the Great, *Chronicle* 11.13 (ed. Chabot, 4.467 = 2.511). Cf. Chapter 1, n. 6.

[10] 'Amr b. Mattā, *Akhbār faṭārikat kursī al-mashriq*, p. 62 (ed. H. Gismondi, *De patriarchis nestorianorum: commentaria. Pars Prior: Maris Textus Arabicus* [Rome, 1899]). The authorial attributions of this chronicle are complicated and contested, but I have followed the arguments of B. Holmberg, 'A Reconsideration of the *Kitāb al-Mağdal*,' *PdO* 18 (1993), pp. 255–73 (also cf. M. Swanson in *CMR*, vol. 2, pp. 627–28) and considered 'Amr b. Mattā the author of this work rather than Marī b. Sulaymān, the figure to whom Gismondi attributed it.

[11] 'Amr b. Mattā, *Akhbār faṭārikat kursī al-mashriq*, p. 62 (ed. Gismondi, *Maris textus Arabicus*). For this point about Isho'yahb III, see Hoyland, *Seeing Islam*, p. 182 and Young, *Patriarch, Shah and Caliph*, p. 90.

[12] See the evidence in Young, *Patriarch, Shah and Caliph*, p. 97; Brock, 'Syriac Views of emergent Islam,' p. 16; Hoyland, *Seeing Islam*, p. 178.

[13] Isho'yahb III, *Letters* I.48 (To various monks), p. 97 (ed. Duval [CSCO: Syr. II.64]; p. 73 [=LT]). On this claim and this letter, see, J.-M. Fiey, 'Īšō'yaw le Grand. Vie du catholicos nestorien Īšō'yaw III d'Adiabène (580–659),' *OCP* 36 (1970), p. 31; Young, *Patriarch, Shah and Caliph*, p. 88; Brock, 'Syriac Views of Emergent Islam,' p. 16; Hoyland, *Seeing Islam*, p. 179.

[14] 'Amr b. Mattā, *Akhbār faṭārikat kursī al-mashriq*, p. 63 (ed. Gismondi, *Maris Textus Arabicus*); the entire saga of Henanisho''s deposition and eventual return to power is interlaced with Christians lobbying of Muslim authorities and their intervention into church affairs; it can be found at 63–65; see also Bar Hebraeus, *Ecclesiastical History* 2.29 (ed. Abbeloos and Lamy, vol. 3, cols. 135, 137, 139).

[15] Michael the Great, *Chronicle* 11.13 (ed. Chabot, 4.436 [Syriac] = 2.456 [French]). For the reading

Before the advent of Arab rule, of course, competition between various Christian groups was already a regular feature of the landscape. We have encountered East Syrian figures like Rabban Qusra, Titus of Hdatta, and Jacob of Beth 'Ābe, who were converting pagans and Miaphysites in the sixth century,[16] and it was in this century that Miaphysites apparently tried to win Nuʿmān, the ruler of Hira, over to their confession after he had been healed by the East Syrian catholicos Sabrishoʿ.[17] Clashes and intense competition between the various confessions continued up to the eve of the conquests: the emperor Heraclius's failed attempt at ecclesiastical union in the late 620s meant violence against Miaphysites and the loss of church properties,[18] and the Monothelete controversy would introduce a new split into the region's churches, sundering the Chalcedonian community in two and leading to violence as well.[19]

Both before and after the conquests, Miaphysites were expanding and encroaching on East Syrian communities.[20] The East Syrian Rabban Qusra had made gains for East Syrians among other Christian groups in Nineveh in the late sixth century, but only decades later, we find Ishoʿyahb III berating East Syrian clergy in Nineveh for their complete inaction in the face of Miaphysite missionary activity that has stolen away church members.[21] Even as East Syrians lost ground to Miaphysites in Nineveh, they were gaining elsewhere: Ishoʿyahb III's contemporary, Rabban Sābūr (d. between 648 and 658), for instance, converted the Kurds near the monastery he had built on Mt. Shustar.[22]

Miaphysite conversionary attempts were aimed at Chalcedonians as well. Writing some time before AD 693–694, the East Syrian John bar Penkaye reported that the reign of Muʿāwiya, which began in 661, had ushered in a time of tranquility and peace in northern Mesopotamia and that Miaphysites seized

ḥaylā, cf. G. Y. Ibrahim, *The Edessa-Aleppo Syriac Codex of the Chronicle of Michael the Great* (Piscataway, N.J., 2009), p. 439. For this, see Hoyland, *Seeing Islam*, p. 182, n. 32, and on Severus, see L. van Rompay's article, 'Severos bar Mashqo,' in *GEDSH*, pp. 367–68.

[16] Rabban Qusra, *Chronicle of Seert* 2.40 (ed. Scher [PO 7.2], p. 107); Titus of Hdatta, *Chronicle of Seert* 2.64 (ed. Scher [and Griveau] [PO 13.4], p. 153); Jacob of Beth 'Ābe, *Chronicle of Seert* 2.56 (ed. Scher [and Griveau] [PO 13.4], p. 142). Cf. Chapter 4, nn. 73–75.

[17] Peter the Monk, *Life of Sabrishoʿ*, p. 323 (ed. Bedjan, *Histoire de Mar-Jabalaha*). Cf. also, Chapter 12, n. 58.

[18] Michael the Great, *Chronicle* 11.3 (ed. Chabot, 4.410 = 2.412); cf. Chapter 1, n. 12.

[19] Michael the Great, *Chronicle* 11.20 (ed. Chabot, 4.460–461 = 2.495) describes the violence and separation that occurred among Chalcedonians in Aleppo.

[20] See the material carefully collected in W. Hage, *Die syrisch-jacobitische Kirche in frühislamischer Zeit. Nach orientalischen Quellen* (Wiesbaden, 1966), pp. 81–82.

[21] Ishoʿyahb III, *Letters* I.48 (To various monks), pp. 93–94 (ed. Duval [CSCO: Syr. II.64]).

[22] *Chronicle of Seert* 2.54 (ed. Scher [and Griveau] [PO 13.4], p. 140).

this moment to expand their communion at the cost of Chalcedonians. 'The accursed heretics,' John wrote,

> taking the situation then as beneficial to themselves, instead of converting and baptising the pagans, in accordance with ecclesiastical canons, started on a retrograde (kind of) conversion, turning almost all the churches of the Byzantines to their own wicked standpoint, reviving and re-establishing something that had been overthrown; (as a result) the majority of the Westerners were regularly using (the addition to the Trisagion of) the words, "... immortal, who was crucified for us.' All the churches became like uncultivated land.[23]

By the late seventh century, we have evidence of Miaphysites worried about Chalcedonians making gains of their own. The *Life* of Theodota of Amid reports that Byzantines were attempting to force Miaphysite refugees on the borders between Byzantine and Arab-ruled territories to convert to Chalcedonianism. Theodota, for his part, did his best to combat this. 'He had had the habit,' the *Life* tells us, 'of writing and sending to the region of the fortresses[24] through the intermediary of his disciple, to the needy who were dwelling there, that they might take hold of the faith of Orthodoxy and that the leaders of the heretics not cause them to deviate from the truth through disturbances or threats.' He threatened the Chalcedonian elites who were forcing needy Miaphysite refugees from the Arabs to change confessions in exchange for aid. In return for a promise from these elites that they would not force Miaphysite refugees to convert, Theodota agreed to pray that God would protect them from an Arab military leader whom they feared.[25] And Theodota himself would be involved in bringing heretical Christians in this region to Miaphysite orthodoxy, though not by force. His *Life* reports that on account of reports of Theodota's miraculous activity and his pious behavior, 'many from among the heretics were cleansed.'[26]

The vast amount of controversial literature written during this period points to the antagonism between different Christian groups. And, perhaps more

[23] John bar Penkaye, *Book of the Main Events*, p. *147 (ed. A. Mingana, *Sources Syriaques*, vol. 1 [Leipzig/Mosul, 1908]; ET taken from S. P. Brock, 'North Mesopotamia in the Late Seventh Century: Book XV of John bar Penkāyē's *Rīš Mellē*,' *JSAI* 9 [1987], p. 63; for a date sometime before 693–694, see p. 52).

[24] I am grateful to Asa Eger for identifying this area for me as what he terms the 'Eastern Thughūr,' that is, the area between the Tigris and the Euphrates that included settlements such as Ḥiṣn Qalawdhiya, Ḥiṣn Ziyād, Ḥiṣn Kamkh, and Samosata; on this area, see his *The Islamic-Byzantine Frontier: Interaction and Exchange among Muslim and Christian Communities* (London, 2015), pp. 102–26, esp. pp. 102, 106.

[25] See St Mark's Jerusalem 199, fols. 554a–b. For the Syriac, see Mardin 275/8, pp. 530–32.

[26] See Mardin 275/8, p. 532: ܘܡܢ ܐܪ̈ܛܝܩܘ ܣܓܝܐܐ ܐܬܕܟܝܘ ܠܗܘܢ For the Karshūnī, see St Mark's Jerusalem 199, fol. 554b.

importantly, the small-scale theological debates we saw in Chapter 4 were another manifestation of competition between groups: these were the on-the-ground clashes that must have accompanied proselytory efforts and inroads. In this environment, the advances of rivals were viewed with utmost seriousness. 'Lord, they persecute us, and fall upon us,' the Miaphysites told Khusro I after their theological debate with the East Syrian catholicos and his supporters in the King's presence,

> and spoil us and uproot our churches and monasteries, and do not permit us to offer up in them our prayers and supplications unto God for the establishment and protection of your life and your kingdom.[27]

Several hundred years later, in the period of Muslim rule, things had not changed all that much: the first time Simeon of the Olives built the Church of Mar Theodore in Nisibis, it was destroyed by Nestorians.[28] I have already mentioned Isho'yahb's ire at the Miaphysite construction of a church in Nineveh;[29] the consternation that the act elicited was enough to provoke him into arguing that the end times were upon him and Gabriel, the metropolitan of Kirkuk, the recipient of his letter.[30]

The arrival and growth of new groups meant construction of new church buildings, something that would be met with alarm and the intense lobbying of authorities to permit or hinder such projects. Isho'yahb attributed Miaphysite success in Tikrit in part to the susceptibility of the authorities to 'silver whispers and gilded petitions,'[31] but from Bar Hebraeus we learn that Isho'yahb himself was able to prevent the construction of a Miaphysite church in Mosul through similar means: he 'spent a great sum in bribes which he presented to the rulers, and stopped the construction.'[32] When the attempts of Simeon of the Olives to build the church of St. Theodore in Nisibis were stymied by Nestorian leaders forbidding their members to work on the project, he went to Gawargī of Anḥel, who held authority over all of Ṭūr 'Abdīn, for help. Gawargī was initially skeptical of Miaphysites (presumably because he was a Chalcedonian), but Simeon eventually won him over to his cause by working

[27] John of Ephesus, *Ecclesiastical History* 6.20 (ed. Brooks [CSCO SS III.3], pp. 317–18; ET taken from Payne Smith, *The Third Part*, p. 419, with my alterations).

[28] See Mardin 8/259, fol. 112v.

[29] See Chapter 3, nn. 49, 56.

[30] Isho'yahb III, *Letters* I.44 (To Gabriel), (ed. Duval [CSCO: Syr. II.64] pp. 81–82 = p. 63 [=LT]). For Gabriel as metropolitan of Kirkuk, cf. Fiey, "Īšō'yaw le Grand,' p. 327.

[31] Isho'yahb III, *Letters* I.44 (To Gabriel), p. 82 (ed. Duval [CSCO: Syr. II.64]).

[32] Bar Hebraeus, *Ecclesiastical History* 2.26 (ed. Abbeloos and Lamy, vol. 3, col. 127). For this footnote and the previous, cf. Young, *Patriarch, Shah and Caliph*, p. 87, and cf. Hoyland, *Seeing Islam*, p. 178.

a miracle; Gawargī was then able to provide three hundred men to help in the construction of the church.[33]

THE SPREAD OF SCHOOLS

One of the most conspicuous forms that interconfessional rivalry took in our period was the construction of educational institutions and the expansion of educational efforts on the part of church leaders. As we have seen, the sixth century saw the beginnings of literacy requirements for ordination. It is at the end of the sixth and into the seventh that we find evidence of an educational arms race between rival churches. For instance: the *Life* of Marutha, the Miaphysite metropolitan of Tikrit (d. 649), reports that in the late sixth century, Nestorians who wished to 'steal the simple people over to their error' were diligently establishing schools in every village and spreading their chanting and hymnody in the region of Beth Nehudra around Nineveh. This prompted a counter movement by zealous Miaphysites to establish a number of their own schools in the same region.[34] The East Syrian catholicos Isho'yahb II (sed. AD 628–645) was known for his concern for doctrine, something that led him to establish schools.[35] After becoming catholicos around 649, Isho'yahb III, his successor, decided to build a school at the monastery of Beth 'Ābe. His plan, Thomas of Marga tells us, was

> to bring to it teachers and masters and expositors, and to gather together many scholars and to provide for them in all things. And he had made ready in his mind, and had resolved and decided to carry out this work in such a way that for every child who was trained and instructed therein the monastery might be near at hand for the purpose of [his] becoming a disciple, so that the school and the monastery might become one; the school to give birth to and rear scholars, and the monastery to teach and sanctify them for the labours of the ascetic life.[36]

[33] See Mardin 8/259, fols. 112v–114r. Also see comments on fol. 113r of Mardin 8/259 about Gawargī being from the West and not trusting the holy men of the Syrians because he had grown up with the Romans. Based on the text of Simeon's *Life*, it seems that Gawargī, though a Christian, held authority under the Arabs.

[34] Denḥā, *Life of Marutha*, pp. 65–66 (ed. Nau [PO 3.1]). On the competition between Miaphysites and East Syrians in the sixth and seventh centuries and the expansion of Miaphysites in the Sasanian empire, see also *Chronicle of Seert* 2.88–89 (ed. Scher [and Griveau] [PO 13.4], pp. 222–25). In general, see M. G. Morony, *Iraq after the Muslim Conquest* (Princeton, 1984), pp. 374–75 and J.-M. Fiey, *Jalons pour une histoire de l'Église en Iraq* (Louvain, 1970), pp. 129-143.

[35] See Bar Hebraeus, *Ecclesiastical History* 2.25 (ed. Abbeloos and Lamy, vol. 3, col. 113).

[36] Thomas of Marga, *Monastic History* 2.7 (ed. Budge, 1.74 [Syriac] = 2.132 [English]). I have used here the translation of Budge.

The Miaphysite Rabban Sabroy was likely a rough contemporary of Isho'yahb III. In addition to writing works responding to Nestorian polemics, he founded a school in a village near Nineveh where some three hundred students studied and which produced a number of teachers. He and his sons also composed an urban office of the liturgy 'on account of the increase and arrogance of the heretics,' as David bar Paulos put it.[37] Such efforts continued into the eighth century: the East Syrian catholicos Pethion (sed. 731–741) was said have founded a school in Tirhan that reportedly reached four hundred students as a result of his gifts and care; other bishops imitated Pethion's church and school-building activities.[38] Thomas of Marga listed twenty-four different schools founded in the region of Marga by Babai of Gebilta in the mid-eighth century, and also cited a report that Babai founded some sixty schools.[39] A bit earlier than this, Simeon of the Olives (d. 734) would build the monastery of Mar Lazarus near the town of Habsenus. In the town itself, he built a school: 'There came to be in Habsenus teachers and chanters and readers and exegetes the likes of which do not exist in the world,' Simeon's *Life* reports, 'for the inhabitants of this village are quick-witted and receivers of instruction, down till today.'[40]

The spread of schools, like the explosion of interconfessional controversial literature, is one of the hallmarks of the post-Chalcedonian confessionalization of the Middle East. We can see the sectarianizing effects of education in another story from Sabrisho''s time as patriarch: three teenage boys, East Syrians, left their ecclesiastical school one day (presumably the School of Seleucia-Ctesiphon) and came across a Marcionite priest—or, as one of the boys' fathers put it, 'a Marcionite from among those whom they call "priests".' The youths stopped the priest and started verbally abusing him. The priest did not turn the other cheek, but instead flew into a fury and came after the boys, two of whom escaped. He seized the third boy and, insulting him, put his hands over the boy's eyes, mouth, and lips. The boy immediately lost his sight and his ability to speak. His work done, the Marcionite 'enchanter' (*sāḥir*), as the blind

[37] See David bar Paulos, *Letter to John the Bishop on Vocalization*, pp. *45–*47 (quote at *47) (ed. Rahmani, *Studia Syriaca*, vol. 1; text also available in F. H. Dolapönu [F. Y. Dolabani], ed., *Egrāteh d-Dawīd bar Pawlos d-metīda' d-Bet Rabban* [Mardin, 1953], pp. 44–49). See also I. A. Barṣawm, *al-Lu'lu' al-manthūr fī ta'rīkh al-'ulūm wa-'l-ādāb al-suryāniyya* (repr. Glane, 1975), p. 287.

[38] See 'Amr b. Mattā, *Akhbār faṭārikat kursī al-mashriq*, p. 66 (ed. Gismondi, *Maris Textus Arabicus*); for the school reaching four hundred students, see Bar Hebraeus, *Ecclesiastical History* 2.33 (ed. Abbeloos and Lamy, vol. 3, col. 151).

[39] For the monasteries, see Thomas of Marga, *Monastic History* 3.2 (ed. Budge, 1.143–44 [Syriac] = 2.296-97 [English]). For the date of Babai's activity, see vol. 1, p. cviii.

[40] Mardin 8/259, fol. 123r.

young man's father would refer to him, departed. Fortunately, Sabrisho' was able to miraculously restore the boy's sight and speech.[41]

Whatever we choose to make of the historicity of such a story, one aspect of it is particularly notable for us here: the boys who stopped the Marcionite priest in the street and treated him with verbal contempt were coming out of a theological school—they had, that is, presumably been made doctrinally and confessionally more aware by what they were learning there than those who had not received such training. In a world of rival churches, education both fueled and was fueled by the competition between them.

Having schools—a place to train one's clergy and to give one's laity a very basic education—was essential if a group or movement was to maintain its existence. It was also the surest way to counter the confused confessional situation we found in Chapter 3, and the most effective means for handling the Middle East's unique mixture of confessional diversity and competition. An educated clergy would mean a firmer control over the sacraments, which in turn would translate into stronger separation between groups. A better-educated clergy might even translate into a laity that was more confessionally aware.[42]

One of the clearest views of the effect a school or schools might have on a particular confession in the post-Chalcedonian world can be found by examining the most important center of Miaphysite learning and study outside of Egypt: Qenneshre.

THE NEST OF EAGLES

The establishment in the late sixth century of rival Nestorian and Miaphysite schools that the *Life of Marutha* reported took place decades after Chalcedonians had carried out several campaigns of expelling Miaphysite monks from monasteries in the region of Antioch, Euphratasia, Osrhoene, and Mesopotamia in the 520s and 530s.[43] Among the monasteries purged of their Miaphysite

[41] *Chronicle of Seert* 2.78 (ed. Scher [and Griveau] [PO 13.4], pp. 175-176).

[42] The critical proviso that needs to be added here is that there had to be a sufficient number of educated clergymen to make these changes. Given the nature of our evidence, it is not possible to know what the numbers of lay and clergy educated in schools were. It would not be unreasonable, however, to assume that increased references to schools in our sources suggest increased efforts at education. In Chapter 9, I will return to the question of the extent and success of efforts at improving clerical training.

[43] For the purge of AD 525–31, see Ps.-Zacharias Rhetor, *Chronicle* 8.5 (ed. Brooks [CSCO 84: SS 39], pp. 80–83; ET available in Hamilton and Brooks, *The Syriac Chronicle Known as that of Zachariah of*

monks at this time was that of St. Thomas at Seleucia-Pieria near Antioch. In about 530, the abbot of the monastery, a man named John bar Aphtonia (d. 537), led a group of Miaphysite monks eastward and established a new monastery called Qenneshre, literally, 'the nest of eagles,' on the eastern bank of the Euphrates, across from the town of Europos (modern Jirbās).[44] We have some evidence that the monastery of St. Thomas was a center of Greek education for Syriac-speaking monks, and the newly-established monastery of Qenneshre continued this tradition.[45] Within decades of Qenneshre's founding, we have evidence that it was already a place where education in the Greek language was probably going on,[46] a place whose monks were being made bishops,[47] and a place that was perhaps very beautiful and a destination for visitors.[48]

By the late sixth century, Qenneshre's importance was becoming more and more conspicuous. In the 117 years between the consecration of Julian I as

---

Mitylene, pp. 209–12). In general, see Menze, *Justinian and the Making of the Syrian Orthodox Church*, pp. 106–44.

[44] Cf. Ps.-Zacharias Rhetor, *Chronicle* 8.5 (ed. Brooks [CSCO 84: SS 39], pp. 79-80; ET available in Hamilton and Brooks, *The Syriac Chronicle Known as That of Zachariah of Mitylene*, pp. 208–10). In the 1990s, Spanish archaeologists claimed to have located the site of Qenneshre, (see A. González Blanco and G. Matilla Séiquer, 'Cristianización: Los Monasterios del Ámbito de Qara Qûzâq,' *Antigüedad y Cristianismo* 15 [1998], pp. 399–415, and A. González Blanco, 'Christianism on the Eastern Frontier,' in *Archaeology of the Upper Syrian Euphrates: The Tishrin Dam Area*, ed., G. del Olmo Lete and J.-L. Montero Fenollós [Barcelona, 1999], pp. 643–62), but their site does not match the literary evidence we possess for the location of Qenneshre, most notably Yāqūt's statement that it is located on the eastern shore of the Euphrates, facing Jirbās (i.e., Europos) (see Yāqūt, *Mu'jam al-Buldān*, vol. 2 [Beirut, 1995], p. 529). More recently, Syrian archaeologist Yusuf al-Dabte has identified a site on the eastern shore of the Euphrates, facing Jirbās, which seems to match quite well the literary evidence we have for the monastery's location and attributes. See 'Iktishāf Dayr Qinnisrīn (Monastery of Qinnisre),' *Mahd al-Ḥaḍarāt* 2 (April, 2007), pp. 83–99. In June of 2008, I spoke with Yousef al-Dabte at the National Museum of Archaeology in Aleppo about the site of Qenneshre, which I have also visited. At the time, al-Dabte hoped to publish additional articles based on the one season of excavation he had done there; analysis he had done on pottery found there suggested that the site was inhabited into the thirteenth century, although the literary sources referring to the monastery go silent after the tenth century. At the time, among the things al-Dabte hoped to publish were Greek inscriptions found at the site of the monastery. These have not, to my knowledge, ever appeared. Cf. also chapter 8, n. 29.

[45] cf. Ps.-Zacharias Rhetor, *Chronicle* 8.5 (ed. Brooks [CSCO 84: SS 39], p. 79; ET available in Hamilton and Brooks, *The Syriac Chronicle Known as that of Zachariah of Mitylene*, p. 208). See also J. W. Watt, 'A Portrait of John Bar Aphtonia, Founder of the Monastery of Qenneshre,' in Drijvers and Watt, eds., *Portraits of Spiritual Authority*, pp. 158–62.

[46] In general, see Watt's 'A Portrait of John Bar Aphtonia,' pp. 155–69.

[47] John of Ephesus, *Lives of the Eastern Saints* 50 (*Lives of James and Theodore*) (ed. and trans. Brooks [PO 19.2], p. 502; see esp. n. 4). For this point, cf. also I. A. Barṣawm, 'Sīrat al-qiddīs Yūḥannā ibn Aftūniyyā,' *Al-Majalla al-Baṭrakiyya al-Suryāniyya* 4:9 (1937), p. 273. See also n. 56 in this chapter.

[48] John of Ephesus, *Lives of the Eastern Saints*, Appendix ('Spurious Life of James') (ed. and trans. Brooks [PO 19.2] [Paris, 1926], pp. 610–11). For this, see Barṣawm, 'Sīrat al-qiddis Yūḥannā ibn Aftūniyyā,' p. 266.

patriarch of Antioch in 591 and the death of the patriarch Julian II in 708, there were seven Miaphysite patriarchs of Antioch, five of whom were from the monastery of Qenneshre or had been trained there in their youth. In the 254 years between Julian I (sed. 591–594) and Dionysius of Tell Mahre (d. 845), something like 136 of them saw patriarchs of Antioch who hailed from Qenneshre.[49]

It is significant that Syriac chroniclers took care to note that many of these patriarchs learned Greek while at Qenneshre.[50] The place was synonymous with Greek education and was a training ground for almost all of the major Miaphysite bishop-scholars of the seventh and eighth centuries. Thomas of Harkel (d. ca. 640),[51] Athanasius II of Balad (d. 683/84),[52] Julian II 'the Roman,' (sed. 687–707/8),[53] Jacob of Edessa (d. 708),[54] and George of Be'eltan (d. 789/90),[55] are all individuals who are explicitly stated to have studied Greek there. There are other figures who were reported to have come from Qenneshre who knew Greek, but for whom we have no specific mention of their studying it there. In the sixth century, Sergius bar Karya was one such figure;[56] in the seventh, Patriarch Athanasius I Gamolo (d. 631), who was elected patriarch after bishops realized he was from Qenneshre, was another.[57] In the ninth century, there was Dionysius of Tell Mahre, another Miaphysite patriarch (d. 845),[58] and Theodosius of Edessa, Dionysius's brother.[59] Conversely, there were individuals

[49] Julian I (591–c. 596), Athanasius I Gamolo (c. 596–631), Theodore (649–667), Athanasius II of Balad (684–687), and Julian II, the Roman (688–708). Dionysius of Tell Mahre was patriarch from 818 to 845. For this, see Barṣawm, 'Sīrat al-qiddīs Yūḥannā ibn Aftūniyyā,' p. 271.

[50] See the evidence cited below.

[51] Michael the Great, *Chronicle* 10.26 (ed. Chabot, 4.391 = 2.381).

[52] Michael the Great, *Chronicle* 11.15 (ed. Chabot, 4.444 = 2.470–471).

[53] Michael the Great, *Chronicle* 11.16 (ed. Chabot, 4.447 = 2.475).

[54] Michael the Great, *Chronicle* 11.15 (ed. Chabot, 4.445 = 2.471).

[55] Michael the Great, *Chronicle* 11.25 (ed. Chabot, 4.475 = 2.525).

[56] For Sergius as being from 'the monastery of Aphtonia,' see John of Ephesus, *Lives of the Eastern Saints* 50 (*Lives of James and Theodore*) (ed. and trans. Brooks [PO 19.2], p. 502 (esp. n. 4); ET taken from Brooks) (cf. n. 47 in this chapter). For Sergius translating John bar Aphtonia's Greek *Life* of Severus of Antioch into Syriac, see PO 2.3, p. 264. The Sergius mentioned by John of Ephesus as being from the monastery of Aphtonia is not explicitly called Sergius bar Karya, but he has traditionally been identified as such by scholars. See, e.g., Barṣawm, *al-Lu'lu' al-manthūr*, pp. 262–63 and Baumstark, *Geschichte*, pp. 184–85.

[57] Bar Hebraeus, *Ecclesiastical History* 1.50 (ed. Abbeloos and Lamy, 1.261). On Athanasius, see also Michael the Great, *Chronicle* 10.24 (ed. Chabot, 4.387–89 [Syriac] = 2.375–77). See also Chapter 4, n. 15 and Chapter 8, n. 14.

[58] For Dionysius being from Qenneshre, see Bar Hebraeus, *Ecclesiastical History* 1.64 (ed. Abbeloos and Lamy, 1.347); Michael the Great, *Chronicle* 12.10 (ed., Chabot, 4.503 = 3.43) and BL Add. 14,726 in *CBM*, v.2, p. 830 [no. 11]). Though no sources state that Dionysius studied Greek at Qenneshre, he did draw upon Greek material when writing his now-lost and very important chronicle; see Michael the Great, *Chronicle* 11.18 (4.452–53 = 2.287–288).

[59] For Theodosius as the brother of Dionysius and the translator of hymns of Gregory Nazianzen

who knew Greek but who are not connected to Qenneshre explicitly in extant sources, though it is likely that they learned it there or spent time there. Such is the case with Paul of Edessa (fl. 623/4),[60] Severus Sebokht (d. 667),[61] and George, Bishop of the Arab Tribes (d. 724).[62] There were also individuals from Qenneshre—e.g., Julian I (sed. 591–594)—about whom we can suggest that they probably knew Greek and possibly studied it there, though solid evidence is lacking on both counts.[63]

Qenneshre, it needs to be emphasized, was a bilingual monastery. John bar Aphtonia, its founder, himself knew Greek and composed works in Greek,[64] as did Jacob, another sixth-century figure who was perhaps abbot of the monastery.[65] John Psaltes, another early abbot of Qenneshre also wrote in Greek and his hymns, like those of John bar Apthonia, would not be translated into Syriac until the seventh century, thanks to the work of Paul of Edessa, who translated them while on Cyprus.[66] In other words, these hymns existed in Greek at Qenneshre for decades before they were finally rendered into Syriac.

---

from Greek into Syriac, see Bar Hebraeus, *Ecclesiastical History* 1.64 (ed. Abbeloos and Lamy, 1.361–63) and Vatican Syriac 96, fol. 96 (Syriac text can be found in *BAV*, vol. 1.2, p. 521 [no.20]).

[60] On Paul's life and his likely connection with Qenneshre, see S. P. Brock, *The Syriac Version of the Pseudo-Nonnos Mythological Scholia* (London, 1971), pp. 28–30.

[61] Severus is referred to as 'Bishop of Qenneshrin' (Bar Hebraeus *Ecclesiastical History* 1.51 [ed. Abbeloos and Lamy, 1.275) and 'of Qenneshrin' (Michael the Great, *Chronicle* 11.8 [4.423 = 2.433]), which could refer to Chalcis, but which might also be understood as a reference to Qenneshre. In the former case, I am unaware of other examples of bishops over monasteries, and Qenneshre itself was the home for at least part of the seventh century to the Miaphysite patriarch of Antioch (see the evidence from the *Life* of Theodota of Amid, Chapter 3, nn. 3, 44). Nevertheless, Athanasius of Balad was the student of Severus (Michael the Great, *Chronicle* 11.15 [4.444 = 2.470]) and it was at Qenneshre that Athanasius learned Greek. See also Baumstark, *Geschichte*, p. 246.

[62] For George and Qenneshre, see K. E. McVey *George, Bishop of the Arabs. A Homily on Blessed Mar Severus, Patriarch of Antioch* (CSCO 531: SS 217) (Louvain, 1993), pp. XXII-XXVII, and my 'Between Christology and Kalām?' pp. 674–77.

[63] For Julian I, see Michael the Great, *Chronicle* 10.23 (ed. Chabot, 4.386 = 2.373), where he is called *mlīlā*, "articulate." Julian was the disciple of Peter of Callinicum, whose disagreements with and writings against Damian of Alexandria as well as his involvement in the Tritheist controversy make it certain that he knew and wrote Greek; see CPG 7250–55; Baumstark, *Geschichte*, p. 177; and L. R. Wickham's article, 'Peter of Kallinikos,' in *GEDSH*, p. 332.

[64] Cf. Baumstark, *Geschichte*, p. 181; Watt, 'A Portrait of John Bar Aphtonia,' p. 160; and S. P. Brock, 'The Conversations with the Syrian Orthodox under Justinian (532),' p. 88, esp. n. 8. For a short Arabic play based on the life of John Bar Aphtonia, see Afrām Būlus, 'Aftūniyyā,' *Al-Majalla al-Baṭrakiyya* 32 (October, 1965), pp. 82–87.

[65] There is a letter by Jacob, 'the leader of the monastery and priests and monks and the rest of the solitaries of Beth Aphtonia' to Theodosius of Alexandria (d. 566) preserved in BL Add. 14,602, fol. 54a (see *CBM*, vol. 2, p. 704, no. 17). Though this survives in Syriac, it must have originally been written in Greek. Barṣawm, 'Sīrat al-qiddīs Yūḥannā ibn Aftūniyyā,' pp. 268–70, did not include this Jacob among the early abbots of Qenneshre whom he was able to identify.

[66] Paul's Syriac translation was later revised by of Jacob of Edessa in 675. See PO 7.5, pp. 389–390.

Qenneshre might also be the final resting place for Greek-speaking Miaphysites who were not from the monastery. Thomas of Germanicia, for example, though not from Qenneshre, was buried there after he died in 542. Thomas was a participant in the Miaphysite-Chalcedonian conversations of 532 in Constantinople, conversations that Qenneshre's founder John bar Aphtonia attended and wrote about.[67] Though there is often an association—perhaps unconscious—of Miaphysitism with Syriac, we should emphasize that the Miaphysite movement in fact continued to have a Greek face into the early eighth century,[68] and even deeper into the eighth and ninth.[69] It was at Qenneshre more than anywhere else that Greek-speaking Miaphysitism gradually came to acquire a Syriac profile.[70]

Many of the scholars whom I have mentioned lived through some of the most dramatic events of the late ancient world—the last great war of antiquity between the Persians and Byzantines in the early seventh century and the Arab conquests and subsequent civil wars that followed. According to the Syriac *Chronicle to 724*, Slavs invaded the island of Crete and other islands in 623, seizing monks from Qenneshre and killing some twenty of them.[71] These

[67] For the conversations, see Ps.-Zacharias Rhetor, *Ecclesiastical History* 9.15 (ed. Brooks [CSCO 84: SS 39], pp. 115–23; ET in Brooks and Hamilton, *The Syriac Chronicle Known as that of Zachariah of Mitylene*, pp. 246–53. John Bar Aphtonia appears on 122 [= 253 English]). On the conversations and what is probably John's account of them, see Brock, 'The Orthodox-Oriental Orthodox Conversations of 532,' and Brock, 'The Conversation with the Syrian Orthodox under Justinian (532).' For Thomas' death in Samosata and burial at Qenneshre, see *Chronicle to 846*, p. 227 (ed. Brooks [CSCO Syr. III.4]). For this information on Thomas, see E. Honigmann, *Évêques et évêchés monophysites d'Asie antérieure au VIe siècle* (Louvain, 1951), pp. 73–74.

[68] On Severus of Antioch as a Greek figure into the eighth century, see van Rompay, 'Severus, Patriarch of Antioch (512–538),' pp. 4–6.

[69] See, e.g., the bilingual Greek and Syriac inscription found at the Monastery of Jacob of Kayshoum, which mentions the patriarch Dionysius of Tell Mahre (sed. 817–845) in L. Jalabert and R. Mouterde, *Inscriptions grecques et latines de la Syrie*, vol. 1 (Paris, 1929), p. 61 (no. 58). Dionysius's predecessor as Syrian Orthodox patriarch, Cyriacus (sed. 793–817), cited the usages of the Greeks in his discussion of the phrase 'we break heavenly bread' in the Miaphysite liturgy,' and was even able to say that it is 'not at all in any Greek manuscript' (Michael the Great, *Chronicle* 12.2 [ed. Chabot, 4.481 = 3.6]). On the controversy over this phrase, see Sauget, 'Vestiges d'une celebration.' More generally, on Middle Eastern/non-Constantinopolitan Greek in late antiquity and the Middle Ages, see the important discussion in S. F. Johnson, 'Introduction: The Social Presence of Greek in Eastern Christianity, 200–1200 CE,' in S. F. Johnson, ed., *Languages and Cultures of Eastern Christianity* (Surrey, England, 2015), pp. 1–122.

[70] On the importance of Qenneshre in the formation of a Syriac-language Miaphysite curriculum of study, see below. I should acknowledge here, too, however, that in the sixth century, Paul of Callinicum was responsible for translating a great deal of the writings of Severus of Antioch into Syriac before Qenneshre was founded. On Paul, see D. King, 'Paul of Callinicum and His place in Syriac literature.'

[71] *Chronicle to 724* (ed. E. W. Brooks, *Chronica Minora II* [CSCO SS III.4] [Paris, 1904], p. 147; ET in A. Palmer, S. P. Brock, and R. Hoyland, *The Seventh Century in the West-Syrian Chronicles* [Liverpool, 1993], p. 18).

monks were likely there fleeing from the brutal conflict between the Romans and the Persians that was raging at the time. Paul of Edessa, for his part, was on the island of Cyprus, 'in flight from the Persians,' in 624 when he translated works by Gregory Nazianzen.[72]

It was scholars trained at Qenneshre who were responsible for much of the Syriac-language intellectual activity that characterized the seventh century, especially in the Miaphysite church, scholarship which contrasts so sharply with the abatement of most secular writing in Greek all over the eastern Mediterranean in the same period. Moreover, scholars trained at Qenneshre were also at the forefront of the Hellenization of the Syriac language. Sebastian Brock has cited George of the Arabs' use in his letters of the greeting *l-meḥdā*—a calque on the Greek χαίρειν—instead of the more traditional *shlām*, as indicative of the 'all pervasive' influence of Greek on Syriac by the seventh century.[73] In fact, usage of *ḥdi, hdāw, ḥdāyēn* ("rejoice!") or *l-meḥdā* (literally, "to rejoice")—the Syriac equivalent of χαῖρε, χαίρετε, or χαίρειν—seems to have been strongly characteristic of writers and translators who were associated with Qenneshre in the seventh century, perhaps exclusively so. Thus, while the East Syrian Isho'yahb III frequently used some version of the traditional *shlām* as a greeting in his letters,[74] his Miaphysite rough contemporaries Athanasius Gamolo,[75] Severus Sebokht,[76] Athanasius of Balad,[77] and Jacob of Edessa[78] all employed some form of this distinctive Hellenizing greeting in

[72] See BL Add. 12,153, fol. 1b, in *CBM*, vol. 2, p. 423. That Paul was 'in flight from the Persians' was noted by Jacob of Edessa in a note in BL Add. 17,134, for which see *CBM*, vol. 1, p. 336 and PO 7.5, pp. 801–802. For all of this, see Brock, *The Syriac Version of the Pseudo-Nonnos Mythological Scholia*, p. 29, and Baumstark, *Geschichte*, p. 190.

[73] See S. P. Brock, 'From Antagonism to Assimilation: Syriac Attitudes to Greek Learning,' in N. Garsoïan, T. Matthews, and R. Thomson, eds., *East of Byzantium: Syria and Armenia in the Formative Period* (Washington, D.C., 1982), p. 29.

[74] See, e.g., Duval, ed., *Īšōʿyahb III Patriarcha: Liber Epistularum* (CSCO: Syr. II.64), pp. 8, 9, 10, 11, 13, 16, 17, 18, 20, 21, 22, 30, 34, 36, 40, 42, 44, 45, 46, 48, 53, 55, 56, 57, 58, 59, 60, 62, 63, 65, 67, 69, 71, 76, 81, 85, 88, 90, 93, 97, 98, 100, 101, 105, 109, 111, 120, 121, 123, 131, 138, 141, 150, 152, 162, 164, 166, 167, 168, etc.

[75] See, e.g., salutations preserved in his encyclical to the Bishops of the East, Michael the Great, *Chronicle* 10.27 (ed. Chabot, 4.400 = 2.394) and in his letter to the monks of Mar Matay (ed. Rahmani, *Studia Syriaca*, vol. 1, p. *29 and Michael the Great, *Chronicle* 11.4 [4.411 = 2.414–15]).

[76] See his *Letter to Yonan the Periodeute*, p. 60 (ed. H. Hugonnard-Roche, 'Questions de logique au VIIe siècle. Les épîtres syriaques de Sévère Sebokht et leurs sources grecques,' *Studia graeco-arabica* 5 (2015); Syriac text from Cambridge Add. 2812, fol. 109b and ET available in *SBI*, p. 282, n. 665).

[77] See F. Nau, 'Littérature canonique syriaque inédite,' p. 128, and Michael the Great, *Chronicle* 10.27 (ed. Chabot, 4.400 = 2.394).

[78] For Jacob's use of *l-meḥdā*, see, e.g., BL Add. 12,172, fol. 81b (*Letter 3*, to John the Priest); fol. 83a (*Letter 4*, to George the Deacon); fol. 85a, (letter 5, to John the Stylite); fol. 97b, (*Letter 9*, to John the Stylite); fol. 99a, (*Letter 10*, to John the Stylite). Also see BL Add. 17,168, fol. 154a (to Simeon the Stylite).

their writings. Thomas of Harkel, who studied at Qenneshre, used the calque in his New Testament translation,[79] as did Paul of Tella in his translation of the Greek Old Testament.[80] In the case of Paul, his usage of the calque is particularly interesting because we do not know where he studied Greek, though his association with Thomas of Harkel and Athanasius Gamolo might suggest that it was at Qenneshre.[81] George of the Arabs also used it—further evidence that he was associated with Qenneshre.[82] Athanasius of Nisibis, a translator who was active in the middle of the seventh century and who may or may not have been the same person as Athanasius of Balad, used this calque in his translation of letters of Severus of Antioch;[83] and so, too, did the anonymous translator of Epiphanius's *Treatise on Weight and Measures*.[84] As this latter work contains much that would be of interest to students of the Bible and also to those interested in biblical translation and the history of biblical translation, it is not hard to imagine that it may have been translated by someone associ-

[79] E.g., see Mt. 26:49, 27:29, 28:9; Mark 15:18; Lk. 1:28; John 19:3; Acts 15:23, 23:26; and James 1:1. For the Harklean Gospels, see J. White, *Sacrorum Evangeliorum versio Syriaca Philoxeniana*... (Oxford, 1778), and for the Harklean Acts and Epistles, see White, *Actuum apostolorum et epistolarum tam catholicarum*... (Oxford, 1799, 1803).

[80] For Paul of Tella's Syro-Hexapla, see, e.g., the use of *l-meḥdā* at 1 Esdras 8:9 (found in Diyarbakir Syriac 1/1, fol. 166r, col. 4, ln. 1). On this manuscript and its Syro-Hexaplar materials, see A. Vööbus, *Discoveries of Very Important Manuscript Sources for the Syro-Hexapla: Contributions to the Research on the Septuagint* (Stockholm, 1970), pp. 11–12.

[81] See the colophon attached to Paul's translation of 4 Kingdoms for Paul's translating at the order of the patriarch Athanasius, in P. de Lagarde, *Veteris testament graeci in sermonem syriacum versi fragmenta octo* (Göttingen, 1892), p. 256. There is a question as to whether Thomas the Syncellus, mentioned in the colophon, is to be identified as Thomas of Harkel; for this debate, see T. M. Law, *Origenes Orientalis: The Preservation of Origen's Hexapla in the Syrohexapla of 3 Kingdoms* (Göttingen, 2011), pp. 20–21.

[82] See *Letter 1* (BL Add. 12,154, fol. 222b): *l-meḥdā*; *Letter 4* (BL Add. 12,154, fol. 245a): *l-meḥdā*; *Letter 6* (BL Add. 12,154, fol. 261a): *l-meḥdā*; *Letter 7* (BL Add. 12,154, fol. 264b): *l-meḥdā*.

[83] Athanasius produced a literal version of the *Sixth Book of the Select Letters* of Severus of Antioch in AD 669; see Baumstark, *Geschichte*, p. 259. Evidence as to the identity of Athanasius of Nisibis is too scanty to make a strong argument either for or against his being the same person as Athanasius II of Balad, though this is assumed in M. Penn's article, 'Athanasios II of Balad,' in *GEDSH*, p. 46. For *l-meḥdā* as a salutation in one of the letters of Severus translated by Athanasius, see Severus of Antioch, *Select Letters* 1.53 (*To the Bishops from Syria Who Are in Alexandria*) (ed. Brooks, 1.1.167, ln. 15).

[84] See Epiphanius, *Treatise on Weights and Measures* (ed. J. E. Dean, *Epiphanius' Treatise on Weights and Measures: The Syriac Version* [Chicago, 1935], p. 93 [52d]). Baumstark, *Geschichte*, pp. 259–60 suggested that this particular translation could have been produced at a monastery like Qarqapta, the home of the West Syrian masoretic tradition (on this, see J. A. Loopstra, 'Patristic Selections in the "Masoretic" Handbooks of the *Qarqaptā* Tradition,' [PhD diss., Catholic University of America, 2009]). Severus bar Mashqa (d. 683/4), who was from the Monastery of Phagimta, also used *l-meḥdā* as a greeting in a letter. See Michael the Great, *Chronicle* 11.14 (ed. Chabot, 4.438 = 2.458); for Severus and Phagimta, see 11.12 [4.435 = 2.453]). The anonymous translator of the letter of Anastasius of Alexandria to Athanasius Gamolo (preserved in Michael the Great, *Chronicle* 10.27 [ed. Chabot, 4.400 = 2.394]), used the Syriac *l-meḥdā* to render what must have been originally χαίρειν.

ated with an important center of studies like Qenneshre, possibly for use by students there.[85]

DIVERSITY AND COMPETITION

Qenneshre is only an example, and a Miaphysite one at that. There is an East Syrian story of schools that can be told, too.[86] This is precisely what we would expect, for in the post-Chalcedonian world the twin factors of diversity and competition—a diversity of Christian confessional factions and intense competition between them for adherents—created an environment in which separating and distinguishing churches from one another and countering confusion among the simple were problems that leaders of all ecclesiastical communions faced.

The impulse to win converts, to protect turf, and to defend one's position in such an unstable landscape was the most important factor driving the proliferation of schools in the sixth, seventh, and eighth centuries. Such considerations were also significant factors fueling the production of texts—and not only polemical ones. Miaphysite translations into Syriac began in the sixth century and intensified, becoming increasingly sophisticated in the seventh, because the situation 'on the ground' meant that if one was to defend and promote one's position ably amid low-level, interconfessional sniping, one had to be dialectically well-equipped and well-informed about the doctrinal bases of one's church.[87] Christian leaders had to concern themselves with the salva-

[85] Alternately, it could have been executed at a monastery like Qarqapta, home of the West Syrian masoretic tradition (see previous note).

[86] See, e.g., A. H. Becker, *Fear of God and the Beginning of Wisdom: The School of Nisibis and Christian Scholastic Culture in Late Antique Mesopotamia* (Philadelphia, 2006), esp. pp. 155–68, and A. Vööbus's classic study, *History of the School of Nisibis* (Louvain, 1965). M. Debié, '"La science est commune": Sources syriaques et culture grecque en Syrie-Mésopotamie et en Perse par-delà les siècles obscurs Byzantins,' *Travaux et mémoires* 21 (2017), pp. 93–114, surveys the various centers of learning in the Syriac-speaking world, in both the Persian and Roman empires (111–14 discusses Qenneshre).

[87] Cf. R. Gottheil's comments in 'The Syriac Versions of the Categories of Aristotle,' *Hebraica* 9 (1893), p. 166. For the argument that the study of logic was not motivated by theological polemic in a late antique and early medieval Syriac context, see D. King, 'Logic in the Service of Ancient Eastern Christianity: An Exploration of Motives,' *Archiv für Geschichte der Philosophie* 97 (2015), pp. 1–33, and King, 'Why Were the Syrians Interested in Greek Philosophy?' in P. Wood, ed., *History and Identity in the Late Antique Near East* (Oxford, 2013), pp. 61–81. On King's arguments in the latter article, see the remarks in Cameron, *Dialoguing in Late Antiquity*, pp. 23–38. King's interest is more narrowly on the question of philosophy and logic, but my interest here is much broader—on Greek literature, both philosophical and theological, in a Syriac context. His skepticism about the existence of disagreement and disputes between members of rival confessions (calling evidence 'circumstantial', p. 81) rests on an overly positiv-

tion of their flock, and in part this meant being able to evaluate and answer the claims of rivals and competitors. 'If you looked in at his council room any day,' we are told of the Chalcedonian John the Almsgiver in early seventh-century Alexandria, 'there was no idle word spoken... but only stories of the holy fathers, or scriptural questions or dogmatic problems due to the multitude of unmentionable heretics who swarmed up in the country.'[88]

One method of dealing with competing religious truth claims was, as we saw in Chapter 2, an appeal to miracles, stories of ordeals, or the authority of a holy man. But not everyone took such a route. And if one were to give a reasoned answer as to why the Council of Chalcedon should not be accepted, one had to have some kind of familiarity with both the specifically Miaphysite tradition and the great writers of the era of Nicaea whose authority both Miaphysites and Chalcedonians would claim.[89] Responding to the question of how to answer a heretic when one did not know how to explain dogma, the Chalcedonian Anastasius of Sinai taught that debate should not be attempted, but rather the heretic should be directed to the church: 'Not only for you, who do not know,' Anastasius wrote,

> but also for those who think they know, it is a danger to talk about the faith. So say to the person questioning you, "I am an unlearned person [ἰδιώτης], but if you really and truly seek to know the truth, go to the Church and there you will learn what is right-minded religion.[90]

---

ist approach to a period in which evidence in general is not as abundant as we would like it to be, though I have attempted to collect in this book material which suggests that disagreements, ranging from (stories of) ordeals, to polemical writings, to actual debates, were part of the landscape of the religiously diverse Middle East in this period. King's arguments are most persusasive on the restricted grounds he sets for himself—looking at the motivation for the study of logic—but they are less convincing when many of the authors are viewed more broadly in the context of the study of not logic specifically, but a curriculum writ large. In general, it cannot be emphasized too strongly that nearly all of the men who translated philosophical (and other) works and who studied them were first and foremost churchmen whose primary concerns on a daily basis would have been pastoral and not scholarly. Therefore, viewing any writer's activity in this period apart from the context of the prayer, worship, and pastoral concern that will have occupied most of his time strips him of the most important context—the communal one—for understanding that activity. The letters of George of the Arabs, discussed above, provide a vivid illustration of how on-the-ground polemics among the simple or less educated will have been an issue that church leaders had to deal with.

[88] Leontius of Neapolis, *Life of John the Almsgiver* 18 (ed. Gelzer, *Leontios' von Neapolis* p. 36; ET taken from Dawes and Baynes, *Three Byzantine Saints*, p. 228). For the 'longer recension,' see Festugière and Rydén, eds., *Vie de Syméon le Fou et Vie de Jean de Chypre*, p. 364 (Greek) = 466 (FT) = Chapter 16.

[89] On the importance of Nicene authors for later theological argumentation, see P.T.R. Gray, '"The Select Fathers": Canonizing the Patristic Past,' *Studia Patristica* 28 (1989), pp. 21-36.

[90] Anastasius of Sinai, *Questions and Answers* 68 (ed. Richard and Munitiz, p. 120; ET taken from Munitiz, *Questions and Answers* p. 182). Cf. Chapter 4, n. 66.

Although many, if not most members of the various rival churches more than likely had little, if any, deep understanding of the issues that separated the communities, for a confessional community—Chalcedonian, Miaphysite, Nestorian, or any other—to survive in the context of rivals, there nevertheless had to be some members, somewhere, who could respond to the sophisticated questions and criticisms of competitors. 'Before all things,' Rabbula of Edessa had ordered monks and ascetics in the fifth century, 'let the sons of the church know the true faith of the holy church, so that heretics not lead them astray.'[91] For there to be the sorts of stories of confessional champions that we encountered in Chapter 4, such champions had to exist. And to survive institutionally, churches needed learned experts. 'When the head of the monastery and the chaste monks saw him,' Denḥā wrote about Marutha of Tikrit's (d. 649) arrival at the monastery of Nardos, near the village of Beth Malūd in northern Mesopotamia,

> that, along with a virtuous way of life, he also possessed a superlative knowledge of the holy Scriptures, they appointed him their master and teacher and scriptural commentator—a model of virtues and image of the blessed ones—by the choice and selection of all of them.[92]

Knowing Scripture and tradition and how these two combined to justify the doctrinal and spiritual identity of a community (as opposed to a rival one) was of fundamental importance if one was to be a leader. While discussing the East Syrian George the Priest's becoming a leading teacher, his biographer Babai the Great asked, 'Who was more able than he and knew how to resolve difficult questions?'[93] The same held true at the end of the eighth century. 'As for that young man who was asking for explanations of the *Categories* from you,' the East Syrian patriarch Timothy I wrote to Sergius of Elam, 'by all means, send him to us, for he will certainly be useful to us.'[94] The highly literate provided soldiers for a church hierarchy concerned with ecclesiastical self-defense and

[91] Rabbula of Edessa, *Rules and Admonitions for Priests and Ascetics* 1 (ed. Overbeck, *S. Ephraemi Syri*, p. 215; translation taken from Connolly, 'Some More Early Syrian Rules,' p. 301 [I have altered Connolly's translation]).

[92] Denḥā, *Life of Marutha*, p. 69 (ed. Nau [PO 3.1]).

[93] Babai the Great, *History of George the Priest*, 491 (ed. Bedjan, *Histoire de Mar-Jabalaha*). 'And within a few years, he became the teacher of monks and the first of those who are regarded as exegetes of the Scriptures. For who is more capable than he and knew how to resolve difficult questions and the doubts about the solitary life from their battle with evil demons?' Of course, not all the questions that George will have had to answer would have been polemical ones from rival churches, but they certainly will have included some inquiries of this nature.

[94] Timothy I, *Letters* 21 (To Sergius of Elam), p. 132 (ed. Braun [CSCO 74–75: SS 30–31], p. 88 = [LT]). Bidawid dates *Letter 21* to the period 799–804; see Bidawid, *Les lettres du patriarche nestorien Timothée I*, p. 75.

offense. Perhaps referring to the same young man, Timothy would write to Sergius in another letter, 'Send me that young man who is a logician.' Here a soldier was about to be made into a general: 'Perhaps I will make him metropolitan of Harew, for there are followers of Severus there, and a strong warrior is needed there.'[95]

Looking at the Miaphysite situation more specifically, we should keep in mind that of the three major distinct Christian confessions in the Middle East—Chalcedonian, (Severan) Miaphysite, and East Syrian—it was the Miaphysites who were, in Syria and Iraq at least, institutionally the weakest and likely the smallest numerically.[96] Chalcedonians had the backing and prestige of the Roman state on their side. The Church of the East was shielded from Roman persecution and attempts at enforcing doctrinal conformity by its location in Sasanian territory, and moreover, had a presence at the Sasanian court from the sixth century,[97] a well-developed school system, and a long-established ecclesiastical hierarchy. East Syrians also had available in translation an very substantial number of works from the Greek-speaking Antiochene tradition.[98] Chalcedonians could point to the enormous prestige of having a Christian emperor who shared their faith, while East Syrians, members of what was in the early Middle Ages perhaps the largest church in the world, would eventually make the claim that Seleucia-Ctesiphon had primacy over all other sees of the Church, even Rome.[99]

Furthermore, in a Roman context, where Chalcedonians enjoyed the great status that came from imperial support, bilingualism and the easy transit of texts across languages, along with the fact that Greek was typically the language of public theological discourse into the seventh century, meant that Syriac-speaking Miaphysite Christians needed both to catch-up and keep-up

[95] Timothy I, *Letters* 25 (To Sergius), pp. 141–42 (ed. Braun [CSCO 74: SS 30]). Bidawid dates this letter to the period AD 799–804; see *Les lettres du patriarche nestorien Timothée I*, p. 75 and cf. p. 27.

[96] See, e.g., John Rufus, *Plerophories* 55 (ed. Nau [PO 8.1] pp. 109–110), for the charge leveled against the Miaphysites that they claimed to be the true church but were small in number: 'To those who say to us, "The whole world goes to church but you alone, who are few, are separated and you call yourselves 'Orthodox' and zealous for the truth . . ."'

[97] See Baumstark, *Geschichte*, pp. 123–25, for East Syrian literature produced in Sasanian court circles.

[98] The *Mēmrā on Ecclesiastical Books* of 'Abdisho' bar Brikha (ed. Assemani, *BO*, 3.1) lists a vast number of Greek works from the Antiochene tradition that were available in Syriac, but which are now no longer extant. These included much more than Theodore of Mopsuestia, but for a discussion of Theodore's works, which relies heavily on 'Abidsho''s *Mēmrā* and the *Chronicle of Seert*, see R. Devreesse, *Essai sur Théodore de Mopsueste* (Rome, 1948), pp. 4–52.

[99] For the importance of the Christian emperor, see the comments of Rabban Isho', reported in Dionysius bar Salibi, *Against the Melkites* 5 (ed. Mingana, p. 77 [Syriac] = 39 [ET]). On Seleucia-Ctesiphon, see Timothy I, *Letters* 26 (To Maranzkā), pp. 148-150 (ed. Braun, *Timothei patriarchae I epistulae* [CSCO 74: SS 30]).

with their opponents.[100] There was also a need to have reliable Syriac versions of the same theological and philosophical resources as were available to Greek-speaking competitors. Squeezed between these two rival and more secure bodies—the Chalcedonian imperial church and the Church of the East—Miaphysites had to develop their own institutions and resources for articulating and defending their Christian confessional identity in a context where their views might be subject to fierce criticism and attack.

EDUCATIONAL CONSEQUENCES OF CHALCEDON

To return to the question we have been asking:What happened when Christian communities were formed on the basis of disagreements about theological speculation that most Christians simply could not understand fully or properly? Here we have another partial answer: Seeking to retain their own members and win those of rivals, the leadership of the various competing confessional movements created educational institutions and sought to raise the level of the theological literacy of their clergy and even laity.

These educational consequences of Chalcedon were not without other notable results as well: It has long been noted that Syriac flourished, especially in the seventh century, when we find a flood of translations and retranslations.[101] The stage has now been set for understanding why.

[100] For examples of polemical theological texts crossing linguistic boundaries, see my 'Between Christology and Kalām? The Life and Letters of George, Bishop of the Arab Tribes.' For Greek-speaking Miaphysitism into the eighth and ninth centuries, see chapter 4, n. 15 and n. 69 in this chapter.

[101] For the wealth of translation taking place in Syriac, see, e.g., L. I. Conrad, 'Varietas Syriaca: Secular and Scientific Culture in the Christian Communities of Syria after the Arab Conquest,' in G. J. Reinink and A. C. Klugkist, eds., *After Bardaisan: Studies on Continuity and Change in Syriac Christianity in Honour of Professor Han J. W. Drijvers* (Louvain, 1999), pp. 85–105, and S. P. Brock, 'The Syriac Commentary Tradition,' in C. Burnett, ed., *Glosses and Commentaries on Aristotelian Logical Texts: The Syriac, Arabic and Medieval Latin Traditions* (London, 1993), pp. 3–18, esp. the chronological table at 9–10.

CHAPTER 7

Education and Community Formation

Having begun with the simple, we now find ourselves, perhaps paradoxically, discussing the learned—or, at least, learning. Like controversial writings and debates, increased attempts at education were also consequences of Chalcedon. What were the nuts and bolts of Christian education in the post-Chalcedonian Middle East?

THE PATH OF STUDY

We can begin by suggesting the pattern found in the Miaphysite *Life* of Simeon of the Olives as typical. Simeon's father, we are told, brought him to the teacher who was in their village church when he was a young boy and Simeon learned letters and began to study the Bible closely. At the age of ten, his father took him to the Monastery of Beth Simon of Qartmin. There was a rule, the *vita* states, which held for the region of Ṭūr ʿAbdīn:

> In the case of each male child that is born in all the region around the monastery, from the age of ten years and above the child is brought by his parents so that he can learn in the school of the holy monastery. Afterwards, if he is willing, he will become a monk or a priest in the world.[1]

It is unlikely that an attempt would be made to educate *all* young Christian boys—the need for child labor in an overwhelmingly agrarian society would have made such a goal difficult to achieve. In fact it was perhaps only in the regions surrounding certain especially strong monasteries, such as Simeon's, that educating all boys was even an ideal. We should, however, still recognize that the spread of Christianity in the Middle East and the post-Chalcedonian increase in educational efforts must have had a positive effect on literacy rates, even if those rates remained quite low.[2] This will have been particularly the

[1] Mardin 8/259, fol. 105a. Syriac also in *SBI*, p. 319, n. 749.

[2] Harris's valuable and provocative *Ancient Literacy* is limited by its lack of Eastern material. Apart from the post-Chalcedonian confessional stimulus to education, Christian missionary activity also included the spread of literacy—see, e.g., *Teaching of Addai*, p. *40, where Addai's spread of Christianity includes building churches in the region of Edessa: 'He adorned and embellished them, set up deacons

case in monastic contexts, where our evidence is the most robust: the canons attributed to Marutha of Maipherqat from the East Syrian Synod of Seleucia-Ctesiphon in 410, for instance, 'reflect a monastic system that expected high levels of literacy,'[3] and John of Tella (d. 538) has left us a canon instructing parents who had a made a vow dedicating their children to a life of asceticism that the children should be 'sent to monasteries to study the Scriptures.'[4] Other anecdotes suggest that efforts to provide young children, even those not bound to become ascetics, with some basic education, were not as isolated as one might suppose. In the late fifth century Syriac *Life* of Simeon Stylites, we find 'young children who were learning letters' being brought by their teachers to the base of Simeon's column, where they sang *Kyrie eleison* responsively in Greek.[5] John of Ephesus wrote of the ascetics Simeon and Sergius teaching two different groups of boys in their village, with the second class having thirty or forty students.[6] Al-Ṭabarī reported that when Khālid b. al-Walīd captured the town of 'Ayn Tamr in Iraq in AH 12, he found 'forty young men learning the Gospel' in the church there.[7]

Simeon was ten when his father took him from the village school to a monastery, and this was a very common age for such a move. A variant reading in the spurious *vita* of Jacob Baradaeus, for instance, reports that

> when he was 2 or 3 years old, they sent [Jacob] to school, and he was taught and instructed in all the learning of the church, in Syriac and Greek. And, when he reached the age of puberty, his father took him with a fitting present and

---

and presbyters in them, taught those who were to read the scriptures in them, and taught the orders of the ministry within and without' (ed. Phillips, trans. Howard, *The Teaching of Addai*, English translation, p. 81; I have used the translation of Howard). For developments in the study of ancient literacy, especially since Harris's landmark study appeared, see S. Werner, 'Literacy Studies in Classics: The Last Twenty Years,' in Johnson and Parker, eds., *Ancient Literacies*, pp. 333–82.

[3] Walker, 'Ascetic Literacy: Books and Readers in East-Syrian Monastic Tradition,' p. 315. See, e.g., *Canons of Marutha* 48.1, 52.6, 54.22–24 (ed. Vööbus, *Syriac and Arabic Documents*, pp. 128, 135, 142–43).

[4] *Canons of John of Tella* 11 (ed. Vööbus, *Syriac and Arabic Documents*, p. 59; translation mine).

[5] Simeon bar Apollon and Bar Ḥaṭār bar Ūdān, *Life of Simeon Stylites*, p. 613 (ed. Bedjan, *AMS*, vol. 4; my translation, but an ET available in F. Lent, 'The Life of St. Simeon Stylites: A Translation of the Syriac Text in Bedjan's *Acta Martyrum et Sanctorum*, Vol. IV,' *JAOS* 35 [1915–1917], p. 178. The translation in R. Doran, *The Lives of Simeon Stylites* [Kalamazoo, Michigan, 1992] is not based on Bedjan's text, unlike Lent [compare Doran's p. 66 with Lent's, pp. 103–108], but nevertheless, for another, more recent ET of this passage, see Doran, p. 156).

[6] John of Ephesus, *Lives of the Eastern Saints* 5 (ed. Brooks [PO 17.1], pp. 89–90). Note that John referred to a class as a 'school' (*eskolā*).

[7] See al-Ṭabarī, *Ta'rīkh*, 1.4, p. 2064 (ed. P. de Jong and E. Prym [Leiden, 1890]). Cf. J. S. Trimingham, *Christianity among the Arabs in Pre-Islamic Times* (London/New York, 1979), p. 177.

brought him to the monastery, and committed him to the hands of Mar Eustace the archimandrite.[8]

We find this same pattern in other Miaphysite contexts: in the sixth century, Ḥabīb began his ascetic training at about the age of ten,[9] and Jacob of Edessa suggested that the proper time for a child to be educated was between the ages of seven and fifteen.[10] Among Chalcedonians, it was roughly the same: the hostile seventh-century Syriac *Life* of Maximus the Confessor reports that Maximus was placed in the monastery of Palaia Lavra about the age of nine and was taught there by the Abbot Pantoleon,[11] and the Quinisext Council stipulated that a monk should be at least ten years of age.[12] In Palestine, the Chalcedonian Stephen of Mar Sabas (d. AD 794) was taken by his uncle to a lavra for instruction at the age of nine or ten.[13]

In other instances, we are not given the precise ages at which people began their studies, but we can nevertheless detect a two-fold pattern similar to that described in Simeon's *vita*: some sort of local instruction followed by more advanced study in a monastery. Jacob of Edessa himself was from a village called ʿAyndābā; in his youth he studied with a periodeute named Cyriacus. When, we are told, he had read all the books of the Old and New Testaments and those of the chief doctors of the Church, he went to the monastery of Qenneshre where he became a monk, learned the Psalms in Greek and the recitation of the Scriptures, and trained intensely in correct language.[14] George of the Arabs also studied with a periodeute—named Gabriel—as a small child.[15]

[8] John of Ephesus, *Lives of the Eastern Saints*, appendix (*The Spurious Life of James*) (ed. and trans. Brooks [PO 19.2], p. 576, n. 2; the translation is that of Brooks, who only printed an ET of this variant and not the Syriac text itself from BL Add. 12,174, dated AD 1197).

[9] John of Ephesus, *Lives of the Eastern Saints* 1 (ed. and trans. Brooks [PO 17.1], p. 7).

[10] Jacob of Edessa, *Hexaemeron*, p. 335 (ed. I.-B. Chabot, *Iacobi Edesseni Hexaemeron* [CSCO 92: SS 44] [Louvain, 1953]). ET available in *SBI*, p. 318, n. 747. This is precisely the period of his life that the fourth-century anchorite John the Arab is supposed to have spent in school in Hira in southern Iraq: see S. P. Brock, 'Notes on Some Monasteries on Mount Izla,' *Abr-Nahrain* 19 (1980–1981), p. 7. On John, see J.-M. Fiey, *Saints syriaques* (Princeton, 2004), pp. 115–16 (no. 238).

[11] Maximus was placed there after his parents had both died: see George of Reshʿayna, *Life of Maximus Confessor* 3 (ed. Brock, 'An Early Syriac Life of Maximus the Confessor,' pp. 303–304 = 314–15 [ET]).

[12] See Council in Trullo, *Canons* 40 (ed. Joannou, *Discipline générale antique*, vol. 1.1, pp. 175-177, esp. 175-176; ET by Percival in *NPNF*, ser. 2, vol. 14, p. 384).

[13] Leontius of Damascus, *Life of Stephen of Mar Sabas* 6.5, 80.3 (ed. and trans. J. C. Lamoreaux, *The Life of Stephen of Mar Sabas* [CSCO 578–78: SA 50–51] [Louvain, 1999], pp. 9, 144 [Arabic] = pp. 9, 129 [ET]).

[14] See Michael the Great, *Chronicle* 11.15 (ed. Chabot, 4.445 = 2.471). Compare Jacob's learning of the Psalms in Greek with John of Tella's (d. 538) learning them in Syriac: Elias, *Life of John of Tella*, p. 43 (ed. Brooks [CSCO III.25]).

[15] See BL Add. 12,154, fol. 261b (Syriac text also in *SBI*, p. 320, n. 754).

Presumably, like Jacob, George eventually moved on to Qenneshre for more advanced instruction. Once Athanasius Gamolo (d. 631) and his brother Severus had received a good education, Athanasius's *vita* reported, their mother Joanna dedicated them to the monastery of Qenneshre, where they received training in the recitation of the Scriptures.[16]

There are variations to be found in this pattern of studying first in a school and then moving to a monastery: most obviously, if a person did not become a monk things likely would be different.[17] But even for monastics, the path could vary. The Miaphysite Marutha of Tikrit (d. 649) was given by his parents to the Monastery of Mar Sergius near Balad; from there, he moved to a newly established Miaphysite school in the same region and then became a teacher at the Monastery of Nardos, before moving to the Monastery of Mar Zakay near Callinicum, where he spent ten years studying the Church Fathers, especially Gregory Nazianzen.[18] In seventh-century Beth Qatraye, once Isaac the Syrian had been educated in the Scriptures and in scriptural exegesis, he became a monk and a teacher (*mallpānā*) himself.[19]

Nevertheless, a two-tiered system seems to have been the most typical course that education took in the late Roman and early medieval Middle East. It was also a durable one: writing in his *Nomocanon* in the thirteenth century, Bar Hebraeus gives us details about Miaphysite education which seem to suggest that a very similar two-tiered system was in place then as well:

> Rule: Let every chief priest, before everything, when there is none, establish a teacher and let him write the names of the children who are suitable for instruction and let him order their parents to enter them into school, even by compulsion. If among them there are needy or poor, let their support come from the church. If the church is poor, then let the steward of the church collect material for their maintenance each Sunday. As for the wages of the teacher, part of it should come from the church and part from the parents of the children.[20]

[16] Michael the Great, *Chronicle* 10.24 (ed. Chabot, vol. 4.388 = 2.376).

[17] See the example of the layman Tribunus in John of Ephesus, *Lives of the Eastern Saints* 44 (ed. and trans. Brooks [PO 18.4], p. 459).

[18] Denḥā, *Life of Marutha*, pp. 64–71 (ed. Nau [PO 3.1]). Marutha would spend time as a teacher in the famous Monastery of Mar Matay (p. 74). Compare Marutha's movements with the note in BL Add. 14,682, fol. 164a, written by Ḥārith bar Sīsīn of Harran ('the Abrahamic city'), in which Ḥārith states that he has collected the material for his commentary on John in part from 'the interpretation of many teachers and from those things which he heard from teachers in whose presence he studied [*qrā*—or 'read'].' For the Syriac text, see *CBM*, vol. 2, p. 609.

[19] *History of Mar Isaac*, p. *33 (ed. Rahmani, *Studia Syriaca*, vol. 1).

[20] Bar Hebraeus, *Nomocanon* 7.9 (ed. Bedjan, *Nomocanon*, p. 107).

Knowing the path of study is significant, but it is perhaps more important to know what exactly it was that students were learning.

SUBJECTS OF STUDY

Fortunately, Bar Hebraeus also wrote of the subjects that were to be studied, and his account is a useful place to begin:

> Rule: In the first place, let them read the Psalms of David, then the New Testament, then the Old Testament, then the Doctors, then the Commentators. If they are not approaching the priesthood, after the Psalms, let them read the yearly lectionary cycle and let them pronounce with expertness. As for those who do not possess a suitable voice, let them not learn any chanting apart from the simple service.[21]

There is in fact evidence that an education in the Scriptures and the liturgy of the type Bar Hebraeus described formed the core of Miaphysite education as far back as at least the early sixth century.[22] Such a pattern of education, however, was not unique to Miaphysites and seems to have persisted over a long period of time. In the sixth century, for instance, when the Nestorian Mar Aba (d. 552) arrived at the school of Nisibis, he first learned the Psalms and then moved on to the rest of the Scriptures.[23] The *History* of Rabban Hormizd, a Nestorian born in the late sixth or early seventh century, reports that his parents took him to a school when he was twelve years old; he remained at the school for six years, at the end of which he knew the Psalms and New Testament by heart. He went on to become a monk.[24] When the East Syrian martyr and convert from Zoroastrianism Isho'sabran (d. 620–621) asked what a person should first learn, he was told that

> a person first learns the letters and then how to read them. Afterwards, he recites the Psalms, and bit by bit, he reads through all the Scriptures. When he has been trained in the recitation of the Scriptures, he sets himself to their interpretation.[25]

[21] Bar Hebraeus, *Nomocanon* 7.9 (ed. Bedjan, *Nomocanon*, p. 107).

[22] See John of Ephesus, *Lives of the Eastern Saints* 16 (*Life of Simeon the Mountaineer*) (ed. Brooks [PO 17.1] p. 246).

[23] *History of Mar Aba*, pp. 216–17 (ed. Bedjan, *Histoire de Mar-Jabalaha*).

[24] Shem'on, *History of Rabban Hormizd* 2 (ed. and trans. E.A.W. Budge, *The Histories of Rabban Hôrmîzd the Persian and Rabban Bar 'Idtâ* [London, 1902], pp. 9–10 [Syriac] = 14 [ET]). See vol. 2.1, p. XII for the approximate date of his birth.

[25] Isho'yahb III, *Life of Isho'sabran*, p. 525 (ed. J.-B. Chabot, 'Histoire de Jésus-Sabran, écrite par

In the eighth century, the East Syrian John Dalyatha 'learned and read the divine scriptures in the church of his village' of Ardamut before eventually becoming a monk in the Monastery of Mar Yozadaq and the disciple of a monk named Stephen.[26]

Crucially, however, some members of the clergy would receive more than just the basic education. In a somewhat cryptic passage, the *Life* of Simeon of the Olives tells us that 'the youth entered school and became the head of the school on account of his wisdom and knowledge. When he had finished the measure (τάξις) of his instruction in three schools, he was trained until he became the chief chanter.'[27] Simeon seems to have studied in at least three different institutions, or perhaps with three different teachers—a 'school' might be a very personal thing, more akin to a small group of students than a physical structure.[28]

I have already cited examples of Athanasius Gamolo and Jacob of Edessa going through several stages of education; George of the Arabs likely did the same. We find this phenomenon of multiple schools or stages in the Church of the East also. At the age of seven in probably the early fifth century, for instance, the famous East Syrian Narsai (d. ca. 500) went to the 'children's school' in his village of 'Ayn Dulba and was reciting the Psalter after only nine months. He would later study at a monastery and also at the School of Edessa.[29] In the sixth century, the East Syrian Sabrisho' first learned the Psalms in his village from a priest named John, and when he had finished that, he went to Nisibis to study the Scriptures at the school there.[30] After converting to

Jésus-Yab d'Adiabène,' *Nouvelles archives des missions scientifiques et littéraires* 7 [1897] FT on p. 491; ET also available in Becker, *Fear of God and the Beginning of Wisdom*, p. 206). I am grateful to Moulie Vidas for bringing this passage to my attention.

[26] *History of Mar John of Dalyatha, Whose Monastery Is in Qardu*, p. *34 (ed. Rahmani, *Studia Syriaca*, vol. 1).

[27] Mardin 8/259, fols. 105b–106a. Syriac text also in *SBI*, p. 326, n. 763.

[28] See the use of *eskolā* in the sense of 'class' or 'group of students' in BL Add. 12,152, fol. 194a (dated to AD 837) (*CBM*, vol. 2, p. 498), and note the similar use of the word *eskolā* by John of Ephesus (see n. 6 in this chapter). In the ninth century, Ḥunayn b. Isḥāq compared the manner of study in medical schools in Alexandria with the manner of study in the East Syrian schools in his own time: 'They would gather every day to read an important work from these and try to understand it, just as our Christian companions today gather every day in the places of instruction which are known as 'school[s]' (*tu'raf bi-'l-askūl*) to [study] an important work from one of the books of the ancients. As for the remaining books, individuals would read them, each one on his own, after instruction in those books which I mentioned, just as our companions today read commentaries on the books of the ancients.' Ḥunayn b. Isḥāq, *Risāla* 20 (ed. G. Bergsträsser, *Ḥunain ibn Isḥāq über die syrischen und arabischen Galen-Übersetzungen* [Leipzig, 1925], pp. *18–*19 = 15 [GT]; with corrections to the Arabic made from Bergsträsser, *Neue materialien zu Ḥunain ibn Isḥāq's Galen-bibliographie* [Leipzig, 1932], p. 17).

[29] For the report of Narsai learning the Psalter at the children's school, see Barhadbshabba, *Ecclesiastical History* 31 (ed. Nau [PO 9.5], p. 106; ET available in Becker, *Sources for the Study of the School of Nisibis*, p. 53). On Narsai, see L. van Rompay's article, 'Narsai,' in *GEDSH*, pp. 303-304.

[30] Peter the Solitary, *Life of Sabrisho'*, p. 291 (ed. Bedjan, *Histoire de Mar-Jabalaha*).

Christianity from Zoroastrianism in the late sixth century, George the Priest (d. 615) studied in an East Syrian school in the village of Beth Rastaq. He began his studies with the Psalms, which he was said to have memorized in a few days. Next, George began to read the Scriptures and to 'listen to their interpretation with understanding.'[31] Later he would give money to found a school, hiring a teacher and gathering monks to learn. George himself, Babai noted, 'began to train his soul in the Scriptures and in the interpretations of the Blessed Theodore.'[32]

CONFESSIONAL DISTINCTIONS

It is in the secondary stage, so to speak, of education, that we catch glimpses of Miaphysites and East Syrians pursuing different objects of study. The *History* of Rabban Bar 'Idta, whose life spanned much of the sixth century (ca. 509–ca. 612), reports that his sister first placed him in a school where he learned the Psalms, chanting, and the art of copying books and writing. Once he had learned these things, she next took him to another school, in a monastery, where he studied the Bible and biblical commentaries. Alone in his room, he would read one book a week. He read and memorized the commentaries of Theodore of Mopsuestia, the works of Aba Isaiah, Mark the Monk, Evagrius, Gregory Nazianzen, Palladius, the 'Sayings of the Fathers,' Basil, and the *Book of Heraclides* of Nestorius, which had been, he tells us, recently translated into Syriac from Greek.[33] Here we have a listing of books that looks something like a curriculum, or at least gives us insight into what it was that some East Syrians were reading in the sixth century.

We have indications on the Miaphysite side as well of what their canon of authorities might have looked like at this time. In the late seventh or early eighth century, Jacob of Edessa would write to John of Litarb that he could not effectively respond to a question he had been asked because he did not

[31] Babai the Great, *History of George the Priest*, p. 442 (ed. Bedjan, Histoire de Mar-Jabalaha).

[32] Babai the Great, *History of George the Priest*, p. 443 (ed. Bedjan, Histoire de Mar-Jabalaha).

[33] Abraham the Priest, *History of Rabban Bar 'Idta*, vol. 1, pp. 117–120 (ed. Budge, *The Histories*, = vol. 2.1, pp. 170-176). NB: the text does not refer explicitly to Palladius's 'Paradise of the Fathers,' or the 'Sayings of the Desert Fathers,' only to 'the Book of Histories,' which Budge, p. 175, n. 5, suggests are these two works. For the dates of Rabban Bar 'Idta's life, see vol. 2.1, p. XXXIII. For this story as illustrative of the system of education, cf. also, F. Nau, 'L'araméen chrétien (syriaque): les traductions faites du grec en syriaque au VIIe siècle,' *Revue de l'histoire des religions* 99 (1929), pp. 244–45. Babai the Great's *History of George the Priest*, p. 491 (ed. Bedjan, *Histoire de Mar-Jabalaha*) notes that George obtained a 'discernment and grasp and comprehension of the holy books and the teachings of the monks and an understanding of all the interpretations of the Blessed Theodore [of Mopsuestia], the universal doctor,' before himself becoming a teacher of other monks and a leading scriptural exegete.

have the books with him that contained the answer. To answer properly, he said, he would have need of the commentaries of doctors like Athanasius, Basil, Gregory of Nyssa, John (Chrysostom), Cyril, Severus, Ephrem, Philoxenus, and Jacob (of Sarugh).[34] Another clue as to who, in Jacob's view, were the proper theological authorities can be found in his version of the liturgy, in which he included prayers of commemoration for Ignatius of Antioch, Dionysius the Areopagite, Basil, Gregory Nazianzen, John Chrysostom, Cyril, Philoxenus, Jacob (of Sarugh), and Jacob (Baradaeus).[35]

It is here at the higher level of education that differences between rival groups became more pronounced, and distinct theological profiles begin to emerge. As was the case with rudimentary education, our fullest testimony as to what constituted a Miaphysite syllabus of study comes from much later, from Bar Hebraeus in his thirteenth-century *Nomocanon.* He offers two lists of the books that are read in the holy church: one of Christian authors, the other of pagan ones. 'Now the books of the doctors which are read in the church,' he begins the first list, 'are the following':

> of Dionysius of Athens: 3 homilies and 10 letters; of Basil: 29 homilies; of Gregory of Nazianzus: two volumes: 47 homilies and 31 various letters; of Severus: three volumes: 124 Cathedral homilies and other letters; of Mar Ephrem and Mar Isaac: 214 *mēmrē*; of Mar Jacob of Sarugh: 182 [*mēmrē*]; and homilies and *mēmrē* of the yearly *ḥudrā,* most of them of Athanasius, Cyril, Theodotus [of Ancyra] and Erechthius [of Antioch of Pisidia], etc.: 155; Histories of the Fathers and Doctors and Martyrs: 125; the Book of Palladius which is called 'The Paradise': three volumes; The *Hexaemeron* of Basil: 9 homilies; [The *Hexaemeron*] of Jacob of Edessa: seven [homilies], and one theological homily and many of his letters; the commentaries of Mar Ephrem and Mar John [Chrysostom] and Moshe Bar Kepha and Bar Ṣalībī.[36]

The second list is comprised mostly of various works of Aristotle. 'From the teachings of the outsiders [sc. pagans],' Bar Hebraeus continues, the following are to be read:

[34] BL Add. 12,172, fols. 100a–b. (Syriac text also in *SBI,* p. 327, n. 765). Also, cf. *CBM,* vol. 2, p. 599.

[35] Cambridge Add. 2887, fol. 33b (Syriac text also in *SBI,* p. 327, n. 766). NB: E. Renaudot's LT of this text, *Liturgiarum Orientalium Collectio,* vol. 2 (2nd ed.; Frankfurt/London, 1847), p. 376, only contains one Jacob, not two.

[36] Bar Hebraeus, *Nomocanon* 7.9 (ed. Bedjan, *Nomocanon,* pp. 105–106). Syriac (with LT) also in Assemani, *BO,* vol. 3.2, pp. 937–38. See also the FT of D.G.K. Taylor, 'L'importance des pères de l'église dans l'oeuvre speculative de Barhebraeus,' *PdO* 33 (2008), pp. 69–71, which is helpful for identifying some of the more obscure names in the list.

The book of Anton of Tikrit; the logical works of Aristotle: *Categories, On Interpretation, Analytika, Apodeitika, Topika* (eight sections), *Sophistical Refutations; On Poetry; On Rhetoric* (three sections); those four Mathematical treatises: they gain elegance for the tongue and training for the mind. As for *Natural Hearing* [sc. the *Physics*] and *Metaphysics*, there is only as much material to be taken as we have taken in our book the *Lamp of the Sanctuary*, and that smaller [volume] of *The Rays*, directed at confuting and disputing those who have known God but who have not glorified him as God. . . .[37]

If we ignore the Syriac names in this list and focus on originally Greek authors and note the time of their translation, it turns out that not only were a number of these books either translated for the first time or retranslated in the seventh century, but the people who were doing the translating and retranslating were associated, so far as we know, almost exclusively with the monastery of Qenneshre. The correlation of time with place is striking.

To make this clearer, I will reproduce the originally Greek works in each list, placing in bold those works that were either translated for the first time or retranslated in the seventh or early eighth century. After each work, I will list the (re-)translator, if known, putting an asterisk by his name if he was associated with Qenneshre. Looking at the originally Greek works of the first list in this way gives us this picture:[38]

Now the books of the doctors which are read in the church are the following:

of Dionysius of Athens: 3 homilies and 10 letters [retranslated by Phocas of Edessa[39] (possibly c. 684–686);[40] NB: Phocas may have been a friend of *Jacob of Edessa?);[41] there may have also been a Syriac version produced by *Athanasius of Balad];[42]

[37] Bar Hebraeus, *Nomocanon* 7.9 (ed. Bedjan, *Nomocanon*, p. 106). Syriac text and LT also available in Assemani, *BO*, vol. 3.2, pp. 938–39. FT of both lists can be found in A. Juckel, 'La reception des pères grecs pendant la «renaissance» syriaque. Renaissance – inculturation – identité,' in A. B. Schmidt and D. Gonnet, eds., *Les pères grecs dans la tradition syriaque* (Paris, 2007), pp. 111–12, but cf. Taylor, 'L'importance des pères de l'église,' p. 70, n. 34.

[38] Taylor, 'L'importance des pères de l'église,' pp. 69–71 attempts to give contemporary bibliographic citations and brief discussion for all the authors on Bar Hebraeus's list of Christian writers.

[39] See J.-M. Hornus, 'Le corpus dionysien en syriaque,' *PdO* 1 (1970), pp. 69–73.

[40] See S. P. Brock, 'Towards a History of Syriac Translation Technique,' in René Lavenant, ed., *III° Symposium Syriacum, 1980: les contacts du monde syriaque avec les autres cultures* (Rome, 1983), p. 3; and Brock, 'Jacob of Edessa's Discourse on the Myron,' p. 21.

[41] See Brock, 'Jacob of Edessa's Discourse on the Myron,' p. 21.

[42] See Timothy I's request to Pethion: 'Please search out and copy for us Dionysius in the translation of Athanasius or that of Phocas' (Timothy I, *Letters* 43.12 [ed. M. Heimgartner, *Die Briefe 42–58 des Ostsyrischen Patriarchen Timotheos I* [CSCO 644: SS 248] [Louvain, 2012], p. 68; ET taken from S. P. Brock, 'Two Letters of the patriarch Timothy from the Late Eighth Century on Translations from Greek,'

of Basil: 29 homilies [translator unknown];[43]

of Gregory of Nazianzus: two volumes: 47 homilies and 31 various letters [revision by *Paul of Edessa;[44] revision by *Athanasius II of Balad[45]];

of Severus: three volumes: 124 Cathedral homilies and other letters [revision by *Jacob of Edessa;[46] NB: *Paul of Edessa translated the *Hymns* of Severus in the early seventh century and *Jacob of Edessa revised them later in the same century[47]];

Homilies and *mēmrē* of the yearly *ḥudrā*, most of them of Athanasius, Cyril, Theodotus and Erechthius etc.: 155;

The Book of Palladius, which is called 'The Paradise': three volumes;

The *Hexaemeron* of Basil: 9 homilies [a second translation made in seventh century by *Athanasius of Balad];[48]

The commentaries of… Mar John [Chrysostom]…

Doing the same for Bar Hebraeus's list of pagan works, yields the following:

The logical works of Aristotle:

Categories [*Jacob of Edessa,[49] *George of the Arabs[50]]

Arabic Sciences and Philosophy 9 [1999], p. 237). Also cf. Barṣawm, *al-Lu'lu' al-manthūr*, p. 590 and Chapter 8, n. 54.

[43] See P. J. Fedwick, 'The Translations of the Works of Basil before 1400,' in Fedwick, ed., *Basil of Caesarea: Christian, Humanist, Ascetic: A Sixteen-Hundredth Anniversary Symposium*, vol. 2 (Toronto, 1981), pp. 449–51 and S. P. Brock, 'Basil's *Homily on Deut. xv 9*: Some Remarks on the Syriac Manuscript Tradition,' in J. Dümmer, ed., *Texte und Textkritik: Eine Aufsatzsammlung* (Berlin, 1987), pp. 62–66. On the homilies, also see S. P. Brock, 'Traduzioni Siriache degli Scritti di Basilio,' in *Basilio tra Oriente e Occidente* (Magnano, BI, 2001), pp. 168–73. The latter article contains valuable information about the manuscript tradition of the works of Basil in Syriac.

[44] For an accessible introduction to Gregory Nazianzen in Syriac, see A. Schmidt, 'The Literary Tradition of Gregory Nazianzus in Syriac Literature and Its Historical Context,' *The Harp* 11–12 (1998–1999), pp. 127–34.

[45] This revision may only have been for the first of the two volumes referred to by Bar Hebraeus, and it is now lost. See J.-C. Haelewyck, *Sancti Gregorii Nazianzeni Opera. Versio Syriaca I: Oratio XL* (CSCG 49: Corpus Nazianzenum 14) (Turnhout/Leuven, 2001), p. ix. See also S. P. Brock, *The Syriac Version of the Pseudo-Nonnos Mythological Scholia*, pp. 30–31. An additional reference to Athanasius as a translator of Gregory Nazianzen can be found in 'Amr b. Mattā, *Akhbār faṭārikat kursī al-mashriq*, p. 65 (ed. Gismondi, *Maris Textus Arabicus*).

[46] See Baumstak, *Geschichte*, p. 251.

[47] See Baumstark, *Geschichte*, pp. 190, 253.

[48] Barṣawm, *al-Lu'lu' al-manthūr*, p. 290, states that references to a translation of Basil's *Hexaemeron* by Athanasius in AD 666–667 can be found in MS Za'farān 241, but cf. also Taylor, 'L'importance des pères de l'église,' p. 70, n. 40.

[49] Baumstark, *Geschichte*, p. 251.

[50] Baumstark, *Geschichte*, p. 257.

On Interpretation [*George of the Arabs[51]]

Analytika [*Athanasius of Balad,[52] *George of the Arabs[53]]

Apodeiktika [*Athanasius of Balad[54]]

***Topika* (eight sections)** [*Athanasius of Balad[55]]

Sophistical Refutations [*Athanasius of Balad[56]]

On Poetry [?][57]

On Rhetoric (three sections) [?][58]

Those four mathematical treatises: they gain elegance for the tongue and training for the mind.

As for *Natural Hearing* [sc. the *Physics*] and *Metaphysics,* there is only as much material to be taken as we have taken in our book the *Lamp of the Sanctuary,* and that smaller [volume] of *The Rays*...

In Bar Hebraeus's first list—books by Christian authors—all of the originally Greek works that were theological in nature were either translated for the first time or retranslated in the seventh century. The originally Greek texts from this list that were not re-translated in the seventh century—the homilies of the *ḥudrā*, Palladius, and the commentaries of Chrysostom—are all notable for not being located at theological pressure points between rival churches,

[51] Baumstark, *Geschichte*, p. 257.

[52] F. E. Peters, *Aristoteles Arabus: The Oriental Translations and Commentaries on the Aristotelian Corpus* (Leiden, 1968), p. 14.

[53] See Baumstark, *Geschichte*, p. 257.

[54] Timothy I, *Letters* 48.4 (ed. Heimgartner [CSCO 644: SS 248], p. 89; ET in Brock, 'Two Letters of the Patriarch Timothy from the Late Eighth Century on Translations from Greek,' pp. 238, cf. 246).

[55] Timothy I, *Letters* 48.10 (ed. Heimgartner [CSCO 644: SS 248], p. 92; ET in Brock, 'Two Letters of the Patriarch Timothy from the Late Eighth Century on Translations from Greek,' pp. 239).

[56] Peters, *Aristoteles Arabus*, p. 23.

[57] The provenance of the Syriac translation of the *Poetics*, which survives only in fragments, is unclear, but based on the extant evidence scholars have argued that it does not have a pre-Islamic origin. See H. Hugonnard-Roche, '*La Poétique. Tradition syriaque et arabe*,' in *DPA*, *Supplément*, pp. 208–11, and the discussion of the question of the Syriac translation by D. Gutas in L. Tarán and D. Gutas, *Aristotle Poetics. Editio maior of the Greek Text with Historical Introductions and Philological Commentaries* (Leiden/Boston, 2012), pp. 77–88, where it is argued that a Syriac translation of the *Poetics* likely did not exist before the ninth century.

[58] Ibn al-Samḥ (d. 1027) knew of a Syriac translation of the *Rhetoric* of Aristotle, but the source of that translation and the question of whether it had a pre-Islamic origin remain uncertain. On the Syriac translation of the *Rhetoric*, see most conveniently, M. Aouad, '*La Rhétorique*. Tradition syriaque et arabe,' in *DPA*, vol. 1, pp. 456–57, and J. Watt, 'Version syriaque,' in *DPA*, *Supplément*, p. 219. G. J. Reinink showed that Severus Sebokht's letter to Yonan the Periodeute cannot be used as evidence for a seventh-century Syriac translation of the *Rhetoric*; see his, 'Severus Sebokts Brief an den Periodeutes Jonan. Einige Fragen zur aristotelischen Logik,' in Lavenant, ed., *III° Symposium Syriacum, 1980*, pp. 97–107.

unlike Ps.-Dionysius, Gregory Nazianzen, Basil, and Severus.[59] It was these latter authors that members of rival churches were studying and seeking to claim for themselves and mobilize against their competitors, or in the case of Severus, to refute. At some point between 785 and 789, for example, Timothy I would write a letter refuting Cyril of Alexandria's attempt to show Nestorius a heretic based on the words of Gregory Nazianzen.[60] As for Bar Hebraeus's second list, of pagan authors, it makes it strikingly clear that the entire *Organon* was translated or retranslated in the seventh century by three men, all of them probably friends,[61] and all probably hailing from Qenneshre.

TRACES OF A CURRICULUM

There seems to be evidence for study of the authors on Bar Hebraeus's two lists —both the Syriac and the Greek authors—in the seventh and early eighth centuries; letters once more can provide us with an indication of what was on the minds of people at this time. Jacob's letters are included in the canon of Bar Hebraeus, for example, and it seems that within decades after his death, they were already beginning to be discussed and studied. George of the Arabs' eighth letter, written in AD 715, seven years after Jacob's death, is a response to a series of questions asked him by John of Litarb about difficult-to-understand passages in a letter Jacob had written to the Stylite.[62] Basil's *Hexaemeron* was among the books Bar Hebraeus included, and we know that it was a work which both Jacob of Edessa[63] and George of the Arabs had read.[64] George was also reading Jacob of Sarugh.[65]

Ephrem, too, made it into Bar Hebraeus's syllabus, and we have evidence suggesting that his *mēmrē*, or at least certain ones of them, were objects of study in the seventh and eighth centuries. George's eleventh letter offers a correspondent named Abraham an explanation of a cryptic passage in Ephrem's

[59] On the importance of Gregory Nazianzen to both Miaphysites and Nestorians, see Schmidt, 'The Literary Tradition of Gregory of Nazianzus in Syriac Literature,' *The Harp* 11–12 (1998–1999), p. 131.

[60] Timothy I *Letters* 39 (To Sergius), pp. 272–79 (ed. Braun [CSCO 74–75: SS 30–31], pp. 189–94 [=LT]). Cf. p. 274: 'And he shows that he is a heretic based on the words of the holy Gregory which are in the letter which is to Cledonius.' For the date of *Letter 39*, see Bidawid, *Les lettres du patriarche nestorien Timothée I*, p. 74.

[61] See my, 'Between Christology and *Kalām*?' pp. 674–77. And cf. below, pp. 202–203,

[62] BL Add. 12,154, fols. 272b–278a.

[63] M. Wilks, 'Jacob of Edessa's Use of Greek Philosophy in His Hexaemeron,' in ter Haar Romeny, *Jacob of Edessa and the Syriac Culture of His Day* (Leiden/Boston, 2008), pp. 223–38, esp. p. 224.

[64] See his citation of it in his *Letter 11*, BL Add. 12,154, fol. 290a.

[65] BL Add. 12,154, fols. 249b, 258a (*Letter 4*).

Hymn 44 *On Faith.*[66] In Jacob's fifth letter to John of Litarb, he responds to a question from John about the meaning of the same Hymn 44, even focusing his attention on precisely the same half dozen or so delphic lines in the Hymn that George would attempt to explain in his letter to Abraham.[67] A common canon or curriculum of study is one possible explanation for this curious coincidence. In the middle of the seventh century, Severus Sebhokt wrote to Yonan the periodeute to answer questions about the meaning of terms in the *On Interpretation* and *Prior Analytics*;[68] he would also write to a priest named Aitilaha of Nineveh explaining the meaning of certain key terms in the *On Interpretation.*[69] Such correspondence suggests that learned Syriac-speaking Miaphysites in the mid-seventh century were studying at least part of the *Organon* of Aristotle. Vatican Syriac 158, likely a ninth century manuscript that contains works of both Porphyry and Aristotle, and has been pointed to as a 'textbook' whose ancestor ultimately goes back to Qenneshre in the eighth or ninth century.[70]

We know that the *Homilies* of Gregory Nazianzen were being studied at this time: in the sixth letter of George of the Arabs, George wrote to his syncellus Jacob to explain two unclear passages in these homilies. In both cases, George offered alternate and superior translations to the Syriac that Jacob had available.[71] We also know that George was familiar with the mythological scholia of Pseudo-Nonnus, a sixth-century composition that explained mythological allusions in four of Gregory's homilies and which, in the manuscript tradition, was attached to and transmitted with the homilies.[72]

George himself seems to have studied the *Homilies* of Gregory Nazianzen with Athanasius II of Balad. In his *Letter 6*, to Jacob, he stated that the meaning of the passage in question was clearer in the way that Patriarch Athanasius had translated it for him.[73] George was also most likely the compiler of a collection of scholia on the *Homilies* of Gregory Nazianzen. Perhaps the strongest

[66] BL Add. 12,154, fols. 290a–290b.

[67] BL Add. 12,172, fols. 85b–87b. Compare esp. fols. 87a–b with George's *Letter 11.*

[68] Cambridge Add. 2812, fol. 109a (Syriac text and ET also in *SBI*, p. 333, n. 797). On this letter and its relation to both Aristotle, Qenneshre, and the Alexandrian commentary tradition, see G. J. Reinink, 'Severus Sebokts Brief an den Periodeutes Jonan. Einige Fragen zur aristotelischen Logik.' The letter has now been published with a FT and detailed analysis in Hugonnard-Roche, 'Questions de logique au VIIe siècle.'

[69] Baumstark, *Geschichte*, p. 246, and Brock, 'The Syriac Commentary Tradition,' p. 13.

[70] King, 'Why Were the Syrians Interested in Greek Philosophy?' pp. 64–65. For a description of the manuscript, see *BAV*, vol. 1.3, pp. 304–307.

[71] BL Add. 12,154, fols. 263a–264b.

[72] Brock, *The Syriac Version of the Pseudo-Nonnos Mythological Scholia*, p. 30, n. 4.

[73] See BL Add. 14,725, fol. 132b and BL Add. 12,154, fol. 263b (Syriac text and ET of both these are available in *SBI*, p. 334, n. 802. Cf. also *SBI*, p. 155, n. 401, and *CBM*, vol. 2, p. 443).

piece of evidence suggesting George as the compiler of this work is a striking parallel between it and George's letters. In explaining a passage in Gregory's *Homily 2,* the compiler of the scholia breaks into the first person and invokes a translation made for him by Patriarch Athanasius II. This passage in Gregory's *Homily 2* is precisely the same passage that caused George to switch to the first person in his *Letter 6* and reference a translation made for him by the patriarch Athanasius.[74] Wright did not recognize the uncanny similarity between the first-person passage in the letters of George and the first-person passage in the collection of scholia, but he was nevertheless able to adduce other reasons for believing that the Bishop of the Arabs was the author of the compilation.[75] This collection of scholia on the *Homilies* of Gregory Nazianzen may very well have been some sort of school text meant to aid students: 'Each homily is preceded by a short introduction,' Wright noted, 'giving an outline of its contents, and a list of the passages of Scripture which are cited in it.' The work also discusses the chronology of the composition of the forty-seven homilies of Gregory.[76]

Not only had Athanasius II of Balad apparently offered George of the Arabs instruction on at least some of the *Homilies*; he had written about them himself. George's collection of scholia preserves a scholion by Athanasius explaining their organization, and Athanasius himself produced a corrected version of the revised translation of Paul of Edessa made in 623–624.[77] Jacob of Edessa, too, has been credited with producing some sort of corrected edition of the *Homilies* of Gregory Nazianzen, but the state of the manuscript evidence is such that it is impossible to tell what exactly it was that Jacob left behind—an improved version, or simply marginalia.[78]

Severus Sebokht, who represented the generation of scholars at Qenneshre before Athanasius II of Balad and who was in fact Athanasius's teacher,[79] was

[74] BL Add. 14,725, fol. 132a (Syriac text also available in *CBM,* vol. 2, p. 443). Compare this passage with BL Add. 12,154, fols. 263a, 263b (the Syriac text and an ET of both these passages is available in *SBI,* p. 334, n. 802).

[75] *CBM,* vol. 2, p. 443.

[76] *CBM,* vol. 2, p. 441.

[77] See BL Add. 14,725, fol. 103a, in *CBM,* vol. 2, p. 441, for the introductory note to the scholia of Athanasius reproduced in the collection of scholia on the *Homilies* of Gregory Nazianzen likely compiled by George of the Arabs. Also see BL Add. 12,153, fol. 121a in *CBM,* vol. 2, p. 441, p. 425 (English translations of both these passages available in *SBI,* p. 335, n. 805). For Athanasius and the *Homilies,* see Brock, *The Syriac Version of the Pseudo-Nonnos Mythological Scholia,* pp. 30–31. It is also worth mentioning again in this context that George of the Arabs was aware of the *Homilies* as well as the *Mythological Scholia* of Ps.-Nonnus, which was attached to the *Homilies* (p. 30 and p. 30, n. 4); Severus Sebokht, too, was aware of the *Homilies,* probably in the translation of Paul of Edessa (p. 29, n. 7).

[78] Brock, *The Syriac Version of the Pseudo-Nonnos Mythological Scholia,* pp. 31–32. On p. 32, n. 1, Brock reproduces the portion of the colophon of BM Or. 8731 that credits Jacob with a 'correction' or 'edition' of the *Homilies* in Syriac.

[79] Bar Hebraeus, *Ecclesiastical History* 1.54 (ed. Abbeloos and Lamy, 1.287).

also concerned with 'the Theologian,' as Gregory was called. In a letter to the periodeute Yonan of Tella, he thanked Yonan for sending along to him a manuscript containing the letters of Basil and Gregory, which he had been trying to obtain from the members of Yonan's monastery for a long time.[80] It is also worth noting that Januarius Candidatus, a contemporary of Severus Sebokht,[81] produced a translation of the poems of Gregory Nazianzen in 665;[82] Wright suggested that Januarius was from Qenneshre.[83] The poems were translated again in 804 by Theodosius of Edessa, likely another product of Qenneshre and the brother of the famous patriarch Dionysius of Tell Mahre, who we know was from Qenneshre.[84]

George, Athanasius, Jacob, Severus, and Januarius were not the only figures who were intensely interested in the *Homilies* of Gregory Nazianzen in the seventh century: the Chalcedonian Maximus the Confessor composed a work on difficult passages in Ps.-Dionysius and Gregory Nazianzen, and scholia in Greek on Ps.-Dionysius[85]—another author on Bar Hebraeus's syllabus and one who was also (re)translated in the seventh century by a Miaphysite possibly connected with Qenneshre, Phocas of Edessa. There was a transconfessional, so to speak, interest in these authors, which raises again the issue of Syriac-speakers needing to have access to the same resources as Greek-speakers. If, in the late eighth century, the Chalcedonian Michael the Syncellus was able to receive a traditional education in grammar, rhetoric, philosophy, poetry, and astronomy in Jerusalem,[86] where might a Syriac-speaking Miaphysite go for something similar? Qenneshre.

These are all hints at what Miaphysites were studying in the seventh and eighth centuries. Combined with the striking fact that so many of the works on Bar Hebraeus's syllabus were translated either for the first time or retranslated in the seventh century by someone who had been trained at Qenneshre,

[80] Severus Sebokht, *Letter to Yonan the Periodeute*, p. 60 (ed. Hugonnard-Roche, 'Questions de logique au VIIe siècle'; Syriac text from Cambridge Add. 2812, fol. 109b and ET available in *SBI*, p. 336, n. 810). NB: Like Severus, George of the Arabs also used the expression ܙܘܓܐ ܐܠܗܝܐ to refer to Basil and Gregory; see BL Add. 12,154, fol. 256a and his *Homily on Blessed Mar Severus*, p. 11, ln. 251 (ed. McVey [CSCO 530: SS 216]).

[81] Michael the Great, *Chronicle* 11.12 (ed. Chabot, 4.435 = 2.453).

[82] For this date, see I. Guidi, 'Di un' Iscrizione Sepolcrale Siriaca e della Versione dei Carmi di S. Gregorio Nazianzeno fatta da Candidato di Âmed,' in *Actes du dixième congrès international des orientalistes. Session de Genève 1894* (Leiden, 1896), p. 78.

[83] W. Wright, *A Short History of Syriac Literature* (London, 1894), p. 156.

[84] Theodosius was the brother of Dionysius of Tell Mahre (see Bar Hebraeus, *Ecclesiastical History* 1.64 [ed. Abbeloos and Lamy, 1.361]) and Dionysius had been from Qenneshre (Bar Hebareus, *Ecclesiastical History* 1.64 = col. 1.347). Cf. chapter 6, n. 59 and chapter 8, n. 69.

[85] See Maximus the Confessor, *Scholia in Corpus Areopagiticum*, PG 4, cols. 15–432, 527–76; *Ambigua ad Thomam*, PG 91, cols. 1032–60; and *Ambigua ad Iohannem*, PG 91, cols. 1061–1417. cf. Beck, *Kirche und Theologische Literatur*, p. 438.

[86] For this, C. Foss, 'Byzantine Saints in Early Islamic Syria,' *AB* 125 (2007), p. 115.

it is tempting to suggest that Bar Hebraeus's thirteenth-century enumeration has as an ancestor a Miaphysite curriculum of study that first took shape hundreds of years earlier, in the seventh century, perhaps at the monastery of Qenneshre or perhaps at Qenneshre and several other important Miaphysite monasteries.[87]

If this is the case, what conclusions can we draw? The testimony of the canons of Jacob and the other bits and pieces I have tried to marshal here suggest that the priest or monk whose education ended after he had learned the Psalms and the lectionary or the Scriptures from his village teacher or at a local monastery was not necessarily sufficiently equipped to defend Miaphysite orthodoxy against the slings and arrows of potential rivals. Nor could such a person always be trusted to maintain the integrity of the boundaries that were supposed to exist between different Christian confessions.

As we have had ample opportunity to see, the leaders of the Miaphysite movement were none too happy about the confused confessional situation on the ground in the seventh and early eighth centuries. At least part of the answer to this messy state of affairs was an institutional one. Just as today some students go on to pursue studies beyond the secondary level, so in this period some young men pursued studies beyond the level of the local village or monastic school. It was at places like Qenneshre and certain other high-powered Miaphysite monasteries, such as Mar Matay, Mar Zakay, and Beth Malka/Eusebona,[88] that the intellectual underpinnings of the seventh-century Syriac-speaking Miaphysite movement were created and maintained. Miaphysite identity radiated most strongly from these centers and from their graduates. The further one traveled from them, the more likely one was to find confessional confusion and mixing. It was at centers like Qenneshre that a graduate school syllabus of study crystallized. It was here that church leaders were trained. The village priest may not have been able to answer the aporetic questions of a confessional rival in a world characterized by low-level theological skirmishing, but he could write a letter to someone who had been

[87] One should make mention here of the monastery of Qarqapta and others like it, from which the 'Syriac Masora,' are said to have emerged. The biblical, patristic and other texts from which these collections of lists of words were drawn and created to use as a study and reading aid also correspond to Bar Hebraeus's syllabus. On the Syriac Massora and the texts covered in it, see most conveniently Baumstark, *Geschichte*, pp. 259–60. But importantly, see now Loopstra, 'Patristic Selections in the "Masoretic" Handbooks of the *Qarqaptā* Tradition,' and Loopstra, 'Jacob of Edessa and Patristic Collections in the "Syriac Masora": Some Soundings,' in D. Bumazhnov and H. R. Seeliger eds., *Syrien im 1.–7. Jahrhundert nach Christus* (Tübingen, 2011), pp. 157–68. (cf. chapter 6, n. 84).

[88] On Mar Matay and Mar Zakay as examples of 'Greco-Syriac' monasteries, see J. Watt, 'Al-Fārābī and the History of the Syriac *Organon*,' in Kiraz, ed., *Malphono w-Rabo d-Malphone*, pp. 759–61. For Beth Malka/Eusebona, see Brock, *The Syriac Version of the Pseudo-Nonnos Mythological Scholia*, p. 10, n.1 (on the identity of these two) and pp. 32–33.

trained at a place like Qenneshre, and he could ask that person for help. This is precisely what we see happening in the letters of George of the Arabs, and also in the letters of Jacob of Edessa.

If this picture is in any way a persuasive one, we might say that the translation and retranslation of texts was being driven by the needs of a syllabus of education that equipped the spiritual and intellectual core of the Miaphysite movement, men who were operating in an environment of unstable and insecure identities and confessional competition. In such an environment, there was a strong need to marginally differentiate themselves[89] from rivals and to assert and draw boundaries between their communities and others.

The continued existence of the Miaphysite church depended on its ability to reproduce a class of leaders who were committed to the doctrinal positions of the Miaphysite movement and who were able to defend those positions against the attacks of rivals. It was also the job of such men to try to counter the confessional confusion that existed among the simple. The clearest example of such attempts we have are the canons of Jacob, which we explored in Chapter 3.

Of the large number of Christian writers who preceded them, members of the Miaphysite movement—like members of the Nestorian and Chalcedonian movements—selected certain authors as spiritual and doctrinal exemplars: Their works were to be studied and their views were to be imitated, taught, and transmitted to subsequent generations. Study was a key to defining who one was.[90] There was of course overlap between the writers deemed 'Fathers' by Miaphysites, Nestorians, and Chalcedonians, but there was also important difference. Rabban Bar 'Idta was reading Nestorius and Theodore of Mopsuestia in his cell, but Jacob of Edessa lamented he did not have his Philoxenus and Severus with him; both men, however, read Basil. In some important sense then, Miaphysite identity, like Nestorian identity, and Chalcedonian identity, was a function of what was being read and taught to and by the leaders of the movement in its intellectual centers.

[89] I use the phrase 'marginal differentiation' here in the modern advertising sense: How does Proctor and Gamble differentiate the different kinds of toothpaste it sells when all the toothpastes have the same basic purpose? Alternately, given that there is great similarity and much overlap between various Christian groups, how does one group distinguish itself from another? See the Sicilian proverb quoted as an epigram at the beginning of Anton Blok's article, 'The Narcissism of Minor Differences,' pp. 115–35, in Blok, *Honour and Violence* (Malden, Mass., 2001). 'Nella stessa faccia, l'occhio destro odiava il sinistro. (In the same face, the right eye hated the left.)' (quote on p. 115).

[90] See, e.g., the story of the Akoimetoi monks and Macedonius and the importance of studying works written in the tradition of Diodore and Theodore and venerating Nestorius in Ps.-Zacharias Rhetor, *Chronicle* 7.7 (ed. Brooks [CSCO 84: SS 39], pp. 39–40; translation available in Hamilton and Brooks, *The Syriac Chronicle Known as That of Zachariah of Mitylene*, pp. 168–69. A more recent translation is available in G. Greatrex et al., *The Chronicle of Pseudo-Zachariah Rhetor: Church and War in Late Antiquity* [Liverpool, 2011], p. 252).

* * *

This then, is the world that Chalcedon created: a region populated by simple believers who (notionally, at least) belonged to churches whose leaders were engaged in attempts to erect boundaries, protect their congregations, and win converts. The Christian Middle East was a fractured and fracturing, confessionally diverse landscape where educational institutions proliferated and, among the Miaphysites, sophisticated translations and retranslations were produced as church leaders sought to impose order on the disorderly world of the simple. This was the world that the Arabs found when they conquered the Middle East in the seventh century.

In the Third Part of this book, we will look at how the Arabs fit into this picture, but before doing so, I want to pause and look at one last consequence of the confessional chaos that Chalcedon wrought in the Middle East: a remarkable cultural continuity. What does this question of continuity, one of the oldest and most venerable in the study of the later Roman Empire, look like when viewed from the perspective of the world we have encountered in Parts I and II?

INTERLUDE

The Question of Continuity

CHAPTER 8

Continuities—Personal and Institutional

What we have studied so far is the ferment that kept the Syrian learned world constantly active. The sectarian diversity and blurry communal lines in Syria and the Middle East more broadly—unique in the entire late Roman Christian world in the extent and depth of its robust confessional differences—led to a proliferation of educational institutions, translation, and learning among the competing Christian communities of the region. Schools were created. Texts were translated. New texts were written. One consequence of this institutional response was a series of continuities across a period of time—the sixth through the ninth centuries—that witnessed some of the most consequential changes in the late ancient world. From a political standpoint, this was a period of dramatic rupture. Regimes changed.

But, in a premodern world of weak states, we should perhaps not read too much significance into a change of regimes. How important was the late Roman state for the preservation and transmission of certain aspects of learned culture if, centuries after it had ended, the population of its former territories (and the territory of its former rival, the Sasanians) was able to translate and transmit an enormous amount of antique and late antique philosophical and scientific material into Arabic? And Baghdad is only the best-known part of that story: discussions of Greco-Arabic translation have tended to focus on the translation of secular material into Arabic in Baghdad, but we should also remember that a great deal of Christian material was translated from Greek into Arabic in Western Syria in the Abbasid period, too, from Antioch to Palestine and the Sinai.[1] What is more, as we have already seen, in the seventh century (and

[1] See the comments in J. Grand'Henry, 'Transmission de textes grecs, spécialement de Grégoire de Nazianze, en milieu arabe,' *PACT News* 19 (1987), pp. 42–43 and, more recently, see A. Treiger, 'Christian Greco-Arabica: Prolegomena to a History of the Arabic Translations of the Greek Church Fathers,' *Intellectual History of the Islamicate World* 3 (2015), pp. 188–227. On translations of secular works into Arabic, see most conveniently, D. Gutas, *Greek Thought, Arabic Culture: the Graeco-Arabic Translation Movement in Baghdad and Early 'Abbāsid Society (2nd–4th/8th–10th centuries)* (New York, 1998); Gutas, 'Greek Philosophical Works Translated into Arabic,' in R. Pasnau, ed., *Cambridge History of Medieval Philosophy*, vol. 2 (Cambridge, 2012), pp. 802–22; and G. Endress, 'Die Wissenschaftliche Literatur,' in H. Gätje, *Grundriß der Arabischen Philologie*. vol. 2: *Literaturwissenschaft* (Wiesbaden, 1987), pp. 400–506. For the suggestion 'that the Roman Empire may not have been the prime mover in the process of Hellenization,' but rather the Christian churches, see Johnson, 'Introduction: The Social Presence of Greek in Eastern Christianity,' p. 13.

before), members of the dissident Miaphysite church were engaged in sophisticated translations from Greek into Syriac of a number of texts. All of these cultural efforts were undertaken apart from the Roman state. What we witnessed in Part II was the development of cultural institutions among Middle Eastern Christian communities that existed and persisted, independently from the state and even despite it. These institutions provided paths by which sophisticated ideas and cultural practices might be transmitted across centuries of great military upheaval and political discontinuity. What we have is a non-state dependent bridge between the world of the late antique Roman-ruled Middle East and the world of medieval Abbasid Baghdad.

Al-Fārābī has left us a celebrated account of ancient philosophy as it was being transmitted to Baghdad via Alexandria and then Antioch. Though both fanciful and misleading, it raises in a vivid way the question of how late Roman traditions were continued after Roman rule ended in the Middle East.[2] I am interested now in the same question of cultural transmission that al-Fārābī was, but rather than his general talk about philosophical instruction being moved from one Mediterranean or Middle Eastern city to the next, the landscape and developments I attempted to sketch out in Part II offer us real and specific human and institutional bridges that spanned the Roman and Arab-ruled worlds and concrete social contexts to explain their growth and development.

Let us take a few examples of the continuities to which I have alluded. Severus Sebokht's association with Qenneshre and Athanasius II of Balad gives us an attested student-teacher line which runs: Severus Sebokht (d. 666/7) → Athanasius of Balad (d. 687) → George of the Arabs (d. 724). Jacob of Edessa (d. 708), who had been elevated to bishop by Athanasius,[3] may very well have been Athanasius's student as well; Jacob certainly belonged to the same milieu and Miaphysite intellectual elite as Severus, Athanasius, and George. It was George who finished Jacob's *Hexaemeron*, probably in the early eighth century, after Jacob died before completing it;[4] both George and Jacob corresponded with John, the Stylite of Litarb (d. 737/8), in the first part of the eighth century and, in the case of Jacob of Edessa, perhaps even in the late

[2] For al-Fārābī's account, see Ibn Abī Uṣaybiʿa, *ʿUyūn al-anbāʾ fī ṭabaqāt al-aṭibbāʾ*, pp. 604–605 (ed. N. Riḍā [Beirut, 1965]). ET available in F. Rosenthal, *The Classical Heritage in Islam* (London/New York, 1975), pp. 50–51. On the Alexandria-to-Baghdad legend, see D. Gutas, 'The "Alexandria to Baghdad" Complex of Narratives: A Contribution to the Study of Philosophical and Medical Historiography among the Arabs,' *Documenti e Studi sulla Tradizione Filosofica Medievale* 10 (1999), pp. 155–93 (pp. 187–88 on the part of the story dealing with the geographic movement instruction). See also, J. W. Watt, 'Al-Fārābī and the History of the Syriac *Organon*,' pp. 751–52.

[3] See Bar Hebraeus, *Ecclesiastical History* 1.54 (ed. Abbeloos and Lamy, 1.289).

[4] Jacob of Edessa, *Hexaemeron*, p. 347 (ed. Chabot [CSCO 92: SS 44]).

seventh century;[5] both Jacob and George also corresponded with a certain Barhadbshabba, possibly the same person.[6]

Furthermore, as I mentioned in the previous chapter, John of Litarb would write to George asking for help in understanding difficult passages in Jacob's letters, and John himself grouped George and Jacob together as authorities along with Severus Sebokht. In John's one extant letter, written in probably the first few decades of the eighth century to an Arab priest named Daniel, his stated aim was not to write out anything new, but only to report what previous authorities had written on the question: '... this is clearly explained and interpreted by chroniclers and even by holy teachers,' he wrote Daniel,

> and is not in need of another explanation and interpretation from a person like us. Since, however, your brotherhood has asked that I make [an explanation] for it, look now, I will set down in brief for it—and only as a reminder of sorts—these things which some of these people inscribed and wrote out at length, neither stating or writing anything of my own.[7]

It is therefore noteworthy that John only cites three texts from the seventh and eighth centuries: a *mēmrā* by Severus Sebokht and letters written by Jacob of Edessa and George of the Arabs.[8] In other words, by John's time in the first part of the eighth century, Severus, Jacob, and George were already being grouped together and associated with one another. Given John of Litarb's connection to George and Jacob, we could rewrite the student-teacher line as follows: Severus Sebokht (d. 666/7) ⟶ Athanasius II of Balad (d. 687) ⟶ George of the Arabs (d. 724) (and Jacob of Edessa? [d. 708]) ⟶ John of Litarb (d. 737/8).

The line from Severus Sebokht (d. 667) to Athanasius of Balad (d. 687), George of the Arabs (d. 724) and then to John of Litarb (d. 737/8) provides more than one hundred years of continuity in intellectual inquiry and study in the Near East. Severus was very likely born before the Arab conquests and may perhaps have even been born before the outbreak of the Byzantine-Persian wars of the early seventh century. The scanty biographical information we

[5] See Baumstark, *Geschichte*, p. 258.

[6] Cf. van Ginkel, "Greetings to a Virtuous Man: The Correspondence of Jacob of Edessa," p. 80, no. 32.

[7] BL Add. 12,154, fol. 291a. Syriac text and ET also in *SBI*, p. 342, n. 823. Severus Sebokht made a similar claim in his letter to Yonan the Periodeute, stating that he would not state anything from himself, but would only speak from those things that had been previously stated by the ancients; see Severus Sebokht, *Letter to Yonan the Periodeute*, p. 60 (ed. Hugonnard-Roche, 'Questions de logique au VIIe siècle'). Such language, was not, of course, unique to George or Severus. For the background to its development, see Gray, "'The Select Fathers'" as well as the comments in Gray, 'Theological Discourse in the Seventh Century: The Heritage from the Sixth Century,' *Byzantinische Forschungen* 26 (2000), pp. 219–28.

[8] For the quotations from these three, see BL Add. 12,154, fols. 292a–293b.

possess about John of Litarb does not allow us to know whether he studied at Qenneshre, but Severus Sebokht, Athanasius II, Jacob, and George were all associated with the place. The generation of scholars associated with Qenneshre before Severus included figures we met in Chapter 6: Paul of Edessa, who revised the Syriac translation of the *Homilies* of Gregory on Cyprus ca. 624, and the important patriarch Athanasius Gamolo (sed. 594/5–631).

It is tempting to speculate that Severus knew both these men and perhaps studied with them: we know, for instance, that by ca. 660, Severus was using Paul of Edessa's revised translation of the *Homilies*, providing us with perhaps its earliest witnesses,[9] and it has been suggested that Athanasius I Gamolo was the patron who commissioned and funded Paul of Edessa's retranslation of the *Homilies.*[10]

Athanasius I was the patron who commissioned Paul of Tella's translation of the Syro-Hexapla[11] and was perhaps behind the ultra-literal New Testament translation of Thomas of Harkel as well.[12] He hailed from a wealthy and elite family in Samosata.[13] Unsurprisingly, he was likely highly educated. The *vita* of Athanasius contained in Michael the Great's *Chronicle* notes that when a group of bishops met Athanasius, who was driving a camel (hence his sobriquet, Gamolo, 'the Camel driver'), 'tasted his knowledge,' and learned that he was from a great (or 'the great') monastery—that is, Qenneshre—they forcefully took him back to the synod of bishops that had gathered at a nearby monastery to elect a new patriarch and ordained him.[14]

Athanasius has been regarded as the author of a *vita* of Severus of Antioch (d. 538).[15] The author of this *Life of Severus* wrote about the connection between his family and the famous patriarch of Antioch:

[9] See Brock, *The Syriac Version of the Pseudo-Nonnos Mythological Scholia*, p. 29.

[10] See Schmidt, 'The Literary Tradition of Gregory of Nazianzus in Syriac Literature,' pp. 132–34.

[11] See Baumstark, *Geschichte*, p. 186, and the colophon to Paul's translation of 4 Kingdoms (cf. n. 18 in this chapter).

[12] See Baumstark, *Geschichte*, p. 188, and cf. Schmidt, 'The Literary Tradition of Gregory of Nazianzus in Syriac Literature,' p. 133. For the classic argument that Thomas of Harkel was Athanasius's syncellus, see J. Gwynn's article 'Thomas Harklensis,' in *A Dictionary of Christian Biography, Literature, Sects and Doctrines; during the First Eight Centuries*, vol. 4 (London, 1887), pp. 1014–21 (on p. 1015 Gwynn makes the argument for identifying Thomas the Syncellus with Thomas of Harkel).

[13] Michael the Great, *Chronicle* 10.24 (ed. Chabot, 4.388 = 2.375).

[14] 'Tasted' here can also mean 'perceived.' Michael the Great, *Chronicle* 10.24 (ed. Chabot, 4.389 = 2.376; compare with election of the patriarch Joseph in 790 [4.483 = 3.10] [cf. Chapter 1, n. 93]). The *History of the Patriarchs of Alexandria* 1.14, refers to him as 'a man who was a monk and a priest and a scholar... exceedingly wise and pure in heart' (translation taken from B. Evetts [PO 1.4], p. 216). On Athanasius, see also Chapter 4, n. 15.

[15] See Baumstark, *Geschichte*, p. 186. Despite the attribution of this work to Athanasius in the manuscript tradition, its actual authorship is uncertain. The text survives in Arabic, Ethiopic, and in fragmentary form in Coptic.

> As for this Father Severus, my brothers, my bodily father would sit with him because he was a priest and my grandfather was also from his city. That old man—I mean, my grandfather—was also a blessed father and was a priest. His name was Athanasius, like my name, and he was a companion of Severus the elder, the bishop in his city, who was the grandfather of Severus the Patriarch. The elder bishop was present at and engaged in controversy in the Council of Ephesus which included two hundred bishops. And this great father Severus, who was the grandfather of the father, the Patriarch Severus, knew my grandfather and was his confidant and would always speak with him at table because the two of them had great brotherly affection.[16]

It possible therefore that Athanasius's father had been friends with Severus of Antioch and that his grandfather had been close friends with the grandfather of Severus.[17] The consequences of this connection are remarkable: if we assume Athanasius I had a connection to Severus Sebokht via Qenneshre,[18] we have an unbroken and continuous line of Miaphysite scholars and intellectuals stretching from the high point of the Miaphysite movement in the time of the Emperor Anastasius into the late Umayyad period. Through the grandfathers, who knew one another, one might even push the beginning of the direct line of continuity back to the time of Theodosius II and the Council of Ephesus.

The existence of such a remarkable person-to-person chain stretching for over two hundred years is partly a matter of speculation and, in the specific case of Severus, unlikely—his own writings suggest that he himself was a pagan convert, from a pagan family, and the *Life of Severus*'s comments on his family history represent an attempt to Christianize his genealogy.[19] Nevertheless, we have in the monastery of Qenneshre, founded about the year 530,[20] an institutional continuity stretching from the heart of the age of

[16] (Ps.-?) Athanasius Gamolo, *Life of Severus* 3 (ed. and trans. Y. N. Youssef, *The Arabic Life of Severus of Antioch attributed to Athanasius of Antioch* [PO 49.4] [Turnhout, 2004], p. 21. The translation is mine, but made with reference to Youssef's. This text is also known as the *Conflict of Severus* and exists in Coptic fragments and also in Ethiopic. For the Ethiopic of this passage, see E. J. Goodspeed and W. E. Crum., ed. and trans., *The Conflict of Severus, Patriarch of Antioch by Athanasius* [PO 4.8] [Paris, 1908], p. 592).

[17] Possible, though in this instance almost certainly unlikely—see below, n. 19, in this chapter.

[18] Though NB: Though Athanasius spent time in Qenneshre in his youth, he resided in the monastery of Mar Zakay in Callinicum as patriarch; see the subscription to the Syro-Hexaplar translation of 4 Kingdoms in P. de Lagarde, ed., *Bibliothecae syriacae* (Göttingen, 1892), p. 256, lns. 28–32.

[19] Allen and Hayward, *Severus of Antioch*, p. 5, doubted the accuracy of the claim that Severus's grandfather had been at the Council of Ephesus, suggesting that Severus's own writings point to his having a pagan family. For evidence of Severus's pagan background, see S. P. Brock and B. Fitzgerald, *Two Early Lives of Severos*, pp. 1–3. Brock (p. 3) noted that the 'process of Christianizing Severos' ancestry' had already begun in his lifetime in the sixth century.

[20] F. Nau demonstrated that Qenneshre must have been founded between 528 and 531. See Nau,

Justinian into the Abbasid period. The political chaos that followed the death of Hārūn al-Rashīd in AH193/AD 809 led to violence which saw the churches of Jerusalem sacked, as well as the desolation of great monasteries and *lavras* in Palestine, such as St. Saba and St. Euthymius.[21] Further north, in Syria, Qenneshre was sacked and torched around AD 811.[22] At the time of its destruction, the monastery had been a continuously functioning center of Miaphysite intellectual activity for some 280 years,[23] a period that straddled the final Roman-Persian war, the Arab conquests, the rise and fall of the Umayyads, and the Abbasid revolution. After its destruction, Qenneshre's monks were dispersed.[24] It was rebuilt around 820.[25] The last great figure to be associated with the monastery, the polymath and patriarch Dionysius of Tell Mahre (d. 845), was trained there before its tragic burning and plunder.[26]

Qenneshre would never return to its former glory of the sixth, seventh, and early eighth centuries. Nevertheless, bishops would still come from there as late as the tenth century,[27] and Arabic Muslim sources indicate that it was an impressive place and a destination for visitors into the time of the Hamdanid

---

'Histoire de Jean bar Aphtonia,' *ROC* 7 (1902), pp. 98–99; also cf. Nau, 'Appendice: Fragments sur le monastère de Qenneshre,' in *Actes du XIV congrès international des orientalistes*, vol. 2 (Paris, 1907), p. 76. See also Chapter 6, nn. 43–44.

[21] The *lavras* of St. Chariton and St. Cyriacus were destroyed as well as the *koinobia* of St. Euthymius and St. Theodosius. See Theophanes, *Chronicle* AM 6301 (ed. de Boor, vol. 1, p. 484; ET available in Mango and Scott, *The Chronicle of Theophanes Confessor*, p. 665).

[22] See Michael the Great, *Chronicle* 12.6 (ed. Chabot, 4.490–91 = vol. 3.23). Michael's text refers to a 'Rabīʿa Naṣrāyā,' or 'Rabīʿa the Naṣrite,' as being behind the plundering and burning of Qenneshre. The Naṣr here referred to is Naṣr b. Shabath al-ʿUqaylī, a leader who emerged in the chaos and civil war that followed the death of Hārūn al-Rashīd in AD 809, and who first shows up in Arabic sources in 811–812, as the leader of gangs of rebels. See C. E. Bosworth's article about him, *s.n.* in *EI2*, vol. 7, p. 1016. The 'Gubbaye' that Michael's text references, who looted the monastery after it was burned, should probably be understood as 'the people of Gubba,' and as being from a nearby location. There is a village 10 kilometers southeast of the location of Qenneshre, called today Jubb al-Faraj, which I suspect may be the origin of these Gubbaye.

[23] Though the report in the *Qenneshre Fragment* that Domitian (d. 602) seized Qenneshre, probably in the late sixth century, would seem to chronicle a brief moment of discontinuity in Miaphysite possession of the monastery. See Penn, 'Demons Gone Wild,' p. 396, n. 135 and cf. Nau, 'Appendice: Fragments sure le monastère de Qenneshre,' p. 77. See also Chapter 3, n. 76. On this text, see G. J. Reinink, 'Die Muslime in einer Sammlung von Dämonengeschichten des Klosters von Qennešrîn,' in R. Lavenant, ed., *VI Symposium Syriacum, 1992: University of Cambridge, Faculty of Divinity, 30 August–2 September 1992* (Rome, 1994), pp. 335–46.

[24] See Bar Hebraeus, *Ecclesiastical History* 1.64 (ed. Abbeloos and Lamy, 1.349).

[25] See Michael the Great, *Chronicle* 12.11 (4.507 [Syriac] = 3.49 [FT]). See also Bar Hebraeus, *Ecclesiastical History* 1.64 (ed. Abbeloos and Lamy, 1.353, 355).

[26] See Bar Hebraeus, *Ecclesiastical History* 1.64 (ed. Abbeloos and Lamy, 1.347) for Dionysius's connection to Qenneshre, and cf. also Chapter 6, n. 58.

[27] See Chabot, *Chronique de Michel le Syrien*, 4.758 = 3.462 (no. 19), for a reference to Aaron of Gisra, the last attested bishop consecrated from Qenneshre.

Sayf al-Dawla in the early tenth century.[28] Preliminary archaeological work suggests that the monastic site was inhabited until the first half of the thirteenth century.[29]

QENNESHRE = A DEAD END?

At the beginning of this chapter, I dismissed al-Fārābī's account of the transmission of late Roman learning from Alexandria to Baghdad, but some might suggest that the continuities I have been speaking of are something of a bridge to nowhere: I have focused on Miaphysite scholars, and my line of continuity stops in the first half of the eighth century. The famous Ḥunayn b. Isḥāq (d. 873) and his celebrated fellow translators lived in the ninth century and the majority of them were East Syrians.[30] Qenneshre was not located in or near Baghdad. I have concentrated on the wrong church and, furthermore, my bridge of continuity does not quite make it from one of the highest points of the Roman period—the Age of Justinian—to one of the highest points of the Arab period—the ninth century.

Such an objection can only gain traction, however, if we assume that members of different churches had no interaction and lived lives sealed off from one another. But this, of course, was not the case at all. These communities were not sealed off from one another, neither at the nonelite level of the 'simple' nor at the level of the learned elite.[31] To focus for now at the learned end of

[28] See Ibn al-ʿAdīm, *Bughyat al-ṭalab fī taʾrīkh Ḥalab*, vol. 10, p. 4489 (ed. S. Zakkār [Beirut, n.d.]).

[29] According to Yousef al-Dabte, the archaeologist who excavated Qenneshre, classification and analysis of the ceramics found at the site suggest that 'without any doubt' the monastery was inhabited until the first half of the thirteenth century. Personal communication, June 30, 2009.

[30] Gérard Troupeau counted 61 different individuals who were engaged in translation from Greek and Syriac into Arabic in Abbasid Baghdad; of these 61, 59 were Christians: 38 Nestorians, 9 Miaphysites, 11 Melkites, and 1 Maronite. See his 'Le rôle des syriaques dans la transmission et l'exploitation du patrimoine philosophique et scientifique grec,' *Arabica* 38 (1991), p. 4.

[31] See S. P. Brock, 'Crossing the Boundaries: An Ecumenical Role Played by Syriac Monastic Literature,' in M. Bielawski and D. Hombergen, eds., *Il monachesimo tra eredità e aperture* (Rome, 2004), pp. 221–38, for examples of spiritual writers who were read across confessional boundaries. For Syrian Orthodox and East Syrian production of philosophical manuscripts containing both East and West Syrian material and the use of Miaphysite texts, such as those written by Sergius of Resh'ayna and Jacob of Edessa, in East Syrian schools, see D. King, *The Earliest Syriac Translation of Aristotle's* Categories*: Text, Translation and Commentary* (Leiden/Boston, 2010), pp. 9–10. For the inclusion of condemned authors in Byzantine (Chalcedonian) Greek exegetical catenae, see Y. Moss, 'Saving Severus: How Severus of Antioch's Writings Survived in Greek,' *Greek, Roman, and Byzantine Studies* 56 (2016), pp. 785–808. H. Teule, 'The Syriac Renaissance,' in H. Teule et al., eds., *The Syriac Renaissance* (Leuven/Paris/Walpole, MA, 2010), pp. 20–23, gives examples of reading across confessional boundaries in the medieval period. See also my 'Greek Kanons and the Syrian Orthodox Liturgy,' for liturgical and other examples of cross-confessional influence and awareness.

the spectrum, and Qenneshre more specifically: the appearance of Athanasius of Balad,[32] and perhaps also Jacob of Edessa,[33] in the marginalia of the Paris *Organon* shows that their work was still being read deep into the period of Arab rule.[34] We might also point out that the famous East Syrian exegete Isho'dad of Merv (fl. 850) quoted from Jacob in his Biblical commentaries;[35] the East Syrian Bar Bahlūl (fl. mid-10th century) cited him in his *Lexicon*;[36] Ibn al-Ṭayyib (d. 1043), one of the last of the great East Syrian philosophers and physicians of medieval Baghdad, cited Jacob's commentary on Matthew;[37] the East Syrian metropolitan Elias bar Shinaya (d. 1046) made use of him in his *Chronography*;[38] and the East Syrian metropolitan 'Abdisho' bar Brikha (d. 1318) knew of Jacob's *Chronicle* and his *Chronicon*.[39] This was all no doubt possible because East Syrians at an earlier period were aware of and reading Miaphysite scholarship produced by people from Qenneshre in the seventh century.

Let us follow these connections. Earlier, I made the argument that the peculiar Syriac calque *l-meḥdā* was used perhaps exclusively by scholars who had spent time at Qenneshre. This was not entirely accurate. I am aware of

[32] See, e.g, the comments of Ibn Suwār about the poor quality of Athanasius's translation of the *Sophistical Refutations* printed (with FT) in Kh. Georr, *Les Catégories d'Aristote dans leurs versions syro-arabes: édition de textes précédée d'une étude historique et critique et suivie d'un vocabulaire technique* (Damascus, 1948), pp. 198–200, and see R. Walzer, 'New Light on the Arabic Translations of Aristotle,' in Walzer, *Greek into Arabic: Essays on Islamic Philosophy* (Cambridge, 1962), p. 83.

[33] Jacob's translation of the *Categories* is possibly cited: see Georr, *Les Catégories d'Aristote dans leurs versions syro-arabes*, p. 380 (Arabic) = 174 (FT), where he is called 'Jacob the Ascetic' (Ya'qūb al-Zāhid). Walzer, 'New Light on the Arabic Translations of Aristotle,' p. 71, and Brock, 'The Syriac Commentary Tradition,' p. 4, n. 4, viewed this Jacob as Jacob of Edessa, but against this identification, see now D. King, *The Earliest Syriac Translation of Aristotle's* Categories (Leiden/Boston, 2010), pp. 22, 27–29. More generally, see Walzer, 'New Light,' pp. 68–69.

[34] On the Paris Organon, see H. Hugonnard-Roche, 'Une ancienne "edition" arabe de l'*Organon* d'Aristote: problems de traduction et de transmission,' in J. Hamesse, ed., *Les Problèmes posés par l'édition critique des textes anciens et médiévaux* (Louvain, 1992), pp. 139–57.

[35] See the examples cited in Kruisheer, 'A Bibliographical Clavis to the Works of Jacob of Edessa (revised and expanded),' pp. 289–90.

[36] Jacob's *Hexaemeron* and his biblical scholia are cited: see R. Duval, ed. *Lexicon syriacum auctore Hassano bar Bahlule*, vol. 3 [Paris, 1888–1901], p. xx—note that he is even called 'Blessed' at one point (vol. 3, col. 779, ln. 25). It should be pointed out that in the Syriac proemium to this work, Bar Bahlūl makes a number of references to Ḥunayn b. Isḥāq, noting that most of the definitions in his work that are unattributed are in fact from Ḥunayn (vol. 1, cols. 2–3). We might take Bar Bahlūl's citations as further potential evidence that Jacob was known and read in medieval Baghdad, by members of rival churches, and quite possibly by Ḥunayn.

[37] See Ibn al-Ṭayyib, *Tafsīr al-mashriqī*, vol. 1, p. 80 (ed. Y. Manqariyūs [Cairo, 1908]) (On the Magi of Matthew 2), and cf. Sachau, *Verzeichniss der syrischen Handschriften der Königlichen Bibliothek zu Berlin*, vol. 1, p. 376 (Berlin Syriac 109).

[38] See L. J. Delaporte, *La chronographie d'Élie Bar-Šinaya, Métropolitain de Nisibe* (Paris, 1910), pp. VII–VIII.

[39] 'Abdisho' bar Brikha, *Mēmrā on Ecclesiastical Books* 165 (ed. Assemani, *BO*, 3.1, p. 229).

one example of the use of this distinctively Hellenizing letter salutation is by a non-Miaphysite: the Nestorian patriarch Timothy I. Timothy's *Letter 40*, written in the year 780–781, contains the distinctive expression in its opening lines.[40] This unique usage suggests that Timothy had been reading and was imitating earlier Miaphysite scholarship, which should come as no surprise: he was an avid consumer of translations produced by Miaphysite philhellenes and actively sought out earlier translations to help him in his own translational endeavors. And this was not something new among East Syrians, either. There was in fact a long tradition, stretching back before the period of Muslim rule, of Christians in the Sasanian empire showing an interest in scholarship from the Roman world, and even of scholars travelling there for study.[41]

[40] Timothy, *Letters* 40.1 (ed. H.P.J. Cheikho, *Dialectique du langage sur Dieu: Lettre de Timothée I (728–823) à Serge. Étude, traduction et édition critique* [Rome, 1983], p. 274 [Syriac] = 185 [FT]): 'To Rabban Mar Sergius, priest and teacher. [From] Timothy: Rejoice in the Lord!' For the date of this letter, see Bidawid, *Les lettres du patriarche nestorien Timothée I*, p. 73. A letter by West Syrian David bar Paulos, a late-eighth century rough contemporary of Timothy I, used forms of this greeting as well; for David using ܚܕܝ in a salutation, see his *Letters* 20 (*On the Numbering Systems of Greeks and Syrians*), in F. J. Dolapönu (Dolabani), ed., *Egrāteh d-Dawid bar Pawlos d-metida' d-Bet Rabban* (Mardin, 1953), p. 76. For David bar Paulos as possibly being from Qenneshre, see S. P. Brock's article, 'Dawid bar Pawlos,' in *GEDSH*, pp. 116–17.

[41] To give only a few examples: in the sixth century, the West Syrian Sergius of Resh'ayna dedicated a variety of medical and philosophical works and translations to Theodore, the bishop of Karkh Juddān in Iraq: see H. Hugonnard-Roche, *La logique d'Aristote du grec au syriaque. Études sur la transmission des textes de l'Organon et leur interprétation philosophique* (Paris, 2004), pp. 125–29, for these various works, and esp. 126, n. 2, for Theodore's identity. In one instance, Theodore had asked Sergius to translate Ps.-Aristotle's *On the World*: see Sergius's comment about Theodore's request in P. de Lagarde, ed., *Analecta Syriaca* (Leipzig, 1858), p. 134. It is clear from Sergius's remarks at the beginning of a treatise on the *Categories* of Aristotle that he and Theodore had worked together translating in the past: *Commentary on the Categories of Aristotle*, Mingana Syriac 606, fol. 52a (ET available in Brock, *A Brief Outline of Syriac Literature*, p. 202). Sergius translated Galen's *De locis affectis* once for Theodore and another time for a certain Elisha: see Ḥunayn b. Isḥāq, *Risāla* 15 (ed. Bergsträsser, *Ḥunain ibn Isḥāq*, p. *12 = 10 [GT]). This Elisha was very possibly Elisha, an East Syrian catholicos (sed. 524–538) who was originally from Ctesiphon but who had spent time in the Roman Empire and learned medicine there (*Chronicle of Seert* 2.25 [ed. Scher (PO 7.2), p. 56]). Joseph, another catholicos (sed. 552–567), spent much of his life in the Roman Empire and studied medicine there (*Chronicle of Seert* 2.84 [PO7.2], p. 84). Mar Aba, as we have already seen, yet another sixth-century catholicos, also traveled to Alexandria (see Ch. 4, n. 48), where he engaged in teaching; Cosmas Indicopleustes wrote of having learned from him (*Christian Topography* 2.2 [ed. W. Wolska-Conus, *Topographie chrétienne* [SC 141] [Paris, 1968], p. 307; see further, Wolska-Conus, *La* Topographie chrétienne *de Cosmas Indicopleustes; théologie et science au VI siècle* [Paris, 1962], pp. 63–73). In the period of Muslim rule, it is worth mentioning that Ḥunayn b. Isḥāq was reported to have studied Greek in Alexandria (Ibn Abī 'Uṣaybi'a, *'Uyūn al-anbā' fī ṭabaqāt al-aṭibbā'*, p. 262) and once went there looking for a copy of Galen's *De demonstratione* (*Risāla* 115 [ed. Bergsträsser, p. 47]). These contacts, of course, are evident because the persons who were doing them ended up leading the East Syrian Church, or in the case of Ḥunayn or Sergius of Resh'ayna, were celebrated figures. There were very likely other contacts occurring beneath these very elite levels—e.g., in the early seventh century, the city of Alexandria was betrayed to the Persians by a certain Peter, who had come to Alexandria in his youth from Beth Qatraye in order to study philosophy: *Khuzistan Chronicle*, pp. 25–26. For

In Timothy's letters, we find him time and again trying to get his hands on books, Christian and pagan, regardless of their confessional provenance.[42] 'Take care to copy out [Pseudo-]Dionysius,' he wrote to the priest Sergius in his *Letter 16*, composed around AD 783–785, '—the version of Athanasius or Phocas.'[43] The 'Athanasius' referred to was Athanasius of Balad, the seventh-century Miaphysite patriarch whose translations of Aristotle also interested Timothy.[44] Athanasius may have made a revision of Ps.-Dionysius, as had Phocas bar Sergius of Edessa (fl. late seventh century);[45] like Athanasius, Phocas belonged to the rival Miaphysite church. Timothy, who also read Severus of Antioch,[46] and who wrote about his successful efforts to get his hands on a copy of the seventh-century Miaphysite translation of the Old Testament today known as the *Syro-Hexapla*,[47] simply had no problem with reading Miaphysite authors or translations.

In fact, translations by the Miaphysite philhellenes of the seventh century were a subject of keen interest for Timothy. 'If possible,' he wrote to the priest Sergius in his *Letter 17*, also written sometime around AD 783–785, 'send the exemplar of the heretics,'—that is, of the Miaphysites—'of Gregory [Nazianzen], from which you copied out two parts. For I have the version which you wrote out, two parts, but they have, however, not at all been corrected. If those of the heretics cannot be sent, send me yours.'[48] Over a decade later, in his *Letter 22*, written to Sergius at some point between 799 and 804, we find Timothy still speaking about the two volumes of Gregory's work in Miaphysite translation. 'We have returned to them,' he wrote Sergius, now metropolitan of Elam,

East Syrian monastic connections to Egypt and Jerusalem, see O. Meinardus, 'The Nestorians in Egypt' and 'A Note on Nestorians in Jerusalem,' *OC* 51 (1967), pp. 112–22, 123-29.

[42] A. McCollum, 'Greek Literature in the Christian East: Translations into Syriac, Georgian, and Armenian,' *Intellectual History of the Islamicate World* 3 (2015), p. 27, gives a brief listing of relevant passages in Timothy's first thirty-nine letters.

[43] Timothy I, *Letter 16* (To Sergius), p. 120 (ed. Braun [CSCO 74: SS 30]). For the date of this letter, see Bidawid, *Les lettres du patriarche nestorien Timothée I*, p. 73.

[44] For Timothy's interest in Athanasius's translation of the *Posterior Analytics*, see *Letters* 48.4, (ed. Heimgartner [CSCO 644: SS 248], p. 89); for his interest in Athanasius's translation of the *Topics*, see *Letters* 48.10 (p. 92).

[45] For a similar request in *Letter 43*, see Chapter 7, n. 42. On Phocas and Athanasius's relationship to the Syriac translation of Ps.-Dionysius, see S. P. Brock, 'Two Letters of the Patriarch Timothy from the Late Eighth Century,' p. 244. Cf. also Chapter 7, nn. 39–42.

[46] For Timothy's citations of Severus, see M. Heimgartner, *Die Briefe 42–58 des Ostsyrischen Patriarchen Timotheos I* (CSCO 645: SS. 249) (Louvain, 2012), p. 123, s.n. 'Severus von Antiochien. '

[47] See Timothy, *Letters* 47.1–15 (ed. Heimgartner [CSCO 644: SS 248], pp. 79–82; ET available in S. P. Brock, *A Brief Outline*, pp. 245–47). And see below, n. 61 in this chapter.

[48] Timothy I, *Letter 17* (To Sergius), pp. 123–24 (ed. Braun [CSCO 74–75: SS 30–31], p. 82 [=LT]). For the date of this letter, see Bidawid, *Les lettres du patriarche nestorien Timothée I*, p. 73.

'the two books of the holy Gregory—the version of Paul [of Edessa] and the revision of Athanasius [of Balad].'[49]

But to read a translation done by a member of a rival church, one had first to get hold of it, and Timothy was aware of the potential manuscript riches that were to be found in Miaphysite monasteries. One such place was Mar Zina, a monastery located 25 kilometers south of Mosul.[50] 'If possible,' Timothy wrote to Sergius in his *Letter 19*, sometime between 783 and 785,

> a list of the books of Mar Zina should be sent to us, for perhaps there is among them something which we are unaware of. And you yourself look over its books personally in order to go over them: every subject and every sort. Perhaps you will find in them the two treatises *On the Poets*—for we have one—or maybe you will find among them a translation of Olympiodorus, of the books on logic, or of Stephanus or Sergius or Alexander. Or ecclesiastical books: of Ambrose, or Amphilochius against Apollinaris, or of Eustathius the Great, or of Flavian, or somebody else. You yourself look for Athanasius the Great—the treatise against the Arians through definite propositions[?], for I have found of it 16 [sections] in number, but I have wondered whether perhaps there might be more of it.... Also seek out for me the dominical letters of Athanasius and that treatise which is an apology for his flight.[51]

But Mar Zina paled in comparison to another monastery in the treasures it might hold: Mar Matay, the seat of the bishop of Nineveh/Mosul and the leading Miaphysite monastery in northern Iraq, was the object of intense

[49] Timothy I, *Letter 22* (To Sergius, Metropolitan of Elam), p. 135 (ed. Braun [CSCO 74–75: SS 30–31], p. 91 [=LT]). For the date of this letter, see Bidawid, *Les lettres du patriarche nestorien Timothée I*, p. 75.

[50] On the location of Mar Zina and the monastery more generally, see J.-M. Fiey, *AC*, vol. 2, pp. 637–39.

[51] Timothy I, *Letter 19* (To Sergius the Teacher), pp. 129-130 (ed. Braun [CSCO 74-75: SS 30-31], p. 86 [=LT]). For the date of this letter, see Bidawid, *Les lettres du patriarche nestorien Timothée I*, p. 73, and cf. also pp. 24–25. On the library of Mar Zina and this passage specifically, including a helpful Italian translation, see V. Berti, 'Libri e biblioteche cristiane nell'Iraq dell'VIII secolo. Una testimonianza dell'epistolario del patriarca siro-orientale Timoteo I (727–823),' in C. C. D'Ancona, ed., *The Libraries of the Neoplatonists* (Leiden/Boston, Brill, 2007), pp. 310–16. NB: BL Add. 18,821, a ninth-century manuscript, perhaps even dating to the life of Timothy I, contains a collection of the poetry and letters of Gregory Nazianzen (including his letter to Amphilochius), as well as part of Olympiodorus's commentary on the *Organon*. See *CBM*, vol. 2 (London, 1871), pp. 775–76. This latter text is published with translation and study in G. Furlani, 'Contributi alla Storia della Filosofia Greca in Oriente: Testi Siriaci III. Frammenti di una versione siriaca del commento di Pseudo-Olimpiodoro alle Categorie d'Aristotele,' *Rivsta degli Studi Orientali* 7 (1916–1918), pp. 131–63. For a description of St. Mark's Jerusalem 126, an eighth-century Syrian Orthodox manuscript, also perhaps from the *Life* of Timothy, which contains Athanasius's *Orations against the Arians*, see S. P. Brock, 'Athanasiana Syriaca: Notes on Two Manuscripts,' *LM* 86 (1973), pp. 437–39, though the *Orations against the Arians* may not have been the specific work Timothy was referencing.

interest on Timothy's part for a period of years.[52] 'Search out books of our Fathers,' he continued in his *Letter 16*, after asking about Ps.-Dionysius, 'at [the monastery] of Mar Matay, and let me know about them. Look for books which are not available, as much as you are able, and provide me with information about them.'[53] Writing later, between 785 and 789, Timothy was still trying to get hold of Ps.-Dionysius from Mar Matay. 'Rabban Sahda has come to us with caution,' Timothy wrote in his *Letter 33*,

> and he brought with him undamaged quires; if, therefore, those others are not needed by you, send them. For barley bread is never useful where pure wheat bread is found and the food of irrational [creatures] is rather more suitable for the irrational than it is for the rational. Along with these things, I ask that you go with care to those of Mar Matay and see the edition of Dionysius of Athanasius or Phocas—whichever is better, have it written out if there is a scribe. If not, send it to us with a trustworthy person and we will send it back quickly.[54]

Ps.-Dionysius was not, however, all that Timothy wanted from the Miaphysites: 'Search at [the monastery of] Matay for the treatise that Athanasius wrote in defense of his flight,' he would tell Sergius in his Letter 39, also likely written between 785 and 789, 'and also for the treatise of the holy Gregory of Nyssa on the burial of Macrina, his sister. Then, look for the book written by Eustathius the Great against the Arians—it is six or seven sections, I don't know which. Be diligent in tracking down these books!'[55] Timothy was conscious that his being the leader of a rival Christian church might make his enquiries unwelcome. 'Let your eminence sagely ask and enquire,' he wrote to Pethion in his *Letter 43*, probably in 782 or 783,

> Whether there is some commentary or scholia by anyone, whether Syriac or not, to this book, the *Topika*, or the *Refutation of the Sophists*, or to the *Rhetorika*, or to the *Poetika*; and if there is, find out by whom and for whom (it was made), and where it is. Enquiries on this should be directed to the Monastery of Mar Matay—but the enquiries should not be made too eagerly, lest the information,

[52] On Mar Matay, see S. P. Brock, ed., *The Hidden Pearl: The Syrian Orthodox Church and its Ancient Aramaic Heritage*, vol. 2: *The Heirs of the Ancient Aramaic Heritage* (Rome, 2001), pp. 159–60; Barṣawm, *al-Lu'lu' al-manthūr*, p. 514; G. Kiraz, 'Matay, Dayro d-Mor,' in *GEDSH*, pp. 280–81.

[53] Timothy I, *Letter 16* (To Sergius), p. 120 (ed. Braun [CSCO 74: SS 30]). For the date of this letter, see Bidawid, *Les lettres du patriarche nestorien Timothée I*, p. 73.

[54] Timothy I, *Letter 33* (To Sergius), p. 156 (ed. Braun [CSCO 74: SS 30]). The Syriac of this passage is in places obscure and Braun's Latin translation ([CSCO 75: SS 31], p. 106) is helpful to consult. For the date of this letter, see Bidawid, *Les lettres du patriarche nestorien Timothée I*, p. 74.

[55] Timothy I, *Letters* 39 (To Sergius), p. 279 (ed. Braun [CSCO 74–75: SS 30–31], p. 194 [=LT]). For the date of this letter, see Bidawid, *Les lettres du patriarche nestorien Timothée I*, p. 74.

(the purpose of the enquiry) being perceived, be kept hidden, rather than disclosed.[56]

Of course Timothy was interested in more than just the Miaphysite monastery of Mar Matay and its books: he was eager to comb the collections of Nestorian monasteries as well. Writing to Sergius in either 794 or 795, he expressed interest in the letters of John Chrysostom to Olympiodorus. 'I once wrote to your chastity,' he began his *Letter 49*,

> about the letters of the holy Mar John which are to the Christ-loving Olympiodorus, making known to your kindness that three letters were known to us that he wrote to him(?): the three of them were after his first captivity—I think. We have the second and third, but we do not have the first. I remember that we were once in the district of Marga. At that time, we were being instructed at the feet of that Christ-clad man—I mean, at the knees of Rabban Mar Abraham. A book came to Rabban from the monastery of Cyprian and these letters of Mar John were in it, along with other things, and Rabban copied them out. See therefore if they are among those books. Set down their incipits: perhaps that first [letter] is there. If you have these [latter] two, examine them [to see] whether the other is there.[57]

Writing later, at some point between 795 and 798, Timothy was still on the lookout for texts. 'Send me the *Apologia* for Origen by Eusebius of Caesaria,' he wrote Sergius, now the metropolitan of Elam in his *Letter 47*,

> so that I may read it and then send it back. Make a search for the *Discousrse on the Soul* by the great patriarch Mar Aba: there are three of them, but only one is available here. And copy out and send the *Homilies* of Mar Narsai, since we have not got them; for Mar Ephrem, of holy memory, wrote to us to say that there is a great deal there with you which is not available here.[58]

[56] Timothy I, *Letters* 43.5–6 (ed. Heimgartner [CSCO 644: SS 248], pp. 66–67; ET taken from Brock, 'Two letters of the Patriarch Timothy,' p. 236. I have slightly altered Brock's spelling). For the date of this letter, see Bidawid, *Les lettres du patriarche nestorien Timothée I*, p. 74.

[57] Timothy I, *Letters* 49.1–4 (ed. Heimgartner [CSCO 644: SS 248], pp. 93–94). For the date of this letter, see Bidawid, *Les lettres du patriarche nestorien Timothée I*, p. 74. For more on the (East Syrian) monastery of Cyprian, see Fiey, *AC*, vol. 1, pp. 296–300. In *Letter 20* (written sometime between 783 and 785), Timothy writes to Sergius about texts of John Chrysostom and Theodore the Great and recalls seeing texts copied out by Rabban Mar Abraham in Marga (ed. Braun [CSCO 74–75: SS 30–31], pp. 130–31 = p. 87 [LT]). For the date of this letter, see Bidawid, *Les lettres du patriarche nestorien Timothée I*, p. 73 and cf. p. 25.

[58] Timothy, *Letters* 47.33–34 (ed. Heimgartner [CSCO 644: SS 248], p. 87; ET taken from Brock, *A Brief Outline*, p. 250. I have added italics to Brock's translation).

Writing later, between 799 and 804, Timothy would still be on the lookout for some of these manuscripts. In *Letter 54*, we find him trying once again to get hold of the writings of Narsai. 'I requested of you,' he wrote once more to Sergius of Elam,

> when you went to Elam and I also sent you a record [ὑπομνηστικόν] of the homilies of Rabban Mar Narsai which we possess so that you could look for his homilies and write out for us their titles and two stanzas from the beginning of each homily. But you promised us and did not complete [the task]: not on account of negligence—your reverence is far from [any] blame—but rather on account of obstacles and ill fortune. Give order, my master, and write for us the incipits of the homilies of the treasury which is in Beth Huzzaye: in monasteries and churches and convents, and send to us so that when we have come to you, if there is something which we do not have, we can inform you and you will copy it out for us. And if there is something which you do not have and which you request, we will write it for you, so that both the abundance and the scarcity [of the texts] will be distributed among one another. Go over the homilies in order to know whether they are spurious or authentic.[59]

And merely having gained access to a translation was not enough for Timothy. Once he had made his own copy, he was eager to collate and correct it. In his *Letter 18*, written sometime between 783 and 785, Timothy brought up with Sergius the issue of the text of Gregory Nazianzen he had been seeking. After his request made in *Letter 16*, he had received the version of Gregory, but not all of it:

> Now, our brother Rabban Aba has arrived safely to us and the final volume of the holy and God-clad Gregory [Nazianzen], along with seven quires from the first, have been written out and come here undamaged; we thank you, O spiritual brother, for sending them. But look now: although I previously wrote to your chastity that you send the entire tome—quires were not to be sent—but given that they have been sent, we have nevertheless gone over them with our copy and we are sending together [to you] both them and the final volume which you sent. For we have this version—[in] two sections—but the [sections] are not collated and these words which are written in Greek are not present in them.[60]

[59] Timothy I, *Letters* 54.10–14 (ed. Heimgartner [CSCO 644: SS 248], pp. 128–29). For the date of this letter, see Bidawid, *Les lettres du patriarche nestorien Timothée I*, p. 74, and for this letter in general, see p. 40. I am grateful to Luke Yarbrough and Joseph Witztum for help with the Syriac of this passage.

[60] Timothy I, *Letters* 16 (ed. Braun [CSCO 74: SS 30], p. 126). For the date of this letter, see Bidawid, *Les lettres du patriarche nestorien Timothée I*, p. 73.

Getting hold of a copy of the Miaphysite Paul of Tella's *Syro-Hexapla* led to a flurry of work in Timothy's scriptorium. He had no less than three copies of this translation of the Greek Old Testament made, employing eight scribes over the course of about six months. The process was arduous and almost physically injurious to him.[61]

What Timothy cared about was the accuracy and quality of a manuscript: he showed no concern for whether the translations he was seeking were made by East Syrians, Miaphysites (or whether they predated the Christological controversies). He was not unique in his lack of concern about the confessional origin of manuscripts, of course—the famous East Syrian Ḥunayn b. Isḥāq, was similarly manuscript thirsty,[62] and a probably fictive story, found in the Armenian version of the *Chronicle* of Michael the Great, has Jacob of Edessa convert to Judaism in an attempt to find new texts he believed Jews to be harboring.[63] What all of this points us to is a simple fact: elite scholars in the early medieval Middle East were more concerned with getting their hands on texts than they were with the precise theological pedigrees of the circles where those texts originated. Timothy's appetite for Miaphysite translations of texts and his imitation of the style of scholars trained at Qenneshre suffice to show that the monastery's influence did in fact stretch to the cultural epicenter of Abbasid Iraq. The bridge to nowhere is no such thing: one of the paths from Alexandria to Baghdad ran through Qenneshre.[64]

(A NON-CIVIC) LATE ANTIQUE *ROMANITAS*

In the transition between the Roman and Arab-ruled Middle East—in the movement from the world of Justinian to that of Hārūn al-Rashīd—the streams and rivers of antique learned culture flowed unbroken. This assertion of continuity, of course, needs to be qualified. The streams flowed without interruption, but they narrowed and passed through a smaller number of channels. Intellectual

[61] See Timothy I, *Letters* 47.4–11 (ed. Heimgartner [CSCO 644: SS 248], pp. 80–81; ET available in Brock, *A Brief Outline*, pp. 246–47). For the date of this letter, see Bidawid, *Les lettres du patriarche nestorien Timothée I*, p. 74.

[62] For examples of Ḥunayn searching for manuscripts, see F. Rosenthal, *The Technique and Approach of Muslim Scholarship* (Rome, 1947), p. 18, and *SBI*, pp. 34–38.

[63] See V. Langlois, *Chronique de Michel le Grand, patriarche des Syriens jacobites* (Venice, 1868), pp. 20–21, 244–45.

[64] Cf. the observation of King, *The Earliest Syriac Translation of Aristotle's* Categories, pp. 10–11: 'It is above all to Qennešre that the building blocks of the Arabic logical tradition can be traced. . . .' See also the remark in F. Briquel Chatonnet and M. Debié, *Le monde syriaque: sur les routes d'un christianisme ignoré* (Paris, 2017), p. 168.

activities such as translation from Greek, philosophical study, history writing, and, to a lesser extent, astrological and medical study—now took place in monasteries and were carried out by Christian clergy. Polymaths like Severus Sebokht, Jacob of Edessa, and George of the Arabs carried the weight of both secular and religious knowledge on their shoulders and represent a concentration of broad and encyclopedic knowledge in single individuals.

Let us examine from a broader perspective what precisely has happened. In the Middle East, traditional Greek learning was no longer the purview of a polis-based urban elite. Athanasius Gamolo, the refined leader of the Miaphysite church in the first three decades of the seventh century was, as I have pointed out, from an elite urban family in Samosata, whereas Jacob of Edessa hailed from a small village in the region of Antioch. Both men, however, were educated at the monastery of Qenneshre, and both had also received educations in urban centers—Jacob in Alexandria and Athanasius most likely in his hometown of Samosata.

The events of Jacob of Edessa's life saw him moving from a small village (ʿAyndābā), to Qenneshre, to Alexandria, to Edessa, to the monasteries of Eusebona, then to Tell ʿAda, and finally back to Edessa; such movements nicely illustrate the flows that people (and information) might take. Jacob was responsible for reviving the study of Greek at the monastery of Eusebona, but he was eventually driven away from it by monks there who 'hated Greeks.' He himself died en route from Edessa to the monastery of Tell ʿAda—as he was returning to Tell ʿAda to fetch his personal library.[65] The *Life* of Theodota of Amid in which the protagonist frequently moves from one monastery to the next also suggests that there was a constant traffic of both laypeople and clergy between monastic centers in the seventh century.

It is important to keep in mind that these centers of culture were connected to one another: Qenneshre stood out as the most important center for Greco-Syriac study and education in the Syriac-speaking Middle East, but it was not unique—places like Beth Malke and Tell ʿAda were also sites of bilingualism and study. Qenneshre existed as the primary and most important node in a network of Miaphysite monasteries that, taken collectively, formed the cultural and intellectual skeleton supporting the muscle and tissue of the body of what eventually would be called the Syrian Orthodox church.[66]

[65] Michael the Great, *Chronicle* 11.15 (ed. Chabot, 4.445–46 = 2.471–72).

[66] Among Chalcedonians, there were centers of Greco-Syriac bilingualism in greater Syria, too, most notably Mar Saba near Jerusalem, St. Catherine's in the Sinai, and the area of Antioch, especially the monasteries of the Black Mountain. For translations from Syriac into Arabic by Chalcedonians in Abbasid Palestine, see A. Treiger, 'Syro-Arabic Translations in Abbasid Palestine: The Case of John of Apamea's Letter on Stillness (Sinai ar. 549),' *PdO* 39 (2014), pp. 81–82. For Syriac on the Black Mountain,

What we have emerging in Syria in the sixth through eighth centuries is an example of what Hervé Inglebert has referred to as an 'antiquité post-romaine, une deuxième phase de l'Antiquité,' characterized by a form of *Romanitas* different from the civic version which so defined the *Romanitas* of the empire.[67] Imperial persecution of Christological dissidents, combined with the diversity and competition that characterized the Christian communities of greater Syria—which we examined in Part II of this book—fueled the development of an alternative, intellectual and cultural elite in the Miaphysite movement, one whose primary basis of operation was in the network of monasteries anchored by Qenneshre. Certain aspects of Roman elite culture were untethered from a civic context, infused with Christianity, and located in monastic centers.

These monasteries existed alongside the older, urban centers of culture which, to be sure, were not as sterile in the seventh century—a period traditionally regarded as something of a cultural nadir—as some might imagine. Jacob did spend part of his life in Edessa, and the eighth-century emergence from Edessa of the Maronite Theophilus of Edessa (d. 785), an astrologer to al-Mahdī, translator of Aristotle, Galen, and Homer into Syriac, and the author of an important chronicle, points to that city's continued status as a center of late Roman culture.[68] Theodosius, the Miaphysite metropolitan of Edessa and brother of the celebrated Miaphysite patriarch Dionysius of Tell Mahre, translated hymns of Gregory Nazianzen from Greek into Syriac while a priest in Edessa in 804,[69] and it was about the year 810 that Michael the Syncellus wrote a Greek grammar in Edessa, at the request of a local deacon named Lazarus.[70] Theodore Abū Qurrah (d. ca. 820), the famous Chalcedonian bishop of Harran,

see S. P. Brock, 'Syriac Manuscripts Copied on the Black Mountain, near Antioch,' in R. Schulz and M. Görg, eds., *Lingua restituta orientalis. Festgabe für Julius Assfalg* (Wiesbaden, 1990), pp. 59–67.

[67] See H. Inglebert, *Histoire de la civilization romaine* (Paris, 2005), p. 483. I am grateful to Peter Brown for alerting me to Inglebert's notion of a second, post-civic phase of Late Antiquity and *Romanitas.*

[68] On Theophilus, see Baumstark, *Geschichte*, pp. 341–42.

[69] See Bar Hebraeus, *Ecclesiastical History* 1.64 (ed. Abbeloos and Lamy, 1.361, 363) for Theodosius as metropolitan of Edessa and brother of Dionysius. A note in Vatican Syriac 96, fol. 97, states that a homily of Gregory Nazianzen on the miracles of the prophet Elijah was translated from Greek into Syriac by "Theodosius the Edessene Priest, from the monastery of Qenneshre" from June to December 804. Cf. chapter 6, n. 59 and chapter 7, n. 84.

[70] Michael's *Peri syntaxeos* is edited and translated in D. Donnet, *Le traité de la construction de la phrase de Michel le syncelle de Jérusalem* (Bruxelles, 1982)—see p. 157 for the information about Michael's writing the work in Edessa at the request of Lazarus, who is identified as a deacon, philosopher, and logothete. On this work, see most recently M. Mavroudi, 'Greek Language and Education under Early Islam,' in B. Sadeghi, A. Q. Ahmed, A. Silverstein, and R. Hoyland, eds., *Islamic Cultures, Islamic Contexts: Essays in Honor of Professor Patricia Crone* (Leiden/Boston, 2015), pp. 329–31.

wrote works in Greek, Syriac, and Arabic and was originally from Edessa,[71] as was Job of Edessa, a physician in Baghdad who translated dozens of works of Galen into Syriac.[72] The precious Chalcedonian Syriac manuscript, British Library Oriental 8606, written in Edessa in AD 723, contains Greek words in Syriac unattested anywhere else,[73] and its colophon indicates that the Chalcedonian cathedral there had two different choirs—one Greek and one Syriac.[74] These are all indications that Edessa continued to be a vibrant bilingual place and an important point for cultural transmission across linguistic lines. Moreover, this particular manuscript, along with the Dyothelete Chalcedonian Theodore Abū Qurrah and the Maronite Theophilus, serve as reminders that it was not just the Miaphysites who were making use of and studying the wisdom of the Greeks. Chalcedonians were an important group as well.

But even Edessa brings us back to monasteries as important nodes of cultural preservation and transmission: part of Edessa's cultural power will eventually have been a function of the fact that it abounded in monasteries. The 'mountain of Edessa,' southwest of the city, was home to monasteries whose names we know from extant manuscript colophons all written, it should be pointed out, under Muslim rule.[75] In fact, according to Ibn Ḥawqal (d. after 973)—himself a native of Nisibis—there were more than three hundred churches and monasteries in Edessa in his day, and most of its inhabitants were Christian. The monasteries, he noted, had elevated cells (*ṣawāmiʿ*) with monks in them, and the cathedral of Edessa was unrivalled among Christian architectural works for its grandeur.[76] Even in important urban areas, monasteries were remarkably durable institutions of cultural production, transmission, and preservation. This was in part because the gradual accumulation of endowments, often from wealthy urban elites, meant that monasteries would come to have their own independent economic bases of survival.[77]

[71] For Theodore being from Edessa, see Michael the Great, *Chronicle* 12.8 (ed. Chabot, 4.495 = 3.32) and Lamoreaux, *Theodore Abū Qurrah*, p. xiii; on Theodore's writing in Greek, Syriac, and Arabic, see pp. xxv–xxvi.

[72] On Job of Edessa, see B. Roggema, 'Job of Edessa,' in CMR, vol. 1, pp. 502–509.

[73] See C. Moss, 'A Syriac Patristic Manuscript,' *JTS* 30 (1929), p. 254.

[74] See R. W. Thomson, 'An Eighth-Century Melkite Colophon From Edessa,' *JTS* n.s., 13 (1962), p. 253: ܘܝܘܚܢܢ ܪܝܫ ܙܡܪܐ ܕܝܘܢܝܐ. ܘܢܝܩܝܢܘܣ ܪܝܫ ܙܡܪܐ ܕܣܘܪܝܝܐ: '. . . And John, the head of the choir of the Greeks, and Nicianos, head of the choir of the Syrians. . . .' (translation Thomson). On British Library Oriental 8606, see further, S. P. Brock, 'The Provenance of BM Or. 8606,' *JTS* 19 (1968), pp. 632–33.

[75] S. P. Brock, 'Manuscripts Copied in Edessa,' in Bruns and Luthe, eds. *Orientalia Christiana*, p. 119.

[76] Ibn Ḥawqal, *Kitāb al-masālik wa-'l-mamālik*, p. 154 (ed. M. J. de Goeje [Leiden, 1872]). On Ibn Ḥawqal, see A. Miquel's article, 'Ibn Ḥawḳal,' in *EI2*, vol. 3, pp. 786–88. For an anecdote about the cathedral of Edessa, see Abū Faraj al-Iṣbahānī, *Kitāb adab al-ghurabā'* 14 (ed. Ṣ. al-Dīn al-Munajjid [Beirut, 1972] pp. 36–37; an ET is available in P. Crone and S. Moreh, *The Book of Strangers: Medieval Arabic Graffiti on the Theme of Nostalgia* [Princeton, 2000], p. 34).

[77] See the discussion of the finances of the East Syrian Monastery of Beth ʿĀbe by Budge in *The Book*

ON CULTURE AND CONTINUITY

Learning continued unbroken through the tumultuous period of the last great Roman-Persian war, the Arab conquests, the Umayyad caliphate, and the Abbasid revolution, but by the seventh and early eighth centuries the texture of the tradition had changed from what it was in the fourth century. Jacob of Edessa's knowledge of the classical Greek tradition was different from that of say, Gregory Nazianzen. In one of his letters, for instance, Jacob cites passages from the now-lost *ὁ πρὸς Νημέρτινον λόγος* of Porphyry. But Jacob's knowledge of Porphyry, at least in this case, is a mediated one: the three passages that Jacob quotes from this lost work can all be found cited in Cyril of Alexandria's *Contra Julianum*. Surely this is no coincidence: Jacob knew Porphyry's work through his reading of Cyril rather than through reading Porphyry himself.[78] Perhaps similarly, part of Severus Sebokht's citation of Plato's *Timaeus* had already been cited by Eusebius in his *Praeparatio Evangelica*.[79] John of Litarb wrote to George of the Arabs, perplexed at allusions in Jacob's letters; he did not, for example, understand what exactly Jacob meant when he rhetorically asked why somebody would bring an owl to Athens.[80] Jacob had also once referred to a story of a monkey, dressed and acting like a human. What exactly was he talking about? George explained the allusion by referring John back to the letter of Gregory of Nyssa to Harmonius. Gregory himself had not seen the monkey dressed and dancing like a human, George notes; it was, rather, a story related by the pagans.[81] The story in fact goes back to Lucian's work

of Governors, vol. 1, pp. lxv–lxix. Eventually, taxes from Muslim authorities caused great economic distress to the monastery. On the funding of monasteries, see C. Villagomez, 'The Fields, Flocks, and Finances of Monks: Economic Life at Nestorian Monasteries, 500–850' (PhD diss, UCLA, 1998) and *SBI*, pp. 360–73.

[78] Jacob cites Porphyry on the issue of divine providence. Cf. BL Add. 12,172, fol. 107b; another passage is cited on fols. 107b–108a; and a third passage from the same treatise is cited on fol. 108a. A. Smith, *Porphyrii Philosophi Fragmenta* (Stuttgart, 1993), pp. 314–18, has collected the fragments of the πρὸς Νημέρτινον λόγος, all of which come from Cyril of Alexandria's *Contra Julianum*. Jacob's first passage corresponds to 280f in Smith's edition, his second passage to Smith's 282f, and his third passage to Smith's 279f. I am grateful to Aaron Johnson for guidance in Porphyrian matters. These portions of the *Contra Julianum* do not appear in the Syriac fragments edited by E. Nestle in C. I. Neumann, *Iuliani Imperatoris Librorum Contra Christianos Quae Supersunt* (Leipzig, 1880), pp. 45–63. See also *CBM*, 2.600.

[79] *Praeparatio Evangelica* 10.4 (ed. Mras and des Places, vol. 1, p. 571); see F. Nau, 'La cosmographie au VIIe siècle chez les Syriens,' *ROC* 5 (15) 1910, p. 250, n. 2.

[80] See BL Add. 12,154, fol. 275b. This was the equivalent of the English expression 'to bring coals to Newcastle.'

[81] See BL Add., 12,154, fols. 275a–b. For Gregory of Nyssa's version of the story, see his *De professione christiana ad Harmonium*, pp. 131–32 (ed. W. Jaeger in *Gregorii Nysseni Opera*, vol. 8.1, *Gregorii Nysseni Opera Ascetica* [Leiden, 1952]; ET available in V. Woods Callahan, *Saint Gregory of Nyssa: Ascetical Works*

The Fisher,[82] but Lucian had now faded away and was only a nameless pagan source. Gregory of Nyssa had known Lucian's text first hand; by the time we arrive at John of Litarb in the eighth century, he has learned of Lucian's story from Jacob and George, who knew it through the medium of Gregory. John is now two or even three layers removed from the pagan Greek original. In the same way, when he explained the meaning of the expression 'to bring an owl to Athens,' George would refer to Severus's using it in his work against John the Grammarian.[83]

Such a mediated knowledge of the classical past was not an exception, but the rule.[84] By the early medieval period, a knowledge of classical culture had become useful as a tool for decoding and understanding the works of the towering theological authorities of the fourth, fifth, and sixth centuries. This trend toward the instrumentalization of classical culture in the service of Christianity is exemplified in the sixth-century composition in Greek of the mythological scholia of Pseudo-Nonnus, whose aim was to explain classical allusions in the homilies of Gregory Nazianzen; the mythological scholia would have at least two Syriac versions.[85] What we have here is a fusion of Christian and pagan learning and the creation of a new set of Christian textual authorities who stand on a par, and indeed above, an older, pagan set. The latter were useful because they helped one understand the former. We are on a road that will lead to the eleventh-century Christian Yaḥyā b. Jarīr writing a marginal note in Syriac and Arabic citing Gregory Nazianzen on a manuscript of a work by al-Fārābī; Ibn al-Nadīm would include Gregory of Nyssa and John Philoponus's refutation of Nestorius among the philosophers in the *Fihrist*; Yaḥyā b. ʿAdī the great (Miaphysite) Christian logician of tenth-century Baghdad would cite Chrysostom, Basil, Gregory Nazianzen and Pseudo-Dionysius among his authorities.[86] 'I am not a Patriarch or a leader, but am rather a lowly

[Washington, D.C., 1967], pp. 82–83). On this story, see W. Jaeger, 'Von Affen und Wahren Christen,' in Jaeger, *Scripta Minora* II (Rome, 1960), pp. 429–39.

[82] See Lucian, *The Fisher* 36 (ed. M. D. Macleod, *Luciani Opera*, vol. 2 [Oxford, 1974], p. 73).

[83] See BL Add. 12,154, fol. 276b.

[84] See the comments and further examples in Brock, 'From Antagonism to Assimilation,' p. 28.

[85] In general, see S. P. Brock's, *The Syriac Version of the Pseudo-Nonnos Mythological Scholia*. The translation and transmission of the *Mythological Scholia* is connected to the translation and transmission of the Gregory's *Homilies*, a very complicated subject. For a third, 'intermediate,' translation of some of Gregory's homilies into Syriac, see A. de Halleux, 'L'homélie baptismale de Grégoire de Nazianze: la version syriaque et son apport au texte grec,' *LM* 95 (1982), pp. 5–40. Athanasius of Balad and Jacob of Edessa also engaged in revision of these translations: Haelewyck, *Sancti Gregorii Nazianzeni Opera. Versio Syriaca I: Oratio XL*, pp. v–vi, gives a succinct summary of the question of Gregory's *Homilies* in Syriac, as does S. P. Brock, 'Charting the Hellenization of a Literary Culture: The Case of Syriac,' *Intellectual History of the Islamicate World* 3 (2015), p. 106. Cf. also Chapter 7, nn. 44–45.

[86] I take all these examples from J. W. Watt, 'Les pères grecs dans le curriculum théologique et

philosopher-monk,' Cosmas, the teacher of John Damascene, is supposed to have told people who asked him what he was.[87] Philosophers were now Christian monks. The municipalities of Athens and Jerusalem had merged.

We return once more to a now-familiar question: What happened when Christian communities were formed on the basis of disagreements about theological speculation that most Christians simply could not understand fully or properly? Here we have found yet another part of the answer: the educational response this situation triggered—as rival confessions competed with one another for simple believers and sought to defend their own turf—contributed to the development of a sophisticated culture of scholarship and translation that reached its fullest expression in ninth-century Baghdad.

* * *

We have traced now some of the implications of thinking of the Middle East as a world of simple believers for understanding the world the Arabs found when they conquered the region in the seventh century: polemics, educational institutions, and scholarship proliferated in response to the confessional chaos among the simple that Chalcedon created. But what does putting the simple at the center of our story do for our understanding of the world the Arab conquests created?[88] For the moment, we can make a slight (and as we will see, provisional) change to the question we have been asking. The question now becomes: What happened when a politically dominant religious rival to Christianity appeared in the Middle East, one whose strongest theological criticisms of Christianity centered on doctrines—the Trinity and the Incarnation—that simple believers could not understand fully or properly?

---

philologique des écoles syriaques,' in A. Schmidt and D. Gonnet, eds., *Les pères grecs dans la tradition syriaque* (*Études Syriaques* 4) (Paris, 2007), p. 38. For Yaḥyā b. Jarīr and al-Fārābī, see R. Walzer, *Al-Farabi on the Perfect State: Abū Naṣr al-Fārābī's Mabādi' Ārā' Ahl al-Madīna al-Fāḍila* (Oxford, 1985), p. 24. Walzer writes that the note refers to 'Gregory of Nyssa or some other Gregory.' Given Gregory Nazianzen's prominence and importance, it is much more likely that the Gregory referred to was Gregory Nazianzen; this, too, is how Watt understood it.

[87] *Life of John of Damascus*, p. 13 (ed. C. Bacha, *Sīrat al-qiddīs Yuḥannā al-Dimashqī* [Harissa, 1912])—though note that the historicity of this source is dubious. On the biography of John Damascene, see S. W. Anthony, 'Fixing John Damascene's Biography: Historical Notes on His Family Background,' *JECS* 23 (2015), pp. 607–27. On what we can know of Cosmas, see A. Kazhdan and S. Gerö, 'Kosmas of Jerusalem: A More Critical Approach to His Biography,' *Byzantinische Zeitschrift* 82 (1989), pp. 122–32.

[88] I refer to the conquests here as 'Arab conquests' for the simple reason that Syriac writers in the seventh century by and large perceived them as such. For Syriac writers understanding the conquerors as Arabs rather than Muslims, see Brock, 'Syriac Views of Emergent Islam,' p. 14. For more on this, see Appendix II.

PART III

Christians and Muslims

CHAPTER 9

A House with Many Mansions

> ʿAlī [b. Abī Ṭālib] used to disapprove of the slaughtered meat of the Christian Banū Taghlib. He would say: 'The only thing they have taken from Christianity is the drinking of wine.'[1]

> Theologische Formeln sind noch nicht die Religion, auch nicht das Wichtigste an der Religion.
>
> Tor Andrae[2]

The most obvious way in which Muslim rule changed the Middle East is that it eventually led to the Arabization and Islamization of the entire region: the very region, in fact, where Christianity was born and from which it spread to the rest of the ancient world. But what was the nature of this conversion? And how does focusing on ordinary Christians (rather than on the learned among their leadership) change the way we see the Middle East under Muslim rule?

Before we can try to answer such questions, we need first to ask the antecedent questions 'What was Islam?' and 'What was Christianity?' For a weakness of discussions of early Christian-Muslim interactions is that they tend to leave unexamined the two most important words in the phrase 'Christian-Muslim interactions'—namely, 'Christian' and 'Muslim'—and instead focus solely on 'interactions,' which in practice usually means 'theological interactions.' For both of these categories, 'Christian' and 'Muslim,' simple, ordinary believers are typically forgotten, and what it meant to be a Christian or to be a Muslim is supplied by the beliefs of theological elites and what might be termed 'confessional entrepreneurs'—that is, people whose aim or intent it was to create a well-formed and well-bounded Christian or Muslim community in a place where a community having that particular constellation of religiously distinctive characteristics had not previously existed.[3]

[1] ʿAbd al-Razzāq, *al-Muṣannaf* (ed. Ḥ. al-Raḥmān al-Aʿẓamī) (Johannesburg/Beirut, 1983), p. 72 (no. 10034).

[2] T. Andrae, 'Zuhd und Mönchtum. Zur Frage von den Beziehungen zwischen Christentum und Islam,' *Le Monde Oriental* 25 (1931), p. 296.

[3] Much as an economic entrepreneur seeks to start a business. I am grateful to Michael Woldemariam for having introduced me to the concept of the 'ethnic entrepreneur' who helps create new ethnicities and which stimulated my thinking on this topic, cf. his 'Why Rebels Collide: Factionalism and Fragmentation in African Insurgencies,' (PhD diss., Princeton 2011), p. 49; and cf. also C. Tilly's notion of

To supply the contents of belief for both Christians and Muslims when discussing Christian-Muslim interactions, therefore, we turn to texts written by what are very unrepresentative figures. A minority is made to speak for the majority. The minority is, to be sure, a learned one, and privileging its views may be useful if we are interested in the history of ideas. But giving this minority pride of place has misleading and distorting results if we are interested in social history and how most people lived. Discussions that set such unrepresentative figures at their center suffer from the same defects as many attempts to describe the nature of Christianity in the Middle East in the wake of Chalcedon. Similar to the patristic seminar run amok that the Middle East can be easily made to resemble in that era, what the Middle East appears to be now, at least when it comes to Christian-Muslim relations in this period, is a region where people obsess over the nature of God's unity, the truth of the Incarnation, and the question of whether Muḥammad was a prophet. The layering of knowledge in the Christian community that I discussed in Part I and the tension between learned and simple understandings of Christianity that we found in Parts I and II are typically nowhere to be found. There is a tacit assumption that everyone in the Middle East in the Middle Ages was well informed about the contents of the theological tradition to which each person belonged—an assumption that would make that period unique in the history of the Christian church.

To be sure, at least so far as concerns Christianity, we can suppose that some of its meanings included the sophisticated doctrinal systems of theological elites such as Athanasius of Balad, Jacob of Edessa, George of the Arabs and Isho'yahb III, figures who have left us extensive writings. But, if we understand 'Christianity' to include what actual Christians were doing and believing, and not just what they were supposed to be doing and believing, 'Christianity' might include many other things as well: the Miaphysite priest who used the Bible as a means of persuading women in his congregation to sleep with him;[4] the Lakhmid King Nu'mān b. al-Mundhir (reg. 580–602), who is said to have made the pilgrimage to Mecca while he was a Christian—and before Muḥammad's prophetic career had even begun;[5] the Christian poet 'Adī b. Zayd (d. AD 587), who would swear by the 'Lord of Mecca and by the Cross'

the 'political entrepreneur' found in *The Politics of Collective Violence* (Cambridge/New York, 2003). For the notion of the 'religious entrepreneur,' see now N. Green, *Terrains of Exchange: Religious Economies of Global Islam* (New York, 2015).

[4] *Questions Which Addai the Priest and Lover of Labors Asked Jacob, the Bishop of Edessa* 49 (ed. Lamy, *Dissertatio*, p. 148). ET available in *SBI*, p. 381, n. 917.

[5] For al-Nu'mān b. Mundhir's pilgrimage, see Ibn al-Faqīh, *Mukhtaṣar kitāb al-buldān* (ed. M. J. de Goeje [Leiden, 1302], p. 19). For this point about al-Nu'mān b. Mundhir and also information about *mawqif al-naṣārā*, 'the station of the Christians,' one of the pilgrimage stops near Mecca, see H. Lam-

in one of his poems;[6] or unnamed individuals who thought it was acceptable to take more than one wife.[7] Jacob of Edessa condemned those who bent needles and threw locks down wells to separate a husband from a wife;[8] those who sought refuge in special trees, springs, sea water, bones, dried animal heads, and herbs when confronted with illness, or who invested thunder, lightning, and comets with meaning and power; those who used the right paw of a wolf or broken pieces of pottery for apotropaic purposes; those who put laurel branches in a field to keep its crops from being scorched by heat.[9] And so on.[10] The people who did these things would have called themselves 'Christians'—presumably they were baptized, attended (at least on occasion) liturgies, and took the Eucharist—and yet, the sort of Christianity they represented and lived out hardly figures in how we have thought about the Christian-Muslim encounter in the seventh century—or indeed any century. But there were presumably many more people engaging in these sorts of behaviors than there were people who had precise understandings of the Trinity or who could articulate a coherent view of the Incarnation.

This is exactly what one would expect in a society where states were weak, religious education and catechesis spotty, clergy often ill-equipped and poorly trained, levels of literacy low, and levels of theological literacy even lower.

---

mens, 'Études sur le règne du calife Omaiyade Mo'awiya Ier,' (part 3), *Mélanges de la Faculté orientale/ Université Saint-Joseph*, 3.1 (1908), p. 267 (for *mawqif al-naṣārā*, see n. 8).

[6] For this, see H. Lammens, 'Études sur le règne du calife Omaiyade Mo'awiya Ier,' (part 3), p. 268. For the poem, see L. Cheikho, *Shu'arā' al-naṣrāniyya qabla al-Islām* (Beirut, 1999), p. 451; an ET can be found in J. Horovitz, "Adi ibn Zeyd, the Poet of Hira,' *Islamic Culture* 4 (1930), p. 45. On this passage and the question of its authenticity, see T. Hainthaler, "Adī ibn Zayd al-'Ibadī, the Pre-Islamic Christian Poet of al-Ḥīrā and His Poem Nr. 3 Written in Jail,' *PdO* 30 (2005), p. 169. For the Christian poet al-Akhṭal swearing by the pagan deity Allāt, see Lammens, 'Études sur le règne du calife Omaiyade Mo'awiya Ier,' (pt. 3), p. 302, n. 3.

[7] For a mid-seventh-century defense of monogamy, see Yonan the Bishop, *Letter to Theodore the Periodeute on Monogamy* in Cambridge Add. 2023, fols. 254b–59a, esp. fol. 254b, where Yonan refers to a debate Theodore had with people wanting arguments against polygamy (for the Syriac text and ET of portions of this letter, see SBI, p. 257, n. 601, and n. 602 for evidence that Christians were advocating polygamy). For Jacob of Edessa condemning Christians who marry more than one wife, Mardin 310, fol. 211b. (Syriac text and ET in *SBI*, p. 258). There is extensive evidence for Christians practicing polygamy in the Middle East, both before and after the Arab conquests—see, e.g., Synod of Isho'yahb I, *Canons* 13 (ed. Chabot, *Synodicon Orientale*, p. 149 = 410 [FT]), and *Canons of Patriarch Dionysius* 6 (ed. and trans. Vööbus, *The Synodicon in the West Syrian Tradition II* [CSCO 375–76: SS 163–64], pp. 30–31 [Syriac] = p. 33 [ET]).

[8] *Questions Which Addai the Priest and Lover of Labors Asked Jacob, the Bishop of Edessa* 40 (ed. Lamy, *Dissertatio*, p. 140; ET in *SBI*, p. 259, n. 605). O.-P. Saar, 'An Incantation Bowl for Sowing Discord,' *Journal of Semitic Studies* 58 (2013), pp. 241–56, discusses a (unique) magic bowl that contains a 'separation spell' aimed at driving a man and woman apart.

[9] *Questions Which Addai the Priest and Lover of Labors Asked Jacob, the Bishop of Edessa* 43 (ed. Lamy, *Dissertatio*, pp. 140, 142). ET available in *SBI*, p. 259, n. 607.

[10] See al-Azmeh, *The Emergence of Islam in Late Antiquity*, p. 260, for more such examples.

Episcopal visitors in Saxony and eastern Germany around the beginning of the seventeenth century, Ramsay MacMullen has pointed out, found that outside of elite company, the level of knowledge of Christianity plummeted markedly. 'Once out of the upper-class circles, however, and even in a time of bitter theological rivalries to concentrate the greatest possible attention on the faith,' he reported,

> the vast bulk of the population are found to have been largely or totally ignorant of the simplest matters of doctrine, rarely or never attending church. They were devoted instead to a 'vigorous religious subculture… beyond the theologian's grasp, the preacher's appeal, or the visitor's power to compel'—that is, they were given over to 'soothsayers, cunning women, crystal gazers, casters of spells, witches, and other practitioners of forbidden arts.'[11]

The content, sophistication, and volume of theological literature being produced in Europe at that time, and specifically in Germany, the epicenter of the Reformation, might easily seduce us into thinking that the concerns over theological speculation that animated the pens of religious leaders were ubiquitous in the Christian community. But then we would be mistaken.

In our period, there was a range of Christian beliefs and a gamut of understandings of what was encouraged, what was acceptable, and what was forbidden by church leaders for Christians to do and to believe. When Arab conquerors rode into the Middle East in the 630s and 640s, the Christianity they would have encountered (and already knew from Arabia) would have included that of all these people, and others as well. In Chapter 3, we looked at some aspects of Christian-Christian relations in the post-Chalcedonian world. In keeping with what we would expect from a world filled with simple believers, the actions of these Christians often fell short of what the doctrinally engaged among the leaders of the various Christian communities expected from their flocks.

But even the leaders of various communities and the prominent learned figures within them might be found engaging in activities that do not sit comfortably with many of our reflexive expectations of what a good Christian should have been. The Sasanian ruler Zamasp (reg. 496–498), for instance,

[11] See R. MacMullen, *Christianizing the Roman Empire (A.D. 100-400)* (New Haven/London, 1984), p. 5. My thinking on the question of the Islamization of the Middle East in the early medieval period has been influenced by MacMullen's arguments in this book. There are a multitude of studies about the prevalence and persistence of 'popular' religion in rural areas in the Europe of the Reformation; see, e.g., C. S. Dixon, 'Popular Beliefs and the Reformation in Brandenburg-Ansbach,' in B. Scribner and T. Johnson, eds., *Popular Religion in Germany and Central Europe, 1400–1800* (Basingstoke/New York, 1996), pp. 119–39 and Dixon, *The Reformation and Rural Society: The Parishes of Brandenburg-Ansbach-Kulmbach, 1528–1603* (Cambridge, 1996), pp. 102–28, 176–207.

reportedly had a Christian astrologer named Moses who played a role in having his relative Babai (sed. 497–502/503) elected catholicos.[12] In the late sixth century, Gregory bar Ruphina, the East Syrian bishop of Nisibis, was driven from his position and replaced 'because he was deeply involved in the movement of the stars and the Zodiac.'[13] In roughly the same period, one of the charges against the controversial head of the School of Nisibis, Henana of Adiabene (d. 610), was that he believed that 'destiny and fate are the cause of everything and that each thing is guided by its star.'[14] Jacob of Edessa's *Hexaemeron* had included arguments against astrology that went back to Basil and, through Basil, to Origen:[15] indeed, Addai had written to Jacob about 'those who blame the stars for their illnesses.'[16] The learned Maronite Theophilus of Edessa (d. 785) was the astrologer of the Caliph al-Mahdī and a strong defender of this art, even on scriptural grounds.[17]

Such reports point us to the fact that some Christians, even among the clergy, did not view practicing a wide variety of forms of divination as incompatible with Christianity.[18] For Christians in the seventh century this compatibilist view, so to speak, might extend to looking to and taking up Zoroastrian astrological practices in attempts to gain insight into future events. This was among the many practices that Jacob of Edessa condemned. 'It is not right,' he wrote,

> for Christians to observe and believe in these things which are called by them '*d-surāde*,' because God is not circumscribed and forced to administer by the decisions of human beings who want to blather foolishness, nor are His mind or His actions comprehended by their examinations [sc., of the stars]. We should rather know that this name which is called '*d-surāde*' is Persian and Magian and is for those days in which they make divinations concerning their error, [days] in which they think that they will have a certain foreknowledge concerning things to come. Magians name them '*d-surāde*', as do insane blabberers among

[12] *Chronicle of Seert*, 2.15 (ed. Scher [PO 7.2], pp. 36–37).

[13] *Khuzistan Chronicle*, p. 17 (ed. Guidi [CSCO Syr. III.4]). Another ET available in Greatrex and Lieu, *The Roman Eastern Frontier and the Persian Wars*, p. 230.

[14] Babai the Great, *History of George the Priest*, p. 496 (ed. Bedjan, Histoire de Mar-Jabalaha).

[15] See Wilks, 'Jacob of Edessa's Use of Greek Philosophy in His Hexaemeron,' pp. 236–38.

[16] *Questions Which Addai the Priest and Lover of Labors Asked Jacob, the Bishop of Edessa* 43 (ed. Lamy, *Dissertatio*, p. 140). See *SBI*, p. 259, n. 607, for an English translation.

[17] See *Catalogus codicum astrologorum graecorum*, vol. 5: F. Cumont and F. Boll, eds., *Codicum Romanorum partem priorem* (Brussels, 1904), pp. 237–38. For the interpretation of the story of the Magi in early Christian thought, see T. Hegedus, *Early Christianity and Ancient Ancient Astrology* (New York, 2007), pp. 201–11.

[18] See the additional evidence for clerical use of divination adduced in Lamy, *Dissertatio*, pp. 245–46.

> the Christians when they imitate them and want to make examinations, they say, and foreknow and foretell—based on their false and empty foreknowledge—idiotic things about future events. They have been made to call it by this pagan and Magian name when they imitate the pagan error of the Magians both in act and word.[19]

What Jacob of Edessa referred to as the '*d-surāde*,' George of the Arabs knew as 'the Examiners' or '*Sūrādē*' or '*Nāsūrdē*'—'I have heard them called by all three of these names,' he wrote. These were terms that referred to the eight days after the rising of Sirius, each of which was supposed to offer insight into the events of a separate month, from October through May.[20] Though George also rejected the practice of astrology, he had a solid understanding of its mechanics.[21]

If we look again to Addai's questions to Jacob, we find him in a number of places criticizing the behaviors of clergymen—not just of the laity—as being outside the bounds of appropriate Christian behavior. Priests and monks were using the Gospels, the Psalter, a work called *The Lot of the Apostles*,[22] and perhaps other books, to make charms—another practice Jacob condemned.[23] Priests and monks would read various types of prognosticatory works in marketplaces and houses for audiences of men and women. Addai gives us several

[19] Jacob of Edessa, *Canons*, Mardin 310, fols. 211b–212a. The Syriac text can also be found in *SBI*, p. 263, n. 615.

[20] See BL Add. 12,154, fols. 278b-279a. The Syriac text can also be found in *SBI*, p. 263, n. 616.

[21] This is evidenced by his detailed discussion of astrology in his *Letter 9* (To John, the Stylite of Litarb), BL Add. 12,154, fols. 278a–284a (esp. 278a–283a). George's *Letter 7* (To John, the Stylite of Litarb) also showed a deep familiarity with astrology and astronomical calculations. See BL Add. 12,154, 264b–272b. The need to make church calendars meant that Christian leaders had to have some familiarity with astronomy/astrology. Before Eusebius's *Chronicon*, the author of the *Chronicle of Seert* remarked, Christians depended on Jews for the information by which they would calculate their feasts, their fasts, and Easter; now that Eusebius had completed his work, however, Christians 'do not need to ever turn to the Jews, or to others—astrologers and mathematicians—for knowledge.' *Chronicle of Seert*, 1.21 (ed. Scher [PO 4.3], pp. 75–76, quote at 76).

[22] A copy of which is preserved in Syriac in BL Or. 4434, from the nineteenth century. G. Furlani published an Italian translation in his 'Una recensione siriaca delle *Sortes apostolorum*,' *Atti del Reale Istituto Veneto di Scienze, Lettere ed Arti* 82.2 (1922–1923), pp. 357–63.

[23] *Questions Which Addai the Priest and Lover of Labors Asked Jacob, the Bishop of Edessa*, Mardin 310, fols. 202a–b. Syriac text and ET in *SBI*, p. 261, n. 611. For other versions of this rule, see Kayser, *Die Canones Jakob's von Edessa*, pp. 2, 21 (Syriac). A shorter version can also be found in *Questions Which Addai the Priest and Lover of Labors Asked Jacob, the Bishop of Edessa*, p. 268 (ed. Vööbus, *The Synodicon in the West Syrian Tradition* I [CSCO 367–68: SS 161–62], p. 244 [ET]). Vööbus understood *nsab petgāmā* to mean 'take an answer,' one possible literal meaning of the two words. If Vööbus's construal is more correct, Jacob's canon would be aimed at forms of bibliomancy that attempted to divine the future based on passages from the Bible (or other books) found randomly, rather than at making charms as I have construed this key phrase, following Manna, *Qāmūs kaldānī-'arabī*, s.v. *nsab*, where the idiom *nsab petgāmā* is defined *raqā ruqyatan*, which means 'to give someone a charm.'

different titles: the *Book of Twitches*, the *Book of the Signs Which Are in the Human Body*, the *Book of Moons* and the *Book of Types of Thunder*.[24] Jacob's canons suggest that priests were engaging in a wide variety of divinatory practices: they spoke incantations, tied knots, made charms, wrote out small texts to drive away headaches and heal tumors. They cast convulsions out of humans and out of animals. They would use the twitterings and movements of birds for auguries; even marks on the human body were being used to divine the future. These priests also interpreted dreams. Jacob had little time for such individuals: 'If it were possible to reckon people who wickedly do one of these things Christians,' he wrote when Addai asked him about such people, 'I would say that they should by all means fall from their rank. But because it is completely impossible to number them among Christians, such a statement is superfluous.'[25]

Writing perhaps about the time that Jacob was quitting his bishopric in response to widespread canonical abuse in the late 680s, the East Syrian John bar Penkaye also lamented the ubiquity of fortune-telling among Christians in northern Mesopotamia. 'For in Egypt, the mother of enchanters,' John observed, 'divination was not as abundant as it is in our time. Indeed, in Babel, augurs and soothsayers were not as numerous as they are now among Christian people.'[26] These practices went on after the seventh century: in 794, the patriarch Cyriacus condemned any clergyman 'who employs magic knots or amulets or goes to charmers or soothsayers or those who mutter incantations or write scraps of writing for fever or other sicknesses.'[27] And they had been going on well before the seventh century as well: in the fifth or sixth century, Isaac of Antioch lamented the active involvement of priests in divination—'the gates of the church, look! They are wide open,' he wrote, 'but no one comes to prayer, for the pastors along with the sheep are running to the door of the

[24] *Questions Which Addai the Priest and Lover of Labors Asked Jacob, the Bishop of Edessa*, Mardin 310, fol. 202b. Syriac text and ET available in *SBI*, p. 261, n. 612.

[25] *Questions Which Addai the Priest and Lover of Labors Asked Jacob, the Bishop of Edessa* 36 (ed. Lamy, *Dissertatio*, pp. 134, 136. ET available in *SBI*, p. 262, n. 614). These practices of course did not cease after the end of late antiquity or the Middle Ages. See, e.g., Mingana Syriac 190, dated to AD 1874, which contains a prayer of the solitary 'Abdisho' for the use of women whose children have died on account of evil spirits and another prayer, attributed to St. Anthony, that protects women from evil spirits. For the description of these two prayers, see A. Mingana, *Catalogue of the Mingana Collection of Manuscripts*, vol. 1 (Cambridge, 1933, 1936, 1939), col. 415 (C and D).

[26] John bar Penkaye, *Book of the Main Events*, p. *151 (ed. Mingana). For the similar idea that divination started in Egypt, then went to Assyria, see Isaac of Antioch, *Second Homily against Those Who Go to Soothsayers*, p. 827, lnn. 13–14 (ed. Bedjan, *Homiliae S. Isaaci, Syri Antiocheni*).

[27] *Canons of Patriarch Cyriacus (AD 794)* 12 (ed. and trans. Vööbus, *The Synodicon in the West Syrian Tradition II* [CSCO 375-376: SS 163–64] [Louvain, 1976], p. 10 [Syriac] = 12 [ET]). I have used the translation of Vööbus.

sorcerers.'[28] When we read in the *Chronicle of Seert* that Catholicos Aḥai (sed. 410–415) had asked church leaders to 'burn every house in which they found any magical arts or instruments of Magianism, for the Christians had mixed with the Marcionites and the Manichaeans and were doing some of their deeds,'[29] we should not be surprised in the slightest: the behaviors Jacob condemned had a long history among Christians in the Middle East and elsewhere. Indeed, even the Apostle Paul had complained to the church in Galatia about its members' astrological practices.[30]

Clergy and monastics engaged in other activities as well that some Christian leaders deemed inappropriate. Among the feats of Theodota of Amid in the seventh century was unmasking a man in the monastery of Barṣawmā who, his *vita* reports, had 'a spirit of sorcery':

> He would repeat both the Old and the New [Testaments], the Psalms, and the [various] liturgies, and the opinion of the Teachers. He was clothed in a demon and he was leading the people astray. He had ascetic feats and vigils and prayers and would teach the people about repentance. He would reveal the sins and hidden things of the people; and all the people of the region began to go astray after him—the priests and the monks and all the people, since they supposed 'The Holy Spirit is in him,' and 'a prophet has been given in our day.'[31]

According to his *vita*, Theodota subsequently drove an evil spirit out of the man and showed him to be a demonic fraud. Nevertheless, what we have here is a concrete example of the sort of person Addai had referred to in his question to Jacob about priests practicing divination: a figure who, although regarded by at least some ecclesiastical elites to be in error and even satanic, still enjoyed a following among lay people and monks. Whatever this man's

[28] Isaac of Antioch, *Homily on Sorcerers, Enchanters, Diviners, and on the End and Consumation*, col. 397 (ed. T. J. Lamy, *Sancti Ephraem Syri hymni et sermones* [Mechlin, 1886], vol. 2). For this homily as the work of Isaac, see Baumstark, *Geschichte*, p. 65, n. 4, and E. G. Mathews, Jr., 'A Bibliographical Clavis to the Corpus of Works Attributed to Isaac of Antioch,' *Hugoye: Journal of Syriac Studies* 5 (2002), p. 11.

[29] *Chronicle of Seert* 1.69 (ed. Scher [PO 5.2], p. 213).

[30] Cf. Galatians 4:10; on this passage, see W. Gundel in *RAC*, vol. 1, col. 825. 'There is no chief of the Jewish synagogue, no Samaritan, no Christian presbyter who is not an astrologer, a soothsayer, or an anointer,' the emperor Hadrian is supposed to have written. Flavius Vopiscus, *Firmus, Saturninus, Proclus, and Bonosus* 8. (ET taken from D. Magie, *The Scriptores Historiae Augustae*, vol. 3 [Loeb Classical Library 263] [Cambridge, MA, 1932], p. 399). This passage was almost certainly not written by the emperor Hadrian. On it, see S. Benko, 'Pagan Criticism of Christianity During the First Two Centuries A.D.,' *Aufstieg und Niedergang der Römischen Welt* II, *Principat*, 23.2 (Berlin/New York, 1980), pp. 1080–81. For Christians and astrology, see Hegedus, *Early Christianity and Astrology*, esp. pp. 261–370. R. B. Barnes, *Astrology and Reformation* (New York, 2015), shows the popularity of astrology even among early Lutheran pastors.

[31] St Mark's Jerusalem 199, fol. 553b. For the Syriac, see Mardin 275/8, pp. 526–27.

self-conception was, he was perceived by others as being holy and his idiom of self-representation was a Christian one. The sorcerer was certainly doing the things that one would expect a holy man to do, at least on the surface.

Addai spoke to Jacob about a similar situation: a priest who claimed an ability to cast demons out of people and animals who had been possessed for less than forty days. For certain animals, like bulls and camels, he would have strong men hold or bind them and then would pray softly in their ear to cast the demon out. Jacob held that such a person was neither a priest, nor a Christian but someone in league with demons to lead 'simple Christians' astray. Such a figure has left us no writings through which he can speak for himself. That he called himself a priest, however, and that he would rub himself with the blessings of the saints the day after the exorcism, and indeed, that Jacob ordered that this priest's Christian followers be punished according to church canons, strongly suggests that the exorcist regarded himself as a Christian and was a respected figure in at least some parts of the Christian community.[32]

The spectrum of what was acceptable and what was not for a Christian could be person-relative and depending on the issue, different Christian authorities might have divergent standards. Theodota's disapproval of a Christian who engaged in magical practices put him in agreement with the stance of Jacob of Edessa on such things; George of the Arabs, too, has left us a canon calling for the excommunication of anyone who made use of magical knots, amulets, or incantations.[33] Theodota's and George's attitudes would, however, conflict on a different topic related to the activities of Christian leaders and holy men. Theodota carried with him a bag of saints' relics as he traveled about, whereas George—who was his younger contemporary—has left us a canon ordering that roving monks who carried such sacks should not be received.[34] George regarded astrology as a 'load of rubbish' and demonic,[35] and yet we find a figure like the eighth- and ninth- century holy man Timothy of

[32] *Questions Which Addai the Priest and Lover of Labors Asked Jacob, the Bishop of Edessa* 39 (ed. Lamy, *Dissertatio*, pp. 136, 138, 140). An ET can also be found in *SBI*, p. 266, n. 622.

[33] Bar Hebraeus, *Nomocanon* 7.8 (ed. Bedjan, *Nomocanon*, p. 102), and compare with Council in Trullo, *Canons* 61 (ed. Joannou, *Discipline générale antique*, vol. 1.1, pp. 196–98; ET by Percival available in *NPNF*, ser. 2, vol. 14, p. 393).

[34] For this point, see A. Palmer, 'Saints' Lives with a Difference: Elijah on John of Tella (d. 538) and Joseph on Theodotos of Amida (d. 698),' in H.J.W. Drijvers et al., eds., *IV Symposium Syriacum, 1984: Literary Genres in Syriac Literature* (Rome, 1987), p. 213, n. 43, and M. M. Mango, 'Monophysite Church Decoration,' in A. Bryer and J. Herrin, eds., *Iconoclasm: Papers Given at the Ninth Spring Symposium of Byzantine Studies, University of Birmingham, March 1975* (Birmingham, 1977), p. 74. For the canons, see Vööbus, *Syriac and Arabic Documents*, p. 99.

[35] See his comments in BL Add. 12,154, fols. 279a–b. Syriac text and ET available in *SBI*, pp. 268–69.

Kākhushtā boasting that he could use the stars to find information about a woman's missing brother, and then proceeding to doing just that.[36]

CHRISTIAN BEHAVIOR, CHRISTIAN BELIEF

Such examples can easily be multiplied, from both before and after the Arab conquests. We read, for instance, of a deacon called Bar Taʿlē, who was punished by his metropolitan in the late sixth or early seventh century after being discovered sacrificing a white cock in a grove outside of Nisibis.[37] The confessional confusion I tried to delineate in Chapter 3 and the behaviors we saw upsetting Jacob in Chapter 5 were only two fronts in the wide-ranging battle to enforce orthodoxy and orthopraxy that (some) church leaders were constantly fighting.[38]

Some may here object, however, that I have mentioned only what might be termed disciplinary abuses and ignored belief and the doctrinal views of these Christians. The two are not the same, it will be noted, and it is differences in belief and doctrine that are of paramount importance in considering the Christian-Muslim encounter.

It may very well have been the case that those whom Jacob of Edessa condemned for engaging in a ceremony that involved declaring a young virgin to be the 'mother' of a locust and then burying it in order to try to rid a garden or a field of such pests[39] at the same time held sophisticated understandings of the Triune nature of the One God—that there was no correlation between apparent disregard for or ignorance of traditional Christian moral teaching and an understanding of the intricacies of sophisticated theological speculation.[40] Nevertheless, it will have been true that just as there was a spectrum

[36] *Life of Timothy of Kākhushtā* 16.1–16.3 ('Saidnaya Version'; ed. Lamoreaux and Cairala [PO 48.4], p. 120 [Arabic] = 121 [ET]).

[37] *Khuzistan Chronicle*, p. 18 (ed. Guidi [CSCO Syr. III.4]; translation available in Greatrex and Lieu, *The Roman Eastern Frontier*, p. 230–31). The metropolitan was Gregory of Kashkar, on whom see Baumstark, *Geschichte*, p. 128.

[38] And church leaders themselves might very well engage in some of these behaviors or, at the least, there might be a view that they could: see, e.g., Sozomen, *Ecclesiastical History* 3.6 (ed. Bidez, p. 108), where Eusebius of Emesa is forced to flee Emesa after being accused of practicing astrology. On this charge, see R. E. Winn, *Eusebius of Emesa: Church and Theology in the Mid-Fourth Century* (Washington, D.C., 2011), pp. 44–45.

[39] *Questions Which Addai the Priest and Lover of Labors Asked Jacob, the Bishop of Edessa* 44 (ed. Lamy, *Dissertatio*, p. 142, 144. ET available in *SBI*, p. 260, n. 609).

[40] It is of course very possible to have a deep knowledge of the Christian theological tradition and also a selective regard for Christian moral teachings. As an example from our period, one can point to the Emperor Justinian, who wrote theological treatises and yet who was seen, or at least charged, in some quarters, as being of very dubious moral character (as witnessed by Procopius's scathingly polemi-

of practices and actions engaged in by Christians, only some of which ecclesiastical authorities deemed acceptable, so there was also a broad spectrum of (doctrinal) beliefs held by Christians. And this spectrum, it should be pointed out, extended well beyond the Christologically-based doctrinal typologies carefully laid out in modern patristic manuals and theological textbooks. One corollary of the poorly defined situation 'on the ground' which I attempted to sketch out in Chapter 3 is that although well-articulated doctrinal positions perhaps existed most strongly among theological elites, beyond highly literate and erudite churchmen in certain monastic centers—that is, among what Jacob referred to as 'simple people' or 'simple Christians'—these labels may not have meant a great deal.

These people, as I suggested earlier, were presumably baptized, took the Eucharist, attended church services (at least on occasion), and would have self-identified as Christians. They would presumably also have believed in Jesus (though they understood what this meant and entailed in various ways). But just as one can believe in gravity without understanding the finer points of Einstein's Theory of General Relativity, or indeed, without ever having heard of Einstein; so, too, one could believe in Jesus without having a coherent view of the Incarnation or a strong opinion on Chalcedon (or any view at all on these matters). If, fifteen hundred years from now, cultural historians of the twentieth and twenty-first century were to point to a widespread belief in gravity and widespread admiration for Einstein as evidence for an equally widespread understanding of General Relativity in our period, a visitor from the present to that future date would simply laugh.[41]

What scholars interested in the history of Christian-Muslim interaction in the medieval period have traditionally taken as their chief objects of study—the learned encounter in a *majlis* (that is, a salon), treatises written by Christians criticizing Islam, or works written by Muslims attacking Christianity[42]—represent in fact only one aspect of the religious landscape of the world dominated by simple believers that I identified in Chapter 4: the importance of learned

cal *Secret History*); on Justinian's theological compositions, see Menze, *Justinian and the Making of the Syrian Orthodox Church*, pp. 251–52. More recently, one could point to the example of the celebrated Protestant theologian Paul Tillich (d. 1965), on whose controversial personal life see R. May, *Paulus: Reminiscences of a Friendship* (New York, 1973), pp. 49–66.

[41] I am grateful to Peter Brown for suggesting the example of gravity to me and stimulating my thoughts on this subject.

[42] For the classic description of the genre of *majlis*-encounter literature, see S. Griffith, 'The Monk in the Emir's *Majlis*: Reflections on a Popular Genre of Christian Literary Apologetics in Arabic in the Early Islamic Period,' in H. Lazarus-Yafeh et al., eds., *The Majlis: Interreligious Encounters in Medieval Islam* (Wiesbaden, 1999), pp. 13–65. The monumental series *Christian-Muslim Relations*, contains entries on an enormous number Christian-Muslim dispute texts and learned religious polemics written by Christians and Muslims.

treatises along with stories of the confessional champion who defeated leading representatives of rival confessions in dialectical contexts. But rather than confessional champions who battled Christians belonging to rival churches, what we now have is a Christian interlocutor, in a *majlis*, confounding a Muslim. Such interreligious confessional champions were not, of course, a development of the period of Muslim rule—Christian confessional champions had (at the literary level, at least) battled pagans, Jews, Manichees, and Magians well before Muḥammad was even born, and stories about these encounters had long been written and circulated, told and retold.

The period of Muslim rule changed very little of the structure that religious belief, its practice, and its justification took. We are still operating in a world of simple believers. The major difference is that a new set of actors has now emerged on the stage.[43] The same problems of poorly trained clergy, spotty catechesis, and low levels of theological literacy that characterized the post-Chalcedonian church were still present after Arabs conquered the Middle East. We spent Chapters 5, 6, 7, and 8 looking at the institutional responses that church leaders made to try to counter the consequences of being in a world of simple believers that was fractured and fracturing on the basis of learned theological speculation, but such efforts will have had, ultimately, limited effect.[44] Mass literacy is something that simply did not exist until much more recent periods of history. And mass theological literacy has arguably never existed at any point in the history of the Christian church.[45]

THE NUMBER AND NATURE OF CLERGY

If we want to think about the varieties of Christian belief and not just about Christian behavior in the early period of Muslim rule, we can start with a suggestion I have made already: a problem confronting church leadership in

[43] Arabs, of course, were not new, but Muslims were: we now have a new religious community with a particular story of God's action in the world that had not just a corpus of revelation but also the patronage of a state.

[44] Note, e.g., the tenth-century report in al-Shābushtī, *Kitāb al-diyārāt*, pp. 171 (ed. K. ʿAwwād [Beirut, 1986]), that at the Nestorian monastery of Dayr Mar Yuḥannā in Tikrit, a certain Melkite monk named ʿAbdūn had built a cell over the monastery's gate and lived there. 'He is now in charge of the monastery,' al-Shābushtī wrote, 'and responsible for those inside.'

[45] The few possible exceptions to this claim that one might point to—most notably, perhaps, colonial New England—will almost all be found in a world where printing existed and Protestantism, especially Calvinism, was culturally hegemonic. But in our period, there was neither printing nor Protestantism. For a description of the high rates of literacy and religious literacy in colonial America and the early United States, especially New England, see S. Prothero, *Religious Literacy: What Every American Needs to Know—and Doesn't* (San Francisco, 2007), pp. 59–86.

the seventh century was one of manpower.[46] It seems that, at least in some rural areas, there were not enough priests to go around. Jacob's canons suggest that on account of a shortage of clergy, Miaphysite priests might escort the funeral processions of deceased Chalcedonians. This also meant that one priest might be called upon to celebrate multiple Eucharists in one day, in a number of different villages. The *Life* of Theodota, as we have seen, reported the holy man coming across a boy in a village who was so sick that his grave had already been dug. The villagers begged Theodota to stay and wait for the boy's death as they had no priest to lead the boy's funeral procession.[47] In the late seventh century, in fact, the Quinisext Council forbade a layperson from giving himself communion when a bishop, priest, or deacon was present, a prohibition that, it has been suggested, implicitly recognized that members of the laity could give themselves the Eucharist if there were no clergy available.[48]

If such a shortage of manpower in rural contexts was real, its potential impact on the meanings Christianity might take for the simple should not be underestimated, especially when coupled with the additional problems that attached to finding well-trained and educated priests, which we encountered in Part I. We should furthermore not assume that a manpower problem was limited to the parish level: at times, it might even extend as high as the episcopacy. The East Syrian catholicos Timothy I has left us a letter in which he bemoaned the lack of qualified church leaders available in Elam and the difficulty of getting people to go there to serve. It was a situation that had gone on for many years. 'Now when we saw your crying out,' he wrote to Sergius, the metropolitan of Elam

> and observed the great desolation that has taken hold of your churches on account of the lack of leaders and when we looked upon the ruin that is born from this for the church, we asked many solitaries and monks and many students and teachers that they give themselves to the task of coming to you. At times we used persuasion and charm and at times [threats of] anathemas and harshness with them—as was the case with Isho'sabran and Isho'rahmeh, who are known to your holiness. But no one at all would bend to our will and our opinion, thinking that they would much rather go to prison than to the [episcopal] throne and that it was to lowly service and slavery that they were called

[46] This may have been partially the result of the continuing effects of the Justinianic plague. I am grateful to Kyle Harper for alerting me to the dramatic and enduring demographic consequences of this epidemic, on which see now his *The Fate of Rome: Climate, Disease, and the End of an Empire* (Princeton, 2017).

[47] For these points, see Chapter 3, nn. 57-59.

[48] Council in Trullo, *Canons* 58 (ed. Joannou, *Discipline générale antique*, vol. 1.1, pp. 194–95). For this suggestion, see Taft, 'Home-Communion in the Late Antique East,' p. 14.

> rather than to the exalted and divine rank [of a bishop] and they would beg off from this.

Timothy gave various reasons why people were refusing to go to Elam to serve: first and foremost, disobedience. But there were other reasons as well: the long distance of travel to Elam and also 'because of the reported poverty and distress of the sees' there, for 'everyone's ear has heard the report of the wasteland that is Elam.'[49]

This situation was not unique to Timothy's day, and it was not confined to Elam, either. A little over a decade after Timothy died in 823, one of his successors as catholicos of the Church of the East, Sabrisho' II (sed. 831–835), would give a depressing report of the state of the clergy in significant portions of the church's jurisdictions. Elam was still an area with problems, but it was not alone: Beth Aramaye, in central Iraq, was in bad shape, as were Fars, Mayshan, and Khurasan. 'In the year 220 of the Arabs [= AD 835],' he wrote,

> when I passed through the region of Beth Aramaye, I saw that all of the villages were bereft of knowledgeable clergy, all the way to where the School of Mar Theodore is and that of Beth Mar Mari and this one of the Mahuze. There was none that remained among them save a remnant of older people and the younger ones did not even know the responsorial hymn of the day. For this reason, the older scholars were forcing their students to learn—either the scripture reading or the tone of the day like a physician who compels a sick person to drink absinthium and myrrh and socotrinum. But the students loathed instruction like a sick person despises drinking socotrinum, for they would only gather together to eat bread and not on account of a love of instruction. I heard the same about the region of Elam and about Mayshan and Fars and Khurasan. I was in mourning and sadness, like a person who has been driven from a sunny eastern region and entered into a house filled with darkness. I discerned that an increase of darkness would be entering upon the church, time after time in the coming generations.[50]

[49] Timothy I, *Letter 52* (quotes from 52.3–5) (ed. Heimgartner [CSCO 644–45: SS 248-249], p. 119–22 [Syriac] = p. 100–102 [GT], quotes on p. 120–21/100-101]. Elam, it should be recalled, was an important ecclesiastical province of the Church of the East. But for other negative assessments of the region, see J.-M. Fiey, 'L'Élam, la première des métropoles ecclésiastiques syriennes orientales,' *Melto* 5 (1969), pp. 224–25. On Elam, see this article and also Fiey, 'L'Élam, la première des métropoles ecclésiastiques syriennes orientales (suite),' *PdO* 1 (1970), pp. 123–53.

[50] Quoted in Abdisho' bar Brikho, *Nomocanon* 6.3 (ed. Mai, *Scriptorum veterum nova collectio e Vaticanis codicibus edita*, vol. 10, p. 274 [Syriac] = 110–11 [Latin translation]). The text can also be found (in a slightly different form) with a Latin translation in Assemani, *BO*, vol. 3.1, pp. 506–507. Sabrisho''s response was to try to change the course of instruction: 'I organized a cycle of responses (*ḥudrā d-'onyātā*) for the Sundays of the year, which I left at the patriarchate—and I admonished the instructor that he should give a copy of it to the priests and readers who are in the villages and to those who are

Problems did not just exist in the Church of the East, either. In the ninth century, when Miaphysite patriarch Dionysius of Tell Mahre visited Egypt with the Caliph al-Ma'mūn, he observed a variety of canonical violations among the Christians there. 'We saw among them,' Michael wrote, 'customs that were not equal to their dignity and that that they were far from Cyril, and Diodore, and Timothy [II/Aelurus], who had established canons for the church.' Some of the problems Michael witnessed related to financial matters, but the quality of the clergy certainly was not a source of happiness:

> One [problem] was that the study of the Holy Scriptures had ceased among them and especially monks were bereft of this grace. As for the venerable among them, this was their work: manual labor and the reading of the Psalms related to it. Those who were expecting to [celebrate] offices were not concerned with knowledge and wisdom but rather with seeking after gold for the price of the elevated position they were going to receive. Without 200 or 300 darics, it was not possible for a person to arrive at being a bishop. If a person is found to have wisdom and a noble conduct of life, but does not possess money so that he might approach the rank of the episcopacy, it is impossible [for this to happen] among them. We criticized and scolded them about this [and] the Pope made a defense to us, saying 'We have come to this situation by means of the debt which the church of Alexandria is drowning in, which we would not be able to pay save through means such as these.' When I made it known that the practice was against the apostolic canons and that whoever draws near to the priesthood through a bribe is worthy of being deposed and so is the one who does the consecration for him, [he said], 'Even if it is foolish to receive something from an ordination, we nevertheless tell [a person] who is drawing near [to the priesthood] to redeem one of the church items that has been set down as a pledge.' As for me, I laughed rather than crying, and said in the face of their simplicity [*biruthon*] that which Christ said to his disciples when they said 'we have two swords.' He answered, 'Enough!' [Luke 22:38].[51]

---

serving in the houses of believers. And because, according to the ancient custom, after the youth study the Psalms, the teachers instruct them in the Law, the *kathismata* prayers, and the Prophets, in accordance with the rite that was in effect in the schools, and when they would arrive at the reading of the New Testament, the youths would leave off and go out and learn a trade, I, Sabrisho', the Patriarch, set down the canonical command that after the youths study the Psalms and the hymns of the service, they should study the Gospel and the Epistles, and then they should study from the Old Testament those portions of the readings that are for Sundays, and feast days, and memorials, which are read on the *bema*. When they have completed these things, let them go to the trades they desire.'

[51] Michael the Great, *Chronicle* 12.17 (ed. Chabot, *Chronique de Michel le Syrien*, 4.525–26 [Syriac] = 3.80–81 [FT]. NB: Chabot's Syriac text contains ambiguities and errors that can be clarified by consulting the superior text available in G. Y. Ibrahim, ed., *The Edessa-Aleppo Syriac Codex of the Chronicle of Michael the Great* [Piscataway, N.J., 2009], pp. 528–29).

In such contexts—where the priests were poorly instructed, where church offices were being purchased, and where the schools were in disappointing condition—what should we expect from the clergy, much less the laity, in terms of the conformity of their belief to an orthodox standard?

When we think about religious belief and practice in the late antique and medieval Middle East, we should keep in mind the experience of places like Jacob's villages where Miaphysite clergy officiated at Chalcedonian services, or Theodota's small country village, or the region of Elam in Timothy's day, or indeed, significant parts of the Church of the East in Sabrisho II's time. Such contexts are usually invisible to historians, for obvious reasons, but a moment's reflection will suggest that they must have been quite common. Perhaps even typical. We need to ask ourselves whether our accounts of Christians and Muslims take the experiences and beliefs of the people living in such areas into consideration or indeed, whether and how we value the experiences of such people at all. If we do, then how do they fit into the stories we tell about the meaning and development of Christianity and Islam in the early medieval period? We need to constantly resist the temptation to make generalizations based on unrepresentative figures and evidence. What will the nature of Christian belief and practice have looked like when viewed from one of these places, rather than a learned exchange in a *majlis*?

THE RELIGIOUS CONSEQUENCES OF CLERICAL LIMITATIONS

We unfortunately have no seventh-century informant or source we can draw upon in order to retrieve some of what people in places poorly served by clergy or served by inadequately trained clergy actually understood their religious identity to mean. The canonical and epistolary material we have just reviewed can give us some intimations of what Christianity outside of centers where Christian institutions were strong may have looked like. Even more striking, however, are saints' *vitae*, which can give us further, at times vivid, clues. Though we should recognize that the purpose of hagiographic narratives was not necessarily to relate accurate reports of social conditions, they can nevertheless provide evocative glimpses of what levels of religious knowledge and instruction may have been like in rural areas, even near major cities.[52] Such suggestive reports are, *faute de mieux*, especially valuable to think with

[52] On hagiography and social history, see the remark of John Haldon in *The Empire That Would Not Die: The Paradox of Eastern Roman Survival* (Cambridge, MA/London, 2016), p. 306, n. 15 (and cf. Appendix I, n. 43).

when we are trying to get a sense for the full spectrum of Christian beliefs and behaviors.

'There was a lake in Alexandria, called Maria,' the *Life* of John the Almsgiver noted, referring to the Mareotic Lake located near Alexandria,

> in which a great quantity of papyrus grew, and the inhabitants of that district had been in the habit of cutting it down and using it as fuel instead of wood. And the boys, whose work it was to cut down the papyrus together with the men dwelling there, practised the vice of sodomy unrestrainedly; and they had no house of prayer, no priest at all, they never heard the Scriptures nor partook of the Divine Mysteries. When the inspired Patriarch heard of these illegal doings and of this pollution, he ordered the boys be brought away from that place and he built houses of prayer for its inhabitants and set apart certain priests whom he appointed to minister to them and teach them.[53]

Even though these people were not far from one of the most ancient and sophisticated centers of Christianity in the entire world, they lacked churches, teaching, and access to the Scriptures and sacraments. Granting the possibility that the *vita* may have exaggerated this picture in order to emphasize the notion that the patriarch John was successful in combating heresy and spreading religious instruction, the anecdote nevertheless points to a situation that someone who read or heard this *vita* in the seventh century would have understood as a real possibility: the existence of nonurban areas where Christianization had shallow roots.[54]

Making similar allowances for the literary shaping characteristic of hagiographic texts, if we look before the seventh century, John of Ephesus's *Life* of Simeon the Mountaineer (d. ca. 541) gives us a similar but much more detailed picture of the some of the effects that a lack of properly trained clergy (or any clergy) would have had. During a sojourn in a mountainous region near Claudia (an area in contemporary southeastern Turkey and one where Theodota of Amid would later spend time in the seventh century), Simeon was surprised to discover people and habitations in such a remote place. Speaking to some

[53] *Life of John the Almsgiver* 8 (ed. Delehaye, 'Une vie inédite de Saint Jean l'Aumonier,' pp. 22–23; ET taken from Dawes and Baynes, *Three Byzantine Saints*, p. 203).

[54] For the argument, based on epigraphic evidence, that 'many Syrian villages would have been Christian for one hundred and fifty years or less' at the time of the Arab conquests in the 630s, see W. Liebeschuetz, 'Problems Arising from the Conversion of Syria,' in D. Baker, ed., *The Church in Town and Countryside* (Oxford, 1979), p. 18, and cf. Liebeschuetz, 'Epigraphic Evidence on the Christianisation of Syria,' in J. Fitz, ed., *Limes: Akten des XI. Internationalen Limeskongresses* (Budapest, 1977), pp. 485–508, esp. p. 498: 'The success achieved by Islam in Syria after the Arab invasions is easier to understand if we bear in mind that over large parts of rural Syria the population had become Christian within the last 150 years or less.'

shepherds he encountered, he asked about their religious background. He was astonished. The men, though they insisted they were Christians, did not know what the benefit of the Eucharist was; indeed, they did not even know what the Eucharist itself was. When Simeon pressed them further, the shepherds admitted that they had heard of the Christian Scriptures from their parents, but they had in fact never laid eyes on them.[55]

The shepherds speaking to Simeon, John of Ephesus informs us, were about thirty years old. Simeon was curious to find out whether their nearly complete ignorance of Christianity was exceptional, or whether it was indicative of the state of knowledge among Christians in the area, so he questioned them further. There were people living in this mountainous region, they claimed, who had only been in a church when they themselves were baptized or when they had baptized their children.[56]

Simeon next came to a village in the same area and was excited to find a church there, taking it as an indication that there were indeed Christians in the region. Upon closer inspection, however, Simeon's delight quickly melted away: the church had fallen into disuse. An old man approached Simeon to receive a blessing, and Simeon took the opportunity to assess the locale's spiritual condition. There was no priest, the old man informed him, and neither were there any monks. A person from the village might only take the Eucharist if he or she had reason to be in a place where there was the possibility to communicate.[57]

The next day, Simeon convened a meeting where every man, woman, and child in the village was present, and he berated the people for their lack of concern over their own salvation. The villagers were shocked and left speechless by Simeon's tongue lashing. 'You can't say anything?' he asked them angrily. They again offered a revealing insight into the nature of Christian belief—at least at the propositional level—among people who lacked proper teaching and instruction. 'What do we have to say to you?' they responded, 'There is no one to speak with us or to teach us and this matter you speak to us about has [never] been heard by us, for the Scriptures are unknown to us.' Simeon began to question them about the basics of the faith: 'Do you know that Our Lord Jesus Christ came down from heaven, and put on our body, from a Virgin, for the sake of our salvation? And that he went around with humans, as a human [himself]?' Knowledge of the Christian story was a function of age in this particular town; there was no priest now, but perhaps a long time ago there had been, for the town's elders, John of Ephesus reported, claimed

[55] John of Ephesus, *Lives of the Eastern Saints* 16 (ed. and trans. Brooks [PO 17.1], pp. 233–34).
[56] John of Ephesus, *Lives of the Eastern Saints* 16 (ed. and trans. Brooks [PO 17.1], p. 235).
[57] John of Ephesus, *Lives of the Eastern Saints* 16 (ed. and trans. Brooks [PO 17.1], pp. 236–37).

that they had heard of the things Simeon asked about.[58] Simeon went on, becoming quite exercised, and asked them rhetorically if they had heard further details of the Christian message. As penance, he ordered the villagers to fast and pray for a week.[59]

This was not the end of the problems Simeon found there, of course. It was the old people in the town who had some familiarity with basic Christian beliefs, and Simeon wanted an explanation for the failure of the youth to receive proper Christian instruction. Why, he asked, had the villagers not made their sons into clergymen and put them to work in the town's church? The demands of rural life, the people responded, often conflicted with proper Christian instruction: the youth were too busy herding goats to receive any instruction. Simeon was confronting the same sort of 'simple people' as Jacob of Edessa and Marutha had dealt with: amazed at their 'simplicity' and disregard, John of Ephesus tells us, he celebrated a Eucharist for them and gave them communion.[60] Simeon next embarked on a project of re-evangelization of the people living in this mountainous region, bringing people to the small village church 'and discipling them anew, as from paganism.'[61] He would go on to tonsure a number of youths for monastic life and would spend a total of twenty-six years teaching and carrying out his work of Christianizing the Christians of this mountainous region.[62]

THE SPECTRUM OF BELIEF

However tempting it might be to write off the image we find in John's *Life* of Simeon as atypical, reflecting only the conditions in an isolated mountain region, or as a hagiographic construct, we can use the brief account of uncatechized Christians living near Alexandria as evidence that, to a late antique audience, it was not implausible for there to be Christians in rural areas, even near important urban centers, who did not know a great deal about Christianity.

That said, John of Ephesus's portrayal of the situation Simeon found was nonetheless likely inaccurate. Even if his mountaineers lacked knowledge and

[58] John of Ephesus, *Lives of the Eastern Saints* 16 (ed. and trans. Brooks [PO 17.1], pp. 238, 239). My translation.

[59] John of Ephesus, *Lives of the Eastern Saints* 16 (ed. and trans. Brooks [PO 17.1], p. 240).

[60] John of Ephesus, *Lives of the Eastern Saints* 16 (ed. and trans. Brooks [PO 17.1], p. 241). My translation.

[61] John of Ephesus, *Lives of the Eastern Saints* 16 (ed. and trans. Brooks [PO 17.1], p. 242). My translation.

[62] For his twenty-six years of ministry, see Brooks, *Lives of the Eastern Saints* (PO 17.1), p. 246.

experience of the rituals and texts most centrally tied to the (to us) more familiar Christianity practiced and propagated by the likes of Simeon (and John himself), they no doubt engaged in practices and held beliefs—perhaps the sorts of things that Jacob condemned and called 'pagan' in his canons—which drew upon Christian symbolic resources. As we saw, when Simeon was entering the forlorn and unused church in the mountain village, an old man had approached him to receive a blessing.[63] A Christian holy man or monk was seen, at least by some of the older generation in that particular village, to possess special powers of some kind. If nothing else, Christian paraphernalia and appurtenances in this context remained highly charged, something which would not have been the case in a purely 'pagan' environment where there had been no previous exposure to Christianity at all.

If these mountain people represent one extreme on the spectrum of possible Christian belief, figures like Simeon the Mountaineer, John of Ephesus, Athanasius Gamolo, Athanasius of Balad, Jacob of Edessa, and George of the Arabs represent the opposite extreme, perhaps equally unrepresentative of what Christianity meant to the mass of people who were Christians in the seventh and eighth centuries when Arab invaders and settlers first encountered the native Christian populations of the Middle East. Between these two opposite ends of the spectrum—sophisticated erudition and nearly complete innocence of the influence of written traditions and church authorities—there was a broad middle ground. But in this middle ground, education and elite status were no guarantors of proper orthodox belief, either. Simeon had asked the shepherds he met whether they were Jews or Christians, and though they apparently knew almost nothing about Christianity, they were adamant that they were Christians. At perhaps roughly the same time, however, Mar Aba (d. 552) met a theological student who, upon questioning, insisted that he was both a Jew *and* a Christian, much to Aba's dismay.[64] The mere fact of education did not translate into a recognizably orthodox pattern of Christian belief.

Two further examples can draw out this point. John, the Stylite of Litarb, once wrote to Jacob of Edessa about *mēmrē* purporting to have been written

[63] John of Ephesus, *Lives of the Eastern Saints* 16 (ed. and trans. Brooks [PO 17.1], p. 237). More generally on the question of the representativeness of this story, see also observations of R. MacMullen, *The Second Church: Popular Christianity, A.D. 200-400* (Atlanta, 2009), p. 109, placing Simeon's encounter in a larger, empire-wide context.

[64] *History of Mar Aba*, pp. 213–14 (ed. Bedjan, *Histoire de Mar-Jabalaha*). Partial ET and discussion of this passage can be found in W. Bauer, *Orthodoxy and Heresy in Earliest Christianity* (Philadelphia, 1971), p. 23; see also D. Boyarin, *Dying for God: Martyrdom and the Making of Christianity and Judaism* (Stanford, 1999), pp. 22–23. An ET of a larger part of this story can be found in *SBI*, p. 391.

by the famous Miaphysite poet Jacob of Sarugh. The metrical homilies in question contained strange doctrinal ideas, many of which seemed to relate to angels and to the idea of the image of God: angels were created on the first day, along with the heavens and the earth; angels were not created in the image of God; Adam was superior to both Michael and Gabriel; a sack with two holes in it, one for putting in and one for taking out, was a representation of what the image of God was; Satan fell on the sixth day, his sin being envy of Adam's glory. Jacob would list other doctrines of this Ps.-Jacob of Sarugh as well, stemming from what he considered an overly literal, 'Jewish' reading of the Scriptures: the pseudonymous author apparently believed that God's words reported in the first chapter of Genesis had been spoken with an audible voice; he had a mistaken understanding of the meaning 'Behemoth' and 'Leviathan' in the book of Job; and he thought that words like 'form' and 'likeness' and 'body' when used of created beings could refer only to literal physical bodies.[65]

Here we have a case not of illiteracy and a complete lack of education leading an individual to deviate from recognized orthodoxies, but rather of literacy in the absence of proper theological oversight or instruction on the part of Ps.-Jacob's authorities leading to improper belief.[66] In many ways, being able to read the Bible and the Fathers was more dangerous than not being able to read them. Taken too literally, or not interpreted properly in light of other Fathers and tradition, a whole host of erroneous ideas might result.

A second example illustrates the importance of such oversight. In 714, George of the Arabs wrote a letter to a figure named Joshua the Hermit, responding to a number of questions Joshua had about Aphrahat, the celebrated Sasanian Syriac author whom George referred to as the 'Persian Sage.' One of Joshua's questions revolved around a passage in Aphrahat's *Demonstrations* in which the fourth-century author suggested that human beings were born with one soul or spirit and then at baptism received a second spirit. Upon death, the natural spirit died, but the new spirit, which had been received

[65] Jacob of Edessa, *Letter 1 to John, the Stylite of Litarb*, pp. 270–71 (ed. R. Schröter, 'Erster Brief Jakob's von Edessa an Johannes den Styliten,' *ZDMG* 24 [1870], pp. 270–71). ET of these passages in *SBI*, p. 392, n. 933.

[66] Viewed from the perspective of proto-orthodox and orthodox writers belonging to the tradition of the Great Church, the ideas found in various apocryphal and pseudepigraphal works can often illustrate well the doctrinal consequences of literacy operating apart from proper theological oversight and instruction. See, e.g., the suggestion of Stephen Shoemaker of reasons why many early Church Fathers may not have made mention of Marian devotion or veneration in *Mary in Early Christian Faith and Devotion*, pp. 6, 24–25, 129, 231–32, and note his detailed analysis of the *Book of Mary's Repose* (discussed at pp. 100–28).

at baptism, went to the presence of Christ.[67] As in the case of Ps.-Jacob of Sarugh's doctrinal aberrations, Aphrahat himself had veered into error. George advised Joshua that he should not wear himself out mentally trying to make sense of everything that Aphrahat wrote in his *Demonstrations.* 'For, although, as we said above,' George continued, '[Aphrahat] was a person with an acute nature who carefully crafted holy books, he was not among those teachers who were approved and who were said to have correct teachings.'

George had a positive view of Aphrahat, but he could not offer an unqualified endorsement. The problems to be found in his writings were the results of a lack of proper ecclesiastical oversight and also perhaps of geography. Aphrahat was not among approved teachers with correct doctrine

> since there was no one in his day in that region who might take notice of him and adjust his thoughts and words to those of approved teachers. For this reason, there are many errors and clumsy passages in that book for one who is knowledgeable and who examines closely what he reads, as it is written [cf. Acts 8:30].

As apparently had been the case also with Ps.-Jacob of Sarugh, Aphrahat had, in the opinion of George, strayed into the wilderness of doctrinal error through reading the Bible too literally. This was the root of the errors and clumsy passages in the *Demonstrations.* 'Among such passages,' George wrote,

> are these things over which at present you have had uncertainty, O Brother. For when he heard Paul the Divine Apostle saying 'It is sown a natural body and rises a spiritual body,' and did not understand the sense and meaning of the passage, he came to write and say, 'when humans are dead, the natural spirit is concealed inside the body and sentience is taken away from it, but the heavenly spirit which they receive goes to its nature in the presence of Christ. Concerning the two of these, the Apostle makes known to us, for he said, "it is buried naturally as a body and it is raised spiritually as a body"' [1 Cor. 15:44].[68]

Merely being able to read or having access to portions of the Scriptures and perhaps some authoritative writings was no guarantee of right belief. What was needed more than anything were properly trained theological authorities who could teach a person what correct Christian belief was.

[67] See BL Add. 12,154, fol. 250b.

[68] BL Add. 12,154, fols. 250b–251a, Syriac text also in *SBI*, p. 394, n. 935: 'Your wisdom, O brother, should not understand or consider that Persian writer among approved writers or their expert compositions, with the result that on account of this you become vexed in your thoughts and weary in your mind [trying to] grasp and know the meaning of all the words that he speaks in that book of *Demonstrations*. . . .'

ON THE GENEALOGY OF WRONG BELIEF

Rather than go on enumerating examples of deviant Christian belief in the period of Muslim rule,[69] what needs emphasizing is that a wide range of Christian beliefs (and not just behaviors) was both to be expected and did in fact exist in this time, and that they did so *within* existing church structures and institutions. We need not strain to uncover previously unknown pockets where ancient 'heresies' or Christian groups who were not part of what is commonly referred to as the Great Church survived in some sort of doctrinal Jurassic Park.[70] Because of the nature of our sources, we only get a faint glimpse of the diversity that must have existed, but like a fuzzy and dim photograph of a rare and endangered animal, such a glimpse is precious indeed if we are seeking to understand what difference Islam made in the seventh and eighth centuries.

Let us take another example as an illustration. In the late eighth century, the East Syrian Maran'ameh was sent by his metropolitan Mar Aḥā into the region of Salakh on account of the strong presence of Magianism there. The people in that area, Thomas of Marga reported, were worshipping the sun, moon and stars; they even worshipped trees.[71] In this region there were also members of the landed aristocracy known in Arabic as the *shahārija*[72] who,

[69] One can get a sense for the number of different possible Christian groups that existed in the early period of Muslim rule—at the rhetorical level at least—by looking at well-known catalogues of erroneous belief, like that of John of Damascus's *On Heresies* (ed. B. Kotter, *Die Schriften des Johannes von Damaskos*, vol. 4 [Berlin/New York, 1981], pp. 19–67) and Chapter 11 of Theodore bar Koni's *Book of the Scholion* (ed. A. Scher, *Theodorus bar Kōnī. Liber Scholiorum* [CSCO Syr. II.66] [Paris, 1912], pp. 284–351). Attempting to discern the connection between such treatises, previous heresiological writings, and actual Middle Eastern Christianity under Muslim rule would take us too far afield. On the genre of heresiology, however, see Av. Cameron, 'How to Read Heresiology,' *Journal of Medieval and Early Modern Studies* 33 (2003), pp. 471–92.

[70] See, e.g., S. Pines's 'Notes on Islam and on Arabic Christianity and Judaeo-Christianity,' *JSAI* 4 (1984), pp. 135–52, where he attempted to offer evidence for Christians showing 'Judaeo-Christian' proclivities in the Middle East on the eve of the Islamic period. Pines's views on Judeo-Christianity came under assault by Samuel Stern—see, notably Stern's "Abd al-Jabbār's Account of How Christ's Religion Was Falsified by the Adoption of Roman Customs,' *JTS* 19 (1968), pp. 128–85. For more on the question of Judaeo-Christianity in this period, see more recently, see P. Crone, 'Jewish Christianity and the Qur'ān (Part One),' *JNES* 74 (2015), pp. 225–53; Crone, 'Jewish Christianity and the Qur'ān (Part Two),' *JNES* 75 (2016), pp. 1–21; and G. G. Stroumsa, *The Making of the Abrahamic Religions in Late Antiquity* (Oxford, 2015), pp. 139–58. On the sharp disagreement between Pines and Samuel Stern over the question of Judaeo-Christianity, see J. G. Gager, 'Did Jewish Christians See the Rise of Islam?' in A. H. Becker and A. Y. Reed, eds., *The Ways That Never Parted: Jews and Christians in Late Antiquity and the Early Middle Ages* (Minneapolis, 2007), pp. 361–72.

[71] Thomas of Marga, *Monastic History* 3.3 (ed. Budge, 1.149–50 [Syriac] = 2.307 [ET]).

[72] The *shahārija* were a class of land-owning aristocrats who sometimes held leadership positions

according to Thomas, 'although they were nominally Christians, made confession that Christ was an ordinary man, and said that "[h]e was one of the Prophets," and the bishops who lived in the country labored among them, but they did not accept the true and orthodox doctrine.'[73] Where bishops had labored and failed, Maran'ameh was more successful. After a miraculous display of light dawned upon them while worshipping in church, these heterodox *shahārija* were willing to confess the divinity of Christ.

In discussing the religious views of the *shahārija*, Chase Robinson entertained and then rejected the notion that their reduced Christology was a function of Islamic influence; he similarly discarded the idea that they had some sort of connection to 'Judaeo-Christianity.' Robinson argued instead for explaining the Christology of this group of landed elites with reference to the ideas of Paul of Samosata, an (in)famous third-century figure who had argued that Jesus was merely a human.[74] I would like to focus for a moment on this last suggestion, for it will take us to one of the most important points to be made about the question of Christianity and Islam with which I began this chapter.

Robinson's concern with supplying the *shahārija* with a proper doctrinal genealogy and connecting them with a notorious figure like Paul of Samosata would have made Epiphanius proud; William of Ockham, however, would not have been as pleased—Robinson did a service by bringing the *shahārija* to the attention of a wider audience, but ultimately advanced a hypothesis about them that was needlessly complicated and complex.[75] Much more economical ways of accounting for the views of the *shahārija* are available: the example of the 'heretical' views of Ps.-Jacob of Sarugh, which Jacob identified, and the erroneous views of Aphrahat picked out by George show that often all that is needed to generate views considered aberrant by church leaders is to read the

in villages. By the period of Muslim rule, they were still found in northern Iraq. On the *shahārija*, see M. G. Morony, 'The Effects of the Muslim Conquest on the Persian Population of Iraq,' *Iran* 14 (1976), p. 45, and C. F. Robinson, *Empire and Elites after the Muslim Conquest* (Cambridge, 2000), pp. 90–108.

[73] Thomas of Marga, *Monastic History* 3.3 (ed. Budge, 1.151 [Syriac] = 2.309–310 [ET]; the translation here is that of Budge).

[74] See Robinson, *Empire and Elites after the Muslim Conquest*, pp. 98–101.

[75] On the practice of providing heretical genealogies to explain the errors in belief of an opponent, see A. de Halleux, 'Die Genealogie des Nestorianismus nach der frühmonophysitischen Theologie,' *OC* 66 (1982), pp. 1–14, which focuses especially on the practice among Miaphysites in the sixth century. On Ephiphanius's method of heresiological writing, including his use of genealogy, see R. Flower, 'Genealogies of Unbelief: Ephiphanius of Salamis and Heresiological Authority,' in C. Kelly, R. Flower, and M. S. Williams, eds., *Unclassical Traditions*, vol. 2: *Perspectives from East and West in Late Antiquity* (Cambridge, 2011), pp. 70–87. On the development of Christian heresiology more generally, see H. Inglebert, *Interpretatio christiana: Les mutations des savoirs, cosmographie, géographie, ethnographie, histoire, dans l'antiquité chrétienne, 30-630 après J.-C.* (Paris, 2001), pp. 393–461.

text of Scripture and take it literally—what Jacob derisively called 'in a Jewish way'; to be more precise, it requires understanding the *wrong* passages of Scripture in a literal fashion, since every biblically based theology is built on some combination of literal and figurative readings of the sacred writ. Looking for the presence of a preexisting, more ancient 'heresy' to explain the origin of each of these 'heresies' (and assuming that all of them were even coherent systems of doctrine and belief and not merely polemical constructs) is simply too much. One required only access to at least portions of the Bible—and such knowledge could have come either through hearing or reading. Even in a world of limited literacy, people who had a degree of familiarity with major events and significant figures in the Christian story will not have been rare, and whatever the nature of people's understanding of the details of sophisticated Christian theological speculation, Christianity's moral teaching and the events of its salvation history, as I pointed out in Part I, had been recognized early on to be simple to grasp.[76] But a familiarity with these basic figures and events is not the same thing as holding beliefs that would be considered orthodox by church authorities of any confession. Orthodoxy is a very unnatural thing and is certainly not a default dogmatic position. This is true even for faithful members of churches that consider themselves to be orthodox or Orthodox.

Orthodoxy, however one capitalizes it, is in fact, no more natural a doctrinal position than being able to play perfectly a piece by Chopin on the piano is the natural starting point for a beginning player—or even for a person who has been playing for years. Like a musical piece, proper orthodox belief requires constant practice, training, instruction, and correction to achieve. If orthodoxy is a fine musical performance and figures like Jacob of Edessa, Athanasius of Balad, Isho'yahb III, Anastasius of Sinai, and John of Damascus were *virtuosi* of the seventh and eighth century Middle East, then we should expect that 'heretical' views would have been as common and as easy as poor, inexperienced, unpracticed piano playing. Rather than being an aberration, 'heresy,' or untuned belief, would be the norm. I should add here that this holds true for 'orthodoxy' however it is defined—be it by reference to the Nicene-Constantinopolitan Creed, the Definition of Chalcedon, or some other definition of faith. It also holds true for Paul of Samosata's understanding of the Incarnation, for that matter, as well as for the variety of beliefs that scholars have attributed to Jewish Christians and other groups. It is the case, in fact, for any doctrinal view that is the result of reflection, study, argument, synthesis, and formal articulation. What is more, in a world of simple believers, it was

[76] See, e.g., the comments attributed to Galen in Walzer, *Galen on Jews and Christians*, pp. 15–16 (Cf. Chapter 1, n. 54).

very likely the case that a number of people were not even attempting to play the piano.

These points cannot be emphasized too strongly. For one might be tempted to suggest that the examples of aberrant belief or ignorance of doctrine that I have adduced in this chapter are only exceptions to an 'orthodox' rule: can we not find many examples of proper (according to this or that church) belief and practice in this period? To be sure, such examples can be found—especially in normative literature written by learned churchmen. But like examples of untuned belief and practice, we must recognize any such examples of orthodox belief and correct practice for what they are: anecdotal.[77] And with no systematic way of gauging and evaluating belief and practice among all Christians in this period (and not just making generalizations based on the words, behavior, and reports of those few whose written texts have survived), the best way to avoid engaging in a battle of dueling anecdotes—citing this example of proper belief and behavior in response to that instance of improper belief and behavior—is to look at the background conditions in which Christians in this world lived and moved and had their being. Given the factors of a largely illiterate, agrarian population and weak catechetical institutions, does 'correct' belief with respect to matters such as the precise nature of the Incarnation or the relationship of members of the Trinity to one another and to the created world seem more or less likely? Does a Christian population that has not only been fully instructed in the moral demands of their particular church but also has fulfilled these expectations seem more or less probable? To ask these questions from the perspective of church history writ large is to answer them.

Achieving a shared understanding of any matter of theological speculation or belief within a group, especially over the course of centuries and across large geographical distances and linguistic boundaries, is not something that just happens naturally. It requires education, institutions, liturgical uniformity, and the human and economic resources that make these possible. Before we invoke this ancient 'heresy' or that non-mainstream (by later lights) Christian group to explain some belief we find popping up in the period of Muslim rule (or in the Qur'ān), we should first ask what institutional, economic, and human means would have been required for that belief to have been transmitted from the late Roman world (often implicitly equated with the world of Epiphanius's *Panarion*) to the Umayyad or Abbasid period and then ask if there is any evidence that such a transmission could have actually happened. In most cases, I would suggest, the answer will be no.

[77] And to the extent that stories of holy men can be seen as exemplary, they should also be viewed as exceptional. See the classic discussion of the holy man as 'Christ made accessible,' in P. Brown, 'The Saint as Exemplar in Late Antiquity,' *Representations* 2 (1983), pp. 1–25 (quote at 10).

So, for instance, we find the Jewish interlocutor in an eighth-century Christian-Jewish Syriac dispute text asserting,

> There are among you some Christians who associate with us in the synagogue and who bring offerings and alms and oil, and at the time of the Passover send unleavened bread (and), doubtless other things also. They are not entirely Christians, and some of our men have said that, if they were truly Christians, they would not associate with us in our synagogue and in our law. And now, because of this, we are all the more scandalized.[78]

Reading this passage, we might begin to think about John Chrysostom's infamous fourth-century sermons against Christians who were taking part in Jewish festivals, holding synagogues in high esteem, making oaths at Jewish shrines, keeping Jewish fasts, and otherwise engaged in Jewish and Judaizing practices,[79] or we might suppose that we had maybe found an example of Judaeo-Christians alive and well in Umayyad Syria—something that would thrill more than one scholar of the Qur'ān. Perhaps.

But perhaps what we have here is only a manifestation of the consequences of weak or nonexistent catechesis and poorly trained clergy in a world where people were making use of the symbolic resources of their own religious tradition and those of others according to the exigencies of their lives. Rather than needing to find evidence of new/old species dwelling in a doctrinal Jurassic Park populated with creatures from late antique heresiographies, it is much easier—though possibly less exciting—to point out that we are dealing with a world of simple believers. Writing maybe half a century before this Christian-Jewish dispute text was composed, Jacob of Edessa had disapproved of Christians who were following Jewish practices. 'Christians should not keep Jewish observances,' he wrote in one place,

> [f]or there are foolish and untrained priests who follow the old law, that of Moses; of keeping a male child out of the church for forty days and a female child eighty days. This they do knowing only how to keep purity or flee pollution in a fleshly and Jewish manner. Those, however, who have a spiritual understanding, know that a midwife should not be kept back from the church even

[78] *Disputation of Sergius the Stylite against a Jew*, 22.1 (ed. and trans. A. P. Hayman, *The Disputation of Sergius the Stylite against a Jew* [CSCO 338–39: SS 152–53] [Louvain, 1973], pp. 73–74 [Syriac] = p. 72 [English]; I have used here Hayman's translation). Hayman [CSCO 338: SS 152] p. ix, dates the dispute to AD 730–770.

[79] John Chrysostom, *Adversos Judaeos orationes* (PG 48, cols. 843–942; ET available in P. W. Harkins, *Discourses against Judaizing Christians* [Washington, D.C., 1979]). Cp. also H.J.W Drijvers's description of Christian attraction to Jewish practices in fourth-century Edessa in 'Jews and Christians at Edessa,' p. 98.

one day, nor should she who gives birth—as soon as she rises from her bed and washes herself.[80]

For Jacob the root cause here was not the existence of some sort of group that would have been familiar to Justin Martyr and Trypho. These people were part of the church. The problem was one of weak teaching institutions and poor catechesis: of foolish and uneducated priests.

Similarly, when the Qur'ān seems to suggest that Christians understood Mary to be part of the Trinity (5:116), we can, as scholars have done, invoke the possible existence of an exotic heretical group like the Collyridians in western Arabia to explain such a curious claim. But in this instance, and in other places where the Qur'ān speaks of Christianity in unfamiliar ways, rather than looking for fourth- or fifth-century groups which held low Christologies, exalted views of Mary, or some other view not typical of the Christian communities most familiar to us now, or seeking to find individual passages in Syriac texts written by theological elites in northern Mesopotamia or Greek writers somewhere in the Mediterranean world which seem to bear resemblance to this or that idea put forth in the Qur'ān,[81] a more fruitful way of understanding the image of Christianity presented therein is to see it as a reflection of and reaction to Christianity as it existed on the ground in the seventh-century Ḥijāz—or wherever it is that one wants to argue is the Qur'ān's original context.[82]

Such a Christianity need not have descended directly from past, 'heretical' groups originating centuries before and hundreds of miles away, but instead was perhaps not all that dissimilar from the untuned Christianity that was ubiquitous throughout the Middle East, differing from it only perhaps in degree as a result of its distance from theological elites like Jacob who were constantly engaged in boundary maintenance and orthodox theological instruction. Rather than sending search parties into the *Patrologia Graeca*, the *Corpus Scriptorum Christianorum Orientalium*, the *Patrologia Orientalis*, and other venerable repositories of late ancient Christian writings, to hunt for the origins of this or that belief that the Qur'ān attributes to Christians, it would be easier

[80] Kayser, *Die Canones Jacob's von Edessa*, p. 3

[81] See for example Neal Robinson's discussion of 'sectarian' Christian influences on the presentation of Jesus in the Qur'ān, where he invokes Nestorianism, Monophysitism, Tritheism, Antideco-Marcianites, Ebionites, Elkasites, Manichaeism, Gnosticism, and Judaism in trying to makes sense of the Quranic evidence, in *Christ in Islam and Christianity* (Albany, 1991), pp. 19–21. See, too, the comments of G. S. Reynolds, 'The Muslim Jesus: Dead or Alive?' *BSOAS* 72 (2009), pp. 252–53.

[82] Cf. the observation of E. Gräf, in 'Zu den Christlichen Einflüsse im Koran,' in *al-Bahit: Festschrift Joseph Henninger zum 70. Geburtstag am 12. Mai 1976*, (St. Augustin bei Bonn, 1976), p. 113, and cf. J. B. Witztum, 'The Syriac Milieu of the Quran: The Recasting of Biblical Narratives' (PhD diss., Princeton University, 2011), p. 50.

and more plausible to remember that the Qur'ān was reflecting and responding to a world of simple Christians. The stories of Noah, Abraham, Isaac, Jacob, Moses, Christ, and others that the Qur'ān mentions, the Christian apologist al-Kindī pointed out in the early ninth century, were tales everyone knows and that Christian children studied in schools (*al-makātib*).[83] Claude Gilliot has shown that all of the proposed Christian and Jewish 'informants' of Muḥammad whom the Muslim tradition itself identifies were foreigners from humble backgrounds—slaves or freed slaves—who knew how to read, and sometimes were even said to be reading either the Torah or the Gospel or both.[84] If any of these informants actually existed and were not invented for the purpose of exegeting the Qur'ān, we should not be astonished if, so far as the Christians among them were concerned, their Christianity was more similar to that of the people Jacob of Edessa criticized than it was to that of Jacob himself. And, the transmission history Qur'ān is such that, unlike essentially every Christian text we have from the late antique and early medieval period, it is a text that has been passed down to us through non-Christian circles. The filter of transmission that causes Christian texts from this period almost invariably to represent the interests and views of theological elites is simply not present with the Qur'ān. Reflected it in, therefore, we can see Christianity from below, as it were, and not from above.

CHRISTIANITY AND THE SIMPLE

A more fruitful approach to understanding Christianity in the seventh and eighth centuries would be one that shifted the focus away from confessional

[83] al-Kindī, *Apology*, p. 96 (*Risālat 'Abd Allāh b. Ismā'īl al-Hāshimī ilā 'Abd al-Masīḥ b. Isḥāq* [London, 1885]. On this text, see Laura Bottini's article, 'The Apology of al-Kindī,' in *CMR*, vol. 1, pp. 585–94). We of course have no evidence for any such Christian schools in Western Arabia, but see Ibn Sa'd, *Kitāb al-ṭabaqāt al-kabīr*, vol. 1.2, p. 84 (ed. E. Mittwoch and E. Sachau [Leiden, 1917]), where, in the delegation from Najran to the Prophet, Abū al-Ḥārith is identified as their bishop, religious authority, leader, and the master of their schools (*usqufuhum wa-ḥibruhum wa-imāmuhum wa-ṣāḥib madārisihim*); ET available in S. M. Haq and H. K. Ghazanfar, *Kitab al-tabaqat al-kabir*, vol. 1 (Karachi, 1967), p. 418. Though dealing with an earlier period, Victor Saxer's study of Biblical citations in the acts of various Christian martyrs is nevertheless useful to invoke here. Saxer suggested that these citations pointed to the existence of both a popular and a learned 'culture biblique' reflected in these texts. The former, he suggested, was the result of private reading, catechetical reading, and liturgical exposure to biblical texts. See *Bible et hagiographie: textes et thèmes bibliques dans les actes des martyrs authentiques des premiers siècles* (Berne/New York, 1986), pp. 170–71.

[84] See C. Gilliot, 'Les «informateurs» juifs et chrétiens de Muḥammad. Reprise d'un problem traité par Aloys Sprenger et Theodor Nöldeke,' *JSAI* 22 (1998), p. 119; also see Gilliot's article, 'Informants,' in *EQ*, vol. 2, pp. 512–18, which is essentially an English summary of this piece. Cf. also Chapter 14, nn. 252–53.

and sectarian typologies and classifications, Christological distinctions, and an emphasis on the doctrinally driven polemical encounter. There were, of course, groups of individuals who were intensely concerned with the subtleties of Christological doctrine. But if we keep in mind that such people were a minority—though a literate and influential one whose writings form the most important basis of our knowledge of this period—we can make better sense of the deep consternation and frustration at abuses and confessional confusion that comes through in the canons and writings of Jacob of Edessa, and of others as well. What made the *shahārija* Christians is the same thing that made all the people condemned in Jacob's canons for 'pagan' practices or for improper uses of the Eucharist Christians: a commitment to and belief in the power of certain shared symbols and rituals that were constitutive of and unique to the Christian community. These included the Eucharist, Baptism, anointing with the Myron, the Cross, belief in Jesus as well as saints and holy men, and the experience of the liturgy (assuming one had access to a church with regular liturgical celebrations).[85]

These symbols and rituals served as focal points for the formation of a community; they did so in part because they provided a repertoire of tools for coping with the sorts of difficulties I spoke about in Chapter 5: worries about health and family, anxieties about crops and cattle, apprehensions about forgiveness, death and eternal life. Their success as symbols around which a community might be able to coalesce was in a certain sense dependent on their ability to be the bearers of multiple and diverse meanings imputed to them by a large number of people of differing backgrounds and levels of sophistication: they were canvases upon which individuals could project their own particular understandings as they sought to deal with the material and spiritual challenges of existence.[86] As symbols and not propositionally laden, precise statements of doctrine, they were less exclusionary and could even

[85] If this understanding perhaps expects too much of any one individual in terms of personal commitment and belief, then it can be further specified that, though levels of conscious personal commitment will have varied from individual to individual, the people who engaged in such behaviors nevertheless belonged to a group—a family, clan, tribe, community, etc.—which had a collective recognition of and commitment to these Christian symbols and as such they made use of these symbolic resources in the course of their lives, particularly in times of conjuncture. These symbols themselves were all uniquely Christian (and not Jewish, Zoroastrian, pagan, or something else) insofar as their authority and perceived efficacy ultimately derived meaning and power by reference to the *kerygma*, that is, the message of the life, death, and resurrection of Jesus. Whatever their differences in doctrine, the message of the life, death, and resurrection of Jesus was proclaimed at every celebration of the Eucharist in late antiquity and the Middle Ages—at least among the Christian groups that have concerned me in this book—regardless of the celebrant's confession.

[86] My thinking here has been influenced by A. P. Cohen, *The Symbolic Construction of Community* (London/New York, 1985).

unite groups that were, doctrinally speaking, at odds: Julianist clergy might have a habit of coming into a Chalcedonian church after services in order to pray and venerate an icon of the Virgin; Maximus the Confessor and Theodore of Caesarea kissed the Gospels, the cross, and icons of Christ and the Virgin at the end of a theological debate that had seen them at doctrinal odds.[87] Shrines to saints could be visited or claimed by Christians belonging to rival churches: for example, Qalʿat Simʿān in Syria.[88] Indeed, the ability of healing and cultic shrines to accommodate and appeal to groups across a theological spectrum has led to the suggestion that imperial authorities in the sixth century promoted such places as one tactic in a larger strategy aimed at repairing Christological rifts between Christians and fostering unity.[89] The Eucharist, of course, was the most prominent such symbol—all Christians partook of it, regardless of confession, and all Christians viewed it as central to the experience of being a Christian.

For Jacob, the Eucharist may have been the Body and Blood of Christ and the Eucharistic celebration something that even angels longed to give thanks in,[90] but from his canons, we have seen that some Christians also viewed it as a thing that could be worn around the neck or in a phylactery to keep sickness at bay. These two understandings of the Eucharist are of course not mutually exclusive, and the latter is no doubt in some sense derivative of the former.

[87] For about one hundred Gaianites (Julianists) coming into a Chalcedonian church and offering *proskynesis* to an icon of the the Virgin: Sophronius of Jerusalem, *Narratio miraculorum ss. Cyri et Iohannis* 12.17 (ed. N. Fernández Marcos, *Los* thaumata *de Sofronio: contribución al estudio de la incubatio cristiana* [Madrid, 1975], pp. 268–69; FT available in J. Gascou, *Sophrone de Jérusalem: Miracles des saints Cyr et Jean (BHGI 477–479)* [Paris, 2006], p. 60); for Maximus and Theodosius kissing the Gospels, cross, and icons after a debate: (Ps-) Anastasius Apocrisarius, *Dialogue of Maximus with Theodore Bishop of Caesarea in Bithynia* 4 (ed. and trans. P. Allen and B. Neil, *Maximus the Confessor and His Companions: Documents from Exile* [Oxford/New York, 2002], p. 100 = 101 [ET]. See pp. 36–37 for discussion of authorship). I have taken these two examples from Mary Charles-Murray, 'Artistic Idiom and Doctrinal Development,' in R. Williams, ed., *The Making of Orthodoxy: Essays in Honour of Henry Chadwick* (Cambridge, 1989), p. 291. On the first example, see, too, Wipszycka, 'How Insurmountable Was the Chasm between Monophysites and Chalcedonians?' pp. 214–15.

[88] See P. Peeters, *Le tréfonds oriental de l'hagiographie byzantine* (Brussels, 1950), pp. 133–36, and the concise and helpful discussion in M. Whitby, *The Ecclesiastical History of Evagrius Scholasticus* (Liverpool, 2000), pp. xlii–xliii.

[89] See W. Mayer, 'Antioch and the Intersection between Religious Factionalism, Place, and Power in Late Antiquity,' in A. Cain and N. E. Lenski, eds., *The Power of Religion in Late Antiquity* (Farnham/Burlington, 2009), pp. 357–67, esp. 362–67, focusing on Michael the Archangel and Cosmas and Damian at Antioch; and P. Booth, 'Orthodox and Heretic in the early Byzantine Cult(s) of Saints Cosmas and Damian,' in P. Sarris, M. Dal Santo, and P. Booth, eds., *An Age of Saints? Power, Conflict, and Dissent in Early Medieval Christianity* (Leiden/Boston, 2011), pp. 114–28, focusing especially on Cosmas and Damian in Constantinople, with a rich collection of other examples at 122–23.

[90] For angels longing to take part in the Eucharistic service, see Jacob's scholion in Harvard Syriac 47, fol. 162v.

What we see, however, in the canons of Jacob or in the condemnations of theological and ecclesiastical elites are attempts at regulating such understandings when they violated the logic of the theological framework worked out by elites to hold the entire system of symbols and rituals together.

For each of these symbols or rituals, theological elites had developed a correct interpretation, or perhaps a small spectrum of acceptable interpretations; this was orthodoxy. But what the evidence I have attempted to present in this chapter and also in Chapters 3 and 5 makes clear is that many Christians, both lay and clergy, both 'simple' and elite, consistently engaged in behaviors that placed their interpretations of these symbols and rituals outside the range held to be acceptable by certain theological leaders. Some elites were aware of this and apparently unperturbed—recall that the patriarch Julian, when confronted by Jacob of Edessa about rampant violations of church canons, told his bishop to go along with the times. Jacob, for his part, was not so sanguine about such violations. And of course, theological elites differed among themselves when it came to which interpretations were correct—hence the more familiar spectrum of different Christological positions, each with a different answer to the question of the number of natures or energies or wills in the Incarnate Christ.

But these well-elaborated views were only the tip of a much larger iceberg. Jacob, George, and the rest of the Christian authors whose names have littered the pages of this book and whose writings fill the shelves of our libraries lived in a world full of untuned Christian belief, not just in rival churches, but in their own churches as well. Many were perhaps not playing the piano, but many of those who were, were playing it badly. As Robinson pointed out, the *shahārija* do not seem to have had an independent set of ecclesiastical institutions, but rather functioned within the existing structures of the Church of the East; in terms of Christian praxis, they were indistinguishable from other East Syrians.[91]

Similarly, the extensive abuses chronicled in Jacob's canons were carried out by individuals and priests who belonged to Jacob's church and not to a rival one. Reports of deviant doctrines existing within putatively orthodox church institutions are common. In the sixth century, for example, the *vita* of Mar Aba reported a story of a heretical nun living in a convent who died on account of her blasphemies.[92] The precise nature of the nun's heresy is never specified, and whether such a nun actually ever existed is not for our purposes important. What is significant is that the problem of incorrect belief, within

[91] See Robinson, *Empire and Elites*, p. 102.

[92] *History of Mar Aba*, pp. 220–21 (ed. Bedjan, *Histoire de Mar-Jabalaha*).

contexts that were supposed to be 'orthodox,' was regularly reported and was clearly something that worried church leaders.[93] In the late seventh century, Catholicos Henanisho' (sed. 685–699) had to investigate charges of Messalianism leveled against certain monks at the monastery of Rabban Sliba. Though these particular charges ultimately proved false, about a century later, at the first synod held by Timothy I in 790, a canon was issued which stipulated that any bishop, monk, or believer who was accused of Messalianism or any other heresy was not to be allowed to serve his office or to take communion before first anathematizing this teaching, in writing, before the church.[94] 'Heretical' notions clearly had a home within the 'Orthodox' church—all of them.

If we assume that what actually united Christians—lay and clergy, rich and poor, common and elite, rural and urban, agrarian and nonagrarian—in the seventh and eighth centuries was a common adherence to a shared set of symbols and rituals and not necessarily a shared set of doctrinal propositions about the precise theological plumbing related to those symbols and rituals, the conclusion that untuned rather than orthodox Christian belief was the natural and majority doctrinal position of most Christians in the seventh and eighth centuries does not seem quite so far-fetched. It was the sacraments and other rituals and symbols that united the learned and the simple as Christians, not competing theories of the Incarnation. This will also bring us back, at last, to the question of the earliest encounters between Christians and Muslims in the seventh and eighth centuries. The Christians that Arab conquerors encountered in this period included highly trained, theologically sophisticated and erudite figures like the denizens of Qenneshre. But such figures were a very, very small minority.

The overwhelming majority of the Christians whom the Arab conquerors came into contact with were likely more similar to the people condemned in Jacob's canons for their 'pagan' practices and abuses of the Eucharist than they were to someone like Jacob himself.[95] After the East Syrian John of Daylam converted thousands of pagans to Christianity in the late seventh century, his *vita* reported that 'over the course of three years he cleansed them of every

[93] See, e.g., the outbreak of Origenism that reportedly occurred in the Judean Desert after the death of Sabas: Cyril of Scythopolis, *Life of Sabas* 83–84 (ed. Schwartz, *Kyrillos von Skythopolis*, 187–89; ET available in Price, *Cyril of Scythopolis: The Lives of the Monks of Palestine*, pp. 196–98).

[94] For Canon 4 from Timothy's Synod of 790 (known as *The First Synod of Timothy I*), see Chabot, ed., *Synodicon Orientale*, p. 602 (Syriac) = p. 607 (French). For Henanisho' investigating charges against the monks Aba, Thomas, and Bar 'Idta, see Thomas of Marga, *Monastic History* 1.28 (ed. Budge, 1.53–56 = 2.93–97 [English]).

[95] Cf. the comments in S. Shaked, 'Popular Religion in Sasanian Babylonia,' *JSAI* 21 (1997), p. 114, about the kind of Zoroastrianism encountered by Arab conquerors in the seventh century. Cf. also the religiously mixed situation Shaked described in 'Manichaean Incantation Bowls in Syriac,' pp. 65–66.

pagan practice and they became true Christians, zealous for the faith.'[96] Such assurances should give us little confidence that all pre- or non-Christian habits and practices had in fact been stripped away.

But even if they had been, or even if they had been imbued with new Christian understandings: what about the countless other places across the rural Middle East that had no similar experiences of intensely supervised depaganization/Christianization? 'Indeed, there was no distinction,' the East Syrian John bar Penkaye, a contemporary of John of Daylam, would lament in perhaps the late 680s, 'between pagan and Christian; Believer was not distinct from Jew and truth was not distinguished from that which leads astray.'[97] The Middle East was filled with Christians whose work, geographic location, and level of education left them with understandings of normative Christianity that were much less nuanced and reflective than those of the clever and dialectically slippery Christian interlocutors who star in Christian-Muslim dialogue and dispute texts, and whose subtle ability to thrust and parry with a Muslim of similar education and sophistication is commonly taken to be representative of what Islam meeting Christianity looked like in the first several centuries of Arab rule. Christianity, then as now, was a multi-layered phenomenon and 'simple Christians' (to use Jacob's phrase) were, like Simeon's shepherds, ubiquitous.

Students of Christian belief and practice in other periods and places will no doubt be quick to point out that the type of things we have seen in this chapter do not in fact differ markedly from what Christians in other regions of the world were doing at the same time and also later.[98] What makes them interesting for us at present is *where* they were doing them and *when*—in the Middle East, in the first regions conquered by armies from western Arabia and in the area which would eventually come to be regarded as the core of the Islamic world. This landscape—confessionally confused and filled with beliefs and activities that church leaders found aberrant, heretical, and simply wrong—was the setting of the Middle East's first Christian-Muslim interactions.

One of the keys therefore to understanding the process of Islamization and to answering the question, 'What difference did Islam make?' is to ask ourselves 'What difference did Islam make, *for whom*?' The traditional focus of scholar-

[96] *Life of John of Daylam* 22 (ed. Brock, pp. 139 = 148 [ET]). I have used here the translation of Brock.

[97] John bar Penkaye, *Book of the Main Events*, p. *151 (ed. Mingana).

[98] See, e.g., E. Cameron, *Enchanted Europe: Superstition, Reason, and Religion, 1250–1750* (Oxford, 2010), pp. 31–40, 50–75; A. de Mier Vélez, 'Supersticiones y horóscopos entre los Cristianos Visigodos y Francos,' *Religión y Cultura* 41 (1995), pp. 811–39 (I am grateful to Molly Lester for this reference); and W. E. Klingshirn, *Caesarius of Arles: The Making of a Christian Community in Late Antique Gaul* (Cambridge, 1994), pp. 218–24. On Caesarius, see most recently L. Grig, 'Caesarius of Arles and the Campaign against Popular Culture in Late Antiquity,' *Early Modern Europe* 26 (2018), pp. 61–81.

ship on the Christian-Muslim encounter has been on the effect Islam had on the learned elite that led Christian communities. But what difference did Islam make for simple Christians? That is the more important question, for it was the conversion of such Christians—farmers, blacksmiths, carpenters, craftsmen, laborers, bakers, and others, person by person, family by family, over the course of decades and centuries—that gradually turned the formerly Roman Middle East into a majority-Muslim society. Numerically, the number of nonelite contacts between ordinary Christians and ordinary Muslims will have vastly outnumbered dealings between the theological elites of the two faiths.

The Christianity these people converted away from was not, I have attempted to suggest, the sort of doctrinally sophisticated faith that we encounter in texts written by theological elites. By the same token, the Islam they converted to was not the sophisticated Islam of ninth-century Baghdad nor even necessarily the Islam used to publicly legitimate the rule of Umayyad Caliphs on coins, in poetry, and through architecture.

Let us therefore now turn to the question of Muslim believing.

CHAPTER 10

A Religion with a Thousand Faces

The wandering Arabs say, 'We believe.' Say: 'You believe not.' But rather say, 'We submit.' For faith has not yet entered into your hearts.

Qur'ān 49:14[1]

Religion they have little, or none. I was informed by our Pilot that it was only here and there on the coast that you met with a man, who could say his prayers, while the Bedwins of the interior were wholly devoid of religion, having no idea of God or devil, of heaven or hell.[2]

In my last chapter, I sought to nuance and broaden the ways in which we think about the import of the word 'Christian' when we are speaking about Christian and Muslim interactions in an early medieval context. 'Christian' might have included people who held to a wide variety of religious beliefs and it could cover people who engaged in a number of different religious practices. Just as no one today would take the *Church Dogmatics* of Karl Barth as representative of the faith and practice of the typical Presbyterian or Reformed Christian in the twentieth century, or the *Theological Investigations* of Karl Rahner as indicative of what the average Catholic believed or of how he or she lived in the world, neither should we take the (written) views of Christian elites in the seventh century and assume that they pointed to how most people were actually behaving and what they were believing. Very few Christians or Muslims were religious experts. What about those who were not in the *majlis* and who, if they had been there, would not have been able to understand or evaluate what was going on?

In this chapter, I will be looking at the other half of the equation in the phrase 'Christian-Muslim interaction.' My goal will be to explore the variety of meanings that 'Islam' and 'Muslim' may have held in the earliest period of Islamic history. Although later Muslim tradition (and popular perception today) would regard the earliest generations of Muslims as the most pious and devout in all of Islamic history, my argument in this chapter will be that most of them

[1] I have altered here the translation of Pickthall.

[2] H. J. Carter, 'Notes on the Mahrah Tribe of Southern Arabia, with a vocabulary of their language, to which are appended additional observations on the Gara Tribe,' *Journal of the Bombay Branch of the Royal Asiatic Society* 2 (1847), p. 341. On literary portrayals of Bedouin religiosity, see S. Binay, *Die Figur des Beduinen in der arabischen Literatur* (Wiesbaden, 2006), pp. 73–74.

had little detailed knowledge of the message of the Prophet and paid scant heed to its implications for how they lived their lives. And even among those who did care about the Prophet's message, there was disagreement as to what exactly it was and shifting opinions about what would later be regarded as matters of central importance. Judged by later standards, most of the earliest followers of Muḥammad—both the *salaf* and those who came after them—will have fallen far short of the expectations and assumptions about them that they have been saddled with for many centuries.[3]

If Christian orthodoxy in the seventh century can be compared to a perfectly executed performance of a piece by Chopin (or Beethoven or Mozart, depending on the Christian group), then we can hardly say that Islamic orthodoxy even had a score in the same period. Indeed, it was in the seventh and eighth centuries that the score that would eventually become orthodoxy in Islam—Sunnī, Shīʿī, Khārijī, or otherwise—was beginning to be written. If we listen to this period, keeping in the forefront of our interest the simple, ordinary adherents who will have been the vast bulk of all Christians and Muslims alive at the time, what we will hear is a lot of music played quite out of tune, as well as some new tunes just beginning to make themselves heard. And we will of course find that a number of people were not even attempting to play music at all.

In other words: just as there was a layering of knowledge in the late antique and early medieval Christian communities of the Middle East, so there was also a layering of knowledge in the Prophet's community in the seventh century (and later). But this was a layering with a twist: in the earliest period of Islamic history, it was complicated by the fact that the competing orthodoxies of medieval Islam had yet to coalesce and crystalize. The spectrum of legitimate and competing attitudes and beliefs among the elite of Muḥammad's followers was broader and more diverse than what would be found in later periods. Recognizing this layering of knowledge and lack of orthodoxy will be key to understanding the religious dynamics in the Middle East in the centuries after the Arab conquests.

THE CHALLENGE OF EARLY ISLAMIC HISTORY

Before proceeding further, however, it should be noted that speaking about the earliest history of the Muslim community inevitably presents the historian with a difficulty: unless he or she chooses to base his or her discussion solely

[3] On the *salaf*, see E. Chaumont's article, 'al-Salaf wa-'l-Khalaf,' in *EI2*, vol. 8, p. 900.

on the text of the Qur'ān, the Arabic sources relating to this period, as we have them now, will date from at least a century (and often much more) after the events they describe.[4] Many of the Syriac and Greek sources that I have made use of in dealing with Christian matters, by contrast, are much closer to—and sometimes contemporary with—the events they portray. What to make of this gap and its implications for our understanding of the origins of Islam have, unsurprisingly, generated a great deal of scholarly literature and disagreement.

My purpose in this chapter (and indeed, this book), is not to enter into these complex debates about the reliability of the early Islamic historical tradition. For this reason, I will assume the not uncontroversial (though nevertheless reasonable and defensible) view that the 'main outlines of the actual events' of early Islamic history, to use the words of Gregor Schoeler, can be known to us.[5] The arguments for radical skepticism about what we can know of the early Islamic tradition, though powerful and at times, very insightful, are ultimately unpersuasive, in part because none of the various reconstructions of early Islamic history that have been proposed to replace some version of the traditional one are more plausible than simply accepting the broad contours of the traditional account, even while readily acknowledging its distortions, contradictions, and manifold problems.[6] One of the secondary arguments of this chapter, in fact, will be that accepting the broad outlines of the traditional account and approaching the history of the early Islamic community while keeping at the forefront of one's interest the question of the beliefs and attitudes of all the members of Muḥammad's community, and not just those members of the elite who were religiously engaged, can help us understand the existence of some of the enigmas that have long puzzled scholars of the early tradition.

[4] The problem of the distance between our extant sources and the events they describe is well known. E.g., for the period preceding the end of the Umayyad Caliphate as 'ein unbeschriebenes Blatt' so far as legal and dogmatic traditions as concerned, see R. Paret, 'Die Lücke in der Überlieferung über den Urislam,' in F. M. Meier, ed., *Westöstliche Abhandlungen. Rudolf Tschudi zum siebzigsten Geburtstag überreicht von Freunden und Schülern* (Wiesbaden, 1954), p. 150.

[5] G. Schoeler, *The Biography of Muḥammad: Nature and Authenticity*, trans. U. Vagelpohl (London/New York, 2011), p. 2. For a critique of Schoeler, see S. J. Shoemaker, 'In Search of 'Urwa's *Sīra*: Some Methodological Issues in the Quest for "Authenticity" in the Life of Muḥammad,' *Der Islam* 85 (2011), pp. 257–344 and see also the response in A. Görke, H. Motzki, and G. Schoeler, 'First Century Sources for the Life of Muḥammad? A Debate,' *Der Islam* 2012 (89), pp. 2–59. On the question of sources, see further Appendix I.

[6] F. M. Donner, *Narratives of Islamic Origins: The Beginnings of Islamic Historical Writing* (Princeton, 1998), pp. 25–31, provides a succinct critique of the skeptical approach to Islamic origins. A. al-Azmeh, *The Arabs and Islam in Late Antiquity: A Critique of Approaches to Arabic Sources* (Berlin, 2014), pp. 1–14, is an insightful discussion of the shortcomings of the radically skeptical position.

In order to get to that point, however, we should first take stock of Muḥammad's community in the mid-seventh century. Why might people have decided to answer the Prophet's call?

'ISLAM' AS A PLACEHOLDER: WHO CONVERTED AND WHEN?

We can begin to answer this question with a simple observation that cannot be emphasized too strongly: although the names of politico-religious elites and sectarian entrepreneurs may easily dominate our understanding of what Islam meant in its earliest stages, we should not forget that it was an anonymous and silent majority that formed the bulk of the Prophet's followers. As Nehemia Levtzion observed, 'The majority of the Arab tribesmen accepted Islam collectively, in what might be described as a passive adhesion to Islam.'[7] And whatever the content of this anonymous majority's belief in and understanding of Muḥammad's message may have been, we should not be astonished if it was neither very profound nor resembled anything like that of the religious leaders of the community—a community that was, we should remember, fractured and beset with dispute, civil wars, and assassinations of prominent figures from a very early period.

Levtzion's point and its implications are worth pondering for a moment: what must have been the overwhelming majority of Muslim Arabs converted to Islam in groups, with their tribes, and not individually in the dramatic and intensely personal way that the later *sīra* literature recounts of those who converted before the emigration to Medina. Such individual conversions, based on the beauty of the Qur'ān or the nobility of Muḥammad's behavior, were the exception and not the rule. They should not be paradigmatic in our understanding of what conversion looked like or meant.[8] In the period before the *hijra*, the number of Muslims was miniscule when compared to the increase it would register in less than a decade. No more than a hundred people are supposed to have emigrated from Mecca to Medina in 622;[9] when Muḥammad

[7] N. Levtzion, 'Toward a Comparative Study of Islamization,' in Levtzion, ed., *Conversion to Islam* (New York, 1979), p. 20.

[8] W. M. Watt, 'Conversion in Islam at the Time of the Prophet,' *Journal of the American Academy of Religion* 47 (Thematic Issue S) (1980), pp. 721–31, is a valuable study of the nature of such conversions, but does not touch at all on the mass conversions that occurred at the end of the Prophet's life.

[9] See W. M. Watt's article, '*Hidjra*' in EI², where Watt puts the number of emigrants—not counting Muḥammad, Abū Bakr, 'Alī, and their wives—at about seventy. For an enumeration of the individuals who made the *hijra*, see column 'H' in the tables provided by Watt in *Muhammad at Mecca* (Oxford, 1953), pp. 170–79.

returned in January 630 to finally conquer Mecca, by contrast, he is said to have led an army of some ten thousand men.[10]

If we believe the traditional sources, after the move of the young community of believers to Medina in 622, Muḥammad engaged in a prolonged conflict with the pagan Qurashīs of Mecca which culminated in the Muslim capture of Mecca in AD 630. One result of this conquest was what is known as the 'Year of the Deputations': AD 630/AH 9 witnessed a number of delegations sent to Muḥammad from various tribes and groups that submitted to Islam. The entry of these tribes into Islam was not portrayed by Ibn Isḥāq as grounded in what might be considered moral or religious factors. It was instead a political choice and represented an act of allegiance and declaration of loyalty to Muḥammad as opposed to the Quraysh of Mecca. And this announcement of fealty came only after Muḥammad's mastery over the Quraysh had been definitively settled. 'In deciding their attitude to Islam,' Ibn Isḥāq reported, 'the Arabs were only waiting to see what happened to this clan of Quraysh and the apostle,'

> [for] Quraysh were the leaders and guides of men, the people of the sacred temple, and the pure stock of Ishmael son of Abraham; and the leading Arabs did not contest this. It was Quraysh who had declared war on the apostle and opposed him; and when Mecca was occupied and Quraysh became subject to him and he subdued it to Islam, and the Arabs knew that they could not fight the apostle or display enmity towards him they entered into God's religion "in batches" [Q 110:1] as God said, coming to him from all directions.[11]

The deputations came from a variety of groups: Banū Tamīm, Banū Sa'd b. Bakr, 'Abd al-Qays, Banū Ḥanīfa, Ṭayyi', Banū Zubayd, Kinda, and the Kings of Ḥimyar, among others.[12] The river of tribal embassies and individual conversions continued to flow the next year as well; among those who converted to Islam were also the cities of Tabāla and Jurash in Yemen.[13]

[10] Ibn Hishām, *Kitāb sīrat rasūl Allāh*, p. 810 (ed. F. Wüstenfeld, *Das Leben Muhammed's nach Muhammed Ibn Ishâk, bearbeitet von Abd el-Malik Ibn Hischâm* [Göttingen, 1858–1860], vol. 1.2; ET available in A. Guillaume, *The Life of Muhammad: A Translation of Isḥāq's Sīrat Rasūl Allāh* [London, 1955], p. 545), cf. W. Montgomery Watt, *Muhammad at Medina* (Oxford, 1956), p. 66.

[11] As related in Ibn Hishām, *Kitāb sīrat rasūl Allāh*, p. 933 (ed. Wüstenfeld, vol. 1.2; ET taken from Guillaume, *The Life of Muhammad*, p. 628).

[12] Ibn Hishām, *Kitāb sīrat rasūl Allāh*, pp. 933–57 (ed. Wüstenfeld, vol. 1.2; ET available in Guillaume, *The Life of Muhammad*, pp. 628–44). L. Caetani, *Annali dell' Islām*, vol. 2.1 (Milan, 1907), pp. 221–302, discussed in detail the embassies and conversions of a number of tribes and portions of tribes in A.H. 9, including: Bāhila part of the Banū Asad b. Khuzayma, Banū Bali, some families of Kalb, Kināna, Thaqīf, the Kings of Himyar, Hamdān, Fazāra, Murra, Banū 'Uqayl b. Ka'b, Banū Kilāb, Banū Ru'ās b. Kilāb, Banū Ja'da, Banū Qushayr b. Ka'b, Banū 'l-Bakkā, Banū Hilāl b. 'Āmir, Taghlib (the pagan members of their embassy embraced Islam, p. 299), Banū Tujīb, Banū Bahrā, Thumāla, and al-Ḥuddān.

[13] For the conversion of Tabala and Jurash, see al-Balādhurī, *Kitāb futūḥ al-buldān*, p. 59 (ed. M. J.

The group conversions of these tribes and even cities to Islam,[14] it is important to remember, came only a few years before the beginnings of the Arab conquests further to the north. Before those conquests could begin in earnest, however, Muḥammad's death intervened in AD 632/AH 11, setting off a period of conflict which has come to be known as the *ḥurūb al-ridda*, or 'Wars of Apostasy.' Tribes, a number of whom had ostensibly converted to Islam, rebelled against the authority of the state that Muḥammad had established in Medina, an act often expressed through the cessation of alms payments.[15] Though it can be difficult to distinguish the political from the religious, the rebellion of some tribes seems to have been political and not to have entailed a rejection of the Prophet's message. But this was not the case across the board: some rebellions had a clearly religious aspect as well. 'When (al-Jārūd) came to his people, he invited them to Islām,' al-Ṭabarī reported,

> whereupon they all responded positively to him. Then it was only a short time before the Prophet died and they apostatized; 'Abd al-Qays said, "If Muḥammad had been a prophet, he would not have died," and they apostatized.[16]

The 'Abd al-Qays eventually resubmitted to Islam, but it would not be a stretch to suggest that most of their members understood the nature and meaning of Islam in ways much different from that of older converts in Medina—and almost certainly radically different from that of Abbasid religious savants.

At this time, a number of prophets appeared, apparently having drawn inspiration from the model of Muḥammad. In the Najd, Ṭalḥa b. Khālid claimed

---

de Goeje, *Liber expugnationes regionum* [Leiden, 1866]; ET available in P. Hitti, *The Origins of the Islamic State*, vol. 1 [New York, 1916], p. 91) and cf. al-Ṭabarī, *Ta'rīkh*, 1.4, 1730–1731 (ed. P. de Jong and E. Prym [Leiden, 1890]; ET available in I. K. Poonawala, *The Last Years of the Prophet* [HṬ 9] [Albany, 1990], pp. 89–90]). For details of the embassies and conversions in AH 10, see Caetani, *Annali dell'Islam*, vol. 2.1, pp. 311–54 (esp. nos. 15 [Banū Khawlān], 20 [Ghāmid], 21 [Azd], 23 [the cities of Jurash and Tabāla in Yemen], 26 [Banū Ghassān], 27 [Banū Bajīla], 28 [Khath'am], 29 [Banū Salāmān], 30 [Banū Ṣadif], 31 [Zubayd], 32 [Murād], 33 [Banū Ḥanīfa], 34 [Kinda], 35 [Ṭayy], 41 [Banū Jarm], 42 [Banū Ujā], 44 [Bakr b. Wā'il], 49 [Banū Muḥārib], 50 [Ju'fī b. Sa'd], 53 [al-Ruhāwiyyūn of the tribe of al-Ruhā], 54 ['Ans], 55 [Azd 'Umān], 56 [Ghāfiq], 57 [Bāriq], 58 [Mahra], and 66 [Jayshān]).

[14] Ibn Sa'd, *Kitāb al-ṭabaqāt al-kabīr*, vol. 1.2, p. 86 (ed. E. Mittwoch and E. Sachau [Leiden, 1917]; translation available in Haq and Ghazanfar, *Kitab al-tabaqat al-kabir*, vol. 1, p. 421), even described a delegation of animals of prey (*wafd al-sibā'*) that approached the Prophet in this period. This reportedly included a wolf that came to Muḥammad and howled in his presence.

[15] Though in many cases the conflicts being fought were not between Muslims and apostates but rather between Muslims and Arab tribes that had not yet converted. See the comments in A. Noth and L. I. Conrad, *The Early Arabic Historical Tradition: A Source-Critical Study*, 2nd ed. (Princeton, 1994), p. 28. On the later Islamic tradition's understanding of the types of rebellion involved, see A. J. Wensinck, *The Muslim Creed: Its Genesis and Historical Development* (New York, 1932), p. 13.

[16] al-Ṭabarī, *Ta'rīkh*, 1.4, p. 1958 (ed. P. de Jong and E. Prym [Leiden, 1890]; ET, with slight alteration, taken from F. Donner, *The Conquest of Arabia* [HṬ 10] [Albany, 1993], p. 135).

to be the prophet of the Banū Asad; in al-Yamāma, Maslama b. Ḥabīb proclaimed himself prophet of the Banū Ḥanīfa; also in the Najd, a woman named Sajāḥ had a following as a prophetess among the Banū Tamīm and Banū Taghlib; in Yemen, Abhala al-ʿAnsī, also known as al-Aswad al-ʿAnsī, was a prophet among the Banū ʿAns; in ʿUmān, Dhū al-Tāj Laqīṭ b. Mālik claimed to be prophet among the Azd.[17] And there were others who claimed to be prophets as well: for example, Ṭulayḥa b. Khuwaylid,[18] and, most famously, Musaylima, whose prophetic ambitions antedated the *hijra*.[19] The appearance of so many prophets in the Arabian peninsula at roughly the same time as Muḥammad raises the question: what was it about seventh-century Arabia that made it such fecund terrain for the sprouting of prophetic claims?[20] The emergence of these prophets and the seeming ease and speed with which tribes all over the Arabian peninsula moved away from putative allegiance to the Prophet Muḥammad and his message to follow them, despite their previous group conversions, suggests that the understanding of the Prophet's message by these tribe members—as well as by the members of tribes elsewhere in the Arabian peninsula who, while continuing as members of the Prophet's community, attempted a political rebellion against Medina—was perhaps not all that much deeper than Simeon the Mountaineer's shepherds' understanding of Christianity.[21]

In other words, when we think about Muslim-Christian contact in the seventh and eighth centuries, we should also be aware of the fact that the overwhelming majority of the earliest followers of the message of Muḥammad were people who had converted, often in groups and not individually, after the Prophet's emigration to Medina and his military successes there; that a number of these left Islam after Muḥammad's death, sometimes to follow other prophets; and that they only returned to the Prophet's community in the face of military force. The consequences of these mass conversions should not be

[17] For all this, see F. Donner, *The Early Islamic Conquests* (Princeton, 1981), pp. 85–87 and the article by M. Lecker, '*al-Ridda*', in *EI2, Supplement*, pp. 692–695. For al-Aswad al-ʿAnsī, also known as ʿAbhala, see W. M. Watt's article, 'al-Aswad,' in *EI2*, vol. 1, p. 728.

[18] On Ṭulayḥa, see E. Landau-Tasseron's article, 'Ṭulayḥa,' in *EI2*, vol. 10, pp. 603–604.

[19] On Musaylima, see Al Makin, *Representing the Enemy: Musaylima in Muslim Literature* (Frankfurt am Main/New York, 2010), and see further M. J. Kister's masterful, 'The Struggle against Musaylima and the Conquest of Yamāma,' *JSAI* 27 (2002), pp. 1–56, which contains information about a number of the prophets I have just mentioned.

[20] Michael Cook reminds me that the existence of these other prophets also suggests that by the end of Muḥammad's life, 'the notion of a Prophet and what he does was widespread in Arabia' (personal communication).

[21] T. W. Arnold, *The Preaching of Islam: A History of the Propagation of the Muslim Faith*, 2nd ed. (London, 1913; repr. New Delhi, n.d.), p. 41, also used the *Ridda* Wars to suggest that the conversion of many Arabs in the seventh century to Islam was not a profound one.

underestimated, underemphasized, or forgotten.[22] What would being a follower of Muḥammad have meant to the simple inhabitant of a city that converted, *en masse*, to Islam not long before the death of the Prophet? What will Islam have meant to a tribesman who became a Muslim when representatives from his tribe converted in 630 or 631?[23]

Several anecdotes can give us an idea. 'What do you have of the Book of God?' Sa'd b. Abī Waqqāṣ reportedly asked 'Amr b. Ma'dīkarib (d. AD 641/AH 21) after the Battle of Qādisiyya, perhaps around 636. 'Amr had converted to Islam in AD 631 (AH 10) and supported another prophetic claimant, al-Aswad al-'Ansī, during the Wars of Apostasy, before eventually returning to the Prophet's community after being captured in battle.[24] His path, in and out of the Prophet's community and then back in again, no doubt followed a common course taken by many notional Muslims in the years after Muḥammad's death. 'I became a Muslim in Yemen,' 'Amr reportedly responded to Sa'd, 'then I took part in military expeditions and I was distracted from memorizing the Qur'ān.'[25] Such a shaky résumé did not prevent 'Amr from being classed among the Companions of the Prophet in the medieval period.[26] Sa'd reportedly next asked Bishr b. Rabī'a what he knew of the Qur'ān. 'In the name of God, the Merciful, the Compassionate,' he replied.[27] In another anecdote, we read of 'Umar b. al-Khaṭṭāb sending Abū Sufyān to see how much Qur'ān inhabitants of the desert could recite; those who could not recite anything were to be

[22] As Caetani, whose detailed account of the various embassies and conversions has not been superseded in Western scholarship, observed, 'Essi però, lo ripeto, erano musulmani solo di nome e per ragioni di oportunismo politico. . . .' See his comments about the enormous role that these late Bedouin converts played in the Arab conquests and how the converts 'mutarono profandamente l'indirizzo dell'Islām': *Annali dell' Islām*, vol. 2.1, pp. 431–32. It is not only modern scholars who have noted the variety of motivations that propelled people into Islam by the end of the Prophet's life. Al-Jāḥiẓ, *al-'Uthmāniyya*, pp. 196–97 (English available in Pellat, *The Life and Works of Jāḥiẓ*, p. 77), listed the various classes (*ṭabaqāt*) of Muslims—their reasons for converting and state of religious knowledge—upon the Prophet's death. According to him, these included everything from knowledgeable believers, to zealous converts with no real knowledge of Islam, to those who had become Muslims to avoid being killed.

[23] An idea of the very basic instruction that will have been given mass converts can be seen in al-Bukhārī, *al-Jāmi' al-ṣaḥīḥ*, vol. 1 (ed. M. al-Dīn al-Khaṭīb) (Cairo, 1400), p. 48 (no. 87), in which a delegation from 'Abd al-Qays comes to Muḥammad and asks for instruction by which they can enter Paradise. The Prophet ordered them to do only a handful of things: believe in God alone, pray, give alms, fast during Ramadan, and pay the fifth of their spoils. He also forbade them from using four different receptacles that were used in the making of wine. The delegation that came to him was to memorize these orders and make them known to members of their tribe who were not present.

[24] See Ch. Pellat's article, "Amr b. Ma'dīkarib,' in *EI2*, vol. 1, p. 453.

[25] Abū al-Faraj al-Iṣbahānī, *Kitāb al-Aghānī*, vol. 14 (Bulaq, 1868–1869), p. 40. On the date of the Battle of Qādisiyya, ca. 636, see L. Veccia Vaglerii in *EI2*, vol. 4, p. 386.

[26] Cf. Ibn Ḥajar al-'Asqalānī, *al-Iṣāba fī tamyīz al-ṣaḥāba*, vol. 7, p. 148 (no. 5966): *yuqāl lahu ṣuḥba* (ed. Ṭ. Muḥammad al-Zaynī [Cairo, 1991]).

[27] Abū al-Faraj al-Iṣbahānī, *Kitāb al-Aghānī*, vol. 14, p. 40.

punished, ʿUmar ordered. Abū Sufyān asked a certain Aws b. Khālid b. Yazīd to recite the Qur'ān. When he was unable to recite anything, Abū Sufyān beat Aws so badly that he died.[28] Unsurprisingly, such stories of ignorance of the Qur'ān among early Muslims can be multiplied,[29] and though the sources in which they are typically found are late ones, these types of anecdotes are nevertheless very suggestive and useful to think with, for they are precisely what we should expect, given the circumstances surrounding so many acts of joining the Prophet's community. Indeed, the Qur'ān itself expresses wariness as to the sincerity of the belief and motives of what it calls *al-aʿrāb*—the Arab tribes or Bedouin—in more than one passage (cf. 9:97–101; 48:11; 49:14).[30]

But it was not just (usually) anonymous tribesmen, the kind of people some might be tempted to write off as minor players in the seventh century, who were late converts. A number of prominent and influential figures in the early Islamic state also converted only a few years before the Prophet's death. If we believe our sources, once elected leader of the community after Muḥammad's death, Abū Bakr relied heavily on a Meccan elite that had until only recently been at war with the Muslim community, and which was now comprised of recent converts; as Elias Shoufani put it, '[T]the newly-converted Meccan aristocracy were the back-bone of Abū Bakr's group of supporters.'[31] It is not clear, however, what level of religious understanding or conviction many of the aristocrats Shoufani referred to actually possessed. Khālid b. al-Walīd, who played an important role in suppressing the rebellions which broke out in Arabia after Muḥammad's death and who was a significant player in the early Muslim conquests, had in fact been the leader of Meccan military forces against the Muslims and did not convert to Islam until AH 6/AD 627 or AH 8/AD 629.[32]

[28] Abū al-Faraj al-Iṣbahānī, *Kitāb al-Aghānī*, vol. 16, p. 58.

[29] I have taken these three from Nöldeke et al. in *History of the Qur'ān*, p. 217, and more anedcotes can be found there.

[30] On the meaning of *al-aʿrāb*, cf. A. A. Ambros, *A Concise Dictionary of Koranic Arabic* (Wiesbaden, 2004), s.v. al-'aʿrābu (p. 307).

[31] E. Shoufani, *Al-Riddah and the Muslim Conquest of Arabia* (Toronto, 1973), p. 61. On the prominent role of late converts, see also the comments in F. M. Donner, *Muhammad and the Believers: At the Origins of Islam* (Cambridge, MA/London, 2010), pp. 95–96. The prominent role that Umayyads were given by Muḥammad, ʿUmar, and Abū Bakr was of course recognized much earlier; see al-Maqrīzī, *Nizāʿ wa-'l-takhāṣum fīmā bayna Banī Umayya wa-Banī Hāshim*, p. 41 (ed. G. Vos, *Die Kämpfe und Streitigkeiten zwischen den Banū 'Umajja und den Banū Hāšim* [Leiden, 1888]; ET available in C. E. Bosworth, *al-Maqrīzī's "Book of Contention and Strife concerning the Relations between the Banū Umayya and the Banū Hāshim"* [Manchester, 1983], pp. 79–80): 'Now just look at how there was not a single representative of the Banū Hāshim amongst the governors appointed by the Messenger of God, Abū Bakr, or ʿUmar. It was this and other occurences which sharpened the fangs of the Banū Umayya, threw open the gates for them, filled their cup to overflowing and twisted firmly their rope for them' (trans. Bosworth).

[32] See Shoufani, *Al-Riddah*, p. 61 and P. Crone's article, 'Khālid b. al-Walīd,' in *EI*², vol. 4, pp. 928–29. Only a few years later, in AH 10, the Prophet sent Khālid to the Banū al-Ḥārith (or Balḥārith) to give

Similarly, ʿAmr b. al-ʿĀṣ, the conqueror of Palestine and Egypt and founder of Fusṭāṭ, converted to Islam in AH 8/AD 629–630. ʿAmr's career and shrewd navigation of the conflicts, battles, and disputes that characterized the Rāshidūn period showed him to have been quite politically savvy.[33] Ibn Abī Sarḥ, the scribe who is supposed to have apostatized from Islam when he saw that he could change the text of the Qur'ān without upsetting Muḥammad, was granted amnesty by the Prophet at the time of the conquest of Mecca and succeeded ʿAmr b. al-ʿĀṣ as governor of Egypt.[34] Abū Sufyān, one of the most prominent leaders of the Meccan opposition to Muḥammad, only converted to Islam at the time of Muḥammad's conquest of Mecca. Within a few years, he would be named the Muslim governor of Najran and possibly also the Hijaz.[35] His sons Yazīd and Muʿāwiya also only converted to Islam at the conquest of Mecca; Yazīd would play an important role in the Muslim conquest of Palestine and would be appointed governor of Syria before his death in AH 18/AD 639. Muʿāwiya would go on to become the fifth leader of the Muslim community and a seminal figure in Islamic history. Muʿāwiya's mother, Hind bt. ʿUtba b. Rabīʿa, was notable for having chewed up part of the liver of Ḥamza, the Prophet's uncle, and then spit it out in an act of desecration committed after the Battle of Uḥud. She reportedly also mutilated the bodies of other Muslims who died there, slicing off their ears and noses.[36]

None of these figures had Islamic religious pedigrees that were long, or worth taking pride in, or which suggested they had become Muslim out of some sort of interior conviction about the truth of the Prophet's message. Of course, even expecting that they—or, for that matter, anyone changing his or her religion in our period—would have converted for reasons of sincerity or

---

them the options of converting to Islam or facing military conflict. The Banū al-Ḥārith converted and Khālid is supposed to have stayed with them to teach them the Qur'ān, the *sunna*, and the precepts of Islam; the Prophet also sent ʿAmr b. Ḥazm al-Anṣārī and a member of the Banū al-Najjār to give them religious instruction. See al-Ṭabarī, *Ta'rīkh*, 1.4, pp. 1724–29 (ed. de Jong and Prym [1890]). As an indication, perhaps, of the success of these efforts at catechism, not long after the Prophet died, the Banū Ḥārith followed al-Aswad al-ʿAnsī, another figure who claimed to be a prophet; see J. Schleifer's article, 'Ḥārith b. Kaʿb,' in *EI2*, vol. 12, p. 223.

[33] See Shoufani, *Al-Riddah*, p. 61 and A. J. Wensinck's article "Amr b. al-ʿĀṣ (al-ʿĀṣī) al-Shāmī,' in *EI2*, vol. 1, p. 451.

[34] Ibn Saʿd, *Kitāb al-ṭabaqāt al-kabīr*, vol. 7.2, pp. 190–91 (ed. E. Sachau, *Biographien Muhammeds, seiner Gefährten und der späteren Träger des Islams bis zum Jahre 230 der Flucht* [Leiden, 1918]; ET available in A. A. Bewley, *The Men of Madina*, vol. 1 [London, 1997], pp. 307-308).

[35] See W. M. Watt's article, 'Abū Sufyān b. Ḥarb b. Umayya,' in in *EI2*, vol. 1, p. 151, and Shoufani, *Al-Riddah*, p. 62; also see nn. 159–60 in this chapter.

[36] Ibn Hishām, *Kitāb sīrat rasūl Allāh*, pp. 580–82 (ed. Wüstenfeld, vol. 1.2; ET taken from Guillaume, *The Life of Muhammad*, pp. 385–86). Also see Shoufani, *Al-Riddah*, p. 62; and C. E. Bosworth's article 'Yazīd b. Abī Sufyān' and M. Hinds's article, 'Muʿāwiya I,' in *EI2*, vol. 11, p. 312 and vol. 7, pp. 263–68, respectively.

spiritual conviction can betray perhaps unconscious expectations that are likely the result more of the First and Second Great Awakenings in North America or of Protestant Pietism than of anything in texts from our period.[37] What we are dealing with here is a number of different Sauls of Tarsus—figures who went from an adversarial or skeptical relationship to a new religious movement to a leadership position in that same new religious movement. But unlike Paul, rather than a dramatic and intensely personal spiritual experience explaining their conversion, we have instead the threat and fear that would have accompanied an imminent military conquest by a rival and enemy and a recognition that relative hegemonies in Western Arabia had shifted. A conversion on the road to Damascus was quite a different matter from a conversion that occurred while Muḥammad was on the road to Mecca, accompanied by a large army.

To be sure, the question of sincerity is raised in our sources,[38] and genuine religious conviction may have played a role in some conversions,[39] especially if one believed that military success was an indication of divine approval and

[37] Though with this said, the criticism of hypocritical or insincere belief is a significant motif in the Qur'ān (e.g. 2:8–20; 3:119, 167, 5:41, 61; 9:8). On this subject, see C. P. Adang's entry, 'Hypocrites and Hypocrisy,' in *EQ*, vol. 2, pp. 468–72; A. Brockett's article, 'al-Munāfiḳūn,' in *EI2*, vol. 7, pp. 561–62; and 'Hypocrites, the,' in M. Mir, *Dictionary of Qur'ānic Terms and Concepts* (New York/London, 1987), pp. 97–98. The Qur'ān's constant worry over insincere belief ('Traditionally, all passages referring to the hypocrites have been considered Medinan, both by Muslim commentators and by modern scholars,' Adang, pp. 468–69) can be taken as an implicit recognition of the complicated nature of incentives for religious conversion and affiliation in contexts where the religious group being joined enjoys political hegemony in a society. R. Szpiech, 'Conversion as a Historiographical Problem. The Case of Zoraya/Isabel de Solís,' in Y. Fox and Y. Yisraeli, eds., *Contesting Inter-Religious Conversion in the Medieval World* (London/New York, 2017), pp. 24–38, attempts to problematize and historicize the idea of 'conversion,' pointing out that, among other things, 'Christian assumptions sometimes creep into considerations of conversion' (p. 30) in historical discussions of the subject.

[38] In addition to the Qur'ānic evidence discussed in the previous note, it is worth mentioning that one also encounters in the sources some version of the expression *ḥasuna Islāmuhu* or *ḥasuna Islāmuhum*, which literally means something to the effect of 'his/their Islam/submission was good' or 'he/they was/were a sincere Muslim,' and which refers to a person having sincere belief, both inwardly and outwardly. Cf. the definition given in Ibn Ḥajar al-ʿAsqalānī, *Fatḥ al-bārī bi-sharḥ Ṣaḥīḥ al-Bukhārī*, vol. 1, p. 99 (ed. ʿA. al-ʿAzīz b. ʿAbd Allāh b. Bāz [Beirut, n.d.]) and see the brief discussion of this expression in E. Landau-Tasseron, *Biographies of the Prophet's Companions and Their Successors* (HṬ 39) (Albany, 1998), p. 93, n. 452. A. Nef's discomfort with historians discussing the subjects of sincerity and levels of religious understanding among converts to Islam is well taken (see 'Conversion et islamisation: quelques réflexions depuis les VIIe-Xe s.' in P. Gelez and G. Grivaud, *Les conversions à l'Islam en Asie Mineure, dans les Balkans et dans le monde musulman: comparaisons et perspectives: actes du colloque de l'École française d'Athènes, 26-28 avril 2012* [Athens, 2016], pp. 231–32), but it needs to be emphasized that concern about such questions are found in medieval sources themselves—beginning with the Qur'ān (see previous note), and therefore should be, at a minimum, raised in any historically responsible discussion of conversion and Islamization.

[39] Or was at least portrayed as having played a role. ʿAmr b. al-ʿĀṣ, for instance, is supposed to have told Muḥammad: 'I did not become a Muslim on account of wealth. I converted, rather, out of a desire

providence.[40] Nevertheless, other factors—e.g., political allegiance and sheer expediency—seem to have been prominent in the decisions of many to become followers of the Prophet. Once Muḥammad and his community in Medina gained hegemony in the Arabian peninsula, the religious incentive structure there was altered, in much the same way that Constantine's conversion to Christianity and Theodosius's eventual proclamation of Christianity as the official religion of the Roman empire affected the meaning and benefits of conversion to Christianity in a late Roman context. How would the history of Christianity have been different if the emperor Theodosius had been a first-century figure and Jesus's leading religious opponents had taken over leadership of his movement a few decades after his death? Given the social, economic, and other advantages that would accrue to a person who adopted the religion of the hegemonic segment of society, and given the mass nature of many

---

for Islam and so that I could be with the Apostle of God.' See Aḥmad b. Ḥanbal, *al-Musnad*, vol. 4, p. 197 (Cairo, 1895).

[40] Cf. e.g., Ibn Sa'd, *Kitāb al-ṭabaqāt al-kabīr*, vol. 1.2, p. 70: 'The Arabs were waiting for the conquest (*al-fatḥ*) [of Mecca] to embrace Islam, saying, "Look! If he triumphs over them, he is truthful and a prophet.' And when word of the conquest reached us, every tribe rushed to embrace Islam' (ed. Mittwoch and Sachau, p. 70; ET also available in Haq and Ghazanfar, *Kitab al-tabaqat al-kabir*, vol. 1, pp. 395–96). Cf. also, Aḥmad b. Ḥanbal, *al-Musnad*, vol. 5, p. 30. On the religious and conversionary consequences of military victory, see the observation of Giovanna Calasso in G. Calasso, 'Récits de conversion, zèle dévotionnel et instruction religieuse dans les biographies des "gens de Baṣra" du *Kitāb al-Ṭabaqāt* d'Ibn Sa'd,' in M. García-Arenal, ed., *Conversions islamiques: identités religieuses en islam méditerranéen/Islamic Conversions: Religious Identities in Mediterranean Islam* (Paris, 2001), p. 44. The idea that divine favor could be known through military success was not of course unique to Western Arabia: on the theology of victory, e.g., in fourth-century Roman Christianity, see F. Heim, *La théologie de la victoire de Constantin à Théodose* (Paris, 1992). The idea that it is God who bears responsibility for military victory and protects his people in conflicts can of course easily be found in the Bible—see, e.g., Exodus 15:3–18; Numbers 10:35; Joshua 1:5–9; 1 Samuel 17:45–47, Psalm 44:1–8, etc.

Also see Watt, *Muhammad at Medina*, pp. 66–67, on the idea of *fatḥ* ('conquest') having the additional semantic connotation of judging between two groups and making a doubtful situation between two parties clear. In the Qur'ān, the verb *fataḥa* often has the meaning 'to decide': see further the comment of J. Scheiner, 'Reflections on Hoyland's *In God's Path*,' *Bustan: The Middle East Book Review* 7 (2016), p. 28, and R. Paret, 'Die Bedeutungsentwicklung von Arabisch *Fatḥ*,' in J.M. Barral, ed., *Orientalia Hispanica, sive studia F.M. Pareja octogenario dictata*, vol. 1 (Leiden, 1974), pp. 537–41.

The Christian charge that Muḥammad was not a true Prophet because he used violence can possibly be seen as a reaction to attitudes and claims that his military success, and later, that of his followers, was proof of the divine origin of his mission. This was a (counter?) charge that appeared very early in the history of Christian-Muslim relations. See, e.g., *Doctrina Jacobi Nuper Baptizati* 16 (ed. V. Déroche, 'Juifs et Chrétiens dans l'Orient du VIIe siècle,' *Travaux et Mémoires* 11 [1991], p. 209), where Muḥammad is called a false Prophet on the basis of his coming with a sword and chariots (on the date of this text, possibly as early as 634, see below, n. 129). When 'Abd al-Malik asked the East Syrian catholicos Henanisho (sed. ca. 686–700) what he made of the religion of the Arabs, the catholicos reportedly replied: 'It is a kingdom which has arisen through the sword and not a faith that is confirmed by divine miracles, like that of Christ and that of the Old [Covenant], through Moses.' See Bar Hebraeus, *Ecclesiastical History* 2.29 (ed. Abbeloos and Lamy, vol. 3, col. 135).

conversions, we should not assume that, for many Arab followers of the Prophet Muḥammad in the seventh century, Islam translated into a well-articulated (or even poorly articulated) and carefully observed code of moral conduct.

MUSLIMS BECOMING… MUSLIM

Predictably, these late and mass conversions had religious consequences for the converts and also for their descendants. We should not be astonished to find reports from the first century that Basrans did not know about the religious duty of paying alms at the end of Ramaḍān (*zakāt al-fiṭr*), or that they had no idea about how to perform prayer and had to be shown, or that the people of Syria did not know that the number of obligatory prayers was five, or that the only person the tribe of ʿAbd al-Ashhal could find to lead their prayers was a slave. Or, that people were reciting Arabic poetry from the pulpits of mosques, mistakenly thinking they were reciting verses from the Qur'ān. Or, that in the time of al-Ḥajjāj and ʿUmar II (d. AH 101/AD 720), people were said not to know when prayer times were.[41] Salima al-Jarmī led the prayers for his tribe at the age of six because they could find nobody who knew more Qur'ān than he did.[42]

There are indications of pre-Islamic and pre-conversionary religious inertia. Musaylima, Muḥammad's rival prophet, reportedly had followers living in Kufa into the time of ʿAbd Allāh b. Masʿūd (d. /AH 32/ AD 652–653); they had their own mosque there and the confession 'There is no god but God and Musaylima is the Prophet of God' was part of their call to prayer.[43] Another

[41] I have taken all these examples from I. Goldziher, *Muslim Studies (Muhammedanische Studien)*, vol. 2, trans. C. R. Barber and S. M. Stern (London, 1971), pp. 39–40. In support of his 'Believers to Muslims' thesis, Fred Donner has collected a variety of reports which suggest that central Islamic religious practices were ill-defined and not uniform well into the Umayyad period: see F. M. Donner, 'Umayyad Efforts at Legitimation: The Umayyads' Silent Heritage,' in A. Borrut and P. M. Cobb, eds., *Umayyad Legacies: Medieval Memories from Syria to Spain* (Leiden/Boston, 2010), pp. 193–201. Such reports can also be seen as evidence of the consequences of factors I have emphasized in this book: mass illiteracy, mass conversion, poor catechesis, and so on.

[42] Ibn Saʿd, *Kitāb al-ṭabaqāt al-kabīr*, vol. 7.1, pp. 63–64 (ed. B. Meissner [Leiden, 1915]; translation available in Bewley, *The Men of Madina*, vol. 1, p. 54). Another way of reading this report would of course be to see it not as a commentary on the low levels of religious learning in Salima's tribe, but rather Salima's extraordinary precociousness. For additional reports on Salima leading prayers at the age of six, see Ibn Sa'd, *Kitāb al-ṭabaqāt al-kabīr*, vol. 1.2, pp. 69–70 (ed. Mittwoch and Sachau; translation available in Haq and Ghazanfar, *Kitab al-tabaqat al-kabir*, vol. 1, pp. 395–96). Al-Jāḥiẓ, *al-Bayān wa-'l-tabyīn*, p. 337 (ed. D. Juwaydī [Beirut, 2013]), gives stories of prominent Muslims in the Umayyad period making grammatical mistakes in their Qur'ānic recitation.

[43] See M. J. Kister's article, 'Musaylima,' in *EQ*, vol. 3, pp. 460–63 (this report is on p. 463).

story has Ibn Mas'ūd summoning a group from the Banū Ḥanīfa (Musaylima's tribe) after receiving a report from a man who prayed in their mosque and heard the imam reciting the words of Musaylima rather than the Qur'ān. 'Abd Allāh called them to repentance, and they all repented, we are told, save Ibn al-Nawwāḥa, whose head 'Abd Allāh had cut off.[44] Probably related to this report is another one in which Ibn Mas'ūd is said to have killed the imam Ibn al-Nawwāḥa for reciting, in a mosque, a text that was not part of Muḥammad's revelation; there were a number of others complicit in Ibn al-Nawwāḥa's recitation, but rather than have them killed, Ibn Mas'ūd had them sent to Syria where, he said, God would either grant them repentance or they would be wiped out by the plague.[45]

Reports of such continuities from the pre-Islamic period or from before a group or individual had converted to Islam can be found also apart from Musaylima and his tribe: One anecdote tells us of people who were receiving governmental stipends and provisions (*al-'aṭā' wa-'l-rizq*) and praying in the mosque, but who were secretly worshipping idols; 'Alī b. Abī Ṭālib put an end to this situation by gathering them all together and burning them alive.[46] Evidence for momentum from the pagan past would continue well beyond the life of 'Alī: 'Umar II, alarmed at reports that women were going out upon the death of somebody and showing their hair and wailing, wrote to his governors that their behavior was 'like the action of the people of the Jahiliyya' and ordered them to crack down hard on this practice.[47]

We have seen already that Christians were engaging in a variety of prognosticatory, divinatory, and magical practices that made Jacob of Edessa none too happy. Early Muslims were doing similar things. Jabala b. al-Azraq reported that the Prophet himself was once stung by a scorpion while praying, 'and so the people used a charm on him (*raqāhu al-nās*). When he recovered, he said, "God healed me, not your spell."'[48] Promises of special privileges in the afterlife for Muslims who did not engage in magical or divinatory practices might also be taken as suggestive that just these sorts of things were widespread among

[44] Ibn Abī Shayba, *al-Muṣannaf*, vol. 11, pp. 288–89 (no. 33284) (ed. Ḥ. b. 'Abd Allāh al-Jum'a and M. b. Ibrāhīm al-Laḥīdān) (Riyad, 2004). And compare this report with no. 33285 (p. 289), which is related to no. 33284, and also the report in 'Abd al-Razzāq (see next note). Another related report has Ibn Mas'ūd call to repentance members of the Banū Ḥanīfa who were spreading and reciting the *ḥadīth* of Musaylima. Some repented, but others did not, and 'Abd Allāh beheaded those who refused (Ibn Abī Shayba, *al-Muṣannaf*, vol. 11, p. 291 [no. 33296]).

[45] 'Abd al-Razzāq, *al-Muṣannaf*, vol. 10, p. 169 (no. 18708).

[46] Ibn Abī Shayba, *al-Muṣannaf*, vol. 11, pp. 289–90 (no. 33287).

[47] Ibn Sa'd, *Kitāb al-ṭabaqāt al-kabīr*, vol. 5, p. 290 (ed. K. V. Zetterstéen [Leiden, 1905]; my translation made with reference to the ET in A. A. Bewley, *The Men of Madina*, vol. 2 [London, 2000], pp. 245–46).

[48] Ibn Sa'd, *Kitāb al-ṭabaqāt al-kabīr*, vol. 7.2, p. 146 (ed. Sachau [Leiden, 1918]; my translation made with reference to the ET in Bewley, *The Men of Medina*, vol. 1, p. 267).

adherents of the new religion. 'My Lord promised me that he would cause seventy thousand people from my community to enter into paradise without reckoning,' Muḥammad is supposed to have stated. 'It was said to him, "Who are those?" He said, 'They are the ones who do not seek to use charms and who do not do evil auguries and who are not cauterized by burning irons, but who rely upon their Lord.'[49] When Muṭarrif b. 'Abd Allāh (d. AH 87/AD 705) had a problem with urine retention, he had his son summoned. The son recited a verse from the Qur'ān to him and brought him a physician. 'My son,' Muṭarrif asked, 'What is this?' 'A doctor,' he replied. 'I forbid you,' Muṭarrif replied, 'to make me carry a charm or to hang a bead upon me.'[50] When Muslims came into the Fertile Crescent, they found themselves surrounded by local practices of divination which were also a cause of worry. 'A letter from 'Umar came to us,' Bajāla b. 'Abada reported, '[saying] "Kill every enchanter and enchantress." His letter,' Bajāla continued, 'was concerning the Magians.'[51] The directive must have not been completely successful, for in the early eighth century, the caliph al-Walīd issued another order that all enchanters (*harrāshē*) be put to death.[52]

We saw in Part II that the confessionally confused situation of the post-Chalcedonian world triggered educational efforts to counteract it. Muslim religious authorities took similar steps to counter catechetical deficits in their new community. 'Umar b. al-Khaṭṭāb sent 'Abd al-Raḥmān b. Ghanm b. Sa'd al-Ash'arī to Syria to give people religious instruction (*yufaqqihu 'l-nās*)[53] and sent ten men to Basra to do the same (*yufaqqihūna 'l-nās*).[54] In Syria, 'Abd al-Raḥmān b. Ghanm had been an acquaintance of Mu'ādh b. Jabal; years before, Mu'ādh had been sent by Muḥammad to Yemen as an administrator and a teacher (*'āmilan wa-mu'alliman*).[55] And Syria, Basra, and Yemen were

[49] Ibn Sa'd, *Kitāb al-ṭabaqāt al-kabīr*, vol. 7.1, p. 52 (ed. Meissner [Leiden, 1915]; my translation made with reference to the ET in Bewley, *The Men of Medina*, vol. 1, p. 44).

[50] Ibn Sa'd, *Kitāb al-ṭabaqāt al-kabīr*, vol. 7.1, pp. 105–106 (ed. B. Meissner [Leiden, 1915], quote on p. 106; my translation made with reference to the ET in Bewley, *The Men of Medina*, vol. 1, p. 93, though in disagreement with her rendering: 'I forbid you to burden me with a charm or puncture me.' *Uḥrij 'alayka an tuḥammilanī 'alā ruqyatan aw tu'alliqa 'alayya kharazatan*).

[51] Ibn Sa'd, *Kitāb al-ṭabaqāt al-kabīr*, vol. 7.1, p. 94 (ed. Meissner [Leiden, 1915]; my translation made with reference to the ET in Bewley, *The Men of Medina*, vol. 1, p. 81).

[52] Michael the Great, *Chronicle* 11.17 (ed. Chabot, 4.451 = 2.481).

[53] Ibn Sa'd, *Kitāb al-ṭabaqāt al-kabīr*, vol. 7.2, p. 152 (ed. Sachau [Leiden, 1918]; my translation made with reference to the ET in Bewley, *The Men of Medina*, vol. 1, p. 273).

[54] See al-Mizzī, *Tahdhīb al-kamāl fī asmā' al-rijāl* (ed. B. 'Awwād Ma'rūf) vol. 26 (Beirut, 1992), p. 174 (report of Ḥasan al-Baṣrī about 'Abd Allāh b. Mughaffal). Cf. W. B. Hallaq, *The Origins and Evolution of Islamic Law* (Cambridge, 2005), p. 31.

[55] Ibn Sa'd, *Kitāb al-ṭabaqāt al-kabīr*, vol. 7.2, p. 114 (ed. Sachau [Leiden, 1918]; ET available in Bewley, *The Men of Madina*, vol. 1, p. 239). For the connection between 'Abd al-Raḥmān and Mu'ādh, see Ibn Sa'd, vol. 7.2, p. 152 (ET available in Bewley, *The Men of Medina*, vol. 1, p. 273).

not alone: ʿUmar also sent ʿAbd Allāh b. Masʿūd to Kufa to be in charge of the treasury there—but also to teach the Kufans the Qur'ān and give them religious instruction (*yufaqqihahum*).[56] It is difficult to know either how these teachers were received and what their results were. For instance: when ʿUmar wrote to one of his governors and told him to give people a stipend for learning the Qur'ān, he received a reply back that people were learning the Qur'ān who had no interest in it and only an interest in getting paid.[57]

ʿUmar sent out religious experts to catechize Muslims because he was no doubt keenly aware of the shallow level of religious knowledge that existed among many in the young community of the Prophet's followers. According to al-Azdī, when ʿUmar was returning to Medina from Syria, he stopped at a watering point of the tribe Judhām where he was told about a man married to two sisters and had the man brought to him. 'Who are these two women you have?' ʿUmar asked. "My two wives,' the man responded. 'What is their relationship?' ʿUmar wanted to know. When the man told ʿUmar that they were sisters, his response was incredulity: 'What is your religion? Aren't you a Muslim?' 'Of course,' the man responded. 'You didn't know that this is forbidden for you!?' ʿUmar answered back, citing Q 4:33 which forbade such marriages. 'No,' the man told ʿUmar, 'I didn't know that and it isn't forbidden for me.'[58]

Another story connected to ʿUmar's return to Medina from Syria had him meet an old man who had agreed to share his wife with a younger man—every other day—in exchange for the younger man's pasturing and watering his animals. ʿUmar had the men brought to him. 'What is your religion?', ʿUmar asked. '[We are] Muslims,' they replied. 'What is this that has reached me concerning you?', ʿUmar asked again. The men did not know what he was talking about; when he told them about the issue of their shared wife, they did not deny it. 'Did you not know,' ʿUmar asked, 'that in the Islamic religion

[56] Al-Masʿūdī, *Murūj al-dhahab wa-maʿādin al-jawhar*, vol. 4, p. 256 (ed. and trans. C. Barbier de Meynard and P. de Courteille, *Les prairies d'or* [Paris, 1865]). Cf. Arnold, *The Preaching of Islam*, p. 51.

[57] M. Ḥamīd Allāh, *Majmūʿat al-wathāʾiq al-siyāsiyya lil-ʿahd al-nabawī wa-ʾl-khilāfa al-rāshida* (Beirut, 1987), p. 510. Any account of religious instruction in this early period should also mention the activities of the *quṣṣāṣ*, popular storytellers and preachers who were known for their interactions with everyday believers and who came to have a mixed reputation in the later medieval Islamic tradition. On the *quṣṣāṣ*, see the classic treatment by Goldziher in *Muslim Studies*, vol. 2, pp. 152–59 and more recently, L. R. Armstrong, *The Quṣṣāṣ of Early Islam* (Leiden/Boston, 2017). See also Chapter 14, n. 204.

[58] al-Azdī, *Taʾrīkh futūḥ al-shām*, pp. 262–64 (ed. ʿAbd Allāh Munʿim ʿAbd Allāh ʿĀmir [Cairo, 1970]). Compare this with another story in which ʿUmar is brought a woman who has married her slave, whereupon he beats her, divorces them, quotes the Qur'ān to her incredulously (70:30), and then writes to the garrison cities that women who marry their slaves or who marry without a witness or an authorized agent should be beaten. Ḥamīd Allāh, *Majmūʿat al-wathāʾiq al-siyāsiyya*, p. 512.

this is forbidden and that it is not appropriate?' 'No, by God,' they answered, 'we didn't know.'[59]

These two incidents are quite similar to Simeon the Mountaineer's encounter with the uneducated Christian shepherds in the mountains. They were Christians but knew very little about normative Christianity. And even if both anecdotes were literary inventions, they nevertheless vividly point to precisely the sort of situations we would expect to have occurred among ordinary, simple Muslims, people who had become Muslim by virtue of mass conversions effected by representatives, or the descendants of such people.[60] Reports of people converting to Islam and then subsequently returning to polytheism can also be taken as indicative of how thin conversion was in some parts of the Muslim community in the early period and how little people understood of just what conversion entailed.[61]

The practical expectations for what a conversion will have meant were low, even in the time of the Prophet. In one anecdote, we learn that Muḥammad was supposed to have sent Khālid b. al-Walīd to investigate the charge that a certain Arab tribe, the Banū al-Muṣṭaliq, had apostatized. After spending a night with the tribe, however, Khālid's spies reported that the tribe was holding to Islam and that they had heard their *adhān* and their prayers. Khālid came the next morning and was happy with what he saw going on among the tribe, we are told, and conveyed all this back to the Prophet.[62] Apart from the claim that they were 'holding to Islam' (*mutamassikūn bi-'l-Islām*) and that Khālid 'saw what he liked,' the most important indicator of a conversion seems to have been that people were praying.[63]

Decades after the Prophet's death, joining his religious community still did not necessarily translate into a solid body of knowledge about the contents and implications of the new faith, such as they were. 'Urwa, we are told, wrote to 'Umar b. 'Abd al-'Azīz about a man who had converted to Islam and then apostatized. 'Umar responded by prescribing a sort of religious examination. 'Ask him,' 'Umar II wrote to 'Urwa, 'about the religious precepts of Islam

[59] al-Azdī, *Ta'rīkh futūḥ al-shām*, pp. 265–66.

[60] For these two anecdotes from al-Azdī and analysis, see N. Khalek, *Damascus after the Muslim Conquest: Text and Image in Early Islam* (Oxford/New York, 2011), pp. 64–65.

[61] For examples of such reports, see, 'Abd al-Razzāq, *al-Muṣannaf*, vol. 10, p. 164 (no. 18693) and pp. 165–66 (no. 18696).

[62] Abū al-Faraj al-Iṣbahānī, *Kitāb al-Aghānī*, vol. 4, p. 185.

[63] Note the report in which 'Umar b. al-Khaṭṭāb writes to his governors and tells them, 'Your most important matter, in my opinion, is prayer. He who observes it and is mindful of it has preserved his religion and he who neglects it is even more neglectful of what is apart from it.' Mālik b. Anas, *al-Muwaṭṭa'*, vol. 1 (ed. M. Fu'ād 'Abd al-Bāqī) (Beirut, 1985), p. 6, no. 6. For the reported importance of prayer to 'Umar b. al-Khaṭṭāb, see G.H.A. Juynboll, *Muslim Tradition* (Cambridge, 1983), pp. 25–26.

(*sharāʾiʿ al-Islām*). If he already knows them, then offer Islam to him—and if he refuses, sever his neck.' Offering apostates a chance to return to Islam was a standard practice. Especially interesting is the second part of 'Umar's response: 'If he does not know them [i.e., the precepts],' he went on, 'then impose the poll-tax on him harshly and leave him be.'[64] Here is an acknowledgement that there were people calling themselves Muslims who did not know what that entailed; they were Muslims in name only—just like Simeon's shepherds. 'Umar b. 'Abd al-'Azīz himself, like 'Umar b. al-Khaṭṭāb, sought to improve the levels of religious knowledge in the Muslim community: he sent, for instance, a *mawlā* named Nāfiʿ to Egypt to teach the people there the traditions of the Prophet (*yuʿallimuhum al-sunan*) and sent Juʿthul b. 'Āhān to North Africa to teach the people there Qur'ānic recitation.[65]

There are other pieces of evidence that suggest an uneven and shallow grasp of the particulars of Muḥammad's religious message among early members of the Prophet's community and a lack of knowledge of, or disregard for, his teaching . No less a figure than Ibn 'Umar (d. AD 693/AH 73), the son of 'Umar b. al-Khaṭṭāb and himself a prominent Companion and important authority in a number of traditions, might not be fully aware of the contents of the Qur'ān. One report has 'Abd al-Raḥmān b. Abī Hurayra ask him about the propriety of eating fish that washed ashore. Ibn 'Umar forbade him from eating such fish, but then, unsure, called for a Qur'ānic codex. When he read 5:96, which declared the fish of the sea *ḥalāl*, he sent to 'Abd al-Raḥmān and told him there was no harm in eating the fish.[66] Ibn 'Umar himself reportedly spent eight years learning Sūrat al-Baqara, the longest extant *sūra* in the Qur'ān.[67] Evidence apart from Ibn 'Umar can be pointed to as well. Though the Qur'ān explicitly ordered cutting off the hands of thieves (5:38) (a view reiterated by later Islamic law) in the first half of the eighth century (AD) John of Damascus would report that Muslims punished thieves with flogging.[68]

[64] 'Abd al-Razzāq, *al-Muṣannaf*, vol. 10, p. 171 (no. 18713).

[65] al-Suyūṭī, *Min ḥusn al-muḥāḍara fī akhbār Miṣr wa-'l-Qāhira*, vol. 1 (Cairo, 1327), p. 119. For this, cf. G. Makdisi, 'Madrasa,' in *EI2*, vol. 5, p. 1124. Al-Mizzī, *Tahdhīb al-kamāl fī asmāʾ al-rijāl*, vol. 5, p. 558, gives his name as Ju'thal b. Hā'ān. For 'Umar II's attempts at Islamic education, see further J. van Ess, *Theologie und Gesellschaft im 2. Und 3. Jahrhundert Hidschra. Eine Geschichte des religiösen Denkens im frühen Islam*, vol. 1 (Berlin/New York, 1991), p. 42 [= *Theology and Society in the Second and Third Centuries of the Hijra: A History of Religious Thought in Early Islam*, vo1. 1 (Leiden/Boston, 2017), p. 49].

[66] Mālik b. Anas, *al-Muwaṭṭaʾ*, vol. 2, p. 494 (no. 9). For this, see Goldziher, *Muslim Studies*, vol. 2, p. 78. On Ibn 'Umar, see L. Veccia Vaglieri's article, ''Abd Allāh b. 'Umar b. al-Khaṭṭāb,' in *EI2*, vol. 1, pp. 53–54.

[67] Mālik b. Anas, *al-Muwaṭṭaʾ*, vol. 1, p. 205, no. 11. (A report from Mālik).

[68] See J. Schacht, *An Introduction to Islamic Law* (Oxford, 1964), p. 18 and the next note.

INTOXICANTS AS A DIAGNOSTIC CASE?

This last example was adduced by Joseph Schacht, perhaps the twentieth century's most important scholar of Islamic law and one of its most influential interpreters of the history of *ḥadīth* literature. Schacht pointed to this question of cutting off the hand of a thief versus flogging him, along with other instances where Umayyad legal practice diverged from Qur'ānic prescriptions, in order to suggest that the Qur'ān was not seen as an important source of law in the first Islamic century, a point that was taken up and expanded after Schacht.[69] At present, I am interested in evidence for confusion about, lack of knowledge of, and disregard for Prophetic and Qur'ānic teaching in the early decades of Muslim rule in the Middle East, and Schacht's suggestion that the Qur'ān may have had some sort of secondary legal status in this period is potentially one way to explain it—at least partially. But Harald Motzki's meticulous and persuasive arguments, against Schacht, that at least some Muslims were in fact appealing to the Qur'ān, as well as to the example of the Prophet, as the basis for conduct in this early period should give us pause before fully embracing such a suggestion.[70]

A perspective that takes seriously the existence of a layering of knowledge within a religious community and the consequences of mass conversion can perhaps offer another way of accounting for the discrepancies between Umayyad practice and Qur'ānic prescription that Schacht identified—and may explain as well other instances when early Muslims seemed unaware of, or only selectively heedful of, the teachings of the Qur'ān or the Prophet. Perhaps the most vivid illustration of the consequences of the phenomena I have emphasized is the question of the consumption of intoxicating drinks by some members of the early Muslim community. Let us therefore pause to examine it.

[69] For the classic statement of the status of the Qur'ān in earliest Islamic legal decisions, see J. Schacht, *The Origins of Muhammadan Jurisprudence* (Oxford, 1950), pp. 190–91, 224–27, esp. p. 224: 'apart from the most elementary rules, norms derived from the Koran were introduced into Muhammadan law almost invariably at a secondary stage.' See P. Crone, 'Two Legal Problems Bearing on the Early History of the Qur'ān,' *JSAI* 18 (1994), pp. 1–37, esp. 10–21, and cf. Hoyland, *Seeing Islam*, p. 550. In a similar vein, as part of his Believers-to-Muslims thesis, F. M. Donner has suggested that the Qur'ān came to have increased importance in a host of contexts around the year 700; see his 'Qur'ânicization of Religio-Political Discourse in the Umayyad Period,' *Revue des mondes musulmans et de la Méditerranée* 129 (2011), pp. 79–92.

[70] Against Schacht and for evidence that 'already in the first/seventh century, people consciously resorted to the Qur'ān and to rulings of the Prophet as sources of the law, if not as extensively as later times,' see H. Motzki, *The Origins of Islamic Jurisprudence: Meccan Fiqh before the Classical Schools*, trans. M. H. Katz (Leiden/Boston/Köln, 2002), pp. 114–17, 125–36, 156–57, etc. (quote at 295).

The Qur'ān expressed an increasingly negative attitude towards wine (*khamr*), one that culminated in its proscription (2:219, 4:43, 5:90),[71] yet the consumption of alcohol seems to have been widespread among early Muslims. Even being an associate of Muḥammad was not necessarily a hindrance: one Companion, al-Walīd b. 'Utba, an eventual governor of Kufa, was famous for his love of wine (*al-khamr*). He was especially given to drinking with Abū Zubayd, a Christian whom al-Walīd eventually induced to convert to Islam.[72] Another Companion, Waḥshī b. Ḥarb al-Ḥabashī, was also said to be the first person beaten on account of wine (*al-khamr*) in Ḥimṣ.[73]

Belonging to a prominent family did not mean one necessarily abstained from alcohol, either. 'Alī b. al-Ḥusayn (d. AH 94/AD 712), the great-grandson of Muḥammad, for instance, is said to have made wine (*yunbidhu*) without dregs in a large leather flask during the two '*īds*.[74] Al-Walīd b. 'Uqba, the brother of 'Uthmān b. 'Affān, once reportedly led the people of Kufa in morning prayers while drunk.[75] 'Abbās b. 'Alī, the grandson of Ibn 'Abbās, the famous Companion, was a well-known consumer of alcohol and a boon companion to al-Akhṭal, the Christian poet.[76] 'Umar b. al-Khaṭṭāb's son 'Abd al-Raḥmān was reported to have imbibed an intoxicating drink in Egypt, an offense that led to his receiving lashes in Egypt and then being sent back to Medina where his father again had him severely whipped.[77] Indeed, the Prophet himself was said to have drunk the intoxicant called *nabīdh*,[78] and

[71] See the article 'Khamr' by A. J. Wensinck in *EI2*, vol. 4, pp. 994–96.

[72] For al-Walīd's love of drinking, especially with Abū Zubayd, see al-Mizzī, *Tahdhīb al-kamāl fī asmā' al-rijāl*, vol. 31, p. 57. For his inducing Abū Zubayd to convert to Islam, see al-Ṭabarī, *Ta'rīkh* 1.5, 2843 (ed. E. Prym [Leiden, 1893]; ET available in R. S. Humphreys, *The Crisis of the Early Caliphate* [HṬ 15] [Albany, 1990], p. 49). Cf. also, C. E. Bosworth's article, 'al-Walīd b. 'Uḳba b. Abī Mu'ayṭ,' in *EI2*, vol. 11, p. 130. Also, see Chapter 14, n. 175.

[73] See Ibn Sa'd, *Kitāb al-ṭabaqāt al-kabīr*, vol. 7.2, p. 137 (ed. Sachau [Leiden, 1918]; ET available in Bewley, *The Men of Madina*, vol. 1, pp. 259–60).

[74] Ibn Sa'd, *Kitāb al-ṭabaqāt al-kabīr*, vol. 5, p. 161 (ed. Zetterstéen [Leiden, 1905]; ET available in Bewley, *Men of Madina*, vol. 2, pp. 140-141).

[75] For this, 'Alī b. Abī Ṭālib had him whipped, with 'Uthmān present. See Ibn 'Abd Rabbih, *al-'Iqd al-Farīd*, vol. 8, p. 61 (ed. 'A. al-Majīd al-Tarḥīnī [Beirut, 1983]). See also, al-Mizzī, *Tahdhīb al-kamāl fī asmā' al-rijāl*, vol. 31, p. 57.

[76] Ibn 'Abd Rabbih, *al-'Iqd al-Farīd*, vol. 8, p. 62. Ibn Qutayba, *Kitāb al-ashriba wa-dhikr ikhtilāf al-nās fīhā*, p. 44 (ed. Y. Muḥammad al-Sawwās [Beirut, 1999]), knows him as al-'Abbās b. 'Abd Allāh b. al-'Abbās.

[77] For this, see N. Abbott, *Studies in Arabic Literary Papyri*, vol. 2: *Qur'ānic Commentary and Tradition* (Chicago, 1967), p. 109. There are also reports of two other sons of 'Umar being punished for drinking: 'Ubayd Allāh and 'Āṣim; see Ibn Qutayba, *Kitāb al-ashriba*, pp. 44–45 and Ibn 'Abd Rabbih, *al-'Iqd al-Farīd*, vol. 8, p. 62 (where 'Ubayd Allāh is 'Abd Allāh).

[78] Ibn Sa'd, *Kitāb al-ṭabaqāt al-kabīr*, vol. 2.1, p. 131 (ed. J. Horovitz [Leiden, 1909]). See the traditions collected in Ibn Qutayba, *Kitāb al-ashriba*, pp. 61–63 and cf. Ibn al-Mu'tazz, *Kitāb fuṣūl al-tamāthīl fī tabāshīr al-surūr*, p. 147 (ed. J. Qanāzi' and F. Abū Khaḍra [Damascus, 1989]). For this point, see I. Gold-

nabīdh was a drink available to pilgrims making the *ḥajj* in Mecca into the ninth century.[79]

In the decades after the Prophet's death, Syria seems to have been associated with drinking: When 'Umar b. al-Khaṭṭāb traveled there, Muslims he met complained of the disease and heaviness of the land and claimed that only drinking alcohol helped ameliorate the situation. 'Umar reportedly tried to suggest they drink honey instead, which they claimed did not improve things.[80] We have several reports of 'Umar I taking measures against Muslims who were drinking wine in Syria. 'It was mentioned to me that 'Abd Allāh and his companions were drinking a drink in Syria,' 'Umar is reported to have said, 'so I asked about it. If it is intoxicating, I will have them whipped.'[81] This was not an isolated action, either. ''Umar b. al-Khaṭṭāb burned down the house of Ruwayshid al-Thaqafī,' Ibrāhīm b. 'Abd al-Raḥmān reported: '[I]t was an inn (*ḥānūtan*) for drinking and 'Umar had forbidden that. I saw it blazing like a coal.'[82] 'Umar's measures led Rabī'a b. Umayya b. Khalaf, who particularly enjoyed drinking (*ṣāḥib sharāb*), to emigrate to Byzantine territory and apostatize from Islam.[83] But even 'Umar himself might be associated with certain kinds of intoxicating beverage: it is reported that after he was stabbed by his assassin in Medina, 'Umar was given an intoxicant (*nabīdh*) to drink.[84]

Many years after 'Umar I's strict attitude, wine was still causing people to leave Muslim-controlled territories: one report claims that 'Umar II's punishment of al-Ṣalt b. al-'Āṣī b. Wābiṣa b. Khālid, the governor (*amīr*) of the Hijaz,

---

ziher, *Introduction to Islamic Theology and Law* (Princeton, 1981), p. 60, n. 68. Wensinck, 'Khamr,' in *EI2*, vol. 4, p. 996, contains a number of citations of reports of the Prophet drinking *nabīdh*.

[79] See P. Heine's article, 'Nabīdh,' in *EI2*, vol. 7, p. 840.

[80] Mālik b. Anas, *al-Muwaṭṭa'*, vol. 2, p. 847, no. 14. For 'Umar being asked about *ṭilā'* in Jerusalem and another unnamed drink in Syria, Ḥamīd Allāh, *Majmū'at al-wathā'iq al-siyāsiyya*, p. 489. NB: there are reports of drinking in places other than Syria. See, e.g., the story of Qudāma b. Maẓ'ūn, a Companion whom 'Umar made governor of Baḥrayn and whom he later had whipped in response to allegations that Qudāma had been seen drinking and drunk: Ibn Ḥajar al-'Asqalānī, *al-Iṣāba fī tamyīz al-ṣaḥāba*, vol. 8, pp. 145–47 (no. 7082), and cf. 'Abd al-Razzāq, *al-Muṣannaf*, vol. 9, pp. 240–43 (nos. 17075–76).

[81] Ibn Abī Shayba, *al-Muṣannaf*, vol. 8, p. 81 (no. 24106).

[82] See Ibn Sa'd, *Kitāb al-ṭabaqāt al-kabīr*, vol. 5, p. 40 (ed. Zettersteen [Leiden, 1905]; my translation made with reference to the ET in Bewley, *The Men of Madina*, vol. 2, p. 36). Cf. also vol. 3.1, p. 202 (ed. E. Sachau [Leiden, 1904]).

[83] 'Umar had first expelled Rabī'a to Khaybar. Ibn Sa'd, *Kitāb al-ṭabaqāt al-kabīr*, vol. 3.1, p. 202 (ed. Sachau [Leiden, 1904]). For this point, see Lammens, 'Études sur le règne du calife Omaiyade Mo'awiya Ier,' (part 3), p. 275, and see 274–75 for examples of Muslim wine-drinking and 'Umar's attempts to suppress it. See, too, the report in al-Nasā'ī, *Kitāb al-sunan al-kubrā*, vol. 5, p. 105 (no. 5166) (ed. Ḥ. 'Abd al-Mun'im Shalabī [Beirut, 2001]).

[84] Ibn Sa'd, *Kitāb al-ṭabaqāt al-kabīr*, vol. 3.1, p. 257 (ed. Sachau [Leiden, 1904]). In Ibn al-Mu'tazz's (d. AH 296/AD 908) version of this story, a physician asked 'Umar what his favorite drink was, and he replied, *nabīdh*; see *Kitāb fuṣūl al-tamāthīl fī tabāshīr al-surūr*, p. 147.

for drinking wine (*al-khamr*) angered al-Ṣalt so much that he emigrated to Constantinople and eventually converted to Christianity.[85] When the people of Medina expelled the Umayyads from their city in AH 63 (AD 682), they made public the vice of the ruler Yazīd b. Muʿāwiya and gave their allegiance to ʿAbd Allāh b. Ḥanẓala. 'O people, fear God alone—He has no partner!' Abū ʿAbd Allāh is reported to have said, 'By God, we only rose up against Yazīd when feared that we would be stoned from heaven: for a man marries mothers and daughters and sisters and drinks wine (*al-khamr*) and forsakes prayer!'[86] It was claimed that during Yazīd's period of rule people were openly drinking in Mecca and Medina.[87]

When Ayyūb b. Shuraḥbīl became governor of Egypt in AH 99 (AD 717), ʿUmar II sent a letter forbidding the drinking of wine (*khamr*) and ordering the destruction of taverns.[88] Another letter, from ʿUmar II to his provinces, indicates that some people during his reign were citing the precedent of ʿUmar I (d. AH 23/AD 644) and other prominent early Muslims to justify drinking the alcoholic *ṭilāʾ*, but he nevertheless forbade *ṭilāʾ* everywhere.[89] At Khunāṣira (near Aleppo), he ordered that wineskins (*ziqāq al-khamr*) be cut open and wine bottles broken.[90] Indeed, Khunāṣira seems to have been a hotbed of intoxication: ʿAbd al-Majīd b. Suhayl reported going there and finding a house known for wine and open revelry where people would gather to drink wine (*khamr*). He reported it to the commander of ʿUmar II's local law enforcement and was told that ʿUmar had been made aware of the situation. 'In the case of

[85] Abū al-Faraj al-Iṣbahānī, *Kitāb al-Aghānī*, vol. 5, p. 184. Another story (p. 185), has al-Wābiṣā [sic] convert as a result of being captured and tortured and eventually marry a Christian woman and have two Christian sons. On Rabīʿa (see n. 83, above) and this al-Ṣalt b. al-ʿĀṣī b. Wābiṣa, see D. Cook, 'Apostasy from Islam: A Historical Perspective,' *JSAI* 31 (2006), pp. 260–61.

[86] Ibn Saʿd, *Kitāb al-ṭabaqāt al-kabīr*, vol. 5, p. 47 (ed. Zetterstéen [Leiden, 1905]; my translation, made with reference to Bewley, *The Men of Madina*, vol. 2, p. 42).

[87] al-Masʿūdī, *Murūj al-dhahab wa-maʿādin al-jawhar*, vol. 5, p. 157. For this, see Lammens, 'Études sur le règne du calife Omaiyade Moʿawiya Ier,' (part 3), pp. 271–72.

[88] al-Kindī, *Kitāb al-wulāh wa-kitāb al-quḍāh*, p. 68 (ed. R. Guest, *The Governors and Judges of Egypt* [London/Leiden, 1912]), and cf. Ibn ʿAbd al-Ḥakam, *Sīrat ʿUmar b. ʿAbd al-ʿAzīz*, pp. 99–102 (ed. A. ʿUbayd) (Damascus, 1964).

[89] See Ibn ʿAbd al-Ḥakam, *Sīrat ʿUmar b. ʿAbd al-ʿAzīz*, pp. 97–98 (ed. A. ʿUbayd [Beirut, 1984]; ET available in H.A.R. Gibb, 'The fiscal rescript of ʿUmar II,' *Arabica* 2 [1955], pp. 5–6) and Ibn Saʿd, *Kitāb al-ṭabaqāt al-kabīr*, vol. 5, p. 256 (ed. Zetterstéen; ET available in Bewley, *The Men of Madina*, vol. 2, p. 216). On ʿUmar I and *ṭilāʾ*, see also Wensinck's article 'Khamr' in *EI2*, vol. 4, p. 995. The report in Mālik's *Muwaṭṭaʾ* about ʿUmar suggesting Muslims in Syria drink honey rather than an intoxicating drink (Mālik b. Anas, *al-Muwaṭṭaʾ*, vol. 2, p. 847, no. 14, cf. above, n. 80) has ʿUmar explicitly condemn *ṭilāʾ*, but only after ordering Syrian Muslims to drink it, and seems to be an attempt to respond to ʿUmar's ambiguous reputation on the question of the permissibility of *ṭilāʾ*.

[90] Ibn Saʿd, *Kitāb al-ṭabaqāt al-kabīr*, vol. 5, p. 269 (ed. Zetterstéen; ET available in Bewley, *Men of Madina*, vol. 2, p. 227).

the one who is hidden by houses,' the caliph is reported to have told the official, 'leave him alone.'[91] 'Umar II undressed and then beat one man eighty times as a *ḥadd* punishment for wine (*khamr*);[92] he had another man who had drunk wine (*shariba khamran*) in the land of the enemy whipped eighty times.[93] 'Umar II also ordered that *dhimmīs* not take wine (*lā yadkhul bi-'l-khamr*) into the garrison cities of Muslims and so, it is reported, they did not.[94] Such a command suggests that *dhimmīs* had been doing precisely this until they were stopped—assuming an early medieval government had the resources to actually put a halt to such a practice. Another report suggests that 'Umar II would take severe measures to try to end the consumption of alcohol: a group of people was drinking, Yaḥyā b. Sa'īd related, and one of them got drunk, so 'Umar had all of them scourged.[95] 'Umar's attitude towards intoxicants, however, does not seem to have been universally negative: *nabīdh*, he is reported to have said, was *ḥalāl*, but he ordered that people drink it from leather flasks.[96]

I have cited a number of instances involving intoxicating drinks and Muslims from 'Umar II's caliphate, but his reign is only an example—a useful one, because his upbringing among devout followers of the Prophet in Medina and his pious reputation and outlook helps bring to the forefront activities that must have been going on before and after his period without raising official ire. The question must be asked, however: can anecdotes such as the ones I have cited really point us to a world where, in the early days of the Prophet's community, the consumption of intoxicants was in fact common among its members?

Those tempted to answer in the negative might point out that I have drawn many of these stories featuring 'Umar II from Ibn Sa'd's *Kitāb al-ṭabaqāt al-kabīr*, a ninth-century work written a century or more after many of the events it purports to describe. What is more, the later legal tradition, it has been ar-

[91] Ibn Sa'd, *Kitāb al-ṭabaqāt al-kabīr*, vol. 5, p. 269 (ed. Zetterstéen [Leiden, 1905]; my translation with reference to the ET in Bewley, *Men of Madina*, vol. 2, p. 227).

[92] Ibn Sa'd, *Kitāb al-ṭabaqāt al-kabīr*, vol. 5, p. 269 (ed. Zetterstéen [Leiden, 1905]; ET available in Bewley, *Men of Madina*, vol. 2, p. 227).

[93] Ibn Sa'd, *Kitāb al-ṭabaqāt al-kabīr*, vol. 5, p. 261 (ed. Zetterstéen [Leiden, 1905]; ET available in Bewley, *Men of Madina*, vol. 2, p. 220).

[94] Ibn Sa'd, *Kitāb al-ṭabaqāt al-kabīr*, vol. 5, p. 269 (ed. Zetterstéen [Leiden, 1905]; ET available in Bewley, *Men of Madina*, vol. 2, p. 227).

[95] Ibn Abī Shayba, *al-Muṣannaf*, vol. 8, p. 83 (no. 24118).

[96] He did this in a letter to the people of Kufa, something which reportedly prompted them all to drink it. See Ibn Sa'd, *Kitāb al-ṭabaqāt al-kabīr*, vol. 5, p. 276 (ed. Zetterstéen [Leiden, 1905]; ET available in Bewley, *Men of Madina*, vol. 2, p. 233). On this, see Gibb, 'The Fiscal Rescript of 'Umar II,' p. 11. Cf. Goldziher, *Introduction to Islamic Theology and Law*, p. 60. While he was caliph, 'Umar was said to have never listened to musical performances, but while he was governor of Medina, it was said that he enjoyed them; see Ps.-Jāḥiẓ, *Kitāb al-Tāj fī akhlāq al-mulūk*, p. 33 (ed. A. Zakī [Cairo, 1914]).

gued, was fond of using 'Umar II to retroject and legitimate its views.[97] The recording of stories like the ones I have cited, someone might therefore suggest, was driven by didactic purposes or the needs of legal debate rather than by some desire to record historical events and social realia.

Denying the historical value of these kinds of reports on such bases, however, would be unwise. The disapproval of intoxicants in legal circles notwithstanding, there is abundant evidence that many Muslims have enjoyed and even celebrated wine-drinking throughout Islamic history.[98] There is no good reason to suppose that medieval and early modern Muslims who were aware of Qur'ānic and Prophetic statements proscribing the consumption of intoxicants but who nevertheless did so were somehow qualitatively different from members of the Prophet's community in its first century of existence. Merely being temporally close to the Prophet did not make people incapable of behaving in ways he would not have approved, or that the later tradition would have thought him to have prohibited. By comparison, any reader of the letters of Paul will know that proximity to the life of Jesus did not mean that his earliest followers always behaved in ways that made their communal leaders happy. Why should we think that early Muslims were somehow incapable of acting in the same ways as later Muslims? And, to acknowledge that the drinking of alcohol might not be uncommon among later Muslims while insisting this was not the case among earlier ones raises the question of explaining an historical caesura: at what point did Muslims begin enjoying wine?

Although the sources are invariably later than we would like, there is a good deal of historical evidence that no such caesura ever existed. Muslims, even from prominent, religiously prestigious families, openly partook of intoxicating drinks of all sorts in this early period, and the anecdotes pointing to this reality extend well beyond stories involving 'Umar I or 'Umar II.[99] To give one more example: Shurayḥ b. al-Ḥārith (d. ca. AH 80/AD 700), a celebrated early *qāḍī*, is said to have been a drinker of a strong form of the alcoholic *ṭilā'*.[100] 'If a *qāḍī* such as Shurayḥ was publicly involved in practices so fla-

[97] See, e.g., P. Crone and M. Hinds, *God's Caliph: Religious Authority in the First Centuries of Islam* (Cambridge, 1986), p. 22.

[98] See, e.g., S. Ahmed, *What Is Islam? The Importance of Being Islamic* (Princeton and Oxford, 2016), pp. 57–71.

[99] And these can be found in sources other than Ibn Sa'd. In *adab* works, especially, it is very common to come across stories of Muslims enjoying alcohol. In addition to what I have already cited in this chapter, see, e.g. 'Abd al-Razzāq, *al-Muṣannaf*, vol. 9, pp. 240–47; Ibn Qutayba, *Kitāb al-ashriba*, pp. 43–47; Ibn 'Abd Rabbih, *al-'Iqd al-Farīd*, vol. 8, pp. 61–65, for a number of examples of prominent early Muslims who were punished for drinking. Lammens, 'Études sur le règne du calife Omaiyade Mo'awiya Ier,' (part 3), pp. 276–80, collected many examples of Muslims enjoying wine—and not just being punished for its consumption—in the first Islamic century.

[100] Wakī', *Akhbār al-quḍāt*, vol. 2 (Beirut, n.d.), pp. 212, 226. For this point, see Hallaq, *The Origins*

grantly contradictory to the Quranic letter and spirit,' Wael Hallaq has written, 'then one can safely assume that, apart from certain highly regulated areas in the Quran (marriage, divorce, inheritance, etc.), there was little concern at that time for an Islamic system of legal morality.'[101] The example of Shurayḥ is significant because he was a figure to whom other early *qāḍīs* turned for advice. 'I have been installed as a judge,' Hishām b. Hubayra al-Ḍabbī wrote to Shurayḥ, 'despite my youth and the paucity of my knowledge in much relating to it, and I cannot do without consulting someone like you.'[102]

But does granting that a number of early members of the Prophet's community were drinking intoxicants necessarily point to the existence of a layering of knowledge in the community? Is this really a symptom of the fact that the vast majority of early Muslims were mass converts? Are we dealing here with evidence of ignorance or of shallow conversions, or is what we are seeing rather evidence of something much more mundane and common in every religious community: sin? To address these questions, several further points should be taken into consideration.

That someone does not heed a rule does not of course mean he or she is unaware of it; I made a similar point in Chapter 3 in regard to communal boundaries—crossing one does not always imply a person did not know that it existed. In many of the instances I have cited above, people were flogged for drinking alcohol and the fact of their punishment can potentially, though not necessarily, be taken as evidence that at least some of them were likely aware that they had transgressed a norm. One need only read through the remarkable and detailed treatise on virtually every aspect of wine and intoxication written Ibn al-Muʿtazz (d. AH 296 /AD 908), an Abbasid prince and poet who was even briefly caliph, to see that members of the Prophet's community, even at its most elite and literate echelons, were able to consider themselves Muslims and drink alcohol without any apparent cognitive dissonance.[103]

---

and Evolution of Islamic Law, p. 40 (and see next note). There are conflicting reports of the date of Shurayḥ's death; for this and further information, see E. Kohlberg's article, 'Shurayḥ,' in *EI2*, vol. 9, pp. 508–509.

[101] Hallaq, *The Origins and Evolution of Islamic Law*, p. 40. And, it might be added, insofar as a systematic and distinctive approach to moral questions based on Qur'ānic and Prophetic teaching and precedent even existed in this earliest period, it seems that there was room for diverse understandings within it.

[102] Ibn Saʿd, *Kitāb al-ṭabaqāt al-kabīr*, vol. 7, pp. 109–110 (ed. Meissner [Leiden, 1915]; my translation made with reference to the ET in Bewley, *The Men of Madina*, vol. 1, p. 96).

[103] And those Muslims who did drink alcohol could defend their behavior by pointing to various aspects of the tradition; see Ibn al-Muʿtazz, *Kitāb fuṣūl al-tamāthīl fī tabāshīr al-surūr*, pp. 147–55. Cf. also the arguments of *aṣḥāb al-nabīdh* reported in Ibn ʿAbd Rabbih, *al-ʿIqd al-Farīd*, vol. 8, p. 48, and the next note. Also see the anecdote in Ahmed, *What Is Islam?*, p. 3.

This recognition leads to another qualification: people who took the Qur'ān and the example of the Prophet very seriously argued over and made distinctions as to the permissibility of alcoholic drinks based on what it was they were made of—grapes, dates, barley, wheat, honey, and otherwise.[104] Examples of 'Umar and of the Prophet drinking the type of alcoholic drink called *nabīdh* were in fact invoked in order to justify imbibing certain kinds of intoxicants, just as Prophetic prohibitions and stories of prominent members of the community being punished for alcohol consumption could be used to justify its proscription.[105] If we choose to read at least some of the anecdotes above as having their proper context in legal discussions, the fact of their composition can point to a second- or third- (AH) / eighth- or ninth- century (AD) world in which some Muslims saw no problem with alcoholic drinks, one in which the example of the Prophet and leading members of the community was invoked to modify, nuance, and circumscribe Qur'ānic proscriptions.

What needs to be realized, however, is that both these qualifications—that lack of observance does not necessarily indicate lack of knowledge and that Muslims debated which kinds of intoxicants, if any, were forbidden by the Qur'ān and Prophetic example—have one thing in common with the suggestion that in the first Islamic century the Qur'ān may not have been utilized as an important source of law: they are all elitist explanations of the phenomenon of the apparently widespread consumption of alcohol among early members of the Muslim community. And to the extent that they are elitist explanations, they are incomplete, for they do not take into account a significant portion of the Muslim community. Another anecdote can serve as an illustration of what I mean.

At one point, having gone out on the *ḥajj*, al-Walīd b. Yazīd (d. AH 126/AD 744) was said to be playing chess with some companions. A man from the tribe of Thaqīf asked permission to enter into the caliph's presence and al-Walīd granted it, covering the chessboard with a cloth before the man came in. Once

[104] Ibn Qutayba, *Kitāb al-ashriba*, pp. 28–29, even reported the arguments of some partisans of *kalām* who argued that the Qur'ān did not in fact prohibit *khamr* categorically, but rather had forbidden it out of disciplinary concern. At 29–34, he records a variety of traditions that reflect various, at times conflicting, attempts to define the meaning of *khamr* and *nabīdh*. For different attitudes toward intoxicants, see the lucid discussion in Goldziher, *Introduction to Islamic Theology and Law*, pp. 59–63. N. Haider, 'Contesting Intoxication: Early Juristic Debates about the Lawfulness of Alcoholic Beverages,' *Islamic Law and Society* 20 (2013), pp. 48–89, is a more recent examination, focusing on the evolving attitudes of Mālikī, Shāfi'ī, and Ḥanafī jurists toward different kinds of intoxicants. Haider includes a chart (p. 54) that very helpfully discusses the differences between various types of alcoholic drinks mentioned in Arabic texts.

[105] See e.g. Ibn al-Mu'tazz, *Kitāb fuṣūl al-tamāthīl fī tabāshīr al-surur*, pp. 146–48 and Ibn Qutayba, *Kitāb al-ashriba*, pp. 34–108. Cf. also n. 103, above.

the man had entered into the caliph's presence and greeted him, al-Walīd asked: 'Have you not read the Qur'ān?' 'No, O Commander of the Faithful,' the man replied, '[v]arious affairs and trifles have distracted me from it.' 'Have you not learned *fiqh*?' al-Walīd next asked. 'No,' the man responded. 'Can you quote any poetry?' the Caliph then asked. 'No,' the man answered again. 'Do you know anything of the stories of the Arabs before Islam (*ayyām al-ʿarab*)?' Yazīd asked him again. 'No,' the man responded once more. At this point, al-Walīd took the cloth off the chessboard and declared, 'Your king!' 'O Commander of the Faithful!' one of his companions, ʿAbd Allāh b. Muʿāwiya, exclaimed—apparently worried about the visitor seeing the caliph playing chess. 'Be quiet,' al-Walīd responded, 'for no one is with us.'[106] This tribesman from Thaqīf did not know any Qur'ān, any law, any history, or any literature. He did not know anything in fact that would have made him an interesting conversation partner for a member of the literate and learned classes. This made him, effectively speaking, invisible to the caliph.

Such people are also, effectively speaking, invisible in our own retellings of the early Islamic period. Although the anecdote in question is almost certainly fictitious, it is nevertheless very suggestive and interesting to ponder. For it is hard to see how a figure like this unnamed and unlearned Thaqīf tribesman could be made to fit into any one of the explanations I have mentioned above if he were a person who drank alcohol. Would he have known any of the passages of the Qur'ān that referred to *khamr*? Would he have known the various Prophetic traditions that might be invoked either in support of the consumption of intoxicants or against it? The legal status of the Qur'ān and the example of the Prophet among legal experts and government administrators in the first Islamic century can be debated by modern scholars, but how important would these normative sources have been to a person who apparently knew very little, if anything, about them? Is it reasonable to suppose that a person like this man from Thaqīf would have been the sort of urbane and sophisticated Muslim who would have composed wine poetry or read and enjoyed a work like the *Fuṣūl al-tamāthīl* of Ibn al-Muʿtazz?

Putting aside examples of *qāḍīs* who drank intoxicants, or Muslims from prominent families doing the same, let us think for a moment about unnamed figures in other anecdotes we have seen: the people drinking in taverns in Egypt in the reign of ʿUmar II, or those who imbibed alcoholic drinks at a well-

[106] Ibn Qutayba, *Kitāb ʿuyūn al-akhbār*, vol. 2, pp. 120–21 (Cairo, 1925–1930). This story can also be found in *Kitāb al-shaṭranj mimmā allafahu al-ʿAdlī wa-'l-Ṣūlī wa-ghayruhumā* (Frankfurt, 1986), p. 24. On objections to the morality of playing chess, see F. Rosenthal, 'Shaṭrandj,' in *EI2*, vol. 9, p. 367. For discussion of this anecdote, see H.J.R. Murray, *A History of Chess* (Oxford, 1913), p. 193.

known spot of revelry in Khunāṣira in Syria, or the unnamed Muslims in garrison cities who were apparently buying intoxicating drinks from *dhimmīs*. Who were these people? Were they more like Ibn al-Muʿtazz and the cosmopolitan Muslims who read his works, or were they more like the Thaqafī in our fictional anecdote? If the overwhelming majority of early conversions to Islam were of a group nature and motivated by a variety of factors, many of them not necessarily related to inner spiritual conviction or even to precise knowledge of the content of Muḥammad's message, figures like him will have belonged to a common and recognizable type.[107] And if Muslims from prominent families were drinking alcohol, for whatever reasons, what can we assume about Muslims like our Thaqafī, who are not nearly so visible in our sources?

One can therefore reasonably make the following suggestions: Some early Muslims likely drank intoxicants because they wanted to, Qur'ānic prohibitions notwithstanding. And some drank because they believed that the type of alcohol they were drinking had not been forbidden. But we can suggest that there were also some—perhaps many—who drank because they either did not know or did not care that this was a practice frowned upon by the Qur'ān and certain religious leaders, for they and their forbears had not joined the community on account of the Qur'ān or the religious teachings of such figures.

Even when nuanced, therefore, the issue of intoxicants points us to by now familiar issues: the inertia of pre-conversionary religious practices, the nature and extent of catechesis, and the layering of knowledge, understanding, and engagement that we have encountered in previous chapters, only this time in the Prophet's community and not just among Christians; it can be used diagnostically to get a sense for broader awareness and understanding of Qur'ānic ordinances and expectations and, importantly, the seriousness with which these were taken. In the context of mass conversion and of elite conversions made for apparently nondoctrinal reasons, reports of early Muslims, even elite ones, drinking *khamr* should astonish us no more than reports of Christian priests engaging in divination. They are, in fact, precisely the sort of phenomena we should expect to find.

[107] Stories of the encounter of a caliph with a Muslim who is religiously unlearned are not hard to find. In addition to the one just cited, as well as above, nn. 58–60, see e.g., al-Jāḥiẓ, *al-Bayān wa-'l-tabyīn*, p. 331, where a man from the Banū Makhzūm approaches al-Walīd b. ʿAbd al-Malik (d. AH 96/AD 715) and asks the caliph to give him his daughter in marriage. 'Have you read [or recited] the Qur'ān?' al-Walīd asks the man. When the man replies in the negative, al-Walīd asks him to draw near and then beats him. For another story, this time involving ʿUmar b. ʿAbd al-ʿAzīz and an Arab woman who wanted to take a Byzantine slave as her concubine, see ʿAbd al-Razzāq, *Muṣannaf*, vol. 7, p. 210 (no. 12,821) (cp. with the alternate version cited in n. 58, above). I am grateful to Michael Cook for this last reference. Cf. also Binay, *Die Figur des Beduinen*, pp. 77–125, esp. 124–25.

'ISLAM,' MUSLIM ELITES, AND THE DIVERSITY OF LEGITIMATE BELIEF

Here some may rightly object that the Prophet's message was about much more than avoiding wine. This is most certainly true. One need not, however, engage in yet another attempt at outlining what precisely the movement that began with Muḥammad really was all about in its first phases[108] to nevertheless make the point that, whatever it meant to be part of Muḥammad's religious community in its earliest period, we have evidence that, even for its spiritual elite—and especially those people who presumably converted for reasons which may have directly related to spiritual or religious concerns—these meanings were varied and changing. To the vertical phenomenon of a layering of knowledge, therefore, we should add a horizontal one of a diversity of viewpoints among the learned elite and a comparative (when viewed from the standpoint of the medieval period) lack of any detailed or agreed upon orthodoxy.

These horizontal and vertical axes—that is, the spectrum of legitimate belief and differing levels of engagement and knowledge—are further complicated by the evolving nature of the Prophet's message and its religious demands, both during Muḥammad's life and after his death. During the Prophet's life, this development and change is witnessed perhaps most easily in the phenomenon of Qur'ānic verses (and *ḥadīth*) that are at variance with one another and whose conflicting precepts the tradition has reconciled by asserting that a later one abrogates, cancels out, or replaces an earlier one.[109]

We can find this change in other places as well, most notably by strictly taking the *sīra* literature uncritically and at face value. In his biography of the Prophet, Ibn Isḥāq reported the incident of the 'Satanic Verses' in which Muḥammad effected a *rapprochement* between the polytheistic Meccans and Muslims through the recitation of Qur'ānic passages that gave honor to three popular local deities, al-Lāt, al-'Uzzā, and Manāt, and granted legitimacy to seeking them as intercessors. In the story as it is told, Muḥammad did not realize there was anything wrong with these statements; he thought they were sent from God, until the angel Gabriel intervened, confronting and correcting

[108] M. Cook and Crone, P. *Hagarism: The Making of the Islamic World* (Cambridge/New York, 1977), and Donner, *Muhammad and the Believers*, represent two of the better known speculative attempts to discuss the evolution of the meaning of Islam across the seventh century. Hoyland, *Seeing Islam*, pp. 546–50, is a circumspect discussion of the early evidence we possess as to what the practice and beliefs of Muḥammad's followers in the first century of the *hijra* may have been.

[109] On the phenomenon of *al-nāsikh wa-'l-mansūkh*, see J. Burton's article, 'Naskh,' in *EI2*, vol. 7, pp. 1009–1012 and his article, 'Abrogation,' in *EQ*, vol. 1, pp. 11–19. Burton treated this topic in greater detail in his *The Sources of Islamic Law: Islamic Theories of Abrogation* (Edinburgh, 1990).

Muḥammad and telling him that Satan had cast these statements into his mouth. Significantly, there was some period of time between Muḥammad's first recitation of the verses and his recognition of them as satanic in origin and their subsequent abrogation.[110] His failure to realize immediately that giving honor to these polytheist deities was problematic has been taken to suggest that, at this point in his prophetic career, Muḥammad was not yet a monotheist, but was rather a henotheist.[111] The uncompromising monotheism of Islam still lay in the future: the meaning of submission, of Islam, was evolving even for the Prophet.

The reception of this story can tell us something about the nature of Muslim belief in the centuries after the Prophet's death. The incident of the Satanic Verses was recorded by Ibn Isḥāq (d. 150/767), the most important of Muḥammad's early biographers, but it was omitted in Ibn Hishām's (d. 215/830) recension of Ibn Isḥāq's work. Similarly, Ibn Hishām omitted Ibn Isḥāq's account of Muḥammad's belief that he may have been a poet or demon-possessed and his consequent plan to kill himself after the shock of receiving his first revelation.[112] Both of these stories in the Prophet's biography were viewed by at least some later Muslims as cause for concern. Shahab Ahmed pointed to changing attitudes among Muslims toward the authenticity of reports of the Satanic Verses as indicative of 'the distinctly fluid and mutable nature of the historical constitution of orthodoxy in Islam.'[113] Similarly, an early report that depicted Muḥammad slaughtering meat for idols and eating it in the time of the *jāhiliyya* did not jibe with later sensibilities and was either explained away or rejected by the subsequent tradition.[114] With the passing of time, the legitimate portion of the spectrum of possible understandings of the significance

[110] cf. Watt, *Muhammad at Mecca*, p. 103.

[111] For Muḥammad as a henotheist, see M. Rodinson, *Mohammed*, trans. A. Carter (New York, 1971), pp. 96–97, 106–107. Also see W. Montgomery Watt's discussion of this incident and whether it shows that Muḥammad was, at this point, some kind of polytheist, in *Muhammad: Prophet and Statesman* (London, 1961), pp. 60–65, and *Muhammad at Mecca*, p. 104 specifically, and more generally, pp. 101–109. On the incident of the Satanic Verses in general, see M. S. Ahmed, 'The Satanic Verses Incident in the Memory of the Early Muslim Community: An Analysis of the early *Riwāyahs* and their *Isnāds*,' (PhD diss., Princeton University, 1997), and now his book *Before Orthodoxy: The Satanic Verses in Early Islam* (Cambridge, Mass., 2017).

[112] For Muḥammad thinking he was possessed (*majnūn*) or a poet, see al-Ṭabarī, *Ta'rīkh*, 1.3, p. 1150 (ed. P. de Jong [Leiden, 1882–1885]); for the Incident of the Satanic Verses in al-Ṭabarī, see 1.3, p. 1192–94 (ed. de Jong). For these incidents omitted from Ibn Hishām's recension of Ibn Isḥāq, see Guillaume, *The Life of Muhammad*, pp. 106, 165–67. Also see the remarks of U. Rubin in his article 'Sīra and the Qur'ān,' in *EQ*, vol. 5, p. 34, and Rubin, *The Eye of the Beholder: The Life of Muḥammad as Viewed by the Early Muslims* (Princeton, 1995), pp. 113–14, 158–66.

[113] See S. Ahmed, 'Ibn Taymiyyah and the Satanic Verses,' *Studia Islamica* 87 (1998), pp. 67–124; quote at p. 122.

[114] See M. J. Kister, '"A Bag of Meat": A Study of an Early *Ḥadīth*,' *BSOAS* 33 (1970), pp. 267–75.

of Muḥammad and his revelation narrowed; earlier devout Muslims had a greater range of legitimate positions available to them than would devout Muslims in the medieval period.

The importance of the oneness of God and the nature of Muḥammad's biography and prophethood would be matters of much more central importance to the eventual identity of Islam than the question of wine-drinking. So, too, would the Qur'ān. I will not go into the history of the text of the Qur'ān in depth here, but it will suffice to point out that a look at this history shows that the early Muslim community was uncertain as to the exact nature of the contents of the Qur'ān, believed that significant portions of it, even entire *sūras*, had been lost, abrogated and therefore not preserved, or not recorded, and was unsure exactly how to vocalize the text of the Qur'ān, an uncertainty that could at times have a legal impact.[115] 'By no means should any one of you say,' Ibn 'Umar is reported to have stated, '"I have learned (*qad akhadhtu*) all of the Qur'ān"—and he does not know what "all of it" is! Much of the Qur'ān has gone away. Instead, let him say: "I have learned what has appeared [in the text]."'[116] Later, a significant portion of the Muslim community—Shī'ī's—would allege that the text itself had been tampered with and corrupted by those who did not want to acknowledge the special role of 'Alī or the Imāms in leading the Muslim community.[117] Christian polemicists would also claim that the Qur'ān had been interpolated by Jews and that Muslims themselves had altered the text in the context of disputes and struggles over leadership in the community.[118]

In this early period, there was also a spectrum of attitudes towards the written text of the Qur'ān itself. The idea that there might be scribal errors in the Qur'ān was not held to be impossible or preposterous by some. When 'Urwa asked 'Ā'isha about three different passages in the Qur'ān that contain

[115] For this, see the evidence in *SBI*, pp. 576–94, and also cf. Burton, *The Sources of Islamic Law: Islamic Theories of Abrogation*, pp. 43–55. For a summary and discussion of a number of recent scholarly ideas about the date of the standardization of the text of the Qur'ān, see S. Shoemaker, *The Death of a Prophet: The End of Muhammad's Life and the Beginnings of Islam* (Philadelphia, 2012), pp. 146–52. On different legal rulings resulting from different vocalizations, see below, n. 151.

[116] al-Suyūṭī, *al-Itqān fī 'ulūm al-Qur'ān* (ed. F. Aḥmad al-Zamarlī) (Beirut, 1999), vol. 1, p. 662. Burton, *The Sources of Islamic Law*, p. 50, translates this passage: 'Let none of you say, "I have the whole Ḳur'ān." How does he know what the whole Ḳur'ān is? Much of the Ḳur'ān has vanished. Rather let him say, "I have what is extant."'

[117] See H. Modarressi's remarkable, 'Early Debates on the Integrity of the Qur'ān: A Brief Survey,' *Studia Islamica* 77 (1993), pp. 5–39, and E. Kohlberg, 'Some Notes on the Imamite Attitude toward the Qur'ān,' in S. M. Stern, A. Hourani, and V. Brown, eds., *Islamic Philosophy and the Classical Tradition: Essays Presented by His Friends and Pupils to Richard Walzer on his Seventieth Birthday* (Oxford, 1972), pp. 209–24.

[118] al-Kindī, *Apology*, pp. 128–38. For charges of corruption made by the *Legend of Sergius Baḥīrā*, see Chapter 2, n. 37. On charges made in the *Letter of Leo III*, see n. 127, below.

apparent grammatical errors (4:162, 5:69, 20:63), her response was frank: 'O son of my sister, this is the work of the scribes,' she said. 'They made errors in the Book.'[119] Ibn 'Abbās read *tasta'dhinū* in 24:27 rather than *tasta'nisū*: 'It's only the error of the scribes,' he is reported to have said.[120] Similarly, Sa'īd b. Jubayr is reported to have said that there are four passages in the Qur'ān that have grammatical errors (5:69, 4:162, 63:10, 20:63); and al-Zubayr b. 'Abd Allāh b. Abī Khālid is said to have asked Abān b. 'Uthmān about the grammatical problem in 4:162.[121] One report has Zayd b. Thābit consult 'Uthmān about the collection of the Qur'ān: initially, 'Uthmān refused and told Zayd, 'You are a people who makes errors in speech (*talḥanūn*),' but after Zayd asked him again, 'Uthmān agreed to be consulted.[122] Another story suggests that 'Uthmān was nonchalant about there being errors in the text of the Qur'ān. When the authoritative Qur'ānic codices that 'Uthmān had ordered produced were copied out and shown to him, al-Dānī (d. AH 444/AD 1053) reported, he found mistakes in them. 'Leave them,' 'Uthmān is supposed to have said, 'for the Arabs will set them right and put them into proper Arabic with their tongue, since the appearance [of the text] points to an error in the consonantal skeleton (*al-rasm*).'[123]

There are other indications of what might be termed an open attitude toward the written text of the Qur'ān in some quarters in the earliest period of Islamic history. Exegetical literature has preserved the story of the apostasy of one of Muḥammad's scribes, 'Abd Allāh b. Sa'd b. Abī Sarḥ, whom we encountered above as a governor of Egypt: this story in particular suggests that the attitude toward the fixedness of the text of the Qur'ān was, at least among some early Muslims, rather liberal. Dictating part of the Qur'ānic revelation to Ibn Abī Sarḥ, Muḥammad included the words '*'azīz, ḥakīm*' ('Mighty, Wise'). Ibn Abī

[119] al-Ṭabarī, *Jāmi' al-bayān 'an ta'wīl āy al-Qur'ān* (ed. 'Abd Allāh b. 'Abd al-Muḥsin al-Turkī) (Cairo, 2003), vol. 7, pp. 680–81. Cf. I. Goldziher, *Schools of Koranic Commentators*, trans. W. H. Behn (Weisbaden, 2006), p. 20. See also, J. Burton, 'Linguistic Errors in the Qur'ān,' *Journal of Semitic Studies* 33 (1988), pp. 181–96, and D. J. Stewart, 'Notes on Medieval and Modern Emendations of the Qur'ān,' in G. S. Reynolds, ed., *The Qur'ān in Its Historical Context* (London/New York, 2008), pp. 225–48.

[120] al-Ṭabarī, *Jāmi' al-bayān 'an ta'wīl āy al-Qur'ān*, vol. 17, p. 240. Cf. Goldziher, *Schools of Koranic Commentators*, p. 20.

[121] Ibn Abī Dāwūd, *Kitāb al-Maṣāḥif*, pp. 33–34.

[122] Ibn Abī Shayba, *al-Muṣannaf*, vol. 10, p. 23.

[123] See 'Uthmān b. Sa'īd al-Dānī, *Kitāb al-muqni' fī rasm maṣāḥif al-amṣār ma'a kitāb al-nuqaṭ* (ed. O. Pretzl) (Istanbul, 1932), p. 124. See also a collection of similar reports in Ibn Abī Dāwūd, *Kitāb al-Maṣāḥif*, pp. 32–33. Cf. Nöldeke et al., *The History of the Qur'ān*, pp. 389–90. NB: That al-Dānī rejects the authenticity of this report (*al-Muqni'*, p. 124) is not important. Regardless of whether 'Uthmān actually made this comment, its very composition and existence shows a diversity of Muslim attitudes towards the nature of the Quranic text. This principle holds true for all the various reports I cite here: their actual occurrence is less important than the sheer fact of their composition and existence as texts which shows that such stories formed part of what some Muslims understood to be sacred history.

Sarḥ, however, changed the text and instead wrote down '*ghafūr, raḥīm*,' ('Forgiving, Merciful'). When Ibn Abī Sarḥ read the changed passage back to Muḥammad, the Prophet's response was, 'Yes, it's the same.' The scribe's reaction was to abandon Islam and return to the Quraysh in Mecca, who were at the time still Muḥammad's polytheist opponents. '"'*Azīz, ḥakīm*," had come down to him,' Ibn Abī Sarḥ is supposed to have told the Meccans, 'and so I changed it and then told him what I had written, and he said, "Yes, it's the same."'[124] Elsewhere, Ibn Abī Sarḥ is reported to have made the statement, 'Muḥammad would only write what I wanted.'[125] Another report combines these two elements but does not explicitly mention Ibn Abī Sarḥ. The unnamed scribe in this version wrote *samīʿan ʿalīman* ('Hearing, Knowing') rather than *samīʿan baṣīran* ('Hearing, Seeing') and *samīʿan baṣīran* rather than *samīʿan ʿalīman*; he later converted to Christianity in disillusionment rather than going back to paganism as Ibn Abī Sarḥ is supposed to have done. Nevertheless, his complaint was the same: 'I would only write what I wanted with Muḥammad.'[126]

Obvious questions of historicity and the soundness of their chains of transmission aside, the mere recording of these anecdotes is a significant reflection of attitudes about the nature of Muḥammad's revelation, its recording, and its preservation that would have been unacceptable to most learned Muslims and religious authorities in later periods. That a matter as important to the subsequent tradition as the actual written contents of the Qur'ān itself, its very words, was contested and open to different and competing answers among elites in the first several centuries after the death of Muḥammad leads to a further question. If Muslim religious elites themselves had evolving and differing attitudes toward something as eventually central as the written text of Muḥammad's revelation, what are we to assume to have been the case among the nonelites, who must have formed the large majority of the Muslim community—and not just with respect to the Qur'ān, but with respect to a whole host of different matters?

The subject of the text of the Qur'ān, however, raises more than just the issue of differing attitudes: it raises the question of the nature and extent of central religious authority and control in the decades after the death of the Prophet. Solidly fixing one version of any text—the Qur'ān, the Bible, the works

[124] al-Ṭabarī, *Jāmiʿ al-bayān ʿan taʾwīl āy al-Qurʾān*, vol. 9, p. 405 (cf. also vol. 14, p. 369).

[125] al-Ṭabarī, *Jāmiʿ al-bayān ʿan taʾwīl āy al-Qurʾān*, vol. 11, p. 288.

[126] Ibn Abī Dāwūd, *Kitāb al-Maṣāḥif*, p. 3. A statement of ʿAbd Allāh b. Masʿūd seems to have been made in partial response to stories like these: 'The error is not that a certain *sūra* enter into another one, nor is it that a verse end with '*ḥakīm ʿalīm*' or '*ʿalīm ḥakīm*' or '*ghafūr raḥīm*.' The error, rather, is that one puts in it what is not from it [sc. the Qur'ān], or that one ends a verse of mercy with punishment, or a verse of punishment with a verse of mercy.' See Abū ʿUbayd al-Qāsim b. Sallām, *Kitāb faḍāʾil al-Qurʾān* (ed. M. al-ʿAṭiyya, M. Kharāba, and W. Taqī al-Dīn) (Damascus, 1995), p. 355.

of Shakespeare—as the authoritative version requires a central authority and considerable power. Stories of a collection of the Qur'ān during the rule of 'Uthmān, or Abū Bakr, or even by the Prophet himself aside, the fact that competing versions of the text of the Qur'ān were still being proscribed and what would eventually be the received text was itself still being subjected to governmental intervention into the eighth century reflects the strength (or weakness) of centralized religious authority in the new religion.[127] What is more, the citation of alternate versions of the Qur'ān that can be found in works of exegesis into the third/ninth century makes clear the (in)ability of the government to regulate this, the most important text in Islam.[128] If the written text of the Qur'ān could not be fully controlled, what about everything else?

If we press the question of the religious elites' knowledge or possession of a strongly defined set of beliefs, we may be mistaken if we assume that it included too much, or that we can identify what exactly it comprised, beyond perhaps the basic affirmations that God was one and that Muḥammad had received a revelation from him.[129] And here we run into the problem of evidence. In discussions of the evolution of Islam in the seventh century, the coin reforms of 'Abd al-Malik and the building of the Dome of the Rock have com-

[127] For evidence of al-Ḥajjāj b. Yūsuf's altering the text of the Qur'ān, see A. Jeffery, 'Ghevond's Text of the Correspondence between 'Umar II and Leo III,' *Harvard Theological Review* 37 (1944), p. 298, n. 48. On a 'Marwanid' rather than an ''Uthmānic' text of the Qur'ān, see C. F. Robinson, *'Abd al-Malik* (Oxford, 2005), pp. 100–104. For an overview of the nature of the early Islamic state, see F. M. Donner, 'Introduction: The Articulation of Early Islamic State Structures,' in Donner, ed., *The Articulation of Early Islamic State Structures* (Farnham, Surrey, 2012), pp. xxiii–xxxii, and his earlier article, 'The Formation of the Islamic State,' reprinted in *ibid.*, pp. 1–14. For the question of the nature of Mu'āwiya's state, see C. Foss, 'Mu'āwiya's State,' in J. Haldon, ed., *Money, Power and Politics in Early Islamic Syria: A Review of Current Debates* (Farnham, Surrey, 2010), pp. 75–96; Foss, 'Egypt under Mu'āwiya, Part I: Flavius Papas and Upper Egypt,' *BSOAS* 72 (2009), pp. 1–24; and Foss, 'Egypt under Mu'āwiya, Part II: Middle Egypt, Fusṭāṭ and Alexandria,' *BSOAS* 72 (2009), pp. 259–78. For a more pessimistic view of the early Islamic state, see, J. Johns, 'Archaeology and the History of Early Islam,' *Journal of the Social and Economic History of the Orient* 46 (2003), pp. 411–36). R. G. Hoyland, 'New Documentary Texts and the Early Islamic State,' *BSOAS* 69 (2006), pp. 395–416, represented an attempt to inject new documentary evidence into the debate between Johns and Foss.

[128] Cf. F. Leemhuis 'Readings of the Qur'ān,' in *EQ*, vol. 4, pp. 354–55.

[129] Whatever one wants to argue about the date and precise provenance of the Qur'ān, already as early as potentially 634, the *Doctrina Jacobi Nuper Baptizati* was referring to reports that a prophet (προφήτης) had appeared among the Saracens. See *Doctrina Jacobi Nuper Baptizati* 16 (ed. Déroche, pp. 208–11). On this text and its date, see most conveniently J. Pahlitzsch in *CMR*, vol. 1, pp. 117–19.

If one is willing to admit the Qur'ān as evidence for the content of earliest Muslim belief, the fundamentals seem to be few and quite basic: belief in God, His angels, His scriptures, His prophets (cf. 2:285) or, alternatively, belief in God, His Messenger, the book sent down to His Messenger, previous revealed scriptures, and the Last Day (cf. 4:136; cp. also 2:177, and see Mir's entry on 'Faith,' in *Dictionary of Qur'ānic Terms and Concepts*, pp. 69–70). Hoyland, *Seeing Islam*, p. 549, gives a succinct statement of the religious beliefs of the Arabs as perceived by non-Muslim authors of the first century AH.

monly been pointed to as marking a new phase in the development and articulation of the religious movement initiated by Muḥammad.[130] But changing numismatic iconography, the use of Qur'ānic slogans on coins, the use of certain formulae in papyri documents, or the erection of certain monumental buildings actually tells very little. Such evidence might help us learn about the public legitimation of a particular regime, but it has not much to offer if what we are curious about are the actual religious beliefs and practices of the community whom the regime represented, the populace that regime ruled, or even the workmen who struck the coins or made the inscriptions and the scribes who wrote religious formulae on papyri—assuming that the scribes or workmen who did these things were even Muslims.[131]

Indeed, if we think of the relationship between rulers and the religious systems they have used to legitimate their rule throughout history, it quickly becomes apparent that we cannot even be sure what something like the Dome of the Rock, a Standing Caliph coin, or an aniconic, post-Reform coin tells us about the actual personal beliefs of 'Abd al-Malik, much less any of his successors or any group of Muslims under his authority. Would inferences about Napoleon's actual religious beliefs, made on the basis of his public proclamations in Egypt, give us deep insight into what the French leader really believed? Would it be responsible historically to go one step further and extrapolate from those public pronouncements to make claims about the religious beliefs of Napoleon's entire army, or all of the population of France, or indeed all of the populations ruled over by Napoleon? Based solely on coins and the inscription on the Arch of Constantine, what conclusions could we draw about the nature of Constantine's personal religious belief in the decade following the Battle of the Milvian Bridge? Would these then be true for all Christians living under his authority? As evidence for belief, coins, milestones, and buildings

[130] Robinson, *'Abd al-Malik*, pp. 1–9, is a good example of the various ideological meanings that have been attributed to the building of the Dome of the Rock, and pp. 78–80 discuss the importance of 'Abd al-Malik's coin reforms. More generally, see Donner, *Muhammad and the Believers*, pp. 194–224, for the argument that it was in the caliphate of 'Abd al-Malik that 'Islam' emerged; Donner has made similar suggestions in other places as well—see, e.g., 'Qur'ânicization of Religio-Political Discourse in the Umayyad Period,' and 'Was Marwan ibn al-Hakam the First "Real" Muslim?' in S. Bowen Savant and H. de Felipe, eds., *Genealogy and Knowledge in Muslim Societies: Understanding the Past* (Edinburgh, 2014), pp. 105–114, where he suggested, based on the names Marwān b. al-Ḥakam gave to his children, that Marwān might be considered the first Muslim (after Muḥammad). Cook and Crone, *Hagarism*, p. 29, also argued for a late-seventh-century emergence of Islam.

[131] See J. Beckwith, *Early Christian and Byzantine Art* (New Haven/London, 1979), pp. 167–68 and the evidence cited there for the suggestion that Byzantine workmen were involved in the construction of the Dome of the Rock, and cf. K. Meinecke, 'The Encyclopaedic Illustration of a New Empire: Graeco-Roman, Byzantine and Sasanian Models on the Façade of Qasr al-Mshatta,' in S. Birk, T. Myrup Mristensen, and B. Poulsen, eds., *Using Images in Late Antiquity* (Oxford/Philadelphia, 2014), p. 294.

do not go very far. Pointing to new inscriptions on coins or milestones and the construction of a new monumental building in the late seventh century does not do much to help us with the well-known conundrums that have long challenged scholars of early Islamic history. The factors I have emphasized in this chapter, however, perhaps can.

CONUNDRUMS AS SYMPTOMS OF A LAYERING OF KNOWLEDGE

It has, for instance, been forcefully argued that there was an important discontinuity between the time of the composition of the Qur'ān and the time of the composition of commentaries on it.[132] This is one obvious way of accounting for the presence in the Qur'ān of words whose precise meanings have eluded commentators, medieval and modern, as well as other enigmas, such as the significance of the seemingly meaningless Arabic letters that begin a number of different *sūras*. The fact that medieval Muslim scholars had to resort to speculation and conjecture to explain these mysterious letters, or the significance of important words like *īlāf*, *kalāla*, *'an yadin*, *ṣamad*, or that the meanings of these letters and words was simply not known suggests that by the time Muslims began trying to interpret the Qur'ān, vital details about its composition and original context had been lost or forgotten.[133] In this vein, the Islamic tradition's many and conflicting attempts to identify the Ṣābi'ūn who, along with Christians, Jews, and Magians, were regarded by the Qur'ān as People of the Book, might also be pointed out. 'It would seem almost incredible,' Arthur Jeffery wrote,

> that when the Qur'ān grants special privilege and protection to four communities as true believers, no exact tradition as to the identity of one of the communities should have survived till the time when the Traditionists and Exegetes began their work of compilation.... [I]f so much uncertainty existed on so important a matter as the identity of a protected community, one can imagine how

[132] Perhaps the strongest such arguments can be found in Crone, 'Two Legal Problems Bearing on the Early History of the Qur'ān.'

[133] Or, alternatively, that these details were not viewed as important. See P. Crone, *Meccan Trade and the Rise of Islam* (Princeton, 1987), pp. 203–210, and M. Cook, *The Koran: A Very Short Introduction* (Oxford/New York, 2000), pp. 138–42. For the difficulties of interpreting the important phrase *'an yadin* in Q 9:29 and *ṣamad* in Q 112:2, see F. Rosenthal, 'Some Minor Problems in the Qur'ān,' in *The Joshua Starr Memorial Volume: Studies in History and Philology* (New York, 1953), pp. 68–83. On *'an yadin*, see also M. J. Kister, "An Yadin (Qur'ān, IX/29): An Attempt at Interpretation,' *Arabica* 11 (1964), pp. 272–78.

> the case stands with regard to unimportant little details which are of profound interest to the philologist to-day, but which, in the early days of Islām, had no doctrinal or political significance to bring them prominently before the attention of the Muslim savants.[134]

There seems to have been some sort of break in continuity between the event of the Qur'ān and later elite Muslim religious discourse.[135] And we have evidence of this at more than just the level of forgotten meanings of words. Joseph Schacht, for example, pointed out that though the Qur'ān expressly accepts written testimony for contracts (2:282), later Islamic law rejects written documents and only accepts witnesses,[136] and there are other important examples of Umayyad legal practice that contradict Qur'ānic law as well, a phenomenon I have already mentioned above.[137] Even central rituals were still being worked out: it has been argued that into the period of the Second Civil war (AH 60–73/AD 680–692) the *ḥajj* itself centered only around 'Arafāt and did not yet have a connection to Mecca and the Ka'ba.[138]

A variety of explanations have been put forth to try to make sense of the various puzzles surrounding the earliest history of Islam.[139] The easiest solution, I suggest, lies right before our faces and is one we have encountered already in the discussion of intoxicants. The problems of early Islamic history that have challenged scholars are nothing more than symptoms of the circumstances I have emphasized: late conversion in the context of the Prophet's military and political success, illiteracy, widespread ignorance of and disregard for the actual contents of Muḥammad's new message, and disagreement as to what those contents were among the, relatively speaking, few followers of the Prophet for whom it was a matter of concern.[140] In other words, an account

[134] See A. Jeffery, *The Foreign Vocabulary of the Qur'ān* (Baroda, 1938), p. 4. For a survey of exegetical attempts at identifying the Ṣābi'ūn, see J. D. McAuliffe, 'Exegetical Identification of the Ṣābi'ūn,' *Muslim World* 72 (1982), pp. 95–106. See also C. Buck, 'The Identity of the Ṣābi'ūn: An Historical Quest,' *Muslim World* 74 (1984), pp. 172–86; F. de Blois's article, 'Sabians,' in *EQ*, vol. 4 (Leiden/Boston, 2004), pp. 511–13; and, more recently, H. Mazuz, 'The Identity of the Sabians: Some Insights,' in R. Jospe and D. Schwartz, eds., *Jewish Philosophy: Perspectives and Retrospectives* (Boston, 2012), pp. 233–54.

[135] See the comments in Cook, *The Koran*, pp. 137–38.

[136] Schacht, *An Introduction to Islamic Law*, pp. 18–19.

[137] See Crone, 'Two Legal Problems,' pp. 10–12.

[138] G. R. Hawting, 'The *ḥajj* in the Second Civil War,' in I. R. Netton, ed., *Golden Roads: Migration, Pilgrimage, and Travel in Medieval and Modern Islam* (Richmond [England], 1993), pp. 31–42.

[139] Cf. n. 108, above.

[140] The number of difficulties that confront the reader of the Qur'ān, medieval and contemporary, can also be taken as indicative of the precision and care with which the text was transmitted from an early date. Cf. the observation of M. Mir, *Verbal Idioms of the Qur'ān* (Ann Arbor, 1989), p. 1: 'In a sense, the Qur'ān is quite easy to follow.... But a serious student soon realizes that the language of this book is only deceptively simple. As is testified by the scores of volumes that exist on Qur'ānic syntax and grammar alone, almost every Qur'ānic verse presents one or more linguistic problems that

of seventh-century Islam that emphasizes a layering of knowledge, understanding, and religious engagement within Muḥammad's community, similar to what would be found in the contemporary Christian community, could make sense of the challenges to historical reconstruction that bedevil this period. In the case of Islam, however, the continuum of possibilities and behaviors was exacerbated by a variety of additional factors particular to a young religious movement: the newness of the Prophet's revelation; the recent mass conversion of most of Muḥammad's followers; sharp, at times violent and bloody disagreements among leaders of the community; and the lack of any agreed upon orthodoxy or common understanding of the full implications of what it meant to acknowledge Muḥammad as a Prophet.

Conundrums about the text of the Qur'ān and questions about the historicity of the actual actions, attitudes, and sayings of Muḥammad that have puzzled later scholars are so intractable precisely because they were not of interest to most early members of the Prophet's community, the great majority of whom had joined for reasons that had nothing to do either with the Prophet's moral and religious example or with the revelation he brought. Already within a relatively short time of the Prophet's death, among those early Muslims who did take an interest in Muḥammad's revelation, confusion could be found: Ṣabīgh b. 'Isl reportedly came to Medina asking about unclear passages of the Qur'ān (*mutashābih al-Qur'ān*); 'Umar b. al-Khaṭṭāb, the Commander of the Faithful, beat him till his head bled and forbade people to sit down with him.[141] By the time many more members of the community had become interested in the Qur'ān and the Prophet's teaching and words, precise answers had been forgotten—if indeed they had ever existed. When asked about a verse from the

claim attention and demand a solution.' Note also the observation of Hoyland, *Seeing Islam*, p. 550, esp. n. 25.

Paradoxically, however, such difficulties can also be taken as evidence that precise details of Muḥammad's earliest revelation could be forgotten by his followers—see, e.g., Witztum's discussion of *al-ḥawāyā* in Q 6:146 which, if emended to *al-jawāyā* makes better sense than the current Qur'ānic reading, 'The Syriac Milieu of the Quran,' pp. 54–57. On the basis of such examples, it can be argued that between Muḥammad's recitation of this passage and the placing of diacritical points on the consonantal skeleton of the written Qur'ānic text, members of the Prophet's community lost the original pronunciation upon which the consonantal skeleton had been based: *al-ḥawāyā* and *al-jawāyā* have the same skeleton and differ by only one diacritical point.

[141] On Ṣabīgh, see Ibn Ḥajar al-'Asqalānī, *al-Iṣāba fī tamyīz al-ṣaḥāba*, vol. 5, pp. 168–69 (no. 4118). This incident has been much discussed and debated; see, e.g., Goldziher, *Muslim Studies*, vol. 2, p. 84; Goldziher, *Schools of Koranic Commentators*, p. 36; H. Birkeland, *Old Muslim Opposition against the Interpretation of the Koran* (Oslo, 1955), p. 14; Abbott, *Studies in Arabic Literary Papyri*, vol. 2: *Qur'ānic Commentary and Tradition*, pp. 106–10; F. Leemhuis, 'Origins and Early Development of the *tafsīr* Tradition,' in A. Rippin, ed., *Approaches to the History of the Interpretation of the Qur'ān* (Oxford, 1988), pp. 16–19; and C. Gilliot, 'The Beginnings of Qur'ānic Exegesis,' in A. Rippin, ed., *The Qur'ān: Formative Interpretation* (Aldershot/Brookfield, VT, 1999), pp. 5–7.

Qur'ān, the reply of 'Abīda b. Qays (d. AD 692/AH 72) perhaps summed up the situation: 'Those who knew what the Qur'ān was sent down about have passed away,' he is supposed to have said, 'so fear God and you must be upright.'[142]

A number of reports, in fact, credit early Muslims with refusing to answer questions about the Qur'ān for which they did not have answers, and even of refusing to offer commentary on the Qur'ān:[143] 'I heard a man asking Sa'īd b. al-Musayyab,' Yaḥyā b. Sa'īd is reported to have said, 'about a verse from the Qur'ān, and he said: "I do not say anything about the Qur'ān."'[144] 'We would ask Sa'īd b. al-Musayyab about what is permitted and forbidden,' Yazīd b. Abī Yazīd was similarly reported to have stated, 'and he was the most learned of people. And if we asked him about the interpretation of a verse from the Qur'ān, he would be quiet, as if he had not heard.'[145] The Sa'īd b. al-Musayyab (d. ca. AD 712/AH 93) referred to here was no ordinary figure, either: he was regarded by some as the most learned Follower of the Prophet's Companions and the greatest religious authority in Medina in his day.[146] The collection and circulation of such statements can be taken as indications that some of those early followers of the Prophet who were actually interested in his message were not always clear about what his revelation meant. These reports can also be understood as attempts to rein in speculation and staunch an inflationary trend in the elaboration of its conflicting interpretations.[147]

Not everyone, however, was as conscientious as 'Abīda b. Qays or Sa'īd b. al-Musayyab in responding to the religious questions that eventually arose.

[142] Ibn Sa'd, *Kitāb al-ṭabaqāt al-kabīr*, vol. 6 pp. 63–64 (ed. Zetterstéen). For this, see Goldziher, *Schools of Koranic Commentators*, p. 37; Birkeland, *Old Muslim Opposition against Interpretation of the Koran*, pp. 11–12; and P. Crone, *Slaves on Horses: The Evolution of the Islamic Polity* (Cambridge, 1980), p. 206, n. 55.

[143] Cf. the early authorities cited in al-Ṭabarī, *Jāmi' al-bayān 'an ta'wīl āy al-Qur'ān*, vol. 1, pp. 79-81, and Ibn Kathīr, *Tafsīr al-Qur'ān al-'aẓīm* (ed. M al-Sayyid Muḥammad et al.) (Giza, 2000), vol. 1, pp. 12–17, where the emphasis is on pious early Muslims refusing to offer their personal opinions on the Qur'ān's meaning or to speak about passages they had no knowledge of. See also, Goldziher, *Schools of Koranic Commentators*, pp. 36–40, and Abbott, *Studies in Arabic Literary Papyri*, vol. 2: *Qur'ānic Commentary and Tradition*, p. 111.

[144] al-Ṭabarī, *Jāmi' al-bayān 'an ta'wīl āy al-Qur'ān*, vol. 1, p. 79.

[145] al-Ṭabarī, *Jāmi' al-bayān 'an ta'wīl āy al-Qur'ān*, vol. 1, pp. 80–81.

[146] On Sa'īd, see al-Mizzī, *Tahdhīb al-kamāl fī asmā' al-rijāl*, vol. 11, pp. 66–75, where his name is vocalized Sa'īd b. al-Musayyib. For al-Musayyab, see W. Caskell, *Ǧamharat an-nasab; das genealogische Werk des Hišam Ibn Muḥammad al-Kalbī* (Leiden, 1966), vol. 2, p. 501, s.n.

[147] Goldziher, *Schools of Koranic Commentators*, p. 40, saw such traditions as aimed against the use of *ra'y* (personal opinion) or *hawā* (personal inclination) in *tafsīr*; cf. also Birkeland, *Old Muslim Opposition*, pp. 30–32. Peter Brown has reminded me that devout monks might also be praised for refusing to offer opinions; what we might be dealing with here could also be instances of pious respect, or the appearance of this late antique *topos*.

With the passing of time, a vast number of different and competing answers was offered to a whole host of problems and queries for which certain answers had been lost. 'They ask us about our opinion,' 'Amr b. Dīnār (d. AD 744/AH 126), a leading religious scholar in eighth-century Mecca, is reported to have said, 'and so we tell them and they write it as if it were inscribed in stone, but perhaps we will go back on it tomorrow.'[148] It is perhaps no coincidence that in the massive Qur'ānic commentary of al-Ṭabarī, whose enormous collection of exegetical traditions has been foundational to understanding the setting and meaning of the Qur'ān's revelation for more than a millennium, the chains of transmission attached to the *ḥadīth* recorded there usually take one no further back than to around AH 100 (AD 718) and typically fall short of the rigorous standards of authenticity expected of *ḥadīth* in other fields of Islamic science.[149]

Answers were not just created in instances when the Prophet's views had been lost—they might also be created for questions the Prophet may well have never addressed. When al-Ḥajjāj asked the religious scholar al-Sha'bī (d. between AD 721–728/AH 103–110) a question about inheritance law, the latter replied that five different Companions of the Prophet of God had disagreed on the issue.[150] The transmission of the text of the Qur'ān itself might not always offer the level of precision that later members of the Prophet's community desired: conflicting answers to a legal issue could be given depending on how one vocalized its text.[151] A context like the one I have attempted to

[148] Ibn Sa'd, *Kitāb al-ṭabaqāt al-kabīr*, vol. 5, p. 353 (ed. K.V. Zetterstéen [Leiden, 1905]. On 'Amr, see H. Motzki's article, "Amr b. Dīnār,' in *EI3*.

[149] See Birkeland, *Old Muslim Opposition*, pp. 16–17, 36 and cf. H. Horst, 'Zur Überlieferung im Korankommentar aṭ-Ṭabarīs,' *ZDMG* 103 (1953), pp. 305–307. For criticism of Horst, see H. Berg, *The Development of Exegesis in Early Islam: The Authenticity of Muslim Literature from the Formative Period* (Richmond, 2000), pp. 66–69. But see also, H. Motzki, 'The Origins of Muslim Exegesis: A debate,' in H. Motzki et al., *Analysing Muslim Traditions: Studies in Legal, Exegetical, and Maghāzī Ḥadīth* (Leiden/Boston, 2010), pp. 231–303, for criticism of Berg, as well as the argument that Qur'ānic exegesis 'began to be established as a scholarly discipline... at the end of the first/seventh and the beginning of the second/eighth centuries' (272–73). Similarly, it has in fact been argued that it was not until around the end of the first century after the *hijra* that the *sunna*, or normative example, of the Prophet began to be emphasized as a resource for solving legal questions; see, e.g., Juynboll, *Muslim Tradition*, pp. 26, 30–36. But saying that Prophetic *sunna* began to be emphasized at this point is not of course to imply that it was not appealed to earlier—see the remarks of Motzki in his *The Origins of Islamic Jurisprudence*, pp. 295–96, and cf. n. 70, above.

[150] 'Abd Allāh, Zayd, 'Alī, 'Uthmān, Ibn 'Abbās. Al-Mas'ūdī, *Murūj al-dhahab*, vol. 5, p. 335. For this point, see Goldziher, *Muslim Studies*, vol. 2, p. 78. On al-Sha'bī, see G.H.A. Juynboll in *EI2*, vol. 9, pp. 162–63.

[151] E.g., *lamastum* vs. *lāmastum* in Q 4:43 and *yaṭhurna* vs. *yaṭṭahharna* in Q 2:222. For these and more, see al-Zarkashī, *al-Burhān fī 'ulūm al-Qur'ān* (ed. M. Abū al-Faḍl Ibrāhīm) (Cairo, 1957), vol. 1, pp. 326–27. For extensive discussion of the legal implications and different views about the vocalization of these two words in these two passages, see al-Qurṭubī, *al-Jāmi' li-aḥkām al-Qur'ān* (ed. 'A. Allāh b.

describe in this chapter, I would suggest, is the easiest explanation for the mass of confusion, contradiction, and ambiguity that can be found in the tradition on so many points.[152] The activities of a small number of scholars aside, significant numbers of the Prophet's community only took a real interest in his example and message long after he and those who knew him, or knew him best, had died.

We find, in fact, an implicit recognition of this in the Islamic tradition itself.[153] At the foundation of a great number of the traditions that provide a significant portion of the information we have about the words of Prophet and the traditional understanding of the Qur'ān are figures who were either very young at the end of Muḥammad's life or only knew him for a brief period. Abū Hurayra (d. AD 678/AH 58), for instance, who transmitted more sound *ḥadīth* than any other figure in the entire Islamic tradition (between 3,500 and 5,300 are attributed to him), only converted to Islam in AD 629 (AH 7) and knew the Prophet for roughly three years before he died.[154] When reading one of the more than one thousand narrations attributed to 'Ā'isha, one of the Prophet's wives and among the most controversial figures in early Islamic

---

'Abd al-Muḥsin al-Turkī) (Beirut, 2006), vol. 3, pp. 486–89 (on 2:222) and vol. 6, pp. 369–77 (on 4:43). For an example of different legal doctrines stemming from alternate versions of the Qur'ānic text, see Schacht, *The Origins of Muhammadan Jurisprudence*, p. 225.

[152] For example: As a strategy for dealing with the multiplicity of textual variants to the 'Uthmānic text, the Sunnī tradition would make a distinction between the Qur'ān (the divine communication [*al-waḥy*] sent down to Muḥammad) and the different readings (*qirā'āt*) of the Qur'ān (the difference in the writing of the words of the communication) (al-Zarkashī, *al-Burhān*, vol. 1, p. 318). A famous statement of Muḥammad provided another way of accounting for these variations: 'The Qur'ān has come down in seven *aḥruf*, all of them clear and sufficient,' the Prophet was reported to have said when approached with differing versions of the same Qur'ānic passage, 'So recite as you wish.' (See, e.g., Ibn Qutayba's invocation of this *ḥadīth* to answer critics of the Qur'ān in *Ta'wīl mushkil al-Qur'ān*, pp. 26–32 [ed. al-Sayyid Aḥmad Ṣaqr (Cairo, 1954)]. For various versions of this *ḥadīth*, see Aḥmad al-Bīlī, *al-Ikhtilāf bayna al-qirā'āt* [Beirut, 1988], pp. 39–43). What exactly *aḥruf* (sing. *ḥarf*) meant in this statement, however, was not exactly clear to later Muslims—al-Suyūṭī was able to list thirty-five different ways that scholars had understood the term—and whatever the text's meaning may have been, its ambiguity allowed it to be invoked almost talismanically by later Muslims seeking to make sense of and find Prophetic legitimation for the potentially confusing and unnerving mass of information about the diversity of the Qur'ānic text (see al-Suyūṭī, *al-Itqān*, vol. 1, pp. 172–83; and cf. al-Zarkashī, *al-Burhān*, vol. 1, p. 212). Crone, *Slaves on Horses*, pp. 3–18 and Crone, *Meccan Trade*, pp. 203–30 are classic statements of the manifold problems that attach to the early Islamic historical tradition.

[153] Cf. the observation in Ibn Sa'd, *Kitāb al-ṭabaqāt al-kabīr*, vol. 2.2 (ed. F. Schwally [Leiden, 1912]), pp. 126, 127, that the number of reports from the more advanced in age of the Prophet's Companions was few 'because they perished before they were sought after.' Most reports came from younger Companions 'because they continued on and their lives were long and people sought after them.' Cp. with the comments of Nöldeke et al. in *History of the Qur'ān*, pp. 317–18, 346.

[154] On Abū Hurayra, see J. Robson's article, 'Abū Hurayra,' in *EI2*, vol. 1, p. 129, and al-Mizzī, *Tahdhīb al-kamāl fī asmā' al-rijāl*, vol. 34, pp. 366–79. See also J.A.C. Brown, *Hadith: Muhammad's Legacy in the Medieval and Modern World* (Oxford, 2009), pp. 18–19. For 3,500, see Robson; for 5,300, see Brown.

history, it is easy to forget that what we have are the purported recollections of someone who knew Muḥammad as a young girl and a teenager—she was married to the Prophet from the age of nine till his death, when she was eighteen.[155] Ibn ʿAbbās, another figure to whom an enormous number of *ḥadīth* have been attributed—1,700 by one count—and who stands at the fountainhead of the Qur'ānic exegetical tradition, was perhaps as young as nine when the Prophet died.[156]

LATE CONVERSION: THE CASE OF THE UMAYYADS

An answer to the puzzles surrounding early Islam would also emphasize the dramatic political consequences of late conversion: about three decades after the Prophet's death, leadership in his religious community was assumed and held through military force by Muʿāwiya, a late convert whose family had been among the fiercest opponents of Muḥammad. Famous for his political skill, Muʿāwiya is also notable for the inscrutability and elusiveness of his actual religious beliefs as portrayed in our extant sources.[157] As a reflection of his checkered reputation in the early community, it can be pointed out that even standard Sunnī *ḥadīth* collections show that no less than the Prophet himself spoke of Muʿāwiya disapprovingly.[158] Muʿāwiya's father, Abū Sufyān, as we have already seen, was one of the leaders of pagan opposition to the

[155] Cf. the comments of Nöldeke et al. in *History of the Qur'ān*, p. 318, and cf. Brown, *Hadith*, pp. 19–20, where he attributes 2,200 *hadīth* to ʿĀ'isha.

[156] See Brown, *Hadith*, p. 19. On Ibn ʿAbbās, see Goldziher, *Schools of Koranic Commentators*, pp. 42–53; Nöldeke et al. in *History of the Qur'ān*, p. 346; F. Sezgin, *Geschichte des Arabischen Schriftums*, vol. 1: *Qur'ānwissenschaften, Ḥadīt Geschichte, Fiqh, Dogmatik, Mystik bis ca. 430 H.* (Leiden, 1967), pp. 25–28; L. Veccia Vaglieri's article, "Abd Allāh b. al-ʿAbbās,' in *EI2*, vol. 1, pp. 40–41; and C. Gilliot's article, "Abd Allāh b. al-ʿAbbās,' in *EI3*. Note Gilliot's comment: 'Ibn ʿAbbās can only have been a Companion of Muḥammad sensu stricto for about thirty months. . . .' The authenticity of reports attributed to Ibn ʿAbbās have, not surprisingly, been the subject of much scholarly interest and skepticism. Berg, *The Development of Exegesis in Early Islam*, pp. 129–37, summarizes a great deal of research on the figure of Ibn ʿAbbās, especially as he relates to the history of *tafsīr*.

[157] On the difficulty of ascertaining Muʿāwiya's religious attitudes, see R. S. Humphreys, *Muʿawiya ibn Abi Sufyan: From Arabia to Empire* (Oxford, 2006), p. 125.

[158] For the (in)famous incident in which a young Muʿāwiya did not come to the Prophet when twice summoned by him, because Muʿāwiya was eating (which prompted the Prophet's exclamation, 'May God not satisfy his stomach!'), see Muslim b. al-Ḥajjāj, *Ṣaḥīḥ*, vol. 4, p. 2010 (no. 96) (ed. M. Fu'ād ʿAbd al-Bāqī) (n.d., n.p.). On this *ḥadīth* and later Sunnī attempts to soften it as well as other negative reports about Muʿāwiya (and the contemporary debate over Muʿāwiya's character), see N. Husayn, 'The Memory of ʿAlī b. Abī Ṭālib in early Sunnī Thought,' (PhD diss., Princeton University, 2016), pp. 62–64. For Muʿāwiya depicted as very overweight as he grew older, see Humphreys, *Muʿawiya ibn Abi Sufyan*, p. 132. For the idea that an unbeliever eats an enormous amount, while a Muslim eats moderately (the Prophet is supposed to have said, 'A Muslim eats in one intestine and an unbeliever eats in seven intes-

Prophet: at one point he in fact had attempted to have Muḥammad murdered and Muḥammad, for his part, had tried to have Abū Sufyān assassinated in response.[159] Abū Sufyān only converted to Islam in 630 at the conquest of Mecca.[160] Muʿāwiya's mother, Hind bt. ʿUtba, as we have seen, reportedly once chewed part of the liver of the Prophet's uncle Hamza out of spite. She is also remembered for having then spit it out, whereupon she cut off more of the liver and used those parts as jewelry. Hind also was said to have made jewelry from the noses and ears she cut off other dead Muslims after the Battle of Uḥud.[161] The military forces of Muʿāwiya's son and successor, Yazīd, would (among other things), decapitate Ḥusayn, the grandson of the Prophet, lay siege to Mecca and bombard the city with war machines in an attack that saw the Kaʿba set on fire.[162] Muʿāwiya himself was famous for his political and military rivalry with ʿAlī, the Prophet's cherished first cousin and son-in-law. He reportedly ordered ʿAlī and his companions vilified and shamed on a regular basis in mosques in Kufa.[163]

In other words, not long after his death, leadership in the Prophet's religious community fell into the hands of a family that had been his enemies for much of his prophetic career and would, in the decades after his death, emerge as the chief nemesis of his family and descendants; they would be accused of killing a number of them.[164]

---

tines,' and 'A Muslim drinks in one intestine and an unbeliever drinks in seven intestines,') see Mālik b. Anas, *al-Muwaṭṭa'*, vol. 2, p. 924, nos. 9 and 10.

[159] M. J. Kister, '"O God, tighten thy grip on Muḍar"... Some Socio-Economic Religious Aspects of an Early *ḥadīth*,' *JESHO* 24 (1981), p. 264.

[160] See W. M. Watt's article, 'Abū Sufyān,' in *EI2*, vol. 1, p. 151. For Abū Sufyān's relations with Muḥammad and eventual reconciliation, see Kister, '"O God, tighten thy grip on Muḍar," pp. 258–67.

[161] See Ibn Hishām, *Kitāb sīrat rasūl Allāh*, pp. 580–82 (ed. Wüstenfeld, vol. 1.2; ET available in Guillaume, *The Life of Muhammad*, pp. 385–86) and al-Maqrīzī, *Nizāʿ wa-'l-takhāṣum fīmā bayna Banī Umayya wa-Banī Hāshim*, p. 15 (ed. Vos; ET available in Bosworth, *al-Maqrīzī's 'Book of Contention and Strife...,'* p. 54) and cf. n. 36, above. On the portrayal of Hind, the question of its historicity, its use to delegitimate the Umayyads, and attempts to repair her reputation, see N. M. El Cheikh, *Women, Islam, and Abbasid Identity* (Cambridge, Mass., 2015), pp. 21, 26–34.

[162] On Yazīd, see G. R. Hawting's, 'Yazīd (I) b. Muʿāwiya,' in *EI2*, vol. 11, pp. 309–11.

[163] al-Ṭabarī, *Ta'rīkh*, vol. 2.1, p. 112 (ed. H. Thorbecke, S. Fraenkel, and I. Guidi [Leiden, 1881–1883]; ET available in M. G. Morony, *Between Civil Wars: The Caliphate of Muʿāwiyah* [HṬ 18] [Albany, 1987], p. 123). Cf. Goldziher, *Muslim Studies*, vol. 2, p. 44.

[164] See al-Maqrīzī, *Nizāʿ wa-'l-takhāṣum fīmā bayna Banī Umayya wa-Banī Hāshim*, pp. 3–4 (ed. Vos; ET available in Bosworth, *al-Maqrīzī's 'Book of contention and strife...*,' p. 44). Traditionally, critics of the Umayyads have dwelt on their poor relations with the Prophet, but it is also worth noting that Muḥammad's uncle, al-ʿAbbās, the forbear of the Abbasid dynasty which overthrew and succeeded the Umayyads, himself only converted around 629/630 and had in fact taken up arms against the Prophet and the Muslims at the Battle of Badr (see Bosworth's comments, pp. 27–28). On al-ʿAbbās, see W. M. Watt's article, 'al-ʿAbbās b. ʿAbd al-Muṭṭalib,' in *EI2*, vol. 1, pp. 8–9.

Given this situation and the fierce opposition to Umayyad rule from groups that judged their claim to rule illegitimate, we should not be astonished to find such traditions, nor should we be surprised that a host of traditions would eventually circulate claiming all manner of Prophetic condemnation against the Umayyads.[165] These included the charge that Muḥammad had asked God to curse Abū Sufyān, Muʿāwiya, and Yazīd (the son of Abū Sufyān); that the Prophet had ordered Muʿāwiya killed if he was ever spotted giving a sermon on his pulpit; and that the Prophet spoke of Muʿāwiya inhabiting the lowest pit of hell—in addition to claiming that the Qur'ān itself had criticized the family (17:60).[166] I have already mentioned the charge that the Qur'ān was altered, an accusation that might have a specifically Umayyad context: both Muslims and non-Muslims accused the Umayyads of changing the Qur'ān.[167] The Christian polemicist al-Kindī, in fact, alleged that al-Ḥajjāj b. Yūsuf (d. AD 714/AH 95), the powerful governor of Iraq during the caliphate of ʿAbd al-Malik and Walīd I, had removed verses from the Qur'ān that mentioned the Umayyad family.[168]

Not just the Sufyānids, but their successors, the Marwānids, too, allegedly had a bad track record with the Prophet. Al-Ḥakam b. Abī al-ʿĀṣī, whose son Marwān b. al-Ḥakam was the first Marwānid caliph, was a figure remembered by critics of the Umayyads for having verbally abused the Prophet, for his opportunistic conversion to Islam at the conquest of Mecca, for having mocked the Prophet even after his conversion, for having spied on the Prophet while he was with one of his wives, and for having been cursed by the Prophet and kicked out of Medina.[169] Al-Ḥakam b. Abī al-ʿĀṣī was one of the grandfathers of ʿAbd al-Malik; his other grandfather, Muʿāwiya b. Abī al-ʿĀṣī, was remembered by critics of the Umayyads for having cut off the nose of Ḥamza after his death at the Battle of Uḥud.[170] Whether Sufyānid or Marwānid, there were

[165] For the potentially Shīʿī origin of anti-Umayyad stories, see most conveniently the comments in Donner, 'Was Marwan Ibn al-Hakam the first "Real" Muslim?' p. 107.

[166] al-Ṭabarī, *Ta'rīkh*, vol. 3.4, pp. 2170–73 (ed. M. J. de Goeje [Leiden, 1890]); ET available in F. Rosenthal, *The Return of the Caliphate to Baghdad* [HṬ 38] [Albany, 1985], pp. 52–58). Cf. Goldziher, *Muslim Studies*, vol. 2, p. 54, and Humphreys, *Muʿawiya ibn Abi Sufyan*, pp. 5–6.

[167] al-Ṭabarī, *Ta'rīkh*, vol. 3.4, pp. 2175–76 (ed. M. J. de Goeje [Leiden, 1890]; ET available in Rosenthal, *The Return of the Caliphate to Baghdad*, p. 61–62); Jeffery, 'Ghevond's Text of the Correspondence between 'Umar II and Leo III,' p. 298 (on this text, see T. Greenwood's, '*The Letter of Leo III* in Ghewond,' in *CMR*, vol. 1, pp. 203–208).

[168] And also verses that mentioned the Abbasid family. See al-Kindī, *Apology*, pp. 137, 138.

[169] al-Maqrīzī, *Nizāʿ wa-'l-takhāṣum fīmā bayna Banī Umayya wa-Banī Hāshim*, pp. 12–14 (ed. Vos; ET available in Bosworth, *al-Maqrīzī's 'Book of contention and strife...,'* pp. 52–54). On these traditions, and the dubious value of some of them, see Bosworth's comments, pp. 123–25.

[170] al-Maqrīzī, *Nizāʿ wa-'l-takhāṣum fīmā bayna Banī Umayya wa-Banī Hāshim*, p. 19 (ed. Vos; ET

many grounds on which to attack the Umayyads' spiritual *bona fides*. Over the course of the nine decades the Umayyad family held onto leadership of the Prophet's community, and long after, their religious credentials would face constant criticism.[171]

The emergence of Islam that some scholars have attempted to identify in the late seventh century[172] was not so much an emergence as it was the increasing official use of Muḥammad's name and message by Umayyads in the legitimation of their rule. This increasingly public appeal to the Prophet and his legacy can be interpreted in various ways, but a simple one (that does not require positing some sort of radical shift in the nature of Islam) would be to see this shift as an Umayyad response to military rebellion and internal critique from other Muslims, as well as an answer to the religious challenge posed by both the Byzantine state and the vast numbers of non-Muslims living under their authority.[173] Faced with ideological challenges from without and within, the Marwānid state 'got religion,' so to speak—at least publicly.

I have in this chapter attempted to emphasize the consequences of late and mass conversion to Islam as results of Muḥammad's increasing military and political hegemony in Western Arabia, and nothing illustrates these consequences quite as clearly as the rise of the Umayyads to power, their leadership over Muḥammad's community, and the support they received from other members of the Prophet's community.[174] Regardless of the negative assessments of the Umayyads written by devout authors in later generations, by

available in Bosworth, *al-Maqrīzī's 'Book of contention and strife . . .,'* p. 58), where this point about 'Abd al-Malik having two grandfathers with very disreputable track records is made.

[171] Cf. the comments in Humphreys, *Mu'awiya ibn Abi Sufyan*, p. 123.

[172] Cf. n. 130, above.

[173] For the Zubayrid introduction of the affirmation that Muḥammad is the messenger of God on coinage in the 680s as a practice the Marwānids copied and continued, see Robinson, *'Abd al-Malik*, pp. 38–39. For an argument that the celebrated shift to aniconic coins with Islamic affirmations on them should be understood in the context of Umayyad religious rivalry with the Byzantines, see J. Walker, *A Catalogue of the Arab-Byzantine and Post Reform Umaiyad Coins* (London, 1956), pp. liv–lv. See also Hoyland, *Seeing Islam*, pp. 552–53, on pressures driving a Marwānid public embrace of Islam in the face of the Zubayrid religious critique of the Umayyads. The notion of Umayyad rulers gradually becoming more devout is of course not new. It can already be found in J. Wellhausen, *The Arab Kingdom and Its Fall*, trans. M. G. Weir (Calcutta, 1927), p. 268.

[174] On supporters of the Umayyads, see P. Crone's article, "Uthmāniyya,' in *EI2*, vol. 10, pp. 952–54, and cf. Goldziher, *Muslim Studies*, vol. 2, pp. 115–20. In AD 915 (AH 303), when the famous *ḥadīth* scholar al-Nasā'ī went to Damascus, he was reportedly asked to narrarate traditions about the virtues of Mu'āwiya. When he could only say negative things about him (e.g., report the tradition in which the Prophet asked that Mu'āwiya's stomach never be satisfied, cf. above, n. 158), al-Nasā'ī was forcibly thrown out of the mosque, trampled on, and taken to al-Ramla, where he died. See Ibn Khallikān, *Wafayāt al-a'yān wa-anbā' abnā' al-zamān* (ed. I. 'Abbās) (Beirut, 1977), p. 77. Among the works of Abū 'Umar Muḥammad b. 'Abd al-Waḥīd al-Zāhid al-Muṭarriz al-Warrāq al-Bāwārdī (d. AH 345 /AD 957) was a work *Fī faḍā'il Mu'āwiya*; see Brockelmann, *GAL*, vol. 1, p. 123.

Abbasid apologists, or by their contemporary rivals, the persistence of Umayyad power and support for the dynasty in the second half of the seventh century and first half of the eighth can be taken as a reflection of the attitudes of many Muslims in this early period.[175] One of the greatest ironies of Islamic history—that not long after his death, the Prophet's staunchest opponents and their descendants assumed leadership of his community—provides therefore a key insight into the nature of early Islam itself: not the Islam of the, relatively speaking, small number of devout scholars, traditionists, Companions, and Followers of Companions, nor that of various pious figures in Mecca or Medina whose purported words and opinions are the subject of most academic inquiry.[176] The Islam of everybody else.

It is this Islam of everybody else that is typically lost in discussions of early Islamic history, to say nothing of discussions of early Christian-Muslim interactions. If we are interested in seeing what belonging to the Prophet's community meant for a late convert in the seventh century, we need only look at the example of Muʿāwiya: as the fifth leader of the Muslim community and a seminal figure in Islamic history, he was the most prominent late convert in the early decades of Muslim rule in the Middle East. A near-contemporary source reported that Muʿāwiya went and prayed at Golgotha and Gethsemane after he was made Commander of the Faithful in Jerusalem in 661.[177] When the bishop Arculf was visiting Jerusalem in the 670s, he reported hearing a

[175] And, it should be emphasized, support for the Umayyads could readily be found among the devout as well. S. C. Judd, *Religious Scholars and the Umayyads: Piety-Minded Supporters of the Marwānid Caliphate* (London/New York, 2014), argued strongly that the traditional picture of the Umayyad dynasty as being nonreligious and opposed by pious Muslims was inaccurate and pointed to scholars such as al-Shaʿbī, al-Zuhrī, al-Awzāʿī, and Sufyān al-Thawrī as being both pro-Marwānid and pious figures respected by and influential in the later tradition. It might be suggested, as well, that the Umayyads benefitted from an early theory of the caliphate and the importance of the imamate, similar to that outlined in Crone and Hind's, *God's Caliph*, esp. pp. 24–42, in which allegiance to a caliph, who was seen as a figure very much like the Prophet in his immense authority (though lacking revelation), was as much a religious as a political act and one on which one's salvation depended. On such a view, levels of individual knowledge and religious engagement among simple Muslims will perhaps have been less important than an individual's choice of which leader to follow. With this said, however, the extent to which everyday, ordinary Muslims will have had the sort of theory of political-religious rulership as can be found in the obsequious, poetic court panegyric that Crone and Hinds relied heavily on to build their case, is hard to know. We run into, again, the problem of the simple believer and the nature of our sources.

[176] Which is not to say that the Umayyads lacked supporters among religious scholars: Goldziher, *Muslim Studies*, vol. 2, pp. 43–52, already highlighted the connection between Umayyad authorities and religious scholars, such as al-Zuhrī, who supported their regime's propaganda needs. For a recent attempt at nuancing the views of Goldziher (and others) on the relationship between scholars and the Umayyads, see Judd, *Religious Scholars and the Umayyads* (see previous note).

[177] *Maronite Chronicle*, p. 71 (ed. Brooks [CSCO III.4]; ET taken from Palmer et al., *The Seventh Century in the West-Syrian Chronicles*, p. 31).

story in which Muʿāwiya arbitrated a dispute between Jewish Christians and Jews over a relic that was supposed to be the cloth that lay over Christ's head in the tomb. The Muslim ruler had a large fire built, took hold of the disputed cloth, and told the battling parties:

> May Christ, the Saviour of the world, who suffered for mankind: Whose head, when he was entombed, was covered by this Cloth which I hold to my breast: Now judge by fire between you, since you are disputing about the Cloth. Thus let us know which of these contentious mobs is the one to which he desires to entrust this great gift![178]

Regardless of whether it actually happened, the story was apparently being widely told and believed even while Muʿāwiya was still Commander of the Faithful—it was, as Adomnan put it, 'affirmed to be true by the whole population of Jerusalem' and had been told to Arculf 'by Christian residents of Jerusalem.'[179] Muʿāwiya was also responsible for rebuilding the Cathedral of Edessa after it was destroyed by an earthquake in 679; his order to have this celebrated Christian structure repaired was allegedly given in response to a dream which indicated, in the report of Michael the Great, 'the destruction of ʿAlī and the confirmation of [Muʿāwiya's] kingdom.'[180] To be sure, Muʿāwiya's actions (and stories that circulated about them among his subjects) will have been influenced and constrained by the fact that most of his subjects in Syria and Palestine were Christians, but they nevertheless represent the reported behaviors of a late convert to Islam who is not anonymous in our sources. What should we assume the Islam of the great mass of other late converts—that is, the vast majority of Muslims—looked like in the seventh century?

If scholars paid more attention to the implications of such considerations, the conundrums that have perplexed students of the early Islamic period might well seem less intractable. The Islamic tradition has preserved the names and prized the memories of a number of Companions and devout members of the early generations of the Prophet's community, but such figures, if the recorded

[178] Adomnan of Iona, *De locis sanctis*, 1.9.13–14 (ed. L. Bieler in P. Geyer et al. eds., *Itineraria et alia geographica* (CSCL 175), pp. 193–94; ET taken from J. Wilkinson, *Jerusalem Pilgrims before the Crusades* [Warminster, 1977], p. 176).

[179] Adomnan of Iona, *De locis sanctis*, 1.9.1 (ed. Bieler, *Itineraria et alia geographica* [CSCL 175], p. 192; ET taken from Wilkinson, *Jerusalem Pilgrims before the Crusades*, p. 175). On Arculf in Jerusalem, see J. Tolan, 'Le pèlerin Arculfe et le roi Mavias: la circulation des informations à propos des "Sarrasins" au VIIe–VIIIe siècles, de Jérusalem à Iona et Yarrow,' in P. Henriet and J. Ducos, eds., *Passages. Déplacements des hommes, circulation des textes et identités dans l'Occident médiéval* (Toulouse, 2009), pp. 175–85, esp. 182–83 on this incident in particular; and for discussion of the historicity of the incident, see further R. G. Hoyland and S. Waidler, 'Adomnán's De Locis Sanctis and the Seventh-Century Near East,' *English Historical Review* 129 (2014), pp. 795–97.

[180] Michael the Great, *Chronicle* 11.13 (ed. Chabot, 4.436–37 = 2.457).

memories of them are in fact reliable, represented a minority within a minority and must have been atypical among their co-religionists.[181] If, to put it bluntly, most early Muslims did not know a great deal about the ideological content and implications of the religious movement to which they ostensibly belonged, and many of those who were in leadership positions in the early Muslim state were late converts who had shown an interest in Muḥammad's religious community only after the Prophet achieved military hegemony in Western Arabia, then nothing I have written here should be astonishing.

Assuming widespread lack of knowledge of the details of the Prophet's message among Arab conquerors may help explain why, for example, Syriac writers tend not to invoke Islam in describing the Arab conquests: '[I]t would be generally true,' Sebastian Brock has observed, 'to say that the Syriac sources of this period see the conquests primarily as Arab, and not Muslim.'[182] Regardless of how Arabic sources written several hundreds of years later by Muslims may have presented the conquests to the conquered, their new rulers and their armies had not presented themselves in a chiefly religious manner—something perhaps to be expected if their decision to join the Prophet's community was motivated by his political and military success (or its apparent religious implications) rather than by the specifically doctrinal and propositional contents of his revelation (which many of them quite probably knew little of).[183]

What would our understanding of seventh-century Islam look like if we took as typical Muslims figures like Muʿāwiya, the late convert-turned-influential-ruler with a dubious history of relations with the Prophet; or Bishr b. Rabīʿa, whose entire knowledge of Muḥammad's revelation consisted in the phrase 'In the name of God, the Merciful, the Compassionate'; or Aws b. Khālid, who knew no Qur'ān at all? What would happen if we placed their experience, and that of those like them, at the center of our story and de-emphasized the experience of men like ʿAlī b. Abī Ṭālib, ʿUmar b. al-Khaṭṭāb, ʿAbd Allāh b.

[181] On the circumstances and the marginal status of the pious among the followers of the Prophet and the devout of Medina under Umayyad rule, see the comments of Goldziher in *Muslim Studies*, vol. 2, pp. 41–42, 75, though Judd, *Religious Scholars and the Umayyads*, has emphasized that the Marwānids enjoyed the support of the 'piety-minded' as well.

[182] See Brock, 'Syriac Views of Emergent Islam,' p. 14, and cf. Penn, 'John and the Emir,' p. 72. Cf., too, the observation of Jean Gascou, 'Arabic Taxation in the Mid-Seventh-Century Greek Papyri,' in C. Zuckerman, ed., *Constructing the Seventh Century* (Paris, 2013), p. 677: 'From the time of the conquest to the beginning of the eighth century, the word Muslim is only attested as a proper name, which is very puzzling. The Greek documents describe the new rulers as Arabs or Saracens (in Syria, Hagarenes), which are ethnic concepts. They also mention μωαγαρῖται an assumed transposition of *muhajirûn*.' On the question of the 'Arab' conquests, see Appendix II.

[183] Though it cannot be argued that non-Muslim authors in general saw the Arab conquerors in strictly nonreligious terms. Hoyland, *Seeing Islam*, pp. 549–50, lists a variety of religious beliefs and practices associated with the Arabs by non-Muslim writers.

Mas'ūd, Ubayy b. Ka'b, or Zayd b. Thābit, whose extensive knowledge of Muḥammad's revelation made them the exception, not the rule? What would happen if we took seriously the notion that there was a layering of knowledge and religious engagement in the early Muslim community?

Scholars who have attempted to find an overarching motivation or a particular interpretation of Muḥammad's message that drove the Arab conquests of the seventh century have not paid enough attention to the many 'Amr b. Ma'dīkaribs of the seventh century—he fought, as we saw above, with the Arab army at Qādisiyya, one of the most consequential battles in Middle Eastern history, and yet he reportedly knew nothing of the Qur'ān because after his conversion he had been too busy with military raiding to memorize any of it.[184] And in overlooking people like 'Amr, scholars have missed a simple fact: a well-articulated and developed ideology—apocalyptic, religious, nativist, or otherwise—is not a necessary precondition for widespread military success over a large geographic area. This is especially the case when the victorious forces are in a position to acquire vast amounts of wealth, slaves, and concubines.[185] Did the Huns, Vikings, or Mongols represent apocalyptic or nativist phenomena? Holding onto territories and governing them as part of an empire, however, once they have been captured, will eventually require some sort of more fully articulated and elaborated ideological justification.[186] Sometimes an effect can be much greater than a cause.

What happened, therefore, when the Arab rulers of a new, diverse, and enormous empire needed to develop a justification for their rule and avoid assimilating into the conquered populations? And what happened when simple members of the Prophet's community—like 'Amr b. Ma'dīkarib—met simple Christians in Syria, Iraq, and Egypt?

The earliest Christian-Muslim interactions took place in a Near East characterized by widespread ignorance of and selective regard—if not outright disregard—for the Qur'ān and for the Prophet's teaching and behavior, even as the understanding of these things and their import among the religiously engaged members of his community were undergoing development and change. It was in such a setting that the notional followers of the Prophet had to answer questions from members of other religious groups and Muslim leaders had to

[184] Cf. above, nn. 24–26.

[185] For the idea that there must have been an ideological motivation for the conquests—though perhaps unknowable given the nature of our sources—and against the notion that the conquests were accidential, see e.g., Donner, 'Qur'ânicization of Religio-Political Discourse in the Umayyad Period,' p. 87. What I am suggesting here is a third way between accounts of the conquest that see it as accidental and accounts that invoke grand ideological justifications.

[186] I am grateful to Peter Brown for this insight.

make cultic and doctrinal decisions about the practical implications of Muḥammad's preaching. It is in the context of these types of encounters and ideological needs that we will find Islam taking on many of the features familiar to us today.

* * *

We have now looked at what 'Christian' and 'Muslim' might have meant in the seventh and eighth centuries. How does this meaning affect how we think about Muslim-Christian interaction?

CHAPTER 11

Joining (and Leaving) a Muslim Minority

A mass of them were baptized, some of them out of religious desire and some of them out of fear of the Emperor.

—*Chronicle of Seert*[1]

Many of these Greeks who decided to accept Christianity did so in name only, as a ward against the difficulties that they now found themselves in, and most of them were caught soon afterward performing their libations and sacrifices and other unholy rites.

—Procopius, *Secret History*[2]

The Jews, for their part, were baptized against their will and then washed off their baptism; and they partook of holy communion on a full stomach and so defiled the faith.

—Theophanes, *Chronicle*[3]

Christian-Muslim interaction can take a number of forms and we will examine some of these in Part 4. What interests me at present, however, is one specific kind of Christian-Muslim interaction, the most consequential: conversion. There were, we saw in Chapter 2, a great number of reasons why a person might belong to, or switch from, one church to another in the post-Chalcedonian world. What many of these reasons shared was that they bore little resemblance to the sort of dramatic and celebrated individual conversions—of Paul, of Augustine, or even of Constantine—that often subtly shape our expectations of what a religious change looks like, or should. If we approach the question of conversion between Christian confessions expecting to find numerous examples of people changing their beliefs because, like John Wesley, they felt their heart to be strangely warmed, we will be disappointed.

[1] *Chronicle of Seert* 2.22 (ed. Scher [7.2], p. 53).

[2] Procopius, *Secret History* 11.32 (ed. J. Haury and G. Wirth, *Procopius. Opera Omnia*, vol. 3: *Historia Arcana*, p. 75; translation taken from Kaldellis, *Prokopios: The Secret History with Related Texts*, pp. 54–55).

[3] Theophanes, *Chronicle* AM 6214 (ed. de Boor, vol. 1, p. 401; ET taken from Mango and Scott, *The Chronicle of Theophanes Confessor*, p. 554; cf. Chapter 14, n. 224).

Thinking about conversion in an intra-Christian context raised questions not only of the role of sincerity and will, but also of the importance of intellectual content and its apprehension in a religious shift. We are now concerned with a similar question: why would a person convert from Christianity to Islam?[4] If we are interested in taking seriously the reality that the world of late Roman and medieval Middle Eastern Christianity was a world of simple believers, we should be more specific: why would a simple Christian make the decision to become a Muslim? How important were doctrinal considerations in such a shift? In the early centuries of Christianity, notable moments of conversion away from Christianity happened in periods of state persecution. In these instances, however, Christian apostasy would typically be followed by a return to Christianity by many who had abandoned their previous faith.[5] After the Arab conquests, did conversion from Christianity to Islam have a similar pattern, or did it represent a new model in the history of conversion away from Christianity and de-Christianization?

These are no small questions, either: the Middle East today is an overwhelmingly Muslim region and even though it contains, relatively speaking, a small percentage of the world's Muslim population—demographically, South Asia and Southeast Asia are much, much more consequential for global Islam—Islam has often been regarded as more indigenous and deeply rooted in a place like Egypt than in a place like Indonesia. But such contemporary (mis)perceptions notwithstanding, can we speak with any confidence about when it became the case that the majority of the inhabitants of the formerly Roman Middle East actually were Muslim and no longer Christian—as opposed to merely being ruled over by Muslims?

Now that we have asked what 'Christian' and 'Muslim' might mean in the early medieval Middle East, we can begin to attempt to address such questions.

[4] The question of why a person would have converted to Christianity in the first place is also an interesting one, but far beyond the scope of this book. For the variety of reasons why this might have happened, see D. König's extremely thorough *Bekehrungsmotive: Untersuchungen zum Christianisierungsprozess im römischen Westreich und seinen romanisch-germanischen Nachfolgern (4.-8. Jahrhundert)* (Husum, 2008), which has a Western focus but nevertheless is useful for scholars interested in late Roman and early medieval conversion, regardless of geographical focus. Av. Cameron, 'Christian Conversion in Late Antiquity: Some Issues,' in A. Papaconstantinou, N. McLynn, and D.L. Schwartz, eds., *Conversion in Late Antiquity: Christianity, Islam, and Beyond: Papers from the Andrew W. Mellon Foundation Sawyer Seminar, University of Oxford, 2009–2010* (Farnham, Surrey/Burlington, 2015), pp. 3–21, is a valuable discussion and overview of a number of important aspects of the question of Christian conversion. For a discussion of theoretical questions that attach to the notion of 'conversion' and how it is represented in written texts, see R. Szpiech, *Conversion and Narrative: Reading Religious Authority in Medieval Polemic* (Philadelphia, 2013), pp. 9–17.

[5] One need only think of the controversies surrounding the Novatian and Donatist Schisms for evidence of this pattern.

They are central to our understanding of the social and religious history of this period and fundamental to any attempt at making sense of the world the Arab conquests created.

SOME (HOSTILE) EXPLANATIONS OF CONVERSION

So why would a simple Christian (or non-Muslim) convert to Islam? The most obvious answer is that there is no single answer: motivations for conversion were sundry. In the last chapter, we focused on the early centuries of Islamic history, but let us for the moment jump forward to see how this question looked later in the medieval period. The Baghdad philosopher Ibn Kammūna (d. 683/1284-5), who was a Jew, had a very no-nonsense and unromantic understanding of reasons for becoming a Muslim. 'Until today,' he wrote,

> We do not see anyone enter into Islam save that he is fearful, or seeking glory, or he is grieved at heavy taxes, or fleeing from low standing, or taken in captivity, or smitten with a Muslim woman, or something like that. We have never seen a man learned in his own religion and in the religion of Islam, honorable, wealthy, and devout, move to the religion of Islam for something other than the reasons mentioned or what is like them.[6]

Christian leaders saw things much the same way. The East Syrian Ḥunayn b. Isḥāq (d. 873),[7] the Chalcedonian Theodore Abū Qurrah, (d. ca. 820),[8] and the Miaphysite Ḥabīb b. Khidma Abū Rā'iṭa (fl. early ninth century)[9] have each

[6] Ibn Kammūna, *Tanqīh al-abḥāth lil-milal al-thalāth*, p. 102 (ed. M. Perlmann, *Sa'd b. Mansūr ibn Kammūna's Examination of the Inquiries into the Three Faiths: A Thirteenth-Century Essay into Comparative Religion* [Berkeley and Los Angeles, 1967]). For this, see J.-M. Fiey, 'Conversions à l'Islam de Juifs et de Chrétiens sous les Abbassides d'après les sources arabes et syriaques,' in ed. J. Irmscher, *Rapports entre Juifs, Chrétiens et Musulmans. Eine Sammlung von Forschungsbeiträgen* (Amsterdam, 1995), p. 16.

[7] Ḥunayn b. Isḥāq, *Kayfiyyat idrāk ḥaqīqat al-diyāna* 1 (ed. S. K. Samir, 'Maqālat Ḥunayn b. Isḥāq fī kayfiyyat idrāk ḥaqīqat al-diyāna,' *al-Machriq* 71 [1997], pp. 352–53; a FT by P. Nwiya of the very similar 'personal recension' of this text can be found in S. K. Samir and P. Nwiya, *Une correspondence Islamo-Chrétienne entre Ibn al-Munağğim, Ḥunayn ibn Isḥāq et Qusṭā ibn Lūqā* [PO 40.4] [Turnhout, 1981], pp. 173–75). On this text and its recensions, as well as the connection between Ḥunayn's ideas in it and Islam, see B. Roggema's article, '*Kayfiyyat idrāk ḥaqīqat al-diyāna*,' in *CMR*, vol. 1, pp. 775–79.

[8] Theodore Abū Qurrah, *On the Confirmation of the Gospel*, p. 71 (ed. C. Bacha, *Mayāmir Thāwdūrus Abī Qurrah Usquf Ḥarrān: aqdam ta'līf 'Arabī Naṣrānī* [Beirut, 1904]; ET available in Lamoreaux, *Theodore Abū Qurrah*, p 49). For Muslims as the audience of this treatise, see Lamoreaux's comment in *CMR*, vol. 1, p. 456. See also Theodore's, *Opusculum 7* (*On the Contending of Christ with the Devil*), PG 97, cols. 1525, 1528 (ET available in Lamoreaux, *Theodore Abū Qurrah*, pp. 238–39). On this text, see Lamoreaux, *CMR*, vol. 1, pp. 479–81.

[9] Abū Rā'iṭa al-Takrītī, *Fī ithbāt dīn al-Naṣrāniyya wa-ithbāt al-thālūth al-muqaddas* 2–9 (ed. and trans. Graf, *Die Schriften des Jacobiten Ḥabīb ibn Ḫidma Abū Rā'iṭa* [CSCO 130–31: SA 14–15], pp. 131–36

left us analyses of what they viewed as legitimate and illegitimate reasons for converting from one religion to another. Though Islam is usually not explicitly mentioned in such discussions, it is clearly in the background, and there is a good deal of overlap in what they had to say. On their view, becoming a Muslim was something that people did out of a number of motivations, some of them more unholy than others: in addition to a desire for material benefits or a drive for status and power, there were family or tribal connections that drew people to convert. There was also an attraction to a religious framework that allowed a greater range of human behaviors and activities—references to permissiveness in these texts should probably be understood as relating to the Muslim sanction of polygamy and divorce and potentially to notions of paradise as a place of physical delights.[10] People might also become Muslims under compulsion. Tellingly, these leaders could not conceive that a person might convert out of sincere religious motivation. Conversions that took place with reference to doctrines or beliefs were seen as cases where people had been deceived or had acted out of a lack of education and ignorance.

The suggestion that one converted to Islam for nonreligious reasons in order to gain worldly benefits was in fact common among non-Muslims.[11] Writing in the early ninth century, the Christian apologist and polemicist known as al-Kindī appealed to an allegedly widely known story that suggested even the caliph was aware of this reality. 'You no doubt recall,' he wrote to his (likely fictional) Muslim correspondent, al-Hāshimī,

> what happened at the salon (*majlis*) of the Commander of the Faithful: It was said to him about a man who was one of his most illustrious companions that he only made an outward showing of Islam, but that his inner beliefs were filthy Magianism. And so he responded with the response you are aware of, saying, 'I certainly know, by God, that so-and-so, and so-and-so'—and he listed a number

---

[Arabic] = 159–66 [GT]; ET in Keating, *Defending the "People of Truth" in the Early Islamic Period*, pp. 83–93).

[10] For Nonnus of Nisibis's (d. ca. 870) view that the Qur'ānic image of paradise as a place of carnal pleasure is something which entices the simple, see S. H. Griffith, 'Disputes with Muslims in Syriac Christian Texts: From Patriarch John (d. 648) to Bar Hebraeus (d. 1286),' in B. Lewis, and F. Niewöhner, eds., *Religionsgespräche im Mittelalter*, p. 266, and C. Hackenburg, 'Voices of the Converted: Christian Apostate Literature in Medieval Islam,' (PhD diss., Ohio State University, 2015), pp. 198–99. The Christian view of the Qur'ānic notion of paradise was a problem for Muslims, too: 'As for the Christians,' al-Zubayr is supposed to have said, 'they have disbelieved in paradise and have said, "There is no food in it or drink"' (al-Bukhārī, *al-Jāmi' al-ṣaḥīḥ*, vol. 3, p. 257 [no. 4767]). For further Christian criticism of Islamic views of paradise, see Roggema, *The Legend of Sergius Baḥīrā*, pp. 121–28.

[11] See the observations on and discussion of many of these same texts in Hoyland, *Seeing Islam*, pp. 541–44. And cf. the comments of Roggema, *The Legend of Sergius Baḥīrā*, p. 27, and the literature cited at n. 51.

> of the leading figures among his companions—'only make a showing of Islam while being devoid of it. They act hypocritically with me and I know that their inner belief most definitely contradicts what they show outwardly because they are people who have entered into Islam, not out of desire for this religion of ours, but because they wanted to get close to us and be honored with the might of our empire. They have no spiritual insight (*baṣīra*) and no desire for the truth of that which they have entered into [sc. Islam]. I know their situation is like that which is spoken of in the popular maxim: "The Jew only observes his Torah's commandments and his Judaism is sound if he makes an outward show of Islam." The situation of these people in their Magianism and their Islam is just like the case of the Jew. I know for sure that so-and-so and so-and-so"—and he enumerated a large number of his companions—"were Christians and converted to Islam reluctantly. They are not Muslims, nor are they Christians, but rather they are deceivers. What should I do? And how can I do it? The curse of God be on all of them! Should they not, since they abandoned unclean and filthy Magianism, which is the most wicked religion and most disgusting set of beliefs, or Christianity, the most submissive to doctrines, for the light of Islam and its radiance and the truth of its belief, have been more vigorous in their devotion to what they entered into than what they superficially left and hypocritically abandoned?'

The unnamed caliph, according to al-Kindī, went on to claim that he took solace in the example of the Prophet, most of whose closest companions and confidants had outwardly acted as his followers and helpers, but who were hypocrites and actually inwardly opposed to how they behaved towards him.[12]

Like other ninth-century Christian authors I have just mentioned, when al-Kindī spoke of why people converted to Islam, he was anything but flattering. Writing anonymously, he was also much more blunt in his assessment of motivations than the Christian authors I have just mentioned. Among converts, there were uninformed and uncouth Aramaic-speaking peasants and riff-raff (*al-anbāṭ wa-'l-asqāṭ*) who were theologically ignorant and knew nothing about either Islam or their previous religion; there were idol-worshippers, Magians, and the lowest elements of the Jews, who simply wanted to glory in the power of the Muslim empire and lord it over others who were better than they; there were doubters, faithless people, and criminals who saw a conversion to Islam as a license to engage in illicit acts and sexual activity that would have been forbidden them had they stayed Christians; there were those who became

[12] al-Kindī, *Apology*, pp. 111–13 (quote on pp. 111–12). ET by A. Tien also available in N. A. Newman, ed., *The Early Christian-Muslim Dialogue: A Collection of Documents from the First Three Islamic Centuries, 632–900 AD* (Hatfield, Penn., 1993), pp. 445–46. FT available in G. Tartar, *Dialogue islamo-chrétien sous le calife Al-Ma'mûn (813–834): les épitres d'Al-Hashimî et d'Al-Kindî* (Paris, 1985), pp. 167–68.

Muslims in order to indulge their bodily passions and enjoy fleeting worldly pleasures; and there were those who entered into Islam for the prospects of economic gain and security that conversion held out.[13] Conversion for reasons of sincerity was not a possibility to be entertained by non-Muslim leaders.

Such accounts are hostile and uncharitable—the religious equivalent of 'sour grapes' spoken about those who had left their communities.[14] Though leaders of non-Muslims might not be eager to highlight it, religious sincerity could motivate a conversion as well: we do, eventually, find stories of conversions to Islam that resulted from intellectual exchange, visions, miracles, and encounters with virtuous Muslims.[15] Nevertheless, the incentive structure of a society in which conversion (despite potentially alienating one from family and community) would yield immediate and palpable material benefits, in addition to perhaps spiritual benefits, means that the former will often overshadow the latter as we look at the historical record. It is hard to disregard a fundamental fact: socially and economically, conversion to Islam was almost always a step up.[16] This reality might lead to certain suspicions hanging over converts. For instance: A work attributed, perhaps spuriously, to the ninth-century al-Jāḥiẓ complained that secretaries (*kuttāb*) made it a priority to criticize the composition of the Qur'ān, pointing out its contradictions, imputing falsehood to historical reports and criticizing the character of *ḥadīth* transmitters. They showed active disregard and dislike for celebrated Muslim role models and much pre-

[13] al-Kindī, *Apology*, pp. 150–52. ET by Tien available in Newman, ed., *The early Christian-Muslim dialogue*, pp. 465–66; FT by Tartar in *Dialogue islamo-chrétien*, pp. 199–201. On the Aramaic-speaking Anbāṭ of Iraq, see J.-M. Fiey, 'Les "Nabaṭ" de Kaskar-Wāsiṭ dans les premiers siècles de l'Islam,' *Mélanges de l'Université Saint-Joseph* 51 (1990), pp. 49–88, and cf. also, M. J. Kister, '...Lā taqra'ū l-qur'āna 'alā l-muṣḥafiyyīn wa-lā taḥmilū l-'ilma 'ani l-ṣaḥafiyyīn ... : Some Notes on the Transmission of Ḥadīth,' *JSAI* 22 (1998), pp. 148–49.

[14] Indeed, one possible reason someone might convert to Islam was as a result of a conflict with leaders within one's own community—a reason that none of these accounts mentions. On conflicts between clergy and laity and conversion to Islam, see the remarks of E. Sachau, 'Studie zur Syrischen Kirchenlitteratur der Damascene,' *Sitzungsberichte der Königlich preussischen Akademie der Wissenschaften zu Berlin* (1899), p. 503, and Fiey, 'Conversions à l'Islam de Juifs et de Chrétiens,' pp. 20–21. More generally, Fiey's article gives an excellent overview of the various factors that motivated conversion to Islam in the Middle Ages. More recently, C. Hackenburg, 'Christian Conversion to Islam,' in D. Thomas, ed., *Routledge Handbook on Christian-Muslim Relations* (London/New York, 2018), pp. 176–84, provides a skilled survey of the reasons driving conversion, as well as of various scholary debates relating to this question.

[15] For examples, see Fiey, 'Conversions à l'Islam de Juifs et de Chrétiens,' pp. 21–22. L. G. Jones, '*Islām al-Kāfir fī Ḥāl al-Khuṭba*: Concerning the Conversion of "Infidels" to Islam during the Muslim Friday Sermon in Mamluk Egypt,' *Anuario de Estudios Medievales* 42 (2012), pp. 53-75 the importance of preaching in the conversion of non-Muslims to Islam.

[16] Though familial and social pressures could offer strong counter-incentives to conversion. See below. On the social benefits that conversion (or even threatening conversion) to Islam might have, see U. Simonsohn, 'Conversion, Exemption, and Manipulation: Social Benefits and Conversion to Islam in Late Antiquity and the Middle Ages,' *Medieval Worlds* 6 (2017), pp. 196–216.

ferred to speak about figures like Ardashir, Anushirwan, and the proper way in which the Sasanians had ruled their lands. No scribe, (Pseudo-?) al-Jāḥīẓ grumbled, had ever been seen taking particular interest in the Qur'ān, or in its exegesis, or in deepening his knowledge of Islam, or in learning Prophetic traditions.[17] The non-Muslim, presumably Zoroastrian, background of such men and the opportunistic nature of their conversions were obvious explanations for their critical stance on Islam and lack of interest in it.[18] Such attitudes are to be expected, too. 'He was a Christian by origin,' one medieval biographical dictionary reported of the important vizier and Christian renegade al-Faḍl b. Marwān (d. AD 860/AH 250), 'with little religious knowledge (*'ilm*) but excellent knowledge of caliphal service.'[19] We do not know what al-Faḍl's personal religious devotion was, if indeed he had any, but it would come as no surprise to learn that his religious views and practices as a Muslim were not all that different from whatever they might have been before his conversion, much as (Pseudo-?) al-Jāḥiẓ's secretaries showed more interest in Sasanian figures than in Arabs.[20] 'The Christian man has become a Muslim out of desire,' the poet Abū al-'Alā' al-Ma'arrī (d. AD 1058/AH 449) wrote,

But not out of a love for Islam
Rather, he craved prestige in his living
Or he feared a blow, sharp bladed and cutting,
Or he wished to marry one like a gazelle, who makes herself known
to onlookers with bracelets and henna.[21]

[17] (Ps.- ?) al-Jāḥiẓ, *Kitāb dhamm akhlāq al-kuttāb*, pp. 192–94 (ed. 'A. al-Salām Muḥammad Hārūn, *Rasā'il al-Jāḥiẓ*, vol. 2 [Cairo, 1964–1979]; ET available in Pellat, *The Life and Works of Jāḥiẓ*, pp. 274–75). For the suggestion that this work contains authentic material from al-Jāḥiẓ but likely represents the work of an unknown writer probably living in Baghdad around the time of al-Jāḥiẓ's death in (AH 255/AD 868–869), see C. Pellat, 'Une charge contre les secretaries d'état attribuée à Ǧāḥiẓ,' *Hespéris* 43 (1956), pp. 29–31.

[18] Cf. the comments of R. Selheim and D. Sourdel in their article, 'Kātib,' in *EI2*, vol. 4, p. 756.

[19] Ibn Khallikān, *Wafayāt al-a'yān wa-anbā' abnā' al-zamān*, vol. 4, p. 45. An ET is also available in W. M. de Slane, *Ibn Khallikan's Biographical Dictionary, Translated from the Arabic*, vol. 2 (Paris, 1843), p. 476. On al-Faḍl, see D. Sourdel's article, 'al-Faḍl b. Marwān,' in *EI2*, vol. 2, p. 730.

[20] Compare with the report of Abū al-'Aynā' asking to see Ṣā'id b. Makhlad (d. AD 889/AH 276), a wazir, and being told that he was praying. 'Every new thing has its pleasure,' was Abū al-'Aynā's response—Ṣā'id had been a Christian before becoming a minister. Here is an example of someone who converted for what were possibly reasons of career advancement but was nevertheless practicing, at least to a certain extent, his new religion. For the report, see Ibn Khallikān, *Wafayāt al-a'yān wa-anbā' abnā' al-zamān*, vol. 4 p. 344, with an ET available in Slane, *Ibn Khallikan's Biographical Dictionary, Translated from the Arabic*, vol. 3, p. 57. For this anecdote, see also al-Mas'ūdī, *Murūj al-dhahab wa-ma'ādin al-jawhar*, vol. 8, pp. 122–23. On Ṣā'id b. Makhlad, see D. Sourdel's article, 'Ibn Makhlad,' in *EI2*, vol. 3, p. 859.

[21] Abū al-'Alā' al-Ma'arrī, *Luzūm mā lā yalzam: al-Luzūmiyyāt*, vol. 2, p. 457 (Beirut, 1961). For this passage and a FT, see Fiey, 'Conversions à l'Islam de Juifs et de Chrétiens sous les Abbassides,' p. 15.

Abū al-ʿAlā'’s short list pointed out many of the most common benefits a person would gain from conversion. Apart from contexts in which conversion meant safety in the face of violence or the threat of violence, among other things, a conversion to Islam would eventually mean that one paid lower taxes, had more employment opportunities, and might achieve greater social prestige.[22] In the case of Christian converts to Islam, renegades had greater freedom to divorce and marry. For Christian men, it also meant that one could marry more than one wife and have religiously legitimated sexual access to slaves.[23]

Among the least powerful in society, a conversion to Islam might also represent something like an escape from a potentially miserable situation: already by the time of Mālik b. Anas (d. AD 796/AH 179), for instance, we find discussion of a Christian or Jewish woman who married a Christian or Jewish man and then converted to Islam before the marriage's consummation,[24] and the case of a Christian who owned a Christian slave who converted to Islam.[25] The experience of slaves, maltreated and otherwise, and of women forced into marriages they did not want to be in is not typically reflected in historical sources from this period or considered in the scholarship based on them, but it is important to take such experiences into account if we want to understand how and why the non-Muslim population of the Middle East eventually con-

[22] For an example of large numbers of Christian elites converting to Islam in Mamluk Egypt for the sake of keeping their jobs, see D. P. Little, 'Coptic Conversion to Islam under the Baḥrī Mamlūks,' *BSOAS* 39 (1976), pp. 557–58. L. B. Yarbrough, 'Islamizing the Islamic State: The Formulation and Assertion of Religious Criteria for State Employment in the First Millennium AH,' (PhD diss., Princeton University, 2012), is a thorough study of the history of Muslim objections to non-Muslim employment by a Muslim state from the eighth to fourteenth centuries (AD).

[23] For an example of differing Christian and Muslim attitudes towards marriage, see the story in Ibn Abī Uṣaybiʿa, *'Uyūn al-anbā' fī ṭabaqāt al-aṭibbā'*, pp. 184–85 (ed. Riḍā), where the Caliph al-Manṣūr gave three Greek slave girls to the Christian physician Jurjis b. Jibrīl on Christmas Day AH 151 (= AD 768) and Jurjis returned them. When the Caliph asked why, Jurjis responded, 'Because we are the Christian community. We do not marry more than one woman and as long as a wife is alive, we do not take someone other than her.' The Caliph had previously known that Jirjis's wife was old and ill. For a Christian version of this story, see Bar Hebraeus, *Chronicle*, pp. 125–26 (ed. Bedjan). On Jurjis, see M. Ullmann, *Die Medizin im Islam* (Leiden, 1970), p. 108. For the opposition of late antique Christian leaders to the common Roman practice of having sex with slaves, see K. Harper, *Slavery in the Late Roman World AD 275–425* (Cambridge, 2011), pp. 281–325.

[24] Mālik b. Anas, *al-Muwaṭṭa'*, vol. 2, p. 528. Mālik said she was not to receive a dowry (*ṣadāq*).

[25] Mālik b. Anas, *al-Muwaṭṭa'*, vol. 2, p. 815. In the case Mālik discusses, the master has already promised to free the slave upon the master's death (*dabbara*). Mālik held that the master was to be separated from the slave and the slave was to pay the master a monthly sum (presumably now working for someone else); the slave was not to be sold against the master's will until the master's circumstances without the slave were clarified. Legal scholars, however, would disagree on what should be done in such a situation: al-Qurṭubī, *al-Jāmi' li-aḥkām al-Qur'ān*, vol. 7, p. 190, summarizes a number of views on the matter.

verted to Islam: there were presumably many more unhappy slaves and women trapped in wretched marital situations in the medieval Middle East than there were people dissatisfied with the Christian understanding of the unity of God in the face of an Islamic critique. The prospect of conversion gave people in these two categories a chance to escape from a station in life that they were otherwise, relatively speaking, helpless to change.

CHANGING REASONS OVER TIME?

But, we should note, Ibn Kammūna lived in the thirteenth century, Abū al-ʿAlāʾ in the tenth and eleventh centuries, Mālik in the eighth century, and our Christian authors in the eighth and ninth centuries. In the previous chapter, my focus was on Muḥammad's community in the seventh and eighth centuries. As Islam developed and the societies ruled by Muslims began slowly to be affected by both the ideology of their rulers and the gradual conversion of local populations, social dynamics will have changed and reasons for conversion will have changed as well. My interest here is in the first three or four centuries of Muslim rule, a period when Muslims will have been a small but growing minority.[26] Later in this book, we will try to understand what effects, if any, that status as a demographic minority might have had on the shape of Islam. For the moment, however, let us ask: did reasons for becoming a Muslim evolve over time?

Changing political circumstances and increased instances of anti-Christian violence will have had an effect on conversion. Christian Sahner has pointed out that the period between 750 and 800 witnessed increased violence against Christians living under Muslim rule, especially in the context of growing conflict with the Byzantines and increasing suspicion of Christian disloyalty to the caliphate.[27] Sahner also emphasized the Abbasids's new manner of stressing Islam in the public legitimation of their rule as creating an environment more conducive to violence against Christians justified on religious grounds. This, along with the fact that conversion was making Islam less ex-

[26] It bears pointing out here that although Muslims were a minority, there may have been certain areas or contexts in which they were more numerous than the members of other religious groups. Cf. the observations in C. Cahen, 'Socio-Economic History and Islamic Studies: Problems of Bias in the Adaptation of the Indigenous Population to Islam,' in Hoyland, ed., *Muslims and Others in Early Islamic Society*, pp. 271–72.

[27] For a description and discussion of hostile actions against Christians undertaken by al-Manṣūr (reg. AH 136–158/AD 754–775), see J.-M. Fiey, *Chrétiens syriaques sous les Abbassides surtout à Bagdad (749–1258)* (Louvain, 1980), pp. 26–28. More generally, van Ess, *Theologie und Gesellschaft*, vol. 3, p. 28 provides bibliographic guidance for the situation of Christians under al-Manṣūr and al-Mahdī.

clusively an Arab and urban phenomenon was, he suggested, slowly changing the meaning and implications of Christian conversion to the new religion.[28]

With the passage of time and the increasing development of Islamic thought, doctrinal considerations and the issue of belief would also come to play a role in some decisions to become Muslim. The seeds for such a shift were certainly present from an early period: the Qur'ān itself criticized certain Christian doctrines and practices,[29] and one of its most prominent themes is the question of belief and unbelief.[30] Evidence of Christian-Muslim oral disagreement centering on doctrinal considerations may have appeared as early as the seventh century;[31] by the late eighth century, we have Muslim polemical literature aimed at Christians.[32] But even if the rhetorical importance of belief and doctrine were present relatively early on, the actual effects of Muslim doctrinal criticism in persuading Christians to convert is hard to gauge—we cannot even be sure how much of the Qur'ān everyday Muslims will have known, and I have attempted to argue that, the interest of modern scholars and theologians notwithstanding, theological speculation was likely not central to the lived experience of most simple Christians. It was, in fact, not until the Christian renegade 'Alī al-Ṭabarī wrote his influential 'Response to the Christians' (*al-radd 'alā al-Naṣarā*) around AD 850 (AH 236), that the Muslim apologetic genre that has been termed 'Christian apostate literature' began.[33] Along these lines,

[28] C. Sahner, 'Christian Martyrs and the Making of an Islamic Society in the Post-Conquest Period,' (PhD diss., Princeton University, 2015), pp. 334–41. Hoyland, *Seeing Islam*, pp. 346–48, made a similar observation.

[29] See S. H. Griffith's article, 'Christians and Christianity,' in *EQ*, vol. 1, pp. 307–316; and see Chapter 12, n. 158.

[30] Cf. C. Adang's article, 'Belief and Unbelief,' in *EQ*, vol. 1, pp. 218–26. From a very early point in the history of the Muslim community, too, the question of belief and unbelief became the source of enormous contention. On the *khawārij* and the question of belief, see T. Izutsu, *The Concept of Belief in Islamic Theology* (Salem, New Hamp., 1988), pp. 1–16.

[31] On the *The Disputation of John and the Emir*, which has traditionally been dated to the middle of the seventh century, see Chapter 4, n. 33.

[32] See, e.g., B. Roggema's article, 'Ibn al-Layth,' in *CMR*, vol. 1, pp. 347–53. As an indication of the atmosphere of the late eighth century, we might point to the report that al-Mahdī (reg. AH 158–169/AD 775–785), was credited with being the first caliph to order that treatises be written against Manicheans and freethinkers (*al-zanādiqa wa-'l-mulḥidīn*); see al-Suyūṭī, *Ta'rīkh al-khulafā'*, p. 274 (ed. W. N. Lees and M. Abd al-Haqq [Calcutta, 1857]). A. Charfi's section on 'Auteurs Musulmans,' in R. Caspar et al., 'Bibliographie du dialogue Islamo-Chrétien,' *Islamochristiana* 1 (1975), pp. 142–52, though now surpassed by *CMR*, remains nevertheless a convenient and easy listing of written Muslim polemics against Christianity. It is noteworthy that the production of this literature does not gain steam until after around the year 800.

[33] 'Christian apostate literature' is the coinage of Clint Hackenburg. See his 'Voices of the Converted: Christian Apostate Literature in Medieval Islam' for a study of this genre, in particular pp. 73–195 on 'Alī al-Ṭabarī (and pp. 2, 337, for his status as the inaugurator of this genre). On *al-Radd 'alā al-Naṣārā*, see also D. Thomas in *CMR*, vol. 1, pp. 671–72.

in a brief study of conversion tales, Richard Bulliet suggested that such stories in the early centuries of Muslim rule typically had little to do with actual Muslim belief and usually focused more on nonreligious factors such as 'attainment or maintenance of social status.'[34] Nevertheless Bulliet detected an eventual shift in the nature of the reasons that were emphasized: 'Late conversion stories have a different flavor . . . ,' he wrote. 'They indicate that knowledge of the faith and belief gradually became more important factors as social distinctiveness declined.'[35] It was only in the fourth century AH, Bulliet suggested, that belief (as opposed to social and political considerations) became a factor in conversion.[36]

ECONOMIC MOTIVATIONS AND CONVERSION

Another factor to consider when attempting to understand conversion is the evolving economic context of non-Muslims. I have already suggested that Muslim hegemony affected the religious incentive structure in areas under Muslim political control: in becoming a Muslim, one obtained immediate and tangible material benefits in addition to whatever spiritual consolations one might also gain. The massive amounts of wealth and the enormous number of slaves that flowed into the Muslim community as a result of its successful and far-flung conquests were unsurprisingly not without effect. 'Every community (*umma*) has an ordeal (*fitna*),' Muḥammad is reported to have said, 'and the ordeal of my community is wealth.'[37]

We can see the role economic incentives played in conversion to Islam in the lifetime of Muḥammad himself. Al-Jārūd, we are told, had been a noble and a Christian in the time of the *jāhiliyya*. He came to Muḥammad as part of a delegation, and Muḥammad invited him to Islam. 'I have had a debt (*dayn*),' he told the Prophet, 'and I am leaving my religion (*dīnī*) for your religion (*li-dīnika*). Will you become responsible for my debt (*daynī*) for me?' Muḥammad, we are told, stated that he would indeed be al-Jārūd's guarantor, telling him that God had guided him to something better. And al-Jārūd converted.[38] Indeed,

[34] R. W. Bulliet, 'Conversion Stories in Early Islam,' in M. Gervers and R. J. Bikhazi eds., *Conversion and Continuity: Indigenous Christian Communities in Islamic Lands, Eighth to Eighteenth Centuries* (Toronto, 1990), p. 131. For a study of conversion stories in Ibn Saʿd that contains valuable insights on the nature of Islamic conversion, see Calasso, 'Récits de conversion.'

[35] Bulliet, 'Conversion Stories in Early Islam,' p. 131.

[36] Bulliet, 'Conversion Stories in Early Islam,' p. 132.

[37] Ibn Saʿd, *Kitāb al-ṭabaqāt al-kabīr*, vol. 7.2, p. 134 (ed. Sachau [Leiden, 1918]; ET taken from Bewley, *The Men of Madina*, vol. 1, p. 257. I have slightly altered Beweley's translation).

[38] Ibn Saʿd, *Kitāb al-ṭabaqāt al-kabīr*, vol. 7.1, p. 61 (ed. Meissner [Leiden, 1915]; my translation with reference to the ET in Bewley, *The Men of Madina*, vol. 1, p. 51).

the Prophet was known for using gifts as a way of solidifying the commitment of wavering converts or persuading people to join his community who had not already converted.[39] Such actions by the Prophet would serve as a model for later Muslims. In the Abbasid period, for instance, Aḥmad b. Ḥanbal would be asked about a case where a promise of money played a role in a conversion to Islam. 'Abū 'Abd Allāh' (sc. Aḥmad), was, we are told, 'asked about a man who said to a Jew: "Convert to Islam so that I give you a thousand dirhams."' And so the Jew converted, but the man did not give him the money. 'The Prophet, God's prayers and peace be upon him,' Aḥmad responded, 'would allure people into embracing Islam.' But, Aḥmad continued, it would be better if the convert were given the money he had been promised.[40]

Perhaps most consequential for anyone other than the wealthiest among non-Muslims, a conversion to Islam would eventually come to mean that one was no longer obliged to pay a poll tax required of all Peoples of the Book. The evidence for early Arab taxation policies is murky and confusing, especially outside of Egypt, and its nature has been much debated.[41] Nevertheless, within a few decades of the conquests, papyri in Egypt suggest that Muslim authorities had instituted a new poll tax on the population there, in a break from Byzantine precedent.[42] In Syria and Iraq, contemporary Syriac sources attest to a poll tax existing by the late seventh century,[43] and later Arabic sources suggest that a poll tax existed even earlier.[44] According to Michael the Great,

[39] See W. M. Watt's discussion of *al-mu'allafa qulūbuhum* in *Muhammad at Medina*, pp. 348–53, and see the article, 'al-Mu'allafa Ḳulūbuhum' in *EI2*, vol. 7, p. 254.

[40] 'But it only pleases me,' Aḥmad's response went, 'that he pay him his due.' See al-Khallāl, *Ahl al-milal wa-'l-ridda wa-'l-zanādiqa wa-tārik 'l-ṣalāt wa-'l-farā'iḍ min Kitāb al-Jāmi'*, vol. 1, p. 64 (ed. I. b. Ḥamad b. Sulṭān [Riyad, 1996]).

[41] See the careful and critical reading of the evidence in A. Papaconstantinou, 'Administering the Early Islamic Empire: Insights from the Papyri,' in Haldon, ed., *Money, Power and Politics in Early Islamic Syria*, pp. 57–74. K. Morimoto, *The Fiscal Administration of Egypt in the Early Islamic Period* (Kyoto, 1981), represented an especially meticulous and clear examination of the sources and issues related to taxation in Egypt, a complex topic that easily perplexes.

[42] See P. M. Sijpesteijn, *Shaping a Muslim State: The World of a Mid-Eighth Century Egyptian Official* (Oxford, 2013), pp. 72–73, on the poll tax's institution 'within one generation' of the Arab conquest (quote at 72).

[43] See: *Synod of Mar George* (AD 676), *Canons* 19 (ed. Chabot, *Synodicon Orientale*, p. 225 [Syriac] = 489–90 [FT]); and Henanisho' I's (d. 699/700) comment in E. Sachau, ed. *Syrische Rechtsbücher*, vol. 2 [Berlin, 1908], p. 18 = 19 [GT]). In Shem'on of Samosata's *Life of Theodota of Amid* (Mardin 275/8, p. 516), Ilusṭrayya, a government official, tells the monks of the Monastery of Mar Sergius the Broad, 'Prepare for me the tribute (*maddātā*) of the ten men who are in your monastery and be on guard because of me, that I not stir up the people of Claudia through you. And do not rely on Theodota, for I am ready to also take from him the tax (*gzitā*).' For these citations, see Crone, *Slaves on Horses*, p. 215, n. 107; Hoyland, *Seeing Islam*, p. 194 and n. 73; C. F. Robinson, 'Neck-Sealing in Early Islam,' *JESHO* 48 (2005), p. 432, n. 151.

[44] See, e.g., F. Løkkegaard, *Islamic Taxation in the Classic Period, with Special Reference to the Circumstances in Iraq* (Copenhagen, 1950), p. 132, and cf. also, Papaconstantinou, 'Administering the Early

in fact, 'Umar I ordered a census taken of his entire realm in AG 951 (=AD 640) and imposed a poll tax on Christians.[45] This tax, whatever its original date, would eventually come to be referred to exclusively as the *jizya*, a word that the Qur'ān (9:29) had used to refer to a tribute to be paid by non-Muslims after they had been defeated in warfare by Muslims.[46] In the medieval period, the payment of the *jizya* was one of the most distinctive features of non-Muslim life under Muslim rule:[47] 'The poll-tax, religiously determined,' Petra Sijpesteijn observed, 'charged together with the land tax at this early period, set the non-Muslim indigenous population apart from the Muslim conquerors.'[48] As the Prophet himself was reputed to have declared: 'There is no *jizya* on Muslims.'[49]

This connection between being a Muslim and reduced taxes would prove fateful for the religious composition of the Middle East. Practices varied regionally in the new Arab empire, but literary evidence suggests that from as early as the reigns of 'Umar I and 'Alī, a conversion to Islam could mean

Islamic Empire,' p. 64: 'One cannot substantiate the claim that it was introduced practically with the campaigning armies, but it is also clear that forms of it existed before 'Abd al-Malik and al-Walīd.' C. Zuckerman argued that this Arab innovation even caught the eyes of the Byzantines, suggesting that 'in the mid-660s Constans II imported into the empire the poll tax freshly created by the Arabs.' ('Learning from the Enemy and More: Studies in "Dark Centuries" Byzantium,' *Millennium* 2 [2005], p. 83); this argument was also made by Gascou, 'Arabic Taxation in the Mid-Seventh-Century Greek Papyri,' p. 677.

[45] Michael the Great, *Chronicle* 11.7 (ed. Chabot, 4.421 = 2.426). See D. C. Dennett, Jr., *Conversion and the Poll Tax in Early Islam* (Cambridge, Mass., 1950), p. 61, who pointed to Greek and Arabic evidence of 'Umar's census and taxation policies. Robinson, *Empire and Elites*, pp. 45–46, rejected the historical value of Michael's statement, however, preferring that of a report from the *Chronicle of Zuqnin* about a poll tax in the later seventh century. For discussion of the development of early Arab taxation policies in northern Syria more generally, see Robinson, pp. 44–50.

[46] On the use of *jizya* and *kharāj* in the early period, see e.g., C. H. Becker, 'The Content of the Papyri on Taxation Practices,' in Donner, ed., *The Articulation of Early Islamic State Structures*, pp. 190–97; Dennett, *Conversion and the Poll Tax in Early Islam*, pp. 12–13; Løkkegaard, *Islamic Taxation in the Classic Period*, pp. 131–32; Morimoto, *The Fiscal Administration of Egypt*, pp. 53–62; Sijpesteijn, *Shaping an Early Muslim State*, p. 177, esp. n. 337; M.A.L. Legendre and K. Younes, 'The Use of Terms ǧizya and ḫarāǧ in the First 200 Years of hiǧra in Egypt,' (Accessed at: http://hum.leiden.edu/lias/formation-of-islam/topics-state/study.html; also available at https://web.archive.org/web/20160730235310/; http://hum.leiden.edu/lias/formation-of-islam/topics-state/study.html); and cf. Papaconstantinou's observations on the ambiguity of Greek and Arabic taxation terms in 'Administering the Early Islamic Empire,' p. 63. For the possibility of *jizya* including *kharāj* in its meaning into the ninth century, see C. Cahen, 'Fiscalité, propriété, antagonismes sociaux en Haute-Mésopotamie au temps des premiers 'Abbāsides, d'après Denys de Tell-Mahré,' *Arabica* 1 (1954), pp. 138–39.

[47] On the *jizya*, see C. Cahen, 'Djizya,' in *EI2*, vol. 2, pp. 559–62; P. L. Heck, 'Poll Tax,' in *EQ*, vol. 4, pp. 151–55; and A. Fattal, *Le statut légal des non-musulmans en pays d'Islam* (Beirut, 1958), pp. 264–91. Gascou, 'Arabic Taxation in the Mid-Seventh-Century Greek Papyri,' p. 676–77, suggests strongly that the early Arab poll tax (διάγραφον) in Egypt was not a religiously determined one and that its conflation with a religiously determined *jizya* did not occur until the late eighth century.

[48] Sijpesteijn, *Shaping a Muslim State*, p. 190.

[49] al-Tirmidhī, *al-Jāmi' al-kabīr*, vol. 3, p. 20 (no. 633) (ed. B. 'Awwād Ma'rūf [Beirut, 1996]).

freedom from certain taxes.[50] But in the earliest period converting to Islam did not always mean that one's tax burden was lightened: the powerful governor al-Ḥajjāj b. Yūsuf (d. AD 714/AH 95) was remembered for having been the first person to make Muslim converts pay the poll tax, which he did in the late seventh century.[51] In due course, however, the connection between conversion and freedom from certain kinds of taxation was made clear and uniform. The reign of 'Umar II (AD 717–720/AH 99–101) has been pointed to as especially significant in terms of the question of taxing converts: in his famous 'fiscal rescript' 'Umar II declared that a convert to Islam would have both the privileges and obligations that a Muslim had, which meant, among other things, that he would not have to pay the *jizya*.[52] Both Muslims and Christians remembered 'Umar II for having lifted the burden of this tax from converts,[53] and it was indeed during his reign that having to pay the poll tax increasingly took on a religious connotation.[54] Speaking of the situation in Egypt, the *History of the Patriarchs of Alexandria* reported that 'Umar II 'commanded that the poll-tax (*al-jizya*) should be taken from all men who would not become

[50] See the evidence for the Sawād collected in Dennett, *Conversion and the Poll Tax*, pp. 32–33, as well as his comments on the situation in Mesopotamia (p. 48) and Egypt (p. 87). P. Crone's review of D. R. Hill, *The Termination of Hostilities in the Early Arab Conquests, A.D. 634–656*, *BSOAS* 35 (1972), p. 360, took a negative view of the historical reliability of the sources Dennett drew upon for such conclusions. Her review more generally gives a good sense for the complicated and thorny nature of the literary evidence surrounding the *jizya* in the post-conquest period.

[51] Dennett, *Conversion and the Poll Tax*, pp. 38–41, 82–84.

[52] Ibn 'Abd al-Ḥakam, *Sīrat 'Umar b. 'Abd al-'Azīz*, pp. 94–95. ET available in Gibb, 'The Fiscal Rescript of 'Umar II,' p. 3 (commentary at pp. 8–9). See further the translation and commentary in A. Guessous, 'The Fiscal Rescript of 'Umar b. 'Abd al-'Azīz: A New Evaluation,' in Donner, ed., *The Articulation of Early Islamic State Structures*, pp. 244–46. For this text being an edict and not a 'rescript,' see Crone and Hinds, *God's Caliph*, p. 46, esp. n. 23. On the importance of 'Umar II, see the comments in P. M. Sijpesteijn, 'Creating a Muslim State: The Collection and Meaning of ṣadaqa,' in B. Palme, ed., *Akten des 23. Internationalen Papyrologenkongresses Wien, 22.–28. Juli 2001* (Vienna, 2007), p. 670 and Sijpesteijn, *Shaping a Muslim State*, pp. 191–92. J. B. Simonsen, *Studies in the Genesis and Early Development of the Caliphal Taxation System* (Copenhagen, 1988), saw the year 720 as a watershed in the development of taxation policy, but resisted giving too much direct credit to 'Umar II specifically (pp. 141–47, esp. 142). G. R. Hawting was cautious as to how much we could know of 'Umar's actual tax policy on non-Muslims: see *The First Dynasty of Islam: The Umayyad Caliphate, AD 661–750*, 2nd ed. (London/New York, 2000), pp. 79–81. For a collection of 'Umar II's orders on the subject of taxation and conversion, see Dennett, *Conversion and the Poll Tax*, pp. 84–85.

[53] See Mālik b. Anas, *al-Muwaṭṭa'*, vol. 1, pp. 279-280 (no. 45), where Mālik speaks of 'Umar writing to his governors and having the *jizya* removed from *jizya*-payers who became Muslims.

[54] On the shift in the meaning of *jizya* from 'tribute' to 'Islamic poll tax' that occurred in early eighth-century Egypt, see Morimoto, *The Fiscal Administration of Egypt* pp. 60–62, 126–39. For a pre-Islamic Sasanian poll tax that began progressively to be levied on religious grounds, eventually falling mainly on non-Zoroastrians, see the discussion in Morony, *Iraq after the Muslim Conquest*, pp. 106–10, where it is suggested that the religious connection between *jizya* and being a non-Muslim in Iraq was established by the first part of the eighth century.

Muslims, even in cases where it was not customary to take it.'[55] 'After a violent earthquake had occurred in Syria,' Theophanes reported, 'Oumar [sc. 'Umar] banned the use of wine in cities and set about forcing the Christians to become converted: those that converted he exempted from tax, while those that refused to do so he killed and so produced many martyrs.'[56] 'He ordered that Christians be afflicted in every way,' Michael the Great similarly wrote of 'Umar II. 'So that they would become Muslims . . . he issued a law that every Christian who became a Muslim not pay the poll tax. And many converted.'[57]

Though we must acknowledge and reject the temptation of falling into a ham-fisted and lazy fiscal determinism as a means of historical explanation, the importance of this situation can nevertheless only be underestimated at the risk of obscuring and distorting our understanding of medieval social realities and ignoring numerous pieces of evidence from writers in this period.[58] The burden of paying taxes could weigh heavily on the population of the Middle East and might drive people to do all sorts of things: al-Manṣūr's onerous demands for taxes in AD 772 led people, Michael the Great reported, to dig up and desecrate graves, looking for gold, silver, and other precious materials which they might use to pay the caliph's tribute;[59] 'he demanded the tax (*gzitā*),' the *Chronicle to 1234* noted of the same event, 'even from windows and doors.'[60] At times, people would simply leave their homes and move somewhere else in order to escape having to pay,[61] a tactic that might

[55] *History of the Patriarchs of Alexandria* 1.17 (ed. Evetts [PO 5.1], p. 326; the translation is that of Evetts). On this passage, see Dennett, *Conversion and the Poll Tax*, p. 110.

[56] Theophanes, *Chronicle* AM 6210 (ed. de Boor, vol. 1, p. 399; ET taken from Mango and Scott, *The Chronicle of Theophanes Confessor*, p. 550).

[57] Michael the Great, *Chronicle* 11.19 (ed. Chabot, 4.456 = 2.489). On this passage, see R. Hoyland, *Theophilus of Edessa's Chronicle and the Circulation of Historical Knowledge in Late Antiquity and Early Islam* (Liverpool, 2011), p. 217, n. 607, and cf. L. Yarbrough, 'Did 'Umar b. 'Abd al-'Azīz Issue an Edict concerning Non-Muslim Officials?' in Borrut and Donner, *Christians and Others in the Umayyad State*, pp. 189–90.

[58] And post-medieval realities as well. For example: F. Armanios, *Coptic Christianity in Ottoman Egypt* (New York, 2011), p. 18, adduced evidence of the burden the *jizya* posed in seventeenth- and eighteenth-century Egypt and the reactions it triggered among Copts.

[59] Michael the Great, *Chronicle* 11.26 (ed. Chabot, 4.477 = 2.526). See the more detailed description of these events in *Zuqnin Chronicle*, pp. 275, 321, 364–66 (ed. Chabot [CSCO 104: SS 53]; ET in Harrak, *The Chronicle of Zuqnīn*, pp. 242, 277–78, 309–10).

[60] *Chronicle to 1234*, p. 340 (ed. Chabot [CSCO SS III.14]). On this passage, see Robinson, 'Neck-Sealing in Early Islam,' p. 433.

[61] Note the comment of the late eighth-century *Zuqnin Chronicle* on a context where the amount of the poll tax was increased: 'During the (early) Arab rule, the tribute did not weigh so heavily upon the Christians that it went beyond their endurance, and so evils of harsh extortions broke out against them. As they had not yet learned to flee from one place to another, the door to paganism [sc. Islam] opened for them.' See *Zuqnin Chronicle*, (ed. Chabot [CSCO 104: SS 53]; ET taken from Harrak, *The Chronicle of*

prompt Muslim authorities to send out agents to track down fugitives, sometimes sometimes ruthlessly.[62]

Christians viewed the *jizya* as particularly onerous: 'in those days,' an apocalyptic passage in the anonymous *Legend of Sergius Baḥīrā*, written perhaps in the early part of the ninth century, lamented, 'people will sell their children for the poll tax, which is extracted mercilessly and is heavy upon them.'[63] Centuries earlier, around AD 691, the *Apocalypse* of Pseudo-Methodius had described in similar terms the burden of what was likely a poll tax on the Christians of northern Mesopotamia: 'A person will sleep in the evening and rise up in the morning,' it stated,

> to find outside his door two or three men who use force as they demand tribute and money. All accounting of what is given and received will disappear from the earth. At that time people will sell their bronze, their iron, and their burial clothes. In that seventh week, when everything else is finished up, they will give their sons and daughters to the unbelievers for money.[64]

Tax collecting led to abuse, literally and figuratively. Various Muslim traditions disapprovingly described non-Muslims being required to stand in the sun or even having oil poured on their heads while standing in the sun on account of not being able to pay the *jizya*.[65] The eighth-century *Zuqnin Chronicle* reported not only people being made to stand in the sun and while oil was poured on them for not paying the *jizya*, but people having their hair and

---

Zuqnīn, p. 321). On tax fugitives, see Sijpesteijn, *Shaping a Muslim State*, p. 190; Hoyland, *Seeing Islam*, p. 340; and Robinson, 'Neck-Sealing in Early Islam,' p. 433.

[62] See the vivid account in *Zuqnin Chronicle*, pp. 268–74 (ed. Chabot [CSCO 104: SS 53]; ET in Harrak, *The Chronicle of Zuqnīn*, pp. 237–41).

[63] *Legend of Sergius Baḥīrā* 17.21 (West Syrian recension; ed. Roggema, p. 356; the ET is that of Roggema, p. 357, but I have slightly altered it). Based on figures in the Aphrodito papyri, Dennett, *Conversion and the Poll Tax*, pp. 86-87, estimated that not having to pay the poll tax could reduce a man's tax burden by between a third and a half.

[64] Ps.-Methodius, *Apocalypse* 13.3–4 (ed. Reinink, *Die syrische Apokalypse des Pseudo-Methodius* [CSCO 540: SS 220], p. 36; ET by S. P. Brock taken from Palmer, *The Seventh Century in the West-Syrian Chronicles*, p. 236). On this passage, see G. J. Reinink, 'Following the Doctrine of the Demons,' in J. N. Bremmer, W. J. van Bekkum, and A. L. Molendijk, eds., *Cultures of Conversions* (Leuven/Dudley, Mass., 2006), p. 130, n. 17. For the census and poll tax (*gzitā*) that the *Apocalypse* was likely responding to, see *Zuqnin Chronicle*, p. 154 (ed. Chabot [CSCO 104: SS 53]; ET in Harrak, *The Chronicle of Zuqnīn*, pp. 147-148). On this incident, see Dennett, *Conversion and the Poll Tax*, pp. 45–47. Compare this passage with a similar one from the roughly contemporary Syriac *Apocalypse of John the Little*, which also states that people will sell their children to pay their tribute. See J. R. Harris, *The Gospel of the Twelve Apostles* (Cambridge, 1900), pp. *18–*19 = 37 (ET). On this text, see L. Greisiger's article, 'The Gospel of the Twelve Apostles,' in *CMR*, vol. 1, pp. 222–25, and on these taxes, see Robinson, *Empire and Elites*, pp. 48–49. For similar complaints, see also Ps.-Samuel of Qalamūn, *Apocalypse*, p. 383.

[65] Abū Yūsuf, *Kitāb al-Kharāj*, p. 125 (Beirut, 1979).

beards shaved as well, or iron shackles placed on different body parts as punishment for nonpayment.[66] Pressure to pay the poll tax could make non-Muslims vulnerable to exploitation. In one report, 'Umar II was asked why prices were higher in his time than they had been previously. 'Those who were before me,' he responded, 'would impose [the tax] on the People of the *Dhimma* above their ability [to pay] and they could find no other recourse but to sell what they possessed at a bad price. But I do not impose [a tax] on someone, save that he can pay it, and so a man will sell as he wishes.'[67] The *Zuqnin Chronicle* told of people profiteering off poor Christians who had to sell their belongings in order to pay the poll tax: 'They rushed to buy the vessels, cattle, and things of the poor who lived in their villages,' it noted, 'and stored them in their houses. They now became wealthy, as they wanted to, lending money at forfeit and with usury without mercy, in such manner that they were near acquiring, as they wanted to, even the children of the poor as slaves and maids.'[68] For poor Christians, the *jizya* could represent an acute challenge and difficult burden, especially in lean years and times of economic difficulty, and conversion offered a way out.

Writing about the later Geniza period, Goitein documented at length the great difficulties the requirement to pay the *jizya* imposed on many non-Muslims and noted his surprise at this. 'In general,' he wrote,

> it has to be emphasized that the subject of the poll tax occupies far more space in the Geniza records than one would anticipate. A very considerable section of the non-Muslim population must have been unable to pay it and often suffered humiliation and privation on its account. Whereas, in the higher circles, the prospects of appointment to leading government posts acted as an inducement for embracing Islam, the mass conversions in the lower classes might well have been caused in part by the intolerable burden of the poll tax.[69]

[66] *Zuqnin Chronicle*, pp. 269–70 (ed. Chabot [CSCO 104: SS 53]; ET in Harrak, *The Chronicle of Zuqnīn*, pp. 237–38).

[67] Abū Yūsuf, *Kitāb al-kharāj*, p. 132. Cf. the FT in E. Fagnan, *Le livre de l'impôt foncier: (Kitâb el-kharâdj)*, (Paris, 1921), p. 203.

[68] *Zuqnin Chronicle*, p. 278 (ed. Chabot [CSCO 104: SS 53]; ET taken from Harrak, *The Chronicle of Zuqnīn*, p. 244).

[69] S. D. Goitein, *A Mediterranean Society: The Jewish Communities of the Arab World as Portrayed in the Documents of the Cairo Geniza.* Vol. II: *The Community* (Berkeley, 1971), pp. 392–93; also, see more generally pp. 380–93. Compare this with his earlier comments on the stark differences between humane literary representations of, and harsh documentary realities of the *jizya* in the Geniza period in Goitein, 'Evidence on the Muslim Poll Tax from Non-Muslim Sources: A Geniza Study,' *JESHO* 6 (1963), pp. 278–79, especially the remark (p. 279), 'This impression proved to be entirely fallacious, for it did not take into consideration the immense extent of poverty and privation experienced by the masses, and in particular their way of living from hand to mouth, the persistent lack of cash, which turned the "season of the tax" into one of horror, dread and misery.'

In the Ottoman period, there are a number of examples of entire Christian villages converting to Islam *en masse* in order to avoid paying the *jizya*; there are even examples of entire Christian villages predicating their conversion to Catholicism on the agreement of Franciscan missionaries to pay the *jizya* on a village's behalf.[70]

For earlier centuries we unfortunately have neither the rich documentary evidence available to Goitein through the Geniza nor the detailed court records Ottoman historians can draw upon. We nevertheless possess indications that, just as would be the case centuries later in the period Goitein was studying, or in the early modern period, in the early centuries of Muslim rule the requirement to pay the poll tax was already motivating people to become Muslims.[71]

Evidence to this effect can be found in a number of sources, from authors of different confessions, writing different languages, across a large geographic area: "Abd Allāh, the king, wrote to his entire realm,' the *History of the Patriarchs of Alexandria* reported, referring to the first Abbasid caliph, al-Saffāḥ (d. AD 754/AH 136),

> that everyone who became a member of his religion and prayed as he prayed would be without the *jizya*. And so, on account of the immensity of the *kharāj* [land tax] and costs upon them, many of the wealthy and the poor denied the religion of Christ and followed him.[72]

Also from Egypt, the Coptic synaxary reported that in the time of Patriarch Khā'īl I (sed. 744–767) some twenty-four thousand Christians denied Christ.[73] The *History of the Patriarchs of Alexandria* reported the conversion of the same number of people at this time and connected this apostasy with Ḥafṣ b.

[70] F. Tramontana, *Passages of Faith: Conversion in Palestinian Villages (17th century)* (Wiesbaden, 2014), pp. 69–70.

[71] For an argument about the importance of changes in administrative personnel (from Christians to Muslims) and the manner in which the Muslim government assessed taxes in the conversion of Egypt to Islam (based on papyri), see, G. Frantz-Murphy, 'Conversion in Early Islamic Egypt: The Economic Factor,' in Hoyland, ed., *Muslims and Others in Early Islamic Society*, pp. 323–29.

[72] *History of the Patriarchs of Alexandria* 1.18 (ed. Evetts [PO 5.1], pp. 443–44; my translation). On this passage, see Dennett, *Conversion and the Poll Tax*, p. 10 and M.S.A. Mikhail, *From Byzantine to Islamic Egypt: Religion, Identity and Politics after the Arab Conquest* (London/New York, 2014), pp. 64–65. On al-Saffāḥ, whose full name was 'Abd Allāh b. Muḥammad b. 'Alī b. 'Abd Allāh b. al-'Abbās, see S. Moscati's article, 'Abū 'l-'Abbās al-Saffāḥ,' in *EI2*, vol. 1, p. 103 and cf. *History of the Patriarchs of Alexandria*, 1.18 (ed. Evetts [PO 5.1], p. 447) for information about this 'Abd Allāh that makes it clear that he is to be identified with al-Saffāḥ.

[73] J. Forget, ed., *Synaxarium Alexandrinum*, vol. 2 (CSCO SA 3:19) (Paris/Leipzig, 1952), p. 30. For this, see Hoyland, *Seeing Islam*, p. 343. On Khā'īl I (i.e., Michael I), see the article 'Khā'īl I' by S. Y. Labib in *CoptEn*, vol. 5, pp. 1410–12.

al-Walīd's lifting of the *jizya* on all converts to Islam: 'by means of this procedure,' it noted, 'Satan did much harm to many people who gave up their religion.'[74] In Palestine, a Samaritan chronicle connected the conversion of non-Muslims in the mid-ninth century to the *jizya*. '[Then] there came a great rise in prices,' it noted,

> And three *'uqqāt* of flour were sold for a *dīnār*. Many people were compelled to take charity because of the pains in their stomach and the hunger. How many left their faith as a result of the terrible rise in prices and because they were exhausted by the *jizya*! Many sons and families who left the faith were lost. [But] God in His mercy watched over him who endured patiently, and comforted him with satiety and well-being.[75]

'Even though he was a tyrant,' Michael the Great reported of the rebel leader Naṣr b. Shabath (d. after AD 824–25/AH 209), one of whose men was responsible for the destruction of Qenneshre,

> He nevertheless loved Christians. So far as those who were becoming Muslims were concerned, he mercilessly was forcing all manner of tribute on them. He would say: "So long as you pay me the *jizya*, let each one take whichever confession he wants." And many returned from mosques to the churches.[76]

Among the events of the eschaton predicted in an apocalyptic portion of the *Legend of Sergius Baḥīrā* was the coming of a king from the east, wearing green, who would punish Muslims and inflict suffering on Christian renegades: 'He will heavily scourge the Christians who apostatized and called themselves Ishmaelites,' the text predicted,

> and he will make them suffer and put on them the heavy yoke [of tax] saying: "Why did you renounce the confession of your fathers and call yourselves Ishmaelites while you are not, and why did you cut the flesh of the foreskin, that you may look like real ones? All this you did in order to be freed and escape

[74] *History of the Patriarchs of Alexandria* 1.18 (ed. Evetts, *History of the Patriarchs of the Coptic Church of Alexandria* [PO 5.1], pp. 370–71; the translation is that of Evetts). On these conversions, see Dennett, *Conversion and the Poll Tax*, p. 86; Hoyland, *Seeing Islam*, p. 343, esp. n. 25; Sijpesteijn, *Shaping a Muslim State*, p. 194, esp. n. 426; and cf. also Mikhail, *From Byzantine to Islamic Egypt*, pp. 64–65.

[75] Translation Milka Levy-Rubin, taken from her *The continuatio of the Samaritan Chronicle of Abū l-Fatḥ Al-Sāmirī Al-Danafī* (Princeton, 2002), p. 95; and see Levi-Rubin, 'New Evidence relating to the Process of Islamization in Palestine in the Early Muslim Period: The Case of Samaria,' *JESHO* 43 (2000), p. 266. For this, see also R. Ellenblum, 'Demography, Geography and the Accelerated Islamisation of the Eastern Mediterranean,' in I. Katzenelson and M. Rubin, eds., *Religious Conversion: History, Experience and Meaning* (Farnham, 2014), p. 68.

[76] Michael the Great, *Chronicle* 12.13 (ed. Chabot, 4.513 = 3.60–61). On Naṣr b. Shabath al-'Uqaylī, see C. E. Bosworth's article, 'Naṣr b. Shabath,' in *EI2*, vol. 7, p. 1016, and cf. Chapter 8, n. 22 above.

from the poll tax. And you abandoned your confession and the noble laws of your fathers and sought refuge with the Sons of Hagar.[77]

These reports all come from non-Muslim sources, but Muslims also associated the conversion of conquered peoples to Islam with payment of the *jizya*. Ḥayyān b. Shurayḥ the governor (*ʿāmil*) of Egypt wrote to ʿUmar II that *dhimmī*s were rushing to convert to Islam and had ceased paying the *jizya*. 'God sent Muḥammad as one who calls people,' ʿUmar wrote back, 'he did not send him as a tax collector. Therefore, if a person of the Book comes to you—if the People of the Covenant are rushing to convert to Islam and cutting off the payment of the *jizya*—then close your tax register (*kitābaka*) and accept them.'[78] ʿUmar II also wrote to his governor in Khurasan, al-Jarrāḥ b. ʿAbd Allāh al-Ḥakamī, and ordered him to summon the people who were paying the *jizya* to Islam. If they converted, ʿUmar commanded, their Islam should be accepted; the *jizya* was to be removed from them and they were to have the same rights and duties as Muslims did. 'By God,' a member of the Khurasani *ashrāf* is reported to have told ʿUmar, 'the only thing calling them to Islam is the removal of the *jizya*. Test them with circumcision!' Presumably, requiring circumcision would serve as something of a test of religious sincerity and weed out those motivated by economic considerations. But ʿUmar would have nothing of it. 'Shall I turn them away from Islam through circumcision?' he is said to have replied. 'If they were to become Muslims and their conversion was a good one, they would be quicker to purity (*ṭuhra*).' ʿUmar's logic was that genuine conversion would eventually lead to a concern with proper Muslim observance and perhaps even circumcision—semantically, *ṭuhra*, 'purity,' evokes the notion of circumcision.[79] Insisting on a convert taking such a dramatic step at the outset might dissuade people who would, with the passing of time, become

[77] *Legend of Sergius Baḥīrā* 17.96–97 (West Syrian recension; ed. and trans. Roggema, *The Legend of Sergius Baḥīrā*, p. 366; the ET is that of Roggema, p. 367, though I have slightly altered it). For analysis of this 'Green king,' see pp. 83–86.

[78] Ibn Saʿd, *Kitāb al-ṭabaqāt al-kabīr*, vol. 5, p. 283 (ed. Zettersteen [Leiden, 1905]; my translation made with reference to the ET in Bewley, *Men of Madina*, vol. 2, p. 239). On this passage, see the remarks of Gibb, 'The Fiscal Rescript of ʿUmar II,' p. 8. Compare with a similar tradition related to ʿUmar II, but this time dealing with the question of lifting the *jizya* on Jews, Christians, and Magians who were converting in Hira: Abū Yūsuf, *Kitāb al-Kharāj*, p. 131.

[79] Cf. Lane, *Arabic-English Lexicon*, s.v. *ṭahara*, where (p. 1887), he notes that *ṭuhra* comes from the substantive *taṭhīr*, a verbal noun that means 'cleansing' but also 'circumcising.' The Prophet was said to have included circumcision (*al-khitān*) as one of the five parts of the *fiṭra* (humanity's natural, created constitution), a *ḥadīth* that Muslim b. al-Ḥajjāj included in his *Kitāb al-ṭahāra, Book of Purity*; see *Ṣaḥīḥ* (ed. M. F. ʿAbd al-Bāqī [n.d., n.p.]) vol. 1, p. 221 (no. 49) (and cf. no. 50 on p. 222, where *ikhtitān*, 'circumcision' or 'self-circumcision' is included in the five things that comprise the *fiṭra*). On the meaning of *fiṭra*, see Lane, s.v. (p. 2416); D. B. MacDonald's article, 'Fiṭra,' in *EI2*, vol. 2, pp. 931–32; and 'Fiṭrah,' in Mir, *Dictionary of Qur'ānic Terms and Concepts*, p. 76.

devout enough to want to undergo circumcision. We do not know whether 'Umar's expectations matched what actually happened in Khurasan, but Ibn Sa'd does report that some four thousand people converted to Islam as a result of his policies on the *jizya* and circumcision.[80] Converting to Islam might also mean that a peasant could leave his land and move to the city, thereby avoiding the land tax. This led to problems during the governorship of al-Ḥajjāj b. Yūsuf (d. AH 95/AD 714) over Iraq: 'The *kharāj* [land tax] is broken,' his agents wrote to him in AH 83 (702), 'and the *dhimmī*s have converted to Islam and gone to the garrison cities.' Al-Ḥajjāj's response was to write to Basra and other places and order those who were from the countryside to return.[81]

The moment at which a conversion took place can furnish us with a strong indication of its motive: 'Umar II ordered that no *jizya* was to be collected from a *dhimmī* who converted to Islam the day before he was to pay it.[82] Those who converted a day before their *jizya* was due could even be said to have planned ahead: apparently, some converts were literally waiting to the last second to change religious allegiance in order to get out of the burden of paying taxes: 'If he becomes a Muslim,' 'Umar II is reported to have stated, 'while the *jizya* is in the weighing pan of the scale, it is not to be taken from him.'[83] If a person converted to Islam, Abū Yūsuf stated, and he still had part of his *jizya* to pay, the remainder was not to be taken from him.[84] Such dynamics would continue for centuries: in 1650, for example, the entire Christian village of Dayr Abān in Palestine converted to Islam. The fact that this mass conversion occurred several days before the village was due to pay its *jizya* has led

[80] Ibn Sa'd, *Kitāb al-ṭabaqāt al-kabīr*, vol. 5, p. 285 (ed. Zetterstéen [Leiden, 1905]; ET available in Bewley, *Men of Madina*, vol. 2, pp. 240–41).

[81] al-Ṭabarī, *Ta'rīkh*, 2.2, pp. 1122–23 (ed. I. Guidi [Leiden, 1883-1885]). For context, see Gibb, 'The Fiscal Rescript of 'Umar II,' p. 16. On the question of the land tax and conversion in southern Iraq and for the point that conversion allowed the peasant to leave his land, see Dennett, *Conversion and the Poll Tax*, pp. 14–42 (38–41 is especially relevant to this passage); for Egypt, see Sijpesteijn, *Shaping a Muslim State*, p. 190, esp. n. 404. On the *kharāj*, see C. Cahen's article, 'Kharādj,' in *EI2*, vol. 4, pp. 1030–34, esp. 1031 on taxation, conversion, and al-Ḥajjāj. On al-Ḥajjāj b. Yūsuf, see A. Dietrich's article, 'al-Ḥadjdjādj b. Yūsuf,' in *EI2*, vol. 3, pp. 39–43. On these Christian peasants, see Fiey, 'Les "Nabaṭ" de Kaskar-Wāsiṭ dans les premiers siècles de l'Islam,' (al-Ḥajjāj's relationship to them is discussed at 76–79).

[82] Ibn Sa'd, *Kitāb al-ṭabaqāt al-kabīr*, vol. 5, p. 262 (ed. Zetterstéen [Leiden, 1905]). Literally, 'who converts to Islam a day before the year [is up].' My translation made with reference to the translation in Bewley, *Men of Madina*, vol. 2, p. 221.

[83] Ibn Sa'd, *Kitāb al-ṭabaqāt al-kabīr*, vol. 5, p. 262 (ed. Zetterstéen [Leiden, 1905]; my translation made with reference to the ET in Bewley, *Men of Madina*, vol. 2, p. 221).

[84] Abū Yūsuf, *Kitāb al-Kharāj*, p. 123. Abū Yūsuf also specified that if a person converted to Islam 'a day or two days or a month or two months, or more or less, before the completion of the year, no part of the *jizya* was to be taken from the convert, if he converted before the completion of the year' (pp. 122–23).

to the suggestion that there was an economic motive behind the inhabitants' embrace of Islam.[85]

We have evidence, in fact, for economically driven conversions taking place among Christians under Muslim rule within decades of the Arab conquests and well before 'Umar II's famous lifting of the poll tax on new Muslims. In an angry letter to Simeon, the Bishop of Revardashir, the East Syrian patriarch Isho'yahb III (d. ca. AD 658) would lament the apparent mass apostasy of Christians in Oman in order to escape having to make a payment of half their possessions to Arab authorities. It would seem that only two members of the clergy had remained Christian. 'How is it,' Isho'yahb would ask,

> that the great people of the Mazzunāyē [sc. Omanīs], having seen neither sword nor fire nor torments, have like lunatics been taken captive by a love of half their possessions and the depths of apostasy have suddenly swallowed them up and they have perished for eternity? Two charred brands with the name of the priesthood have been rescued from the blaze of wickedness, but they have amounted to nothing. Oh, oh, oh, the pain! Not one small Eucharist has been consecrated to God as a personal sacrifice on behalf of a true faith by the many thousands of people who were called Christians.[86]

Isho'yahb was so extremely upset by the voluntary mass apostasy in Oman that he would return to the issue later in the same letter. 'How on earth could your Mazzunāyē,' he asked Simeon again

> leave their faith on their own account? And this [they did] when, as the Mazzunāyē themselves will say, the Arabs did not force them to leave their faith. They only told them to let go of half their possessions and to keep their faith. But they have left their faith forever and held on to half their possessions for a small time. And it is that faith which all the nations have bought and are buying with the blood of their necks and through which they inherit eternal life, [life] that your Mazzunāyē have not bought with half their possessions.[87]

Isho'yahb's letter gives us evidence that the same dynamic operating in the early second/eighth century during the reign of 'Umar II and later in Goitein's

[85] Tramontana, *Passages of Faith*, pp. 76–77.

[86] Isho'yahb III, *Letters* III.14 (To Simeon of Revardashir), p. 248 (ed. Duval [CSCO: Syr. II.64]). On the Mazzunāyē, see J. P. Margoliouth (Smith), *Supplement to the Thesaurus Syriacus of R. Payne Smith, S.T.P.* (Oxford, 1927), s.v. ܡܙܘܢܝܐ. (p. 200) .

[87] Isho'yahb III, *Letters* III.14 (To Simeon of Revardashir), p. 251 (ed. Duval [CSCO: Syr. II.64]). Young, *Patriarch, Shah, and Caliph*, pp. 94–96, contains an ET of the two passages from the letter of Isho'yahb I have cited here, as well as historical discussion. Young (p. 96) suggested that the payment in question should not be confused with a *jizya*.

Geniza period was at work already in the very earliest period of post-conquest Arab rule. When faced with the choice of converting to Islam or making payments to Muslim authorities, some people chose to change their religion. Tellingly perhaps, some Muslim authors expected Muslims living under Byzantine rule after the Byzantine reconquest of parts of Syria to apostatize once the Christians had imposed a version of the *jizya* on Muslims—and some Muslims did in fact convert.[88]

LEAVING ISLAM?

If people were undertaking conversions out of a variety of motives, many or most of them nondoctrinal and nonpropositional, it should come as no surprise that some of those shifts were impermanent and that renegades went back to their previous religions when the circumstances that had prompted the initial conversion changed: a religious version, as it were, of buyer's remorse.[89] Although the conversion of nearly the entire Christian population of the Middle East to Islam over the course of the past fourteen hundred or so years, and contemporary experience as well, lead us to expect that Christians converted to Islam and not the other way around, there is in fact a good deal of evidence to suggest that conversion, especially in the early centuries of Muslim rule, was a two-way street and that some Christian conversions to Islam simply did not not stick.

For instance: a group of people in the region of the Jazira converted to Islam, we are told in one report, but after only a little while they apostatized. When informed of this, ʿUmar b. ʿAbd al-ʿAzīz simply ordered that the *jizya* be reimposed on them and they be left alone.[90] Earlier in this chapter, I quoted the *Apocalypse* of Pseudo-Methodius decrying Christian apostasy to Islam in the late seventh century, but Muslims themselves were producing apocalyptic laments about apostasy at about the same time. At the time of the death of Yazīd b. Muʿāwiya in AD 683/AH 64—a little less than a decade before Ps.-Methodius was writing—al-Ḍaḥḥāk b. Qays wrote a letter to Qays b. al-Haytham in which he reported apocalyptic sentiments he attributed to Muḥammad. 'I heard the Prophet of God…', al-Ḍaḥḥāk wrote, 'saying that at

[88] See T. Carlson, 'The Contours of Conversion: The Geography of Islamization in Syria, 600–1500,' *JAOS* 134 (2015), p. 803.

[89] On the phenomenon of Muslims converting to Christianity under the Umayyads and Abbasids, see C. C. Sahner, 'Swimming against the Current: Muslim Conversion to Christianity in the Early Islamic period,' *JAOS* 136 (2016), pp. 265–84.

[90] ʿAbd al-Razzāq, *al-Muṣannaf*, vol. 10, p. 171 (no. 18714).

the Hour [there will be] calamities like clouds of smoke (*qiṭaʿ al-dukhān*), in which a man's heart dies just as his body dies. A man will wake up a Believer and in the evening be an infidel; in the evening he will be a Believer and in the morning an infidel. People will sell their portion of happiness and their religion for a fleeting benefit of the world.'[91]

Most early Muslims, I suggested in Chapter 10, were late converts or members of tribes who had converted, *en masse*, at the end of the Prophet's life; most will likely have had only the most superficial understanding of the Prophet's message and its implications for their lives. In such a context, the specter of a convert or group of converts leaving Islam for his or their earlier religion was a real one. A Muslim army sent by ʿAlī b. Abī Ṭālib in the year AH 38 (AD 658), for example, found that the Banū Nājiya were comprised of three different groups: one which had been Christian and converted to Islam, another that was firm in its Christianity, and yet another that had been Christian, had converted to Islam, and then returned to Christianity. 'We were a people (*qawm*) who were Christians and then became Muslims,' this last group told the Muslim army, 'but we have not seen a religion which is better than our first one.' When these apostates refused to go back to Islam, the Muslim army surprised and killed all of their fighters and took their children as captives.[92]

The Christian reverts of the Banū Nājiya had reportedly left Islam for Christianity because they had come to the conclusion that Christianity was better (*afḍal*) than Islam, though they did not specify in what respect Christianity was superior. But there were other factors apart from the view that their previous religion was better that were driving peoples' decisions to switch back and forth from Islam. We can see this in another story involving ʿAlī. ʿAlī, we are told, had brought him an old man who had been a Christian, then converted to Islam, and then apostatized and went back to Christianity. The first motivation ʿAlī considered was a monetary one: 'You have perhaps committed apostasy,' ʿAlī is said to have asked him, 'only in order to obtain an inheritance—then you will return to Islam?' 'No,' the man replied. Next, ʿAlī tried another reason—maybe there was a woman behind the man's religious change: 'Then perhaps you were betrothed to a woman and they refused to marry you to her,' ʿAlī continued, 'so you wanted to marry her and then return to Islam?' Once again, the man replied in the negative. With Marx, as it were, and Freud having failed him as explanations of the apostate's behavior,

[91] Ibn Saʿd, *Kitāb al-ṭabaqāt al-kabīr*, vol. 7.2, p. 131 (ed. Sachau [Leiden, 1918]; my translation made with reference to the ET in Bewley, *Men of Madina*, vol. 1, p. 255).

[92] al-Ṭabarī, *Ta'rīkh*, 1.6, pp. 3434–35 (ed. E. Prym). Another version of this story is in ʿAbd al-Razzāq, *al-Muṣannaf*, vol. 10, pp. 171–72 (no. 18715).

'Alī resorted to a bald exhortation: 'Then come back to Islam!' No, the man responded again, 'Until I meet Christ [i.e., until I die],' he went on, 'No!' 'Alī reacted by ordering that the man's head be cut off and his inheritance be given to his Muslim children.[93] As in the accounts of conversion given by Ibn Kammūna and Christian leaders of the ninth century, what is notable here is the absence of any mention that doctrine or some sort of spiritual conviction may have played a motivating role in these religious movements from Islam to Christianity.

Statements about penalties for Muslims apostatizing in the early period also point to this simple fact, that people were converting to Islam and then having second thoughts.[94] 'Cut off the head of any Christian who embraces Islam and then returns to Christianity,' the Prophet is supposed to have ordered.[95] 'Repentance is to be sought from the apostate for three days,' 'Umar II is reported to have ordered, 'if he repents [then he is to be let go], otherwise, his neck should be severed.'[96] 'Umar gave a similar order in response to a group (*qawm*) of former Christians that had similarly left Islam.[97] One report has Abū Mūsā al-Ash'arī approach Mu'ādh b. Jabal (d. AH 2/AD 624) in Yemen accompanied by a man who had been a Jew, then converted to Islam, and then returned to Judaism. Abū Mūsā and others had been trying to bring him back to Islam for two months. 'By God,' Mu'ādh is supposed to have told Abū Mūsā, 'I will not sit down until you sever his neck.' And so, the anecdote continues, the man's head was cut off.[98] Ibn Mas'ūd is said to have taken hold of a group of people who had apostatized from Islam in Iraq and written to 'Umar about them. 'Show them the religion of truth,' 'Umar replied, 'and the testimony "There is no God but God." If they accept it, leave them go. But if they don't, kill them.' Some of these people accepted, we are told, and Ibn Mas'ūd let them be, but others did not, and so he killed them.[99] There are other stories as well involving converts to Islam who went back to their original religion: al-Mustawrid al-'Ijlī was killed by 'Alī b. Abī Ṭālib for reverting to Christianity after he had converted to Islam. It is reported that 'Alī asked him to repent

[93] 'Abd al-Razzāq, *al-Muṣannaf*, vol. 10, pp. 169–70 (no. 18709).

[94] U. Simonsohn, '"Halting between Two Opinions": Conversion and Apostasy in Early Islam,' *Medieval Encounters* 19 (2013), pp. 342–70, uses Muslim, Christian, and Jewish material to look at this question.

[95] Ibn Abī Shayba, *al-Muṣannaf*, vol. 11, pp. 289–90 (no. 33293). This prescription from Muḥammad reportedly was prefaced by his observation that it was not right for there to be two religious communities in Medina.

[96] Ibn Sa'd, *Kitāb al-ṭabaqāt al-kabīr*, vol. 5, p. 259 (ed. Zetterstéen [Leiden, 1905]; my translation made with reference to the ET in Bewley, *Men of Madina*, vol. 2, p. 218).

[97] Ibn Abī Shayba, *al-Muṣannaf*, vol. 11, p. 290 (no. 33288).

[98] 'Abd al-Razzāq, *al-Muṣannaf*, vol. 10, p. 168 (no. 18705).

[99] 'Abd al-Razzāq, *al-Muṣannaf*, vol. 10, pp. 168–69 (no. 18707).

and cut a cross off his neck. When the Christians wanted al-Mustawrid's body, 'Alī had it burned.[100] In the case of another man who had converted to Islam and then apostatized, 'Alī is said to have spent a month asking him to repent before finally killing him.[101] Another report has 'Alī brought a man who had been a Christian, converted to Islam, and then went back to Christianity. 'Alī approached the apostate, we are told, and kicked him, at which point other people present set upon the man and beat him to death.[102] 'Uthmān b. 'Affān asked a man who had converted to Islam and then apostatized to repent three times and then killed him when he refused.[103] 'Umar b. al-Khaṭṭāb sent an armed contingent out and when they found an individual who had been a Muslim and then converted to Christianity after his embrace of Islam, the men killed him. In this instance, however, the men did not first summon the apostate back to Islam. When 'Umar found out that they had not, he declared himself not responsible before God for the man's blood.[104]

Christian sources also indicate that there was movement into and out of Islam in this early period. If a person becomes a Muslim or a pagan, John the Stylite wanted to know from Jacob of Edessa, and then after a time repents and comes back from his paganism to Christianity, should he be baptized again?[105] The Armenian chronicler Sebeos, writing in the mid-seventh century, reported that in Egypt during the First Civil War, a Muslim army of fifteen thousand men converted to Christianity and was baptized.[106] In his *Narrations*

[100] For various reports on 'Alī and al-Mustawrid, see 'Abd al-Razzāq, *al-Muṣannaf*, vol. 10, p. 170. Note that in one version of this story (no. 18711) 'Alī only strikes al-Mustawrid with his foot and then al-Mustawrid is killed 'by the people.' Cp. the burning of al-Mustawrid's body with the burning of the body of Elias of Heliopolis (d. 799), a Christian who was accused of converting to Islam and then reverting to Christianity. After Elias had been executed and miraculous stories associated with his body began, the Muslim ruler of Damascus ordered that 'before the story of these visions spread, the saint's body should be taken down from the cross and burned with fire, so, he said, Christians may not take it and build churches and perform feasts celebrating his memory.' *Life of Elias of Heliopolis* 25 (ed. A. Papadopoulos-Kerameus, *Syllogē Palaistinēs kai Syriakēs hagiologies*, vol. 1 [St. Petersburg, 1907], pp. 57–58; ET taken from S. McGrath, 'Elias of Heliopolis: The Life of an Eighth-Century Syrian Saint,' in J. W. Nesbitt, ed., *Byzantine Authors: Literary Activities and Preoccupations: Texts and Translations Dedicated to the Memory of Nicolas Oikonomides* [Leiden/Boston, 2003], p. 106). For a detailed analysis of the story of Mustawrid, see also, Sahner, 'Christian Martyrs and the Making of an Islamic Society,' pp. 62–71. Sahner argues that the story has little actual historical value.

[101] 'Abd al-Razzāq, *al-Muṣannaf*, vol. 10, p. 164 (no. 18691).

[102] Ibn Abī Shayba, *al-Muṣannaf*, vol. 11, p. 288 (no. 33282).

[103] 'Abd al-Razzāq, *al-Muṣannaf*, vol. 10, p. 164 (no. 18692).

[104] Ibn Abī Shayba, *al-Muṣannaf*, vol. 11, pp. 287–88 (no. 33281).

[105] Jacob of Edessa, *Additional Questions of John the Stylite to Jacob* 15 (ed. Vööbus, *The Synodicon in the West Syrian Tradition* I [CSCO 367–68; SS 161–62], p. 253 [Syriac] [= pp. 231–32 (ET)]. See also Bar Hebraeus, *Nomocanon* 2.1 (ed. Bedjan, *Nomocanon*, p. 22) and cf. Kayser, *Die Canones Jacob's von Edessa*, pp. 8, 13. For an ET of all these passages, see *SBI*, p. 447, n. 1057.

[106] See R. W. Thomson, trans., with J. Howard-Johnson and T. Greenwood, *The Armenian History attributed to Sebeos*, vol. 1 (Liverpool, 1999), p. 154, and see commentary in vol. 2, p. 287.

Profitable for the Soul, composed ca. AD 690, Anastasius of Sinai told of a certain Christian named Moses who, five years after his father died, 'denied the faith of Christ' and became a Muslim. Condemned by his friends for apostasy, Moses reconverted to Christianity, but after a short while, returned to Islam; his goings back and forth between religions, Anastasius noted, earned Moses the further censure of his friends—a clear example of the sort of social pressures that might play a role in bringing converts to reconsider their decisions. Anastasius himself, having been a friend of Moses as well as an old friend of Moses's father, Azarias, found Moses living as a Muslim in the town of In and rebuked him for his infidelity. 'What can I do, reverend Father,' Moses asked him,

> for insofar as I turn and become a Christian, the demon harasses me and when I become an apostate again, he does not bother me at all? But the spirit has appeared to me a number of times and commanded me, saying: "Do not bow down to Christ and I will not harass you. Do not confess him as God and the Son of God and I will not draw near to you. Do not take communion and I will not trouble you. Do not make the sign of the cross and I will love you."[107]

Anastasius has also left us a brief account of a martyr known as George the Black who was likely killed in the 650s. Taken captive while a young boy, George renounced Christianity when he was eight years old and became a Muslim. When he became an adolescent and possessed of knowledge, we are told, George went back to his original Christianity, caring nothing, Athanasius noted, for the fear of any human. This act did not go unnoticed: one of George's fellow slaves, an apostate himself whom Anastasius called a 'Christ-hater' (μισόχριστος), slanderously reported George's reversion to Christianity to their master. The master sent for George and questioned him, urging the now-Muslim apostate to pray with him, but George refused.[108] The punishment was a harsh one: he was hung in the air from his hands and feet, with his stomach facing the ground and his master cut him in half with a sword. The inhabitants of Damascus, Anastasius reported, took George's remains and placed them in a special memorial chapel.[109] Elias of Heliopolis was accused of converting

[107] Anastasius of Sinai, *Narrations Beneficial for the Soul* II.13 (ed. Binggeli, p. 1.233 [Greek] = 2.548–49 [FT] [= C-8 in Heid, ed., 'Die C-Reihe erbaulicher Erzählungen des Anastasios vom Sinai,' pp. 91–92]). For the date of these *Narrations* as ca. AD 690, see Hoyland, *Seeing Islam*, p. 99.

[108] For the point that praying is one way for an apostate to reaffirm his Islam, see the discussion in Ibn Qudāma, *al-Mughnī*, vol. 12 (ed. 'A. Allāh b. 'Abd al-Muḥsin al-Turkī and 'A. al-Fattāh Muḥammad al-Ḥulw) (Riyad, 1997), pp. 290–91.

[109] Anastasius of Sinai, *Narrations Beneficial for the Soul* II.22 (ed. Binggeli, p. 1.252 [Greek] = 2.567 [FT] [= C-13 in Heid, ed. 'Die C-Reihe erbaulicher Erzählungen des Anastasios vom Sinai,' pp. 102–103]).

from Christianity to Islam and then going back to Christianity, a charge which he denied since he claimed to have never converted to Islam in the first place. Nevertheless, he was beaten, imprisoned, and eventually executed for his apostasy from Islam. Before his death Elias was taken before the Muslim ruler of Damascus, a nephew of the caliph al-Mahdī, who informed him of a caliphal edict that is of interest to us as it points to Christians going back and forth between Christianity and Islam in the late eighth century as well: '... those who convert to the faith of the Arabs and then immediately convert back again to Christianity,' the ruler told Elias, 'must be imprisoned, and if then, in spite of exhortations, they do not apostatize from the faith of Christ, they should be put to death.'[110]

Sometimes the return to Christianity would take place only when the renegade was on his deathbed. Is it lawful for a priest, Addai asked Jacob, to grant absolution to one who has converted to Islam or paganism if he is at the point of death?[111] Regardless of the point in life when they took place, however, reconsiderations of conversion were happening. 'Many of the sons of the church will stray from the truth,' an apocalyptic section in the *Legend of Sergius Baḥīrā* stated of a period in which an eschatological figure from South Arabia would emerge, 'and they will follow him in order to worship demons and bring sacrifices to them.' Unlike other passages where Christian apostasy to Islam is decried, however, in this instance there is an acknowledgement that some apostates might come back to Christianity: 'And those who repent are one in ten,' the text continued.[112] Movements back to Christianity from Islam were common enough, in fact, that eventually various churches would develop specific rites for Christian apostates who wanted to return.[113]

Hoyland, *Seeing Islam*, p. 352, suggests that George converted to Islam ca. 640 and was martyred in the 650s.

[110] *Life of Elias of Heliopolis* 10–15, quote in section 15 (ed. A. Papadopoulos-Kerameus, *Syllogē Palaistinēs kai Syriakēs hagiologies*, vol. 1, pp. 48–52, quote at 52; ET taken from McGrath, 'Elias of Heliopolis: The Life of an Eighth-Century Syrian Saint,' pp. 97–101, quote at 100–101).

[111] *Questions Which Addai the Priest and Lover of Labors Asked Jacob, the Bishop of Edessa* 21 (ed. Vööbus, *The Synodicon in the West Syrian Tradition I* [CSCO 367–68; SS 161–62], p. 261 [= p. 238 (ET)]).

[112] *Legend of Sergius Baḥīrā* (East Syrian recension) 17.80 (ed. Roggema, p. 292; the ET is that of Roggema, p. 293). Compare this with the West Syrian recension (p. 364 = 365 [ET]), where the proportion one in ten or one in one hundred refers to those who do not convert rather than apostates who return to Christianity. On the identity of the figure in question, see Roggema's discussion, pp. 77–81.

[113] For Coptic renegades returning to Christianity, see L.S.B. MacCoull, 'The Rite of the Jar: Apostasy and Reconciliation in the Medieval Coptic Orthodox Church,' in D. Wolfthal, ed., *Peace and Negotiation: Strategies for Coexistence in the Middle Ages and the Renaissance* (Turnhout, 2000), pp. 145–62. For Greek rites of conversion and reconversion from Islam to Christianity, see D. J. Sahas, 'Ritual of Conversion from Islam to the Byzantine Church,' *Greek Orthodox Theological Review* 36 (1991), pp. 57–69. For a Chalcedonian Syriac rite for a Christian who became a Muslim and then returned to Christianity, see the sixteenth-century Paris Syriac 100, fols. 30v–35r (described in Zotenberg, *Manuscrits orientaux*, p.

CONVERSION, APOSTASY, AND THE LIMITS OF OUR SOURCES

The threat of death or imprisonment for a person who converted from Islam to Christianity meant that such (re-)conversions, when they happened, would not necessarily have received the attention—publicly, much less in written sources—that conversion from Christianity to Islam might have received in Muslim-ruled territories.[114] Indeed, for Christians living in an Islamic state, engaging in the open preaching of Christianity aimed at Muslims could be a very dangerous act,[115] and in some versions of the so-called 'Pact of 'Umar' (the *shurūṭ 'Umar,* or 'conditions of 'Umar'), Christians promised not to proselytize.[116] Importantly, the relative absence of written evidence about Muslim conversions to Christianity does not mean that such conversions did not take place.[117] In AH 124/AD 741–742, for instance, Sulaymān b. Hishām led an army against a Byzantine fort in Asia Minor, only to have the plague strike his forces. A number died of illness, hunger set in, and a Byzantine assault killed even more men and most of their horses. The result of these unhappy events was a religious shift in the remaining troops: 'a great number of them sought refuge with the Romans,' Maḥbūb b. Qusṭanṭīn reported, 'and they became Christians on account of the calamity that had gotten hold of them.'[118]

Important in this anecdote is the fact that these renegades were no longer living under Muslim rule. When we hear about such conversions in Islamic texts, the same is the case: renegades are usually no longer living in Muslim-ruled lands. At another Byzantine fortress, for example, we find in the *Kitāb al-aghānī* the story of an Arab *ghāzī* who fell in love with a Christian girl and converted to marry her. When the Muslims who meet him asked if he would leave if they paid his ransom, he thinks for a moment and then tells them to

58). More generally and for more detail, see Sahner, 'Christian Martyrs and the Making of an Islamic Society in the Post-Conquest Period,' p. 136.

114 On the legal implications and consequences of apostasy, see W. Heffening's article, 'Murtadd,' in *EI2*, vol. 7, pp. 635–36.

115 A notable example of a Christian killed for such behavior is Peter of Capitolias (d. 715), for whom see Theophanes, *Chronicle* AM 6234 (ed. de Boor, vol. 1, p. 416; ET available in Mango and Scott, *The Chronicle of Theophanes Confessor,* pp. 577–78). For a summary of Peter's *Passion,* see P. Peeters, 'La Passion de S. Pierre de Capitolias († 13 janvier 715),' *AB* 57 (1939), pp. 299–333. See also S. Efthymiadias's article, 'The Martyrdom of Peter of Capitolias,' in *CMR,* vol. 1, pp. 419–22. For an ET of the *Passion,* see S. Shoemaker, *Three Christian Martyrdoms* (Provo, 2016) pp. 2–65.

116 Ibn Qayyim al-Jawziyya, *Aḥkām ahl al-dhimma,* vol. 2, p. 113 (ed. Ṭ. 'Abd al-Ra'ūf Sa'd [Beirut, 1995]): *wa-lā nuraghghib fī dīninā wa-lā nad'ū ilayhi aḥadan.*

117 Cf. the observations in Cook, 'Apostasy from Islam,' p. 251.

118 Maḥbūb b. Qusṭanṭīn, *Kitāb al-'Unwān,* p. 249 (ed. Vasiliev [PO 8.3]). For the date of this event, see L. Caetani, *Chronographia Islamica,* vol. 5 (Paris, 1912), p. 1559, no. 10.

leave. 'May God accompany you,' he is supposed to have said.[119] In fact, this renegade's physical transfer away from a Muslim community seems typical of Muslim apostates—at least those who lived openly as non-Muslims—from nearly the very beginning of Islamic history. 'Ubayd Allāh b. Jaḥsh, one of the Muslims who emigrated to Abyssinia early in the Prophet's ministry, apostatized from Islam there and became a Christian; he would die there a Christian.[120]

Though the Qur'ān had nothing explicit to say about Muslim apostates, the Prophet was credited with ordering death as the punishment for a Muslim who changed his religion.[121] One possible way of interpreting the harshness of this penalty is to see it as a reflection of anxieties that shallow conversions, undertaken for the sort of expedient reasons that we have encountered—as a means of social gain, for the sake of marriage, to escape taxes, and so on—would not stick.[122] By making death the punishment for leaving Islam once one had converted, Muslim religious authorities were attempting to keep the walls of their community from springing leaks as converts seeped back into their previous communities—which were older, better established, much more numerous, and populated by friends and relatives. The death of the Prophet itself, we should recall, triggered widespread rebellion and apostasy among the Muslims of Arabia, the great majority of whom had, as we have also seen, converted *en masse*, late in the Prophet's life. There is no reason to think that the possibility of or temptation to apostasy will have ended simply with the conclusion of the Wars of Apostasy. These involved military action and violence, not 'hearts and minds' campaigns of religious persuasion and instruction.

Scholars who have focused on Christian anxieties about apostasy to Islam have seen only part of the story and usually have done so out of a certain unwitting teleology. Because Muslims eventually achieved numerical supremacy in the Middle East—a centuries-long process—we look for and assume that conversion away from Christianity would cause consternation within the

[119] Abū al-Faraj al-Iṣbahānī, *Kitāb al-Aghānī*, vol. 5, pp. 185–86. For a similar story and the theme of 'apostasy for the sake of love,' see Cook, 'Apostasy from Islam,' pp. 266–68.

[120] 'Ubayd Allāh was also married to Umm Ḥabība, who would eventually be one of the Prophet's wives. See Ibn Sa'd, *Kitāb al-ṭabaqāt al-kabīr*, vol. 8, pp. 157–58 (ed. C. Brockelmann [Leiden, 1904]; ET available in A. Bewley, *The Women of Madina* [London, 1995], p. 153) and cf. vol. 3.1 (ed. Sachau), p. 62.

[121] See the article 'Apostasy' by F. Griffel in *EI3*. For prophetic *hadīth* on apostasy, see, e.g., 'Abd al-Razzāq, *al-Muṣannaf*, vol. 10, p. 168 (no. 18706). In general, see Ibn Qudāma, *al-Mughnī*, vol. 12, pp. 264–306. For death as the punishment for apostasy in Zoroastrianism, see chapter 4, n. 7.

[122] In this respect, mass conversions, where an entire family, clan, tribe, village, or city became Muslim at the same time, though potentially quite shallow doctrinally, ironically might be more immune to the threat of apostasy than an individual conversion which threatened to alienate someone from his or her family and community. I am grateful to Luke Yarbrough for this point.

Christian community, which it did. But Christians and Muslims in the seventh and eighth centuries had no way of knowing about Islam's eventual demographic triumph in the Middle East. There was, in the early period, a real and present danger that some Muslim converts might leave Islam (or simply not follow any of its precepts), just as there was a real possibility that a non-Muslim might convert to Islam—though the political and economic context would suggest the latter shift was the more likely.

Such were some of the reasons why a person might have chosen either course. Over the long term, however, the trend was strongly in the direction of those who joined the Prophet's community. But when did conversion actually happen?

WHEN DID PEOPLE CONVERT?

Even though the medieval Middle East is typically treated as an Islamic place—effectively an Arab Muslim nation state rather than a multireligious empire—and medieval Middle Eastern history is routinely conflated with Islamic history, Muslims likely remained a numerical minority in the Middle East for centuries after the conquests. For much of the Middle Ages, in fact, the ruler with the largest subject Christian population in the world will have been an Umayyad or an Abbasid caliph, not the Byzantine or Holy Roman Emperor. It is quite possible in fact, even probable, that Muslims remained a demographic minority in most parts of the formerly Roman Middle East at least until the Mamluk period (AD 1250–1517/AH 648–922), when harsh discriminatory measures, large-scale state-sponsored violence targeting Christians, and the widespread destruction of churches led to conversions that may have made Muslims a majority population.[123]

[123] The Black Death also likely played a role in devastating the Christian population of the Middle East in the Mamluk period. A convenient summary of the Christian situation under the Mamluks can be found in J. Nasrallah, *Histoire du mouvement littéraire dans l'Eglise melchite du Ve au XXe siècle*, vol. 3.2 (Louvain/Paris, 1981), pp. 37–43, and A. S. Atiya, 'Mamluks and Copts,' in *CoptEn*, vol. 5, pp. 1517–18. See, too, M. Perlmann, 'Notes on anti-Christian Propaganda in the Mamlūk Empire,' *BSOAS* 10 (1942), pp. 843–61; Little, 'Coptic Conversion to Islam under the Baḥrī Mamlūks'; and M. Megally's articles, 'Waq'at al-Kanā'is,' and 'Waq'at al-Naṣārā,' in *CoptEn*, vol. 7, pp. 2313–16, and 2316–19, respectively, as well as Jones, *'Islām al-Kāfir fī Ḥāl al-Khuṭba*: Concerning the Conversion of "Infidels" to Islam during the Muslim Friday Sermon in Mamluk Egypt,' *Anuario de Estudios Medievales* 42 (2012), pp. 65–70. Cf. also the short summary in Armanios, *Coptic Christianity in Ottoman Egypt*, pp. 16–17, including (p.16), the observation: 'Some have estimated that the Coptic population was reduced by half or two-thirds between the fourteenth and seventeenth centuries.' I am grateful to Luke Yarbrough for some of these bibliographical references. See also the observations of J.-M. Fiey on the importance of the Black Death,

The evidence for this assertion is, admittedly, thin. But the evidence for the contrary, that Muslims were a demographic majority in the Middle East in Syria, Palestine, and Egypt within two or three centuries of the conquests, is even thinner. The question of conversion, much like the debates over literacy we saw in Chapter 1 or questions related to the ancient economy, can quickly slip into an imprecise, inexact, and impressionistic world, one where scholarly consensus often serves as a substitute for hard evidence and the constant repetition of poorly substantiated assumptions becomes the basis for fact.

The rate of Islamization in the eastern Mediterranean seems to have increased from the mid-tenth to the late eleventh centuries,[124] but there is no way to gauge the relative numbers of Christians and Muslims there over this period of time. Until the end of the eleventh century in Palestine, 'apart from the days of al-Ḥākim, we have no explicit evidence of mass conversion of Christians to Islam.'[125] In Egypt there is only evidence for one major wave of Coptic conversion to Islam—in the eighth/fourteenth century[126] and it has been suggested on the basis of papyri 'that much of the population was Coptic through the 12th century.'[127] Building—or the lack thereof—can also point to the slow growth of the Muslim community: it was only at the beginning of the twelfth century, for instance, that Damascus and Aleppo experienced the first construction of significant new Islamic monuments since the erection of their congregational mosques under the Umayyads about five hundred years earlier, something that Stephen Humphreys pointed to as possibly indicating a relatively small size for Muslim communities in these two cities for many centuries after the beginnings of Muslim rule.[128] Language can be taken as

---

Tīmūr, and the situation of Christians under Mongol rule once the Mongols began to convert to Islam in the late thirteenth century in *EI2*, vol. 7, p. 973; and cf. the Conclusion to this volume, n. 10.

[124] Ellenblum, 'Demography,' combines a wider range of impressive textual and climatic evidence to support this claim.

[125] M. Gil, *A History of Palestine, 634–1099* (Cambridge, 1992), p. 222. Ellenblum, 'Demography,' p. 72, cited Gil approvingly, with the exception of an attempted forced conversion in the 840s. Levy-Rubin, 'New Evidence relating to the Process of Islamization in Palestine in the early Muslim Period', p. 262, summarized reasons for thinking the Islamization of Palestine proceeded slowly in the first centuries of Muslim rule.

[126] T. El-Leithy, 'Coptic Culture and Conversion in Medieval Cairo, 1293–1524 A.D.,' pp. 13–30, gives a very useful overview of studies of Coptic conversion to Islam in Egypt. For only one major wave of medieval Coptic conversion, see p. 23. S. I. Gellens, 'Egypt, Islamization of,' in *CoptEn*, vol. 3, pp. 936–42, can be taken as representative of earlier views which saw pre-Mamluk waves of conversion as well.

[127] J. Iskander, 'Islamization in Medieval Egypt: The Copto-Arabic "Apocalypse of Samuel" as a Source for the Social and Religious History of Medieval Copts,' *Medieval Encounters* 4 (1998), p. 219, n. 1. For this, see H. Munt, 'What did Conversion to Islam Mean in Seventh-Century Arabia?' in A.C.S. Paecock, ed., *Islamisation: Comparative Perspectives from History* (Edinburgh, 2017), p. 83, n. 2.

[128] See the observation of R. S. Humphreys in 'Christian Communities in Early Islamic Syria and Northern Jazira: the Dynamics of Adaption,' in Haldon, ed., *Money, Power and Politics in Early Islamic*

another clue pointing to late conversion: Tamer el-Leithy has suggested that the late conversion of Egypt to Islam was 'likely a pre-condition' that allowed it to be Arabized in a way that Iran, which converted to Islam earlier, never was: 'had significant religious conversion taken place earlier, bilingualism may have occurred on a wider scale—allowing Coptic to survive as a language *of* Islam, as Persian did.'[129] Judged by this measure, the ultimate victory of Arabic over Aramaic/Syriac and Greek in other formerly Roman areas, like Syria and Palestine, could be taken, along with the absence of large-scale waves of conversions in these regions, as evidence for Christian majorities existing there into the second millennium.

Nearly forty years ago, Richard Bulliet published a groundbreaking book on conversion in the Islamic world that remains in many ways the best study on this subject. Bulliet built his estimates of conversion rates on the examination of name changes that could be found in the genealogies of scholars listed in medieval biographical dictionaries. The first appearance of a Muslim name listed among an individual's forbears was taken to indicate the point at which a conversion to Islam had occurred: a Muslim name meant that a parent had become a Muslim.[130] If we accept Bulliet's estimate, it was around AH 275/AD 888 that Syria became majority Muslim.[131] On this account, Syria will have remained a majority-Christian region for nearly two hundred and fifty years after the conquests. For all its importance and the impressiveness of the quantitative methods that he employed, however, Bulliet's suggestion suffered from fatal methodological flaws. Though still very valuable, the book's weaknesses are indicative of the problems that attach to efforts to ascertain the pace of conversion, as well as to common assumptions about the nature of Middle Eastern society in the period of Muslim rule. Let us pause for a moment, therefore, to examine it.

Syria, pp. 47–48. Humphreys, p. 47, notes two exceptions to the lack of new Islamic building in Aleppo in this period: a burial shrine built in the tenth century and a new minaret added to Aleppo's great mosque in the eleventh century.

[129] El-Leithy, 'Coptic Culture and Conversion in Medieval Cairo, 1293–1524 A.D.,' p. 25. Cf. also the observations in S. M. Ayyad, 'Regional Literature: Egypt,' in J. Ashtiany et al., eds., *Abbasid Belles Lettres* (Cambridge, 1990), p. 413.

[130] R. Bulliet, *Conversion to Islam in the Medieval Period: An Essay in Quantitative History* (Cambridge, MA/London, 1979), pp. 18–19, 21. Bulliet has recently reaffirmed confidence in his method of analysis and offered a defense of it against objections. See his 'The Conversion Curve Revisited,' in Peacock, ed., *Islamisation*, pp. 69-79.

[131] Bulliet, *Conversion to Islam*, p. 109. P. Fargues, 'The Arab Christians of the Middle East: A Demographic Perspective,' in A. Pacini, ed., *Christian Communities in the Middle East: The Challenge of the Future* (Oxford, 1998), pp. 48–66, while not focusing specifically on the medieval period as Bulliet does, nevertheless provides very interesting and insightful analysis on the nature and size of the Christian population of the Middle East in the period after the Arab conquests.

Apart from the urban and elite bias of the biographical dictionaries that formed the backbone of his study—more than 80 percent of Syria's population, Alan Walmsley has estimated, lived in rural settlements,[132] and the religious experience of this population is typically invisible in medieval sources, biographical dictionaries, and otherwise—Bulliet's use of Islamic names as indicators of conversion in biographical dictionaries was deeply problematic.[133] Name changes can indeed reflect religious changes,[134] and the religious and social importance of names in the Middle East is obvious to anyone familiar with the experience of religious minorities in the region: in Levantine Christian communities, the connection between name and confessionial identity and confessional (in)visibility is a well-known part of life and the choice of a more or less confessionally indicative name can reflect (though not necessarily) one's broader religious and cultural attitudes.[135] What is more, many Christians, especially in Egypt, will often give their children religiously 'neutral' names in order to avoid the discrimination, social and economic difficulties, and problems in dealing with government offices that can attend having an explicitly Christian name.[136]

Given the social and even economic importance of onomastic choices, we should not be astonished to find that Christians were in fact taking Muslim names in the medieval Middle East. The evidence for this is manifold. There are specific instances of Christians who had names that were associated with important figures in early Islamic history—a priest named al-Ḥasan b. Yūsuf,

[132] A. Walmsley, *Early Islamic Syria: An Archaeological Assessment* (London, 2007), p. 72.

[133] Though for Bulliet's defense against the charge of an urban bias, see 'The Conversion Curve Revisited,' p. 71.

[134] See, e.g., former pagans taking the names of biblical prophets in Eusebius of Caesarea, *History of the Martyrs of Palestine* , pp. *29–*30, *43 (ed. W. Cureton, *History of the Martyrs of Palestine, Discovered in a Very Antient Syriac Manuscript* [London/Edinburgh, 1861], pp. 27–28, 40 [ET]). For an attempt to apply Bulliet's methodology to the question of the Christianization of pagan Egypt, see R. S. Bagnall, 'Religious Conversion and Onomastic Change in Early Byzantine Egypt,' *Bulletin of the American Society of Papyrologists* 19 (1982), pp. 105–24.

[135] Note the remarks of the Lebanese author Elias Khoury: 'I remember Emile Habibi, the great Palestinian novelist, once said to me, How dare you give the characters of your novels Christian or Muslim names? Habibi was a Christian like me, of course. I said to him, But that's the way our society is. You know that we can often tell a person by their name. And he said, You should give them neutral names. It's what I do. So I said, Your own name isn't neutral, it's Emile! Are you going to change that?' See Robyn Creswell, 'Elias Khoury, The Art of Fiction No. 233,' *Paris Review* 220 (Spring, 2017) (available at https://www.theparisreview.org/interviews/6940/elias-khoury-the-art-of-fiction-no-233-elias-khoury).

[136] George Kiraz reminds me that among the Syrian Orthodox of contemporary Iraq, one also finds names such as ʿAmr and Ḥassān, which are more commonly associated with Islam than with Christianity. As an example of the ideological nature of onomastic choices in a contemporary context: the use by Christians of names more traditionally associated with the Islamic tradition can indicate, for instance, an identification with Arab nationalism.

for example,[137] or a monk named Abū al-Ḥasan ʿAlī b. ʿUbayd.[138] There are also complaints about Christians using Muslim names: in his *Answer to the Christians*, al-Jāḥiẓ (d. AH 225/AD 868–9) complained that Christians had taken the names al-Ḥasan, al-Ḥusayn, al-ʿAbbās, al-Faḍl and ʿAlī. 'It only remains for them to be named Muḥammad and have the *kunya* "Abū al-Qāsim,"' he wrote.[139] Hundreds of years later, Ibn Qayyim al-Jawziyya (d. AH 751/AD 1350), would also bemoan the fact that in his time Christians (and Jews) were taking Muslim *kunyas*, such as Abū al-ʿAlāʾ, Abū al-Faḍl, and Abū al-Ṭayyib, and names like Ḥasan and Ḥusayn and ʿUthmān and ʿAlī.[140] Ibn al-Qayyim's contemporary, Ibn al-Ukhuwwa (d. AH 729/AD 1329), made similar complaints: 'If Umar b. al-Khaṭṭāb were now to see Jews and Christians!' he wrote, listing among their violations of the stipulations of ʿUmar (i.e., the 'Pact of ʿUmar') their use of epithets associated with caliphs, such as al-Rashīd, and their taking *kunyas* associated with famous Muslims such as Abū al-Ḥusayn and Abū al-Faḍl.[141] Some Christians were also unhappy that their coreligionists were giving their children names associated with a rival religion: in the tenth century, Ps.-Samuel of Qalamūn complained that Christians were 'naming their children with their [i.e., Muslims'] names and forsaking the names of the angels, the Prophets, the Apostles, and the Martyrs.'[142] Egyptian papyri from the ninth and tenth centuries (AD) even give us examples of people who had two sets of names—one Christian and one Muslim—which they apparently used in different contexts.[143]

[137] See G. Graf, *Geschichte der christlichen arabischen Literatur*, vol. 2 (Rome, 1947), p. 153, for al-Ḥasan's twenty-eight questions to Yūḥannā b. ʿĪsā.

[138] Graf, *Geschichte der christlichen arabischen Literatur*, vol. 2, p. 159, records a note that a preface and commentary were 'für den Mönch, Schreiber und Philosophen Abu 'l-Ḥasan ʿAlī ibn ʿUbaid gefertigt.'

[139] See al-Jāḥiẓ, *Fī 'l-radd ʿalā al-Naṣārā*, p. 317 (ed. ʿA. al-Salām Muḥammad Hārūn, *Rasāʾil al-Jāḥiẓ*, vol. 3 [Beirut, 1991]). For the Prophet forbidding the use of his *kunya*, see al-Bukhārī, *al-Jāmiʿ al-ṣaḥīḥ*, vol. 1, p. 55 (no. 110).

[140] Ibn Qayyim al-Jawziyya, *Aḥkām Ahl al-Dhimma*, vol. 2, p. 189.

[141] Abū al-Ḥusayn being ʿAlī b. Abī Ṭālib and Abū al-Faḍl being al-ʿAbbās, the uncle of the Prophet. See Ibn al-Ukhuwwa, *Maʿālim al-qurba fī aḥkām al-ḥisba*, p. *42 (ed. R. Levy [London, 1938]; ET at p. 15. I have used here Levy's translation).

[142] Ps.-Samuel of Qalamūn, *Apocalypse*, p. 379.

[143] M. Legendre, 'Perméabilité linguistique et anthroponymique entre copte et arabe: l'exemple de comptes en caractères coptes du Fayoum Fatimide,' in A. Boud'hors, A. Delattre, C. Louis, and T. Sebastian Richter, eds., *Coptica argentoratensia* (Paris, 2014), p. 350. In much earlier periods of Egyptian history, the phenomenon of 'double names'—a person having both an Egyptian and a Greek name—was a common one, with people using different names depending on the context. For this phenomenon as undermining the use of 'onomastic criterion in establishing the ethnic origin of persons in government service,' see W. Clarysse, 'Greeks and Egyptians in the Ptolemaic Army and Administration,' *Aegyptus* 65 (1985), pp. 57–66 (quote from p. 65). I am grateful to Jacco Dieleman for making me aware of this article. For double names in Spain, see T. E. Burman, *Religious Polemic and the Intellectual History of the Mozarabs* (Leiden/New York/Köln, 1994), p. 29.

The practice of Christians using Muslim names is also suggested by the clause in the 'Pact of 'Umar,' where People of the Book pledge that they will not take the *kunya*s of Muslims.[144] Ibn al-Qayyim in fact offered a typology of three different kinds of names in his exposition of the *shurūṭ 'Umar*: names specific to Muslims (e.g., Muḥammad, Aḥmad, Abū Bakr, 'Umar, 'Uthmān, 'Alī, Ṭalḥa, al-Zubayr), names specific to infidels (e.g., George, Peter, John, Matthew), and shared names (e.g., Yaḥyā, 'Īsā, Ayyūb, Dāwūd, Sulaymān, Zayd, 'Abd Allāh, 'Aṭiyya, Mawhūb, Salām, and [even though he also lists it as being only for Muslims], 'Umar).[145] *Ḥadīth* that focused on the question of the propriety of giving a non-Muslim a *kunya* can also be taken as evidence for the fact that Muslims were doing precisely this.[146]

There is also the problem that a convert might falsify his genealogy to cover up his Christian heritage, as did, for instance, the great poet Abū Tammām, whose father had been a Christian named Thādhūs but who claimed his father had actually been named Aws and that he belonged to the tribe Ṭayyi',[147] and as did the Banū Wahb, who were of East Syrian Christian origin, but who claimed that they were Arabs from Najrān.[148] In an environment where there was social and economic benefit to having a Muslim name and a Muslim genealogy, we simply cannot assume that a person bearing a name that, on the face of it, seems Islamic, was actually a Muslim.[149] For the Islamization of Iran, the most important region for Bulliet's study, a methodology focused on name changes may have a firmer basis—attitudes towards non-Muslim names there may have been different. But it is not clear that such attitudes were the same across all Muslim-ruled territories, nor is it obvious that a methodology that is effective in an Iranian context would be equally useful in a Syrian or Egyptian one. What is more, once we realize that a name change does not necessarily signal a change of religion, and that there was incentive to falsify and Islamize genealogies, studying name changes as a way to ascertain religious allegiance becomes a risky proposition.[150]

[144] Ibn Taymiyya, *Iqtiḍā' al-ṣirāṭ al-mustaqīm mukhālafat aṣḥāb al-jaḥīm*, pp. 121, 122 (ed. M. Ḥāmid al-Fiqī [Cairo, 1950]).

[145] Ibn Qayyim al-Jawziyya, *Aḥkām ahl al-dhimma*, vol. 2, pp. 186–88.

[146] For a collection of such *ḥadīth*, see 'Abd al-Razzāq, *al-Muṣannaf*, vol. 6, pp. 122–23 (nos. 10195–99).

[147] See H. Ritter's article, 'Abū Tammām Ḥabīb b. Aws,' in *EI2*, vol. 1, p. 153.

[148] See C. E. Bosworth's article, 'Wahb', in *EI2*, vol. 11, pp. 33–34, esp. p. 33. Bulliet, *Conversion to Islam*, p. 19, noted the possibility of fabricated genealogies and allowed that 'in most cases there is no way of detecting such fabrications.'

[149] There are parallel cases where there were incentives to falsify genealogies for material benefits: How many of the many people in the Ottoman period who claimed to be descended from the Prophet and who could produce genealogies to prove it were actually genetic descendants of Muḥammad?

[150] Ḥ. Zayyāt, 'Al-asmā' wa-'l-kunā wa-'l-alqāb al-naṣrāniyya fī 'l-Islām,' *Al-Machriq* 42 (1948), pp.

Bulliet's efforts to quantify conversion based on name changes in biographical dictionaries, as creative and notable as they were, ultimately failed to convince. The evidentiary base he used was too unrepresentative and limited to justify broad generalization across all Muslim-ruled lands and a methodology based on name-changes is simply not reliable. In raising the question of conversion and its consequences in such a vivid way, however, Bulliet nevertheless highlighted perhaps the most important and elusive question in the social history of the medieval Middle East. After the Arab conquest, the Middle East is treated by scholars and nearly everyone else, implicitly or even explicitly, as a predominantly Muslim region. But how Muslim was it?

In the absence of persuasive evidence for massive waves of conversion to Islam in the three or four centuries after the Arab conquests and in the face of the weaknesses of attempts to show large numbers of people leaving Christianity in this period,[151] we can suggest as an alternative a model where conversions occurred at a slow and incremental pace, with individuals choosing to become Muslim for the mixture of reasons we have reviewed, and perhaps for others as well. In addition to this slow drip, periods of state-sponsored anti-Christian violence and persecution, such as occurred under al-Ḥākim, during the Mamluk period, or under the Mongols, will have witnessed a marked increase in the rate of Christian conversion. After these episodes, the specter of death for apostasy meant that many, but not all of the Christians who converted under duress remained Muslim even after the period of threat had ended—a religious 'ratchet effect,' as it were.[152]

It is important here also to keep in mind the social aspects of religious change in this period, for thinking of conversion only in strongly individualistic

1–21, gives extensive evidence for Christian use of Muslim names in the medieval period. Carlson, 'The Contours of Conversion,' offers a judicious approach to the question of the Islamiziation of Syria, including a critique of Bulliet's views (pp. 812–14). For further criticism of Bulliet's methodology, see el-Leithy, 'Coptic Culture and Conversion in Medieval Cairo,' pp. 21–22; J.-M. Fiey in *EI2*, vol. 7, p. 972; and Hackenburg, 'Christian Conversion to Islam,' p. 178.

[151] This is not to say that instances of large-scale conversions in this period cannot be identified; see, for example, Hoyland, *Seeing Islam*, p. 343, for two examples. Cahen, 'Socio-Economic History and Islamic Studies,' p. 270, saw no evidence of mass conversions before the Ṭulunid period, i.e., roughly the second half of the ninth century (AD).

[152] For talk of a 'ratchet effect' in the context of conversion and the gradual disappearance of Middle Eastern Christian communities, see P. Jenkins, *The Lost History of Christianity: The Thousand-Year Golden Age of the Church in the Middle East, Africa, and Asia—and How It Died* (New York, 2008), p. 211. Note that Fargues, 'The Arab Christians of the Middle East,' p. 51, stresses the importance of mixed marriages (a Muslim man marrying a non-Muslim woman, with the children being Muslim, or a Christian man converting to marry a Muslim woman) in the Islamization of the Middle East: 'A simulation shows that over the period in question, covering a thousand years, mixed marriages alone, and the conversion required for men in half of these cases, would have sufficed to create a proportion of Muslims around 90 per cent.'

terms and highlighting the personal advantages it might offer—economic, marital, social, political, or otherwise—misses the reality that familial and communal pressure could represent strong headwinds that any potential convert would have to sail against. In other words, for all its potential personal benefits, an individual conversion might also come at great social cost: the convert risked alienating himself from his family and religious community.[153] This point should not to be downplayed, either, for membership in a religious community became an increasingly important part of personal identity over the course of medieval period.[154] It is perhaps for this reason that some versions of the 'Pact of 'Umar' have Christians promise to not prevent relatives who want to 'enter into Islam' from conversion.[155] At times, we can even find concrete examples of such pressure: we have already seen the story of the seventh-century Christian renegade Moses, whose movements between Christianity and Islam were in part apparently influenced by criticism from his friends. In the tenth century (AD), the Christian renegade al-Ḥasan b. Ayyūb would write that his connection to his Christian family and friends had been a factor weighing against his contemplated conversion.[156] In much later periods, there are vivid examples of families attempting to prevent the conversion of individuals to Islam.[157] Keeping such social pressures in mind leads to the

[153] In the case of Christian women who converted to Islam to get out of marriages, such alienation from (at least some) family may have been precisely the thing desired. But the social results of conversion will have been complex. On social pressures against conversion, see Cahen, 'Socio-Economic History and Islamic Studies,' p. 265. On the case of Jewish renegades and the status of their marriages to Jews after conversion, see U. Simonsohn, 'The Legal and Social Bonds of Jewish Apostates and their Spouses according to Gaonic Responsa,' *The Jewish Quarterly Review* 105 (2015), pp. 417–39.

[154] Michael Morony argued that a personal identity in which one's religious communal membership was a primary component had already begun, in Iraq at least, in the Sasanian period. See his 'Religious Communities in Late Sasanian and early Muslim Iraq,' *JESHO* 17 (1974), pp. 113–35, and his *Iraq after the Muslim Conquest*, pp. 277–79. For discussion, see A. Papaconstantinou, 'Confrontation, Interaction, and the Formation of the Early Islamic *Oikoumene*,' *Revue des études Byzantines* 63 (2005), pp. 173–74 and for more on the transformation of ecclesiastical communities into social groupings, see Papaconstantinou, 'Between *Umma* and *Dhimma*: The Christians of the Middle East under the Umayyads,' *Annales islamologiques* 42 (2008), pp. 127–56.

[155] Ibn Qayyim al-Jawziyya, *Aḥkām ahl al-dhimma*, vol. 2, p. 113.

[156] See Hackenburg, 'Voices of the Converted: Christian Apostate Literature in Medieval Islam,' pp. 12, 198. Compare also the case of the twelfth-century Jewish convert to Islam, Samwāl b. Yaḥyā al-Maghribī, who delayed his conversion out of regard for his father; see M. García-Arenal, 'Dreams and Reason: Autobiographies of Converts in Religious Polemics,' in García-Arenal, ed., *Conversions islamiques*, p. 95. The late eighth-century *Zuqnin Chronicle* depicts people who converted to Islam as not giving heed to the reproof of their pastors or others; when a certain deacon decided to convert to Islam, 'all the notables and priests of the village seized him and begged him at length not to apostatise, but he was not persuaded.' See *Zuqnin Chronicle*, pp. 383, 390 (ed. Chabot [CSCO 104: SS 53]; ET taken from Harrak, *The Chronicle of Zuqnin*, pp. 323, 327 [quote at 390/327]).

[157] See, e.g., the nineteenth-century story of a trader whose father pleaded with him not to convert to Islam in A. N. Kefeli, *Becoming Muslim in Imperial Russia: Conversion, Apostasy, and Literacy* (Ithaca/

suggestion that it was people whose personal situation had removed them from family and communal networks—most notably, captives and slaves—who were perhaps more likely to convert. And it is the factors of familial and communal pressure that can explain why it is that we find stories of entire communities converting to Islam from the Umayyad period until Ottoman times, and also why it is that dramatic periods of widespread anti-Christian violence are so important in explaining the region's eventual conversion to Islam. It was in such contexts that the familial and communal pressures against conversion, so important in maintaining the religious status quo after the Arab conquests, were suspended or superseded by other considerations.

A proposed scenario of punctuated equilibria in religious demographics means that numerically, the Christian community will have remained substantial in formerly Roman areas for much longer than is commonly assumed. Demographically speaking, much of the early and high medieval Middle East—Egypt, Syria, Palestine, and perhaps northern Iraq—was a Christian region.

To this, a related observation should be added. Other phenomena, such as conversion and reversion, which we have already seen, and religiously-mixed families, which we will see, mean that even among the portion of the Middle East's population that had converted to Islam, an intimate and familiar knowledge and experience of Christianity could be found. Not only was the region a majority Christian one, but for many among its non-Christian Muslim minority, Christianity will have been a reality familiar to them from their homes. Any understanding of the medieval Middle East that does not take these demographic realities into consideration profoundly misses an important aspect of the region's social and cultural identity.

DEMOGRAPHICS AND THE QUESTION OF POWER

Such considerations aside, however, it must be acknowledged that focusing on numbers and on when exactly it was that Muslims achieved a demographic majority in the Middle East can itself be a misleading endeavor, tainted by concerns that are more at home in the political dynamics of democratic states in our contemporary world than in the period in question.[158] In the Middle

London, 2014), p. 1. Kefeli's converts to Islam from Christianity in a Russian imperial context represent an interesting case of conversion to Islam under Christian rule, and despite social pressures militating against conversion. In our period, the political context was reversed: we have Christians converting to Islam under Muslim, not Christian, rule.

[158] See the comments of Carlson, 'The Contours of Conversion,' pp. 813–14. R. S. Lissak, *When and How the Jewish Majority in the Land of Israel was Eliminated: Are the Palestinians Descendants of Islamized*

Ages, demography was not as significant as political power. What was important was that from the mid-seventh century onward, the followers of the Prophet belonged to a religion of winners: 'And this is the sign that God loves us, and is pleased with our religion,' the Muslim interlocutor in an early eighth-century Syriac dispute text is made to say, 'that he has given us authority over all faiths and all peoples. And behold, they are our slaves and subjects!'[159] 'Do not think, my beloved children,' Ps.-Samuel of Qalamūn admonished his tenth-century readers in Egypt, 'that this nation is honored in the sight of God because he has handed over this land to their hands.'[160] Christians, however, numerous they may have been, could not compete: 'They seek help from Saint Sergius and his son, after the Cross,' the poet Jarīr (d. ca. 728), wrote mockingly of the Christian Arab tribe of Taghlib, 'but they have no helper.'[161] Writing in the late seventh century, Ps.-Methodius would describe the Arabs, or Children of Ishmael, bragging about their military successes over a variety of different peoples. 'They will be dressed as bridegrooms,' he wrote, 'and adorned as brides; they will blaspheme, saying, "The Christians have no Saviour."'[162]

Al-Hāshimī, the Muslim correspondent in the early ninth-century *Apology* of al-Kindī, referred to the debate tactics of the 'rabble, ignorant, riff-raff, commoners, and foolish among those of our religion' whose manner of discussing and disputing with Christians was uncouth and did not rely on reason; their way of speaking was to be contentious, arrogant, and domineering, he noted, based on 'the power of the empire, without knowledge or argument.'[163] That al-Hāshimī's portion of the *Apology* was probably written by a Christian points to how the attitudes of at least some Muslims towards religious others in the context of interreligious discussion, especially outside of learned religious circles, were perceived. In Part I, we saw that Chalcedonians might

Jews (Illinois, 2015), is an example of the sort of controversial and nationalistic concerns that can easily enter into such questions.

[159] *Disputation between a Muslim and a Monk of Bēt Ḥālē* 9 (ed. Taylor, in 'The Disputation between a Muslim and a Monk of Bēt Ḥālē,' p. 209; the translation is that of Taylor). Cf. Roggema, *The Legend of Sergius Baḥīrā*, p. 22. Cp. also with *Khuzistan Chronicle*, p. 38 (ed. Guidi [CSCO Syr. III.4]): 'The victory of the Sons of Ishmael, who prevailed over and subdued these two mighty kingdoms, was from God.' (cf. Brock, 'Syriac Views of Emergent Islam,' p. 201, n. 25). Note, too, the view of the *qāḍī* Abū 'Abd Allāh b. al-Murābiṭ reported in 'Iyāḍ b. Mūsā (d. AD 1149/AH 544), *Shifā bi-ta'rīf ḥuqūq al-Muṣṭafā*, vol. 2, (ed. 'A. Muḥammad al-Bajāwī) (Beirut, 1984), pp. 941–42, that anyone who said that the Prophet had been routed and put to flight (*huzima*) should be given the opportunity to repent and, if he did not repent, should be killed.

[160] Ps.-Samuel of Qalamūn, *Apocalypse*, p. 376.

[161] Jarīr, *Dīwān*, p. 238 (Beirut, 1986).

[162] Ps.-Methodius, *Apocalypse* 13.6 (ed. Reinink [CSCO 540: SS 220], pp. 37–38; the ET here is by S. P. Brock, taken from Palmer, *The Seventh Century in the West-Syrian Chronicles*, p. 237).

[163] al-Kindī, *Apology*, pp. 11–12. ET by Tien also available Newman, ed., *The Early Christian-Muslim Dialogue*, pp. 387–88. FT available in Tartar, *Dialogue islamo-chrétien*, p. 93.

simply appeal to the fact of who it was that controlled the holy places as a way to trump other Christians in debate; now, a Muslim similarly might point to the might of the Muslim state as proof of the truth of the Prophet's message. The political domination of Muslims over non-Muslims and the divine favor this implied was what mattered, not numerical hegemony. Indeed, when the Andalusian jurist Ibn Ḥazm (d. AH 456/AD 1064) discussed notions of *dār al-islām* and *dār al-shirk*, the 'abode of Islam' and the 'abode of polytheism,' he noted that a region or area or place (*dār*) 'is only named for the one who is dominant over it and who governs it and possesses it.'[164] Since the medieval period, Westerners and Western scholars have adopted this view, too, something which has had a homogenizing effect on how the actual religious demographics of the region have been viewed and has obscured the enormous non-Muslim presence there.

MUSLIMS AS A MINORITY

Political power notwithstanding, however, demographic realities remained: even Jarīr wrote of visiting monasteries in his poems, in fact seeking healing at one of them.[165] After the conquests, members of the Prophet's community found themselves living in a context where their numbers were small. From this point onward, historians of the Middle East typically shift their focus to the activities of this community, its conflicts, ideological development, legal activities, and practices of writing about its past. But the amount of attention such events, places, and people receive is seductively distorting if we are interested in the Middle East writ large and not just a small segment of its population. 'The total number of Arabs who left their homes can hardly have exceeded, or even totaled, five hundred thousand,' Patricia Crone has written of the period after the conquests in the Middle East: 'The conquered peoples numbered perhaps twenty to thirty million.'[166]

[164] *al-dār innamā tunsabu lil-ghālib 'alayhā wa-'l-ḥākim fīhā wa-'l-mālik lahā*. Ibn Ḥazm, *al-Muḥallā* (ed. A. Muḥammad Shākir et al.) (Cairo, 1347–1352), vol. 11, p. 200. I am grateful to Cole Bunzel for drawing my attention to this passage.

[165] He was quoted by Yāqūt in *Mu'jam al-buldān*, vol. 2, p. 497, speaking about Dayr Arwā: 'We asked healing of her, but she did not heal us. . . .' Yāqūt thought Dayr Arwā was in the *bādiya*, but was not sure of its precise location. For poetry by Jarīr on the Monastery of Peter and the Monastery of Paul outside of Damascus, see p. 520, and for Jarīr writing about Dayr al-Lujj outside of Hira, see pp. 530–31; for his allusion to Dayr al-Walīd in a line of poetry, see p. 540.

[166] P. Crone, 'The Early Islamic World,' in K. Raaflaub and N. Rosenstein, eds., *War and Society in the Ancient and Medieval World: Asia, the Mediterranean, Europe, and Mesoamerica* (Washington, D.C., 1999), p. 314. See also the additional numbers given by Crone in *The Nativist Prophets of Early Islamic Iran* (New York, 2012), p. 8. Claude Cahen suggested that in the seventh century perhaps a hundred thousand and

The questions to which such a setting will have given rise were said to have already been anticipated in the life of Muḥammad: 'We are a travelling people,' Abū Tha'laba al-Khushanī is supposed to have told the Prophet, 'we pass by Jews, Christians, and Magians, and we find nothing but their vessels.' In other words, only non-Muslim vessels were available for use when travelling in non-Muslim regions. The Prophet is said to have replied, 'If you have not found anything other than these, wash them with water, then eat in them and drink.'[167]

There were many other vessels, so to speak, that Muslims in the seventh century and later would wash off and use: this question of what to wash off and use, metaphorically speaking, and what not to wash off and not to use was one of the fundamental challenges that the small and fledgling community faced. 'I asked the Prophet about the food of the Christians,' Qabīṣa b. al-Hulb reported on the authority of his father, Hulb, one of the Prophet's Companions, 'and he said, "Do not let any food which you think resembles that of the Christians cause any doubt at all in your heart." '[168] In a world where Muslims were few and Christians many, and where there was much food to be found with a Christian origin, such a statement had obvious prudential value. 'You have settled among Persians and Nabateans,' 'Abd Allāh b. Mas'ūd said, 'therefore when you buy meat, if it is slaughtered by a Jew or a Christian, then eat it, but if a Magian slaughtered it, do not eat it.'[169] Questions would arise for those Muslims engaged in military activities in Christian areas as well: 'Amr b. al-Ḍurays al-Asadī asked al-Sha'bī (d. after AH 100/AD 718), 'We are fighting in the land of Armenia—a Christian land—what do you think of their slaughtered meat and their food?' 'If we launched military attacks on a country,' al-Sha'bī replied, 'we would ask about its inhabitants. If they said, "Jews or Christians," we would eat their slaughtered meat and food and we would cook in their vessels.'[170]

But the Prophet's followers had to deal with more than just matters related to food. This question of how his community would define itself vis-à-vis Christians and Jews was wide-ranging and fundamental to its very identity.

---

and no more than two hundred thousand Arabs occupied 'most of the territory between the Hind[u] Kush and the Atlas Mountains.' See Cahen, 'Socio-Economic History and Islamic Studies,' p. 264.

[167] al-Tirmidhī, *al-Jāmi' al-kabīr*, vol. 3, p. 133 (no. 1464).

[168] al-Tirmidhī, *al-Jāmi' al-kabīr*, vol. 3, p. 224 (no. 1565) and see, too, Ibn Abī Shayba, *Muṣannaf*, vol. 11, p. 276 (no. 33233).

[169] Ibn Abī Shayba, *Muṣannaf*, vol. 11, p. 276 (no. 33235). Cf: 'Abd al-Razzāq, *al-Muṣannaf*, vol. 6, pp. 117–18 (no. 10176), also attributed to Ibn Mas'ūd: 'You have settled in a land in which Muslims do not butcher, but Nabateans and Persians do. If therefore you buy meat, ask—if it is the slaughtering of a Jew or a Christian, then eat it, for their food is permitted to you.'

[170] Ibn Abī Shayba, *Muṣannaf*, vol. 11, p. 277 (no. 33237).

And it was made more pressing by the fact that, with time, most Muslims in the Middle East would be the descendants, wholly or partially, of converts, the great majority of whom had likely joined the Prophet's community for reasons that had little to do with the spiritual or religious content of Muḥammad's message. In formerly Roman territories (and in some parts of the previously Sasanian world), these converts will have been for the most part simple Christians. We have now looked at some of the reasons why a simple Christian might have chosen to become a Muslim (and perhaps subsequently to return to Christianity). We have also attempted to look at the question of when conversion was happening. But once conversion did happen and became permanent, what was its result? What did the conversion of simple Christians to Islam look like?

CHAPTER 12

Conversion and the Simple

The More Things Change, the More They Stay the Same

> Most of the descendants of most of the men and women who in the year 600 believed that Jesus of Nazareth was the son of God now profess a belief in Allah and in Muḥammad as his messenger.
>
> Richard Bulliet[1]

At the end of Chapter 8, I raised a question: What happened when a politically-dominant, religious rival to Christianity appeared in the Middle East, one whose strongest theological criticisms of Christianity centered on doctrines (the Trinity and the Incarnation) that simple believers could not understand fully or properly? By now it will have become clear why I called that question a provisional one. Traditional approaches to Christian-Muslim relations have stressed the doctrinal encounter, but the considerations I have attempted to raise in the past three chapters (and indeed, in this entire book)—the fact of mass illiteracy, poor and spotty catechesis, largely agrarian populations, mass conversions, the non-representative character of sources that typically have urban and/or elite biases, and so on—have the cumulative effect of suggesting to us that we step back from such a perspective, much like my earlier suggestion that we step back from a heavily doctrinal view of inter-Christian relations in the post-Chalcedonian Middle East. Stepping back does not mean, of course, stepping away from doctrine altogether, but we must recognize that any attempt to understand the religious landscape that Chalcedon created or that resulted from the Arab conquests that takes sophisticated theological doctrine as its primary focus is one that does not properly take into account large swaths of the Christian and Muslim communities. At best, such an attempt will yield an incomplete picture of the religious landscape of this period. Done clumsily, it will give the misleading impression that the population of the Middle East was concerned primarily with proving or disproving the doctrine of the Trinity or the idea that God could have taken on human flesh.

[1] R.W. Bulliet, 'Process and Status in Conversion and Continuity,' in Gervers and Bikhazi eds., *Conversion and Continuity*, p. 2; punctuation slightly altered.

Ibn Kammūna, as we saw in the previous chapter, observed that he had never seen a person who was actually learned in both his own religious tradition and in the Islamic tradition convert for anything other than nontheological reasons.[2] Most Christians and Muslims were not learned in their own religious tradition, much less in that of a rival religion, and will have been ill-equipped or simply unable to discuss and debate religious difference at the level of sophisticated theology in a proper and informed way.[3] For this reason, if when speaking about Christian-Muslim relations, our focus is on difference at the level of doctrinal theology, we will gain only a distorted understanding of seventh- and eighth-century (as well as later) realities. We will overlook the existence of a layering and continuum of knowledge in the Christian community and fail to take into account the reality that most conversions by Christians to Islam will have been conversions of simple Christians into simple Muslims. Focusing on theological difference points us away from other types of interaction and exchange that will have been much more common.

If we step back and ask what sorts of interaction these might be, what we are left with is a situation not unlike what we encountered in Part II when seeking to understand the religious landscape of the Middle East in the wake of Chalcedon. Just as there was a spectrum of ways that Christians engaged the question of Chalcedon, stretching from composing erudite polemics and engaging in learned disputes before a ruler, to telling stories of miraculous vindications of one church's views over another, there was a similar range of ways in which Christians and Muslims dealt with religious disagreement and difference.

One notable way of dealing with religious difference, which we encountered in Part II, was simply not to disagree. People could also choose to ignore differences or to pay them only selective heed. We now find much the same situation. For instance: We saw in Chapter 3 that some members of the Church of the East had no objection to helping build a Miaphysite church, something that raised the ire of church leaders; we similarly have a report, probably from the middle part of the seventh century, of Christians, including an archdeacon named John, who in the time of Patriarch Sophronius (d. 641) willingly helped the Arabs clear off the Temple Mount and build a mosque there. Sophronius was, needless to say, reportedly not happy about this behavior.[4] Christian-

[2] Compare with the similar comments of al-Kindī, *Apology*, p. 152.

[3] Though it should be pointed out that not all doctrinally focused Christian-Muslim dispute texts operate at the same levels of sophistication; see S. H. Griffith, *The Church in the Shadow of the Mosque: Christians and Muslims in the World of Islam* (Princeton/Oxford, 2008), pp. 101–102, for the distinction between 'popular genres of apologetics and the more scholarly exercises in controversial theology, the *kalām* texts, and the words of philosophical theology' (quote on p. 101).

[4] Ps.-John Moschus, *Spiritual Meadow* (Georgian Appendix) 19 (ed. and trans. B. Flusin, 'L'esplanade

Muslim relations also of course took the familiar forms that scholars typically write about: there was violence, for example, when the Caliph al-Mahdī forced 5,000 men of the Christian Arab tribe of Tanūkh to convert to Islam in AD 779,[5] and the anti-Christian brutality and forced conversions of rulers like al-Ḥākim (reg. AH 386–411/AD 996–1021)[6] and Baybars (reg. AH 658–676/AD 1260–1277) later in the medieval period are infamous.

There were other ways, as well. As with Chalcedon, people elaborated narratives that vindicated the truth of their side. In response to Christian criticisms of Muḥammad's prophetic profile as lacking miracles, Muslims developed and told stories of him doing just that,[7] casting his biography into forms clearly inspired by biblical models,[8] or possibly even by accounts of late antique Christian holy men.[9] It is in this context of polemical counter-narratives that

---

du temple a l'arrivée des Arabes, d'après deux récits byzantins,' in J. Raby and J. Johns, eds., *Bayt al-Maqdis: 'Abd al-Malik's Jerusalem*, vol. 1 [Oxford, 1992], pp. 19–22). On this text, see B. Roggema, 'The Chapters of the Miracles, 19,' in *CMR*, vol. 1, pp. 148–50, and Hoyland, *Seeing Islam*, pp. 62–64.

[5] Michael the Great, *Chronicle* 12.1 (ed. Chabot, 4.478–79 [Syriac] = 3.1 [FT]); their wives continued to be Christians.

[6] On al-Ḥākim, see A. Ferré, 'Ḥākim bi-Amr-Illāh Abū 'Alī Manṣūr, al-,' in *CoptEn*, vol. 4, pp. 1201–03; and for detailed discussions of his anti-Christian violence and persecution, see Y. Lev, 'Persecutions and Conversion to Islam in Eleventh-Century Egypt,' *Asian and African Studies* 22 (1988), pp. 73–91. For the report that al-Ḥākim had 1,030 churches pulled down in Syria and Eypt over one two-year period (though he later was said to want them to be reconstructed), see R. J. Gottheil, 'Dhimmis and Muslims in Egypt,' in R. F. Harper, F. Brown, and G. F. Moore, eds., *Old Testament and Semitic Studies in Memory of William Rainey Harper*, vol. 2 (Chicago, 1908), p. 365.

[7] J. Horovitz, 'The Growth of the Mohammed Legend,' *The Moslem World* 10 (1919), pp. 49–58, and cf. D. J. Sahas, 'The Formation of Later Islamic Doctrines as a Response to Byzantine Polemics: The Miracles of Muhammad,' *Greek Orthodox Theological Review* 27 (1982), pp. 307–24, for a similar argument, made independently of Horovitz. Cf. also the classic C. H. Becker, 'Christian Polemic and the Formation of Islamic Dogma,' in Hoyland, ed., *Muslims and Others in Early Islamic Society*, pp. 241–57.

[8] See P. Jensen, 'Das Leben Muhammeds und die David-Sage,' *Der Islam* 12 (1922), pp. 84–97, which should be read with J. Horovitz, 'Biblische Nachwirkungen in der Sira,' *Der Islam* 12 (1922), pp. 184–89. Also see A. J. Wensinck, 'Muḥammad and the Prophets,' in U. Rubin, ed., *The Life of Muḥammad* (Aldershot, 1998), pp. 339–40 (reprint of 'Muhammed und die Propheten,' *Acta Orientalia* 2 [1924], pp. 168–98); Z. Maghen, 'Intertwined Triangles: Remarks on the Relationship between Two Prophetic Scandals,' *JSAI* 33 (2007), pp. 17–92 and Maghen, 'Davidic Motifs in the Biography of Muḥammad,' *JSAI* 35 (2008), pp. 91–139. Cf. I. Goldziher, 'Influences chrétienes dans la litérature religieuse de l'Islam,' in J. Desomogyi, ed., *Ignaz Goldziher: Gesammelte Schriften*, vol. 2 (Hildesheim, 1968), p. 304. For the suggestion that Ibn Isḥāq's *sīra* 'appears to have had a Jewish and Christian audience in mind,' and an elaboration of the consequences, see G. D. Newby, *The Making of the Last Prophet: A Reconstruction of the Earliest Biography of Muhammad* (Columbia, S.C., 1989), pp. 16–25 (quote at 21). For more bibliography on research into the Christian and Jewish traditions' effects on the *sīra*, see L. I. Conrad, 'The *mawālī* and Early Arabic Hstoriography,' in M. Bernards and J. Nawas, eds., *Patronate and Patronage in Early and Classical Islam* (Leiden, 2005), p. 375, n. 21.

[9] In biblical writers, the presence or absence of rain was an indication of Israel's obedience to God (Deuteronomy 11:13–17, cf. Leviticus 26:3–4, 1 Kings 8:35–36, 2 Chronicles 6:26–27, Psalm 68:6,9, Isaiah 5:6, Jeremiah 3:3, Ezekiel 22:24, Amos 4:7, Zechariah 14:17–18). For futher discussion, see P. Reymond, *L'eau, sa vie, et sa signification dans l'Ancien Testament* (Leiden, 1958), pp. 112–17. Elijah prayed success-

we should view the various anecdotes relating to Christians that can be found in the *sīra* of Muḥammad. We hear, for example, of Waraqa b. Nawfal, the cousin of Muḥammad's wife Khadīja, 'who had become a Christian and read the scriptures and learned from those that follow the Torah and the Gospel,' providing an important early confirmation of the divine origin of Muḥammad's prophetic call.[10] And we hear also of a group of Abyssinian or Najrānī Christians who converted to Islam after speaking with Muḥammad in Mecca—'They recognized in him the things which had been said of him in their scriptures.'[11] As in the case of Chalcedon, there might be dueling versions of these kinds of stories: the monk Baḥīrā, 'well versed in the knowledge of Christians,' recognized Muḥammad as foretold in Christian books while Muḥammad was still a boy, but Christians had their own version of the story of Baḥīrā, one in which it was the Christian monk, not Gabriel, who gave the Prophet religious teach-

---

fully for rain (1 Kings 18:41–45; cf. James 5:17–18) and so did Samuel (1 Samuel 12:16–18). Though it was not an influential book in the late antique period, among the powers of the Two Witnesses of the book of Revelation was their ability to prevent rain (Revelation 11:6); Jesus himself rebuked the wind and calmed a storm (Mark 4:35–41; cf. Ps. 65:7, 89:9). Christian holy men who were depicted as being able to successfully pray for rain included Simeon Stylites (d. 459), Theodore of Sykeon (d. 613), and Abba Xoius, a fourth- or fifth-century Desert Father. There are depicitions, too, of at least five different Jewish holy men who successfully prayed for rain: see C. A. Evans, *Ancient Texts for New Testament Studies: A Guide to the Background Literature* (Grand Rapids, 2005), pp. 424–30, NB esp. 429; and see also the comparative discussion in M. Bar-Asher Siegal, *Early Christian Monastic Literature and the Babylonian Talmud* (Cambridge/New York, 2013), pp. 112–17, and further A. J. Avery-Peck, 'The Galilean Charismatic and Rabbinic Piety: The Holy Man in the Talmudic Literature,' in A.-J. Levine, D. C. Allison, Jr., and J. D. Crossan, eds., *The Historical Jesus in Context* (Princeton, 2006), pp. 149–65. For Simeon Stylites and rain, see Simeon bar Apollon and Bar Ḥaṭār bar Ūdān, *Life of Simeon Stylites*, pp. 610–14 (ed. Bedjan, *AMS*, vol. 4; ET available in Lent, 'The Life of St. Simeon Stylites,' pp. 177–79, cf. Doran, *The Lives of Simeon Stylites*, pp. 155–57). For Theodore of Sykeon praying for rain, see *Life of Theodore of Sykeon* 14, 50, 51, 56 (where Theodore does not pray for rain, but prays to alter where exactly the rain is falling), 101 (ed. Th. Ioannou, *Mnēmeia hagiologika* [Venice, 1884], pp. 373–74 408, 409; ET available in Dawes and Baynes, *Three Byzantine Saints*, pp. 97, 124, 125, 128, 154–56, 450–52). For Abba Xoius, see *Apophthegmata Patrum*, PG 65, cols. 312D–313A (ET available in B. Ward, *The Sayings of the Desert Fathers: The Alphabetical Collection* [Kalamazoo, Michigan, 1975], pp. 158–59). Muḥammad, too, was depicted as successfully praying for rain: for his praying successfully for rain on behalf of delegations from the tribe of Fazāra and the tribe of Murra, see Ibn Sa'd, *Kitāb al-ṭabaqāt al-kabīr*, vol. 1.2, pp. 42–43 (ed. Mittwoch and Sachau; translation available in Haq and Ghazanfar, *Kitab al-tabaqat al-kabir*, vol. 1, pp. 352–53). For the Prophet and rain, see also Goldziher, *Muslim Studies*, vol. 2, pp. 106–107, 285. On the caliphs and rain, see p. 69 and 345 (on rain being sought through 'Abd al-Malik). For 'Abd al-Malik and rain, see also, Robinson, *'Abd al-Malik*, pp. 84, 90–91.

[10] Ibn Hishām, *Kitāb sīrat rasūl Allāh*, pp. 153–54, quote at 153 (ed. Wüstenfeld, vol. 1.1; ET taken from Guillaume, *The Life of Muhammad*, p. 107). On Waraqa, see C. F. Robinson's article, 'Waraḳa b. Nawfal,' in *EI2*, vol. 11, pp. 142–43.

[11] Ibn Hishām, *Kitāb sīrat rasūl Allāh*, p. 259 (ed. Wüstenfeld, vol. 1.1; ET taken from Guillaume, *The Life of Muhammad*, p. 179). See Crone, *Meccan Trade*, pp. 219–20 for a listing of fifteen different such stories and a negative assessment of their historicity.

ing.[12] Here we have in writing tales that almost certainly had their origins in oral tellings and retellings—indeed, Christians across the Middle East still tell versions of the Baḥīrā story to this day, most of them unaware of its early medieval origins.[13]

Importantly, deemphasizing a doctrinal perspective on Christian-Muslim relations does not mean that we should completely abandon the importance of doctrine. As I suggested in Chapter 4, we should avoid a starkly binary vision of this world, one where there were two groups, the informed and the uniformed, those who cared about theological ideas and those who did not. We should think, rather, in terms of a spectrum or continuum of engagement with and understanding of religious ideas and doctrines, and we should not assume that theological illiteracy meant an absence of theological curiosity. Between sophisticated thinkers, Christian and Muslim, and adherents who were largely unfamiliar with the (written) content of their own tradition (much less that of others), we can suggest that there existed a middle ground—the 'simpler' believers I pointed to in Chapter 4.

In Chapter 4, one piece of evidence I cited for the existence of such people—theologically aware and interested but lacking a depth of theological learning—was the phenomenon of small-scale debates and discussions. This world did not simply vanish with the entrance of Arabs from Western Arabia onto the scene. On the contrary, one more voice was added: there were now also learned debates, written and oral, with Muslims eventually developing their own confessional champions who did battle against both non-Muslims and Muslims alike in disputations.[14] And, in the centuries after the Arab conquests,

[12] Ibn Hishām, *Kitāb sīrat rasūl Allāh*, pp. 115–17, quote at 115 (ed. Wüstenfeld, vol. 1.1; ET taken from Guillaume, *The Life of Muhammad*, pp. 79–81, quote at 79). For the figure of Baḥīrā in the Islamic tradition, see B. Roggema, 'Baḥīrā,' in *EI3*, and especially, Roggema, *The Legend of Sergius Baḥīrā*, pp. 37–60 (and 29–35 for the use of 'counterhistory' in the Christian-Muslim polemical encounter). For the story of Baḥīrā outside the specific Baḥīrā legend texts, see 151–201. More generally, Roggema edits and analyzes Syriac and Arabic versions of the Christian Baḥīrā story. In addition to Roggema's foundational work, K. Szilágyi, 'Muḥammad and the Monk: the Making of the Christian Baḥīrā Legend,' *JSAI* 34 (2008), pp. 169–214, is an important study of the relationship between the rival Christian and Muslim versions of the Baḥīrā story.

[13] And the medieval 'Baḥīrā' becomes in these modern retellings 'Buḥayra.' Much later (and better-documented) periods can be very interesting to think with when it comes to the subject of storytelling as a means of interreligious polemic and religious instruction. Kefeli, *Becoming Muslim in Imperial Russia, passim*, but see pp. 60–116 and esp. 103–14, gives vivid examples of popular Islamic stories that, though in this instance often printed and from the nineteenth century, give a good sense for the role such stories played in both religious catechesis and in the encounter between the illiterate and semi-literate Christian and Muslim peasantry.

[14] See S. Pines, 'A Note on an Early Meaning of the Term *mutakallim*,' *Israel Oriental Studies* 1 (1971), pp. 224–40. Note p. 232, where Pines suggests that the '*raison d'être* of Kalām' was 'to defend Islam against the argument of non-Muslims.' Christian-Muslim debates and disputes have been exhaustively

it has been suggested, debate and disputation played a key role in the propagation of Islam.[15] I proposed in Chapter 4 that we see written examples of intra-Christian debates as the learned tip of the iceberg, and we can make the same suggestion here. Though the ghosts of these Christian-Muslim conversations past have now also vanished, we can occasionally still find their traces: in AD 755–756, for instance, an Abbasid governor ordered 'that Christians should not discourse with Arabs on matters of religion.'[16]

In the letters of George, Bishop of the Arab tribes, we encountered a distinctive aporetic style of theological questioning that presented its target with a relentless set of disjunctive dilemmas aimed at confounding him. This style of questioning would eventually come into widespread use in Islamic dialectical theology and its Christian origin has been persuasively argued.[17] If we are interested in locating a middle ground of theological engagement, the use of aporetic styles of questioning is important because of its performative nature: even if someone could not fully understand the precise issues being debated, he or she might get a general sense of which side in the dispute was winning (or losing) based on a debater's ability to handle the dilemmas posed to him. This style of questioning, therefore, provided avenues for people who were not theological elites to take part, indirectly, in more rarified discussions.[18] Likewise, the existence of confessional champions—Muslim and Christian—provided a similar avenue for vicarious participation. A person might not be able to defend his or her confessional stance dialectically, but knowing that a great person in the past had or that a learned person in the present could, provided its own intellectual satisfaction.

These two avenues might also converge: Confessional champions could use aporetic questioning in their disputes. Bar Hebraeus recorded the story of a

---

documented in the volumes of *Christian-Muslim Relations*, but there were also debates between Muslims and non-Christians. For an example of a Muslim-Jewish disputation, see the debate between al-Naẓẓām and a Jew named Yassā over the abrogation of religious precepts, edited in L. Cheikho, *Vingt traités théologiques d'auteurs arabes chrétiens (IXe-XIIIe)* (Beirut, 1920), pp. 68–70.

[15] See van Ess, *Theologie und Gesellschaft*, vol. 1, pp. 47–56, esp. 47–48 [= *Theology and Society*, vol. 1, pp. 55–65, esp. 55]. van Ess, 'Disputationspraxis in der Islamischen Theologie: Eine Vorläufige Skizze,' *Revue des études islamiques* 44 (1976), pp. 23–60, is an important overview of debates and disputation in Islamic theology.

[16] Theophanes, *Chronicle* AM 6248 (ed. de Boor, vol. 1, p. 430; ET taken from Mango and Scott, *The Chronicle of Theophanes Confessor*, p. 594).

[17] For the Christian origin of this technique of disputation, see M. Cook, 'The Origins of "*Kalām*."' On its widespread use and for further discussion of the question of origins, see van Ess, *Theologie und Gesellschaft*, vol. 1, pp. 54–55 (= *Theology and Society*, vol. 1, pp. 62–63). This Christian style of disputation may have been introduced to Muslim usage either by converts or in the context of Christian-Muslim discussions, with Muslims adopting the practice after having been subjected to it by Christian interlocutors.

[18] I am grateful to Michael Cook for this point.

disputation between the East Syrian catholicos Isho' bar Nun (sed. 823–828) and a Miaphysite priest named Papa over the nature of the Incarnation: disjunctive questioning was used, the Bible was cited, and Gregory Nazianzen was quoted. In Bar Hebraeus's brief description of this dispute, we get a sense for the importance of the audience in such encounters: 'But when the catholicos heard that the words of Papa were more agreeable to those listening,' he wrote, 'being from the Holy Scriptures and not like his sophistries'—presumably a reference allusion to the aporetic question that Isho' bar Nun had asked Papa—the catholicos himself quoted the Bible (Malachi 3:6). But Isho' bar Nun's attempts at using Scripture did not help his case. 'Because Papa saw that the catholicos was distressed,' Bar Hebraeus noted, 'he cut off the words of the dispute.'[19] A story told by a Miaphysite chronicler in which a Miaphysite priest defeats the head of the East Syrian Church in a dispute should neither astonish nor should its reliability be accepted uncritically. Nevertheless, these two points—the importance of the reaction of those watching the debate and the dismay of a struggling disputant—were no doubt common features of both Christian-Christian and Christian-Muslim dialectical encounters.[20]

ENCOUNTERS OUTSIDE THE *MAJLIS*

But doctrine, however it was understood, experienced, and met with, was not everything. And here it should be emphasized that stepping back—but not away—from doctrine when thinking about Christian-Muslim relations does not mean ceasing to view these interactions through a religious lens. When we approach the question of how most actual Christians related to most actual Muslims on a religious level, however, it will be more fruitful to think instead in terms of commitments to rituals and symbols, along the lines I suggested in Chapter 9. For many, perhaps most Christians, Christianity was not a series of doctrines to be believed or a set of precisely articulated propositions to affirm, but a commitment to certain symbols and rituals that structured their lives, families, and communities. Moreover, it provided access to sacred power, thereby offering means for coping with some of the most fundamental challenges in human existence. We have seen the central importance and enormous power that these symbols were believed to hold.

[19] Bar Hebraeus, *Ecclesiastical History* 2.38 (ed. Abbeloos and Lamy, vol. 3, cols. 185, 187).

[20] Note the allusion to Matthew 22:46 ('And no one was able to answer him a word, nor from that day did anyone dare to ask him any more questions' [ESV]), used in the context of describing the results of Severus of Antioch's composition of his *Philalethes* in Ps.-John bar Aphtonia, *Life of Severus* p. 153 (ed. Kugener [PO 2.3]).

It should not, therefore, be surprising that in the boundary lines between Christianity and Islam that were gradually erected and reinforced, it was precisely these symbols that became highly charged points, the rejection or acceptance of which placed a person solidly in one community or another. In Chapter 5, I cited Anastasius of Sinai's story about John of Bostra, a chartularius from Damascus who interviewed four demon-possessed young women in the district of Antioch. The three things they feared most from Christians, the demons told John, were the Cross, Baptism, and the Eucharist, and of these three things, the Eucharist was the most powerful. This revelation, however, was not the end of the back and forth between John and the young women: the exchange would continue beyond Christianity to cover other religions. 'Which faith do you love,' John asked the women, 'out of all those which exist in the world today?' The women did not mention any one religion specifically, but offered a set of beliefs that their favorite religion(s) lacked: 'They say to him: "Those which neither have anything of the three [things] of which we spoke to you [i.e., the Cross, Baptism, and the Eucharist] nor confess either God or the Son of God, the son of Mary.'[21]

There may have been a number of faiths that lacked the sacraments and denied that Jesus was the Son of God, but to a Christian audience living under Muslim rule, one faith certainly stuck out. This story is found in Anastasius' *Narrations Beneficial for the Soul*, a work that was written about AD 690, and Robert Hoyland has pointed out that one significant theme in this text is an anxiety about Christian apostasy to Islam.[22] Writing at nearly the exact same time, ca. 690–691, the *Apocalypse* of Pseudo-Methodius decried Christians converting to Islam. Here again we can see the centrality of the acceptance or rejection of certain Christian symbols for marking communal belonging and participation. 'Many people who were members of the Church will deny the true Faith of the Christians,' the anonymous author wrote, 'along with the holy Cross and the awesome Mysteries: without being subjected to any compulsion or lashings or blows, they will deny Christ, putting themselves on a par with the unbelievers.'[23] Bringing simple believers into our picture means recognizing that it was precisely these things—the Cross and the sacraments—that for most people were central to what it meant to be a Christian. In practical

[21] Anastasius of Sinai, *Narrations Beneficial for the Soul* II.20 (ed. Binggeli, p. 1.250 [Greek] = 2.565 [FT] [= §53 in Nau, ed. 'Le texte grec des récits utiles à l'âme d'Anastase (le Sinaïte),' p. 79; French summary available in Nau, 'Les récits inédits du moine Anastase,' p. 144]).

[22] Hoyland, *Seeing Islam*, pp. 99–100.

[23] Ps.-Methodius, *Apocalypse* 12.3 (ed. Reinink [CSCO 540: SS 220], p. 33; the ET here is by S. P. Brock, taken from Palmer, *The Seventh Century in the West-Syrian Chronicles*, p. 235. For Brock's dating of this apocalypse, see p. 225).

religious terms, conversion to Islam meant that one's relationship to these things would change. Or did it?

If we keep our focus on the simple, what we find in fact is that it was possible for one to be a Muslim and yet make use of many distinctively 'Christian' religious elements in one's everyday existence. Later periods in Islamic history are much better documented in this regard. F. W. Hasluck has pointed to numerous and wide-ranging examples of the continuation of Christian practices and persistent use of Christian symbols by Muslims into the medieval and Ottoman periods: a cross marked on a stone used for curing; bread inscribed with crosses before baking; cross tattoos; phylacteries with the name 'wood of the Cross;' a cross placed in the minaret of a mosque to defend against bad luck; Muslim women having their babies baptized for protection; the name of Jesus or a cross or the first lines of the Gospel of John worn in protective amulets, for example.[24] Similarly, Manolis Peponakis has collected evidence of a deep and extensive persistence of former Christian practices among rural converts to Islam in Crete: they wore the same clothes; they 'drank wine and ate pork; they invoked the Virgin, calling her 'Meire-Mana' (Μεϊρέ-μάνα); they revered Christ, Saint John, and Saint Spiridon and took ex-voto offerings to the Monastery of St. George, whose feast day coincided with the Bektashis's spring festival. They carried small lamps to country chapels, accepted the blessings of priests and called to the Virgin for help, [asking] that she give comfort to pregnant women. . . .' They also took part in rites Christians performed to drive away plague and would even still act as Godparents, paying for Christian baptisms, though they themselves would not be present at the actual performance of the rite.[25] Writing about the Balkans, Speros Vryonis noted a host of Christian survivals among Muslim communities there: not only did Muslims have their children baptized, they also venerated Christian holy men and saints. What is more:

> Many observed Easter by taking colored eggs from the Christians, which, they believed, would assure good health. In connection with health, they brought ill children to church on Good Friday, visited the local *ayasma* [sacred spring], sought the blessing of the priest in church on feast days, and took holy water from the priest for the benefit of the family members and the livestock. They made offerings to church icons, frequently and covertly kept church books and icons in their houses, and continued to perform animal sacrifices in the courtyards of certain churches and monasteries.

[24] F. W. Hasluck, *Christianity and Islam under the Sultans*, vol. 1 (Oxford, 1929), pp. 30–37.

[25] For this, see M. Peponakis, *Εξισλαμισμοί και επανεκχριστιανισμοί στην Κρήτη* (1645–1899) (Rethymno, 1997), pp. 75–76.

Muslim wedding ceremonies used pre-Islamic elements, Vryonis noted, Muslims continued celebrating the feast days of the saints who had been their family patrons when they were Christian, and they celebrated the feasts of Christian saints such as George, John, Peter, and Barbara.[26]

While Crete, the Balkans, and Anatolia were all unique landscapes with hundreds of years of history behind them,[27] and we cannot assume that the experience of early medieval and medieval Syria was precisely the same, their examples are nevertheless very suggestive of what may have happened in the Middle East centuries earlier: survivals of much the same sort can also be found in other places where Christian populations converted to Islam.[28] We have no reason to believe that in the earliest centuries of Islamic history, when the script of Islamic orthodoxy was still being hammered out, the situation would have been any less complicated and mixed-up than it was in the later periods that scholars like Hasluck, Peponakis, and Vyronis studied. In fact, because what would become the central institutions, rites, texts, and habits of later Islamic orthodoxies either did not yet exist (or were in their very earliest stages of development), we should rather assume that the level of mixing in this early period was even greater, especially if the large majority of Muslims

[26] See S. Vryonis, 'Religious Changes and Patterns in the Balkans, 14th–16th Centuries,' in H. Birnbaum and S. Vryonis, Jr., eds., *Aspects of the Balkans: Continuity and Change. Contributions to the International Balkan Conference held at UCLA, October 23–28, 1969* (The Hague/Paris, 1972), pp. 173–76, quote on p. 175. My thinking about the role of religious syncretism in Christian-Muslim conversion has been influenced by Vryonis's ideas, both in this article and in his *The Decline of Medieval Hellenism in Asia Minor and the Process of Islamization from the Eleventh through the Fifteenth Century* (Berkeley/Los Angeles/London, 1971), pp. 351–402. For more on the question of the Islamization of Anatolia, see now A.C.S. Peacock, B. de Nicola, and S.N. Yildiz, eds., *Islam and Christianity in Medieval Anatolia* (Farnham, Surrey, and Burlington, Vt., 2015) and also the literature cited in the next note.

[27] A good overview of the issues and debates that have characterized the extensive and sophisticated research into Christian conversion in the Ottoman Empire can be found in T. Krstić, *Contested Conversions to Islam: Narratives of Religious Change in the Early Modern Ottoman Empire* (Stanford, 2011), pp. 1–25. The scholarly conversation about conversion to Islam in an Ottoman context is much more advanced than it is for the early medieval period, in part due to the existence of rich archival material that scholars of earlier periods in the Middle East, alas, do not possess (apart from a few notable exceptions, such as the Cairo Geniza). See also the enormous amount of scholarly literature surveyed and discussed in G. Grivaud and A. Popovic, *Les conversions à l'islam en Asie mineure et dans les Balkans aux époques seldjoukide et ottomane: bibliographie raisonnée* (1800-2000) (Athens, 2011), as well as the studies in Gelez and Grivaud, *Les conversions à l'Islam en Asie Mineure.* For Christian conversion to Islam and Muslim conversion to Christianity in the early modern Mediterranean and Middle East more generally, see C. Norton, ed., *Conversion and Islam in the Early Modern Mediterranean: The Lure of the Other* (London/New York, 2017).

[28] For the example of Muslims in Palestine with amulets proclaiming that there is no victor save God and that Muḥammad is his Prophet—and which also have a cross on them; see E. Peterson, *Eis Theos. Epigraphische, formgeschichtliche und religionsgeschichtliche Untersuchungen* (Göttingen, 1926), p. 154.

had joined the Prophet's religious community through group conversion and possessed little profound acquaintance with the content, such as it was, of their new religion. For all our labels—Miaphysite, Chalcedonian, Nestorian, Zoroastrian, Jew, Muslim, pagan, etc.—all the people we are dealing with in the seventh, eighth, and later centuries had one fundamental and inescapable fact in common: they were human beings, and as such shared the same worries and anxieties over health, safety, their families, death and the afterlife.

Such concerns were 'interfaith' in the broadest sense of the word, and many showed a pronounced willingness to be equally interfaith when it came to dealing with these anxieties. Part of the growth and development of Christianity had entailed the working out of a repertoire of tools for addressing and dealing with such pressing concerns; and many Muslims, quite understandably, suffered no great qualms in availing themselves of such resources. What is more, many Christian converts to Islam seemed to see no great contradiction or tension in continuing to draw upon them once they had crossed over into a different religion.[29] This is the dynamic underlying the mixing of religious practices that we see in the Ottoman period.

This phenomenon was not a late development in the history of Islam in the Middle East, either. Indeed, if we go over our sources from the seventh and eighth centuries, we will find traces and hints of precisely the same sort of Muslim veneration of Christian symbols and rituals that is so abundantly documented for later periods. The Arabs, Isho'yahb III would write in the middle of the seventh century, 'are not only not opposed to Christianity, they also sing the praises of our Faith and honor priests and the saints of Our Lord and aid churches and monasteries.'[30] At the end of the same century, John bar Penkaye would attribute the coming of Arab rule to God's care for Christians. 'We should not think of the advent (of the children of Hagar) as something ordinary,' he wrote,

> but as due to divine working. Before calling them (God) had prepared them beforehand to hold Christians in honour; thus they also had a special commandment from God concerning our monastic station, that they should hold it in honour.[31]

[29] Note Drijvers's comments on competition between Christians, Jews, Manicheans, pagans, and others in the area of healing in fourth-century Edessa, 'Jews and Christians at Edessa,' p. 99.

[30] Isho 'yahb III, *Letters* III.14 (To Simeon of Revardashir), p. 251 (ed. Duval [CSCO: Syr. II.64]): 'For the Arabs, also, to whom God has given in this time authority over the world, [who] indeed, as you know, are with us and are not only not against Christianity but are people who praise our faith and who honor our priests and the saints of Our Lord and people who give aid to churches and monasteries. . . .'

[31] John bar Penkaye, *Book of the Main Events*, p. *141 (ed. Mingana; ET taken from Brock, 'North Mesopotamia in the Late Seventh Century,' p. 57).

A number of pieces of evidence corroborate these general statements of Isho'yahb III and John. Some of these come from Christian sources that date much closer to the events they describe than the Muslim Arabic sources we have for this period. Despite their (at times) chronological proximity, however, we should acknowledge that they are Christian sources, written by non-Muslims, describing in often positive ways the politically powerful Muslim minority in their midst. But they were written, it needs to be emphasized, for a Christian audience, not a Muslim one, and we should assume that they dealt with situations that would have seemed plausible and possible to their readers and therefore can point us to the realities and expectations of the societies in which they were produced. Let us now turn to them.

THEODOTA OF AMID AND CHRISTIAN HOLY MEN

We can see the honor that (at least some) early Muslims showed Christians and Christianity in considerable detail in the *vita* of Theodota of Amid (d. AD 698), a text that remains available only in manuscript. Theodota was a holy man who was active in northern Mesopotamia over the course of the second half of the seventh century, and in his *vita* we find more than just broad statements expressing a generally positive Muslim disposition towards Christianity or Christians. What we find are a number of instances where Muslims show respect, deference, and even reverence for Christian figures, symbols and institutions. When the Miaphysite patriarch Theodore died ca. AD 649, for example, we are told that 'his disciples and the members of his monastery wept, as did the cities and villages and the believing peoples and the Arabs.'[32] In

[32] St Mark's Jerusalem 199, fol. 548b. For the Syriac, see Mardin 275/8, p. 491. For Theodore's date of death, see Hage, *Die syrisch-jacobitische Kirche in frühislamischer Zeit,* (table insert). The Syriac here for 'Arabs' is *ṭayyāyē*, and we have examples of pre-Islamic Arabs, or *ṭayyāyē*, showing an interest in Christian holy men (e.g., Simeon bar Apollon and Bar Ḥaṭār bar Ūdān, *Life of Simeon Stylites*, pp. 545, 596–98 [ed. Bejdan, *AMS*, vol. 4]), as well as Christian Arabs in the early period of Muslim rule showing an awareness of stylites (cf. al-Akhṭal, *Dīwān*, p. 71.6 [ed. A. Ṣāliḥānī, *Dīwān al-Akhṭal*, (Beirut, 1891) and cf. S. Seppälä, *In Speechless Ecstasy: Expression and Interpretation of Mystical Experience in Classical Syriac and Sufi Literature* [Helsinki, 2003], pp. 20–21). In the abstract, it is possible that the *ṭayyāyē* referred to here are pagans or Christians, but in this particular text, *ṭayyāyē* always refers to Muslims: see e.g., Mardin 275/8, pp. 508 (the Blessed One saved many souls from the *ṭayyāyē* and the Romans [sect. 74]); 530 (fleeing from the privation and troubles caused by the *ṭayyāyē* [sect. 115]); 531 (the *ṭayyāyē* seeking to enter that region [sect. 115]), 539 ('in the war of the *ṭayyāyē*' [sect. 126]); 544 (the Christians and the *ṭayyāyē* went out to meet him [sect. 133]); 547 (a certain man of the *ṭayyāyē* was in Amid [sect. 135]); 548 (all the *ṭayyāyē* cavalry [sect. 135]); 548 (all the *ṭayyāyē* made a great cry [sect. 135]); 548 (prominent figures from the townspeople and the *ṭayyāyē* [sect. 135]); 549 ('Christians and *ṭayyāyē* and pagans were being blessed by him' [sect. 137]); 550 (the *ṭayyāyē* and all the cavalry, who were giving good things to the city [sect. 138]); 551 (the Christians and the *ṭayyāyē* were gathered to

other words, within decades of the Arab conquest of Syria, a Christian patriarch held a position of honor for Muslims such that his death was mourned by them and by Christians alike. Arab reverence for the Patriarch Theodore was no isolated incident, either. Later in the *Life* we find the patriarch Julian II (sed. AD 687–708) receiving similar treatment. Theodore 'entered Amid with great honor,' the *Life* states, 'and the Christians and the Arabs who were present in Amid went out to meet him.' If the Arabs who celebrated Julian's entry along with the Christians of Amid were bothered by the lamps, crosses, and incense that the *Life* informs us were present there, their displeasure was not noted by the *Life*.[33]

Theodota, for his part, was a charismatic holy man who could work miracles. His ecumenical appeal and power extended to Jews, Muslims, pagans and heretical (i.e., non-Miaphysite) Christians, and we see a number of occasions where Arab Muslims act reverentially towards this Christian saint; Theodota's *Life* even credits him with saving 'many souls from among the Arabs and Romans' in the border area between the Caliphate and Byzantium.[34] In this early period, Christians might still hold positions of authority over certain cities or even regions,[35] and in this *vita*, we find authorities, both Muslim and non-Muslim, attracted to Theodota. The governor of Dara, called Ilusṭrayya and possibly a Christian,[36] was keen to meet Theodota, and when the holy man and his disciple, Joseph, passed near the city, we are told that this official and 'his wife went out along with their children and they prostrated before them and were blessed by him.' Eager to have Theodota stay in his region, Ilusṭrayya promised the holy man that he would pay the tax of the monastery

see him [sect. 143]); 576 (a certain *ṭayyāyā* came to the holy man [sect. 195]). The incident in question is part of a clear pattern in the *vita* of Muslims seeking out this particular Christian holy man; see below for more detailed discussion of most of these passages. Cf. also the observation of A. Palmer, 'Āmīd in the Seventh-Century Syriac Life of Theodūṭē,' in E. Grypeou et al., *The Encounter of Eastern Christianity with Early Islam* (Leiden, 2006), p. 25 (and see below, n. 139), on the meaning of *ṭayyāyā* in this text.

[33] St Mark's Jerusalem 199, fol. 556a. For the Syriac, see Mardin 275/8, p. 544.

[34] St Mark's Jerusalem 199, fol. 551a. For the Syriac, see Mardin 275/8, fol. 248r (p. 503), and *SBI*, p. 457, n. 1072.

[35] Michael the Great (*Chronicle* 11.16 [ed. Chabot, 4.449 = 2.774]) reported that into the late seventh century 'Christian leaders were in charge in the cities and in the country areas.' In the *Passion* of Peter of Capitolias, an official named 'Zora,' that is, the Syriac, *z'orā* ('little, small'), is the government official over Trichora who investigates Peter's attacks on Islam on behalf of the Muslim state; see Peeters, 'La Passion de S. Pierre de Capitolias († 13 janvier 715),' p. 306: 'c'était un Syrien arabisé, renégat ou descendant de chrétiens passés à l'islam.'

[36] As suggested by his name, but Palmer, 'Āmīd in the Seventh-Century Syriac Life of Theodūṭē,' p. 118, n. 10 and p. 126, n. 26, understood him to be a pagan, not a Christian, and sought to restrict the meaning of Michael the Great's statement about Christians having authority (see previous footnote), a passage which ultimately goes back to the now-lost *Chronicle* of Dionysius of Tell Mahre. Though used as a name in the *vita*, Ilūsṭrayya very obviously derives from the title ἰλλούστριος (cp. *vir illustris*).

of Mar Abay at Qeleth out of his own pocket at Theodota's request. Theodota settled at Mar Abay and built a cell there,[37] and Ilusṭrayya later helped Theodota build his monastery at the end of the holy man's life.[38] Earlier, while Theodota was staying at the Monastery of Mar Shem'ūn in Qartmin, the governor (ἄρχων) of Ṭūr 'Abdīn came to visit him and sought to be blessed by him and to enjoy his conversation. But Theodota demurred. He later relented and visited the governor in his camp. When the holy man approached him, 'the governor rose up and prostrated to him,' we are told

> and said, 'You are Theodota, whose report has gone out.' Then the Blessed One said to him, 'What you have heard about me is a lie, for I am weak and a sinner. And I have gone out weeping over my sins.' The governor said, 'Look! Truly you are a disciple of Jesus and a Blessed One among the people!'[39]

Theodota had had the option of saying no to the official who wanted to speak with him and receive his blessing, but this does not always seem to have been the case for Christian clergy who were being sought out by Muslim officials.[40] What should be done, Addai asked Jacob, if an emir commands the steward of a monastery to eat with him from the same dish? Should the man eat or should he refuse? 'I do not permit him,' Jacob replied, 'but necessity does.'[41]

[37] St Mark's Jerusalem 199, fol. 555b; for the Syriac, see Mardin 275/8, pp. 540–41. The tax is referred to as both *maddātā* and *gzitā*.

[38] St Mark's Jerusalem 199, fol. 560b. For the Syriac, see Mardin 275/8, p. 576. The Syriac is lacunose and needs to be supplemented by the Karshūnī translation. See *SBI*, p. 463, n. 1099. The Karshūnī translation makes it explicit that Ilusṭrayya greatly loved Theodota, but the Syriac is ambiguous and could also be read, 'For the Blessed One greatly loved him (sc. Ilusṭrayya).'

[39] St Mark's Jerusalem 199, fol. 555b. In Syriac, the governor is called both ܐܪܟܘܢ and ܐܪܟܘܢܐ. For the Syriac text, see Mardin 275/8, p. 539.

[40] The official is never explicitly stated to be a Muslim, though the *vita* notes that Theodota went to visit the governor in his camp, because 'in the war of the Arabs, he had been wounded by an arrow when they attacked Nisibis' (Mardin 275/8, pp. 539–40).

[41] *Questions Which Addai the Priest and Lover of Labors Asked Jacob, the Bishop of Edessa* 57 (ed. Lamy, *Dissertatio*, p. 156; ET in *SBI*, p. 458, n. 1075). See also Mardin 310, fols. 204a–b (pp. 405–406). Compare Jacob's response and Theodota's behavior with the report in the *History of the Patriarchs of Alexandria* (1.14) that Miaphysite patriarch Benjamin I (sed. 622–661) publicly prayed for 'Amr b. al-'Āṣ, the conqueror of Egypt, (at 'Amr's request) and 'pronounced an eloquent discourse, which made Amr and those present with him marvel, and which contained words of exhortation and much profit for those that heard him; and he revealed certain matters to Amr and departed from his presence honoured and revered' (translation taken from Evetts [PO 1.4], p. 233). Also see the incident involving Isaac of Alexandria (sed. 686–689) and 'Abd al-'Azīz, the governor of Egypt, eating a meal together in Mena of Nikiou, *History of the Patriarch Isaac*, pp. 67–71 (ed. E. Amélineau, *Histoire du patriarche copte Isaac: étude critique, texte et traduction* [Paris, 1890]; English available in D. N. Bell, *The Life of Isaac of Alexandria; and The Martyrdom of Saint Macrobius* [Piscataway, N.J., 2009], pp. 71–72). On this *vita* and for a suggested date around 700, perhaps the exact time when Jacob and Addai were writing, see H. Suermann's, 'Mēna of Nikiou,' in *CMR*, vol. 1, pp. 219–21.

The Arab official who had wanted to see Theodota had sought him out because of his reputation, but Theodota's reception among administrators in the Muslim government was not uniformly positive, at least initially. Because the holy man had written a letter to people living in Byzantine territory, an unnamed Arab who was in authority over Amid had Theodota seized and accused him of being a friend of the Byzantines. This action upset not only the entire city, we are told, but also all of the Arab cavalry there. Theodota was dragged to the local mosque and when the accusing Arab kicked him and he fell to the ground, 'all the Arabs cried out with a great shout and there was great pain in the Church of Our Lord.' The Arabs, like the Christians, were clearly not happy at the way Theodota was being treated. The Arab leader, however, was soon humbled: God took his sight away. Desperate, he sent for Theodota:

> He fell down, prostrating to him and said, 'O Friend of God, have mercy on me! And give me leave for what I have sinned against you; and give me the light of my eyes which you have taken from me!

Theodota healed the Muslim authority by making the sign of the cross in the name of Jesus over his eyes.[42] This was a moment of great triumph for the Christian holy man. He went out from the ruler's presence, we are told, in a great procession, and 'Christians, Arabs and pagans were blessed by him.' The leader who had persecuted him was soon recalled from his position and, as he was leaving Amid, fell from his horse and died from his injury. 'And so the people feared God and feared His servant,' the *Life* tells us.[43] Not long after this, Theodota was made bishop of Amid. Everyone in the city rejoiced, including its administrators, possibly Muslims, who were 'radiant in every adornment,' as well as 'the Arabs and all the cavalry, who were giving pleasing things to the city.'[44] Later in his life, Theodota would be given authority over the legal affairs of all the Christians of Amid, and it seems that the Christian bishop had the respect and obedience of local Muslim administrators: 'So the fear of the Blessed One was upon all the people; and on the chief men and administrators and those who stand before the officers of the ruler of this world. They were obeying his command and the city and its territory were preserved from evils.'[45] Also late in life, Theodota passed through Edessa where, we are told, the chief men and administrators 'rejoiced when they heard about

[42] St Mark's Jerusalem 199, fol. 556b. For the Syriac text, see Mardin 275/8, pp. 547–49.

[43] St Mark's Jerusalem 199, fols. 556b–557a. For the Syriac text, see Mardin 275/8, p. 549.

[44] St Mark's Jerusalem 199, fol. 557a. For the Syriac, see Mardin 275/8, p. 550 (also *SBI*, p. 459, n. 1078).

[45] St Mark's Jerusalem 199, fol. 558a. For the Syriac, see Mardin 275/8, p. 561.

the Holy Theodota and they sought to see him with every effort. They went out to him and they greeted him and he prayed for them.'[46]

As these vivid examples (and others)[47] show, attraction to the power of the Christian holy man transcended all sectarian and confessional boundaries—this was as true for Christian-Christian relations as it was for Christian-Muslim relations.[48] Though Theodota was a Miaphysite, we find a Nestorian in pain seeking him out for healing and prayer;[49] Chalcedonians at one point ask him to come to their monastery and pray for them in the hope that they would have eternal life through his faith.[50] Muslims, too, approached Theodota for help: 'A certain Arab came to the Holy One,' the *Life* states.

> He had been seized by a difficult pain and was unable to walk. He therefore fell before the feet of the Holy One. His disciple begged him to pray for him, so he gave an order and a blessing came, then he rubbed him with it. And he went away healthy and thanking God.[51]

[46] St Mark's Jerusalem 199, fol. 560a and Mardin 275/8, p. 572. A little while later (St Mark's Jerusalem 199, fol. 560b and Mardin 275/8, pp. 575–76), we learn that the 'leaders and nobles' (ܡܕܒܪ̈ܢܐ ܘܚܐܪ̈ܐ) of Mardin, Dara, Tur 'Abdin, and Ḥesnā d-Kifā (= Stone Fortress) were eager to come out and meet Theodota and be blessed by him. Some of these may have been Muslims, some may have been Christians.

[47] E.g., according to Theophanes, the caliph Hishām was friends with a monk from Syria named Stephen ('who was rather simple, but pious'), whom he allowed the Christians to elect as patriarch of Antioch, ending a forty-year period in which permission to elect a patriarch had not been granted by Muslim authorities. Theophanes, *Chronicle* AM 6234 (ed. de Boor, vol. 1, p. 416; ET taken from Mango and Scott, *The Chronicle of Theophanes Confessor*, p. 577).

[48] The holy man whose appeal transcended confessional and even religious boundaries can readily be found in Syriac literature—e.g., the fifth-century *Teaching of Addai* claimed that pagans and Jews also mourned at the death of the Christian apostle (*Teaching of Addai*, p. *49; ed. Phillips/trans. Howard = p. 99) and in the eleventh century, the Byzantine governor of Antioch, who was afflicted by leprosy, sought and received healing from the Syrian Orthodox patriarch, John bar 'Abdūn (sed. 1004–1030) (Michael the Great, *Chronicle* 13.6 [3.139 = 4.562]; I am grateful to David Gyllenhaal for bringing this example to my attention). For more such examples, see my 'Greek Kanons and the Syrian Orthodox Liturgy,' pp. 161–64.

This cross-over appeal should not be written off as a mere literary *topos* with no connection to reality: The Miaphysite martyrology of Rabban Sliba would include a number of Chalcedonian saints among those it commemorated; see. P. Peeters, 'Le martyrologe de Rabban Sliba,' *AB* 27 (1927), p. 134; and in the Syriac translation of Leontius of Neapolis's *Life of Simeon the Holy Fool*, made between the seventh and tenth centuries, the Chalcedonian Simeon is turned into a Miaphysite, and Miaphysites are understood to be Orthodox and Chalcedonians heretics, an inversion of the understandings in the Greek original; see L. van Rompay, 'The Syriac Version of the "Life of Symeon Salos": First Soundings,' in A. Schoors and P. van Deun, eds., *Philohistôr: Miscellanea in honorem Caroli Laga Septuagenarii* (Leuven, 1994), pp. 387–88.

[49] St Mark's Jerusalem 199, fol. 560b. For the Syriac, see Mardin 275/8, p. 576.

[50] St. Mark's Jerusalem, fol. 560a = Mardin 275/8, p. 572. The *mushāqiqīn* of the Karshūnī ('schismatics') translates the Syriac ܣܘܢܕܝܩܘ *sunādiqu.*

[51] St Mark's Jerusalem 199, fol. 560b. For the Syriac, see Mardin 275/8, p. 576.

Stories of Christian holy men healing Muslims are not unique to this particular *vita*. Rabban Khudhāwī was said to have healed the withered limb of one of the Muslim ruler Mu'āwiya's daughters by baptizing her.[52] When 'Ubayd Allāh b. Ziyād (d. AH 67/AD 686), the governor of Iraq, was suffering from a pain in his leg so severe that he could not stand on it, he was said to have sent to the Christian holy man 'Abdā b. Ḥanīf for help. Mar 'Abdā sent 'Ubayd Allāh his staff with the advisory that when he used it for support, he would be healed; sure enough, once he had used the staff, 'Ubayd Allāh was cured immediately.[53] In the mid-seventh century, 'Utba, the governor of the province of Beth Garmai reportedly asked Sabrisho', the area's metropolitan, to pray for two of his daughters who were afflicted by Satan. After seven days of his constant fasting, the girls were healed.[54] Also in the seventh century, John of Daylam reportedly visited 'Abd al-Malik in Damascus. The Caliph 'asked him to pray for his daughter, who was tried by demons. She was healed, and the king, delighted, gave him royal gifts.' John, however, did not want gifts: what he wanted was permission to build churches and monasteries, so 'Abd al-Malik obliged, giving an order that John be permitted to build churches and monasteries wherever he wanted and at the ruler's expense, no less.[55] According to a verse panegyric on John of Daylam, however, it was 'Abd al-Malik's son, not his daughter that John healed: 'John washed his cross (in water) and signed it over the child's head, whereupon he was healed.'[56] The Chalcedonian Stephen of Mar Sabas (d. 794) was another figure with interfaith appeal. 'Every request brought to him, he fulfilled,' his *Life* tells us, 'whether it be of the spirit or the body. He denied no one, but received all with the same respect, not favoring one above another. He showed mercy and compassion not only to Christians but also to Muslims. These he would feed with abundant food of diverse kinds.'[57]

Such stories appear in Christian sources and have a certain literary or even legendary quality about them. We should remember here that reports of holy men who healed sick non-Christian rulers or sick members of a non-Christian

[52] *Chronicle of Seert* 2.98 (ed. Scher [and Griveau] [PO 13.4], p. 274). For this, see S. Qāshā, *Aḥwāl naṣārā al-'Irāq fī khilāfat banī Umayya*, vol. 3 (Beirut, 2005), p. 584.

[53] *Chronicle of Seert* 2.97 (ed. and trans. A. Scher [and Griveau] [PO 13.4], p. 269). For this, see Qāshā, *Aḥwāl naṣārā al-'Irāq fī khilāfat banī Umayya*, vol. 3, p. 584.

[54] *Chronicle of Seert* 2.109 (ed. Scher [and Griveau] [PO 13.4]), p. 312). For this, see Qāshā, *Aḥwāl naṣārā al-'Irāq fī khilāfat banī Umayya*, vol. 3, p. 584. For Sabrisho' as possibly a contemporary of Isho'yahb III, see PO 13.4, p. 312, n. 1.

[55] *Life of John of Daylam* 26–30 (ed. Brock, p. 139–40 [Syriac] = 148–49 [ET]. The translation is that of Brock, at p. 148).

[56] Translation Brock in 'A Syriac Life of John of Dailam,' p. 165.

[57] Leontius of Damascus, *Life of Stephen of Mar Sabas* 81.5 (ed. and trans. Lamoreaux, *The Life of Stephen of Mar Sabas*, p. 146 [Arabic] = p. 131 [ET]). The translation here is that of Lamoreaux.

ruler's family had a long pedigree in Syriac hagiography.[58] With this said, however, we should not be too quick to write off as mere literary commonplaces accounts of Muslim rulers seeking healing help from Christian figures. John of Daylam was reported to visit the famous Muslim governor al-Ḥajjāj b. Yūsuf, whom, according to the same panegyric, he cured of cancer; and Arabic sources offer possible corroboration of this account.[59] Dayr Saʿīd, a monastery near the Tigris, to the west of Mosul, was, according to Yāqūt, named for Saʿīd b. ʿAbd al-Malik b. Marwān—that is, for the caliph's son. During his father's caliphate, Saʿīd had been put in authority over the province of Mosul. He fell ill and when his Christian doctor, also named Saʿīd, healed him, the Muslim prince reportedly said to him, 'Choose what you wish.' The physician asked for a piece of land outside of Mosul where he might build a monastery and was given it.[60]

And even though our sources for many of the stories of Christian holy men healing prominent Muslims are texts written long after the purported event, as I have already pointed out, one explanation for their existence is that they described events Christian audiences found familiar and plausible.[61] We have evidence in fact from the late seventh or early eighth century that Muslims in this period were seeking out the healing help of Christians: Was it right, John of Litarb had asked Jacob of Edessa, for a priest to give the blessings of

[58] Especially East Syrian hagiography. For example: ʿAqbalaha healed the daughter of Abraham, the son of Shapur II, who was tormented by a demon; see *History of Karka d-Beth Slokh*, pp. 516–17 (ed. Bedjan, *AMS*, vol. 2). Shapur's wife was healed from demonic affliction by the anointing of oil that had been sent to her by Shabbay; see *Life of Shabbay* 7 (ed. Brock, 'A West Syriac Life of Mar Shabbay (Bar Shabba), Bishop of Merv,' p. 274 [Syriac] = 266 [English], and cf. *Chronicle of Seert* 1.40 [ed. Scher (PO 5.2), p. 142]). The catholicos Yahbalaha I (sed. 415–20) prayed over Yazdgird I and healed him of a headache that doctors had been unable to cure; see *Chronicle of Seert* 1.71 (ed. Scher [PO 5.2], pp. 215–16). Buzaq, bishop of al-Ahwāz, healed Qawad I and his daughter from an ailment they both had; *Chronicle of Seert* 2.19 (ed. Scher [PO 7.2], p. 44). Nuʿmān III and all those with him denied their gods and broke their idols and wanted to receive baptism after the East Syrian Sabrishoʿ (d. 604) healed the king from being tormented by a demon through praying for him; see Peter the Solitary, *Life of Sabrishoʿ*, pp. 322–23 (ed. Bedjan, *Histoire de Mar-Jabalaha*; cf. above, Chapter 6, n. 17. Nuʿmān, his wives, his children, and all the members of his house are eventually baptized, p. 327). By contrast, the *Chronicle of Seert* reports that when Valens refused to have his sick son baptized by Nicenes but had Arians do it instead, the son died; see *Chronicle of Seert* 1.51 (ed. Scher [PO 5.2], pp. 168–169). Cp. also *Chronicle of Seert* 2.27, where Justinian sends a doctor—not a holy man—named Ṭrīkhūmā to treat Khusro, who had fallen gravely ill (ed. Scher [PO 7.2], p. 69). Jesus, of course, was celebrated for having sent Addai to heal Abgar, the ruler of Edessa; see *Teaching of Addai*, p. *4-*7 (ed. Phillips in Howard, *The Teaching of Addai*).

[59] See Brock, 'A Syriac Life of John of Dailam,' p. 168.

[60] Yāqūt, *Muʿjam al-buldān*, vol. 2, p. 515.

[61] It also bears pointing out that there would eventually be stories of Christians greatly distraught at the death of prominent Muslim scholars, the implication being that these men had been held in high esteem by Christians in their lifetimes; see M. Q. Zaman, 'Death, Funeral Processions, and the Articulation of Religious Authority in Early Islam,' *Studia Islamica* 93 (2001), pp. 38, 45, and cf. p. 49, n. 125.

the saints to Hagarenes and pagans who were afflicted by evil spirits, that they might rub them and thereby be healed? Jacob had been unequivocal in his response: it was by all means right to do so, and such things should be given without restraint.[62] Muslims, too, would later show a latitudinarian attitude in their approach to problems and afflictions that crossed religious borders. When he was asked, Aḥmad b. Ḥanbal (d. AH 241/AD 855) saw no harm in People of the Book making supplication for rain (*istisqā'*) alongside Muslims.[63]

THE EUCHARIST

The attraction that holy men held for Muslims is only one example: we have extensive evidence that other Christian objects, symbols, and rituals were held in esteem by Muslims from a very early period as well—just as they would be in later periods. The Eucharist, as we saw in Chapter 5, was of central importance to Christians in the seventh century and, unsurprisingly, we have indications that at least among some Muslims in the early period there was a fascination with and belief in its power.

At times, this fascination could manifest itself in sacrilegious and coarse ways—Muslims were very aware of Christian sacraments, but they might not always treat or use them in the way that a Christian, simple or not, would. 'Is it necessary that the doors of the church be shut when the Eucharist is being celebrated?' John, the Stylite of Litarb, asked Jacob of Edessa. It is indeed necessary, Jacob responded, 'especially on account of the Hagarenes, lest they enter into the church and mix with the believers and disturb them and mock the holy mysteries.'[64] What should happen to a holy *ṭablitā*, Addai asked Jacob, referring to a consecrated block of wood placed on the altar for the Eucharistic celebration, which the Arabs have eaten meat upon and left with stains and defiled with fat? A *ṭablitā* upon which pagans have eaten, Jacob responded, is no longer an altar. It can be washed and used for other purposes, or perhaps broken up and buried in the earth, but it will be retired from Eucharistic duties.[65] In his *Questions and Answers*, Anastasius of Sinai, Jacob's contemporary,

[62] Jacob of Edessa, *Letter to John, the Stylite of Litarb*, p. 52 (ed. Rignell). Cf. Ch. 5, n. 73.

[63] See al-Khallāl, *Ahl al-milal*, vol. 2, p. 120.

[64] *Questions of All Kind, Which John the Stylite Asked the Venerable Jacob, the Teacher* 9 (ed. Vööbus [CSCO 367–68: SS 161–62] p. 237 [= p. 219 (ET)]). NB: Vööbus renders *mhaggrāyē* as 'perverts to Islam,' rather than simply 'Muslims.' This is my translation; see also *SBI*, p. 466, n. 1111.

[65] *Questions Which Addai the Priest and Lover of Labors Asked Jacob, the Bishop of Edessa* 25 (ed. Lamy, *Dissertatio*, pp. 126, 128). The Syriac text in Mardin 310, fol. 200a is superior; for this text and ET, see *SBI*, p. 467, n. 1113. An alternate and shorter version of this is found in Rignell, *A Letter from Jacob*

wrote about Arabs defiling Christian altars and holy places[66] and, similarly, in his *Narrations Profitable for the Soul* Anastasius wrote about twenty-four Arab families living in and defiling a church dedicated to the martyr Theodore and located in a village named Karsatas outside of Damascus: one of the Arabs even shot an arrow at the image of St Theodore in the church.[67]

Other narrative sources put a fuller face on what can seem rather abstract when read in Jacob or Anastasius. 'They will make a sacrifice of those who minister in the sanctuary,' Ps.-Methodius complained of the Arabs in the late seventh century,

> and they will even sleep with their wives and with captive women inside the sanctuary. They will appropriate the sacred vestments as clothing for themselves and their children. They will tether their cattle to the sarcophagi of the martyrs and to the graves of holy men.[68]

During the life of the East Syrian Mar Yohannan (d. AD 692), we are told that an 'Ishmaelite leader' came and made his dwelling among the hovels of the monks at Mar Yohannan's monastery. The saint asked the Arab to leave two times but, indignant, he refused. As a result, the saint cursed him; the Arab's wife then gave birth to 'two people that were in one body, stuck together,' that is, conjoined twins. Humbled, the Arab asked Mar Yohannan to give the order that the child die, lest he have shame before his friends and fellow tribesmen on its account. 'And with the word of that man of the Lord, Mar Yohannan,' the *History of the Monastery of Sabrisho'* continued, 'the body died and that Arab went quickly away.'[69] While he was still a Muslim, Rawḥ al-Qurashī (d. AD 799), actually lived in the Monastery of St Theodore in Damascus. Rawḥ was, we are told, very fond of the church there, though he expressed his fondness in curious ways: he would steal its Eucharist and eat it, would drink what remained of the consecrated wine in the cup. He would take crosses from their places, tear up altar coverings and frequently show up when the priest and congregation were in the church. Rawḥ's sitting room overlooked the church

---

of Edessa to John the Stylite, pp. 61, 63. I am grateful to Sebastian Brock for giving me this definition of a *ṭablitā*. Manna, *Qāmūs kaldānī-'arabī*, s.v. ܛܒܠܝܬܐ (p. 274), notes that a *ṭablitā* can also be a rock.

[66] Anastasius of Sinai, *Questions and Answers* 100 (ed. Richard and Munitiz, p. 161… θυσιαστήρια θεοῦ πάλιν καὶ τόπους τιμίους μολύνοντες ....).

[67] Anastasius of Sinai, *Narrations Beneficial for the Soul* II.2 (ed. Binggeli, p. 1.220 [Greek] = 2.532 [FT] [= §44 in Nau, ed., 'Le texte grec des récits utiles à l'âme d'Anastase (le Sinaïte),' p. 64).

[68] Ps.-Methodius, *Apocalypse* 11.18 (ed. Reinink [CSCO 540: SS 220], p. 332; the ET here is by S. P. Brock, taken from Palmer, *The Seventh Century in the West-Syrian Chronicles*, p. 234). Cf. also Ps.-Samuel of Qalamūn, *Apocalypse*, p. 382.

[69] *History of the Monastery of Sabrisho'*, p. 199 (ed. A. Mingana, *Sources Syriaques*, vol. 1 [Mosul, 1908], pp. 247–48 [= FT]). Cf. also Hoyland, *Seeing Islam*, p. 210.

and on Sundays he would drink alcohol and watch the Christian liturgy taking place below him.[70]

Though such reports come from Christian sources, we have evidence of this sort of irreverent behavior from Muslim texts as well: the Caliph al-Walīd b. Yazīd (reg. AH 125–126 /AD 743–744) reportedly spent a day in drinking and revelry at Dayr Bawannā, near Damascus; in a poem he wrote about his time there, al-Walīd spoke mockingly of making Peter *khalīfat Allāh*, the deputy of God, and John God's counselor and, though he and his entourage were unbelievers, of taking the Eucharist and bowing before the monastery's crosses.[71]

The Muslims in such stories were portrayed as irreverent, sometimes recklessly so, in their conduct in a Christian church, but such oafish and disrespectful behavior carried with it an implicit recognition that the things being defiled were of great value to Christians. And significantly, not all Muslims were so cavalier when it came to the Eucharist. Jacob of Edessa spoke of Muslims who took Eucharistic elements and brought them back from the land of the Greeks. Ultimately, their conscience led them to turn the host over to Jacob. He in turn restored it to the possession of Chalcedonians.[72] What is revealing here is that Muslims had focused on the Eucharist as an item of value. The fact that they would take the trouble to remove the Eucharistic elements, transport them long distances, and then for reasons of conscience turn them over, presumably intact, to a member of the Christian clergy suggests that at least some Muslims, like Christians, viewed those elements as possessing distinct and special powers, even if it is not clear from such a report that they sought to use the Christian Eucharist in any ritualistic way.[73] What is more, Muslims were marrying

[70] *Passion of Anthony of Rawḥ* 1 (ed. I. Dick, 'La passion arabe de S. Antoine Ruwaḥ: néo-martyr de Damas († 25 déc. 799),' *LM* 74 [1961], p. 119 [FT on p. 127] = 'recension A'; J.-P. Monferrer-Sala, '*Šahādāt al-qiddīs Mār Anṭūniyūs*. Replanteamiento de la 'antigüedad' de las versiones sinaíticas a la luz del análisis textual,' *Miscelánea de estudios árabes y hebraicos. Sección de árabe-Islam* 57 (2008), p. 258 = 'recension B'). On the vocalization of Anthony's Arabic/pre-baptismal name Rawḥ and on his name in general, see S. K. Samir, 'Saint Rawḥ al-Qurašī: etude d'onomastique arabe et authenticité de sa passion,' *LM* 105 (1992), pp. 343–59. An ET by John Lamoreaux of this martyrdom is now available in A. Treiger and S. Noble, eds., *The Orthodox Church in the Arab World, 700–1700: An Anthology of Sources* (De Kalb, 2014), pp. 117–23; for discussion of 'recension A' vs. 'recension B', see p. 114. On this text more generally, see D. Vila's article, 'The Martyrdom of Anthony (Rawḥ al-Qurashī),' in *CMR*, vol. 1, pp. 498–501.

[71] Yāqūt, *Mu'jam al-buldān*, vol. 2, p. 502. On the title *khalīfat Allāh* and the Umayyads (as well as others), see Crone and Hinds, *God's Caliph*, pp. 4-23.

[72] *Questions of All Kind, Which John the Stylite Asked the Venerable Jacob, the Teacher* 23 (ed. Vööbus [CSCO 367: SS 161] pp. 243–44 [= 224 (ET)]). (Cf. chapter 3, n. 53).

[73] Contrast this reported behavior by Muslims with other possible ways of dealing with the Eucharistic elements of a group in which one was not a member: e.g., the report in the *Chronicle of Seert* 2.22 (ed. Scher [PO 7.2], p. 50) that 'heretics' (i.e., Miaphysites) in the time of Justin were taking the Eucharist and throwing it away. On the basis of this report, Scher (p. 50, n. 6), raised the possibility that Miaphy-

Christian women already in the seventh century, and once a Christian woman had married a Muslim man, we find evidence that her husband might be concerned that she still have access to the Eucharist—another indication that some Muslims ascribed value to the Eucharist. Addai asked Jacob about 'a Christian woman who of her own will marries a Hagarene: whether it is appropriate for priests to give her the Eucharist? And if there is a specific canon about this?' A husband might resort to extraordinary measures to make sure his wife could take communion: 'And if her husband threatens to kill him if he does not give her the Eucharist,' Addai continued, 'if it is right for him to agree for a time while he is seeking that he be killed, or whether for him to agree will be a sin for him? Or if it is better that he give her the Eucharist and she not become a Hagarene and have her husband be friendly to the Christians?' For Jacob, preventing Christian apostasy was the preeminent concern when dealing with this situation. Addai had answered his own question when asking it: 'You have solved all your perplexities which are in this question,' Jacob wrote,

> with what you have said, namely, 'whether it is appropriate that the Eucharist be given to her and she not become a Hagarene.' On account of her not becoming a Hagarene—even if it means that the priest was sinning when he gave [it] to her, and even if her husband was not threatening—it is right for him to give her the Eucharist and he will not have a sin on account of giving to her. Now as for the last thing you said, namely, whether there is a specific canon concerning this, you should be guided in this way: if it is the case that there is no fear of apostasy, and her husband is not threatening, so that there be fear for other [women], that they too not stumble, and for the purpose of admonishing her, she should fall under the [punishment of the] canon so long as she seems to those in power able to bear it.[74]

JESUS

The only thing more central to Christianity than the Eucharist is the figure of Christ himself, and Jesus, too, was held in esteem among Muslims: apart from his appearance and relatively exalted status in the Qur'ān, the Islamic tradition

sites who had feigned reconciliation with Chalcedonians were acting as if they were communicating while in church but actually only putting the element in their mouth and later discarding it on the ground or some other place.

[74] *Further Questions Which the Priest Addai Asked*, Mardin 310, fols. 213b–214a (Syriac text also in *SBI*, p. 470, n. 1120). Cf. the ET in Hoyland, *Seeing Islam*, pp. 604–605. For discussion of this canon, see U. Simonsohn, 'Communal Membership despite Religious Exogamy: A Critical Examination of East and West Syrian Legal Sources of the Late Sasanian and Early Islamic Periods,' *JNES* 75 (2016), pp. 262–63.

preserved a number of Jesus's sayings, attributing them to Jesus himself.[75] Other saying and parables ascribed to Jesus in the Gospels came to be attributed to Muḥammad in the *ḥadīth* literature.[76] Arabic inscriptions written by Muslims and dating between the late first and late second centuries AH (roughly the eighth century AD) in the Negev ask forgiveness from the 'Lord of Jesus' (*[ra]bb [ʿĪ]sā*), the 'Lord of Jesus and Moses' (*rabb ʿĪsā wa-Mūsā*) and the 'Lord of Moses and Jesus' (*rabb Mūsā wa-ʿĪsā*); one even refers to God as the 'Lord of Aaron and Jesus' (*rabb Hārūn wa-ʿĪsā*).[77]

BAPTISM

Baptism of Muslims was also not unknown in this early period. Rabban Khudhāwī had reportedly healed Muʿāwiya's daughter by baptizing her and, as we saw earlier, in the Ottoman period, there is evidence that Muslims were having their children baptized by priests. There is no reason to suppose that Muslims were not having their children baptized from the earliest post-conquest period. By the middle of the twelfth century AD, the Miaphysite bishop John of Marde would issue a canon forbidding the baptism of Muslim

[75] See D. Cook, 'New Testament Citations in the Ḥadīth Literature and the Question of Early Gospel Translations into Arabic,' in Grypeou et al. *The Encounter of Eastern Christianity with Early Islam*, pp. 206–18.

[76] See e.g., Goldziher, *Muslim Studies*, vol. 2, pp. 346–56 and A. Guillaume, *The Traditions of Islam* (repr. New York, 1980), pp. 138–42. Cf. also chapter 13, nn. 104–105.

[77] Appeals are also made to the 'Lord of Moses,' and God is once called the 'Lord of Moses and Abraham' and once 'Lord of Muḥammad and Abraham.' See the lists of prophets in inscriptions in Y. D. Nevo, Z. Cohen, and D. Heftman, *Ancient Arabic Inscriptions from the Negev*, vol. 1, (Jerusalem, 1993), pp. 141–42. There are references to 'Lord of Issa': MA 487(10), MA 489(10); 'Lord of Moses': MA 401D(07), MA 4114(12), MA 4137(12), MA 4168(13), MA 4271(19), MA 4293(21), MA 4293(21), MA 4295(21), MA 4342(22), MA 4428(23), MA 4501(25), MA 4509(25), and MA 4513(25); 'Lord of Jesus and Moses': MA 4204A(14), MA 4340(22); 'Lord of Muḥammad and Abraham': HS 3155(06); 'God of Moses and Abraham': MM113(01); 'Lord of Moses and Jesus': MA 4210(16), MA 4269(19), MA 4467(24), MA 4508(25); MA 4516(26); 'Lord of Moses and Aaron': SC303(03), SC305(03), YA3112(05); and 'Aaron and Jesus': HL4900(27). See also, Cook, 'New Testament Citations in the Ḥadīth Literature,' p. 189; R. G. Hoyland, 'The Content and Context of Early Arabic Inscriptions,' *JSAI* 21 (1997), pp. 78–79; and S. Ory, 'Aspects religieux des textes épigraphiques du de l'Islam,' *Revue du monde musulman et de la Méditerranée* 58 (1990), pp. 34–35. Y. D. Nevo and J. Koren, *Crossroads to Islam: The Origins of the Arab Religion and the Arab State* (Amherst, NY, 2003), pp. 197–200, 297–336, argued that these inscriptions represented the work of people following an 'indeterminate monotheism' that developed into Islam, rather than that of Muslims. Their proposal, while creative, is unconvincing; for discussion of the nature of Muslim identity reflected in these inscriptions, see the comments of Hoyland, 'The Content and Context,' p. 96, and see F. Imbert, 'L'Islam des pierres: l'expression de la foi dans les graffiti arabes des premiers siècles,' *Revue des mondes musulmans et de la Méditerranée* 129 (2011), pp. 57–78, where Nevo and Koren's ideas are discussed with reference to Arabic inscriptions from Arabia and not just the Negev. I am grateful to Sean Anthony for alerting me to this article.

infants in the same laver as Christian infants. 'In the case of the children of Muslims,' John's canon stated,

> we carefully order you and speak to you with an apostolic commandment that there is no authority from God for priests to baptize them with the children of believers and in our holy font. Instead, let them have a different baptism, apart, on a different day, either before or after, in ordinary [i.e., nonconsecrated] water.

Rather than a Christian baptism, John prescribed that Muslim children were to be given a different baptism, one for the remission of sins—what he called the 'baptism of John [the Baptist]':

> There shall only be for them a service of repentance, that is: a cycle and a prayer and a hymn of repentance, etc. Let the priest baptize the children of the Arabs as he says the following: I baptize this so-and-so in the name of the Lord with this baptism of John for the forgiveness of trespasses and the remission of sins. Amen. And let them anoint them with unconsecrated (*shḥimā*) oil.[78]

What we have here is an attempt to regulate and control what must have been a practice known across the Middle East: At roughly the same time as John of Marde was writing, it was common for Turks in Anatolia to have their children baptized, a practice which Balsamon reported. 'The Agarenes suppose that their children will be possessed of demons and will smell like dogs if they do not receive Christian baptism,' he wrote. 'Accordingly they do not invoke baptism as a cathartic of all spiritual sordidness and as the provider of holy light and sanctification, but rather as a remedy or magical charm.'[79]

THE CROSS

One last major Christian symbol remains to be discussed: the Cross. Whatever we make of the historical reliability of the saying attributed to Muḥammad

[78] *Canons of John of Marde* 25 (ed. Vööbus, *The Synodicon in the West Syrian Tradition II* [CSCO 375–76; SS 163–64] [Louvain, 1976], p. 246 [Syriac] [= p. 259 (ET)]; my translation). I am grateful to David Taylor for bringing this passage to my attention; see now his 'The Syriac Baptism of St John: A Christian Ritual of Protection for Muslim Children,' in R. G. Hoyland, ed., *The Late Antique World of Early Islam: Muslims among Christian and Jews in the East Mediterranean* (Princeton, 2015), pp. 437–59.

[79] For the Greek text of Balsamon see G. A. Ralles and M. Potles, *Syntagma tōn theiōn kai hierōn kanonōn tōn te hagiōn kai paneuphēmōn apostolōn*, vol. 2 (Athens, 1852), p. 498. The ET here is that of S. Vryonis, taken from *The Decline of Medieval Hellenism*, p. 487. See the evidence for Turkish Muslims being baptized collected by Vryonis more generally at 487–89. For further discussion of this phenomenon, which is attested in Greek sources relating to Anatolia from the ninth to fifteenth centuries, see R. Shukurov, *The Byzantine Turks, 1204–1461* (Leiden/Boston, 2016), pp. 59–62.

that Jesus's actions when he returns to judge mankind will include breaking the Cross,[80] we can be sure that by a very early point in the period of Arab rule, the Cross had become a target of objections from Muslims in positions of power.[81] Nevertheless, in later periods, there is a divergence between normative Islamic antipathy towards the Cross and evidence of its use by Muslims for apotropaic purposes such as have been documented by Hasluck and others. And even with our scanty and problematic evidentiary base in this early period, we have some small pieces of information suggesting that there was a spectrum of Muslim attitudes toward what was perhaps the most distinctive and divisive of all Christian symbols in the early centuries of Arab rule, just as there would be in later centuries.[82]

There was, to be sure, negative treatment of the Cross: 'Why is the Cross being insulted?' Sophronius asked on Epiphany in 636 or 637, listing a number of unhappy developments that had accompanied the Arab invasions going on even as he preached.[83] Not long after, 'Umar's attempt to build a mosque on the site of the Temple of Solomon in the late 630s or early 640s was reported to have been accompanied by an act of cross removal and a subsequent rise in antagonism toward the Cross throughout the regions of Arab rule.[84] Such

[80] al-Bukhārī, *al-Jāmiʿ al-ṣaḥīḥ*, vol. 2, p. 490 (no. 3448).

[81] Cf. S. H. Griffith, 'Anastasios of Sinai, the *Hodegos*, and the Muslims,' *Greek Orthodox Theological Review* 32 (1987), pp. 345–46; Griffith, 'Theodore Abū Qurrah's Arabic Tract on the Christian Practice of Venerating Images,' *JAOS* 105 (1985), pp. 59–60; and Griffith, 'Images, Islam and Christian Icons: A Moment in the Christian/Muslim Encounter in Early Islamic Times,' in P. Canivet and J.-P. Rey-Coquais, eds., *La Syrie de Byzance à l'islam, VIIe-VIIIe siècles* (Damascus, 1992), pp. 121–38.

[82] Ḥ. Zayyāt, *al-Ṣalīb fī 'l-Islām* (Beirut, 2005), is a foundational work on the question of the Cross in medieval Islamic texts.

[83] Πόθεν σταυρὸς ἐνυβρίζεται; Sophronius of Jerusalem, *Homilia in theophaniam* 10 (ed. A. Papadopoulos-Kerameus, *Analekta hierosolymitikēs stachiologias*, vol. 5 [St. Petersburg, 1898], p. 166). For the date of this text, see Hoyland, *Seeing Islam*, p. 71; an ET of the entire passage is available at pp. 72–73.

[84] Michael the Great, *Chronicle* 11.8 (ed. Chabot, 4.421 = 2.431). Theophanes placed 'Umar's initial desire to build a sanctuary at the site of Solomon's Temple in 634–635 (*Chronicle* AM 6127 [ed. de Boor, vol. 1, p. 339; ET available in Mango and Scott, *The Chronicle of Theophanes Confessor*, p. 471) and this incident in particular in 642–643 (AM 6135 [ed. de Boor, p. 342 = Mango and Scott, p. 476]), but on these two dates, see C. Mango, 'The Temple Mount AD 614–638,' in Raby and Johns, eds., *Bayt al-Maqdis*, vol. 1, pp. 1–2. Similarly to Mango (p. 2), Flusin, 'L'esplanade du temple a l'arrivée des Arabes,' placed the construction of the 'Mosque of 'Umar' around 638. Elias bar Shinaya placed 'Umar's building of a mosque on the site of the Temple of Solomon in AH 17/23 January AG 949 (= AD 638)—which was, though he does not note it, the first day of the *hijrī* year 17 (cf. V. Grumel, *La chronologie* [Paris, 1958], p. 247); see Elias bar Shinaya, *Chronography*, pp. 132–33 (ed. E. W. Brooks, *Opus chronologicum* [CSCO III.7] [Paris, 1910]).

For a detailed examination of 'Umar's visit to Jerusalem, see H. Busse, ''Omar b. al-Ḫaṭṭāb in Jerusalem,' *JSAI* 5 (1984), pp. 73–119, and for the development of Muslim stories linking 'Umar to the conquest of Jerusalem, see Busse, ''Omar's Image as the Conqueror of Jerusalem,' *JSAI* 8 (1986), pp. 149–68. A. Kaplony, *The Ḥaram of Jerusalem, 324–1099: Temple, Friday Mosque, Area of Spiritual Power* (Stuttgart,

stories, however, do not mean that there was a uniform hostility to the Cross among Muslims in this early period: one saying attributed to the Prophet has him forbid Muslims from praying in a garment that has a cross on it,[85] a tradition that surely would not have been circulated if such actions had been unknown. Even prominent members of the community were reported to be seen wearing a garment with a cross on it.[86] In the late seventh century, the poet al-Akhṭal boasted of the Christian Taghlib marching into battle with the Cross and Saint Sergius (on a banner?) held high;[87] Henri Lammens connected this striking line of poetry to the actions of Taghlib soldiers under the command of Muslim b. ʿUqba when he put down a rebellion in Medina and captured the city in AH 63/AD 683 on behalf of the ruler Yazīd I, something which, if true, would make it extraordinary.[88] Perhaps even more remarkable is the report that in Egypt in AD 750, Khurasani soldiers—Muslims—pursuing the last Umayyad Caliph, Marwān II, had gold and silver crosses on the necks of their horses.[89] Here it is also worth recalling the several instances we cited above of Christians displaying the cross prominently while Muslims were present or Christians using the sign of the Cross in the course of healing a sick Muslim. We saw how Theodota restored the Muslim official's sight by making the sign of the Cross over his eyes and invoking the name of Jesus; John of Daylam using a cross to make the sign of the Cross over the head of ʿAbd al-Malik's son who was ill; and we noted Arabs present at the patriarch Julian II's entry into Amid, a celebration where there were many crosses on display.

2002), pp. 23–31, discusses the pre-Marwānid character of the area of the Temple Mount and the nature of ʿUmar's mosque. See also below, n. 115.

[85] Ibn al-Athīr, *al-Nihāya fī gharīb al-ḥadīth wa-'l-athar*, vol. 3, p. 44 (ed. Ṭ. Aḥmad al-Zāwī and M. Muḥammad al-Ṭanāḥī) (n.d., n.p.). For discussion of this *ḥadīth*, see also *al-Mawsūʿa al-fiqhiyya* (Kuwait, 1988), vol. 12, p. 84. Cf. Zayyāt, *al-Ṣalīb fī 'l-Islām*, p. 12.

[86] For al-Ḥasan (b. ʿAlī b. Abī Ṭālib?) seen wearing such a garment, see Ibn al-Athīr, *al-Nihāya fī gharīb al-ḥadīth wa-'l-athar*, vol. 3, p. 44, and ʿAbd al-Razzāq, *al-Muṣannaf*, vol. 11, p. 76 (no. 19957). Cf. Zayyāt, *al-Ṣalīb fī 'l-Islām*, p. 12.

[87] al-Akhṭal, *Dīwān*, p. 309 (ed. A. Ṣāliḥānī [Beirut, 1891]).

[88] See H. Lammens, *La Syrie, précis historique* (Beirut, 1921), p. 73, and cf. Lammens, 'Études sur le règne du calife Omaiyade Moʿawiya Ier,' (part 3), p. 299; and Lammens, 'Un poète royal a la cour des omiades de Damas,' *ROC* 8 (1903), p. 355. See also the comments in E. K. Fowden, *The Barbarian Plain: Saint Sergius between Rome and Iran* (Berkeley, 1999), pp. 179–80. On Muslim b. ʿUqba, see H. Lammens's article, 'Muslim b. Uḳba,' in *EI2*, vol. 7, pp. 693–94. Lammens's suggested context, however, does not seem to have any basis in the poem itself, which only refers to the Qays and which is supposed to be about the conflict between Qays and Taghlib, on which see Ṣāliḥānī's note in al-Akhṭal, *Dīwān*, p. 308, fn. e.

[89] *History of the Patriarchs of Alexandria* 1.18 (ed. Evetts [PO 5.1], p. 440). Only three years later, the Abbasid rulers of Egypt raised taxes on Christians, '[f]or the two secretaries aforesaid and the Khorassanians forgot that it was God who had given them the government, and neglected the holy Cross which had gained them victory' (trans. Evetts, p. 443).

To be sure, a number of these examples come from Christian saints' lives and some may represent hagiographic commonplaces or reflect the agendas of Christian sources written in the context of Muslim political power. More notable, however, and more historically likely is that report of Muʿāwiya's decision upon being made Commander of the Faithful to go and pray at Golgotha and Gethsemane, an event that the *Maronite Chronicle* reported only a few years after it happened. It would be difficult to imagine two places more closely associated with the crucifixion of Jesus, an event whose historicity Muslims have traditionally denied (cf. Q 4:157) and to which the Cross points.[90] We should, however, balance this report (and that of Arculf encountered in the previous chapter) with other moments in Muʿāwiya's period of rule: only a few months later in the same year that he prayed at the sites of the Agony and Crucifixion, in AH 41/AD 660, Muʿāwiya tried to mint gold and silver coins without crosses on them, but this omission meant that people refused to use them.[91] Arab-Byzantine coins that displayed crosses, even when sometimes also bearing affirmations of the prophethood of Muḥammad, also reflect the ideological tension between Muʿāwiya's public philo-Christian acts and his removal of the Cross from coins.[92] As Clive Foss has pointed out, however, an official Greek inscription in the baths at Hammat Gader, rebuilt under Muʿāwiya in 662, is preceded by a cross and contains Muʿāwiya's name. Muslims used these baths and it is not improbable that Muʿāwiya himself visited there as well: 'In other words, public display of the cross was not incompatible with the official life of the Umayyad state.'[93]

Indeed, the tension between hostility to the Cross and its veneration might have existed in a single person. In response to the criticisms of al-Hāshimī, his Muslim interlocutor, al-Kindī pointed out that in various moments of distress—when falling from an animal, fleeing from danger, encountering a lion—

[90] See Humphreys' discussion of this event in *Muʿawiya ibn Abi Sufyan*, p. 84. Cf. Chapter 10, n. 177.

[91] See *Maronite Chronicle*, p. 71 (ed. Brooks [CSCO III.4]). For an ET, see Palmer, *The Seventh Century in the West-Syrian Chronicles*, p. 32.

[92] See C. Foss, *Arab-Byzantine Coins: An Introduction, with a Catalogue of the Dumbarton Oaks Collection* (Cambridge, Mass, 2008), pp. 117–18 for a discussion of the ideological tension represented by crosses appearing on Islamic coins, and *ibid.*, p. 63 for a coin bearing a cross as well as an Arabic inscription reading 'Muḥammad, the Prophet of God.'

[93] Foss, *Arab-Byzantine Coins*, p. 118. For the inscription in question, see Y. Hirschfeld, *The Roman Baths of Hammat Gader: Final Report* (Jerusalem, 1997), pp. 238–40. On this inscription and Muʿāwiya's building accomplishments more generally, see D. Whitcomb, 'Notes for an Archaeology of Muʿāwiya: Material Culture in the Transitional Period of Believers,' in A. Borrut and F. M. Donner, eds., *Christians and Others in the Umayyad State* (Chicago, 2016), pp. 11–27. See also Y. al-Shdaifat, A. Al-Jallad, Z. al-Salameen, and R. Harahsheh, 'An Early Christian Arabic Graffito Mentioning "Yazīd the King," ' *Arabian Archaeology and Epigraphy* 28 (2017), pp. 315–24, for a recently discovered Arabic graffito in Jordan which asks that God remember a certain Yazīd the King. The inscription is preceded by a cross and the authors argue that the 'Yazīd' it refers to is Yazīd b. Muʿāwiya.

al-Hāshimī himself had invoked the Cross for protection. 'Why have you said that the worship of the Cross does harm and does not benefit?,' al-Kindī asked. 'I wish I knew what harm befell you when you sought refuge in the Cross!'[94] As with other instances of al-Kindī's interactions with the likely fictional al-Hāshimī, the effectiveness of such an argument lay in its appeal to types of behavior that would have been familiar to al-Kindī's audience.

Al-Kindī's charge against al-Hāshimī serves as an important reminder: Whatever expressions of antipathy towards the Cross we might find in the Islamic tradition, be it in official ideology or in the writings of religious leaders and polemicists, we should not confuse such opposition with hostility toward the Cross by most individual Muslims on a day-to-day basis.[95] What is more, Christian converts to Islam and their descendants might still look to the Cross as an object with special power and importance. According to the historian 'Arīb b. Sa'd (d. ca. AD 980/AH 370), for instance, the tenth-century Abbasid vizier al-Ḥusayn b. al-Qāsim, a Muslim, would reportedly approach Christian scribes and tell them, 'My family is from among you and my forefathers were among your notables.' A cross fell from the hand of 'Ubayd Allāh b. Sulaymān (d. AD 901/AH 288), al-Ḥusayn's grandfather, in the days of al-Mu'taḍid (reg. AD 892–902/AH 279–289), 'Arīb went on, 'When people saw it, ['Ubayd Allāh] said: "This is something which our old folks (*'ajā'izunā*) seek blessing from and they place it in our clothing without our knowing."' Al-Ḥusayn would tell this to the Christian secretaries, 'Arīb claimed, as a way to curry favor with them.[96]

CHURCHES AND MONASTERIES

The Cross, like the Eucharist, was strongly associated with Christian churches and monasteries, and there is abundant evidence that some early Muslims had a great interest in, and even veneration for these places (as would later Muslims). 'We will not raise our voices in prayer or in [scriptural] recitation,' the Christians promised in a clause in one version of the so-called 'Pact of 'Umar',

[94] al-Kindī, *Apology*, p. 210. An ET by Tien is available in Newman, ed., *The Early Christian-Muslim Dialogue*, p. 493. For this, see Zayyāt, *al-Ṣalīb fī 'l-Islām*, pp. 34–35.

[95] M. N. Swanson, *Folly to the Ḥunafā': The Cross of Christ in Arabic Christian-Muslim Controversy in the Eighth and Ninth Centuries A.D.* (Excerpta ex dissertation ad doctoratum; Cairo, 1995), traces the theological argument between Christians and Muslims over the Cross in the eighth and ninth centuries.

[96] *Taqarruban ilayhim.* See 'Arīb b. Sa'd, *Ṣilat ta'rīkh al-Ṭabarī*, p. 164 (ed. M. J. de Goeje [Leiden, 1897]). For this point, see Zayyāt, *al-Ṣalīb fī 'l-Islām*, p. 37. On this family, see C. E. Bosowrth's article, 'Wahb,' in *EI2*, vol. 11, pp. 33–34.

'in our churches while Muslims are present.'[97] Other versions of the 'Pact of 'Umar' had clauses in which Christians promised not to forbid Muslims from staying in churches, night or day, and in which they agreed to open their doors to travelers and wayfarers.[98]

Like the Sasanians before them,[99] Muslim rulers patronized churches and monasteries. Writing not long after the conquests, the East Syrian Isho'yahb III (d. ca. AD 658), spoke of the Arabs helping out churches and monasteries,[100] and there is evidence for such activity throughout the medieval period.[101] Umayyad caliphs and officials would also give permission to Christians to build new churches. Around 689, for instance, 'Abd al-'Azīz b. Marwān, the governor of Egypt and brother of 'Abd al-Malik, gave the go-ahead to two of his chamberlains, who were Chalcedonians, to build a church dedicated to Mar Girgis in Ḥulwān.[102] A few years later, 'Abd al-'Azīz allowed one of his scribes, a Miaphysite named Athanasius, to build two churches, Mar Jirjis and Abū Qīr.[103] In both these instances, 'Abd al-'Azīz merely granted permission for the building of churches, but in other instances he seems even to have

[97] *wa-lā narfa'u aṣwātanā fī 'l-ṣalāt wa-lā al-qirā'a fī kanā'isinā fīmā yaḥḍuruhu al-Muslimūn.* See Ibn Taymiyya, *Iqtiḍā'*, p. 121.

[98] See the two versions of the *shurūṭ 'Umar* (stipulations of 'Umar) recorded in Ibn Qayyim al-Jawziyya, *Aḥkām ahl al-dhimma*, vol. 2, pp. 113, 114.

[99] Ibn al-Nadīm mentioned a Christian physician named Theodorus for whom Shapur II or Bahram V was supposed to have built churches (*Fihrist*, vol. 1, p. 303 (ed. Flügel [Leipzig, 1871–1872]). For Khusro II building a monastery during the patriarchate of Sabrisho' I (sed. 596–604) in the name of his Christian wife Shirin, see Peter the Solitary, *Life of Sabrisho'*, p. 306 (ed. Bedjan, *Histoire de Mar-Jabalaha*). Khusro was even careful, Peter noted, to obtain holy books from Edessa; for the importance of Edessa as a center of Syriac manuscripts, see S.P. Brock, 'Manuscripts Copied in Edessa,' in Bruns and Luthe, eds., *Orientalia Christiana: Festschrift für Hubert Kaufhold zum 70. Geburtstag*, p. 119.

[100] Isho'yahb III, *Letters* III.14 (To Simeon of Revardashir), p. 251 (ed. Duval [CSCO: Syr. II.64]; see Chapter 12, n. 30 for a translation of this passage).

[101] Examples of Muslim rulers giving land or money to Christian monasteries or churches in Egypt (from later in the medieval period) can be found in Abū al-Makārim, *Ta'rīkh al-kanā'is wa-'l-adyira*, vol. 2, pp. 7 (fol. 7a), 78 (fol. 62a), 116 (fol. 88b) (ed. al-Anbā Ṣamū'īl, *Ta'rīkh Abū al-Makārim* [n.d., n.p.]; ET in B.T.A. Evetts, *The Churches and monasteries of Egypt* [Oxford, 1895], pp. 15, 183, 248). For Abū al-Makārim as the actual author of this text and for its dates of composition being in the period AD 1177 to 1204, see most conveniently A. S. Atiya in *CoptEn*, vol. 1, p. 23, and J. Den Heijer and P. Pilette in *CMR*, vol. 3, pp. 983–88. For more detail, and on the relationship between Evett's translation and the available Arabic edition, see U. Zanetti, 'Abū l-Makārim et Abū Ṣāliḥ,' *Bulletin de la societé d'archéologie Copte* 34 (1995), pp. 85–138.

More generally, Fattal, *Le statut légal des non-musulmans en pays d'Islam*, pp. 180–203, gives a detailed survey of the treatment of Christian churches from the earliest period of Muslim rule through the Crusades.

[102] Sa'īd b. Biṭrīq, *Kitāb al-Ta'rīkh*, p. 41 (ed. L. Cheikho, B. Carra de Vaux, and H. Zayyat, *Eutychii patriarchae alexandrini annales II* [CSCO SA III.7] [Beirut, 1909]). Caetani, *Chronographia islamica*, vol. 4, p. 825, no. 18, placed this in AH 70 (= AD 689).

[103] Sa'īd b. Biṭrīq, *Kitāb al-Ta'rīkh*, p. 41 (ed. Cheikho, Carra de Vaux, and Zayyat [CSCO SA III.7]).

ordered the construction of new churches, though Christians had to pay for the buildings themselves.[104] What is more, ʿAbd al-ʿAzīz was also remembered by Christians for building churches and monasteries on account of his love for Christians.[105]

Throughout Syria, churches were turned into mosques after the conquests, or partitioned to serve as places of worship for both Christians and Muslims.[106] In the *vita* of Theodota we even find Arabs present at one of the holy man's homilies.[107] Various *ḥadīth* attributed to ʿUmar b. al-Khaṭṭāb have him refusing to go into churches on account of the images (*ṣuwar* or *tamāthīl*) present in them, and Ibn ʿAbbās, we are told, disapproved of praying in churches if there were images (*tamāthīl*) in them.[108] The existence of such reports suggests, of course, that some Muslims had no such qualms, and even in normative Islamic sources we can find intimations of a spectrum of attitudes towards Muslim prayer in Christian places of worship, which we can also infer from reports of such activities in Christian texts. The last *ḥadīth* listed by ʿAbd al-Razzāq in his section on 'Prayer in a Church' has Salmān al-Fārisī—himself a Christian renegade—seeking a place to pray. 'Seek a pure heart,' a foreign woman (*ʿilja*) told him, 'and pray where you will.'[109] Another report has Salmān and Hudhayfa at one point staying with a Nabatean (that is, Aramaic-speaking) woman. 'Is there a place here where we can pray?' they are said to have asked her. 'Purify your heart,' she is supposed to have said. 'And so one of them said to the other, "Take it—it is wisdom from the heart of an unbeliever." '[110] Such reports would seem to indicate that some foreign converts to Islam were perhaps open to using their former places of worship for Islamic prayer.

[104] *History of the Patriarchs of Alexandria* 1.16 (ed. Evetts [PO 5.1], p. 296). Caetani, *Chronographia Islamica*, vol. 4, p. 939, no. 18, placed this in AH 79 (= AD 698).

[105] Mena of Nikiou, *History of the Patriarch Isaac*, pp. 62–63 (ed. E. Amélineau, *Histoire du patriarche copte Isaac* [Paris, 1890]; ET available in Bell, *The Life of Isaac of Alexandria; and the Martyrdom of Saint Macrobius*, p. 69).

[106] See K.A.C. Creswell, *A Short Account of Early Muslim Architecture* (repr. Beirut, 1968), p. 7; Fattal, *Le statut légal des non-musulmans en pays d'Islam*, p. 184; M. Guidetti, *In the Shadow of the Church: The Building of Mosques in Early Medieval Syria* (Leiden/Boston, 2017), pp. 36–70. On the phenomenon of Muslim prayer in churches, especially in the first several centuries AH, see also S. Bashear, 'Qibla Musharriqa and Early Muslim Prayer in Churches,' *Muslim World* 81 (1991), pp. 267–82.

[107] St Mark's Jerusalem 199, fol. 557a: 'On Sunday, the entire city assembled to convey the Holy One up to the church. And he spoke to them from the pulpit; when he ascended for his homily, the Arabs and the Christians gathered to see him and the church was filled inside and out and there was an enormous multitude. At the end of his homily, he fell down on his face before all of them above the pulpit and there was a great cry and much weeping.' For the Syriac, see Mardin 275/8, p. 551.

[108] For these reports, see ʿAbd al-Razzāq, *al-Muṣannaf*, vol. 1, pp. 411–12 (ʿUmar b. al-Khaṭṭāb: nos. 1610, 1611; Ibn ʿAbbās: no. 1608).

[109] ʿAbd al-Razzāq, *al-Muṣannaf*, vol. 1, p. 412 (no. 1612).

[110] al-Sakhāwī, *al-Maqāṣid al-ḥasana fī bayān kathīr min al-aḥādīth al-mushtahira ʿalā al-alsina*, p. 119 (no. 119) (ed. M. ʿUthmān al-Khisht) (Beirut, 1985).

Churches also held attractions for Muslims who were not Christian converts. ʿĀmir b. ʿAbd Allāh b. ʿAbd al-Qays, who died at some point during the reign of Muʿāwiya, was famous for his ascetic ways:[111] when Kaʿb al-Aḥbār saw ʿĀmir in Syria, for instance, he said of him, 'This is the monk of this community.'[112] Ibn Saʿd records a story in which ʿĀmir and a group of others made a raid. Afterwards, the Muslims camped in a certain spot, but ʿĀmir went away and alighted at a church. Placing a man at the church's door, he gave a stern order that no one was to be allowed to enter in to his presence. When the commander of the raid asked to be allowed to come in, ʿĀmir agreed. 'I implore you by God, may He remind you,' ʿĀmir told him, 'to make me desire this world or make me renounce the next.'[113] Given his ascetic profile, ʿĀmir's decision to visit this church and his wish for solitude there seem hardly to have been coincidental.[114]

State patronage of and involvement in church and monastery construction may explain why, writing even as the Dome of the Rock was under construction by ʿAbd al-ʿAzīz's brother, ʿAbd al-Malik, Anastasius of Sinai reported the story of his own personal realization that demons had been at work clearing rubble off the Temple Mount thirty years previously: he considered it necessary to write such things down 'on account of those who think and say that what is being built right now in Jerusalem is a temple of God.' In other words, while the Dome of the Rock was being built at least some Christians believed that it was some sort of Christian edifice. The Dome of the Rock's physical similarity to other Christian structures might also have played a role in this belief among Christians that ʿAbd al-Malik was building a church. After all, only a few miles from Jerusalem was the fifth-century Church of the Kathisma, an octagonal structure, built around a sacred rock (where the Virgin had reportedly sat to rest on two different occasions—hence the church's name), which had undergone restoration in the early seventh century and contained mosaics, some of which resembled those of the Dome of the Rock.[115] Whatever

[111] For ʿĀmir, see al-Mizzī, *Tahdhīb al-kamāl fī asmāʾ al-rijāl*, vol. 14, pp. 64–65.

[112] Ibn Saʿd, *Kitāb al-ṭabaqāt al-kabīr*, vol. 7.1, p. 79 (ed. Meissner [Leiden, 1915]; ET taken from Bewley, *The Men of Madina*, vol. 1, p. 68).

[113] Ibn Saʿd, *Kitāb al-ṭabaqāt al-kabīr*, vol. 7.1, p. 79 (ed. Meissner [Leiden, 1915]; my translation made with reference to the ET in Bewley, *The Men of Madina*, vol. 1, p. 68).

[114] For more on ʿĀmir's ascetic profile, see Andrae, 'Zuhd und Mönchtum,' p. 311.

[115] On the Church of the Kathisma and the Dome of the Rock, see O. Grabar, *The Dome of the Rock* (Cambridge, Mass./London, 2006), pp. 104–106. Grabar, p. 106, was cautious in accepting the idea that the Church of the Kathisma served as a model for the Dome of the Rock. I am not, however, making such a suggestion here, but am rather speculating that the resemblance between the two structures may have caused some to think that ʿAbd al-Malik's new structure would be a church like the nearby Church of the Kathisma. On the Kathisma church, see also R. Avner, 'The Kathisma: A Christian and Muslim Pilgrimage Site,' *Aram* 18–19 (2006–2007), pp. 541–57 and Avner, 'The Recovery of the Kathisma Church and Its Influence on Octagonal Buildings,' in G. C. Bottini, L. Di Segni, and L. D. Chrupcata, eds., *One*

the cause of these Christian rumors that ʿAbd al-Malik was building a church on the Temple Mount, Anastasius was certain the caliph was doing no such thing: 'For how could a temple of God be built in that place?' he asked, citing Christ's statement that the area would be a wasteland (Mt. 23:38).[116]

The idea that the Dome of the Rock was a church also may be related to an interest in churches and monasteries that seems to have been common among members of the Umayyad dynasty. As we have already seen, the mid-seventh century *Maronite Chronicle* reported that after being made leader of the Muslim community in Jerusalem, Muʿāwiya prayed in several famous churches there;[117] and when an earthquake destroyed the ciborium and two walls of the church of Edessa in AH 59/AD 679, Muʿāwiya ordered them rebuilt, as we saw in Chapter 10.[118] ʿAbd al-Malik, as we have also seen, is supposed to have offered to pay for whatever churches and monasteries John of Daylam wanted to build. A monastery in the *ghūṭa* of Damascus was called Dayr Bishr on account of Bishr b. Marwān (d. ca. AH 74/AD 693–694), the son of the Umayyad caliph Marwān.[119] Yazīd I was in Dayr al-Murrān near Damascus when he learned that a Muslim military force had been taken captive and killed in Byzantine territory.[120] Yazīd I's grandson, Saʿīd b. Muḥammad b. Ibn Abī ʿAbd Allāh, and Saʿīd's son, Khālid, lived in Dayr Qays in the *ghūṭā* near Damascus;[121] ʿUmar b. Muḥammad, a great grandson of Yazīd I, lived in a monastery near Damascus known as Dayr Sābur;[122] and ʿAbd al-Karīm b. Abī Muʿāwiya, a great-great grandson of Yazīd I lived in Dayr al-Hind in a village outside of Damascus.[123] In fact, ʿAbd al-Karīm's father, Abū Muʿāwiya, had been associated with Dayr al-Hind as well.[124]

Land, Many Cultures: Archaeological Studies in honour of Stanislao Loffreda OFM (Jerusalem, 2003), pp. 173–86.

[116] Anastasius of Sinai, *Narrations Beneficial for the Soul* II.7 (ed. Binggeli, p. 1.225 [Greek] = 2.538 [FT] [= C-3 in Heid, ed. 'Die C-Reihe erbaulicher Erzählungen des Anastasios vom Sinai,' p. 82]). See also Flusin, 'L'esplanade du temple a l'arrivée des arabes,' p. 25–26.

[117] *Maronite Chronicle*, p. 71: He "went up and sat down on Golgotha; he prayed there, and went to Gethsemane and went down to the tomb of the blessed Mary to pray in it' (ed. Brooks [CSCO III.4]; ET taken from Palmer, *The Seventh Century in the West-Syrian Chronicles*, p. 31).

[118] Michael the Great, *Chronicle* 11.13 (ed. Chabot, 4.436–37 = 2.457).

[119] Yāqūt, *Muʿjam al-buldān*, vol. 2, p. 500. On Bishr, see L. Veccia Vaglieri's article, 'Bishr b. Marwān,' in *EI2*, vol. 1, pp. 1242–43.

[120] Yāqūt, *Muʿjam al-buldān*, vol. 2, p. 534.

[121] Yāqūt, *Muʿjam al-buldān*, vol. 2, p. 529 and cf. E. Campbell, 'A Heaven of Wine: Muslim-Christian Encounters at Monasteries in the Early Islamic Middle East' (PhD diss., University of Washington, 2009), p. 292.

[122] Yāqūt, *Muʿjam al-buldān*, vol. 2, p. 514.

[123] Yāqūt, *Muʿjam al-buldān*, vol. 2, p. 543. Cf. Campbell, 'A Heaven of Wine,' p. 281.

[124] Ibn ʿAsākir, *Taʾrīkh madīnat Dimashq*, vol. 67 (ed. ʿU. b. Gharāma al-ʿAmrawī) (Beirut, 1998), p. 245 (no. 8846).

This interest was not restricted to minor figures in the ruling family. In a short report, Ismāʿīl b. Rāfiʿ spoke of visiting ʿUmar b. ʿAbd al-ʿAzīz in a church after he was made caliph[125]—though it is not clear whether this was directly after ʿUmar had been made caliph. If it was, it would have been an act reminiscent of Muʿāwiya's visits to churches in Jerusalem after becoming Commander of the Faithful. ʿUmar in particular is an interesting figure when it comes to the relationship of members of the Umayyad clan to Christianity. Though celebrated for his deep Muslim piety, that piety could be described in terms reminiscent of Christian devotion, as when someone speaking of ʿUmar's gait observed that ʿUmar ʿwalked as monks do.'[126] There was even a claim that ʿUmar would put on a hair shirt and wear an iron collar he kept in a box and spend his nights in a special alcove in his house that nobody else was allowed to enter, praying fervently and weeping.[127] ʿUmar was in fact reported to have died in a monastery (in the region of Apamea).[128] Further examples of his apparent fondness for Christianity can easily be adduced.[129]

Monasteries might acquire new names as a result of their connection to Muslim figures: Dayr Ṣalībā, a mile from the eastern gate of Damascus, came to be called Dayr Khālid for Khālid b. Walīd, who was said to have stayed there during his siege of the city,[130] and Dayr Muḥammad, in the region of Damascus, was given its name on account of Muḥammad b. al-Walīd b. ʿAbd Allāh, the nephew and son-in-law of Yazīd I.[131] Another monastery near Damascus, originally dedicated to St. Michael, came to be called Dayr al-Bukht on account of a certain Central Asian camel that the caliph ʿAbd al-Malik kept there.[132] The

[125] Ibn Saʿd, *Kitāb al-ṭabaqāt al-kabīr*, vol. 5, p. 284 (ed. Zettersteen [Leiden, 1905]; ET in Bewley, *Men of Madina*, vol. 2, p. 240).

[126] Ibn Saʿd, *Kitāb al-ṭabaqāt al-kabīr*, vol. 5, p. 244 (ed. Zettersteen). Cf. Andrae, 'Zuhd und Mönchtum,' p. 299.

[127] Ibn al-Jawzī, *Sīrat wa-manāqib ʿUmar b. ʿAbd al-Azīz* (ed. N. Zarzūr) (Beirut, 1984), p. 210. Cf. Andrae, 'Zuhd und Mönchtum,' p. 301.

[128] The monastery was called ܐܒܪܘܢܬܐ. See *Chronicle to 846*, p. 234 (ed. Brooks [CSCO Syr. III.4]). Yāqūt, *Muʿjam al-buldān*, vol. 2, p. 517, has the story of ʿUmar buying a spot to be buried in Dayr Simʿān, as well as poetry connecting him to the place. Another place ʿUmar was said to be buried was Dayr Murrān near Kafar Ṭāb (p. 534), as was the monastery Dayr al-Naqīra near al-Maʿarra. For a survey of Muslim traditions about ʿUmar's death and burial in a monastery—often associated with Dayr Simʿān, see J. Nasrallah, 'Le couvent de Saint Siméon l'alépin. Témoignages littéraires et jalons sur l'histoire,' *PdO* 1 (1970), pp. 348–52. See, too, A. Borrut, *Entre mémoire et pouvoir: l'espace syrien sous les derniers Omeyyades et les premiers Abbassides (v. 72-193/692-809)* (Leiden/Boston, 2011), pp. 304–305. I am grateful to Dina Boero and Adam Bursi for this last reference.

[129] See Yarbrough, 'Did ʿUmar b. ʿAbd al-ʿAzīz Issue an Edict concerning non-Muslim Officials?' p. 185.

[130] Yāqūt, *Muʿjam al-buldān*, vol. 2, pp. 507, 519 and cf. al-Balādhurī, *Kitāb futūḥ al-buldān*, p. 129 (ed. de Goeje).

[131] Yāqūt, *Muʿjam al-buldān*, vol. 2, p. 533.

[132] Yāqūt, *Muʿjam al-buldān*, vol. 2, p. 500, cf. p. 538.

Monastery of the Castrates (*dayr al-khiṣyān*) in the Balqa valley between Damascus and Jerusalem received its name when Sulaymān b. ʿAbd al-Malik, who was staying there, heard a man praising the beauty of one of his female slaves; in response, the Umayyad prince had the man castrated there at the monastery.[133]

RELIGIOUS CONVERSION, RELIGIOUS INERTIA

When combined with the reality that the formerly Roman Middle East was a region populated with simple Christians, the attitudes (at least among some Muslims) that we have seen here in the early centuries of Muslim rule—toward Christian holy men, churches, the Eucharist, Baptism, Jesus, and perhaps even the Cross—were such that one could join Muḥammad's community and yet give up little of what one had previously been committed to on a religious level. A person could become a Muslim and yet maintain veneration for many Christian symbols and rituals. One could move into a new house, so to speak, but bring along much of the comfortable furniture from one's previous habitation. This will have been especially true since the level of religious knowledge among the mass of early Muslims, most of whom had joined the Prophet's community through group conversions, will not have been very high, nor had the institutions and texts that eventually became sources of normativity in Islam crystallized, or in some cases, even been born. It is not surprising, for example, that a late seventh- or early eighth-century Greek graffito from Bawit, preceded by a cross and asking the 'Lord God Jesus Christ' for help, speaks of George, the son of Sergius, who has become ʿAbd Allāh ibn ʿAmr, and Moager, who has become Abu Saleen.[134] A recent alternative reading of this graffito, suggests that it should instead be read as referring to a Christian and a Muslim visitor to the monastery where it was found, rather than to two converts.[135] Regardless of which reading is better, either interpretation fits well in the world I have tried to suggest existed—this was a context in which both Chris-

[133] Yāqūt, *Muʿjam al-buldān*, vol. 2, p. 507.

[134] Γεωργις ιεος Σεργιου γενομενου Μαλεκ Αβδαλα ϊεος Αμρου. For this reading, see S. J. Clackson, *Coptic and Greek Texts relating to the Hermopolite Monastery of Apa Apollo* (Oxford, 2000), pp. 23–24.

[135] Γεώργις ἱεὸς Σεργίου γενομένου, μαυλε Αβδηλα ἱεὸς Αμρου Μαογερ ἱεὸς Ηεγλαν γενομένου ἀπὸ Σαλεεν. For this reading, see J.-L. Fournet, 'Conversion religieuse dans un graffito de Baouit? Revision de *SB* III 6042,' in A. Boud'hors et al., eds., *Monastic Estates in Late Antique and Early Islamic Egypt: Ostraca, Papryi, and Essays in Memory of Sarah Clackson (P. Clackson)*, (Cincinnati, 2009), pp. 141–47 (picture of the graffito on p. 141). Note that Fournet suggests (p. 146) the possibility that the graffito should be dated prior to 685 and that the ʿAbd Allāh b. Amr it refers to is the son of ʿAmr b. al-ʿĀṣ.

tian converts to Islam and Muslims might show veneration for Jesus and also for the Cross.

Continuing to maintain ties to the Christian community and to avail oneself of Christian symbols and rituals will have been common in an environment where conversion occurred for a variety of reasons, most of them having little to do with doctrinal conviction or intense inner spiritual experience. A later period provides an interesting anecdote that we might consider in this regard. Yaḥyā b. Saʿīd reported that in AH 411 (= AD 1021) a group of Muslims complained on a number of occasions to the Fatimid caliph al-Ḥākim that Christians were meeting and praying and celebrating the Eucharist in their houses and 'present with them was a group of Christians who had converted to Islam and they were participating in the taking of the Eucharist.' Al-Ḥākim, Yaḥyā noted, did not disapprove of this and ignored those who were making the denunciations.[136] Previously, in AH 404 (= AD 1013), when al-Ḥākim permitted Jews and Christians in Egypt and Syria to emigrate to Byzantine territory in safety, a great number of Christians who had previously converted to Islam as a result of his policies emigrated to Laodicea, Antioch, and other Byzantine-controlled areas.[137] It would not be surprising if, prior to this emigration, these converts had maintained many of the practices and even beliefs that they had held before their conversion to Islam.

We find indications that precisely the sorts of behaviors we saw in the Ottoman examples at the beginning of this chapter were going on also in the earliest period of Muslim rule. At one point in the *Life* of Theodota, we meet the holy man going up into his pulpit and ordering that money be given to help ransom captives. 'Our Lord was giving zeal to their hearts,' we are told, 'and they were fulfilling His commandment, Christians along with Hagarenes (*mhaggrāyē*).'[138] Since the *Life* of Theodota usually refers to Arabs as *ṭayyāyē*, the use of *mhaggrāyē* here has led Andrew Palmer to suggest that the phrase refers to Christian converts to Islam.[139] If his hypothesis is correct, it constitutes

[136] Yaḥyā b. Saʿīd, *Kitāb al-dhayl*, p. 64 (ed. I. Kratchkovsky, *Histoire de Yahya-ibn-Saʿīd d'Antioche* [PO 47.2] [Turnhout, 1997]; FT by F. Micheau and G. Troupeau at p. 65). On converts to Islam continuing as crypto-Christians, see Cook, 'Apostasy from Islam,' p. 253–54, esp. nn. 18–19.

[137] Yaḥyā b. Saʿīd, *Kitāb al-dhayl*, p. 311 (ed. and trans. I. Kratchkovsky and A. Vasiliev, *Histoire de Yahya-ibn-Saʿīd d'Antioche, continuateur de Saʿīd-ibn-Bitriq* [PO 23.3] [Paris, 1932]). For Muslim converts to Christianity escaping to monasteries—in Wadi Natrun or near the Red Sea—for safety, see Mikhail, *From Byzantine to Islamic Egypt*, p. 67.

[138] St. Mark's Jerusalem 199, fol. 557b. Syriac text in Mardin 275/8, p. 554 (the Syriac text can also be found in *SBI*, p. 471, n. 1123).

[139] A. Palmer, 'The Garshūnī Version of the Life of Theodotos of Amida,' *PdO* 16 (1990–1991), p. 256, suggests that *mhaggrāyē* may mean 'those who have become sons of Hagar.' In other words, he believes that *mhaggrāyē* in this text 'means converts to Islam,' since Muslims are referred to as *ṭayyāyē* (personal communication). See also, Palmer, 'Āmīd in the Seventh-Century Syriac Life of Theodūṭē,' pp. 125–26,

evidence for Christian renegades attending church services and following the orders of Christian leaders. Similarly, the *Life* also reports that 'Hagarenes (*mhaggrāyē*), heretics and the Orthodox feared [Theodota], and everything that he would command, they were receiving joyfully.'[140]

A homily by Pseudo-Theophilus of Alexandria, perhaps written in the late seventh or early eighth century—that is, almost exactly contemporary to the composition of the *Life* of Theodota—is also very suggestive in this regard. The homily includes a dialogue between Athanasius the Great and St. Peter and alludes to Christians who have converted to Islam in a way that possibly implies they were trying to maintain some connections to their former religious practices and community: 'A Christian who has left Christianity and walks and mixes with the nations in their faith has no part with the Christians [just] because he, too, has been baptized,' the homily has Athanasius affirm. Were some renegades pointing to their baptism as grounds for keeping a connection to the Christian church? If this was the case, the homily plainly attempts to shut the door after them and not let them back in: 'When they have confessed Christ in their hearts,' Athanasius asks St. Peter, 'but they do not confess him with their mouths on account of fear of people, will it be forgiven them or not?' What should those remaining in the Christian community make of those who still regard themselves as Christians but who outwardly behave as non-Christians? Peter dismissed such people:

> The Lord Jesus has said, 'The one who denies me before people, I will deny before my Father who is in heaven and all the angels' [cf. Matthew 10:33]. There will be, O Athanasius, a time on the earth [in which] many will deny their faith in Christ and they will mix with the nations and they will say, 'We worship God the Father,' and they do not have the Son [because] they seek ease for their bodies for a short period, but their souls have inherited the everlasting fire that will never be extinguished for eternity.[141]

The phenomenon of Christians continuing previous religious practices after their conversion to Islam, which can be seen so clearly in the Ottoman period,

---

where he discusses this issue and writes, 'I shall preserve this uncertainty in translation by writing Muslims/converts to Islam.'

[140] St. Mark's Jerusalem 199, fol. 557b. The Syriac text in Mardin 275/8, p. 555 is lacunose, and needs to be restored on the basis of the Karshūnī translation. (The Syriac text can also be found in *SBI*, p. 472, n. 1125).

[141] Ps.-Theophilus of Alexandria, *Homily on SS Peter and Paul*, p. 397 (ed. H. Fleisch, *ROC* 30 (1935-1936); FT at p. 396. Translation made with reference to *errata* in Fleisch, *Mélanges de l'université Saint Joseph* 28 (1948–1950), pp. 351–52. On this text and its dating, see J. van Lent's article, 'The Arabic Homily of Pseudo-Theophilus of Alexandria,' in *CMR*, vol. 1, pp. 256–60, and van Lent, 'Réactions coptes au défi de l'Islam: L'Homélie de Théophile d'Alexandrie en l'honneur de Saint Pierre e de Saint Paul,' in A. Boud'Hors and C. Louis, eds., *Études coptes XIII: quinzième journée d'études* (Paris, 2015), pp. 133–48.

was there from the beginning; we are dealing with a case of turtles all the way down.[142]

DOCTRINE VS. PRACTICE?

A final caveat should be appended to this discussion of conversion: doctrine and practice should not be set too strictly against one another. Properly understanding the religious landscape we are dealing with requires that we constantly keep before us all points on the spectrum of theological awareness and engagement; this means acknowledging that doctrine was important for some people and played a role in some conversions. For instance: the author of the anonymous *Chronicle of Zuqnin*, who seems to have written his work over the course of the years spanning 743 to 775, spoke bitterly of a large number of Christians converting to Islam in the later part of the eighth century. He understood leaving Christianity as an abandonment of Jesus, Baptism, the Myron, and the Eucharist—in other words, it was a matter of giving up a particular set of symbols and rituals.[143] Later in the same text, however, the author described the act of Christian apostasy not just in terms of the rejection of symbols, but also in doctrinal terms: Christian renegades who were going over to Islam were portrayed as professing a new, lower Christology, denying Christ's divinity, and describing him in Qur'ānic language as a Prophet and the Word and Spirit of God.[144] In this text, when a deacon from the region of Edessa decides to convert, the *Chronicle* has him approach an Arab and explicitly affirm the Prophethood of Muḥammad and deny the divinity of Christ.[145] Here was a conversion in which the explicit rejection of Christian teaching was important.

The dramatic nature of such an account, however, should not cause us to forget what I have previously attempted to show—it is not clear that all who called themselves Christians in the seventh or eighth centuries necessarily had a consciously high, orthodox Christology to begin with or, in fact, even a

[142] It was likely there for non-Christian converts as well. In the ninth century, al-Kindī spoke of the convert who 'claimed Islam verbally with his tongue while in his heart there is still a certain sickness from his Judaism or Magianism' (*Apology*, p. 150).

[143] *Zuqnin Chronicle*, pp. 381–82 (ed. Chabot [CSCO 104: SS 53]; translation in A. Harrak, *The Chronicle of Zuqnīn*, pp. 321–22. For the date of the *Chronicle of Zuqnin*'s composition, see Harrak, *The Chronicle of Zuqnīn*, p. 31).

[144] *Zuqnin Chronicle*, p. 389 (ed. Chabot [CSCO 104: SS 53]; translation in Harrak, *The Chronicle of Zuqnīn*, p. 327).

[145] *Zuqnin Chronicle*, p. 390 (ed. Chabot [CSCO 104: SS 53]; an English translation is available in Harrak, *The Chronicle of Zuqnīn*, p. 328). On these incidents from the *Zuqnin Chronicle*, cf. also Chapter 11, n. 156.

consciously low one—the affirmations of creedal formulae aside, in practice they may not have had any detailed Christology apart from a belief in a glorified and powerful Jesus who had a unique and special relationship to God and was able to answer prayers and petitions. And although Muslims professed belief in a non-divine Jesus, their Jesus was still an exalted one, born of a Virgin and called the Word of God.[146]

Another apologetic story embedded in the *sīra* can serve to illustrate this point. With most of the young community of Muslims reportedly having fled across the Red Sea to Abyssinia in order to escape the persecution of the Quraysh, two Qurashīs came after them and sought to cause problems for them with the Negus in order to have them sent back to Mecca. Their point of attack was Christ: these Muslims, the Negus was told, say awful things about Jesus. Summoned to give an account of Muslim beliefs, Jaʿfar b. Abī Ṭālib gave a summary of the Qur'ān's Christology: 'We say about him that which our prophet brought, saying, he is the slave of God, and His apostle, and His spirit and His word, which He cast into Mary the blessed virgin.' The Negus was duly impressed: '[He] took a stick from the ground and said, 'By God, Jesus, son of Mary, does not exceed what you have said by the length of this stick.'[147] Such stories were clearly circulated with Christians, ex-Christians, and Muslims living among Christians in mind, and if we presume the ubiquity of belief that church leaders would have considered aberrant among the simple Christians of the Middle East, the shift to Islam by such Christians living under Arab Muslim rule may perhaps not have been much of a shift at all. To Christians like Simeon's goat herders, such a high, though not divine, view of Jesus may not have struck them as particularly problematic.[148]

Again, a period a bit later than our own can offer us help us in understanding the ideological dynamics that were no doubt at work from a very early point. In a text popular among both Copts and Melkites, known as the *Kitāb al-īḍāḥ*, or 'Book of Illumination,' and traditionally ascribed to the tenth-

[146] For an argument that the Qur'ān does not deny the crucifixion of Jesus, but that this notion is the result of the readings of later exegetes, see Reynolds, 'The Muslim Jesus: Dead or Alive?'

[147] Ibn Hishām, *Kitāb sīrat rasūl Allāh*, pp. 220–21 (ed. Wüstenfeld, vol. 1.1; ET taken from Guillaume, *The Life of Muhammad*, p. 152. I have slightly altered Guillaume's capitalizations).

[148] Paradoxically, we should also remember that the presence of Christians, Jews, Zoroastrians, and other converts in prominent positions among the Ghulāt has been proposed as an explanation for some of these 'extremist' Islamic views; see M. Hodgson's article 'Ghulāt,' in *EI2*, vol. 2, pp. 1093–95, especially his comments on p. 1094. As Hodgson notes, Goldziher pointed out long ago that the idea of a light that passed down through generations of prophets, from Adam to Muḥammad, is a notion that appears in the Pseudo-Clementine *Homilies*; see 'Neuplatonische und gnostiche Elemente im Ḥadīṯ,' *Zeitschrift für Assyriologie* 22 (1909), p. 337. On this notion, cf. also Uri Rubin's article, 'Nūr Muḥammadī,' in *EI2*, vol. 8, p. 125, and also U. Rubin, 'Pre-existence and Light: Aspects of the Concept of Nūr Muḥammad,' *Israel Oriental Studies* 5 (1975), pp. 62–119, esp. p. 108.

century Coptic bishop Severus ibn al-Muqaffaʿ, the author, perhaps actually writing in the early eleventh century, spoke of the level of knowledge of the doctrine of the Trinity to be found among Christians of his day. It was not good. 'I say that the reason for the concealment of this mystery from believers in this time,' he wrote

> is their mixing with foreigners (*ajānib*) and the loss of their original Coptic language by which they used to know their way of believing. It has come to the point that they do not hear mention of the Trinity among themselves, save only a bit, and 'Son of God' has no mention among them save metaphorically. Instead, what they mostly hear is that God is unique and everlasting (*fard ṣamad*) and the rest of the way of speaking that the others use. And so the believers have grown accustomed to it and been brought up with it so that it has become the case that it is difficult for them to mention 'Son of God' and 'Son of the Virgin Mary.' They think that His beginning was from the Virgin Mary, just as the others suppose that we say, and they do not know that he was eternally with God, begotten from him before Mary and before the ages.[149]

The author of the *Kitāb al-īḍāḥ* assigned part of the blame for peoples' poor understanding of the Trinity to the shift from Coptic to Arabic, but it is not obvious that simple Christians ever had a strong understanding of the Trinity in any language: John Chrysostom, as we saw in Chapter 1, speaking in Greek to native Greek speakers, not long after the doctrine of the Trinity had reached its classic articulation, in Greek, even explicitly stated that he did not dwell at length on certain aspects of Trinitarian teaching so as not to confuse people.[150] What we have is one of the consequences of a world that was largely illiterate, under-catechized, and served by priests who likely had only a weak theological formation. In such contexts, we should not be astonished if sophisticated doctrines fell prey to easy misunderstanding and critique, or if Christians themselves, as (Ps-) Severus complained, came to have Islamic understandings of Christian doctrines rather than the traditional Christian understandings of those doctrines.[151]

[149] (Ps.-?) Severus b. al-Muqaffaʿ, *Kitāb al-Īḍāḥ*, p. 10–11 (ed. Murqus Jirjis, *al-Durr al-thamīn fī īḍāḥ al-dīn* [Cairo, n.d.]; my translation, made with reference to the ET in M. Swanson, 'The Specifically Egyptian Context of a Coptic Arabic Text: Chapter Nine of the *Kitāb al-Īḍāḥ* of Sawīrūs ibn al-Muqaffaʿ,' *Medieval Encounters* 2 (1996), p. 216. Swanson's translation is based on manuscript witnesses that are superior to the published uncritical edition that I have used). For the reading *ḥunafāʾ* (i.e., Muslims) rather than *ajānib* (foreigners) in this passage, see also S. J. Davis, *Coptic Christology in Practice: Incarnation and Divine Participation in Late Antique and Medieval Egypt* (Oxford/New York, 2008), p. 202, n. 3. On this text, see M. Swanson's article in *CMR*, vol. 3, pp. 265–69.

[150] See chapter 1, n. 79.

[151] And even here, I should note that I use 'traditional' in the sense of being in accord with views

For simple Christians in such a world, if becoming a Muslim would have meant only the abjuration of certain doctrines, like the Trinity, which were only partially understood, or not understood at all and therefore incompletely believed (if at all), and which, moreover, played no part in their lives, and if, at the same time, conversion held out the possibility of maintaining adherence to many familiar and cherished Christian symbols and rituals while escaping certain economic burdens or possibly gaining social benefits, then the change that becoming a Muslim presented would have been potentially as attractive as it was small—which is to say, very.[152]

We should be careful, too, not to let our understanding of the ease with which simple Christians could transition into an ideologically thin (for most of its adherents) Islam be obscured by the sources we have, which tend to valorize and champion individuals who refused to convert, or who came back to Christianity once they had converted. Such individuals are the exceptions that prove the rule. The long-term religious demographic trend of the region shows that they were quite a small minority in terms of their attitude towards

articulated by the great councils of the fourth century, rather than what most Christians have actually believed. It should also be added that mass literacy is, of course, no guarantor of widespread theological literacy. Polls done of Christians in the United States commonly find widespread ignorance of basic traditional Christian doctrines. For example, a recent survey found that 74% of American Evangelical Christians agreed with the statement, 'Jesus is the first and greatest being created by God.' See 'Our Favorite Heresies,' *Christianity Today* 60.9 (November 2016), p. 19. In the ninth century, the idea that Christ's divine nature died on the Cross (in addition to his human nature) spread among large numbers of Christians in Upper Egypt, including their bishops: *History of the Patriarchs of Alexandria*, pp. 20–21 (ed. and trans. Y. 'Abd al-Masīh, O.H.E. Burmester, and Antoine Khater, *History of the Patriarchs of the Egyptian Chruch* [Cairo, 1943], vol. 2.1, pp. 29–30 [ET]). Pointing to this incident, Maged Mikhail noted, 'A pervasive belief in such a nonsensical doctrine betrays a Christian population only marginally aware of Christian principles.' See *From Byzantine to Islamic Egypt*, pp. 73–74, for discussion of this anecdote.

[152] Cf. the similar observations in Mikhail, *From Byzantine to Islamic Egypt*, pp. 74–75. There is also, it should be noted, the possibility that by this point one should consider doctrines such as the Trinity and the Incarnation not only as sets of propositions, but also as symbols themselves—the idea that Jesus was equally divine with God the Father was something that had been debated and attacked for many centuries by the time of the Arab conquests, and the doctrine of the Trinity, too, had been the subject of fierce controversy. If we regard the Trinity and the Incarnation as having achieved the status of symbols by the period of Muslim rule, then conversion to Islam would have required jettisoning these important symbols. But, while there is no place in traditional Islamic thought for belief in the Trinity, there is, nevertheless, room for understanding Jesus as a powerful and important—albeit nondivine—figure. In practical terms, this veneration of Christ would have made the conversion from Christianity to Islam perhaps less dramatic, in terms of specific religious attitudes and behaviors, than one might *prima facie* expect. A modern parallel might be helpful here: an American Evangelical who converts to Mormonism will, formally at least, at the doctrinal level, have made a radical shift in terms of his or her triadology and Christology. But in practice, much of his or her beliefs about God and Christ likely will not have changed much—indeed, most Christians, Evangelical and non-, have no idea what triadology even refers to.

conversion. Anastasius of Sinai, for instance, described in a few lines the unsuccessful attempt of local Arab Christians to fight off 'Saracen' invaders at Mt. Sinai in the middle part of the seventh century; when it became clear that they could not hold off the mass of Muslims, they made a treaty with them and 'believed with them,' i.e., converted.

Anastasius, however, focused most of his attention on the one Arab Christian there who sought to flee through a precipitous and dangerous area 'choosing rather for himself the death of the body than to give up the faith of Christ and be in spiritual danger.' Before he could flee, the man's wife stopped him, weeping, and pleaded with him 'in the Arabic language' to offer her and their children up as sacrifices to God, as Abraham had done, rather than letting them stay to fall into the hands of 'these wolves.' Before his flight, therefore, the man took out a sword and killed his wife and children to spare them a forced conversion to Islam.[153]

The dramatic nature of such a story should not distract us from what is most historically significant in the narrative: the other Arab Christians apparently did convert upon their capitulation to the Muslim army. In Michael the Great's account of the forced conversion of five thousand Christian Arabs from the tribe of Tanūkh, only one—a man named Layth—suffered martyrdom.[154] We have no solid evidence as to what Islam would have meant or looked like to such Christian converts (or indeed, for the members of the Muslim army they fought), but my argument has been that very little actually changed—or to put it slightly differently, much remained the same—for them religiously once they did become Muslims. Did they hold to some or many of their previous Christian ways?

It would be surprising if they did not: the Jabaliyya Bedouin are the tribe that has traditionally protected St. Catherine's Monastery in the Sinai, and they claim descent in part from Roman soldiers sent there in the sixth century by Justinian. As late as 1517, there were still Christians among the Jabaliyya, and it was not until 1750 that the last Christian Jabaliyya—a woman—died.[155] As recently as the nineteenth and early twentieth centuries, European visitors to the Sinai noted that the Jabaliyya, though Muslim, made use of the Cross in a variety of ways: in their clothing, on tombstones, in circumcision ceremonies, and in religious processions, among other contexts. When the German

[153] Anastasius of Sinai, *Narrations Beneficial for the Soul* II.8 (ed. Bingelli, pp. 1.226–228 = 2.540–543 [FT] [=§41 in Nau, ed., 'Le texte grec des récits utiles à l'âme d'Anastase (le Sinaïte),' pp. 87–88]; French summary available in Nau, 'Les récits inédits du moine Anastase,' p. 129–132). ET available in Caner, *History and Hagiography from the Late Antique Sinai*, pp. 196–199.

[154] Michael the Great, *Chronicle* 12.1 (ed. Chabot, 4.478–79 = 3.1).

[155] For the Jabaliyya's conversion to Islam, see J. J. Hobbs, *Mount Sinai* (Austin, 1995), p. 159.

scholar Constantine von Tischendorf visited the Sinai in the 1840s, he was amazed to find Muslim Jabaliyya attending and taking part in the liturgy of Pentecost at the monastery. As recently as the late twentieth century, members of the tribe would pray before icons in the monastery.[156]

AN ECUMENICAL MONOTHEIST MOVEMENT?

The evidence I have adduced in this chapter should not be taken to mean that I am arguing for the emergence in seventh-century Arabia of some sort of ideologically motivated monotheistic ecumenism that later disappeared and was replaced by what we now call 'Islam.' Here it should be emphasized that a number of factors could have caused a receptivity to people who belonged to other religious traditions, even rival and competing ones: religious indifference and ignorance of one's own tradition; sheer pragmatism that grew from everyday human interaction; the realities of governing an empire that was overwhelmingly non-Muslim; and, in the case of a political elite that was made up of Muḥammad's staunchest opponents and their descendants, a possible lack of deep religious commitment and conviction. Though in practical terms, an openness that resulted from a receptivity rooted in one (or some combination) of these is much the same as that which would have stemmed from a consciously inclusive ideology, we should not mistake an inclusiveness that stemmed from the first set of factors with an openness that grew from an explicitly ecumenical ideology.

For this reason, the image of an 'ecumenical' early Islam, such as has recently been advocated,[157] is unpersuasive. Insofar as this new perspective points to instances of Christian-Muslim boundary crossing, congenial interreligious attitudes, and shared activities, it is helpful in opening up our understanding of the religious possibilities of the seventh and eighth centuries. But pushed too far, such an image ultimately mistakes symptoms for causes by attributing the consequences of the factors I have emphasized in this book to a top-down ideology of religiously motivated tolerance.[158] As we have

[156] For all these examples, see Hobbs, *Mount Sinai*, p. 162.

[157] Donner, *Muhammad and the Believers*; Donner, 'From Believers to Muslims: Confessional Self-Identity in the Early Islamic Community,' *al-Abhath* 50–51 (2002–2003), pp. 9–53; Donner, 'Muhammad und die frühe islamische Gemeinschaft aus historischer Sicht,' *Asia* 68 (2014), pp. 439–51; and Penn, *Envisioning Islam*, pp. 142–82.

[158] Any view of an 'ecumenical' Believers movement or of an Islam that is not religiously distinct from Christianity or Judaism in the seventh century also has to explain pieces of evidence that suggest the ideology underpinning Muḥammad's community, even in this period, could be decidedly particular, sectarian, and critical of both Judaism and Christianity. So, for instance, the Qur'ān criticizes the Chris-

seen, however, many of the same behaviors that can be pointed to as occurring between Christians and Muslims in the early period of Arab rule can also be seen in the relations between different Christian confessional groups in the post-Chalcedonian world. And such behaviors continued to occur in the Middle East throughout the Middle Ages. So far as intergroup relations were concerned, the seventh century was not a unique moment in Middle Eastern interconfessional interaction in the first millennium AD. It was utterly typical.

Like traditional approaches to Christian-Muslim relations, which have focused heavily on doctrinal matters such as the Trinity and the Incarnation, the notion of an 'ecumenical' early Islam, too, is one-dimensional and lacking in texture. It does not acknowledge the layering of knowledge that characterizes religious communities, nor does it take into account the consequences of such a layering. Rather than assuming, as many traditional approaches implicitly do, that all Christians and Muslims in the seventh and eighth centuries were maximally informed about and concerned with this or that matter of theological speculation, such an approach assumes that all Muslims in this period were maximally informed about the content and implication of the Prophet's message and takes as reflective of the actual nature of what Muḥammad taught behaviors that can more easily be explained by factors such as mass conversion, religious ignorance, selective religious regard, or religious indifference.

---

tian belief in the divinity of Jesus (5:116) and has Jesus tell Christians he wanted them to worship God (5:117). It orders Christians to not speak of 'three' when speaking of God and criticizes the idea that God might have offspring (4:171). It also calls speaking of Christ as divine disbelief (5:72); calls speaking of God as three unbelief and promises painful torture for those who persist in doing so (5:73); calls Christ only an apostle (5:75); denies that he was killed or crucified (4:157); criticizes Christians for calling Jesus the Son of God and Jews for calling Ezra the Son of God (9:30); accuses rabbis and monks of blocking people from the path of God (9:34); and states that those who pursue a religion other than Islam will be counted among the losers in the next life (3:85). The Children of Israel are accused of distorting Scripture and forgetting some of what they have been told (5:13; cf. 4:46, 5:41); Christians have also forgotten some of what they have been reminded of and God has caused dissension among them (5:14). Moreover, the Qur'ānic Messenger has come in part to clarify what the People of the Book have hidden in their Scriptures (5:15). The People of the Book are portrayed as skeptical, asking Muḥammad to bring a Scripture down from heaven (4:153), and members of the Prophet's community are told they will surely hear much abuse from those already in possession of a Scripture and from those who associate with God (3:186). Those who believe are ordered not to take Jews or Christians as allies (5:51). If the People of the Book had believed, the Qur'ān affirms, it would have been good for them; only a few believe, however, and most do not (3:110; cf. 3:199, 4:155, 5:66).

Outside the Qur'ān, an ecumenical hypothesis needs to account for mid-seventh-century reports of Arab hostility to the Cross (see n. 83 and cf. also n. 84 in this chapter); the mid-seventh-century report that in the early 660s Mu'āwiya tried unsuccessfully to remove crosses from coins (n. 91 in this chapter); and the mid-to-late-seventh-century report that Mu'āwiya wrote to Constans II, calling on him to abandon Christianity and turn from Jesus to worship the God of Abraham (see Thomson, trans., *The Armenian History attributed to Sebeos*, vol. 1, p. 144).

But an explicit ideology of religious tolerance, just like one of explicit religious intolerance—or any religious doctrine for that matter—is something that needs to be imparted and transmitted, and it can only, therefore, be as effective as the catechetical institutions of a religious community. If, for the sake of argument, it is granted that the Prophet's original message was one of tolerant and inclusive monotheism, the question of the extent to which most members of his community will have known about and internalized this message and used it as the basis for personal conduct will persist; for the challenges of catechesis in a community that was largely comprised of mass converts and simple adherents will also persist, regardless of whatever it is one wants to argue the Prophet's original message actually was. We should additionally remember that a top-down tolerance is not the same thing as the sort of informal, ad hoc, and everyday acts of co-existence that inevitably spring up in contexts where people live side-by-side and are poorly instructed in religious teachings that might otherwise negatively affect and discourage normal human interaction. Saying that the early medieval Middle East was a world of simple believers is not the same as saying that it was a world of Believers who had consciously articulated views of religious inclusion toward other monotheists and a strict code of personal piety, or that, following certain models of the Christian-Jewish 'parting of the ways,' it would take two to three centuries before Christianity and Islam came to have distinct boundaries in the Middle East.[159] Again, the sorts of behaviors found in this chapter are in fact to be found throughout Middle Eastern history, into the present day,[160] and scholars working on later periods have spoken of 'rough tolerance' and 'folk toleration' to describe them.[161] What we are dealing with is something different from a doctrinally inspired tolerance that is preached and taught by religious authorities.[162]

[159] Penn, *Envisioning Islam*, p. 182.

[160] See, e.g., the description of the Coptic moulid of Mār Barsūm in Upper Egypt in J. W. McPherson, *The Moulids of Egypt (Egyptian Saints-Days)* (Cairo, 1941), pp. 170–73, esp. p. 173, where McPherson describes Muslim participation in the moulid. For a more recent example, one can point to the large numbers of Muslims regularly attending and seeking exorcisms at exorcism services held at the Kanīsa al-Murqusiyya in el-Azbakeya and the church of St. Simeon in Mokattam/Ḥayy al-Zabbalīn in today's Cairo (I am thankful to Mourad Takawi for bringing this to my attention).

[161] For 'rough tolerance,' see C. MacEvitt, *The Crusades and the Christian World of the East: Rough Tolerance* (Philadelphia, 2008), pp. 21–25; for 'folk toleration,' see Grehan, *Twilight of the Saints*, pp. 181–87.

[162] For an example of a nonelitist history of religious toleration, 'from below,' see S. B. Schwartz, *All Can Be Saved: Religious Tolerance and Salvation in the Iberian Atlantic World* (New Haven/London, 2008).

Rather than ask what happened when Christians first met Muslims,[163] we should first ask which (and what kind of) Christians were meeting which (and what kind of) Muslims, and we must recognize that, in a world where most religious believers belonged to the 'simple,' any 'ecumenical' behavior should not astonish. It should rather be expected. It is precisely what we saw happening in Chapter 3 when we looked at some of the consequences of Chalcedon. In a context, too, where Muslims held political authority, examples of 'ecumenical' behavior should also be viewed against the background of potential violence stemming from asymmetries of power: a Christian refusal to indulge a Muslim's efforts at availing himself of this or that Christian resource could result in injury or even death for the Christian.[164] Such considerations, in addition to a layered perspective on religious communities, offer a more plausible explanation of our evidence for early Christian-Muslim interactions.

THE SHAPE OF ISLAM

We return therefore to by-now familiar themes: the various challenges represented by the mass conversion of most members of the Prophet's community in the last few years of his life, the reality that the world the Arabs found was one filled with simple believers, and the sheer presence of demographic super-majorities of non-Muslims in post-conquest, early Muslim-ruled societies. To be satisfying, any account of the nature of early Christian-Muslim relations and the shape Islam eventually came to have must deal squarely with these factors.

In particular, if we do not take seriously the question of how Muslims related to and appropriated the cultural traditions of the large conquered populations

[163] Cf. M. Penn, *When Christians First Met Muslims: A Sourcebook of the Earliest Syriac Writings on Islam* (Oakland, 2015).

[164] See, e.g., the story in Yāqūt, *Muʿjam al-buldān*, vol. 5, p. 538, of the Ḥimṣī poet al-Baṭīn, a contemporary of Abū Nuwās (ca. AH 137–199/AD 754–814). Al-Baṭīn fell ill and was taken to the monastery to be healed. When the monks of the monastery ignored him, he urinated in front of the tomb of the martyr there and died a short time later. The people of Ḥimṣ, Yāqūt reported, 'came to the monastery to tear it down and they said, "A Christian kills a Muslim? We will not accept this unless you hand over to us the bones of the martyr so we can burn them!" And the Christians bribed the emir of Ḥimṣ so that he would remove the mob from them.' This story is likely fictitious—al-Baṭīn is said to have actually died in Alexandria—but it raises a question: If al-Baṭīn had been a Jew, a Magian, or a pagan, would his treatment have triggered a similar response? Not likely. On al-Baṭīn b. Umayya al-Bajalī, see Ibn al-Jarrāḥ, *al-Waraqa*, pp. 10–12 (ed. ʿA. al-Wahhāb ʿAzzām and ʿA. al-Sattār Aḥmad Farrāj [Egypt, 1967]). For the example from Jacob of Edessa's canons of a Muslim husband threatening a priest with murder if the priest refused the Eucharist to the Muslim's Christian wife, see above, n. 74.

they found themselves ruling over by the middle part of the seventh century, our narrative and understanding of early medieval Middle Eastern and Islamic history will be a depressingly familiar one and predictably narrow in its focus: quarrels and battles over booty and succession disputes between different interest groups within a small conquering elite concentrated in only a handful of places. One's mental map of the Middle East will be reduced to Medina, Damascus, Kufa, Basra, and perhaps Khurasan[165]—that is, to the handful of places where Muslims may (or may not) have been in the majority or represented a religious plurality—and one's cast of historical characters will be reduced to the names that appear in Muslim historical chronicles like al-Ṭabarī's, or in this or that biographical dictionary of legal experts or *ḥadīth* transmitters. Much as the post-Chalcedonian world can be easily mistaken for a patristics seminar run amok, the early period of Muslim rule can at times seem to be little more than pious Muslims transmitting accounts of the Prophet's behavior, planting the seeds of an unbelievably rich medieval legal tradition, writing now-lost historical works whose existence scholars today debate and strain to recover, and warring against one another over who should be leader of their community.

But focusing on such issues, however important they may be, will distract us from the massive shift that was happening in Middle Eastern society even as Islam was reaching its classical articulation. In the period after the conquest, we saw in the last chapter, there were likely several hundred thousand Muslims—many, perhaps most of them will little knowledge of the particulars of the Prophet's message—living among perhaps twenty or thirty million non-Muslims. Narrowing our focus to Syria, we find that Ottoman tax registers show that 'in the sixteenth century the Muslim population of Syria formed an overwhelming majority in the countryside and a large majority in most towns and cities.'[166] In other words, by nine hundred or so years after the Arab conquests, most of the population of Syria had become Muslim. A similar transformation happened across the formerly Roman Middle East over the same period. If conversion in the medieval Middle East was not, for the most part, a matter of doctrinal reflection, personal spiritual crisis, or an individualistic quest for meaning, what effect did this massive shift in religious allegiance have on the religion of the Prophet?

To come back now to the factors I have just mentioned: in this period, Muslim religious authorities faced two challenges with respect to the non-

[165] On the geographical biases and limitations of early Muslim sources, see the discussion in P. M. Cobb, 'Community versus Contention: Ibn ʿAsākir and ʿAbbāsid Syria,' in J. E. Lindsay, ed., *Ibn ʿAsākir and Early Islamic History* (Princeton, 2001), pp. 101–106.

[166] Carlson, 'Contours of Conversion,' pp. 791–92.

Muslim heritage of the societies in which they lived. First, Islam was a minority religion, surrounded by ancient and rival communities which, though they were largely comprised of simple believers, nevertheless might include highly sophisticated, very learned figures in their leadership. Second, the Muslim community was one where most members were converts, or the descendants of converts who had joined the Prophet's movement for a variety of reasons, most of them non-doctrinal and most probably having little to do with the spiritual claims of the actual contents of the Prophet's revelation and message.

How might this situation be dealt with? And what did it mean for Islam and for the Middle East that the medieval Muslim community was made up of non-Muslim converts and their descendants?

CHAPTER 13

Finding Their Way

The Mosque in the Shadow of the Church

> You will surely follow the customs (*sunan*) of those who were before you, measure by measure and cubit by cubit, to the point that if they entered into the hole of a lizard, you would enter it. We said, 'O Apostle of God, the Jews and the Christians?' He said, 'Who else?'[1]

Political power over a variety of religious groups and spectacular military success may have influenced how some people viewed the truth of the Prophet's message,[2] but they did not free his followers from the very real task of figuring out how their religious traditions related to those of the people they now ruled over, especially Jews and Christians. These were two groups who had, long before the rise of Islam, developed answers to a whole host of religious questions that Muslims now had also to confront. And the answers, traditions, antiquity, and confidence of these communities meant that though the followers of the Prophet enjoyed political power, in the realm of religion, the communities they ruled over had a certain deep historical experience and authority that Muslims did not. For decades after the Arab conquests, Muslims only needed to look at the images of crosses (or slightly transformed pseudo-crosses) and Roman emperors on the coins they used in formerly Roman territories for a quick reminder of the spiritual history and inertia of the area they now ruled.

What were the consequences of Muslims being a religious minority, and a young one at that? And how did Muslim religious leaders deal with the sort of behaviors we saw in the previous chapter?

RELIGIOUS COMPETITION

One notable result of these circumstances was a need to assert Muslim precedence over non-Muslim alternatives and competitors. I have just mentioned

[1] al-Bukhārī, *al-Jāmiʿ al-ṣaḥīḥ*, vol. 2, p. 492 (no. 3456); the same tradition is related in vol. 4, p. 367 (no. 7320), and a similar one, which speaks in terms of following the Romans and the Persians rather than Jews and Christians, can be found in vol. 4, p. 367, no. 7319. ET also in Guillaume, *Traditions*, p. 135.

[2] Cf. chapter 10, n. 40 and chapter 11, nn. 159–162.

coins, but the ideological and social challenge of older, sophisticated religions would persist in a variety of ways long after 'Abd al-Malik changed the Islamic state's coinage in the late seventh century. Writing in the ninth century, al-Jāḥiẓ gave a number of reasons why ordinary, everyday Muslims held Christians (wrongly, he thought) in high esteem. They had a king (i.e., the Byzantine emperor),[3] there were many Arab Christians, and it was the daughters of Byzantines who were the mothers of Muslim rulers. Christians were dialectical theologians (*mutakallimīn*), physicians, astronomers—which made Muslims view them as intellectuals and wise philosophers. Christians were also the secretaries and chamberlains of authorities and kings, and physicians to aristocrats, among other distinctions. They were wealthy, wore fine clothing, enjoyed refined pastimes, and had servants.[4] Elsewhere, al-Jāḥiẓ would colorfully describe a Muslim doctor who was unable to get work—even in a time of plague—because people preferred Christian physicians to Muslim ones.[5] Al-Jāḥiẓ wrote in a period regarded as one of the highest points of medieval Islamic achievement; it is significant that even in this context Christians enjoyed great social and intellectual prestige and could be viewed as public competitors.[6]

The Christian challenge should come as no surprise, however. The Middle East was a place where, quite literally, the mosque was in the shadow of the Church, or better yet, Churches.[7] In a world where impressive architecture was seen as a religious boon and public symbol of the importance of one's community,[8]— this was certainly how at least some Muslims viewed the mat-

[3] But note that for Lazarus bar Sābtā, the Miaphysite Bishop of Baghdad in the early ninth century (he was deposed in 829), Ethiopia and Iberia represented places with Orthodox (i.e., Miaphysite) kings; see J.-M. Fiey, 'Diptyques Nestoriens du XIVe siècle,' *AB* 81 (1963), p. 407. On Lazarus, see L. van Rompay's article, 'Lo'ozar bar Sobhto' in *GEDSH*, pp. 251–52.

[4] al-Jāḥiẓ, *Fī 'l-radd 'alā al-Naṣārā*, pp. 312–13, 316–17 (an ET is available: J. Finkel, 'A Risāla of al-Jāḥiẓ, *JAOS* 47 [1927], pp. 326–28. A partial translation is available in Pellat, *The Life and Works of Jāḥiẓ*, pp. 87–88). These were all reasons that ordinary Muslims—whom al-Jāḥiẓ refers to (p. 316) as *al-'awāmm* and *al-ṭaghām*—held Christians in higher regard than Jews.

[5] al-Jāḥiẓ, *Kitāb al-bukhalā'* (ed. Ṭ. al-Ḥājirī) (Cairo, 1967), p. 102. FT available in C. Pellat, *Le livre des avares de Ğahiz* (Paris, 1951), pp. 147–48. Cp. with the later complaint of Ibn al-Ukhuwwa that 'many a town has no physician who is not a dhimmī,' and that Muslims devoted themselves to law rather than medicine: see *Ma'ālim al-qurba fī aḥkām al-ḥisba*, p. *166 (ed. Levy; ET at pp. 56-7. I have used the translation of Levy).

[6] Samir, 'Liberté religieuse et propogation de la foi chez les théologiens arabes chrétiens du IXe siècle et en Islam,' pp. 105–111, discusses the sociological status of Christians in the ninth century on the basis of these texts (and others) from al-Jāḥiẓ.

[7] Cf. Griffith, *The Church in the Shadow of the Mosque*, (Princeton/Oxford, 2008).

[8] When the *Zuqnin Chronicle* described the magnificence of the enormous pagan temple in Baalbek, it tied its grandeur to pagan believing: 'Erring pagans, while misled by the strength of this building, were especially proud of it, and slaughtering, vows, and endless burnt sacrifices for demons used to take place continually in this temple. And, indeed, no one was able to destroy it or to bring to an end in it the error of the servants of idols. But God, who saw the deviation and erring of people because of the magnificence of this temple, suddenly kindled fire from heaven in it.... As for all the Christians who

ter, too, and the presence of Churches could pose a problem. 'It is not right,' the Prophet was supposed to have said, 'that there be two *qibla*s in one land';[9] medieval jurists would appeal to this statement when they discussed whether churches and synagogues could be erected in pre-Islamic settlements that had been forcibly conquered by Muslims.[10] The medieval geographer al-Maqdisī (d. AH 380/AD 990?) wrote of how he had once spoken to his paternal uncle, questioning the wisdom of building the Umayyad Mosque in Damascus. The money, he thought, would have been better spent on what today might be termed 'infrastructure projects.' But al-Maqdisī's uncle disagreed.

> Said he: 'You simply do not understand, my dear son. Al-Walīd was absolutely right, and it was open to him to do a worthy work. For he saw that Syria was a country settled by the Christians, and he noted there their churches so handsome with their enchanting decorations, renowned far and wide, such as are the Qumāma,[11] and the churches of Ludd (Lydda) and al-Ruhā [Edessa]. So he undertook for the Muslims the building of a mosque that would divert their attention from the churches, and make it one of the wonders of the world. Do you not realize how 'Abd al-Malik, seeing the greatness of the dome of the Qumāma and its splendour, fearing lest it should beguile the hearts of the Muslims, hence erected, above the Rock, the dome you now see there?'[12]

Whatever the cultic purpose of the Dome of the Rock, the polemical intent of many of its inscriptions vis-à-vis Christianity is clear.[13] Christians, too, re-

---

saw or heard about what had happened to that temple, they rejoiced and exulted, while marveling at this sign of wonder that God had performed' (pp. 130, 131 [ed. Chabot [CSCO 104: SS 53]; ET taken from Harrak, *The Chronicle of Zuqnīn*, p. 127).

[9] al-Tirmidhī, *al-Jāmiʿ al-kabīr*, vol. 3, p. 20 (no. 633). For other versions of this *ḥadīth*, see A. J. Wensinck, J.P. Mensing, and J. Brugman, *Concordance et indices de la tradition musulmane*, vol. 5 (Leiden, 1965), p. 263.

[10] Cf. Ibn Qayyim al-Jawziyya, *Aḥkām ahl al-dhimma*, vol. 2, p. 130.

[11] That is, the *Qiyāma*, or Church of the Resurrection (Anastasis). Qumāmā means 'dunghill.' For another example of this pejorative and mocking usage, see, e.g., Ibn Taymiyya, *Majmūʿat al-fatāwā*, vol. 27, p. 12, and for more on the Muslim practice of referring to the Church of the Resurrection (*Kanīsat al-qiyāma*) as the *Qumāma*, see K.A.C. Creswell, *Early Muslim Architecture: Umayyads, Early ʿAbbāsids and Ṭūlūnids*. Part One: *Umayyads. AD 622–750* (Oxford, 1932), p. 24.

[12] al-Maqdisī, *Kitāb aḥsan al-taqāsīm fī maʿrifat al-aqālīm*, p. 159 (ed. M. J. de Goeje, 2nd ed. [Leiden, 1906]; ET taken from B. A. Collins, *The Best Divisions for Knowledge of the Regions: A Translation of* Ahsan al-Taqasim fi Maʿrifat al-Aqalim [Reading, 1994], p. 146). For this quote, see Creswell, *Early Muslim Architecture*, vol. 1, p. 101. On al-Maqdisī, see A. Miquel's article, 'al-Muḳaddasī,' in *EI2*, vol. 7, pp. 492–93.

[13] For the anti-Christian (and other) inscriptions, see C. Kessler, 'Abd al-Malik's Inscription on the Dome of the Rock: A Reconsideration,' *Journal of the Royal Asiatic Society of Great Britain and Ireland* 1 (1970), pp. 2–14. An ET is available in Hoyland, *Seeing Islam*, pp. 696–99, and Donner, *Muhammad and the Believers*, pp. 234–35.

membered Umayyad construction in terms of religious competition, but they interpreted caliphal actions less charitably than al-Maqdisī's uncle had. Writing in the early ninth century, Theophanes portrayed al-Walīd as jealous of the Christians' attractive structure: 'In this year [AD 706–707],' he wrote, 'Oualid [sc. Walīd] seized the most holy cathedral of Damascus. The wretched man did this out of envy of the Christians, because this church was surpassingly beautiful.'[14] For Michael the Great, al-Walīd was even more sinister: 'This Walīd,' he wrote, 'hated the Christians and uprooted their churches. At first, he tore down the great church which is in Damascus and built in its place a mosque and [then] did the same in many places.'[15]

The element of competition influenced more than just how places of worship were built: it extended to the ritual choices that early Muslims made. Christians and Jews had special days of the week when they would gather for their services, for example, and Muslims would select a day, too—with reference to Christian and Jewish practice. Friday was given as the day of special religious observance, the Prophet is reported to have said, but there was disagreement about that, and for this reason, 'People follow us in this matter. The Jews have tomorrow [Saturday] and the Christians after tomorrow [Sunday].'[16] the question of precedence, chronological, but also theological, played a role here: 'we, the last,' as the Prophet had reportedly prefaced these remarks about the proper day of special religious observance, 'have precedence on the Day of Resurrection even though they were given the Book before us.'[17]

This notion that Muslims had precedence over Christians and Jews extended to everyday manifestations of religion: Maslama b. Mukhallad (d. AH 62/AD 682), al-Maqrīzī informs us, heard the loud wooden clappers (*nawāqīs*) of the Christians of Fusṭāṭ in the night and was not happy. He told Shuraḥbīl b. ʿĀmir (d. 65 AH/AD 684) about his displeasure and Shuraḥbīl extended the length of the *adhān* from midnight to about the time of the first morning prayer (*fajr*), and Maslama forbade the Christians from beating their clappers while the

[14] Theophanes, *Chronicle* AM 6199 (ed. de Boor, vol. 1, pp. 375–76; ET taken from Mango and Scott, *The Chronicle of Theophanes Confessor*, p. 524). For the treatment of churches and monasteries under medieval Muslim rule, see the evidence amassed in A. S. Tritton, *The Caliphs and Their Non-Muslim Subjects: A Critical Study of the Covenant of ʿUmar* (London, 1930), pp. 37–60.

[15] Michael the Great, *Chronicle* 12.17 (ed. Chabot, 4.451 = 2.481).

[16] al-Bukhārī, *al-Jāmiʿ al-ṣaḥīḥ*, vol. 1, p. 280 (no. 876). See also the lengthy report in ʿAbd al-Razzāq, *al-Muṣannaf*, vol. 3, pp. 159–60 (no. 5144). Note also the Prophetic statement (in a report said to be transmitted by Ḥudhayfa), that God had guided Muslims to Friday but led those who were before them (i.e., Jews and Christians), away from it: Muslim b. al-Ḥajjāj, *Ṣaḥīḥ*, vol. 2, p. 586 (no. 23—and compare with the similar report, no. 22, also p. 586). For this report from Muslim and many other parallel references, see the discussion in Ibn Ḥajar al-ʿAsqalānī, *Fatḥ al-bārī bi-sharḥ Ṣaḥīḥ al-Bukhārī*, vol. 2, pp. 353–56.

[17] al-Bukhārī, *al-Jāmiʿ al-ṣaḥīḥ*, vol. 1, p. 280 (no. 876).

adhān was taking place.[18] The drive to show Islamic supremacy even extended beyond religious matters to something as basic as one's dwelling place. In some versions of the 'Pact of 'Umar', Christians promised that they would not look down on Muslims in their houses,[19] an idea that can be glossed by noting that jurists would make the point that a non-Muslim's house was not allowed to be higher than a Muslim's house if they were neighbors.[20] 'Islam is exalted,' the Prophet is supposed to have said, 'and is not topped.'[21]

More profoundly, the presence of non-Muslims could even affect the public face of the ruling Muslim regime. At the level of the religious legitimation of Muḥammad's community, it has been long observed that Muḥammad's prophethood was not publicly proclaimed until the time of the Marwānids, that is, the late seventh century. '[I]t is clear from the context in which [the Marwānids] made their public affirmation of [Muḥammad's] status,' Crone and Hinds observed, 'that they were motivated more by a desire to establish the credentials of Islam over and above other faiths (notably Christianity) than by a wish to emphasise his continuing importance within the Islamic world.'[22] The public display of the Muslim profession of faith in the Marwānid period was possibly affected by the nature of the non-Muslim context as well. In Egypt and Syria, where there were large Christian populations, the *shahāda* included phrases like *lā sharīka lahu*, 'He has no partner,' whereas in the Islamic East such expressions were lacking—perhaps because the Christian presence was not as large.[23] Once confronted with the Christianity of the Fertile Crescent, the categories Muslims used to speak about non-Muslims changed, too. Though the Qur'ān accused Christians of unbelief, it never labeled them *mushrikūn*, or 'associators.' This was a category reserved for the

[18] al-Maqrizī, *al-Mawā'iẓ wa-'l-i'tibār fī dhikr al-khiṭaṭ wa-'l-āthār*, vol. 4.1 (ed. A. Fu'ād Sayyid) (London, 2003), p. 83. Cf. J. Pedersen in *EI2*, vol. 6, p. 676.

[19] *wa-lā nuṭli'u 'alayhum fī manāzilihim*. See, e.g., Ibn Qayyim al-Jawziyya, *Aḥkām ahl al-dhimma*, vol. 2, p. 114.

[20] See the discussion of various views and scenarios in Ibn Qayyim al-Jawziyya, *Aḥkām ahl al-dhimma*, vol. 2, pp. 142–46.

[21] *al-Islām ya'lū wa-lā yu'lā*. al-Dāraquṭnī, *Sunan*, vol. 4, p. 371 (no. 3620) (ed. Sh. Arna'ūṭ, Ḥ. 'Abd al-Mun'im Shalabī, et al. *Sunan al-Dāraquṭnī* [Beirut, 2004]); and al-Bukhārī, *al-Jāmi' al-ṣaḥīḥ*, vol. 1, p. 415 (no. 1353[b] = *Kitāb al-janā'iz*, *bāb* 79). Cf. Ibn Qayyim al-Jawziyya, *Aḥkām ahl al-dhimma*, vol. 2, p. 143. This *ḥadīth* was also used as part of the explanation for why a Muslim female could not marry a male from among the People of the Book; see Ibn Taymiyya, *Majmū'at al-fatāwā*, vol. 32, p. 117 (ed. 'Ā. al-Jazzār and A. al-Bāz [al-Manṣūra, 2005]). For further discussion of this *ḥadīth*, see A. M. Emon, *Religious Pluralism and Islamic Law: Dhimmīs and Others in the Empire of Law* (Oxford, 2012), pp. 127–29, and cf. also, Y. Friedmann, *Tolerance and Coercion in Islam: Interfaith Relations in the Muslim Tradition* (Cambridge, 2003), pp. 113–14.

[22] Crone and Hinds, *God's Caliph*, p. 26.

[23] For this argument, see J. L. Bacharach and S. Anwar, 'Early Versions of the *shahāda*: A Tombstone from Aswan of 71 A.H., the Dome of the Rock, and Contemporary Coinage,' *Der Islam* 89 (2012), pp. 60–69, esp. 67.

Prophet's polytheist opponents.[24] By the middle part of the eighth century, however, we find John Damascene reporting that Muslims in his day were calling Christians 'associators' on account of their belief that Jesus is the Son of God.[25]

THE ANXIETY OF INFLUENCE

So far as concerns being a minority, however, perhaps more important than the element of competition was the fact that Muslim authorities had an anxiety of influence when it came to Christians and Jews.[26] This was perhaps in part because there was so much that these groups shared in common: belief in one God, prophets, revealed scripture, and the biblical tradition more generally, in addition to rituals and practices like prayer, fasting, and almsgiving, to name only the most obvious areas of similarity. Given this shared repertoire of doctrines and practices, there was a need to develop a specifically Islamic assemblage. Various *ḥadīth* attribute to the Prophet injunctions that Muslims should not imitate non-Muslims: 'He who imitates a people is one of them,'[27] and 'He who imitates others does not belong to us, do not imitate Jews and Christians.'[28] Another, related group of *ḥadīth* have Muḥammad enjoining Muslims to act differently from (*khālifū*) Jews and Christians.[29] To Albrecht

[24] See D. Gimaret, 'Shirk,' in *EI2*, vol. 9, p. 485.

[25] Πῶς λοιδορεῖτε ἡμᾶς ὡς ἑταιριαστάς; John of Damascus, *On Heresies* 100 (ed. Kotter, pp. 63–64). See further the discussion of whether the People of the Book were to be considered *mushrikūn* in Ibn Taymiyya, *Majmūʿat al-fatāwā*, vol. 32, pp. 113–15.

[26] Similar worries can be found in the Jewish tradition; see G. Vajda, 'Juifs et Musulmans selon le Ḥadīṯ,' *JA* 229 (1937), p. 63, n. 1, and E. Russ-Fishbane, *Judaism, Sufism, and the Pietists of Medieval Egypt* (Oxford, 2015), pp. 76–77 on the question of *ḥuqqot ha-goyim*, imitating the nations, in Judaism. For Christian aversion to imitating non-Christians, see, e.g., Ishoʿyahb III, *Life of Isho'sabran*, p. 525 (ed. Chabot), where the young Isho'zeka tells the convert Isho'sabran not to do as the Magians do when he is praying. Mention might also be made of contrasts given by George of the Arabs between how pagans and Christians referred to certain logical terms (*Letters* 8 [BL Add. 12,154, fols. 273a-274a]) as well as contrasts between pagan and Christian names for heaven (in his conclusion to Jacob of Edessa's *Hexaemeron*, p. 355 [ed. Chabot, CSCO 92: SS 44]). Cf. also Matthew 6:2, 5, 7–8, 16.

[27] Abū Dāwūd, *Sunan*, vol. 6, p. 144 (no. 4031) (ed. Sh. Al-Arna'ūṭ and M. Kāmil Qarah Balilī) (Damascus, 2009).

[28] al-Tirmidhī, *al-Jāmiʿ al-kabīr*, vol. 4, p. 425 (no. 2695). Cf. This report ascribed to Ibn ʿAbbās; 'When the Prophet of God, may God pray for him and grant him peace, conquered Mecca, he said: "God, to whom belongs power and glory, and his Prophet forbade you wine (*khamr*) and its price; they forbade you improperly slaughtered meat and its price; and they forbade you pigs, eating pork, and its price." And he said, "Cut your mustaches and let your beards grow out and do not walk in the markets save with a garment on covering your legs (*wa-ʿalaykum al-izr*), for he who engages in the custom of others is not one of us."' al-Ṭabarānī, *al-Muʿjam al-kabīr*, vol. 11, p. 152 (no. 11335) (ed. Ḥ. ʿAbd al-Majīd al-Salafī [Cairo, 1404]).

[29] al-Bukhārī, *al-Jāmiʿ al-ṣaḥīḥ*, vol. 2, p. 493 (no. 3462). For other *ḥadīth* where the Prophet orders

Noth belongs the insight that these regulations stemmed from a fear of being swallowed up by the conquered peoples in the post-conquest world; Noth connected such injunctions, as well as stipulations on non-Muslim dress in the so-called 'Pact of 'Umar' (the *shurūṭ 'Umar*), with the fragile and threatened situation Muslims found themselves in in the post-conquest period: '… the dress rules (etc.) for non-Muslims can also (or only?) be understood as protecting the Muslim conquerors who began to settle in the conquered territories, but who were still a small minority in an alien environment,' he wrote; in trying to draw sharp lines between Muslim and non-Muslim by regulating what sort of headgear, footwear, hairstyle, and means of transportation non-Muslims used, the Pact of 'Umar was attempting to 'protect Muslim identity.'[30] Indeed, such was the impulse to be different from non-Muslims that a variety of traditions were circulated suggesting that those Muslims who engaged in or held to certain Christian and Jewish-like activities or doctrines would be turned into apes and pigs in the hereafter.[31]

We can look at the issue of prayer as an example of this drive to develop a distinctly Muslim way of doing things. A report attributed to Ibn 'Umar (d. AD 693/AH 73) has been used to explain the beginnings of the call to prayer: 'When Muslims came to Medina,' he is supposed to have said,

> they would gather together and would try to know the time of prayer—a summons to it was not made. And so one day, they were speaking about this. One person said, 'Take a wooden clapper (*nāqūsan*) like the wooden clapper of the Christians. Another person said: '[Take] rather a trumpet, like the horn of the Jews.' But 'Umar said, 'And you would not send a man who will summon to prayer?' And so the Prophet, may God pray for him and grant him peace, said 'O Bilāl, get up and call to prayer!'[32]

---

his followers to be different (*khālifū*) from others, including Magians and polytheists, see A. J. Wensinck et al., *Concordance et indices de la tradition musulmane*, vol. 2, p. 65.

[30] See A. Noth, 'Problems of Differentiation between Muslims and Non-Muslims: Re-reading the "Ordinances of 'Umar" (*Al-Shurūṭ al-Umariyya*),' in Hoyland, ed., *Muslims and Others in Early Islamic Society*, pp. 119–21 (where Noth points out the *hadīth* on imitation and differentiation I have just cited above) and p. 118 (quotes). On the question of the Pact of 'Umar, much has been written. In addition to Noth, the following are especially important contributions: Tritton, *The Caliphs and their non-Muslim Subjects*, pp. 5–17; Fattal, *Le statut légal des non-musulmans en pays d'Islam*, pp. 60–69; M. Cohen, 'What Was the Pact of 'Umar? A Literary-Historical Study,' *JSAI* 23 (1999), pp. 100–57; D. E. Miller, 'From Catalogue to Codes to Canon: The Rise of the Petition in 'Umar among Legal Traditions Governing Non-Muslims in Medieval Islamicate Societies,' (PhD diss., University of Missouri-Kansas City, 2000); M. Levy-Rubin, 'The Pact of 'Umar,' in *CMR*, vol. 1, pp. 360–64; and Levy-Rubin, *Non-Muslims in the Early Islamic Empire: From Surrender to Coexistence* (Cambridge, 2011).

[31] U. Rubin, 'Apes, Pigs, and the Islamic Identity,' *Israel Oriental Studies* 17 (1997), pp. 89–105.

[32] al-Bukhārī, *al-Jāmi' al-ṣaḥīḥ*, vol. 1, p. 205 (no. 204) and see, too, 'Abd al-Razzāq, *Muṣannaf*, vol. 1, pp. 456–57 (no. 1776).

Though the idea of summoning a community to shared prayer at a set time was, at a deep level, very similar to the practices of Jews and Christians, when confronted with the question of how this common ritual should look, the Muslim community sought a third way, so to speak, one that was different from Jewish and Christian practices.

Other versions of this story make the need to find an independent Muslim path more apparent. In the version we have just seen, it is only an unnamed individual who suggested the use of the *nāqūs*, a wooden clapper beaten to summon to prayer, which is strongly associated with Christianity in the Islamic tradition. In another version of the same story, however, it is the Prophet himself who gave the order to use the *nāqūs* before a dream led the community toward the custom of using a call to prayer.[33] The Prophet's role in making this suggestion dropped out in other versions, presumably because some viewed it as untoward that he might suggest following a Christian practice. In another tradition, the Christian *nāqūs* was in fact decided upon as the means to summon to prayer, and ʿUmar b. al-Khaṭṭāb intended to buy two pieces of wood to make one, but before he could do so, he was told in a dream not to make a *nāqūs* and was instead given the idea of the call to prayer.[34]

In yet another version of the story, the logic of differentiation is set out even more clearly. The Prophet, we are told, consulted with people about the matter of prayer: 'They mentioned [using] a horn, but he disapproved of it on account of the Jews. Then they mentioned [using] a wooden clapper [*nāqūs*] and he disapproved of it on account of the Christians.'[35] To return to the question we saw in Chapter 11, about which vessels to use and which ones to wash off, we now find Muslims forming their own vessels, so to speak, rather than repurposing those of Christians and Jews.

This pattern of seeking a third way can be found in a number of places and at a number of junctures.[36] The Prophet ordered that no one should dress in

[33] Ibn Mājah, *Sunan*, vol. 2 (ed. B. ʿA. Maʿrūf) (Beirut, 1998), p. 33 (no. 706). Versions of this tradition appear elsewhere: see, e.g., ʿAbd al-Razzāq, *Muṣannaf*, vol. 1, pp. 455–56 (no. 1774), where the Muslim community looks for something to help them gather for prayer and considers using a wooden clapper (or *nāqūs*), or a horn, but is given the 'better' idea of the call to prayer in dreams delivered at the same time to different prominent figures.

[34] ʿAbd al-Razzāq, *Muṣannaf*, vol. 1, p. 456 (no. 1775). (cf. also no. 1787, pp. 460–61).

[35] As in other versions, the idea of using a summons to prayer is given in a dream to two people, and that is the solution to the issue of finding a way to gather people together for prayer. See Ibn Mājah, *Sunan*, vol. 2, pp. 35–36 (no. 707) (quote on p. 35).

[36] For extensive examples and documentation of this theme, see Vajda, 'Juifs et Musulmans selon le Ḥadīṯ,' and I. Goldziher, 'Usages Juifs d'après la littérature religieuse des musulmans,' in J. Desomogyi, ed., *Ignaz Goldziher: Gessamelte Schriften*, vol. 3 (Hildesheim, 1969), pp. 322–41. NB: p. 327: 'Bien des lois, bien des rites et même bien des usages de la vie ordinaire n'ont d'autre raison d'être, d'après l'exposé des motifs, que le désir, chez les Musulmans, de ne pas imiter les autres croyants et de se dis-

prayer as the Jews do, wearing only one garment: 'let he who has two garments dress himself and then pray.'[37] Fasting was something that Jews, Christians, and Muslims all engaged in, so it was one area of ritual where there was the potential of resembling another group. All groups would break fasts, for example, but Muslims were to do so in a distinctive way: 'Religion will continue to be ascendant so long as people rush to break the fast, for the Jews and Christians delay,' Muḥammad was supposed to have stated.[38] When the Prophet was fasting for Ashura, the tenth day of the month of Muḥarram, and gave the command that people should fast, one report has unnamed Muslims object: 'O Prophet of God, it [Ashura] is a day that the Jews and the Christians reverence.' Muḥammad's response was to suggest a change in the fast by one day: 'In the coming year,' he answered, 'God willing, we will fast the ninth day.'[39] The type of fasting known as *wiṣāl* fasting, where a person abstained for food for more than one day without breaking the fast was frowned upon because doing so was reminiscent of Christian practices.[40]

There were other areas of differentiation as well: According to one report relating to the collection of the text of the Qur'ān, once the text had been gathered, people discussed what the book should be called. One person suggested referring to it as '*al-sifr*' ('the book') but a *mawlā* of Abū Ḥudhayfa (d. AD 633/AH 12) named Sālim (who was credited in this report with the text's collection) averred: 'That is a word,' he is supposed to have said, 'which the Jews use as a name,' and so the people gathered there disapproved of it. Instead, Sālim suggested that they use the word '*muṣḥaf*' ('codex') as he had seen a similar book in Ethiopia and that was the word used to refer to it there; this was the label that everyone agreed on.[41] After the conquest of Jerusalem, 'Umar b. al-Khaṭṭāb, the leader of the Muslim community, prayed on the Temple

---

tinguer d'eux le plus possible.' Similarly, H. Mazuz, *The Religious and Spiritual Life of the Jews of Medina* (Leiden/Boston, 2014), pp. 25–67, argued that a wide range of Islamic practices and attitudes, as found in the *ḥadīth* literature, can be shown to be consciously articulated with the aim of differentiating the practices of Muḥammad's community from that of Talmudic Judaism.

[37] 'Abd al-Razzāq, *al-Muṣannaf*, vol. 1, p. 358 (no. 1390).

[38] Abū Dāwūd, *Sunan*, vol. 4, p. 37 (no. 2353).

[39] The Prophet died, the report notes, before the coming year arrived. See Muslim b. al-Ḥajjāj, *Ṣaḥīḥ*, vol. 2, pp. 797–98 (text on p. 797) (no. 133). On this tradition, see J. Burton, 'Notes towards a Fresh Perspective on the Islamic Sunna,' in H. Motzki, ed., *Ḥadīth: Origins and Developments* (Aldershot/Burlington, VT, 2004), pp. 39–53.

[40] On *wiṣāl* fasting and its disapproval, see G.H.A. Juynboll, *Encyclopedia of Canonical Ḥadīth* (Leiden/Boston, 2007), p. 331.

[41] al-Suyūṭī, *Itqān*, vol. 1, p. 209. For *sifr* as 'book' in Hebrew and Jewish Aramaic, cf. F. Brown, S. R. Driver and C. A. Briggs, *A Hebrew and English Lexicon of the Old Testament* (Boston/New York, 1907), s.v. ספר (pp. 706–707), and M. Sokoloff, *A Dictionary of Jewish Palestinian Aramaic of the Byzantine Period* (Ramat Gan, 1990), s.v. ספר (p. 387). For *muṣḥaf* in Ge'ez, cf. *maṣ(ə)ḥaf* in W. Leslau, *Comparative Dictionary of Ge'ez (Classical Ethiopic)* (Wiesbaden, 1987), s.v. *ṣaḥafa* (p. 552).

Mount and then asked the Jewish convert Kaʿb al-Aḥbār where they should put a new mosque. Kaʿb suggested putting it behind the Rock on the Temple Mount in order to combine both the direction of prayer of Moses and that of Muḥammad. ʿUmar rejected this idea: ʻO Kaʿb,' he said, ʻyou are imitating the Jewish religion! I have seen you taking off your shoes.'[42]

This story involving ʿUmar and Kaʿb points us to the fact that the anxieties about following the practices of Jews and Christians that the Islamic tradition placed in the life of the Prophet were equally well-founded in the post-conquest period as well. In fact, they were likely even more pressing after the conquests than they had been during Muḥammad's life. There was a real worry that Muslims would be physically indistinguishable from non-Muslims: another clause in the ʻPact of ʿUmar' had the Christians promise not to imitate Muslim dress in any way, or to wear similar footwear, or to part their hair in like manner.[43] When travelling from al-Jābiya to Jerusalem ʿUmar b. al-Khaṭṭāb was supposed to have encountered some companions of Abū ʿUbayda who asked him to ride a certain kind of horse (*al-birdhawn*) and wear white clothing—it would look better on him, they told ʿUmar, ʻand we do not like for the People of the *dhimma* to see you in the sort of style (*al-hay'a*) we see you in.' ʿUmar did not take up the white clothes, but rode the horse for a while before getting rid of it. When members of his entourage tried to get him to wear the white clothes and ride the horse again, he refused. Once he arrived in Jerusalem, some Muslim men came to him ʻhaving dressed,' al-Azdī tells us, ʻin the clothing of the Byzantines and imitated them in their appearance (*hay'atihim*).' ʻStir up dust in their faces,' ʿUmar commanded, ʻuntil they return to our look (*hay'atinā*) and our custom and our clothing!'[44]

[42] al-Ṭabarī, *Ta'rīkh*, 1.5, p. 2408 (ed. E. Prym [Leiden, 1893]; ET taken from Y. Friedmann, *The Battle of al-Qādisiyyah and the Conquest of Syria and Palestine* [HṬ 12] [Albany, 1992], p. 195. See especially Friedmann's comments, p. 195, n. 723.) For this, see Hoyland, *Seeing Islam*, p. 564. For changing early Muslim attitudes toward prayer in shoes relating an anxiety about imitating Jewish practices, see M. J. Kister, ʻ"Do not assimilate yourselves…" *Lā tashabbahū*,' *JSAI* 12 (1989), pp. 340–49.

[43] Ibn Taymiyya, *Iqtiḍā'*, pp. 121, 122. On the question of the *ghiyār* and the difficulty of placing its historical origins in the post-conquest, Umayyad, or even Abbasid periods, see L. Yarbrough, ʻOrigins of the *ghiyār*,' *JAOS* 134 (2014), pp. 113–21, which should be read in tandem with Levy-Rubin, *Non-Muslims in the Early Islamic Empire*, pp. 88–98.

[44] al-Azdī, *Ta'rīkh futūḥ al-shām*, pp. 252–53. For this, see N. Khalek, ʻFrom Byzantium to Early Islam. Studies on Damascus in the Umayyad Era' (PhD diss., Princeton, 2006), pp. 171–72 and cf. Khalek, *Damascus after the Muslim Conquest: Text and Image in Early Islam*, p. 64. Worries about dressing like a non-Muslim would continue: Badr al-Rashīd (d. AH 768/AD 1366), for example, considered it unbelief if a Muslim put on a *zunnār* (that is the distinctive belt that Jews and Christians were supposed to wear); if he put a rope around his waist and called it a *zunnār*; if he put on a *zunnār* and went to non-Muslim lands (*dār al-ḥarb*) to engage in commerce; if he put on the headgear (*qalansuwa*) of a Magian seriously and not in jest. If a Muslim, however, put on a *zunnār* to save captives, it was not considered unbelief. For these opinions (and others) about the acceptability of dressing like non-

Certain forms of salutation were to be used for Muslims alone, and if Christians dressed in the same way as Muslims did, this might lead to people being greeted in a way that violated the Prophet's example. One anecdote has 'Uqba b. 'Āmir al-Juhanī (d. AH 58/AD 679), one of the Prophet's Companions, pass by a man who looked like a Muslim (*hay'atuhu hay'at Muslim*). The man greeted him with peace and, we are told, 'Uqba wished peace back upon him as well as the mercy and blessings of God. When, however, a slave told 'Uqba that the man was actually a Christian, 'Uqba went back and followed the man till he caught up with him: 'The mercy of God and his blessings are on Believers,' he said, 'but may God give you a long life and increase your possessions and children.'[45]

The temptation for Muslims to take up the practices of those whom they now settled among will have been a constant one. 'If I die and you bring me out,' 'Imrān b. al-Ḥuṣayn b. 'Ubayd (d. AH 53/AD 673) is reported to have ordered, 'hurry as you walk and do not go slowly as the Jews and Christians walk slowly and do not cause fire and wailing (*ṣawtan*) to follow me.'[46] In one of the provisos of the so-called 'Pact of 'Umar,' Christians had promised not to raise their voices (*aṣwātanā*) over their dead,[47] and 'Imrān's request about how his funeral should be conducted suggests that some Muslims (perhaps converts?) had been following this Christian practice. The potential of adopting local customs extended to more than just funerary practices. 'These foreigners (*al-a'ājim*),' 'Umar II wrote to one of his governors,

> amuse themselves with things which Satan has adorned for them. Therefore, drive those Muslims who are near you away from that. By my life, it is appropriate for them to leave that [sort of thing], in accordance with what they read from the Book of God. So scold them away from what is vain and wanton in terms of singing and things like it. If they do not stop, then punish those of them who undertake it as an example with a chastisement which is not unjust.[48]

Muslims, see his *Alfāẓ al-kufr*, pp. 82–83 (ed. M. b. 'Abd al-Raḥmān al-Khumayyis in *al-Jāmi' fī alfāẓ al-kufr* [Kuwait, 1999]).

45 al-Bukhārī, *al-Adab al-mufrad*, p. 286 (no. 1112) (ed. M. Fu'ād 'Abd al-Bāqī [Cairo, 1375]).

46 Ibn Sa'd, *Kitāb al-ṭabaqāt al-kabīr*, vol. 7.1, p. 6 (ed. Meissner [Leiden, 1915]; my translation is made with reference to ET in Bewley, *Men of Madina*, vol. 1, p. 6). Abū Hurayra forbade his funerary procession to be followed with fire, and Mālik disapproved of the practice (Mālik b. Anas, *al-Muwaṭṭa'*, vol. 1, p. 226, no. 13). For the idea that 'the dead person is tortured by the weeping of the living' and the Prophet telling a Jewish family who were crying over a dead woman that she was being tortured in her grave, see *al-Muwaṭṭa'*, vol. 1, p. 234 (no. 37). On traditions condemning weeping for the dead, see Juynboll, *Muslim Tradition*, pp. 96–108 and see further the discussion in El Cheikh, *Women, Islam, and Abbasid Identity*, pp. 38–58.

47 *wa-lā narfa'u aṣwātanā ma'a mawtānā*. See Ibn Taymiyya, *Iqtiḍā'*, p. 121.

48 Ibn Sa'd, *Kitāb al-ṭabaqāt al-kabīr*, vol. 5, p. 290 (ed. Zetterstéen [Leiden, 1905]; my translation is made with reference to the ET in Bewley, *The Men of Madina*, vol. 2, pp. 245–46).

'Umar wrote these lines in a letter in which he also he decried Muslim women who were engaging in mourning practices from the *jāhiliyya.* The caliph was dealing with a situation in which Muslims were both still engaged in pre-Islamic practices and adopting the behaviors of the conquered peoples around him. He was none too pleased on either account.

'DO NOT SPEAK TO THE PEOPLE OF THE BOOK'

Beyond questions of religious practice and imitation, however, the presence of Muslims living among Christians and Jews raised questions about contact with non-Muslims. The propriety of social interactions with people of different religious communities had occupied religious authorities before Islam: the New Testament enjoined that false teachers should not be received into one's house or even greeted (2 John 10; cf. also 3 John 10), and Christian leaders across the confessional spectrum discouraged any sort of association or interaction with heretics. As we saw in Chapter 3, Jacob of Edessa was upset at members of his church for having close contacts with members of rival confessions, an aversion that had a long and ecumenical pedigree in the Christian world:[49] 'Let not the Sons of the Church have intercourse with heretics,' Rabbula of Edessa (d. 435/6) had enjoined, 'neither in word nor in deed';[50] Severus of Antioch wrote that 'one should not even offer a simple greeting to those who bring another doctrine and do not teach the orthodox faith.'[51] And this could also extend to non-Christians: 'Why do you, a Christian, keep company with pa-

[49] The evidence is abundant. See, e.g., Athanasius, *Life of Anthony* 68, 89 (Syriac text in R. Draguet, *La vie primitive de S. Antoine conservée en syriaque* [CSCO 417: SS 183] [Louvain, 1980] pp. 113, 142. For the Greek, see PG 26, cols. 940–41, 968 = Bartelink, ed. [SC 400], pp. 314, 354); Athanasius' *Letter to Monks*, PG 26, cols. 1185–88; Lucifer of Calaris, *De non conveniendo cum haereticis* (ed. G. F. Diercks, *Luciferi Calaritani Opera quae supersunt: ad fidem duorum codicum qui adhuc extant necnon adhibitis editionibus veteribus* [CCSL 8] [Turnhout, 1978], pp. 165–92); Synod of Laodicea, *Canons*, 31–34 (ed. Joannou, *Discipline générale antique*, vol. 1.2, pp. 142–43); John Rufus, *Plerophories* 40 (ed. Nau [PO 8.1], p. 91); John Moschus, *Spiritual Meadow* 12 (PG 87, col. 2861); and *Letter of the Venerable Orthodox Bishops to the Monks in the Congregation of Amid and All of Its Province*, p. *26.11–13 (ed. Rahmani, *Studia Syriaca*, vol. 1; On the dating of this letter, see Rahmani's comments, p. 60, where he places it between 519 and 560. R. Draguet published a longer version of this later, based on the mutilated BL Add. 14,663, and suggested ca. 530 as a date; see R. Draguet, 'Une pastorale antijulianiste des environs de l'année 530,' *LM* 40 [1927], pp. 75–92. Draguet's version has very little overlap with that of Rahmani).

[50] Rabbula of Edessa, *Rules and Admonitions for Priests and Ascetics* 47 (ed. Overbeck, *S. Ephraemi Syri*, p. 220; ET, with very slight alteration, taken from Connolly, 'Some More Early Syrian Rules,' p. 305).

[51] Severus of Antioch, *Select Letters* 4.10 (*To Caesaria*) (ed. Brooks, 1.2.304–306 [Syriac] [quotation at 304–305]). I have used here the translation from Allen and Hayward, *Severus of Antioch*, pp. 146–48, but have slightly modified it (quotation at p. 146).

gans?' an old monk asked Ephrem in the *Life of Ephrem*.[52] Muslim leaders showed a similar impulse: 'Do not learn the barbarous language (*raṭāna*) of the foreigners (*al-a'ājim*),' 'Umar b. al-Khaṭṭāb is said to have ordered, 'and don't enter into their presence in their churches on the day of their feast, for wrath will come down upon them.'[53] The Qur'ān itself, we should also remember, could show an aversion to believers taking Jews and Christians as allies (5:51).

Of particular concern and importance was the potential for learning new religious information from non-Muslims. Just as Christians such as Origen and Jerome had looked to Jewish texts and informants for greater insight into the Scriptures,[54] so Muslims turned to Jews and Christians to learn more about the biblical figures and stories that appeared in Muḥammad's new revelation. Reading the works of religious rivals was something that some Christians had also been wary of: in the third century, Dionysius of Alexandria (d. ca. AD 265) wrote that another Christian had tried to restrain and frighten him away from reading the books of heretics—'… he said I should ruin my soul, and, as I perceived, there was truth in what he said'[55]—and in early 480s, when the monk Ḥabīb accused Philoxenus of not reading 'other books,' Philoxenus accepted the charge. 'Look,' he wrote, 'you have been made a pagan and godless by the reading of many books, of which you are so proud. You speak with every religion and change yourself to every creed and become everything to everyone, when you yourself are one thing: a demon incarnate….' 'For faith,' Philoxenus would add, 'does not teach the reading of many books, O faithless one, but rather simple obedience (*shem'ā pshiṭā*) and a mind that is filled with sincerity.'[56]

Similar concerns could be found among Muslims when it came to learning from non-Muslims. Even though the Qur'ān itself had admonished Believers

[52] *Life of Ephrem* 13a (ed. J.P. Amar, *The Syriac Vita Tradition of Ephrem the Syrian* [CSCO 629–630: SS 242–43] [Louvain, 2011], 26 [Syriac text] = 30 [Amar's translation, which I have used]). In another version, the old monk asks Ephrem after seeing him debate pagans, 'My son, how is it appropriate for you to be mixing with pagans when you are a Christian? Do you have a desire to be in the world?' (translation Amar). In the recension I have quoted, the monk does not witness a debate and simply asks, 'Where are you from, young man? Why do you, a Christian, keep company with pagans?' (translation Amar). See also, *Teaching of Addai*, pp. *43, *44, where Addai admonishes, 'Beware, therefore, of the crucifiers [sc. Jews] and do not be friends with them, lest you be responsible with those whose hands are full of the blood of the Messiah…. beware of pagans… avoid them because they worship things that are created and made' (ed. Phillips, translation by Howard, taken from *The Teaching of Addai*, pp. 87, 89).

[53] 'Abd al-Razzāq, *al-Muṣannaf*, vol. 1, p. 411 (no. 1609).

[54] On Origen and Jerome's use of Jewish texts and contacts with Jews (as well as similar contacts by other Christian scholars), see A. Salvesen, 'A Convergence of the Ways? The Judaizing of Christian Scripture by Origen and Jerome,' in Becker and Reed, eds., *The Ways That Never Parted*, pp. 233–57.

[55] Dionysius of Alexandria, *Letter to Philemon* 1 (ed. C.L. Feltoe, *The Letters and Other Remains of Dionysius of Alexandria* [Cambridge/New York, 1904], pp. 52–53; ET taken from Feltoe, *St. Dionysius of Alexandria: Letters and Treatises* [London/New York, 1918], p. 57).

[56] Philoxenus of Mabbug, *Mēmrē against Ḥabīb*, 10.189-190 (ed. Brière and Graffin [PO 40.2], pp. 150, 152).

who were in doubt about what God had revealed to ask those who had read Scripture before them (Q 10:94), the Prophet is reported to have said: 'I do not doubt and I do not ask.'[57] A variety of *ḥadīth* reflect such ambivalence. 'Narrate concerning the children of Israel for there is no sin (*lā ḥaraja*) in that,' the Prophet is supposed to have said, a tradition that had legitimated Muslims taking up Jewish and Christian materials.[58] But seeking out Jews or Christians for information triggered criticism from some quarters: 'How do you ask them about something,' Ibn 'Abbās is supposed to have said, referring to the People of the Book, 'when the Book of God is in your midst?'[59] Other versions of this report suggest that Muslim religious leaders were not happy at all that believers were asking Christians and Jews about what was in their Scriptures and were ignoring the revelation brought by Muḥammad: 'You ask the People of the Book about their books,' Ibn 'Abbās said, 'while you have with you the Book of God? You should read it as the closest of the Scriptures in knowledge of God, one in which imperfection has not been mixed.'[60] A still longer version of this same report has Ibn 'Abbās not only asserting the superiority of Muḥammad's revelation, but also attacking the reliability of previous scriptures: 'How do you ask the People of the Book about something,' he is supposed to have said,

> when your Book, which God sent down to his Prophet... is among you? He [sc. Muḥammad] introduced the books [sic] out of knowledge of his Lord and did not mix in imperfection. Has God not informed you in His Book that they have changed the Book of God and altered it and written the Book with their hands and then said, "This is from God" in order to exchange it for a small price (cf. Q 2:79). Has not the knowledge which comes from asking them been forbidden? By God, we have never seen a man from among them asking you about what God has sent down to you![61]

Ibn 'Abbās's reported criticisms of Muslims who asked Christians and Jews for information from their scriptures, at least in this longer report, seemed to have at least in part come from dismay at the lack of reciprocity in interest: People of the Book were not equally curious to find out what the Qur'ān had to say.

[57] 'Abd al-Razzāq, *al-Muṣannaf*, vol. 6, pp. 125–126 (no. 10211).

[58] al-Bukhārī, *al-Jāmi' al-ṣaḥīḥ*, vol. 2, p. 493 [no. 3461]. On this tradition and on Isrā'īliyyāt, see Kister's marvellously rich and classic study, '*Ḥaddithū 'an banī isrā'īla wa-la ḥaraja*: A Study of an Early Tradition,' *Israel Oriental Studies* II (Tel Aviv, 1972), pp. 216–39. NB: I have followed Kister in rendering *ḥaddithū 'an* as 'narrate concerning' (pp. 215–16), but it might also be rendered as 'narrate from.'

[59] Ibn 'Abd al-Barr, *Jāmi' bayān al-'ilm wa-faḍlihi*, vol. 2, p. 51 (ed. 'A. al-Raḥmān Muḥammad 'Uthmān [Medina, 1968]).

[60] Ibn 'Abd al-Barr, *Jāmi' bayān al-'ilm wa-faḍlihi*, vol. 2, p. 53.

[61] Ibn 'Abd al-Barr, *Jāmi' bayān al-'ilm wa-faḍlihi*, vol. 2, p. 52, and cf. al-Bukhārī, *al-Jāmi' al-ṣaḥīḥ*, vol. 4, pp. 374–75 (no. 7363).

But there was more than just a worry about asymmetry at play—there was the charge that Christians and Jews had corrupted their Scriptures, purposefully, so as to trade the truth for an easier life here and now.[62] Ironically, Christians had, centuries before, leveled similar charges of scriptural alteration against Jews.[63] In part, distrust of seeking information from Jews and Christians stemmed also from a suspicion that non-Muslims might try to trick and deceive Muslims or to contradict Muḥammad's message: Abū Namla spoke of sitting with Muḥammad when 'a man from the Jews' came to the Prophet. 'O Muḥammad,' the Jew asked, 'does this corpse speak?' 'God knows best,' was Muḥammad's reply. 'I bear witness,' the Jew responded, 'that it speaks!' And so, we are told, Muḥammad ordered Muslims: 'Do not speak to the People of the Book! Neither believe them nor consider them liars, but say, "We believe in God and his books and his prophets." That way, if [what they say] is true, you have not called them liars, and if it is false, you have not believed them.'[64] There was also the worry that Muslims would be attracted to the scripture and teachings of prophets who preceded Muḥammad: 'By the One in whose hand is Muḥammad's soul,' the Prophet was supposed to have said to Muslims, 'if Moses were to appear to you and you were to follow him and leave me, you would have truly gone astray. You are my portion from among the nations and I am your portion among the prophets.'[65]

Even the tradition that sees Muḥammad encouraging Muslims to narrate about the Children of Israel took different forms and was not always quite so positive on the subject of Muslims getting information from Jews and Christians. 'Do not ask the People of the Book about anything,' the Prophet is sup-

[62] On the Muslim charge that Jews and Christians had corrupted their scriptures, see in H. Lazarus-Yafeh, 'Taḥrīf,' in *EI2*, vol. 10, pp. 111–12; G. D. Newby, 'Forgery,' in *EQ*, vol. 2, pp. 242–44; and S. Lowin, 'Revision and Alteration,' in *EQ*, vol. 4, pp. 448–51.

[63] E.g., Justin Martyr, *Dialogue with Trypho* 71.2, 72.1–2, 4, 73.1, 5–6 (ed. G. Archambault, *Dialogue avec Tryphon*, vol. 1 [Paris, 1909], pp. 344, 346, 348, 350, 354), and cf. Irenaeus of Lyons, *Against Heresies*, 3.21.1 (ed. and trans. N. Brox, *Irenäeus von Lyon. Adversus Haereses/Gegen die Häresien*, vol. 3 [Freiburg im Breisgau, 1995], pp. 252–55). See, too, Ps.-Justin Martyr, *Cohortatio ad Graecos* 13 (PG 6, col. 268), where the author anticipates the possibility that some might accuse the Christians of falsifying their Scriptures. Clement of Alexandria, *Stromateis* 1.22 (149.3) (ed. O. Stählin, *Clemens Alexandrinus*, vol. 2, p. 92 [Leipzig, 1906]), held that the original Jewish scriptures had been destroyed in the Babylonian Captivity. See further, W. Adler, 'The Jews as Falsifiers: Charges of Tendentious Emendation in Anti-Jewish Christian Polemic,' in *Translation of Scripture* (Philadelphia, 1990), pp. 1–27, esp. p. 2, n. 2, for additional literature on this Christian charge as well as the Jewish charge that Samaritans had altered the text of the Bible. For a number of examples of the charge that Christian heretics altered the biblical text, see E. Nestle, *Einführung in das Griechische Neue Testament*, 3rd ed. (Göttingen, 1909), pp. 219–26. For seventh-century Christian charges of forgery against other Christians, see S. Wessel, 'Forgery and the Monothelete Controversy: Some Scrupulous Uses of Deception,' *Greek, Roman, and Byzantine Studies* 42 (2001), pp. 201–20.

[64] Ibn 'Abd al-Barr, *Jāmi' bayān al-'ilm wa-faḍlihi*, vol. 2, p. 51.

[65] Ibn 'Abd al-Barr, *Jāmi' bayān al-'ilm wa-faḍlihi*, vol. 2, p. 52.

posed to have said, according to one version of this tradition, 'for they will not give you guidance, having led their own souls astray.' In response to this pronouncement, Muḥammad was reportedly asked, 'O Apostle of God, are we not to narrate concerning the Children of Israel?' 'He said,' the report continued, 'Narrate—there is no sin.'[66] Another version of this tradition has the Prophet admonishing: 'Do not ask the People of the Book about anything, for they will not guide you, having led their own souls astray. And so you will deny the truth or affirm what is false.' Despite this suspicion of the motivations of the Christians and Jews, Muḥammad reportedly expressed a confidence that, deep down inside, they knew that the message of Islam was right: 'There is no one among the People of the Book,' the Prophet continued, 'who does not have something in the back of his heart (*illā fī qalbihi tāliya*) which calls him to God and His Book.'[67]

'DO YOU KNOW SYRIAC WELL?'

Notwithstanding such reservations about seeking out information from non-Muslims, learning their language and studying their scriptures, at least some Muslims were doing just this and traditions circulated showing that it was an activity with Prophetic sanction. 'Do you know Syriac well?' Muḥammad was supposed to have asked his secretary, Zayd b. Thābit, 'for letters are coming to me!' 'I said, "No,"' Zayd reported. The Prophet's response? 'Then learn it!' 'So I learned it,' Zayd continued, 'in nineteen days.'[68] There were several variations on this *ḥadīth* in circulation, and 'Syriac' and 'Hebrew' seemed to have been interchangeable. 'Letters (*kutub*) which I do not want everyone to read are coming to me,' the Prophet told Zayd in a similar report, 'could you therefore learn Hebrew (or Syriac) writing?' 'I said yes,' the report went on, 'and I learned it in seventeen nights.'[69]

We have other indications of early Muslims seeking information either from the books of the People of the Book or from actual Christian or Jewish informants.[70] 'Abd Allāh b. Salām, a Jewish convert to Islam, is reported to have once approached the Prophet: 'I have recited the Qur'ān and the Torah,'

[66] See 'Abd al-Razzāq, *al-Muṣannaf*, vol. 10 (no. 19209) pp. 311–12. I am grateful to Luke Yarbrough for help understanding this *ḥadīth*. On this more suspicious version of the *ḥaddithū* tradition, see Kister, '*Ḥaddithū 'an banī isrā'īla*,' p. 219.

[67] See 'Abd al-Razzāq, *al-Muṣannaf*, vol. 10 (no. 19212) pp. 312–13.

[68] *fa-inna-hā ta'tīnī kutub*. Ibn Abī Dāwud, *Kitāb al-maṣāḥif*, p. 3.

[69] al-Mizzī, *Tahdhīb al-kamāl fī asmā' al-rijāl*, vol. 10, p. 28.

[70] See Abbott, *Studies in Arabic Literary Papyri*, Vol. 2: *Qur'ānic Commentary and Tradition*, pp. 7–10, for a number of illustrative reports.

he told him. 'Recite this one night,' Muḥammad responded, 'and this one the next.'[71] Sharīk b. Khalīfa reported seeing 'Abd Allāh b. 'Amr b. al-'Āṣ, a Companion of the Prophet and the son of the famous Muslim general, reading Syriac.[72] 'Abd Allāh b. 'Amr was supposed to have gotten hold of two animal-loads of books from the People of the Book at the Battle of Yarmuk and he would use them to teach people.[73] Al-Aqra', the *mu'adhdhin* of 'Umar b. al-Khaṭṭāb, reported that 'Umar 'summoned the bishop and said, "Do you find in your books. . . .?" '[74] Such anecdotes can be multiplied: 'I came to the mountain,' said Abū Hurayra (d. AH 58 or 59/AD 678), perhaps the most prolific of all *ḥadīth* transmitters from Muḥammad, reportedly said, 'and I found there Ka'b [al-Aḥbār]. He and I stayed a day—with me telling him about the Prophet and him telling me about the Torah. . . . '[75] Another *ḥadīth* has Abū Hurayra report that 'The People of the Book would read the Torah in Hebrew and explain it in Arabic to the people of Islam.'[76] No less than the caliph Hishām was said to have had the Miaphysite patriarch Athanasius III (sed. AD 724–739) build his episcopal residence next to the caliphal salon-room in order to hear his prayers and his scriptural reading.[77]

Above, I cited a report attributed to Ibn 'Abbās in which he urged Muslims not to read Christian and Jewish texts because they had been willfully changed to conceal God's truth. Another report, however, has 'Umar give his blessing to reading the Torah—so long as one knew it was free from alteration. 'If you know that it is the Torah which God sent down to Moses, the Son of 'Imrān,'—i.e., that it is not some later, corrupted version—'read it day and night.'[78] Another report has 'Umar approach Muḥammad and give him a book: 'O Apostle of God,' he is supposed to have said, 'I have obtained an excellent book from

[71] *Iqra' hādhā laylatan wa-hādhā laylatan.* al-Dhahabī, *Kitāb tadhkirat al-ḥuffāẓ*, vol. 1 (Hyderabad/Deccan, 1955–1958), p. 27. For this example, see R. Na'nā'a, *al-Isrā'īliyyāt wa-atharuhā fī kutub al-tafsīr* (Damascus/Beirut, 1970), p. 160, n. 1.

[72] Ibn Sa'd, *Kitāb al-ṭabaqāt al-kabīr*, vol. 7.2, p. 189 (ed. Sachau [Leiden, 1918]; an ET is available in Bewley, *The Men of Madina*, vol. 1, p. 306). 'Abd Allāh b. 'Amr b. al-'Āṣ was only eleven years younger than his celebrated father and was famous himself for the number of *ḥadīth* he transmitted. On 'Abd Allāh b. 'Amr b. al-'Āṣ, see al-Mizzī, *Tahdhīb al-kamāl fī asmā' al-rijāl*, vol. 15, pp. 357–62.

[73] For this, see Na'nā'a, *al-Isrā'īliyyāt wa-atharuhā fī kutub al-tafsīr*, p. 146.

[74] Ibn Sa'd, *Kitāb al-ṭabaqāt al-kabīr*, vol. 7.1, p. 73 (ed. Meissner [Leiden, 1915]; my translation made with reference to the ET in Bewley, *The Men of Madina*, vol. 1, p. 62).

[75] al-Nasā'ī, *Kitāb al-sunan al-kubrā*, vol. 2, p. 292 (no. 1766). For this, see Na'nā'a, *al-Isrā'īliyyāt wa-atharuhā fī kutub al-tafsīr*, pp. 137. On Abū Hurayra, see J. Robson's article, 'Abū Hurayra al-Dawsī al-Yamānī' in *EI2*, vol. 1, p. 129.

[76] Which is supposed to have prompted the Prophet to reply, 'Do not believe them and do not accuse them of lying, but say: 'We believe in God and what he has sent down to us and what was sent down to you' (Q 29:46). See al-Bukhārī, *al-Jāmi' al-ṣaḥīḥ*, vol. 4, p. 374 (no. 7362).

[77] *History of the Patriarchs of Alexandria* 1.17 (ed. Evetts [PO 5.1], p. 328).

[78] Ibn 'Abd al-Barr, *Jāmi' bayān al-'ilm wa-faḍlihi*, vol. 2, p. 53.

a certain one of the People of the Book!'[79] 'Umar himself was said to own a piece of property in the upper part of Medina; every time he would go to it, he would pass by a Jewish hall of study and would stop and listen. He might also debate with the Jews there.[80] According to a report in Ibn Sa'd, Abū al-Jald al-Jawnī 'used to read books.'[81] 'My father,' Abū al-Jald's daughter reminisced, 'used to recite the Qur'ān every seven days and would finish the Torah in six—he would recite it while looking at it. And if it was the day when he was finishing it [sc. the Torah], people would gather for that reason. He would say, "It was said that mercy descends upon its completion [sc. the finishing of the recitation of the Torah]."'[82] Tubay', the son of the wife of Ka'b al-Aḥbar, we are told, was a learned man who read books and gained much knowledge by listening to Ka'b.[83]

Ka'b (d. AH 32/AD 652-653) himself was a Yemeni Jew who converted to Islam and was an important vector through which Jewish materials entered the Islamic tradition.[84] Ka'b did not convert to Islam till after the death of Muḥammad, perhaps around AH 17/AD 638, and the story of Ka'b's conversion, like the story of the monk Baḥīra, allowed Muslims to understand their religion as being foretold in and confirmed by previous religions which had grown from the soil of the Hebrew Bible. 'What prevented you from becoming Muslim in the time of the Apostle of God… and of Abū Bakr,' al-'Abbās is supposed to have asked Ka'b, 'up till the present in the time of 'Umar?' Ka'b's purported answer reflected the suspicion, which we have already encountered, that Jews and Christians were hiding parts of their Scriptures which bore witness to the truth of Muḥammad's message. 'My Father,' Ka'b reportedly said,

[79] Muḥammad's response was anger. 'Are they not perplexed at [their own books], O son of al-Khaṭṭāb?!' the Prophet is supposed to have responded. 'By the One in whose hand is my soul, I have brought you a spotless saying concerning them [sc. the Scriptures of the People of the Book]: "Do not ask them about anything, for they will speak to you of something true and you will regard it false, or of something false and you will regard it true.' As with a tradition I referenced above, this particular report contained a counterfactual claim aimed both at keeping Muslims away from Jewish and Christian scriptures and assuring them that Muḥammad's revelation was in line with what had come before: 'By the One in whose hand is my soul,' the Prophet continued, 'if Moses were alive, he would only be able to follow me.' See Ibn 'Abd al-Barr, *Jāmi' bayān al-'ilm wa-faḍlihi*, vol. 2, pp. 52–53. Compare this claim with Jesus's statement against Jewish opponents that Abraham had seen his ministry and rejoiced at it (John 8:56).

[80] Ibn 'Abd al-Barr, *Jāmi' bayān al-'ilm wa-faḍlihi*, vol. 2, pp. 123–24.

[81] Ibn Sa'd, *Kitāb al-ṭabaqāt al-kabīr*, vol. 7.1, p. 161 (ed. Meissner [Leiden, 1915]).

[82] Ibn Sa'd, *Kitāb al-ṭabaqāt al-kabīr*, vol. 7.1, p. 161 (ed. Meissner [Leiden, 1915]; my ET made with reference to Bewley, *The Men of Madina*, vol. 1, p. 140).

[83] Ibn Sa'd, *Kitāb al-ṭabaqāt al-kabīr*, vol. 7.2, p. 160 (ed. Sachau [Leiden, 1918]).

[84] On Ka'b, see M. Schmitz, 'Ka'b al-Aḥbār,' in *EI2*, vol. 4, pp. 316–17.

wrote a book for me from the Torah and turned it over to me and said, 'Work with this,' and put a seal on the rest of his books. He restrained me, with the right of a father over his son, from breaking the seal. When it came to the present and I saw Islam appear and saw no harm [in it], my soul said to me: 'Perhaps your Father has concealed knowledge from you—he has hidden from you! If you were to read it. . . .' So I broke the seal and I read it and I found in it a description of Muḥammad and his community and have therefore now come as a Muslim.[85]

The story of Ka'b, like that of Baḥīra, is another indication that Muslims did in fact have a keen interest in seeing how Muḥammad's new text related to previous scriptures and believed that Muḥammad's claims would be verified there.[86] Abū al-Jald's recitation of the Torah alongside the Qur'ān had apparently been something of public interest and Ka'b himself, we are told, went so far as to study Torah in the mosque: Ḥuṣayn b. Abī al-Ḥurr al-'Anbarī reported going into the mosque in Syria, in what must have been the earliest post-conquest period, and seeing there Ka'b and 'Āmir b. 'Abd Allāh b. 'Abd al-Qays. 'Between them was one of the books of the Torah,' Ḥuṣayn narrated, 'and Ka'b was reading. When [Ka'b] came to something that pleased him, he explained it to ['Āmir].'[87]

The number of *ḥadīth* and the range of subjects they cover is vast. Similarly large are the complex debates—stretching from the medieval period to the present—concerning the authenticity of sayings of the Prophet and other early prominent members of his community that the Islamic tradition has transmitted. Such questions, though very interesting, are not germane to what has occupied me in this chapter. It simply does not matter whether Muḥammad or 'Umar or Ibn 'Abbās or anyone else actually uttered any of the statements cited above. It is the traditions and the sentiments they express that are important, because they reflect precisely the tensions between an openness to and interest in Judaism and Christianity and an aversion to information coming from these groups that one would expect if Muslim religious leaders were concerned about keeping their young community, many of whose members

[85] Ibn Sa'd, *Kitāb al-ṭabaqāt al-kabīr*, vol. 7.2, p. 154 (ed. Sachau [Leiden, 1918]; my ET made with reference to Bewley, *The Men of Madina*, vol. 1, p. 277).

[86] See the remarks of S. H. Griffith, 'Arguing from Scripture: The Bible in the Christian/Muslim Encounter in the Middle Ages,' in T. J. Heffernan and T. E. Burman, eds., *Scripture and Pluralism: Reading the Bible in the Religiously Plural Worlds of the Middle Ages and Renaissance* (Leiden/Boston, 2005), p. 32 on biblical citations in Muslim authors of the eighth and ninth centuries AD, and see, too, the more lengthy discussion in Griffith, *The Bible in Arabic: The Scriptures of the "People of the Book" in the Language of Islam* (Princeton/Oxford, 2013), pp. 176–198.

[87] Ibn Sa'd, *Kitāb al-ṭabaqāt al-kabīr*, vol. 7.1, pp. 78-79 (ed. Meissner [Leiden, 1915]; my ET made with reference to the ET in Bewley, *The Men of Madina*, vol. 1, p. 68).

did not have a profound acquaintance with or understanding of Muḥammad's message, from assimilating into the more ancient and numerically superior communities surrounding them. Though largely comprised of simple believers, these communities could, at their elite level, boast of highly sophisticated and complex systems of doctrine and thought.[88] Whether their origin is to be found in the seventh, eighth, or even the ninth centuries, the reports I have highlighted here, and others like them, when circulated, could serve as either warning signs to Muslims to avoid the religious literature of Christians and Jews, or alternately, could provide legitimation for their not doing so. What we see reflected here are competing views and differing attitudes among early Muslims with regard to the question of how to deal with—reject? accept? accept with qualification?—the traditions of the communities the Muslims found themselves ruling over, living alongside, and with whom they were now discussing religious matters.

ISLAM AND THE TRADITIONS OF CONQUERED COMMUNITIES

If we are interested in understanding how Arabs from the Hijaz related to the communities they now ruled over, the existence of statements attributed to both the Prophet and other important early Muslim authorities attempting to discourage Muslims from speaking to and learning from Christians and Jews can be taken to suggest that precisely this was happening. What we are dealing with are attempts to regulate and even put a stop to practices that certain religious leaders viewed unfavorably. But, precisely as one would expect, such attempts did not succeed. Muslims were in fact seeking out, speaking with, and learning from non-Muslims on a host of issues. The evidence for this is manifold.

Al-Hāshimī, the Muslim correspondent in the famous early ninth-century *Apology* of al-Kindī, claimed to have read a number of Christian books. He had read the Old and New Testaments, he asserted, and studied them, and discussed them with the East Syrian catholicos Timothy I, as well as other Christians—Nestorian, Melkite, and Jacobite.[89] Although this particular piece of evidence is dubious, given that it was likely written by a Christian, the pseudonymous al-Kindī was likely basing al-Hāshimī's claim on the reality of Muslims showing interest in Christian writings and Scripture, for we can

[88] I am influenced by Goldziher's use of *ḥadīth* in *Muslim Studies*, vol. 2, pp. 89–125, as a reflection of ideological and political conflicts in the Muslim community in its first centuries.

[89] al-Kindī, *Apology*, pp. 6-8.

point to the mixed reputations of Muslim scholars who did indeed look to Christians and Jews for information: Certain people, we are told, avoided the Qur'ānic commentary of Mujāhid b. Jabr (d. AH 100–104/AD 718–722) because he had been seen asking the People of the Book questions;[90] one criticism of Muqātil b. Sulaymān (d. AH 150/AD 767), an early exegete of the Qur'ān, was that he learned about the Qur'ān from Jews and Christians in a way that agreed with their Scriptures;[91] Mālik b. Anas (d. AH 179/AD 796), we read, disapproved of Ibn Isḥāq's reliance on the children of converted Jews for information about the Prophet's military campaigns, the story of Khaybar, and other matters, without verifying their information;[92] Ibn Isḥāq would, Ibn al-Nadīm noted, transmit from Jews and Christians, and refer to them in his books as the 'People of the Original Knowledge' (*ahl al-'ilm al-awwal*).[93] And it was not only Muslim scholars who had an interest in Christianity. 'He was honored by Caliphs and rulers,' the East Syrian *Book of the Tower* observed of the catholicos Timothy I

> on account of the abundance of his knowledge and his virtues and the fineness of his responses to the questions they would pose him and press him with concerning religion and doctrines and other things. The Caliph al-Hādī would, most days, summon him and debate religion with him and discuss with him and argue with him about many things. He would present numerous questions, problems, and powerful objections. And [Timothy] would respond to all of them with decisive and silence-inducing answers. . . .

[90] Ibn Sa'd, *Kitāb al-ṭabaqāt al-kabīr*, vol. 5, p. 344 (ed. Zetterstéen [Leiden, 1905]). For this, see A. Rippin's article, 'Mudjāhid b. Djabr al-Makkī,' in *EI2*, vol. 7, p. 293 and D. S. Powers, *Muḥammad Is Not the Father of Any of Your Men: The Making of the Last Prophet* (Philadelphia, 2009), p. 198, though NB: Goldziher, *Schools of Koranic Commentators*, p. 45, n. 64, understood *yattaqūna* here in the sense of 'honor' rather than 'fear and avoid.'

[91] That is, he presumably was interpreting Qur'ānic references to biblical figures in light of what the Bible had to say about them. See al-Mizzī, *Tahdhīb al-kamāl fī asmā' al-rijāl*, vol. 28, p. 540. On Muqātil, see M. Plessner and A. Rippin's article, 'Muḳātil b. Sulaymān,' in *EI2*, vol. 7, pp. 508–509. For this, cf. Powers, *Muḥammad Is Not the Father of Any of Your Men: The Making of the Last Prophet*, p. 198, and also Goldziher, *Schools of Koranic Commentators*, p. 38.

[92] Ibn Ḥajar al-'Asqalānī, *Tahdhīb al-tahdhīb*, vol. 3 (ed. I. al-Zaybaq and 'Ā. Murshid) (n.d., n.p.), p. 507. For the suggestion that Ibn Isḥāq's grandfather was perhaps a Christian, see C. Gilliot, 'Christians and Christianity in Islamic exegesis,' in *CMR*, vol. 1, p. 37.

[93] Ibn al-Nadīm, *Fihrist*, vol. 1, p. 92 (ed. G. Flügel [Leipzig, 1871–1872]). But there were nevertheless also contexts in which Jews and Christians could be used as sources of information that religious conservatives would find less objectionable: in his description of Rome, for instance, Ibn al-Faqīh (fl. 3rd/9th century) cited as one of his sources 'a certain monk from among those who entered it and dwelt in it for a year' (see Ibn al-Faqīh, *Mukhtaṣar kitāb al-buldān*, pp. 149–50. On this passage and its relationship to Yāqūt and al-Jayhānī, see A. Baumstark, 'Orientalische Rombeschreibungen,' *OC* 1 [1901], p. 384). Ibn al-Nadīm's description of China relied in part upon a conversation he had with an East Syrian monk who had spent seven years there (Ibn al-Nadīm, *Fihrist*, vol. 1, p. 349 [ed. Flügel]).

Timothy would, we are told, do the same with Hārūn al-Rashīd and in his time as catholicos was close to al-Hādī, al-Amīn, and al-Ma'mūn.[94] In such instances, we have the names of people who violated the putatively prophetic proscription against speaking with the People of the Book. In a host of other instances, however, though we cannot point to any names, we can point to the effects of such interactions.

One notable example is the question of the origins of Muslim dialectical theology, or *kalām*, which I alluded to in the previous chapter. In a short but very significant article, Michael Cook demonstrated that Muslim *kalām* took a form borrowed directly from pre-Islamic Christian styles of theological argumentation. Cook took what is perhaps the oldest-known example of *kalām* we have—the *Questions* of al-Ḥasan b. Muḥammad b. al-Ḥanafiyya (d. ca. AH 100/AD 718)—a text which already displayed the distinctive, aporetic style of questioning employed in Muslim disputation, and showed that this style of dilemma-based questioning was characteristic of an entire genre of Christian theological works that had nothing to do with Islam, and indeed was being written before Muḥammad received his first revelation. The similarities in genre between the Christian texts and the later Islamic texts were simply too striking to be coincidence.[95]

Cook's discovery raises the question of the terminology we use in speaking about such a phenomenon. Scholars may disagree about the suitability of a word like 'borrowing' and prefer instead to use other less provocative phrases, such as 'appropriation' or 'absorption,' or to speak rather in terms of Muslims continuing a pre-Islamic tradition of dialectical dispute.[96] At a certain level, however, such semantic variance is immaterial for my present task: what I am interested in is the sheer fact that a cultural practice which existed before the Islamic conquests, and indeed before the birth of Muḥammad, reappeared in the Arab period in Islamic garb, speaking Arabic, as it were, and being used

[94] Ṣalībā,' *Akhbār faṭārikat kursī al-mashriq*, pp. 65–66 (ed. H. Gismondi, *Maris Amri et Slibae. De patriarchis Nestorianorum commentaria. Pars altera, Amri et Slibae Textus* [Rome, 1896]). I have followed the arguments of Bo Holmberg, 'A Reconsideration of the *Kitāb al-Mağdal*,' and attributed this work to Ṣalībā, rather than to 'Amr b. Mattā and Ṣalībā, as its editor Gismondi did. On the question of the contested attributions of this work, cf. chapter 6, n. 10.

[95] See Cook, 'The Origins of "*Kalām*,"' and Cook, *Early Muslim Dogma: A Source-Critical Study* (Cambridge, 1981), pp. 156–57. See also my article, "Between Christology and Kalām? The Life and Letters of George, Bishop of the Arab Tribes," and more recently, A. Treiger, 'Origins of *Kalām*,' in S. Schmidtke, ed., *The Oxford Handbook of Islamic Theology* (Oxford, 2016), pp. 27–43.

[96] For an example of an essay that focuses on what one might called nomenclature or procedural framing of the question of the relationship between Islam and older religions, see M. Pregill, 'The Hebrew Bible and the Quran: The Problem of the Jewish "Influence" on Islam,' *Religion Compass* 1/6 (2007), pp. 643–59. On the idea of 'influence' more generally, P. Y. Lee, 'Modern Architecture and the Ideology of Influence,' *Assemblage* 34 (1997), pp. 6-29, has interesting historical observations.

by Muslims. Eventually, it came to be seen as Islamic to the extent that Cook's discovery of an unmistakable pre-Islamic ancestor could count as a discovery at all. Its pre-Islamic pedigree had been lost and forgotten. It is the social context of this process that interests me, not debates over what words we should use to name it or clumsy civilizational apologetics and precedence claims or crude attempts at (de)legitimation.

This particular continuity—in the form that *kalām* took—is but one of a myriad of continuities between the pre- and post-conquest periods. In swallowing up the Middle East, the conquerors from western Arabia also ingested and took over a great many of the cultural practices that were there when they arrived, and historians have suggested any number of such continuations of previous, pre-Islamic traditions in the Islamic period.[97] The various reports expressing hesitation or displeasure with Muslims speaking with or reading the books of non-Muslims that we reviewed in this chapter should be read with these survivals in mind and should not be understood apart from this context. In order to get a sense for the wide-ranging extent of these continuities, let us take up a few more examples.

Other aspects of *kalām* have been seen to reflect late antique Christian theological practices,[98] but *kalām* is just one area where religious continuities can be detected. When we look at the biography of Muḥammad, or *sīra*, there is clear evidence that the Muslim community sought to portray its Prophet using motifs and elements from the sacred histories of the groups around it:[99] striking and clearly identifiable parallels between traditional Muslim accounts of the life of Muḥammad and biblical portrayals of Jesus,[100] David,[101] and others[102] have been noted by a variety of scholars. Related to this is the fact that

[97] For more detail, see *SBI*, pp. 493–504.

[98] See S. Pines, 'Some Traits of Christian Theological Writing in Relation to Moslem *Kalām* and Jewish Thought,' in S. Stroumsa, ed., *The Collected Works of Shlomo Pines*, vol. 3, *Studies in the History of Arabic Philosophy* (Jerusalem, 1996), pp. 79–99. N. Aradi, 'The Origins of the *kalām* Model of Discussion on the Concept of *tawḥīd*,' in *Arabic Sciences and Philosophy* 23 (2013), pp. 135–66, is a more recent defense and elaboration of Pines's view. More generally, Treiger, 'Origins of *Kalām*,' takes up the question of the origin of *kalām* and the beginnings of the controversy over *qadar* in its late antique Christian context.

[99] See Newby, *The Making of the Last Prophet*, pp. 16–25 and cf. chapter 12, n. 8, above.

[100] See Wensinck, 'Muḥammad and the Prophets,' pp. 339–40, and note Jensen, 'Das Leben Muhammeds und die David-Sage,' pp. 93–94. See also Conrad, 'The *mawālī* and Early Arabic Historiography,' p. 375, n. 21, and cf. chapter 12, n. 8.

[101] Maghen, 'Intertwined Triangles,' pp. 17–92, and Maghen, 'Davidic Motifs in the Biography of Muḥammad,' and cf. chapter 12, n. 8.

[102] Jensen, 'Das Leben Muhammeds und die David-Sage,' pp. 84–93 for the Old Testament connections, especially those between the story of David and the life of Muḥammad (and see the previous footnote). Jensen's article, however, should be read alongside J. Horovitz, 'Biblische Nachwirkungen in der Sira' (cf. Chapter 12, n. 8.).

a large amount of biblically inspired material found its way into Muslim *ḥadīth* and *tafsīr* literature; although the sources of this material were both Jewish and Christian, it eventually came to be known as 'Isrā'īliyyāt.'[103] To take one figure: The Islamic tradition contains a great deal of material attributed to Jesus,[104] as we have already seen, and conversely contains material clearly drawn from the Gospels that has been detached from its original context and attributed to Muḥammad—the Lord's Prayer, for example, occurs in the *ḥadīth.*[105]

Outside the realm of Prophetic biography and *ḥadīth*, we also find parallels, connections, and similarities between Muslim asceticism and Christian asceticism that have long been noted by scholars[106] as have evidence of contacts between Christians and Muslim ascetics.[107] So far as Sufism, a later phenomenon, is concerned, it has long been suggested that the word 'Ṣūfī' refers to

[103] For a definition of 'Isrā'īliyyāt,' see Muḥammad Wahīb 'Allām, *al-Isrā'īliyyāt fī tafsīr al-Qur'ānī* (Beirut, 2007), pp. 53–54, and see the various definitions offered in Na'nā'a, *al-Isrā'īliyyāt wa-atharuhā fī kutub al-tafsīr*, pp. 71-75. See also the article 'Isrā'īliyyāt,' by G. Vajda in *EI2* (vol. 4, pp. 211–12) for a definition and discussion of Isrā'īliyyat, though Vajda focuses more on Isrā'īliyyat as a Jewish phenomenon. On the question of *Masīḥiyyāt*, see G. Levi della Vida, 'Leggende agiografiche Cristiane nell'Islam,' in *Atti del convegno internazionale sul tema L'oriente cristiano nella storia della civiltà* (Rome, 1964), p. 147, n. 29.

[104] See T. Khalidi, *The Muslim Jesus: Sayings and Stories in Islamic Literature* (Cambridge, Mass./London, 2001). M. Asín y Palacios, 'Logia et agrapha Domini Jesu apud Moslemicos scriptores, asceticos praesertim, usitata,' (PO 13.3) (Paris, 1919), pp. 327–431 and (PO 19.4) (Paris, 1926), pp. 529–601 contains a classic collection of 225 sayings of Jesus preserved in a variety of Islamic texts. Most recently, see the rich collection and commentary assembled in S. Chialà, ed., and I. de Francesco, trans., *I detti islamici di Gesù* (Rome, 2009). See also the following note.

[105] See S. K. Bukhsh, *Contributions to the History of Islamic Civilization*, vol. 1 (2nd ed., Calcutta, 1929), p. 9 and pp. 5–12 for examples of elements of the Gospels that were given an Islamic pedigree in Muslim literature. For sayings of Jesus attributed to Muḥammad, M. Asín y Palacios, 'Influencias evangélicas en la literatura religiosa del Islam,' in T. W. Arnold and R. A. Nicholson, eds., *A Volume of Oriental Studies Presented to Edward G. Browne… on his 60th Birthday* (Cambridge, 1922), pp. 8–27, has a collection of forty-five such sayings. Goldziher also collected a number of examples of sayings of Jesus from the Gospels, or ones clearly inspired by evangelical pronouncements, attributed to Muḥammad. See his 'Influences chrétienes dans la littérature religieuse de l'Islam,' in J. Desomogyi, ed., *Ignaz Goldziher: Gesammelte Schriften*, vol. 2 (Hildesheim, 1968), pp. 305–307, 312–13.

[106] See the comments in L. Massignon, *Essay on the Origins of the Technical Language of Islamic Mysticism*, trans. B. Clark, (Notre Dame, 1997), pp. 50–52, and Andrae, 'Zuhd und Mönchtum.' The literature on this subject is vast: more recently, see, e.g., G. G. Blum, 'Christlich-orientalische Mystik und Sufismus: Zu Grundproblemen ihres Kontaktes und ihrer gegenseitigen Beeinflussung,' in Lavenant, ed., *IIIo Symposium Syriacum*, pp. 261–71 and Blum, *Die Geschichte der Begegnung christlich-orientalischer Mystik mit der Mystik des Islams* (Wiesbaden, 2009). Sufism and early Islamic asceticism should not to be conflated; against the notion of Islamic mysticism's dependence on Neo-Platonic and Christian sources and connections, see the comments in A. Schimmel, 'Sufismus,' in H. Gätje, ed., *Grundriß der Arabischen Philologie*, vol. 2 (Wiesbaden, 1987), p. 338.

[107] See, e.g., O. Livne-Kafri, 'Early Muslim Ascetics and the World of Christian Monasticism,' *JSAI* 20 (1996), pp. 105–29; Livne-Kafri limited herself to an earlier period and collected a number of parallels between practices of early *zuhhād*—renunciants or ascetics—and Christian monks, and did not look at the question of connections between Sufis and Christian ascetics and mystics.

woolen garments worn by Muslim ascetics, perhaps in imitation of the Christian monks with whom they interacted.[108] Indeed, Muslims themselves made the connection between Sufism and Christianity in the medieval period: 'Ḥammād b. Abī Sulaymān went up to Basra,' Abū Nuʿaym al-Iṣbahānī (d. AH 430/AD 1038) reported, 'and Farqad al-Sabakhī [d. AH 131/AD 748] came to him and on him was a garment of wool (*thawb ṣūf*), and so Ḥammād said to him: 'Remove from yourself this Christianity of yours!''[109]

When it came to sacred places, Muslims took over and sometimes expanded an enormous number of Jewish and Christian traditions that associated specific biblical figures and events with particular places in Syria, Palestine, Jordan, Mesopotamia, Iraq, Egypt, and South Arabia.[110] Architecturally, the practice of turning churches into mosques was widespread and is well known,[111] and suggestions have been made that various classic features of the mosque can be traced to pre-Islamic traditions of church construction—notably the minaret,[112] the minbar,[113] and the *miḥrāb*.[114] The design of the Dome of the Rock, perhaps the most famous of all early Islamic structures, follows the plan of late antique Christian martyria and mausolea; and the Church of the Kathisma, referred to in my previous chapter, is just one example, the most dramatic, of a number of pre-Islamic Christian structures that seem to be architectural forbears of ʿAbd al-Malik's new building in Jerusalem.[115]

[108] See M. Smith, *The Way of the Mystics: the Early Christian Mystics and the Rise of the Sūfīs (London, 1976)*, pp. 158–60, and A. Schimmel, *Mystical Dimensions of Islam* (Chapel Hill, 1975), pp. 34–35. Cf. the report where Jesus's disciples ask him what he wears and he responds, 'Wool' (*al-ṣūf*): Ibn Abī Shayba, *al-Muṣannaf*, vol. 12, p. 134 (no. 35232). For traditions about Moses and Muḥammad also wearing wool, cf. G. Ogén, 'Did the Term 'ṣūfī' Exist before the Sufis?' *Acta Orientalia* 43 (1982), p. 48. On the meaning of the word *ṣūfī*, see also the classic T. Nöldeke, 'Ṣûfī,' *ZDMG* 48 (1894), pp. 45–48.

[109] Abū Nuʿaym al-Iṣbahānī, *Ḥilyat al-awliyāʾ wa-ṭabaqāt al-aṣfiyāʾ* (Beirut, 1988), vol. 4, pp. 221–22. On Farqad, see al-Mizzī, *Tahdhīb al-kamāl fī asmāʾ al-rijāl*, vol. 23, pp. 164–69; for two reports from Farqad speaking about his reading the Torah, see *ibid.*, p. 168. For this story about Ḥammād and Farqad and others that show Muslims making a (negative) connection between the woolen garment of Sufis and Christianity, see Livne-Kafri, 'Early Muslim Ascetics and the World of Christian Monasticism,' p. 113.

[110] For this, see H. Busse, 'Der Islam und die biblischen Kultstätten,' *Der Islam* 42 (1966), pp. 113–47. Busse provides a listing, by city and region and based on medieval sources, pp. 137–42, of sites associated with biblical figures which become part of the Islamic tradition. See also, H. Schwarzbaum, *Biblical and Extra-Biblical Legends in Islamic Folk-Literature* (Walldorf-Hessen, 1982), pp. 69–72.

[111] See, e.g., the numerous examples adduced in J. Pedersen's article, 'Masdjid,' in *EI2*, vol. 6, pp. 649–50 and cf. Bashear, 'Qibla Musharriqa,' pp. 267–68, esp. 267, n. 1.

[112] See Creswell, *Early Muslim Architecture*, vol. 1, pp. 38–40, and R. Hillenbrand's article 'Manāra, Manār,' in *EI2*, vol. 6, esp. pp. 362–64. Cf. also the arguments in H. Lammens, 'Phares, minarets, clochers, et mosques: leur origine, leur architecture,' *Revue de questions historiques* 46 (1911), pp. 5–27.

[113] See Creswell, *Early Muslim Architecture*, vol. 1, pp. 31–32. See also J. Pedersen's article, 'Minbar,' in *EI2*, vol. 7, pp. 73–76, and cf. Caetani, *Annali dell' Islām*, vol. 2.1, pp. 68–69 (no. 79), on the Greek or Coptic slave named Bāqūm or Bāqūl who is supposed to have built the first minbar in Medina.

[114] See Creswell, *Early Muslim Architecture*, vol. 1, pp. 98–99

[115] See Grabar, *The Dome of the Rock*, pp. 98–106. See also the extensive discussion in Creswell, *Early*

In the case of the Mosque of the Prophet in Medina, we have several accounts of a reconstruction undertaken of it by al-Walīd (reg. AD 705–715/AH 86–96) that illustrate vividly the way in which Roman traditions of ecclesiastical construction were applied in an Islamic context. Al-Walīd is said to have written to the Byzantine emperor asking for workers and mosaic tiles to help in the building of the mosque, and the emperor obliged him, sending between twenty and one hundred workmen (depending on the account) and a load of materials for making mosaics. According to Ibn Zabāla (d. after AH 199/AD 814), one of the Rūm mosaicists is supposed to have said of their work on the mosque: 'We made it in accordance with pictures we have found of the trees of paradise and its palaces.'[116]

Although it has been argued that reports of actual workmen coming from Byzantium are historically dubious—there was an indigenous Syrian tradition of sophisticated mosaic-making and a caliph could have much more easily drawn upon the skill of workers living under his own authority[117]—such stories carry with them a recognition that by the late seventh century, mosque construction was utilizing elements commonly associated with churches. As Abān b. 'Uthmān is reported to have answered al-Walīd when asked about the newly reconstructed Prophet's Mosque: 'We built it as one builds mosques, but you built it as one builds churches.'[118] Even the Prophet was made to weigh in on these developments: 'I see you,' Muḥammad was credited with saying, 'that you will make your mosques illustrious after me, just as the Jews have honored their synagogues and the Christians their churches.'[119] 'I was not commanded to raise mosques up high,' another tradition has the Prophet say, to which Ibn

---

Muslim Architecture, vol. 1, pp. 70–90, of the architectural background of fourteen different aspects of the Dome of the Rock.

[116] As reported in al-Samhūdī, *Wafā' al-wafā bi-akhbār dār al-muṣṭafā*, vol. 2, p. 519 (ed. M. Muḥyī al-Dīn 'Abd al-Ḥamīd [Beirut, 1984]). More generally, on 518–19 al-Samhūdī gives various accounts of the numbers sent. Cf. also Ṭabarī, *Ta'rīkh*, 2.2, p. 1194 (ed. Guidi [Leiden, 1883–1885]) and Balādhurī, *Kitāb futūḥ al-buldān*, pp. 6–7 (ed. M. J. de Goeje [Leiden, 1866]). J. Sauvaget, *La Mosquée omeyyade de Médine; étude sur les origines architecturales de la mosquée et de la basilique* (Paris, 1947), pp. 111–14 discusses the differences between the various Arabic accounts that survive.

[117] See the discussion of the various traditions relating to al-Walīd, Byzantine and Coptic workmen, and the reconstruction of the Prophet's Mosque in Medina and an evaluation of their historicity in G. I. Bisheh, 'The Mosque of the Prophet at Madīnah throughout the First-Century A.H. with Special Emphasis on the Umayyad Mosque,' (PhD diss., University of Michigan, 1979), pp. 201–11, and cf. the comments in Lammens, 'Phares, minarets, clochers, et mosques,' pp. 11–12, and Sauget, *La Mosquée omeyyade de Médine; étude sur les origines architecturales de la mosquée et de la basilique*, p. 112. See, too, the discussion in H. Munt, *The Holy City of Medina: Sacred Space in Early Islamic Arabia* (New York, 2014), p. 107.

[118] al-Samhūdī, *Wafā' al-wafā bi-akhbār dār al-muṣṭafā* (ed M. Muḥī al-Dīn 'Abd al-Ḥamīd), vol. 2, p. 523. Note that an alternate tradition (also reported on p. 523) has Abān tell this to 'Umar b. 'Abd al-'Azīz, who was the governor of Medina when al-Walīd had the Prophet's Mosque rebuilt.

[119] Ibn Mājah, *Sunan*, vol. 2, p. 61 (no. 740).

'Abbās is supposed to have commented, 'Surely you will ornament them [sc. mosques] as the Jews and Christians have adorned [their places of worship].'[120]

To such continuities, any number of others might be added—in the areas of food,[121] language,[122] administration,[123] and so on.[124] We are dealing in fact with the whole of human culture.[125] And none of this should astonish us. The practice of Islamizing pre-Islamic traditions had an excellent pedigree,[126] and medieval Muslims themselves recognized that certain pre-Islamic practices had been continued in Islam while others had been abandoned.[127] The Qur'ān itself used names for God that were in use among pre-Islamic inhabitants of Arabia;[128] certain *talbiyas* used by Muslims as part of the *ḥajj* likely repre-

[120] Abū Dāwūd, *Sunan*, vol. 1, p. 336 (no. 448). For a similar tradition (without the reference to Jews and Christians), see 'Abd al-Razzāq, *Muṣannaf*, vol. 3, p. 152 (no. 5127).

[121] See M. Rodinson's article Ghidhā' in *EI2*, vol. 2, pp. 1057–72, esp. p. 1062, and cf. the observation of D. Waines about the relationship between the ancient food traditions of Mesopotamia and that of medieval, Muslim-ruled Iraq in his 'Introduction,' in Waines, ed., *Patterns of Everyday Life* [Aldershot, England/Burlington, VT, 2002], p. xxxiii.

[122] On the question of substrate influences in modern Arabic dialects, see W. Diem, 'Studien zur Frage des Substrats im Arabischen,' *Der Islam* 56 (1979), pp. 12–80 (the question of Iraq and greater Syria covered at 41–49); J. Retsö, 'Aramaic/Syriac Loanwords,' pp. 178–82 in K. Versteegh, ed., *Encyclopedia of Arabic Language and Linguistics*, vol. 1 (Leiden/Boston, 2006); and M. Neishtadt, 'The Lexical Component in the Aramaic Substrate of Palestinian Arabic,' in A. M. Butts, ed., *Semitic Languages in Contact* (Leiden/Boston, 2015), pp. 280–311.

[123] For a good treatment of the administrative continuities and discontinuities in Egypt in the first fifty years after the conquest, see P. M. Sijpesteijn, 'New Rule over Old Structures: Egypt after the Muslim Conquest,' in H. Crawford, ed., *Regime Change in the Ancient Near East and Egypt: From Sargon of Agade to Saddam Hussein* (*Proceedings of the British Academy* 136) (Oxford, 2007), pp. 183–200. For the Umayyad administrative *ajnād* in Greater Syria being based on late Roman administrative structures, see J. Haldon, 'Seventh-Century Continuities: the *Ajnād* and the "Thematic Myth,"' in Av. Cameron, ed., *The Byzantine and Early Islamic Near East*, vol. 3: *States, Resources and Armies* (Princeton, 1995), pp. 379–423. See also, Walmsley, *Early Islamic Syria*, p. 73.

[124] A. Treiger, 'Mutual Influences and Borrowings,' in Thomas, ed., *Routledge Handbook on Christian-Muslim Relations* pp. 194–206, gives a useful survey of both Muslim appropriation of Christian material and Christian appropriation of Muslim material. There exist a number of studies—of varying quality and sometimes polemical in intent—along similar lines, for which J. Henninger, 'L'influence du Christianisme oriental sur l'islam naissant,' in *Atti del convegno internazionale sul tema L'oriente cristiano nella storia della civiltà (Roma 31 marzo - 3 aprile 1963) (Firenze 4 aprile 1963)* (Rome, 1964), pp. 379–411 and R. Bell, *The Origin of Islam in Its Christian Environment: The Gunning Lectures. Edinburgh University*, 1925 (London, 1926), can be taken as representative.

[125] Cf. the observation in Cahen, 'Socio-Economic History and Islamic Studies,' in Hoyland, ed., *Muslims and Others*, pp. 260–61.

[126] Rubin, *The Eye of the Beholder*, pp. 183, 183–85, gives examples of pre-Islamic practices being turned into Islamic ones by 'gaining the sanction of traditions attributed to the Prophet.'

[127] See the discussion of various *jāhiliyya* customs (*sunan*) that were either kept or dropped by Islam in Ibn Ḥabīb (d. AH 245/AD 860), *Kitāb al-muḥabbar* (ed. I. Lichtenstädter) (Hyderabad, 1942), pp. 309–340. Cf. also Ibn 'Abd Rabbih, *al-'Iqd al-Farīd*, vol. 3, p. 268; ET available in I. J. Boullata, *The Unique Necklace (al-'Iqd al-Farīd)*, vol. 3 (Reading, 2011), p. 230.

[128] For the names 'Abd al-Wāḥid, 'Abd al-Raḥmān, 'Abd al-A'lā, 'Abd al-Malik, 'Abd al-Ḥamīd, and others used in the pre-Islamic period, see L. Cheikho, *al-Naṣrāniyya wa-ādābuhā bayna 'arab al-*

sented pre-Islamic, pagan acclamations that had been altered and made acceptable to Muslim belief;[129] and the *ḥajj* itself, one of the most celebrated ritual aspects of Islam, was transformed by the Prophet from a pagan ritual into a Muslim pilgrimage.[130] Indeed, the Prophet himself was said to 'love to agree with the People of the Book in that which he had not been commanded,' a statement which can be seen as providing justification for and implicit recognition of all manner of Christian and Jewish traditions that continued on into Islamic tradition.[131] Similarly, one of the sources of religious guidance 'Umar b. al-Khaṭṭāb was said to have pointed Muslims to at the end of his life was the *Ahl al-Dhimma*.[132] Such widespread appropriation was not without precedent or parallel: Christians, too, had a longstanding habit of absorbing and repurposing pre- and non-Christian traditions and imbuing them with new meanings.[133]

ENTERING THE BLOODSTREAM

The continuities I have attempted to lay out in this chapter suggest that, despite the best efforts of some Muslim religious leaders to staunch the flow of non-Muslim ideas into their young community, much non-Muslim material did in fact 'enter the bloodstream of Islam,' to use Patricia Crone's expression.[134] The

jāhiliyya, vol. 2 (Beirut, 1989), pp. 237–38. Note also that in Q 43:9, pagans refer to Allāh as *al-'azīz* and *al-'alīm*, two names that the Qur'ān also uses to refer to Allāh.

[129] See M. J. Kister, 'Labbayka, Allāhuma, Labbayka... On a monotheistic aspect of a Jāhiliyya practice,' *JSAI* 2 (1980), pp. 33–57.

[130] Cf. A. J. Wensinck's contribution to the article 'Ḥadjdj,' ('The origin of the Islamic Ḥadjdj,') in *EI2*, vol. 3, p. 33. For the debate on the *ḥajj* before Muḥammad and especially Muslim views on this subject, see P. Webb, 'The Hajj before Muhammad: Journeys to Mecca in Narratives of Pre-Islamic History,' in V. Porter and L. Saif, eds., *The Hajj: Collected Essays* (London, 2013), pp. 6–14.

[131] al-Bukhārī, *al-Jāmi' al-ṣaḥīḥ*, vol. 4, p. 76 (no. 5917). Note that this *ḥadīth*, which suggests that the Prophet both let his hair hang down (like the People of the Book) and then parted it (like the *mushrikūn*), sits in tension with other *ḥadīth* that suggest Muslims were to be different from non-Muslims. Another report that shows a similar tension with the impulse to differentiate has the Prophet state that he had intended to forbid the practice of a woman nursing while she was sexually active (*al-ghīla*), 'until I remembered that the Romans and the Persians do that and it does not harm their children'; see Mālik b. Anas, *al-Muwaṭṭa'*, vol. 2, pp. 607–608 (no. 16).

[132] Ibn Sa'd, *Kitāb al-ṭabaqāt al-kabīr*, vol. 3.1, p. 243. For this, see Juynboll, *Muslim Tradition*, p. 26. The other sources were the Book of God (i.e., Qur'ān), the Muhājirūn, the Anṣār, and the A'rāb (i.e., Bedouin).

[133] For the Christian habit of adopting and Christianizing pagan practices and its Manichean criticism, see Jones, *Between Pagan and Christian*, pp. 98–100. Christians outside the Roman Empire adopted and Christianized pre-Christian practices, too. See, e.g., S. H. Taqizadeh, 'The Iranian Festivals Adopted by the Christians and Condemned by the Jews,' *BSOAS* 10 (1940), pp. 632–53.

[134] A phrase I have taken from Patricia Crone's introductory remarks at the 'Islamic Freethinking

Arabs were not immune to the same processes of cultural absorption, adaptation, and appropriation that have occurred throughout history whenever a new religious movement, ethnic group, or political entity has emerged and developed. Again, none of this should astonish us. If the world the Arabs found was a world of simple believers and this world gradually converted to Islam for largely non-doctrinal reasons, then what this world was, was a world ripe for such continuities.

The most obvious way that Muslim rule changed the Middle East, I suggested at the beginning of Chapter 9, was that it lead to the eventual Islamization of the entire region and the Arabization of much of it outside Anatolia and Iran. But, if we recognize the large number of pre-Islamic elements that came to be regarded as Islamic, deemphasize a *majlis* model of Christian-Muslim relations, and think of the formerly Roman Middle East as still a largely Christian one until several centuries into the second millennium AD (though nevertheless dominated politically by Muslims), we will find ourselves confronting a slightly different question. Did Islam change the Middle East or did the Middle East change Islam?

If our interest is in Christian-Muslim relations and in how a politically dominant Muslim minority related to the religious traditions of the populations it ruled over, one of the most interesting questions that arises is that of the mechanisms by which non-Muslim material became Islamicized. What were the vectors through which so many pre-Islamic, late antique things came to wear a Muslim badge and leave an Arabic calling card? The social context of these transfers will take us to the heart of the making of the medieval Middle East—the world the Arab conquests created—and it is the final question I will take up.

---

and Western Radicalism' conference held at the Institute for Advanced Study, Princeton, New Jersey, April 21–24, 2008.

PART IV

The Making of the Medieval Middle East

CHAPTER 14

Rubbing Shoulders

A Shared World

Any model we put forth in an effort to understand the process by which much that was simply late antique Christian, Jewish, Zoroastrian, or Middle Eastern tradition or culture came to be regarded as (distinctively) Islamic must recognize that there were multiple mechanisms of transmission at work. For the flow of information into Muslim communities and into Muslim normative texts from older, non-Muslim communities moved through a variety of channels.[1] Historians have a weakness for the written, but if we focus only on this one mode of transmission—essentially looking for evidence that some (anonymous?) Muslim directly copied an idea or practice from a Christian or Jewish text—we will blind ourselves to the fact that there must have been a significant oral layer of diffusion as well: Muslims and non-Muslims living together, side-by-side and having a shared existence.[2] This was the case in Syria from the earliest period of Muslim rule. Arab Muslim immigrants settled in preexisting towns and cities and al-Jābiya and al-Ramla, two well-known Arab encampments, never took off as significant places of Muslim habitation.[3]

[1] E. van Donzel and A. Schmidt, *Gog and Magog in Early Christian and Islamic Sources: Sallam's Quest for Alexander's Wall* (Leiden/Boston, 2010), pp. 175–81, is an example of an attempt to trace the appearance of late antique Christian notions in an Islamic context by looking for concrete paths of transmission. D.G. König, *Arabic-Islamic Views of the Latin West: Tracing the Emergence of Medieval Europe* (Oxford, 2015), pp. 27–71, looks at the flow of information between the Muslim-ruled world and the Latin west.

[2] To take a Christian-Jewish example, in the ninth century the Jewish al-Qirqisānī spoke of asking the bishop Yasū' Sakā, who was in 'Ukbara, a question and said the bishop was the least dishonest Christian scholar or philosopher he had met; see *Kitāb al-anwār wa-'l-marāqib*, vol. 2 (ed. L. Nemoy) (New York, 1940), p. 220, and cf. S. P. Brock, 'Jewish Traditions in Syriac Sources,' *Journal of Jewish Studies* 30 (1979), p. 230, where the bishop is identified as the East Syrian bishop Isho'zeka of 'Ukbara.

[3] See Donner, *The Early Islamic Conquests*, pp. 245–50. On al-Jābiya, see H. Lammens and J. Sourdel-Thomine's article, 'al-Djābiya,' in *EI2*, vol. 2, p. 360; on al-Ramla, see E. Honigmann's article, 'al-Ramla,' in *EI2*, vol. 8, pp. 423–24. On Muslim settlement patterns in Syria, see D. Whitcomb, 'Amṣār in Syria? Syrian Cities after the Conquest,' *Aram* 6 (1994), pp. 13–33, and Walmsley, *Early Islamic Syria*, pp. 71–112. Against the view that Muslims did not establish new towns and for a discussion of various garrison cities (e.g., Ayla, 'Anjar, al-Ramla), as well as the desert palaces, see Walmsley, pp. 90–104. For an increase in contacts between Muslims and Christians toward the end of the seventh century, see R. Hoyland, 'Jacob of Edessa on Islam,' in G. J. Reinink and A. C. Klugkist, eds., *After Bardaisan: Studies on*

GARRISON CITIES AND THE OUTSIDE WORLD

Outside Syria, we must also remember that the garrison cities in which Arab immigrants settled were themselves not hermetically sealed off from the populations around them: I have already cited a letter of 'Umar II forbidding Christians from selling wine in garrison cities, and one might also mention another letter of 'Umar II ordering the churches in the garrison cities of the Muslims be destroyed.[4] Similarly, al-Ḥasan al-Baṣrī (d. AH 110/AD 728) is reported to have said that the *sunna* dictated destroying churches in the garrison cities, both new and old.[5]

Basra, which along with Kufa was perhaps the garrison city *par excellence*, was known before its refoundation in 638 as Prath Mayshan; we have evidence for Christian bishops there starting in 310 and continuing for centuries after the Arab conquests.[6] As late as the twelfth century, a Christian physician in Basra named Yaḥyā b. Sa'īd b. Mārī (d. AD 1193/AH 589) would write a series of *maqāmāt* in imitation of the famous *Maqāmāt* of al-Harīrī (d. AD 1122/AH 516); Ibn Mārī's were known as *al-Maqāmāt al-masīḥiyya*, the Christian *maqāmāt*.[7] Kufa, for its part, was known in Syriac as 'Aqulā.[8] In the early seventh century, Marutha of Tikrit built a monastery dedicated to St. Sergius, filling it with both monks and liturgical books. It was, his *vita* reported, a

---

Continuity and Change in Syriac Christianity in Honour of Professor Han J. W. Drijvers (Leuven, 1999), pp. 152–53.

[4] See Ibn Qayyim al-Jawziyya, *Aḥkām ahl al-dhimma*, vol. 2, p. 122. Though see Yarbrough, 'Did 'Umar b. 'Abd al-'Azīz Issue an Edict concerning non-Muslim Officials?' for 'Umar also supporting Christian churches in certain contexts.

[5] See Ibn al-Durayhim, *Manhaj al-ṣawāb fī qubḥ istiktāb ahl al-kitāb*, p. 166 (ed. S. Kasrawī [Beirut, 2002]), and also 'Abd al-Razzāq, *al-Muṣannaf*, vol. 10, p. 319 (no. 19231).

[6] See the evidence collected in J.-M. Fiey, *Pour un Oriens Christianus Novus*, pp. 59–60, and *AC*, vol. 3, pp. 266–71. On various dates for Basra's foundation, see C. Pellat, *Le milieu baṣrien et la formation de Ǧāḥiẓ* (Paris, 1953), p. 2.

[7] His full name was Abū al-'Abbās Yaḥyā b. Sa'īd b. Mārī al-Baṣrī. On this work, see Brockelmann, *GAL*, vol. 1, p. 329 and vol. S1, p. 489. A description of it can be found in G. Flügel, *Die arabischen, persischen und türkischen Handschriften der Kaiserlich-königlichen Hofbibliothek zu Wien*, vol. 1 (Vienna, 1865), pp. 358–59; an edition of its introduction and first *maqāma* can be found in A. al-Karmalī, 'al-Maqāmāt al-Naṣrāniyya li-Ibn Mārī,' *al-Machriq* 3 (1900), pp. 591–98; an edition of its twelfth and fiftieth *maqāmas* can be found in Ṣ. Ṣādiq, 'Baghdād min khilāl al-maqāmāt,' *al-Mawrid* 8 (1979), pp. 585–88. For more on Yaḥyā, see Yāqūt, *Mu'jam al-udabā': irshād al-arīb ilā ma'rifat al-adīb*, vol. 6 (ed. I. 'Abbās) (Beirut, 1993), p. 2835 (no. 1245), where he is called Yāḥyā b. Yaḥyā b. Sa'īd and is said to have been known as Ibn Mārī al-Masīḥī; see also, Ibn al-Qifṭī, *Ta'rīkh al-ḥukamā'*, pp. 320–21 (ed. J. Lippert [Leipzig, 1903]), where it is noted that he was also known as al-Masīḥī ('the Christian'). On the work's reception, see D. Stewart, 'The *Maqāma*,' in R. Allen and D. S. Richards, ed., *Arabic Literature in the Post-Classical Period* (Cambridge, 2008), p. 153.

[8] Payne Smith, ed. *Thesaurus Syriacus*, vol. 2, col. 2964.

stopping point and a 'harbor' for people passing through the desert to 'Aqulā.[9] In the period of Muslim rule, there was a Christian church in Kufa before AD 660, the year in which the church was apparently destroyed,[10] and even though 'Alī b. Abī Ṭālib reportedly objected to any Jew, Christian, or Magian living in Kufa, the very fact that he is supposed to have had such a prohibition announced daily suggests that it was not being followed.[11] Indeed, Christianity was openly practiced in Kufa: we even have a report of al-Akhṭal (d. AH 92/ AD 710), the famous Christian poet, mediating a dispute at the gate of Kufa's main mosque while wearing a gold cross.[12]

Only three miles from Kufa was Hira, perhaps the preeminent center of pre-Islamic Arabic-speaking Christianity and an important Christian center more generally;[13] when 'Alī's herald would announce each day that Jews, Christians, and Magians were not to live in Kufa, he also announced that it was to Hira or al-Zurāra (a village outside of Kufa) that they should go instead.[14] To some medieval writers at least, the connection between Hira and Kufa was so close that they were essentially identical.[15] A large number of Christian monasteries could be found in Hira and its environs,[16] and a series of colorful stories claimed that prominent early Muslims—al-Ḥajjāj b. Yūsuf,

[9] Denḥā, *Life of Marutha*, p. 86 (ed. Nau [PO 3.1]).

[10] Fiey, *AC*, vol. 3, p. 207.

[11] al-Subkī, *Fatāwā al-Subkī*, vol. 2, p. 381 (Beirut, n.d.). Cf. Friedmann, *Tolerance and Coercion*, p. 93, and S. Ward, 'A Fragment from an Unknown Work by Al-Ṭabarī on the Tradition "Expel the Jews and Christians from the Arabian Peninsula (and the Lands of Islam)",' *BSOAS* 53 (1990), pp. 414, 417.

[12] For Christians in Islamic Kufa, see Qāshā, *Aḥwāl naṣārā al-'Irāq fī khilāfat banī Umayya*, vol. 2, pp. 409–21. Lammens, 'Études sur le règne du calife Omaiyade Mo'awiya Ier,' (part 3), pp. 299–301, also contains information about the presence of Christians in Kufa and the open practice of Christianity there. For al-Akhṭal at the mosque in Kufa, wearing a golden cross, see pp. 299–301 and Lammens, *Le chantre des Omiades: notes biographiques et littéraires sur le poète arabe chrétien Aḥṭal* (Paris, 1895), pp. 81–82. Cf. also Abū al-Faraj al-Iṣbahānī, *Kitāb al-Aghānī*, vol. 7, p. 187, and see, too, al-Akhṭal, *Diwān*, p. 156, n. a.

[13] On Christians and Hira, see Fiey, *AC*, vol. 3, pp. 203–43; Qāshā, *Aḥwāl naṣārā al-'Irāq fī khilāfat banī Umayya*, vol. 2, pp. 395–409; E.C.D. Hunter, 'The Christian Matrix of al-Hira,' in C. Jullien, ed., *Controverses des chrétiens dans l'Iran sassanide (Chrétiens en terre d'Iran* II*)* (Paris, 2008), pp. 41–56; Hunter, 'Reconstructing Christianity in South-West Iraq: Reassessing Hira,' *The Harp* 24 (2009), pp. 411–23; P. Wood, 'Hira and Her Saints,' *AB* 132 (2014), pp. 5–20; and I. Toral-Niehoff, *Al-Ḥīra: Eine arabische Kulturmetropole im spätantiken Kontext* (Leiden/Boston, 2014), pp. 151–211. Fiey, *Pour un Oriens Christianus Novus*, pp. 90-91, discusses the bishops of Hira going back to the fourth century.

[14] al-Subkī, *Fatāwā al-Subkī*, vol. 2 p. 381 (cf. n. 11, above).

[15] 'Suwaid had designs regarding al-Baṣrah similar to those of al-Muthanna regarding al-Kūfa, which at that time was not called al-Kūfah but al-Ḥīrah.' See al-Balādhurī, *Kitāb futūh al-buldān*, p. 241 (ed. de Goeje); ET taken from Hitti, *The Origins of the Islamic State*, vol. 1, p. 388). For this point, see Fiey, *AC*, vol. 3, p. 205, n. 9.

[16] Toral-Niehoff, *Al-Ḥīra*, p. 175, estimates there were forty churches and monasteries in and around al-Ḥīra in the Abbasid period; Fiey, *AC*, vol. 3, pp. 212–21, attempted to survey what could be known of these.

Sa'd b. Abī Waqqāṣ, and al-Mughīra b. Shu'ba—all visited Dayr al-Hind in Hira in the decades after the Arab conquests.[17] As for Kufa, Balādhurī included in his list of points of interest there a number of monasteries.[18] The large number of Christian structures in the area of Kufa might be one explanation for the apparent similarity between its main mosque and Christian churches: 'Their minaret is of a different shape from that at Baṣra,' al-Jāhiẓ wrote in the ninth century, 'being modeled on the bell-towers of the Melkites and Jacobites.'[19] With this said, however, there were monasteries in and around Basra as well.[20] Taxation also points to the presence of non-Muslims in garrison cities: in his discussion of the *jizya*, Abū Yūsuf (d. AD 798/AH 182) spoke of how one should go about collecting the poll tax on non-Muslims in garrison cities such as Baghdad, Kufa, and Basra, and other places like them.[21] It has also been argued that traditions crediting 'Umar b. al-Khaṭṭāb with refusing to employ a Christian in government work had their origins in late Sufyānid Kufa.[22]

Ibn 'Abbās's reported disapproval of People of the Book settling alongside Muslims in garrison cities is yet another piece of evidence that precisely this was occurring,[23] and we have other indications of Christians in areas of Muslim settlement, such as Ayla.[24] Wāsiṭ was founded in the late seventh century across the Tigris from the important Christian center of Kashkar; this location, it has been suggested, meant that the Muslims living there would have come into regular contact with Christians. After 713, in fact, Christians were permitted to live in Wāsiṭ, and two monasteries were founded there around this time.[25] There were even apparently Christians in Medina, the capital city of

[17] al-Shābushtī, *al-Diyārāt*, pp. 244–45; an ET is available in A. Talib, 'Topoi and Topography in the Histories of al-Ḥīra,' in Wood, ed., *History and Identity in the Late Antique Near East*, pp. 145–47.

[18] al-Balādhurī, *Kitāb futūḥ al-buldān*, pp. 283–84 (ed. de Goeje; ET available in Hitti, *The Origins of the Islamic State*, vol. 1, p. 443): these included Dayr Qurra, Dayr al-Sawā, Dayr al-Jamājim, Dayr Ka'b, and Dayr Hind. He also mentioned the Church of the Banū 'Adī.

[19] Jāḥiẓ, *Kitāb al-amṣār wa-'ajā'ib al-buldān*, p. 199 (ed. C. Pellat, 'Al-Jāḥīẓ rā'id al-jughrāfiyya al-insāniyya,' *al-Mashriq* 60 [1966]; translation taken from Pellat, *The Life and Works of Jāḥiẓ*, p. 193).

[20] Yāqūt (*Mu'jam al-buldān*, vol. 2) also gives the names of several monasteries located near Basra: Dayr Jābīl (p. 503) was near Basra, and Dayr al-Dihdār (p. 509) was a monastery of pre-Islamic origins in the area of Basra.

[21] Abū Yusūf, *Kitāb al-Kharāj*, p. 123.

[22] See L. Yarbrough, 'Upholding God's Rule: Early Muslim Juristic Opposition to the State Employment of Non-Muslims,' *Islamic Law and Society* 19 (2012), pp. 11–85.

[23] al-Subkī, *Fatāwā al-Subkī*, vol. 2 p. 381; for this, see Fridemann, *Tolerance and Coercion*, p. 93. See also Ibn Abī Shayba, *al-Muṣannaf*, vol. 11, p. 286 (no. 33278).

[24] For Ayla as founded next to a Byzantine town with a similar name, whose bishop was reputed to have been in contact with the Prophet, see D. Whitcomb, 'The Miṣr of Ayla: New Evidence for the Early Islamic City,' in Donner, ed., *The Articulation of Early Islamic State Structures*, p. 370.

[25] On Wāsiṭ, see M. Sakly, 'Wāsiṭ,' in *EI2*, vol. 11, pp. 165–69 (for Kashkar and Wāsiṭ connected from the latter's foundation by a pontoon bridge, see p. 166). For Kashkar's Christian history, see Fiey, *AC*, vol. 3, pp. 151–87 (for Christians living in Wāsiṭ after 713 and the foundation of two monasteries there,

the earliest caliphs.[26] Apart from such signals of a Christian presence in these areas of Muslim settlement, there must have been more generally a large number of non-Muslims in these places: by the ninth century, for example, al-Jāḥiẓ was pointing to non-Arabic (Persian) words that could be found in the Arabic dialects of Medina, Kufa, and Basra.[27] It would be safe to assume that the number of non-Muslim slaves and concubines in the garrison cities must have been substantial:[28] Bashshār b. Burd can serve as an example. Born in Basra around AH 95–96 (AD 715–716), his father had been a slave and his grandfather was a Central Asian captive who had been brought to Iraq in the seventh century. We know of Bashshār and his family history because he became one of the most celebrated poets of the eighth century,[29] but given the remarkable successes of Arab armies and their reputation for taking slaves, how many other captives and descendants of freed captives must have populated places like Basra and Kufa in the seventh and eighth centuries? Patricia Crone has in fact suggested that non-Muslims likely outnumbered Muslims in garrison cities not long after they were founded.[30]

If we have Muslims and Christians living in such close proximity—and not protected from one another by any sort of quarantine—we find ourselves

---

see p. 170) and Y. Y. Maskūnī, 'Naṣārā Kaskar wa-Wāsiṭ qubayla al-Islām,' *al-Mashriq* 58 (1964), pp. 633–47. On Christians and Muslims at Kashkar, see S. H. Griffith, 'Chapter Ten of the Scholion: Theodore Bar Kônî's Apology for Christianity,' *OCP* 47 (1981), p. 161.

[26] See the evidence assembled by Lammens for Christians in Medina in 'Études sur le règne du calife Omaiyade Moʿawiya Ier,' (part 3), p. 268, and his argument that the number of Christians in Medina *increased* after the death of Muḥammad such that ʿUmar would lament their large number there on his deathbed (p. 269) (cf. ʿUmar's charge against Ibn ʿAbbās that he and his father wanted to see an increase in the number of *al-ʿulūj*—unbelieving foreigners—in Medina: Ibn al-Athīr, *al-Nihāya fī gharīb al-ḥadīth wa-'l-athar*, vol. 3, p. 286). More recently, see H. Munt, '"No Two Religions": Non-Muslims in the Early Islamic Ḥijāz,' *BSOAS* 78 (2015), pp. 249–69, esp. 259–64.

[27] al-Jāḥiẓ, *al-Bayān wa-'l-tabyīn*, p. 19.

[28] I am grateful to Peter Brown for this point. For slaves and *mawālī* likely accompanying the Arab tribes who settled in Basra, see Pellat, *Le milieu baṣrien et la formation de Ǧāḥiẓ*, p. 34. It was a Persian slave, Abū Lu'lu'a, who killed ʿUmar b. al-Khaṭṭāb in Medina in 644, which is reported to have prompted al-Hurmuzān to exclaim, 'I will not leave in Medina or elsewhere a Persian, save I have killed him!' (al-Masʿūdī, *Murūj al-dhahab*, vol. 4, p. 353; and cf. L. Veccia Vaglieri in *EI2*, vol. 3, p. 587). In the early seventeenth century, Antonio de Sosa provided a description of Algiers that can be useful to think with in this context: 'The inhabitants of this city are generally divided into three kinds: Moors, Turks, and Jews. We do not speak of Christians, although there is an infinite number of them of every stripe and nation, because they ordinarily arrive here as captives and slaves, including the more than 25,000 who row in the galleys or who remain on land. Christians, therefore, count as neither inhabitants nor neighbors of Algiers. Nor do we include Christian merchants as inhabitants, since very few are based here: their business done and their merchandise sold, each man returns to his own land.' Translation by D. de Armas Wilson taken from M. A. Garcés, ed., *An Early Modern Dialogue with Islam: Antonio de Sosa's* Topography of Algiers *(1612)* (Notre Dame, 2011), p. 119.

[29] On Bashshār, see R. Blachère's article, 'Bashshār b. Burd,' in *EI2*, vol. 1, pp. 1080–82.

[30] Crone, *Nativist Prophets*, p. 8.

confronted once again with the problem of the ghosts of conversations past which I took up earlier in this book. We saw in Chapter 4 that there will have been an enormous layer of non-elite religious discussion that has been lost to us. My focus in that chapter was on a Christian context, but the same will have held true for Muslims. 'If a scholar stands up in the main street or the marketplace,' al-Jāḥiẓ complained, in language reminiscent of Gregory of Nyssa's famous description of Constantinople half a millennium earlier,

> and discusses grammar and prosody, or discourses on the law or astronomy, mathematics, medicine, geometry or the crafts, only specialists will gather around and dispute with him. But let him say so much as a word about predestination, or mention the Knowledge and Will [of God], or "capacity" and responsibility, or consider whether or not God created unbelief, and there will be no fool of a porter, no down-and-out wretch, no tongue-tied idiot or ignorant blockhead who will not stop and argue and contribute his approval or criticism... These sort of people ought not to associate with the aristocracy; and furthermore, however good their intentions may be, they lack the attainments needed for understanding and discrimination.[31]

We have no reason to think that the same will not have also held true for exchanges between Christians and Muslims, for acknowledging that this was a world where theological illiteracy was rampant does not preclude us from acknowledging that theological curiosity was widespread as well: every Muslim, al-Jāḥiẓ complained elsewhere, regarded himself a dialectical theologian (*mutakallim*) and that there was no one more qualified at debating religious deviants.[32] Christians had discussed and debated religious questions with each other, as well as with Jews, Zoroastrians, and pagans. They were doing the same now with Muslims: as we have already seen, in AD 755–756, for instance, a Muslim governor ordered Christians not to discuss matters of faith with Arabs.[33] Such an order was hardly enforceable, and the circumstances triggering it are not hard to imagine. In the ninth century, al-Jāḥiẓ began his letter in *Response to the Christians* (*Radd ʿalā al-Naṣārā*) by noting that his correspondent had written to him about confusion entering into the hearts of young and weak Muslims on account of Christians. Christians had been pointing out to Muslims, al-Jāḥiẓ's correspondent noted, that they did not believe that Mary was a god, as the Qur'ān claimed they did (5:116), and that Jews did not believe Ezra was the Son of God, as the Qur'ān also claimed (9:30). In these and other

[31] al-Jāḥiẓ, *al-ʿUthmāniyya*, pp. 254–55 (ET taken from Pellat, *The Life and Works of Jāḥiẓ*, p. 79).

[32] al-Jāḥiẓ, *Fī 'l-radd ʿalā al-Naṣārā*, p. 320. For this, see van Ess, *Theologie und Gesellschaft*, vol. 1, p. 54 [= *Theology and Society*, vol. 1, p. 62].

[33] Theophanes, *Chronicle* AM 6248 (ed. de Boor, vol. 1, p. 430; ET available in Mango and Scott, *The Chronicle of Theophanes Confessor*, p. 594). See chapter 12, n. 16.

cases, the Qur'ān was making charges, these Christians asserted, that did not correspond to reality.[34]

Here we have a theological example, but the range of such contacts and interactions much have included much more than simply controversial encounters. And because the conversations, discussions, stories, disagreements, and debates through which Muslims came into contact with the traditions of the non-Muslims over whom they ruled have largely vanished and are unknown to us, we cannot recover what must have been one of the most important vectors by which Muslims learned of non-Muslim ideas and practices.[35]

MILIEUX OF CONTACT AND TRANSMISSION

What we can do, however, is attempt to sketch out some of the concrete social milieux of contact where Muslims and non-Muslims rubbed shoulders and where Muslims would have encountered pre-Islamic traditions.[36] In other words, we can turn this question of intellectual and cultural history into one of social history in order to try to understand the nuts and bolts of the formation of what, eventually, would be understood to be 'Islam' and 'Islamic society.' In what remains of this chapter, I will attempt to suggest some of the social milieux of exchange and vectors by which Muslims came into contact with non-Muslims, milieux where through shared settings and shared experiences non-Muslim ideas and practices came to be taken up by Muslims. In Chapter 12, I dealt with one important area of contact—the relationship between Muslims and Christian holy men and sacraments. And now, from among the many further points of contact which must have existed, I will narrow my focus to the following: religiously mixed families, daily interactions in towns and cities, Christian monasteries and religious festivals, religious converts, and prisoners of war. I will take each of these up in turn.

RELIGIOUS INTERACTION BEGINS . . . AT HOME

Many of the mixed religious practices I attempted to adduce evidence for in Chapter 12 no doubt were the result of marriages between Muslim men and

[34] al-Jāḥiẓ, *Fī 'l-radd 'alā al-Naṣārā*, pp. 303–304.

[35] There is a visual aspect to keep in mind, too: Muslims could have learned about Christian ideas, stories, and practices simply by seeing churches and the images and objects they contained and by observing rituals, such as Christian processions, weddings, and funerals.

[36] I have been influenced here by the remarks and ideas of Patricia Crone at the 'Islamic Freethinking and Western Radicalism' conference; cf. chapter 13, n. 134.

Christian women, or of marriages in which a man would convert to Islam but his wife would remain Christian.[37] Muslim men were allowed to marry the women of the People of the Book (cf. Q 5:5), and we have evidence that this was an attractive prospect to such an extent that it even caused problems for some Muslim women who could not find spouses. For instance, after Muslim forces captured al-Madā'in in Iraq, Ḥudhayfa was appointed by 'Umar b. al-Khaṭṭāb as its governor. When 'Umar saw that the number of Muslim women without husbands was on the rise in the area, he ordered Ḥudhayfa to divorce his wife, who was not a Muslim. Ḥudhayfa wrote to the caliph, asking whether he was permitted to marry a member of the People of the Book: 'It is indeed permissible,' 'Umar responded, 'but the non-Arab women are captivating, and if you draw near to them they will wrest you from your wives.'[38] Arab soldiers might also marry non-Muslim women simply because there were no Muslim women to be found in places far from home: 'I participated in the battle of al-Qādisiyyah with Sa'd,' Jābir reported, 'We married women from the People of the Book, as we did not find many Muslim women. When we returned, some of us divorced them and some of us kept them.'[39]

There was, of course, Prophetic precedent for marrying women from the People of the Book: numbered among Muḥammad's eleven wives was Ṣafiyya bint Ḥuyayy b. Akhṭab,[40] a Jew, and the mother of Muḥammad's only son,

[37] On the subject of interreligious marriage in the period in question, see more generally Simonsohn, 'Communal Membership despite Religious Exogamy.' Though there are obvious difficulties in projecting the circumstances of modern interfaith marriage back into the medieval period, contemporary treatments of the subject can nevertheless be useful to explore. See, e.g., E. B. Seamon, *Interfaith Marriage in America: the Transformation of Religion and Christianity* (New York, 2012), esp. 113–72, and H. Richmond, *Blessed and Called to Be a Blessing: Muslim-Christian Couples Sharing a Life Together* (Oxford, 2015). See also the document produced by the Pontifical Council for Interreligious Dialogue and the World Council of Churches' Office on Inter-Religious Relations' on 'Reflections on Interreligious Marriage. A Joint Study Document,' *Pro Dialogo* 96 (1997), pp. 325–39, in particular its observations about the various ways the children of interreligious marriages potentially can relate to the different religious traditions of their parents ('Bringing Up Children in an Interreligious Marriage,' 334–36).

[38] al-Ṭabarī, *Ta'rīkh*, 1.5, p. 2375 (ed. E. Prym [Leiden, 1893]; ET taken from Friedmann, *The Battle of al-Qādisiyyah and the Conquest of Syria and Palestine*, p. 159). 'Umar's son, Ibn 'Umar, disapproved of marrying Christian and Jewish women, see al-Bukhārī, *al-Jāmi' al-ṣaḥīḥ*, vol. 3, p. 408 (no. 5275): 'If Ibn 'Umar was asked about marrying a Christian or a Jewish woman, he said: "God has forbidden polytheistic women (*al-mushrikāt*) from Believers and I know no bigger case of *shirk* than for a woman to say her Lord is Jesus, he being a servant among the servants of God.'

[39] al-Ṭabarī, *Ta'rīkh*, 1.5, p. 2375 (ed. E. Prym [Leiden, 1893]; ET taken from Friedmann, *The Battle of al-Qādisiyyah and the Conquest of Syria and Palestine*, p. 159).

[40] Ibn Hishām, *Kitāb sīrat rasūl Allāh*, pp. 758, 763, 766 (ed. Wüstenfeld, vol. 1.2; ET available in Guillaume, *The Life of Muhammad*, pp. 511, 514–15, 516–17). On Ṣafiyya, see the article by V. Vacca and R. Roded, 'Ṣafiyya bt. Ḥuyayy b. Akhṭab,' in *EI2*, vol. 8, p. 817. On the Prophet and Ṣafiyya, as well as Rayḥāna bt. Sham'ūn bt. Zayd, another Jewish woman whom he may have married, see Friedmann, *Tolerance and Coercion*, pp. 183–84.

Ibrāhīm, was a Coptic slave named Mary, who was a concubine.[41] Muḥammad gave Mary's sister, Sīrīn, to Ḥassān b. Thābit, and she bore him a son named ʿAbd al-Raḥmān.[42] Early leaders of the community would follow Muḥammad's lead: ʿUthmān b. ʿAffān, for instance, had a Christian wife named Nāʾila b. al-Furāfiṣa, and Muʿāwiya famously had a Christian wife named Maysūn.[43]

We should not forget that the demographic realities of the early Muslim-ruled Middle East offered plenty of opportunities for Muslim-Christian interaction of this kind. Muḥammad b. Abī Bakr wrote to ʿAlī and asked him about the case of a Muslim man who had fornicated with a Christian woman: the Muslim, ʿAlī responded, should receive the *ḥadd* punishment, and the woman should be turned over to her religious community.[44] And though I will focus here on Muslim men marrying non-Muslim, especially Christian, women, we should not imagine that there was no sexual interaction between non-Muslim men and Muslim women: 'If a man from the People of the Book,' Ibn Jurayj (d. AH 150/AD 768) stated, 'fornicates with a Muslim woman or steals something from a Muslim man, [a punishment] should be established against him and the imam should not turn away from it.'[45] Similarly, Jacob of Edessa himself had dealt with the question of whether a Christian man or woman who committed adultery with a pagan was to receive the same punishment as a Christian who committed adultery with a Christian.[46] A letter from the patriarch Athanasius of Balad (d. AD 687), written perhaps in 684, condemned 'wretched' Christian women who were 'unlawfully and inappropriately' marrying pagan

[41] al-Ṭabarī, *Taʾrīkh*, 1.3, p. 1561 (ed. de Jong [Leiden, 1882–1885]) and Ibn Saʿd, *Kitāb al-ṭabaqāt al-kabīr*, vol. 8, pp. 153–56 (ed. Brockelmann [Leiden, 1904]; ET available in Bewley, *The Women of Madina*, pp. 148–51). On Māriya, see F. Buhl's article, 'Māriya,' in *EI2*, vol. 6, p. 575, and on Ibrāhīm's birth, see Caetani, *Annali dell' Islam*, vol. 2.1, pp. 211–12.

[42] See Ibn Saʿd, *Kitāb al-ṭabaqāt al-kabīr*, vol. 5, p. 196 (ed. Zettersteen [Leiden, 1905]; an ET is available in Bewley, *The Men of Madina*, vol. 2, p. 166).

[43] See Qāshā, *Aḥwāl al-naṣārā fī 'l-khilāfat banī Umayya*, vol. 1, p. 126. On Maysūn, see H. Lammens's article, 'Maysūn' in *EI2*. For Nāʾila's father as a Christian, see Abū Faraj al-Iṣbahānī, *Kitāb al-aghānī*, vol. 15, p. 70; for Nāʾila as a Christian, see Ibn ʿAsākir, *Taʾrīkh Madīnat Dimashq*, vol. 70, p. 138. For the common practice among the Umayyads of marrying women from the Christian tribe of Kalb, see H. Lammens, 'Études sur le règne du calife Omaiyade Moʿawiya Ier,' (part 3), p. 157; but note, too, J. W. Fück, 'Kalb b. Wabara,' in *EI2*, vol. 4, pp. 492–93, who states that the Kalb were a Christian tribe but converted to Islam en masse in 629. On Companions with Jewish or Christian wives, see S. Spectorsky, 'Problems of Intermarriage in Early *fiqh* Texts,' in B. H. Hary, J. L. Hayes, and F. Astern, eds., *Judaism and Islam: Boundaries, Communications, and Interaction: Essays in Honor of William M. Brinner* (Leiden/Boston, 2000), p. 273; see further Friedmann, *Tolerance and Coercion*, p. 181, and for the legal debate on interfaith marriage, pp. 160–93 more generally.

[44] ʿAbd al-Razzāq, *al-Muṣannaf*, vol. 10, p. 321 (no. 19236).

[45] ʿAbd al-Razzāq, *al-Muṣannaf*, vol. 10, p. 323 (no. 19243).

[46] *Questions Which Addai the Priest and Lover of Labors Asked Jacob, the Bishop of Edessa* 69 (ed. Lamy, *Dissertatio*, pp. 166, 168). For the Syriac text of Mardin 310, fol. 206a (p. 409), with an ET, see *SBI*, p. 526, n. 1256.

men (*ḥanpē*); these *ḥanpē* may have in fact been Muslims, or were, at the very least, understood as such by the later tradition.[47] In the late seventh or early eighth century, Jacob of Edessa, as we have already seen, dealt with a question from Addai about whether a Christian woman who had freely married a Muslim man (implying that there were instances where Christian women had done so unwillingly) could receive the Eucharist; Addai also raised the possibility that the Muslim man might threaten the priest with death in order to secure Eucharistic access.[48] By the middle of the eighth century, the Miaphysite patriarch George of Beʿeltan (sed. AD 758–789/790) had issued a canon explicitly aimed at women who were marrying Muslims and pagans: 'So far as women who marry pagans (*ḥanpē*) or Hagarenes (*mhaggrāyē*) are concerned,' he wrote, 'the holy synod has ordered that they shall not enter the church. Neither shall they take the Eucharist.'[49]

Only a few years before Athanasius of Balad wrote his letter, the East Syrian Synod of Mar George, held in 676, admonished Christian women to 'be on guard with all their strength against marriage with pagans (*ḥanpē*), because marriage with them produces in them practices which are foreign to the fear of God.' The synod went on to declare 'distant from the church and from all honor of the Christians' any woman who lived with pagans (*ḥanpē*).[50] The East

[47] Athanasius of Balad, *Letter on Eating the Sacrifices of the Hagarenes*, p. 129 (Syriac text and FT in Nau, 'Littérature canonique syriaque inédite'). This is a passage that has been much studied: text and translation also available in Ebied, 'The Syriac Encyclical Letter of Athanasius II,' p. 172 = 173 (ET). An ET and discussion of this text is available in M. P. Penn, *When Christians First Met Muslims: A Sourcebook for the Earliest Syriac Writings on Islam* (Oakland, Calif., 2015), pp. 79–84. A full translation is available in *SBI*, p. 469, n. 1119, and a partial ET in Hoyland, *Seeing Islam*, p. 148.

The incipit of the letter (p. 128) states that it concerns the Hagarenes (ܡܗܓܪ̈ܝܐ) who currently hold power, a statement that was already included with the letter in its earliest ms., Mardin 310 (fol. 183b/p. 366), which dates from the eighth century. This explanatory rubric, however, may be a later addition. Cf. Hoyland's discussion of this issue in his *Seeing Islam*, pp. 148–49, and later, M. P. Penn, 'Monks, Manuscripts, and Muslims: Syriac Textual Changes in Reaction to the Rise of Islam,' *Hugoye* 12 (2009), pp. 244–46 and Penn, *Envisioning Islam*, 165–66. NB: Scholars typically take *ḥanpē* in this context to mean either 'pagan' or 'Muslim,' but in East Syrian texts of the sixth century (and before), it is a common way to refer to Zoroastrians (see chapter 4, n. 70). Athanasius's letter was primarily concerned with Christians eating with pagans, but note that one of the charges against Mar Aba was that he was ordering Christians to stop eating meat consecrated by Magians; see *History of Mar Aba*, p. 229 (ed. Bedjan, *Histoire de Mar-Jabalaha*). Aba himself states (p. 232) that he admonished Christians 'to keep themselves from all the pollution of sacrifices,' and at p. 238, it is demanded that Aba stop preventing Christians from eating meat that Magians have prayed over. Apart from social realities that would have forced these issues on Christian leaders, one obvious background to such discussions is 1 Corinthians 8-10; cf. also Acts 15:29.

[48] See chapter 12, n. 74.

[49] *Canons of the Patriarch George* 13 (ed. Vööbus, *The Synodicon in the West Syrian Tradition II* [CSCO 375–76: SS 163–64], p. 4 [Syriac] = p. 5 [ET]; the translation is mine).

[50] Synod of Mar George, *Canons* 14 (ed. Chabot, *Synodicon Orientale*, pp. 223–24 [= 488 (FT)]).

Syrian catholicos Mar Aba (d. AD 552) had declared that any man who married a pagan woman (*ḥanptā*) should not only be held back from communion, but should also be prevented from entering church or mixing with other Christians.[51] In this latter instance, 'pagan' cannot have meant 'Muslim,' but in the case of the letter of Athanasius and the Synod of Mar George in 676, regardless of whether we should interpret the *ḥanpē* they refer to as pagans or as Muslims, these condemnations point to a simple fact: in the seventh and eighth centuries, as now, the heart was often blind to sectarian affiliation.[52]

The problem of marrying members of rival churches, or even non-Christians, was one that would not go away, either. In 785, the Miaphysite patriarch George of Beʿeltan excommunicated Christians who married their daughters to pagans, Hagarenes, or Nestorians in the same synod in which he had forbidden women who had married pagans or Hagarenes from entering church and from taking the Eucharist.[53] In 846, a synod convened by the Miaphysite patriarch John III excommunicated any man or woman who married their daughter off to a 'pagan or a Jew or a Magian,' as well as any woman who 'of her own will' married a member of one of these groups.[54] By this point, *ḥanpā*, 'pagan,' likely meant Muslim.[55] The appearance of Muslims in an already diverse religious landscape simply added one more group that Christians might potentially marry.

The combination of demographics—Muslims existing as a small minority in a sea of non-Muslims—and permissive religious regulations—Muslim men could have up to four wives and were allowed to marry women from the People of the Book—meant that it was only inevitable that religious intermarriage would take place. The fact that Muslim men were permitted to have sex with female slaves would have been another factor in encouraging this most basic type of Muslim-Christian interaction.[56] And when we read accounts of Muslims holding various Christian symbols and rituals in high esteem—baptism, Jesus,

[51] Mar Aba, *Letter On the Politeia of Correct Behavior*, p. 83 (ed. Chabot, *Synodicon Orientale* = [p. 336 (French)]).

[52] Perhaps less romantically, mention can be made of Anastasius of Sinai speaking about Arabs forcing elderly female ascetics who were virgins into marriage. *Questions and Answers* 101 (ed. Richard and Munitiz, p. 162).

[53] *Canons of the Patriarch George* 12, 13 (ed. Vööbus [CSCO 375–76: SS 163–64], pp. 4 [Syriac] = p. 5 [ET]).

[54] *Canons of the Patriarch John* 23 (ed. Vööbus, *The Synodicon in the West Syrian Tradition* II [CSCO 375–76: SS 163–64], pp. 45 [Syriac] = p. 47 [ET]; I have used Vööbus' translation but made my own alterations).

[55] See the comment of H.G.B. Teule, 'Yaʿḳūbiyyūn,' in *EI2*, vol. 11, p. 261. More generally, I have relied on Teule's article, p. 261, and its concise enumeration of the evidence of Christian/non-Christian marriage for the information in this paragraph.

[56] For various views on the permissibility of marrying Jewish or Christian women and a discussion of releavant *ḥadīth* and Qur'ānic verses, see Ibn Ḥazm, *al-Muḥallā*, vol. 9, p. 445–49 (no. 1817).

the Eucharist, saints, holy men—we should remember that many of these Muslims were no doubt married to Christian women, had Christian concubines, were the children of Christian mothers, or were descended from people who had been any or all of these things.[57]

What were the effects of intermarriage on everyday life, belief, and practice? At times, we can find indications. In tenth-century Egypt, for instance, we read about a certain Muzāḥim, the son of a Bedouin Muslim man and a Christian woman. Muzāḥim would go to church with his mother and he became very fond of Christians, eventually asking his mother to give him the Eucharist. She replied that it was not possible for an unbaptized person to communicate, but nevertheless gave him some of the antidoron, which tasted like honey to him when he ate it, something that caused him to wonder how the Eucharist itself might taste in comparison. At this point, Muzāḥim began to desire to become a Christian. When he grew older, he married a Christian woman. At her encouragement, he was baptized taking Jirjis (that is, George) as his new name. Muzāḥim/Jirjis would eventually be killed for his apostasy.[58] The fondness for Christianity that Muzāḥim had as a result of his Christian mother was surely not unique or uncommon among the Muslim children of religiously mixed marriages, and as is the case with so many phenomena from the early medieval Middle East, we can get a clearer picture of what these marriages quite possibly looked like and of their effects on children by looking to later periods. Examining closely the importance and effects of religious intermarriage, especially in the Seljuk harem, Rustam Shukorov has argued that, so far as society in medieval Anatolia was concerned, 'Christianity and the Greek language were not exterior to local Muslim culture but rather formed some of its constituent elements.'[59]

[57] We forget easily that very famous figures often had mothers who belonged to religions different from the one with which they are most strongly associated. The notoriously anti-Christian al-Ḥākim at times made kind gestures to Christians and it has been speculated that this may have been somehow connected to the fact that his mother had been a Christian; see M. Canard's article, 'al-Ḥākim bi-Amr Allāh,' in *EI2*, vol. 3, p. 78. Throughout Islamic history, many rulers, especially in the Ottoman period, had Christian mothers. The question of the influence of mothers belonging to a different religion on the religious behavior and policies of their sons who become caliphs or sultans is one that has scarcely been explored. See, e.g., the comments in T. Nöldeke, *Geschichte der Perser und Araber zur Zeit der Sasaniden* (Leiden, 1879), p. 51, n. 3, about the apparent influence of Shapur II's mother on his attitudes towards Judaism (the note continues on to p. 52, where the comment in question can be found).

[58] A short account of Muzāḥim/Jirjis's conversion and martyrdom can be found in the Coptic Synaxary on 19 Ba'ūna /13 June. See R. Basset, ed., *Le synaxaire arabe Jacobite. V. Les mois de Baounah, Abib, Mésoré et jours complémentaires* (PO 17.3) (Paris, 1923), pp. 578–80. For more on this martyrdom, see M. N. Swanson in *CMR*, vol. 2, pp. 461–63.

[59] R. Shukurov, 'Harem Christianity: The Byzantine Identity of Seljuk Princes,' in A.C.S. Peacock and S. N. Yıldız, eds., *The Seljuks of Anatolia: Court and Society in the Medieval Middle East* (London/New York, 2013), p. 133.

In the case of mixed Christian-Muslim marriages, it is likewise not clear whether the Muslim males had actually been born Muslim or whether they themselves were converts. As we have already seen, for instance, in AD 779, the caliph al-Mahdī forced five thousand men of the Christian Arab tribe of Tanūkh to convert to Islam, but their wives continued to be Christians.[60] One suspects that the type of Islam practiced by these men likely included the continuation of a number of practices and beliefs from their Christian past. This is something we would in fact expect, given a mass involuntary conversion and, presumably, little in the way of religious instruction.

We saw in Chapter 12 that in the late seventh and early eighth century, the threat of force was used to induce priests to give Christian wives of Muslim men the Eucharist. Similarly, a threat of force also seems to have been used to motivate Christian priests to teach Muslim children. Is it appropriate, Addai asked Jacob, for a priest to teach the children of the Hagarenes who have the authority to hurt him if he does not teach?[61] Jacob saw no problem in this and indeed noted that it might very well have beneficial results. The practice of having Christians teach the children of Muslims was not unique to Jacob's circle or area—Sa'd b. Abī Waqqāṣ, one of the Prophet's Companions, brought a Christian named Jufayna from Hira to Medina to teach his children and other people how to read and do arithmetic (*al-kitāb wa-'l-ḥisāb*).[62] In the case of Jacob, at least, one possibility is that these children were the product of marriages between Muslim men and Christian women, which would explain why a Muslim father might have been keen to have his children taught by a Christian priest.[63] In the twelfth century, in fact, Balsamon would explicitly link the

[60] Michael the Great, *Chronicle* 12.1 (ed. Chabot, 4.478–79 = 3.1).

[61] *Questions Which Addai the Priest and Lover of Labors Asked Jacob, the Bishop of Edessa* 58 (ed. Lamy, *Dissertatio*, p. 158; ET available in *SBI*, p. 471, n. 1121).

[62] al-Balādhurī, *Ansāb al-ashrāf*, vol. 2, pp. 205–206 (ed. M. al-Fardūs al-'Aẓm [Damascus, n.d]) (for this, cf. W. Madelung, *The Succession to Muḥammad: A Study in the Early Caliphate* [Cambridge, 1997], p. 69, n. 46). This pattern continued: see also the story of Dāwūd b. 'Abd al-Raḥmān (AH 100–174/AD 718–790), a Christian doctor from Syria who came to Mecca, settled there, married and had children. They all converted to Islam and he taught them to read the Qur'ān and *fiqh*; Ibn Sa'd, *Kitāb al-ṭabaqāt al-kabīr*, vol. 5, p. 345 (ed. Zettersteén [Leiden, 1905]). Cf. Lammens, 'Études sur le règne du calife Omaiyade Mo'awiya Ier,' (part 3), p. 270. On the legendary nature of stories that Khālid b. Yazīd (d. AH 85 or 90/AD 704 or 709) studied alchemy with a Byzantine monk, see M. Ullmann's article, 'Khālid b. Yazīd b. Mu'āwiya,' in *EI2*, vol. 4, pp. 929–30. For Abū Yūsuf Ya'qūb b. Isḥāq b. al-Sikkīt (d. ca. AH 243/AD 857), who was likely of Aramaean heritage and whom al-Mutawakkil had teach his son, al-Mu'tazz, see Brockelmann, *GAL*, vol. 1, p. 120.

[63] Though the example of 'Abd al-Malik having Athanasius bar Gummaye teach his younger brother 'Abd al-'Azīz can serve as a contemporary example of a Christian tutoring a Muslim whose mother was not necessarily a Christian. See Michael the Great, *Chronicle* 11.16 (ed. Chabot, *Chronique* 4.447–48 [Syriac] = 2.475–76 [FT]). For 'Abd al-'Azīz's mother as Laylā b. Zabbān b. al-Aṣbagh al-Kalbī, see al-Balādhūrī, *Kitāb jumal min ansāb al-ashrāf*, vol. 6 (ed. S. Zakkār and R. Ziriklī) (Beirut, 1996), p. 307.

baptism of Muslims in Anatolia with the efforts of their Christian mothers.[64] Similarly, in the fifteenth century, the Christian pilgrim Bertrandon de la Brocquière wrote of a Turkoman prince whose Christian mother had had him baptized.[65] Some women who married Muslim men converted upon marriage, but others remained Christians.[66] Ibn Rusta, writing in the third/tenth century, produced a list of early Muslim notables (*ashrāf*) whose mothers were Christians.[67] Before him, Ibn al-Kalbī (d. AH 204/AD 819 or AH 206/AD 821) composed a book, *Mathālib al-ʿArab* (*Faults of the Arabs*), which provided lists of Arabs who fell into a number of categories, often dubious: sodomites, thieves, bastards, fornicators, men who married their stepmothers; also included were five chapters devoted to notable men who were the children of different kinds of non-Muslim women: Ethiopians, Byzantines, Sindis, Nabateans, and Jews.[68] Before any debates or disputations held in the presence of a caliph or emir took place, and before letters were sent back and forth between learned controversialists, there was this different and much, much more common type of Muslim-Christian interaction. This was a world where Muslim-Christian religious exchanges began at home.

The power of religious intermarriage to effect religious change should not be underestimated. We need only look at the spread of Christianity in the Sasanian empire to see what might result when people wed across religious lines. One fourth-century martyr, Pusai, was the son of a Christian who had been deported and resettled in Sasanian territory by Shapur II and a Persian mother, whom his father had converted to Christianity and had had baptized after they were married. The author of the account of Pusai's martyrdom made the following observation about the importance of religious intermarriage:

[64] See Rhalles and Potles, eds., *Syntagma tōn theiōn kai hierōn kanonōn tōn te hagiōn kai paneuphēmōn apostolōn*, p. 498. Quoted with ET in Vryonis, *The Decline of Medieval Hellenism*, pp. 487–88 (cf. chapter 12, n. 79, above).

[65] See Taylor, 'The Syriac Baptism of St John,' p. 440.

[66] See, e.g., the report in ʿAbd al-Razzāq, *Muṣannaf*, vol. 7, pp. 160–61 (no. 12616), where ʿAbd al-Ḥamīd al-Anṣārī speaks of how his grandfather converted to Islam but his Christian wife did not. The wife had a young son by the grandfather. The Prophet is said to have sat the father in one place and the mother in another and given the child the choice to go to one or the other. The child reportedly went to his (Muslim) father.

[67] See Ibn Rusta, *al-Mujallad al-sābiʿ min Kitāb al-aʿlāq al-nafīsa*, p. 213 (ed. M.J. de Goeje [Leiden, 1892]). For this point, see Lammens, 'Études sur le règne du calife Omaiyade Moʿawiya Ier,' (part 3), p. 161; for discussion of the identities of these men, see *ibid.*, 162.

[68] See Ibn al-Kalbī, *Mathālib al-ʿArab* (ed. N. al-Ṭāʿī) (Beirut/London, 1998), pp. 103–10. See also Ibn Ḥabīb, *Kitāb al-muḥabbar*, pp. 305–309, for lists of men whose mothers were Christians or Abyssinians (cf. Crone, *Slaves on Horses*, p. 206, n. 53).

> Shapur (II) built the city of Karka d-Ladan, brought captives from various places and settled them there. He also had the idea of bringing about thirty families apiece from each of the ethnic groups living in the cities belonging to his realm, and settling them among the deported captives, so that through intermarriage the latter should become tied down by the bonds of family and affection, thus making it less easy for them to slip away gradually in flight and return to areas from which they had been deported. Such was Shapur's crafty plan, but God in his mercy turned it to good use, for thanks to intermarriage between the deported population and the native pagans, the latter were brought to knowledge of the faith.[69]

In the context of Muslim rule, however, the religions would change, but the dynamics would stay the same: Muslim men marrying Christian, Jewish, and Zoroastrian women was an important mechanism in the gradual conversion of the Middle East's population to Islam.

Religiously mixed households and families presented Muslims with a host of challenges whose echoes we can hear in legal discussions. How did one negotiate the shoals of religious difference when members of one's immediate and extended family belonged to a different community? In the ninth century, for example, the jurist Aḥmad b. Ḥanbal (d. AH 241/AD 855) was asked about the case of a Muslim man who had *dhimmī* relatives whom he would greet with the Arabic *al-salāmu ʿalaykum*; such a man, Aḥmad held, should greet them in Persian and should not initiate contact with them with this (Islamic) greeting.[70]

Families that were multi-religious presented children with potentially thorny issues at the end of life. Muḥammad b. al-Ashʿath, for example, asked ʿUmar and ʿUthmān what he should do about a paternal aunt of his who had died and who was Jewish.[71] At issue, probably, was whether and how he should take part in her funeral procession. In roughly the exact same period, Addai was asking Jacob of Edessa whether it was permissible for Christian women to take part in the funeral processions of pagan Harranians and Jews, some-

[69] *Martyrdom of Pusai*, pp. 208–209 (quotation taken from p. 209) (ed. Bedjan, *AMS*, vol. 2; ET taken from S. P. Brock, 'Christians in the Sassanian Empire: A Case of Divided Loyalties,' in S. Mews, ed., *Religious and National Identity* [Oxford, 1982], p. 4). The importance of interreligious marriage in affecting religious practice can of course be found much earlier and is a subject that is treated in the Bible: see, e.g., Deuteronomy 7:1–4; Judges 3:5–7; 1 Kings 11:1–8; 2 Corinthians 6:14, and cf. 1 Corinthians 7:12–16, etc.

[70] al-Khallāl, *Ahl al-milal*, vol. 2, pp. 462–63 (nos. 1110–12).

[71] Ibn Saʿd, *Kitāb al-ṭabaqāt al-kabīr*, vol. 5, p. 46 (ed. Zetterstéen [Leiden, 1905]; an ET is available in Bewley, *The Men of Madina*, vol. 2, p. 41). For the aunt as either a Jew or a Christian, see Mālik b. Anas, *al-Muwaṭṭa'*, vol. 2, p. 519 (no. 12).

thing that Jacob permitted on account of love and human custom.[72] Jacob also permitted pagans and Jews to take part in Christian funeral processions.[73]

On the Islamic side of things, the treatment of the case of al-Ḥārith b. ʿAbd Allāh b. Abī Rabīʿa provides an example of the different ways in which Muslims dealt with taking part in such funeral processions. Al-Ḥārith had a Muslim father and a Christian mother—Ibn Saʿd tells of him that 'in him was blackness, because his mother was a Christian Abyssinian'[74]—and there survive a number of varying reports about what exactly al-Ḥārith did upon his mother's death. According to one, members of Quraysh and other Muslims came to be present at her funeral procession, but al-Ḥārith told them that God had taken the obligation to attend away from them, and that it would be more appropriate for members of her religious community to take part in it than for them; as a result, they all left. Another report has al-Ḥārith finding out that his mother was a Christian only after her death, when a female servant secretly tells him that they discovered his mother wearing a cross when they undressed her to wash her body; in this report, it is after al-Ḥārith finds out about his mother's true identity that he tells Muslims that God has satisfied the obligation on their behalf and that it would be better for them to let her coreligionists be in the funeral procession. According to this version, al-Ḥārith's reputation increased for his having done this. Yet another report has the Companions of the Prophet in the funeral procession, and al-Ḥārith tells them that she has coreligionists other than them; in this report, however, there is no mention of Muslims departing from the procession, nor is there mention of al-Ḥārith's reputation increasing as a result of his actions.[75] One last account, from Ibn Saʿd, has al-Ḥārith and a number of Muslims taking part in the funeral procession, in addition to a number of Christians, but the two groups are separate from one another.[76]

[72] *Questions Which Addai the Priest and Lover of Labors Asked*, Mardin 310, fol. 205a. Syriac text and ET in *SBI*, p. 528, n. 1265. Syriac text and LT also available in Lamy, *Dissertatio*, pp. 162–63. Cf. the report in the *Chronicle of Seert* 2.38 (ed. Scher [PO 7.2], p. 103), where the Christians who had been deported from Antioch to the Sasanian empire by Khusro gave honor to the dead king's body and processed around it with candles and censers up to the spot where it was buried.

[73] *Questions Which Addai the Priest and Lover of Labors Asked*, Mardin 310, fol. 205a. Syriac text and ET in *SBI*, p. 529, n. 1266. See also Kayser, *Die Canones Jacob's von Edessa*, p. 19 (ET in *SBI*, p. 529, n. 1266).

[74] Ibn Saʿd, *Kitāb al-ṭabaqāt al-kabīr*, vol. 5, p. 19 (ed. Zettersteén [Leiden, 1905]; an ET is available in Bewley, *The Men of Madina*, vol. 2, p. 15).

[75] These reports are all collected in al-Mizzī, *Tahdhīb al-kamāl fī asmāʾ al-rijāl*, vol. 5, pp. 241–43. Quraysh present: from al-Zubayr b. Bakkār (p. 241); al-Ḥārith discovers his mother is a Christian: also from al-Zubayr b. Bakkār (pp. 241–42); Companions of the Prophet accompany the body: from al-Bukhārī (p. 242).

[76] This report is contained in al-Mizzī, *Tahdhīb al-kamāl fī asmāʾ al-rijāl*, vol. 5, p. 243, but the text

These various permutations on what al-Ḥārith and other Muslims did about his Christian mother's funeral make it clear that there were varying answers to the question of how a Muslim should act when confronted by a question of whether and how to participate in funeral rituals when a non-Muslim family member had passed away: depending on the report one took as authoritative, one might not take part in the funeral procession at all or one might attend, but be separate from non-Muslims. In the Abbasid period, when asked whether a Muslim could attend the funeral of a polytheist, Aḥmad b. Ḥanbal would cite the example of al-Ḥārith attending but standing to one side as precedent for permitting Muslims to participate.[77]

Ibn Ḥanbal's view was recorded in a collection of his legal opinions made by al-Khallāl (d. AH 311/AD 923), and the range of questions asked there on just this one issue of funerals and burial reflects a society in which Muslim and non-Muslim lives were intertwined at the most intimate levels: A Jewish man dies who has a Muslim son, how should the son act? Abū Wā'il's (d. after AH 82/ AD 701) mother died a Christian and he asked 'Umar what he should do. Qays b. Shammās's mother died a Christian and he wanted to attend her funeral; he asked the Prophet how he should act.[78] Beyond the question of taking part in the funeral processions of non-Muslim family members, Aḥmad would be asked nearly identical questions to those Addai had asked Jacob perhaps 150 years previously: Could a man who had a Muslim neighbor with a Christian mother follow along in the mother's funeral procession? How about watching the funeral of neighbors who were Christians? Could a Muslim man with a Christian mother follow along in her funeral procession? A Muslim man whose father died a Christian?[79]

Religious intermarriage or interreligious concubinage raised other interesting problems that can be tracked in various *ḥadīth* that address them. A Muslim could make a Christian an executor:[80] Ṣafiyya, the wife of Muḥammad, made one of her relatives who was a Christian an executor of her will;[81] she also

---

in Ibn Sa'd, *Kitāb al-ṭabaqāt al-kabīr*, vol. 5, p. 19 (ed. Zetterstéen [Leiden, 1905]), is slightly better, reading *'alā ḥida* rather than *'alā ḥaddihi*. An ET can be found in Bewley, *The Men of Madina*, vol. 2, p. 15).

[77] al-Khallāl, *Ahl al-milal*, vol. 1, p. 297. For a broader perspective on the attendance of funerals, see Zaman, 'Death, Funeral Processions, and the Articulation of Religious Authority in Early Islam.'

[78] All of these examples can be found in al-Khallāl, *Ahl al-milal*, vol. 1, pp. 298–99. The answers to such questions involve taking part in the funeral procession but riding ahead of it on an animal and not being behind it. The concern seems to be with maintaining both the separateness and the social precedence of the Muslim participant in the funeral procession. On Abū Wā'il, see al-Mizzī, *Tahdhīb al-kamāl fī asmā' al-rijāl*, vol. 12, pp. 549–54.

[79] al-Khallāl, *Ahl al-milal*, vol. 1, p. 301.

[80] 'Abd al-Razzāq, *al-Muṣannaf*, vol. 10, p. 353 (no. 19341).

[81] 'Abd al-Razzāq, *al-Muṣannaf*, vol. 10, p. 353 (no. 19342).

made a Jewish relative an executor.[82] A Muslim could not be the heir of an unbeliever (*kāfir*), and an unbeliever could not be the heir of a Muslim.[83] A paternal aunt of al-Ash'ath b. Qays died; she was a Jew. Al-Ash'ath went to 'Umar b. al-Khaṭṭāb to seek her inheritance. 'Umar, however, refused to give it to him and instead granted it to Jews.[84] Death brought out in other vivid ways some of the conundrums intermarriage might raise: Where should a Christian woman who dies while pregnant with a Muslim's child be buried—in a Muslim cemetery or in a Christian one?[85]

Non-Muslim wives or slave girls who maintained their Christian (or Jewish) observance might represent a religious predicament for Muslim husbands or masters. Al-Awzā'ī (d. AH 157/AD 774), a Syrian legal expert whose views represent some of the earliest legal opinions preserved in the Islamic tradition,[86] was asked about a Muslim man who had a Christian slave girl. Could he forbid her from going to church, or should he permit her to do so? Was it possible for him to forbid her from making pilgrimage to Christian holy places (*al-ziyārāt*), or should he give her permission? Al-Awzā'ī's response allowed the master plenty of freedom: he saw no harm in forbidding her from doing these things; equally, however, he also saw no harm in giving her permission to do them, either. Aḥmad b. Ḥanbal, on the other hand, while holding that the Muslim master should not forbid her from taking part in pilgrimages (*lā yamna'uhā min ahl al-ziyārāt*), maintained that the master should not give the slave girl permission to go to church.[87]

A series of questions posed to Aḥmad offer us a glimpse of some of the issues that a Muslim husband might expect to deal with if he took a Christian for his wife. Could the Muslim husband, Aḥmad was asked, forbid his wife from drinking wine? He could order her to not drink wine, Aḥmad responded; if she refused to accept his order, however, the husband could not prevent her from drinking. Another question: Could the husband forbid the wife from leaving the house to go to church? 'As for her leaving [the house],' Aḥmad held, 'it is not right for her to go out and he has the right to forbid her, because it is not appropriate for her to leave, save with his permission.' Could the

[82] 'Abd al-Razzāq, *al-Muṣannaf*, vol. 10, pp. 353–54 (no. 19344).

[83] 'Abd al-Razzāq, *al-Muṣannaf*, vol. 10, p. 341 (nos. 19303–304). See pp. 341–43 (nos. 19305, 19309, 19310) for more *ḥadīth* on questions of inheritance between Muslims and non-Muslims, esp. Jews and Christians.

[84] 'Abd al-Razzāq, *al-Muṣannaf*, vol. 10, p. 342 (no. 19306).

[85] al-Khallāl, *Ahl al-milal*, vol. 1, pp. 302–304. The responses that were given to this question included: she could be buried in a Muslim cemetery; she could be buried in a Christian cemetery; she could be buried separately in a place between Christian and Muslim cemeteries.

[86] See J. Schacht's article 'al-Awzā'ī, Abū 'Amr 'Abd al-Raḥmān b. 'Amr,' in *EI2*, vol. 1, pp. 772-773.

[87] al-Khallāl, *Ahl al-milal*, vol. 2, p. 431 (no. 1001).

husband forbid his Christian wife from bringing a cross into the house? As in the case of drinking wine, Aḥmad held that the husband might order her not to bring a cross in, but if the Christian wife did not accept his order, he could not prevent her. One solution, which Aḥmad thought was a good one, was to stipulate before marriage that the Christian wife not drink wine or go to church.[88]

In addition to questions about going to church, wine, and crosses, there was the issue of whether a Muslim husband should let his Christian wife go to festivals celebrating Christian saints—Aḥmad said no.[89] Related to the issue of a Christian wife was the issue of a Christian slave girl: when Aḥmad was asked whether a Muslim should grant permission to his Christian slave girl to go the celebration of Christian feast days, or to church, or to Christian gatherings, he held that her master should not permit her to do so.[90] What is more, the Muslim master or husband should not buy a *zunnār*—the belt that People of the Book were required to wear—for his Christian wife or slave girl; she should go out and buy it herself.[91]

In the fourteenth century, Ibn Qayyim al-Jawziyya (d. AH 751/AD 1350) would expand Aḥmad b. Ḥanbal's discussions about what a Muslim husband or master could or could not control in the religious observation of his non-Muslim wife. According to Ibn al-Qayyim, the Muslim husband was not permitted to forbid his non-Muslim wife from undertaking fasts that she believed were obligatory (even if it meant that he could not have sex with her when he wanted), nor could he forbid her from praying toward the east in his house. The Muslim husband was not permitted to compel his Jewish wife to break the Sabbath, and he could not force his wives to eat food that their religions forbade; as to whether he could forbid his wife from eating pork, there were two different opinions. Similarly, there were two opinions on whether he could forbid her—if she wanted—from observing the fast of Ramadan with him. And so it went. Among other things the Muslim husband could not prevent the non-Muslim wife from doing, according to Ibn al-Qayyim, was reading her Scripture, so long as she did not raise her voice as she did.[92]

Intermarriage between Muslim men and non-Muslim women no doubt played a significant role in introducing a number of non- and pre-Islamic religious practices into the bloodstream of everyday Islam. Khālid al-Qasrī (d. AH 126/AD 743–744), for example, was the governor of Iraq and had a Christian

[88] al-Khallāl, *Ahl al-milal*, vol. 2, p. 430 (no. 997).

[89] al-Khallāl, *Ahl al-milal*, vol. 2, p. 431 (no. 1000).

[90] al-Khallāl, *Ahl al-milal*, vol. 2, p. 430 (no. 998).

[91] al-Khallāl, *Ahl al-milal*, vol. 2, p. 431 (no. 1002).

[92] For these points (and others), see Ibn Qayyim al-Jawziyya, *Aḥkām ahl al-dhimma*, vol. 1, p. 316.

mother. While governor, Khalid built her a church in Kufa, located behind the great mosque; the sounds of the *nāqūs* and chanting from Khālid's church would reportedly compete with the call to prayer and the preaching in the mosque.[93] What is more, after building a fountain in that mosque, Khālid was said to have had a priest bless it on the reported grounds that the priest's prayer would be more effective than even that of ʿAlī; Khālid was also charged with having stated that Christianity was a better religion than Islam and was alleged to have favored Christians and other non-Muslims over Muslims in appointments to public office and in adjudicating disputes.[94] It was also claimed that Khālid showed special deference to the patriarch of the Church of the East and even requested his prayers.[95] 'Has not the Merciful made repugnant the back of the beast who, swaggering from Damascus, brought us Khālid?' the poet al-Farazdaq wrote.

> How can one whose mother believes that God is not One lead the people?
> He built a church for his mother, inside of which is a cross, but out of hatred he pulls down the minarets of mosques.[96]

'He was accused of Manichaeism (*al-zandaqa*),' Ibn al-Nadīm wrote of Khālid, 'and his mother was a Christian.'[97]

There are other examples. Maysūn, the Christian wife of Muʿāwiya whom I mentioned above, was the mother of Yazīd, who succeeded his father as ruler of the Arab empire. Yazīd was raised in the area of Palmyra, among the Arabs of his mother's tribe, Kalb, which was composed of Christians and recent converts to Islam; this formation has been connected to Yazīd's later behavior as caliph.[98] According to the *Kitāb al-Aghānī*, Yazīd's boon companions were Sarjūn (perhaps the father of John of Damascus) and the Christian poet al-Akhṭal; Yazīd was also said to have been the first caliph in Islam to introduce musical instruments, to welcome singers, and to behave immorally in public and drink wine.[99]

[93] For this, see Tritton, *The Caliphs and Their Non-Muslim Subjects*, pp. 45–46. By the time of Balādhurī (d. ca. AD 892/AH 278), Khālid's church had been turned into a post-office; see Balādhurī, *Kitāb futūḥ al-buldān*, p. 286 (ed. de Goeje; ET available in Hitti, *The Origins of the Islamic State*, vol. 1, p. 445).

[94] For all these points, see G. R. Hawting's article, 'Khālid b. 'Abd Allāh al-Ḳasrī' in *EI2*, vol. 4, pp. 925–27. See also Lammens, 'Études sur le règne du calife Omaiyade Mo'awiya Ier,' (part 3), p. 162.

[95] ʿAmr b. Mattā, *Akhbār faṭārikat kursī al-mashriq*, p. 66 (ed. Gismondi, *Maris textus arabicus*). For this, see Yarbrough, 'Islamizing the Islamic State,' pp. 76–77. More generally, Yarbrough, 75–79, gives an expert discussion of Khālid's Christian connections.

[96] Ibn Khallikān, *Wafayāt al-aʿyān wa-anbā' abnā' al-zamān*, vol. 2, pp. 228–29. An ET is also available in de Slane, *Ibn Khallikan's Biographical Dictionary*, vol. 1, p. 485.

[97] Ibn al-Nadīm, *Fihrist*, vol. 1, p. 338 (ed. Flügel).

[98] See Lammens, 'Études sur le règne du calife Omaiyade Mo'awiya Ier,' (part 3), p. 190.

[99] '*Awwal man sanna al-malāhī fī 'l-Islām min al-khulafā'* might also mean 'the first of the Caliphs to pursue amusements in Islam.' See *Kitāb al-aghānī*, vol. 16, p. 70. Lammens, 'Études sur le règne du

The traditional concern of most students of Islam and Christianity, however, has not been ritual and practice, popular or otherwise, but rather doctrine and belief, a focus that reflects the common assumption that doctrine is the most important part of a religious system. For this reason, a more controversial question, one that is perhaps unanswerable, concerns the effect that widespread intermarriage between Muslim men and non-Muslim women had on the normative, textual Islam that forms the focus of much of Islamic studies in the West and in the Muslim world. It would not be surprising if close interaction with Christians affected the religious beliefs of certain Muslims, even among the literate elite. It has been argued, for example, that writings of al-Qāsim b. Ibrāhīm (d. AD 860/AH 246), a Zaydī imam and 'the earliest Muslim *kalām* theologian of whose treatises a broad range is extant,' was not only clearly aware of the theological argumentation of Christians like Theodore Abū Qurrah but also influenced by Christian ideas.[100] Scholars have also raised the possibility that the spread and success of Ibāḍism in North Africa may have had something to do with the region's Donatist Christian population and certain similarities between Ibāḍī and Donatist thought.[101] Ibn al-Rāwandī (d. fourth century AH/tenth century AD) wrote that no less a figure than the great al-Naẓẓām (d. AH 221/AD 836), 'the head of the Mu'tazilites, despite the elevation of his level in theology (*kalām*) and his ability and authority in knowledge' composed a book on the superiority of Trinitarianism over unitarianism for a Christian boy whom he loved passionately (*'ashiqahu*) as a means of acquiring from the boy 'what God had forbidden.'[102] Al-Jāḥiẓ, the student of al-Naẓẓām, certainly held that Christianity was a fertile breeding ground for all sorts of unbelief. 'Their religion,' he said of the Christians,

> ... resembles Manichaeism (*al-zandaqa*) and in certain aspects is like the doctrine of the materialists (*al-dahriyya*). They are among the causes of all confusion and doubt. The proof of this is that we have never seen a religious group which is more unbelieving (*akthar zandaqatan*) than the Christians—or more confused or befuddled than they. Such is the situation of all who have looked

calife Omaiyade Mo'awiya Ier,' (part 3), p. 247, saw this as an exaggeration and an anti-Syrian/Umayyad slander (also, cf. his translation [along with his note] on p. 272, n. 1). On the complicated question of John Damascene and his family history, see S. W. Anthony, 'Fixing John Damascene's Biography: Historical Notes on His Family Background,' *Journal of Eastern Christian Studies* 23 (2015), pp. 607–27.

[100] W. Madelung, 'al-Qāsim ibn Ibrāhīm and Christian Theology,' *ARAM* 3 (1991), pp. 35–44 (quote at 35).

[101] W. Madelung, ''Īsā ibn 'Umayr's Ibāḍī Theology and Donatist Christian Thought,' in R. Hansberger, M. Afifi al-Akiti, and C. Burnett, eds., *Medieval Arabic Thought: Essays in Honour of Fritz Zimmerman* (London/Turin 2012), pp. 99–103.

[102] See Ibn Ḥazm, *Ṭawq al-ḥamāma* (ed. Ḥ. Kāmil al-Ṣīrfī) (Cairo, 1950), p. 130. Cf. J. van Ess's article, 'Abū Esḥāq Ebrāhīm b. Sayyār b. Hāne' al-Naẓẓām,' in *Encyclopaedia Iranica*, vol. 1 (London/Boston/Henley, 1985), pp. 275–80, story cited on p. 276, and C. Brockelmann, *GAL*, vol. S1, p. 339. On the probability that this story is baseless polemic, see D. Thomas's remarks in *CMR*, vol. 1, pp. 619–20.

> into obscure matters with weak intellects. Consider the fact that most of those who have been killed for unbelief (*zandaqa*)—of those who profess Islam and show it externally—are those whose fathers and mothers are Christians.[103]

The 'Pact of 'Umar' had Christians promising that they would neither speak the language of the Muslims nor show crosses or any of their religious books in the streets of the Muslims or in their markets. Again, a safe assumption would be that Christians were doing just this.[104] We have already seen that Jacob of Edessa saw no harm in Christian priests teaching the children of Hagarenes (he had no problem, either, with priests teaching the children of Jews and pagan Harranians),[105] a phenomenon which I suggested could in part be attributed to families where at least one parent was a Christian or where the parents were converts to Islam who held on to much of their previous Christian baggage, so to speak. By the time we get to Aḥmad b. Ḥanbal in third/ninth century Baghdad, we find him being asked about a Muslim who was teaching Qur'ān to the children of a Magian, a Jew and a Christian, something that did not please Aḥmad.[106]

It was widely held that the children of Muslim men should be Muslims,[107] but this might not have always been the case,[108] and, to repeat a point I have

[103] See al-Jāḥiẓ, *Fī 'l-radd 'alā al-Naṣārā*, p. 315–16.

[104] *Wa-lā natakallamu bi-kalāmihim... wa-lā nuẓhiru ṣalīban wa-lā kutuban min kutub dīninā fī shay' min ṭuruq al-Muslimīn wa-lā aswāqihim.* See Ibn Taymiyya, *Iqtiḍā'*, p. 121.

[105] *Questions Which Addai the Priest and Lover of Labors Asked Jacob* 59 (ed. Lamy, *Dissertatio*, p. 158; ET in *SBI*, p. 537, n. 1296).

[106] al-Khallāl, *Ahl al-milal*, vol. 1, pp. 120–21. On the question of non-Muslims studying the Qur'ān, see C. Wilde, '"We shall neither learn the Qur'ān nor teach it to our children": The Covenant of 'Umar on Learning,' in J. Scheiner and D. Janos, eds., *The Place to Go: Contexts of Learning in Baghdād, 750–1000 CE* (Princeton, 2014), pp. 237–65.

[107] Many jurists also maintained this view in situations where the mother was a Muslim and the father a non-Muslim. The underlying idea was that the child of a Muslim parent should be a Muslim, a notion based on the principle that a child, when its parents belong to different religions, should follow the better religion, i.e., Islam (*al-walad yatba'u khayra al-abawayn dīnan*). See, e.g., Ibn Qudāma, *al-Mughnī*, vol. 12, pp. 284–85, and al-Sarakhsī, *Sharḥ Kitāb al-siyar al-kabīr li-Muḥammad b. al-Ḥasan al-Shaybanī*, vol. 5, p. 1846 (no. 3706), 1994 (no. 3995) (ed. Ṣ. Al-Dīn al-Munajjid [Cairo, 1971–1972]; see, too, al-Shaybanī's comments from *Kitāb al-siyar* at p. 2268 [no. 4523] and pp. 2209–10 [no. 4377], along with al-Sarakhsī's accompanying commentary). For a modern discussion see *al-Mawsū'a al-fiqhiyya* (Kuwait, 1983), vol. 45, pp. 193–94. This evidence (and more) is dicussed in Friedmann, *Tolerance and Coercion*, pp. 174–75 (NB, 174: 'According to most views, the children follow the parent whose religion is "better..."').

[108] Note that Sufyān al-Thawrī (d. AH 161/AD 778) held the view that when the child reached maturity it was to be allowed to choose between the religion of its father and the religion of its mother (Ibn Qudāma, *al-Mughnī*, vol. 12, p. 285), and cf. the example of the Prophet in Abū Dāwūd, *Sunan*, vol. 3, p. 559 (no. 2244). More generally, there was some disagreement about the principle that a child should follow the better religion when its parents' religions differed: see, e.g., the views of Mālik b. Anas, who held that the father's religion should be followed, whatever it was, in Ibn Qudāma, *al-Mughnī*, vol. 12, pp. 284–85. For discussion of these and a number of other opinions, see Friedmann, *Tolerance and Coercion*, pp. 113–15, 175.

already made, we should not underestimate the importance and role Christian mothers played in the formation of their Muslim children's religious identities. At a very basic level, the jurist Mālik b. Anas (d. AH 179/AD 796) did not like the idea of using Christian women as foster mothers—they drank wine and ate pork, he said, and he feared that they would give these things to children to eat; he disliked using them as wet nurses on similar grounds.[109] Questions of food aside, Muslim authorities recognized the considerable influence a non-Muslim mother might exert over her Muslim child. Depending on the legal school, in the case of separation, divorce, or death, a Christian or Jewish mother might be denied custody of her children with a Muslim man, or she would only be allowed to keep custody so long as she did not attempt to influence her children away from Islam.[110]

We should not let the eventual overwhelming Islamization of the Middle East, something which people in the seventh, eighth and ninth centuries had no way of foreseeing, mislead us into thinking that each conversion to Islam meant that an irrevocable step had been taken or that contemporaries viewed such conversions as having permanent effects. We have already seen the possible effects of a Christian mother in the case of Muzāḥim/Jirjis, but other examples can be found. The story of the martyr Bacchus the Younger provides a late eighth-century example from Maiouma in Palestine of the kinds of conflicts and mixed identities which might result from conversions and inter-religious marriages. Bacchus's mother was a Christian and his father had been one, too, 'but having been ensnared and drawn in with Satanic enticements, he abandoned the holy worship of the Christians and drew near to the foul worship of the Hagarenes.'[111] After his conversion, the renegade would go on to have seven children whom he raised and taught in accordance with the customs of his new religion; his wife, however, was distressed at the new confession and would regularly attend Christian churches in secret where she would, the martyrdom reports, beseech God that she be separated from her husband and that she and her children be joined to the Christian church. Bacchus himself was the third of the seven children and was given the name Ḍaḥḥāk at birth. He remained unmarried, according to the martyrdom, not because he refused to have anything to do with marriage, but because he

[109] Saḥnūn, *al-Mudawwana al-kubrā*, vol. 2, pp. 303–304 (Beirut, 1994). Cf. A. S. Tritton, 'Non-Muslim Subjects of the Muslim State,' *Journal of the Royal Asiatic Society of Great Britain and Ireland* 1 (1942), p. 38.

[110] See Y. Linant de Bellefonds's article, 'Ḥaḍāna,' in *EI2*, vol. 3, pp. 16–19, esp. p. 18.

[111] *Life and Martyrdom of the Holy Neo-Martyr Bacchus the Younger*, p. 344 (ed. F. A. Demetrakopoulou, '῞Αγιος Βάκχος ὁ Νέος,' *Epistēmonikē epetēris tēs Philosophikēs Scholēs tou Panepistēmiou Athēnōn* 26 [1977-1978]). For a summary of this martyrdom/life, see Foss, 'Byzantine Saints in Early Islamic Syria,' pp. 116–17, and S. Efthymiadis's article in *CMR*, vol. 1, pp. 598-599.

wanted to become a Christian and by taking up the monastic way of life be married to Christ. Bacchus's desire to become a Christian no doubt had something to do with his mother's secret Christianity and her wish that her children convert to Christianity from Islam. When his father died, Bacchus reported his yearning to become a Christian to his mother, who rejoiced at what he told her. Bacchus then went to Jerusalem where he met a monk at the Church of the Resurrection, a meeting which eventually led to his being baptized at the lavra of St. Sabas and receiving his new, Christian name.[112] Later, Bacchus's mother came to Jerusalem to see the True Cross and also out of a desire to see her son, whom she found. Bacchus told her of his conversion to Christianity, his baptism, and his taking up of the monastic garment: 'At last,' he said, 'by means of your prayers, O mother, I put into effect everything I long for without obstruction.'[113]

When Bacchus's mother returned to Maiouma, she reported to her other children everything she had seen and told them of his holy ways: 'He suffers greatly and is grieved,' she told them, 'at our false doctrine.'[114] At this point, they sold their belongings and all moved to a different region where they were baptized, along with their wives and children. The wife of one of Bacchus's brothers, however, did not go along with this family conversion, but instead left and 'made everything clear to the unbelievers.' This news of apostasy, we are told, outraged the Muslims, who paid a man, who according to the martyrdom was thought to be a Christian but was really a renegade, to go about churches and monasteries searching for Bacchus.[115] Having been tasked with finding Bacchus/Ḍaḥḥāk, the crypto-Muslim headed for Jerusalem, where, 'secretly and deceitfully walking up and down its squares,' he looked about for Bacchus. At last the man spotted Bacchus, who, having offered up a prayer, was entering the Church of the Resurrection. 'He is one of us!' the agent shouted out, grabbing him by the shoulder and the back, 'He felt a disgust at our faith and has become a Christian. Look! He is even clothed with a monastic garment!'[116] At this point, the martyrdom takes a predictable path: Bacchus is put in prison and eventually taken before a Muslim ruler who tries unsuccessfully to persuade him to come back to his 'ancestral faith.' In the end, Bacchus was beheaded for his apostasy.

[112] Though the name 'Bacchus' may sound pagan, thanks to the famous Syrian Saints Sergius and Bacchus (BHO 1052-1055) it could also be regarded as a Christian one by this point.

[113] *Life and Martyrdom of the Holy Neo-Martyr Bacchus the Younger*, p. 347.

[114] *Life and Martyrdom of the Holy Neo-Martyr Bacchus the Younger*, p. 347.

[115] *Life and Martyrdom of the Holy Neo-Martyr Bacchus the Younger*, p. 347.

[116] *Life and Martyrdom of the Holy Neo-Martyr Bacchus the Younger*, pp. 347 (first quote), 348 (second quote).

Worries about how literally we should be reading such accounts should not deter us from recognizing that this one martyrdom presents us with a whole spectrum of possible Christian responses to the religious opportunities presented by Islam in the early period of Muslim rule: Ḍaḥḥāk/Bacchus's father, who converted for unspecified reasons; his mother, who followed her husband into Islam but clung to a secret Christian observance; the children whose subsequent paths in life suggest that their religious identities were, if not confused, then not rock solid. If Bacchus's mother was actually a secret Christian, as the martyrdom reports, it would be hard to imagine that her children would not be aware of their mother's attachment to her previous religion. The children themselves had an obvious affection for Christianity, due no doubt at least partially to their mother's influence: Ḍaḥḥāk/Bacchus was baptized and became a monk and credited his mother's prayers with helping him achieve what he desired. Moreover, all the rest of his siblings followed his example and were baptized as well. This same pattern of tensions created by Christian-Muslim marriages played itself out at the other end of the Muslim-ruled world, in al-Andalus, where we also find a number of Christian martyrs who came from religiously mixed families.[117]

Perhaps most interestingly, the particular martyrdom in question provides us with another example of a possible Christian response to Islam—namely, the Christian who, as it were, played it both ways—being a Christian when it suited him and being a Muslim when it suited him, in this case in exchange for money from the Muslim rulers. Here we have an example of a confessional code-switcher like we encountered in Chapter 3, but rather than switching identities between different versions of Christianity, this figure was switching between Christianity and Islam as expediency dictated.[118] The advent of Islam, therefore, did not invent the phenomenon of one person inhabiting more than one religious identity, or to put it differently, making use of the spiritual and symbolic resources of more than one religious tradition. This had been going on for a long time. Such code-switching would have been aided and abetted by the fact that in a world of simple believers—Christians, Muslims, Jews, Zoroastrians, and pagans—while theological curiosity may have been a regular feature, for many, the nature of religious identity was nevertheless not necessarily tightly bound up with doctrinally heavy understandings of what religious belonging entailed.

[117] A. Christys, *Christians in Al-Andalus (711-1000)* (Richmond, 2002), pp. 52–53.

[118] I spoke of Bacchus as a 'confessional code switcher' in *SBI*, p. 541. A. Chrysostomides, '"There is No God but God": Islamisation and Religious Code-Switching, Eighth to Tenth Centuries,' in Peacock, ed., *Islamisation*, pp. 123–25, has now analyzed his *vita* using the similar notion of 'religious code-switching.'

We should also not forget that as time progressed and conversions gradually piled up, the Muslim community of the early medieval and medieval Middle East became increasingly a convert community. What is more, if the arguments of my Part III were in any way persuasive, this is how we should view the Muslim community in the Middle East from the very beginning of the conquest period. The shifting allegiances and mixed identities that can be seen in the martyrdom of Bacchus must have been commonplace.

THE PRACTICE OF EVERYDAY LIFE

Apart from intermarriage and religiously mixed families, however, everyday life presented a myriad of other opportunities for Muslims to come into contact with non-Muslims on a constant basis. Given the demographic realities I have stressed, such contact must in fact have been almost unavoidable for Muslim settlers and immigrants living in garrison cities and pre-Islamic settlements throughout the Fertile Crescent. These Muslims would often have been a small minority, even in areas of Muslim settlements, which perhaps explains why conquest treaties sometimes specify that the local non-Muslim population should show hospitality to Muslims, give them advice, or offer them guidance if they are lost.[119] And everyday contacts will have continued well after the initial conquest period: The famous early legal scholar al-Awzāʿī, we are told, stayed with a Christian family during the caliphate of al-Manṣūr (reg. AH 136–158/AD 754–775) and was treated hospitably. In gratitude for their hospitality, al-Awzāʿī attempted to help them with the excessive taxes that were being extorted from them.[120] Ibn Ḥayyūs (d. AD 1081), a leading Syrian poet of the eleventh century, had the habit of visiting the house of Paul the Christian and holding salons there.[121]

Worries about everyday greetings can be taken as indications of the demographic situation that interests us. Even though the tradition showed a discomfort with Muslims greeting Christians and Jews with 'Peace,' this was bound to occur, even accidentally. Mālik was asked if a Muslim who had greeted a Jew or a Christian with a wish of peace should seek pardon for having done

[119] See, e.g. Ḥamīd Allāh, *Majmūʿat al-wathāʾiq al-siyāsiyya*, vol. 1: the people of Ḥimṣ were to give hospitality to Muslims (pp. 467–68, hospitality p. 468); or the Bishop of Edessa was to offer advice to Muslims (p. 495); the people of Edessa were to give guidance to the lost Muslim (p. 495).

[120] Ibn Abī Ḥātim, *Taqdimat al-maʿrifa li-kitāb al-jarḥ wa-ʾl-taʿdīl* (Hyderabad, 1952), pp. 210–11. For this, see Judd, *Religious Scholars and the Umayyads*, p. 74.

[121] Ibn Khallikān, *Wafayāt al-aʿyān wa-anbāʾ abnāʾ al-zamān*, vol. 4, pp. 439–40. An ET is also available in de Slane, *Ibn Khallikan's Biographical Dictionary*, vol. 3, p. 140. On Ibn Ḥayyūs, see the article, 'Ibn Ḥayyūs,' in *EI2*, vol. 3, p. 790.

so: 'He said,' we are told, '"No."'[122] Contact between the newcomers, their descendants, and the local population was of the most literal kind as well: in his collection of *ḥadīth*, 'Abd al-Razzāq included a section on 'Taking the Hand of the People of the Book' (*muṣāfaḥat ahl al-kitāb*): there was, it seems, a question as to whether it was appropriate for Muslim and Christian to do just this when greeting a person.[123] 'Abd Allāh b. Muḥayrīz (d. early second century AH/eighth century AD), for example, was seen in Damascus taking the hand of a Christian.[124] Some saw no harm in taking the hands (*muṣāfaḥa*) of Jews or Christians, but other Muslims disapproved of eating with them or engaging in such hand clasping.[125]

Despite disapproval from some quarters, the very existence of the question and of an anecdote like the one reporting the behavior of 'Abd Allāh b. Muḥayrīz points to the reality that such interreligious physical contact was happening and that Christians and Muslims were speaking to one another in the streets—in the case of 'Abd Allāh b. Muḥayrīz, another version of the same

[122] Mālik b. Anas, *al-Muwaṭṭa'*, vol. 2, p. 960. One only need read the *ḥadīth* before this one—where the Prophet speaks of Jews greeting Muslims with *al-sāmu 'alaykum* ('poison be upon you') rather than *al-salāmu 'alaykum* ('peace be upon you') for a classic example of ambivalence about offering 'peace' as a greeting to non-Muslims. Ibn Abī Shayba, *al-Muṣannaf*, vol. 8, pp. 470–71 (no. 26264–67), contains various *ḥadīth* further illustrating this ambivalence. On this question of only greeting those who are members of one's religious community, contrast this ambivalence with Matthew 5:47, and cp. with H. L. Strack and P. Billerbeck, *Kommentar zum Neuen Testament aus Talmud und Midrasch*, vol. 1: *Das Evangelium nach Matthäus erläutert aus Talmud und Midrasch* (München, 1922), pp. 380–85, esp. p. 384, nn. M and N, and W. D. Davies and D. C. Allison, *A Critical and Exegetical Commentary on the Gospel according to Saint Matthew*, vol. 1 (Edinburgh, 1988), p. 559. Cf. also Luke 10:4, which some have seen as an echo of 2 Kings 4:29. In the post-Chalcedonian world, the question of receiving greetings from heretics came up: see John of Tella, *Canonical Answers* 26 (ed. Lamy, *Dissertatio*, pp. 80, 82), where the disciple is made to ask the teacher whether it is blameworthy if a heretic gives a greeting to believers—likely a Chacledonian greeting Miaphysites—'from natural love,' even though their doctrines disagree. Since it was on account of love, the teacher thought there was no harm, so long as the heretics did not give a kiss with their mouth to the hand or head of the believer.

[123] Cf. the *ḥadīth* collected in Ibn Abī Shayba, *al-Muṣannaf*, vol. 8, pp. 445–46 (nos. 26109–17) on the question of taking a person's hand when greeting him. According to Ibn al-Athīr, *al-Nihāya fī gharīb al-ḥadīth wa-'l-athar*, vol. 3, p. 34, *muṣāḥafa*, when used in the context of meeting, included not just the joining of hands but also the touching of faces together.

[124] 'Abd al-Razzāq, *al-Muṣannaf*, vol. 6, p. 117 (no. 10173), and cf. Ibn Abī Shayba, *al-Muṣannaf*, vol. 8, p. 446 (no. 26118). On 'Abd Allāh b. Muḥayrīz, see al-Mizzī, *Tahdhīb al-kamāl fī asmā' al-rijāl*, vol. 16, pp. 106–10. He died either in the caliphate of 'Umar b. 'Abd al-'Azīz or in the caliphate of al-Walīd b. 'Abd al-Malik.

[125] 'Abd al-Razzāq, *al-Muṣannaf*, vol. 6, p. 117 (disapprove: no. 10174; approve: 10175). Similar to 'Abd al-Razzāq, Ibn Abī Shayba included a section in his collection of *ḥadīth* on 'Taking the Hand of a Polytheist' when greeting (*al-Muṣannaf*, vol. 8, pp. 446–47). In addition to the report of 'Abd Allāh b. Muḥayrīz taking the hand of a Christian (see below), there is a report that al-Ḥasan disapproved of a Muslim taking the hand of a Jew or a Christian, as well as a report that al-Ḥasan regarded polytheists as unclean and therefore advised doing ablutions if one had taken their hand in greeting. A final report from 'Aṭā' expresses disapproval of taking the hand of a Magian.

report has him taking the hand of a Christian in the mosque of Damascus.[126] Similarly, despite disapproval in some quarters of Muslims eating with Christians and Jews, it seems that Muslims, as we saw in Chapter 12, were at times initiating such interaction: Addai wrote to Jacob of Edessa to ask how the steward of a monastery should proceed if he were commanded by an emir to eat with him from the same bowl.[127] We can also point to the memorable story of Isaac, the Miaphysite patriarch of Alexandria (sed. AD 686–689), sharing a high-stakes meal with ʿAbd al-ʿAzīz, a governor whose great respect and affection for the Christian leader had raised the ire of some of his fellow Muslims.[128] Such encounters were happening at all levels of society.

There were other points of quotidian contact. In addition to families in which Muslims and non-Muslims lived together, Muslims and non-Muslims who were not connected by marriage also were living together. In the second/eighth century in Ayla, Yazīd b. Abī Sumayya was known as a person who would pray the entire night while weeping. 'There was living with him in [his] abode (*fī 'l-dār*),' Ibn Saʿd reported, 'a Jewish woman who would weep out of mercy for him. And so one night in his supplication he said, "O God, this Jewish woman has wept out of mercy for me and her religion disagrees with mine. How much more then should *you* have mercy on me!"'[129] Living in Basra in the second/eighth century, ʿAbd Allāh b. ʿAwn b. Arṭabān had a large dwelling in the marketplace in which Christians and Muslims both lived; he lived there as well. 'He would say,' according to Ibn Saʿd, '"Let Christians be below me; Muslims should not be below me." And he dwelt in the top of his abode (*dārihi*).'[130] ʿUmar b. al-Khaṭṭāb is supposed to have washed with warm water from the house of a Christian woman.[131] But ʿUmar is also supposed to have been dismayed to hear that believing women and women from the *muhājirūn* were entering into baths with women from the People of the Book and wanted the practice stopped.[132]

[126] Ibn Abī Shayba, *al-Muṣannaf*, vol. 8, p. 446 (no. 26118).

[127] See Chapter 12, n. 41.

[128] See Mena of Nikiou, *History of the Patriarch Isaac*, pp. 67–71 (ed. Amélineau; ET in Bell, *The Life of Isaac of Alexandria*, pp. 71–72), and cf. Chapter 12, n. 41.

[129] *Fa-anta awlā bi-raḥmatī.* I am grateful to Joseph Witztum and Luke Yarbrough for helping me with this translation. See Ibn Saʿd, *Kitāb al-ṭabaqāt al-kabīr*, vol. 7.2, p. 206 (ed. Sachau [Leiden, 1918]; my translation made with reference to the ET in Bewley, *The Men of Madina*, vol. 1, p. 322). On Yazīd b. Abī Sumayya, see al-Mizzī, *Tahdhīb al-kamāl fī asmāʾ al-rijāl*, vol. 32, pp. 151–52. Al-Mizzī does not give a date for Yazīd's death, but I take him as a second/eighth century figure based on the people from whom he transmitted, e.g., ʿUmar b. ʿAbd al-ʿAzīz.

[130] Ibn Saʿd, *Kitāb al-ṭabaqāt al-kabīr*, vol 7.2, p. 26 (ed. Sachau [Leiden, 1918]; my translation made with reference to the ET in Bewley, *The Men of Madina*, vol. 1, p. 163).

[131] al-Bukhārī, *al-Jāmiʿ al-ṣaḥīḥ*, vol. 1, p. 83 (*Kitāb al-wuḍūʾ*, *bāb* 43).

[132] ʿAbd al-Razzāq, *al-Muṣannaf*, vol. 1, p. 295 (no. 1134).

Without going into too great detail, one could mention scribes,[133] sailors and workmen,[134] interreligious debates,[135] and even the important role that Christians played as copyists of the Qurʿān in the early period as further examples of the host of other points of everyday interaction that must have been typical.[136] Christians might also be in the army:[137] 'When our citadel on the frontiers was being attacked by those from the outside,' Addai wrote Jacob,

> the Arabs who were ruling inside ordered that everyone go out to the wall for the battle and they did not leave behind anyone whom they did not bring out, not even priests. In the case of a priest or a deacon who, when the battle grew fierce, threw a stone from the wall and struck and killed one of the fighters who was attempting to go up the wall, what does he deserve from the canons? Does he have a sin [in this]? I want to learn. Or, with respect to him, or other priests and monks who, unwillingly were tied up with the ropes of a war machine (μαγγανικόν) and were throwing rocks and killing some opposing warriors,

[133] See the biographical dictionary of Christian scribes and wazirs compiled by L. Cheikho and C. Hechaïmé, *Wuzarāʾ al-naṣrāniyya wa-kuttābuhā fī ʾl-Islām: 622–1517* (Jouniyeh, Lebanon, 1987). A read through al-Jahshiyārī's (d. AH 331) *Kitāb al-wuzarāʾ wa-ʾl-kuttāb* (ed. M. al-Saqā, I. al-Ibyārī, and ʿA. al-Ḥafīẓ Shalabī) (Cairo, 1938), shows many examples of scribes who were Christians or *mawālī*. Tritton, *The Caliphs and Their Non-Muslim Subjects*, pp. 18–36 presented a large amount of evidence from a variety of sources of widespread Christian participation in Muslim administration. On the development of the Sunnī discourse around the employment of non-Muslims in Muslim administrations, see Yarbrough, 'Islamizing the Islamic State.'

[134] See H. I. Bell and W. E. Crum, eds., *Greek Papyri in the British Museum: Catalogue, with Texts*. Vol. IV: *The Aphrodito Papyri* (London, 1910), pp. 435–50, for Coptic papyri showing men being conscripted and sent to serve as sailors on Muslim ships that were engaged in raiding in the Mediterranean and also to serve in official government building projects; pp. xxxii–xxxv, explains how the *cursus* worked and the mixture between Arab fighters and Egyptian sailors on board the ships. For Egyptian sailors in the Arab navy, see Sijpesteijn, *Shaping a Muslim State*, p. 76.

[135] For a listing of such debates and their records, see the various bibliographies in the periodical *Islamochristiana*, beginning with R. Caspar, A. Charfi, M. de Epalza, A. T. Khoury and P. Khoury, 'Bibliographie du dialogue islamo-chrétien,' *Islamochristiana* 1 (1975), pp. 125–81, and R. Caspar, A. Charfi, A.T. Khoury and K. Samir, 'Bibliographie du dialogue islamo-chrétien,' *Islamochristiana* 2 (1976), pp. 187-249, etc. These have now been superceded by *Christian-Muslim Relations: A Bibliographical History*, vols. 1–11.

[136] For this, see M. J. Kister, '*Lā yamassuhu illā ʾl-muṭahharūn*...: Notes on the Interpretations of a Qurʾānic Phrase,' *JSAI* 34 (2008), pp. 330–31. Cf. also Chapter 3, n. 34.

[137] E.g., Crone, *Slaves on Horses*, pp. 37–38; Lammens, 'Études sur le règne du calife Omaiyade Moʿawiya Ier,' (part 3), p. 299, and most recently and comprehensively, W. al-Qāḍī, 'Non-Muslims in the Early Muslim Conquest Army in Early Islam,' in Borrut and Donner, eds., *Christians and Others in the Umayyad State*, pp. 83–127. Related to the question of Christian participation is that of non-Arab participation in the Arab armies, on which see A.M.M. al-Faouri, 'Dawr al-ʿanāṣir ghayr al-ʿarabiyya fī ʾl-futūḥāt al-Islāmiyya fī ʾl-ʿaṣr al-Umawī,' *Jordan Journal for History and Archaeology* 8 (2014), pp. 51–75.

> should they serve in the priesthood, or is it right that for a short time they be [. . .] the canon?[138]

Christians might even take part in Muslim razzias against non-Muslims: 'among them,' the East Syrian John bar Penkaye wrote of Arab raiders outside the caliphate in the late seventh century, 'were also Christians in no small numbers: some belonged to the heretics, while others to us.'[139] What is more, when Christians had disputes with one another, they had the option of going before Muslim rulers for adjudication: perhaps unsurprisingly, the austere Jacob of Edessa issued a canon forbidding the clergy from taking their disagreements before worldly authorities: 'It is not right for clergymen or monks who lose something,' he wrote,

> to bring those against whom they have a claim before the rulers of the world or before the pagans, as they have taken that which has been lost, nor to turn them over to whippings and scourgings. Instead, they should adjudicate and try their matter modestly and chastely and with justice and piety and as is meet for brothers in Christ, apart from all disturbance and blows, before members of the Church, according to the commandment of the Holy Apostle [1 Corinthians 6:1-6]. For criticizing and reprimanding them, he says to those who are foolishly making an error like this, 'Has one of you acted brazenly when, having a case against his brother, they have gone to court before the outsiders and not before the Church?' And although he was saying these things to Christian laymen, if he was commanding Christian laypeople in this way, how much more in the case of clergy and monks is it not right that they should take their legal adversaries before secular rulers? How can he speak of everything which is right if

[138] *Further Questions Which the Priest Addai Asked* Mardin 310, fols. 215b–16a (pp. 428–29) (Syriac text and ET of the full passage in *SBI*, p. 543, n. 1310). For a canon of Rabbula, forbidding priests, deacons, and ascetics from joining the *comitatus* without permission of the bishop, see Rabbula of Edessa, *Rules and Admonitions for Priests and Ascetics* 37 (ed. Overbeck, *S. Ephraemi Syri*, p. 219; translation available in Connolly, 'Some More Early Syrian Rules,' p. 304). For Basil of Caesarea ordering the deposition of clergymen who go out to battle bandits, see his third letter to Amphilochius (*Epistle 217*), Canon 55 (ed. Joannou, *Discipline générale antique*, vol. 2, p. 144). (I am grateful to Peter Brown for this last reference). For the different attitudes Christian Arab tribes took vis-à-vis the Arab conquests, see M. A. Khrīsāt, 'Dawr al-'Arab al-mutanaṣṣira fī 'l-futūḥāt,' in *Proceedings of the Second Symposium on the History of Bilad al-Sham during the Early Islamic Period up to 40 A.H./640 A.D.*, vol. 2, ed. M. A. Bakhit and I. Abbas (Amman, 1987), pp. 135–64.

[139] John bar Penkaye, *Book of the Main Events*, p. *147 (ed. Mingana; translation taken from Brock, 'North Mesopotamia in the Late Seventh Century,' p. 61, who suggests [n. a] that members of the Ghassanid and Lakhmid tribes were being referred to). See also the series of questions about whether *dhimmī*s who take part in raids (*ghazā*) with Muslims get a share in the spoils, in al-Khallāl, *Ahl al-milal*, vol. 2, pp. 317–19. Yarbrough, 'Upholding God's Rule,' p. 70, n. 180, contains further references to discussion among Muslim authorities on the question of non-Muslims receiving a share in booty acquired through raiding.

> it is the case that it is monks who are the ones who have a legal case and it is not at all right that they should demand their justice? Instead, if there is love among them, if he has some kind of case like this—be he a clergyman or a monk, who has destroyed something of his—and he dares to bring his case before secular judges and to turn his brother over to blows and scourging, he should be judged as an enemy of the law of Christ, and he should receive from the ecclesiastical canons a rebuke which is fitting for his error.[140]

But Christians were doing just this: "Umar wrote to 'Udayy b. 'Udayy,' one report states, '"If the People of the Book come to you, judge between them."'[141] By the Geniza period a whole host of business partnerships between Muslims and non-Muslims had become utterly commonplace,[142] a phenomenon that no doubt had its beginnings much earlier.

MONASTERIES AND FESTIVALS

> I went with my father to Syria and they began to pass by monastic cells (*ṣawāmiʿ*) in which there were Christians. And they were greeting [the Christians] with "peace."
>
> Suhayl b. Abī Ṣāliḥ[143]

Another important place where Muslims regularly came into contact not just with Christians, but also with Christian religious institutions and practices,

[140] Jacob of Edessa, *Canons*, Mardin 310, fols. 212a–b (Syriac text also in *SBI*, p. 544, n. 1315; cp. with Canon 24 in Vööbus ed. and trans. [CSCO 367–68: SS 161–62], p. 272 [Syriac] = 247 [ET]). I am grateful to Joseph Witztum for suggestions on improving this translation.

[141] See ʿAbd al-Razzāq, *al-Muṣannaf*, vol. 10, p. 322 (no. 19241). For a detailed examination of the phenomenon of Christians appearing before Muslim judges, see U. Simonsohn, *A Common Justice: The Legal Allegiances of Christians and Jews under Early Islam* (Philadelphia, 2011), esp. Chapters 3 and 5. The use of Islamic courts by non-Muslims is another factor that should be remembered when thinking about conversion—the shift in legal status entailed by a conversion will not have been so great in a setting where Christians were already using Muslim courts. For the development of civil law in an East Syrian legal context in response to judicial competition from Muslim courts, see Simonsohn, 'The Introduction and Formalization of Civil Law in the East Syrian Church in the Late Sasanian-Early Islamic Periods,' *History Compass* 14 (2016), pp. 231–43.

[142] For this, see Goitein, *A Mediterranean Society: The Jewish Communities of the World as Portrayed in the Documents of the Cairo Geniza*, vol 3: *The Community*, pp. 293–98.

[143] Abū Dāwūd, *Sunan*, vol. 7, pp. 497–98 (no. 5205). The report continues: 'Then my father said: "Do not initiate 'Peace' with them, for Abū Hurayra related to us from the Prophet, may God pray for him and grant him peace, he said: 'Do not say "Peace" to them first and if you meet them on the road, force them to the narrowest part of the road." ' On Suhayl b. Abī Ṣāliḥ, see al-Mizzī, *Tahdhīb al-kamāl*, vol. 12, pp. 223–28. On the issue of greeting non-Muslims, see n. 122 in this chapter.

was the monastery. 'I have met a large number of monks known for the forcefulness of their asceticism and the abundance of their knowledge,' 'Abd Allāh b. Ismā'īl al-Hāshimī, the Muslim correspondent of the Christian apologist al-Kindī, wrote. 'And I have entered into many cloisters and monasteries and churches and attended their prayers—the lengthy seven which they call "the prayers of the hours."' Al-Hāshimī would go on to name and describe the different offices of the hours and Christian feast days and sacraments: 'For this, all of it, I have been present and witnessed its practitioners and known and been aware of it.'[144] Although the letter of al-Hāshimī may have actually been written by a Christian using a pseudonym and not by a Muslim, the familiarity with monasteries and interest in Christianity which the letter shows was not uncommon. The geographer al-Bakrī (d. AH 487/AD 1094) preserved an anecdote attributed to the poet al-Ḥusayn b. al-Ḍaḥḥāk (AH 250/AD 864) in which the latter spoke of spending the night with some other Muslim visitors in Qullāyat 'Umr, a monastery in Samarra. 'The monk read one of their books (*sifran min asfārihim*) until the dawn broke,' al-Ḥusayn is supposed to have said, 'his speech was mournful and he chanted with an intonation in his voice the likes of which I have never heard.'[145]

The encounter between Christian monks and Muslims might even be portrayed as having didactic and not merely aesthetic aspects: 'I saw a mountain upon which there was a monk,' Mālik b. Dīnār (d. ca. AH 130/AD 747–748), a figure regarded as an early ascetic, is reported to have said,

> So I called him and I said: 'Teach me something by which you will cause me to forsake the world!' He said: 'Do you not have the Qur'ān and God's revelation (*al-furqān*)?' I said, 'Of course! But I want you to teach me something of yours by which I can renounce the world. He said: 'If you can make a wall of iron between you and your passions, do it.'[146]

[144] Al-Hāshimī continues to describe his intimate knowledge of Christianity after this, but I will not belabor the point. For the quotes, see al-Kindī, *Apology*, pp. 10, 11.

[145] al-Bakrī, *Mu'jam mā ista'jama min asmā' al-bilād wa-'l-mawāḍi'*, vol. 3, p. 1090 (ed. M. al-Saqqā [Beirut, n.d.]).

[146] Abū Nu'aym al-Iṣbahānī, *Ḥilyat al-awliyā' wa-ṭabaqāt al-aṣfiyā'*, vol. 2, p. 265. For this passage, see Livne-Kafri, 'Early Muslim Ascetics and the World of Christian Monasticism,' p. 108. For the translation of a number of passages where a Muslim ascetic asks a Christian monk for direction, see S. A. Mourad, 'Christian Monks in Islamic Literature: A Preliminary Report on Some Arabic *Apophthegmata Patrum*,' *Bulletin of the Royal Institute for Inter-faith Studies* 6 (2004), pp. 91–92. On Mālik b. Dīnār, see C. Pellat's article, 'Mālik b. Dīnār,' in *EI2*, vol. 6, pp. 266–67. Pellat regards most of the sayings attributed to Mālik by Abū Nu'aym as inauthentic. For this same saying attributed to another monk who spoke with 'Abd al-Wāḥid b. Zubayd, see Mourad, 'Christian Monks in Islamic Literature,' p. 93 (no. 18).

Importantly, there are reports that Muslim ascetics would even read Christian books: 'I was eager for books that I might look into,' Mālik b. Dīnār also reportedly said,

> And so I entered into a certain monastery during the nights of the pilgrims and they brought out one of their books and I examined it. There was in it: 'O son of man, why do you seek knowledge of what you do not know when you do not practice what you do know?'[147]

Though such reports may have more literary than historical value, they are nevertheless suggestive. We have already seen extensive evidence for Muslim interest in churches and what was going on in them, and even examples of Muslims living in or very close to churches. Such contacts go back to the earliest period of Arab rule.[148] What is more, contacts between Muslim ascetics and Christian monks have been well documented, as we have seen,[149] and inspired by stories like these, Sabino Chialà was able to adduce a number of examples of Christian *apophthegmata* that appear in Muslim ascetic literature, though transformed there into Islamic edifying anecdotes. This led him to suggest that at least some Muslim ascetics were in fact reading the sayings of the Desert Fathers and that a systematic study of Islamic spiritual literature would eventually turn up more such examples of appropriation.[150] Goitein, too, has pointed out how common it is to find in the writings of Muslim ascetics references to having spoken with and learned from monks in Jerusalem.[151]

[147] Abū Nuʿaym al-Iṣbahānī, *Ḥilyat al-awliyā' wa-ṭabaqāt al-aṣfiyā'*, vol. 2, p. 275. For this passage, see Livne-Kafri, 'Early Muslim Ascetics and the World of Christian Monasticism,' p. 108 and S. Chialà, 'Les mystiques musulmans lecteurs des écrits chrétiens. Quelques échos d'Apophtegmes,' *Proche-Orient Chrétien* 60 (2010), p. 358, esp. n. 18, where Chialà tries to identify its origin in Christian ascetic literature.

[148] See See Chapter 12, pp. 371–373, 384–386.

[149] See Livne-Kafri, 'Early Muslim Ascetics and the World of Christian Monasticism,' and also the collection of texts assembled, for example, in Y. Ṣādir, *Ruhbān 'arab fī ba'ḍ siyar al-mutaṣawwifīn al-Muslimīn* (Beirut, 2009). See also T. Andrae, *In the Garden of Myrtles: Studies in Early Islamic Mysticism*, trans. B. Sharpe (Albany, 1987), pp. 9–15, and B. M. Landron, 'Les rélations originelles entre chrétiens de l'Est (Nestoriens) et Musulmans,' *PdO* 10 (1981–1982), pp. 201–207 (on monasteries as a locus of contact).

[150] See his fascinating 'Les mystiques musulmans lecteurs des écrits chrétiens.' Andrae, 'Zuhd und Mönchtum,' p. 319, contains another example of an *apopthegmatum* transmited and transformed in an Islamic context, cf. also p. 326–27. Blum, 'Christlich-Orientalische Mystik und Sufismus,' p. 268, suggested that literary dependence between Sufi and Eastern Christian texts can at most be rarely shown, and that Eastern Christian influence on Sufi writings and practice will have been largely through example and through conversation ('durch Vorbild und Gespräch').

[151] See S. D. Goitein, 'The Historical Background of the Erection of the Dome of the Rock,' *JAOS* 70 (1950), p. 108.

The information that was exchanged could of course be about more than just spiritual and ascetic practices: it might also be philosophical: It was at Dayr al-Fārūs in Latakiya, for instance, that the famously skeptical poet Abū 'Alā' al-Ma'arrī (D. AH 449/AD 1058) was said to have met a monk educated in Greek philosophy. And it was hearing sayings of the ancient philosophers from this monk that aroused religious doubt in Abū 'Alā's mind.[152] Muslims might also gather material from other Christian institutions: 'From al-Ḥīra's churches,' Ibn al-Kalbī (d. AH 204/AD 819 or AH 206/AD 821) the great genealogist and scholar reported, 'I used to obtain data about the Arabs, the genealogy of the family of Naṣr b. Rabī'a, the dates of their service to the Persian emperors and the chronicle of their years. For in those churches is a record of their kingdom and all their affairs.'[153]

If expecting every Muslim to have an intellectualized and deep interest in Christianity of the type that al-Hāshimī showed, or to have been attracted to the spiritual and ascetic aspects of monasteries as Mālik b. Dīnār reputedly was, is perhaps unrealistic and asking more of Muslims than one would ask of non-Muslims, it is salutary to remember that there were other attractions to be had in these Christian institutions. Ibn al-Ḥaddād (d. AH 480/AD 1088), the Maghribi poet, is one example. He planned to make the *ḥajj* via Egypt, going up the Nile to the town of Qūṣ with the goal of crossing the Red Sea through the port of 'Aydhāb. At the monastery of Rīfa, however, located above al-Suyūṭ, he saw a nun named Nuwayra and this changed everything. He stopped his pilgrimage and stayed in al-Rīfa so he could see Nuwayra more. 'One day,' Ibn Faḍl Allāh (d. AD 1349/AH 749) reported, 'he saw her among her friends, like the night bringing the moon out among the stars.' Ibn al-Ḥaddād would go on to compose a number of poems to her.[154]

Apart from the pulchritude of some of their inhabitants and the pleasantness and respite of their gardens and vineyards, monasteries had at least two things that were of interest to Muslims and non-Muslims alike: wine and the

[152] Ibn al-Qifṭī, *Inbāh al-ruwāh 'alā anbāh al-nuhāh*, vol. 1, p. 84 (ed. M. Abū al-Faḍl Ibrāhīm [Cairo/Beirut, 1986]). On this incident, see P. Smoor's article, 'al-Ma'arrī,' in *EI2*, vol. 5, p. 927. Brockelmann, *GAL*, vol. S1, p. 451, wrote that this story was 'wohl eine Sage.'

[153] al-Ṭabarī, *Ta'rīkh*, 1.2, p. 770 (ed. J. Barth and Th. Nöldeke [Leiden, 1881–1882]; ET taken from M. Perlmann, *The Ancient Kingdoms* [HṬ 4] [Albany, 1987], p. 150; I have slightly altered Perlmann's spelling). For this, see W. Atallah in *EI2*, vol. 4, p. 495 (part of his article, 'al-Kalbī').

[154] See Ibn Faḍl Allāh al-'Umarī, *Masālik al-abṣār fī mamālik al-amṣār*, vol. 1, pp. 403–405, quote from p. 404 (ed. K. Salmān al-Jubūrī [Beirut, 2010]). On Ibn al-Ḥaddād and his poetry written to Nuwayra, see H. Monés' article, 'Ibn al-Ḥaddād,' in *EI2*, vol. 3, pp. 775–76. On al-Rīfa, see Abū al-Makārim, *Ta'rīkh al-kanā'is wa-'l-adyira*, vol. 2, p. 97 (fol. 77b) (ET in Evetts, *The Churches & Monasteries of Egypt*, p. 214). For the connection between Christian churches, monasteries, clergy, physical beauty, and sex in the Islamic tradition, see J. E. Montgomery, 'For the Love of a Christian Boy: A Song by Abū Nuwās,' *Journal of Arabic Literature* 27 (1996), pp. 115–24, esp. 124.

festivals of saints. Even before the coming of Islam, Arabs would go to Christians in order to get hold of wine. Aʿshā, for example, was a pre-Islamic Arab poet (d. AD 629) who became a Christian through his contact with the Christian Arabs of Hira in southern Iraq who were known as the ʿIbād: 'He would go to them and buy wine from them,' the *Kitāb al-Aghānī* reported, 'and so they taught him [Christianity].'[155] Wine was made in monasteries, and it could even be bought there. Dayr al-ʿAdhārā, located somewhere between Mosul and Raqqa, had wine shops (*ḥānāt khamr*);[156] there were many vineyards, taverns, and wine sellers in Dayr Sābur near Baghdad;[157] Dayr Qūṭā, also near Baghdad, had numerous taverns (*ḥānāt*) and was a place where drink was said to be abundantly available;[158] Dayr Ashmūnā, again near Baghdad, had taverns, too;[159] in neighboring Dayr Mar Jirjis in Baghdad there were wine taverns;[160] the lands of Dayr Sarjis between Kufa and Qādisiyya were surrounded with vineyards, trees, and taverns;[161] Dayr Zurāra, near Kufa, was a place of many taverns and plentiful drink,[162] and the village of Zurāra was known as a place where wine was sold.[163] At Dayr al-Sūsī (also known as Dayr Maryam) near Samarra, people would drink in the gardens.[164] And so on.

A number of monasteries were known for the wine they produced: the wine of Dayr Aḥwīshā in Seert was carried to surrounding regions on account of its quality;[165] wine from Dayr al-Zaʿfarān in Nisibis was taken to Nisibis and to other places as well;[166] Dayr Akmun, located near Mt. Jūdī, was known for the high quality of its celebrated wine.[167] Dayr al-Zurnūq in Jazīrat Ibn ʿUmar in northern Iraq (modern Cizre in Turkey) was known to produce a great deal

[155] See Cheikho, *Shuʿarāʾ al-Naṣrāniyya qabla al-Islām*, p. 358, and see Abū al-Faraj al-Iṣbahānī, *Kitāb al-Aghānī*, vol. 8, p. 79. For this, see G. Rothstein, *Die dynastie der Lahmiden in al-Hîra: Ein Versuch zur arabisch-persischen Geschichte zur Zeit der Sasaniden* (Halle, 1899), p. 26. On Hira, see n. 13 in this chapter.

[156] Yāqūt, *Muʿjam al-buldān*, vol. 2, p. 522; see Campbell, 'A Heaven of Wine,' p. 273.

[157] al-Shābushtī, *al-Diyārāt*, p. 54; cf. Campbell, 'A Heaven of Wine,' p. 294.

[158] al-Shābushtī, *al-Diyārāt*, p. 62; cf. Campbell, 'A Heaven of Wine,' p. 293.

[159] al-Shābushtī, *al-Diyārāt*, p. 46.

[160] al-Shābushtī, *al-Diyārāt*, p. 69.

[161] al-Shābushtī, *al-Diyārāt*, p. 233. This was also known as Dayr Sarjis wa-Bakkus (Sergius and Bacchus) (Yāqūt, *Muʿjam al-buldān*, vol. 2, p. 514). cf. Campbell, 'A Heaven of Wine,' p. 296.

[162] al-Shābushtī, *al-Diyārāt*, p. 247; cf. Campbell, 'A Heaven of Wine,' p. 301.

[163] Yāqūt, *Muʿjam al-buldān*, vol. 3, p. 135.

[164] al-Shābushtī, *al-Diyārāt*, p. 149. For this monastery also known as Dayr Maryam, see Yāqūt, *Muʿjam al-buldān*, vol. 2, p. 518.

[165] al-Shābushtī, *al-Diyārāt*, p. 198, and Yāqūt, *Muʿjam al-buldān*, vol. 2, p. 497; cf. Campbell, 'A Heaven of Wine,' p. 273.

[166] al-Shābushtī, *al-Diyārāt*, p. 191; cf. Campbell, 'A Heaven of Wine,' p. 300.

[167] Yāqūt, *Muʿjam al-buldān*, vol. 2, p. 499; cf. Campbell, 'A Heaven of Wine,' p. 274.

of wine.[168] At least some of the time, it was monks who were serving wine to Muslim visitors at monasteries. Referring, for example, to his experience in the curiously named Dayr al-Shayāṭīn (Monastery of Demons), which was located between Balad and Mosul, al-Khabbāz al-Baladī, a poet of perhaps the fourth/tenth century, wrote that

Monks of a monastery gave me pure wine to drink
Like demons, in the Monastery of Demons.[169]

The laity could also get hold of wine with apparent ease in some Christian establishments. In an anecdote contained in Abū Faraj al-Iṣbahānī's *Kitāb adab al-ghurabā'*, we find the father of a young Christian girl bringing high-quality wine from a storeroom where Eucharistic elements were kept (*bayt al-qurbān*) to his daughter and the caliph al-Mutawakkil. The caliph had become smitten with her when he saw her walking through a church in Ḥimṣ and would eventually induce her to convert to Islam and marry him.[170]

The easy access monasteries provided to alcohol, along with the fact that wine was used in the Eucharist, meant that in the period of Muslim rule, non-Muslims and especially Christians would become associated with wine.[171] 'The one who steals wine from the People of the Book,' 'Aṭā' (d. ca. AH 115/AD 733) is supposed to have said, 'should have his head cut off.'[172] 'We will not sell different kinds of wine (*khumūr*),' the Christians promised in the 'Pact of 'Umar.'[173] But they were in fact doing just this. In a letter supposed to have

[168] Yāqūt, *Mu'jam al-buldān*, vol. 2, p. 511; cf. Campbell, 'A Heaven of Wine,' p. 301.

[169] al-Shābushtī, *al-Diyārāt*, p. 198 (on al-Khabbāz, see n. 3), and Yāqūt, *Mu'jam al-buldān*, vol. 2, p. 518.

[170] Abū Faraj al-Iṣbahānī, *Kitāb adab al-ghurabā'* 51 (ed. al-Munajjid, pp. 67–68; ET in Crone and Moreh, *The Book of Strangers*, p. 61–62, where they render *bayt al-qurbān* as 'the communion store' [61]).

[171] For the association of Christians and monasteries with wine, see the evidence in, e.g., A. Schippers, *Spanish Hebrew Poetry and the Arab Literary Tradition: Arabic Themes in Hebrew Andalusian Poetry* (Leiden/New York, 1994), p. 115.

[172] 'Abd al-Razzāq, *al-Muṣannaf*, vol. 10, p. 365 (no. 19503). On 'Aṭā' b. Abī Rabāḥ, see al-Mizzī, *Tahdhīb al-kamāl fī asmā' al-rijāl*, vol. 20, pp. 69–86. For different dates of his death, see al-Mizzī, pp. 84–85. Thomas asked Jacob of Edessa if it was appropriate for a Christian to knowingly drink wine that came from Jews; see (the damaged) Harvard Syriac 93, fols. 35b–37a, and see further *The Questions of Thomas the Hermit, Which He asked Jacob of Edessa* 3 (Vööbus, ed. and trans. [CSCO 367–368: SS 161–162], pp. 257–58 [Syriac] = 235 [ET]); for a roughly contemporaneous condemnation of Christians rushing to drink wine at Jewish taverns (*ḥānwātā*) after taking the Eucharist, and the mention that there are Christian taverns available, too, see Synod of Mar George (AD 676), *Canons* 17 (ed. Chabot, *Synodicon Orientale*, p. 225 [Syriac] = 489 [FT]). Muslim jurists had differing views about what, if any, obligation a Muslim who destroyed the wine of a *dhimmī* had. For instance: Mālik stated that the Muslim who destroyed the wine of a *dhimmī* should pay for its value, but al-Shāfi'ī held that a Muslim who destroyed the wine of a *dhimmī* or killed a pig of his was under no financial obligation; see al-Ṭabarī, *Ikhtilāf al-fuqahā'*, (Ed. F. Kern [Beirut, 1999]), p. 184.

[173] Ibn Taymiyya, *Iqtiḍā'*, p. 121.

been written by ʿUmar b. ʿAbd al-ʿAzīz to Ayyūb b. Shuraḥbīl and the people of Egypt, which dealt with the prohibition of wine, the caliph took up the case of people who claimed the drink *ṭilāʾ* was different from wine in taste and temper and that there was no harm in drinking it. 'Those [people] only imbibe their drink—which they want to claim as licit (*alladhī yastaḥillūna*)—,' he wrote, 'at the hands of the Christians, who love to have Muslims go astray in their religion and have them enter into what is not licit for them, along with that which adds to the good sale of their wares and the easing of the burden on them.'[174] Abū Zubayd was a Christian Arab related to the Christian tribe of Taghlib on his mother's side. Friends with al-Walīd b. ʿUqba, whom ʿUmar I had appointed a fiscal official in the Jazira, Abū Zubayd eventually converted to Islam as a result of the entreaties of al-Walīd in AH 30 (AD 650). Enemies of al-Walīd would charge him with drinking alcohol with Abū Zubayd: 'Do you know that al-Walīd is drinking with Abū Zubayd?' they asked subversively: 'This man is your emir; Abū Zubayd is his chosen intimate, and they are both devotees of wine.'[175] Though al-Ṭabarī's account of Abū Zubayd and al-Walīd does not make an explicit connection, one wonders whether Christian renegades such as Abū Zubayd fell under the suspicion of being wine drinkers; one also wonders how many of them actually did continue to drink wine once they had converted to Islam, especially given the wide variety of attitudes towards wine in the early period which we saw in Chapter 10.

Christian feast days provided opportunities for wine and also for the mixing of men and women. Well before the birth of Muḥammad, the festivals of saints had become associated with revelry and impurity. In the fifth century, Theodoret would write of one holy man, Maris, who had been virtuous from his youth. 'This he told me plainly,' Theodoret wrote, 'informing me that his body had remained chaste, just as it had left his mother's womb, and this although he had taken part in many festivals of martyrs when young, and captivated the crowds with the beauty of his voice....' Though Maris had been a cantor, 'neither his bodily beauty nor his brilliance of voice nor his mixing with the multitude injured his beauty of soul....'[176] It was possibly worries about the untoward things that might happen at such celebrations that motivated Rabbula, also in the fifth century, to issue a regulation to monks stipulating that

[174] See Ibn ʿAbd al-Ḥakam, *Sīrat ʿUmar b. ʿAbd al-ʿAzīz*, p. 101.

[175] al-Ṭabarī, *Taʾrīkh*, 1.5, p. 2843 (ed. E. Prym [Leiden, 1893]; ET taken from Humphreys, *The Crisis of the Early Caliphate*, pp. 48–49, quotes from p. 49). And cf. chapter 10, n. 72.

[176] Theodoret of Cyrrhus, *Historia religiosa* 20.2 (ed. P. Canivet and A. Leroy-Molinghen, *Histoire des moines de Syrie: Histoire Philothée* [SC 257] [Paris, 1977], pp. 64-66; ET taken from R. M. Price, *A History of the Monks of Syria* [Kalamazoo, 1985], p. 131). I am grateful to Nick Marinides for bringing this passage to my attention.

'Commemorations in monasteries should not take place with gatherings of people, but rather only with the brothers of the monastery [present].'[177] Importantly, men were not the only ones who would attend the festivals of saints. It was at an Easter celebration in the latter part of the sixth century that Mariya, the servant of Hind, the famous Lakhmid princess and daughter of Nuʿmān III (reg. 580–602), had seen the poet ʿAdī b. Zayd and fallen in love with him.[178]

Precisely because women and men would come into close contact in these contexts, festivals were the cause of concern among church leaders who feared these occasions would enable sin. 'But as for you, O women who love God,' Theodota of Amid would write in his final prayer at the very end of the seventh century,

> I command you, I, Theodota, the sinner, that when you have come to the commemoration of the saints, that you do not wear alluring adornments and radiant clothing and refined shoes on account of the thought of the world. For you will become stumbling blocks to those who look upon you, despite the fact that they fast and pray and hold vigils for their sins and for their afflictions. For looking at your fancy adornment they will be reproached and will become cut off from the help of the Saints. And, instead of them, you will receive hell with the demons. Rather than receiving help and prayers for you and for your households, you will take destruction and loss for your souls, which are the image of God.[179]

At the time of the Arab conquests, a number of people were taken captive while celebrating the festival of St. Simeon at the site of his famous pillar. Michael the Great blamed their capture on the improper behavior that went on at such celebrations: 'After these things,' he wrote,

> when the Arabs heard of the festival that took place at the Monastery of Mar Simeon the Stylite, which is in the territory of Antioch, they came and took captive a great mass of people, men, women, boys, and girls without number, and the Christians began to despair. Some people were saying: "Why did God permit this to happen?" But the discerning person [will understand]: righteousness permitted this to take place, for instead of fasting and keeping watch and singing psalms, the Christians engage in debauchery and drunkenness and revelry and other kinds of wantonness and dissipation at the festivals of the saints

[177] Rabbula of Edessa, *Admonitions concerning Monks* 8 (ed. Overbeck, *S. Ephraemi Syri*. . ., p. 213. My translation, but another ET is available in R. H. Connolly, 'Some Early Rules for Syrian Monks,' *Downside Review* 25 [1906], p. 156).

[178] See Horovitz, ''Adi ibn Zeyd, the Poet of Hira,' p. 58.

[179] St Mark's Jerusalem 199, fol. 563b. For the Syriac, see Mardin 275/8, p. 596 (the Syriac is lacunose).

and provoke God. Therefore, it is with justice that He reproves and chastises us for the purpose of correction.[180]

In the period of Muslim rule, Muslims would join Christians in celebrating feast days at monasteries. The most vivid testimony to this is a small genre of *kutub al-diyārāt*, books of monasteries, of which only one, that of al-Shābushtī (d. AH 388/AD 998), survives in any significant size.[181] Organized into chapters, each named for a different monastery, it contains a wealth of poetry, much of it written about or inspired by monasteries, and anecdotes in which we see the elite of Abbasid society, including even caliphs, visiting monasteries for diversion, amusement, and debauchery. That Muslim elites would go to monasteries was well known: mention of famous monasteries has reached us, Ibn Faḍl Allāh noted, through the poetry of the Arabs or from when caliphs, princes, men of letters, and other famous people entered into them, and works like that of al-Shābushtī, which Ibn Faḍl Allāh relied upon when he himself wrote about famous monasteries, can be seen as ways of organizing and explaining the poetic remains and allusions that resulted from frequent visits to these Christian places.[182] Each chapter of al-Shābushtī's work begins with a description of a different monastery and its location and sometimes even provides information about its feast day. 'This monastery is to the east of Baghdad,' a typical description (this one of the monastery of Samālū) begins,

at the al-Shammāsiyya gate, on the al-Mahdī Canal; there are water mills [there] and gardens, trees and palm trees surround it. It is a pleasant spot, of fine construction, inhabited by those who visit it and its monks. At Easter in Baghdad there is an amazing spectacle there, for every Christian comes and takes com-

[180] Michael the Great, *Chronicle* 11.6 (ed. Chabot, 4.417 = 2.422).

[181] On Christian monasteries in the Muslim-ruled Middle East, see Ḥ. Zayyāt, 'al-Diyārāt al-naṣrāniyya fī 'l-Islām,' *al-Machriq* 36 (1938), pp. 289–417. On *kutub al-diyārāt* and al-Shābushtī's *Kitāb al-diyārāt* more specifically, and on the social implications of this genre, see G. Troupeau, 'Les couvents chrétiens dans la littérature arabe,' *La nouvelle Revue du Caire* 1 (1975), pp. 265–79; H. Kilpatrick, 'Monasteries through Muslim Eyes: The *Diyārāt* Books,' in D. Thomas, ed., *Christians at the Heart of Islamic Rule: Church Life and Scholarship in 'Abbasid Iraq* (Leiden/Boston, 2003), pp. 19–37; Kilpatrick, 'al-Shābushtī,' in *CMR*, vol. 2, pp. 565–69; and T. Sizgorich, 'Monks and Their Daughters: Monasteries as Muslim-Christian Boundaries,' in M. Cormack, ed., *Muslims and Others in Sacred Space* (Oxford, 2013), pp. 193–216. Also see Campbell, 'A Heaven of Wine.' For an Italian paraphrase of parts of al-Shābushtī's *Kitāb al-diyārāt*, see L. Capezzone, *Il libro dei monasteri* (Milan, 1993). For Ibn Abī Dunyā's (d. AH 281/AD 894) extract from an otherwise-lost *Kitāb al-Ruhbān* (*Book of Monks*), the author of which is unknown, see S. al-Munajjed, 'Morceaux choisis du livre des moines,' *Mélanges de l'Institut Dominicain d'Études Orientales du Caire* 3 (1956), pp. 349–58. Abū Faraj al-Iṣbahānī's *Kitāb adab al-ghurabā'* contains three anecdotes recording visits of Muslims to Christian monasteries; on the relationship between this work and the genre of books of monasteries, see Crone and Moreh, *The Book of Strangers*, pp. 150–52.

[182] See Ibn Faḍl Allāh's comments in *Masālik al-abṣār*, vol. 1, p. 298.

munion in it and every Muslim who loves pleasure and amusement heads there to stroll about. It is among Baghdad's celebrated places for excursion and known areas of revelry.[183]

The pleasures available in monasteries made them attractive places for some Muslim visitors. We have already met the poet al-Ḥusayn b. al-Ḍaḥḥāk listening to a monk chant the scriptures through the night at Qullāyat 'Umr in Samarra. It was a place he apparently visited often. Next to the monastery there was a wine merchant named Joshua who had a son who was beardless, possessed of a handsome face—and who was also a deacon. 'Al-Ḥusayn would visit the wine seller,' al-Bakrī noted, 'on account of his son, out of love for him.'[184] 'Abd Allāh b. al-'Abbās b. al-Faḍl b. al-Rabī', a ninth-century poet, wrote about the delight he found in Dayr Qūṭā, a monastery on the banks of the Tigris near Baghdad. According to a poem 'Abd Allāh wrote about the monastery and its enchantments, an unnamed young beauty dwelt there, the likes of which his eyes had never seen, either among Arabs or non-Arabs. This *shādin*, gazelle, was a powerful attraction to the place:

I dwelt in the monastery until it became a home to me
    On his account, and I wore a hair shirt and crosses.
Its deacon became my friend and brother
    And its priest became a parent and father.[185]

Abū 'Alī, a son of Hārūn al-Rashīd, would spend time drinking in Dayr al-Midyān in Baghdad. He had a group of female singers whom he would bring with him, and he would stay for days, not growing tired of song and revelry. Such was Abū 'Alī's behavior that visitors to the monastery complained about him. Al-Shābushtī records a vivid anecdote in which a government official rode out to the monastery at night and demanded that Abū 'Alī be brought out. He emerged drunk and wearing an elaborately colored, perfumed robe. The official ordered that a rug be rolled out over the threshold of the monastery's gate; Abū 'Alī was thrown down on it and beaten twenty times with a whip.[186]

Such stories could be easily multiplied and at times it can be difficult to know what their relationship to reality is. On the first Sunday of Lent at Dayr al-Khuwāt (in 'Ukbarā in Iraq), for example, something called the 'night of *al-māshūsh*' was said to take place. According to al-Shābushtī, this was 'a night

[183] al-Shābushtī, *al-Diyārāt*, p. 14.

[184] See al-Bakrī, *Mu'jam mā ista'jama min asmā' al-bilād wa-'l-mawāḍi'*, vol. 3, p. 1090, and cf. H. Lammens, 'Un poète royal a la cour des omiades de Damas,' *ROC* 9 (1904), p. 38.

[185] al-Shābushtī, *al-Diyārāt*, p. 63.

[186] al-Shābushtī, *al-Diyārāt*, pp. 34–35.

on which women mix with men and no one holds his hand back from anything and no one holds anyone else back from anything.'[187] Other references to the 'night of *al-māshūsh*' can be found in medieval literature, and the story was almost certainly a legendary invention and slander that began circulating probably in the ninth century.[188] Nevertheless, the existence of such a charge points to the associations between monasteries and drinking that had developed by this point in time.

Muslims might also attend Christian weddings. One controversial work written by Theodore Abū Qurrah has as its framing device a question he was asked by a Muslim while attending a Christian wedding in rural Syria.[189] They might also simply attend Christian parties. Everyday life presented its own opportunities for mixing: according to the Ḥanafī Badr al-Rashīd (d. AH 768/AD 1366), a Muslim had become an unbeliever if he passed by a Christian street, saw Christians drinking wine and enjoying stringed instruments and female singers, and said, 'This is a fun social street. A person should tie a piece of rope around his waist [i.e., in imitation of a *zunnār*] and enter in among them and delight in this world!'[190]

What is more, as books of monasteries abundantly attest, Muslims would attend Christian religious festivals, and at least some members of the Muslim religious elite were none-too-happy about Muslims taking part in such events. Al-Maqrīzī (d. AH 845/AD 1442) left a lengthy description of Coptic feasts in Egypt, but he was careful to preface his account with a series of *ḥadīth* which discouraged Muslims from taking part in such activities and from learning the language of non-Muslims.[191] Ibn al-Ḥājj (d. AH 737/AD 1336) was a Mālikī jurist who devoted a section of his book *al-Madkhal* to discussing some of the feasts of the People of the Book.[192] Among the prohibitions he made was that a Muslim could not sell a Christian anything—meat, vegetables, clothing—that

[187] al-Shābushtī, *al-Diyārāt*, p. 93.

[188] See the criticisms against its historicity leveled by Zayyāt in 'al-Diyārāt al-naṣrāniyya fī 'l-Islām,' pp. 297–300 (he referred to it as 'an ugly charge which certain of the adversaries of Christianity unjustly use against the monks of monasteries,' p. 297), and see the discussion of F. de Blois in his '*Laylat al-Māšūš*: Marginalia to al-Bayrūnī, Abū Nuwās and other authors,' *Journal of Semitic Studies* 29 (1984), pp. 81–96; on de Blois and this subject, cf. also, Campbell, 'A Heaven of Wine,' pp. 150–51.

[189] Theodore Abū Qurrah, *Statements against the Outsiders*—This text is unpublished, but see the description of it by J. C. Lamoreaux in *CMR* 1, p. 470.

[190] Badr al-Rashīd, *Alfāẓ al-Kufr*, p. 85

[191] For al-Maqrīzī's account excerpted from the *Khiṭaṭ*, with a FT, see R. Griveau, 'Les Fêtes des coptes,' (PO 10.4), (Paris, 1915), pp. 313–43. Statements discouraging Muslim participation occur at the beginning, on p. 316.

[192] He was not unique in taking up this topic, for Ibn Taymiyya's discussion of Christian feasts and the translation of a section of his *Iqtiḍā'*, see G. Troupeau, 'Les fêtes des chrétiens vues par un juriste musulman,' in *Mélanges offerts à Jean Dauvillier* (Toulouse, 1979), pp. 795–802.

might help him celebrate his feast, nor could he help the Christian's animal, or assist him in any way in his religion, 'for this is something which honors their polytheism and aids their unbelief.'[193] Most interestingly perhaps, Ibn al-Ḥājj began his discussion of these festivals by discussing just which Muslims were taking part in these events: 'There remains to talk about the festivals which most of them are accustomed to,' he wrote.

> and they know that they are festivals which are particular to the People of the Book; and so certain people of this age imitate (*fa-tashabbaha*) them in them and participate with them in venerating them [sc. the festivals]. Would that it were only among the common people! You will see, however, a certain person who claims connection to religious knowledge (*ʿilm*) doing this in his house [i.e., celebrating a festival] and helping them in it and being pleased at it [happening] among them. He will bring choice things to those—great or small—in his house, distributing coins and clothing according to what he thinks; some of them add that they give presents to the People of the Book during their festivals and send to them what they have need of for their feast days and thereby help to increase their unbelief. Some of them send sheep and some of them send green melons and some send dates and other things which are in season. And perhaps most of them agree with that, but this, all of it, contradicts the noble divine law.[194]

Muslim attendance and participation in Christian festivals was not limited, it seems clear, to only the uneducated and religiously uninformed. Writing in the first half of the eleventh century, Yaḥyā b. Saʿīd has left us a description of the celebration of the Feast of the Epiphany in Cairo in which the Christians (especially the Melkites) processed around the city and to the banks of the Nile. Even though the head of the police would go around the city announcing that Muslims should not mix with Christians on this particular night, or hinder their celebration, the ruler of Egypt himself, al-Ḥākim, is supposed to have attended the festival for a number of years, incognito. 'The people of Cairo,' Yaḥyā wrote, 'had delight and joy on this feast day which they did not have on any of the other days or feasts of the year.' In AH 404 (= AD 1009), however, al-Ḥākim would completely forbid the celebration of the feast, proscribing even its mention.[195]

[193] Ibn al-Ḥājj, *al-Madkhal*, vol. 2, p. 49 (Egypt, 1960).

[194] Ibn al-Ḥājj, *al-Madkhal*, vol. 2, p. 48.

[195] Yaḥyā b. Saʿīd, *Kitāb al-dhayl*, p. 286 (ed. Kratchkovsky and Vasiliev [PO 23.3]). Al-Ḥākim was succeeded as Fatimid Caliph by al-Ẓāhir. For al-Ẓāhir and his harem watching the festival of the Epiphany, see Maqrīzī, *Ittiʿāẓ al-ḥunafāʾ bi-akhbār al-aʾimmah al-Fāṭimīyīn al-khulafāʾ*, vol. 2 (ed. M. Ḥilmī Muḥammad Aḥmad) (Cairo, 1996), pp. 162–63.

When thinking about Muslim attendance at the celebrations of Christian feast days and Muslim interest in Christian churches, monasteries and monks, it is important to remember that many of these Muslims, if not most, were descended from Christian converts: al-Ḥākim himself, for all the notorious brutality he showed to the Christians under his rule, likely had a Christian mother.[196] Yāqūt (d. AD 1229/AH 626) reported that he had heard that the monks of the Monastery of Barṣawmā near Melitene would pay the Byzantine Emperor 10,000 dinars every year on behalf of Muslims who had made vows there.[197] It is quite likely that a significant number of these Muslims were simply continuing practices that their Christian forbears had engaged in. When we encounter stories of Muslims visiting monasteries or celebrating Christian festivals, at least part of what we are dealing with is how a society handles religious change: we are looking at a sort of spiritual path dependency. One way of seeing such interest and visits is as another mixed practice—like baptizing one's child—that resulted from conversion. As with so many religious dynamics we have encountered in this book, such spiritual continuities were nothing new: Christian leaders in late antiquity had complained about Christians continuing to engage in pagan practices.[198]

CONVERTS

Certainly one of the most important vectors by which the conquerors and their new religion assimilated late antique ideas and practices was through converts.[199] In the previous chapter, I cited the story of Ḥammād b. Abī Sulaymān rebuking Farqad al-Sabakhī in the eighth century for wearing a woolen garment, something which was redolent of Christian asceticism.

[196] On al-Ḥākim, see M. Canard's article, 'al-Ḥākim bi-Amr Allāh,' in *EI2*, vol. 3, pp. 76–82, especially the comment, p. 78, on al-Ḥākim's Christian mother and the caliph's treatment of Christians; on al-Ḥākim's Christian mother, see also Ferré, 'Ḥākim bi-Amr-Illāh,' in *CoptEn*, vol. 4, p. 1203. P. E. Walker, *Caliph of Cairo: Al-Hakim bi-Amr Allah, 996–1021* (Cairo/New York, 2009), pp. 18–20, provides a detailed discussion of the question of 'al-Hākim's Christian mother. Cf. also Chapter 12, n. 6.

[197] See Yāqūt *Mu'jam al-buldān*, vol. 2, p. 500. For this point, see Mourad, 'Christian Monks in Islamic Literature,' p. 84.

[198] See, e.g., Joshua the Stylite's criticism of Edessenes for taking part in pagan celebrations in the late fifth century in his *Chronicle* 27, 30, 33, 46 (ed. W. Wright, *The Chronicle of Joshua the Stylite Composed in Syriac A.D. 507* [Cambridge, 1882], pp. 21–23, 24–26, 27, 42–43; ET available in F. R. Trombley and J. W. Watt, *The Chronicle of Pseudo-Joshua the Stylite* [Liverpool, 2000], pp. 24–26, 28–29, 32, 47–49, and see the discussion at xv–xvii). On the continuation of paganism in the Syriac-speaking world, cf. also H.J.W. Drijvers, 'The Persistence of Pagan Cults and Practices in Christian Syria,' in Garsoian, Mathews, and Thomson, eds., *East of Byzantium*, pp. 35–44.

[199] By comparison, for Jewish converts to Christianity as a source of Jewish traditions in Syriac literature, see the evidence in Brock, 'Jewish Traditions in Syriac Sources,' p. 230.

Ḥammād told Farqad to 'take off that Christianity' of his. Farqad himself, we learn in another place, 'was a weaver from among the Christians of Armenia,'[200] and one wonders whether Farqad's Christian past had anything to do with the way in which he chose to articulate his own renunciant ways as a Muslim. The case of Farqad also raises an interesting conceptual point for historians. Converts who brought familiar stories, practices, and ideas with them into their new religious context are one reason why it is difficult to find adequate language to speak about pre-Islamic religious elements present in Islam: If Farqad had been a Christian who was interested in asceticism and had worn a wool cloak and continued to do so once he became a Muslim, would it make sense to say that he had 'borrowed' this practice from Christianity?[201]

An *isnād* from al-Ṭabarī's exegesis of Q 17:7 illustrates nicely what I mean. 'Ibn Ḥumayd related to us,' it begins:

> He said: 'Salama related to us on the authority of Ibn Isḥāq, on the authority of Abū 'Attāb—a man from the Taghlib, he had been a Christian for a period of his life, then afterwards, he converted to Islam and then he read the Qur'ān and became versed in religion and he was, according to what was said of him, a Christian for forty years, then he lived in Islam for forty years—he said. . . .[202]

Al-Ṭabarī continued with a story about the last prophet of Israel. What is important for us here is that this 'Attāb had lived much of his life as a Christian Arab and then became a Muslim and from there, eventually ended up teaching in a Muslim context material he had no doubt learned as a Christian. What we have here is essentially the Christian tradition of biblical exegesis and understanding continuing under a different label.

Tamīm b. Aws (d. AH 40/AD 660) was a Christian who converted to Islam in AH 9 (AD 630). Originally from Palestine, he serves as another good example of a convert who is thought to have brought Christian ideas and practices into an Islamic context when he converted. Tamīm's Christian background has been pointed to explain a number of things he has been held responsible for introducing into Islam: It is said that he was the first to light lamps in mosques; that he was involved in the construction of the first *minbar*, built on Christian models; that it was he who told Muḥammad the story of the Beast (*al-jassāsa*) and the Antichrist (*al-dajjāl*); and, moreover, that Muḥammad himself taught

[200] See al-Bukharī, *Kitāb al-ta'rīkh al-kabīr*, vol. 4.1, p. 131 (no. 592) (Hyderabad, n.d).

[201] I am grateful to Lena Salaymeh for this point.

[202] al-Ṭabarī, *Jāmi' al-bayān 'an ta'wīl āyy al-Qur'ān*, vol. 14, p. 502. For this example, see Goldziher, *Schools of Koranic Commentators*, p. 59. On the line of transmission Ibn Ḥumayd – Salamah – Ibn Isḥāq, see F. Rosenthal, *General Introduction, and, From Creation to the Flood* (HṬ 1) (Albany, 1989), pp. 18–19.

these things on Tamīm's authority. Tamīm was also reputed to have been the first person to act as a *qāṣṣ*, or popular storyteller—he sought permission to do so, the story goes, from 'Umar b. al-Khaṭṭāb and was granted it[203]—and it is the *quṣṣāṣ* who have been credited with introducing a large amount of invented exegetical and historical material into the Islamic tradition, material they created for both edifying reasons and also for mere entertainment without regard for historical accuracy.[204]

This brings us back to the issue of Isrā'īliyyāt, which I have spoken of previously. Here is another area where large amounts of Jewish and Christian material were taken up into the Islamic tradition. One need only read the names in the *isnāds* of al-Ṭabarī's massive Qur'ānic commentary to encounter, over and over again, certain figures whose teaching and acts of transmission infused the Islamic tradition with stories from the Jewish and Christian traditions. Scholars have sifted through historical and exegetical works, in addition to biographical dictionaries, and picked out some of the most important individuals responsible for bringing this biblical material into a Muslim context.[205] Some of these names have already come up in the course of this chapter: Tamīm al-Dārī, whom I have just mentioned, and 'Abd Allāh b. 'Amr b. al-'Āṣ, who reportedly knew how to read Syriac. Ibn 'Abbās, perhaps the most important person in Islamic history for Qur'ānic exegesis, was also credited with transmitting much Jewish and Christian material. Such was his erudition that he was called 'the rabbi of the Arabs' (*ḥibr al-'arab*).[206] Ibn 'Abbās and 'Abd Allāh

[203] For all this information about Tamīm, see M. Lecker's article 'Tamīm al-Dārī' in *EI2*, vol. 10, p. 176, and G. Levi Della Vida's article, 'Tamīm al-Dārī,' in *EI1*. His conversion is also reported as having taken place in AH 7 (AD 628). See also Ibn Ḥajar al-'Asqalānī, *al-Iṣāba fī tamyīz al-ṣaḥāba*, vol. 1, pp. 304–305 (no. 833) and Ibn al-Athīr, *Usd al-ghāba fī ma'rifat al-ṣaḥāba*, vol. 1, pp. 428–29 (ed. 'A. Muḥammad Mu'awwad and 'Ā. Aḥmad 'Abd al-Mawjūd [Beirut, 1994]). On *Hikayat Tamim al-Dari*, a Malay folk tale centering on the deeds of Tamīm al-Dārī, see R. Winstedt, *A History of Classical Malay Literature* (New York/London/Melbourne, 1969), pp. 107–11.

[204] See Crone, *Meccan Trade*, pp. 215–30; Goldziher, *Muslim Studies*, pp. 150–59. See also C. Pellat's article, 'Ḳāṣṣ' in *EI2*, vol. 4, pp. 733–35, and Armstrong, *The Quṣṣāṣ of Early Islam*. See also Chapter 10, n. 57.

[205] I am thinking particularly of Na'nā'a, *al-Isrā'īliyyāt wa-atharuhā fī kutub al-tafsīr*, pp. 132–97. Mention might also be made of M. W. 'Allām, *al-Isrā'īliyyāt fī 'l-tafsīr al-Qur'ānī* (Beirut, 2007), pp. 65–74.

[206] al-Ṭabarī, *Ta'rīkh*, 1.1, p. 461 (ed. J. Barth [Leiden, 1879–1881]; ET taken from W. M. Brinner, *The Children of Israel* [HṬ 3] [Albany, 1991], p. 46). *Ḥibr* (or *ḥabr*) might also refer to a religiously learned non-Muslim or even a bishop; see, e.g., A. Biberstein-Kazimirski, *Dictionnaire arabe-français*, vol. 1. (Cairo, 1875), p. 466, s.v.; J. G. Hava, *al-Faraid, Arabic-English Dictionary*, 5th ed. (Beirut, 1982), p. 108, s.v; and cf. Lane, *Arabic-English Lexicon*, p. 498, s.v. See also Chapter 9, n. 83, above, for its use to refer to a Christian religious leader. For *ḥibr/ḥabr* in a ninth-century translation of the letters of Paul as the equivalent of the Syriac *kumrā*, see M. Eskult, 'Translation Technique in the Epistle to the Hebrews as Edited by Edvard Stenij from Codex Tischendorf,' in M.L. Hjälm, ed., *Senses of Scripture, Treasures of Tradition: The Bible in Arabic among Jews, Christians and Muslims* (Leiden/Boston, 2017), p. 432.

b. ʻAmr b. al-ʻĀṣ serve as reminders that not all the prominent transmitters of Jewish and Christian lore were converts from these two religions, or the descendants of converts, but certainly some significant transmitters were.

Mention might also be made of a few more individuals. We have previously met in this chapter Kaʻb al-Aḥbār, a Jewish convert who transmitted large amounts of Jewish material into the Islamic tradition.[207] Alongside him should be set ʻAbd Allāh b. Salām (d. AH 43/AD 663–664), a Jew whose original name was al-Ḥusayn and who converted to Islam when Muḥammad made his flight to Medina, another figure responsible for injecting large amounts of Jewish material into the Islamic tradition.[208] Ibn Jurayj (d. AH 150/AD 767), the son of a Greek slave named ʻJurayjʼ (ʻGeorgiosʼ or ʻGregoriosʼ) and reputed to be the first person to compose books in the Ḥijāz, was another prominent transmitter of Isrāʼīliyyāt with a direct Jewish or Christian connection.[209] Wahb b. Munabbih (d. AH 110/AD 728 or AH 114/AD 732) was not a Jewish convert, but was nevertheless an important vector through which biblical traditions from Kaʻb and ʻAbd Allāh were passed down.[210] ʻI have read ninety-two books,ʼ Wahb is supposed to have said, ʻall of them sent down from heaven. Seventy-two of them are in churches and in the possession of people and twenty only a few know of.ʼ[211] ʻI have read thirty books,ʼ Wahb is also reported to have said, ʻwhich were sent down to thirty prophets.ʼ[212] Wahb would also be associated with non-biblical traditions that found their way into Muslim texts: a story originally found in chapter 60 of John Moschus's *Spiritual Meadow* can even be found in the Islamic tradition, attributed to Wahb.[213]

[207] On Kaʻb's importance for introducing Jewish traditions into the bloodstream of Islam, see also R. Tottoli, *Biblical Prophets in the Qurʼān and Muslim Literature* (London/New York, 2002), pp. 89–92.

[208] See ʻAllām, *al-Isrāʼīliyyāt fī ʼl-tafsīr al-Qurʼānī*, pp. 71–73, and Naʻnāʻa, *al-Isrāʼīliyyāt wa-atharuhā fī kutub al-tafsīr*, pp. 159–60. On ʻAbd Allāh, see Ibn al-Athīr, *Usd al-ghāba*, vol. 3, pp. 265–66, and J. Horovitz's article "ʻAbd Allāh b. Salām' in *EI2*, vol. 1, p. 52. For ʻAbd Allāh called a *ḥibr*, see al-Dhahabī, *Kitāb tadhkirat al-ḥuffāẓ*, vol. 1, p. 26.

[209] On Ibn Jurayj, see al-Mizzī, *Tahdhīb al-kamāl fī asmāʼ al-rijāl*, vol. 18, pp. 338–54; for his father Jurayj as a slave and his Rūmī origin, p. 339; as *awwal man ṣannafa al-kutub*—along with Ibn Abī ʻArūba—p. 341. Also on Ibn Jurayj, see C. Pellat's article ʻIbn Djuraydj,ʼ in *EI2, Supplement*, p. 386. For all this and for Ibn Jurayj as prominent transmitter of Isrāʼīliyyāt, see Naʻnāʻa, *al-Isrāʼīliyyāt wa-atharuhā fī kutub al-tafsīr*, pp. 193–95, and cf. also, Brockelmann, *GAL*, vol. S1, p. 255.

[210] Though note that Ibn al-Nadīm, *Fihrist*, vol. 1, p. 22, lists Wahb as among those of the People of the Book who converted to Islam. More generally on Wahb, see R. G. Khoury's article, ʻWahb b. Munabbih,ʼ in *EI2*, vol. 11, pp. 34–36, and Naʻnāʻa, *al-Isrāʼīliyyāt wa-atharuhā fī kutub al-tafsīr*, pp. 183–92. On Ibn al-Nadīm's report that Wahb had been a member of the People of the Book before converting, see J. Horovitz's comments in ʻThe Earliest Biographies of the Prophet and Their Authors,ʼ *Islamic Culture* 1 (1927), p. 553–54.

[211] Ibn Saʻd, *Kitāb al-ṭabaqāt al-kabīr*, vol. 5, p. 395 (ed. Zetterstéen).

[212] Ibn Saʻd, *Kitāb al-ṭabaqāt al-kabīr*, vol. 5, p. 396 (ed. Zetterstéen). See Horovitz, ʻThe Earliest Biographies of the Prophet,ʼ p. 555, on the doubtful authenticity of these statements.

[213] See Levi della Vida, ʻLeggende agriografiche cristiane nell'Islam,ʼ p. 148 and cf. Chialà, ʻLes mys-

We have the names of other converts who introduced ideas and practices into the Islamic tradition as well. The Qadarite controversy—the dispute over human freedom and divine predestination—was one of the earliest theological issues to arise in Islam. And the first person to speak about *qadar* was supposed to have been a Christian from Iraq named SWSR, or Sawsan, who converted to Islam and then reconverted to Christianity. Maʿbad al-Juhanī, a famous early Qadarite, is said to have learned from Sawsan, and Ghaylān al-Dimashqī, another famous Qadarite, is said to have learned from Maʿbad. Ghaylān himself was a Coptic convert to Islam.[214] Scholars have noted similarities between arguments adduced in favor of free-will by Qadarites and Christian theologians; they have also noted apparent Syriac calques in Qadarī vocabulary and other indications of Christian elements in Qadarism and Islamic theology more broadly.[215] People we have names for, however, are the exception: there will have been countless unnamed converts who acted as important vectors of information: 'A certain one of the Rūm,' Masʿūdī began one anecdote, 'who had converted to Islam and he was sincere in his religion (*ḥasuna Islāmuhu*), told me that the Rūm had depicted ten individuals in one of their churches. . . .'[216]

CAPTIVES

We cannot speak about converts without also talking about captives. The early medieval period saw a constant flow of population into and out of Muslim-controlled areas in the form of prisoners of war. From early on, Muslim armies and governments had a reputation among Christians for trafficking in captives. 'Let us not fast like the God-killing Jews,' the Coptic *Panegyric of the Three*

tiques musulmans lecteurs des écrits chrétiens,' p. 360. Note, however, that Levi della Vida thought it difficult to attribute the story as it currently stands in Arabic to Wahb.

[214] For this report, see Ibn ʿAsākir, *Taʾrīkh madīnat Dimashq*, vol. 48, p. 192. See also C. Pellat's article 'Ghaylān b. Muslim,' in *EI2*, vol. 2, p. 1026, and J. van Ess's article 'Maʿbad al-Djuhanī,' in *EI2*, vol. 5, pp. 935–36. For Ghaylān and Maʿbad, see R. Caspar, *A Historical Introduction to Islamic Theology: Muḥammad and the Classical Period*, trans. P. Johnstone (Rome, 1998), p. 158, n. 32. For Maʿbad as the first person to speak about *qadar* and then Ghaylān after him, see Ibn Qutayba, *al-Maʿārif*, p. 484 (ed. Th. ʿUkāsha [Cairo, 1960]). For a discussion of other accounts from the Islamic tradition concerning the question of the origins of Qadarism and a questioning of the connection between Ghaylān's Christian background and his alleged heresy, see van Ess, *Theologie und Gesellschaft*, vol. 1, pp. 72–74 [= *Theology and Society*, vol. 1, pp. 82–84].

[215] See J. van Ess's article, 'Ḳadariyya' in *EI2*, vol. 4, pp. 368–72; see also Cook, *Early Muslim Dogma*, pp. 146–52, and A. S. Tritton, 'Foreign Influences on Muslim Theology,' *BSOAS* 10 (1942), pp. 837–42. Caspar, *A Historical Introduction to Islamic Theology*, pp. 158–61, lists Christian elements in Islamic theology, but seeks to de-emphasize any Christian 'influence' on the earliest theological debates in Islam.

[216] Al-Masʿūdī, *Murūj al-dhahab wa-maʿādin al-jawhar*, vol. 8, p. 74. An ET is also available in P. Lunde and C. Stone, *The Meadows of Gold* (London/New York, 1989), p. 319.

Holy Children of Babylon urged, perhaps in the 640s, 'nor fast like the Saracens who are oppressors, who give themselves up to prostitution, massacre and lead into captivity the sons of men saying, "We both fast and pray."'[217] Decades later, at the end of the seventh century, the *Apocalypse of John the Little* would speak of Ishmael—that is, the kingdom of the Arabs: 'He will take a great captivity among all the nations of the earth and they will plunder greatly. And all quarters of the earth will toil [in] servitude.'[218] Around the same time, among the unflattering characterizations of the ruling Muslims that John bar Penkaye would use was that they were a people 'whose wish it is to take captives and deport.' Taking foreign captives and slaves was a yearly ritual:

> Their robber bands went annually to distant parts and to the islands, bringing back captives from all the peoples under the heavens. Of each person they required a tribute, allowing him to remain in whatever faith he wished.[219]

Reading through the early medieval portions of various chronicles bears out John's observation—we encounter, over and over again, references to raids and to captives being taken.[220] There is evidence, in fact, for Muslim raids into Byzantine territory literally every year, just as John claimed.[221]

The movement of population must have been constant. This was not always due to wars and military raiding, either: in 686–687, Syria witnessed a famine with the result that 'many men migrated to the Roman country.'[222] In 690–691, Justinian tried to move the inhabitants of Cyprus to Byzantine territory, but many of them drowned in transit; those who did not drown went back to Cyprus.[223] Around 721–722, Leo III's persecution of Jews and Montanists in

[217] *Panegyric of the Three Holy Children of Babylon*, p. 100 (ed. and trans. H. de Vis, *Homélies Coptes de la Vaticane*, vol. 2 [Louvain, 1990]; ET taken from Hoyland, *Seeing Islam*, p. 121). On this text, also see H. Suermann, 'Copts and the Islam of the Seventh Century,' in Grypeou et al., eds., *The Encounter of Eastern Christianity with Early Islam*, pp. 107–108, and see Suermann, 'The Panegyric of the Three Holy Children of Babylon,' in *CMR*, vol. 1, pp. 128–29.

[218] *Apocalypse of John the Little*, p. *18 (ed. Harris; ET at p. 37 but this is my translation). On this text, see most conveniently, L. Greisiger's article, 'The Gospel of the Twelve Apostles,' in *CMR*, vol. 1, pp. 222–25.

[219] John bar Penkaye, *Book of the Main Events*, pp. *145, *147 (ed. Mingana; translation taken from Brock, 'North Mesopotamia in the Late Seventh Century,' pp. 60 [first quote], p. 61 [second quote]).

[220] See the evidence gathered in *SBI*, pp. 556–59.

[221] See the material collected in E. W. Brooks, 'The Arabs in Asia Minor (641–750), from Arabic Sources,' *Journal of Hellenic Studies* 18 (1898), pp. 182–208. Crone, *Nativist Prophets*, p. 7, adduces further evidence of the enormous number of captives taken in the decades after the Arab conquest of the Middle East.

[222] Theophanes, *Chronicle* AM 6179 (ed. de Boor, vol. 1, p. 364; ET taken from Mango and Scott, *The Chronicle of Theophanes Confessor*, p. 507).

[223] Theophanes, *Chronicle* AM 6183 (ed. de Boor, vol. 1, p. 365; English available in Mango and Scott, *The Chronicle of Theophanes Confessor*, p. 509). On the transfer of people into and out of the Byzantine Empire in the early medieval period, see C. Mango, *Byzantium: The Empire of New Rome* (New York,

Byzantine territory and his attempts to force them to receive baptism resulted in many of them fleeing to the caliphate.[224] Around 742–743, al-Walīd II forced the people of Cyprus to choose between moving either to Syria or to Byzantine territory. Part of the population, al-Ṭabarī reported, chose to live with Muslims and part chose to go to the land of the Romans.[225]

Such movements of people were not lacking in social ramifications: this was a society in which the issue of captives was of concern to many people, across religious lines. Redeeming captives was seen by many Muslims as a shared religious duty.[226] 'The ransom of Muslim captives [should come] from the treasury (*bayt al-māl*),' 'Umar b. al-Khaṭṭāb is supposed to have said.[227] Mālik and 'Umar II, among others, held that if possible, Muslim captives should be ransomed.[228] 'Umar II wrote a letter to Muslim captives in Constantinople sending them money and someone to ransom them[229] and was portrayed as showing great concern for the plight of even individual Muslim captives in the Byzantine capital.[230] He was said once to have ransomed a man, woman, slave, and *dhimmī* from Aden.[231] When thinking about captives, we should not forget, either, the communities and individuals left behind in the wake of raiding and warfare.[232]

The question of captives might even arise in interreligious polemic: in the *Trophies of Damascus*, a Christian-Jewish dispute text likely written in the

---

1980), pp. 25–26, and cf. also P. Charanis, 'The Transfer of Population as a Policy in the Byzantine Empire,' *Comparative Studies in Society and History* 3 (1961), pp. 140–54.

[224] See Michael the Great, *Chronicle* 11.19 (ed. Chabot, 4.457 = 2.489–490), and Theophanes, *Chronicle* AM 6214 (ed. de Boor, vol. 1, p. 401; English available in Mango and Scott, *The Chronicle of Theophanes Confessor*, pp. 554–55; cf. chapter 11, n. 3).

[225] al-Ṭabarī, *Ta'rīkh*, 2.3, p. 1769 (ed. I. Guidi, D. H. Müller, and M. J. de Goeje [Leiden, 1885–1889]); Theophanes, *Chronicle* AM 6234 (ed. de Boor, vol. 1, p. 417; English available in Mango and Scott, *The Chronicle of Theophanes Confessor*, pp. 554–55). Cf. Caetani, *Chronographia Islamica*, vol. 5, p. 1575, no. 16.

[226] Cf. E. Gräf, 'Religiöse und Rechtliche Vorstellungen über Kriegsgefangene in Islam und Christentum,' *Die Welt des Islams* 8 (1963), p. 111, and Ibn Qudāma, *al-Mughnī*, vol. 13, pp. 135–36. See also Ibn Baṭṭāl, *Sharḥ Ṣaḥīḥ al-Bukhārī*, vol. 5, p. 210 (ed. Abū Tamīm Yāsir b. Ibrāhīm [Riyad, 2000]).

[227] Ibn Baṭṭāl, *Sharh Ṣaḥīḥ al-Bukhārī*, vol. 5 p. 210.

[228] Gräf, 'Religiöse und rechtliche Vorstellungen über Kriegsgefangene in Islam und Christentum,' p. 111, and Ibn Qudāma, *al-Mughnī*, vol. 13, p. 135.

[229] Ibn 'Abd al-Ḥakam, *Sīrat 'Umar b. 'Abd al-'Azīz*, pp. 163–64 (ed. 'Ubayd).

[230] See n. 279 in this chapter.

[231] Ibn Sa'd, *Kitāb al-ṭabaqāt al-kabīr*, vol. 5, p. 260 (ed. Zetterstéen). For another example of 'Umar's concern for captives, see Jeffery, 'Ghevond's Text of the Correspondence between 'Umar II and Leo III,' p. 271.

[232] See, e.g., the report that John of Mardē (d. AD 1165) 'fixed, restored and bound many volumes of books (left) by captives. They were mutilated a long time ago,' raises our awareness to the phenomenon of saving and salvaging the things that remained in the wake of a military raid by an opposing state's forces. See *Concerning John of Mardē*, p. 208 (ed. Vööbus, *The Synodicon in the West Syrian Tradition II* [CSCO 375–76: SS 163–64], p. 208 [Syriac] = p. 219 [I have used Vööbus's translation with a slight alteration]).

second half of the seventh century, the Christian at one point compared the successes and spread of Christianity to the Jews' comparative misfortunes and their lack of control over holy places like Jerusalem and Mt. Sinai, and offered the contrast as proof that Christians were increasing and Jews were decreasing. But, 'if these things are the case, as you say,' the Jew responded to the Christian, 'Where have all the captives that are coming to you come from? Whose are the regions that have been made desolate?'[233]

With their armies on the march and their territory expanding, Muslim-ruled lands in the seventh century must have been awash in prisoners of war: The Miaphysite patriarch of Alexandria Agathon (sed. AD 661–677) ransomed and set free many Christian captives that Arabs had brought to Egypt from Sicily, because he 'was sad at heart when he saw his fellow-Christians in the hands of the Gentiles.'[234] The fact that the captives in question would have belonged to a church with which Agathon was not in communion apparently did not affect his decision to buy and emancipate them.

Concern for captives was not only an issue for elites. In his *Life* of Marutha (d. AD 649), Denḥā gave a lengthy description of the virtues of the people of Tikrit, a list which included honoring their parents, helping to meet the needs of solitaries and monks, building churches and monasteries, giving alms to the poor—and 'delivering captives and prisoners.'[235] In the seventh century, freeing captives was a good deed. Theodota of Amid's *Life*, written in the early eighth century, picked out his compassion for captives and efforts to ransom them as one of the many signs of his holiness. 'He would speak to each person in accordance with their stature,' we are told,

> and was pained over those taken into captivity. He would stand in the pulpit of the church and speak on account of them. He would speak in the following way: 'My brothers, today, Our Lord asks of you through my hands. Give me, each one of you, ten *fals*; I have confidence in the Lord that He will reward you with His blessings instead of me.' And Our Lord was giving zeal to their hearts and they were fulfilling His commandment, Christians along with Muslims. He was saving captives and sending them away. And they would go, blessing and rejoicing and praying for Amid and for Theodota her Bishop.[236]

[233] *Trophies of Damascus* 2.3.1 (ed. Bardy, *Les trophées de Damas: controverse judéo-chrétienne du VIIe siècle* [PO 15.2], p. 50). On the date of the *Trophies*, see Hoyland, *Seeing Islam*, pp. 85–86.

[234] *History of the Patriarchs of Alexandria* 1.15 (ed. Evetts [PO 5.1], p. 258; the translation is that of Evetts).

[235] Denḥā, *Life of Marutha*, pp. 81–83, captives and prisoners mentioned p. 83 (ed. Nau [PO 3.1])

[236] For the Syriac text, see Mardin 275/8, pp. 554–55 (Syriac text also in *SBI*, p. 559, n. 1377). For the Karshūnī, see St Mark's Jerusalem 199, fol. 557b.

At roughly the same time, we find Jacob of Edessa disapproving of the practice of melting down ecclesiastical plate to create money that could be used to ransom captives.[237]

Such grassroots efforts at ransoming points to a simple fact: captives were to be found everywhere and came from all segments of society: in AD 739–740, the caliph Hishām 'put to death the Christian prisoners in all the towns of his realm.'[238] When the Mardaites revolted in 676–677, their mountain strongholds across the western Levant became a magnet for people in search of sanctuary: 'Many slaves, captives and natives took refuge with them,' Theophanes tells us, 'so that in a short time they grew to many thousands.'[239] In 653–654, two Christian brothers in Tripoli in Lebanon 'rushed to the city prison, where there was a multitude of Roman captives.' They broke into the prison, freed the captives, and together killed the Muslim ruler of the city.[240]

The presence of captives in society raised questions that religious leaders had to confront.[241] Since we see certain female captives transgressing, a question directed at Anastasius of Sinai asked, what should we say about them? Those who transgress from pleasure and wantonness, he replied, fall under a greater judgment than those who sin out of difficulty and necessity, just as the one who steals food from hunger commits a smaller sin than the one who does not need and still steals. Women who are beautifully adorned have a different allowance than those women in their midst who are wearing

[237] *Questions of All Kind, Which John the Stylite Asked the Venerable Jacob, the Teacher* 27 (ed. Vööbus [CSCO 367–68: SS 161–62], p. 245 [= p. 225 (ET)]). Contrast this with *Codex Justinianus* 1.2.21.2 (ed. Krueger, *Corpus Iuris Civilis*, vol. 2: *Codex Iustinianus*, p. 16), which allowed for the sale of church vessels in order to ransom captives. For more on the issue of selling church plate for this purpose, see Chadwick, *The Role of the Christian Bishop*, p. 9.

[238] Theophanes, *Chronicle* AM 6232 (ed. de Boor, vol. 1, p. 413; ET taken from Mango and Scott, *The Chronicle of Theophanes Confessor*, p. 573). Michael the Great placed this event in AD 731 (AG 1042) and suggested that Hishām was engaged in a mistaken act of tit-for-tat—he had falsely believed that the Byzantine Emperor Leo had had all of his Arab captives executed: See Michael the Great, *Chronicle* 11.21 (ed. Chabot, 4.463 [date on 462] = 2.501). 'Umar II was said to disapprove of killing captives—they would either be enslaved or freed (Ibn Sa'd, *Kitāb al-ṭabaqāt al-kabīr*, vol. 5, p. 231 [ed. Zetterstéen]; but compare this to Ibn Qudāma, *al-Mughnī*, vol. 13, p. 45, where 'Umar is named as a person who killed captives). When Leo IV and al-Mahdī both came to power within a month of one another, they both freed prisoners; Leo freed his Muslim prisoners and al-Mahdī freed his Christian prisoners. See Bar Hebraeus, *Chronicle*, p. 126 (ed. P. Bedjan, *Gregorii Barhebraei: Chronicon Syriacum* [Paris, 1890]), and cf. *Chronicle to 813*, p. 248 (ed. E. W. Brooks, *Chronica Minora* III [CSCO 3.4] [Paris, 1905]) and Michael the Great, *Chronicle* 12.1 (ed. Chabot, 4.478 = 3.1).

[239] Theophanes, *Chronicle* AM 6169 (ed. de Boor, vol. 1, p. 355; ET taken from Mango and Scott, *The Chronicle of Theophanes Confessor*, p. 496).

[240] Theophanes, *Chronicle* AM 6146 (ed. de Boor, vol. 1, p. 345; ET taken from Mango and Scott, *The Chronicle of Theophanes Confessor*, p. 482).

[241] See, e.g., 'Abd al-Razzāq, *al-Amālī fī āthār al-Ṣaḥāba*, pp. 66–67 (ed. M. al-Sayyid Ibrāhīm [Cairo, n.d.]): 'The Muslim should not be shackled with a slave or a *dhimmī*' (attributed to 'Ikrima).

chains.[242] Muslims also worried about what captives from their own ranks might do when in non-Muslim lands: In the eighth century, the Syrian jurist al-Awzāʿī would be asked about what should be done to a Muslim captive who had been ransomed and who had fornicated, or drunk wine, or committed murder, or been accused of something, or injured another Muslim while in captivity.[243]

I am interested in 'information flows'[244] here, however, and movements of people unsurprisingly had effects in this area as well. If we look, we can find examples of information being disseminated by these people, but given the numbers of captives who were moving and the constancy of their movement, we should assume that such traces as we have are only the faint outlines of what must have been a much larger phenomenon. When people moved, they took their ideas, customs, habits, and culture with them, and they contributed these things to the communities and networks they were now entering.[245]

This was a well-established pattern by the time the Arabs conquered the Middle East. Over the course of late antiquity, the Sasanians engaged in a number of mass and even spectacular deportations of populations from Roman territory.[246] Jundishapur/Beth Lapaṭ, a place that would later become renowned for producing famous Christian doctors in the Abbasid period, had been populated by Shapur I with Christian captives taken from Antioch in 256. Shapur settled the captives in several other cities as well and gave them lands. 'For this reason,' the *Chronicle of Seert* noted, 'Christians increased in the land of the Persians and monasteries and churches were built. There were among them priests who had been taken captive in Antioch. They settled in Jundishapur

[242] Anastasius of Sinai, *Questions and Answers* 76 (ed. Richard and Munitiz, *Anastasii Sinaitae: Quaestiones et Responsiones*, pp. 127–28).

[243] See al-Ṭabarī, *Ikhtilāf al-fuqahā'*, pp. 60–61 (ed. J. Schacht, *Das Konstantinopler Fragment des Kitāb iḫtilāf al-fuqahā' des Abū Ǧaʿfar Muḥammad ibn Ǧarīr aṭ-Ṭabarī* [Leiden, 1933]), and cf. Gräf, 'Religiöse und rechtliche Vorstellungen über Kriegsgefangene in Islam und Christentum,' p. 116.

[244] I owe this language to John-Paul Ghobrial. See his *The Whispers of Cities: Information Flows in Istanbul, London, and Paris in the Age of William Trumbull* (Oxford, 2013).

[245] On the importance of captives and slaves for the spread of information, see N. Lenski, 'Captivity, Slavery, and Cultural Exchange between Rome and the Germans from the First to Seventh Century CE,' in C. M. Cameron, ed., *Invisible Citizens: Captives and Their Consequences* (Salt Lake City, 2008), pp. 80–109.

[246] See the masterful survey of Sasanian deportations by E. Kettenhofen in his article, 'Deportations: ii. In the Parthian and Sasanian Periods,' in *Encyclopaedia Iranica*, vol. 7, pp. 297-308, as well as M. G. Morony, 'Population Transfers between Sasanian Iran and the Byzantine Empire,' in *Convegno internazionale La Persia e Bisanzio: Roma, 14-18 ottobre 2002* (Rome, 2004), pp. 161–79. More recently, see K. Smith, *Constantine and the Captive Christians of Persia* (Oakland, 2016), pp. 125–53, for discussion of the importance of captivity and deportations for the spread of Christianity and for Christian identity in the Sasanian world.

and they chose Azdoq and made him bishop over them.'[247] The presence of captives from Roman lands in Sasanian territory meant that Greek was more widely known: at one place in Fars, the Christians built two churches, one of which was known as 'the Church of the Romans.' 'They would pray in it in Greek and Syriac,' the *Chronicle of Seert*, noted, 'and God made up to the Romans for the captivity and servitude that had overtaken them inasmuch as they were in a good condition in it.'[248]

This was not an isolated incident. Captives were one of the ways that Christianity spread in the later Roman world. The people of Iberia, Jacob of Edessa's *Chronology* informs us, were 'attracted to Christianity by means of a certain Christian woman, who had gone to that country as a captive.'[249] Ps.-Zacharias Rhetor reported that the arrival of prisoners of war taken from Roman territory by the Huns had been a key moment in the eventual translation of the Christian Scriptures into Hunnic. Ps.-Zacharias related the story on the authority of John of Resh'ayna and a tanner named Thomas, both of whom had themselves been taken captive by the Sasanian king Kawad and then sold to the Huns. 'They spent more than thirty years in their country, marrying and begetting children there,' he noted.[250]

Captives and slaves would continue spreading information into the time of the Prophet.[251] Muḥammad was known to sit and talk to a young Christian slave named Jabr, Ibn Hishām reported, 'and they used to say "The one who teaches Muhammad most of what he brings is Jabr the Christian, slave of the B. al-Ḥaḍramī."'[252] Jabr and Yasār, another of the various 'informants' of

[247] *Chronicle of Seert* 1.2 (ed. A. Scher and J. Périer [PO 4.3] [Paris, 1908], p. 11). Cf. Also S. P. Brock's article, 'Beth Lapaṭ,' in *GEDSH*, p. 72.

[248] *Chronicle of Seert* 1.2 (ed. Scher and Périer [PO 4.3], p. 12). For Greeks in the Sasanian empire and more on the cultural consequences of the Sasanian deportations, see C. Jullien, 'La minorité chrétienne "grecque" en terre d'Iran à l'époque sassanide,' in R. Gyselen, ed., *Chrétiens en terre d'Iran: Implantation et acculturation* (Paris, 2006), pp. 105–42. See Smith, *Constantine and the Christian Captives of Persia*, p. 131, for cautions on the use of the *Chronicle of Seert* for reconstructing some aspects of the deportations, and Morony, 'Population transfers,' pp. 165–67, on problems of anachronism in this passage specifically.

[249] Jacob of Edessa, *Chronicle*, p. 289 (ed. E.W. Brooks, *Chronica Minora, pars tertia* [CSCO III.4] [Paris, 1905; ET taken from E. W. Brooks, 'The Chronological Canon of James of Edessa,' *ZDMG* 53 [1899], pp. 309–310).

[250] Ps.-Zacharias Rhetor, *Chronicle* 12.7 (ed. Brooks [CSCO 84: SS 39], pp. 215–16; ET taken from Brock, *A Brief Outline of Syriac Literature*, p. 212).

[251] On slave taking and slave raiding among Arabic-speaking groups before the rise of Islam, with a view toward the continuation of these practices by early Muslims, see N. Lenski, 'Captivity and Slavery among the Saracens in Late Antiquity (ca. 250–630 CE),' *Antiquité tardive* 19 (2011), pp. 237–66.

[252] Ibn Hishām, *Kitāb sīrat rasūl Allāh*, p. 260 (ed. Wüstenfeld, vol. 1.1; ET taken from Guillaume, *The Life of Muhammad*, p. 180). Note that Jabr likely comes from the Aramaic *gabrā*, meaning simply 'man.' This was first pointed out to me by Aron Zysow, but cf. also the observation in A. Jeffery, 'Had Muḥammad a Scripture Teacher?' in L. G. Leary, ed., *From the Pyramids to Paul: Studies in Theology,*

Muḥammad identified by the Islamic tradition, were thought in at least some quarters to have been captured by the Byzantines and turned into slaves.[253] Such stories may have their origin in the fact that the Qur'ān itself alludes to a foreigner who was friends with Muḥammad and was alleged to have fed him the contents of his revelation: 'We know very well that they say, "Only a mortal is teaching him,"' the Qur'ān acknowledges, but '[t]he speech of him whom they hint is foreign (*a'jamī*) and this is clear Arabic speech.'[254] Slaves continued to be conduits of information, too: originally a slave from Yemen, perhaps with Indian forbears, Abū Ma'shar (d. AH 170/AD 787) eventually attained his freedom and would pass from Medina to Baghdad. Al-Ṭabarī would eventually draw upon his work for material—including biblical stories—included in his celebrated *Ta'rīkh*.[255]

Learning from foreign captives was a common experience. 'This we heard from men who had been taken as captives to Khuzhastan, [from] Tachkastan,' the Armenian historian Sebeos (or perhaps his source) writes at one point, '[h]aving been themselves eyewitnesses of these events, they gave this account to us.'[256] Captives and refugees were vectors by which theological opin-

---

Archaeology and Related Subjects, Prepared in Honor of the Seventieth Birthday of George Livingstone Robinson (New York, 1935), p. 99. For Jabr as a Jew and not a Christian, see T. Nöldeke, 'Hatte Muḥammad christliche Lehrer?' *ZDMG* 12 (1858), p. 703, and see p. 704 for Nöldeke's observation about all of the suggested teachers of Muḥammad, save Waraqa b. Nawfal, being either slaves, freedmen, or workmen.

[253] For this, see C. Gilliot, 'Les «informateurs» juifs et chrétiens de Muḥammad,' p. 110, and Gilliot's article more generally on the question of the 'informants' of Muḥammad. Various exegetes reported that Jabr and Yasār were said to be two slaves in Mecca who made swords and who would read the Gospel; when the Prophet would pass by them, he might stop and listen, which led to this charge. See, e.g., al-Zamakhsharī, *al-Kashshāf*, vol. 4, p. 474 (ed. 'A. Aḥmad 'Abd al-Mawjūd and 'A. Muḥammad Mu'awwaḍ [Riyadh, 1998]) and al-Suyūṭī, *al-Durr al-manthūr fī 'l-tafsīr bi-'l-ma'thūr*, vol. 9, p. 116 (ed. 'A. Allāh b. 'Abd al-Muḥsin al-Turkī [Cairo, 2003]). Qur'ānic commentaries will contain information about the various individuals referred to in 16:103. For example, al-Ṭabarī, *Jāmi' al-bayān 'an ta'wīl āy al-Qur'ān*, vol. 14, pp. 365–69, discusses the various individuals who were thought to be candidates for the unnamed person referred to in 16:103, among whom were a certain Bal'ām, Ya'īshu, Salmān al-Fārisī, and one of Muḥammad's scribes.

Of course, both Jabr and Yasār, like some of the other suggested informants who, apart from Salmān al-Fārisī, are otherwise little known, could have been fabrications invented to interpret Q 16:103. But even if Jabr or Yasār never existed, the fact that it might be suggested that they had been captives suggests something about associations which must have existed, at least in some portions of the Middle Ages, about the information-carrying functions captives might have. On the question of Muḥammad's unnamed 'teacher,' see also the previous note and cf. chapter 9, n. 84.

[254] Q 16:103 (and cf. 6:104-105, 25:4-5, 44:13-14). Translation Arberry, with slight alteration. al-Ṭabarī understood the person being referred to here by the Qur'ān to be a Byzantine slave (*'abd rūmī*). See, al-Ṭabarī, *Jāmi' al-bayān 'an ta'wīl āyy al-qur'ān*, vol. 14, p. 364. More generally, see the previous two notes.

[255] See J. Horovitz and F. Rosenthal's article, 'Abū Ma'shar,' in *EI2*, vol. 1, p. 140.

[256] Translated by R. W. Thomson in *The Armenian History attributed to Sebeos*, vol. 1, p. 102. At 102,

ions might move about also. In the 630s, refugee Miaphysite monks in North Africa, fleeing the Arab conquests, stirred up the ire of church leaders by spreading their heretical views.[257] If we are to believe Michael the Great, the Monothelete understanding of the number of Christ's wills was the dominant one in Syria until an influx of captives from the Byzantine Empire changed things:

> Now, while this doctrine [sc. Dyotheletism] had held sway in the regions of the Romans from the time of Constantine [IV], in the regions of Syria it was not accepted at all. At this time, however, it was planted by means of the captives and exiles who came and settled in Syria because of Arab raids. Increasingly, city dwellers and their bishops and their leaders were corrupted and accepted this doctrine on account of esteem for the Roman Empire.[258]

Famously, Theophanes laid part of the blame for the iconoclast activities of Leo III at the feet of a figure named Beser—that is, Bishr—'a former Christian who had been taken captive in Syria, who had abjured the Christian faith and become imbued with Arab doctrines and who, not long before, had been freed from their servitude and returned to the Roman state.'[259] Constantine V's deportation of Miaphysite Christians from Muslim-ruled Claudia to Constantinople led to theological discussions between Miaphysites and Chalcedonians

n. 634, Thomson suggests that these lines come from Sebeos's source. J.-H. Johnson and T. Greenwood, *The Armenian History Attributed to Sebeos*. Part II: *Historical Commentary* (Liverpool, 1999), vol. 2, pp. 248–49, suggest the same. For this, see Hoyland, *Seeing Islam*, pp. 125, 593.

[257] See V. Grumel, *Les regestes des actes du patriarcat de Constantinople*, vol. 1, fasc. 1, 2nd ed. (Paris, 1972), p. 220 (no. 291a). Cf. p. 215, no. 280b: around 620, Sergius I donated a monastery in Constantinople to nuns who had fled to the capital from the convent of the Ascension in Melitene after the Persians conquered it. Paul of Edessa engaged in important translation activity while on Cyprus in the early 620s, also in flight from the Persians (see chapter 6, n. 66 and n. 72). The capture of monks from Qenneshre and the killing of twenty of them during a Slavic attack on Crete and other islands, reported in the *Chronicle to 724* as having happened in AG 934 (= AD 623), may have also been the ultimate result of flight and emigration due to the Roman-Persian war that was going on at the time. See *Chronicle to 724*, p. 147 (ed. Brooks, *Chronica Minora* II [CSCO SS III.4]; ET available in Palmer, *The Seventh Century in the West-Syrian Chronicles*, p. 18; cf. Chapter 6, n. 71). Cp. With Dayr al-Rūm in Baghdad, which was given its name on account of Byzantine captives who had been settled by al-Mahdī in eastern Baghdad. The monastery, though Nestorian, took its name from the area, which had been called after the captives: Yāqūt, *Muʿjam al-buldān*, vol. 2, p. 511. Similarly, Dayr Samālū in Baghdad was built by residents of Ṣamālū, located near Tartus on the Syrian frontier, who had come to Baghdad in AH 163 (AD 780) after Hārūn al-Rashīd attacked Ṣamālū and granted some of its residents protection. See Yāqūt, vol. 2, p. 516 (on Dayr Samālū), and vol. 3, p. 423 (on Ṣamālū—for unexplained reasons, the residents changed the spelling of the monastery so that it differed from the spelling of their hometown).

[258] Michael the Great, *Chronicle*, 4.457–58 (Syriac) = 2.492 (FT).

[259] Theophanes, *Chronicle* AM 6215 (ed. de Boor, vol. 1, p. 402; ET taken from Mango and Scott, *The Chronicle of Theophanes Confessor*, p. 555; on Beser's name, see 556, n. 2)

and a captive-mediated attempt to achieve a union between the imperial church and the Miaphysites of Syria.[260]

But it was not just theological views that captives spread—they were disseminators of information more broadly conceived. In the Arabic *Life* of John Damascene, John was educated by Cosmas, a Calabrian 'philosopher monk' who was brought to Damascus with a group of captives taken in a raid at sea.[261] Hārūn al-Rashīd had a Byzantine slave girl who taught a young slave boy Greek literature, how to read Greek books, and how to speak Greek;[262] al-Rashīd put Yūḥannā b. Māsawayh in charge of translating ancient books found in Ankara, Amorium, and other Byzantine cities when Muslims took captives from them.[263] Theophanes credited an architect from Heliopolis in Syria who was a refugee in the Byzantine Empire with the invention of the famous naval weapon known as 'Greek Fire.'[264] In 693–694, refugee Slavs from the Byzantine Empire used their knowledge of their former home to help a Muslim army successfully raid there.[265] A prisoner captured in Asia Minor claimed to be the son of the emperor Justinian; the Arabs outfitted him with regal trappings and had him tour about Syria in order to scare the Byzantines with the threat of a pretender to their throne.[266] Taken captive by Byzantines in Ascalon in the late ninth or early tenth century, Hārūn b. Yaḥyā would eventually write a celebrated Arabic description of Constantinople based on what he saw after being taken there and before his eventual release.[267]

There was also movement of individuals who were not captives: al-Ḥārith b. Kalada (d. AH 13/AD 634–635), the famous Arab doctor who counted

[260] Michael the Great, *Chronicle* 11.25 (ed. Chabot, 4.473-474 = 2.523)

[261] *Life of John of Damascus*, p. 12. For Cosmas as an example of information flowing through captives, see J. Herrin, 'Aspects of the Process of Hellenization in the Early Middle Ages,' *Annual of the British School at Athens* 68 (1973), p. 118. As with most of the sources I use in this chapter, and indeed throughout this book, whether the events described in them actually took place and whether they were actually written at the time they purport to be composed, is irrelevant. Even as fictional narratives, they still reflect expectations and possibilities indicative of what was considered possible and plausible in the early medieval and medieval periods. For more, see Appendix I.

[262] Ibn Abī Uṣaybiʿa, *'Uyūn al-anbā'*, p. 258.

[263] Ibn Abī Uṣaybiʿa, *'Uyūn al-anbā'*, p. 246.

[264] Theophanes, *Chronicle* AM 6165 (ed. de Boor, vol. 1, p. 354; ET available in Mango and Scott, *The Chronicle of Theophanes Confessor*, p. 494—but see also n. 5, which calls into question crediting Callinicus with this invention).

[265] Theophanes, *Chronicle* AM 6186 (ed. de Boor, vol. 1, p. 367; ET available in Mango and Scott, *The Chronicle of Theophanes Confessor*, p. 513).

[266] Theophanes, *Chronicle* AM 6229 (ed. de Boor, vol. 1, p. 411; ET available in Mango and Scott, *The Chronicle of Theophanes Confessor*, p. 570).

[267] For what survives of Hārūn's description, see Ibn Rusta, *al-Mujallad al-sābiʿ min Kitāb al-aʿlāq al-nafīsa*, pp. 119–30. For an ET, see A. Vasiliev, 'Harun-Ibn-Yahya and His Description of Constantinople,' *Seminarium Kondakovianum* 5 (1932) pp. 149–63. On Hārūn, see in M. Izzedin's article, 'Hārūn b. Yaḥyā' in *EI2*, vol. 3, p. 232.

Muḥammad among his patients, was said to have studied medicine in Persia and in Yemen.[268] Ananias of Shirak (d. ca. AD 650) could not find the instruction he wanted in Armenia and so traveled to Greece, Constantinople, Alexandria, Jerusalem, Rome, and Athens.[269] Maximus the Confessor spread his teaching while travelling from Palestine to North Africa (where he found eighty-seven Nestorian students from Nisibis who eventually moved to Rome), then to Sicily, Rome, Constantinople, and finally he was exiled to Lazika.[270] Jacob of Edessa went to Alexandria from northern Mesopotamia in order to 'gather wisdom.'[271] Archbishop Theodore (d. AD 690) moved from Tarsus to Rome to Canterbury, with stops in Constantinople and (it is presumed) Antioch and Edessa along the way; the wide learning he brought with him to England has been credited with helping to create in Canterbury one of the most exciting centers of education of the early medieval period.[272] Already in the Middle Ages, it was recognized that travelling for trade was one way in which the pre-Islamic Arabs learned about other peoples,[273] and travelling for trade did not stop once the Arabs had conquered the Middle East. The Christian scholar and translator Abū 'Alī b. Zur'a (d. AH 398/AD 1008), for instance, was known to travel to Byzantium as a merchant.[274]

But here my focus is captives and their role as vectors for spreading information: this was the case, in part, because slaves seem to have been integrated into Muslim-ruled society rather than isolated from it.[275] Captives can help us understand not only the movement of information in this early medieval world, but also religious change, for captives, removed from their homes, families, and communities, and enslaved, might be prime candidates for conversion to a different religion.[276] 'Umar b. 'Abd al-'Azīz wrote about a Muslim who was

[268] See Ṣā'id b. Aḥmad al-Andalusī (d. AH 462/AD 1069), *Kitāb ṭabaqāt al-umam*, p. 47 (ed. L. Cheikho [Beirut, 1912]). Pellat was skeptical about the claim that al-Ḥārith had studied in Yemen; see his article, 'al-Ḥārith b. Kalada,' in *EI2*, *Supplement*, pp. 354–55.

[269] See F. C. Conybeare, trans., 'Ananias of Shirak (A.D. 600–650 c.)', *Byzantinische Zeitschrift* 6 (1897), pp. 572–74.

[270] These movements are traced out in George of Resh'ayna, *Life of Maximus Confessor* (ed. Brock).

[271] Michael the Great, *Chronicle* 11.15 (ed. Chabot, 4.445 = 2.471).

[272] See M. Lapidge, 'The Career of Archbishop Theodore,' in Lapidge, ed., *Archbishop Theodore: Commemorative Studies on His Life and Influence* (Cambridge, 1995), pp. 1–29.

[273] Ṣā'id al-Andalusī, *Kitāb ṭabaqāt al-umam*, p. 44 (ed. Cheikho).

[274] See Ibn Abī Uṣaybi'a, *'Uyūn al-anbā'*, p. 319. See also the article 'Ibn Zur'a,' in *EI2*, vol. 3, pp. 979–80.

[275] Note the comment of R. Brunschvig in his article ''Abd,' in *EI2*, vol. 1, p. 33: 'But it must be emphasized that medieval Islam seems scarcely to have known the system of large-scale rural exploitation based on an immense and anonymous labour-force.' The Zanj of ninth-century Iraq are a well-known exception that proves the rule in this case.

[276] Cf. the comments in P. Crone, *God's Rule: Government and Islam: Six Centuries of Medieval Islamic Political Thought* (New York, 2004), pp. 372–73. Note Antonio de Sosa's hostile comment about Christian

captured and then converted to Christianity: if this became known, his wife would be free of him and should undertake a waiting period of three menstrual cycles; his money was to be given to his Muslim heirs.[277] ʿAbd Allāh b. Abī Rabīʿa, the father of al-Ḥārith b. ʿAbd Allāh, captured al-Ḥārith's mother, we are told, along with six hundred other Ethiopians. Once in captivity, she made three different requests of ʿAbd Allāh, all of which he granted; her second request was that he not force her to change her religion.[278]

Indeed, those who resisted conversion were heroes. One story tells of a messenger from caliph ʿUmar II who came upon a blind Muslim captive in Byzantine territory. Given the choice between having his eyes gouged out and converting to Christianity, he told the caliph's messenger, 'I chose my religion over my sight.' When the messenger returned to ʿUmar and told him of the story, the caliph began weeping even before he had finished; he wrote to the Byzantine Emperor demanding that the blinded Muslim be sent to him and promising he would not return any captured troops if the man was not released.[279] Anastasius of Sinai wrote of a seventeen-year-old Jew on Cyprus 'from the east' who had been rescued from captivity and now sincerely wanted to receive baptism and become a Christian.[280] A theme, however, which characterizes Anastasius's late-seventh-century *Narrations Profitable for the Soul* is the difficult challenges faced by Christian captives under Muslim rule.[281]

What became of all these captives who were being moved around the eastern Mediterranean? Though conversion and manumission were not always associated with one another,[282] the pattern these individuals followed seems

---

renegades in Algiers in the early seventeenth century: 'What moves some of these men to forsake the true path of God, at such great peril to their souls, is nothing more than the fainthearted refusal to take on the work of slavery. Others are attracted by pleasure, by the good life of fleshly vice in which the Turks live. Still others are addicted since childhood to the wickedness of sodomy imposed on them by their masters. And together with all the fuss the Turks make over them—more than over their own women—these men turn Turk in their youthful ignorance, understanding neither what they are disowning nor what they are adopting. And the Turks willfully turn them into renegades, persuading themselves that, as good Turks, they do this to serve both God and Muhammad. Those who have already adopted that way of life or profession naturally want others to follow and approve of their deceits, from which, in general, they all profit.' Translation by D. de Armas Wilson taken from Garcés, ed., *An Early Modern Dialogue with Islam: Antonio de Sosa's* Topography of Algiers *(1612)*, p. 119.

[277] ʿAbd al-Razzāq, *al-Muṣannaf*, vol. 10, p. 338 (no. 19292). See also the report of a man being taken captive and converting to Christianity in vol. 7, p. 161 (no. 12619).

[278] al-Mizzī, *Tahdhīb al-kamāl fī asmāʾ al-rijāl*, vol. 5, p. 241.

[279] For the story, see Ibn ʿAbd al-Ḥakam, *Sīrat ʿUmar b. ʿAbd al-ʿAzīz*, pp. 168–69.

[280] Anastasius of Sinai, *Narrations Beneficial for the Soul* II.17 (ed. Binggeli, p. 1.240 [Greek] = 2.555 [FT] [=§51 in Nau, ed. 'Le texte grec des récits utiles à l'âme d'Anastase (le Sinaïte),' p. 71]).

[281] For this, see Hoyland, *Seeing Islam*, p. 100.

[282] Cf. the observation in van Ess, *Theologie und Gesellschaft*, vol. 1, p. 39, n. 4 [= *Theology and Society*, vol. 1, p. 45, n. 4].

regularly to have been captivity, enslavement, conversion, manumission.[283] And in the early period, it has been asserted, most (non-Arab) converts to Islam were freedmen.[284] Once manumitted, a former slave would be the *mawlā*, or client, of the one who had freed him. And though some might complain that the children of prisoners of war were the causes of heresies in Islam,[285] the reality is that, as Goldziher pointed out long ago, many of the most important figures in Islamic history had as their forbears Persian captives.[286] A study of the position and importance of *mawālī* in Islamic society and in the development of Islam itself is well beyond the scope of this work, but the importance of *mawālī*—both those who became clients of Muslims through conversion and those who became clients through manumission—can hardly be overemphasized. As an example, we might take an anecdote told by Ibn Shihāb al-Zuhrī (d. AH 124/AD 742) in which the caliph ʿAbd al-Malik asked about who was in charge of Mecca, Yemen, Egypt, Syria, the Jazira, Khurasan, and Basra, and was exasperated to learn that of all of these, only Basra had an Arab as its leader. The rest were run by *mawālī*.[287] A similar anecdote, attributed to Ibn Abī Laylā (d. AH 148/AD 765), points to the same reality. Asked by ʿĪsā b. Mūsā (d. AH 167/AD 783–784) about the jurists in Basra, Mecca, Medina, Yemen, Khurasan, Syria, and the Jazira, Ibn Abī Laylā informed him that they were all *mawālī*; in reaction to his questioner's growing anger at these responses, however, Ibn Abī Laylā incorrectly told ʿĪsā that two Arabs were the jurists of Kufa in order to placate him.[288] Having been conquered by the Arabs,

[283] See Crone, 'The Early Islamic World,' p. 314, and cf. Crone, *Nativist Prophets*, pp. 8–11. On the different types of *walāʾ*, see Crone, *Roman, Provincial and Islamic Law: The Origins of the Islamic Patronate* (Cambridge, 1987), pp. 35–40. For conversion and manumission, cf. R. Brunschvig's article, ''Abd,' in *EI2*, vol. 1, pp. 26, 29–30. Note the statement attributed by Ibn ʿAbd Rabbih to anonymous partisans of the Arabs against the criticisms of the Shuʿūbiyya: 'If we had done nothing for the *mawlā* in freeing him and doing him good but the fact that we have saved him from unbelief, and brought him out of the abode of polytheism to the abode of belief—as in the *ḥadīth*, "Some people are led to their good fortunes by leashes," and as he said "Our Lord is astonished at a people led to Paradise by chains," [it would be sufficient].' *Al-ʿIqd al-Farīd*, vol. 3, p. 360; the translation is taken from Boullata, *The Unique Necklace*, vol. 3, p. 305, with slight modification.

[284] Crone, *Roman, Provincial and Islamic Law*, p. 90. NB: Crone asserts this but offers no evidence to support such a claim. Cf. also van Ess, *Theologie und Gesellschaft*, vol. 1, p. 39 [= *Theology and Society*, vol. 1, p. 45]. Cahen, 'Socio-Economic History and Islamic Studies,' p. 265, similarly identified slaves (who had been prisoners of war) as representing a significant proportion of converts.

[285] Tritton, 'Foreign Influences,' p. 838.

[286] Goldziher, *Muslim Studies*, vol. 1, p. 109.

[287] See Abū Ḥayyān al-Tawḥīdī, *al-Baṣāʾir wa-'l-dhakhāʾir*, vol. 2.2 (ed. I. al-Kīlānī) (Damascus, n.d. [1964?]), pp. 414–17. For this anecdote, see R. Hoyland, 'Arabic, Syriac, and Greek Historiography in the First ʿAbbasid Century: An Inquiry into Inter-Cultural Traffic,' *Aram* 3.1–2 (1991), p. 231, and van Ess, *Theologie und Gesellschaft*, vol. 1, p. 40, n. 8a [= *Theology and Society*, p. 46, n. 9].

[288] Ibn ʿAbd Rabbih, *al-ʿIqd al-Farīd*, vol. 3, pp. 363-364. ET available in Boullata, *The Unique Necklace*, vol. 3, pp. 308–309.

it was these *mawālī* who eventually came to dominate the new society that resulted from the conquests.[289] *Graecia capta ferum victorem cepit.*

[289] On the *mawālī*, their importance in Islamic society and for the development of Islam, and on the institution of *walā'*, see the excellent article 'Mawlā' by P. Crone (and A. J. Wensinck) in *EI2.*, vol. 6, pp. 874–82. For an analysis of the meaning of *'mawla,'* see further D. Pipes, 'Mawlas: Freed Slaves and Converts in Early Islam,' in J. R. Willis, ed., *Slaves and Slavery in Muslim Africa*, vol. 1: *Islam and the Ideology of Enslavement* (London/Totowa, N.J., 1985), pp. 199–247. To get a sense of the profound importance of the economic and social roles played by *mawālī* in all aspects of Islamic society, see J. Judah, 'The Economic Conditions of the *Mawālī* in Early Islamic Times,' in M. G. Morony, ed., *Manufacturing and Labour* (Ashgate, 2003), pp. 167–97.

CONCLUSION

Dark Matter and the History of the Middle East

What has become an open question is: Are there experiences of the past that cannot be captured by the methods of the discipline, or which at least show the limits of the discipline?

Dipesh Chakrabarty[1]

The people of this village [Ṭamrīs] are Christians and Muslims. They speak the Coptic language.

Abū al-Makārim[2]

In many ways, this book has been an experiment: how would our understanding of the religious and social history of the Middle East be different if we challenged and changed a few basic assumptions that have often (perhaps subconsciously) dictated how scholars have approached the region in the centuries after Chalcedon and in the centuries after the life of the Prophet?

Two different authors, one from the twentieth century, one from the thirteenth, can help illustrate the consequences of contrasting assumptions for how we think about the region and its inhabitants. 'The German became Romanized as soon as he entered "Romania,"' Henri Pirenne wrote in one of the twentieth century's most famous works of early medieval history:

> The Roman, on the contrary, became Arabized as soon as he was conquered by Islam. It is true that well into the Middle Ages certain small communities of Copts, Nestorians and, above all, Jews, survived in the midst of the Musulman world. Nevertheless, the whole environment was profoundly transformed. There was a clean cut: a complete break with the past.[3]

Next to Pirenne, we can set Burchard of Mt. Zion, a German Dominican living in Palestine in the late thirteenth century who has left us a work entitled

[1] D. Chakrabarty, *Provincializing Europe: Postcolonial Thought and Historical Difference* (Princeton/Oxford, 2008), p. 107.

[2] Abū al-Makārim, *Ta'rīkh al-kanā'is wa-'l-adyira*, vol. 1, p. 59 (fol. 44b).

[3] H. Pirenne, *Mohammed and Charlemagne* (trans. B. Miall) (repr. New York, 1957), p. 152. On this passage, see B. Effros, 'The Enduring Attraction of the Pirenne Thesis,' *Speculum* 92 (2017), p. 190.

Description of the Holy Land.[4] At one point in his *Description*, Burchard turned his attention to the question of the number of Christians living in the Middle East. 'Now it must be noted as a matter of fact,' he wrote,

> albeit some, who like to talk about what they have never seen, declare the contrary, that the whole East beyond the Mediterranean Sea, even unto India and Ethiopia, acknowledges and preaches the name of Christ, save only the Saracens and some Turcomans who dwell in Cappadocia, so that I declare for certain, as I have myself seen and have heard from others who knew, that always in every place and kingdom, besides Egypt and Arabia, where Saracens and other followers of Mahomet chiefly dwell, you will find thirty Christians and more for one Saracen.

Even in the High Middle Ages, it seems, some Westerners were confusing the official religious ideology of a state and its most prominent officials with the religion of the majority of its subjects. 'But the truth is,' he continued,

> all the Christians beyond the sea are Easterns by nation, and albeit they are Christians, yet, as they are not much practised in the use of arms, when they are assailed by the Saracens, Turks, or any other people soever, yield to them and buy peace and quiet by paying tribute, and the Saracens, or other lords of the land, place their bailiffs and tax-gatherers therein. Hence it arises that their kingdom is said to belong to the Saracens, whereas, as a matter of fact, all the people are Christians save those bailiffs and tax-gatherers and their families, as I have seen with my own eyes in Cilicia and Lesser Armenia. . . .

The Christians of the region, he noted, were not quite the same as Western Christians. And it seemed that a number of Westerners viewed them through the prism of post-Chalcedonian categories of heresies. But seeing them in terms of these labels was, Burchard thought, misleading. 'Many, too,' he wrote,

> are frightened when they are told that in parts beyond the seas there dwell Nestorians, Jacobites, Maronites, Georgians, and other sects named after heretics whom the church has condemned, wherefore these men are thought to be heretics, and to follow the errors of those after whom they are called. This is by no means true. God forbid! But they are men of simple and devout life; yet I do not deny there may be fools among them, seeing that even the Church of Rome is not free from fools.[5]

[4] On whom, see most conveniently, J. Prelog's 'Burchardus de Monte Sion,' in *Lexikon des Mittelalters*, vol. 2 (München/Zurich, 1981), col. 953.

[5] Burchard of Mt. Zion, *Description of the Holy Land* 13.8 (ed. J.C.M. Laurent, *Peregrinatores medii aevi quatuor* [Leipzig, 1864], pp. 90–91; ET taken from A. Stewart, *Burchard of Mount Sion* [London,

Burchard was inaccurate and just plain wrong in many of the particulars of what he wrote in the passages quoted above. Southwestern Asia, from the Mediterranean to India, was never fully Christianized, for instance, and there are many ways we can interpret his ratio of 30:1, but to take it literally probably would not be the most prudent one this many centuries after the Arab conquests.

Nevertheless, Burchard's comments anticipated many of the themes that have underlain the preceding pages. What if, broadly speaking, Burchard of Mt. Zion's view of the medieval Middle East was more accurate than that of Pirenne? What if it was a region populated by simple Christians and these simple Christians remained a significant portion of the inhabitants, even a majority, well into the period of the Crusades? What would this mean for our understanding of the religious history of the Middle East, both Christian and Muslim?

At the level of demography at least, a view like Burchard's strikes us as being, on the face of it, wildly implausible. But the reasons why we find it to be such are not very good ones: 'In contrast to previous assessments that mass conversion was complete before the eleventh century,' archaeologist Gideon Avni has recently written, for instance: '... the survey of sites shows that most Christian settlements in Palestine and Jordan preserved their identity up to the Crusader period.... Islamization gained real momentum only after the conquest of Saladin in 1187 and the expulsion of the Franks.'[6] A hesitation to think of the formerly Roman Middle East as a largely Christian region into the eleventh, twelfth, or even thirteenth century will often be rooted more in inchoate impressions that have developed out of our own library- and classroom-based experiences of reading and learning about the medieval Middle East (or projections back into the medieval period rooted in our experiences in the region today) than they are in Umayyad or Abbasid or Mamluk census materials (which do not exist) or in thinking carefully about the nature of the evidence we have from the region in this period—and the evidence that has been lost or destroyed—and what sorts of inferences we can make from it. Should we not take, someone might suggest, the enormous amount of medieval Islamic literature written in Arabic as indicative of the nature of the population of the region? It is this rich and vast body of material that has delighted and occupied historians of the Middle East for generations.[7]

1896], pp. 106–107). For this quote, cf. Ellenblum, 'Demography, Geography and the Accelerated Islamisation of the Eastern Mediterranean,' p. 61.

[6] G. Avni, *The Byzantine-Islamic Transition in Palestine: An Archaeological Approach* (Oxford, 2014), p. 336.

[7] Note the observation of Claude Cahen in *Jean Sauvaget's Introduction to the History of the Muslim*

But the existence of a few centers of concentrated Muslim population—Medina, Baghdad, Kufa, Basra, Wāsiṭ, Fusṭāṭ, etc.—where Islamic texts might be written, or the presence of rulers who used an Islamic idiom to legitimate their sovereignty and whose court patronized certain kinds of literature and art, does not mean that the entire Middle East had itself converted to Islam. And, even more importantly, there is no direct or necessary connection between the size of a religious community and the volume of literature that its adherents produce, especially when those adherents hold political power. Nor is there a necessary connection between the size of a religious community in a certain period and the amount of literature that has survived to the present from that community. The number of pagans in the fourth-century Roman Empire almost certainly dwarfed the number of Christians, but this is not something that one would be able to surmise based solely on the metrics of the relative amounts of surviving literature produced by these two different groups or on the relative amount of scholarly attention these two groups have traditionally received.[8] And, to take another Roman example, the dramatic increase in the number of identifiable Christian writers composing in Greek in Asia Minor and Constantinople in the first three Christian centuries and then between the fourth and fifth Christian centuries—from 3 to 10 to 49—is a vivid illustration of the importance of a court, a capital, and an official religion for the production of literature.[9] What if the amount of medieval literature we possess from one group as opposed to another is a function of their relative political dominance and wealth (both in the period and, even more importantly, after it) rather than demographic heft?

The amount of literature that a particular confession's adherents produced is in fact only indirectly related to the amount of literature that has been preserved up till the present. And, there is no necessary connection between the amount of literature a community produces and its size. Moments of radical discontinuity also distort what survives: we should not forget the devastation visited on Middle Eastern Christian communities, their monasteries, and their manuscripts by the Mamluks, Timur Lenk, and others in the High and

East: A Bibliographical Guide (Berkeley, 1965; repr. Westport, Conn., 1982), p. 22: 'Even though the historian of Islam is at a definite disadvantage with respect to archives, he at least has access to a large quantity of literary resources, larger perhaps than any other civilization has produced until modern times.'

[8] I am grateful to Peter Brown for this example. Cf. the remarks of H.J.W. Drijvers about the presence of large numbers of pagans in Edessa for a longer time than most scholars assume, 'Jews and Christians at Edessa,' p. 89.

[9] See the indices of *CPG*, vol. 5, pp. 286–88. In the first three Christian centuries, by contrast, there are only three authors writing in Greek associated with Asia Minor (p. 286).

late Middle Ages.[10] Manichean literature and Middle Persian literature, both of which have largely vanished, are further instructive examples, as is, for that matter, pre-Abbasid Arabic literature, which has mostly been lost to us in its original forms. Indeed, that there is, in the early medieval Middle East, little connection between the survival of manuscripts and literature and the size of a religious community holds true for Christians, Muslims, Jews, Zoroastrians, pagans, and others.

The existence and survival of a large amount of Islamic literature in Arabic, dating from the ninth century and later, can in fact point to a number of things: the increasing importance of the new religion in legitimating rule, the growing self-awareness of various competing parts of the Muslim community and their attempts to narrate identity in ways that would legitimate their positions and delegitimate those of others, the importance of imperial and state patronage for the production and preservation of certain kinds of literature, the needs of a religiously legitimated state for a system of law by which to run its affairs, and rivalry with the Christian East Romans, not to mention rivalry with indigenous Christians now living under minority Muslim rule. None of these factors, however, necessitates a marked and rapid decline in Christian population or Muslim numerical hegemony in the Middle East.

In the end, all scholars of the medieval Middle East fall into the class of people whom Burchard, a person who had actually lived there, referred to as those 'who like to talk about what they have never seen.' In writing this book, I have certainly placed myself among those against whom Burchard might lay such a charge. No serious scholar of the medieval Middle East today would endorse a vision of the region like that of Pirenne—indeed, treating Islam as a late antique phenomenon has gone from being an interesting hypothesis to

[10] On the fate of the Church of the East between 1318 and 1552, see most conveniently, D. Wilmshurst, *The Martyred Church: A History of the Church of the East* (London, 2011), pp. 277–315; see also the brief comments in J.-M. Fiey, *Chrétiens syriaques sous les Mongols (Il-Khanat de Perse, XIIIe–XIVe s.)* (Louvain, 1975), pp. 83–84. Fiey also credited the Black Death with dealing a significant blow to Christian communities. For a description of the destruction of Antioch, the killing of seventeen thousand Christians there, and the capture of a hundred thousand more by the Mamluk Sultan Baybars in May 1268, see E. S. Bouchier, *A Short History of Antioch, 300 B.C.- A.D. 1268* (Oxford, 1921), p. 269, and cf. C. Cahen, *La Syrie du nord à l'époque des croisades et la principauté franque d'Antioche* (Paris, 1940), pp. 713–21, esp. 716, n. 14, where the number of killed at Antioch is placed between seventeen thousand and forty thousand. For the effect of this event (and previous military conflicts in northern Syria) on Christian manuscripts, see the comments in Grand'Henry, 'Transmission de textes grecs,' pp. 43–44. L. Bréhier, 'Bibars l'Arbalétrier,' in *DHGE*, vol. 8, cols. 1388–1401, esp. 1393–97, succinctly describes Baybar's campaigns against Christian Crusader communities in Western Syria. For the destruction of the Christian population of Irbil in AD 1309, see the remarks of Fiey in *EI2*, vol. 7, p. 973. On the fate of Christian communities under the Mamluks, see also chapter 11, n. 123, above.

simply standard scholarly practice.[11] Nevertheless, views like Pirenne's are widespread at the popular level. And even beyond the popular level, at the level of academic publishing, college course offerings, and, importantly, of the hiring decisions of universities all over Europe and North America—not to mention the way Middle Eastern history is taught and spoken about in the Middle East itself—there is a common understanding that the history of the medieval Middle East is a history of the politically-dominant Muslim demographic minority that ruled over the region.[12] This book has been an argument that such a view is misleading. By effectively making medieval Middle Eastern history a sectarian one, it distorts both how people in the West and how people in the Middle East view the region's religious past, and it has consequences for how Christian communities in the region are seen (or, as the case may be, not seen) today, both in the West and, most importantly, in the Middle East itself.

And though viewing the Arab conquests as marking a discontinuity in the stark terms that Pirenne used may no longer be acceptable, softer versions of discontinuity are still to be found: understanding the conversion of the Middle East's population from Christianity to Islam as an example of 'mass ideological change'[13] would raise fewer eyebrows today than Pirenne's notion that the Arab conquests marked a 'complete break.' This book has been an argument that even a more supple view, such as the latter, is equally inaccurate, at least when it comes to the conversion of the simple Christians of much of the Middle

[11] See, e.g., T. Sizgorich, 'Narrative and Community in Islamic Late Antiquity,' *Past and Present* 185 (2004), pp. 9–42; R. Hoyland, 'Early Islam as a Late Antique Religion,' in S. F. Johnson, ed., *The Oxford Handbook of Late Antiquity* (Oxford/New York, 2012), pp. 1053–77; and Holyand, ed., *The Late Antique World of Early Islam.* Note also the comments on the notion of 'Islamic late antiquity,' in H. Kennedy, 'The Middle East in Islamic Late Antiquity,' in A. Monson and W. Scheidel, eds., *Fiscal Regimes and the Political Economy of Premodern States* (Cambridge, 2015), p. 390, and L. Salaymeh, 'Taxing Citizens: Socio-legal Constructions of Late Antique Muslim Identity,' *Islamic Law and Society* 23 (2016), pp. 336-337. For additional historiographic perspective, see Papaconstantinou, 'Confrontation, Interaction, and the Formation of the Early Islamic *oikoumene*,' and Cameron, 'Patristic Studies and the Emergence of Islam.'

[12] And it also bears pointing out that such assumptions can be found deep within the DNA of the field itself and underlying some of its most basic and venerable *instrumenta studiorum.* See, e.g., Hilary Kilpatrick's discussion of the attitudes towards Christian Arabic literature and the assumption that Arabic literature is an Islamic literature in Carl Brockelmann's foundational *Geschichte der arabischen Litteratur* in 'Brockelmann, Kaḥḥâla & Co: Reference Works on the Arabic Literature of Early Ottoman Syria,' *Middle Eastern Literatures* 7 (2004), pp. 34–36. Note, too, the comments of S. Khalil, 'La "*Geschichte des arabischen Schrifttums*" et la littérature arabe chrétienne,' *OCP* 44 (1978), pp. 470–71, on the mention and non-mention of a particular author's religious membership in Fuat Sezgin's monumental *Geschichte des arabischen Schrifttums.* See also R. G. Khoury, 'Quelques réflexions sur la première ou les premières Bibles arabes,' in T. Fahd, ed., *L'Arabie préislamique et son environnement historique et culturel: actes du Colloque de Strasbourg, 24–27 juin 1987* (Leiden, 1989), p. 549, esp. n. 1.

[13] See e.g., Bulliet, *Conversion to Islam in the Medieval Period,* p. 4.

East. Conversion for these people was quite often anything but ideological and often may not have represented much of a change at all in their lived religious life, however consequential it may eventually have been at a social or economic level. Thinking critically about the reasons and nature of conversion in a world of simple believers—in a largely agrarian society, one where print, television, satellite television, social media, and attempts at universal education were nonexistent and large numbers of books not widely available, and where levels of literacy were low and theological literacy even lower—affects markedly how we understand what a shift in Christian confession or even a change in religion would have meant in practical terms by dethroning doctrine as the primary prism through which we view cross-confessional and interreligious interaction in the post-Chalcedonian and post-conquest periods. And understanding Islam as having crystalized in the context of a largely non-Muslim world, even as it absorbed large numbers of converts, is fundamental for understanding the shape it eventually came to take at the level of normative texts, and most especially, what it looked like when it came to everyday lived experience.

If we accept that the Middle East maintained a very significant population of Christians for as much as half a millennium (or even more) after the Arab conquests and then look at the way the study of the medieval Middle East takes place institutionally today, it quickly becomes clear that in attempting to understand the world the Arabs found, and especially the world the Arab conquests created, we stand before a subject where historical disciplines that have been influenced by the politics of the nation-state are unable to do justice to the period in question. Crudely put, Byzantinists, who typically focus on Greek (and occasionally, Armenian) sources, shift their focus away from the Middle East after the seventh century, and Byzantium is henceforth treated as a nation-state of Greek-speaking (Chalcedonian) Orthodox Christians and the forerunner of modern Greece; the 'Byzantine Commonwealth,'[14] if it is spoken of, traditionally includes Christians in Slavic-speaking areas, but not those in Arabic- or Aramaic- speaking ones, even though a large number of the latter would be identified from eighth century onwards as *Rūm*, 'Romans,' despite being subjects of a Muslim ruler.[15]

[14] Cf. D. Obolensky, *The Byzantine Commonwealth: Eastern Europe, 500–1453* (New York, 1971).

[15] Dyothelete Chalcedonian Christians in the Middle East were being called 'Romans' perhaps as early as the late eighth century: see the letter of Ephrem, metropolitan of Elam (fl. 782) to Gabriel b. Bukhtisho' (d. 828) which warns that one should not take communion from Jacobites or 'Romans.' Mingana Syriac 587, fols. 357b–360a (cf. also A. Mingana, *Catalogue of the Mingana Collection of* Manuscripts, vol. 1 [Cambridge, 1933], col. 1119) and see above, Chapter 1, n. 9. On the *Rūm*, see further Ḥ. Zayyāt, *al-Rūm al-Malakiyyūn fī 'l-Islam* (Ḥarīsā, 1953).

Post-conquest, medieval Middle Eastern history is inevitably conflated with Islamic history, and Islamicists focus on the political intrigues and protean beliefs of the region's rulers, issues related to the Qur'ān, Islamic law, *ḥadīth*, the rise of sectarianism, the nature and development of the Muslim historical tradition, or other questions related to the communal ordering or religion of the Arabic-speaking, Muslim minority of the region. In the subjects that are studied, the books that are published, the languages that are taught, and the areas of specialization of the people who are hired to teach, the medieval Middle East is treated, in effect, as a nation-state of Arab Muslims.

But what about the mass of people still living there, who did not flee with the Emperor Heraclius, and who did not convert to Islam and begin to speak Arabic as soon as they found themselves under Arab political authority? What about the people who are the ancestors of much of the population of today's Middle East, Christian and non-Christian? With no modern nation state that looks to these people as their forbears,[16] this population has traditionally been left in silence outside of the small, specialized, and heavily theological parallel universe of Eastern Christian and Christian Arabic studies.[17] Apart from this world, they have only the occasional Islamicist or Byzantinist to speak for them, and then usually only in the context of research questions connected to the region's Muslim minority: Eastern Christian studies is treated as the handmaiden of Islamic history.[18] In this context, even though they vastly outnum-

[16] Lebanon represents a possible exception, but civil war, its small size and comparative lack of wealth, and the reality that it has been more of a failed state than a functioning one for much of its existence, complicate its status—not to mention the fact that it has not been a majority Christian state for many decades.

[17] A small world but one, it should be emphasized, that has an enormously rich tradition of scholarship stretching back to the Assemanis of the eighteenth century and, before them, to figures like Ibrāhīm al-Ḥāqilānī. It is this deep and ancient tradition of scholarship that has made this study possible. Indeed, the current increase in scholarly work on Christians in the late antique and medieval Middle East would not be possible without the fundamental contributions of scholars such as Joseph Assemani, William Wright, Anton Baumstark, Louis Cheikho, Ḥabīb Zayyāt, Filoksenos Dolabani, Afram Barsawm, Addai Scher, Ignatius Afram Rahmani, Alphonse Mingana, Ignazio Guidi, Eduard Sachau, Theodor Nöldeke, Ernest Walter Brooks, Jean-Baptiste Chabot, François Nau, Georg Graf, Carl Brockelmann, Sebastian Brock, Jean-Maurice Fiey, Joseph Nasrallah, Samir Khalil, Sidney Griffith, Lucas van Rompay, and many others who have toiled in the vineyards of Eastern Christian studies.

[18] Much like the study of Syriac, which had a long tradition of being treated as an auxiliary science for Biblical textual criticism in many parts of the English-speaking world before the field was transformed in the final decades of the twentieth century and first part of the twenty-first century, in no small part due to the prolific and profoundly learned scholarship of Sebastian Brock. J. J. Scheiner, *Die Eroberung von Damaskus: Quellenkritische Untersuchung zur Historiographie in klassisch-islamischer Zeit* (Leiden/Boston, 2010), pp. 423–51, is an example of the increasing practice of Islamicists of making use of Christian sources. More generally, if Cook and Crone's *Hagarism* was responsible for making English-speaking Islamicists in the late twentieth century aware of the importance of non-Muslim sources, it was the publication of Andrew Palmer's *The Seventh Century in the West-Syrian Chronicles* and Robert

bered Muslims, Christians, and non-Muslims more generally, are often spoken of in anachronistic nation-state language as 'minorities,'[19] and their usefulness is often in corroborating information in this or that Islamic text or providing context for this or that passage in the Qur'ān: they are made into modern day Baḥīrās or Waraqa b. Nawfals. Though these 'minorities' comprised the bulk of the Middle East's population for much of the Middle Ages, in universities across North America, Europe, and the Middle East, the study of Eastern Christianity leads a very precarious existence outside religious establishments.[20] When thinking about the world the Arab conquests created, the experience of a great deal of the region's population is relegated to a bit part and minor role in the telling of the region's story, or simply falls through the cracks.[21] How can we catch it?

My attempt has relied on several inversions of perspective: How will our understanding of the religious landscape of the Middle East in the centuries after Chalcedon change if we put simple, ordinary Christians at the center of our story? How will our understanding of the medieval Middle East change if we focus on its non-Muslim majority rather than its small but growing Muslim population? How will our understanding of the formation of Islam and Christian-Muslim relations change if we take into account simple Christians

---

Hoyland's *Seeing Islam* that provided the tools for many outside the small field of Eastern Christian studies to actually do so. F. Donner, review of *In God's Path. The Arab Conquests and the Creation of an Islamic Empire* by R. Hoyland, *Al-ʿUṣūr al-Wusṭā* 23 (2015), p. 135, provides a useful list of examples of scholars who have used non-Muslim sources in the reconstruction of Islamic history.

[19] See B. T. White, *The Emergence of Minorities in the Middle East: The Politics of Community in French Mandate Syria* (Edinburgh, 2011), esp. pp. 21–37, for an 'argument that majority and minority are not meaningful concepts outside the context of a modern nation-state' and E. Kedourie, 'Ethnicity, Majority, and Minority in the Middle East,' in M. J. Esman and I. Rabinovich, eds., *Ethnicity, Pluralism and the State in the Middle East* (Ithaca, 1988), pp. 25–31, for notions of 'minority' and 'majority' being imported to the Middle East from Western political discourses. Cf. also el-Leithy, 'Coptic Culture and Conversion in Medieval Cairo, 1293–1524 A.D.,' p. 27, esp. n. 71, and R. S. Humphreys, *Islamic History: A Framework for Inquiry*, rev. ed. (London/New York, 1991), pp. 255–56.

[20] See, e.g., the report on the endangered state of Eastern Christian studies in Germany—once the most important center of Eastern Christian studies in the West—found in M. Marx, J. Pahlitzsch, and D. Weltecke, 'Östliches Christentum in Geschichte und Gegenwart—Perspektiven und Hindernisse der Forschung,' *Der Islam* 88 (2012), pp. 1–10.

[21] The introduction to Eugen Weber's *Peasants into Frenchmen: The Modernization of Rural France, 1870–1914* (Stanford, 1976), lays out similar problems of representation with respect to traditional ways of thinking about the cultural history of nineteenth-century France and is very helpful to think with by analogy here. '[A]t the turn of the century,' Weber wrote (in Chapter 1), 'the great debate in and around the university turned on whether the teaching of Latin and Greek should take precedence over French, completely ignoring the problems posed by and the lessons to be drawn from the still-current conflict between French and local speech. Among the spate of surveys that marked the fin-de-siècle and the early twentieth century, none looked beyond Paris and what went on there. And this without reservations, confident that the views and aspirations of a tiny minority taking itself for *all* did indeed represent all' (pp. 8–9).

and all members of the Prophet's community, not just its religious and political elite?

All of these inversions have been motivated by a discomfort with many traditional approaches to the cultural history of the period between Chalcedon and the Crusades as elitist and exclusionary. The views and experiences of people who were highly literate, dwelling in major urban centers, or closest to political power have been taken as representative and reflective of the views and experience of all the inhabitants of the region.[22] But in making them representative we create a misleading picture of the past. We implicitly buy into the assumption that the study of the past should be the study of the politically powerful. We miss the fundamental reality that differing levels of understanding, knowledge, and awareness exist in religious communities. We fail to see those who were not in the *majlis* and overlook those who did not get exercised over the question of how many natures or *prosopa* or energies or wills there were in the Incarnate Christ and those who simply could not understand it. Outside the academy, the twentieth and twenty-first centuries have been filled with political groups whose utopian and at times violent visions of reestablishing the seventh century in the present are similarly blind to the implications of what such a layered perspective would mean for the nature of their idealized early Muslim community, how it related to non-Muslims and their traditions, and what it meant for the practice and development of Islam from its earliest days as a newcomer in Western Arabia and later, in the entire Middle East.[23] In contrast to such approaches—both academic and political/theological—I have sought to ask, over and over: What does the world that results from Chalcedon and the world that results from the Arab conquests look like if we take seriously the existence of a layering of knowledge in religious communities, Christian and Muslim, and then relentlessly seek to understand the historical consequences of such a layering?

I have suggested that we cannot understand learned Christianity in late antiquity if we do not see it in the context of the great mass of simple believers and adherents. And we cannot understand Islam in the early medieval and

[22] I borrow the notions of such history as elitist and exclusionary from Khaled Fahmy's critique of histories of nineteenth- and twentieth-century Alexandria that focus only on the cosmopolitanism of its European minority. See K. Fahmy, 'For Cavafy, with Love and Squalor: Some Critical Notes on the History and Historiography of Modern Alexandria,' and 'Towards a Social History of Modern Alexandria,' in A. Hirst and M. Silk, eds., *Alexandria, Real and Imagined* (Ashgate, 2004), pp. 263–80 and 281–306.

[23] See, e.g., the Islamic State's article, 'Break the Cross,' in *Dabiq* 15 (Shawwal, 1437), pp. 46–63, which (pp. 47–48) takes the Prophet's *ḥadīth* about Muslims following the customs of Jews and Christians, even to the point of following them down a hole (cf. chapter 13, n. 1), as predictive of deviations and apostasy in the Muslim community, and contains a picture, presumably from a *moulid*, with the caption, 'Sufis imitating Christians by celebrating the Prophet's birthday.'

medieval period unless we see it in the context of the great mass of non-Muslims—in formerly Roman areas, most of whom will have been simple Christians—and their gradual conversion to Islam. We let these groups slip through our fingers to our own detriment: they are the Dark Matter that makes everything else in our universe intelligible, for it is in looking at the relationship between the groups that historians usually focus on and the groups they do not—how the simple related to the learned, how simple Christians became simple Muslims, how learned Muslims related to simple Christians and to Muslims who were descended from simple Christians, and so on—that we gain a more textured perspective on late antique and medieval Christianity and Islam and learn to see them in a new light.

These groups whose existence I have attempted to push to the center have a tendency to dwell quietly and unnoticed at the edges of the subjects we study unless we consciously attempt to keep them in focus and look for their shadows in the texts we read: When we think about medieval mosques, for instance, would we pause to consider the role that Christians may have played in their everyday outfitting if we did not read in passing the disapproval a Muslim religious scholar expressed of monks entering a mosque to spread out woven mats they had made for it?[24] Given demographic and social realities, such points of quotidian contact and of Christian, and more broadly, non-Muslim, contribution to what are commonly assumed to be 'Islamic' subjects must have been ubiquitous.[25] The same can be suggested when we read in a late twelfth or early thirteenth century text about the custom of Christians chanting in Coptic at Muslim weddings and marching before the groom as he passed through the streets in Esneh in Upper Egypt, or large numbers of both Christians and Muslims lighting candles and lamps and burning wood there on Christmas Eve.[26] One of my assumptions in this book has been that the Christians and Muslims of Esneh will have been more typical of the medieval Middle East than the rulers, legal theorists, historians, and religious scholars who commonly occupy our time.

Whether we speak in terms of a 'complete break,' 'mass ideological change,' or are simply writing a syllabus for an undergraduate lecture course, the Arab

[24] Ibn al-Ḥājj, *al-Madkhal*, vol. 2, pp. 232–33. Cf. J. Pedersen in *EI2*, vol. 6, p. 654.

[25] Ibn ʿAbd Rabbih relates a story where a *mawlā* of ʿUthmān b. ʿAffān said to ʿĀmir b. ʿAbd al-Qays, 'May God not have many like you among us,' to which ʿĀmir responded, 'May God rather have many like you among us.' When asked to explain these kind words, ʿĀmir stated in part, 'They [i.e., *mawālī*] pave our roads, they mend our sandals and they weave our clothes.' For this, see *al-ʿIqd al-Farīd*, vol. 3, pp. 361–62; ET taken from Boullata, *The Unique Necklace*, vol. 3, p. 307.

[26] Abū al-Makārim, *Taʾrīkh al-kanāʾis wa-ʾl-adyira*, vol. 2, p. 137 (fols. 102a–102b). ET in Evetts, trans., *The Churches & Monasteries of Egypt*, pp. 278–79. For this, cf. Smith, *The Way of the Mystics*, p. 122.

conquests loom as one of the largest and most convenient boundary markers in world history. The seventh century has traditionally been seen as being a time of great discontinuity and transformation, a time of beginnings and endings: the end of the ancient world, the death of the classical city, the end of Rome and the beginning of Byzantium, the beginning of Islam. And so on. But the story I have attempted to tell has been one of cultural continuity. The continuity I have tried to suggest existed (and which still exists) can perhaps most clearly be illustrated by another example, pointed out by Goitein long ago in a little-cited yet fascinating article.

There exists, Goitein showed, a large number of common proverbs shared by Arabic speakers from the Gulf to Morocco; these have been sedulously recorded and documented by scholars and anthropologists. Somewhat similarly, in the medieval period, Muslim scholars collected and wrote down thousands of classical Arabic proverbs, often pre-Islamic in origin. A comparison of these medieval collections of proverbs with their modern counterparts from all over the Arab world shows that there is almost no overlap at all between the two large bodies of material. The pre-Islamic and classical Arabic proverb has had no afterlife in modern Arabic-speaking societies.

What is striking, however, is that there is considerable overlap between the proverbs used in modern Arabic-speaking societies and the pre-Islamic Near Eastern proverbs that one finds recorded in Hebrew and Aramaic in Jewish sources. These pre-Islamic proverbs, Goitein stressed, were not specifically Jewish but were rather part of a stock of proverbs common to all throughout the Middle East before the advent of Islam. What is especially fascinating is that originally Aramaic proverbs occur in roughly the same percentages in Arabic-speaking countries with no Aramaic background (like Yemen or Egypt or in the Maghrib) as they do in countries where Arabic replaced Aramaic as the language of the common people. This points, Goitein suggested, to an early appropriation by Arabic speakers of the pre-Islamic Near Eastern heritage. The larger import of his discovery of a continuity between modern Arabic proverbs and pre-Islamic Aramaic and Hebrew proverbs and a simultaneous discontinuity between modern Arabic proverbs and classical Arabic proverbs is worth keeping in mind: 'The new society of the Middle Eastern civilization,' he wrote, 'differed widely from anything that had preceded it, but still had much more in common with the Hellenized Aramaic speaking Ancient East than with the Bedouin civilization of pre-Islamic Arabia.'[27]

[27] All of this information can be found in Goitein's article 'The Present-Day Arabic Proverb as a Testimony to the Social History of the Middle East,' in S. D. Goitein, *Studies in Islamic History and Institutions* (Leiden, 1968), pp. 361–79. Quote taken from p. 379.

A moment's reflection will bear out the utterly unsurprising nature of Goitein's conclusion: although the Aramaic-, Coptic-, and Greek-speaking majority population of the Middle East fades to the background or fades away completely in our histories of the region after the Arab conquests (and even before), it did not disappear. The Middle East is still populated with its descendants, though many, if not most of them, no longer identify with these forbears. Nevertheless, the ghost of the deceased later Roman world can be readily seen in medieval Islam, dwelling in what were Rome's wealthiest and most important provinces. And those with eyes to see will recognize that the later Roman world never really died.

In writing about the eastern background to Byzantine hagiography, the great Bollandist Paul Peeters wrote of a Late Antique *Syrie bilingue*, a place where stories of Aramaic-speaking saints were effortlessly Hellenized and transferred into Greek. The movement of stories across linguistic frontiers was not, Peeters argued, the result of the efforts of a school or the activities of a certain library. It was the outcome of a shared life between Greek speakers and Aramaic speakers: 'Ce fut plutôt une conséquence de la symbiose qui avait réuni sur le meme territoire deux ou plusieurs races différentes,' he wrote. 'Les influences dont elles ont béneficié ou pâti l'une et l'autre se sont produites par un jeu naturel de la vie.'[28] Byzantine and oriental hagiography, composed in separate languages, had a deceptive, *prima facie* difference: the closer one looked, the more similarities one found between them,

> la séparation suffisamment nette si on la réduit à la question des langues, le paraît moins quand on essaie d'entrer un peu plus avant dans le fond des choses. En beaucoup d'endroits, la frontière commune se réduit à une ligne fictive, ou plutôt elle s'élargit en une zone indécise, sur laquelle les deux cultures ont un droit égal ou peu s'en faut. La diplomatie appellerait cela un *condominium*.[29]

In other words, late Roman Syria was a place where linguistic frontiers did not translate into cultural boundaries. The Arab conquests of the seventh century did not change this; instead, the prestige their new scripture enjoyed added a third literary language, Arabic, to the mix of a region with an already

[28] 'This was rather a consequence of the symbiosis that had brought together in the same territory two or more different races. The influences from which they benefitted or which they both underwent took place through a natural interplay of life.' See Peeters, *Le tréfonds oriental de l'hagiographie byzantine*, p. 71.

[29] 'The distinction, clear enough if one reduces it to the question of languages, seems less when one attempts to enter in a bit more deeply into things. In many places, the common border is reduced to a fictional line, or instead, it widens out into an indistinct area in which the two cultures have equal rights—or just about. Diplomacy would call this a *condominium*.' See Peeters, *Le tréfonds oriental de l'hagiographie byzantine*, p. 137.

rich history of intercultural exchange. Peeter's *Syrie bilingue* became a *Syrie trilingue*. There was no clean break. There was nothing like a mass ideological change. Religious dynamics continued as they had for centuries—viewed against the background of post-Chalcedonian Christian-Christian interaction, the scope and nature of Christian-Muslim interaction looks very familiar. This was not a new game: the playbook and objectives were the same. Short-term, the biggest change was that a new player had joined the field; long-term, that player's political power would eventually change the game, but the game, to extend the metaphor, would dramatically change the player as more people joined his team and as he learned to play with and against more seasoned competitors.

In trying to place the existence of the Middle East's population of simple Christians not just into this story, but at its center, it has been my hope to capture some of the excitement and interest of this process in a way that does justice to all of the people living there, not just a small subset of them. And thereby perhaps, in some small way, to affect how we understand it today. For '[t]he simple, indeed,' as Tertullian wrote, '... always constitute the majority of believers.'[30] To ignore the simple is not only to engage in an elitist retelling of the past. It is to miss the largest part of the story.

[30] *Simplices enim quique, ne dixerim imprudentes et idiotae, quae maior semper credentium pars est....* Tertullian, *Against Praxeas* 3. (Latin text available in E. Evans, *Q. Septimii Florentis Tertulliani Adversus Praxean liber. Tertullian's treatise against Praxeas* [London, 1948], p. 91 = 132 [ET]; I have used the ET by P. Holmes taken from ANF, vol. 3: *Latin Christianity: Its Founder, Tertullian*, pp. 598–99).

APPENDIX I

Approaching the Sources

Fully dealing with the question of sources I have used here would take an entire book (or perhaps several books).[1] Rather than add extensive additional material to a volume that is already rather lengthy, I will try to offer here some comments on the approach to sources that I have taken in these pages.

This book centers around a series of related problems: how we think about the full spectrum of religious believers and adherents in the late antique and early medieval Middle East; how non-elite Christians related to the teachings and symbols of their tradition and how they related to the religious claims of their communal leaders and political rulers; what conversion of these non-elites to the religious tradition of their rulers will have meant; the effects of mass conversion at the end of Muḥammad's life on Christian-Muslim relations and the shape Islam came to have; and how the demographic Muslim minority, elite and non-, of the Middle East related to the traditions of the autochthonous majority population of the region.

In attempting to investigate these questions, I have found it most helpful to separate questions of literary and theological influence, authenticity, and historical usefulness. These three issues are, to be sure, all of greatest interest and also in some ways related. But they are not the same thing. And confusing or conflating them ultimately will hobble the task of historical inquiry and make answering the questions that have interested me impossible. Underlying the research in this book are, therefore, several basic assumptions: Texts can be literary or theological and still be 'true,' pointing to a world beyond the page. They can likewise be inauthentic—that is, in an Islamic context, a statement or an action can be attributed to a person who never actually did or said it—but nevertheless communicate important social realities and attitudes; and for this reason they may be considered historically reliable and historically useful.

[1] Indeed, such books have been written, though no single volume fully covers the period and precise subjects I have been concerned with in this book. Nevertheless, see e.g., Hoyland, *Seeing Islam*; L. Brubaker and J. Haldon, *Byzantium in the Iconoclast Era (ca. 680-850): The Sources* (Aldershot, 2001); J. D. Howard-Johnston, *Witnesses to a World Crisis: Historians and Histories of the Middle East in the Seventh Century* (Oxford/New York, 2010). Less comprehensive is the recent, Penn, *When Christians First Met Muslims*, which focuses only on Syriac sources that refer to Muslims. Mention can also be made of the monumental series, *Christian-Muslim Relations: a Bibliographical History*, edited by David Thomas.

Let me take one example from this current book to illustrate my methodological assumptions and their possible concomitant perils. A historian interested in how early followers of the Prophet related to Christian rituals, Christian symbols, Christian holy men, and the religiously rooted ways of dealing with illness that were well established in the Christian community by the time of the arrival of Arab rule, might point to a story in the *vita* of Theodota of Amid (d. AD 698), likely an early eighth-century text, where we find this Christian holy man restoring a Muslim's ability to walk and also healing a Muslim official's sight. On this basis, he or she might suggest that members of the Prophet's community from an early period sought help from Christian figures reputed to have healing powers.[2] A critical reader of just this one piece of hagiography might be tempted to write the incident off as a *topos*—after all, perhaps the most famous incident in all of Syriac hagiography was the story of Jesus promising to send a disciple to heal Abgar, the ruler of Edessa,[3] and various healing stories from the Bible could also be adduced as possibly providing inspiration.[4] A similar reaction might be expected if the story of John of Daylam, another seventh-century Christian holy man, healing the son of the Umayyad Caliph ʿAbd al-Malik were cited in an attempt to answer this question.[5] John of Daylam was an East Syrian, it could be pointed out, and there was a long pre-Islamic tradition of stories about East Syrian holy men healing people in power.[6] Even though the examples of Theodota and John appear in roughly contemporary texts written in different ecclesiastical traditions—Miaphysite and East Syrian—and date, relatively speaking, from quite early in the period of Arab rule, it might be asserted that we are dealing with nothing but well-established Christian hagiographic *topoi*, being applied now in Islamic contexts.

In the face of such concerns, it might then be countered that Jacob of Edessa (d. AD 708), another contemporary of Theodota and John of Daylam, fielded a question from one of his correspondents who wanted to know whether it was appropriate for a Christian priest to provide the blessings of the saints or

[2] See chapter 12, n. 51 (ability to walk); n. 42 (sight).

[3] On this story, see H.J.W. Drijvers, 'The Abgar Legend,' in W. Schneemelcher, ed., *New Testament Apocrypha*, vol. 1: *Gospels and Related Writings*. Trans. R. McL. Wilson. Rev. ed. (Louisville/London, 1991), pp. 492–500, and B. Chevallier-Caseau, 'La lettre de Jésus à Abgar d'Édesse,' in F.-M. Humann and J.-N. Pérès, eds., *Apocryphes chrétiens des premiers siècles. Mémoire et traditions* (Paris, 2009), pp. 15–45.

[4] For stories of Jesus healing people in positions of power, see Matthew 8:5–13 and John 4:43–54. For a non-Jew seeking healing from Jesus, see Matthew 15:21–28. The story of Naaman and Elisha (2 Kings 5) also comes to mind.

[5] See chapter 12, n. 56.

[6] See chapter 12, n. 58.

a special kind of anointing oil to Muslims or pagans in a healing context.[7] But how do we know, it will be asked, that this question asked of Jacob reflects reality? Jacob's canons (about which I will say more in a moment), represent, it will be alleged, hypothetical situations, or reflect his own self-aggrandizing agenda, or are simply extreme cases and have nothing to do with reality.

In response, additional evidence can then be supplied, now from Muslim sources: the story of an Umayyad prince healed by a Christian doctor,[8] for example, or the fact that the story of John of Daylam's healing of the famous al-Ḥajjāj b. Yūsuf is possibly alluded to in another Islamic text.[9] When the Caliph al-Manṣūr fell ill in AD 765 (AH 148), did he not summon Jurjis b. Jibrīl, a Christian doctor from Jundishapur, for treatment?[10] But, it may be countered, we cannot trust any specific story—Christians had a reputation for being doctors more generally and were prominent doctors at the Sasanian court in the pre-Islamic period; these Islamic texts are merely echoing what are literary *topoi* common in Christian texts. After all, didn't Jesus promise to send someone to heal Abgar?

And so it goes. This imagined back-and-forth is something of a caricature for the purposes of *reductio ad absurdum*. As a parlor game or an exercise in a graduate seminar, such exchanges can have their own amusements and be pedagogically useful. For a time-tested (and easy) mode of scholarly critique is simply to argue that someone with whom one disagrees has misread his or her sources, or has read them in a naïve manner, or that he or she has not been fully aware of this or that authorial agenda or of the conventions of a certain genre. No scholar wants to be pinned with the charge of credulity in the use of evidence, of confusing literary convention with reality, of engaging in eisegesis rather than exegesis, of understanding a trope in a crudely literal fashion, or of taking a fiction composed centuries after an event as illustrating an actual event or phenomena from an earlier period.

Acknowledging these pitfalls, however, this imagined exchange can point to another one: the dangers of what might be called literary Pyrrhonism when it comes to reading our sources.[11] This is the excess, as it were, to the defect

[7] See chapter 12, n. 62.

[8] See chapter 12, n. 60.

[9] See chapter 12, n. 59.

[10] Ibn Abī Uṣaybi'a, *'Uyūn al-anbā' fī ṭabaqāt al-aṭibbā'*, pp. 183–84. On Jurjis, see also chapter 11, n. 23, above.

[11] Nowhere can this tendency be seen so clearly as in New Testament studies, where the move from showing that a text is literary in nature, contains allusions, or employs typology, to arguing that it is non-historical is a familiar one. See, e.g., Rudolf Bultmann's use of literary analysis to dissolve the historicity of nearly the entire Passion narrative of the Synoptics in *The History of the Synoptic Tradition* (New York, 1963), pp. 262–84, and John Dominic Crossan's explanation of what he means by 'prophecy

of credulity. And here the above exchange can lead us to an important distinction: while literary analysis is a valuable tool, literary skepticism is a dead end if one wants to write social history or to do something other than establish textual filiations, study a specific philological question, examine a particular genre of writing, or engage in discursive and literary analysis. It needs to be emphasized that though our surviving texts are often saturated in *topoi*, tropes, and allusions, the mere presence of these and other literary devices does not mean that a particular event or phenomenon never occurred.[12] More broadly, recognizing the literary nature of the texts we have does not preclude their use as historical sources.[13] To argue the contrary would be to make any attempt at large-scale synthesis exceedingly difficult, if not impossible, for places and periods lacking in rich supplies of documentary evidence—that is to say, for

---

historicized,' in *Who Killed Jesus: Exposing the Roots of Anti-Semitism in the Gospel Story of the Death of Jesus* (San Francisco, 1995), pp. 1–6. For this and for further discussion of Crossan, Bultmann, and others' views of the historicity of the Passion narratives, see D. C. Allison, Jr., *Constructing Jesus: Memory, Imagination, and History* (Grand Rapids, 2010), pp. 387–92. It is no coincidence that John Wansbrough, whose skeptical views towards the reliability of the early Islamic tradition have been among the most notable in recent decades, was indebted in his approach to biblical scholarship.

[12] Like a green bay tree, this idea has spread and indeed flourished in many quarters of scholarship. But its wide acceptance does not increase its plausibility. The move from recognizing a text as literary to concluding that it is therefore not historical is only persuasive on the questionable assumption that authors and historical actors could not consciously use allusions and tropological or typological framing in their own self-representation or in their writing about important figures or events. The truth of such an assumption, however, is by no means obvious. To use a contemporary example: Would identifying the clear allusions in George W. Bush's use of the phrase 'Axis of Evil'—to a World War II alliance and to the language Ronald Reagan used to speak of the Soviet Union—be sufficient grounds to argue that Bush never used this phrase or made a speech employing it? Simply to point out the literary nature of a text or the existence of a trope, *topos*, or allusion is not enough to prove that something never occurred. And it is *a fortiori* far from sufficient in arguing against the value of using a literary text for the purposes of social history. Cf. the observation in D. C. Allison, Jr., *The New Moses: A Matthean Typology* (Minneapolis, 1993), pp. 267, esp. n. 321: '. . . the presence of a typology does not, despite widespread presumption to the contrary, settle, without further ado, the historical question. Typology did often contribute to fictional narratives (as in *4 Ezra*). But it also sometimes *interpreted* historical facts. Notwithstanding Eusebius's Moses typology, Constantine did win a dramatic victory at the Milvian bridge; and Gregory of Nyssa's eulogy of his brother Basil, full of *synkrisis*, is an eye-witness account.' See, too, *Constructing Jesus*, p. 389 ('To biblicize is not necessarily to invent.'), and see further Allison's discussion of the allusive nature of Christian and Jewish texts in *Scriptural Allusions in the New Testament: Light from the Dead Sea Scrolls* (North Richland Hills, Tex., 2000), pp. 1–8, in particular, the use of allusive language in the speeches of Martin Luther King, Jr. What would we make of a scholar who argued for their nonhistoricity on the basis of their at times highly allusive nature?

A phenomenon often driving inferences from the literary nature of a text to its nonhistorical status (usually followed by an assumption that ahistorical means 'not useful for historical reconstruction'), is a certain scholarly fondness for 'parallelomania.' On this impulse, see Samuel Sandmel's classic, 'Parallelomania,' *Journal of Biblical Literature* 81 (1962), pp. 1–13.

[13] H. I. Marrou's discussion in *Le pédagogue [par] Clement d'Alexandrie.* Livre I. *Texte grec* (SC 70) (Paris, 1960), pp. 87–91, is a model for showing how a text that might be regarded *prima facie* as highly rhetorical and of little worth for historical reconstruction can be shown to have real historical value.

most places outside of Egypt in the pre-Ottoman Middle East. All that is solid would threaten to melt into air.

Conscious of the literary nature of the texts I have used, I have done my best throughout the book to make a cumulative case: to assemble as much evidence as possible, from as many sources as possible, to support my arguments, with the hope that it will become evident that we are dealing with more than just a collection of artlessly and uncritically reified examples of *topoi*, rhetorical artifices, and theological agendas. The thickness of the evidence across time, place, and language is evidence itself for historical veridicality. Our texts point to social realities.[14]

* * *

A few examples from the present work will give a fuller picture of this cumulative approach. In this book, I have attempted to put everyday, ordinary, non-elite Christians at the center of my story. But these people have, by definition, left us no sources that we might draw upon. We cannot hear their voices and must rely on the words and descriptions of sometimes hostile, patronizing, or unsympathetic religious elites to describe them. Is not our picture therefore distorted?

This issue of lost voices and unsympathetic representation is not unique to this particular subject: the study of slaves[15] in late antiquity is a notable example with many of the same challenges. Similarly, relative to their proportion of the population of the late Roman world, we have what amounts to a lamentably small handful of texts written by women,[16] and in an adjoining period, we have very little first-hand material from the peasants who formed the great mass of the population of medieval Europe.[17] None of this, however, means

[14] Dale Allison's approach to recovering the teaching of the historical Jesus is useful to think with, by analogy: 'certain themes, motifs, and rhetorical strategies recur again and again throughout the primary sources,' he has written, 'and it must be in those themes and motifs and rhetorical strategies—which, taken together, leave some distinct impressions—if it is anywhere, that we will find memory.' See Allison, *Constructing Jesus*, pp. 15–17 (quote at 15). See further Allison's comments on his method, as well as his critique of the traditional criteria used by New Testament scholars looking for 'authentic' sayings of Jesus in *The Historical Christ and the Theological Jesus* (Grand Rapids/Cambridge, 2009), pp. 54–78. Allison's ideas are very suggestive and provide a way forward for other areas outside of New Testament which are, as it were, haunted by questions of authenticity.

[15] Note the observation in Harper, *Slavery in the Late Roman World*, p. 22.

[16] Cf. the remarks in A. Kadel, *Matrology: A Bibliography of Writings by Christian Women from the First to the Fifteenth Centuries* (New York, 1995), and see his listing of late antique Christian works written by women, pp. 31–50. Even if extant writings by non-Christian women from this period are included, the amount of written material we have from what was half of the population of the late antique world is almost vanishingly small.

[17] See P. Freedman, *Images of the Medieval Peasant* (Stanford, 1999), p. 8.

that we should hold back from writing about slaves, women, or peasants in this period or any other—and indeed scholars have not refrained from doing so. In much the same way, the lack of material written by members of the illiterate agrarian majority of the late Roman and early medieval Middle East does not mean seeking to capture something of their attitudes and behaviors is impossible. It means only that we must find ways to access such people indirectly.[18]

The way to do so is not mysterious, and I have already alluded to it above: it is to put a wide array of sources, of as many types as possible, into conversation with one another so that together they yield an idea of how such people related to, understood, and made use of the symbols, teachings, and norms of the religious traditions to which they belonged. This is precisely what I have attempted, however imperfectly, to do. The sources that are available to us for such a task are the ones I have tried to utilize—canonical material, saints' lives, letters, historical chronicles, and more. Within these, a certain hierarchy may be said to exist: some texts may bring us closer to the 'simple' than others. Graffiti, certain kinds of papyri, or the famous lead curse tablets from Bath can bring us closer to the everyday world of an ordinary, non-elite inhabitant of the Roman empire, for example, than a highly rhetorical text written in a linguistic register that few will have had the training to fully understand or appreciate. In the context of this book, it is Jacob of Edessa's canonical material that is particularly useful for getting a sense for what was happening among ordinary Christians 'on the ground.'

The behaviors this material records so vividly is unique in its specificity, so far as I can tell, in the early medieval Middle East for helping to form a detailed profile of the behaviors engaged in by ordinary Christians (and the reactions these provoked in religious leaders). Such a profile can in turn help us evaluate, understand, and use material related to simple, non-elite religious believers found in other sources. To take an example from the research and writing of this book: my understanding of the *vita* of Theodota of Amid, a north Syrian contemporary of Jacob's, has been deeply influenced by reading Jacob's canonical *responsa*. Many of the same issues of confessional identity that appear in Jacob show up also in Theodota's *vita*, a text perhaps written around end of Jacob's life. I read Jacob's canonical material in both printed

[18] See the observations on this problem and apposite prescriptions in Haldon, *The Empire That Would Not Die*, pp. 57–58, and note also Weber's observation about a similar problem in *Peasants into Frenchmen*, pp. xi–xii. Peter Burke's discussion of the challenges of accessing the 'elusive quarry' of early modern popular culture in Europe and the use of 'oblique approaches' to do so is also useful to think with; see his *Popular Culture in Early Modern Europe*, rev. ed., (Aldershot/Burlington, Vt., 1994), pp. 65–87.

editions and unedited manuscript form, having previously read Theodota's *Life* in manuscript as well. After reading through Jacob's canonical *responsa*, I returned to the *Life* of Theodota and saw it in a different light. I saw other texts differently, too. Jacob's *responsa* raised for me in a striking manner the issue of how ordinary believers navigated confessional differences; reading across a wide variety of sources with this particular question in mind, I realized that the same sorts of issues Jacob dealt with regularly appear in quite a number of other texts. Much of the evidence I found is gathered in the pages of this book.

But do Jacob's questions disclose information about the world of Jacob's mind or actual events in the world in which Jacob lived? I have now given a partial answer: taken on their own, one might suggest that the canons should be understood as exaggerated or reflecting the inner life of an obstreperous and obsessed churchman who wanted to play up differences between different Christian groups[19] or, alternatively, that Jacob chose extreme examples so as to illustrate rules and norms as clearly as possible.[20] But taken alongside corroborating material from additional sources, that is, other saints' *vitae*, chronicles, letters, and other church canons—in other words, the sorts of evidence I adduce over the course of the book—we have, I suggest, reason to believe that Jacob is a reasonably reliable source for information about how some non-elite Christians were behaving in the seventh and eighth centuries.

Moreover, Jacob's biography, I attempt to argue in Chapter 3, suggests that church discipline (and rules more generally, as can be seen in his *Letter on Orthography* or his writing of a grammar of Syriac) was of great concern to him. That he was reported to have clashed with clergy under his authority while bishop over their uncanonical actions, drove people out of the church on account of their behavior, and ultimately quit his position as bishop of Edessa in anger at the patriarch Julian's lax attitude toward the enforcement of church discipline, all point to the seriousness with which he took the implementation of church norms. Jacob's strict notion of canonical discipline offers a partial explanation, as well, for why we have the quantity of material from him that we do. It was a topic that exercised him and he wrote about it.

Two further points support the contention that Jacob's canons are rightly viewed as reflecting actual behaviors. The first is that most of what are referred to as Jacob's 'canons' are not really canons at all. To be sure, Jacob did issue prescriptive regulations in an attempt to order the behavior of the Christians

[19] A possibility suggested to me by Robert Hoyland.

[20] A possibility suggested to me by Uriel Simonsohn.

under his spiritual authority,[21] and the medieval tradition would later refer to Jacob's rule-making writings as 'canons,' even excerpting and transmitting them in canonical collections.[22] Nevertheless, most of Jacob's 'canons' are more accurately answers to questions that were asked to him in letters written by correspondents.[23] What is more, the information they convey about actual behaviors is most typically contained not in his answers but in the questions that Jacob's correspondents asked; the behaviors were not reported by Jacob himself. Jacob's response is usually (and predictably) to condemn whatever activity is at issue.

It cannot simply be argued that Jacob's questioners were inventions, either: we know almost nothing about Addai the Priest, but the manner in which he is described is very similar to how Jacob's other correspondents are spoken of in his other letters, as well as how the correspondents are described in our closest set of Syriac epistolary comparanda—the letters of George of the Arabs, Jacob's younger contemporary and possibly his student. John, the Stylite of Litarb, Jacob's other major correspondent[24] on canonical questions, is a figure whom we do know about from other sources: he corresponded with George of the Arabs, and composed his own works in Syriac, some of which we still possess in independent form. One of these is a letter in which he himself answers questions that were asked of him by a priest.[25] In other words, Jacob, a prominent bishop and leader, was writing answers to real people in leadership positions—a priest and an intellectually active stylite—about questions they asked him regarding the appropriateness of a variety of activities, many of which we can find similar examples of in other texts.

The second reason for treating Jacob's canons as reliable sources of information is a diachronic one: there is abundant evidence throughout the history of Christianity in the Middle East (and outside of it), down to the present, for

[21] These are prefaced in Harvard Syriac 93, fol. 18a, and Mardin 310, fol. 208a, with the rubric 'of the venerable Jacob, on his own' and 'of Jacob, on his own,' respectively. That is, they are rules he issued not in response to a question posed to him.

[22] See the fundamental discussion of the nature of Jacob's canonical material and its transformation by the later tradition in Teule, 'Jacob of Edessa and Canon Law,' pp. 86–90. Cf. also Hoyland, *Seeing Islam*, pp. 605–606.

[23] See the short and helpful discussion in Penn, *When Christians First Met Muslims*, pp. 160–61. Note Penn's positive assessment of the historical value of Jacob's canonical responses.

[24] Jacob's correspondents on canonical questions also included Thomas the Hermit and Abraham the Hermit; see most conveniently Kaufhold, 'Sources of Canon Law in the Eastern Churches,' p. 249. On Jacob's correspondence wth Abraham, see A. Vööbus, 'The Discovery of New Cycles of Canons and Resolutions Composed by Ja'qōb of Edessa,' *OCP* 34 (1968), p. 419; Hoyland, *Seeing Islam*, p. 610; and Vööbus, *The Synodicon in the West Syrian Tradition I* (CSCO 368: SS 162), pp. 233–34. In this book, however, I have drawn most extensively on Jacob's answers to questions posed by Addai and John.

[25] See chapter 8, n. 7.

the occurrence of the sorts of behavior that Jacob condemns. Be it fourth-century Egypt,[26] sixth-century Egypt,[27] sixth- and seventh-century Egypt,[28] eighteenth-century Egypt,[29] the late Ottoman Middle East more generally,[30] or areas outside the Middle East, such as sixth-century Iberia[31] or early modern Europe,[32] in environments characterized by a plurality of Christian confessions, partitioning members of rival groups off from one another has regularly proven to be difficult. Looking at late antique evidence from Syria in the light of the experience of other contexts suggests that the behaviors depicted in canonical material were indeed actual possibilities and can be taken as evidence for social realities. They need not be relegated to the realm of pure discourse. Indeed, anyone familiar with Christian communities in the contemporary Middle East and their relations with one another on a day-to-day basis at the lay level will not find anything terribly surprising in the picture that emerges in Jacob's canonical responses.[33] A similar point can be made about Jacob's consternation

[26] See B. Palme, 'Political Identity versus Religious Distinction? The Case of Egypt in the Later Roman Empire,' in W. Pohl, C. Ganter, and R. Payne, eds., *Visions of Community in the Post-Roman World: The West, Byzantium and the Islamic World, 300-1100* (Farnham, Surrey/Burlington, Vt., 2012), p. 89, for the example of the fourth-century bishop Theodorus who shifted from Nicene to Arian, and then back to Nicene Christianity over the course of several decades.

[27] Palme, 'Political Identity versus Religious Distinction?,' pp. 90–91, gives the example of Eulogius, a sixth-century Melitian monk who became Orthodox and who, while Orthodox, sold his monk's cell to Melitian monks. Compare with the *Canons* of Ps.-Athanasius, dated between 350 and 500, which forbid Orthodox churches from singing 'the writings of Meletius and of the ignorant' (ET 24). The canons also forbid priests from giving communion to 'wizards or conjurers or soothsayers' and order the doorkeepers of churches to seat these types with the catechumens if they enter a service; these doorkeepers are also charged with watching the outer door of the church to make sure that 'they that enter in unto the church may have no community with the enemies of the church,' a seeming reference to Melitians. See Ps.-Athanasius, *Canons* 12, 25 (ed. W. Riedel and W. E. Crum, *The Canons of Athanasius of Alexandria* [London, 1904], pp. 18, 23–24 [Arabic] = 24, 30 [ET]; I have used Riedel's translation).

[28] See Wipszycka, 'How Insurmountable Was the Chasm between Monophysites and Chalcedonians?'.

[29] On Copts and Catholics, see Armanios, *Coptic Christianity in Ottoman Egypt*, pp. 131, 136–38.

[30] See the various examples in L. Valensi, 'Inter-communal Relations and Changes in Religious Affiliation in the Middle East (Seventeenth to Nineteenth Centuries),' *Comparative Studies in Society and History* 39 (1997), pp. 255–60.

[31] See the rich evidence for Nicene-Arian boundary crossing in Iberia collected in M. Lester, 'The Word as Lived: The Practice of Orthodoxy in Early Medieval Iberia, c. 500–711,' (PhD diss., Princeton University, 2017), chapter 1.

[32] See B. J. Kaplan, *Divided by Faith: Religious Conflict and the Practice of Toleration in Early Modern Europe* (Cambridge, Mass., 2007), pp. 237–332, for various types of confessional coexistence, on a day-to-day level, in confessionally mixed areas of early modern Europe.

[33] In addition to the abundant anecdotal confirmation offered by one's personal experience (and that of many friends and family) to confirm this assertion, written examples of elite consternation at such interactions are not hard to find, either. See, e.g., A. Badrāwī, 'al-Kanīsa al-Urthūduksiyya tarfuḍ itmām zawāj Qibṭī li-khidmatihi fī 'l-Injīliyya,' 24 October 2016, (http://www.shorouknews.com/news/view.aspx?cdate=24102016&id=f65f854c-0297-4a78-9981-ca339c1a5966), reporting a case in which the

over things like Christians engaging in divinatory practices or the evidence his *responsa* provide for Christians and Muslims leading lives that intersected in various ways. It is not difficult to find similar practices and patterns of behavior throughout Christian history and throughout the history of Christian-Muslim relations.[34]

If the evidence in Jacob's canons is taken in isolation, therefore, one might be tempted to write it off or downplay it as exaggerated, hypothetical, literary, or in some way not representative of the situation among ordinary Christians. But read in the light of an abundance of other texts from the period and, even more broadly, in the light of the entirety of Christian history, what we find in Jacob's canons does not seem unique. In fact, read in light of Christian history writ large, one would expect the sorts of behaviors that Jacob condemns to be taking place, given that he was living in a confessionally plural environment and in a period when the various rival Christian communities had not yet fully solidified and indeed, were still forming.[35] We are fortunate that such a rich record of their occurrence has been preserved in his writings.

Homilies can serve as another illustration of my approach to using literary sources as historical evidence. It goes without saying that sermons are, by definition, highly rhetorical in nature, and that we must be careful in using them as sources for social history. And yet, there is a long tradition of doing just this.[36] Chrysostom in particular has for over a century been recognized as providing an especially rich supply of information on all aspects of everyday life, and though the biases in his preaching are clear, it has nevertheless been argued that his reporting of social realities is reliable.[37] To take one example

---

Coptic Orthodox Church refused to allow a man to be married in the Orthodox church due to complaints that the man had been active in the Evangelical church. This, despite the fact that the man had already completed parts of the marriage process in Orthodox institutions.

[34] On divination, in addition to Chapter 9, nn. 18–30, see e.g., Armanios, *Coptic Christianity in Ottoman Egypt*, pp. 143–45. T. de Bruyn, *Making Amulets Christian: Artefacts, Scribes, and Contexts* (Oxford, 2017), pp. 17–42, is a rich discussion of conflicting Christian attitudes toward and use of amulets and incantations. On Christian-Muslim interaction, see e.g., Chapter 12, n. 160.

[35] Jacob's life, which likely spanned much of the seventh century and ended in 708, witnessed, in addition to the rise of Islam, the Monothelete controversy, which split the Chalcedonian church of Syria into rival and competing groups.

[36] W. Mayer, 'Homiletics,' in S. A. Harvey and D. G. Hunter, eds., *The Oxford Handbook of Early Christian Studies* (Oxford, 2008), pp. 566–67, lists notable studies that draw upon homilies for 'social and cultural information.' David W. Sabean's observation, 'Anyone who has sat in church long enough knows how difficult it is to draw conclusions about the social life of parishoners from the message of the preacher,' is much too pessimistic (see *Power in the Blood: Popular Culture and Village Discourse in Early Modern Germany* [New York, 1984], p. 199); one might argue, in fact, that the opposite is true.

[37] J. M. Vance, *Beiträge zur Byzantinischen Kulturgeschichte am Ausgange des IV. Jahrhunderts aus den Schriften des Johannes Chrysostomus* (Jena, 1907), p. 3, listed various 'Tendenzen' and emphases in Chrysostom's preaching but also affirmed that 'In seinen Schilderungen zeigt es sich aber klar, dass er

from this book: did John Chrysostom exaggerate when he charged his congregation with having Christian books but not reading them?

We can grant that there is good evidence that early church leaders exhorted Christians to read edifying material privately,[38] and also allow that John's statement should not be taken completely literally and applied to everyone in his audience, but nevertheless still make room for the suggestion that merely possessing Christian books was no guarantee that the relatively small percentage of Christians who could read were in fact reading them. We can even hold out the likelihood that a significant portion of them were in fact not reading them. And at least three points should incline us to believe that John was motivated by something other than rhetorical and hortatory conceit when he made this charge. First, there is the sheer fact that he would even make such a complaint in a public sermon, to a real audience; second, there is the fact that he made it in more than one sermon;[39] and third, like grumbling about confessional boundary crossing or the use of divination, the lament that Christians lacked interest in reading the Bible is one that can be found in other late antique and medieval authors as well.[40]

Hagiographic narratives can serve as a final illustration of my approach. As with homilies, there is a strong tradition of scholars drawing upon the *vitae* of saints for insights into the social world of the late antique and early medieval periods.[41] It is also undeniable that hagiographic works can be highly literary, frequently filled with tropes, and colored by the theological aims of

---

die Tatsachen selber nicht falsch angibt. Die Tatsachen sind vielmehr die Ausgangspunkte, an welche er seine Ermahnungen anknüpft.'

[38] See the discussion in Gamble, *Books and Readers*, pp. 231–37, and note his conclusion, p. 237. Harnack, *Bible Reading in the Early Church*, adduced extensive evidence to make such an argument, but for criticism of his Protestant biases and other problems in the work, see Gamble, *Books and Readers*, p. 332, n. 90.

[39] Harnack, *Bible Reading in the Early Church*, pp. 117–18 made this point, arguing in favor of taking these complaints as accurate. See a similar observation in Gamble, *Books and Readers*, p. 233.

[40] Harnack, *Bible Reading in the Early Church*, pp. 117–21, adduces examples from various authors. In addition to these, see the evidence cited above, chapter 1, nn. 64–66; see also Haines-Eitzen, *Guardians of Letters*, p. 26, for a non-Christian parallel.

[41] See, e.g., the classic discussion on hagiography and the writing of history in F. Graus, *Volk, Herrscher und Heiliger im Reich der Merowinger: Studien zur Hagiographie der Merowingerzeit* (Praha, 1965), pp. 13–139. R. Aigrain, *L'Hagiographie; ses sources, ses méthodes, son histoire* (Mayenne, 1953), remains the best introduction to the genre. S. A. Harvey, 'Martyr Passions and Hagiography,' in Harvey and Hunter, eds., *The Oxford Handbook of Early Christian Studies*, pp. 603–27, is a good overview of the history of the scholarly study and use of hagiography. E. Patlagean, 'Ancient Byzantine Hagiography and Social History,' in S. Wilson, ed., *Saints and their Cults: Studies in Religious Sociology, Folklore, and History* (Cambridge, 1983), pp. 101–22, is a fundamental discussion of hagiography and social history. On the question of history vs. hagiography, see also F. Lifshitz, 'Beyond Positivism and Genre: "Hagiographical" Texts as Historical Narrative,' *Viator* 25 (1994) pp. 95–113. I am grateful to Christian Sahner for some of these references.

their authors.[42] Acknowledging this, however, does not make them useless or otherwise drastically diminish their value for the historian concerned with things other than rhetorical or theological analyses. Like every other genre discussed in this appendix, such considerations mean only that we must be careful when we use these texts. The strategies I have outlined above in discussing other examples can help us here, too. We can recognize potential elements of exaggeration or literary shaping in the depiction of a particular anecdote, but at the same time affirm that the social reality it presents would have been recognized as possible and plausible to its audience. And we can, moreover, cite both synchronic and diachronic corroborating evidence which suggests that the phenomenon in question might reasonably have occurred.[43] To construe 'literary' to mean 'historically unreliable' or 'not useful for historical reconstruction' is to adopt a reductionist stance that impoverishes the resources we have available for understanding the past.

Let us now look at several concrete examples from this present work. How should we rate the reasonableness of John of Ephesus's depiction of Simeon the Mountaineer finding Christians in a mountain village who knew astonishingly little about Christianity, or the accuracy of Sophronius and John Moschus's description in the *vita* of John the Almsgiver of an area near Alexandria with no priests, no churches, and where the people had no real knowledge of Christianity? Allowing that John of Ephesus, Sophronius of Jerusalem, and John Moschus were all interested in more than providing sixth- or seventh-century ethnographies of Christian communities in non-urban or remote areas, the circumstances these anecdotes describe are precisely what we would expect in rural areas poorly served by clergy or far from strong episcopal oversight.

A more recent case may help to illustrate this point. The island of Socotra, off the coast of Yemen and Somalia, had a Christian population in the medieval

[42] For an example of a literary analysis of *vitae* and passion narratives, see A. G. Elliott, *Roads to Paradise: Reading the Lives of the Early Saints* (Hanover, N. Hamp., 1987). For three different and contrasting perspectives on the usefulness of hagiography in historical reconstruction, see D. Frankfurter, 'Hagiography and the Reconstruction of Local Religion in Late Antique Egypt: Memories, Inventions, and Landscapes,' J. van der Vliet, 'Bringing Home the Homeless: Landscape and History in Egyptian Hagiography,' and P. van Minnen, 'Saving History? Egyptian Hagiography in Its Space and Time,' in J. Dijkstra and M. van Dijk, eds., *The Encroaching Desert: Egyptian Hagiography and the Medieval West* (Leiden/Boston, 2006), pp. 13–37, 39–55, 57–91, respectively.

[43] Note the observation of John Haldon, *The Empire That Would Not Die*, p. 306, n. 15: 'Although many of these lives are full of literary topoi and rhetorical artifice and not to be taken at face value, they nevertheless reflected a recognizable reality for their listeners or readers, and there is no reason to doubt that the general situations they describe are more or less accurate.'

period whose origins went back as far as perhaps the fourth or fifth century.[44] By the early modern period, however, its Christian community had apparently fallen on hard times. 'Each village had a priest called *kashi*,' Francis Xavier wrote of it:

> No man could read. The *kashis* repeated prayers in a forgotten tongue, frequently scattering incense. A word like Alleluia often occurred. For bells they used wooden rattles. They assembled in their churches four times a day, and held St. Thomas in great veneration. The *kashis* married, but were very abstemious. They had two lents, and fasted from meat, milk, and fish.[45]

In 1615, speaking about the Christians of Socotra, Thomas Roe reported that his travel companion, Humpherey Boughton,

> saw an old Church of theirs in the way to Tamara, left desolate, the doore shut, but onely tyed, being desirious to enter it, the Sheck his guide told him it was full of Spirits, yet he adventured in and found an Altar with Images, and a crosse upon it, which he brought out, then the Shecke told him that they were people of another religion ....[46]

Another seventeenth-century traveler, the Italian priest Vincenzo Maria, has left us the last description we have of the Christians of Socotra. 'The people still retained a perfect jumble of rites and ceremonies,' he wrote,

> sacrificing to the moon, circumcising, and abominating wine and pork. They had churches called *moquame*, dark and dirty, and they daily anointed with butter an altar. They had a cross, which they carried in procession, and a candle. They assembled three times a day and three times a night; the priests were called *odambo*. ... If rain failed they selected a victim by lot and prayed round him to the moon, and if this failed they cut off his hands. All the women were called Maria.[47]

To be sure, such notices by highly educated Western Christians in the era of the Reformation and Counter-Reformation, outsiders who could not speak the local language and whose observations were inflected by their own prejudices

[44] See T. Bent and M.V.A. Bent, *Southern Arabia* (London, 1900), p. 344, and B. Doe, *Socotra: Island of Tranquility* (London, 1992), pp. 31–32.

[45] Quote taken from Bent and Bent, *Southern Arabia*, p. 355, and see Doe, *Socotra*, p. 32.

[46] S. Purchas, *Hakluytus Posthumus, or, Purchas his Pilgrimes*, vol. 4 (Glasgow, 1905), p. 321, and Doe, *Socotra*, p. 32. H. Yule, *Cathay and the Way Thither*, vol. 1 (London, 1866), p. 168, n. 4 (which covers pp. 168–70) offers a thorough résumé of travel reports relating to Socotra and its Christians.

[47] Quote taken from Bent and Bent, *Southern Arabia*, p. 355, and see Doe, *Socotra*, p. 32. The Italian text can be found in V. Maria, *Il viaggio all'Indie orientali* (Rome, 1672), p. 132.

and biases, present their own problems of interpretation. If we were able to somehow speak with these Christians in Socotra and gain a sort of insider's perspective on their religious life, we would likely find that their activities had an inner logic, purpose, and coherence that an unsympathetic clerical observer of the sixteenth or seventeenth century easily could miss.[48] Nevertheless, as with the late antique reports from the *vitae* of Simeon the Mountaineer and John the Almsgiver, these early modern reports highlight the fact that lay Christian communities in rural and remote places (or in the case of Socotra, far from what may be termed the Christian metropole), lacked access to the doctrinal and catechetical resources that were available in major centers of Christianity, and that this had consequences for their practice and understanding of the kind of Christianity more familiar in those centers.

The challenges of catechizing such out-of-the-way communities, seen in the *Life* of Simeon the Mountaineer, is also something we would expect. In a modern context, one can find non-religious parallels. In Yugoslavia in the 1930s, for instance, communists seeking to spread their ideas faced the problem of high rates of illiteracy among a peasant population, which acted as a barrier to people understanding what they were trying to communicate: 'It was a difficult task to present the party's program to this kind of audience, to adjust the Marxist-Leninist jargon to understandable concepts,' Jeléna Batinić observed, 'and to win over the local people for the Partisan cause.'[49] Simeon's *vita* is extremely valuable in part because it is portrays in a striking way how the geographical and educational limitations and challenges we know must have existed in rural areas may have looked to, and been understood by, Christian leaders in late antiquity.

* * *

So much for Christian sources. What now of Islamic ones? Early Islamic history is a period whose sources have been subject to levels of searching doubt and systematic scholarly incredulity unknown in fields of history outside of biblical studies. The problems swirling around early Islamic history—a function of a source-base that is late, tendentious, and contradictory—are in fact so well known, and the battles have been so hard fought, that there exists a small genre of literature whose aim it has been to review and evaluate various aspects

[48] We could also compare such accounts with other accounts of early modern Europeans encountering religious practices in places like Peru, India, or the Philippines to put these reports in a broader context.

[49] J. Batinić, *Women and Yugoslav Partisans: A History of World War II Resistance* (New York, 2015), pp. 33–35 (quote at 34).

of these controversies.[50] The works of scholars such as Ignaz Goldziher,[51] Henri Lammens,[52] Joseph Schacht,[53] John Wansbrough,[54] Patricia Crone,[55] Herbert Berg,[56] and others[57] have combined to form something like a Great Wall of Skepticism that circles around the first centuries of Islamic history, a wall that

[50] To give only a few examples, see F. E. Peters, 'The Quest of the Historical Muhammad,' *International Journal of Middle East Studies* 23 (1991), pp. 291–315; Humphreys, *Islamic History: A Framework for Inquiry*, pp. 69–103; J. Koren and Y. D. Nevo, 'Methodological Approaches to Islamic Studies,' *Der Islam* 68 (1991), pp. 87–107; Donner, *Narratives of Islamic Origins*, pp. 1–31 (the best single overview available); Donner, 'Modern Approaches to Early Islamic History,' in C. F. Robinson, ed., *The New Cambridge History of Islam*, vol. 1: *The Formation of the Islamic World, Sixth to Eleventh Centuries* (Cambridge/New York, 2010), pp. 625–47; C. Melchert, 'The Early History of Islamic Law,' in H. Berg, ed., *Method and Theory in the Study of Islamic Origins* (Leiden/Boston, 2003), pp. 293–324; H. Motzki, 'The Question of the Authenticity of Muslim Traditions Reconsidered: A Review Article,' in Berg, ed., *Method and Theory in the Study of Islamic Origins*, pp. 211–57; Motzki, 'Dating Muslim Traditions: A Survey,' *Arabica* 52 (2005), pp. 204–53; R. Hoyland, 'Writing the Biography of the Prophet Muhammad: Problems and Solutions,' *History Compass* 5 (2007), pp. 1–22; H. Berg, 'The Implications of, and Opposition to, the Methods and Theories of John Wansbrough,' *Method and Theory in the Study of Religion* 9 (1997), pp. 3–22; Berg, *The Development of Exegesis in Early Islam*, pp. 6–64; Berg, 'The Needle in the Haystack: Islamic Origins and the Nature of the Early Sources,' in C.A. Segovia and B. Lourié, eds., *The Coming of the Comforter: When, Where, and to Whom? Studies on the Rise of Islam in Memory of John Wansbrough* (Piscataway, N.J.: 2012), pp. 271–302; Berg, 'Failures (of Nerve?) in the Study of Islamic Origins,' in W. E. Arnal et al., eds., *Failure and Nerve in the Study of Religion: Working with Donald Wiebe* (London, 2012), pp. 112–28; Brown, *Hadith*, pp. 197–239; and S. J. Shoemaker, 'Muḥammad and the Qur'ān,' in S. F. Johnson, ed., *The Oxford Handbook of Late Antiquity* (Oxford/New York, 2012), pp. 1078–1108.

[51] See especially Goldziher, *Muslim Studies*, vol. 2.

[52] See, e.g., H. Lammens, 'Qoran et tradition: comment fut composée la vie de Mahomet,' *Recherches de science religieuse* 1 (1910), pp. 27-51, and Lammens, *Fāṭima et les filles de Mahomet: notes critiques pour l'étude de la sīra* (Rome, 1912).

[53] See J. Schacht, 'A Revaluation of Islamic Traditions,' *The Journal of the Royal Asiatic Society of Great Britain and Ireland* 2 (1949), pp. 143–54; Schacht, *The Origins of Muhammadan Jurisprudence*; Schacht, 'On Mūsā ibn 'Uqba's Kitāb al-Maghāzī,' *Acta Orientalia* 21 (1953), pp. 288–300; and Schacht, *An Introduction to Islamic Law* (Oxford, 1964).

[54] J. E. Wansbrough, *Quranic Studies: Sources and Methods of Scriptural Interpretation* (Oxford, 1977); and Wansbrough, *The Sectarian Milieu: Content and Composition of Islamic Salvation History* (Oxford/New York, 1978).

[55] Crone was the most prominent and formidable representative of a skeptical approach to early Islamic history in the last decades of the twentieth century and first decade and a half of the twenty-first. Two classic statements of her view of the reliability of the Islamic tradition's information about its earliest period are *Slaves on Horses*, pp. 3–17, and *Meccan Trade and the Rise of Islam*, pp. 203–30. More recently, her essay 'What Do We Actually Know about Mohammed?' (https://www.opendemocracy.net/faith-europe_islam/mohammed_3866.jsp) can be taken as reflecting her views in the twenty-first century. Her book *Hagarism: The Making of the Islamic World*, written with Michael Cook, combined high levels of erudition and sharp skepticism with an implausible reconstruction of Islamic origins.

[56] H. Berg, *The Development of Exegesis in Early Islam: The Authenticity of Muslim Literature from the Formative Period* (Richmond, 2000).

[57] Among many other skeptical or revisionist approaches to early Islamic history, G. R. Hawting, *The Idea of Idolatry and the Emergence of Islam: From Polemic to History* (Cambridge/New York, 1999), Shoemaker, *The Death of a Prophet*, and M. Cook, 'Eschatology and the Dating of Traditions,' *Princeton Papers in Near Eastern Studies* 1 (1992), pp. 23–47, might be mentioned.

grows stronger and more forbidding the closer one gets to the life of the Prophet himself. As a result, the task of writing an account of early Islamic history that avoids the charges of either uncritically parroting the problematic reports of the sources or, alternatively, of creating an improbable and fantastic replacement for the traditional account, a quite difficult one. A history of early Islam that evades one accusation quite often is open to the other.

I have no interest here in re-litigating the historiographic debates of the past forty years or adding another entry to this particular bibliography, but I will offer the following observations. There have long been scholars who were skeptical of the Great Wall of Skepticism which surrounds early Islamic history,[58] and the Great Wall, as foreboding as is it, has not been without its cracks.[59] It was arguably breached in the late twentieth century by Harald Motzki, who made a powerful case that it was possible in fact to trace the circulation of some *ḥadīth* reports to the late seventh century AD/end of the first century AH, and even further back, to the time of the Prophet's Companions.[60] Motzki identified the *Muṣannafs* of 'Abd al-Razzāq (d. AH 211/AD 827) and Ibn Abī Shayba (d. AH 235/AD 849–850) in particular, as being collections of early *ḥadīth* that could give us information from the first century of Islamic history.[61] Similarly, focusing on the biography of the Prophet, Gregor Schoeler argued that it was in fact possible to identify material about the Prophet's life from the first century AH, going so far as to suggest that we could obtain information that was collected thirty to sixty years after Muḥammad's death.[62] Even with the Great Wall's foundations shaken, however, there is nevertheless a certain stalemate that currently exists in debates over the origins of Islam.[63]

[58] Abbot, *Studies in Arabic Literary Papyri*, vol. 2, pp. 1–83; F. Sezgin, *Geschichte des Arabischen Schriftums*, vol. 1 (Leiden, 1967), pp. 53–84; and M. M. al-Azami, *On Schacht's Origins of Muhammadan Jurisprudence* (repr. Oxford/Cambridge, 1996). The force of these alternate and more traditional views of the early Islamic tradition, however, has not typically been accepted by most scholars working in Western academic contexts. See also Motzki, *The Origins of Islamic Jurisprudence*, pp. 28–29, and Motzki, 'Introduction,' in Motzki, ed., *Ḥadīth: Origins and Developments* (Aldershot/Burlington, Vt., 2004), pp. xxiv–xxv.

[59] See e.g., M. Lecker, 'The Death of the Prophet Muḥammad's Father: Did Wāqidī Invent Some of the Evidence?,' *ZDMG* 145 (1995), pp. 9–27, and and D. S. Powers, 'On Bequests in Early Islam,' *JNES* 48 (1989), pp. 185–200.

[60] See H. Motzki, 'The Muṣannaf of 'Abd al-Razzāq al-Ṣan'ānī as a Source of Authentic *Aḥādīth* of the First Century A. H.,' *JNES* 50 (1991), pp. 1–21; and Motzki, *The Origins of Islamic Jurisprudence*.

[61] Motzki, 'The Muṣannaf of 'Abd al-Razzāq al-San'ānī,' p. 21 and Motzki, *The Origins of Islamic Jurisprudence*, 51–74.

[62] Schoeler, *The Biography of Muḥammad*, see esp. p. 16.

[63] Cf. H. Berg, 'Competing Paradigms in the Study of Islamic Origins: Qur'ān 15:89–91 and the Value of *Isnāds*,' in Berg, ed., *Method and Theory in the Study of Islamic Origins*, pp. 259–90. Glen Bowersock has recently called for their conclusion. See the discussion in G. W. Bowersock, *The Crucible of Islam* (Cambridge, MA/London, 2017), pp. 12–13.

As interesting and important as these controversies are, my goal here has been, so far as possible, simply to step outside of them. They are not relevant for my project. I have instead sought to orient my inquiry along a different set of axes, engaging in an alternate set of problems. For what concerns me in the present book is not the development of legal thought in Muḥammad's community, the historical genesis of its ways of interpreting the Qur'ān, or the evolution of its methods of remembering the past. I am not particularly interested in issues of the authenticity of this report or that—the question of whether Muḥammad or ʿUmar I or ʿUmar II actually uttered this statement or engaged in that act at some point in the seventh or eighth century. These are all, to be sure, subjects of enormous importance, but engaging them directly is not particularly helpful for the task I have undertaken.

My interest centers around everyday believers and religious adherents, how they related to one another, how they related to elite discourses, how elite discourses related to them, and how they dealt with confessional and religious difference and conversion. In an Islamic context, perceptive historians have long acknowledged that the vast majority of early followers of Muḥammad must have been illiterate with very little knowledge of the precise contents of the Prophet's message.[64] Placing these ordinary religious adherents and believers at the center of one's understanding of the early period of Muslim rule means taking their mass conversions and the religious consequences of these mass conversions seriously. Taken by numbers, these believers and adherents, not the authors of the scholarly discourses or literary works that students of Islamic history have traditionally studied, embodied what it most typically meant to be a Muslim in the early medieval period.

Prescinding from debates about authenticity is possible in this volume because to investigate the questions that interest me in the earliest periods of Islamic history, one need only hold that the outlines of the traditional story of Islamic origins are accurate. Such a position is defensible on both internal grounds (through meticulous study of Islamic sources)[65] and external ones

[64] See Goldziher, *Muslim Studies*, vol. 2, pp. 39–40 (cf. Chapter 10, n. 41); Nöldeke et al. in *The History of the Qur'ān*, p. 217 (cf. Chapter 10, n. 29); Donner, *Muhammad and the Believers*, p. 77; Humphreys, *Islamic History*, p. 89; cf. also L. Caetani, 'The Art of War of the Arabs and the Supposed Religious Fervor of the Arab Conquerors,' in F. M. Donner, ed., *The Expansion of the Early Islamic State* (Aldershot/Burlington, Vt., 2008), pp. 9–10; and Wensinck, *The Muslim Creed*, pp. 11–14. Patricia Crone raised this as a possible explanation for the seeming lack of connection between Qur'ānic norms and Umayyad practice, but rejected it; see her 'Two Legal Problems Bearing on the date of the Qur'ān,' p. 11. Cf. also the observation of van Ess, *Theologie und Gesellschaft*, vol. 1, p. 43 [= *Theology and Society*, vol. 1, p. 49].

[65] For an argument that the 'main outlines' of early Islamic history can be known, see Schoeler, *The Biography of Muḥammad.* Cf. also the comments in Donner, *Narratives of Islamic Origins*, pp. 28–29.

(through careful examination of non-Muslim materials).[66] Dealing with the questions that interest me can provide new and alternative ways of thinking about the issues of authenticity, as I tried to suggest in Chapter 10, but engaging my questions does not have as its immediate goal trying to solve the various conundrums that result from the close study and analysis of the earliest Islamic legal, exegetical, and historical traditions.

For my purposes, when dealing with controverted Islamic texts, it is most helpful simply to distinguish between the issue of historical authenticity and that of historical reliability or usefulness for the reconstruction of social history and assert that these are not the same thing.[67] The Prophet may never have actually predicted that his followers would follow the customs of those who were before them—Christians and Jews (or Romans and Persians)[68]—and he may very well never have encouraged his followers to be different from Christians and Jews,[69] but the attitudes underlying such statements point to a world in which some Muslim leaders worried about precisely these sorts of issues. It is the existence of such an anxiety that is important to me, not necessarily the identity of the individual who 'really' uttered it or put a tradition in question into circulation. 'Umar II may or may not have actually written to his governors ordering them to keep Muslims from adopting the customs of local non-Muslims,[70] and 'Umar I may or may not have had certain followers of the Prophet whipped for drinking intoxicants,[71] but when these incidents are viewed in context of the questions as to the religious consequences of mass conversion, Muslim interactions with the indigenous majority population of the Middle East, and why Arabs settlers were not eventually assimilated into the religious traditions of these populations, neither incident is *a priori* unlikely. And, more importantly, the existence and circulation of both stories points to real disciplinary problems that some Muslim religious leaders faced in the first several centuries of Muslim rule in the Fertile Crescent.

It is undeniable that 'Umar I and 'Umar II eventually became exemplary and idealized figures—the 'favourite mouthpieces' of later Muslim scholars, as Patricia Crone and Martin Hinds once put it[72]—whom, it has been argued, the later tradition utilized as canvasses upon which to project back and legitimate

[66] In addition to archaeology and numismatic materials. See the remarks in Hoyland, *Seeing Islam*, pp. 545–59, esp. 546–50. And see also Hoyland, 'Early Islam as a Late Antique Religion,' pp. 1056–57.

[67] Note the comment in M. Cooperson, review of *Method and Theory in the Study of Islamic Origins*, ed. H. Berg, *Islamic Law and Society* 15 (2008), p. 269.

[68] See above, chapter 13, n. 1.

[69] See above, chapter 13, n. 29.

[70] See chapter 13, n. 48, above.

[71] See chapter 10, nn. 92–93.

[72] Crone and Hinds, *God's Caliph*, p. 22. They also included Abū Bakr as one of these 'mouthpieces.'

their views when trying to make historical and legal arguments.[73] But looking at incidents involving ʿUmar I or ʿUmar II strictly in terms of authenticity and in the context of a paradigm that concerns itself with how legal scholars of the second Islamic century may have attempted to use exemplary figures to backdate and legitimate their positions, misses the larger point that there was in fact someone in the first century or two of Islamic history who felt the need to put these stories into circulation. It is that need which is interesting to me, not necessarily who it was who responded to it through the circulation of a tradition. And discarding or discounting any report over which a cloud of 'inauthenticity' hangs risks losing very valuable witnesses for the task of historic reconstruction. In the same way that a piece of hagiography or a homily can be influenced by literary and theological agendas and yet nevertheless be 'true' for the purposes of social history, *ḥadīth* can be inauthentic and yet historically reliable for certain historical questions and useful for understanding the societies in which they were recorded. The question of the historicity of a particular event aside, both types of sources can point us what sorts of behaviors and attitudes were possible and plausible in a certain context.

I have, to be sure, made frequent use of ʿAbd al-Razzāq's *Muṣannaf*, and I have also made use, to a lesser extent, of Ibn Abī Shayba's *Muṣannaf*: both of these have been recognized as important repositories of early traditions and are therefore of special value. But I have additionally cited al-Bukhārī (d. AH 256/AD 870), Muslim (d. AH 261/AD 875), al-Tirmidhī (d. AH 279/AD 892), al-Nasāʾī (d. AH 393/AD 915), Abū Dāwūd (d. AH 275/AD 889), and Ibn Mājah (d. ca. AH 275/AD 889). All of these authors, like Ibn Saʿd, a figure whom I use extensively, were writing in the ninth or tenth century AD (third or fourth century AH), and these dates provide a *terminus ante quem* for the reports that they record, many of which certain critical approaches would likely date to some point in the eighth century.[74] Importantly for me, these authors were writing in a period when Muslims were still a demographic minority in the Middle East and therefore their reports, whether ultimately dating to the sev-

[73] See, e.g., Schacht, *The Origins of Muhammadan Jurisprudence*, pp. 70, 206, for references to ʿUmar II as fictitious and for ʿUmar as the idealized object of retrojection, and cf., too, pp. 25–26, 34, 192. Also cf. Goldziher, *Muslim Studies*, vol. 2, pp. 195–96. Borrut, *Entre mémoire et pouvoir*, pp. 283–320, examines the creation of an idealized image of ʿUmar II; see esp. 309–15 for ʿUmar II and law.

[74] Though note also Motzki's observation on Ibn Saʿd in *The Origins of Islamic Jurisprudence*, p. 291 and n. 1025. For a classic statement suggesting that the detailed information about the *sunna* of the Prophet found in legal material should be dated to the middle of the second century A.H. and that historical material, similarly, dates to the second century A.H., see Schacht's conclusions, 'A Revaluation of Islamic Traditions,' pp. 153–54; cf. also, *The Origins of Muhammadan Jurisprudence*, p. 176; Schacht even argued that a large number of Islamic traditions only came into circulation post-Shāfiʿī (d. AH 204/AD 820), p. 4, examples on pp. 146–49. NB: the second century AH corresponds to roughly AD 718–816.

enth, eighth, or even ninth centuries, and whether or not 'authentic' (understood to mean actually uttered by the person to whom they were attributed), relay important historical information about social dynamics and cultural attitudes among Muslim religious leaders in the Middle East in this period. In fact, arguing that the traditions these works contain should be dated to the eighth century rather than the seventh, makes them more useful to me than dating them to the seventh century, for it makes their actual context the post-conquest societies of the Fertile Crescent that interest me in this study, not the seventh-century Hijaz, which is of secondary concern in this book.

* * *

'Jede Epoch ist unmittelbar zu Gott,' Leopold van Ranke once famously stated.[75] A further assumption underlying the composition of this book has been just this: that every epoch is equally immediate to God. I have also assumed its converse: that every epoch is equally distant from God. That is to say, the challenges that religious leaders faced in catechizing all of the members of their communities—widespread illiteracy, largely agrarian populations, weak states and weak institutions more generally, difficulties in communication and coordination over long distances, poorly trained clergy, a lack of easy access to sophisticated books and higher-level theological education in rural areas, and so on—were not somehow suspended during a certain period because later eras looked back on it as some sort of 'age of spirituality' or came to see it as a golden, foundational period in their religious community's history and idealized a small number of individuals living in it from among the wider group of adherents. It is because such educational, occupational, and geographic limitations were built-in to the world studied in this book, throughout the centuries here covered, that I have at times cited evidence that ranges widely over time and place. No location in our period was immune to these constraints.

In making such an assumption, I have been strongly anti-exceptionalist in my approach to the past: even in periods when world-historical religious *virtuosi* lived, there were no privileged moments, no time or place in which rates of literacy and levels of catechesis reached levels only achievable in more recent periods when factors like printing, mass communication, universal education, urbanization, and now the Internet, have introduced a new religious ecosystem. To assume the opposite, whether consciously or unconsciously, would be to adopt a romantic and ahistorical posture that is difficult to defend on empirical grounds.

[75] L. von Ranke, *Über die Epochen der neueren Geschichte* (Leipzig, 1906), p. 18.

APPENDIX II

The ‘Arab’ Conquests

The word Syriac writers of the seventh century most typically use to refer to the conquerors is *ṭayyāyē*, and it is increasingly common to point out that this term can also mean ‘nomad’ and so should not be carelessly translated as ‘Arab.’[1] Admitting the danger of retrojecting contemporary ethnic understandings into the early medieval period, it is nevertheless worth pointing out that by the sixth century, *ṭayyāyā* and *ṭayyāyē* commonly meant more than simply ‘nomad’ and might refer to Arabic speakers living in a settled polity or living non-nomadic lives and who were not members of the tribe of the Banū Ṭayy. As such, seventh-century Syriac references to conquerors and rulers from the Ḥijāz should be understood in light of this pre-Islamic Syriac usage. Let me offer the following pieces of evidence to support this decision.

Although the Lakhmids were not members of the Banū Ṭayy,[2] Mundhir III is called ‘king of the Ṭayyāyē’ by Pseudo-Zacharias Rhetor[3] and also by John of Ephesus.[4] The *History of Mar Aba* refers to the ‘king of the Ṭayyāyē’ coming to prostrate before the Sasanian King of Kings.[5] Peter the Solitary’s *Life of Sabrisho‘* speaks of the report of Sabrisho‘’s miracles reaching ‘all nations, even the barbarian race of the Ṭayyāyē’ (*gensā barbrāyā d-ṭayyāyē*). Nu‘mān is the ‘leader of all their kings, the line of whose race (*d-genseh*) was descended from the prophecy of the blessing of Ishmael,’ and Nu‘mān is located in Hira,

[1] See e.g., Penn, *Envisioning Islam*, p. 20: ‘Originally a designation for a specific tribe, prior to the conquests, *ṭayyāyē* … was the term usually used to speak of people living in Arabia, especially those seen as nomadic.’ (See also the remarks at 57–58); Donner, review of *In God’s Path*, p. 138; cf. P. Webb, review of *The Emergence of Islam in Late Antiquity: Allāh and His People* by ‘Aziz al-Azmeh, *Al- Al-‘Uṣūr al-Wusṭā* 23 (2015), p. 152; Scheiner, ‘Reflections on Hoyland’s *In God’s Path*,’ pp. 26–28; and F. Millar, *Religion, Language and Community in the Roman Near East: Constantine to Muhammad* (Oxford, 2013), pp. 162–63. Note that by the medieval period, Syriac writers themselves were clearly equating *ṭayyāyē* and Arab—see, e.g., Bar Hebraeus, *Chronicle*, p. 85.17 (ed. Bedjan), where he speaks of there being two divisions in the sixth century among the ‘*ṭayyāyē*, that is, the Arabs’ (*ṭayyāyē aw kit Arbāyē*).

[2] cf. I. Shahid’s article, ‘Ṭayyi’’ in *EI2*, vol. 10, pp. 402–403 and Shahid, ‘Lakhmids’, *EI2*, vol. 5, pp. 632–34, as well as H. Lammens and I. Shahid, ‘Lakhm,’ in *EI2*, vol. 5, p. 632.

[3] Ps.-Zacharias Rhetor, Chronicle 8.5 (ed. Brooks [CSCO 84: SS 39], p. 77).

[4] ‘Mundhir bar Ḥārith, king of the Ṭayyāyē’; see John of Ephesus, *Ecclesiastical History* 4.21, 4.26, 4.39 (ed. Brooks [CSCO SS III.3], pp. 208, 216, 218).

[5] *History of Mar Aba*, p. 270.

his capital city (*mdinat malkuteh*).[6] Later in the *vita*, Nuʿmān is referred to as the 'King of the Ṭayyāyē.'[7] The early sixth-century *Chronicle of Joshua the Stylite* also called Nuʿmān the 'King of the Ṭayyāyē,'[8] and already in the late fifth century, the Synod of Barṣawmā in 494 was referring to the 'king of the Ṭayyāyē' obeying the order of the Sasanian King of Kings.[9] Lest it be thought that this title was only applied in pre-Islamic Syriac usage to rulers of Hira and clients of the Sasanians, we can point to John of Ephesus calling the famous Ghassanid ruler Ḥārith b. Jabala (d. 569) 'the great king of the Ṭayyāyē',[10] and Ps.-Zacharias Rhetor spoke of another Ghassanid, Aṭfar, as a 'Ṭayyāyā king' (*mlek Ṭayyāy*).[11] We can also mention Paul of Edessa's translation of a hymn by John Psaltes on the Himyarite martyrs, carried out probably in the 620s and revised by Jacob of Edessa in 675, which includes in its preface the explanation that it refers to a point in time when 'the Christians [in Najran] were being persecuted by Masrūq, king of the Arabs (*malkā d-ṭayyāyē*), who was a Jew by religion.'[12] Jacob, for his part, in his early eighth-century *Chronicle*, noted that 'the kingdom of the Arabs (*malkutā da-rabāyē*), whom we call the Ṭayyāyē began' in the eleventh year of Heraclius, king of the Romans, and the thirty-first year of Khusro, king of the Persians.[13]

There are also references to the language of the *ṭayyāyē*. Simeon, for instance, the East Syrian bishop of Hira, spoke to Nuʿmān in the 'Ṭayāyā language' (*b-leshshānā Ṭayyāyā*),[14] and Simeon of Beth Arsham in the sixth cen-

[6] Peter the Solitary, *Life of Sabrishoʿ*, pp. 321–22.

[7] Peter the Solitary, *Life of Sabrishoʿ*, p. 327.

[8] (Ps-) Joshua the Stylite, *Chronicle* 58 (ed. Wright, p. 55).

[9] See Chabot, *Synodicon Orientale*, p. 527.

[10] John of Ephesus, *Lives of the Eastern Saints* 50 [*Lives of James and Theodore*] (ed. and trans. Brooks [PO 19.2], p. 499). Cf. the comments in T. Hainthaler, 'Christian Arabs before Islam: A Short Overview,' in N. Al Jallad, *People from the Desert: Pre-Islamic Arabs in History and Culture* (Wiesbaden, 2012), p. 34.

[11] Ps.-Zacharias Rhetor, *Chronicle* 9.2 (ed. Brooks [CSCO 84: SS 39], p. 93). NB: Ps.-Zacharias's ܡܠܟ ܛܝܝ might also be construed not as a noun in the absolute followed by an attributive adjective in the absolute, but rather in the construct state, that is, as *mlek Ṭayy*, in which case it should be understood to mean 'king (or ruler) of the Ṭayy,' though I am unaware of any other example in Syriac of tribe known in Arabic as the Ṭayy or Ṭayyi' being referred to as Ṭayy in Syriac. I am grateful to George Kiraz for help with this grammatical point. On this Aṭfar and for the argument that he should be identified with Jabala b. Ḥārith, see I. Shahid, *The Martyrs of Najrân: New Documents* (Bruxelles, 1971), pp. 273–76.

[12] E. W. Brooks, ed. and trans. *James of Edessa. The Hymns of Severus of Antioch and Others* (PO 7.5), p. 201; I have used Brooks' translation but slightly changed the spelling. On the use of the title MLK in pre-Islamic inscripitions and texts, see U. Avner, L. Nehmé, and C. Robin, 'A Rock Inscription Mentioning Tha'laba, an Arab King from Ghassān,' *Arabian Archaeology and Epigraphy* 24 (2013), pp. 249–53; for 'leader' as a better translation in pre-Islamic contexts, see al-Shdaifat et al., 'An Early Christian Arabic Graffito,' p. 319. NB: Masrūq's primary language was likely not Arabic.

[13] Jacob of Edessa, *Chronicle*, p. 326 (ed. Brooks [CSCO III.4]). On this passage, see Hoyland, *Seeing Islam*, p. 165, and Millar, *Religion, Language and Community*, p. 163.

[14] Peter the Solitary, *Life of Sabrishoʿ*, p. 326 (ed. Bedjan, *Histoire de Mar-Jabalaha*).

tury gave the name of a place as it was called 'in the Ṭayyāyā language' (*wa-b-leshshānā Ṭayyāyā*).[15] By comparison, writing in the period of Muslim rule, Timothy I spoke of Aristotle's *Topics* being translated to the *leshshānā Ṭayyāyā* from Syriac,[16] Thomas of Marga could speak of 'Ṭayyāyā letters,'[17] and 'Abdisho' wrote of translating from 'Ṭayyāyā speech into the language of the Syrians.'[18] A manuscript written in AD 936 contains a note stating that a saint's *vita* had been translated from the 'Ṭayāyā language' (*leshshānā Ṭayyāyā*) to the Syriac language.[19] As is the case with other uses of *ṭayyāyē* and *ṭayyāyā*, we have, therefore, references to the *leshshānā Ṭayyāyā* from before the rise of Islam well into the period in which Muslims ruled the Middle East.

We find a similar continuity of naming practice when it comes to identifying Hira, the capital of the Lakhmids. Though *ḥirtā d-ṭayyāyē*, 'camp of the Arabs,' might also be used to refer to a non-Lakhmid (e.g., Ghassanid) encampment,[20] already in fifth-century Syriac texts, the Lakhmid capital was being called Ḥirtā of the Ṭayyāyē': present at the Synod of Dadisho' in 424 was Simeon, bishop of Ḥirtā of the Ṭayyāyē.[21] This practice carried on into the

[15] Simeon of Beth Arsham, *Letter to Simeon, Abbot of Gabula*, p. 365 (ed. Assemani, *BO*, vol. 1). NB: Guidi's edition of this letter reads *b-leshshaneh da-trā ṭayyāyā*, 'in the Arabic language [or dialect] of the region' ('La lettera di Simeone vescovo di Bêth-Arśâm sopra i martiri omeriti,' *Atti della Reale Accademia Nazionale dei Lincei, Serie Terza: Memorie della Classe di Scienze morali, storiche e filologiche* 7 [1881], p. 502), and Bedjan (*AMS*, vol. 1, p. 373), reads the same, though offers a variant which would make it *b-leshshāneh da-trā wa-b-leshshānā ṭayyāyā*, 'in the language of the region and in the Ṭayyāyā language.' For an ET of Guidi's text, see A. Jeffery, 'Christianity in South Arabia,' *Moslem World* 36 (1946), pp. 193–216 (the passage in question is at 204). The version of this letter preserved in Ps.-Zacharias Rhetor, *Chronicle* 8.3 (ed. Brooks [CSCO 84: SS 39], p. 64; ET in Hamilton and Brooks, p. 193), has *wa-b-leshshānā ṭayyāyā*.

On the question of the authenticity of these letters, see Y. Shitomi, 'Réexamen des deux lettres attribuées à Siméon de Bêth Aršâm, relatives à la persécution des chrétiens de Nagrân,' in *Études sud-arabes. Recueil offert à Jacques Ryckmans* (Louvain-la-Neuve, 1991), pp. 207–24 and D.G.K. Taylor, 'A Stylistic Comparison of the Syriac Ḥimyarite Martyr Texts Attributed to Simeon of Beth Arsham,' in J. Beaucamp, F. Briquel-Chatonnet, and C. J. Robin, eds., *Juifs et Chrétiens en Arabie aux Ve et VIe siècles. Regards croisés sur les sources* (Paris, 2010), pp. 143–76.

[16] Timothy I, *Letters* 48.10 (ed. Heimgartner [CSCO 644: SS 248] [Louvain, 2012], p. 92).

[17] Thomas of Marga, *Monastic History* 5.2 (ed. Budge, 1.254 [Syriac] = 2.469 [English]; my translation). See also *BO*, 3.2, p. XVI.

[18] *mpashsheq (e)nā men mamllā ṭayyāyā l-bā(r)t qālā d-suryāyē*. 'Abdisho' bar Brikho, *Nomocanon* 3 (ed. Mai, p. 221 [Syriac] = 55 [Latin translation]).

[19] BL Add. 14,645, fol. 90b. Syriac text printed in *CBM*, vol. 3, p. 1116.

[20] For the pre-Islamic use of *ḥirtā d-ṭayyāyē*, 'encampment of the Arabs,' to refer to Ghassanid settlement, see John of Ephesus, *Lives of the Eastern Saints* 50 [*Lives of James and Theodore*] (ed. and trans. Brooks [PO 19.2], p. 154, esp. n. 1) and John of Ephesus, *Ecclesiastical History* 4.36 (ed. Brooks, p. 216). Cf. the comments in Hainthaler, 'Christian Arabs before Islam,' p. 34.

[21] See Chabot, ed., *Synodicon Orientale*, p. 43. John the Ṭayyāyā was a fourth-century ascetic from a prominent family in Hira: See Brock, 'Notes on Some Monasteries on Mount Izla,' pp. 6–11, and Fiey, *Saints syriaques*, pp. 115–16 (no. 238), and cf. chapter 7, n. 10. In the Syriac *vita* of Simeon Stylites, Nu'mān I is reported to say: 'Some of our Ṭayyāyē have begun going up to [Simeon] and these notables

period of Muslim rule: in the seventh century, Isho'yahb III mentioned Ḥirtā of the Ṭayyāyē;[22] in the late eighth century, Theodore bar Koni also made reference to Ḥirtā of the Ṭayyāyē;[23] and in the ninth century, Thomas of Marga refered to Hira as 'the great city of the Ṭayyāyē.'[24]

We also have references to there being *ṭayyāyē* monastics before the rise of Islam: John of Ephesus mentioned a John, 'Bishop of the *ṭayyāyē* monks of Hawarin,' who had to flee from persecution after Severus was driven from the see of Antioch in 518.[25] Among the signatories of a letter written in 567 was a certain 'Antioch, abbot of the Monastery of the Ṭayyāyē,'[26] and Antioch appears again as abbot of the 'Monastery of the Ṭayyāyē,' in letter found in the same manuscript.[27] Similarly, the signatories of a letter written in 571 include a 'John, abbot of the Monastery of the Ṭayyāyē.'[28] Sergius, 'of the monastery of the Ṭayyāyē,' wrote a treatise against the supporters of Paul of Beth Ukkame, probably in the late sixth century.[29] We find another example of Ṭayyāyē monastics when two 'blessed Ṭayyāyē monks' escape from Khusro's Antioch, the city he had built and populated with an enormous number of deported Roman captives.[30] A note in BL Add. 14,458, a manuscript Wright dated to the sixth or seventh century, states that it was collated by 'Qashish,

have come to my Hira [or camp] and said to me ….' (ed. Bejdan, *AMS*, vol. 4, p. 597). The Syriac *ḥirtā* can also refer more generally to an encampment, and here Nu'mān's statement may be referring to a camp he had apparently made near Damascus rather than the Lakhmid city in southern Iraq. Cf. also Severus of Antioch, *Letter* 23 (*To Jonathan, Samuel, and John* [ed. Brooks [PO 12.2], p. 45), where the city of Hira is referred to as 'Ḥīrta of Nu'mān' in the rubric.

[22] *Letters* II.32 (*To Isaac of Nisibis, concerning Jerusalemites*) (ed. Duval [CSCO: Syr. II.64], p. 216, ln. 21).

[23] Theodore bar Koni, *Book of the Scholion*, p. 346.27 (ed. Scher [CSCO Syr. II.66]); for an ET of this passage, see D. Kruisheer, 'Theodor bar Koni's Ketābā d-'Eskolyon as a Source for the Study of Early Mandaeism,' *Jaarbericht Ex Oriente Lux* 33 (1993–1994), p. 167. Theodore was likely relying on a now-lost sixth-century text; see S. Gerö, 'Ophite Gnosticism according to Theodore bar Koni's Liber Scholiorum,' in H.J.W. Drijvers et al., eds., *IV Symposium Syriacum, 1984: Literary Genres in Syriac Literature* (Rome, 1987), pp. 265–66.

[24] Thomas of Marga, *Monastic History* 1.9 (ed. Budge, p. 1.28 [Syriac] = 2.51 [ET]; I have used Budges's translation but slightly altered its spelling).

[25] Quoted in Michael the Great, *Chronicle* 9.13 (ed. Chabot, 4.267 = 2.172). On this John, see T. Hainthaler, *Christliche Araber vor dem Islam: Verbreitung und konfessionelle Zugehörigkeit: eine Hinführung* (Leuven/Dudley, Mass., 2007), p. 59.

[26] BL Add., 14,602, fol. 66a. Syriac text printed in *CBM*, vol. 2, p. 706, c. 1, ln. 15–16.

[27] Also in BL Add. 14,602. Syriac text in *CBM*, vol. 2, p. 708, c. 2, ln. 17–18.

[28] Also in BL Add., 14,602. Syriac text in *CBM*, vol. 2, p. 707, c. 1, ln. 30.

[29] BL 12,155, fol. 125b, Syriac text in *CBM*, vol., 2, p. 941, no. IX.1; cf. Baumstark, *Geschichte*, p. 185. Michael the Great also has a reference to a certain bishop George, 'from the monastery of the Ṭayyāyē' (ed. Chabot, 4.753 = 3.452) as well as a metropolitan named Abraham, also from the 'monastery of the Ṭayyāyē' (4.755 = 3.455). For a thorough discussion of monasteries associated with the Ghassanids, see I. Shahid, *Byzantium and the Arabs in the Sixth Century*, vol. 2.1: *Toponymy, Monuments, Historical Geography, and Frontier Studies* (Washington, DC, 2002), pp. 183–217.

[30] John of Ephesus, *Ecclesiastical History* 6.19 (ed. Brooks [CSCO SS III.3] p. 315).

the Ṭayyāyā priest of Nahra d-Qastra, along with his syncellus, who worked diligently with him, Mar John the Ṭayyāyā, bar Daniel and Mar John the deacon, who is from AWMRA, who is an Arab (*'arbāyā*) by race (*b-gensā*).'[31] Translating *ṭayyāyā* or *ṭayyāyē* as 'nomad,' 'nomads,' or even 'tent dwellers' in these contexts, I would suggest, does not do their contexts the same justice as simply rendering them as 'Arab,' 'Arabs,' or even 'Arabic-speaker(s).'[32]

In various places we can see *ṭayyāyā* or *ṭayyāyē* used to qualify a specific tribe. In the sixth century, Simeon of Beth Arsham wrote of 'pagan and Ma'add Ṭayyāyē' (*Ṭayyāyē ḥanpē w-Ma'ādāyē*),[33] and the early eighth-century bishop Joseph was referred to as Joseph of the Taghlibite *ṭayyāyē*,[34] also as 'Joseph of the Taglibites,' and simply as 'Joseph of the *ṭayyāyē*.'[35] A fly-leaf written in the eighth century speaks of 'the priest Abraham, the *ṭayyāyā*, from the believing nation of the Ṭu'āyē.'[36] The most famous bishop over Arab tribes was George (d. AD 724), the celebrated polymath who has appeared a number of times in this book. George is referred to as 'Bishop of the Tanukāyē, the Ṭū'āyē and the 'Aqulāyē,'[37] but he is also referred to as George, 'Bishop of the *ṭayyāyē* nations (*'ammē*) and the Ṭu'āyē and 'Aqulāyē,'[38] as well as George, 'Bishop of the *ṭayyāyē* nations' (*'ammē*).[39] In fact, perhaps the most common way of referring to George was simply as George 'of the nations (*'ammē*).'[40] And George was not the only figure referred to in Syriac as 'Bishop of the nations' or 'Bishop of the Arab nations': the mid-seventh century Trokos was bishop of the 'Arab nations,'[41] and there was a late seventh-century Nonnus 'of the nations.'[42]

[31] Syriac text in *CBM*, vol. 1, p. 48.

[32] Although it comes from the period of Muslim rule, it is perhaps nevertheless useful also to point to Bar Yeshū', 'Bishop of the Ṭayyāyē of the Jazira,' mentioned in an eighth or ninth-century manuscript (BL Add. 14,629, fol. 5a; see *CBM*, vol. 2, p. 754)

[33] Simeon of Beth Arsham, *Letter to Simeon, Abbot of Gabula*, p. 365 (ed. Assemani = Guidi, ed., p. 502). Cf. Ps.-Zacharias Rhetor, *Chronicle* 8.3 (ed. Brooks [CSCO 84: SS 39], p. 64).

[34] Bar Hebraeus, *Ecclesiastical History* 1.35 (ed. Abbeloos and Lamy, 1.295).

[35] Michael the Great, *Chronicle* 11.16 (ed. Chabot, 4.448 = 2.475 [Joseph of the Taglibites] and 476 [Joseph of the *ṭayyāyē*]).

[36] BL Add. 17,217, fol. 59. Syriac text in *CBM*, vol. 3, p. 1195.

[37] See BL Add., 12,154, fols. 222a, 245a.

[38] Jacob of Edessa, *Hexaemeron*, p. 347 (ed. Chabot [CSCO 92: SS 44]).

[39] Bar Hebraeus, *Ecclesiastical History* 1.34, 1.57 (ed. Abbeloos and Lamy, 1.293, 1.303).

[40] See, e.g., BL Add. 12,144, fol. 180a (*CBM*, vol. 2, p. 909, no. 8); BL Add., 12,154, fol. 264b; BL 12,165, fol. 262b (*CBM*, vol. 2, p. 848, no. 78); BL Add. 14,538, fols. 17a and 17b (see *CBM*, vol. 2, p. 1005). Mingana Syriac 106 (see Mingana, *Catalogue of the Mingana Collection*, vol. 1, col. 261, B); Mingana Syriac 292 (Mingana, *Catalogue of the Mingana Collection*, vol. 1, col. 563, B), Berlin Syriac 236 (Sachau 121) (Sachau, *Verzeichniss der syrischen Handschriften der Königlichen Bibliothek zu Berlin*, vol. 2, p. 720); Vatican Syriac 103, fol. 306a (*BAV*, vol. 1.3, p. 22, no. 12), etc.

[41] *d-'ammē ṭayyāyē*. Michael the Great, *Chronicle* 11.12 (ed. Chabot, 4.435 = 2.453).

[42] Michael the Great, *Chronicle* 11.14 (ed. Chabot, 4.438 = 2.459). On Trokos and Nonnus, see Hage, *Die syrisch-jacobitische Kirche in frühislamischer Zeit*, p. 96.

If it be objected that all the references I have so far adduced to bishops over 'Arab tribes,' or 'of the nations,' come from the period of Muslim rule,[43] we can point also to a letter from the Miaphysite patriarch Athanasius Gamolo (d. AD 631), preserved by Michael the Great, in which Athanasius speaks of the consecration of Aḥā as the bishop of lower Peroz Shapur 'and of the Arab people of the Namarāyē' (*wa-d-ʿammā ṭayyāyē d-namarāyē*).[44] What is more, Jacob of Sarugh (d. AD 521) had a disciple who was called George 'of the Nations' (*d-ʿammē*).[45] Even before this, we can look to the *acta* of the Council of Chalcedon to find a bishop named John, referred to as both 'John of the Saracens'[46] and 'John of the Saracen nations.'[47] There was also a Eustathius who was referred to as 'Eustathius of the Saracens'[48] and 'Eustathius of the Saracen nations.'[49] Syriac references to bishops of the 'Arab nations' or bishops of the 'nations' from the period of Muslim rule merely continue this pre-Islamic tradition of naming.

Before and after the period of Muslim rule, therefore, *ṭayyāyā* and *ṭayyāyē* functioned as both nouns and adjectives and applied to non-nomadic Arabic speakers—monks, priests, bishops, and rulers—who were not from the Banū Ṭayy, but from other Arabic-speaking tribes, tribes that were sometimes even specified.[50] Although when we look at neighboring languages like Greek and Christian Palestinian Aramaic, we find that *ṭayyāyā* and *ṭayyāyē* can have as

[43] See also Michael the Great, *Chronicle* (ed. Chabot), 4.757 = 3.460 (John, Bishop of the *ʿammē*) and 4.759 = 3.463 (Athanasius, Bishop of the *ʿammē*).

[44] Michael the Great, *Chronicle* 11.4 (ed. Chabot, 4.413 = 2.416). This is the tribe of Banū Namir.

[45] Bar Hebraeus, *Ecclesiastical History* 1.42 (ed. Abbeloos and Lamy, vol. 1, col. 191). Cf. J.-B. Abbeloos, *De vita et scriptis Sancti Jacobi, Batnarum Sarugi in Mesopotamia episcopi* (Louvain/Bonn, 1867), p. 24, and see the comment in S. P. Brock, 'Jacob of Serugh: A Select Bibliographical Guide,' in G. A. Kiraz, ed., *Jacob of Serugh and His Times: Studies in Sixth-Century Syriac Christianity* (Piscataway, N.J., 2010), p. 239.

[46] Ἰωάννου Σαρακηνῶν. See E. Schwartz, ed., *Acta conciliorum oecumenicorum: Concilium universale Chalcedonense* (Berlin/Leipzig, 1932–1938) (= *ACO*), vol. 2.1.1: p. 59.22, and vol. 2.1.2: p. 134.3.

[47] Ἰωάννου ἔθνους Σαρακηνῶν: *ACO*, vol. 2.1.2, pp. 73.13 and p. 87.41

[48] Εὐσταθίου Σαρακηνῶν. *ACO*, 2.1.2, p. 6.15, Εὐστάθιος Σαρακηνῶν: p. 33.2

[49] Εὐσταθίου ἔθνους Σαρακηνῶν. *ACO*, vol. 2.1.1, p. 64.33; vol. 2.1.2: pp. 77.34, 92.5, 138.14.

[50] Greg Fisher's definition of 'Arab'—'the most common and convenient label to refer to those peoples from the general geographical region of the Arabian peninsula, including the frontier regions bordering on northern Arabia, whom the soldiers, writers, monks, priests, and others of the Roman Empire encountered and described as such, without any desire to express a particular opinion on ethnicity, nationality, or identity'—can also serve as a good working definition of *ṭayyāyā*, though *ṭayyāyē* in Syriac texts are easily found as far north as northern Mesopotamia. For this quote, see *Between Empires: Arabs, Romans, and Sasanians in Late Antiquity* (Oxford, 2011), p. 2. Little systematic work has been done on the question of the precise meaning of *ṭayyāyē* in Syriac. J. B. Segal, 'Arabs in Syriac Literature before the Rise of Islam,' *JSAI* 4 (1984), pp. 89–123, remains a foundational discussion devoted specifically to Arabs in Syriac sources; G. Fisher, P. Wood, et al., 'Arabs and Christianity,' in G. Fisher, ed., *Arabs and Empires before Islam* (Oxford, 2015), pp. 276–372, contains an abundance of useful references to and discussions of relevant Syriac texts.

their equivalents 'Saracen,'[51] 'Arab' seems an equally useful and less provocative translation.[52] For all these reasons, I have preferred to refer to the seventh-century conquests as 'Arab,' following the usage of the Aramaic speakers among the conquered peoples whose perspective I have tried to place at the center of this book.[53]

[51] For the equivalence of *ṭayyāyē* and 'Saracen' in Syriac and Greek by the fifth century, see J. Retsö, *The Arabs in Antiquity: Their History from the Assyrians to the Umayyads* (London/New York, 2003), p. 520. For the use of 'Saracen' to refer to Bedouin in the Christian Palestinian Aramaic translation of the *Forty Martyrs of Sinai*, see C. Müller-Kessler and M. Sokoloff, ed. and trans., *The Forty Martyrs of the Sinai Desert, Eulogios, the Stone-Cutter, and Anastasia* (Groningen, 1996), s.n. ܣܪܩܐ, (p. 129) (Note that in the Syriac translation of the *Forty Martyrs*, 'barbarian' [= *barbrāyē*], not 'Saraceṇ,' or *ṭayyāyē* is used; see, e.g., BL Add. 14,645, fols. 111a, 113a, and 118b; though compare this with the Acts of the Second Council of Ephesus's reference to 'Ṭayyāyē barbarians,' *Ṭayyāyē barbrāyē*, in Flemming, ed., *Akten der Ephesinischen Synode vom Jahre 449*, p. 58.23; cf. also M.-A. Kugener, 'Sur l'emploi en Syrie, au VIe siècle de notre ère, du mot "barbare" dans le sens de "arabe,"' *Oriens Christianus* 7 [1907], pp. 408–12). 'Saracen' can also be found in Syriac texts where one might normally expect *Ṭayyāyā*—see e.g., *BAV*, vol. 1.3, p. 409 (Vatican Syriac 111), where a translation of a logical work of Avicenna is said to have been done *men leshshānā sarqāyā l-seprā suryāyā*, 'from the Saracen language to the Syriac language.' Hainthaler, 'Christian Arabs before Islam,' pp. 31–34, is a convenient discussion of the term 'Saracen.'

[52] We should also remember that the Middle Persian *tāzīg*, used already in the pre-Islamic period to refer to Bedouin and Arabs, is likely derived from the Syriac/Aramaic *ṭayyāyā*/*ṭayyāyē*; see W. Sundermann, 'An Early Attestation of the Name of the Tajiks,' in W. Skalmowski and A. van Tongerloo, eds., *Medioiranica* (Leuven, 1993), p. 171 and cf. T. Nöldeke, *Geschichte des Artachšîr i Pâpakân, aus dem Pehlewî übersetzt* (Göttingen, 1879), p. 52, n. 1.

[53] The question of whether the seventh-century conquerors from the Ḥijāz would have viewed themselves as 'Arabs' is a separate one which is perhaps ultimately unanswerable. Recent attempts to deal with this question of Arab identity before the rise of Islam include M.C.A. Macdonald, 'Arabs, Arabias, and Arabic before Late Antiquity,' *Topoi* 16 (2009), pp. 277–332; Fisher, *Between Empires*, pp. 128-172; P. Webb, *Imagining the Arabs: Arab Identity and the Rise of Islam* (Edinburgh, 2016), and cf. also, J. Retsö, 'The Nabateans—Problems of Defining Ethnicity in the Ancient World,' in Pohl, Gantner, and Payne, eds., *Visions of Community*, pp. 73–79. R. G. Hoyland, 'Reflections on the Identity of the Arabian Conquerors of the Seventh-Century Middle East,' *Al-'Uṣūr al-Wusṭā* 25 (2017), pp. 113–40 offers a circumspect perspective on this question. My own view is that it is not clear that the limited sources we have to try to answer this question—inscriptions, the Qur'ān, and the problematic corpus of pre-Islamic poetry—are an evidentiary base strong enough to support any solid conclusions or broadly applicable generalizations.

Acknowledgments

It is right, and a good and joyful thing to thank all the people who have helped one complete a project such as this one. But it is also something that causes a bit of anxiety: so many people have contributed over the years that I fear I will fail to acknowledge help that has been gratefully received.

This book is a revised and expanded version of part of a doctoral dissertation that was written and researched at Princeton University. A number of people were helpful in its creation, but Shahab Ahmed, Tom Boeve, Sara Brooks, Mark Cohen, Michael Cook, Danny Ćurčić, Jeremy Friedman, Dimitri Gondicas, John Haldon, George Hatke, Norman Itzkowitz, Jaimiaal Jordan, William Chester Jordan, Nancy Khalek, Markus Kohl, Maria Mavroudi, Karam Nachar, Richard Payne, Dan Schwartz, Lena Salaymeh, Larry Stratton, Yossi Witztum, and Aron Zysow all helped and influenced me in different and important ways. During my time at Dumbarton Oaks, my horizons were expanded by many conversations with Irfan Shahid and Margaret Mullett was a wonderful mentor.

Bishop Yohanna Ibrahim showed me memorable hospitality in Aleppo and made it possible for me to visit Qenneshre in 2008, at the conference he held in honor of the thirteen hundredth anniversary of the death of Jacob of Edessa. Bishop Hanna's visit to my home in Princeton, after I had returned to teach here, is something I look back upon with both happiness and sadness. I can only hope that the mystery of his kidnapping in the context of the tragic Syrian Civil War will eventually be solved.

I have profited greatly from years of conversations with Thomas Carlson, Nicholas Marinides, Christian Sahner, Lev Weitz, and Luke Yarbrough on many of the topics in this book.

Some of the ideas in Part I of this book were presented at the Central European University in Budapest, the Johannes Gutenberg University in Mainz, the Kulturwissenschaftliches Kolleg in Konstanz, and the Institute for Advanced Study in Princeton. I am grateful to Aziz el-Azmeh, Volker Menze, Johannes Pahlitzsch, Sabine Schmidtke, and Guy Stroumsa for giving me these fora in which to receive feedback.

Part II of this book first saw life in a paper I presented at a seminar organized by Philip Wood at Corpus Christi College, Oxford. A revised version of this paper was later published in Philip's volume *History and Identity in the Late*

Antique Near East (Oxford/New York: Oxford University Press, 2013). What is published here in the chapters of Part II expands and refines the ideas found in that original presentation and the subsequent publication.

Patricia Crone was generous to me as a graduate student and similarly generous to me when I came back to Princeton to teach. Part IV of this book was in many ways inspired by the challenging and insightful opening remarks she gave at a conference at the Institute for Advanced Study in April 2008. While writing this book, I often thought of the piercing and keen criticisms that Patricia would no doubt level at it (and inwardly winced). Like so many others, I mourn her passing.

I have also presented ideas found in this book at the Catholic University of America, Georgetown University, and the University of Oklahoma, and am grateful to audiences there for generous and helpful feedback. At OU, Scott Johnson and Kyle Harper were remarkable and engaging hosts and, most graciously, did not hold my studies at the University of Texas against me.

In many ways, the path that took me to Qenneshre started in Sebastian Brock's office at the Oriental Institute in Oxford in 2003, when he suggested to me that I edit and translate some of the letters of George, Bishop of the Arab Tribes, as part of my master's thesis. It has been my good hap to have not only Sebastian as a teacher, but also David Taylor. Most of what I know about the Syriac language and tradition comes from their tutelage, both at Oxford and in the long time since I left. George Kiraz has for years answered many questions about arcane points of Syriac grammar and usage with the grace, patience, and liberality of a truly great *malfono.* One of the joys of studying Syriac is the kind-heartedness that pervades the field. Sebastian, David, and George embody this virtue.

I am grateful to Bishop Sawiros Malki and Abouna Shemoun Jan for the hospitality they showed me at St. Mark's Monastery in Jerusalem and for allowing me to photograph the Karshūnī *Life* of Theodota of Amid.

Without the amazing efforts at manuscript digitization of Columba Stewart and the Hill Monastic Museum and Library, this book would have looked much different. I am grateful to Columba not only for these efforts, but also for years of friendship and support.

I am grateful to Father Justin of the Sinai for first showing me the manuscript of *The Heavenly Ladder* from which an illumination has been taken to make the cover of this book and to St. Catherine's Monastery for giving me permission for its use. I am also deeply grateful to Father Justin for his friendship, support, and encouragement over the years and over the course of writing this book.

At Princeton University Press, Fred Appel, Thalia Leaf, and Debbie Tegarden deserve treasure in heaven for the patience and good will they have shown me as they shepherded this obstinate volume (and its author) through the stages on its life's way.

Leslie Boctor, Muriel Debié, David Jenkins, Helmut Reimitz, Jeannette Rizk, Philip Rizk, Christian Sahner, and Candace Tannous provided me with very helpful feedback on all or parts of this book. A discussion with John Haldon on historical methodology at a key moment was similarly very helpful and stimulating. Luke Yarbrough's breathtakingly thorough reading of a draft not only provided me with a bounty of helpful and insightful remarks, but also saved me from a number of errors. Michael Cook's meticulous reading and perceptive comments prevented additional embarrassing mistakes and pointed me to places where sharpening and refinement were needed. I am grateful to Michael for his kindness to me, first as a student and now as a colleague, and for the way in which he has transmitted the absolute joy of working in the incredibly rich Islamic scholarly tradition to his students.

Robert Hoyland gave me a wealth of challenging and insightful feedback and came to Princeton to spend an afternoon in my office discussing and debating my ideas after he had read my manuscript. Uriel Simonsohn also gave me remarkably generous comments and later spent the better part of a day taking me around Haifa and discussing this book with me. I am deeply grateful to both Uri and Robert for the time they devoted to helping me improve it. The comments and suggestions of a third anonymous reader for Princeton University Press were also a tremendous help.

I am grateful to Jolyon Pruszinski for making this book's maps.

This book would not have been completed had I not spent a sabbatical year working on it at the University of Konstanz's Kulturwissenschaftliches Kolleg. I could not have asked for better hosts than Fred Girod and the Kuko team, or for a more ideal (and beautiful) work environment. One of the highlights of my time in Konstanz was learning from Dorothea Weltecke and having her as an interlocutor.

A perennial challenge to those working in Syriac and Eastern Christian studies is that of accessing important but hard-to-get publications and editions. David Taylor, Muriel Debié, Hidemi Takahashi, and Kristian Heal have for years been incredibly generous in helping me obtain rare books and articles, and more recently, Sergey Minov has joined them in this role. I am grateful to these *abdai ktabe* for all their assistance. I am also grateful to David Jenkins and James Weinberger, as well as the staff of Firestone Library, for their supererogatory efforts in procuring all manner of obscure references for me.

Of my many debts, two stand out. Since I first met him in 2002, John-Paul Ghobrial has been a kindred spirit, a constant source of intellectual stimulation and delight, and an unfailing and reliable spring of encouragement. Our countless discussions about the subjects dealt with in this book, in Princeton, Konstanz, and Oxford, and his generous comments on a draft of it have benefitted me enormously. I am grateful to John-Paul for many things, but most of all, for his friendship: Φίλου πιστοῦ οὐκ ἔστιν ἀνταλλάγμα, καὶ οὐκ ἔστιν σταθμὸς τῆς καλλονῆς αὐτοῦ.

My greatest debt is to my teacher, Peter Brown, who tirelessly read through many drafts of this work and debated me over seemingly every point with an enthusiasm and patience that was nothing less than biblical. Our regular *majālis* at the Panera Bread on Nassau Street have always been lively, challenging, encouraging, and invariably left me with much food for thought. Peter's legendary generosity and kindness have been a very present help in trouble and in calm for years.

I am only too conscious of the manifold shortcomings and problems that remain in this book, and none of the people who have helped me along the way should be held responsible for what are my faults alone.

I could not have finished a project such as this without the support of my family. My parents, Boulos and Candace Tannous, and my brother and sister, Issa and Kathryn, have been my greatest supporters, throughout my life. Members of the Tannous, Mantoufeh, and Barsha families in Beirut and Jaffa have shown me enormous hospitality and generosity and taught me many things about the Middle East.

In Cairo, Maged and Judith Rizk opened their home to me with the greatest warmth. My understanding of Middle Eastern Christianity has been deeply influenced by many discussions with Maged about Christianity in Egypt and Upper Egypt. In Maasara, Oum Hani's hospitality was remarkable; but even more than her food, I benefitted from conversations with her about life and Christianity, Orthodox and Protestant, in Egypt. After this book had been completed, when we saw her in Cairo, she told me *al-ṭu'ūs mukhtalifa bas al-imān wāḥid*, and the words have stayed with me since.

A final debt, one too great to repay, is owed to my dear wife, Jeannette Rizk, who has lived with this book for too long. I am unworthy of her long-suffering, good humor, unflagging support, and grace. Τιμιωτέρα δέ ἐστιν λίθων πολυτελῶν ἡ τοιαύτη, indeed. Many discussions with Jeannette about her two years spent living with the Jabaliyya Bedouin of the Sinai and her work in women's economic development in rural areas of Egypt have profoundly affected how I think about the societies I study and opened me to blind spots in the assumptions I make about the audiences of the texts I read. Our children, Eleanor and Elias, have been a constant source of joy and wonder, and in the final stages of this book have never ceased to provide a much-needed distraction and escape from both the seventh century and the twenty-first.

Abbreviations

AB = *Analecta Bollandiana*

AC = Jean-Maurice Fiey, *Assyrie chrétienne. Contribution à l'étude de l'histoire et de la géographie ecclésiastiques et monastiques du nord de l'Iraq*. 3 vols. (Beirut, 1965–1968).

ACO = *Acta conciliorum oecumenicorum*

Add. = *Additional (manuscript)*

AMS = Paul Bedjan, ed., *Acta martyrum et sanctorum*. 7 vols. (Paris/Leipzig, 1890–1897).

ANF = Alexander Roberts, James Donaldson, and A. Cleveland Coxe, eds., *The Ante-Nicene fathers: Translations of the Writings of the Fathers down to A.D. 325*. 10 vols. (Buffalo, 1885–1896) [American edition].

BAV = Stefano Evodio Assemani and Joseph Simon Assemani, *Bibliothecae Apostolicae Vaticanae codicum manuscriptorum catalogus*, vols. 1.2–1.3 (Rome, 1758–1759).

BHG = François Halkin, *Bibliotheca hagiographica graeca*. 3 vols. 3rd ed. (Brussels, 1957).

BHO = Paul Peeters, *Bibliotheca hagiographica orientalis* (Brussels, 1910).

BL = British Library (London)

BO = Joseph S. Assemani, *Bibliotheca orientalis Clementino Vaticana: in qua manuscriptos codices syriacos, arabicos, persicos, turcicos, hebraicos, samaritanos, armenicos, aethiopicos, graecos, aegyptiacos, ibericos, & malabaricos*. 3 vols. in 4 (Rome, 1719–1728).

BSOAS = *Bulletin of the School of Oriental and African Studies*

CBM = William Wright, *Catalogue of Syriac Manuscripts in the British Museum, Acquired since the Year 1838*. 3 vols. (London, 1870–1872).

CMR = David Thomas et al., eds., *Christian Muslim Relations: A Bibliographic History*. 11 vols. (Leiden/Boston, 2009–).

CCSL = Corpus Christianorum. Series Latina.

CoptEn = Aziz S. Atiya, ed., *The Coptic Encyclopedia*. 8 vols. (New York/Toronto, 1991).

CPG = Maurice Geerard, ed., *Clavis patrum Graecorum*. 6 vols. (Turnhout, 1974–1998).

CPL = Eligius Dekkers, *Clavis patrum Latinorum: qua in Corpus Christianorum edendum optimas quasque scriptorum recensiones a Tertulliano ad Bedam* (Steenbrugis, in Abbatia Sancti Petri, 1995).

CCSG = Corpus Christianorum Series Graeca

CSCO = Corpus Scriptorum Christianorum Orientalium

CSEL = Corpus Scriptorum Ecclesiasticorum Latinorum

DACL = Fernand Cabrol et al., eds., *Dictionnaire d'archaéologie chrétienne et de liturgie*. 15 vols in 30 (Paris, 1907–1953).

DCA = William Smith and Samuel Cheetham, eds., *A Dictionary of Christian Antiquities.* 2 vols. (London, 1880).
DSp = Marcel Viller et al., eds., *Dictionnaire de spiritualité: ascétique et mystique, doctrine et histoire.* 17 vols. in 20 (Paris, 1932–1995).
DECL = Siegmar Döpp and Wilhelm Geerlings, eds., *Dictionary of Early Christian Literature.* Trans. Matthew O'Connell. (New York, 2000).
DHGE = Alfred Baudrillart et al., eds. *Dictionnaire d'histoire et de géographie ecclésiastiques.* 32 vols. (Paris, 1912–).
DPA = Richard Goulet, ed., *Dictionnaire des philosophes antiques.* 6 vols. in 7 [+ supplement]. (Paris, 1989–2016).
EI1 = Martijn Th. Houtsma, et al., eds. E. J. Brill's First Encyclopaedia of Islam, 1913–1936. 9 vols. 1st ed. (Leiden/New York, 1987).
EI2 = Hamilton A. R. Gibb et al., eds. *The Encyclopaedia of Islam: Prepared by a Number of Leading Orientalists,* 13 vols. 2nd ed. (Leiden, 1954–2009).
EI3 = *Encylopedia of Islam Three* (Leiden/Boston, 2007).
EQ = Jane D. McAuliffe, ed., *Encyclopedia of the Qur'ān.* 5 vols. (Leiden/Boston, 2006).
ESV = English Standard Version
ET = English translation
FT = French translation
GAL = Carl Brockelmann, *Geschichte der arabischen Litteratur.* 6 vols. (Leiden/Boston, 2012).
GT = German translation
GEDSH = Sebastian P. Brock, Aaron M. Butts, George A. Kiraz, and Lucas van Rompay, eds., *The Gorgias Encyclopedic Dictionary of the Syriac Heritage* (Piscataway, N.J., 2011).
HṬ = Ehsan Yar-Shater, ed., *The History of al-Ṭabarī*
JA = *Journal Asiatique*
JAOS = *Journal of the American Oriental Society*
JECS = *Journal of Early Christian Studies*
JESHO = *Journal of the Economic and Social History of the Orient*
JNES = *Journal of Near Eastern Studies*
JSAI = *Jerusalem Studies in Arabic and Islam*
JTS = *Journal of Theological Studies*
LM = *Le Muséon*
LT = Latin translation
NPNF = Philip Schaff and Henry Wace, eds., *A Select Library of Nicene and Post-Nicene Fathers of the Christian Church*
OC = *Oriens Christianus*
OCP = *Orientalia Christiana Periodica*
PdO = *Parole de l'Orient*
PG = Jacques-Paul Migne, ed., *Patrologiae cursus completus, seu, Bibliotheca universalis, integra, uniformis, commoda, oeconomica: omnium SS patrum, doctorum scriptorumque ecclesiasticorum. . .: series græca.* 161 vols. (Paris, 1857–1889).
PO = *Patrologia Orientalis*
RAC = Franz J. Dölger et al., eds., *Reallexikon für Antike und Christentum: Sachwörterbuch zur Auseinandersetzung des Christentums mit der antiken Welt.* 27 vols. (Stuttgart, 1950–).

ROC = *Revue de l'Orient chrétien*
SBI = Jack Tannous, 'Syria between Byzantium and Islam: Making Incommensurables Speak.' PhD diss., Princeton University, 2010.
SA = Scriptores Arabici
SC = Sources chrétiennes
SS = Scriptores Syri
ZDMG = *Zeitschrift der Deutschen Morgenländischen Gesellschaft*

Works Cited

MANUSCRIPTS CITED

Berlin Syriac 109 (Sachau 16)
Berlin 236 (Sachau 121)
Cambridge Add. 2812
Codex Syriacus I
BL Add. 12,139
BL Add. 12,144
BL Add. 12,148
BL Add. 12,152
BL Add. 12,153
BL Add. 12,155
BL Add. 12,165
BL Add. 14,490
BL Add. 14,491
BL Add. 14,492
BL Add. 14,533
BL Add. 14,538
BL Add. 14,602
BL Add. 14,629
BL Add. 14,645
BL Add. 14,682
BL Add. 14,725
BL Add. 17,134
BL Add. 17,217
BL Add. 17,923
BL Add. 18,821
Milan Chabot 34
Mingana Syriac 106
Mingana Syriac 190
Mingana Syriac 281
Mingana Syriac 292
Paris Syriac 100
St. Mark's Jerusalem 126
Vatican Syriac 96
Vatican Syriac 103
Vatican Syriac 111
Vatican Syriac 158

PRIMARY SOURCES I: IN MANUSCRIPT

1 Esdras [Syro-Hexapla]. Diyarbakir Syriac 1/1, fols. 164r–167r.

Anathemas for Those Returning from Heresies. BL Add. 12,156, fols. 61a–61b.

Ephrem, Metropolitan of Elam, *Letter to Gabriel b. Bukhtīshūʿ on Intercommunion.* Mingana Syriac 587, fols. 357b–360a.

Forty Martys of Sinai, BL Add. 14,645, fols. 110b–118b.

George, Bishop of the Arab Tribes, *Letters.* BL Add. 12,154, fols. 222a–290a. German translation in Victor Ryssel, *Georgs des Araberbischofs Gedichte und Briefe, aus dem Syrischen übersetzt und erläutert* (Leipzig, 1891).

——, [?] *Scholia on the Homilies of Gregory Nazianzen.* BL Add. 14,725, fols. 100b–215.

Jacob of Edessa, *Canons and Questions*:

Mardin 310:

Fols. 195a–212b (pp. 387–413) = *Questions of Addai* [= *Questions Which Addai the Priest and Lover of Labors Asked* (beginning missing)]

Fols. 208a–212b (pp. 413–22) = *Canons* of Jacob [= 'Jacob, on His Own']

Fols. 212b–16a (pp. 422–29) = *Other Questions of Addai* [=*Further Questions Which the Priest Addai Asked*]

Fol. 216b–(end missing) (pp. 429–) = *Questions Which Thomas the Priest Asked* [=*The Questions of Thomas the Hermit, Which He Asked Jacob of Edessa*]

Harvard Syriac 93 (formerly Cod. Syr. Harris 85):

Fols. 1a–18a = *Questions of Addai* [= *Questions Which Addai the Priest and Lover of Labors Asked*]

Fols. 18a–25a = *Canons* of Jacob [= 'of the Venerable Jacob, on His Own']

Fols. 25a–33b = *Other Questions of Addai* [=*Further Questions Which the Priest Addai Asked*]

Fols. 33b–37a = *Questions Which Thomas the Priest Asked* [=*The Questions of Thomas the Hermit, Which He Asked Jacob of Edessa*]

Fols. 37a–44b = *Other Questions Which John, the Stylite of the Village Litarb, Asked*

[NB: The contents of Mardin 310 and Harvard Syriac 93 are described by Robert Hoyland in *Seeing Islam*, pp. 601–610, and by Herman Teule in *CMR*, vol. 1, pp. 227–31.]

——, *Letter to the Chalcedonians of Harran* [Syriac fragments with Karshūnī translation]. Cambridge Add. 2889, fols. 272b–273b [quoted in a letter of Makkikā, Metropolitan of Mosul].

——, *Letter to the Deacon Barhadbshabba, against the Chalcedonians.* BL Add. 16,631, fols. 14b–16b.

——, *Letters to John, the Stylite of Litarb.* BL Add. 12,172, fols. 79a-134b.

——, *Letter to Simeon the Stylite.* BL Add. 17,168, fols. 154–62a.

——, *Scholion on Communion.* Harvard Syriac 47, fols. 162r–63v.

——. *Liturgy.* Cambridge Add. 2887, fols. 31a-35a. LT in Eusebius Renaudot, *Liturgiarum Orientalium Collectio*, vol. 2 (2nd ed.; Frankfurt/ London, 1847), pp. 370-379.

Job of Beth Manʿam, *Life of Simeon of the Olives.* Mardin 8/259, pp. 203–247 (fols. 105r–127r). Paris Syriac 375, fols. 152r–210r.

John of Litarb, *Letter to Daniel, an Arab Priest.* BL Add. 12,154, fols. 291a–94b.

Life of Barṣawmā. Contained in an unnumbered manuscript held in the Syrian Orthodox Church of St. George, Aleppo. Available at https://www.wdl.org/en/item/7075/view/1/1/, and described at https://www.wdl.org/en/item/7075/.

Sergius bar Karya, *Letter fragment.* BL Add. 17,193, fol. 36a.

Sergius of Reshʿayna, *Commentary on the Categories of Aristotle, Addressed to Theodore.* Mingana Syriac 606, fols. 52s–140b. Partial translation in Brock, *A Brief Outline of Syriac Literature*, pp. 201–204. [See Brock, 'The Syriac Commentary Tradition,' p. 12, 2.2.1–2.2.2 for Sergius's two commentaries on the *Categories*]

Shemʿon of Samosata, *Life of Theodota of Amid* [Syriac]. Mardin 275, fols. 237a–296b (pp. 481–600).

——, *Life of Theodota of Amid* [Karshūnī]. St Mark's Jerusalem 199, fols. 547a–564b. [I am working on an edition and translation of the Karshūnī version of the *Life* of Theodota, to be published with Andrew Palmer's Syriac edition by Brigham Young University Press and Gorgias Press.]

Solutions to Manichaean Blasphemies Written by One of the Followers of Julian, from the Village of Saqra. Vatican Syriac 135, fols. 80b–87a.

Timothy II (Aelurus), *Prayer for Those Turning Back from Communion with Those Who Say 'Two natures,' Those Who Have Accepted the Council.* BL Add 12,156, fol. 61b.

Yonan the Bishop, *Letter to Theodore the Periodeute on Monogamy.* Cambridge Add. 2023, fols. 254b–259a.

PRIMARY SOURCES II: TEXTS AND TRANSLATIONS

ʿAbdishoʿ bar Brikho, *Mēmrā on Ecclesiastical Books*. Ed. Joseph S. Assemani, *BO* 3.1, pp. 3–362. English translation in George P. Badger, *The Nestorians and Their Rituals*, vol. 2 (London, 1852), pp. 361–79.

——, *Nomocanon*. Ed. and trans. Angelo Mai, *Scriptorum veterum nova collectio e Vaticanis codicibus edita*, vol. 10 (Rome, 1838), pp. 1–168 (Latin) = 169–331 (Syriac).

ʿAbd al-Razzāq, *al-Amālī fī āthār al-Ṣaḥāba*. Ed. Majdī al-Sayyid Ibrāhīm (Cairo, n.d).

——, *al-Muṣannaf*. Ed. Ḥabīb al-Raḥmān al-Aʿẓamī. 11 vols. (Johannesburg/Beirut, 1983).

Abraham the Priest, *History of Rabban Bar ʿIdta* (BHO 137). Ed. and trans. Ernest A. Wallis Budge, *The Histories of Rabban Hôrmîzd the Persian and Rabban Bar ʿIdtâ*. 3 vols in 2. (London, 1902), vol. 1, pp. 3–109 (Syriac) = vol. 2.1, 161–304 (ET).

Abū al-ʿAlāʾ al-Maʿarrī, *Luzūm mā lā yalzam: al-Luzūmiyyāt*. 2 vols. (Beirut, 1961).

Abū Dāwūd, *Sunan*. Ed. Shuʿayb al-Arnaʾūṭ and Muḥammad Kāmil Qarah Balilī. 7 vols. (Damascus, 2009).

Abū al-Faraj al-Iṣbahānī, *Kitāb adab al-ghurabāʾ*. Ed. Ṣalāh al-Dīn al-Munajjid (Beirut, 1972). English translation in Patricia Crone and Shmuel Moreh, *The Book of Strangers: Medieval Arabic Graffiti on the Theme of Nostalgia* (Princeton, 2000).

——, *Kitāb al-Aghānī*. 20 vols. in 6 (Bulaq, 1868–1869). [Vol. 21 = Rudolph E. Brünnow, *The Twenty-First Volume of the Kitâb al-Aghânî, Being a Collection of Biographies Not Contained in the Edition of Bûlâq; edited from Manuscripts in the Royal Library of Munich* (Leiden, 1888)].

Abū Ḥayyān al-Tawḥīdī, *al-Baṣāʾir wa-ʾl-dhakhāʾir*. Ed. Ibrāhīm al-Kīlānī. 4 vols. in 6. (Damascus, 1964–1966).

Abū al-Makārim, *Taʾrīkh al-kanāʾis wa-ʾl-adyira*. Ed. al-Anbā Ṣamūʾīl, usquf Shībīn al-Qanāṭir, *Taʾrīkh Abū al-Makārim (Taʾrīkh al-kanāʾis wa-ʾl-adyira fī ʾl-qarn al-thānī ʿashar bi-ʾl-wajh al-baḥrī)*. 4 vols. (n.d., n.p.). English translation of vol. 2 in Basil T. A. Evetts, *The Churches and Monasteries of Egypt and Some Neighboring Countries, attributed to Abû Ṣâliḥ, the Armenian; Translated from the Original Arabic* (Oxford, 1895).

Abū Nuʿaym al-Iṣbahānī, *Ḥilyat al-awliyāʾ wa-ṭabaqāt al-aṣfiyāʾ*. 10 vols (Beirut, 1988).

Abū Rāʾiṭa al-Takrītī, Ḥabīb b. Khidma, *Fī ithbāt dīn al-Naṣrāniyya wa-ithbāt al-thālūth al-muqaddas*. Ed. Georg Graf, *Die Schriften des Jacobiten Ḥabīb ibn Ḫidma Abū Rāʾiṭa*. CSCO 130–31, SA 14–15. (Louvain, 1951), pp. 131–61 (Arabic) = 159–94 (GT). English translation in Sandra Toenies Keating, *Defending the 'People of Truth' in the Early Islamic Period: The Christian Apologies of Abū Rāʾiṭah* (Leiden/Boston, 2006), pp. 82–145.

——, *Min qawl Abī Rāʾiṭa al-Takrītī al-Suryānī usquf Naṣībīn mustadillan bihi ʿalā ṣiḥḥat al-Naṣrāniyya*. Ed. Georg Graf, *Die Schriften des Jacobiten Ḥabīb ibn Ḫidma Abū Rāʾiṭa*. CSCO 130–31, SA 14–15 (Louvain, 1951), pp. 162 (Arabic) = 197 (GT). English translation in Sandra Toenies Keating, *Defending the 'People of Truth' in the Early Islamic Period: the Christian Apologies of Abū Rāʾiṭah* (Leiden/Boston, 2006), p. 342 (Arabic) = 343 (ET).

Abū ʿUbayd al-Qāsim b. Sallām, *Kitāb faḍāʾil al-Qurʾān*. Ed. Marwān al-ʿAṭiyya, Muḥsin Kharāba, and Wafāʾ Taqī al-Dīn (Damascus/Beirut, 1995).

Abū Yūsuf, *Kitāb al-Kharāj* (Beirut, 1979). English translation by Aharon Ben Shemesh, *Abū Yūsuf's Kitāb al-kharāj* (Leiden/London, 1969). FT in Edmond Fagnan, *Le livre de l'impôt foncier: (Kitâb el-kharâdj)*, (Paris, 1921).

Acts of the Second Council of Ephesus. Ed. and trans. Johannes P.G. Flemming, *Akten der Ephesinischen Synode vom Jahre 449: Syrisch. Abhandlungen der Königlichen Gesellschaft der Wissenschaften zu Göttingen, Philologisch-Historische Klasse*, N.F. 15.1. (Berlin, 1917). English translation in Samuel G.F. Perry, *The Second Synod of Ephesus, together with Certain Extracts relating to it, from Syriac Mss. Preserved in the British Museum* (Dartford, 1881).

Adomnan of Iona, *De locis sanctis*. Ed. L. Bieler in *Itineraria et alia geographica*. CSCL 175 (Turnhout, 1965), pp. 177–234. ET in John Wilkinson, *Jerusalem Pilgrims before the Crusades* (Warminster, 1977), pp. 167–206.

Aḥmad b. Ḥanbal, *al-Musnad*. 6 vols. (Cairo, 1895).

al-Akhṭal, *Dīwān*. Ed. Anṭūn Ṣāliḥānī, *Dîwân al-Aḫṭal: texte arabe publié pour la première fois d'après le manuscrit de St. Pétersbourg et annoté* (Beirut, 1891). English translation in Arthur Wormhoudt, *Diwan al Akhtal, Abu Malik Giyath ibn Gauth al Taglibi: The Recension of al-Sukkari of the Text of Ibn al Arabi d. 231 heg.* (Oskaloosa, Iowa, 1973).

ʿAmr b. Mattā, *Akhbār faṭārikat kursī al-mashriq*. Ed. and trans. Henricus Gismondi, *Maris, Amri, et Slibae. De patriarchis nestorianum commentaria ex codicibus Vaticanus. Pars Prior.* 2 vols. [Maris textus arabicus and Maris versio latina] (Rome, 1899). [On correcting the attribution of this work, see Bo Holmberg, 'A Reconsideration of the *Kitāb al-Mağdal*,' *PdO* 18 (1993), pp. 255–73].

ʿAnanishoʿ, *The Book of Paradise*. Ed. and trans. Ernest A. W. Budge, *The Book of Paradise, Being the Histories and Sayings of the Monks and Ascetics of the Egyptian Desert by Palladius, Hieronymus and Others: The Syriac Texts, according to the Recension of ʿAnân-Îshôʿ of Bêth ʿÂbhê*. 2 vols (London, 1904).

(Ps-?) Anastasius Apocrisarius, *Dialogue of Maximus with Theodore Bishop of Caesarea in Bithynia* [Acta in primo exsilio seu dialogus Maximi cum Theodosio episcopo Caesareae in Bithynia] (CPG 7735). Ed. and trans. P. Allen and B. Neil, *Maximus the Confessor and His Companions: Documents from Exile* (Oxford/New York, 2002), pp. 76–119.

Anastasius of Sinai, *Homilia de sacra synaxi* (CPG 7750). PG 89, cols. 825–49

——, *Narrations Beneficial for the Soul* [Narrationes] (CPG 7758). Ed. and trans. André Binggeli, 'Anastase le Sinaïte: récits sur le Sinaï et récits utiles à l'âme. Édition, traduction, commentaire.' 2 vols. (PhD diss., Paris, 2001). Partial ed. and trans. in Stefan Heid, 'Die C-Reihe erbaulicher Erzählungen des Anastasios vom Sinai im *Codex Vaticanus Graecus* 2592,' *OCP* 74 (2008), pp. 71–114. Partial ed. in François Nau, 'Le texte grec des récits utiles à l'âme d'Anastase (le Sinaïte),' *OC 3* (1903), pp. 56–90. Partial French translation and summary in Nau, 'Les récits inédits du moine Anastase. Contribution à l'histoire du Sinai au commencement du VIIe siècle (traduction française),' *Revue de l'institut catholique de Paris* 1 (1902), pp. 1–25, 110–51. Partial edition and French translation in Bernard Flusin, 'L'esplanade du temple a l'arrivée des Arabes, d'après deux récits byzantins,' in Julian Raby and Jeremy Johns, eds., *Bayt al-Maqdis: ʿAbd al-Malik's Jerusalem*. Part One (Oxford, 1992), pp. 25–26.

Partial English translation in Daniel F. Caner, *History and Hagiography from the Late Antique Sinai* (Liverpool, 2010), pp. 196–99.

——, *Questions and Answers* [Quaestiones et responsiones] (CPG 7746). Ed. Marcel Richard and Joseph A. Munitiz, *Anastasii Sinaitae Quaestiones et responsiones* (Turnhout/Leuven, 2006). English translation in Joseph A. Munitiz, *Anastasios of the Sinai: Questions and Answers* (Turnhout, 2011).

Anonymous Rules for Monks. Ed. and trans. Arthur Vööbus, *Syriac and Arabic Documents Regarding Legislation Relative to Syrian Asceticism* (Stockholm, 1960), pp. 110–12.

Aphrahat, *Demonstrations.* Ed. Jean Parisot, *Aphraatis Sapientis Persae Demonstrationes.* Patrologia Syriaca 1.1, 1.2 (cols. 1–150) (Paris, 1894–1907).

Apocalypse of John the Little. Ed. J. Rendel Harris, *The Gospel of the Twelve Apostles together with the Apocalypses of Each One of Them* (Cambridge, 1900), pp. *15–*21 (Syriac) = 34–39 (ET) [Part of the *Gospel of the Twelve Apostles*].

Apophthegmata Patrum [Collectio alphabetica] (CPG 5560). PG 65, cols. 71–440. English translation in Benedicta Ward, *The Sayings of the Desert Fathers: The Alphabetical Collection* (Kalamazoo, Michigan, 1975).

Apostolic Church Order (Greek) [Canones ecclesiastici apostolorum] (CPG 1739). Ed. and trans. Alistair Stewart Sykes, *The Apostolic Church Order: The Greek Text with Introduction, Translation and Annotation* (Strathfield, NSW, 2006).

Apostolic Church Order (Syriac). Ed. and trans. J. P. Arendzen, 'An Entire Syriac Text of the "Apostolic Church Order,"' *Journal of Theological Studies* O.S. 3 (9) (1901), pp. 59–80.

Apostolic Constitutions (CPG 1740). Ed. and trans. Marcel Metzger, *Les Constitutions apostoliques.* SC 320, 329, 336. (Paris, 1985–1986). English translation by William Whiston (revised by James Donaldson) in *ANF*, vol. 7, pp. 391–505.

ʿArīb b. Saʿd, *Ṣilat taʾrīkh al-Ṭabarī.* Ed. Michael J. de Goeje, *Arîb. Tabarî continuatus* (Leiden, 1897).

Ps.-Aristotle, *On the World.* Ed. Paul de Lagarde, *Analecta Syriaca* (Leipzig, 1858), pp. 134-158. [Translated into Syriac by Sergius of Reshʿayna]

Athanasius, *Epistle to the Monks* [Epistula ad monachos] (CPG 2108). PG 26, cols. 1185–88. English translation by John-Henry Newman and Archibald Robertson in *NPNF*, ser. 2, vol. 4, p. 564.

——, *Life of Anthony* (Greek) [Vita Antonii] (CPG 2101/BHG 140). PG 26, cols. 837-976. Also ed. and trans. by G.J.M. Bartelink, *Vie d'Antoine.* SC 400 (Paris, 1994). English translation by Robert C. Gregg in *The Life of Antony and the Letter to Marcellinus* (Mahwah, N.J., 1980), pp. 29–99.

——, *Life of Anthony* (Syriac). Ed. and trans. René Draguet, *La vie primitive de S. Antoine conservée en syriaque.* CSCO 417–18, SS 183–84 (Louvain, 1980).

——, *Orations against Arians* [Orationes contra Arianos iii] (CPG 2093, 2230). PG 26, cols. 12-468 (Orations 1–3). English translation by John-Henry Newman and Archibald Robertson in *NPNF*, ser. 2, vol. 4 (New York, 1892), pp. 306–432 (*Orations* 1–3). [Oration 4 *Against the Arians* (CPG 2230) = PG 26, cols. 468–525, ET in *NPNF*, ser. 2, vol. 4, 433–47].

(Ps.-?) Athanasius/Apollinaris of Laodicea (?), *Ad Iouianum* (CPG 3665). Ed. by Hans Lietzmann, *Apollinaris von Laodicea und seine Schule*, pp. 250–53.

Ps.-Athanasius, *Canons* (CPG 2302). Ed. and trans. Williams Riedel and Walter E. Crum,

The Canons of Athanasius of Alexandria: The Arabic and Coptic Versions (London, 1904).

Athanasius of Balad, *Letter on Eating the Sacrifices of the Hagarenes.* Ed. and trans. François Nau, 'Littérature canonique syriaque inédite. Concile d'Antioche; lettre d'Italie; canons "des saints Pères," de Philoxène, de Théodose, d'Anthime, d'Athanase,' *ROC* 14 (1909), pp. 128–30. Ed. and trans. Rifaat Y. Ebied, 'The Syriac Encyclical Letter of Athanasius II, Patriarch of Antioch, Which Forbids the Partaking of the Sacrifices of the Muslims' in Bruns and Luthe, eds., *Orientalia Christiana: Festschrift für Hubert Kaufhold zum 70. Geburtstag*, pp. 169–74. English translation in Michael P. Penn, *When Christians First Met Muslims: A Sourcebook of the Earliest Syriac Writings on Islam* (Oakland, Calif., 2015), pp. 82–84.

Athanasius Gamolo, *Letter to the Monks of Mar Matay.* Ed. and trans. Ignatius Ephrem Rahmani, *Studia Syriaca*, vol. 1, pp. *29–*31 (Syriac) = 28–30 (LT).

(Ps-?) Athanasius Gamolo, *Life of Severus* [Arabic] (BHO 1062). Ed. and trans. Youhanna Nessim Youssef, *The Arabic Life of Severus of Antioch attributed to Athanasius of Antioch.* PO 49.4 (Turnhout, 2004).

——, *Life of Severus* [Coptic and Ethiopic] (BHO 1062). Ed. and trans. Edgar J. Goodspeed and Walter E. Crum, *The Conflict of Severus, Patriarch of Antioch by Athanasius.* PO 4.8. (Paris, 1908).

Athenagoras, *Supplicatio pro Christianis* (CPG 1070). Ed. and trans. Bernard Pouderon, *Supplique au sujet des chrétiens; et, Sur la résurrection des morts.* SC 379 (Paris, 1992). English translation by B. P. Pratten in *ANF*, vol. 2 (New York, 1885), pp. 123–48.

Augustine, *City of God* [De ciuitate Dei] (CPL 313). Ed. Bernhard Dombart and Alfons Kalb, with FT by Gustave Combès in *La cite de Dieu.* Oeuvres de Saint Augustin 33–37 (Paris, 1959–1960). English translation in R. W. Dyson, *Augustine: The City of God against the Pagans* (Cambridge/New York, 1998).

——, *Confessions* (CPL 251). Ed. Lucas Verheijen, *Sancti Augustini Confessionum libri XIII.* CCSL 27. Turnhout, 1981. English translation in Henry Chadwick, *Saint Augustine: Confessions* (Oxford, 1991).

——, *On the Catechizing of the Uninstructed* [De catechizandis rudibus] (CPL 297). Ed. J. Bauer in *Sancti Aurelii Augustini De fide rerum invisibilium: Enchiridion ad Laurentium, de fide et spe et caritate: De catechizandis rudibus: Sermo ad catechumenos de symbolo: Sermo de disciplina christiana: Sermo de utilitate ieiunii: Sermo de excidio urbis Romae: De haeresibus.* CCSL 46 (Turnhout, 1969), pp. 121–78. English translation by Joseph P. Christopher, *The First Catechetical Instruction (De Catechizandis Rudibus)* (Westminster, Md./London, 1962).

al-Azdī, *Ta'rīkh futūḥ al-shām.* Ed. 'Abd Allāh Mun'im 'Abd Allāh 'Āmir (Cairo, 1970).

Babai the Great, *History of George the Priest* (BHO 323). Ed. Paul Bedjan, *Histoire de Mar- Jabalaha* (Paris, 1895), pp. 416–571.

Badr al-Rashīd, *Alfāẓ al-kufr.* Ed. Muḥammad b. 'Abd al-Raḥmān al-Khumayyis in *al-Jāmi' fī alfāẓ al-kufr* (Kuwait, 1999), pp. 13–134.

al-Bakrī, *Mu'jam mā ista'jama min asmā' al-bilād wa-'l-mawāḍi'.* Ed. Muṣṭafā al-Saqqā. 4 vols. (Beirut, n.d.).

al-Balādhurī, *Ansāb al-ashrāf.* Ed. Maḥmūd al-Fardūs al-'Aẓm. 26 vols. (Damascus, 1996–2010).

——, *Kitāb futūḥ al-buldān.* Ed. Michael J. de Goeje, *Liber expugnationis regionum auctore Imámo Ahmed ibn Jahja ibn Djábir al-Beládsorí* (Leiden, 1866). English translation in Hitti, *The Origins of the Islamic State, Being a Translation from the Arabic Accompanied with Annotations, Geographic and Historic Notes of the Kitâb futûḥ al-buldân of al-Imâm abu-l 'Abbâs Aḥmad ibn-Jâbir al-Balâdhuri.* 2 vols. (New York, 1916–1924). [Vol. 1, trans. by Philip K. Hitti; vol. 2, trans. by Francis Clark Murgotten].

——, *Kitāb jumal min ansāb al-ashrāf.* Ed. Suhayl Zakkār and Riyāḍ Ziriklī. 13 vols. (Beirut, 1996).

Barhadbshabba, *The Cause of the Foundation of the Schools.* Ed. and trans. Addai Scher, *Mar Barhadbšabba 'Arbaya, évêque de Halwan (VIe siècle). Cause de la fondation des écoles.* PO 4.4. (Paris, 1908). English translation in Adam H. Becker, *Sources for the History of the School of Nisibis* (Liverpool, 2008), pp. 86–160.

——, *Ecclesiastical History.* Ed. and trans. François Nau, *La seconde partie de l'Histoire de Barhadbešabba 'Arbaïa et controverse de Théodore de Mopsueste avec les Macédoniens.* PO 9.5 (Paris, 1913). English translation in Adam H. Becker, *Sources for the History of the School of Nisibis* (Liverpool, 2008), pp. 40–85.

Bar Hebraeus, *Book of the Dove.* Ed. Paul Bedjan, *Ethicon; seu, Moralia Gregorii Barhebraei* (Paris/Leipzig, 1898). English translation in Arent J. Wensinck, *Bar Hebraeus's Book of the Dove, together with Some Chapters from his Ethikon* (Leiden, 1919).

——, *Chronicle.* Ed. Paul Bedjan, *Gregorii Barhebraei: Chronicon Syriacum* (Paris, 1890). English translation in Ernest A. W. Budge, *The Chronography of Gregory Abû'l Faraj, the Son of Aaron, the Hebrew Physician, Commonly Known as Bar Hebraeus, Being the First Part of His Political History of the World* (London, 1932).

——, *Ecclesiastical History.* Ed. and trans. Jean-Baptiste Abbeloos and Thomas J. Lamy, *Gregorii Barhebraei Chronicon ecclesiasticum: quod e codice Musei britannici descriptum conjuncta opera ediderunt, Latinitate donarunt annotationibusque...* 3 vols. (Louvain, 1872–1877). English translation in David Wilmshurst, *Bar Hebraeus: The Ecclesiastical Chronicle* (Piscataway, N.J., 2016).

——, *Nomocanon.* Ed. Paul Bedjan, *Nomocanon Gregorii Barhebraei* (Pairs/Leipzig, 1898).

Basil of Caesarea, *Homilies on the Hexaemeron* [Homiliae in hexaemeron] (CPG 2835). Ed. Emmanuel Amand de Mendieta and Stig Y. Rudberg, *Basilius von Caesarea: Homilien zum Hexaemeron* (Berlin, 1997). French translation in Stanislas Giet, *Homélies sur l'Hexaéméron [par] Basile de Césarée.* 2nd ed. SC 26 (Paris, 1968).

——, *Letter 217* [Epistula 217] (cf. CPG 2901.1). Ed. and trans. Périclès-Pierre Joannou, *Discipline générale antique,* vol. 2, pp. 140–59.

al-Bukhārī, *al-Adab al-mufrad.* Ed. Muḥammad Fu'ād 'Abd al-Bāqī (Cairo, 1375).

——, *al-Jāmi' al-ṣaḥīḥ.* Ed. Muḥibb al-Dīn al-Khaṭīb. 4 vols. (Cairo, 1400).

——, *Kitāb al-ta'rīkh al-kabīr.* 4 vols. in 8 (Hyderabad, [1958–1964]).

Burchard of Mt. Zion, *Description of the Holy Land.* Ed. Johann C. Moritz, *Peregrinatores medii aevi quatuor: Burchardus de Monte Sion, Ricoldus de Monte Crucis, Odoricus de Foro Julii, Wibrandus de Oldenborg* (Leipzig, 1864), pp. 19–94. English translation in Aubrey Stewart, *Burchard of Mount Sion: A.D. 1280* (London, 1896).

Canons of Isho' bar Nun. Ed. and trans. Arthur Vööbus, *Syriac and Arabic Documents regarding Legislation Relative to Syrian Asceticism* (Stockholm, 1960), pp. 191–204.

Canons of John of Marde. Ed. and trans. Arthur Vööbus, *The Synodicon in the West Syr-*

ian Tradition II. CSCO 375–76, SS 163–64 (Louvain, 1976), pp. 233–55 (Syriac) = 247–68 (ET).

Canons of John of Tella. Ed. and trans. Arthur Vööbus, *Syriac and Arabic Documents Regarding Legislation Relative to Syrian Asceticism* (Stockholm, 1960), pp. 57–59.

Canons of Marutha. Ed. and trans. Arthur Vööbus, *Syriac and Arabic Documents Regarding Legislation Relative to Syrian Asceticism* (Stockholm, 1960), pp. 119–49.

Canons for Nuns. Ed. and trans. Arthur Vööbus, *Syriac and Arabic Documents Regarding Legislation Relative to Syrian Asceticism* (Stockholm, 1960), pp. 64–68.

Canons of Patriarch Cyriacus (AD 794). Ed. and trans. Arthur Vööbus, *The Synodicon in the West Syrian Tradition II.* CSCO 375–76, SS 163–64 (Louvain, 1976), pp. 25–34 (Syriac) = 27–36 (ET).

Canons of Patriarch Dionysius. Ed. and trans. Arthur Vööbus, *The Synodicon in the West Syrian Tradition II.* CSCO 375–76, SS 163–64 (Louvain, 1976), pp. 6–17 (Syriac) = 7–18 (ET).

Canons of the Patriarch George. Ed. and trans. Arthur Vööbus, *The Synodicon in the West Syrian Tradition II.* CSCO 375–76, SS 163–64 (Louvain, 1976), pp. 1–6 (Syriac) = 2–7 (ET).

Canons of the Patriarch John. Ed. and trans. Arthur Vööbus, *The Synodicon in the West Syrian Tradition II.* CSCO 375–76, SS 163–64 (Louvain, 1976), pp. 34–45 (Syriac) = 37–48 (ET).

Chapters Written by the Easterners [Who] Presented Their Questions to the Holy Fathers. Ed. and trans. Ignatius Ephrem Rahmani, *Studia Syriaca*, vol. 3 (Charfeh, 1908), pp. *5–*23 (Syriac) = 30–47 (LT).

Chronicle to 724. Ed. Ernest Walter Brooks, *Chronica Minora, Pars Secunda.* CSCO III.4 (Paris/Leipzig, 1904), pp. 77–156. Partial English translation in Palmer et al., *The Seventh Century in the West-Syrian Chronicles*, pp. 13–23, 43.

Chronicle to 813. Ed. Ernest Walter Brooks, in Ernest Walter Brooks, Ignazio Guidi, and Jean-Baptiste Chabot, eds., *Chronica Minora, Pars Tertia.* CSCO SS 3.4 (Paris, 1905), pp. 243–60. Previous edition, with English translation, in Ernest Walter Brooks, 'A Syriac Fragment,' *ZDMG* 54 (1900), pp. 195–230.

Chronicle to 819. Ed. Aphram Barsaum, *Chronicon anonymum ad A.D. 819 pertinens.* CSCO Ser. III.14 (Paris, 1920), pp. 3–22.

Chronicle to 846. Ed. Ernest Walter Brooks, *Chronica Minora, Pars Secunda.* CSCO III.4. (Paris/Leipzig, 1904), pp. 157–238. English translation in Ernest Walter Brooks, 'A Syriac Chronicle of the Year 846,' *ZDMG* 51 (1897), pp. 569–88.

Chronicle to 1234. Ed. and trans. Jean-Baptiste Chabot, *Chronicon anonymum ad annum Christi 1234 pertinens.* CSCO Ser. III.14–15 [= CSCO 81–82, SS 36, 37] (Paris, 1916–1920); CSCO 109 SS 56 (Paris, 1937). Partial FT by Albert Abouna and Jean-Maurice Fiey in CSCO 354, SS 154 (Louvain, 1974).

Chronicle of Seert. Ed. and trans. Addai Scher, *Histoire nestorienne (Chronique de Séert).* PO 4.3, 5.2, 7.2, 13.4. (Paris, 1908–1919).

Clement of Alexandria, *Stromateis* [Stromata] (CPG 1377). Ed. Otto Stählin, *Clemens Alexandrinus*, vols. 2–3 (Leipzig, 1906–1909).

Codex Justinianus. See Justinian, *Codex.*

Concerning John of Mardē. Ed. and trans. Arthur Vööbus, *The Synodicon in the West Syrian Tradition II.* CSCO 375–76, SS 163–64 (Louvain, 1976), pp. 201–208 (Syriac) = 212–20 (ET).

Coptic Synaxary. Ed. and trans. René Basset, *Le Synaxaire arabe jacobite (redaction copte)*. PO 1.3, 3.3., 11.5, 16.2, 17.3, 20.5 (Paris, 1907–1929).

Cosmas Indicopleustes, *Christian Topography* [Topographia christiana] (CPG 7468). Ed. Wanda Wolska-Conus, *Topographie chrétienne*. SC 141, 159, 197 (Paris, 1968–1973).

Council of Nicaea, *Canons* (CPG 8513). Ed. and trans. Périclès-Pierre Joannou, *Discipline générale antique*, vol. 1.1, pp. 23–41. ET by Henry Percival in *NPNF*, ser. 2, vol. 14, pp. 9–49.

Council in Trullo, *Canons* (CPG 9444). Ed. and trans. Périclès-Pierre Joannou, *Discipline générale antique*, vol. 1.1, pp. 111–241. ET by Henry R. Percival, in *NPNF*, ser. 2, vol. 14 (New York, 1905), pp. 359–408.

Cyril of Scythopolis, *Life of Euthymius* (Vita Euthymii) (CPG 7535/BHG 648). Ed. Eduard Schwartz, *Kyrillos von Skythopolis* (Leipzig, 1939), pp. 5–85. English translation in Richard M. Price, *The Lives of the Monks of Palestine by Cyril of Scythopolis* (Kalamazoo, Mich., 1991), pp. 1–83.

——, *Life of Sabas* [Vita Sabae] (CPG 7536/BHG 1608). Ed. Eduard Schwartz, *Kyrillos von Skythopolis* (Leipzig, 1939), pp. 85–200. English translation in Richard M. Price, *The Lives of the Monks of Palestine by Cyril of Scythopolis* (Kalamazoo, Mich., 1991), pp. 93–209.

Cyrillona, *Homilies*. Ed. and trans. Carl Griffin, *The Works of Cyrillona* (Piscataway, N.J., 2016).

al-Dānī, *Kitāb al-muqniʿ fī rasm maṣāḥif al-amṣār maʿa kitāb al-nuqaṭ*. Ed. Otto Pretzl (Istanbul, 1932).

al-Dāraquṭnī, *Sunan*. Ed. Shuʿayb Arnaʾūṭ, Ḥasan ʿAbd al-Munʿim Shalabī, et al. 6 vols. (Beirut, 2004).

David bar Paulos, *Letter to John the Bishop on Vocalization*. Ed. and trans. Ignatius Ephrem Rahmani, *Studia Syriaca*, vol. 1 (Charfeh, 1908), pp. *45–*47 = 44–46 (LT). Also edited in F. H. Dolapönu [Filoksinos Yuhanna Dolabani], *Egrāteh d-Dawid bar Pawlos d-metidaʿ d-Bet Rabban* (Mardin, 1953), pp. 44–49.

Debate of Theodore Abū Qurrah with al-Maʾmūn. Ed. Ignace Dick, *Mujādalat Abī Qurrah maʿa al-mutakallimīn al-muslimīn fī majlis al-khalīfa al-Maʾmūn* (Aleppo, 2007).

Denḥā, *Life of Marutha* (BHO 719). Ed. and trans. François Nau, *Histoires d'Ahoudemmeh et de Marouta, métropolitains jacobites de Tagrit et de l'Orient (VIe et VIIe siècles), suivies du traité d'Ahoudemmeh sur l'homme*. PO 3.1 (Paris, 1905), pp. 61–96.

al-Dhahabī, *Kitāb tadhkirat al-ḥuffāẓ*. 4 vols. (Hyderabad/Deccan, 1955–1958).

Dionysius of Alexandria, *Letter to Philemon* [Epistula ad Philemonem presbyterum Romanum] (CPG 1557). Ed. Charles L. Feltoe, *The Letters and Other Remains of Dionysius of Alexandria* (Cambridge/New York, 1904), pp. 52–55. ET in Charles L. Feltoe, *St. Dionysius of Alexandria: Letters and Treatises* (London/New York, 1918), pp. 56–58.

Dionysius bar Salibi, *Against the Melkites*. Ed. and trans. Alphonse Mingana, *Woodbrooke Studies*, vol. 1 (Cambridge, 1927), pp. 17–95.

Disputation between John and the Emir. Ed. and trans. François Nau, 'Un colloque du patriarche Jean avec l'émir des Agaréens,' *JA* 11 (1915), pp. 248–56 (Syriac) = 257–67 (FT). Ed. and trans. Michael P. Penn, 'John and the Emir: A New Introduction, Edition and Translation,' *LM* 121 (2008), pp. 65–91.

Disputation between a Muslim and a Monk of Bēt Ḥālē. Ed. and trans. David G. K. Taylor, in 'The Disputation between a Muslim and a Monk of Bēt Ḥālē: Syriac Text and Annotated English Translation,' in Sidney H. Griffith and Sven Grebenstein, eds., *Christsein in der islamischen Welt: Festschrift für Martin Tamcke zum 60. Geburtstag* (Wiesbaden, 2015), pp. 187–242.

The Disputation of Sergius the Stylite against a Jew. Ed. and trans. Allison Peter Hayman, *The Disputation of Sergius the Stylite against a Jew.* CSCO 338–39, SS 152–53 (Louvain, 1973).

Doctrina Jacobi Nuper Baptizati (CPG 7793). Ed. and trans. Vincent Déroche, 'Juifs et Chrétiens dans l'Orient du VIIe siècle,' *Travaux et Mémoires* 11 (1991), pp. 71–273.

Doctrina Patrum (CPG 7781). Ed. Franz Diekamp, *Doctrina patrum de incarnatione verbi; ein griechisches Florilegium aus der Wende des siebenten und achten Jahrhunderts* (Münster in Westf., 1907).

Elia, *Apologetic Letter.* Ed. and trans. Albert van Roey, *Eliae epistula apologetica ad Leonem, syncellum Harranensem.* CSCO 469–470, SS 201–202 (Leuven, 1985).

Elias, *Life of John of Tella.* Ed. Ernest Walter Brooks, *Vitae virorum apud Monophysitas celeberrimorum. Pars prima.* CSCO SS III.25 (Paris, 1907), pp. 31–95. English translation in Joseph R. Ghanem, 'The Biography of John of Tella (d. A.D. 537) by Elias: Translated from the Syriac with a Historical Introduction and Historical and Linguistic Commentaries' (PhD diss., University of Wisconsin, 1970).

Elias bar Shinaya, *Chronology.* Ed. Ernest Walter Brooks and trans. Jean-Baptiste Chabot, *Opus chronologicum.* 2 vols. in 4. CSCO 62-62a, 63-63a, SS III.7-8 (Paris, 1910). FT available in Louis J. Delaporte, *La chronographie d'Élie Bar-Šinaya, Métropolitain de Nisibe* (Paris, 1910).

Ephrem the Syrian, *Commentary on the Diatessaron.* Trans. Louis Leloir, *Commentaire de l'Évangile concordant ou Diatessaron.* SC 121 (Paris, 1966).

Epiphanius, *Treatise on Weights and Measures* [De mensuris et ponderibus] (CPG 3746). Ed. and trans. James E. Dean, *Epiphanius' Treatise on Weights and Measures: The Syriac Version* (Chicago, 1935).

Eubulus of Lystra, *Against Athanasius, the Pseudo-Bishop of the Severans* [Aduersus Athanasium pseudepiscopum Seuerianorum] (CPG 7685). Ed. Franz Diekamp, *Doctrina Patrum* (Münster in Westf., 1907), pp. 141–48.

Eusebius, *Ecclesiastical History* (CPG 3495). Ed. Eduard Schwartz, Theodor Mommsen, [and Friedhelm Winkelmann]. *Die Kirchengeschichte. Eusebius Werke* 2.2. 2nd ed. (Berlin, 1999).

——, *History of the Martyrs of Palestine* (CPG 3490/BHO 710). Ed. and trans. William Cureton, *History of the Martyrs of Palestine, Discovered in a Very Antient Syriac Manuscript* (London/Edinburgh, 1861).

——, *Preparation for the Gospel* [Praeparatio euangelica] (CPG 3486). Ed. Karl Mras and Édouard des Places, *Die Praeparatio Evangelica* (*Eusebius Werke* 8.1–8.2). 2 vols. (Berlin, 1982–1983). English translation in Edwin H. Gifford, *Preparation for the Gospel* (Oxford, 1903).

First Synod of Timothy I. Ed. and trans. Jean-Baptiste Chabot, *Synodicon Orientale*, pp. 599–603 (Syriac) = 603–608 (French).

Flavius Vopiscus, *Firmus, Saturninus, Proclus, and Bonosus* [*Historia Augusta* 29]. Ed.

and trans. David Magie, *The Scriptores Historiae Augustae*, vol. 3. Loeb Classical Library 263 (Cambridge, MA, 1932), pp. 386–415.

Florilegium Edessenum. Ed. Ignaz Rucker, *Florilegium Edessenum anonymum (syriace ante 562)* (Munich, 1933).

Gennadius of Marseilles, *Lives of Illustrious Men* [De uiris inlustribus] (CPL 957). Ed. Ernest C. Richardson, *Hieronymus liber De viris inlustribus; Gennadius liber De viris inlustribus* (Leipzig, 1896), pp. 57–97.

George, Bishop of the Arab Tribes, *Commentary on the Liturgy*. Ed. and trans. Robert H. Connolly and Humphrey W. Codrington, *Two Commentaries on the Jacobite Liturgy by George Bishop of the Arab Tribes and Moses Bar Kepha, together with the Syriac Anaphora of St. James and a Document Entitled The Book of Life* (London/Oxford, 1913), pp. 11-23 (translation), *3-*15 (text).

——, *Homily on Blessed Mar Severus*. Ed. and trans. Kathleen E. McVey, *George, Bishop of the Arabs. A Homily on Blessed Mar Severus, Patriarch of Antioch*. CSCO 530–31, SS 216–17. (Louvain, 1993).

George of Resh'ayna, *Life of Maximus Confessor*. Ed. and trans. Sebastian P. Brock, 'An Early Syriac *Life* of Maximus the Confessor,' *Analecta Bollandiana* 91 (1973), pp. 299–346.

Gregory of Nazianzus, *Orations* [Orationes] (CPG 3010). PG 35–36, cols. 12–664. Partial English translation by Charles G. Browne and James E. Swallow in *NPNF*, ser. 2, vol. 7 (New York, 1894), pp. 203–434, and partial translation in Martha Vinson, *Select Orations. St. Gregory Nazianzus* (Washington, D.C., 2003).

——, *Orations 20–23*. Ed. and trans. Justin Mossay. *Grégoire de Nazianze. Discours 20–23*. SC 270 (Paris, 1980).

——, *Orations* 32–37. Ed. Claudio Moreschini, trans. Paul Gallay, *Grégoire de Nazianze. Discours* 32–37. SC 318. (Paris, 1985). Other orations are edited and translated in SC 247 [1–3], 250 [27–31], 284 [24–26], 309 [4–5], 318 [32–37], 358 [38–41], 384 [42–43], 405 [6–12] (Paris, 1978–).

Gregory of Nyssa, *Apologia in hexaemeron* (CPG 3153). Ed. and trans. Gregory H. Forbes, *Sancti Patris Nostri Gregorii Nysseni, Basilii M. fratris, quae supersunt omnia*, vol. 1 (Burntisland, 1855), pp. 1–95.

——, *De professione christiana ad Harmonium* (CPG 3163). Ed. Werner Jaeger in *Gregorii Nysseni Opera*, vol. 8.1, *Gregorii Nysseni Opera Ascetica* (Leiden, 1952), pp. 129–42. English translation in Virginia Woods Callahan, *Saint Gregory of Nyssa: Ascetical Works* (Washington, D.C., 1967), pp. 81–89.

——, *Oration on the Divinity of the Son and the Holy Spirit* [De deitate filii et spiritus sancti] (CPG 3192). Ed. Ernestus Rhein in Ernestus Rhein, Friedhelm Mann, Dörte Teske, and Hilda Polack, eds., *Gregorii Nysseni Opera* 10.2 (Leiden/New York/København/Köln, 1996), pp. 117-144.

History of Karka d-Beth Slokh (BHO 705). Ed. Paul Bedjan, *AMS*, vol. 2 (Paris, 1891), pp. 507–535.

History of Mar Aba (BHO 595). Ed. Paul Bedjan, *Histoire de Mar-Jabalaha* (Paris, 1895), pp. 206–74.

History of Mar Isaac [Isaac the Syrian/Isaac of Nineveh] (BHO 540). Ed. Rahmani, *Studia Syriaca*, vol. 1, p. *33.

History of Mar John of Dalyatha, Whose Monastery Is in Qardu (BHO 510). Ed. and trans. Rahmani, *Studia Syriaca*, vol. 1, p. *34 = 33–34 (LT).

History of Mar Yazdpaneh (BHO 431–32). Ed. Paul Bedjan, *Histoire de Mar-Jabalaha* (Paris, 1895), pp. 394–415.

History of the Monastery of Sabrisho' (BHO 874). Ed. and trans. Alphonse Mingana, *Sources Syriaques*, vol. 1 (Mosul, 1908), pp. 171–220 (Syriac) = 221–67 (FT).

History of the Patriarchs of Alexandria ['vulgate recension']. Ed. and trans. Basil T. A. Evetts, *History of the Patriarchs of the Coptic Church of Alexandria*. PO 1.2, 1.4, 5.1, 10.5 (Paris, 1904–1915). Ed. and trans. Yassā 'Abd al-Masīh, O.H.E. Burmester, and Antoine Khater, *History of the Patriarchs of the Egyptian Church: Known as the History of the Holy Church*. 7 vols. (Cairo, 1943–1974).

Ḥunayn b. Isḥāq, *Kayfiyyat idrāk ḥaqīqat al-diyāna*. Ed. Samir Khalil Samir, 'Maqālat Ḥunayn b. Isḥāq fī kayfiyyat idrāk ḥaqīqat al-diyāna,' *al-Machriq* 71 (1997), pp. 345–63. Cf. the French translation in [Samir] Khalil Samir and Paul Nwiya, *Une correspondence Islamo-Chrétienne entre Ibn al-Munağğim, Ḥunayn ibn Isḥāq et Qusṭā ibn Lūqā*. PO 40.4. (Turnhout, 1981).

——, *Risāla*. Ed. and trans. Gotthelf Bergsträsser, *Hunain ibn Ishāq über die syrischen und arabischen Galenübersetzungen* (Leipzig, 1925). Corrections and new collations in Bergsträsser, *Neue materialien zu Ḥunain ibn Isḥāq's Galen-bibliographie* (Leipzig, 1932). Newly edited and translated in John C. Lamoreaux, *Ḥunayn ibn Isḥāq on his Galen Translations: A parallel English-Arabic Text* (Provo, 2016).

Hypatius of Ephesus, *Miscellaneous Enquiries* [Quaestiones miscellaneae] (CPG 6806). Ed. Franz Diekamp, *Analecta Patristica. Texte und Abhandlungen zur Griechischen Patristik* (Rome, 1938), pp. 127–29. English translation in Paul J. Alexander, 'A Note on Image Worship in the Sixth Century,' *Harvard Theological Review* 45 (1952), pp. 178–81.

Ibn 'Abd al-Barr, *Jāmi' bayān al-'ilm wa-faḍlihi*. Ed. 'Abd al-Raḥmān Muḥammad 'Uthmān. 2 vols. (Medina, 1968).

Ibn 'Abd al-Ḥakam, *Sīrat 'Umar b. 'Abd al-'Azīz 'alā mā rawāhu al-Imām Mālik b. Anas wa-aṣḥābuh*. Ed. Aḥmad 'Ubayd (Beirut, 1984).

Ibn 'Abd Rabbih, *al-'Iqd al-Farīd*. Ed. Mufīd Muḥammad Qumayḥa and 'Abd al-Majīd al- Tarḥīnī. 9 vols. in 8. (Beirut, 1983). Partial English translation in Issa J. Boullata, *The Unique Necklace* (*al-'Iqd al-Farīd*). 3 vols. (Reading, UK, 2006–2011).

Ibn Abī Dāwūd, *Kitāb al-masāḥif*. Ed. Arthur Jeffery (Miṣr, 1936).

Ibn Abī Ḥātim, *Taqdimat al-ma'rifa li-kitāb al-jarḥ wa-'l-ta'dīl* (Hyderabad, 1952) [= vol. 1 of Ibn Abī Ḥātim, *Kitāb al-jarḥ wa-'l-ta'dīl*. 9 vols. (Hyderabad, 1952–1953)].

Ibn Abī Shayba, *al-Muṣannaf*. Ed. Ḥamad b. 'Abd Allāh al-Jum'a and Muḥammad b. Ibrāhīm al-Laḥīdān. 16 vols. (Riyad, 2004).

Ibn Abī Uṣaybi'a, *'Uyūn al-anbā' fī ṭabaqāt al-aṭibbā'*. Ed. Nizār Riḍā (Beirut, 1965).

Ibn al-'Adīm, *Bughyat al-ṭalab fī ta'rīkh Ḥalab*. 12 vols. Ed. Suhayl Zakkār (Beirut, 1988).

Ibn 'Asākir, *Ta'rīkh madīnat Dimashq*. Ed. 'Umar b. Gharāma al-'Amrawī. 80 vols. (Beirut, 1995–2001).

Ibn al-Athīr, *al-Nihāya fī gharīb al-ḥadīth wa-'l-athar*. 5 vols. Ed. Ṭāhir Aḥmad al-Zāwī and Maḥmūd Muḥammad al-Ṭanāḥī (n.d., n.p.).

——, *Usd al-ghāba fī ma'rifat al-ṣaḥāba*. Ed. 'Alī Muḥammad Mu'awwaḍ and 'Ādil Aḥmad 'Abd al-Mawjūd. 8 vols. (Beirut, 1994).

Ibn Baṭṭāl, *Sharḥ Ṣaḥīḥ al-Bukhārī*. Ed. Abū Tamīm Yāsir b. Ibrāhīm. 10 vols. (Riyad, 2000).

Ibn al-Durayhim, *Manhaj al-ṣawāb fī qubḥ istiktāb ahl al-kitāb*. Ed. Sayyid Kasrawī (Beirut, 2002).

Ibn Faḍl Allāh al-ʿUmarī, *Masālik al-abṣār fī mamālik al-amṣār*. Ed. Kāmil Salmān al-Jubūrī. 27 vols. in 15. (Beirut, 2010).

Ibn al-Faqīh, *Mukhtaṣar kitāb al-buldān*. Ed. Michael J. de Goeje, *Compendium libri kitāb al-boldān: auctore Ibn al-Fakīh al-Hamadhānī* (Leiden, 1885).

Ibn Ḥabīb, *Kitāb al-muḥabbar*. Ed. Ilse Lichtenstädter (Hyderabad, 1942).

Ibn Ḥajar al-ʿAsqalānī, *Fatḥ al-bārī bi-sharḥ Ṣaḥīḥ al-Bukhārī*. Ed. ʿAbd al-ʿAzīz b. ʿAbd Allāh b. Bāz. 13 vols. (Beirut, n.d.).

——, *al-Iṣāba fī tamyīz al-ṣaḥāba*. Ed. Ṭahā Muḥammad al-Zaynī. 13 vols. (Cairo, 1992–1993).

——, *Tahdhīb al-tahdhīb*. Ed. Ibrāhim al-Zaybaq and ʿĀdil Murshid. 4 vols. (n.d., n.p.).

Ibn al-Ḥājj, *al-Madkhal*. 4 vols. (Egypt, 1960).

Ibn Ḥawqal, *Kitāb al-masālik wa-'l-mamālik*. Ed. Michael Jan de Goeje, *Viae et regna. Descriptio ditionis Moslemicae* (Leiden, 1873).

Ibn Ḥazm, *al-Muḥallā*. Ed. Aḥmad Muḥammad Shākir, et al. 11 vols. (Cairo, 1347–1352).

——, *Ṭawq al-ḥamāma*. Ed. Ḥasan Kāmil al-Ṣirfī. (Cairo, 1950).

Ibn Hishām, *Kitāb sīrat rasūl Allāh*. Ed. Ferdinand Wüstenfeld, *Das Leben Muhammed's nach Muhammed Ibn Ishâk, bearbeitet von Abd el-Malik Ibn Hischâm*. 2 vols. in 3 (Göttingen, 1858–1860). English translation in Alfred Guillaume, *The Life of Muhammad: A Translation of Isḥāq's Sīrat Rasūl Allāh* (London, 1955).

Ibn al-Jarrāḥ, *al-Waraqa*. Ed. ʿAbd al-Wahhāb ʿAzzām and ʿAbd al-Sattār Aḥmad Farrāj (Egypt, 1967).

Ibn al-Jawzī, *Sīrat wa-manāqib ʿUmar b. ʿAbd al-Azīz*. Ed. Naʿīm Zarzūr (Beirut, 1984).

Ibn al-Kalbī, *Mathālib al-ʿArab*. Ed. Najāḥ al-Ṭāʾī (Beirut/London, 1998).

Ibn Kammūna, *Tanqīh al-abḥāth lil-milal al-thalāth*. Ed. Moshe Perlmann, *Saʿd b. Mansūr ibn Kammūna's Examination of the Inquiries into the Three Faiths: A Thirteenth-Century Essay into Comparative Religion* (Berkeley and Los Angeles, 1967). English translation in Moshe Perlmann, *Ibn Kammūna's Examination of the Three Faiths: A Thirteenth-Century Essay in the Comparative Study of Religion* (Berkeley, 1971).

Ibn Kathīr, *Tafsīr al-Qur'ān al-ʿaẓīm*. Ed. Muṣṭafā al-Sayyid Muḥammad, et al. 15 vols. (Giza, 2000).

Ibn Khallikān, *Wafayāt al-aʿyān wa-anbā' abnā' al-zamān*. Ed. Iḥsān ʿAbbās. 8 vols. (Beirut, 1977). English translation in William MacGuckin de Slane, *Ibn Khallikan's Biographical Dictionary, Translated from the Arabic*. 4 vols. (Paris, 1842–1871).

Ibn Mājah, *Sunan*. Ed. Bashshār ʿAwwād Maʿrūf. 6 vols. (Beirut, 1998).

Ibn Mārī, *al-Maqāmāt al-Masīḥiyya*. Partial edition (introduction and first *maqāma*) in Anastās al-Karmalī, 'al-Maqāmāt al-Naṣrāniyya li-Ibn Mārī,' *al-Machriq* 3 (1900), pp. 591–98. Partial edition (the twelfth and fiftieth *maqāmas*) in Ṣabīḥ Ṣādiq, 'Baghdād min khilāl al-maqāmāt,' *al-Mawrid* 8 (1979), pp. 581–88.

Ibn al-Muʿtazz, *Kitāb fuṣūl al-tamāthīl fī tabāshīr al-surūr*. Ed. Jurj Qanāziʿ and Fahd Abū Khaḍra (Damascus, 1989).

Ibn al-Nadīm, *Fihrist*. Ed. Gustav Flügel, *Kitâb al-fihrist, mit Amnerkungen*. 2 vols. (Leipzig, 1871–1872).

Ibn Qayyim al-Jawziyya, *Aḥkām ahl al-dhimma*. Ed. Ṭāhā 'Abd al-Ra'ūf Sa'd. 2 vols. in 1 (Beirut, 1995).

Ibn al-Qifṭī, *Inbāh al-ruwāh 'alā anbāh al-nuhāh*. Ed. Muḥammad Abū al-Faḍl Ibrāhīm. 4 vols. (Cairo/Beirut, 1986).

——, *Ta'rīkh al-ḥukamā'*. Ed. Julius Lippert, *Ibn al-Qifṭī's Ta'rīḫ al-ḥukamā': auf Grund der Vorarbeiten Aug. Müller's*. (Leipzig, 1903).

Ibn Qudāma, *al-Mughnī*. Ed. 'Abd Allāh b. 'Abd al-Muḥsin al-Turkī and 'Abd al-Fattāh Muḥammad al-Ḥulw. 15 vols. (Riyad, 1997).

Ibn Qutayba, *Kitāb al-ashriba wa-dhikr ikhtilāf al-nās fīhā*. Yāsīn Muḥammad al-Sawwās (Beirut, 1999).

——, *Kitāb 'uyūn al-akhbār*. 4 vols. in 2 (Cairo, 1925-1930).

——, *al-Ma'ārif*. Ed. Tharwat 'Ukāsha (Cairo, 1960).

——, *Ta'wīl mushkil al-Qur'ān*. Ed. al-Sayyid Aḥmad Ṣaqr (Cairo, 1954).

Ibn Rusta, *al-Mujallad al-sābi' min Kitāb al-a'lāq al-nafīsa*. Ed. Michael J. de Goeje (Leiden, 1892).

Ibn Sa'd, *Kitāb al-ṭabaqāt al-kabīr*. Ed. Eduard Sachau, Eugen Mittwoch, et al. *Biographien Muhammeds, seiner Gefährten und der späteren Träger des Islams*. 15 vols. in 9. (Leiden, 1905–1940). English translation of vols. 5 and 7 in Aisha Bewley, *The Men of Madina*. 2 vols. (London, 1997–2000). English translation of volume 8 in Aisha Bewley, *The Women of Madina* (London, 1995). English translation of volumes 1.1–2.2 in Syed Moinul Haq and H. K. Ghazanfar, *Kitab al-tabaqat al-kabir*. 2 vols. (repr. New Delhi, 2009).

Ibn Taymiyya, *Iqtiḍā' al-ṣirāṭ al-mustaqīm mukhālafat aṣḥāb al-jaḥīm*. Ed. Muḥammad Ḥāmid al-Fiqī (Cairo, 1950).

——, *Majmū'at al-fatāwā*. Ed. 'Āmir al-Jazzār and Anwār al-Bāz. 37 vols. (al-Manṣūra, 2005).

Ibn al-Ṭayyib, *Tafsīr al-mashriqī*. Ed. Yūsuf Manqariyūs. 2 vols. (Cairo, 1908–1910).

Ibn al-Ukhuwwa, *Ma'ālim al-qurba fī aḥkām al-ḥisba*. Ed. and trans. Reuben Levy, *The Ma'ālim al-qurba fī aḥkām al-ḥisba of Ḍiyā' al-Dīn Muḥammad ibn Muḥammad al-Qurashī al-Shāfi'ī, known as Ibn al-Ukhuwwa* (London, 1938).

Irenaeus of Lyons, *Against Heresies* [Aduersus Haereses] (CPG 1306). Ed. and trans. Norbert Brox, *Epideixis; Adversus haereses. Darlegung der apostolischen Verkündigung; Gegen die Häresien*. 5 vols. (Freiburg/New York, 1993-2001).

Isaac of Antioch, *Homilies*. Ed. Paul Bedjan, *Homiliae S. Isaaci, Syri Antiocheni* (Paris/Leipzig, 1903).

——, *Homily on Sorcerers, Enchanters, Diviners, and on the End and Consumation*. Ed. and trans. Thomas J. Lamy, *Sancti Ephraem Syri hymni et sermones*, vol. 2, cols. 393–426. [For this homily as the work of Isaac (and not Ephrem), see Baumstark, *Geshichte*, p. 65, n. 4, and Mathews, 'A Bibliographical Clavis,' p. 11.]

Isho'dnaḥ of Basra, *The Book of Chastity*. Ed. and trans. Jean-Baptiste Chabot, *Le livre de la chasteté composé par Jésusdenah, évêque de Baçrah* (Rome, 1896).

Isho'yahb III, *Letters*. Ed. and trans. Rubens. Duval, *Išō'yahb III Patriarcha: Liber Epistularum*. CSCO Ser II.64. (Paris, 1904–1905).

——, *Life of Isho'sabran* (BHO 451). Ed. Jean-Baptiste Chabot, 'Histoire de Jésus-Sabran, écrite par Jésus-Yab d'Adiabène,' *Nouvelles archives des missions scientifiques et littéraires* 7 (1897), pp. 485–584.

ʿIyāḍ b. Mūsā, *Shifā bi-taʿrīf ḥuqūq al-Muṣṭafā*. Ed. ʿAlī Muḥammad al-Bajāwī. 2 vols. (Beirut, 1984). English translation in Aisha Bewley, *Muhammad, Messenger of Allah.* Ash-Shifa *of Qadi Iyad* (Inverness, 2011).

Jacob of Edessa, *Additional Questions of John the Stylite to Jacob*. Ed. and trans. Arthur Vööbus, *The Synodicon in the West Syrian Tradition* I. CSCO 367–68, SS 161–62 (Louvain, 1975), pp. 245–54 (Syriac) = 225–33 (English).

——, *Canons*. Ed. and trans. Arthur Vööbus, *The Synodicon in the West Syrian Tradition I.* CSCO 367–368, SS 161–62 (Louvain, 1975), pp. 269 (Syriac) = 245–47 (ET).

——, *Chronicle*. Ed. and trans. Ernest Walter Brooks, *Chronica Minora, pars tertia*. CSCO III.4 (Paris, 1905–1907), pp. 261–330 (Syriac) = 197–258 (LT). Partial edition and ET (of Jacob's Chronological Canon) in Ernest Walter Brooks, 'The Chronological Canon of James of Edessa,' *ZDMG* 53 (1899), pp. 261–327.

——, *Hexaemeron*. Ed. Jean-Baptiste Chabot, *Iacobi Edesseni Hexaemeron*. CSCO 92, SS 44 (Louvain, 1953). Latin translation in Arthur Vaschalde, *Iacobi Edesseni Hexaemeron*. CSCO 97, SS 48 (Louvain, 1953). Arabic translation in Gharīghūriyūs Ṣalībā Shamʿūn, *al-Ayyām al-Sitta* (Aleppo, 1990).

——, *Letter 1 to John, the Stylite of Litarb*. Ed. and trans. Robert Schröter, 'Erster Brief Jakob's von Edessa an Johannes den Styliten,' *ZDMG* 24 (1870), pp. 261-300.

——, *Letter 12 and 13* to John, the Stylite of Litarb [Syriac text]. Ed. William Wright, 'Two Epistles of Mār Jacob, Bishop of Edessa,' *Journal of Sacred Literature and Biblical Record* 10 (1867), pp. 430-460. Translation in François Nau, 'Traduction des lettres XII et XIII de Jacques d'Édesse,' *ROC* 10 (1905), pp. 197-208, 258-282.

——, *Letter to Domeṭ* (fragment). Ed. and trans. Sebastian P. Brock and Lucas van Rompay, *Catalogue of the Syriac Manuscripts and Fragments in the Library of Deir al-Surian, Wadi al-Natrun (Egypt)* (Leuven, 2014), pp. 397–98.

——, *Letter to John, the Stylite of Litarb, from BL Add. 14,493*. Ed. and trans. Karl-Erik Rignell, *A Letter from Jacob of Edessa to John the Stylite of Litarab concerning Ecclesiastical Canons Edited from Ms. Br. Mus. Add. 14,493 with Introduction, Translation and Commentary. Syriac Text with Introduction, Translation and Commentary* (Lund, 1979).

——, *Letter on Orthography*. Ed. and trans. George Phillips, *A Letter by Mār Jacob, Bishop of Edessa, on Syriac Orthography* (London, 1869). This work is supplemented by George Phillips, *Mār Jacob and Bar Hebraeus on Syriac Accents &c:* Appendix III (London, 1870).

——, *Letter on Orthography*. Ed. and trans. Jean-Pierre Paulin Martin, *Jacobi episcopi Edesseni Epistola ad Gregorium episcopum Sarugensem de orthographia syriaca* (Leipzig, 1869).

——, *Mēmrā on Faith and Against Nestorians*. Ed. and trans. Marianus Ugolini, *Iacobi Edesseni de fide adversus Nestorium Carmen* (Rome, 1888). Ed. and trans. Aho Shemunkasho, 'A Verse-Homily Attributed to Jacob of Edessa: On Faith and Contra Nestorius,' in Gregorius Y. Ibrahim and George A. Kiraz, eds., *Studies on Jacob of Edessa* (Piscataway, N.J., 2010), pp. 107–141.

——, *Questions Which Addai the Priest and Lover of Labors Asked Jacob, the Bishop of Edessa*. Ed. Paul Anton de Lagarde, *Reliquiae Iuris Ecclesiastici Antiquissimae Syriace* (Leipzig, 1856), pp. *117–*43. Ed. Thomas J. Lamy, *Dissertatio de Syrorum fide et disciplina in re eucharistica* (Louvain, 1859), pp. 98–171. Ed. and trans. Arthur Vööbus, *The Synodicon in the West Syrian Tradition* I. CSCO 367–68, SS 161–62. (Louvain, 1975), pp. 258–69 (Syriac) = 235–44 (ET). GT in Carl Kayser, *Die Canones Jacob's von Edessa übersetzt und erläutert* (Leipzig, 1886), pp. 11–33. FT of Lamy's edition in François Nau, *Les canons et les résolutions canoniques de Rabboula, Jean de Tella, Cyriaque d'Amid, Jacques d'Édesse, Georges des Arabes, Cyriaque d'Antioche, Jean III, Théodose d'Antioche et des Perses* (Paris, 1906), pp. 38–66.

Jacob of Edessa, *Questions of All Kind, Which John the Stylite Asked the Venerable Jacob, the Teacher.* Ed. and trans. Ed. and trans. Arthur Vööbus, *The Synodicon in the West Syrian Tradition I.* CSCO 367–68, SS 161–62 (Louvain, 1975), pp. 233–45 (Syriac) = 215–25 (English).

——, *The Questions of Thomas the Hermit, which he asked Jacob of Edessa.* Ed. and trans. Arthur Vööbus, *The Synodicon in the West Syrian Tradition I.* CSCO 367–368, SS 161–62 (Louvain, 1975), pp. 256–58 = 234–35 (ET).

——, *Treatise against Those Who Transgress Ecclesiastical Canons* [Chapter 12]. Ed. and trans. Michael Penn, 'Jacob of Edessa's Defining Christianity: Introduction, Edition, and Translation,' *Journal of Eastern Christian Studies* 64 (2012): 175–99.

Jacob of Sarugh, *Homilies.* Ed. Paul Bedjan, *Homiliae Selectae Mar-Jacobi Sarugensis.* 5 vols. (Paris/Leipzig, 1905–1910).

——, *Homily on Mar Ephrem.* Ed. and trans. Joseph Amar, *A Metrical Homily on Holy Mar Ephrem by Mar Jacob of Sarug: Critical Edition of the Syriac Text, Translation and Introduction.* PO 47.1 (Turnhout, 1995)

al-Jāḥiẓ, *al-Bayān wa-'l-tabyīn.* Ed. Darwīsh Juwaydī. 3 vols. in 1 (Beirut, 2013).

——, *Fī 'l-radd 'alā al-Naṣārā.* Ed. 'Abd al-Salām Muḥammad Hārūn, *Rasā'il al-Jāḥiẓ*, vol. 3 (Beirut, 1991), pp. 303–51. English translation in Joshua Finkel, 'A Risāla of al-Jāḥiẓ,' *Journal of the American Oriental Society* 47 (1927), pp. 311–34. Partial English translation in Pellat, *The Life and Works of Jāḥiẓ*, pp. 86–91.

——, *Kitāb al-amṣār wa-'ajā'ib al-buldān.* Ed. Charles Pellat, 'Al-Jāḥīẓ rā'id al-jughrāfiyya al-insāniyya,' *al-Mashriq* 60 (1966), pp. 169-205. Partial English translation in Pellat, *The Life and Works of Jāḥiẓ*, pp. 188–195.

——, *Kitāb al-bukhalā'.* Ed. Ṭāḥa al-Ḥājirī (Cairo, 1967). FT in Charles Pellat, *Le livre des avares de Ğahiz* (Paris, 1951).

——, *al-Uthmāniyya.* Ed. 'Abd al-Salām Muḥammad Hārūn (Miṣr, 1955). Partial English translation in Pellat, *The Life and Works of Jāḥiẓ*, pp. 72–82.

Ps.-Jāḥiẓ, *Kitāb dhamm akhlāq al-kuttāb.* Ed. 'Abd al-Salām Muḥammad Hārūn, *Rasā'il al-Jāḥiẓ*, vol. 2 (Cairo, 1964–1979), pp. 183–209. Partial English translation in Pellat, *The Life and Works of Jāḥiẓ*, pp. 273–75.

——, *Kitāb al-Tāj fī akhlāq al-mulūk.* Ed. Aḥmad Zakī (Cairo, 1914).

Jahshiyārī, *Kitāb al-wuzarā' wa-'l-kuttāb.* Ed. Muṣṭafā al-Saqqā, Ibrāhīm al-Ibyārī, and 'Abd al-Ḥafīẓ Shalabī (Cairo, 1938).

Jarīr b. 'Aṭiyya, *Diwān* [Diwān Jarīr]. (Beirut, 1986).

Ps.-John bar Aphtonia, *Life of Severus.* Ed. and trans. Marc-Antoine Kugener, *Sévère, patriacrhe d'Antioche, 512–518: textes syriaques publiés, traduits et annotés.* Pt. 2: *Vie de Sévère par Jean, supérieur du monastère de Beith-Aphtonia, avec divers textes syriaques, grecs et latins.* PO 2.3 (Paris, 1904). English translation by Sebastian P. Brock in Sebastian P. Brock and Brian J. Fitzgerald, *Two Early Lives of Severos, Patriarch of Antioch* (Liverpool, 2013), pp. 101–39.

John bar Penkaye, *Book of the Main Events.* Partial edition in Alphonse Mingana,

Sources Syriaques, vol. 1 (Leipzig/Mosul, 1908), pp. *2–*171. Partial English translation available in Sebastian P. Brock, 'North Mesopotamia in the Late Seventh Century: Book XV of John bar Penkāyē's Rīš Mellē,' *Jerusalem Studies in Arabic and Islam* 9 (1987), pp. 51–75.

John Cassian, *Conferences* (CPL 512). Ed. Michael Petschenig, *Iohannis Cassiani Conlationes XXIIII* (Vienna, 1886). English translation by Edgar C. S. Gibson in *NPNF*, ser. 2, vol. 11, pp. 291–546.

John Chrysostom, *Adversos Judaeos orationes* (CPG 4327). PG 48, cols. 843–942. English translation in Paul W. Harkins, *Discourses against Judaizing Christians* (Washington, D.C., 1979).

——, *Baptismal Instructions* [Catecheses ad illuminandos (series tertia)] (CPG 4465–72). Ed. and trans. Antoine Wenger, *Huit catéchèses baptismales inédites*. SC 50. (Paris, 1957). English translation by Paul W. Harkins, *St. John Chrysostom: Baptismal Instructions* (Westminster, MD/London, 1963).

——, *De baptismo Christi* (CPG 4335), PG 49, cols. 363–72.

——, *Homilies on the Acts of the Apostles* [In acta apostolorum homiliae] (CPG 4426), PG 60, cols. 13-384. English translation by J. Walker, J. Sheppard, H. Browne, and George B. Stevens in *NPNF*, ser. 1, vol. 11 (New York, 1889), pp. 1–330.

——, *Homilies on First Corinthians* [In epistulam i ad Corinthos argumentum et homiliae] (CPG 4428). PG 61, cols. 9–382. English translation by Talbot W. Chambers in *NPNF*, ser. 1, vol. 12, pp. 1–269.

——, *Homilies on John* [In Iohannem homiliae] (CPG 4425). PG 59, cols. 23-482. English translation by G.T. Stupart in *NPNF*, ser. 1, vol. 14 (New York, 1889), pp. 1-334.

——, *Homilies on Matthew* [In Matthaeum homiliae] (CPG 4424), PG 57-58, cols. 13-794. English translation by George Prevost in *NPNF*, ser. 1, vol. 10.

——, *Homilies on the Statues* [Ad populum Antiochenum homiliae (*De statuis*)] (CPG 4330). PG 49, cols. 15–222. English translation by W.R.W. Stephens in *NPNF* (New York, 1889), ser. 1, vol. 9, pp. 317–489.

——, *In Illud:* Pater, si possibile est, transeat (CPG 4369). PG 51, cols. 31–40. English translation by W.R.W. Stephens in *NPNF*, ser. 1, vol. 9, pp. 201–207.

——, *On the Incomprehensible Nature of God* [De incomprehensibili dei natura homiliae] (CPG 4318). Ed and trans. Anne-Marie Malingrey, *Jean Chrysostome: Sur l'incompréhensibilité de Dieu. t. 1. Homélies I-V.* SC 28bis. (Paris, 1970). Translated into English by Paul W. Harkins, *St. John Chrysostom: On the Incomprehensible Nature of God* (Washington, D.C., 1982).

——, *De Sanctis Martryibus* (CPG 4357), PG 50, cols. 645–54.

John of Damascus, *On Heresies* [De haeresibus] (CPG 8044). Ed. Bonifatius Kotter, *Die Schriften des Johannes von Damaskos*, vol. 4: *Liber de haeresibus. Opera Polemica* (Berlin/New York, 1981), pp. 19–67.

John of Ephesus, *Ecclesiastical History*. Ed. and trans. Ernest Walker Brooks, *Iohannis Ephesini historiae ecclesiasticae pars tertia.* 2 vols. CSCO III.3. (Paris, 1935–1936). Partial English translation in Robert Payne Smith, *The Third Part of the Ecclesiastical History of John Bishop of Ephesus* (Oxford, 1860).

——, *Lives of the Eastern Saints.* Ed. and trans. Ernest Walter Brooks, *John of Ephesus. Lives of the Eastern Saints.* PO 17.1, 18.4, 19.2 (Paris, 1923–1925).

John Moschus, *Spiritual Meadow* [Pratum spirituale] (CPG 7376). PG 87, cols. 2852–

3112. English translation in John Wortley, *The Spiritual Meadow* (Collegeville, MN, 1992).

Ps.-John Moschus, *Spiritual Meadow* (Georgian Appendix), Chapter 19. Ed. and trans. Bernard Flusin, 'L'esplanade du temple a l'arrivée des Arabes, d'après deux récits byzantins,' in Raby and Johns, eds., *Bayt al-Maqdis: 'Abd al-Malik's Jerusalem*, vol. 1 (Oxford, 1992), pp. 19–22.

John Rufus, *Plerophories* [Plerophoriae] (CPG 7507). Ed. and trans. François Nau, *Jean Rufus, évêque de Maïouma. Plérophories.* PO 8.1 (Paris, 1912).

John of Tella, *Canonical Answers.* Ed. and trans. Thomas J. Lamy, *Dissertatio de Syrorum fide et disciplina in re eucharistica* (Louvain, 1859), pp. 62–97.

(Ps.-?) Joshua the Stylite, *Chronicle.* Ed. and trans. William Wright, *The Chronicle of Joshua the Stylite Composed in Syriac A.D. 507* (Cambridge, 1882). ET in Frank R. Trombley and John W. Watt, *The Chronicle of Pseudo-Joshua the Stylite* (Liverpool, 2000).

Justin Martyr, *Dialogue with Trypho* [Dialogus cum Tryphone Iudaeo] (CPG 1076). Ed. Georges Archambault, *Dialogue avec Tryphon.* 2 vols. (Paris, 1909). English translation in Thomas B. Falls and Thomas P. Halton, *Dialogue with Trypho* (Washington, DC, 2003).

Ps.-Justin Martyr, *Cohortatio ad Graecos* (CPG 1083). PG 6, cols. 241–312.

Justinian, *Codex.* Ed. Paul Krueger, *Corpus Iuris Civilis*, vol. 2: *Codex Iustinianus* (Berlin, 1906). English translation based on the work of Fred Blume in Bruce W. Frier, ed., *The Codex of Justinian: A New Annotated Translation, with Parallel Latin and Greek Text based on a Translation by Justice Fred H. Blume.* 3 vols. (Cambridge, 2016).

——, *Contra Monophysitas* (CPG 6878). PG 86, cols. 1104–46.

——, *Novels.* Ed. Rudolf Schoell and Wilhelm Kroll, *Corpus Iuris Civilis*, vol. 3: *Novellae* (Berlin, 1912). English translation by Fred Blume available at: http://www.uwyo.edu/lawlib/justinian-novels/.

al-Khallāl, *Ahl al-milal wa-'l-ridda wa-'l-zanādiqa wa-tārik 'l-ṣalāt wa-'l-farā'iḍ min Kitāb al-Jāmi'.* Ed. Ibrāhīm b. Ḥamad b. Sulṭān. 2 vols. (Riyad, 1996).

Khuzistan Chronicle. Ed. Ignazio Guidi, *Chronica minora, Pars prior.* CSCO Syr. III.4. (Paris, 1903), pp. 15–39. Partial English translation by Geoffrey Greatrex in Geoffrey Greatrex and Samuel N. C. Lieu, *The Roman Eastern Frontier and the Persian Wars. Part II: AD 363–630. A Narrative Sourcebook* (London/New York, 2002), pp. 229–37.

al-Kindī, *Apology.* [Ed. Anton Tien,] *Risālat 'Abd Allāh b. Ismā'īl al-Hāshimī ilā 'Abd al-Masīḥ b. Isḥāq* (London, 1885). English translation by Anton Tien in N. A. Newman, ed., *The Early Christian-Muslim Dialogue: A Collection of Documents from the First Three Islamic Centuries, 632–900 AD* (Hatfield, Penn., 1993), pp. 365–545. FT in Georges Tartar, *Dialogue islamo-chrétien sous le calife Al-Ma'mûn (813–834): les épitres d'Al-Hashimî et d'Al-Kindî* (Paris, 1985).

al-Kindī, Abū 'Umar Muḥammad b. Yūsuf. *Kitāb al-wulāh wa-kitāb al-quḍāh.* Ed. Rhuvon Guest, *The Governors and Judges of Egypt* (London/Leiden, 1912).

Kitāb al-shaṭranj mimmā allafahu al-'Adlī wa-'l-Ṣūlī wa-ghayruhumā (Frankfurt, 1986).

Legend of Sergius Baḥīrā. Ed. and trans. Barbara Roggema in *The Legend of Sergius Baḥīrā. Eastern Christian Apologetics and Apocalyptic in Response to Islam* (Leiden/Boston, 2009), pp. 254–309 (= East Syrian recension); 312–73 (= West Syrian recension).

Leontius of Damascus, *Life of Stephen of Mar Sabas* (BHG 1670). Ed. and trans. John C.

Lamoreaux, *The Life of Stephen of Mar Sabas*. CSCO 578–79, SA 50–51 (Louvain, 1999).

Leontius of Jerusalem, *Testimonies of the Saints*. Ed. and trans. Patrick T. R. Gray, *Leontius of Jerusalem. Against the Monophysites: Testimonies of the Saints and Aporiae* (Oxford, 2006).

Leontius of Neapolis, *Life of John the Almsgiver* (BHG 886). Ed. Heinrich Gelzer, *Leontios' von Neapolis Leben des heiligen Johannes des Barmherzigen, Erzbischofs von Alexandrien* (Freiburg/Leipzig, 1893), pp. 1–103. English translation in Dawes and Baynes, *Three Byzantine Saints*, pp. 207–62. The Greek text of the 'long recension' has been edited in André J. Festugière and Lennart Rydén, eds. and trans., *Vie de Syméon le Fou et Vie de Jean de Chypre* (Paris, 1974), pp. 343–409 (Greek) = 439–524 (FT).

Letter of the Bishops and Priests of Armenia to Proclus, Bishop of Constantinople (CPG 5898). Ed. Paul Bedjan in *Nestorius. Le Livre d'Héraclide de Damas* (Paris/Leipzig, 1910), pp. 594–96.

Letter of Tansar. Trans. Mary Boyce, *The Letter of Tansar* (Rome, 1968).

Letter of the Venerable Orthodox Bishops to the Monks in the Congregation of Amid and All of Its Province. Ed. and trans. Ignatius Ephrem Rahmani, *Studia Syriaca*, vol. 1, pp. *25–*26 (Syriac) = 24–25 (LT). Cf. also Draguet, 'Une pastorale antijulianiste des environs de l'année 530,' *LM* 40 (1927), pp. 75–92.

Libanius, *Orations*. Ed. Richardus Foerster, *Libanii opera*. 12 vols. in 13. (*Orations* are in vols. 1–4). (Leipzig, 1903–1927). English translation of *Oration* 11 available in Albert F. Norman, *Antioch as a Centre of Hellenic Culture as Observed by Libanius* (Liverpool, 2000), pp. 3–65.

Life of Elias of Heliopolis (BHG 578–79). Ed. Athanasios Papadopoulos-Kerameus, *Syllogē Palaistinēs kai Syriakēs hagiologies*, vol. 1 (St. Petersburg, 1907) pp. 42-59. English translation in Stamatina McGrath, 'Elias of Heliopolis: The Life of an Eighth-Century Syrian Saint,' in John W. Nesbitt, ed., *Byzantine Authors: Literary Activities and Preoccupations. Texts and Translations dedicated to the Memory of Nicolas Oikonomides* (Leiden/Boston, 2003), pp. 85–107.

Life of Ephrem. Ed. and trans. Joseph P. Amar, *The Syriac Vita Tradition of Ephrem the Syrian*. CSCO 629-630, SS 242–43 (Louvain, 2011). [= BHO 269, 270 + a previously unpublished recension]

Life of John the Almsgiver (BHG 887v). Ed. Hippolyte Delehaye, 'Une vie inédite de Saint Jean l'Aumonier,' *AB* 45 (1927), pp. 19–73. Partial English translation in Dawes and Baynes, *Three Byzantine Saints*, pp. 199–206. French translation in Festugière Lennart Rydén, *Vie de Syméon le Fou et Vie de Jean de Chypre*, pp. 321–29.

Life of John of Damascus. Ed. Constantine Bacha, *Sīrat al-qiddīs Yuḥannā al-Dimashqī* (Harissa, 1912).

Life of John of Daylam. Ed. and trans. Sebastian P. Brock, 'A Syriac Life of John of Dailam,' *PdO* 10 (1981–1982), pp. 123–89.

Life and Martyrdom of the Holy Neo-Martyr Bacchus the Younger (BHG 209). Ed. F. A. Demetrakopoulou, ''Άγιος Βάκχος ὁ Νέος,' *Epistēmonikē epetēris tēs Philosophikēs Scholēs tou Panepistēmiou Athēnōn* 26 (1977–1978), pp. 331–63 [344–50 is an edition of the epitome of the *vita* and martyrdom of Bacchus contained in Athens 2108].

Life of Shabbay. Ed. and trans. Sebastian P. Brock, 'A West Syriac Life of Mar Shabbay (Bar Shabba), Bishop of Merv,' in Dmitrij Bumazhnov, Emmanouela Grypeou, Timothy B. Sailors, and Alexander Toepel, eds., *Bibel, Byzanz und Christlicher Orient: Festschrift für Stephen Gerö zum 65. Geburtstag* (Leuven, 2011), pp. 259–79.

Life of Theodore of Sykeon (BHG 1748). Ed. Theophilou Ioannou, *Mnēmeia hagiologika* (Venice, 1884), pp. 361–495. English translation available in Dawes and Baynes, *Three Byzantine Saints*, pp. 88–185.

The Life of Timothy of Kākhushtā. Ed. and trans. John C. Lamoreaux and Cyril Cairala, *The Life of Timothy of Kākhushtā: Two Arabic Texts*. PO 48.4 (Turnhout, 2000). ['Paris Version' = pp. 38–95; 'Saidnaya Version' = 96–183].

Lot of the Apostles. Trans. Giuseppe Furlani, 'Una recensione siriaca delle *Sortes apostolorum*,' *Atti del Reale Istituto Veneto di Scienze, Lettere ed Arti* 82.2 (1922-1923), pp. 357-363.

Lucian, *The Fisher*. Ed. M. D. Macleod, *Luciani Opera*, vol. 2 (Oxford, 1974), pp. 51–85.

Lucifer of Calaris, *De non conveniendo cum haereticis* (CPL 112). Ed. Gerardus F. Diercks, *Luciferi Calaritani Opera quae supersunt: ad fidem duorum codicum qui adhuc extant necnon adhibitis editionibus veteribus*. CCSL 8 (Turnhout, 1978), pp. 165–92.

Maḥbūb b. Qusṭanṭīn [Agapius of Manbij], *Kitāb al-ʿUnwān*. Ed. and trans. Alexandre A. Vasiliev, *Kitab al-ʿunvan (histoire universelle, écrite par Agapius de Menbidj)*. PO 5.4, 7.4, 8.3, 11.1 (Paris, 1910–1947).

Mainyo-i-khard. Ed. and trans., Edward W. West, *The Book of the Mainyo-i-khard; The Pazand and Sanskrit Texts (in Roman characters) as arranged by Neriosengh Dhaval in the fifteenth century; with an English translation, a glossary of the Pazand text, containing the Sanskrit, Persian and Pahlavi equivalents, a sketch of Pazand grammar, and an introduction* (Stuttgart/London, 1871).

Mālik b. Anas, *al-Muwaṭṭa'*. Ed. Muḥammad Fu'ād ʿAbd al-Bāqī. 2 vols. (Beirut, 1985). English translation in Aisha Abdurrahman Bewley, *Al-Muwatta of Imam Malik ibn Anas: The First Formulation of Islamic law* (London/New York, 1989).

al-Maqdisī, *Kitāb aḥsan al-taqāsīm fī maʿrifat al-aqālīm*. Ed. Michael J. de Goeje, *Descriptio imperii Moslemici, auctore al-Moqaddasi*. 2nd ed. (Leiden, 1906). ET in Basil A. Collins, *The Best Divisions for Knowledge of the Regions: A Translation of* Ahsan al-Taqasim fi Maʿrifat al-Aqalim (Reading, 1994).

al-Maqrīzī, *Ittiʿāẓ al-ḥunafā' bi-akhbār al-a'immah al-Fāṭimīyīn al-khulafā'*. Ed. Jamāl al-Dīn al-Shayyāl and Muḥammad Ḥilmī Muḥammad Aḥmad. 3 vols. (Cairo, 1996).

——, *al-Mawāʿiẓ wa-'l-iʿtibār fī dhikr al-khiṭaṭ wa-'l-āthār*. Ed. Ayman Fu'ād Sayyid. 7 vols. in 8 (London, 2003). Partial edition and translation of section on 'The Feasts of the Copts' in Robert Griveau, ed. and trans., 'Les fètes des Coptes,' in PO 10.4, pp. 313–43 (Paris. 1915).

——, *Nizāʿ wa-'l-takhāṣum fīmā bayna Banī Umayya wa-Banī Hāshim*. Ed. Geerhardus Vos, *Die Kämpfe und Streitigkeiten zwischen den Banū 'Umajja und den Banū Hāšim* (Leiden, 1888). ET available in Clifford E. Bosworth, *al-Maqrīzī's 'Book of Contention and Strife concerning the Relations between the Banū Umayya and the Banū Hāshim'* (Manchester, 1983).

Mar Aba, *Letter on the Politeia of Correct Behavior*. Ed. and trans. Jean-Baptiste Chabot, *Synodicon Orientale*, pp. 80–85 (Syriac) = 332–38 (French). Also edited by Paul Bedjan in *Histoire de Mar-Jabalaha*, pp. 274–88, with the title, 'On the Ordering of Believers.'

Maronite Chronicle. Ed. Ernest Walter Brooks, *Chronica minora, Pars secunda*. CSCO Syr. III.4 (Paris, 1904), pp. 43–74. Partial English translation by Andrew Palmer in Palmer et al., *The Seventh Century in the West-Syrian Chronicles*, pp. 29–35. [Additional, newly-discovered material likely from the *Maronite Chronicle* has been edited and translated in Sebastian P. Brock and Lucas van Rompay, *Catalogue of the Syriac Manuscripts and Fragments in the Library of Deir al-Surian, Wadi al-Natrun (Egypt)* (Leuven, 2014), pp. 373–75 (and see also 358–59).]

Martyrdom of Gregory Pirangushnasp (BHO 353). Ed. Paul Bedjan, *Histoire de Mar-Jabalaha* (Paris, 1895), pp. 347–94.

Martyrdom of Pusai (BHO 993). Ed. Paul Bedjan, *AMS*, pp. 208–32.

Mar Zadoy, *History of Mar Yawnan* (BHO 527–30). Ed. Paul Bedjan, *AMS*, vol. 1, pp. 466–525. English translation by Sebastian P. Brock in 'The History of Mar Yawnan,' in Mario Kozah et al., eds., *An Anthology of Syriac Writers from Qatar in the Seventh Century* (Piscataway, N.J., 2015), pp. 1–42.

al-Masʿūdī, *Murūj al-dhahab wa-maʿādin al-jawhar*. Ed. and trans. Charles Barbier de Meynard and Pavet de Courteille, *Les prairies d'or*. 9 vols. (Paris, 1861–1877). Partial ET in Paul Lunde and Caroline Stone, *The Meadows of Gold* (London/New York, 1989).

Maximus the Confessor, *Ambigua ad Iohannem* (CPG 7705.2). PG 91, cols. 1061–1417. Ed. and trans. Nicholas Constas, *On Difficulties in the Church Fathers. The Ambigua*, vol. 1 (Cambridge, MA/London, 2014), pp. 61–451, and vol. 2.

——, *Ambigua ad Thomam* (CPG 7705.1). PG 91, cols. 1032–60. Ed. and trans. Nicholas Constas, *On Difficulties in the Church Fathers. The Ambigua*, vol. 1 (Cambridge, MA/London, 2014), pp. 1–59.

——, *Scholia in Corpus Areopagiticum* (CPG 7708), PG 4, cols. 15–432, 527–76.

Mena of Nikiou, *History of the Patriarch Isaac* (BHO 539). Ed. Emile Amélineau, *Histoire du patriarche copte Isaac: étude critique, texte et traduction* (Paris, 1890), pp. 1–80. English translation in David N. Bell, *The Life of Isaac of Alexandria; and The Martyrdom of Saint Macrobius* (Piscataway, N.J., 2009), pp. 43–76.

Ps.-Methodius, *Apocalypse*. Ed. and trans. Gerrit J. Reinink, *Die syrische Apokalypse des Pseudo-Methodius*. CSCO 540–41, SS 220–21. Partial English translation by Sebastian P. Brock available in Palmer et al., *The Seventh Century in the West-Syrian Chronicles*, pp. 230–42. English translation available in Paul J. Alexander, *The Byzantine Apocalyptic Tradition* (Berkeley, 1985), pp. 36–51.

Michael the Great, *Chronicle*. Ed. and trans. Jean-Baptiste Chabot, *Chronique de Michel le Syrien: patriarche jacobite d'Antioche (1166–1199)*. 4 vols. (Paris, 1899–1910).

——, *Chronicle*. Edited by Gregorios Y. Ibrahim, *The Edessa-Aleppo Syriac Codex of the Chronicle of Michael the Great: a Publication of the St. George Parish and the Edessan Community in Aleppo* (Piscataway, N.J., 2009). English translation in Matti Moosa, *The Syriac Chronicle of Michael Rabo (the Great): A Universal History from the Creation* (Teaneck, N.J., 2014).

——, *Chronicle* [Armenian]. Trans. Victor Langlois, *Chronique de Michel le Grand, patriarche des Syriens jacobites* (Venice, 1868).

Michael Syncellus, *Peri syntaxeos*. Ed. and trans. Daniel Donnet, *Le traité de la construction de la phrase de Michel le syncelle de Jérusalem: histoire du texte, édition, traduction et commentaire* (Bruxelles, 1982).

Minucius Felix, *Octavius* (CPL 37). Ed. Bernhard Kytzler, *M. Minuci Felicis. Octavius* (Stuttgart, 1992). English translation in G.W. Clarke, *The Octavius of Marcus Minucius Felix* (New York/Paramus, N.J., 1974).

al-Mizzī, *Tahdhīb al-kamāl fī asmāʾ al-rijāl*. Ed. Bashshār ʿAwwād Maʿrūf. 35 vols. (Beirut, 1982–1992).

Moshe bar Kepha, *Commentary on the Liturgy*. Ed. and trans. Robert H. Connolly and Humphrey W. Codrington, *Two Commentaries on the Jacobite Liturgy by George Bishop of the Arab Tribes and Moses Bar Kepha, together with the Syriac Anaphora of St. James and a Document Entitled The Book of Life* (London/Oxford, 1913), pp. 24–90 (translation), *26–*86.

Muslim b. al-Ḥajjāj, *Ṣaḥīḥ*. Ed. Muḥammad Fu'ād 'Abd al-Bāqī. 5 vols. (n.d., n.p.).

al-Nasā'ī, *Kitāb al-sunan al-kubrā*. Ed. Ḥasan 'Abd al-Mun'im Shalabī. 12 vols. (Beirut, 2001).

Nestorius, *Bazaar of Heracleides*. Ed. Paul Bedjan, *Nestorius. Le Livre d'Héraclide de Damas* (Paris/Leipzig, 1910). English translation in Godfrey R. Driver and Leonard Hodgson, *The Bazaar of Heracleides* (Oxford, 1925).

Nonnus of Nisibis, *Apologetic Treatise*. Ed. Albert van Roey, *Nonnus de Nisibe. Traité apologétique* (Louvain, 1948).

Origen, *Contra Celsum*. Ed. and trans. Marcel Borret, *Contra Celse*. 5 vols. SC 132, 136, 147, 150, 227. Paris, 1967–1976. Revised and corrected edition of SC 132 (Paris 2005). English translation by Henry Chadwick, *Contra Celsum* (Cambridge, 1953).

———, *Homilies on Ezekiel* [In Ezechielem homiliae] (CPG 1441). Ed. Willem A. Baehrens and trans. Marcel Borret, *Homélies sur Ezéchiel*. SC 352 (Paris, 1989). English translation in Thomas P. Scheck, *Origen: Homilies 1–14 on Ezekiel* (New York/Mahwah, N.J., 2010).

Palladius, *Lausiac History* [Historia Lausiaca] (CPG 6036). Ed. Cuthbert Butler, *The Lausiac History of Palladius: The Greek Text*. Texts and Studies 6.2 (Cambridge, 1904). English translation in Robert T. Meyer, *Palladius: The Lausiac History* (Westminster, Md., 1965).

Panegyric of the Three Holy Children of Babylon. Ed. and trans. Henri de Vis, *Homélies coptes de la Vaticane*, vol. 2 (Louvain, 1990), pp. 64–120.

Passion of Anthony of Rawḥ ['Recension A']. Ed. and trans. Ignace Dick, 'La passion arabe de S. Antoine Ruwaḥ: néo-martyr de Damas († 25 déc. 799),' *LM* 74 (1961), pp. 109–33. ['Recension B']. Ed. Juan-Pedro Monferrer-Sala, '*Šahādāt al-qiddīs Mār Anṭūniyūs*. Replanteamiento de la "antigüedad" de las versiones sinaíticas a la luz del análisis textual,' *Miscelánea de estudios árabes y hebraicos. Sección de árabe-Islam* 57 (2008), pp. 237–67. English translation of 'recension B' by John C. Lamoreaux in Alexander Treiger and Samuel Noble, eds., *The Orthodox Church in the Arab World, 700-1700: An Anthology of Sources* (De Kalb, 2014), pp. 117–23.

Passion of Peter of Capitolias. ET by Stephen Shoemaker available in Shoemaker, *Three Christian martyrdoms from early Islamic Palestine: Passion of Peter of Capitolias*, Passion of the Twenty Martyrs of Mar Saba, Passion of Romanos the Neomartyr (Provo, Utah, 2016), pp. 2–65. [written by John of Damascus?; Shoemaker also includes a revised version of Korneli Kekelidze's Georgian edition].

Paul the Persian, *Dispute with Photinus the Manichaean* [Disputatio cum Manichaeo] (CPG 7010). PG 88, cols. 529–52.

Peter the Solitary, *Life of Sabrisho'* (BHO 1032). Ed. Paul Bedjan, *Histoire de Mar-Jabalaha* (Paris, 1895), pp. 288–331.

Philostorgius, *Church History* [Historia ecclesiastica] (CPG 6032). Ed. Joseph Bidez and Friedhelm Winkelmann, *Philostorgius Kirchengeschichte*. 3rd edition. Berlin, 1981. English translation by Philip R. Amidon, *Philostorgius: Church History* (Atlanta, 2007).

Philoxenus of Mabbug, *Discourses*. Ed. and trans. Ernest A.W. Budge, *The Discourses of Philoxenus Bishop of Mabbôgh, A.D. 485–519, Edited from Syriac Manuscripts of the*

Sixth and Seventh Centuries, in the British Museum, with an English Translation. 2 vols. (London, 1894). ET in Robert A. Kitchen, *The Discourses of Philoxenos of Mabbug: A New Translation and Introduction* (Collegeville, MN, 2013).

——, *Mēmrē against Ḥabīb.* Ed. and trans. Maurice Brière and François Graffin, *Sancti Philoxeni episcopi Mabbugensis dissertationes decem de Uno e sancta Trinitate incorporato et passo (Mêmrê contre Habib).* PO 15.4, 38.3, 39.4, 40.2. (Turnhout, 1920–1980).

Procopius, *Secret History.* Ed. Jakob Haury and Gerhard Wirth, *Procopius Caesariensis: Opera Omnia,* vol 3: *Historia quae dicitur Arcana* (Leipzig, 2001). English translation in Anthony Kaldellis, *Prokopios: The Secret History with Related Texts* (Indianapolis, 2010).

Qenneshre Fragment. Ed. and trans. Michael P. Penn, 'Demons Gone Wild: An Introduction, and Translation of the Syriac Qenneshre Fragment,' *OCP* 79 (2013), pp. 367–99. Ed. and trans. François Nau, 'Appendice: Fragments sure le monastère de Qenneshre,' in *Actes du XIV congrès international des orientalistes,* vol. 2 (Paris, 1907), pp. 76–135.

al-Qirqisānī, *Kitāb al-anwār wa-'l-marāqib.* Ed. Leon Nemoy. 2 vols. (New York, 1939–1943).

al-Qurṭubī, *al-Jāmi' li-aḥkām al-Qur'ān.* Ed. 'Abd Allāh b. 'Abd al-Muḥsin al-Turkī. 24 vols. (Beirut, 2006).

Rabbula of Edessa, *Admonitions concerning Monks.* Ed. J. Josephus Overbeck, *S. Ephraemi Syri, Rabulae episcopi Edesseni, Balaei aliorumque Opera selecta e codicibus syriacis manuscriptis in museo Britannico et bibliotheca Bodleiana asservatis primus edidit* (Oxford, 1865), pp. 212–14. Translated by Robert H. Connolly, 'Some Early Rules for Syrian Monks,' *Downside Review* 25 (1906), pp. 152–62.

——, *Rules and Admonitions for Priests and Ascetics.* Ed. J. Josephus Overbeck, *S. Ephraemi Syri, Rabulae episcopi Edesseni, Balaei aliorumque Opera selecta e codicibus syriacis manuscriptis in museo Britannico et bibliotheca Bodleiana asservatis primus edidit* (Oxford, 1865), pp. 215–21. Translated by Robert H. Connolly, 'Some More Early Syrian Rules,' *Downside Review* 25 (1906), pp. 300–306.

——, *Rules for Monks in Persia.* Ed. and trans. Arthur Vööbus, *Syriac and Arabic Documents Regarding Legislation Relative to Syrian Asceticism* (Stockholm, 1960), pp. 89–92.

Rufinus, *Ecclesiastical History* [continuation: Books 10 and 11]. Ed. Theodor Mommsen, in Eduard Schwartz, Theodor Mommsen, [and Friedhelm Winkelmann], eds., *Die Kirchengeschichte. Eusebius Werke 2.2.* 2nd ed. (Berlin, 1999), pp. 957–1040. English translation in Philip R. Amidon, *Rufinus of Aquileia: History of the Church* (Washington, D.C., 2016).

Saḥnūn, *al-Mudawwana al-kubrā.* 5 vols. (Beirut, 1994).

Ṣā'id b. Aḥmad al-Andalusī, *Kitāb ṭabaqāt al-umam.* Ed. Louis Cheikho (Beirut, 1912).

Sa'īd b. Biṭrīq, *Kitāb al-Ta'rīkh.* [Eutychius of Alexandria, *Annales*] Ed. Louis Cheikho, Bernard Carra de Vaux, and Ḥabīb Zayyāt, *Eutychii Patriarchae Alexandrini. Annales,* CSCO SA III.6 and CSCO III.7, pp. 1–88 (Beirut, 1906–1909).

Sa'īd b. Yūsuf [Saadiya Gaon], *Kitāb al-amanāt wa-'l-i'tiqādāt.* Ed. S. Landauer, *Kitâb al-amânât wa'l-I'tiqâdât* (Leiden, 1880). English translation in Samuel Rosenblatt, *The Book of Beliefs and Opinions* (New Haven, 1948).

al-Sakhāwī, *al-Maqāṣid al-ḥasana fī bayān kathīr min al-aḥādīth al-mushtahira 'alā al-alsina.* Ed. Muḥammad 'Uthmān al-Khisht (Beirut, 1985).

Ṣalībā, *Akhbār faṭārikat kursī al-mashriq*. Ed. and trans. Henricus Gismondi, Maris, Amri, et Slibae. *De patriarchis nestorianum commentaria ex codicibus Vaticanus. Pars Altera*. 2 vols. [*Amri et Slibae textus* and *Amri et Slibae textus versio latina*] (Rome, 1896). [On correcting the attribution of this work, see Bo Holmberg, 'A Reconsideration of the *Kitāb al-Maǧdal*,' PdO 18 (1993), pp. 255–73].

al-Samhūdī, *Wafā' al-wafā bi-akhbār dār al-muṣṭafā*. Ed Muḥammad Muḥyī al-Dīn 'Abd al-Ḥamīd. 4 vols. (Beirut, 1984).

Ps.-Samuel of Qalamūn, *Apocalypse*. Ed. and trans. J. Ziadeh, 'L'Apocalypse de Samuel, supérieur de Deir-el-Qalamoun,' *Revue de l'orient Chrétien* 20 (1915–1917), pp. 374–404.

al-Sarakhsī, *Sharḥ Kitāb al-siyar al-kabīr li-Muḥammad b. al-Ḥasan al-Shaybanī*. Ed. Ṣalāḥ al-Dīn al-Munajjid. 5 vols. (Cairo, 1971–1972).

Second Council of Nicaea, *Canons*. Ed. and trans. Périclès-Pierre Joannou, *Discipline générale antique*, vol. 1.1, pp. 242–85. ET by Henry Percival in *NPNF*, ser. 2, vol. 14, pp. 555–70.

Severus of Antioch, *Ad Nephalium*. Ed. and trans. Joseph Lebon, *Severi Antiocheni orations ad Nephalium. Eiusdem ac Sergii Grammatici epistulae mutuae*. CSCO 119–20. Syr. IV.7.(Louvain, 1949). Partial English translation of *Oration 2* in Pauline Allen and C.T.R. Hayward, *Severus of Antioch* (London/New York, 2004), pp. 59–66.

——, *Cathedral Homilies*. Ed. and trans. Rubens Duval, Maurice Brière, François Graffin, Marc-Antoine Kugener, et al., *Les Homiliae Cathedrales de Sévère d'Antioche: traduction syriaque de Jacques d'Édesse*. 17 vols. PO 4.1, 8.2, 12.1, 16.5, 20.2, 22.2, 23.1, 25.1, 25.4, 26.3, 29.1, 35.3, 36.1, 36.3. 36.4, 38.2 (Paris/Turnhout, 1908-1976).

——, *Hymns*. Ed. and trans. Ernest Walter Brooks, *The Hymns of Severus and Others in the Syriac Version of Paul of Edessa as revised by James of Edessa*. PO 6.1, 7.5 (Paris, 1909, 1911).

——, *Letters*. Ed. and trans. Ernest Walter Brooks, *A Collection of Letters of Severus of Antioch, from Numerous Syriac Manuscripts*. PO 12.2, 14.1 (Paris, 1919, 1920).

——, *Select Letters*. Ed. and trans. Ernest Walter Brooks, *The Sixth Book of the Select Letters of Severus, Patriarch of Antioch, in the Syriac Version of Athanasius of Nisibis*. 2 vols. in 4. (London, 1902–1904).

(Ps.-?) Severus b. al-Muqaffa', *Kitāb al-Īḍāḥ*. Ed. Murqus Jirjis, *al-Durr al-thamīn fī īḍāḥ al-dīn* (Cairo, n.d.).

Severus Sebokht, *Letter to Yonan the Periodeute*. Ed. and trans. Henri Hugonnard-Roche, 'Questions de logique au VIIe siècle. Les épîtres syriaques de Sévère Sebokht et leurs sources grecques,' *Studia graeco-arabica* 5 (2015), pp. 53–104.

al-Shābushtī, *Kitāb al-diyārāt*. Ed. Kūrkīs 'Awwād (Beirut, 1986). Italian paraphrase in Leonardo Capezzone, *Il libro dei monasteri* (Milan, 1993).

al-Shaybanī, *Kitāb al-siyar*. Ed. Ṣalāḥ al-Dīn al-Munajjid in al-Sarakhsī, *Sharḥ Kitāb al-siyar al-kabīr li-Muḥammad b. al-Ḥasan al-Shaybanī*. 5 vols. (Cairo, 1971–1972).

Shem'on, *History of Rabban Hormizd* (BHO 383). Ed. and trans., Ernest A. Wallis Budge, *The Histories of Rabban Hôrmîzd the Persian and Rabban Bar 'Idtâ*. 3 vols in 2. (London, 1902), vol. 1, pp. 3–109 (Syriac) = vol. 2.1, 3–160 (ET).

Simeon bar Apollon and Bar Ḥaṭār bar Ūdān, *Life of Simeon Stylites* (BHO 1121). Ed. Paul Bedjan, *AMS*, vol. 4, pp. 507–644. English translation in Frederick Lent, 'The *Life* of St. Simeon Stylites: A Translation of the Syriac Text in Bedjan's *Acta Martyrum et Sanctorum*, vol. IV,' *Journal of the American Oriental Society* 35 (1915–1917), pp. 103–98. English translation (based on Vatican Syriac 160 and Stefano Evodio

Assemani, *Acta sanctorum martyrum orientalium et occidentalium*, vol. 2 [Rome, 1748], pp. 268–398]) in Robert Doran, *The Lives of Simeon Stylites* (Kalamazoo, Michigan, 1992), pp. 103–98.

Simeon of Beth Arsham, *Letter to Simeon, Abbot of Gabula*. Ed. and trans. J. S. Assemani in *BO*, vol. 1, pp. 364–79. Ed. and trans. Ignazio Guidi, 'La lettera di Simeone vescovo di Bêth-Arśâm sopra i martiri omeriti,' *Atti della Reale Accademia Nazionale dei Lincei, Serie Terza: Memorie della Classe di Scienze morali, storiche e filologiche* 7 (1881), pp. 471–514. ET of Guidi's text in Arthur Jeffery, 'Christianity in South Arabia,' *Moslem World* 36 (1946), pp. 204–16. Also ed. Paul Bedjan in *AMS*, vol. 1, pp. 372–97.

Socrates, *Ecclesiastical History* [Socrates Scholasticus, *Historia ecclesiastica*] (CPG 6028). Ed. Günther C. Hansen, *Sokrates Kirchengeschichte* (Berlin, 1995). English translation by E. Walford (?) and A. C. Zenos in *NPNF*, ser. 2, vol. 2 (New York, 1890), pp. 1–178.

Sophronius of Jerusalem, *Homilia in theophaniam* (CPG 7643). Ed. Athanasius Papadopoulos-Kerameus, *Analekta hierosolymitikēs stachiologias*, vol. 5 (St. Petersburg, 1898), pp. 151–68.

———, *Narratio miraculorum ss. Cyri et Iohannis* (CPG 7646/BHG 477–79i). Ed. Natalio Fernández Marcos, *Los* thaumata *de Sofronio: contribución al estudio de la incubatio cristiana* (Madrid, 1975), pp. 241–400; FT available in Jean Gascou, *Sophrone de Jérusalem: Miracles des saints Cyr et Jean (BHGI 477–479)* (Paris, 2006).

———, *Synodical Letter* [Epistula synodica ad Sergium CPolitanum] (CPG 7635). Ed. Rudolf Riedinger and trans. Pauline Allen in Pauline Allen, *Sophronius of Jerusalem and Seventh-Century Heresy: the Synodical Letter and Other Documents* (Oxford/New York, 2009), pp. 66–157.

Sozomen, *Ecclesiastical History* [Sozomenus, *Historia ecclesiastica*] (CPG 6030). Ed. Joseph Bidez and Günther C. Hansen, *Sozomenus Kirchengeschichte* (Berlin, 1960). English translation by Chester D. Hartranft in *NPNF*, ser. 2, vol. 2, pp. 239–427.

Statement of Faith of 612. Ed. and trans. Jean-Baptiste Chabot, *Synodicon Orientale*, pp. 564–67 (Syriac) = 581–85 (French).

al-Subkī, *Fatāwā al-Subkī*. 2 vols. (Beirut, n.d.).

al-Suyūṭī, *al-Durr al-manthūr fī 'l-tafsīr bi-'l-ma'thūr*. Ed. 'Abd Allāh b. 'Abd al-Muḥsin al-Turkī. 17 vols. (Cairo, 2003).

———, *al-Itqān fī 'ulūm al-Qur'ān*. Ed. Fawwāz Aḥmad al-Zamarlī. 2 vols. (Beirut, 1999).

———, *Min ḥusn al-muḥāḍara fī akhbār Miṣr wa-'l-Qāhira*. 2 vols. in 1. (Cairo, 1327).

———, *Ta'rīkh al-khulafā'*. Ed. W. N. Lees and Mawlawi Abd al-Haqq, *The Taríkh al-kholfáa: or, History of the Caliphs, from the Death of Mohammad to the year 900 of the Hijrah* (Calcutta, 1857).

Synesius of Cyrene, *Letters* [Epistulae] (CPG 5640). Ed. Antonio Garzya and trans. Denis Roques, *Synésios de Cyrène*, vols. 2 and 3: *Correspondence* (Paris, 2000–2003). English translation in Augustine FitzGerald, *The Letters of Synesius of Cyrene, Translated into English with Introduction and Notes* (London, 1926).

Synod of Barṣawmā. Ed. and trans. Jean-Baptiste Chabot, *Synodicon Orientale*, pp. 61 (Syriac) = 308–309 (French).

Synod of Dadisho'. Ed. and trans. Jean-Baptiste Chabot, *Synodicon Orientale*, pp. 43–52 (Syriac) = 285–98 (French).

Synod of Ezekiel. Ed. and trans. Jean-Baptiste Chabot, *Synodicon Orientale*, pp. 110–29 (Syriac) = 368–89 (French).

Synod of Isho'yahb I. Ed. and trans. Jean-Baptiste Chabot, *Synodicon Orientale*, pp. 130–64 (Syriac) = 390–455 (French).

Synod of Laodicea, Canons [Canones] (CPG 8607). Ed. and trans. Périclès-Pierre Joannou, *Discipline générale antique*, vol. 1.2, pp. 130–55.

Synod of Mar George. Ed. and trans. Jean-Baptiste Chabot, *Synodicon Orientale*, pp. 215–26 (Syriac) = 480–514 (French).

Synod of Mar Isaac. Ed. and trans. Jean-Baptiste Chabot, *Synodicon Orientale*, pp. 17–36 (Syriac) = 252–75 (French).

al-Ṭabarānī, *al-Mu'jam al-kabīr.* Ed. Ḥamdī 'Abd al-Majīd al-Salafī. 25 vols. (Cairo, 1404).

al-Ṭabarī, *Ikhtilāf al-fuqahā'.* Ed. Friedrich Kern (Beirut, 1999). Ed. Joseph Schacht, *Das Konstantinopler Fragment des Kitāb iḫtilāf al-fuqahā' des Abū Ǧa'far Muḥammad ibn Ǧarīr aṭ-Ṭabarī* (Leiden, 1933).

——, *Jāmi' al-bayān 'an ta'wīl āy al-Qur'*ān. Ed. 'Abd Allāh b. 'Abd al-Muḥsin al-Turkī. 26 vols. (Cairo, 2001–2003).

——, *Ta'rīkh* [= *Ta'rīkh al-rusul wa-'l-mulūk*]. Ed. Michael Jan de Goeje et al., *Annales quos scripsit Abu Djafar Mohammed ibn Djarir at-Tabari.* 15 vols. (Leiden, 1879–1901). English translation available in Ehsan Yar-shater, ed., *The History of al-Ṭabarī: An Annotated Translation.* 40 vols. (Albany, 1985–2007). [See Primary Sources III for individual volumes cited in this book.]

Tatian, *Oratio ad Graecos* (CPG 1104). Ed. Miroslav Marcovich, *Tatiani Oratio ad Graecos, Theophili Antiocheni Ad Autolycumi* (Berlin/New York, 1995), pp. 7–75. English translation by J. E. Ryland in *ANF*, vol. 2 (Buffalo, 1885), pp. 65–83.

Teaching of Addai [by (Ps-?) Labubna bar Senaq] (BHO 24). Ed. George Phillips, trans. George Howard, in George Howard, *The Teaching of Addai* (Chico, Calif., 1991).

Teaching of the Apostles [Didascalia apostolorum] (CPG 1738). Ed. and trans. Arthur Vööbus, *The Didascalia Apostolorum in Syriac.* CSCO 401–402, 407–408. SS 175–76, 179–80 (Louvain, 1979).

Tertullian, *Against Praxeas* [Aduersas Praxean] (CPL 26). Ed. and trans. Ernest Evans, *Q. Septimii Florentis Tertulliani Adversus Praxean liber. Tertullian's Treatise against Praxeas* (London, 1948), pp. 89–129 (Latin) = 130–79 (ET). ET by Peter Holmes also available in *ANF*, vol. 3, 597–627.

Testament of Our Lord [Testamentum Domini] (CPG 1743). Ed. and trans. Arthur Vööbus in *The Synodicon in the West Syrian Tradition* I. CSCO 367–68, SS 161–62 (Louvain, 1975), pp. 1–49 (Syriac) = 27–64 (English). Also ed. and trans.: Paul de Lagarde, *Reliquiae Iuris Ecclesiastici Antiquissimae* (Vienna, 1856), pp. 2–19; Ignatius E. Rahmani, *Testamentum Domini Nostri Jesu Christi* (Moguntiae, 1899); John P. Arendzen, 'A New Syriac Text of the Apocalyptic Part of the "Testament of the Lord,"' *JTS* (1901), pp. 401–16; Françoios Nau, 'Fragment inédit d'une traduction syriaque jusqu'ici inconnue du *Testamentum D.N. Jesu Christi*,' *JA* 17 (1901), pp. 233–56

Theodore Abū Qurrah, *On the Confirmation of the Gospel* [*Maymar fī taḥqīq al-Injīl wa-anna kullamā lā yuḥaqqiquhu al-Injīl fa-huwa bāṭil*]. Ed. Constantine Bacha, *Mayāmir Thāwdūrus Abī Qurrah Usquf Ḥarrān: aqdam ta'līf 'Arabī Naṣrānī* (Beirut, 1904), pp. 71–75. English translation in John C. Lamoreaux, *Theodore Abū Qurrah* (Provo, Utah, 2005), pp. 49–53.

——, *Opusculum 7* (*On the Contending of Christ with the Devil*), PG 97, cols. 1523–528. English translation in John C. Lamoreaux, *Theodore Abū Qurrah* (Provo, 2005), pp. 237–39.

Theodore bar Koni, *Book of the Scholion.* Ed. Addai Scher, *Theodorus bar Kōnī. Liber Scholiorum.* CSCO Syr. II.65–66. (Paris, 1910–1912).

Theodoret of Cyrrhus, *Historia religiosa* (CPG 6221). Ed. and trans. P. Canivet and A. Leroy-Molinghen, *Histoire des moines de Syrie: Histoire Philothée.* SC 257 (Paris, 1977). English translation in Richard M. Price, *A History of the Monks of Syria* (Kalamazoo, 1985).

——, *Letters* (CPG 6239–6240a). Ed. and trans. Yvan Azéma, *Théodoret de Cyr. Correspondence.* SC 40, 98, 111, 429 (Paris, 1995–1998). English translation by Blomfield Jackson in *NPNF*, ser. 2, vol. 3, pp. 250–348.

Theophanes, *Chronicle.* Ed. Carolus de Boor, *Theophanis: Chronographia.* 2 vols. (Leipzig, 1883–1885). English translation in Cyril Mango and Roger Scott, *The Chronicle of Theophanes Confessor: Byzantine and Near Eastern History, AD 284–813* (Oxford, 1997).

Ps.-Theophilus of Alexandria, *Homily on SS Peter, Paul, Repentance, and Anba Athanasius.* Ed. and trans. H. Fleisch, 'Une homélie de Théophile d'Alexandrie en l'honneur de St Pierre et de St Paul,' *Revue de l'Orient chrétien* 30 (1935–1936), pp. 371–416. Errata in *Mélanges de l'université Saint Joseph* 28 (1948–1950), pp. 351–52.

Ps.-Theopistus, *History of Dioscorus* (BHO 257–58). Ed. and trans. François Nau, 'Histoire de Dioscore,' *JA* 10 (1903), pp. 5–108, 241–310.

Thomas of Kafarṭāb, *The Ten Chapters* [al-Maqālāt al-ʿashr]. Ed. and trans. Charles Chartouni, *Le traité des dix chapitres de Thomas de Kfarṭāb: un document sur les origines de l'Église maronite* (Beirut, 1986).

Thomas of Marga, *Monastic History.* Ed. and trans. Ernest A. Wallis Budge, *The Book of Governors: The Historia Monastica of Thomas, Bishop of Margâ, A.D. 840. Edited from Syriac Manuscripts in the British Museum and Other Libraries.* 2 vols. (London, 1893).

Timothy I, *Disputation with al-Mahdī* (*Letter 59*). Ed. and trans. M. Heimgartner, *Timotheos I., Ostsyrischer Patriarch. Disputation mit dem Kalifen al-Mahdī.* CSCO 631–32, SS 244–45 (Louvain, 2011). ET in Alphonse Mingana, *Woodbrooke Studies,* vol. 2: *Timothy's Apology for Christianity; The Lament of the Virgin; The Martyrdom of Pilate* (Cambridge, 1928), pp. 15–90.

——, *Extracts on Whether to Rebaptize Jacobites and Marcionites, from Various Letters.* Ed. Oscar Braun, *Timothei Patriarchae I: Epistulae* (Paris, 1914–1915), pp. 30–34 (Syriac) = 18–21 (LT).

——, *Letter 43 and Letter 48.* Trans S. P. Brock, 'Two Letters of the Patriarch Timothy from the Late Eighth Century on Translations From Greek,' *Arabic Sciences and Philosophy* 9 (1999), pp. 233–46. Syriac text also edited in in Henri Pognon, *Une version syriaque des aphorisms d'Hippocrate,* (Leipzig, 1903), pp. xvi–xviii, xxi–xxii.

——, *Letter to the Monks of Mar Marūn.* [Letter 41] Ed. and trans. Raphaël J. Bidawid, *Les lettres du patriarche nestorien Timothée I. Studi e Testi* 187 (The Vatican, 1956), pp. 91–125, ܐ-ܡܙ (*1-*47).

——, *Letters.* [Letters 1–39]. Ed. and trans. Oscar Braun, *Timothei Patriarchae I: Epistulae.* CSCO 74–75: SS 30–31 (Paris, 1914–1915).

Timothy I, *Letters.* [Letter 40]. Ed. and trans. ed. Hanna P. Jajou Cheikho, *Dialectique du langage sur Dieu: Lettre de Timothée I (728–823) à Serge. Étude, traduction et édition critique* (Rome, 1983), pp. 274–331 (Syriac) = 185–273 (French).

Timothy I, *Letters.* [Letters 42-58]. Ed. and trans. Martin Heimgartner, *Die Briefe 42-58 des Ostsyrischen Patriarchen Timotheos I.* CSCO 644–45, SS 248–49 (Louvain, 2012).

——, *Order of Reconciliation.* Ed. and trans. Oscar Braun, *Timothei Patriarchae I: Epistulae.* CSCO 74-75: SS 30-31. (Paris, 1914-1915), pp. 33-34 (Syriac) = 20-21 (LT).

Timothy II (Aelurus), *Letter to the City of Alexandria* [Epistula ad Alexandrinos] (CPG 5477). Ed. and trans. Rifaat Y. Ebied and Lionel R. Wickham, 'A Collection of Unpublished Syriac Letters of Timothy Aelurus,' *JTS* 21 (1970), pp. 337–41 (Syriac) = 357–62 (ET).

——, *Letter to Claudianus* [Epistula ad Claudianum presbyterum] (CPG 5481). Ed. and trans. Rifaat Y. Ebied and Lionel R. Wickham, 'A Collection of Unpublished Syriac Letters of Timothy Aelurus,' *JTS* 21 (1970), pp. 344–46 (Syriac) = 366–69 (ET).

——, *Letter to Egypt, Thebaid, and Pentapolis* [Epistula ad Aegyptum, Thebaidem et Pentapolim] (CPG 5479). Ed. and trans. Rifaat Y. Ebied and Lionel R. Wickham, 'A Collection of Unpublished Syriac Letters of Timothy Aelurus,' *JTS* 21 (1970), pp. 341–43 (Syriac) = 362–64 (ET).

——, *Letter to Faustinus the Deacon* [Epistula ad Faustinam diaconum] (CPG 5480). Ed. and trans. Rifaat Y. Ebied and Lionel R. Wickham, 'A Collection of Unpublished Syriac Letters of Timothy Aelurus,' *JTS* 21 (1970), pp. 343–44 (Syriac) = 364–66 (ET).

Timothy, Presbyter of Constantinople, *De iis qui ad ecclesiam accedunt* (CPG 7016), PG 86, cols. 12–74.

al-Tirmidhī, *al-Jāmiʿ al-kabīr.* Ed. Bashshār ʿAwwād Maʿrūf. 6 vols. (Beirut, 1996).

Trophies of Damascus [Trophaea Damasci. Dialogus contra Iudaeos] (CPG 7797). Ed. and trans. Gustave Bardy, *Les trophées de Damas: controverse judéo-chrétienne du VIIe siècle.* PO 15.2 (Paris, 1920).

Wakīʿ, *Akhbār al-quḍāt.* 3 vols. (Beirut, n.d.).

Yaḥyā b. ʿAdī, *Maqāla fī tabyīn al-wajh alladhī ʿalayhi yaṣiḥḥu al-qawl fī ʾl-Bārīʾ, jalla wa-taʿālā, innahu jawhar wāḥid dhū thalāth khawāṣṣ tusammīhā al-Naṣārā aqānīm.* Ed. and trans. Augustin Périer, *Petits traités apologétiques de Yaḥyâ ben ʿAdî: texte arabe: édité pour la priemière fois d'après les manuscrits de Paris, de Rome et de Munich* (Paris, 1920), pp. 44–62.

Yaḥyā b. Saʿīd, *Kitāb al-dhayl.* Ed. and trans. Ignace Kratchkovsky and Alexandre A. Vasiliev, *Histoire de Yahya-ibn-Saʿīd d'Antioche, continuateur de Saʿīd-ibn-Bitriq.* PO 18.5, 23.3 (Paris, 1932–1957). Ed. Ignace Kratchkovsky, trans. Françoise Micheau and Gérard Troupeau, *Histoire de Yahya-ibn-Saʿīd d'Antioche.* PO 47.4 (Turnhout, 1997). Ed. Louis Cheikho, Bernard Carra de Vaux, and Habib Zayyat, *Annales Yahia Ibn Saīd Antiochensis.* CSCO SA III.7 (Beirut, 1909), pp. 91–273.

Yāqūt, *Muʿjam al-buldān.* 7 vols. (Beirut, 1995).

——, *Muʿjam al-udabāʾ: irshād al-arīb ilā maʿrifat al-adīb.* 7 vols. Ed. Iḥsān ʿAbbās (Beirut, 1993).

Ps.-Zacharias Rhetor, *Chronicle.* Ed. and trans. Ernest Walter Brooks, *Historia Ecclesiastica Zachariae Rhetori vulgo adscripta.* CSCO 83–84, 87–88. SS 38–39, 41–42 (Louvain, 1953). English translation by Frederick J. Hamilton and Ernest Walter Brooks, *The Syriac Chronicle Known as That of Zachariah of Mitylene* (London, 1899). English translation also by Geoffrey Greatrex, Robert R. Phenix, and Cornelia B. Horn, *The Chronicle of Pseudo-Zachariah Rhetor: Church and War in Late Antiquity* (Liverpool, 2011).

al-Zamakhsharī, *al-Kashshāf.* Ed. ʿĀdil Aḥmad ʿAbd al-Mawjūd and ʿAlī Muḥammad Muʿawwaḍ. 6 vols. (Riyadh, 1998).

al-Zarkashī, *al-Burhān fī 'ulūm al-Qur'ān*. Ed. Muḥammad Abū al-Faḍl Ibrāhīm. 4 vols. (Cairo, 1957).

Zuqnin Chronicle. Ed. and trans. Jean-Baptiste Chabot, *Incerti auctoris chronicon anonymum Pseudo-Dionysianum vulgo dictum*. CSCO 91, 104, SS 43, 53 (Paris, 1927–1933). FT of CSCO 104, SS 53 in Robert Hespel, *Chronicon anonymum Pseudo-Dionysianum vulgo dictum*. CSCO 507, SS 213 (Louvain, 1989). English translation in Amir Harrak, *The Chronicle of Zuqnīn*, Parts III and IV: *A.D. 488–775* (Toronto, 1999) and in Witold Witakowski, *Pseudo-Dionysius of Tel-Mahre: Chronicle* Part III (Liverpool, 1996). [NB: This chronicle is also known as the *Chronicle of Pseudo-Dionysius of Tel Mahre.*]

PRIMARY SOURCES III

Collections and Other

Abbeloos, Jean-Baptiste. *De vita et scriptis Sancti Jacobi, Batnarum Sarugi in Mesopotamia episcopi* (Louvain/Bonn, 1867).

Abramowski, Luise and Alan E. Goodman, ed. and trans., *A Nestorian Collection of Christological Texts: Cambridge University Library ms. Oriental 1319*. 2 vols. (Cambridge, 1972).

Allen, Pauline and C.T.R. Hayward, *Severus of Antioch* (London/New York, 2004).

Arberry, Arthur J. *The Koran Interpreted: A Translation*. 2 vols. in 1. (New York, 1996).

Asín y Palacios, Michaël. 'Logia et agrapha Domini Jesu apud Moslemicos scriptores, asceticos praesertim, usitata.' PO 13.3, 19.4 (Paris, 1919–1926).

Becker, Adam. *Sources for the Study of the School of Nisibis* (Liverpool, 2008).

Bedjan, Paul. *Histoire de Mar-Jabalaha, de trois autres patriarches, d'un prêtre et de deux laïques nestoriens* (Paris, 1895).

Bell, Harold I. and Walter E. Crum, eds., *Greek Papyri in the British Museum: Catalogue, with Texts*, vol. IV: *The Aphrodito Papyri* (London, 1910).

Bettiolo, Paolo. *Una raccolta di opuscoli Calcedonensi: Ms. Sinaï Syr. 10*. CSCO 403: SS 177. (Louvain, 1979).

Brinner, William M. *The Children of Israel*. HṬ 3 (Albany, 1991).

Brock, Sebastian P. and Brian J. Fitzgerald, *Two Early Lives of Severos, Patriarch of Antioch* (Liverpool, 2013).

Caskell, Werner. *Ǧamharat an-nasab; das genealogische Werk des Hišam Ibn Muḥammad al-Kalbī*. 2 vols. (Leiden, 1966).

Catalogus codicum astrologorum graecorum. 12 vols. (Brussels, 1898–1924).

Chabot, Jean-Baptiste, ed. and trans. *Synodicon Orientale, ou recueil de synodes nestoriens* (Paris, 1902).

Cheikho, Louis. *al-Naṣrāniyya wa-ādābuhā bayna 'arab al-jāhiliyya*. 2 vols. (Beirut, 1989).

——. *Shu'arā' al-naṣrāniyya qabla al-Islām* (Beirut, 1999).

——. *Vingt traités théologiques d'auteurs arabes chrétiens (IXe–XIIIe)* (Beirut, 1920).

Clackson, Sarah J. Clackson, *Coptic and Greek Texts relating to the Hermopolite Monastery of Apa Apollo* (Oxford, 2000).

Conybeare, Frederick C. 'Ananias of Shirak (A.D. 600–650 c.),' *Byzantinische Zeitschrift* 6 (1897), pp. 572–84.

Dawes, Elizabeth and Norman H. Baynes, *Three Byzantine Saints: Contemporary Biographies Translated from Greek* (Oxford, 1948).
de Lagarde, Paul Anton. *Analecta Syriaca* (Leipzig, 1858).
———. *Bibliothecae syriacae* (Göttingen, 1892).
———. *Veteris testament graeci in sermonem syriacum versi fragmenta octo* (Göttingen, 1892).
Donner, Fred M. *The Conquest of Arabia.* HṬ 10 (Albany, 1993).
Draguet, René. 'Une pastorale antijulianiste des environs de l'année 530,' *LM* 40 (1927), pp. 75–92.
Duval, Rubens, ed. *Lexicon syriacum auctore Hassano bar Bahlule.* 3 vols. (Paris, 1888–1901).
Evetts, Basil Thomas Alfred, trans. *The Churches and Monasteries of Egypt and Some Neighbouring Countries Attributed to Abû Ṣâlih, the Armenian; Translated from the Original Arabic* (Oxford, 1895).
Forget, Jacques, ed. *Synaxarium Alexandrinum.* CSCO 47–49, 67, 78, 90, SA III.18–19. 2 vols. in 6 (Beirut, 1905–1926).
Friedmann, Yohanan. *The Battle of al-Qādisiyyah and the Conquest of Syria and Palestine.* HṬ 12 (Albany, 1992).
Furlani, Giuseppe. 'Contributi alla Storia della Filosofia Greca in Oriente: Testi Siriaci III. Frammenti di una versione siriaca del commento di Pseudo-Olimpiodoro alle Categorie d'Aristotele,' *Rivsta degli Studi Orientali* 7 (1916–18), pp. 131–63.
Garcés, María Antonia, ed. *An Early Modern Dialogue with Islam: Antonio de Sosa's* Topography of Algiers *(1612).* Trans. Diana de Armas Wilson (Notre Dame, 2011).
Georr, Khalil. *Les Catégories d'Aristote dans leurs versions syro-arabes: édition de textes précédée d'une étude historique et critique et suivie d'un vocabulaire technique* (Damascus, 1948).
Harris, J. Rendel. *The Gospel of the Twelve Apostles together with the Apocalypses of each one of them* (Cambridge, 1900).
Ḥamīd Allāh, Muḥammad. *Majmū'at al-wathā'iq al-siyāsiyya lil-'ahd al-nabawī wa-'l-khilāfa al-rāshida* (Beirut, 1987).
Hoyland, Robert G. *Theophilus of Edessa's Chronicle and the Circulation of Historical Knowledge in Late Antiquity and Early Islam* (Liverpool, 2011).
Humphreys, R. Stephen. *The Crisis of the Early Caliphate.* HṬ 15 (Albany, 1990).
Jalabert, Louis and René Mouterde. *Inscriptions grecques et latines de la Syrie,* vol. 1 (Paris, 1929).
Joannou, Périclès-Pierre, ed. *Discipline générale antique.* 3 vols. in 4. (Grottaferrata [Rome], 1962–1964).
Kayser, C. *Die Canones Jakob's von Edessa* (Leipzig, 1886).
Kessler, Christel. 'Abd al-Malik's Inscription on the Dome of the Rock: A Reconsideration,' *Journal of the Royal Asiatic Society of Great Britain and Ireland* 1 (1970), pp. 2–14.
Lamoreaux, John C. *Theodore Abū Qurrah* (Provo, 2005).
Lamy, Thomas J., ed. and trans. *Sancti Ephraem Syri hymni et sermones.* 4 vols. (Mechlin, 1882–1902).
Landau-Tasseron, Ella. *Biographies of the Prophet's Companions and Their Successors.* HṬ 39 (Albany, 1998).

Levy-Rubin, Milka. *The continuatio of the Samaritan Chronicle of Abū l-Fatḥ Al-Sāmirī Al-Danafī* (Princeton, 2002).

Morony, Michael G. *Between Civil Wars: The Caliphate of Mu'āwiyah* (HṬ 18) (Albany, 1987).

Müller-Kessler, Christa and Michael Sokoloff, ed. and trans. *The Forty Martyrs of the Sinai Desert, Eulogios, the Stone-Cutter, and Anastasia* (Groningen, 1996).

al-Munajjed, Ṣalaḥuddin. 'Morceaux choisis du livre des moines,' *Mélanges de l'Institut Dominicain d'Études Orientales du Caire* 3 (1956), pp. 349–58.

Nau, François. 'Littérature canonique syriaque inédite. Concile d'Antioche; lettre d'Italie; canons "des saints Pères," de Philoxène, de Théodose, d'Anthime, d'Athanase,' *ROC* 14 (1909), pp. 1–49, 113–30.

———. 'Résumé de monographies syriaques: Barṣauma, Abraham de la Haute Montagne, Siméon de Kefar 'Abdin, Yaret l'Alexandrin, Jacques le reclus, Romanus, Talia, Asia, Pantaléon, Candida, Sergis et Abraham de Caškar,' *ROC* 18 (1913), pp. 270–76, 379–89; 19 (1914), pp. 113–34, 278–89; 20 (1915–1917), pp. 3–32.

Neumann, Carolus Ioannes [Karl Johannes]. *Iuliani Imperatoris Librorum Contra Christianos Quae Supersunt* (Leipzig, 1880).

Nevo, Yehuda D., Zemira Cohen, and Dalia Heftman, *Ancient Arabic Inscriptions from the Negev*, vol. 1, (Jerusalem, 1993).

Nöldeke, Theodor. *Geschichte des Artachšîr i Pâpakân, aus dem Pehlewî übersetzt* (Göttingen, 1879).

Palmer, Andrew, Sebastian Brock, and Robert Hoyland, *The Seventh Century in the West-Syrian Chronicles* (Liverpool, 1993).

Peeters, Paul. 'Le martyrologe de Rabban Sliba,' *AB* 27 (1927), pp. 129–200.

Pellat, Charles. *The Life and Works of Jāḥiẓ*. Trans. D. M. Hawke (London, 1969).

Penn, Michael P. 'John and the Emir: A New Introduction, Edition and Translation,' *LM* 121 (2008), pp. 65–91.

———. *When Christians First Met Muslims: A Sourcebook of the Earliest Syriac Writings on Islam* (Oakland, Calif., 2015).

Perlmann, Moshe. *The Ancient Kingdoms*. HṬ 4 (Albany, 1987).

Pickthall, Mohammed Marmaduke. *The Meaning of the Glorious Koran: An Explanatory Translation* (New York, n.d.).

Poonawala, Ismail K. *The Last Years of the Prophet*. HṬ 9 (Albany, 1990).

Rahmani, Ignatius Ephrem. *Studia Syriaca: seu, collectio documentorum hactenus ineditorum ex codicibus Syriacis*. 4 vols. (Charfeh, 1904–1909).

Ralles, Georgios A. and Michael Potles, *Syntagma tōn theiōn kai hierōn kanonōn tōn te hagiōn kai paneuphēmōn apostolōn: kai tōn hierōn oikoumenikōn kai topikōn synodōn, kai tōn kata meros hagiōn paterōn, ekdothen, syn pleistais allais tēn ekklēsiastikēn katastasin diepousais diataxesi, meta tōn archaiōn exēgētōn*. 6 vols. (Athens, 1852–1859).

Rosenthal, Franz. *The Classical Heritage in Islam* (London/New York, 1975).

———. *General Introduction, and, From Creation to the Flood*. HṬ 1 (Albany, 1989).

———. *The Return of the Caliphate to Baghdad*. HṬ 38 (Albany, 1985).

Sachau, Eduard. *Syrische Rechtsbücher*. 3 vols. (Berlin, 1907–1914).

Scholefield, James, ed. *The Works of James Pilkington, B.D., Lord Bishop of Durham* (Cambridge, 1842).

Schwartz, Eduard. *Concilium universale Chalcedonense. Acta conciliorum oecumenicorum*, t. 2, vol. 1–6 (Berlin/Leipzig, 1932–1938).
———. *Kyrillos von Skythopolis* (Leipzig, 1939).
Smith, Andrew. *Porphyrii Philosophi Fragmenta* (Stuttgart, 1993).
Thomson, Robert W., trans., with James Howard-Johnston and Tim Greenwood, *The Armenian History attributed to Sebeos.* 2 vols. (Liverpool, 1999).
Vasiliev, Alexandre. 'Harun-Ibn-Yahya and His Description of Constantinople,' *Seminarium Kondakovianum* 5 (1932) pp. 149–63.
Vööbus, Arthur. *The Synodicon in the West Syrian Tradition.* 2 vols. in 4. (CSCO 367–68, 375–76, SS 161–62, 163–64 (Louvain, 1975–1976).
———. *Syriac and Arabic Documents Regarding Legislation Relative to Syrian Asceticism* (Stockholm, 1960).
White, Joseph. *Actuum apostolorum et Epistolarum tam Catholicarum quam Paulinarum, versio Syriaca Philoxeniana ex Codice Ms Ridleinao in Bibl. Coll. Nov. Oxon. reposito, nunc primum edita cum interpretatione et annotationibus.* 2 vols. (Oxford, 1799, 1803).
———. *Sacrorum Evangeliorum versio Syriaca Philoxeniana: ex codd. mss. Ridleianis in Bibl. Coll. Nov. Oxon. repositis nunc primum edita.* 2 vols. (Oxford, 1778).

SECONDARY SOURCES

Abbott, Nabia. *Studies in Arabic Literary Papyri.* 3 vols. (Chicago, 1957–1972).
Adler, William. 'The Jews as Falsifiers: Charges of Tendentious Emendation in Anti-Jewish Christian Polemic,' in *Translation of Scripture: Proceedings of a Conference at the Annenberg Research Institute, May 15–16, 1989* (Philadelphia, 1990), pp. 1–27.
af Hällström, Gunnar. *Fides Simpliciorum* according to Origen of Alexandria (Helsinki, 1984).
Ahlwardt, Wilhelm. *Verzeichnis der arabischen Handschriften der Königlichen Bibliothek zu Berlin.* 10 vols. (Berlin, 1887–1899).
Ahmed, Shahab. *Before Orthodoxy: The Satanic Verses in Early Islam* (Cambridge, Mass., 2017).
———. 'Ibn Taymiyyah and the Satanic Verses,' *Studia Islamica* 87 (1998), pp. 67–124.
———. 'The Satanic Verses Incident in the Memory of the Early Muslim Community; An Analysis of the early *Riwāyahs* and their *Isnāds*,' (PhD diss., Princeton University, 1997).
———. *What Is Islam? The Importance of Being Islamic* (Princeton and Oxford, 2016).
Aigrain, René. *L'Hagiographie; ses sources, ses méthodes, son histoire* (Mayenne, 1953).
'Allām, Muḥammad Wahīb. *al-Isrāʾīliyyāt fī tafsīr al-Qurʾānī* (Beirut, 2007).
Allen, Pauline. 'The Homilist and the Congregation: A Case-Study of Chrysostom's Homilies on Hebrews,' *Augustinianum* 36 (1996), pp. 397–421.
———. 'Severus of Antioch as a Source for Lay Piety in Late Antiquity,' in Mario Maritano, ed. *Historiam perscrutari. Miscellanea di studi offerti al prof. Ottorino Pasquato* (Rome, 2002), pp. 711–21.
Allen, Pauline, and C.T.R. Hayward. *Severus of Antioch* (London/New York, 2004).
Allen, Pauline and Wendy Mayer. 'Computer and Homily: Accessing the Everyday Life of Early Christians,' *Vigiliae Christianae* 47 (1993), pp. 260–80.

Allison, Dale C. *Constructing Jesus: Memory, Imagination, and History* (Grand Rapids, 2010).
———. *The Historical Christ and the Theological Jesus* (Grand Rapids/Cambridge, 2009).
———. *The New Moses: A Matthean Typology* (Minneapolis, 1993).
———. *Scriptural Allusions in the New Testament: Light from the Dead Sea Scrolls* (North Richland Hills, Texas, 2000).
Alpi, Frédéric. 'Sévère d'Antioche, prédicateur et polémiste: qualification et disqualification des adversaires dogmatiques dans les *Homélies cathédrales*,' in Piroska Nagy, Michel-Yves Perrin, and Pierre Ragon, *Les controverses religieuses entre débats savants et mobilisations populaires: monde chrétien, antiquité tardive - XVIIe siècle* (Mont-Saint-Aignan, 2011), pp. 33-45.
Ambros, Arne A. *A Concise Dictionary of Koranic Arabic* (Wiesbaden, 2004).
Amstutz, Joseph. *Haplotēs; eine begriffsgeschichtliche Studie zum jüdisch-christlichen Griechisch* (Bonn, 1968).
Andrae, Tor. *In the Garden of Myrtles: Studies in Early Islamic Mysticism*, trans. Birgitta Sharpe (Albany, 1987).
———. 'Zuhd und Mönchtum. Zur Frage von den Beziehungen zwischen Christentum und Islam,' *Le Monde Oriental* 25 (1931), pp. 296–327.
Anthony, Sean W. 'Fixing John Damascene's Biography: Historical Notes on His Family Background,' *Journal of Eastern Christian Studies* 23 (2015), pp. 607–27.
Aradi, Naomi. 'The Origins of the *kalām* Model of Discussion on the Concept of *tawḥīd*,' in *Arabic Sciences and Philosophy* 23 (2013), pp. 135–66.
Arendzen, John P. 'A New Syriac Text of the Apocalyptic Part of the "Testament of the Lord,"' *JTS* (1901), pp. 401–16.
Armanios, Febe. *Coptic Christianity in Ottoman Egypt* (New York, 2011).
Armstrong, Lyall R. *The Quṣṣāṣ of Early Islam* (Leiden/Boston, 2017).
Arnold, Thomas Walker. *The Preaching of Islam: A History of the Propagation of the Muslim Faith*, 2nd ed. (London, 1913; repr. New Delhi, n.d.).
Asín y Palacios, Michaël. 'Influencias evangélicas en la literatura religiosa del Islam,' in Thomas W. Arnold and Reynold A. Nicholson, eds., *A Volume of Oriental Studies Presented to Edward G. Browne ... on his 60th Birthday* (Cambridge, 1922), pp. 8–27.
Avery-Peck, Alan J. 'The Galilean Charismatic and Rabbinic Piety: The Holy Man in the Talmudic Literature,' in Amy-Jill Levine, Dale C. Allison, Jr., and John Dominic Crossan, eds., *The Historical Jesus in Context* (Princeton, 2006), pp. 149–65.
Avner, Uzi, Laïla Nehmé, and Christian Robin. 'A Rock Inscription Mentioning Tha'laba, an Arab King from Ghassān,' *Arabian Archaeology and Epigraphy* 24 (2013), pp. 237–56.
Avner, Rina. 'The Kathisma: A Christian and Muslim Pilgrimage Site,' *Aram* 18–19 (2006–2007), pp. 541–57.
———. 'The Recovery of the Kathisma Church and Its Influence on Octagonal Buildings,' in G. Claudio Bottini, Leah Di Segni, and L. Daniel Chrupcata, eds., *One Land, Many Cultures: Archaeological Studies in Honour of Stanislao Loffreda OFM* (Jerusalem, 2003), pp. 173–86.
Avni, *The Byzantine-Islamic Transition in Palestine: An Archaeological Approach* (Oxford, 2014).
Ayyad, S. M. 'Regional Literature: Egypt,' in Julia Ashtiany et al., eds., *Abbasid Belles Lettres* (Cambridge, 1990), pp. 412–41.

Al-Azami, Muhammad Mustafa. *On Schacht's Origins of Muhammadan Jurisprudence* (repr. Oxford/Cambridge, 1996).

al-Azmeh, Aziz. *The Arabs and Islam in Late Antiquity: A Critique of Approaches to Arabic Sources* (Berlin, 2014).

———. *The Emergence of Islam in Late Antiquity: Allāh and His People* (New York, 2014).

Bacharach, Jere L. and Sherif Anwar, 'Early Versions of the *shahāda*: A Tombstone from Aswan of 71 A.H., the Dome of the Rock, and Contemporary Coinage,' *Der Islam* 89 (2012), pp. 60–69.

Bagnall, Roger S. *Everyday Writing in the Graeco-Roman East* (Berkeley/Los Angeles/London, 2011).

———. 'Religious Conversion and Onomastic Change in Early Byzantine Egypt,' *Bulletin of the American Society of Papyrologists* 19 (1982), pp. 105–24.

Barnes, Robin B. *Astrology and Reformation* (New York/Oxford, 2015).

Barṣawm, Ighnāṭyūs Afrām [Aphram Barsaum]. *al-Lu'lu' al-manthūr fī tā'rīkh al-'ulūm wa-'l-adab al-suryāniyya* (repr. Glane, Holland, 1987).

———. 'Sīrat al-qiddīs Yūḥannā ibn Aftūniyyā,' *Al-Majalla al-Baṭrakiyya al-Suryāniyya* 4:9 (1937) pp. 265–78.

Bashear, Suliman. 'Qibla Musharriqa and Early Muslim Prayer in Churches,' *Muslim World* 81 (1991), pp. 267–82.

Batinić, Jelena. *Women and Yugoslav Partisans: A History of World War II Resistance* (New York, 2015).

Bauer, Walter. *Orthodoxy and Heresy in Earliest Christianity* (Philadelphia, 1971).

Baumstark, Anton. *Geschichte der syrischen Literatur, mit Ausschluss der christlich-palästinensischen Texte* (Bonn, 1922).

———. *On the Historical Development of the Liturgy*, trans. Fritz West (Collegeville, MN, 2011).

———. 'Orientalische Rombeschreibungen,' *OC* 1 (1901), pp. 382–87.

Beck, Hans-Georg. *Kirche und theologische Literatur im Byzantinischen Reich* (Munich, 1959).

Becker, Adam H. *Fear of God and the Beginning of Wisdom: The School of Nisibis and Christian Scholastic Culture in Late Antique Mesopotamia* (Philadelphia, 2006).

Becker, Adam and Annette Yoshiko Reed, eds., *The Ways That Never Parted: Jews and Christians in Late Antiquity and the Early Middle Ages* (Minneapolis, 2007).

Becker, Carl Heinrich. 'Christian Polemic and the Formation of Islamic Dogma,' in Hoyland, ed., *Muslims and Others in Early Islamic Society*, pp. 241–57.

———. 'The Content of the Papyri on Taxation Practices,' in Donner, ed., *The Articulation of Early Islamic State Structures*, pp. 187–215.

Beckwith, John. *Early Christian and Byzantine Art* (New Haven/London, 1979).

Bell, Richard. *The Origin of Islam in its Christian Environment: The Gunning Lectures.* Edinburgh University, 1925 (London, 1926).

Benin, Stephen D. 'The "Cunning of God" and Divine Accommodation,' *Journal of the History of Ideas* 45 (1984), pp. 179–91.

———. *The Footprints of God: Divine Accommodation in Jewish and Christian Thought* (Albany, N.Y., 1993).

———. 'Sacrifice as Education in Augustine and Chrysostom,' *Church History* 52 (1983), pp. 7–20.

Benko, Stephen. 'Pagan Criticism of Christianity During the First Two Centuries A.D.,'

Aufstieg und Niedergang der Römischen Welt II, *Principat,* 23.2 (Berlin/New York, 1980), pp. 1055–1118.

Bent, Theodore and Mabel V. A. Bent. *Southern Arabia* (London, 1900).

Berg, Herbert. 'Competing Paradigms in the Study of Islamic Origins: Qur'ān 15:89–91 and the Value of *Isnāds*,' in Berg, ed., *Method and Theory in the Study of Islamic Origins*, pp. 259–90.

———. *The Development of Exegesis in Early Islam: The Authenticity of Muslim Literature from the Formative Period* (Richmond, 2000).

———. 'Failures (of Nerve?) in the Study of Islamic Origins,' in William E. Arnal, Willi Braun, and Russell T. McCutcheon, eds., *Failure and Nerve in the Study of Religion: Working with Donald Wiebe* (London, 2012), pp. 112–28.

———. 'The Implications of, and Opposition to, the Methods and Theories of John Wansbrough,' *Method and Theory in the Study of Religion* 9 (1997), pp. 3–22.

———, ed. *Method and Theory in the Study of Islamic Origins* (Leiden/Boston, 2003).

———. 'The Needle in the Haystack: Islamic Origins and the Nature of the Early Sources,' in Carlos Segovia and Basil Lourié, eds., *The Coming of the Comforter: When, Where, and to Whom? Studies on the Rise of Islam in Memory of John Wansbrough* (Piscataway, N.J.: 2012), pp. 271–302.

Bertaina, David. 'An Arabic Account of Theodore Abu Qurra in Debate at the Court of Caliph al-Ma'mun: A Study in Early Christian and Muslim Literary Dialogues' (PhD diss., Catholic University of America, 2007).

Berti, Vittorio. 'Libri e biblioteche cristiane nell'Iraq dell'VIII secolo. Una testimonianza dell'epistolario del patriarca siro-orientale Timoteo I (727–823),' in Costa C. D'Ancona, ed., *The Libraries of the Neoplatonists: Proceedings of the Meeting of the European Science Foundation Network "Late Antiquity and Arabic Thought. Patterns in the Constitution of European Culture" Held in Strasbourg, March 12–14, 2004* (Leiden/Boston, Brill, 2007), pp. 307–17.

Biberstein-Kazimirski, Albert de. *Dictionnaire arabe-français.* 4 vols. (Cairo, 1875).

Bidawid, Raphaël J. *Les lettres du patriarche nestorien Timothée I. Studi e Testi* 187 (The Vatican, 1956).

al-Bīlī, Aḥmad. *al-Ikhtilāf bayna al-qirā'āt* (Beirut, 1988).

Biller, Peter. 'Intellectuals and the Masses: Oxen and She-Asses in the Medieval Church,' in John H. Arnold, ed., *The Oxford Handbook of Medieval Christianity* (Oxford, 2014), pp. 323–39.

Binay, Sara. *Die Figur des Beduinen in der arabischen Literatur. 9. 12. Jahrhundert* (Wiesbaden, 2006).

Bingham, Joseph. *Origines ecclesiasticae: or, The Antiquities of the Christian Church.* 2 vols. (London, 1856).

Birkeland, Harris. *Old Muslim Opposition against the Interpretation of the Koran* (Oslo, 1955).

Bisheh, Ghazi I. 'The Mosque of the Prophet at Madīnah throughout the First-Century A.H. with Special Emphasis on the Umayyad Mosque,' (PhD diss., University of Michigan, 1979).

Blachère, Régis. *Introduction au Coran*, 2nd ed. (Paris, 1959).

Blok, Anton. ''The Narcissism of Minor Differences,' in Anton Blok, *Honour and Violence* (Malden, Mass., 2001), pp. 115–35.

Blum, Georg G. *Die Geschichte der Begegnung christlich-orientalischer Mystik mit der Mystik des Islams* (Wiesbaden, 2009).

Blum, Georg G. 'Christlich-orientalische Mystik und Sufismus: Zu Grundproblemen ihres Kontaktes und ihrer gegenseitigen Beeinflussung,' in Lavenant, ed., *IIIo Symposium Syriacum*, pp. 261–71.

Booth, Phil. *Crisis of Empire: Doctrine and Dissent at the End of Late Antiquity* (Berkeley, 2014).

———. 'Orthodox and Heretic in the early Byzantine Cult(s) of Saints Cosmas and Damian,' in Peter Sarris, Matthew Dal Santo, and Phil Booth, eds., *An Age of Saints?: Power, Conflict, and Dissent in Early Medieval Christianity* (Leiden/Boston, 2011), pp. 114–28.

Borrut, Antoine. *Entre mémoire et pouvoir: l'espace syrien sous les derniers Omeyyades et les premiers Abbassides (v. 72–193/692–809)* (Leiden/Boston, 2011).

Borrut, Antoine and Fred Donner, eds., *Christians and Others in the Umayyad State* (Chicago, 2016).

Bouchier, Edmund S. *A Short History of Antioch, 300 B.C.– A.D. 1268* (Oxford, 1921).

Bowersock, Glen W. *The Crucible of Islam* (Cambridge, MA/London, 2017).

Boyarin, Daniel. *Dying for God: Martyrdom and the Making of Christianity and Judaism* (Stanford, 1999).

Briquel Chatonnet, Françoise and Muriel Debié, *Le monde syriaque: sur les routes d'un christianisme ignoré* (Paris, 2017).

Brock, Sebastian P. 'Athanasiana Syriaca: Notes on Two Manuscripts,' *LM* 86 (1973), pp. 437–42.

———. 'Basil's *Homily on Deut. xv 9*: Some Remarks on the Syriac Manuscript Tradition,' in Jürgen Dümmer, ed., *Texte und Textkritik: Eine Aufsatzsammlung* (Berlin, 1987), pp. 57–66.

———. *A Brief Outline of Syriac Literature* (Kottayam, 1997).

———. 'Charting the Hellenization of a Literary Culture: The Case of Syriac,' *Intellectual History of the Islamicate World* 3 (2015), pp. 98–124.

———. 'Christians in the Sassanian Empire: A Case of Divided Loyalties,' in Stuart Mews, ed., *Religious and National Identity: Papers Read at the Nineteenth Summer Meeting and the Twentieth Winter Meeting of the Ecclesiastical History Society* (Oxford, 1982), pp. 1–19.

———. 'Clothing Metaphors as a Means of Theological Expression in Syriac Tradition,' in M. Schmidt and C. Friedrich, *Typus, Symbol, Allegorie bei den östlichen Vätern und ihren Parallelen im Mittelalter. Internationales Kolloquium, Eichstätt 1981* (Regensburg, 1982), pp. 11–38.

———. 'The Conversations with the Syrian Orthodox under Justinian (532),' *OCP* 47 (1981), pp. 87–121.

———. 'Crossing the Boundaries: An Ecumenical Role Played by Syriac Monastic Literature,' in Maciej Bielawski and Daniel Hombergen, eds., *Il monachesimo tra eredità e aperture. Atti del simposio "Testi e Temi nella Tradizione del Monachesimo Cristiano" per il 50⁰ anniversario dell'Istituto Monastico di Sant'Anselmo; Roma, 28 maggio –1⁰ giugno 2002* (Rome, 2004), pp. 22–238.

———. 'From Antagonism to Assimilation: Syriac Attitudes to Greek Learning,' in Garsoïan, Matthews, and Thomson, eds., *East of Byzantium*, pp. 17–34.

———, ed. *The Hidden Pearl: The Syrian Orthodox Church and its Ancient Aramaic Heritage*. 4 vols. (Rome, 2001).

———. 'Jacob of Edessa's Discourse on the Myron,' *OC* 63 (1979), pp. 20–36.

———. 'Jacob of Serugh: A Select Bibliographical Guide,' in George A. Kiraz, ed., *Jacob of Serugh and His Times: Studies in Sixth-Century Syriac Christianity* (Piscataway, N.J., 2010), pp. 219–44.

———. 'Jewish Traditions in Syriac Sources,' *Journal of Jewish Studies* 30 (1979), pp. 212–32.

———. *The Luminous Eye: The Spiritual World Vision of Saint Ephrem*, rev. ed. (Kalamazoo, 1992).

———. 'Manuscripts Copied in Edessa,' in Bruns and Luthe, eds. *Orientalia Christiana: Festschrift für Hubert Kaufhold zum 70. Geburtstag*, pp. 109-128.

———. 'Miaphysite, Not Monophysite!', *Cristianesimo nella storia* 37 (2016), pp 45-54.

———. 'The "Nestorian" Church: A Lamentable Misnomer,' *Bulletin of the John Rylands University Library of Manchester* 78 (1996), pp. 23–35.

———. 'Notes on Some Monasteries on Mount Izla,' *Abr-Nahrain* 19 (1980–1981), pp. 1–19.

———. 'The Orthodox-Oriental Orthodox Conversations of 532,' *Apostolos Varnavas* 41 (1980), pp. 219–28.

———. 'The Provenance of BM Or. 8606,' *JTS* 19 (1968), pp. 632–33.

———. 'The Syriac Commentary Tradition,' in Charles Burnett, ed., *Glosses and Commentaries on Aristotelian Logical Texts: The Syriac, Arabic and Medieval Latin Traditions* (London, 1993), pp. 3–18.

———. 'Syriac Manuscripts Copied on the Black Mountain, near Antioch,' in Regine Schulz and Manfred Görg, eds., *Lingua restituta orientalis. Festgabe für Julius Assfalg* (Wiesbaden, 1990), pp. 59–67.

———. *The Syriac Version of the Pseudo-Nonnos Mythological Scholia* (London, 1971).

———. 'Syriac Views of Emergent Islam,' in Gautier H. A. Juynboll, ed., *Studies in the First Century of Islamic Society* (Carbondale and Edwardsville, Ill., 1982), pp. 9–21.

———. 'The Thrice-Holy Hymn in the Liturgy,' *Sobornost/Eastern Churches Review* 7 (1985), pp. 24–34.

———. 'Towards a History of Syriac Translation Technique,' in René Lavenant, ed., *III° Symposium Syriacum*, pp. 1–14.

———. 'Traduzioni Siriache degli Scritti di Basilio,' in *Basilio tra Oriente e Occidente: convegno internazionale 'Basilio il Grande e il monachesimo orientale,' Cappadocia, 5–7 ottobre 1999* (Magnano, BI, 2001), pp. 165–180.

Brooks, Ernest Walter. 'The Arabs in Asia Minor (641-750), from Arabic Sources,' *Journal of Hellenic Studies* 18 (1898), pp. 182–208.

Brown, Francis, Samuel R. Driver, and Charles A. Briggs, *A Hebrew and English Lexicon of the Old Testament* (Boston/New York, 1907).

Brown, Jonathan A. C. *Hadith: Muhammad's Legacy in the Medieval and Modern World* (Oxford, 2009).

Brown, Peter. 'Augustine and a Practice of the *imperiti*,' in Goulven Madec, ed., *Augustin Prédicateur (395–411): actes du Colloque International de Chantilly (5-7 septembre 1996)* (Paris, 1998), pp. 367–75.

———. 'Images as a Substitute for Writing,' in Evangelos Chrysos and Ian Wood, eds. *East and West: Modes of Communication: Proceedings of the First Plenary Conference at Merida* (Leiden/Boston, 1999), pp. 15–34.

———. *Power and Persuasion in Late Antiquity: Towards a Christian Empire* (Madison, Wisc., 1992).

———. 'The Saint as Exemplar in Late Antiquity,' *Representations* 2 (1983), pp. 1–25.

———. *The World of Late Antiquity* (London, 1971).

Bruns, Peter. 'Beobachtungen zu den Rechtsgrundlagen der Christenverfolgungen im Sasanidenreich,' *Römische Quartalschrift für christliche Altertumskunde und für Kirchengeschichte* 103 (2008), pp. 82–112.
Bruns, Peter. 'Wer war Paul der Perser?' *Studia Patristica* 45 (2010), pp. 263–68.
Bruns, Peter and Heinz O. Luthe, *Orientalia Christiana: Festschrift für Hubert Kaufhold zum 70. Geburtstag* (Wiesbaden, 2013).
Buck, Christopher. 'The Identity of the Ṣābi'ūn: An Historical Quest,' *Muslim World* 74 (1984), pp. 172–86.
Bukhsh, S. Khuda. *Contributions to the History of Islamic Civilization.* 2 vols. 2nd ed. (Calcutta, 1929–1930).
Bulliet, Richard W. 'The Conversion Curve Revisited,' in Peacock, ed., *Islamisation*, pp. 69–79.
———. *Conversion to Islam in the Medieval Period: An Essay in Quantitative History* (Cambridge, MA/London, 1979).
———. 'Conversion Stories in Early Islam,' in Gervers and Bikhazi, eds., *Conversion and Continuity*, pp. 123–33.
———. 'Process and Status in Conversion and Continuity,' in Gervers and Bikhazi eds., *Conversion and Continuity*, pp. 1–12.
Bultmann, Rudolf. *The History of the Synoptic Tradition.* Translated by John Marsh (New York, 1963).
Būlus, Afrām. Aftūniyyā,' *Al-Majalla al-Baṭrakiyya* 32 (October, 1965), pp. 82–87.
Burke, Peter. *Popular Culture in Early Modern Europe*, rev. ed., (Aldershot/Burlington, Vt., 1994).
———. *What is Cultural History?* (Cambridge/Malden, MA, 2004).
Burman, Thomas E. *Religious Polemic and the Intellectual History of the Mozarabs, c. 1050–1200* (Leiden/New York, 1994).
Burr, Viktor. 'Der byzantinische Kulturkreis,' in Fritz Milkau and Georg Leyh, eds., *Handbuch der Bibliothekswissenschaft*, vol. 3.1: *Geschichte der Bibliotheken* (Wiesbaden, 1955), pp. 146–87 (= §70–§78).
Burton, John. 'Linguistic Errors in the Qur'ān,' *Journal of Semitic Studies* 33 (1988), pp. 181-196.
———. 'Notes towards a Fresh Perspective on the Islamic Sunna,' in H. Motzki, ed., *Ḥadīth: Origins and Developments* (Aldershot/Burlington, VT, 2004), pp. 39–53.
———. *The Sources of Islamic Law: Islamic Theories of Abrogation* (Edinburgh, 1990).
Busse, Heribert. 'Der Islam und die biblischen Kultstätten,' *Der Islam* 42 (1966), pp. 113–47.
———. ''Omar's Image as the Conqueror of Jerusalem,' *JSAI* 8 (1986), pp. 149–68.
———. ''Omar b. al-Ḫaṭṭāb in Jerusalem,' *JSAI* 5 (1984), pp. 73–119.
Cadoux, Cecil J. *The Early Church and the World* (reprint, Edinburgh/New York, 1955).
Caetani, Leone. *Annali dell' Islām.* 10 vols. (Milan, 1905–1926).
———. 'The Art of War of the Arabs and the Supposed Religious Fervor of the Arab Conquerors,' in Fred M. Donner, ed., *The Expansion of the Early Islamic State* (Aldershot/Burlington, Vt., 2008), pp. 1–13.
———. *Chronographia Islamica; ossia, Riassunto cronologico della storia di tutti i popoli musulmani dall'anno 1 all'anno 922 della Higrah (622–1517 dell'èra volgare). Corredato della bibliografia di tutte le principali fonti stampate e manoscritte.* 5 vols. (Paris, 1912).
Cahen, Claude. 'Fiscalité, propriété, antagonismes sociaux en Haute-Mésopotamie au

temps des premiers ‘Abbāsides, d’après Denys de Tell-Mahré,’ *Arabica* 1 (1954), pp. 136–52.

———. ‘Socio-Economic History and Islamic Studies: Problems of Bias in the Adaptation of the Indigenous Population to Islam,’ in Hoyland, ed., *Muslims and Others in Early Islamic Society*, pp. 259–76.

———. *La Syrie du nord à l’époque des croisades et la principauté franque d’Antioche* (Paris, 1940).

Calasso, Giovanna. ‘Récits de conversion, zèle dévotionnel et instruction religieuse dans les biographies des “gens de Baṣra” du *Kitāb al-Ṭabaqāt* d’Ibn Sa‘d,’ in Mercedes García-Arenal, ed., *Conversions islamiques: identités religieuses en islam méditerranéen/Islamic Conversions: Religious Identities in Mediterranean Islam* (Paris, 2001), pp. 20–47.

Cameron, Alan. *Circus Factions: Blues and Greens at Rome and Byzantium* (Oxford, 1976).

Cameron, Averil, ‘Byzantines and Jews: Some Recent Work on Early Byzantium,’ *Byzantine and Modern Greek Studies* 20 (1996), pp. 249–74.

———. ‘Christian Conversion in Late Antiquity: Some Issues,’ in Arietta Papaconstantinou, Neil McLynn, and Daniel L. Schwartz, eds., *Conversion in Late Antiquity: Christianity, Islam, and Beyond: Papers from the Andrew W. Mellon Foundation Sawyer Seminar, University of Oxford, 2009–2010* (Farnham, Surrey/Burlington, 2015), pp. 3–21.

———. *Dialoguing in Late Antiquity* (Washington, D.C., 2014).

———. ‘How to Read Heresiology,’ *Journal of Medieval and Early Modern Studies* 33 (2003), pp. 471–92.

———. ‘The Jews in Seventh-Century Palestine,’ *Scripta Classical Israelica* 13 (1994), pp. 75–93.

———. ‘Patristic Studies and the Emergence of Islam,’ in Brouria Bitton-Ashkelony, Theodore de Bruyn, and Carol Harrison, eds., *Patristic Studies in the Twenty-First Century* (Turnhout, 2015), pp. 249–78.

Cameron, Euan. *Enchanted Europe: Superstition, Reason, and Religion, 1250–1750* (Oxford, 2010).

Campbell, Elizabeth. ‘A Heaven of Wine: Muslim-Christian Encounters at Monasteries in the Early Islamic Middle East’ (PhD diss., University of Washington, 2009).

Cancik, Hubert. ‘Antike Religionsgespräch,’ in Günther Schörner, Darja S. Erker, eds., *Medien religiöser Kommunikation im Imperium Romanum* (Stuttgart, 2008), pp. 15–25.

Carcione, Filippo. ‘Il “De iis qui ad ecclesiam accedunt” del presbitero constantinopolitano Timoteo. Una nuova proposta di datazione,’ *Studi e ricerche dull’Oriente cristiano* 14 (1991), pp. 309–20.

Carlson, Thomas. ‘The Contours of Conversion: The Geography of Islamization in Syria, 600–1500,’ *Journal of the American Oriental Society* 134 (2015), pp. 791–816.

Carpenter, H. J. ‘Popular Christianity and the Theologians in the Early Centuries,’ *Journal of Theological Studies* 14 (1963), pp. 294–310.

Carter, H. J. ‘Notes on the Mahrah Tribe of Southern Arabia, with a Vocabulary of Their Language, to Which Are Appended Additional Observations on the Gara Tribe,’ *Journal of the Bombay Branch of the Royal Asiatic Society* 2 (1847), pp. 339–70.

Caspar, Robert. *A Historical Introduction to Islamic Theology: Muḥammad and the Classical Period*, trans. P. Johnstone (Rome, 1998).

Caspar, Robert, et al., 'Bibliographie du dialogue Islamo-Chrétien,' *Islamochristiana* 1 (1975), pp. 125–81.

Cassin, Matthieu. '*De deitate filii et spiritus sancti et in Abraham*,' in Volker H. Drecoll and Margitta Berghaus, eds., *Gregory of Nyssa: The Minor Treatises on Trinitarian Theology and Apollinarism* (Leiden/Boston, 2011), pp. 277–311.

Chadwick, Henry. 'Eucharist and Christology in the Nestorian Conflict,' *JTS* 2 (1951), pp. 145–64.

——. 'John Moschus and his friend Sophronius the Sophist,' *Journal of Theological Studies* 25 (1974), pp. 41–74.

——. *The Role of the Christian Bishop in Ancient Society* (Berkeley, 1980).

Chakrabarty, Dipesh. *Provincializing Europe: Postcolonial Thought and Historical Difference* (Princeton/Oxford, 2008).

Charanis, Peter. 'The Transfer of Population as a Policy in the Byzantine Empire,' *Comparative Studies in Society and History* 3 (1961), pp. 140–54.

Charles-Murray, Mary. 'Artistic Idiom and Doctrinal Development,' in Rowan Williams, ed., *The Making of Orthodoxy: Essays in Honour of Henry Chadwick* (Cambridge, 1989), pp. 288–307.

El Cheikh, Nadia Maria. *Women, Islam, and Abbasid Identity* (Cambridge, Mass., 2015).

Cheikho, Louis and Camille Hechaïmé, *Wuzarā' al-naṣrāniyya wa-kuttābuhā fī 'l-Islām: 622–1517* (Jouniyeh, Lebanon, 1987).

Chevallier-Caseau, Béatrice. 'La lettre de Jésus à Abgar d'Édesse,' in François-Marie Humann and Jacques-Noël Pérès, eds., *Apocryphes chrétiens des premiers siècles. Mémoire et traditions* (Paris, 2009), pp. 15–45.

Chialà, Sabino. 'Les mystiques musulmans lecteurs des écrits chrétiens. Quelques échos d'Apophtegmes,' *Proche-Orient Chrétien* 60 (2010), pp. 352–67.

Chialà, Sabino, ed., and Ignazio de Francesco, trans., *I detti islamici di Gesù* (Rome, 2009).

Christys, Ann. *Christians in Al-Andalus: (711-1000)* (Richmond, 2002).

Chrysostomides, Anna. '"There is No God but God": Islamisation and Religious Code-Switching, Eighth to Tenth Centuries,' in Peacock, ed., *Islamisation*, pp. 118–33.

Clark, E. G. 'Pastoral Care: Town and Country in Late-Antique Preaching,' in Thomas S. Burns and John W. Eadie, eds., *Urban Centers and Rural Contexts in Late Antiquity* (East Lansing, 2001), pp. 265–84.

Clarke, Elizabeth A. *The Origenist Controversy: The Cultural Construction of an Early Christian Debate* (Princeton, 1992).

——. *Reading Renunciation: Asceticism and Scripture in Early Christianity* (Princeton, 1999).

Clarysse, W. 'Greeks and Egyptians in the Ptolemaic Army and Administration,' *Aegyptus* 65 (1985), pp. 57–66.

Cobb, Paul M. 'Community versus Contention: Ibn 'Asākir and 'Abbāsid Syria,' in J. E. Lindsay, ed., *Ibn 'Asākir and Early Islamic History* (Princeton, 2001), pp. 100–26.

Cohen, Anthony P. *The Symbolic Construction of Community* (London/New York, 1985).

Cohen, Mark. 'What Was the Pact of 'Umar? A Literary-Historical Study,' *JSAI* 23 (1999), pp. 100–57.

Conrad, Lawrence I. 'The *mawālī* and Early Arabic Historiography,' in Monique Bernards and John Nawas, eds., *Patronate and Patronage in Early and Classical Islam* (Leiden, 2005), pp. 370–425.

——. 'Varietas Syriaca: Secular and Scientific Culture in the Christian Communities of Syria after the Arab Conquest,' in Gerrit J. Reinink and Alexander C. Klugkist, eds., *After Bardaisan: Studies on Continuity and Change in Syriac Christianity in Honour of Professor Han J.W. Drijvers* (Louvain, 1999), pp. 85–105.

Cook, David. 'Apostasy from Islam: A Historical Perspective,' *Jerusalem Studies in Arabic and Islam* 31 (2006), pp. 248–88.

——. 'New Testament Citations in the Ḥadīth Literature and the Question of Early Gospel Translations into Arabic,' in Grypeou et al., *The Encounter of Eastern Christianity with Early Islam*, pp. 185–23.

Cook, Michael A. *Early Muslim Dogma: A Source-Critical Study* (Cambridge, 1981).

——. 'Eschatology and the Dating of Traditions,' *Princeton Papers in Near Eastern Studies* 1 (1992), pp. 23–47.

——. *The Koran: A Very Short Introduction* (Oxford/New York, 2000).

——. 'The Origins of "Kalām,"' *BSOAS* 43 (1980), pp. 32–43.

Cook, Michael A., and Patricia Crone, *Hagarism: The Making of the Islamic World* (Cambridge/New York, 1977).

Cooperson, Michael. Review of *Method and Theory in the Study of Islamic Origins*, ed. H. Berg, *Islamic Law and Society* 15 (2008), 268–74.

Creswell, Keppel A. C. *Early Muslim Architecture: Umayyads, Early 'Abbāsids & Ṭūlūnids*. 2 vols. (Oxford, 1932–1940).

——. *A Short Account of Early Muslim Architecture* (repr. Beirut, 1968).

Creswell, Robyn. 'Elias Khoury, The Art of Fiction No. 233,' *Paris Review* 220 (Spring, 2017): Available at https://www.theparisreview.org/interviews/6940/elias-khoury-the-art-of-fiction-no-233-elias-khoury.

Crone, Patricia. 'The Early Islamic World,' in Kurt Raaflaub and Nathan Rosenstein, eds., *War and Society in the Ancient and Medieval World: Asia, the Mediterranean, Europe, and Mesoamerica* (Washington, D.C., 1999), p. 309–32.

——. *God's Rule: Government and Islam: Six Centuries of Medieval Islamic Political Thought* (New York, 2004).

——. 'Jewish Christianity and the Qur'ān (Part One),' *JNES* 74 (2015), pp. 225–53.

——. 'Jewish Christianity and the Qur'ān (Part Two),' *JNES* 75 (2016), pp. 1–21.

——. *Meccan Trade and the Rise of Islam* (Princeton, 1987).

——. *The Nativist Prophets of Early Islamic Iran* (New York, 2012).

——. *Roman, Provincial and Islamic Law: The Origins of the Islamic Patronate* (Cambridge, 1987).

——. *Slaves on Horses: The Evolution of the Islamic Polity* (Cambridge, 1980).

——. Review of D. R. Hill, *The Termination of Hostilities in the Early Arab Conquests, A.D. 634–656, BSOAS* 35 (1972), p. 360–62.

——. 'Two Legal Problems Bearing on the Early History of the Qur'ān,' *JSAI* 18 (1994), pp. 1–37.

Crone, Patricia and Martin Hinds, *God's Caliph: Religious Authority in the First Centuries of Islam* (Cambridge, 1986).

Crossan, John D. *Who Killed Jesus: Exposing the Roots of Anti-Semitism in the Gospel Story of the Death of Jesus* (San Francisco, 1995).

al-Dabte, Yousef, 'Iktishāf Dayr Qinnisrīn (Monastery of Qinnisre),' *Mahd al-Ḥaḍarāt* 2 (April, 2007), pp. 83–99.

Davies, William D. and Dale C. Allison, *A Critical and Exegetical Commentary on the Gospel according to Saint Matthew*. 3 vols. (Edinburgh, 1988–1997).

Davis, Stephen J. *Coptic Christology in Practice: Incarnation and Divine Participation in Late Antique and Medieval Egypt* (Oxford/New York, 2008).

Debié, Muriel. 'Christians in the Service of the Caliph: Through the Looking Glass of Communal Identities,' in Borrut and Donner, *Christians and Others*, pp. 53–71.

———. '"La science est commune": Sources syriaques et culture grecque en Syrie-Mésopotamie et en Perse par-delà les siècles obscurs Byzantins,' *Travaux et mémoires* 21 (2017), pp. 87–127.

Debié, Muriel and David G. K. Taylor, 'Syriac and Syro-Arabic Historical Writing, c. 500–c. 1400,' in Sarah Foot and Chase F. Robinson, eds., *The Oxford History of Historical Writing*, vol. 2: *400–1400* (Oxford, 2012), pp. 155–79.

de Blois, François. '*Laylat al-Māšūš*: Marginalia to al-Bayrūnī, Abū Nuwās and other Authors,' *Journal of Semitic Studies* 29 (1984), pp. 81–96.

de Bruyn, Theodore. *Making Amulets Christian: Artefacts, Scribes, and Contexts* (Oxford, 2017).

Decker, Michael. *Tilling the Hateful Earth: Agricultural Production and Trade in the Late Antique East* (Oxford/New York, 2009).

de Halleux, André. 'Die Genealogie des Nestorianismus nach der frühmonophysitischen Theologie,' *OC* 66 (1982), pp. 1–14.

———. 'L'homélie baptismale de Grégoire de Nazianze: la version syriaque et son apport au texte grec,' *LM* 95 (1982), pp. 5–40.

———. *Philoxène de Mabbog. Sa vie, ses écrits, sa théologie* (Louvain, 1963).

de Mier Vélez, Antonio. 'Supersticiones y horóscopos entre los Cristianos Visigodos y Francos,' *Religión y Cultura* 41 (1995), pp. 811–39.

Dennett, Jr., Daniel C. *Conversion and the Poll Tax in Early Islam* (Cambridge, Mass., 1950).

Déroche, Vincent. 'La polémique anti-judaïque au VIe et au VIIe siècle un mémento inédit, les *Képhalaia*,' *Travaux et mémoires* 11 (1991), pp. 275–311.

Devreesse, Robert. *Essai sur Théodore de Mopsueste* (Rome, 1948).

Dictionnaire de théologie catholique, contenant l'exposé des doctrines de la théologie catholique, leurs preuves et leur histoire. Edited by Alfred Vacant, Eugène Vacant, et al. 15 vols. in 23. (Paris, 1899–1950).

Diem, Werner. 'Studien zur Frage des Substrats im Arabischen,' *Der Islam* 56 (1979), pp. 12–80.

Dijkstra, Jitse and Mathilde van Dijk. *The Encroaching Desert: Egyptian Hagiography and the Medieval West* (Leiden/Boston, 2006).

Dixon, C. Scott. 'Popular Beliefs and the Reformation in Brandenburg-Ansbach,' in Bob Scribner and Trevor Johnson, eds., *Popular Religion in Germany and Central Europe, 1400–1800* (Basingstoke/New York, 1996), pp. 119–39.

———. *The Reformation and Rural Society: The Parishes of Brandenburg-Ansbach-Kulmbach, 1528-1603* (Cambridge, 1996).

Doe, Brian. *Socotra: Island of Tranquility* (London, 1992).

Donner, Fred M. ed., *The Articulation of Early Islamic State Structures* (Farnham, Surrey, 2012).

———. *The Early Islamic Conquests* (Princeton, 1981).

———. 'From Believers to Muslims: Confessional Self-Identity in the Early Islamic Community,' *al-Abhath* 50–51 (2002–2003), pp. 9–53.
———. 'The Formation of the Islamic State,' reprinted in Donner, ed., *The Articulation of Early Islamic State Structures*, pp. 1–14
———. 'Introduction: The Articulation of Early Islamic State Structures,' in Donner, ed., *The Articulation of Early Islamic State Structures*, pp. xiii–xxxii.
———. 'Modern Approaches to Early Islamic history,' in Chase F. Robinson, ed., *The New Cambridge History of Islam*, vol. 1: *The Formation of the Islamic World, Sixth to Eleventh Centuries* (Cambridge/New York, 2010), pp. 625–47.
———. *Muhammad and the Believers: At the Origins of Islam* (Cambridge, Mass./London, 2010).
———. 'Muhammad und die frühe islamische Gemeinschaft aus historischer Sicht,' *Asia* 68 (2014), pp. 439–51.
———. *Narratives of Islamic Origins: The Beginnings of Islamic Historical Writing* (Princeton, 1998).
———. 'Qur'ânicization of Religio-Political Discourse in the Umayyad Period,' *Revue des mondes musulmans et de la Méditerranée* 129 (2011), pp. 79–92.
———. Review of *In God's Path: The Arab Conquests and the Creation of an Islamic Empire* by R. Hoyland, *Al-'Uṣūr al-Wusṭā* 23 (2015), pp. 134–40.
———. 'Umayyad Efforts at Legitimation: The Umayyads' Silent Heritage,' in Antoine Borrut and Paul M. Cobb, eds., *Umayyad Legacies: Medieval Memories from Syria to Spain* (Leiden/Boston, 2010), pp. 187–211.
———. 'Was Marwan ibn al-Hakam the First "Real" Muslim?' in Sarah Bowen Savant and Helena de Felipe, eds., *Genealogy and Knowledge in Muslim Societies: Understanding the Past* (Edinburgh, 2014), pp. 105–14.
Dossey, Leslie. *Peasant and Empire in Christian North Africa* (Berkeley, 2010).
Draguet, René. *Julien d'Halicarnasse et sa controverse avec Sévère d'Antioche sur l'incorruptibilité du corps du Christ. Études d'histoire littéraire et doctrinale, suivie des fragments dogmatiques de Julien* (Louvain, 1924).
Dreuzy, Agnes de. *The Holy See and the Emergence of the Modern Middle East: Benedict XV's Diplomacy in Greater Syria (1914–1922)* (Washington, D.C., 2016).
Drijvers, Han J. W. 'The Abgar Legend,' in Wilhelm Schneemelcher, ed., *New Testament Apocrypha*, vol. 1: *Gospels and Related Writings*. Trans. Robert McL. Wilson. Rev. ed. (Louisville/London, 1991), pp. 492–500.
———. *Bardaiṣan of Edessa* (Assen, 1966).
———. 'Jews and Christians at Edessa,' *Journal of Jewish Studies* 36 (1985), pp. 88–102.
———. 'The Persistence of Pagan Cults and Practices in Christian Syria,' in Garsoian, Matthews, Thomson, eds., *East of Byzantium* pp. 35–44.
———. 'The Testament of Our Lord: Jacob of Edessa's Response to Islam,' *Aram* 6 (1994), pp. 104–14.
Duncan-Jones, Richard P. 'Age-Rounding, Illiteracy and Social Differentiation in the Roman Empire,' *Chiron* 7 (1977), pp. 333–53.
———. 'Age-Rounding in Greco-Roman Egypt,' *Zeitschrift für Papyrologie und Epigraphik* 33 (1979), pp. 169–177.
Dunn, John 'The Politics of Locke in England and America in the Eighteenth Century,'

in John W. Yolton, ed., *John Locke: Problems and Perspectives: A Collection of New Essays* (London, 1969), pp. 45–80.

Effros, Bonnie. 'The Enduring Attraction of the Pirenne Thesis,' *Speculum* 92 (2017), pp. 184–208.

Eger, A. Asa. *The Islamic-Byzantine Frontier: Interaction and Exchange among Muslim and Christian Communities* (London, 2015).

Ellenblum, Ronnie. 'Demography, Geography and the Accelerated Islamisation of the Eastern Mediterranean,' in Ira Katzenelson and Miri Rubin, eds., *Religious Conversion: History, Experience and Meaning* (Farnham, 2014), pp. 61–80.

El-Leithy, Tamer. 'Coptic Culture and Conversion in Medieval Cairo, 1293–1524 A.D.,' (PhD diss., Princeton, 2005).

Elliott, Alison G. *Roads to Paradise: Reading the Lives of the Early Saints* (Hanover, N. Hamp., 1987).

Emon, Anver M. *Religious Pluralism and Islamic Law: Dhimmīs and Others in the Empire of Law* (Oxford, 2012).

Encyclopaedia Iranica, ed. Ehsan Yarshater (London/Boston, 1982–).

Endress, Gerhard. 'Die Wissenschaftliche Literatur,' in Helmut Gätje, *Grundriß der Arabischen Philologie*, vol. 2: *Literaturwissenschaft* (Wiesbaden, 1987), pp. 400–506.

Eskult, Mats. 'Translation Technique in the Epistle to the Hebrews as Edited by Edvard Stenij from Codex Tischendorf,' in Miriam L. Hjälm, ed., *Senses of Scripture, Treasures of Tradition: the Bible in Arabic among Jews, Christians and Muslims* (Leiden/Boston, 2017), pp. 425–35.

Evans, Craig A. *Ancient Texts for New Testament Studies: A Guide to the Background Literature* (Grand Rapids, 2005).

Fahmy, Khaled. 'For Cavafy, with Love and Squalor: Some Critical Notes on the History and Historiography of Modern Alexandria,' in Anthony Hirst and Michael Silk, eds., *Alexandria, Real and Imagined* (Ashgate, 2004), pp. 263–80.

———. 'Towards a Social History of Modern Alexandria,' in Anthony Hirst and Michael Silk, eds., *Alexandria, Real and Imagined* (Ashgate, 2004), pp. 281–306.

al-Faouri, Amjad Mamdouh Mohammad. 'Dawr al-ʿanāṣir ghayr al-ʿarabiyya fī 'l-futūḥāt al- Islāmiyya fī 'l-ʿaṣr al-Umawī,' *Jordan Journal for History and Archaeology* 8 (2014), pp. 51–75.

Fargues, Phillipe. 'The Arab Christians of the Middle East: A Demographic Perspective,' in Andrea Pacini, ed., *Christian Communities in the Middle East: The Challenge of the Future* (Oxford, 1998), pp. 48–66.

Fattal, Antoine. *Le statut légal des non-musulmans en pays d'Islam* (Beirut, 1958).

Fedwick, Paul J. 'The Translations of the Works of Basil Before 1400,' in Paul J. Fedwick, ed., *Basil of Caesarea: Christian, Humanist, Ascetic: A Sixteen-Hundredth Anniversary Symposium*, vol. 2 (Toronto, 1981), pp. 439–512.

Fiey, Jean-Maurice. *Chrétiens syriaques sous les Abbassides surtout à Bagdad (749–1258)* (Louvain, 1980).

———. *Chrétiens syriaques sous les Mongols (Il-Khanat de Perse, XIIIe–XIVe s.)* (Louvain, 1975).

———. 'Conversions à l'Islam de Juifs et de Chrétiens sous les Abbassides d'après les sources arabes et syriaques,' ed. Johannes Irmscher, *Rapports entre Juifs, Chrétiens et Musulmans. Eine Sammlung von Forschungsbeiträgen* (Amsterdam, 1995), pp. 13–28.

———. 'Diptyques Nestoriens du XIVe siècle,' *AB* 81 (1963), pp. 371–413.

———. 'L'Élam, la première des métropoles ecclésiastiques syriennes orientales,' *Melto* 5 (1969), pp. 221–67.

———. 'L'Élam, la première des métropoles ecclésiastiques syriennes orientales (suite),' *PdO* 1 (1970), pp. 123–53.

———. 'Īšō'yaw le Grand: Vie du caltholicos nestorien Īšō'yaw III d'Adiabène (580–659),' *OCP* 35 (1969), pp. 305–333; vol. 36 (1970), pp. 5–46.

———. *Jalons pour une histoire de l'Église en Iraq* (Louvain, 1970).

———. 'Les "Nabaṭ" de Kaskar-Wāsiṭ dans les premiers siècles de l'Islam,' *Mélanges de l'Université Saint-Joseph* 51 (1990), pp. 49–88.

———. *Pour un Oriens Christianus Novus. Répertoire des diocèses syriaques orientaux et occidentaux.* (Beirut/Stuttgart, 1993).

———. Saints syriaques (Princeton, 2004).

Fisher, Greg. *Between Empires: Arabs, Romans, and Sasanians in Late Antiquity* (Oxford, 2011).

Fisher, Greg, Philip Wood, et al., 'Arabs and Christianity,' in Greg Fisher, ed., *Arabs and Empires before Islam* (Oxford, 2015), pp. 276–72.

Flower, Richard. 'Genealogies of Unbelief: Ephiphanius of Salamis and Heresiological Authority,' in Christopher Kelly, Richard Flower, and Michael Stuart Williams, eds., *Unclassical Traditions*, vol. 2: *Perspectives from East and West in Late Antiquity* (Cambridge, 2011), pp. 70–87.

Flügel, Gustav. *Die arabischen, persischen und türkischen Handschriften der Kaiserlich-königlichen Hofbibliothek zu Wien*, 3 vols. (Vienna, 1865–1867).

Flusin, Bernard. 'L'esplanade du temple a l'arrivée des Arabes, d'après deux récits byzantins,' in Raby and Johns, eds., *Bayt al-Maqdis*, vol. 1, pp. 17–31.

Forness, Philip M. 'Preaching and Religious Debate: Jacob of Serugh and the Promotion of His Christology in the Roman Near East.' PhD diss., Princeton Theological Seminary, 2016.

Foss, Clive. *Arab-Byzantine Coins: An Introduction, with a Catalogue of the Dumbarton Oaks Collection* (Cambridge, Mass, 2008).

———. 'Byzantine Saints in Early Islamic Syria,' *AB* 125 (2007), pp. 93–119.

———. 'Egypt under Mu'āwiya, Part I: Flavius Papas and Upper Egypt,' *BSOAS* 72 (2009), pp. 1-24.

———. 'Egypt under Mu'āwiya, Part II: Middle Egypt, Fusṭāṭ and Alexandria,' *BSOAS* 72 (2009), pp. 259-278.

———. 'Mu'āwiya's State,' in Haldon, ed., *Money, Power and Politics in Early Islamic Syria: A Review of Current Debates*, pp. 75–96.

Fournet, Jean-Luc. 'Conversion religieuse dans un graffito de Baouit? Revision de *SB* III 6042,' in Anne Boud'hors, et al., eds., *Monastic Estates in Late Antique and Early Islamic Egypt: Ostraca, Papryi, and Essays in Memory of Sarah Clackson (P. Clackson)*, (Cincinnati, 2009), pp. 141–47.

Fowden, Elizabeth K. *The Barbarian Plain: Saint Sergius between Rome and Iran* (Berkeley, 1999).

Fowden, Garth. *Before and After Muḥammad: The First Millennium* (Princeton, 2014).

Frankfurter, David. 'Hagiography and the Reconstruction of Local Religion in Late Antique Egypt: Memories, Inventions, and Landscapes,' in Dijkstra and van Dijk, *The Encroaching Desert*, pp. 13–37.

Frantz-Murphy, Gladys. 'Conversion in Early Islamic Egypt: The Economic Factor,' in Robert Hoyland, ed. *Muslims and Others in Early Islamic Society* (Aldershot, 2004), pp. 323–329.

Freedman, Paul. *Images of the Medieval Peasant* (Stanford, 1999).

Frend, W.H.C. 'Popular Religion and Christological Controversy in the Fifth Century,' in G. J. Cuming and Derek Baker, eds., *Studies in Church History*, vol. 8 (Cambridge, 1971), pp. 19–29. Reprinted in W.H.C. Frend, *Religion Popular and Unpopular in the Early Christian Centuries* (London, 1976), no. XVII.

——. *The Rise of the Monophysite Movement: Chapters in the History of the Church in the Fifth and Sixth Centuries* (Cambridge, 1972).

Friedmann, Yohanan. *Tolerance and Coercion in Islam: Interfaith Relations in the Muslim Tradition* (Cambridge, 2003).

Gager, John G. 'Did Jewish Christians See the Rise of Islam?' in Becker and Reed, eds., *The Ways that Never Parted*, pp. 36–72.

Galadza, Daniel. 'Liturgical Byzantinization in Jerusalem: Al-Biruni's Melkite Calendar in Context,' *Bollettino della Badia Greca di Grottaferrata* 7 (2010), pp. 69–85.

——. *Worship of the Holy City in Captivity: The Liturgical Byzantinization of the Orthodox Patriarchate of Jerusalem after the Arab Conquests (8th–13th c.)* (Excerpta ex dissertation ad doctoratum; Rome, 2013).

Galvão-Sobrinho, Carlos R. *Doctrine and Power: Theological Controversy and Christian Leadership in the Later Roman Empire* (Berkeley, 2013).

Gamble, Harry Y. *Books and Readers in the Early Church: A History of Early Christian Texts* (New Haven/London, 1995).

Garceau, Michelle E. 'God and his Saints in Medieval Catalunya: A Social History,' (PhD diss., Princeton University, 2009).

García-Arenal, Mercedes. 'Dreams and Reason: Autobiographies of Converts in Religious Polemics,' in Mercedes García-Arenal, ed., *Conversions islamiques: identités religieuses en islam méditerranéen/Islamic Conversions: Religious Identities in Mediterranean Islam* (Paris, 2001), pp. 89–118.

Garsoïan, Nina G., Thomas F. Matthews, and Robert W. Thomson, eds. *East of Byzantium: Syria and Armenia in the Formative Period* (Washington, D.C., 1982).

Gascou, Jean. 'Arabic Taxation in the Mid-Seventh-Century Greek Papyri,' in Constantin Zuckerman, ed., *Constructing the Seventh Century* (Paris, 2013), pp. 671–77.

Gatier, Pierre-Louis. 'Villages du Proche-Orient protobyzantin (4ème-7ème s.). Étude régionale,' in G.R.D. King and Averil Cameron, eds., *The Byzantine and Early Islamic Near East* II: *Land Use and Settlement Patterns* (Princeton, 1994), pp. 17–48

Geary, Patrick J. 'L'humiliation des saints,' *Annales. Histoire, Sciences sociales* 34 (1979), pp. 27–42.

——. *The Myth of Nations: The Medieval Origins of Europe* (Princeton, 2002).

Géhin, Paul. 'Manuscrits sinaïtiques dispersés III: les fragments syriaques de Londres et de Birmingham,' *OC* 94 (2010), pp. 14–57.

Gelez, Philippe and Gilles Grivaud, *Les conversions à l'Islam en Asie Mineure, dans les*

Balkans et dans le monde musulman: comparaisons et perspectives: actes du colloque de l'École française d'Athènes, 26-28 avril 2012 (Athens, 2016).

Gerö, Stephen. 'Galen on the Christians: A Reappraisal of the Arabic Evidence,' *OCP* 56 (1990) pp. 371–411.

———. 'Ophite Gnosticism according to Theodore bar Koni's Liber Scholiorum,' in Han J. W. Drijvers et al., eds., *IV Symposium Syriacum, 1984: Literary Genres in Syriac Literature* (Rome, 1987), pp. 265–66.

Gervers, Michael and Ramzi Jibran Bikhazi eds., *Conversion and Continuity: Indigenous Christian Communities in Islamic Lands, Eighth to Eighteenth Centuries* (Toronto, 1990).

Ghobrial, John-Paul. *The Whispers of Cities: Information Flows in Istanbul, London, and Paris in the Age of William Trumbull* (Oxford, 2013).

Gibb, Hamilton A. 'The Fiscal Rescript of 'Umar II,' *Arabica* 2 (1955), pp. 1–16.

Gil, Moshe. *A History of Palestine, 634–1099* (Cambridge, 1992).

Gilliot, Claude. 'The Beginnings of Qur'ānic Exegesis,' in A. Rippin, ed., *The Qur'ān: Formative Interpretation* (Aldershot/Brookfield, VT, 1999), pp. 1–27.

———. 'Christians and Christianity in Islamic exegesis,' in *CMR*, vol. 1, pp. 31–56.

———. 'Les «informateurs» juifs et chrétiens de Muḥammad. Reprise d'un problem traité par Aloys Sprenger et Theodor Nöldeke,' *JSAI* 22 (1998), pp. 84–126.

Goitein, Shelomo Dov. 'Evidence on the Muslim Poll Tax from Non-Muslim Sources: A Geniza Study,' *JESHO* 6 (1963), pp. 278–95.

———. 'The Historical Background of the Erection of the Dome of the Rock,' *JAOS* 70 (1950), pp. 104–108.

———. *A Mediterranean Society: The Jewish Communities of the Arab World as Portrayed in the Documents of the Cairo Geniza.* 6 vols. (Berkeley, 1967–1993).

———. 'The Present-Day Arabic Proverb as a Testimony to the Social History of the Middle East,' in Shelomo Dov Goitein, *Studies in Islamic History and Institutions* (Leiden, 1968), pp. 361–79.

Goldfeld, Isaiah. 'The Illiterate Prophet (*Nabī Ummī*): An Inquiry into the Development of a Dogma in Islamic Tradition,' *Der Islam* 57 (1980), pp. 58–67.

Goldziher, Ignaz. 'Influences chrétienes dans la litérature religieuse de l'Islam,' in Joseph Desomogyi, ed., *Ignaz Goldziher: Gesammelte Schriften*, vol. 2 (Hildesheim, 1968), pp. 302–21.

———. *Introduction to Islamic Theology and Law*, trans. Andras and Ruth Hamori, (Princeton, 1981).

———. *Muslim Studies (Muhammedanische Studien)*. Ed. Samuel M. Stern. Trans. C. R. Barber and Samuel M. Stern. 2 vols. (London, 1967–1971).

———. 'Neuplatonische und gnostiche Elemente im Ḥadīṯ,' *Zeitschrift für Assyriologie* 22 (1909), pp. 317–44.

———. *Schools of Koranic Commentators*, trans. Wofgang H. Behn (Weisbaden, 2006).

———. 'Usages Juifs d'après la littérature religeuse des musulmans,' in Joseph Desomogyi, ed., *Ignaz Goldziher: Gessamelte Schriften*, vol. 3 (Hildesheim, 1969), pp. 322–41.

González Blanco, Antonio. 'Christianism on the Eastern Frontier,' in Gregorio del Olmo Lete and Juan-Luis Montero Fenollós, eds., *Archaeology of the Upper Syrian Euphrates: The Tishrin Dam Area* (Barcelona, 1999), pp. 643–62.

González Blanco, Antonio and Gonzalo Matilla Séiquer, 'Cristianización: Los Monasterios del Ámbito de Qara Qûzâq,' *Antigüedad y Cristianismo* 15 (1998), pp. 399–415.

Görke, Andreas, Harald Motzki, and Gregor Schoeler, 'First Century Sources for the Life of Muḥammad? A Debate,' *Der Islam* 2012 (89), pp. 2–59.

Gottheil, Richard. 'Dhimmis and Muslims in Egypt,' in Robert Francis Harper, Francis Brown, and George Foot Moore, eds., *Old Testament and Semitic Studies in Memory of William Rainey Harper*, vol. 2 (Chicago, 1908), pp. 353–414.

———. 'The Syriac Versions of the Categories of Aristotle,' *Hebraica* 9 (1893), pp. 166–215.

Grabar, Oleg. *The Dome of the Rock* (Cambridge, Mass./London, 2006).

Gräf, Erwin. 'Religiöse und rechtliche Vorstellungen über Kriegsgefangene in Islam und Christentum,' *Die Welt des Islams* 8 (1963), pp. 89–139.

———. 'Zu den Christlichen Einflüsse im Koran,' in *al-Bahit: Festschrift Joseph Henninger zum 70. Geburtstag am 12. Mai 1976* (St. Augustin bei Bonn, 1976), pp. 111–44.

Graf, Georg. *Geschichte der christlichen arabischen Literatur*. 5 vols. (Rome, 1944–1953).

Grand'Henry, Jaques. 'Transmission de textes grecs, spécialement de Grégoire de Nazianze, en milieu arabe,' *PACT News* 19 (1987), pp. 42–45.

Graus, František. *Volk, Herrscher und Heiliger im Reich der Merowinger: Studien zur Hagiographie der Merowingerzeit* (Praha, 1965).

Gray, Patrick T. R. 'From Eucharist to Christology: The Life-Giving Body of Christ in Cyril of Alexandria, Eutyches and Julian of Halicarnassus,' in István Perczel, Réka Forrai, and György Geréby, eds., *The Eucharist in Theology and Philosophy: Issues of Doctrinal History in East and West from the Patristic Age to the Reformation* (Leuven, 2005), pp. 23–35.

———. '"The Select Fathers": Canonizing the Patristic Past,' *Studia Patristica* 28 (1989), pp. 21–36.

———. 'Theological Discourse in the Seventh Century: The Heritage from the Sixth Century,' *Byzantinische Forschungen* 26 (2000), pp. 219–28.

Green, Nile. *Terrains of Exchange: Religious Economies of Global Islam* (New York, 2015).

Gregg, Robert C. and Dennis E. Groh, 'The Centrality of Soteriology in Early Arianism,' *Anglican Theological Review* 59 (1977), pp. 260–78.

———. *Early Arianism: A View of Salvation* (Philadelphia, 1981).

Grehan, James. *Twilight of the Saints: Everyday Religion in Ottoman Syria and Palestine* (New York, 2014).

Gribomont, Jean. 'Documents sur les origines de l'Église Maronite,' *Parole de l'Orient* 5 (1974), pp. 95–132.

Griffin, Carl. *Cyrillona: A Critical Study and Commentary* (Piscataway, N.J., 2016).

Griffith, Sidney H. 'Anastasios of Sinai, the *Hodegos*, and the Muslims,' *Greek Orthodox Theological Review* 32 (1987), pp. 341–58.

———. 'Arguing from Scripture: The Bible in the Christian/Muslim Encounter in the Middle Ages,' in Thomas J. Heffernan and Thomas E. Burman, eds., *Scripture and Pluralism: Reading the Bible in the Religiously Plural Worlds of the Middle Ages and Renaissance: Papers Presented at the First Annual Symposium of the Marco Institute for Medieval and Renaissance Studies at the University of Tennessee, Knoxville, February 21–22, 2002* (Leiden/Boston, 2005), pp. 29–58.

———. *The Bible in Arabic: The Scriptures of the "People of the Book" in the Language of Islam* (Princeton/Oxford, 2013).

———. 'Chapter Ten of the Scholion: Theodore Bar Kônî's Apology for Christianity,' *OCP* 47 (1981), pp. 158–88.

———. *The Church in the Shadow of the Mosque: Christians and Muslims in the World of Islam* (Princeton/Oxford, 2008).

———. 'Disputes with Muslims in Syriac Christian Texts: From Patriarch John (d. 648) to Bar Hebraeus (d. 1286),' in Bernard Lewis and Friedrich Niewöhner, eds., *Religionsgespräche im Mittelalter*, pp. 251–73.

———. 'Images, Islam and Christian Icons: A Moment in the Christian/Muslim Encounter in Early Islamic Times,' in Pierre Canivet and Jean-Paul Rey-Coquais, eds., *La Syrie de Byzance à l'islam, VIIe-VIIIe siècles* (Damascus, 1992), pp. 121–38.

———. '"Melkites," "Jacobites" and the Christological Controversies in Arabic in Third/Ninth-Century Syria,' in David R. Thomas, ed., *Syrian Christians under Islam: The First Thousand Years* (Leiden/Boston/Köln, 2001), pp. 9–55.

———. 'The Monk in the Emir's *Majlis*: Reflections on a Popular Genre of Christian Literary Apologetics in Arabic in the Early Islamic Period,' in Hava Lazarus-Yafeh et al., eds., *The Majlis: Interreligious Encounters in Medieval Islam* (Wiesbaden, 1999), pp. 13–65.

———. 'The Prophet Muhammad, His Scripture and His Message according to Christian Apologies in Arabic and Syriac from the First Abbasid Century,' in Toufic Fahd, ed., *La vie du prophète Mahomet. Colloque de Strasbourg, octobre 1980* (Paris, 1983), pp. 99–146.

———. 'Theodore Abū Qurrah's Arabic Tract on the Christian Practice of Venerating Images,' *Journal of the American Oriental Society* 105 (1985), pp. 53–73.

Grig, Lucy. 'Caesarius of Arles and the Campaign against Popular Culture in Late Antiquity,' *Early Modern Europe* 26 (2018), pp. 61–81.

Grillmeier, Alois [Theresia Hainthaler et al.] *Christ in Christian Tradition.* 5 vols. in 2. (London, 1975–2013).

Grivaud, Gilles and Alexandre Popovic, *Les conversions à l'islam en Asie mineure et dans les Balkans aux époques seldjoukide et ottomane: bibliographie raisonnée* (1800–2000) (Athens, 2011).

Grumel, Venance. *La chronologie* (Paris, 1958).

———. *Les regestes des actes du Patriarcat de Constantinople*, vol. 1, fasc. 1: *Les regestes de 381 à 715* (Paris, 1972).

Grypeou, Emmanouela, Mark Swanson, and David Thomas, eds., *The Encounter of Eastern Christianity with Early Islam* (Leiden, 2006).

Gryson, Roger 'The Authority of the Teacher in the Ancient and Medieval Church,' *Journal of Ecumenical Studies* 19 (1982), pp. 176–87.

Guessous, Azeddube. 'The Fiscal Rescript of 'Umar b. 'Abd al-'Azīz: A New Evaluation,' in Donner, ed., *The Articulation of Early Islamic State Structures*, pp. 241–64.

Guidetti, Mattia. *In the Shadow of the Church: The Building of Mosques in Early Medieval Syria* (Leiden/Boston, 2017).

Guidi, Ignazio. ''Di un' Iscrizione Sepolcrale Siriaca e della Versione dei Carmi di S.

Gregorio Nazianzeno fatta da Candidato di Âmed,' in *Actes du dixième congrès international des orientalistes. Session de Genève 1894. Troisième partie, section II: langues sémitiques* (Leiden, 1896), pp. 75–82.

Guillaume, Alfred. *The Traditions of Islam* (repr. New York, 1980).

Guillaumont, Antoine. 'Un colloque entre orthodoxes et théologiens nestoriens de Perse sous Justinien,' *Comptes-rendus des séances de l'Académie des Inscriptions et Belles-Lettres, Paris* (1970), pp. 201–207.

———. 'Justinien et l'Église de Perse,' *Dumbarton Oaks Papers* 23 (1969–1970), pp. 39–66.

Gutas, Dimitri. 'The "Alexandria to Baghdad" Complex of Narratives: A Contribution to the Study of Philosophical and Medical Historiography among the Arabs,' *Documenti e Studi sulla Tradizione Filosofica Medievale* 10 (1999), pp. 155–93.

———. 'Greek Philosophical Works Translated into Arabic,' in Robert Pasnau, ed., *The Cambridge History of Medieval Philosophy*, vol. 2 (Cambridge, 2012), pp. 802–22.

———. Greek Thought, Arabic Culture: The Graeco-Arabic Translation Movement in Baghdad and Early 'Abbāsid Society (2nd–4th/8th–10th centuries) (New York, 1998).

Gwynn, John. 'Thomas Harklensis,' in William Smith and Henry Wace, eds., *A Dictionary of Christian Biography, Literature, Sects and Doctrines; during the First Eight Centuries*, vol. 4 (London, 1887), pp. 1014–21.

Hackenburg, Clint. 'Christian Conversion to Islam,' in D. Thomas, ed., *Routledge Handbook on Christian-Muslim Relations* (London/New York, 2018), pp. 176–84.

———. 'Voices of the Converted: Christian Apostate Literature in Medieval Islam,' (PhD diss., Ohio State University, 2015).

Haelewyck, Jean-Claude. *Sancti Gregorii Nazianzeni Opera. Versio Syriaca I: Oratio XL* (CSCG 49, Corpus Nazianzenum 14 (Turnhout/Leuven, 2001).

Hage, Wolfgang. *Die syrisch-jacobitische Kirche in frühislamischer Zeit. Nach orientalischen Quellen* (Wiesbaden, 1966).

Haider, Najam. 'Contesting Intoxication: Early Juristic Debates about the Lawfulness of Alcoholic Beverages,' *Islamic Law and Society* 20 (2013), pp. 48–89.

Haines-Eitzen, Kim. 'Girls Trained in Beautiful Writing: Female Scribes in Roman Antiquity and Early Christianity,' *Journal of Early Christian Studies* 6 (1998), pp. 629–46.

———. *Guardians of Letters: Literacy, Power, and the Transmitters of Early Christian Literature* (Oxford, 2000).

Hainthaler, Theresia. ''Adī ibn Zayd al-'Ibadī, the Pre-Islamic Christian Poet of al-Ḥīrā and His Poem Nr. 3 Written in Jail,' *PdO* 30 (2005), pp. 157–72.

———. 'Christian Arabs before Islam: A Short Overview,' in Nader Al Jallad, *People from the Desert: Pre-Islamic Arabs in History and Culture* (Wiesbaden, 2012), pp. 29–44.

———. *Christ in Christian Tradition*, vol. 2, pt. 3: *The Churches of Jerusalem and Antioch from 451 to 600.* Trans. Marianne Ehrhardt (Oxford, 2013).

———. *Christliche Araber vor dem Islam: Verbreitung und konfessionelle Zugehörigkeit: eine Hinführung* (Leuven/Dudley, Mass., 2007).

Haldon, John F. *The Empire That Would Not Die: The Paradox of Eastern Roman Survival* (Cambridge, Mass. /London, 2016).

——. ed., *Money, Power and Politics in Early Islamic Syria: A Review of Current Debates* (Farnham, Surrey, 2010).

——. 'Seventh-Century Continuities: the *Ajnād* and the "Thematic Myth,"' in Averil Cameron, ed., *The Byzantine and Early Islamic Near East* III: *States, Resources and Armies* (Princeton, 1995), pp. 379–423.

——. 'The Works of Anastasius of Sinai: A Key Source for the History of Seventh-Century East Mediterranean Society and Belief,' in Averil Cameron and Lawrence I. Conrad, eds., *The Early Medieval Near East: Problems in the Literary Source Material* (Princeton, 1990), pp. 107–47.

Haldon, John and Leslie Brubaker, *Byzantium in the Iconoclast Era (ca. 680-850): The Sources* (Aldershot, 2001).

Hallaq, Wael. *The Origins and Evolution of Islamic Law* (Cambridge, 2005).

Hanna, Nelly. 'Literacy among Artisans and Tradesmen in Ottoman Cairo,' in Christine Woodhead, ed., *The Ottoman World* (Milton Park, Abingdon, Oxford/New York, 2012), pp. 319–31.

Hanson, Richard P. C. *The Search for the Christian Doctrine of God: The Arian Controversy, 318–381* (Edinburgh, 1988).

Harnack, Adolf von. *Bible Reading in the Early Church.* Trans. J. R. Wilkinson (London/New York, 1912).

Harper, Kyle. *The Fate of Rome: Climate, Disease, and the End of an Empire* (Princeton, 2017).

——. *Slavery in the Late Roman World AD 275–425* (Cambridge, 2011).

Harris, William V. *Ancient Literacy* (Cambridge, Mass., 1989).

Harvey, Susan Ashbrook. 'Martyr Passions and Hagiography,' in Susan A. Harvey and David G. Hunter, eds., *The Oxford Handbook of Early Christian Studies* (Oxford, 2008), pp. 603–27.

Hasan-Rokem, Galit. *Web of Life: Folklore and Midrash in Rabbinic Literature* (Stanford, 2000).

Hasluck, F. W. *Christianity and Islam under the Sultans.* 2 vols. (Oxford, 1929).

Hava, J. G. *al-Faraid, Arabic-English Dictionary*, 5th ed. (Beirut, 1982).

Hawting, Gerald R. *The First Dynasty of Islam: The Umayyad Caliphate, AD 661–750*, 2nd ed. (London/New York, 2000).

——. 'The *ḥajj* in the Second Civil War,' in Ian Richard Netton, ed. *Golden Roads: Migration, Pilgrimage, and Travel in Medieval and Modern Islam* (Richmond [England], 1993), pp. 31–42.

——. *The Idea of Idolatry and the Emergence of Islam: From Polemic to History* (Cambridge/New York, 1999).

Hegedus, Tim. *Early Christianity and Ancient Astrology* (New York, 2007).

Heim, François. *La théologie de la victoire de Constantin à Théodose* (Paris, 1992).

Henninger, Joseph. 'L'influence du Christianisme oriental sur l'islam naissant,' in *Atti del convegno internazionale sul tema L'oriente cristiano nella storia della civiltà (Roma 31 marzo–3 aprile 1963) (Firenze 4 aprile 1963)* (Rome, 1964), pp. 379–411.

Herrin, Judith. 'Aspects of the Process of Hellenization in the Early Middle Ages,' *Annual of the British School at Athens* 68 (1973), pp. 113–26.

Hezser, Caroline. *Jewish Literacy in Roman Palestine* (Tübingen, 2001).

Hill, Robert C. *Reading the Old Testament in Antioch* (Atlanta, 2005).

Hiltbrunner, Otto. *Latina Graeca: Semasiologische Studien über Lateinische Wörter im Hinblick auf ihr Verhältnis zur griechischen Vorbildern* (Bern, 1958).

Hirschberg, Martin. *Studien zur Geschichte der simplices in der Alten Kirche. Ein Beitrag zur Problem der Schichtungen in der menschlichen Erkenntnis* (Berlin, 1944).

Hirschfeld, Yizhar. *The Roman Baths of Hammat Gader: Final Report* (Jerusalem, 1997).

Hobbs, Joseph J. *Mount Sinai* (Austin, 1995).

Holmberg, Bo. 'A Reconsideration of the *Kitāb al-Mağdal*,' *PdO* 18 (1993), pp. 255–73.

Honigmann, Ernst. *Évêques et évêchés monophysites d'Asie antérieure au VIe siècle* (Louvain, 1951).

Hopkins, Keith. 'Conquest by Book,' in John Humphrey, ed., *Literacy in the Roman World*, pp. 133–58.

Horn, Cornelia B. *Asceticism and Christological Controversy in Fifth-Century Palestine: The Career of Peter the Iberian* (Oxford, 2006).

Hornus, Jean-Michel. 'Le corpus dionysien en syriaque,' *PdO* 1 (1970), pp. 69–93.

Horovitz, Josef. ''Adi ibn Zeyd, the Poet of Hira,' *Islamic Culture* 4 (1930), pp. 31–69.

——. 'Biblische Nachwirkungen in der Sira,' *Der Islam* 12 (1922), pp. 184–89.

——. 'The Earliest Biographies of the Prophet and Their Authors,' *Islamic Culture* 1 (1927), pp. 535–59.

——. 'The Growth of the Mohammed Legend,' *Moslem World* 10 (1919), pp. 49–58.

Horsfall, N. 'Statistics or State of Mind?' in Humphrey, ed., *Literacy in the Roman World*, pp. 59–76.

Horsley, G.H.R. *New Documents Illustrating Early Christianity: A Review of the Greek Inscriptions and Papyri Published in 1979* (North Ryde, N.S.W., 1987).

Horst, Heribert. 'Zur Überlieferung im Korankommentar aṭ-Ṭabarīs,' *ZDMG* 103 (1953), pp. 290–307.

Houston, George W. 'Papyrological Evidence for Book Collections and Libraries in the Roman Empire,' in William A. Johnson and Holt N. Parker, eds., *Ancient Literacies: The Culture of Reading in Greece and Rome* (Oxford/New York, 2009), pp. 243–67.

Howard-Johnston, James D. *Witnesses to a World Crisis: Historians and Histories of the Middle East in the Seventh Century* (Oxford/New York, 2010).

Hoyland, Robert G. 'Arabic, Syriac, and Greek Historiography in the First 'Abbasid Century: An Inquiry into Inter-Cultural Traffic,' *Aram* 3 (1991), pp. 211–33.

——. 'The Content and Context of Early Arabic Inscriptions,' *JSAI* 21 (1997), pp. 77–102.

——. 'Early Islam as a Late Antique Religion,' in Scott F. Johnson, ed., *The Oxford Handbook of Late Antiquity* (Oxford/New York, 2012), pp. 1053–77.

——. 'Jacob of Edessa on Islam,' in Gerrit J. Reinink and Alex C. Klugkist, eds., *After Bardaisan: Studies on Continuity and Change in Syriac Christianity in Honour of Professor Han J.W. Drijvers* (Leuven, 1999), pp. 149–60.

——, ed. *The Late Antique World of Early Islam: Muslims Among Christians and Jews in the East Mediterranean* (Princeton, 2015).

——. ed., *Muslims and Others in Early Islamic Society* (Aldershot, 2004).

——. 'New Documentary Texts and the Early Islamic State,' *BSOAS* 69 (2006), pp. 395–416.

——. 'Reflections on the Identity of the Arabian Conquerors of the Seventh-Century Middle East,' *Al-'Uṣūr al-Wusṭā* 25 (2017), pp. 113–40.

———. *Seeing Islam as Others Saw It: A Survey and Evaluation of Christian, Jewish, and Zoroastrian Writings on Early Islam* (Princeton, 1997).

———. 'Writing the Biography of the Prophet Muhammad: Problems and Solutions,' *History Compass* 5 (2007), pp. 1–22.

Hoyland, Robert G. and Sarah Waidler, 'Adomnán's De Locis Sanctis and the Seventh-Century Near East,' *English Historical Review* 129 (2014), pp. 787–807.

Hugonnard-Roche, Henri. 'Une ancienne "edition" arabe de l'*Organon* d'Aristote: problems de traduction et de transmission,' in Jacqueline. Hamesse, ed., *Les Problèmes posés par l'édition critique des textes anciens et médiévaux* (Louvain, 1992), pp. 139–57.

———. *La logique d'Aristote du grec au syriaque. Études sur la transmission des textes de l'Organon et leur interprétation philosophique* (Paris, 2004).

Huijgen, Arnold. *Divine Accommodation in John Calvin's Theology: Analysis and Assessment* (Göttingen, 2011).

Humphrey, John, ed. *Literacy in the Roman World* (Ann Arbor, 1991).

Humphreys, R. Stephen. 'Christian Communities in Early Islamic Syria and Northern Jazira: the Dynamics of Adaption,' in Haldon, ed., *Money, Power and Politics in Early Islamic Syria*, pp. 45–56.

———. *Islamic History: A Framework for Inquiry*. Rev. ed. (London/New York, 1991).

———. *Mu'awiya ibn Abi Sufyan: From Arabia to Empire* (Oxford, 2006).

Hunter, Erica C. D. 'The Christian Matrix of al-Hira,' in Christelle Jullien, ed., *Controverses des chrétiens dans l'Iran sassanide (Chrétiens en terre d'Iran* II*)* (Paris, 2008), pp. 41–56.

———. 'Reconstructing Christianity in South-West Iraq: Reassessing Hira,' *The Harp* 24 (2009), pp 411–23.

Husayn, Nebil. 'The Memory of 'Alī b. Abī Ṭālib in Early Sunnī Thought,' (PhD diss., Princeton University, 2016).

Husmann, Heinrich. 'Eine alte orientalische christliche Liturgie: Altsyrisch-Melkitisch,' *OCP* 42 (1976), pp. 156–96.

Imbert, Frédéric. 'L'Islam des pierres: l'expression de la foi dans les graffiti arabes des premiers siècles,' *Revue des mondes musulmans et de la Méditerranée* 129 (2011), pp. 57–78.

Inglebert, Hervé. *Histoire de la civilization romaine* (Paris, 2005).

———. *Interpretatio christiana: Les mutations des savoirs, cosmographie, géographie, ethnographie, histoire, dans l'antiquité chrétienne, 30–630 après J.-C* (Paris, 2001).

Ioan, Ovidiu. 'Martyrius-Sahdona: la pensée christologique, clé de la théologie mystique,' in Alain Desreumaux, ed., *Les mystiques syriaques* (Paris, 2011), pp. 45–61.

Iskander, John. 'Islamization in Medieval Egypt: The Copto-Arabic "Apocalypse of Samuel" as a Source for the Social and Religious History of Medieval Copts,' *Medieval Encounters* 4 (1998), pp. 219–27.

Izutsu, Toshihiko. *The Concept of Belief in Islamic Theology* (Salem, New Hamp., 1988).

Jaeger, Werner. 'Von Affen und Wahren Christen,' in Werner Jaeger, *Scripta Minora* II (Rome, 1960), pp. 429–39.

Janeras, S. 'Les Byzantins et le Trisagion christologique,' in *Miscellanea liturgica in onore di sua eminenza il Cardinale Giacomo Lercaro, arcivescovo di Bologna, presidente del 'Consilium' per l'applicazione della costituzione sulla sacra liturgia*, vol. 2 (Rome/New York, 1967), pp. 469–99.

Janeras, S. 'Le Trisagion: une formule brève en liturgie comparée,' in Robert F. Taft and Gabriele Winkler, eds., *Comparative Liturgy Fifty Years after Anton Baumstark (1872–1948): Acts of the International Congress, Rome, 25–29 September 1998* (Rome, 2001), pp. 495–562.

Jeffery, Arthur. *The Foreign Vocabulary of the Qur'ān* (Baroda, 1938).

——. 'Ghevond's Text of the Correspondence between 'Umar II and Leo III,' *Harvard Theological Review* 37 (1944), pp. 269–332.

——. 'Had Muḥammad a Scripture Teacher?' in Lewis G. Leary, ed., *From the Pyramids to Paul: Studies in Theology, Archaeology and Related Subjects, Prepared in Honor of the Seventieth Birthday of George Livingstone Robinson* (New York, 1935), pp. 95–118.

Jenkins, Philip. *The Lost History of Christianity: The Thousand-Year Golden Age of the Church in the Middle East, Africa, and Asia—and How It Died* (New York, 2008).

Jensen, P. 'Das Leben Muhammeds und die David-Sage,' *Der Islam* 12 (1922), pp. 84–97.

Johns, Jeremy. 'Archaeology and the History of Early Islam,' *JESHO* 46 (2003), pp. 411–36.

Johnson, Scott F. 'Introduction: The Social Presence of Greek in Eastern Christianity, 200–1200 CE,' in Scott F. Johnson, ed., *Languages and Cultures of Eastern Christianity* (Surrey, England, 2015), pp. 1–122.

Johnson, Trevor. 'Blood, Tears and Xavier-Water: Jesuit Missionaries and Popular Religion in the Eighteenth-Century Upper Palatinate,' in Bob Scribner and Trevor Johnson, eds., *Popular Religion in Germany and Central Europe, 1400–1800* (Basingstoke/New York, 1996), pp. 182–203.

Jones, Christopher P. *Between Pagan and Christian* (Cambridge, Mass., 2014).

Jones, Linda G. 'Islām al-Kāfir fī Ḥāl al-Khuṭba: Concerning the Conversion of "Infidels" to Islam During the Muslim Friday Sermon in Mamluk Egypt,' *Anuario de Estudios Medievales* 42 (2012), pp. 53–75.

Juckel, Andreas. 'La reception des pères grecs pendant la «renaissance» syriaque. Renaissance – inculturation – identité,' in Andrea Schmidt and Dominque Gonnet, eds., *Les pères grecs dans la tradition syriaque* (Paris, 2007), pp. 89–125.

Judah, Jamal. 'The Economic Conditions of the *Mawālī* in Early Islamic Times,' in Michael G. Morony, ed., *Manufacturing and Labour* (Ashgate, 2003), pp. 167–97.

Judd, Steven C. *Religious Scholars and the Umayyads: Piety-Minded Supporters of the Marwānid Caliphate* (London/New York, 2014).

Jullien, Christelle. 'La minorité chrétienne "grecque" en terre d'Iran à l'époque sassanide,' in Rika Gyselen, ed., *Chrétiens en terre d'Iran: Implantation et acculturation* (Paris, 2006), pp. 105–42.

Juynboll, Gautier H.A. *Encyclopedia of Canonical Ḥadīth* (Leiden/Boston, 2007).

——. *Muslim Tradition* (Cambridge, 1983).

Kadel, Andrew. *Matrology: A Bibliography of Writings by Christian Women from the First to the Fifteenth Centuries* (New York, 1995).

Kaldellis, Anthony. *Prokopios: The Secret History with Related Texts* (Indianapolis, 2010).

Kaplan, Bejamin J. *Divided by Faith: Religious Conflict and the Practice of Toleration in Early Modern Europe* (Cambridge, Mass., 2007).

Kaplony, Andreas. *The Ḥaram of Jerusalem, 324–1099: Temple, Friday Mosque, Area of Spiritual Power* (Stuttgart, 2002).

Katalog 487 Manuscripte vom Mittelalter bis zum XVI. Jahrhundert (Karl Hiersemann) (Leipzig, 1921). [partially authored by Anton Baumstark; also known as *Hiersemann 487*]

Katalog 500: Orientalische Manuskripte (Karl Hiersemann) (Leipzig, 1922). [authored by Anton Baumstark; also known as *Hiersemann 500*]

Kaufhold, Hubert. 'Sources of Canon Law in the Eastern Churches,' in Wilfried Hartmann and Kenneth Pennington, eds., *The History of Byzantine and Eastern Canon Law to 1500* (Washington, D.C., 2012), pp. 215–342.

Kazhdan, Alexander and Stephen Gerö, 'Kosmas of Jerusalem: A More Critical Approach to His Biography,' *Byzantinische Zeitschrift* 82 (1989), pp. 122–32.

Kedourie, Elie. 'Ethnicity, Majority, and Minority in the Middle East,' in Milton J. Esman and Itamar Rabinovich, eds., *Ethnicity, Pluralism and the State in the Middle East* (Ithaca, N.Y., 1988), pp. 25–31.

Kefeli, Agnès Nilüfer. *Becoming Muslim in Imperial Russia: Conversion, Apostasy, and Literacy* (Ithaca, N.Y./London, 2014).

Kelly, Christopher. 'Emperors, Government and Bureaucracy,' in Averil Cameron and Peter Garnsey, eds., *The Cambridge Ancient History*, vol. 13: *The Late Empire, A.D. 337–425* (Cambridge, 1998), pp. 138–83.

Kennedy, Hugh. 'Islam.' In Glen W. Bowersock, Peter Brown, and Oleg Grabar, eds., *Late Antiquity: A Guide to the Postclassical World* (Cambridge, Mass./London, 1999), pp. 219–37.

———. 'The Middle East in Islamic Late Antiquity,' in Andrew Monson and Walter Scheidel, eds., *Fiscal Regimes and the Political Economy of Premodern States* (Cambridge, 2015), pp. 390–403.

Khalek, Nancy. *Damascus after the Muslim Conquest: Text and Image in Early Islam* (Oxford/New York, 2011).

———. 'From Byzantium to Early Islam. Studies on Damascus in the Umayyad Era' (PhD diss., Princeton, 2006).

Khalidi, Tarif. *The Muslim Jesus: Sayings and Stories in Islamic Literature* (Cambridge, Mass. /London, 2001).

Khalil, Samir. [See Samir, Khalil]

Khoury, R. G. 'Quelques réflexions sur la première ou les premières Bibles arabes,' in Toufic Fahd, ed., *L'Arabie préislamique et son environnement historique et culturel: actes du Colloque de Strasbourg, 24–27 juin 1987* (Leiden, 1989), pp. 549–61.

Khrīsāt, Muḥammad 'Abd al-Qādir. 'Dawr al-'Arab al-mutanaṣṣira fī 'l-futūḥāt,' in Muḥammad 'Adnān Bakhit and Iḥsān 'Abbās, eds., *Proceedings of the Second Symposium on the History of Bilad al-Sham during the Early Islamic Period up to 40 A.H./640 A.D.*, vol. 2 (Amman, 1987), pp. 135–64.

Kilpatrick, Hilary. 'Brockelmann, Kaḥḥâla & Co: Reference Works on the Arabic Literature of Early Ottoman Syria,' *Middle Eastern Literatures* 7 (2004), pp. 33–51.

———. 'Monasteries through Muslim Eyes: The *Diyārāt* Books,' in David Thomas, ed., *Christians at the Heart of Islamic Rule: Church Life and Scholarship in 'Abbasid Iraq* (Leiden/Boston, 2003), pp. 19–37.

King, Daniel. *The Earliest Syriac Translation of Aristotle's Categories: Text, Translation, and Commentary* (Leiden/Boston, 2010).

King, Daniel. 'Logic in the Service of Ancient Eastern Christianity: An Exploration of Motives,' *Archiv für Geschichte der Philosophie* 97 (2015), pp. 1–33

King, Daniel. 'Paul of Callinicum and his Place in Syriac Literature,' *LM* 120 (2007), pp. 327–49.

——. 'Why Were the Syrians Interested in Greek Philosophy?' in Philip Wood, ed., *History and Identity in the Late Antique Near East* (Oxford, 2013), pp. 61–81.

Kinzig, Wolfram. 'The Creed in the Liturgy: Prayer or Hymn?' in Albert Gerhards and Clemens Leonhard, eds., *Jewish and Christian Liturgy and Worship: New Insights into Its History and Interaction* (Leiden/Boston, 2007), pp. 229–46.

Kiraz, George A., ed. *Malphono w-Rabo d-Malphone: Studies in Honor of Sebastian P. Brock* (Piscataway, N.J., 2008).

Kister, M. J. '"A Bag of Meat": A Study of an Early *Ḥadīth*,' *BSOAS* 33 (1970), pp. 267–75.

——. ''An Yadin (Qur'ān, IX/29): An Attempt at Interpretation,' *Arabica* 11 (1964), pp. 272–78.

——. '"Do not assimilate yourselves..." *Lā tashabbahū*,' *JSAI* 12 (1989), pp. 321–71.

——. '*Ḥaddithū 'an banī isrā'il wa-la ḥaraja*: A Study of an Early Tradition,' *Israel Oriental Studies* II (Tel Aviv, 1972), pp. 216–39.

——. 'Labbayka, Allāhuma, Labbayka ... On a monotheistic aspect of a Jāhiliyya practice,' *JSAI* 2 (1980), pp. 33–57.

——. '...Lā taqra'ū l-qur'āna 'alā l-muṣḥafiyyīn wa-lā taḥmilū l-'ilma 'ani l-ṣaḥafiyyīn ... : Some Notes on the Transmission of Ḥadīth,' *Jerusalem Studies in Arabic and Islam* 22 (1998), pp. 127–62.

——. '*Lā yamassuhu illā 'l-muṭahharūn...*: Notes on the Interpretations of a Qur'ānic Phrase,' *JSAI* 34 (2008), pp. 309–34.:

——. '"O God, tighten thy grip on Muḍar" ... Some Socio-Economic Religious Aspects of an Early *ḥadīth*,' *JESHO* 24 (1981), pp. 242–73.

——. 'The Struggle against Musaylima and the Conquest of Yamāma,' *JSAI* 27 (2002), pp. 1–56.

Klingshirn, William E. *Caesarius of Arles: The Making of a Christian Community in Late Antique Gaul* (Cambridge, 1994).

Kohlberg, Etan. 'Some notes on the Imamite Attitude toward the Qur'ān,' in Samuel M. Stern, Albert Hourani, and Vivian Brown, eds., *Islamic Philosophy and the Classical Tradition: Essays Presented by his Friends and Pupils to Richard Walzer on His Seventieth Birthday* (Oxford, 1972), pp. 209–24.

König, Daniel G. *Arabic-Islamic Views of the Latin West: Tracing the Emergence of Medieval Europe* (Oxford, 2015).

——. *Bekehrungsmotive: Untersuchungen zum Christianisierungsprozess im römischen Westreich und seinen romanisch-germanischen Nachfolgern (4.-8. Jahrhundert)* (Husum, 2008).

Koren, Judith and Yehuda Nevo, 'Methodological Approaches to Islamic Studies,' *Der Islam* 68 (1991), pp. 87–107.

Krausmüller, Dirk. 'Leontius of Jerusalem: A Theologian of the Seventh Century,' *JTS* 52 (2001), pp. 637–57.

Krstić, Tijana. *Contested Conversions to Islam: Narratives of Religious Change in the Early Modern Ottoman Empire* (Stanford, 2011).

Kruisheer, Dirk. 'A Bibliographical Clavis to the Works of Jacob of Edessa (revised and expanded),' in Bas ter Haar Romeny, ed., *Jacob of Edessa and the Syriac Culture of His Day* (Leiden/Boston, 2008), pp. 265–93.

———. 'Theodor bar Koni's Ketābā d-'Eskolyon as a Source for the Study of Early Mandaeism,' *Jaarbericht Ex Oriente Lux* 33 (1993–1994), pp. 151–69.

Landron, Benedicte. 'Les rélations originelles entre chrétiens de l'Est (Nestoriens) et Musulmans,' *PdO* 10 (1981-1982), pp.191–222.

Kugener, Marc-Antoine, 'Sur l'emploi en Syrie, au VIe siècle de notre ère, du mot "barbare" dans le sens de "arabe,"' *Oriens Christianus* 7 (1907), pp. 408–12.

Lammens, Henri. *Le chantre des Omiades: notes biographiques et littéraires sur le poète arabe chrétien Aḫṭal* (Paris, 1895).

———. 'Études sur le règne du calife Omaiyade Mo'awiya Ier,' *Mélanges de la Faculté orientale/Université Saint-Joseph*, 3.1 (1908), pp. 145–312. [Part 3]

———. *Fāṭima et les filles de Mahomet: notes critiques pour l'étude de la sīra* (Rome, 1912).

———. 'A propos d'un colloque entre le patriarche Jacobite Jean 1er et 'Amr ibn al-'Āṣi,' *JA* 11 (1919), pp. 97–110.

———. 'Phares, minarets, clochers, et mosques: leur origine, leur architecture,' *Revue de questions historiques* 46 (1911), pp. 5–27.

———. 'Qoran et tradition: comment fut composée la vie de Mahomet,' *Recherches de science religieuse* 1 (1910), pp. 27–51.

———. 'Un poète royal a la cour des omiades de Damas,' *ROC* 8 (1903), pp. 325–55, *ROC* 9 (1904), pp. 32–57.

———. *La Syrie, précis historique* (Beirut, 1921).

Lampe, Geoffrey W.H. *A Patristic Greek Lexicon* (Oxford/New York, 1961).

Landron, Benedicte. 'Les rélations originelles entre chrétiens de l'Est (Nestoriens) et Musulmans,' *PdO* 10 (1981–1982), pp. 191–222.

Lane, Edward William. *An Arabic-English Lexicon: Derived from the Best and Most Copious Eastern Sources.* 8 vols. (London, 1863–1893).

Lange, Christian. 'Dioscurus of Alexandria in the Syriac *vita* of Theopistus,' *The Harp* 19 (2006), pp. 341–351.

Lapidge, Michael. 'The Career of Archbishop Theodore,' in Lapidge, ed., *Archbishop Theodore: Commemorative Studies on His Life and Influence* (Cambridge, 1995), pp. 1–29.

Laudan, Rachel. *Cuisine and Empire: Cooking in World History* (Berkeley, 2013).

Lavenant, René. ed., *IIIe Symposium Syriacum, 1980: les contacts du monde syriaque avec les autres cultures: Goslar 7–11 Septembre 1980* (Rome, 1983).

Law, Timothy M. *Origenes Orientalis: The Preservation of Origen's Hexapla in the Syrohexapla of 3 Kingdoms* (Göttingen, 2011).

Lecker, Michael. 'The Death of the Prophet Muḥammad's Father: Did Wāqidī Invent Some of the Evidence?,' *ZDMG* 145 (1995), pp. 9–27.

Lee, Paula Young. 'Modern Architecture and the Ideology of Influence,' *Assemblage* 34 (1997), pp. 6–29.

Leemhuis, Fred. 'Origins and Early Development of the *tafsīr* Tradition,' in Andrew Rippin, ed., *Approaches to the History of the Interpretation of the Qur'ān* (Oxford, 1988), pp. 13–30.

Legendre, Marie. 'Perméabilité linguistique et anthroponymique entre copte et arabe: l'exemple de comptes en caractères coptes du Fayoum Fatimide,' in Anne Boud'hors,

Alain Delattre, Catherine Louis, and Tonio Sebastian Richter, eds., *Coptica argentoratensia: textes et documents de la troisième université d'été de papyrologie copte (Strasbourg, 18–25 juillet 2010): (P. Stras. Copt.)* (Paris, 2014), pp. 325–87.

Legendre, M.A.L. and K. Younes, 'The Use of Terms ǧizya and ḫarāǧ in the First 200 Years of hiǧra in Egypt,' (Accessed at: http://hum.leiden.edu/lias/formation-of-islam/topics-state/study.html; also available at: https://web.archive.org/web/20160730235310/http://hum.leiden.edu/lias/formation-of-islam/topics-state/study.html).

Lehmhaus, Lennart. '"Were not understanding and knowledge given to you from Heaven?" Minimal Judaism and the Unlearned "Other" in *Seder Eliyahu Zuta*,' *Jewish Studies Quarterly* 19 (2012), pp. 230–58.

Lenski, Noel. 'Captivity and Slavery among the Saracens in Late Antiquity (ca. 250–630 CE),' *Antiquité tardive* 19 (2011), pp. 237–66.

——. 'Captivity, Slavery, and Cultural Exchange between Rome and the Germans from the First to Seventh Century CE,' in Catherine M. Cameron, ed., *Invisible Citizens: Captives and their Consequences* (Salt Lake City, 2008), pp. 80–109.

Leslau, Wolf. *Comparative Dictionary of Geʿez (Classical Ethiopic)* (Wiesbaden, 1987).

Lester, Molly. 'The Word as Lived: The Practice of Orthodoxy in Early Medieval Iberia, c. 500– 711,' (PhD diss., Princeton University, 2017).

Lev, Yaacov. 'Persecutions and Conversion to Islam in Eleventh-Century Egypt,' *Asian and African Studies* 22 (1988), pp. 73–91.

Levi della Vida, Giorgio. 'Leggende agiografiche Cristiane nell'Islam,' in *Atti del convegno internazionale sul tema L'oriente cristiano nella storia della civiltà: Roma 31 marzo–3 aprile 1963, Firenze 4 aprile 1963* (Rome, 1964).

Levtzion, Nehemia. 'Toward a Comparative Study of Islamization,' in Levtzion, ed., *Conversion to Islam* (New York, 1979), pp. 1–23.

Levy-Rubin, Milka. 'New Evidence relating to the Process of Islamization in Palestine in the Early Muslim Period: The Case of Samaria,' *JESHO* 43 (2000), pp. 257–76.

——. *Non-Muslims in the Early Islamic Empire: From Surrender to Coexistence* (Cambridge, 2011).

Lewis, Clive S. 'Rejoinder to Dr. Pittenger,' *The Christian Century* 75 (November 26, 1958), pp. 1359–61.

Lexikon des Mittelalters. Ed. Robert Auty et al. 9 vols. (Munich/Zurich, 1977–1999).

Liebeschuetz, Wolfgang. 'Epigraphic Evidence on the Christianisation of Syria,' in Jenö Fitz, ed., *Limes: Akten des XI. Internationalen Limeskongresses* (Budapest, 1977), pp. 485–508.

——. 'Problems Arising from the Conversion of Syria,' in Derek Baker, ed., *The Church in Town and Countryside* (Oxford, 1979), pp. 17–24.

Lietzmann, Hans. *Apollinaris von Laodicea und seine Schule: Texte und Untersuchungen* (Tübingen, 1904).

Lieu, Samuel N.C. *Manichaeism in the Later Roman Empire and Medieval China: A Historical Survey* (Manchester and Dover, NH, 1985).

Lifshitz, Felice. 'Beyond Positivism and Genre: "Hagiographical" Texts as Historical Narrative,' *Viator* 25 (1994) pp. 95–113.

Lim, Richard. *Public Disputation, Power, and Social Order in Late Antiquity* (Berkeley, 1995).

Lissak, Rivka Shpak. *When and How the Jewish Majority in the Land of Israel Was Eliminated: Are the Palestinians Descendants of Islamized Jews* (Illinois, 2015).

Little, Donald P. 'Coptic Conversion to Islam under the Baḥrī Mamlūks,' *BSOAS* 39 (1976), pp. 552–69.

Livne-Kafri, Ofer. 'Early Muslim Ascetics and the World of Christian Monasticism,' *JSAI* 20 (1996), pp. 105–29.

Løkkegaard, Frede. *Islamic Taxation in the Classic Period, with Special Reference to the Circumstances in Iraq* (Copenhagen, 1950).

Loopstra, Jonathan A. 'Jacob of Edessa and Patristic Collections in the "Syriac Masora": Some Soundings,' in Dimitrij Bumazhnov and Hans Reinhard Seeliger eds., *Syrien im 1.–7. Jahrhundert nach Christus* (Tübingen, 2011), pp. 157–68.

———. 'Patristic Selections in the "Masoretic" Handbooks of the *Qarqaptā* Tradition,' (PhD diss., Catholic University of America, 2009).

Louth, Andrew. *Modern Orthodox Thinkers: From the* Philokalia *to the Present* (Downer's Grove, 2015).

Luisier, Phillipe. 'Il miafisismo, un termine discutibile della storiografia recente. Problemi teologici ed ecumenici,' *Cristianesimo nella storia* 35 (2013), pp. 297–307.

McAuliffe, Jane Dammen. 'Exegetical Identification of the Ṣābi'ūn,' *Muslim World* 72 (1982), pp. 95–106.

McCollum, Adam C. 'Greek Literature in the Christian East: Translations into Syriac, Georgian, and Armenian,' *Intellectual History of the Islamicate World* 3 (2015), pp. 15–65.

McCormick, Michael. 'Emperor and Court,' in Averil Cameron, Bryan Ward-Perkins, and Michael Whitby, eds., *The Cambridge Ancient History*, vol. 14: *Late Antiquity: Empire and Successors, A.D. 425–600* (Cambridge, 2000), pp. 135–63.

MacCoull, Leslie S.B. 'The Rite of the Jar: Apostasy and Reconciliation in the Medieval Coptic Orthodox Church,' in Diane Wolfthal, ed., *Peace and Negotiation: Strategies for Coexistence in the Middle Ages and the Renaissance* (Turnhout, 2000), pp. 145–62.

Macdonald, Michael C.A. 'Arabs, Arabias, and Arabic before Late Antiquity,' *Topoi* 16 (2009), pp. 277–332.

———. 'Literacy in an Oral Environment,' in Piotr Bienkowski, Christopher Mee, and Elizabeth. Slater, eds., *Writing and Ancient Near Eastern Society: Papers in Honour of Alan R. Millard* (New York/London, 2005), pp. 45–114.

McDowell, Andrea G. 'Daily Life in Ancient Egypt,' *Scientific American* 275.6 (1996), pp. 100–105.

MacEvitt, Christopher. *The Crusades and the Christian World of the East: Rough Tolerance* (Philadelphia, 2008).

McGrath, Alistar. *The Genesis of Doctrine: A Study in the Foundation of Doctrinal Criticism* (Grand Rapids/Cambride/Vancouver, 1997).

McKitterick, Rosamond, ed. *The Uses of Literacy in Early Mediaeval Europe* (Cambridge/New York, 1990).

McLynn, Neil. 'Christian Controversy and Violence in the Fourth Century,' *Kodai* 3 (1992), pp. 15–44.

MacMullen, Ramsey. *Christianizing the Roman Empire (A.D. 100-400)* (New Haven/London, 1984).

MacMullen, Ramsey. 'The Historical Role of the Masses in Late Antiquity,' in MacMullen, *Changes in the Roman Empire: Essays in the Ordinary* (Princeton, 1990), pp. 250–76, 385–93.

MacMullen, Ramsey. 'The Preacher's Audience (AD 350–400),' *Journal of Theological Studies* 40 (1989), pp. 503–11.

——. *The Second Church: Popular Christianity, A.D. 200–400* (Atlanta, 2009).

McPherson, Joseph W. *The Moulids of Egypt (Egyptian Saints-Days)* (Cairo, 1941).

Madelung, Wilferd. ''Īsā ibn 'Umayr's Ibāḍī Theology and Donatist Christian Thought,' in Rotraud Hansberger, M. Afifi al-Akiti, and Charles Burnett, eds., *Medieval Arabic Thought: Essays in Honour of Fritz Zimmerman* (London/Turin 2012), pp. 99–103.

——. 'al-Qāsim ibn Ibrāhīm and Christian Theology,' *ARAM* 3 (1991), pp. 35–44.

——. *The Succession to Muḥammad: A Study in the Early Caliphate* (Cambridge, 1997).

Maghen, Ze'ev. 'Davidic Motifs in the Biography of Muḥammad,' *JSAI* 35 (2008), pp. 91–139.

——. 'Intertwined Triangles: Remarks on the Relationship between Two Prophetic Scandals,' *JSAI* 33 (2007), pp. 17–92.

Makdisi, Ussama S. *Artillery of Heaven: American Missionaries and the Failed Conversion of the Middle East* (Ithaca, N.Y., 2008).

Makin, Al. *Representing the Enemy: Musaylima in Muslim Literature* (Frankfurt am Main/New York, 2010).

Mango, Cyril. 'The Availability of Books in the Byzantine Empire, A.D. 750-850,' in Cyril Mango and Ihor Ševčenko, eds., *Byzantine Books and Bookmen: A Dumbarton Oaks Colloquium* (Washington, D.C., 1975), pp. 29–45.

——. *Byzantium: The Empire of New Rome* (New York, 1980).

——. 'The Temple Mount AD 614–638,' in Raby and Johns, eds., *Bayt al-Maqdis*, vol. 1, pp. 1–16.

Mango, Marlia Mundell. 'Monophysite Church Decoration,' in Anthony Bryer and Judith Herrin, eds., *Iconoclasm: Papers Given at the Ninth Spring Symposium of Byzantine Studies, University of Birmingham, March 1975* (Birmingham, 1977), pp. 59–74.

Manna, Ya'qūb A. *Qāmūs kaldānī-'arabī* (Beirut, 1975).

Margoliouth, Jesse P. *Supplement to the Thesaurus Syriacus of R. Payne Smith, S.T.P.* (Oxford, 1927).

Maria, Vincenzo. *Il viaggio all'Indie orientali* (Rome, 1672).

Marinides, Nicholas. 'Lay Piety in Byzantium, ca. 600-730' (PhD diss., Princeton University, 2014).

Marrou, Henri I. *Le pédagogue [par] Clement d'Alexandrie. Livre I. Texte grec.* SC 70 (Paris, 1960).

Martens, Peter W. *Origen and Scripture: The Contours of the Exegetical Life* (Oxford/New York, 2012).

Marx, Michael, Johannes Pahlitzsch, and Dorothea Weltecke, 'Östliches Christentum in Geschichte und Gegenwart—Perspektiven und Hindernisse der Forschung,' *Der Islam* 88 (2012), pp. 1–10.

Maskūnī, Yusūf Ya'qūb. 'Naṣārā Kaskar wa-Wāsiṭ qubayla al-Islām,' *al-Mashriq* 58 (1964), pp. 633–47.

Massignon, Louis. *Essay on the Origins of the Technical Language of Islamic Mysticism*, trans. Benjamin Clark, (Notre Dame, 1997).

Mathews, Edward G., Jr. 'A Bibliographical Clavis to the Corpus of Works Attributed to Isaac of Antioch,' *Hugoye: Journal of Syriac Studies* 5 (2002), pp. 3–14.

Mavroudi, Maria, 'Greek Language and Education Under Early Islam,' in Behnam Sadeghi, Asad Q. Ahmed, Adam Silverstein, and Robert Hoyland, eds., *Islamic Cultures, Islamic Contexts: Essays in Honor of Professor Patricia Crone* (Leiden/Boston, 2015), pp. 295–342.

al-Mawsūʻa al-fiqhiyya. 45 vols. (Kuwait, 1983–2006).

Maxwell, Jaclyn L. 'The Attitudes of Basil and Gregory of Nazianzus toward Uneducated Christians,' *Studia Patristica* 47 (2010), pp. 117–22.

———. *Christianization and Communication in Late Antiquity: John Chrysostom and His Congregation in Antioch* (Cambridge/New York, 2006).

———. 'Popular Theology in Late Antiquity,' in Lucy Grig, ed., *Popular Culture in the Ancient World* (Cambridge, 2017), pp. 277–95.

May, Rollo. *Paulus: Reminiscences of a Friendship* (New York, 1973).

Mayer, Wendy. 'Antioch and the Intersection between Religious Factionalism, Place, and Power in Late Antiquity,' in Andrew Cain and Noel E. Lenski, eds., *The Power of Religion in Late Antiquity* (Farnham/Burlington, 2009), pp. 357–67.

———. 'Homiletics,' in Susan A. Harvey and David G. Hunter, eds., *The Oxford Handbook of Early Christian Studies* (Oxford, 2008), pp. 565-583.

———. 'John Chrysostom and His Audiences: Distinguishing Different Congregations at Antioch and Constantinople,' *Studia Patristica* 31 (1997), pp. 70–75.

Mazuz, Haggai. 'The Identity of the Sabians: Some Insights,' in Raphael Jospe and Dov Schwartz, eds., *Jewish Philosophy: Perspectives and Retrospectives* (Boston, 2012), pp. 233–54.

———. *The Religious and Spiritual Life of the Jews of Medina* (Leiden/Boston, 2014).

Meinardus, Otto. 'The Nestorians in Egypt' and 'A Note on Nestorians in Jerusalem,' *OC* 51 (1967), pp. 112–22, 123–29.

Meinecke, Katharina. 'The Encyclopaedic Illustration of a New Empire: Graeco-Roman, Byzantine and Sasanian Models on the Façade of Qasr al-Mshatta,' in Stine Birk, Troels Myrup Mristensen, and Birte Poulsen, eds., *Using Images in Late Antiquity* (Oxford/Philadelphia, 2014), pp. 283–300.

Melchert, Christopher. 'The Early History of Islamic Law,' in Berg, ed., *Method and Theory in the Study of Islamic Origins*, pp. 293–324.

Menze, Volker L. *Justinian and the Making of the Syrian Orthodox Church* (Oxford, 2008).

Michelson, David A. 'A Bibliographic Clavis to the Works of Philoxenos of Mabbug,' *Hugoye* 13 (2010), pp. 273–338.

———. *The Practical Theology of Philoxenos of Mabbug* (Oxford, 2014).

Milbank, John. *Theology and Social Theory: Beyond Secular Reason.* 2nd ed. (Oxford/Malden, Mass., 2006).

Millar, Fergus. 'The Evolution of the Syrian Orthodox Church in the Pre-Islamic Period: From Greek to Syriac?' *Journal of Early Christian Studies* 21 (2013), pp. 43–92.

———. *Religion, Language and Community in the Roman Near East: Constantine to Muhammad* (Oxford, 2013).

Millard, Alan R. *Reading and Writing in the Time of Jesus* (New York, 2000).

Miller, Daniel E. 'From Catalogue to Codes to Canon: The Rise of the Petition in 'Umar among Legal Traditions Governing Non-Muslims in Medieval Islamicate Societies,' (PhD diss., University of Missouri-Kansas City, 2000).

Mikhail, Maged S. A. *From Byzantine to Islamic Egypt: Religion, Identity and Politics after the Arab Conquest* (London/New York, 2014).

Mingana, Alphonse. *Catalogue of the Mingana Collection of Manuscripts: Now in the Possession of the Trustees of the Woodbrooke Settlement, Selly Oak, Birmingham.* 4 vols. (Cambridge, 1933–1964).

Mir, Mustansir. *Dictionary of Qur'ānic Terms and Concepts* (New York/London, 1987).

——. *Verbal Idioms of the Qur'ān* (Ann Arbor, 1989).

Modarressi, Hossein. 'Early Debates on the Integrity of the Qur'ān: A Brief Survey,' *Studia Islamica* 77 (1993), pp. 5–39.

Montgomery, James E. 'For the Love of a Christian Boy: A Song by Abū Nuwās,' *Journal of Arabic Literature* 27 (1996), pp. 115–24.

Morgan, Teresa. *Literate Education in the Hellenistic and Roman Worlds* (Cambridge, 1998).

——. *Popular Morality in the Early Roman Empire* (Cambridge, 2007).

Morimoto, Kosei. *The Fiscal Administration of Egypt in the Early Islamic Period* (Kyoto, 1981).

Morony, Michael G. 'The Effects of the Muslim Conquest on the Persian Population of Iraq,' *Iran* 14 (1976), pp. 41–59.

——. *Iraq after the Muslim Conquest* (Princeton, 1984).

——. 'Population Transfers between Sasanian Iran and the Byzantine Empire,' in *Convegno internazionale La Persia e Bisanzio: Roma, 14–18 ottobre 2002* (Rome, 2004), pp. 161–79.

——. 'Religious Communities in Late Sasanian and early Muslim Iraq,' *JESHO* 17 (1974), pp. 113–35.

Moss, Cyril. 'A Syriac Patristic Manuscript,' *JTS* 30 (1929), pp. 249–54.

Moss, Yonatan. *Incorruptible Bodies: Christology, Society, and Authority in Late Antiquity* (Oakland, Calif., 2016).

——. 'The Rise and Function of the Holy Text in Late Antiquity: Severus of Antioch, The Babylonian Talmud, and Beyond,' in Brouria Bitton-Ashkelony, Theodore S. de Bruyn, and Carol Harrison, eds., *Patristic Studies in the Twenty-First Century*, pp. 521–46.

——. 'Saving Severus: How Severus of Antioch's Writings Survived in Greek,' *Greek, Roman, and Byzantine Studies* 56 (2016), pp. 785–808.

Motzki, Harald. 'Dating Muslim Traditions: A Survey,' *Arabica* 52 (2005), pp. 204–53.

——, ed. *Ḥadīth: Origins and Developments* (Aldershot/Burlington, Vt., 2004).

——. 'The *Muṣannaf* of 'Abd al-Razzāq al-Ṣan'ānī as a Source of Authentic *Aḥādīth* of the First Century A. H.,' *JNES* 50 (1991), pp. 1–21.

——. *The Origins of Islamic Jurisprudence: Meccan Fiqh before the Classical Schools.* Trans. Marion H. Katz (Leiden/Boston/Köln, 2002).

——. 'The Origins of Muslim Exegesis. A Debate,' in H. Motzki et al., *Analysing Muslim Traditions: Studies in Legal, Exegetical, and Maghāzī Ḥadīth* (Leiden/Boston, 2010), pp. 231–303.

——. 'The Question of the Authenticity of Muslim Traditions Reconsidered: A Review Article,' in Berg, ed., *Method and Theory in the Study of Islamic Origins*, pp. 211–57.

Mourad, Suleiman A. 'Christian Monks in Islamic Literature: A Preliminary Report on Some Arabic *Apothegmata Patrum*,' *Bulletin of the Royal Institute for Inter-faith Studies* 6 (2004), pp. 81–98.

Mullett, Margaret. 'Writing in Early Mediaeval Byzantium,' in Rosamond McKitterick, ed., *The Uses of Literacy in Early Medieval Europe* (Cambridge, 1990), pp. 156–85.
Munt, Harry. *The Holy City of Medina: Sacred Space in Early Islamic Arabia* (New York, 2014).
———. '"No Two Religions": Non-Muslims in the Early Islamic Ḥijāz,' *BSOAS* 78 (2015), pp. 249–69.
———. 'What did Conversion to Islam Mean in Seventh-Century Arabia?' in Peacock, ed., *Islamisation*, pp. 83–101.
Murray, Harold J.R. *A History of Chess* (Oxford, 1913).
Naʿnāʿa, Ramzī. *al-Isrāʾīliyyāt wa-atharuhā fī kutub al-tafsīr* (Damascus/Beirut, 1970).
Nasrallah, Joseph. 'Le couvent de Saint Siméon l'alépin. Témoignages littéraires et jalons sur l'histoire,' *PdO* 1 (1970), pp. 327–56.
———. *Histoire du mouvement littéraire dans l'Eglise melchite du Ve au XXe siècle.* 3 vols. in 6. (Louvain/Paris, 1979–1989).
———. 'La liturgie des Patriarcats melchites de 969 à 1300,' *OC* 71 (1987), pp. 156–81.
———. 'The Liturgy of the Melkite Patriarchs from 969 to 1300,' in Scott F. Johnson, ed., *Languages and Cultures of Eastern Christianity: Greek* (Surrey, England, 2015), pp. 507–32.
Nau, François. 'Appendice: Fragments sur le monastère de Qenneshre,' in *Actes du XIV congrès international des orientalistes*, vol. 2 (Paris, 1907), pp. 76–135.
———. 'L'araméen chrétien (syriaque): les traductions faites du grec en syriaque au VIIe siècle,' *Revue de l'histoire des religions* 99 (1929), pp. 232–87.
———. 'Un colloque du patriarche Jean avec l'émir des Agaréens,' *JA* 11 (1915), pp. 225–79.
———. 'La cosmographie au VIIe siècle chez les Syriens,' *ROC* 5 (15) 1910, pp. 225–54.
———. 'Histoire de Jean Bar Aphtonia,' *ROC* 7 (1902), pp. 97–135.
Nef, Annliese. 'Conversion et islamisation: quelques réflexions depuis les VIIe-Xe s.' in P. Gelez and G. Grivaud, *Les conversions à l'Islam en Asie Mineure, dans les Balkans et dans le monde musulman: comparaisons et perspectives: actes du colloque de l'École française d'Athènes, 26-28 avril 2012* (Athens, 2016), pp. 229–44.
Neishtadt, Mila. 'The Lexical Component in the Aramaic Substrate of Palestinian Arabic,' in Aaron M. Butts, ed., *Semitic Languages in Contact* (Leiden/Boston, 2015), pp. 280–311.
Nestle, Eberhard. *Einführung in das Griechische Neue Testament*, 3rd ed. (Göttingen, 1909), pp. 219–26.
Neuwirth, Angelika. *Der Koran als Text der Spätantike: ein europäischer Zugang* (Berlin, 2010).
———. 'Locating the Qur'an' and Early Islam in the "Epistemic Space" of Late Antiquity,' in Carol Bakhos and Michael Cook, eds., *Islam and Its Past: Jahiliyya, Late Antiquity, and the Qur'an* (Oxford, 2017), pp. 165–85.
Nevo, Yehuda D. and Judith Koren, *Crossroads to Islam: The Origins of the Arab Religion and the Arab State* (Amherst, N.Y., 2003).
Newby, Gordon Darnell. *The Making of the Last Prophet: A Reconstruction of the Earliest Biography of Muhammad* (Columbia, S.C., 1989).
Newman, John-Henry. 'On Consulting the Faithful in Matters of Doctrine,' *Rambler* 1 (N.S.) (1859), pp. 219–27.
Nock, Arthurd D. *Sallustius: Concerning the Gods and the Universe* (Cambridge, 1926).

Nock, Arthurd D. 'Studies in the Graeco-Roman Beliefs of the Empire,' *The Journal of Hellenic Studies* 45 (1925), pp. 84–101.

Nöldeke, Theodor. *Geschichte der Perser und Araber zur Zeit der Sasaniden (Leiden, 1879).*

———. 'Hatte Muḥammad christliche Lehrer?,' *ZDMG* 12 (1858), pp. 699–708.

———. 'Ṣûfî,' *ZDMG* 48 (1894), pp. 45–48.

Nöldeke, Theodor, Friedrich Schwally, Gotthelf Bergsträsser, and Otto Pretzl, *The History of the Qur'ān.* Trans. Wolfgang H. Behn (Leiden/Boston, 2013).

Norton, Claire, ed. *Conversion and Islam in the Early Modern Mediterranean: The Lure of the Other* (London/New York, 2017).

Noth, Albrecht. 'Problems of Differentiation between Muslims and Non-Muslims: Re-reading the "Ordinances of 'Umar" (*Al-Shurūṭ al-Umariyya*),' in Hoyland, ed., *Muslims and Others in Early Islamic Society*, pp. 103–24.

Noth, Albrecht and Lawrence I. Conrad, *The Early Arabic Historical Tradition: A Source-Critical Study*, trans. Michael Bonner. 2nd ed. (Princeton, 1994).

Obolensky, Dimitri. *The Byzantine Commonwealth: Eastern Europe, 500–1453* (New York, 1971).

Ogén, Göran. 'Did the Term 'ṣūfī' Exist before the Sufis?,' *Acta Orientalia* 43 (1982), pp. 38–48.

Olivar, Alexandre. *La predicación cristiana antigua* (Barcelona, 1991).

Orlandi, Tito. *Koptische Papyri theologischen Inhalts* (Vienna, 1974).

———. 'Un frammento delle Pleroforie in Copto,' *Studi e Ricerche sull'Oriente Cristiano* 2 (1979), pp. 3–12.

Ory, Solange. 'Aspects religieux des textes épigraphiques du de l'Islam,' *Revue du monde musulman et de la Méditerranée* 58 (1990), pp. 30–39.

Outtier, Bernard. 'Le sort des manuscrits du "Katalog Hiersemann 500,"' *AB* 93 (1975), pp. 377–80.

Palme, Bernhard. 'Political Identity versus Religious Distinction? The Case of Egypt in the Later Roman Empire,' in Walter Pohl, Clemens Ganter, and Richard Payne, eds., *Visions of Community in the Post-Roman World. The West, Byzantium and the Islamic World, 300-1100* (Farnham, Surrey/Burlington, VT, 2012), pp. 81–98.

Palmer, Andrew. 'Āmīd in the Seventh-Century Syriac Life of Theodūṭē,' in Grypeou et al., *The Encounter of Eastern Christianity with Early Islam*, pp. 111–38.

———. 'The Garshūnī Version of the Life of Theodotos of Amida,' *PdO* 16 (1990–1991), pp. 253–60.

———. 'Saints' Lives with a Difference: Elijah on John of Tella (d. 538) and Joseph on Theodotos of Amida (d. 698),' in Han J. W. Drijvers, René Lavenant, Corrie Molenberg and Gerrit J. Reinink, eds., *IV Symposium Syriacum, 1984: Literary Genres in Syriac Literature,* (Rome, 1987), pp. 203–16.

———. 'The West-Syrian Monastic Founder Barṣawmo: A Historical Review of the Scholarly Literature,' in Bruns and Luthe, eds., *Orientalia Christiana: Festschrift für Hubert Kaufhold zum 70. Geburtstag*, pp. 399–414.

Papaconstantinou, Arietta. 'Administering the Early Islamic Empire: Insights from the Papyri,' in Haldon, ed., *Money, Power and Politics in Early Islamic Syria*, pp. 57–74.

———. 'Between *Umma* and *Dhimma*: The Christians of the Middle East under the Umayyads,' *Annales islamologiques* 42 (2008), pp. 127–56.

———. 'Confrontation, Interaction, and the Formation of the early Islamic *oikoumene*,' *Revue des études Byzantines* 63 (2005), pp. 167–81.

———. '"They Shall Speak the Arabic Language and Take Pride in It": Reconsidering the Fate of Coptic after the Arab Conquest,' *Le Muséon* 120 (2007), pp. 273–99.

Paret, Rudi. 'Die Bedeutungsentwicklung von Arabisch *Fatḥ*,' in J. M. Barral, ed., *Orientalia Hispanica, sive studia F.M. Pareja octogenario dictata*, vol. 1 (Leiden, 1974), pp. 537–541.

———. *Der Koran: Kommentar und Konkordanz* (Stuttgart, 1980).

———. 'Die Lücke in der Überlieferung über den Urislam,' in Fritz M. Meier, ed., *Westöstliche Abhandlungen. Rudolf Tschudi zum siebzigsten Geburtstag überreicht von Freunden und Schülern* (Wiesbaden, 1954), pp. 147–53.

Patlagean, Evelyne. 'Ancient Byzantine Hagiography and Social History,' in Stephen Wilson, ed., *Saints and their Cults: Studies in Religious Sociology, Folklore, and History* (Cambridge, 1983), pp. 101–22.

Patterson, Paul A. *Visions of Christ: The Anthropomorphite Controversy of 399 CE* (Tübingen, 2012).

Paverd, Frans van de. *St. John Chrysostom, The Homilies on the Statues: An Introduction* (Rome, 1991).

Payne Smith Margoliouth, Jessie. *A Compendious Syriac Dictionary* (Oxford, 1903).

———. *Supplement to the Thesaurus Syriacus of R. Payne Smith, S.T.P.* (Oxford, 1927). [Jesse Payne Smith = Jesse Payne Margoliouth]

Payne Smith, Robert. *Thesaurus Syriacus.* 2 vols. (Oxford, 1879–1901).

Peacock, Andrew C. S., ed. *Islamisation: Comparative Perspectives from History* (Edinburgh, 2017).

Peacock, Andrew C. S., Bruno de Nicola, and Sara N. Yildiz, eds., *Islam and Christianity in Medieval Anatolia* (Farnham, Surrey, and Burlington, Vt., 2015).

Peeters, Paul. Peeters, 'La Passion de S. Pierre de Capitolias († 13 janvier 715),' *AB* 57 (1939), pp. 299–333.

———. *Le tréfonds oriental de l'hagiographie byzantine* (Brussels, 1950).

Pellat, Charles. 'Une charge contre les secretaries d'état attribuée à Ǧāḥiẓ,' *Hespéris* 43 (1956), pp. 29–50.

———. *Le milieu baṣrien et la formation de Ǧāḥiẓ* (Paris, 1953).

Penn, Michael P. *Envisioning Islam: Syriac Christians and the Early Muslim World* (Philadelphia, 2015).

———. 'Monks, Manuscripts, and Muslims: Syriac Textual Changes in Reaction to the Rise of Islam,' *Hugoye* 12 (2009), pp. 235-257.

Peponakis, Manolis G. *Εξισλαμισμοί και επανεκχριστιανισμοί στην Κρήτη* (1645–1899) (Rethymno, 1997). [= Manolēs G. Peponakēs, *Exislamismoi kai epanekchristianismoi stēn Krētē (1645–1899)*]

Perlmann, Moshe. 'Notes on Anti-Christian Propaganda in the Mamlūk Empire,' *BSOAS* 10 (1942), pp. 843–61.

Perrin, Michel-Yves. 'À propos de la participation du peuple fidèle aux controversies doctrinales dans l'antiquité tardive: considerations introductives,' *Antiquité tardive* 9 (2001), pp. 179–99.

Peters, Francis E. *Aristoteles Arabus: The Oriental Translations and Commentaries on the Aristotelian* Corpus (Leiden, 1968).

Peters, Francis E. 'The Quest of the Historical Muhammad,' *International Journal of Middle East Studies* 23 (1991), pp. 291–315.

Peterson, Erik. *Eis Theos. Epigraphische, formgeschichtliche und religionsgeschichtliche Untersuchungen* (Göttingen, 1926).

Pines, Shlomo. 'A Note on an Early Meaning of the Term *mutakallim*,' *Israel Oriental Studies* 1 (1971), pp. 224–40.

——. 'Notes on Islam and on Arabic Christianity and Judaeo-Christianity,' *JSAI* 4 (1984), pp. 135–52.

——. 'Some Traits of Christian Theological Writing in Relation to Moslem *Kalām* and Jewish Thought,' in Sarah Stroumsa, ed., *The Collected Works of Shlomo Pines*, vol. 3, *Studies in the History of Arabic Philosophy* (Jerusalem, 1996), pp. 79–99.

Pipes, Daniel. 'Mawlas: Freed Slaves and Converts in Early Islam,' in John Ralph Willis, ed., *Slaves and Slavery in Muslim Africa*, vol. 1: *Islam and the Ideology of Enslavement* (London/Totowa, N.J., 1985), pp. 199–247.

Pirenne, Henri. *Mohammed and Charlemagne.* Trans. Bernard Miall (repr. New York, 1957).

Plathottathil, Stephen. "Themes of Incarnation in the Sedrē for the Period of Sūborō-Yaldō according to Mosul Fenqitho," *PdO* 36 (2011): 287–97.

Pontifical Council for Interreligious Dialogue and the Office on Inter-Religious Relations, World Council of Churches, 'Reflections on Interreligious Marriage. A Joint Study Document,' *Pro Dialogo* 96 (1997), pp. 325–39.

Possekel, Ute. 'Christological Debates in Eighth-Century Harran: The Correspondence of Leo of Harran and Eliya,' in Maria E. Doerfler, Emanuel Fiano, and Kyle R. Smith, eds., *Syriac Encounters: Papers from the Sixth North American Syriac Symposium, Duke University, 26–29 June 2011* (Leuven, 2015), pp. 345–68.

Powers, David S. *Muḥammad Is Not the Father of Any of Your Men: the Making of the Last Prophet* (Philadelphia, 2009).

——. 'On Bequests in Early Islam,' *JNES* 48 (1989), pp. 185–200.

Pregill, Michael. 'The Hebrew Bible and the Quran: The Problem of the Jewish "Influence" on Islam,' *Religion Compass* 1/6 (2007), pp. 643–59.

Prothero, Stephen. *Religious Literacy: What Every American Needs to Know—and Doesn't* (San Francisco, 2007).

Purchas, Samuel. *Hakluytus Posthumus, or, Purchas his Pilgrimes: Contayning a History of the World in Sea Voyages and Lande Travells by Englishmen and Others.* 20 vols. (Glasgow, 1905–1907).

al-Qāḍī, Wadād. 'Non-Muslims in the Early Muslim Conquest Army in Early Islam,' in Borrut and Donner, eds., *Christians and Others in the Umayyad State*, pp. 83–127.

Qāshā, Suhayl. *Aḥwāl naṣārā al-ʿIrāq fī khilāfat banī Umayya.* 3 vols. (Beirut, 2005).

Raby, Julian and Jeremy Johns, eds., *Bayt al-Maqdis: ʿAbd al-Malik's Jerusalem.* 2 vols. (Oxford, 1992).

Rapp, Claudia. *Holy Bishops in Late Antiquity* (Berkeley, 2005).

Rebillard, Éric. *Christians and Their Many Identities in Late Antiquity, North Africa, 200–450 CE* (Ithaca, NY/London, 2012).

Reinink, Gerrit J. 'Babai the Great's Life of George and the Propagation of Doctrine in the Late Sasanian Empire,' in J. W. Drijvers and J. W. Watt, eds., *Portraits of Spiritual Authority: Religious Power in Early Christianity, Byzantium and the Christian Orient* (Leiden, 1999), pp. 171–94.

———.'The Beginnings of Syriac Apologetic Literature in Response to Islam,' *OC* 77 (1993), pp. 171–87.

———. 'Following the Doctrine of the Demons,' in Jan N. Bremmer, Wout J. van Bekkum, and Arie L. Molendijk, eds., *Cultures of Conversions* (Leuven/Dudley, Mass., 2006), pp. 127–38.

———. 'Die Muslime in einer Sammlung von Dämonengeschichten des Klosters von Qennešrîn,' in René Lavenant, ed., *VI Symposium Syriacum, 1992: University of Cambridge, Faculty of Divinity, 30 August–2 September 1992* (Rome, 1994), pp. 335–46.

———. 'Severus Sebokts Brief an den Periodeutes Jonan. Einige Fragen zur aristotelischen Logik,' in Lavenant, ed., *III Symposium Syriacum*, pp. 97–107.

———. 'Tradition and the Formation of the 'Nestorian' Identity in Sixth- to Seventh-Century Iraq,' *Church History and Religious Culture* 89 (2009), pp. 217–50.

Retsö, Jan. *The Arabs in Antiquity: their History from the Assyrians to the Umayyads* (London/New York, 2003).

———. 'Aramaic/Syriac Loanwords,' in Kees Versteegh, ed., *Encyclopedia of Arabic Language and Linguistics*, vol. 1 (Leiden/Boston, 2006), pp. 178–82.

———. 'The Nabateans—Problems of Defining Ethnicity in the Ancient World,' in Walter Pohl, Clemens Gantner, and Richard Payne, eds., *Visions of Community in the Post-Roman World: The West, Byzantium and the Islamic World, 300–1100* (Farnham, Surrey/Burlington, Vt.), pp. 73–79.

Reymond, Phillipe. *L'eau, sa vie, et sa signification dans l'Ancien Testament* (Leiden, 1958).

Reynolds, Gabriel S. 'The Muslim Jesus: Dead or Alive?' *BSOAS* 72 (2009), pp. 237–58.

———., ed. *New Perspectives on the Qur'ān: The Qur'ān in Its Historical Context* 2 (London/New York, 2011).

———., ed. *The Qur'ān in Its Historical Context* (London/New York, 2008).

Richmond, Helen. *Blessed and Called to Be a Blessing: Muslim-Christian Couples Sharing a Life Together* (Oxford, 2015).

Robinson, Chase F. *'Abd al-Malik* (Oxford, 2005).

———. *Empire and Elites after the Muslim Conquest* (Cambridge, 2000).

———. 'Neck-Sealing in early Islam,' *JESHO* 48 (2005), pp. 401–441.

Robinson, Neal. *Christ in Islam and Christianity* (Albany, 1991).

Robinson, Thomas A. *Who Were the First Christians? Dismantling the Urban Thesis* (New York, 2017).

Rodinson, Maxime. *Mohammed*, trans. Anne Carter (New York, 1971).

Roggema, Barbara. *The Legend of Sergius Baḥīrā. Eastern Christian Apologetics and Apocalyptic in Response to Islam* (Leiden/Boston, 2009).

———. 'Pour une lecture des dialogues islamo-chrétiens en syriaque à la lumière des controverses internes à l'islam,' in Flavia Ruani, ed., *Les controverses religieuses en syriaque* (Paris, 2016), p. 261–94.

Rosenthal, Franz. 'Some Minor Problems in the Qur'ān,' in *The Joshua Starr Memorial Volume: Studies in History and Philology* (New York, 1953), pp. 67–84.

———. *The Technique and Approach of Muslim Scholarship* (Rome, 1947).

Rothstein, Gustav. *Die dynastie der Lahmiden in al-Hîra: Ein Versuch zur arabisch-persischen Geschichte zur Zeit der Sasaniden* (Halle, 1899).

Rousseau, Philip. '"The Preacher's Audience": A More Optimistic View,' in T. W. Hillard, R. A. Kearsley, C.E.V. Nixon, and Alana M. Nobbs, eds., *Ancient History in a*

Modern University, vol. 2: *Early Christianity, Late Antiquity and Beyond* (New South Wales/Grand Rapids/Cambridge, 1998), pp. 391–400.
Ruani, Flavia, ed., *Les controverses religieuses en syriaque* (Paris, 2016).
Rubin, Uri. 'Apes, Pigs, and the Islamic Identity,' *Israel Oriental Studies* 17 (1997), pp. 89–105.
———. *The Eye of the Beholder: The Life of Muḥammad as Viewed by the Early Muslims* (Princeton, 1995).
———. 'Pre-existence and Light: Aspects of the Concept of Nūr Muḥammad,' *Israel Oriental Studies* 5 (1975), pp. 62–119.
Russ-Fishbane, Elisha. *Judaism, Sufism, and the Pietists of Medieval Egypt* (Oxford, 2015).
Saar, Ortal-Paz. 'An Incantation Bowl for Sowing Discord,' *Journal of Semitic Studies* 58 (2013), pp. 241–56.
Sabean, David W. *Power in the Blood: Popular Culture and Village Discourse in Early Modern Germany* (New York, 1984).
Sachau, Eduard. 'Studie zur Syrischen Kirchenlitteratur der Damascene,' *Sitzungsberichte der Königlich preussischen Akademie der Wissenschaften zu Berlin* (1899), pp. 502–28.
———. *Verzeichniss der syrischen Handschriften der Königlichen Bibliothek zu Berlin*. 1 vol. in 2. (Berlin, 1899).
Ṣādir, Yūḥannā. *Ruhbān 'arab fī ba'ḍ siyar al-mutaṣawwifīn al-Muslimīn* (Beirut, 2009).
Sahas, Daniel J. 'The Formation of Later Islamic Doctrines as a Response to Byzantine Polemics: The Miracles of Muhammad,' *Greek Orthodox Theological Review* 27 (1982), pp. 307–24.
———. 'Ritual of Conversion from Islam to the Byzantine Church,' *Greek Orthodox Theological Review* 36 (1991), pp. 57–69.
Sahner, Christian. 'Christian Martyrs and the Making of an Islamic Society in the Post-Conquest Period,' (PhD diss., Princeton University, 2015).
———. 'Swimming against the Current: Muslim Conversion to Christianity in the Early Islamic Period,' *Journal of the American Oriental Society* 136 (2016), pp. 265–84.
Salaymeh, Lena. 'Taxing Citizens: Socio-legal Constructions of Late Antique Muslim Identity,' *Islamic Law and Society* 23 (2016), pp. 333–67.
Salvesen, Alison. 'A Convergence of the Ways? The Judaizing of Christian Scripture by Origen and Jerome,' in Becker and Reed, eds., *The Ways That Never Parted*, pp. 233–57.
Samir, Khalil. 'La "*Geschichte des arabischen Schrifttums*" et la littérature arabe chrétienne,' *OCP* 44 (1978), pp. 463–72.
———. 'Liberté religieuse et propogation de la foi chez les théologiens arabes chrétiens du IXe siècle et en Islam,' *Tantur Yearbook* (1980–1981), pp. 93–164.
———. 'Saint Rawḥ al-Qurašī: etude d'onomastique arabe et authenticité de sa passion,' *LM* 105 (1992), pp. 343–59.
Sandmel, Samuel. 'Parallelomania,' *Journal of Biblical Literature* 81 (1962), pp. 1–13.
Sauget, Joseph-Marie. 'Deux homéliaires syriaques de la Bibliothèque Vaticane,' *OCP* 27 (1961), pp. 327–424.
———. 'Vestiges d'une célébration gréco-syriaque de l'Anaphore de Saint Jacques,' in Carl Laga, Joseph A. Munitiz, and Lucas van Rompay, eds., *After Chalcedon: Studies*

in Theology and Church History Offered to Professor Albert Van Roey for His Seventieth Birthday (Leuven, 1985), pp. 309–45.

Sauvaget, Jean. *La Mosquée omeyyade de Médine; étude sur les origines architecturales de la mosquée et de la basilique* (Paris, 1947).

Sauvaget, Jean and Claude Cahen, *Jean Sauvaget's Introduction to the History of the Muslim East: A Bibliographical Guide* (Berkeley, 1965; repr. Westport, Conn., 1982).

Saxer, Victor. *Bible et hagiographie: textes et thèmes bibliques dans les actes des martyrs authentiques des premiers siècles* (Berne/New York, 1986).

Schacht, Joseph. *An Introduction to Islamic Law* (Oxford, 1964).

———. 'On Mūsā ibn 'Uqba's Kitāb al-Maghāzī,' *Acta Orientalia* 21 (1953), pp. 288-300.

———. *The Origins of Muhammadan Jurisprudence* (Oxford, 1950).

———. 'A Revaluation of Islamic Traditions,' *The Journal of the Royal Asiatic Society of Great Britain and Ireland* 2 (1949), pp. 143–54.

Scheidel, Walter. 'Demography,' in Walter Scheidel, Ian Morris, and Richard Saller, eds., *The Cambridge Economic History of the Greco-Roman World* (Cambridge, 2008), pp. 38–86.

Scheiner, Jens. *Die Eroberung von Damaskus: Quellenkritische Untersuchung zur Historiographie in klassisch-islamischer Zeit* (Leiden/Boston, 2010).

———. 'Reflections on Hoyland's *In God's Path*,' *Bustan: The Middle East Book Review* 7 (2016), pp. 19–32.

Scher, Addai. *Catalogue des manuscrits syriaques et arabes conservés dans la bibliothèque épiscopale de Séert (Kurdistan)* (Mosul, 1905).

Schimmel, AnneMarie. *Mystical Dimensions of Islam* (Chapel Hill, 1975).

———. 'Sufismus,' in Helmut Gätje, ed., *Grundriß der Arabischen Philologie*, vol. 2 (Wiesbaden, 1987), pp. 338–57.

Schippers, Arie. *Spanish Hebrew Poetry and the Arab Literary Tradition: Arabic Themes in Hebrew Andalusian Poetry* (Leiden/New York, 1994).

Schmidt, Andrea B. 'The Literary Tradition of Gregory of Nazianzus in Syriac Literature and Its Historical Context,' *The Harp* 11–2 (1998–1999), pp. 127–34.

Schmidt, Nora, Nora K. Schmid, and Angelika Neuwirth, eds., *Denkraum Spätantike: Reflexionen von Antiken im Umfeld des Koran* (Wiesbaden, 2016).

Schoeler, Gregor. *The Biography of Muḥammad: Nature and Authenticity*, trans. Uwe Vagelpohl (London/New York, 2011).

Schwartz, Daniel L. *Paideia and Cult: Christian Initiation in Theodore of Mopsuestia* (Washington, D.C., 2013).

Schwartz, Stuart B. *All Can Be Saved: Religious Tolerance and Salvation in the Iberian Atlantic World* (New Haven/London, 2008).

Schwarzbaum, Haim. *Biblical and Extra-Biblical Legends in Islamic Folk-Literature* (Walldorf-Hessen, 1982).

Seamon, Erika B. *Interfaith Marriage in America: the Transformation of Religion and Christianity* (New York, 2012).

Segal, Judah B. 'Arabs in Syriac Literature before the Rise of Islam,' *JSAI* 4 (1984), pp. 89–123.

Seppälä, Serafim. *In Speechless Ecstasy: Expression and Interpretation of Mystical Experience in Classical Syriac and Sufi Literature* (Helsinki, 2003).

Sezgin, Fuat. *Geschichte des Arabischen Schriftums*. 17 vols. (Leiden, 1967–).

Shahid, Irfan. *Byzantium and the Arabs in the Sixth Century*. Vol. 2.1: *Toponymy, Monuments, Historical Geography, and Frontier Studies* (Washington, D.C., 2002).

———. *The Martyrs of Najrân: New Documents* (Bruxelles, 1971).

Shaked, Shaul. 'Manichaean Incantation Bowls in Syriac,' *JSAI* 24 (2000), pp. 58–92.

———. 'Popular Religion in Sasanian Babylonia,' *JSAI* 21 (1997), pp. 103–17.

al-Shdaifat, Younis, Ahmad Al-Jallad, Zeyad al-Salameen, and Rafe Harahsheh, 'An Early Christian Arabic Graffito Mentioning "Yazīd the King,"' *Arabian Archaeology and Epigraphy* 28 (2017), pp. 315-24.

Shitomi, Yuzo. 'Réexamen des deux lettres attribuées à Siméon de Bêth Aršâm, relatives à la persécution des chrétiens de Nagrân,' in *Études sud-arabes. Recueil offert à Jacques Ryckmans* (Louvain-la-Neuve, 1991), pp. 207–24.

Shoemaker, Stephen J. *The Death of a Prophet: The End of Muhammad's Life and the Beginnings of Islam* (Philadelphia, 2012).

———. *Mary in Early Christian Faith and Devotion* (New Haven/London, 2016).

———. 'Muḥammad and the Qur'ān,' in Scott F. Johnson, ed., *The Oxford Handbook of Late Antiquity* (Oxford/New York, 2012), pp. 1078–1108.

———. 'In Search of 'Urwa's *Sīra*: Some Methodological Issues in the Quest for "Authenticity" in the Life of Muḥammad,' *Der Islam* 85 (2011), pp. 257–344.

Shoufani, Elias. *Al-Riddah and the Muslim Conquest of Arabia* (Toronto, 1973).

Shukurov, Rustam. *The Byzantine Turks, 1204–1461* (Leiden/Boston, 2016).

———. 'Harem Christianity: The Byzantine Identity of Seljuk Princes,' in Andrew C.S. Peacock and Sara N. Yıldız, eds., *The Seljuks of Anatolia: Court and Society in the Medieval Middle East* (London/New York, 2013), pp. 115–50.

Siegal, Michal Bar-Asher. *Early Christian Monastic Literature and the Babylonian Talmud* (Cambridge/New York, 2013).

Sijpesteijn, Petra M. 'Creating a Muslim State. The Collection and Meaning of *ṣadaqa*,' in Bernhard Palme, ed., *Akten des 23. Internationalen Papyrologenkongresses Wien, 22.–28. Juli 2001* (Vienna, 2007), pp. 661–73.

———. 'New Rule over Old Structures: Egypt after the Muslim Conquest,' in Harriet Crawford, ed., *Regime Change in the Ancient Near East and Egypt: From Sargon of Agade to Saddam Hussein* (*Proceedings of the British Academy* 136) (Oxford, 2007), pp. 183–200.

———. *Shaping a Muslim State: The World of a Mid-Eighth Century Egyptian Official* (Oxford, 2013).

Simonsen, Jørgen Baek. *Studies in the Genesis and Early Development of the Caliphal Taxation System* (Copenhagen, 1988).

Simonsohn, Uriel. *A Common Justice: The Legal Allegiances of Christians and Jews under Early Islam* (Philadelphia, 2011).

———. 'Communal Membership Despite Religious Exogamy: A Critical Examination of East and West Syrian Legal Sources of the Late Sasanian and Early Islamic Periods,' *JNES* 75 (2016), pp. 249–66.

———. 'Conversion, Exemption, and Manipulation: Social Benefits and Conversion to Islam in Late Antiquity and the Middle Ages,' *Medieval Worlds* 6 (2017), pp. 196–216.

———. '"Halting between Two Opinions": Conversion and Apostasy in Early Islam,' *Medieval Encounters* 19 (2013), pp. 342–70.

——. 'The Introduction and Formalization of Civil Law in the East Syrian Church in the Late Sasanian-Early Islamic Periods,' *History Compass* 14 (2016), pp. 231–43.

——. 'The Legal and Social Bonds of Jewish Apostates and their Spouses according to Gaonic Responsa,' *The Jewish Quarterly Review* 105 (2015), pp. 417–39.

Sizgorich, Thomas. 'Monks and Their Daughters: Monasteries as Muslim-Christian Boundaries,' in Margaret Cormack, ed., *Muslims and Others in Sacred Space* (Oxford, 2013), pp. 193–216.

——. 'Narrative and Community in Islamic Late Antiquity,' *Past and Present* 185 (2004), pp. 9–42.

Smith, Kyle. *Constantine and the Captive Christians of Persia* (Oakland, 2016).

Smith, Margaret. *The Way of the Mystics: The Early Christian Mystics and the Rise of the Ṣūfīs* (London, 1976).

Smoller, Laura A. '"Popular" Religious Culture(s),' in John H. Arnold, ed., *The Oxford Handbook of Medieval Christianity* (Oxford, 2014), pp. 340–56

Sokoloff, Michael. *A Dictionary of Jewish Palestinian Aramaic of the Byzantine Period* (Ramat Gan, 1990).

——. *A Syriac Lexicon: A Translation from the Latin, Correction, Expansion, and Update of C. Brockelmann's Lexicon Syriacum* (Winona Lake, Ind. /Piscataway, N.J., 2009).

Speck, Paul. 'ΓΡΑΦΑΙΣ Η ΓΛΥΦΑΙΣ. Zu dem Fragment des Hypatios von Ephesos über die Bilder,' in Ralph Johannes Lilie and Paul Speck, eds., *Varia* I (Bonn, 1984), pp. 211–72.

Spectorsky, Susan A. 'Problems of Intermarriage in Early *fiqh* Texts,' in Benjamin H. Hary, John L. Hayes, and Fred Astern, eds., *Judaism and Islam: Boundaries, Communications, and Interaction: Essays in Honor of William M. Brinner* (Leiden/Boston, 2000), pp. 269–78.

Stern, Samuel. ''Abd al-Jabbār's Account of How Christ's Religion Was Falsified by the Adoption of Roman Customs,' *JTS* 19 (1968), pp. 128–85.

Stewart, Columba. *Cassian the Monk* (New York/Oxford, 1998).

Stewart, Devin J. 'The *Maqāma*,' in Roger Allen and Donald S. Richards, ed., *Arabic Literature in the Post-Classical Period* (Cambridge, 2008), pp. 145–58.

——. 'Notes on Medieval and Modern Emendations of the Qur'ān,' in Reynolds, ed., *The Qur'ān in Its Historical Context*, pp. 225–48.

Strack, Hermann L. and Paul Billerbeck, *Kommentar zum Neuen Testament aus Talmud und Midrasch*. 6 vols in 7 (München, 1922–1961).

Strothmann, Werner. 'Die orientalischen Handschriften der Sammlung Mettler (Katalog Hiersemann 500),' in Wolfgang Voigt, ed., XIX. *Deutscher Orientalistentag vom 28. September bis 4. Oktober 1975 in Freiburg im Breisgau: Vorträge* (Wiesbaden, 1977), pp. 285–93.

Stroumsa, Guy G. *The Making of the Abrahamic Religions in Late Antiquity* (Oxford, 2015).

Suermann, Harald. 'Copts and the Islam of the Seventh Century,' in Grypeou et al., eds., *The Encounter of Eastern Christianity with Early Islam*, pp. 95–109.

——. 'The Old Testament and the Jews in the Dialogue between the Jacobite Patriarch John I and 'Umayr ibn Sa'd al-Anṣārī,' in Juan Pedro Monferrer-Sala, ed., *Eastern Crossroads: Essays on Medieval Christian Legacy* (Piscataway, N.J., 2007), pp. 131–41.

Sundermann, Werner. 'An Early Attestation of the Name of the Tajiks,' in Wojciech

Skalmowski and Alois van Tongerloo, eds., *Medioiranica* (Leuven, 1993), pp. 163–71.

Swanson, Mark N. 'A Copto-Arabic Catechism of the Later Fatimid Period: "Ten Questions That One of the Disciples Asked His Master,"' *PdO* 22 (1997), pp. 473–501.

———. *Folly to the Ḥunafāʾ: The Cross of Christ in Arabic Christian-Muslim Controversy in the Eighth and Ninth Centuries A.D.* (Excerpta ex dissertation ad doctoratum; Cairo, 1995).

———. 'The Specifically Egyptian Context of a Coptic Arabic text: Chapter Nine of the *Kitāb al-Īḍāḥ* of Sawīrūs ibn al-Muqaffaʿ,' *Medieval Encounters* 2 (1996), pp. 214–27.

Szilágyi, Krisztina. 'Muḥammad and the Monk: The Making of the Christian Baḥīrā Legend,' *JSAI* 34 (2008), pp. 169–214.

Szpiech, Ryan. *Conversion and Narrative: Reading and Religious Authority in Medieval Polemic* (Philadelphia, 2013).

———. 'Conversion as a Historiographical Problem: The Case of Zoraya/Isabel de Solís,' in Yaniv Fox and Yosi Yisraeli, eds., *Contesting Inter-Religious Conversion in the Medieval World* (London/New York, 2017), pp. 24–38.

———. 'Introduction' in Ryan Szpiech, ed., *Medieval Exegesis and Religious Difference: Commentary, Conflict, and Community in the Premodern Mediterranean* (New York, 2015), pp. 1–16.

Taft, Robert F. *Beyond East and West: Problems in Liturgical Understanding* (Washington, D.C., 1984).

———. 'The Decline of Communion in Byzantium and the Distancing of the Congregation from the Liturgical Action: Cause, Effect, or Neither?' in Sharon E. J. Gerstel, ed., *Thresholds of the Sacred: Architectural, Art Historical, Liturgical, and Theological Perspectives on Religious Screens, East and West* (Washington, D.C., 2006), pp. 27–50.

———. *The Great Entrance: A History of the Transfer of Gifts and Other Pre-Anaphoral Rites of the Liturgy of St. John Chrysostom* (Rome, 1975).

———. 'Home-Communion in the Late Antique East,' in Clare V. Johnson, ed., *Ars Liturgiae: Worship, Aesthetics and Praxis: Essays in Honor of Nathan D. Mitchell* (Chicago, 2003), pp. 1–25.

Talib, Adam. 'Topoi and Topography in the Histories of al-Ḥīra,' in Wood, ed., *History and Identity in the Late Antique Near East*, pp. 123–47.

Tanner, Norman and Sethina Watson, 'Least of the Laity: The Minimum Requirements for a Medieval Christian,' *Journal of Medieval History* 32 (2006), pp. 395–423.

Tannous, Jack. 'Between Christology and Kalām? The Life and Letters of George, Bishop of the Arab Tribes' in George A. Kiraz, ed., *Malphono w-Rabo d-Malphone: Studies in Honor of Sebastian P. Brock* (Piscataway, N.J., 2008) pp. 671–716.

———. "Greek Kanons and the Syrian Orthodox Liturgy," in Brouria Bitton-Ashkelony and Derek Krueger, eds. *Prayer and Worship in Eastern Christianities, 6th to 11th Centuries* (London/New York, 2017), pp. 151–80.

———. 'In Search of Monotheletism,' *Dumbarton Oaks Papers* 68 (2014), pp. 29–67.

———. 'The Life of Simeon of the Olives: A Christian Puzzle from Islamic Syria,' in Jamie Kreiner and Helmut Reimitz, eds., *Motions of Late Antiquity: Essays on Religion, Politics, and Society in Honour of Peter Brown* (Turnhout, 2016), pp. 309–30.

———. 'Syria between Byzantium and Islam: Making Incommensurables Speak.' (PhD diss., Princeton University, 2010).

———. 'You Are What You Read: Qenneshre and the Miaphysite Church in the Seventh Century,' in Philip J. Wood, *History and Identity in the Late Antique Near East* (Oxford/New York, 2013), pp. 83–102.

Taqizadeh, S. H. 'The Iranian Festivals Adopted by the Christians and Condemned by the Jews,' *BSOAS* 10 (1940), pp. 632–53.

Tarán, Leonardo and Dimitri Gutas, *Aristotle Poetics. Editio maior of the Greek Text with Historical Introductions and Philological Commentaries* (Leiden/Boston, 2012).

Taylor, David G. K. 'The Authorship of the Apocalyptic Section of the *Testament of Our Lord* Reconsidered,' (forthcoming).

———. 'The Christology of the Syriac Psalm Commentary (AD 541/2) of Daniel of Salah and the "Phantasiast" Controversy,' *Studia Patristica* 35 (2001), pp. 508–15.

———. 'The Great Psalm Commentary of Daniel of Salah,' *The Harp* 11–12 (1998–1999), pp. 33–42.

———. 'L'importance des pères de l'église dans l'oeuvre speculative de Barhebraeus,' *PdO* 33 (2008), pp. 63–86.

———. 'The Patriarch and the Pseudepigrapha: Extra-Biblical Traditions in the Writings of Cyriacus of Tagrit (793–817),' in François Briquel-Chatonnet, ed., *Sur les pas des Araméens chrétiens. Mélanges offerts à Alain Desreumaux* (Paris, 2010), pp. 35-61.

———. 'A Stylistic Comparison of the Syriac Ḥimyarite Martyr Texts Attributed to Simeon of Beth Arsham,' in Joëlle Beaucamp, François Briquel-Chatonnet, and Christian J. Robin, eds., *Juifs et Chrétiens en Arabie aux Ve et VIe siècles. Regards croisés sur les sources* (Paris, 2010), pp. 143–76.

———. 'The Syriac Baptism of St John: A Christian Ritual of Protection for Muslim Children,' in Robert G. Hoyland, ed., *The Late Antique World of Early Islam: Muslims among Christians and Jews in the East Mediterranean* (Princeton, 2015), pp. 437–59.

ter Haar Romeny, Bas, ed. *Jacob of Edessa and the Syriac Culture of His Day* (Leiden/Boston, 2008).

Teule, Herman G. B. 'It Is Not Right to Call Ourselves Orthodox and the Other Heretics: Ecumenical Attitudes in the Jacobite Church in the Time of the Crusaders,' in Krijnie N. Ciggaar and Herman G. B. Teule, eds., *East and West in the Crusader States: Context – Contacts – Confrontations* II. *Acta of the Congress Held at Hernen Castle in May 1997* (Leuven, 1999), pp. 13–27.

———. 'Jacob of Edessa and Canon Law,' in ter Haar Romeny, ed., *Jacob of Edessa and the Syriac Culture of His Day* (Leiden/Boston, 2008), pp. 83–100.

———. 'The Syriac Renaissance,' in Herman Teule et al., eds., *The Syriac Renaissance* (Leuven/Paris/Walpole, MA, 2010), pp. 1–30.

Thomas, David, ed. *Routledge Handbook on Christian-Muslim Relations* (London/New York, 2018).

Thomas, David, et al., eds., *Christian-Muslim Relations: A Bibliographical History.* 11 vols. (Leiden/Boston, 2009-).

Thomas, Keith. 'The Meaning of Literacy in Early Modern England,' in Gerd Baumann, ed., *The Written Word: Literacy in Transition.* (Wolfson College Lectures 1985) (Oxford, 1986), pp. 97-131.

Thomson, Robert W. *A Bibliography of Classical Armenian Literature to 1500 AD* (Turnhout, 1995).

Thomson, Robert W. 'An Eighth-Century Melkite Colophon From Edessa,' *JTS* n.s., 13 (1962), pp. 249–58.

Tilly, Charles. *The Politics of Collective Violence* (Cambridge/New York, 2003).

Toenies Keating, Sandra. *Defending the "People of Truth" in the Early Islamic Period: The Christian Apologies of Abū Rā'iṭah* (Leiden/Boston, 2006).

Tolan, John. 'Le pèlerin Arculfe et le roi Mavias: la circulation des informations à propos des "Sarrasins" au VIIe–VIIIe siècles, de Jérusalem à Iona et Yarrow,' in Joëlle Ducos and Patrick Henriet, eds., *Passages. Déplacements des hommes, circulation des textes et identités dans l'Occident médiéval* (Toulouse, 2009), pp. 175–85.

Toral-Niehoff, Isabel. *Al-Ḥīra: Eine arabische Kulturmetropole im spätantiken Kontext* (Leiden/Boston, 2014).

Tottoli, Roberto. *Biblical Prophets in the Qur'ān and Muslim Literature* (London/New York, 2002).

Tramontana, Felicita. *Passages of Faith: Conversion in Palestinian Villages (17th century)* (Wiesbaden, 2014).

Treiger, Alexander. 'Christian Greco-Arabica: Prolegomena to a History of the Arabic Translations of the Greek Church Fathers,' *Intellectual History of the Islamicate World* 3 (2015), pp. 188–227.

———. 'Mutual Influences and Borrowings,' in David Thomas, ed., *Routledge Handbook on Christian-Muslim Relations* (London/New York, 2018), pp. 194–206.

———. 'Origins of *Kalām*,' in Sabine Schmidtke, ed., *The Oxford Handbook of Islamic Theology* (Oxford, 2016), pp. 27–43.

———. 'Syro-Arabic Translations in Abbasid Palestine: The Case of John of Apamea's Letter on Stillness (Sinai ar. 549),' *PdO* 39 (2014), pp. 79–131.

Trimingham, John Spencer. *Christianity among the Arabs in Pre-Islamic Times* (London/New York, 1979).

Tritton, Arthur S. *The Caliphs and Their Non-Muslim Subjects: A Critical Study of the Covenant of 'Umar* (London, 1930).

———. 'Foreign Influences on Muslim Theology,' *BSOAS* 10 (1942), pp. 837–42.

———. 'Non-Muslim Subjects of the Muslim State,' *Journal of the Royal Asiatic Society of Great Britain and Ireland* 1 (1942), pp. 36–40.

Trombley, Frank R. 'The Council in Trullo (691–92): A Study in the Canons Relating to Paganism, Heresy, and the Invasions,' *Comitatus: A Journal of Medieval and Renaissance Studies* 9 (1978), pp. 1–18.

Troupeau, Gérard. 'Les couvents chrétiens dans la littérature arabe,' *La nouvelle Revue du Caire* 1 (1975), pp. 265–79.

———. 'Les fêtes des chrétiens vues par un juriste musulman,' in *Mélanges offerts à Jean Dauvillier* (Toulouse, 1979), pp. 795–802.

———. 'Le rôle des syriaques dans la transmission et l'exploitation du patrimoine philosophique et scientifique grec,' *Arabica* 38 (1991), pp. 1–10.

Ullmann, Manfred. *Die Medizin im Islam* (Leiden, 1970).

Vajda, Georges. 'Juifs et Musulmans selon le Ḥadīṯ,' *JA* 229 (1937), pp. 57–127.

Valensi, Lucette. 'Inter-communal Relations and Changes in Religious Affiliation in the Middle East (Seventeenth to Nineteenth Centuries),' *Comparative Studies in Society and History* 39 (1997), pp. 251–69.

Vance, James M. *Beiträge zur Byzantinischen Kulturgeschichte am Ausgange des IV. Jahrhunderts aus den Schriften des Johannes Chrysostomus* (Jena, 1907).
van der Vliet, Jacques. 'Bringing Home the Homeless: Landscape and History in Egyptian Hagiography,' in Dijkstra and van Dijk, *The Encroaching Desert*, pp. 39–55.
van Donzel, Emeri and Andrea Schmidt, *Gog and Magog in Early Christian and Islamic Sources: Sallam's Quest for Alexander's Wall* (Leiden/Boston, 2010).
van Esbroeck, Michel. 'The Memra on the Parrot by Isaac of Antioch,' *JTS* 47 (1996), pp. 464–76.
van Ess, Josef. 'Disputationspraxis in der Islamischen Theologie: Eine Vorläufige Skizze,' *Revue des études islamiques* 44 (1976), pp. 23–60.
———. *Theologie und Gesellschaft im 2. Und 3. Jahrhundert Hidschra. Eine Geschichte des religiösen Denkens im frühen Islam.* 6 vols. (Berlin/New York, 1991–1997). [= *Theology and Society in the Second and Third Centuries of the Hijra: A History of Religious Thought in Early Islam*, trans. John O'Kane (Leiden/Boston, 2017–)].
van Ginkel, Jan. 'Greetings to a Virtuous Man: The Correspondence of Jacob of Edessa,' in ter Haar Romeny, ed., *Jacob of Edessa and the Syriac Culture of His Day*, pp. 67–81.
van Lent, Jos. 'Réactions coptes au défi de l'Islam: L'Homélie de Théophile d'Alexandrie en l'honneur de Saint Pierre e de Saint Paul,' in Anne Boud'Hors and Catherine Louis, eds., *Études coptes XIII: quinzième journée d'études (Louvain-la-Neuve, 12–14 mai 2011)* (Paris, 2015), pp. 133–48.
van Minnen, Peter. 'Saving History? Egyptian Hagiography in Its Space and Time,' in Dijkstra and van Dijk, *The Encroaching Desert*, pp. 57–91.
van Roey, Albert. 'La lettre apologétique d'Élie à Léon, syncelle de l'évêque chalcédonien de Harran,' *LM* 57 (1944), pp. 1–52.
———. *Traité apologétique: étude, texte et traduction* (Louvain, 1948).
———. 'Trois auteurs chalcédoniens syriens: Georges de Martyropolis, Constantin et Léon de Harran,' *Orientalia Lovaniensia Periodica* 3 (1972), pp. 125–53.
van Rompay, Lucas. 'The Martyrs of Najran: Some Remarks on the Nature of the Sources,' in Jan Quaegebeur, ed., *Studia Paulo Naster oblata II: Orientalia Antiqua* (Leuven, 1982), pp. 301–309.
———. 'Severus, Patriarch of Antioch (512–538), in the Greek, Syriac, and Coptic Traditions,' *Journal of the Canadian Society for Syriac Studies* 8 (2008), pp. 3–22.
———. 'The Syriac Version of the "Life of Symeon Salos": First Soundings,' in Antoon Schoors and Peter van Deun, eds., *Philohistôr: Miscellanea in Honorem Caroli Laga Septuagenarii* (Leuven, 1994), pp. 381–98.
Vasiliev, Alexandre A. *Justin the First: An Introduction to the Epoch of Justinian the Great* (Cambridge, Mass., 1950).
Villagomez, Cynthia. 'The Fields, Flocks, and Finances of Monks: Economic Life at Nestorian Monasteries, 500–850' (PhD diss., UCLA, 1998).
von Ranke, Leopold. *Über die Epochen der neueren Geschichte* (Leipzig, 1906).
Vööbus, Arthur. *Discoveries of Very Important Manuscript Sources for the Syro-Hexapla: Contributions to the Research on the Septuagint* (Stockholm, 1970).
———. 'The Discovery of New Cycles of Canons and Resolutions Composed by Ja'qōb of Edessa,' *OCP* 34 (1968), pp. 412–19.
———. *History of the School of Nisibis* (Louvain, 1965).

Vööbus, Arthur. *Syrische Kanonessammlungen: Ein Beitrag zur Quellenkunde,* I: *Westsyrische Originalurkunden,* 1, A-B. CSCO 308, 317, Subsidia 35, 38 (Louvain, 1970).

Vryonis, Jr., Speros. *The Decline of Medieval Hellenism in Asia Minor and the Process of Islamization from the Eleventh through the Fifteenth Century* (Berkeley/Los Angeles/London, 1971).

Vryonis, Jr., Speros. 'Religious Changes and Patterns in the Balkans, 14th–16th Centuries,' in Henrik Birnbaum and Speros Vryonis, Jr., eds., *Aspects of the Balkans: Continuity and Change. Contributions to the International Balkan Conference held at UCLA, October 23–28, 1969* (The Hague/Paris, 1972), pp. 151–76.

Waines, David, 'Introduction,' in David Waines, ed., *Patterns of Everyday Life* (Aldershot, England/Burlington, VT, 2002), pp. xi–xlviii.

Wainwright, Geoffrey. *Doxology: The Praise of God in Worship, Doctrine, and Life: A Systematic Theology* (New York, 1980).

Walker, Joel T. 'Ascetic Literacy: Books and Readers in East-Syrian Monastic Tradition,' in Henning Börm and Josef Wiesehoefer, eds., *Commutatio et Contentio: Studies in the Late Roman, Sasanian, and Early Islamic Near East in Memory of Zeev Rubin* (Düsseldorf, 2010), pp. 307–45.

———. *The Legend of Mar Qardagh: Narrative and Christian Heroism in Late Antique Iraq* (Berkeley, 2006).

Walker, John. *A Catalogue of the Arab-Byzantine and Post Reform Umaiyad Coins* (London, 1956).

Walker, Paul E. *Caliph of Cairo: Al-Hakim bi-Amr Allah, 996–1021* (Cairo/New York, 2009).

Walmsley, Alan. *Early Islamic Syria: An Archaeological Assessment* (London, 2007).

Walzer, Richard. *Al-Farabi on the Perfect State: Abū Naṣr al-Fārābī's Mabādi' Ārā' Ahl al-Madīna al- Fāḍila* (Oxford, 1985).

———. *Galen on Jews and Christians* (Oxford, 1949).

———. 'New Light on the Arabic Translations of Aristotle,' in Richard Walzer, *Greek into Arabic: Essays on Islamic Philosophy* (Cambridge, 1962), pp. 60–113.

Wansbrough, John E. *Quranic Studies: Sources and Methods of Scriptural Interpretation* (Oxford, 1977).

———. *The Sectarian Milieu: Content and Composition of Islamic Salvation History* (Oxford/New York, 1978).

Ward, Seth. 'A Fragment from an Unknown Work by Al-Ṭabarī on the Tradition "Expel the Jews and Christians from the Arabian Peninsula (And the Lands of Islam)",' *BSOAS* 53 (1990), pp. 407–20.

Watt, John W. 'Al-Fārābī and the History of the Syriac *Organon*,' in Kiraz, ed., *Malphono w-Rabo d-Malphone*, pp. 751–78

———.'Les pères grecs dans le curriculum théologique et philologique des écoles syriaques,' in Andrea Schmidt and Dominique Gonnet, eds., *Les pères grecs dans la tradition syriaque* (*Études Syriaques* 4) (Paris, 2007), pp. 27–41.

———. 'A Portrait of John Bar Aphtonia, Founder of the Monastery of Qenneshre,' in Jan Willem Drijvers and John W. Watt, eds., *Portraits of Spiritual Authority: Religious Power in Early Christianity, Byzantium and the Christian Orient* (Leiden, 1999), pp. 155–69.

Watt, W. Montgomery. 'Conversion in Islam at the Time of the Prophet,' *Journal of the American Academy of Religion* 47 (Thematic Issue S) (1980), pp. 721–31.

———. *Muhammad at Mecca* (Oxford, 1953).
———. *Muhammad at Medina* (Oxford, 1956).
———. *Muhammad: Prophet and Statesman* (London, 1961).
Webb, Peter. 'The Hajj before Muhammad: Journeys to Mecca in Narratives of Pre-Islamic History,' in Venetia Porter and Liana Saif, eds., *The Hajj: Collected Essays* (London, 2013), pp. 6–14.
———. *Imagining the Arabs: Arab Identity and the Rise of Islam* (Edinburgh, 2016).
———. Review of *The Emergence of Islam in Late Antiquity: Allāh and His people* by 'Aziz al-Azmeh, *Al- Al-'Uṣūr al-Wusṭā* 23 (2015), pp. 149–53.
Weber, Eugen. *Peasants into Frenchmen: The Modernization of Rural France, 1870–1914* (Stanford, 1976).
Wellhausen, Julius. *The Arab Kingdom and Its Fall.* Trans. Margaret Graham Weir (Calcutta, 1927).
Wendel, Carl and Willi Göber. 'IV. Die Kirche auf Griechisch-Römischem Boden,' in Fritz Milkau and Georg Leyh, eds., *Handbuch der Bibliothekswissenschaft*, vol. 3.1: *Geschichte der Bibliotheken* (Wiesbaden, 1955), pp. 12–39 (= §57–§64).
Wensinck, Arent J. 'Muḥammad and the Prophets,' in U. Rubin, ed., *The Life of Muḥammad* (Aldershot, 1998), pp. 319–43.
———. *The Muslim Creed: Its Genesis and Historical Development* (Cambridge, 1932).
Wensinck, Arent J., et al., *Concordance et indices de la tradition musulmane: les six livres, le Musnad d'al-Dārimī, le Muwaṭṭa' de Mālik, le Musnad de Aḥmad ibn Ḥanbal.* 8 vols. (Leiden, 1936–1988).
Werner, Shirley. 'Literacy Studies in Classics: The Last Twenty Years,' in Johnson and Parker, eds., *Ancient Literacies*, pp. 333–82.
Wessel, Susan. 'Forgery and the Monothelete Controversy: Some Scrupulous Uses of Deception,' *Greek, Roman, and Byzantine Studies* 42 (2001), pp. 201–20.
West, Martin L. 'The Metre of Arius' *Thalia*,' *Journal of Theological Studies* 33 (1982), pp. 98–105.
Whitby, Mary. *The Ecclesiastical History of Evagrius Scholasticus* (Liverpool, 2000).
Whitcomb, Donald. 'Amṣār in Syria? Syrian Cities after the Conquest,' *Aram* 6 (1994), pp. 13–33.
———. 'The Miṣr of Ayla: New Evidence for the Early Islamic City,' in Donner, ed., *The Articulation of Early Islamic State Structures*, pp. 369–87.
———. 'Notes for an Archaeology of Mu'āwiya: Material Culture in the Transitional Period of Believers,' in Borrut and Donner, eds., *Christians and Others in the Umayyad State*, pp. 11–27.
White, Benjamin T. *The Emergence of Minorities in the Middle East: The Politics of Community in French Mandate Syria* (Edinburgh, 2011).
Whittow, Mark. 'How Much Trade Was Local, Regional, and Inter-regional? A Comparative Perspective on the Late Antique Economy,' *Late Antique Archaeology* 10 (2013), pp. 133–65.
Wickham, Chris. *Framing the Early Middle Ages: Europe and the Mediterranean 400–800* (Oxford/New York, 2005).
Wilde, Claire. '"We shall neither learn the Qur'ān nor teach it to our children": The Covenant of 'Umar on Learning,' in Jens Scheiner and Damien Janos, eds. *The Place to Go: Contexts of Learning in Baghdād, 750–1000 CE* (Princeton, 2014), pp. 237–65.
Wilks, Marina. 'Jacob of Edessa's Use of Greek Philosophy in His Hexaemeron,' in ter

Haar Romeny, *Jacob of Edessa and the Syriac Culture of His Day* (Leiden/Boston, 2008), pp. 223–38.

Wilmshurst, David. *The Martyred Church: A History of the Church of the East* (London, 2011).

Wilson, Nigel G. 'Books and Readers in Byzantium,' in Cyril Mango and Ihor Ševčenko, eds., *Byzantine Books and Bookmen: A Dumbarton Oaks Colloquium* (Washington, D.C., 1975), pp. 1–15.

———. 'Libraries in Byzantium and the West,' in *St Catherine's Monastery at Mount Sinai: Its Manuscripts and their Conservation. Papers Given in Memory of Professor Ihor Ševčenko* (London, 2011), pp. 17–19.

Winkler, Dietmar W. 'Miaphysitism: A New Term for Use in the History of Dogma and in Ecumenical Theology,' *The Harp* 10 (1997), pp. 33–40.

Winn, Robert E. *Eusebius of Emesa: Church and Theology in the Mid-Fourth Century* (Washington, D.C., 2011).

Winstedt, Richard. *A History of Classical Malay Literature* (New York/London/Melbourne, 1969).

Wipszycka, Ewa. 'How Insurmountable Was the Chasm between Monophysites and Chalcedonians?' in Luca Arcari, ed., *Beyond Conflicts: Cultural and Religious Cohabitations in Alexandria and Egypt between the 1st and the 6th century CE* (Tübingen, 2017), pp. 207–226.

Witakowski, Witold. 'Sources of Pseudo-Dionysius for the Third Part of his Chronicle,' *Orientalia Suecana* 40 (1991), pp. 252–75.

———. *The Syriac Chronicle of Pseudo-Dionysius of Tel-Maḥrē: A Study in the History of Historiography* (Uppsala, 1987).

Wittgenstein, Ludwig. *Culture and Value*, ed. Georg Henrik von Wright and Heikki Nyman, trans. Peter Winch, rev. ed. (Oxford, 1998).

Witztum, Joseph B. 'The Syriac Milieu of the Quran: The Recasting of Biblical Narratives' (PhD diss., Princeton University, 2011).

Woldemariam, Michael. 'Why Rebels Collide: Factionalism and Fragmentation in African Insurgencies' (PhD diss., Princeton 2011).

Wolfson, Harry A. 'Saadia on the Trinity and the Incarnation,' in Meir Ben-Horin, Bernard D. Weinryb, and Solomon Zeitlin, eds., *Studies and Essays in Honor of Abraham A. Neuman president, Dropsie College for Hebrew and Cognate Learning, Philadelphia* (Leiden, 1962), pp. 547–68.

Wolska-Conus, Wanda. *La* Topographie chrétienne *de Cosmas Indicopleustes; théologie et science au VI siècle* (Paris, 1962).

Wood, Philip. 'The Chorepiscopoi and Controversies over Orthopraxy in Sixth-Century Mesopotamia,' *Journal of Ecclesiastical History* 63 (2012), pp. 446–57.

———. 'Christian Authority under the Early Abbasids: The Life of Timothy of Kakushta,' *Proche-Orient Chrétien* 61 (2011), pp. 258–74.

———. 'Hira and Her Saints,' *AB* 132 (2014), pp. 5–20.

Woolf, Greg. 'Literacy,' in Alan K. Bowman, Peter Garnsey, and Dominic Rathbone, eds., *The Cambridge Ancient History*, vol. 11: *High Empire, A.D. 70–192.* 2nd ed. (Cambridge, 2008), pp. 875–97.

Wright, William. *A Short History of Syriac Literature* (London, 1894).

Yarbrough, Luke B. 'Did 'Umar b. 'Abd al-'Azīz Issue an Edict concerning Non-Muslim

Officials?' in Borrut and Donner, *Christians and Others in the Umayyad State*, pp. 173–206.

———. 'Islamizing the Islamic State: The Formulation and Assertion of Religious Criteria for State Employment in the First Millennium AH,' (PhD diss., Princeton University, 2012).

———. 'Origins of the *ghiyār*,' *JAOS* 134 (2014), pp. 113–21.

———. 'Upholding God's Rule: Early Muslim Juristic Opposition to the State Employment of Non-Muslims,' *Islamic Law and Society* 19 (2012), pp. 11–85.

Young, William G. *Patriarch, Shah and Caliph* (Rawalpindi, 1974).

Yule, Henry. *Cathay and the Way Thither: Being a Collection of Medieval Notices of China.* 2 vols. (London, 1866).

Zahra, Tara. 'Imagined Noncommunities: National Indifference as a Category of Analysis,' *Slavic Review* 69 (2010), pp. 93–119.

Zaman, Muhammad Qasim. 'Death, Funeral Processions, and the Articulation of Religious Authority in Early Islam,' *Studia Islamica* 93 (2001), pp. 27–58.

Zanetti, Ugo. 'Abū l-Makārim et Abū Ṣāliḥ,' *Bulletin de la societé d'archéologie Copte* 34 (1995), pp. 85–138.

Zayyāt, Ḥabīb. 'Al-asmā' wa-'l-kunā wa-'l-alqāb al-naṣrāniyya fī 'l-Islām,' *al-Machriq* 42 (1948), pp. 1–21.

———. 'al-Diyārāt al-naṣrāniyya fī 'l-Islām,' *al-Machriq* 36 (1938), pp. 289–417.

———. *al-Rūm al-Malakiyyūn fī 'l-Islam* (Ḥarīsā, 1953).

———. *al-Ṣalīb fī 'l-Islām* (Beirut, 2005).

Zotenberg, Hermann. *Manuscrits orientaux. Catalogues des manuscrits syriaques et sabéens (mandaïtes) de la Bibliothèque nationale* (Paris, 1874).

Zuckerman, Constantine. 'Learning from the Enemy and More: Studies in "Dark Centuries" Byzantium,' *Millennium* 2 (2005), pp. 79–135.

Zwemer, Samuel M. 'The "Illiterate" Prophet: Could Mohammed Read and Write?' *Moslem World* 11 (1921), pp. 344–63.

Permissions

I gratefully acknowledge permissions I have received to use the following quotations:

The first epigraph of Chapter 2 (page 46), taken from *Oration 32* of Gregory Nazianzen, was translated by Martha Vinson in *Gregory of Nazianzus: Select Orations* (Washington, D.C.: Catholic University Press, 2003). Copyright © 2003 Catholic University of America Press. Used by permission of Catholic University of America Press.

The second epigraph of Chapter 2 (page 46), taken from the *Questions and Answers* of Anastasius of Sinai, was translated by Joseph A. Munitiz in *Anastasios of Sinai: Questions and Answers* (Turnhout: Brepols, 2011). Copyright © 2011 Brepols Publishers. Used by permission.

The third epigraph of Chapter 2 (page 46), taken from the *Commentary on the Diatessaron* by Ephrem the Syrian, was translated by Sebastian P. Brock in *The Luminous Eye: The Spiritual World Vision of Saint Ephrem*, Rev. ed. (Kalamazoo, 1992). Copyright 1992 by Cistercian Publications, Inc. © 2008 by Order of Saint Benedict, Collegeville, Minnesota. Used with permission.

The fourth epigraph of Chapter 2 (page 46), taken from Ludwig Wittgenstein's *Culture and Value*, revised second edition (Oxford: Basil Blackwell, 1998), was translated by Peter Winch. Copyright © Basil Blackwell 1998. Used by permission of John Wiley & Sons, Ltd.

The epigraph of Chapter 3 (page 85), taken from the *Secret History* of Procopius was translated by Anthony Kaldellis and taken from his *Prokopios: The Secret History with Related Texts* (Indianapolis: Hackett Pub. Co., 2010). Copyright © 2010 Hackett Publishing Company, Inc. Used with permission.

The quotation in Chapter 5 (pages 139–40) from Cyrillona's poem, *On the Scourges*, was translated by Carl Griffin and taken from his, *The Works of Cyrillona* (Piscataway, NJ: Gorgias Press, 2016). Copyright © 2016 Gorgias Press. Used with permission.

The epigraph of Chapter 12 (page 353) is a quotation from Richard Bulliet's article, 'Process and Status in Conversion and Continuity,' in Michael Gervers and Ramzi Jibran Bikhazi, eds., *Conversion and Continuity: Indigenous Christian Communities in Islamic Lands, Eighth to Eighteenth Centuries* (Toronto: Pontifical Institute of Mediaeval Studies, 1990). Copyright © 1990 Pontifical Institute of Mediaeval Studies. Used with permission.

The epigraph of the Conclusion (page 491) is a quotation from Dipesh Chakrabarty's *Provincializing Europe: Postcolonial Thought and Historical Difference* (Princeton: Princeton University Press, 2008). Copyright © 2010 Princeton University Press. Used with permission.

Portions of Part II: The Consequences of Chalcedon, originally appeared in Jack Tannous, 'You are What You Read: Qenneshre and the Miaphysite Church in the Seventh Century,' in Philip Wood, ed., *History and Identity in the Late Antique Near East* (Oxford/New York, 2013), pp. 83–1025. Copyright © 2013, Oxford University Press. This material has been used with the permission of Oxford University Press. What appears in this book represents a revised and expanded version of this original publication.

Index

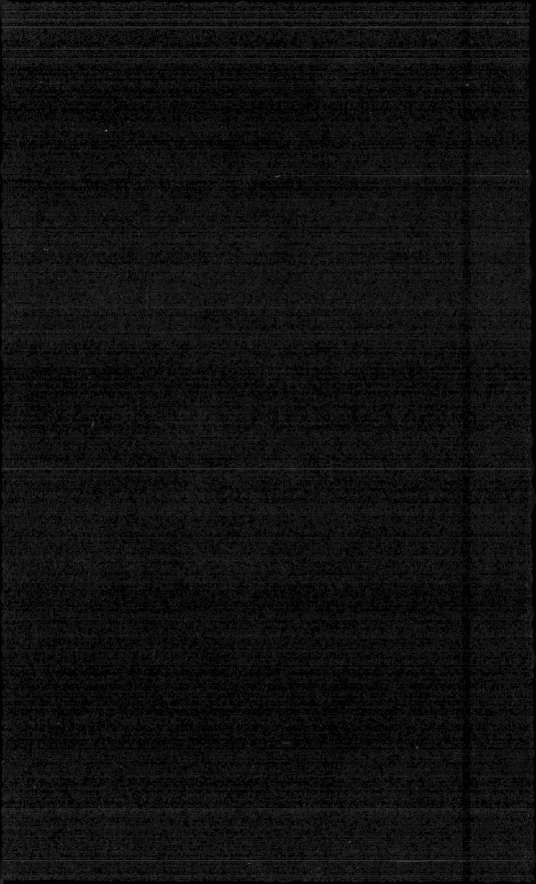